Educational Measurement

Educational Measurement

SECOND EDITION

Edited by Robert L. Thorndike

William H. Angoff
Alexander W. Astin
Frank B. Baker
William V. Clemans
William E. Coffman
William W. Cooley
Lee J. Cronbach
Junius A. Davis
Robert Fitzpatrick
Robert Glaser
Sten Henryssen

John R. Hills
Lyle V. Jones
David R. Krathwohl
Edward J. Morrison
Anthony J. Nitko
Robert J. Panos
David A. Payne
Paul A. Schwarz
Julian C. Stanley
Robert L. Thorndike
Sherman N. Tinkelman
Alexander G. Wesman

AMERICAN COUNCIL ON EDUCATION
WASHINGTON, D.C.

*The preparation of this publication
was made possible by the grant of funds
by The Grant Foundation, Inc., New York.*

Contents

v

List of Figures

List of Tables

Foreword

THE FIRST EDITION of this work was published two decades ago. Its appearance reflected the interests of the American Council on Education in continuous appraisal of the effectiveness and usefulness of testing instruments. The reception accorded the book, which has gone through seven printings since publication, indicates the acceptance the volume has received from workers in the field.

Several years ago those concerned with testing recognized the need for a thoroughgoing revision of the earlier work. With the assistance of the American Educational Research Association, the American Council on Education appointed an Advisory Committee and selected Robert L. Thorndike, Teachers College, Columbia University, to oversee the preparation of a second edition. Financial assistance was given by the Grant Foundation, which had provided the subsidy for the preparation of the earlier edition. The work of the writers, collaborators, and the editor, as for the first edition, was contributed as a professional service without compensation. I want to express the Council's thanks to the members of the Advisory Committee, to the many authors, and to their collaborators for their contributions to this volume. Dr. Thorndike as editor brought wide experience, sound scholarship, a broad point of view, and the devotion necessary to an enterprise of this nature. I am sure this work will receive the same recognition as the earlier volume.

Logan Wilson, *President*
American Council on Education

Editor's Preface

THIS BOOK is the result of some four years of effort to which a host of educators and psychologists have made contributions of varying kinds and sizes. The impetus for this second edition came jointly from the American Council on Education and the American Educational Research Association. Planning started at a meeting called by the AERA in October 1964, at which time the present editor agreed to take on general editorial responsibilities.

An Editorial Advisory Committee was set up to help the editor formulate the book's general plan and recruit chapter authors and critics. The committee was quite active and very helpful in these planning and recruiting functions. Members of the committee, with their affiliations at the time of appointment, are noted opposite the title page.

Funds to defray the costs of preparing the book were provided in part by the Grant Foundation, which had supported the preparation of the first edition. In part, the costs were borne by the American Council on Education, using funds from sales of the first edition.

It was a matter of policy that a new author be picked for any chapter corresponding to a chapter in the original edition. With this in mind, several individuals were invited to critique each chapter in the 1951 book. In a number of cases, it was then possible to identify a promising author for the second edition. The other chapter reviewers frequently served as reviewers and critics of that chapter in the second edition. In addition, a chapter author often circulated drafts of his manuscript for suggestions and criticism. Thus, in total, a very large number of individuals made contributions, ranging widely in extent, to the final manuscript.

Authors were not constrained in their use of material from the first edition. In some instances, the present chapter is clearly a revision, following closely the plan and even the wording of the original but bringing it up to date and supplementing it with knowledge of the current author. In other cases, either the chapter was completely rewritten, with no more than occasional reference to the original, or there was no cognate chapter in the first edition. In the acknowledgments that follow, the author of the corresponding first edition chapter is indicated, whenever such a chapter existed. In one or two instances, the major responsibility of the first edition author is acknowledged for text still included in the second edition.

The sequence and organization of chapters has been rather drastically revised, so that the matching of chapters in the two editions is never a one-to-one matter and is sometimes difficult. In what follows, the most nearly matching chapter is identified when the correspondence seems close enough to make such a cross-reference appropriate.

Chapter 2. Defining and assessing educational objectives by David R. Krathwohl, Syracuse University, and David A. Payne, University of Georgia. Cognate first edition chapter: chapter 5, Preliminary considerations in objective test construction by E. F. Lindquist.

The following individuals contributed, through their comments and criticisms, to the preparation of the chapter: Robert F. McMorris, State University of New York at Albany, Dale P. Scannell, University of Kansas, and Robert J. Solomon, Educational Testing Service.

Chapter 3. Planning the objective test by Sherman N. Tinkelman, New York State Education Department. Cognate first edition chapter: chapter 6, Planning the objective test by K. S. Vaughn.

The following individuals contributed, through their comments and criticisms, to the preparation of the chapter: Alexander W. Astin, American Council on Education, and Dale P. Scannell, University of Kansas.

Chapter 4. Writing the test item by Alexander G. Wesman, Psychological Corporation. Cognate first edition chapter: chapter 7, Writing the test item by Robert L. Ebel.

In this chapter, Dr. Wesman has chosen to follow quite closely the structure and language of the first edition, and he expresses his primary indebtedness to Dr. Ebel.

In addition, the chapter was reviewed by, and suggestions received from, George A. Prescott, University of Maine.

Chapter 5. Gathering, analyzing, and using data on test items by Sten Henryssen, University of Umeå, Umeå, Sweden. Cognate first edition chapter: chapter 9, Item selection techniques by Frederick B. Davis and, in part, chapter 8, The experimental tryout of test materials by Herbert S. Conrad.

The following individuals contributed, through their comments and criticisms, to the preparation of the chapter: Lewis R. Aiken, Jr., Guilford College, Leonard S. Feldt, University of Iowa, Albert N. Hieronymus, University of Iowa, Kenneth D. Hopkins, University of Colorado, Jason Millman, Cornell University, and Lynnette B. Plumlee, Sandia Corporation, Albuquerque, New Mexico.

The material on item characteristic curves was supplemented somewhat by the editor.

Chapter 6. Reproducing the test by Robert L. Thorndike. Cognate first edition chapter: chapter 11, Reproducing the test by Geraldine Spaulding.

The second edition chapter follows closely Miss Spaulding's chapter in the first edition, differing primarily in its addition of material on new reproduction techniques.

The following individuals contributed, through their comments and criticisms, to the preparation of the chapter: Dorothy M. Clendenen, Psychological Corporation, Robert Quick, American Council on Education, William B. Michael, University of Southern California, and Paul A. Schwarz, American Institutes for Research.

Chapter 7. Test administration by William V. Clemans, Science Research Associates, Cognate first edition chapter, in part: chapter 10, Administering and scoring the objective test by Arthur E. Traxler.

Suggestions and comments relating to the preparation of this chapter were provided by: William W. Cooley, Learning Research and Development Center, University of Pittsburgh, Douglas Pidgeon, National Foundation for Educational Research in England and Wales, London, Wimburn L. Wallace, Psychological Corporation, and Williard G. Warrington, Michigan State University.

Chapter 8. Automation of test scoring, reporting, and analysis by Frank B. Baker, University of Wisconsin. There was no really cognate chapter in the first edition, although some overlap exists with chapter 10, Administering and scoring the objective test by Arthur E. Traxler.

The chapter was reviewed and important suggestions and criticisms were provided by: Carmen J. Finley, National Assessment of Educational Progress, Ann Arbor, Michigan, Gene V. Glass, University of Colorado, E. F. Lindquist, University of Iowa (emeritus), and William J. Moonan, National Computer Systems, Minneapolis, Minnesota.

Chapter 9. Performance and product evaluation by Robert Fitzpatrick, American Institutes for Research, and Edward J. Morrison, Ohio State University. Cognate first edition chapter: chapter 12, Performance tests of educational achievement by David G. Ryans, and Norman Frederiksen.

The following individuals contributed through their suggestions and criticisms to the preparation of the chapter: John K. Hemphill, Far West Laboratory of Educational Research and Development, Berkeley, California, and William G. Mollenkopf, Procter and Gamble Company, Cincinnati, Ohio.

Chapter 10. Essay examinations by William E. Coffman, State University of Iowa. Cognate first edition chapter: chapter 13, The essay type of examination by John M. Stalnaker.

The following individuals contributed, through their suggestions and criticisms, to the preparation of the chapter: John B. Carroll, Paul B. Diederich, Henry S. Dyer, and Frederick I. Godshalk, Educational Testing Service, and Ellis B. Page, University of Connecticut.

Chapter 11. Prediction instruments for educational outcomes by Paul A. Schwarz, American Institutes for Research. There was no comparable chapter in the first edition.

The chapter was reviewed by, and valuable suggestions were received from, John C. Flanagan, American Institutes for Research.

Chapter 12. The nature of measurement by Lyle V. Jones, University of North Carolina. Cognate first edition chapter: chapter 14, The fundamental nature of measurement by Irving Lorge.

Drafts of the chapter were read by and useful suggestions and criticisms were received from: Gerald C. Helmstadter, Arizona State University, Dorothy L. Jones, University of Pennsylvania, Samuel Mayo, Loyola University, Chicago, Phillip R. Merrifield, New York University, Lincoln E. Moses, Stanford University, Amnon Rapoport, University of North Carolina,

John Schapler, University of North Carolina, James P. Kahan, University of Southern California, and Franklin M. Henry, University of California, Berkeley.

Preparation of the chapter was partially supported by a research grant from the National Institutes of Health, No. M-10006.

Chapter 13. Reliability by Julian C. Stanley, Johns Hopkins University. Cognate first edition chapter: chapter 15, Reliability by Robert L. Thorndike.

Extensive comments on drafts of the chapter were provided by: Lee J. Cronbach, Stanford University, and Gene V. Glass, Laboratory of Educational Research, University of Colorado.

The following individuals also contributed to the preparation of the chapter through their suggestions and criticisms: Edward E. Cureton, University of Tennessee, Frederick B. Davis, University of Pennsylvania, Eric F. Gardner, Syracuse University, Gerry L. Hendrickson, Johns Hopkins University, John R. Hills, Florida State University, Lloyd G. Humphreys, University of Illinois, Richard Jaeger, United States Office of Education, William Kruskal, University of Chicago, Frederick M. Lord, Princeton University and Educational Testing Service, Warren T. Norman, University of Michigan, Melvin R. Novick, Educational Testing Service, David V. Tiedeman, Harvard University, John W. Tukey, Princeton University, and James L. Wardrop, University of Illinois.

Assistance in proofing the manuscript and galleys was furnished by the following individuals, then graduate students at Johns Hopkins University: Joan M. Finucci, Gerry L. Hendrickson, Samuel A. Livingston, Claire C. Owens, Robert Q. Pollard, Sheldon L. Shubert, Carol Vale, and Marilyn D. Wang.

Typists of the manuscript were Agnes Page and Virginia Grim.

Chapter 14. Test validation by Lee J. Cronbach, Stanford University. Cognate first edition chapter: chapter 16, Validity by Edward E. Cureton.

Assistance in preparation of the manuscript was provided by Thomas J. Quirk, Educational Testing Service.

The following individuals contributed to the preparation of the chapter through their suggestions and criticisms: Hubert E. Brogden, Purdue University, William E. Coffman, University of Iowa, and Richard Darlington, Cornell University.

Chapter 15. Scales, norms, and equivalent scores by William H. Angoff, Educational Testing Service. Cognate first edition chapter: chapter 17, Units, scores, and norms by John C. Flanagan.

The following individuals contributed through their suggestions and criticisms to the preparation of the chapter: Anne Anastasi, Fordham University, Jerome E. Doppelt, Psychological Corporation, John A. Keats, University of Newcastle, New South Wales, Australia, Richard S. Levine, Educational Testing Service, E. Elizabeth Stewart, Educational Testing Service, and Richard W. Watkins, Far West Laboratory for Educational Research and Development, Berkeley, California.

Valuable suggestions were gained in discussions with Frederic M. Lord, Princeton University and Educational Testing Service.

Chapter 16. Techniques for considering multiple measurements by William W. Cooley, Learning Research and Development Center, University of Pittsburgh. Cognate first edition chapter: chapter 18, Batteries and profiles by Charles I. Mosier.

The following individuals contributed through their suggestions and criticisms to the preparation of the chapter: Benjamin Fruchter, University of Texas, Paul R. Lohnes, State University of New York at Buffalo, and David V. Tiedeman, Harvard University.

The preparation of this chapter was supported in part by funds from the United States Office of Education, Department of Health, Education, and Welfare. The opinions expressed do not necessarily reflect the position or policy of the Office of Education, and no official endorsement by the Office of Education should be inferred.

Chapter 17. Measurement in learning and instruction by Robert Glaser and Anthony J. Nitko, Learning Research and Development Center, University of Pittsburgh. The most nearly cognate first edition chapters, though not closely paralleling the present chapter, were chapter 1, The functions of measurement in the facilitation of learning, Walter W. Cook, and chapter 2, The functions of measurement in improving instruction by Ralph W. Tyler.

The authors acknowledge important editorial assistance from Mary Louise Marino, University of Pittsburgh.

Draft versions of the chapter were read and criticized by: John R. Bormath, University of Chicago, Richard C. Carlson, University of Pittsburgh, Robert L. Ebel, Michigan State University, Richard L. Ferguson, University of Pittsburgh, Robert M. Gagne, Florida State University, Gene V. Glass, University of Colorado, Wells Hively II, University of Minnesota, Richard T. Johnson, American Institutes for Research, C. Mauritz Lindvall, Learning Research and Development Center, Pittsburgh, Pennsylvania, and W. James Popham, University of California at Los Angeles.

Critiques of the cognate chapters in the first edition were provided by: Jack C. Merwin, University of Minnesota, and Warren W. Willingham, College Entrance Examination Board.

The preparation of this chapter was supported by the Personnel and Training Branch, Psychological Sciences Division, Office of Naval Research, and by the Learning Research and Development Center supported as a research and development center by funds from the United States Office of Education, Department of Health, Education, and Welfare.

Chapter 18. Use of measurement in student planning and guidance by

Junius A. Davis, Educational Testing Service. Cognate first edition chapter: chapter 3, The functions of measurement in counseling by John G. Darley and Gordon V. Anderson.

The first edition chapters parallel to this and the following chapter were read and suggestions for revision were provided by: Ralph F. Berdie, University of Minnesota, John R. Hills, Florida State University, and Henry Weitz, Duke University.

Chapter 19. Use of measurement in selection and placement by John R. Hills, Florida State University. Cognate first edition chapter: chapter 4, The functions of measurement in educational placement by Henry Chauncey and Norman Frederiksen.

The author acknowledges help that he received from fellow authors Julian C. Stanley (chapter 13) and Lee J. Cronbach (chapter 14). Other individuals who contributed to the chapter through their suggestions and criticisms included: William H. Angoff, Educational Testing Service, Hazen A. Curtis, Florida State University, Benjamin Cameron and Benjamin Gibson, College Entrance Examination Board, Robert E. Dear, San Fernando Valley State College, H. Paul Kelley, University of Texas, and Kenneth M. Wilson, Vassar College.

Editing and typing assistance was provided by Myra Hills.

Chapter 20. The evaluation of educational programs by Alexander W. Astin, American Council on Education, and Robert J. Panos, National Computer Systems, Minneapolis, Minnesota. There was no chapter closely paralleling this in the first edition.

The following individuals contributed, through their suggestions and criticisms, to the preparation of the chapter: Leonard S. Cahen, Educational Testing Service, Ralph W. Tyler, Center for Advanced Study in the Behavioral Sciences (emeritus), and Merlin C. Wittrock, University of California at Los Angeles.

My secretary, Linda Israel, has cheerfully endured the growls of a crochety editor and the temperaments of twenty authors and has shown a continuing commitment to the project of bringing this book into being. Mrs. Jane Newman served as copy editor for the manuscript, smoothing over many rough edges of expression and contributing importantly to unity of style and coherence of thought. Camille Jones, at the American Council on Education, was responsible for shepherding the manuscript through the successive stages of manufacture. Robert Quick, Director of Publications for the Council, provided unwavering interest in and support for the enterprise and made the road of the editor as smooth as possible in the inherently rugged terrain through which he had to travel.

ROBERT L. THORNDIKE

Educational Measurement

1. Educational Measurement for the Seventies

Robert L. Thorndike
Teachers College, Columbia University

In 1951, when the first edition of this book was published, educational testing had already come of age. Objective forms of tests had been in use for thirty years or more—some of them in large volume. Tests had been developed for most of the skill and content areas from the primary grades to college. Tests to identify educational and vocational potential had mushroomed, under the force-feeding of two world wars, and had been widely used in schools and colleges during the period between those wars. Critical evaluation of the existing tests had been crystallized in the first three of the series of Mental Measurements Yearbooks. Evaluation of educational programs had developed from Learned and Wood's (1938) survey of accomplishments in the colleges of Pennsylvania to the elaborate and comprehensive appraisal of outcomes in the Progressive Education Association's Eight-Year Study (Smith, Tyler, & The Evaluation Staff, 1942). Technology had made initial inroads through the IBM 805 test-scoring machine, which had helped to give the four- or five-choice multiple-choice item a preeminent place among item formats. Objective testing for college admissions was firmly entrenched in the program of the College Entrance Examination Board. It was appropriate that a handbook be written that summarized the theory and practice of educational testing and made existing knowledge and technique available to the student and to the educational practitioner.

After a lapse of some twenty years, it now seems desirable to stand back and take another look at the techniques, the theory, and the issues underlying educational measurement for the 1970s. What developments have taken place during the past twenty years? How have approaches to measurement problems changed? What new technologies have emerged, and how have they modified the testing enterprise? How have the concepts underlying measurement theory developed? What new issues and problems have arisen with changing concepts of social functioning and of education's role in it?

This chapter will take a general look at the "state of the art" as background for more detailed examination of specific topics in the chapters that follow. Developments will be examined under three broad headings: (*a*) technological developments and their reverberations and implications, (*b*) conceptual developments, and (*c*) social and political issues impinging upon the testing enterprise. The boundary lines between these rubrics become blurred as technology influences practice, modified practice raises new theoretical issues, changes in theory make new demands upon practice and technology, and all raise issues of social and educational policy and are in turn influenced by social attitudes and political pressures. However, the division will help to provide a focus for the discussion.

THE IMPACT OF TECHNOLOGICAL DEVELOPMENT

The most dramatic changes in educational testing during the past twenty years have been those that have stemmed from technological progress, especially the development of optical scanners and computers. Whereas in 1950 a clerk working at an IBM 805 test-scoring machine could record in an hour up to three scores on each of two or three hundred answer sheets, in 1970 an optical scanner can easily read, and a computer score, a hundred times as many sheets, recording ten times as many different scores on each one. With the tabulating equipment available in 1950, one could prepare listings of names and scores at a reasonable speed and arrange to compute summary statistics for particular groups as these were needed. In 1970, listings, press-on labels, statistics by class, school, district, and state are routinely ground out by test-processing organizations at a speed equaling the rate the test papers whip through the optical scanner. In 1950, a research worker could if necessary do the computations to obtain a 30×30 correlation matrix and carry out a subsequent factor analysis, but it was a substantial undertaking. In 1970, undergraduates do similar analyses overnight as class exercises. The impacts of the information-processing explosion upon educational testing have been many and diverse. Several are especially worthy of consideration.

Large-scale Testing Programs

Facilitated by the improved test-processing techniques that use an optical scanner and a computer and made necessary by mushrooming high school and college enrollments, large-scale testing programs have come to occupy a much more prominent role in the past twenty years. In 1948, the College Entrance Examination Board Scholastic Aptitude Test was administered to about 20,000 candidates. In 1963–64 the number was some 1,200,000, and in 1967, it was reported to be about 1,750,000. In 1948, there was no American College Testing Program; by 1967, it was beginning to challenge the volume of the SAT. Various citywide and statewide testing programs have come into being, all made practical by the advances in the technology for processing examinee responses.

As large-scale testing programs become more common, questions tend to be raised about them. What part should they play in the educational enterprise? Do they tend to become too powerful in shaping the curriculum? in determining a student's future? How can and should the results be used by colleges in selecting their students? Do the tests tend to be overvalued by those who take them and those who use them? How can the results of such testing be interpreted to communities, to school systems, to parents and pupils, so that the results are used constructively to improve education, rather than being used competitively and punitively?

The increased saliency of tests in the educational scene, resulting from the numerous external testing programs to which students are exposed, has resulted in a wave of critical re-examination of objective tests and testing programs. An array of publications, ranging from the somewhat petulant examination of minutiae of item writing by Hoffman (1962) to the wide-ranging studies of parent and teacher attitudes toward and information about tests and testing carried out by the Russell Sage Foundation (Brim, Neulinger, & Glass, 1965), has expressed a renewed concern lest tests distort the educational process or unfairly deprive individuals of a chance to continue their exposure to it. But a good deal of the public discussion has been fair and friendly, recognizing that testing programs are a response to the truly massive character of the American educational enterprise.

Large-scale Psychometric Research Projects

The information-processing technology that has made it practical to carry out, on a large scale, testing programs for college admissions or for feedback to the schools has also made feasible research studies on a scale not previously contemplated. These are projects on a grand scale both in the data collection and the data analysis. Mention may be made of Project Talent (Flanagan, Dailey, Shaycoft, Orr, & Goldberg, 1962), in which almost a half-million secondary school students were given a two-day battery of ability and personality measures. The resulting test scores are available in a data bank and have been used for analyses requested by many different research workers, while at the same time a continuing follow-up study is being carried out by the Project Talent staff.

The Equality of Educational Opportunity Survey (Coleman, Campbell, Hobson, McPartland, Mood, Weinfeld, & York, 1966) gathered data on first-, third-, sixth-, ninth-, and twelfth-grade students in some 4,000 schools. Attention was focused on individual and school variables associated with student achievement, especially as these were related to the problems of education for minority groups. The National

Assessment (Merwin & Womer, 1969) represents a continuing program to appraise the achievements of students countrywide, with results and trends being analyzed by region and type of community.

Surveys on a massive scale have even spilled across national boundaries, and the International Association for the Evaluation of Educational Achievement has been set up to carry out studies that will provide an empirical base for comparative education. An international study of achievement in mathematics has been completed and the results published (Husén, 1967); studies in other subject areas are currently under way.

Instructional Systems

Another development, stemming in part from reinforcement learning theory, as interpreted by B. F. Skinner and his followers, and in part from the availability of computer technology, has been the application of testing in what may broadly be called *instructional systems*. Instructional systems include quite a wide variety of enterprises, having, as a common feature, testing incorporated as an integral part of instruction.

In programmed instruction, it is sometimes difficult to tell what is instruction and what is testing, for each "frame" of instruction culminates in a test task in which the individual selects or produces the response to a task or question. As the successive steps in presenting and developing a concept or skill are planned, the items that test mastery of the acquisition are defined at the same time. One must then inquire what role, if any, exists for testing as an enterprise having some independence from the step-by-step process of instruction, and what kind of a test is required to fill that role. Since appraisal of retention and of transferability of learnings will still be needed, this may be the role that separate testing will play in this type of instructional system.

A second type of instructional system is one that undertakes to individualize the rate and timing, and perhaps the content of instructional sequences. The idea of self-paced and self-directed learning is not something new.

The Winnetka plan of the 1920s called for students to progress at their own rate, testing themselves periodically, and proceeding to new materials as the test results indicated to the teacher that they were ready to do so. But this program had to be monitored by the teacher, and the load of record keeping, test processing, and decision making apparently proved too burdensome for already harried teachers. Current proponents of individualized learning programs avow that the computer has changed all this. The computer will score unit tests; its memory will keep a cumulative record of test results; and its program will include decision rules to tell the teacher or student whether to recycle to a review unit, to move on to the next unit in the regular series, or to switch to an accelerated sequence.

Clearly, the types of tests needed in the management of such an instructional system are markedly different from the standardized tests that have been used in the past to assess an individual's level of competence in some broad aspect of schooling and to place him in relation to his fellows. In the first place, each test needs to be quite specific in content, appraising mastery of a limited segment of instruction. In the second place, the information that each test is asked to supply has to do with level of mastery—the term employed is *criterion referenced*—rather than with standing relative to others. The question asked is one that relates only to the specific individual and the materials of instruction. Will it be more advantageous for Johnny to continue with unit X or unit Y? The decision called for is an absolute one; it involves no one other than Johnny. The implications for test construction of this use of test results are still only partially explicated.

Sequential Testing

Testers have long been fascinated by the possibility of efficiently tailoring testing to each specific individual being tested. In the usual group test, there are likely to be a good many items that are so easy for a given examinee that he solves them without effort or else a good many so difficult that he cannot begin to attack them. An ideal is that each test item help to define the precise limits of an examinee's competence. This is done to some extent in an individually administered test such as the Binet. The level at which the testing is started is determined by the individual's age and anything that is known about his previous test performance. If the items first administered are failed, the examiner retreats to easier levels of the test, determining a floor and then advancing to a ceiling level for each examinee. The technology of scanners and computers raises the possibility of bringing the same flexibility to large-scale testing.

The simplest form of adaptation is to provide tests in multilevel format, including in a single test booklet items covering the whole range of difficulty from, for example, easy nine-year-old to difficult sixteen-year-old level. By specifying the point at which each individual is to enter the test and the point at which he is to stop, test difficulty can be adjusted by small gradations to match his level of competence. A number of practical problems arise in handling this type of individualization on a large scale. These include (a) organizing previous information about the individual to provide guidance as to the test difficulty level that would be most appropriate for him, (b) communicating to each examinee on an individual basis instructions as to just where in the test he is to start and stop, and (c) programming the computer to identify for each single answer sheet the subset of items that has been responded to and then to apply the proper scoring key and norms table. However, it seems likely that these problems will be solved in the next few years and that it will be practical to give each examinee in a class or a larger group the level of test that is most efficient for measuring his level of aptitude or achievement.

If the examinee can be placed in direct interaction with the computer, a more completely individualized form of testing becomes possible. By storing in the computer's memory an adequate stock of test items and an appropriate set of decision rules it will be possible to carry out *sequential testing*, in which the item to be presented at any stage will be determined by the individual's history of successes and failures on previous items. Thus, the individual will be started with an item of moderate difficulty. If he passes it, he will be given a more difficult item, while if he fails it he will be given an easier one. If he passes the first and second items, the difficulty will continue to increase; if he passes the first but fails the second, the third will be of a difficulty intermediate between the first two. Basing the selection of each new item upon the individual's history of successes and failures up to that point will make it possible to bracket his ability level efficiently and to get the maximum amount of information from each additional item administered to him. The theory for this type of sequential testing is beginning to be formulated, but it is still incomplete.

Item Banks and Computer-generated Tests

The large memory storage available in modern computers makes it possible for testing organizations to prepare files classified by content and level in which large numbers of test items can be stored. Stored with each item can be all the summary statistics describing its properties of difficulty and discrimination. When a test is then desired having certain specifications of content coverage and difficulty level, an appropriate inquiry can be addressed to the computer, and it will select and display items that meet the specifications. Final assembly of the test from among the items offered from the library of items in the computer's memory storage can be made by the test editor. The time, however, may come when, for large-scale testing programs with frequent administrations of alternate forms of a test, the assembly of complete test forms will be left almost entirely to the computer. The obvious application of this technology is to large-scale testing programs with frequent test administrations, such as those of the College Entrance Examination Board and the American College Testing Program. But in some state universities with enrollments of thousands of students each semester in a course such as Psychology I, a technique like this—that is, one that would quickly, simply, and automatically generate equivalent test forms for course examinations without the touch of human hands—might become quite attractive.

Procedures for Test Analysis

The analysis of test data was the point at which computer technology was most immediately felt in psychometrics. In the 1930s and 1940s, data reduction was one of the most laborious and tedious aspects of psychometric research. Because of the then almost impossible burden of computing such standard statistics as biserial and point-biserial correlations, tables of item correlations and covariances, and so forth, computationally simpler but less powerful statistics were developed for examining item characteristics. Now, where adequate computer facilities are available, these problems no longer exist. It is literally true that any type of statistical analysis that is worth doing can be done in a reasonable time and at a reasonable cost. The compromises involved in shortcut techniques are no longer necessary or justifiable. The bind in test development shifts from adequate data analysis to adequate data collection. Given that the investigator has had the wisdom and the time to collect adequate data to begin with he can always manage to carry through the appropriate and fruitful analyses of those data.

One impact of improved computing capabilities is on the internal analysis of tests and of test items. As indicated above, standard correlational statistics can now be used in evaluating the degree to which each item measures the same function that the test does as a whole. It is practical to obtain these correlations not only for the correct answer but also for each of the wrong options, thus providing a profile of discrimination for each of the error choices. It is practical to obtain the complete set of item intercorrelations, where these seem likely to be useful, and to select subsets of items on the basis of their correlations or covariances. In order to determine whether the items can be thought of as all measuring one common factor or as defining several different factors or subfactors, factor analyses of pools of test items have become quite possible.

Increased computational capability has gone hand in hand with developments in the theory and application of multivariate analysis to batteries of tests (and other variables). Factor analysis was already a well-developed branch of psychometrics by 1950, but its development has continued and has been facilitated by improved data-processing techniques. Matrices can readily be handled of a size that were unmanageable twenty years ago, and objective, analytic procedures are conveniently available for estimating communalities of variables and for carrying out factor rotations. In addition, the theory and technology of multiple discriminant analysis has been developed. Discriminant analysis examines the differences between categories of individuals and combines tests in such a way as to maximize the group differences. This makes it possible to supplement predictions of an individual's success within an occupation (by multiple regression procedures) with statements about his resemblance to those in one or another of the groups for which data are available. Such statements seem potentially valuable in a field such as guidance, in which an individual must consider a wide range of educational and job possibilities.

Objective Item Format

The first impact of technology on testing tended to stereotype item construction in one or another variation of the multiple-choice format. The focus on multiple-choice items was not solely a response to the IBM 805 test-scoring machine; this type of item has many inherent virtues as a mode of testing application and understanding as well as information. But the readiness with which the format fitted into the commercially available answer sheets tended to focus test makers' attention upon this format to the exclusion of all others.

Scanners and document readers of the new generation are more versatile than the old scoring machines, and their capabilities are continuously increasing. They can read marks and combinations of marks in a wide range of locations on the answer page. Moreover, the speed of present scanners makes it possible to feed the complete test booklet through the scanner so that the examinee can mark directly on the test materials themselves. He can underline words in a sentence, mark locations on a map, or mark the set of numerals that constitutes a quantitative answer to a problem. As character readers are developed, he will be able to produce the answer by writing a set of numerals or letters. It can be anticipated that during the next twenty years these developments will result in a considerable increase in the diversity of test tasks including the greater use of constructed rather than recognition types of items.

Item Weighting and Option Weighting

From time to time, test makers have toyed with plans for weighting test items or specific choices within an item. The gain from these procedures has not been great; and when the weighting had to be done by hand or with crude devices, the labor involved made the procedures of questionable value. With the advent of computer scoring of tests, however, weighting becomes a much more practical undertaking and renewed interest in weighting schemes can be expected. At times in the past, there have been attempts to build tests in which one choice on an item represented a particular category of erroneous response, such as a reversal error in word recognition or an error of overgeneralization in a reasoning test. With computerized processing of tests, multiple scoring to give counts of the frequency of specific categories of errors becomes quite practical and thus may play a greater role in testing in the future.

CONCEPTUAL DEVELOPMENTS

Accompanying the technological developments, which have made possible several quantum leaps in the volume of testing and test analysis, have been a number of expansions and shifts of emphasis in testing theory and rationale. A few of the more important ones will be briefly mentioned.

Formulation of Educational Objectives in Behavioral Terms

Central to any test development enterprise, and in fact to any educational enterprise, is a clear, explicit statement of the objectives that the program is designed to achieve and that, in consequence, the test should be expected to assess. In recent years there has been a strong reaffirmation that the goals of education are to be found in changes in students—in what they can do and in what they choose to do. The emphasis has been upon identifying these behaviors so explicitly and defining them so specifically that there can be little question as to whether the objectives have been achieved. Such an approach fits perfectly into the needs of the test constructor, since specifically stated behavioral objectives become clear guides to a test blueprint and to item construction.

Related to the concern with objectives have been attempts to develop comprehensive taxonomies to provide a conceptual framework within which all the specific goals can fit. The taxonomy for cognitive objectives was developed first (Bloom, 1956), and a body of research has emerged undertaking to appraise the usefulness of the taxonomy as a system for classifying test tasks. More recently a taxonomy of affective objectives has been published (Krathwohl, Bloom, & Masia, 1964), but little has appeared so far on uses made of this schema.

Emphasis on the Meaning of Test Scores

In 1950, test validity was expressed largely either in terms of (a) how faithfully the test represented some domain of content or (b) how accurately the test predicted some specific criterion measure. Then, at mid-decade Cronbach and Meehl (1955) published their first presentation of the notion of construct validity. They stressed the point that many tests are used in varied settings and for various purposes and that to be able to decide when and where a test should be used, whether for research or for practical inferences about a person, one needs an understanding of what the test score means, of what it signifies about an individual.

The formulations of construct validity have been set out and discussed most fully in relation to tests of behavioral traits. A trait such as spatial visualizing, associative memory, or dominance is, after all, a construct, that is, a conception that is formulated in order to account for patterns and consistencies in behavior. When a test is developed that is to measure such an attribute, understanding and appraisal of the test will stem from knowledge about the whole network of relationships into which it fits. Information is needed, therefore, not simply on the nature of the test content nor on its correlation with a single, preselected criterion measure, but rather on the whole network of relationships into which the test fits so that understanding of what the test score signifies about the individual is as complete as possible.

Achievement tests can also be thought of as "trait" tests. *Reading comprehension* is an attribute of an individual, as is *understanding of scientific method*. Appraisal of a test as a measure of either of these attributes requires an understanding of what the test is in fact measuring, an understanding that cannot be gained solely from an examination of the content of the test items. This meaning is explicated by the whole array of correlates of the test as well as by its responsiveness to various manipulations of testing conditions or prior training.

Domain Sampling

One concern of test makers from the early days of testing has been that their tests measure reliably and that the test user know how reliably the test does measure. Classical discussions of reliability were formulated in terms of *true score* and *error* or in terms of a definition of *parallel* test forms. A somewhat different conception has been offered in recent years, the conception of a domain of admissible tasks from which the test was drawing one sample. Reliability is then conceived as the accuracy with which the sample represents the complete domain from which it was drawn. The domain may be a domain of arithmetic reasoning tasks or a domain of word knowledge items. It may be conceived of as tasks that might be presented at a single point in time or as a domain that extends over occasions as well as tasks. The domain can be sampled as a whole, or a stratified sample of tasks can be drawn from subdomains of tasks defined in terms of

area of content, type of intellectual process required, or level of difficulty. Though it is often difficult to formulate a clear definition of the domain in specific cases, the conception of a test as sampling from a domain often seems to provide a useful way of thinking about a test and about the issues of precision of measurement with which the test maker is concerned.

Response Set and Stylistic Factors in Testing

During the twenty years just past, test makers have become increasingly interested in and concerned about factors of response set and cognitive style as determiners of individual responses to tests. These factors have been of special concern to makers of self-descriptive devices designed for appraisal in the affective domain. However, the possibility continues to be explored that such personal qualities as "field dependence" (Witkin, Dyk, Faterson, Goodenough, & Karp, 1962) or tendency to "leveling" versus "sharpening" of the figures in the field may exercise significant influence on the manner of responding to cognitive tasks. These issues have had relatively little impact upon educational test design to date but may have a significant impact in the future.

Placement and Classification as Opposed to Selection

In the military and industrial context, the distinctive requirements of tests for personnel classification as opposed to personnel selection became clear in the testing programs of World War II and the immediate postwar period. With a selection objective, one is concerned solely with maximizing validity of the tests or other procedures for one single category of training or work. With a classification objective one is concerned with maximizing *differential* validity, so that decisions ("assign to job A rather than job B") will be made with a maximum of accuracy. When there are a number of possibilities for assignment, it is important that each test show a wide dispersion of validity coefficients. Each test should show validity for some but not all jobs; each job should be predicted by some but not all tests;

and no two jobs should be predicted by exactly the same tests in the battery.

The conception of tests as serving primarily a classification and/or guidance function implies the need for a battery of distinct and relatively uncorrelated tests of discrete psychological functions. Test batteries designed to serve this type of function were just appearing when the first edition of this book was written. Research has continued explicating the model of the ideal classification battery and its use, and developing tests of more limited and specific abilities and traits.

During the past twenty years, psychometricians and research workers in education have become more conscious that many of the educational assignments that are made on the basis of test data are classification decisions rather than selection decisions. There are, of course, the admissions decisions by specific colleges and universities, in which the goal is to maximize some criterion of desirability in those who are admitted. But there are many other decisions in which the options are not acceptance versus rejection, but rather treatment A versus treatment B versus treatment C. The different treatments may be majoring in different subject-matter fields, assignment to different sections of a common course taught in different manners or at different levels, or moving ahead to different units in a course sequence after completing unit X. For such decisions, the logic of classification holds, and a test or test battery must be evaluated in terms of its differential validity for the alternate treatments. Recognition of the crucial role of differential validity has gradually spread from research workers concerned with personnel classification in jobs to those concerned with guidance of choices of field of study and on to those concerned with placement of students in differentiated treatments within some one course or program. As awareness of the requirements for the placement and classification use of tests in education increases, a different criterion will be applied to tests for these purposes—the criterion of differential validity.

One essential for differential validity is that the several treatments be genuinely differ-ent. Only then can a test be expected to relate differentially to them. An active program of research has grown up in recent years through which the investigators hope to identify treatments that are genuinely and importantly different and tests that are differentially related to them. The yield from this work seems modest to date (Cronbach & Snow, 1969), but the search is a busy one and seems likely to attract considerable attention in the years ahead.

Item Sampling

In the large-scale survey studies that have become practical in recent years, the concern is often to describe groups rather than individuals—groups such as the students in a particular school, a particular community, or a particular region. For this purpose, it is often desirable to have a very broad sampling of test content as well as a representative sampling of students. However, it is *not* necessary that every student be tested with every task. If the tasks are assigned to students in some random manner so that each task is attempted by a random subsample of examinees, it is possible to estimate item parameters and from them the parameters of total scores based on groups of items.

In an item-sampling approach, it is possible to broaden the sampling of content without at the same time making the load of testing for any single examinee impossibly burdensome. One trades off length of test against number of examinees, testing a larger total number for a shorter period of time, a trade off that can often be quite advantageous. However, one does lose by the trade a good deal of the precision of measurement for individuals and, consequently, the possibility of studying individual correlates of the test score. The models by which item-sampling procedures can be applied are actively being developed, and the uses and limitations of the models are still only partially understood.

Tab Test

One interesting technique of testing, which has been actively developed during the past twenty years, has been the test in which the examinee follows through a chain of reasoning, eliciting bits of information as he goes. An early form covered the information with paper tabs that could be torn off by the examinee, hence the name. The test context might be electronics troubleshooting or medical diagnosis. If so, the examinee would have the immediate symptoms of a malfunction or a patient's illness described to him. A number of steps that he might take in search of information would also be described in the test paper. If the examinee decided to carry out a specific diagnostic test, he would tear off the corresponding tab, at which point the result of the test would be made known to him.

The examinee would continue to seek information until he felt that he had all the information he needed. At that point, he would proceed to the next stage, in which various possible corrective actions would be listed. He would choose what he considered to be the appropriate corrective action and, once again, remove the cover from the stated outcome of his action (either by erasing a protective ink covering or tearing off the paper cover). He would continue making corrective attempts until he was told either that he had succeeded or that "the patient just died; get another patient." He would be scored on the efficiency and appropriateness of his search for information and on the speed with which he reached a correct solution. Problems of scoring and evaluating such sequences of behavior are very real, but the richness of the behavior that is sampled seems quite promising.

SOCIAL AND POLITICAL ISSUES

During the past twenty years, testing has been the subject of renewed public pressure and concern. To some extent this has been a by-product of its success. The expansion and proliferation of testing programs and the widespread use of tests by government and industry as a basis for personnel decisions have brought tests very much into public view. Concern has been expressed about the impact of testing upon the educational enterprise, about the invasion of individual privacy, and about the "fairness" of tests to underprivileged and minority groups. Concern about the quality and use of tests has been expressed also by the testing specialists, and they have moved to safeguard the quality of test production and test use.

Impact of Testing upon Education

Concerns about testing's impact have been of two kinds. One type of concern is that there is too much testing and that too much weight is given to it. The other is that objective tests of the sort that are widely used tend to pervert the learning process, either because they are poorly constructed or because they inherently measure limited and trivial educational outcomes.

The outcry about overtesting has tended to come from administrators in secondary education (Joint Committee on Testing, 1962), who have been particularly exposed to the burden of external testing programs. And there can be no question that at certain times and places the schedule of multiple testing has become administratively burdensome. College Boards, American College Testing Program admissions tests, National Merit Scholarship exams, statewide scholarship tests, statewide achievement tests have followed one another in a wearying succession. Many represent by-products of the rapid expansion of collegiate education and the pressure of youth and their parents to gain access to that higher education under the most favorable conditions. Thus, in part, it would seem to be the general social scene rather than testing that has been the culprit.

The expressed concern that too much reliance has been placed on tests in such decisions as college admissions is almost impossible to evaluate, either pro or con, because the situation is highly specific to individual institutions and their own particular admissions procedures. Decisions must be made. All types of information have their limitations, and it would be easy to overweight any one element in the picture. Since admissions committees are very human, it is likely that misweighting of many kinds does in fact occur.

The impact of a testing program upon the educational process is also something that is quite specific. To the extent that the test exercises included in a testing program represent a wise and thoughtful definition of educational objectives and to the extent that results from the testing program are available to a teacher, school, or school system for constructive use in behalf of students, the testing program can provide a leaven to the educational enterprise. To the extent that specialists in the teaching of a subject are intimately involved in the design and construction of achievement tests, they can represent an enlightened definition of teaching objectives. This is the goal toward which the better test-making agencies strive, though obviously they sometimes fall short of achieving it.

Invasion of Privacy

The issue of invasion of privacy has arisen primarily in relation to personality assessment rather than with aptitude and achievement tests and more in the context of employment than in the context of education. However, educators are concerned about the affective as well as the cognitive outcomes of schooling. Also, relatively personal information is often sought in the context of diagnostic and remedial work with pupils who are having problems in their adaptation to instruction or to the social scene of the school. Moreover, personal information is sought from relatively young and immature individuals, who may not be fully aware of the import of the information that they are giving. The fact that this information is usually gathered so that it may be used in the individual's behalf is an ameliorating factor. However, it seems clear that educational testers and educational research workers are going to have to be a good deal more sensitive than they have in the past to problems of invasion of privacy and take precautions to protect the legitimate interests and concerns of students and their families. Sensitive information will have to be gathered sparingly and used with discretion.

Fair Use of Tests with Minority Groups

It has become abundantly clear throughout the history of ability testing that some groups do less well on tests than others. Children from remote rural areas, children from economically and culturally deprived homes, and children of ethnic minorities—the Negro, the Mexican-American, the Indian—have typically performed less well than the general American population on which test norms have been based. The use of test results with these groups has been questioned more and more insistently in recent years as court decisions and legislation have focused attention on civil rights and the demands of minority groups.

The main focus of concern in the use of tests with minority groups has been in the use of tests as predictors. What predictive inferences can legitimately be drawn from a test score for a minority group member? Does a specific level of test performance have the same significance for him that it does for a middle-class white examinee? How shall we define "fair" use of test results? Neither the definitions of fairness nor the stock of evidence upon which judgments of fairness can be based are in very satisfactory condition at the present time. The evidence (Kirkpatrick, Ewen, Barrett, & Katzell, 1968) is meager in part because previous pressures to avoid discrimination had made it difficult to get evidence on tests and training or job performance separately for different religious or ethnic subgroups within a group of students or employees. Work on the problem is currently more active, and clarification of concepts and expansion of the data base from which conclusions may be drawn can be expected in the near future.

When achievement tests are viewed not as screening devices but as measures of the *outcomes* of education, their application to minority groups would seem less in question. However, the question can be raised, and to some extent is raised by some minority group spokesmen, as to whether the objectives of education for minority group children are or should be identical with those of the white majority. To the extent that this point of view of unique and distinctive educational objectives takes hold, one may expect the standard measures of achievement also to be challenged by minority group members. If such a point of view of unique and different educational objectives were accepted, it would pose very difficult problems not only for test makers but for educators generally.

Maintenance of Test Quality

Concern about the quality of tests and their wise use has been as prominent within the professions of educational and psychological measurement as among their critics. This concern has expressed itself concretely in several ways. Critical test reviews have continued to appear in successive editions of the *Mental Measurements Yearbooks* appearing in 1953, 1959, and 1965. In addition, the American Psychological Association and the National Council on Measurement in Education have prepared, and subsequently revised, statements of standards for the preparation and publication of psychological and educational tests (APA, 1966). These publications are the most tangible signs of a concern for sound construction and wise use that is also expressed in textbooks and teaching, in articles and symposia, and in all the media by which test makers communicate with one another and with the public.

CONTINUITY IN SPITE OF CHANGE

The focus of this chapter has been on what is different in 1970 as compared with 1950. But in truth, testing is like an iceberg. The part that shows as change is the one-ninth of the berg that is above water level, and the part that remains much the same is the vast underwater bulk. Test and item formats have changed little over the twenty-year span. The range of content and objectives measured by current tests has not been greatly extended over what was included twenty years ago. The basic techniques of test construction are much as they were then. Developments in test theory have been evolutionary rather than revolutionary. The reader of the chapters that follow will find a good deal that is written as it was or might have been in 1950, and, by the same token, much that appears in the first edition of this book is as applicable today as when it was written. But there is also a good deal that is new, as the brief statement in this chapter has tried to indicate. The art is changing and growing, but it is the same basic art. The details of that art and the concepts that lie back of it are set forth in the chapters that follow.

REFERENCES

American Psychological Association. *Standards for educational and psychological tests and manuals.* Washington: APA, 1966.

Bloom, B. S. (Ed.) *Taxonomy of educational objectives.* Handbook I. *The cognitive domain.* New York: David McKay, 1956.

Brim, O. G., Jr., Neulinger, J., & Glass, D. G. *The use of standardized tests in American secondary schools and their impact on students, teachers, and administrators.* New York: Russell Sage Foundation, 1965.

Coleman, J. S., Campbell, E. Q., Hobson, C. J., McPartland, J., Mood, A. M., Weinfeld, F. D., & York, R. L. *Equality of educational opportunity.* Washington: U.S. Government Printing Office, 1966.

Cronbach, L. J., & Meehl, P. E. Construct validity in psychological tests. *Psychological Bulletin,* 1955, **52,** 281–302.

Cronbach, L. J., & Snow, R. E. *Final report: Individual differences in learning ability as a function of instructional variables.* Stanford, Calif.: Stanford University School of Education, 1969.

Flanagan, J. C., Dailey, J. T., Shaycoft, M. F., Orr, D. B., & Goldberg, I. *The talents of American youth.* Vol. 1. *Design for a study of American youth.* Boston: Houghton Mifflin, 1962.

Hoffman, B. *The tyranny of testing.* New York: Crowell Collier, 1962.

Husén, T. (Ed.) *International study of achievement in mathematics.* New York: Wiley, 1967.

Joint Committee on Testing. *Testing, testing, test-*

ing. Washington: American Association of School Administrators, 1962.

Kirkpatrick, J. J., Ewen, R. B., Barrett, R. S., & Katzell, R. A. *Testing and fair employment*. New York: New York University Press, 1968.

Krathwohl, D. R., Bloom, B. S., & Masia, B. *Taxonomy of educational objectives*. Handbook II. *The affective domain*. New York: David McKay, 1964.

Learned, W. S., & Wood, B. D. *The student and his knowledge*. New York: Carnegie Foundation for the Advancement of Teaching, 1938.

Merwin, J. C., & Womer, F. B. *Evaluation in assessing the progress of education to provide bases of public understanding and public policy*. In *Educational evaluation: New roles, new means* (68th yearbook of the National Society for the Study of Education). Chicago: The Society, 1969.

Smith, E. R., Tyler, R. W., & The Evaluation Staff of the Commission on the Relation of School and College of the Progressive Education Association. *Appraising and recording student progress*. New York: Harper, 1942.

Witkin, H. A., Dyk, R. B., Faterson, H. F., Goodenough, D. R., & Karp, S. A. *Psychological differentiation*. New York: Wiley, 1962.

Test Design, Construction, Administration, and Processing

PART ONE

2. Defining and Assessing Educational Objectives

David R. Krathwohl and David A. Payne
Syracuse University

Educational objectives are the goals and purposes that it is hoped will be realized through a system of education. To the extent that these objectives are defined clearly, it can be determined whether or not the system is doing what one wishes it to do.

Clarity of objectives is important in the educational enterprise at a number of levels and in a number of contexts. Clear objectives give direction to the curriculum maker in choosing from the wide range of content and from the multiplicity of media for presenting that content. They give direction to the teacher in planning a unit of instruction. They provide focus for the evaluator and test maker whose concern is to determine the extent to which the purposes of an educational program are being achieved. It is especially important in a volume devoted to test making that the nature and role of objectives and the process of formulating them be explicitly considered.

A DEFINITION OF EDUCATION

Just as many problems are most easily solved if they are approached from certain directions and with particular prior assumptions, so the formulation of educational objectives, as well as the construction of tests of those objectives, is facilitated if what is meant by *education* is defined in a certain way. Such facilitation occurs if education is defined as a process designed to change the behavior of students. Students enter the educational system—be it kindergarten, any grade level, a unit, or a day's class session—with an array of probabilities of behaving in certain ways. The intent of that segment of education is to change some of these probabilities: certain behaviors defined as "desirable" are to increase in probability of occurrence and certain "undesirable" behaviors are to decrease.

The teacher's task is to create an environment that brings about the desired changes in the probabilities of selected behaviors. He may do this through interacting with the students individually or in groups, through creating groups in which the students interact with one another, or through having the students interact with instructional materials either individually or in groups. In each instance he is controlling aspects of the student's environment (e.g. text, audiovisual aids, or the instructor himself), in such a way as to maximize the student's achievement of the intended goals of instruction.

The first-grade teacher has the goal, among others, of teaching his pupils all the sums of pairs of numbers from 1 through 9. The pupils come to him with certain entry behaviors—that is, behaviors already learned to certain levels of probability—that are required for mastery of the new behavior. For this exercise, the entry behaviors probably would be a perfect or near-perfect recognition of the numerals and what they stand for. The teacher's task is to use the most efficient and effective teaching techniques (lecture, demonstration, games, or whatever) in order to modify the pupil's response to $3+5$, for example, so that the child has a very high probability of responding with 8.

The educational process consists of providing a series of environments that permit the student to learn new behaviors or modify or eliminate existing behaviors and to practice these behaviors to the point that he displays them at some reasonably satisfactory level of competence and regularity under appropriate circumstances. The statement of objectives becomes the description of behaviors that the student is expected to display with some regularity. The evaluation of the success of instruction and of the student's learning becomes a matter of placing the student in a sample of situations in which the different learned behaviors may appropriately occur and noting the accuracy and regularity with which they do occur.

BEHAVIORAL OBJECTIVES AND CURRICULUM DECISIONS

Defining education as a process of *changing student behavior* to achieve certain specified goals orients one toward some facets of education more than to others. The facets thus made prominent are an important positive feature of this definition in contrast to other possible definitions. For example, other possibilities include defining education as the course of study described in an outline of the essential material to be covered. This emphasizes covering certain subject matter in a given time unit and assumes the student will be properly affected by that coverage. Similarly, one can detail the teacher's behavior in terms of particular lectures, demonstrations, and discussions. This emphasizes the teacher's activities on the assumption that the student will attend and learn from them. But, by contrast with these points of view, describing education as a process that changes a student's behavior into certain specified patterns is more likely to lead to an education program in which:

1. There is an emphasis on what is actually to be achieved by education, namely changes in the student. Coverage of content and teacher activities are means toward those goals that may or may not be successfully reached.

2. There is a greater emphasis on content *usage* and on content *application* than on content *recall*. The stress is on what a student *does* with the content he learns rather than on his being able to remember it on demand. Content learned in the context of its use is more resistant to forgetting than if learned more or less by rote as a series of relatively unrelated facts.

3. There is, as a result of the accent on content *use*, greater emphasis given to learning methods for processing data, for solving problems, and for decision making. In themselves, these skills are even more resistant to forgetting than the content with which they are useful.

Furthermore, as electronic retrieval systems become increasingly available, the skills and abilities for processing data are critical behaviors and are a key to continued learning and to effective problem solving.

4. There is a concentration of greater teacher effort on complex skills and abilities that means that the teacher's time and talents are being used to teach the parts of the curriculum most difficult to learn without teacher modeling and guidance. Much simple material can be self-taught, or nearly so, from suitably prepared texts and programmed materials. It is much more difficult to build such materials to teach complex skills and fewer good materials are available for this purpose in most fields. Focusing a larger portion of teaching at the complex levels is an important side effect of this approach.

5. It becomes apparent, as one concentrates attention on student behaviors, that such behaviors are useful, not only in the context in which they were learned, but also in a variety of other circumstances. Thus there is greater emphasis on the transferability of learned behavior. Prominence is given to the display of learned behaviors in the wide array of situations and problems to which they are appropriately applicable but in which their applicability was not directly taught.

6. The cumulative effect of emphasizing the achievement of skills is the development, through the integration of relevant, previously learned behaviors, of complex thinking abilities required in the most intricate problems.

Ultimate vs. Immediate Objectives

When concern focuses on behavioral change, education is not an end in itself but rather it is a means to the development of the educated person.[1] By the specification of the behaviors that define the educated person, who is to be

[1] There are some who see education as intrinsically valuable as a growth experience for the individual. In economic terms it is a consumer rather than a producer good. In humanistic terms it is an experience of value in and of itself. This point of view, in our pluralistic society, is legitimate and desirable, but unless held to the exclusion of other viewpoints does not negate the point made here.

the result of our schooling, the ultimate objectives of the instructional process are specified. In order to provide guidance for the activities to be incorporated in a school program, a grade level, a subject course, or a class session, there is need to derive immediate objectives that are related to those ultimate objectives. As Lindquist (1951) noted in the first edition of this book:

Many of the basic objectives of school instruction cannot possibly be fully realized until long after the instruction has been concluded. For guidance in specific courses of instruction, however, it is common practice to set up less remote objectives—objectives which are capable of immediate attainment. Ideally, these immediate objectives should in every instance have been clearly and logically derived from accepted ultimate objectives, in full consideration of all relevant characteristics of the pupils who are to receive the instruction. Ideally, also, the immediate objectives should be supported by dependable empirical evidence that their attainment will eventually lead to or make possible the realization of the ultimate objectives. Finally, the content and methods of instruction should, ideally, be logically selected, devised, and used with specific reference to these immediate and ultimate objectives, and should likewise be supported by convincing experimental evidence of their validity [p. 121].

As Lindquist himself noted next, "Unfortunately, this ideal relationship among ultimate objectives, immediate objectives, and the content and methods of instruction has only rarely been approximated in actual practice [p. 121]." Too rarely does one have empirical evidence that certain required educational experiences do lead to the ultimate objectives intended (e.g. that the study of Shakespeare leads to more reading of good literature). In the main, educators have had to rely on their own application of deductive and inferential logic to descend from ultimate to immediate objectives or ascend from ideas of what is good education to a modified definition of the educated person. Much work is needed to improve the process of building the flights of steps by which to move from ultimate goals to immediate outcomes and hence to what represents a sound curriculum.

But even though limited mainly to logical tools, a focus upon desired ultimate behaviors should provide for greater relevance in the content of education—a need that has always been great but which appears to be particularly serious in the closing third of the twentieth century. Without the guidance of ultimate objectives, much subject matter may be included in the curriculum because it "completes the logic of an area" or "has always been taught" rather than because it contributes to some future behavioral goal.

Lindquist made this point with respect to the subject-matter orientation to education:

Unfortunately, a portion of the present content of school instruction is there only by reason of the organization of the curriculum by "subjects," and because of the practice of introducing new materials in intact subject units, or subject by subject, often without any careful selection of the detailed content of those subjects. As a result of this practice many detailed elements which have no relationship whatever to any ultimate objectives have entered the curriculum simply because they "belonged" in the same broad category of knowledge, or in the same subject, with other content which could be readily justified, and because of which the subject as a whole was selected [p. 121].

As an example of this point, Lindquist noted that a considerable portion of the factual content in courses in United States history had been included on this basis. He noted that "many historical facts are included in the school textbooks for apparently no better reason than that they are of interest to historians or that they are a part of 'American history' and many otherwise useful facts are taught in such a way as to minimize their contribution to desirable educational objectives [p. 122]." He noted, of course, that the same point could be made with more or less justification about every school subject in the curriculum.

Continuing his discussion of the problems of justifying education in terms of subject matter, Lindquist illustrated a problem of particular concern; namely, relating ultimate and immediate objectives:

. . . it is frequently true that, instead of the content and immediate objectives of instruction having been derived from any accepted ultimate objectives, just the reverse of this relationship obtains. That is, many of the immediate objectives were actually derived from, or adapted to, the traditional content; and their claimed relationships to ultimate objectives—as well, sometimes, as the ultimate objectives themselves—were "thought up" in an effort to rationalize the continued teaching of the traditional content. It has been claimed, for example, that knowledge of Latin will contribute to improved reading comprehension in the vernacular, through developing a better understanding of English words and phrases of Latin origin, or through developing a more accurate grammatical sense, and so forth. While there may be some truth in these claims, they are clearly made in an effort to justify the perpetuation of Latin in the school curriculum, rather than to justify its selection in preference to all known alternative and more direct ways of improving English reading comprehension. Again, of course, Latin has been used only as a convenient example. For any subject in the school curriculum, particularly for the long-established subjects, many of the immediate objectives claimed for them have a similar origin [p. 122].

As Lindquist's discussion makes clear, ultimate goals may be rationalizations derived from accepted immediate goals. The reverse also can occur. Derivation from an ultimate objective of more immediate subobjectives that have clear behavioral referents can result in a wide range of behavioral possibilities, not all of which are equally central to their base of origin nor lead as directly back to it. Careful logic and a clear reading of the original intent is required to choose from among these possibilities those that will culminate in the achievement of the original ultimate objective. Once subobjectives with clear behavioral referents have been identified, the way is open to plan for collection of empirical evidence to support this choice between alternative approaches. Thus, if a subobjective is mastery of a sizable English vocabulary, the effectiveness of instruction in Latin and through direct vocabulary building units can be compared.

Behavioral Objectives and the Test Maker

Education has been defined here as the process of creating behavioral changes which taken as a whole serve to produce the educated person whose ways of acting are described by education's ultimate objectives. How does this relate to the making of a test? How does the test maker begin to construct his instrument? He could presumably simply sit down and begin

to write test items that ask questions about the content that has been taught. If the instructor himself is writing the test, presumably the types of questions that easily come to mind will be those that deal with outcomes high on his list of priorities. Hopefully, he will be wise enough to realize that the most salient content is that which was most recently covered. If his test is to be a fair one, he will have to examine his set of test exercises to be sure that content and behavioral applications are covered in proportion to his intended emphasis. This is the beginning of a deliberate analytic approach to test building. If one follows this approach, the sequence of steps is approximately as follows:

1. Specify the ultimate goals of the educational process.

2. Derive from these the goals of the portion of the system under study.

3. Specify these goals in terms of expected student behavior. If relevant, specify the acceptable level of successful learning.

4. Determine the relative emphasis or importance of various objectives, their content and their behaviors.

5. Select or develop appropriate situations that will elicit the desired behavior in the appropriate context or environment, assuming the student has learned it.

6. Assemble a sample of such situations so that together they best represent the emphasis on content and behavior previously determined.

7. Provide for the recording of responses in a form that will facilitate scoring but that does not change the nature of the behavior elicited so that it is no longer a true sample or an accurate index of the behavior desired.

8. Establish scoring criteria and guides to provide objective and unbiased judgments.

9. Try out the instrument in preliminary form.

10. Revise the sample of situations on the basis of tryout information.

11. Analyze reliability, validity, and score distribution in accordance with purposes of score use.

12. Develop test norms and a manual, and reproduce and distribute test.

These steps give an overview of where and

how behavioral objectives fit in the process of test construction (cf. chap. 3, p. 51). Michael and Metfessel (1967) have proposed eight comparable steps for the evaluation of educational programs which the reader may wish to compare with the above 12.

The place of objectives as the first stages of test construction and thus as guides to the total process makes clear that their formulation is important. The earlier discussion from Lindquist (1951) and steps 1 and 2 above show that specification of objectives in at least two levels of specificity is important and useful. Actually, for practical purposes, it is useful to delineate three levels of generality along a continuum from highly abstract to very concrete statements (Krathwohl 1964, 1965). A fourth level of specificity is formed by the instructional materials and test items themselves.

LEVELS OF EDUCATIONAL OBJECTIVES

Three Main Levels

The first level of educational objectives, the most abstract level, includes the long-term global goals of education that describe the end product of a complete education or the broad goals toward which a sizable block of training, such as college, high school, or elementary school, might strive. Examples of objectives at this level would be:

1. The student shall develop the fundamental skills of reading and writing.

2. The student shall become a citizen who is informed about the major political issues of the day and who uses this information to act for the betterment of the community.

3. The student shall learn an appropriate masculine or feminine social role.

4. The student shall develop a conscience, morality, and a scale of values.

5. The student shall be prepared to enter a vocation on graduation from high school if he so wishes.

At a second and more concrete level are the statements that are the translation of the global goals into specific behaviors that form the terminal performance capabilities of students successfully completing an instructional unit in a course, a course itself, and, in some instances, a sequence of courses.

As applied to pupils completing the elementary school, the first of the general objectives might break down into narrower and more concrete objectives such as:

1. Can name and recognize the letters of the alphabet

2. Can write legibly at X words per minute

3. Can write a simple letter or paragraph with no more than Y errors of spelling or punctuation

4. Reads with understanding material that appears in simple newspaper stories and in books for children

5. Adapts reading techniques to a specific purpose (e.g. entertainment, finding an item of information, or following an argument).

Deduced from the previous level is the third, characterized by still greater specificity and detail, that provides the guidance needed to create or to choose specific instructional items. When used for development of a linear sequence of programmed instruction, for instance, such objectives at this level would describe, at the unit or course level of specificity, a succession of way stations, each of which would be a behavior more sophisticated than the previous one.

For example, from the second-level objective that the child be able to name the letters of the alphabet, one could derive at the third level several highly specific objectives describing the child's ability to discriminate between pairs of similar and easily confused letters, for example, the child shall distinguish P from R, he shall distinguish O from Q, he shall distinguish C from G, etc. These specific objectives might lead to giving the child practice in recognizing these letters in isolation or choosing between them when they are presented in pairs.

Third-level objectives can be useful, not only for specifying the instructional materials and experiences needed for learning, but also to guide construction of measures of very fine-grain increases in pupil competence. This is the level of measures used in programs of individualized instruction such as the Oakleaf Project

(Cox & Graham, 1966) in which the pupil is tested for mastery as he completes each instructional unit. Mastery tests for units of programmed instruction determine whether to recycle the student through the material, to route him to remedial loops of materials, or to route him on to new material. Thus objectives even at this most specific level serve a purpose of guiding test construction just as at the more general level.

The Necessity of Using All Three Levels

Specification of objectives at all three levels is important. Specification at the most general level is important for it is there that educators can most meaningfully communicate the goals of the instructional process to the public and develop some general understanding of what teachers and educators are trying to do. There is a danger here that these statements can become too global and too full of Madison-Avenue terms to be meaningful. Thus Henry Dyer (1967) cited the following paragraph from the 1947 report of the President's Commission on Higher Education as an example of "word magic."

The first goal in education for democracy is the full, rounded, and continuing development of the person. The discovery, training, and utilization of individual talents is of fundamental importance in a free society. To liberate and perfect the intrinsic powers of every citizen is the central purpose of democracy, and its furtherance of individual self-realization is its greatest glory [p. 9].

As Dyer noted, "it sings to our enthusiasms," but it is not couched in terms that permit one to fathom when educators have "liberated and perfected the intrinsic powers of a citizen." Neither does this level of statement help to tease out how to "calibrate the roundness of his development." But a statement at this level which, for instance, indicates that "each student graduating from high school shall, if he desires it, be adequately prepared to enter a vocation" has very concrete implications for vocational areas.

The public school curriculum since the inception of free public education has been a battleground for special-interest groups and for differing educational philosophies, each seeking to change the emphasis or to substitute one orientation for another. Statements of objectives at a general level thus become important for they provide a basis for the decision makers of education to make the judgments that are necessary for the system to maintain its forward momentum and to provide a curriculum for tomorrow as well as today.

Besides objectives at the most general level, objectives at several levels of abstraction are needed for a variety of reasons. One of the most important is so that the interrelation of the meaning at one level to that at another can be examined.

When developing a curriculum, educators try to get those involved in the decision to agree at as specific a level as possible, but complete agreement usually can be reached only at the more abstract levels. For example, it is possible to get general agreement that students should be good citizens, but it is harder to get agreement on the specifics that this broad objective includes. To some teachers, good citizenship may signify engagement in some kind of political action—ringing doorbells at election time, writing Congressmen, even demonstrating and picketing; to other teachers the meaning may be confined to voting and attempting to understand issues and discussing them with others. As society, knowledge, teachers, and pressures change, it helps to have agreed-upon general objectives to which curriculum builders and evaluators can refer.

While honest differences in interpretation of the more abstract statements may exist with respect to their meaning for more specific goals, a given statement at a more abstract level can act as a homing beacon for alternative instructional routes, since each would be described by different educational objectives at the more specific levels. Specifically, each alternative instructional pattern and its objectives though proposed in different terms may be a legitimate route to the same more global goal. Lindquist (1951) made this point, in the quotation used earlier, with respect to the teaching of Latin as a means to building vocabulary in contrast to the use of vocabulary units in English classes.

As another example, consider the very general level-one objective, preparation to enter a vocation, as it applies to the TV repair field. It might be approached by the alternative routes of first learning the general principles of electricity and electronics and later applying them or of first being taught to operate certain kinds of diagnostic electronic equipment and then to read the circuit diagrams that permit one to apply the equipment to a variety of sets. Similarly, one could teach the recognition of the alphabet through discrimination exercises, such as those noted earlier, or through learning a variety of pictorial associates ("*B* for ball," "*C* for cat," etc.).

The choice between alternative routes such as the above may depend both on their relative effectiveness in reaching the more general objective and on other important factors. Among such other factors are the facilitation of the generalizability and transferability of learning, the relative effectiveness of one set of antecedent behaviors in leading to more complex behaviors, the kind of cognitive organizers in one route in contrast to another as a precursor to more complex learning, the relative efficiency of one route of learning as well as its effectiveness, etc. In most instances, not all the considerations for choice are known and the instructional specialist and teacher precede the psychologist and sociologist into areas where students must learn, but, in all these instances, choices must be made. The specification of objectives at the more general level can provide a reference for evaluating alternative routes and subgoals by defining the common global aim.

Some, but not all, objectives can be meaningfully translated into a complete set of subgoals at the third and most specific level. For these objectives, the universe of behaviors can be completely detailed. They are designated *mastery objectives*, for these objectives require that the student master all or a certain specified sample of behaviors at relatively high levels of accuracy. Consider, for example, the objective that the student shall be able to recall the sums of pairs of numbers 0 through 9. There are only 45 such sums, each of which could be specified as a specific third-level objective. Learning the

letters of the alphabet is another example.

In many of our objectives, however, we want the student to learn a principle or a process that he can use in a variety of situations beyond those in which he learned it. These are *transfer objectives*. An objective such as the ability to differentiate value judgments from predictions of consequences is so open ended that the number of such situations is infinite, and the third-level objectives can only be samples of the more general behavior. Similarly, there is no way of describing the limits of the range of transfer of the application of a principle like Boyle's law nor of specifying the number of situations to which the student should be able to apply it. Specification of objectives at the second level is clearly necessary for transfer objectives, both for testing and instruction to provide an accurate general description of the behavior being sought and as a basis for choosing appropriate third-level objectives.

A Fourth Level

The three levels so far discussed have proven themselves useful in curriculum and test construction. It is worth noting, however, that, though not statements of objectives themselves, the test items and instructional materials form a fourth and most specific level of all. They describe the situations in which the behaviors to be learned actually are displayed and are the operational definitions of previous levels of specificity. This fourth level is important because, as has already been noted and shall be seen later, in some instances one proceeds to develop instructional materials and even test items before being able to formulate clearly the general objective. This is not to say that teachers do not know what they want to teach, but rather that often a teacher can assemble materials that have a particular quality and flavor about them so that they seem to express what the teacher wants though he cannot verbalize it. If he finds these materials interesting and motivating to children, this reinforces the teacher's enthusiasm for this particular collection of teaching devices. In such a situation, the determination of what broad and sweeping first-level goals are achieved is fairly easy. The second- and third-level goals are the problem, and they are usually focused by a process of working back and forth between first-level goals and the instructional materials as one observes the behaviors elicited. This process provides goal statements at the intermediate levels that the teacher will frequently find helpful in guiding him to better uses of the materials. Often it will lead him to revise the materials or to form a new composition of them that will permit still better attainment once the goal target is clear.

The process of stating objectives is an iterative one whereby each level helps one understand levels above and below it. Developments at one level frequently have implications for those at other levels, and one obtains the most complete understanding, particularly once the major developmental lines are clear, by working back and forth among the various levels. Thus, for both testing and curriculum building, it is clear that objectives can and must be stated at a variety of levels of specificity, each level important to an understanding and interpretation of the other levels.

THE IDENTIFICATION AND SELECTION OF OBJECTIVES

Sources of Objectives

Specific objectives at the second or third level, which are deduced from more abstractly stated objectives, result from a rational process. Similarly, the formulation of the most abstract levels of objectives is best guided by a rational scheme. Official and semiofficial bodies, namely the various presidential commissions on higher education, the American Council on Education, the Educational Policies Commission of the National Education Association, and others, have provided a number of guideposts. For example, in the American Council on Education's (1944) *A Design for General Education* over 200 objectives were presented, which are reasonably clearly defined in terms of student behavior and rather broad descriptive subject-matter content, and were grouped under 10 broad outcomes.

Many of these efforts have been phrased in broad descriptive terms such as the early *Cardinal Principles of Secondary Education* (1918):

1. Good health
2. Command of fundamental processes
3. Worthy home membership
4. Vocational efficiency
5. Good citizenship
6. Worthy use of leisure time
7. Ethical character

The statements of objectives described by the Educational Policies Commission of the National Education Association provided one broad socially oriented set (1938) and one cognitively oriented set (1961):

1938	1961
1. Self-realization	1. Recalling and imagining
2. Human relationship	2. Classifying and generalizing
3. Economic efficiency	3. Comparing and evaluating
4. Civic responsibility	4. Analyzing and synthesizing
	5. Deducing and inferring

Complete and detailed collections of objectives for the elementary and secondary schools were an outgrowth of the work of the Mid-Century Committee on Outcomes in Elementary Education (Kearny, 1953) and of a similar effort for the secondary level by French (1957). While neither of these reports provides an overall rationale for the collections, each represents the pooled wisdom of numerous subcommittees and groups. The volume for elementary education uses the categories of (*a*) knowledge and understandings, (*b*) skills and competencies, (*c*) attitudes and interests, and (*d*) action patterns. These four general categories were related separately to ethical behaviors, standards, and values at one extreme and to quantitative relationships at the other. The secondary school level objectives are classified under the three maturity goals of self-realization, interpersonal relationships, and large group memberships and leaderships, as well as under the four behavioral areas of intellectual development, cultural integration, physical and mental health, and economic competence.

Different sets of objectives will be identified

depending upon whether one emphasizes the socialization of the individual or general societal needs. A list of individual-oriented objectives might look something like Havighurst's (1953) list of developmental tasks (pp. 25–41):

1. Learning physical skills necessary for ordinary games
2. Building wholesome attitudes toward oneself as a growing organism
3. Learning to get along with age-mates
4. Learning an appropriate masculine or feminine social role
5. Developing fundamental skills in reading, writing, and calculating
6. Developing concepts necessary for everyday living
7. Developing conscience, morality, and a scale of values
8. Achieving personal independence
9. Developing attitudes toward groups and institutions.

A more society-oriented view of education might formulate a set of objectives like (Hand, Hoppock, & Zlatchin, 1948):

1. To keep the population healthy
2. To provide physical protection and guarantees against war
3. To conserve natural resources and use them wisely
4. To provide opportunity for people to make a living
5. To rear and educate the young
6. To provide wholesome and adequate recreation
7. To enable the population to realize aesthetic and spiritual values
8. To provide a sufficient body of commonly held beliefs and aspirations to guarantee social integration
9. To organize and govern in harmony with beliefs and aspirations.

While these statements of official bodies and committees and these analyses by talented individuals are extremely helpful, in many instances an individual or group may wish to make its own choices from among these or to develop its own list from basic sources rather than depend on the work of others. Tyler (1964) has proposed a process for the development and selection of objectives that has proven very effective for first-level objectives and has been used to go directly to second-level objectives as well. Tyler named three sources of objectives that should be routinely considered in the process of objectives development. They are: (*a*) studies of the needs of the individual in his society, (*b*) studies of the needs of the society which the school must serve, and (*c*) statements by those trained in specific subject matter as to the contributions of their specialty to the area of education under consideration. For the purposes here, Tyler's sources can be treated as a series of questions:

1. *What suggestions for objectives are gained from our information about the needs of students?* Here consideration is given to the characteristics of students that bear upon their needs at particular ages—their concerns, their interests, their background and preparation in relevant areas. This information will assist in suggesting or choosing objectives that have relevance, that permit one to build on student interests and motivation, and that, therefore, have a greater chance of being effective. In some instances, this consideration of the needs of students at a particular age will raise a question about the readiness of an individual for certain objectives. Have his previous educational experiences prepared him for a particular field of study? An example of this latter question arises in the articulation of high school and college level work in mathematics, where the appearance of the new math and other instructional innovations have produced mathematical sophistication in college freshmen far above that of the past. College and university faculties will have to change their objectives to fit the changed needs of these students. As innovations and expanding information increase student sophistication at all ages, educators will need to reevaluate their objectives in many other fields as well.

Also of concern here are such basic needs as those of love, food, and self-preservation. Studies of these needs will be relevant as well as studies of the need for personal integrity and self-actualization. The school may not necessarily meet all such needs directly but may do so through providing the skills that make need fulfillment possible. Vocational education, for example, through providing a number of skills for earning a living makes possible the fulfillment of a number of needs.

2. *What suggestions are gained from studies of the needs of the individual for effective functioning in our contemporary society and culture?* As noted previously, an analysis of the culture, particularly of its demands on young people and adults and the opportunities it provides them, may yield valuable insights into the needs of its individual members. What are the activities individuals are expected to perform? What problems are they likely to encounter? What opportunities are they likely to have for service and self-realization? Answers to these and similar questions provide a background against which to judge suggested objectives or provide a basis for suggesting objectives. As an example of the questions raised, consider the objective of fluency in speaking a foreign tongue used to support teaching foreign languages in the early grades. If one views our society as a relatively U.S.-bound culture, is the command of a foreign language a worthwhile skill? Practical considerations in terms of opportunity to use the language on the one hand and the attitudinal orientation toward foreign cultures that go with learning such a language on the other would be of paramount concern in evaluating such a practice.

3. *What suggestions are gained from the present state of knowledge insofar as that knowledge contributes to the education of the nonspecialist or the typical citizen? (Or to the education of the specialist, if that is the more relevant question?)* The continuing "knowledge explosion" will certainly influence educators to assess periodically their teaching goals. As new ideas, understandings, and facts become available, probably at an ever-increasing rate, mastery of them becomes an enormous problem; and specialists can be helpful in selecting from their area that which will be most useful to the citizen and have the greatest transferability to the problems he is likely to face.

Similarly, specialists know what the new breed of specialist needs. Furthermore, new alignments of faculty to formulate and select objectives for new specialties are necessary as the communication problems and desirability of cooperation across disciplines become accentuated. New specialties, such as the combination of biology and physics to form biophysics, have important implications for specialists and nonspecialists alike. Consider the implications for citizen and specialist of the unraveling of the mystery of heredity by biophysicists. The advances in space science over the last ten years alone would serve to illustrate the need for continual reappraisal and refinement of our educational objectives from the subject-matter point of view.

Thus statements and lists of objectives prepared by various study committees, published analyses by persons with special expertise, and original analyses by the educator of social and individual needs provide varied choices from among which the curriculum or test developer may choose objectives upon which to focus his work.

Choice of Objectives

It must be apparent that many more objectives will be proposed by various interested parties and derived from first-level objectives than the school is able to achieve. The final decision about which objectives will be selected will be dictated in part by the intended function of the school, the assigned role of that portion of the curriculum being developed, the practicalities of what can be accomplished, and the level of abstraction appropriate to the level of curriculum being developed. Tyler (1964) has discussed two criteria that embody the major considerations in the choice of objectives. These are (*a*) the philosophy of education of the person or institution involved in the selection and (*b*) the extent to which the objectives fit known psychological realities of what can be taught at a given student age in the light of the time available and the previous learning.

Is the objective consistent with the school's philosophy of education? This criterion is concerned with the values emphasized in a given school situation. Selection will involve such concerns as the school's view of the satisfying and effective life for an individual in our society. What are the important values? What is the proper relation between man and society? What are the proper relations between man and man? Should there be different education for different segments of society? Answers to these and other similar questions relating to a school's philosophy clearly have a considerable impact on what is ruled out, what is chosen, and what is emphasized.

Is the objective consistent with accepted knowledge and theories about learning and instruction? Knowledge about theories of learning and instruction also will assist in determining whether objectives should be chosen for particular grades, or particular learning sequences, or where in grade placement they are most appropriately placed. It will help keep one realistic about which objectives can be appropriately selected for short-term emphasis and which ones require much longer periods of building and growth to attain. It can help one determine which entry behaviors are most appropriate and which follow-up behaviors should be practiced. It can help one distinguish those objectives that are less amenable to teaching from those that are more responsive to the instructional process.

No doubt there are other questions that can be raised with respect to this framework, first formulated by Tyler in the 1930s, and there are of course other orientations to curriculum building. The above framework, however, has stood the test of time as a useful and usable orientation to test and curriculum construction.

Once objectives have been selected, the next problems concern formulating and stating them so that they provide maximum guidance for curriculum construction and evaluation.

The Explicit Statement of Objectives

The orientation expressed throughout this chapter is that statements of educational objectives be descriptions of behavior. What does this mean when one gets down to cases? Typically the objectives that one first tries to formulate are those that deal with the recall of facts and knowledge. These objectives are to develop the basic behaviors on which all the more complex thinking behaviors are built. Objectives to achieve these basic behaviors would be stated in the form of: The student shall be able to recall the _____, and the blank can then be filled in endlessly, from "letters of the alphabet" through "definition of a set" or "names of the cranial nerves."

But recall is only a part of what is meant when an educator states he wants a student to know a subject. And it is here that the value of stating objectives in terms of the student's behavior becomes particularly apparent. The term *to know* comes to have many meanings when the educator begins to consider the operations involved in a student's demonstration that he *really* knows a subject. To some educators, knowing is adequately demonstrated by being able to recall the material in its original learned form or by recognizing it in a list; e.g. pick the most appropriate definition of Gresham's law. But to others, it means that the student not only can pick the item from a list, but that he can tell you about it in his own words, elaborating in such a way that it is clear that he understands how, for example, Gresham's law works in abstract terms and that he is able to describe its workings in a historical or contemporary example. Thus, the term *to know* may mean to be able to recall, to be able to describe in other terms, to be able to illustrate by analogy, or to be able to apply to a new example. It could mean all of these and more.

Ebel (1965), in describing the fuller meaning of *to know*, stated: "To have command of knowledge is to have ready access to it and full comprehension of its scope, its limitations, and its implications. . . . The knowledge a person understands he has command of, and the knowledge he commands he also understands [pp. 41–42]." Translating *to know* into its behavioral manifestations lends a greater specificity to both teaching and testing. If the teacher means that for the student to know he shall be able to apply the knowledge to new situations, then the teacher needs to give the student opportunity to practice with this behavior in a variety of situations so that the student will be able to demonstrate his knowledge through appropriate test items.

Lindvall (1964) provides an example of how a group moves from abstract and general objectives to behaviorally stated ones. He noted that in a seventh-grade curriculum project developing a social studies unit on Africa, the teachers began with such questions as: What have the students previously learned about Africa? What basic social studies abilities and skills might be developed here (e.g. read maps)? What basic principles or streams provided meaningfulness to previous units that are relevant? What material prerequisite to later units should be included? These considerations resulted in statements such as:

Determine how geography has affected politico-socio-economic development
Recognize past accomplishments and present problems
Understand, accept, and appreciate differences among people
Understand the ever-increasing importance of Africa in the world community
Understand the difficulties faced by the United States in forming African policies [p. 14].

Each of these statements needed to be further defined to communicate meaningfully what was meant. Lindvall noted that teachers complained that "such specificity . . . is unnecessary. Teachers will know what is meant by these general statements and supply their own specifics [p. 15]." An hour of discussion and dispute ensued as the teachers explored the specifics and then came up with a short list of objectives.

While Lindvall did not indicate the content of that dispute, the fact that it existed indicated that teachers did not unanimously "know what is meant by these general statements." He noted that such discussion resulted in objectives such as these to specify further how "geography affected politicio-socio-economic development":

To be able to describe the geography of the various regions of Africa
To be able to explain how geography has affected the economic development of at least one country from each major geographic division of Africa

To be able to explain how geography has affected the social and political development of the same selected countries [p. 15].

In the same way the goal statement "recognize past accomplishments and present problems" translated as:

To be able to describe, for each African country, its major sources of income and what must be done if income is to be increased
To be able to describe past and present social conditions and the problems associated with these conditions [p. 15].

This example is quite typical, with respect to both process and product, of how changes in formulation take place. It should be noted that for a *very detailed* test that would measure achievement of the objectives in *depth*, this statement of objectives would need still further detailing and specification to guide adequately test construction. But the last formulation has moved toward considerable behavioral specificity in comparison with the first statements.

The translation of objectives into behavioral terms is no longer new to measurement specialists. This process has been successfully completed often enough that aids for those formulating objectives have been developed. A programmed book by Mager (1962) will help the novice through the process. In addition, there are several classification systems that are suggestive of the kinds of categories and terms that may be useful in working through such a translation and that may be used to provide a structure within which to fit specific objectives. Such a category system may be useful in communicating to others about one's work, in developing instructional methods, and in devising evaluation techniques.

THE TAXONOMY OF EDUCATIONAL OBJECTIVES

One attempt to provide a framework for the entire panorama of educational objectives is the *Taxonomy of Educational Objectives*, so called because it is a hierarchical classification scheme. Since the *Taxonomy*'s authors were much concerned with the holistic nature of learning, the universe of educational objectives is divided, solely for purposes of convenience, into three domains—cognitive, affective, and psychomotor. The cognitive and affective domains contain the bulk of the objectives for conventional courses, and a framework has been developed for each of these (Bloom, 1956; Krathwohl, Bloom, & Masia, 1964). A tentative framework for the psychomotor domain also has been developed (Simpson, 1966). These frameworks are hierarchical in nature—the lowest level of behavior in the hierarchy is believed to be the simplest and least complex and its achievement is presumed to be the key to successful achievement at the next higher level in the structure.

The structure proposed in the *Taxonomy* is educationally, logically, and psychologically consistent insofar as the authors were able to make it so. Thus, it makes distinctions that teachers, supervisors, and educators make in their discussions of objectives. It is consistent with the way educators think in the field. It is intended to be logically, internally consistent with terms that are defined as precisely as possible. In some instances, stipulative definitions are used although these were avoided insofar as possible and most terms are used in their common descriptive meanings (this was more possible in the cognitive than the affective domain). Terms once defined in the *Taxonomy* are used consistently in accord with that definition.

The Cognitive Domain Taxonomy
The structure of the cognitive domain

The cognitive domain has categories arranged from simple to complex and from concrete to abstract. A brief description of the major categories and a sample objective for each category follows (Bloom, 1956, pp. 201–207):[2]

Knowledge. Recall or recognition in an appropriate context of material whether it be specific facts, universal principles, methods, process patterns, structures, or settings. Little is required besides bringing to mind the appropriate material; e.g. recall of major facts about particular cultures.

Comprehension. This is the lowest level of

what is commonly called "understanding" and requires that the individual be able to paraphrase knowledge accurately, to explain or summarize it in his own words, or to show logical extensions in terms of implications or corollaries; e.g. skill in translating verbal descriptions of mathematical material into symbolic statements and vice versa.

Application. The ability to select a given abstraction (idea, rule of procedure, or generalized method) appropriate for a new situation and to correctly apply it; e.g. the ability to predict the probable effect of a change in a factor, such as food supply, on a biological situation previously at equilibrium.

Analysis. The ability to break apart a communication or concept into its constituent elements to show the hierarchy or other internal relation of ideas, to show the basis for organization, and to indicate how it conveys its effects; e.g. the ability to recognize form and pattern in literary and artistic works as a way of understanding their meaning.

Synthesis. The arrangement and combination of pieces, parts, elements, etc., in such a way as to constitute a pattern or structure not there before; e.g. ability to tell a personal experience effectively.

Evaluation. Qualitative and quantitative judgment about the extent to which material and methods satisfy criteria determined by teacher or student; e.g. the ability to compare a work with the highest known standards in its field—especially with other works of recognized excellence.

To the extent possible, the *Taxonomy* structure was made consistent with psychological knowledge about the phenomena under consideration. But, since in most instances teachers go beyond "hard" psychological knowledge to teach what they are expected to include in the curriculum, any taxonomy that is all inclusive speculatively leaps considerably beyond the realm of known psychological theory.

There have been several attempts to validate one particular claim of the *Taxonomy*. This is the claim of hierarchical structure which if validated would mean that achievement at a higher level of behavior would be dependent

[2] Figure 3.1 (p. 51) reproduces the outline of these categories.

upon achievement at a previous level. Thus, Ayers (1966); Kropp, Stoker, and Bashaw (1966); Johnson (1966); and Miller (1965)—all have obtained empirical evidence that gives at least mild support to the order of the first three categories of the cognitive domain. Support for the order of the more complex categories has largely failed to appear in these studies. All of the investigators encountered difficulties in developing measures, particularly objective ones, at the most complex end of the continuum. The complications of classifying accurately an item in a higher-level category are compounded by the fact that the student's prior experience with the material on which the item is based may have resulted in his learning by rote a problem that would be complex if new to the student. Such a problem would drop into a lower category, such as *Knowledge*, for the student who learned it by rote, whereas it would be a measure of more complex behavior for the student who met it afresh.

The usefulness of the cognitive domain taxonomy

The comprehensive nature of the framework of the *Taxonomy* has made it useful in analyzing whether or not a formulated set of objectives includes objectives at all levels of the *Taxonomy* appropriate to the curriculum under consideration. The *Taxonomy*, like a periodic table of elements or a check-off shopping list, provides a panorama of possible objectives. As the *Taxonomy* provides many examples of objectives at the more complex levels, it has frequently been suggestive of behavior that previously had been omitted or given insufficient emphasis.

The *Taxonomy* also has been used in the analysis of examinations and teaching practices to compare the emphasis given to various of its categories in the statements of course objectives with the emphasis on these same categories in analyses of the test questions or of instruction (McGuire, 1963; Scannell & Stellwagen, 1960). As might be expected, too frequently the balance between factual knowledge and the complex ways of thinking about and using it called for in the statement of objectives fails to appear when one examines items from the

examination or the materials and nature of instruction. The heavy emphasis on memorizing knowledge is dramatized by a comparison of the proportionate use of the *Knowledge* category versus all the others combined. It is not unusual to find that the time spent on knowledge instruction or the items so categorized is 50 to 90 percent of the total. The problem is made obvious by this technique.

Frequently, when searching for ideas in building a curriculum, the work of others is most helpful. Where one's own work and that of others are both phrased in terms of the *Taxonomy* categories, comparison is markedly facilitated. Translation of objectives into the *Taxonomy* framework can provide a basis for more precise comparison. Furthermore, where similarities exist, it becomes possible to trade experiences regarding the values of certain learning experiences with more confidence that there is a firm basis for comparison and that the other person's experience will be truly relevant.

It is perhaps also important to note the implications of the hierarchical nature of the *Taxonomy* for curriculum building. If the analysis is correct, then a hierarchy of objectives in a given subject-matter area suggests a readiness relationship that exists between those objectives lower in the hierarchy and those higher. Thus, the *Taxonomy* may be suggestive of the order in which objectives should be sequenced in the curriculum.

As indicated previously, objectives may be stated at a variety of levels of abstraction. It is at the second level of abstraction, previously defined relative to the specifications of objectives, that the *Taxonomy* may find one of its most significant applications. To assist this application, Metfessel, Michael, and Kirsner (1969) have provided a series of verbal guidelines useful in operationalizing specific levels of the *Taxonomy*.

The *Taxonomy* is intended to assist those operating at the unit and course level. For the statement of objectives for smaller portions of instruction, such as is required in the development of instructional materials like programmed books that are used in teaching machines or with computers, a finer category system, such as that of Gagné's (1965), is needed.

Gagné's Learning Hierarchy

Gagné's structure, which was used in the American Association for the Advancement of Science and National Science Foundation sponsored curriculum—*Science—A Process Approach*—is a blending of behavioristic and cognitive psychology. It is intended to distinguish those types of behaviors from one another which are learned under different conditions. Since it is also a hierarchical scheme, each capability depends on having learned the next simpler one. Gagné's categories, in order, are:

Signal learning. This refers to the general, diffuse, and emotional reaction which involuntarily results as a learned reaction to certain stimuli. Fear of water or of heights, or the pleasurable feeling on entering an art gallery, would be examples of this kind of learning.

Stimulus-response learning. This learning involves a precise skeletal muscle response to a particular complex of stimulation. This form of learning, for example, appears to govern the acquisition of a new vocalization habit by a young child.

Chaining. Chaining results from connecting in sequence two previously learned stimulus-response behaviors. Our language is filled with chains of verbal sequences (e.g. horse and buggy). Motor acts such as starting a car or properly putting a specimen under a microscope are also chains.

Verbal association. This type of learning is a subvariety of chaining which depends on a code or clue that provides the link between the learned responses in the chain. Gagné gives the example of the French student who uses the word *illuminate* as his code or clue. As the student visualizes the illumination of the flame of a match, it provides the clue to *allumette*, the French word for match.

Multiple discrimination. This type of learning occurs when a number of learned chains interfere with one another so that retention of certain individual chains is shortened and forgetting occurs. Multiple discrimination learning occurs when the teacher is learning to call each

of his students by his right name.

Concept learning. Concept learning requires response to stimuli in terms of abstract properties such as shape, color, position, or number. Examples of such concepts are up and down, near and far, and right and left.

Principle learning. Learning a principle requires the chaining of two or more concepts. It is exemplified by the acquisition of the "idea" contained in such propositions as "gases expand when heated."

Problem solving. The chaining of principles into new combinations to fit particular circumstances is the heart of problem solving. Examples would include the solution of simple problems such as the reorganization of an office staff to fit the space available in a new building or the abstract manipulation of physics principles to derive a new theory.

Alternative Conceptual Frameworks

In addition to the *Taxonomy* and Gagné's framework, there have been a number of other attempts to provide ways of conceptualizing the range of educational objectives. Some of these schemes are summarized in table 2.1. These particular classifications range from the very general (Smith & Tyler, 1942) to the specific (Walbesser, 1965).

The Affective Domain Taxonomy

The major efforts at test construction and curriculum building have been predominantly in the cognitive areas of achievement, yet criticism of the schools shows concern about students' "poor" attitudes, "low" motivation to achieve, slovenly work habits, and the lack of commitment to societal values. Thus affective goals and objectives seem to have high saliency and high concern for educators and noneducators alike. Furthermore, affective objectives have long-range importance for they deal not with whether a student can do but whether he wants to and indeed *does* behave in certain educationally desirable ways. Unfortunately, there is little *formal* recognition of this long-range importance of affective outcomes in the school's curricula nor are there often measures for evaluation of these outcomes. Thus, the

TABLE 2.1

Ways of Conceptualizing Educational Objectives

Smith and Tyler (1942)	Raths (1938)	Ebel (1965)	Walbesser (1965)
Development of effective thinking methods	Functional information	Terminology—understanding of terminology, vocabulary	Identifying
Cultivation of useful work habits and study skills	Various aspects of thinking	Understanding of fact or descriptive detail	Distinguishing
The inculcation of social attitudes	Attitudes	Ability to explain or illustrate	Naming
Acquisition of wide range of significant interests	Interests, aims, purposes, appreciations	Ability to calculate	Ordering
Appreciation of aesthetic experience	Study skills and work habits	Ability to predict under specified conditions	Describing
Development of social sensitivity	Social adjustments and sensitivity	Ability to recommend appropriate action	Applying rules
Personal social adjustment	Creativeness	Ability to make an evaluative judgment	Stating rules
Acquisition of important information	Functional social philosophy		Demonstrating
Development of physical health			Interpreting
Development of consistent life philosophy			

SOURCE: Payne, 1968.

development of a structure for the affective area similar to those discussed above may be even more critical for progress than it was for the cognitive area. The definition of terms in such a structure is especially needed because the confusion of meanings of terms in the affective area is even greater than in the cognitive.

If there is confusion about whether a term like *really understand* means ability to define, to apply, or whatever, consider the variety of meanings of a term like *appreciation.* When teachers say that they want a child to *appreciate* art, do they mean that he should be aware of a work of art? Should he be willing to give it some attention when it is around? Do they mean that he should seek it out—go to the museum on his own, for instance? Do they mean that he should regard works of art as having positive value? Should he experience an emotional "kick" or thrill when he sees a work of art? Should he be able to evaluate it and to know why and how it is effective? Should he be able to compare its aesthetic impact with that of some other art form (e.g. music)?

This list could be extended, but it is enough to suggest that the term *appreciation* covers a wide variety of meanings. And worse, not all of these are distinct from the terms *attitude* and *interest.* Thus, if appreciation has the meaning that the student should like a work of art well enough to seek it out, how would one distinguish such behavior from an interest in art—or are interests and appreciations, as these words are used, the same thing? If the student *values* art, does he have a favorable *attitude* toward it? Are appreciation objectives the same as, overlapping with, or, in some respects, distinct from, attitude objectives?

Structure and categories of affective domain

Although the authors of the *Taxonomy* felt it was possible to structure the cognitive domain on the basis of simple to complex and concrete to abstract, the authors of the affective domain taxonomy found that it required the addition of the *dimension of internalization* to provide a meaningful hierarchical structure. *Internalization* refers to the process by which behavioral control consistent with things that are positively valued increasingly is dominantly exerted from inside the individual. At first, this incorporating into oneself, or adopting as one's own behavior, may be limited to isolated manifestations but gradually it comes to dominate one's thinking and motivation so that the person is seen as acting in ways consistent with his professed value orientation.

Internalization refers to the inner growth that occurs as the individual becomes aware of and then adopts attitudes, principles, codes, and sanctions that are basic to his value judgments and to guiding his conduct. It has many elements in common with the term *socialization*. Internalization may be best understood by looking at the categories in the affective domain of the *Taxonomy* structure. Stripped of their definitions, the category and subcategory titles appear in sequence as follows (Krathwohl et al., 1964, pp. 34–35):

1.0 Receiving (attending)
  1.1 Awareness
  1.2 Willingness to receive
  1.3 Controlled or selected attention
2.0 Responding
  2.1 Acquiescence in responding
  2.2 Willingness to respond
  2.3 Satisfaction in response
3.0 Valuing
  3.1 Acceptance of a value
  3.2 Preference for a value
  3.3 Commitment (conviction)
4.0 Organization
  4.1 Conceptualization of a value
  4.2 Organization of a value system
5.0 Characterization by a value or a value complex
  5.1 Generalized set
  5.2 Characterization

[The lowest level of behavior in the structure is the individual's awareness] . . . of the stimuli which initiate the affective behavior and which form the context in which the affective behavior occurs. Thus, the lowest category is 1.0 *Receiving*. It is subdivided into three categories. At the 1.1 *Awareness* level, the individual merely has his attention attracted to the stimulus, e.g. he develops some consciousness of the use of shading to portray depth and lighting in a picture. The second subcategory, 1.2 *Willingness to receive*, describes the state in which he has differentiated the stimulus from others and is willing to give it his attention, e.g. he develops a tolerance for bizarre uses of shading in modern art. At 1.3 *Controlled or selected attention*, the student looks for the stimulus, e.g. he is on the alert for instances where shading has been used both to create a sense of three-dimensional depth and to indicate the lighting of the picture; or he looks for picturesque words in reading.

At the next level, 2.0 *Responding*, the individual is perceived as responding regularly to the affective stimuli. At the lowest level of responding, 2.1 *Acquiescence in responding*, he is merely complying with expectations, e.g. at the request of his teacher, he hangs reproductions of famous paintings in his dormitory room; he is obedient to traffic rules. At the next higher level, 2.2 *Willingness to respond*, he responds increasingly to an inner compulsion, e.g. voluntarily looks for instances of good art where shading, perspective, color, and design have been well used or has an interest in social problems broader than those of the local community. At 2.3 *Satisfaction in response*, he responds emotionally as well, e.g. works with clay, especially in making pottery, for personal pleasure. Up to this point, he has differentiated the affective stimuli; he has begun to seek them out and to attach emotional significance and value to them.

As the process unfolds, the next levels of 3.0 *Valuing* describe increasing internalization, as the person's behavior is sufficiently consistent that he comes to hold a value: 3.1 *Acceptance of a value*, e.g. continuing desire to develop the ability to write effectively and hold it more strongly; 3.2 *Preference for a value*, e.g. seeks out examples of good art for enjoyment of them to the level where he behaves so as to further this impression actively; and 3.3 *Commitment*, e.g. faith in the power of reason and the method of experimentation.

As the learner successively internalizes values, he encounters situations for which more than one value is relevant. This necessitates organizing the values into a system, 4.0 *Organization*. And since a prerequisite to interrelating values is their conceptualization in a form which permits organization, this level is divided in two: 4.1 *Conceptualization of a value*, e.g. desires to evaluate works of art which are appreciated or to find out and crystallize the basic assumptions which underlie codes of ethics; and 4.2 *Organization of a value system*, e.g. acceptance of the place of art in one's life as one of dominant value, or weighs alternative social policies and practices against the standards of public welfare.

Finally, the internalization and the organization processes reach a point where the individual responds very consistently to value-laden situations with an interrelated set of values, a structure, a view of the world. The *Taxonomy* category that describes this behavior is 5.0 *Characterization by a value or value complex*, and it includes the categories 5.1 *Generalized set*, e.g. views all problems in terms of their aesthetic aspects, or readiness to revise judgments and to change behavior in the light of evidence, and 5.2 *Characterization*, e.g. develops a consistent philosophy of life.

Implications of the affective domain taxonomy

The existence of an affective domain taxonomy raises questions about the relation of cognitive to affective objectives. Usually the typical statement of objectives is concerned with specifying behavior in only one domain at a time. No doubt this results from the typical analytic approaches to building curricula. Only occasionally do we find a statement like "the student should learn to analyze a good argument with pleasure," which suggests not only the cognitive behavior but also the affective aspect that accompanies it.

In spite of this lack of explicit formulation, however, nearly all cognitive objectives have an affective component if one searches for it. For example, most instructors hope their students will develop a continuing interest in and certain attitudes toward the phenomena dealt with or toward the way in which problems are approached. But they leave these goals unspecified. This means that many of the objectives that are classified in the cognitive domain have an implicit but unspecified affective component that could be concurrently classified in the affective domain. Where such an attitude or interest objective refers, as it most often does, to the content of the course as a whole or at least to a sizable segment of it, it may be most convenient to specify it as a separate objective. Many such affective objectives—the interest objectives, for example—become the affective components of all or most of the cognitive objectives in the course. (For example, the instructor holds as a goal not only "ability to apply principles such as Boyle's or Hook's law," but also "interest in further pursuing the major topics of the course.")

In the cognitive domain, the concern is that the student shall be able to do a task when requested. In the affective domain, the concern is that he *does do* it when it is appropriate after he has learned that he *can do* it. Even though the whole school system rewards the student more on a *can do* than on a *does do* basis, it is the latter that every instructor seeks, for first-level objectives are nearly always oriented to what the individual *does do* as a result of his education. By emphasizing this aspect of the affective components, the affective domain brings to light an extremely important and often missing element in cognitive objectives.

Like the cognitive frameworks, the heuristic value of the affective *Taxonomy* may be its most important contribution. By its very existence, it may encourage greater development of the affective components of cognitive objectives. It may encourage people to attempt more completely to operationalize their objectives in this domain. The article (Metfessel et al., 1969) referred to earlier contains suggestions which are helpful in operationalizing the categories of the affective as well as the cognitive domain.

This area should not be left without noting an important difference between the two domains that often remains obscure. In both the cognitive and affective domains, the concern is with both overt and covert behavior. Because the covert behavior is by definition unobservable and because the teacher, both to guide learning and to determine whether it has indeed occurred, must deal with the observable, the approach to both teaching and evaluation has assumed that all covert behaviors—e.g. thinking certain ways—have certain overt consequences that can be sensed. This is particularly easy to demonstrate in the cognitive domain where certain thinking results in "right" answers, or at least in certain approaches to problems that result in demonstrable abilities to perform in certain ways. This is often true in the affective domain as well where, for example, if students like or enjoy a course, certain behaviors no longer need be required but are engaged in spontaneously and enjoyed during the period of instruction (attending concerts, reading books in the area, talking to others about the subject, etc.).

However, in other instances the link between covert and overt behavior is much less direct, less immediate, and thus less observable in the affective domain. Feelings of pleasure in reading, for instance, may have no immediate overt manifestations whatsoever, and if they occur at a low level it may be a long time before they change the probabilities of such overt action as, for example, increased reading. Thus, realistically the attempt to state goals in the affective domain in observable behavioral terms often may be impossible. It may be necessary to phrase objectives in terms of internal states that are immediate objectives and which over time will have overt behavioral consequences. This suggests the importance of stating long-term goals and of evaluating complete programs as well as single units and courses.

COMPLEX OBJECTIVES IN PROGRAM PLANNING AND EVALUATION

The fact that complex objectives are achieved only over a period of years has important implications for, in particular, program planning and evaluation. The bulk of the testing in schools is of the short-range unit and semester kind that helps teachers and students know relatively promptly whether or not they were successful. But usually such success can be judged only in terms of change in the simple behaviors of the cognitive and affective domains. Rarely does a teacher have the same students over a period of time that is sufficient for them to show changes in the more complex cognitive and affective behaviors that grow slowly and develop over a period of years. The most complex cognitive and affective domain behaviors are the product of all or a major portion of the student's years of schooling. Most measures of these complex behaviors are not sensitive enough to sense a semester's or a year's change.

This suggests that the more complex cognitive and affective goals should be matters for consensus among teachers in a major instructional unit, such as the elementary, the junior high, or the senior high school. Once this consensus has been achieved, all should consciously attempt to move the child toward these goals; and evaluation should be based on a sufficient block of learning experiences (total junior high years, for example) so that the changes may be large enough to be observable and measurable.

Such planned efforts are to be found in some school systems, but most longitudinal testing is a function of whatever commonality of complex cognitive objectives across grades exists in the commercial achievement tests used at the year's beginning and end in successive grades of the system. Similar efforts with affective objectives are rare or nonexistent.

Perhaps the use of the standardized tests provides enough stimulation with respect to assuring some continuing emphasis on the growth of cognitive skills over the grades. But long-term emphasis on any of the complex objectives, whether cognitive or affective, where little tangible evidence of success can be seen, tends to erode relatively soon unless there is reinforcement of a social kind, as in the case of a group supporting each other's efforts as a result of a commitment to a given complex goal, or the reinforcement that comes from tangible success, as in the case of being able to find measurable gains over a program.

This erosion-of-effort effect is particularly likely to occur with affective objectives. The conceptual structure of nearly all new efforts at curriculum building includes affective objectives in some important way. But as the structure is developed, such objectives cease to influence the direction of instruction, the choice of activities, or what students learn. As objectives to be achieved concomitantly with cognitive objectives, they are *not* taught directly, and it is often merely hoped that they will be achieved with no concentrated effort on them. Furthermore, teaching for affective objectives is perceived as difficult, in part because it is not as well understood as teaching for cognitive objectives. Teaching for affective objectives is, therefore, less likely to be included in the focus of new or less skilled teachers who have a struggle just to get the cognitive material across.

An additional important factor is that students will typically seek to learn those aspects of a course that will earn them a good grade, and affective objectives rarely play any significant part in grading. This results, not only from the already noted covert nature and slow growth of these behaviors, but also from the difficulty of witnessing *does do* behavior, which must be observed in the variety of circumstances in which it occurs, in contrast to *can do* behavior, which the teacher can elicit at his convenience in the classroom. Thus, special efforts are probably required to assure that affective behaviors, particularly the complex ones, are a part of the evaluation process. Such special efforts are more likely to be fruitful in the context of examining a total program. The unit and course evaluation which results from the efforts of a single teacher over short periods of time is unlikely to suffice.

This same necessity for program planning and evaluation applies as well to complex cognitive objectives. As any college English instructor will readily testify, the ability to write well grows slowly and growth continues for many persons well into the adult years. The presence or absence of significant changes in ability to think through and plan a composition are probably most appropriately identified as the cumulative result of several years of instruction. This is equally true of certain kinds of problem-solving abilities and of the ability to work creatively in certain areas. Thus, program planning and evaluation for complex cognitive skills, which are nearly as absent as for affective objectives, are considerations that are most important, but that have not so far been given anywhere near sufficient emphasis.

It may be useful to consider three levels of planning and evaluation:

1. Achievement in a school system or one of its major programs
2. Achievement in a specific course
3. Achievement within a specific instructional unit.

It would be expected that complex cognitive objectives and some relatively simple, as well as complex, affective objectives would be quite prominent at the program level. In terms of expecting significant changes these same objectives would not apply to the unit level. The emphasis at the course level would be between that at the first and third.

Because a student seeks to learn what he expects to be tested upon, complex objectives should appear, of course, at the second and third levels. This will assure that they are practiced and that further growth can build on skill developed in previous units and courses. But evidence of achievement should be looked for primarily in measures at the first level, and coordinated efforts over the span of time necessary to bring about that achievement should be provided by the planning of the curriculum that takes place at the first level.

TEST DEVELOPMENT PROBLEMS CREATED BY OBJECTIVES APPROACH

While many feel that the explicit formulation of behavioral objectives is a very useful approach, that feeling is not universal. For one thing, one always prefers to take the simplest approach to any problem. By contrast, the behavioral objectives approach moves from simple general statements to a complex array of detailed objectives. Second, because of the difficulty of stating complex objectives and ease of stating simple objectives, the objectives approach tends to focus attention on the simpler knowledge objectives, thereby causing curriculum developers to lose sight of the complex but important goals that were often their first concern. Third, the approach places the emphasis on the student when emphases on the teacher or subject matter may be more salient or more appropriate to the curriculum revision proposed. Fourth, and most importantly, such a series of steps may be quite irksome to those concerned primarily with spontaneous creativity as a way of developing curriculum. Fifth and finally, it may be impossible to state common outcomes. The foregoing are important concerns which must be discussed further. This discussion will separate those that are an integral part of the process from those that arise because of improper use of the objectives approach.

The Complexities of Stating and Analyzing Objectives

When one embarks on the route to curriculum and test development being described, one is very quickly struck with the complexity of the educational process. For example, some glimpse of the tasks involved in developing third-level objectives can be gained from the example noted earlier with respect to teaching reading. In that example, it was noted that in learning the alphabet there would be a series of third-level objectives that would give the student practice in recognizing the letters of the alphabet in isolation and, in particular, in discriminating one from another letters that are likely to be confusing. In this relatively small segment of education one can see that there are a wide variety of subobjectives, and for that matter a variety of alternatives about how to teach the alphabet, among which the educators must choose (e.g.: Should skill in tactile recognition of the letters as well as visual be included? Should the letters always be taught in conjunction with a related concept or other letters? Etc.).

Thus one concern with this approach is that complexity results. Whether the objectives approach is really more complex than any other careful and analytical approach to teaching is debatable. But the significant question is empirical: Does better instruction result? Some evidence on this point emerges from the results of programmed instruction in which an extremely detailed analysis of subobjectives is required. Programmed instruction texts vary in quality, as does all instructional material. Nevertheless it has been repeatedly demonstrated that, with successive tryouts and modification, it is possible to engineer programmed materials that consistently teach a large percentage of the students to attain a very high probability of accurate responses. Furthermore, those constructing programmed material have indicated that the analysis of the material taught which resulted from the objectives ap-

proach was one of the most important ingredients in the success of the method.

Emphasis on What Can vs. What Should Be Specified as Objectives

An important objection to the approach in terms of behavioral objectives is that the trivial learner-behaviors are the easiest to translate into behavioral objectives, particularly those dealing with *Knowledge* (Ausubel, 1967). Effort tends to be placed on these objectives and the important complex objectives are underemphasized or omitted. Atkin (1968a) made this point as a follow-up to considering the problem of complexity dealt with above. He used the example of a child studying a mealworm's reaction to a stream of warm air. He noted that the child is "learning about interaction of objects, forces, humane treatment of animals, his own ability to manipulate the environment, structural characteristics of the larval form of certain insects, equilibrium, the results of doing an experiment at the suggestion of the teachers [p. 28]," and he continued this list to great length. He then pointed out that we should:

Multiply learning outcomes from the mealworm activity by all the various curriculum elements we attempt to build into a school day. Then multiply this by the number of days in a school year, and you have some indication of the oversimplification that *always* occurs when curriculum intents or outcomes are articulated in any form that is considered manageable. If my argument has validity to this point, the possible implications are potentially dangerous. If identification of all worthwhile outcomes in behavioral terms comes to be commonly accepted and expected, then it is inevitable that, over time, the curriculum will tend to emphasize those elements which have been thus identified. Important outcomes which are detected only with great difficulty and which are translated only rarely into behavioral terms tend to atrophy. They disappear from the curriculum because we spend all the time allotted to us in teaching explicitly for the more readily specifiable learning to which we have been directed [p. 29].

It is interesting that Atkin in his objections to the procedure stated the very concern noted earlier in this chapter about the atrophy of important objectives. But the problem is not inherent in the process; it is related to its implementation. As Popham (1968) pointed out in rebuttal:

There is the danger that because of their ready translation to operational statements, teachers will tend to identify too many trivial behaviors as goals. But the very fact that we can make these behaviors explicit permits the teacher and his colleagues to scrutinize them carefully and thus eliminate them as unworthy of our educational efforts. Instead of encouraging unimportant outcomes in education, the use of explicit instructional objectives makes it possible to identify and reject those objectives which are unimportant.

The problem then becomes one of concentrating efforts on the goals that really are important, of specifying these as well as one can, and of working with them to state them better. It is questionable if emphasis can really be given to nonoperationally defined objectives. If teachers do not know how to translate them into student behaviors, how will they recognize whether the student is indeed learning them?

Orientation to Student Behavior vs. Orientation to Teacher Behavior or Subject Matter

As noted earlier, there are alternative ways of defining education. Most curriculum reformers view it from the standpoint of subject matter or teacher behavior. Others view certain kinds of pupil-teacher interaction, such as are involved in the discovery approach, as the heart of education. For both of these groups, being forced to start with educational goals and objectives seems a backward step when one group is concerned with working out how the structure of an area is translated into curriculum and the other with how to implement the "inquiry approach" to learning. Their enthusiasm frequently stems from a sudden awareness that what is being taught their children is hopelessly out of date and they want to remedy this situation as quickly as possible.

Such enthusiasm tends to build the curriculum on the basis of whatever is new and outstanding about the approach, and this is sufficient to guide the work far down the developmental road. In the past, though less so recently, it sometimes was not until the evaluator was called in to start looking at the often nearly finished product that the matter of elaboration

of goals and objectives came to the fore. The possibility of fads preceding objectives is ever present.

When the process of starting with objectives is put forward for consideration, the curriculum reformers may feel that it results in the wrong emphasis. Consider two examples, one showing a wrong emphasis and one an excessive emphasis. As an example of the former, efforts to advance the discovery or "inquiry method" of teaching emphasize student behavior as a means rather than an end. The reformers assume that if the students approach physics as physicists do, they may later behave more like scientists in dealing with scientific problems.

But viewing student behavior as an end rather than a means would suggest that if one wishes students to act as scientists do, then the appropriate question is how do such persons act? What are the behaviors to be displayed? Then one may determine whether the inquiry teaching method is indeed the best way of helping students to learn to act in this manner.

In another instance the objectives approach may lead to what is perceived by those who are subject matter oriented as an overemphasis on the complex skills and abilities (sometimes called the process approach to curriculum). Here is a criticism of such a curriculum by Atkin (1968b):

[In this curriculum] it is postulated that there are certain fundamental "skills" required in most scientific activities . . . [that] can be developed in relative isolation from the context of specific science disciplines, but that they can be applied later in the study of *any* science discipline. . . . Perhaps fewer critics would find flaws in this program if the "skills" were developed as children attempted to understand the broad science concepts (content, if you wish). But such is not the case. In this program there is only casual attention to the continuity of content. There is indeed elaborate and detailed attention to sequencing, but the sequencing is based on a conception of the scientific process. Content is present, of course. But it is present solely as a vehicle for achieving a process-oriented purpose. It is chosen on an opportunistic basis for its assumed potential in developing process learnings.

The above quotation may leave the impression that Atkin's concern is that the process approach is faulty, but as a later part of his article makes clear, this is not true. He noted (1968b) "that there is something called 'process' which can be extracted from the fabric of science and which can be taught for its own sake in isolation from content continuity." Rather, his concern was with the way the goals were developed and here he made an important point worth noting in the use of the objectives approach. He argued that part of the artificiality that this curriculum displays results from the fact that when representatives of an academic discipline (in his example, scientists) are pressed to come up with a list of behavioral goals, they tell you " . . . all that they learned about scientific method in Chapter 1 of their high school science textbook in biology or in physics. An idealized, dispassionate, methodical, lifeless picture of science is likely to result. This particular method of attempting to uncover some of the *human* elements associated with science succeeds only in providing a curriculum that is emasculated, mechanical and *dehumanized*. In point of fact, it is a caricature of science."

He then argued that a desirable alternative approach is not to ask scientists what they do but actually to observe the scientists' behavior. His caveat appears to make good sense and applies to the manner in which objectives are identified rather than the fact of identifying them.

Spontaneous Originality vs. Planned Creativity

Perhaps the most serious objection is one that is difficult, but perhaps not impossible, to eliminate from the process. This is the argument that there is a basic incompatibility between spontaneous originality and planning. A term such as "planned creativity" as used in the title of this section would, to those who raise this concern, be meaningless.

Imagine yourself a musician concerned about the paucity of chamber music to which students are exposed. You are enthusiastic about developing a curriculum that can unlock the mysteries of chamber music, can help the student to find its unusual and variously haunting, plaintive, vibrant, melodic, and even dis-

cordant characteristics, and can bring the student to "truly appreciate it." You have been eagerly selecting chamber music recordings, writing material about them, getting narrators to tape their analyses, getting teachers who are equally enthusiastic to try out and modify the material. Then a specialist concerned with evaluation says, "What do you mean by 'truly appreciate it'? How does a student act differently if he appreciates chamber music?"

While such a question may make sense to the behavioral engineer constructing a test, it is easy to see how disconcerting it would be to a person not so oriented. Atkin (1968b) suggested that the timing of these disconcerting questions may be quite important. He (1968a) stated:

Scholars who do not talk a behavioral-change language are expected to describe their goals at a time when the intricate intellectual subleties of their work may not be clear, even in the disciplinary language with which they are familiar. At the other end, the educational evaluator, the behavioral specifier, typically has very little understanding of the curriculum that is being designed—understanding with respect to the new view of the subject field that it affords. It is too much to expect that the behavioral analyst, or anyone else, recognize the shadings of meaning in various evolving economic theories, the complex applications of the intricacies of wave motion, or the richness of nuance reflected in a Stravinsky composition.

After [the scholar] . . . has produced a program that seems pleasing, it might then be a productive exercise for the behavioral analyst to attempt with the curriculum developer to identify *some* of the ways in which children seem to be behaving differently [p. 29].

Atkin (1968a) then argued that the objectives approach may interfere with classroom spontaneity as well. He pointed out that there are many pervasive ideas in science, like equilibrium, symmetry, entropy, etc., with a broad range of application.

These ideas are taught with the richest meaning only when they are emphasized repeatedly in appropriate and varied contexts. Many of these contexts arise in classroom situations that are unplanned, but that have powerful potential. It is detrimental to learning not to capitalize on the opportune moments for effectively teaching one idea or another. Riveting the teacher's attention to a few behavioral goals provides him with blinders that may limit his range. Directing him to hundreds of goals leads to a confusing, mechanical pedagogic style with a concomitant loss of desirable spontaneity [p. 29].

Popham (1968) answered this point:

Serendipity in the classroom is always welcome but, and here is the important point, *it should always be justified in terms of its contribution to the learner's attainment of worthwhile objectives. . . .* Prespecification of explicit goals does not prevent the teacher from taking advantage of unexpectedly occurring instructional opportunities in the classroom, it only tends to make the teacher justify these spontaneous learning activities in terms of worthwhile instructional ends [p. 2].

Popham might have added that if the teacher knows what his goals are, he is better able to select spontaneously arising opportunities and to take appropriate advantage of them.

Perhaps the best answer on both counts (curriculum and classroom creativity) is to question whether planning really acts as a deterrent to creativity or as a director of it. All creativity takes place within certain bounds. While it is true that one can prescribe the options too tightly for some artists, it is truly amazing what artists have done within tight bounds. Consider the creativity that poets have displayed within the limits of tight structures such as sonnets or in writing haiku, or that Bach displayed in his music. Of the latter, existentialist Jean Paul Sartre is said to have observed, "He taught how to find originality within an established discipline; actually— how to live." The discipline of planning through objectives may be too strict for some individuals, but, considering the values to be gained in using this approach, whether it is in fact too strict should be a tested rather than a foregone conclusion.

Other Objections
to the Behavioral-Objectives Approach

Arnstine (1964) suggested that the programmed instruction movement, which has a strong behavioral orientation, is basically undemocratic because it spells out in advance how the learner is to behave after instruction. Komisar and McClellan (1965) rebutted this charge by noting that under this definition

teaching by its very nature is undemocratic and that to imply democracy reigns in the classroom would not be true. Teachers have the responsibility for helping the young develop, and this implies some knowledge and wisdom about what constitutes "desirable" behavior. Society uses the schools to perpetuate itself and will remove support from schools that deviate too far.

The point of view presented in this chapter represents, qualified as it is, a rather conventional measurement point of view. Just as there are many who argue that nobody actually follows Dewey's paradigm of problem solving, so one may argue that this set of suggested steps is more an "ideal" than a practical model. Thus, several have argued that teachers just will not specify their objectives. Jackson (1966) argued that since this is the way the world is, we ought to recognize it. Raths (1968) noted that "even some exponents of writing behavioral objectives occasionally teach courses without bothering to write specific objectives for their teaching."

Popham (1968) pointed out that: "There is obviously a difference between identifying the status quo and applauding it. Most of us would readily concede that few teachers specify their instructional aims in terms of measurable learner behaviors; *but they ought to. . . .* The way teaching really is at the moment just isn't good enough."

Finally Popham (1968) stated, answering still another objection:

Some fear that if we cleave to behaviorally stated objectives which must be specified prior to designing an instructional program, we will overlook certain outcomes of the program which were not anticipated yet which may be extremely important. They point out that some of the relatively recent "new curricula" in the sciences have had the unanticipated effect of sharply reducing pupil enrollments in those fields. In view of the possibility of such outcomes, both unexpectedly good and bad, it is suggested that we really ought not spell out objectives in advance, but should evaluate the adequacy of the instructional program after it has been implemented.

Such reasoning, while compelling at first glance, weakens under close scrutiny. In the first place, really dramatic unanticipated outcomes cannot be overlooked by curriculum evaluators. They certainly should not be. We should judge an instructional sequence not only by whether it attains its prespecified objectives, but also by any unforeseen consequences it produces. But what can you tell the would-be curriculum evaluator regarding this problem? "Keep your eyes open" doesn't seem to pack the desired punch. Yet, it's about all you can say. For if there is reason to believe that a particular outcome may result from an instructional sequence, it should be built into the set of objectives for the sequence; then behavioral objectives can be devised which reveal whether the instructional sequence has effectively counteracted this affective outcome.

Implementing
the Behavioral-Objectives Approach

Atkin (1968b) pointed out with respect to the problem of spontaneity that part of the problem may lie in the timing of the confrontation of the evaluator and the curriculum developer. After the curriculum is developed he may be more amenable to assisting in objectives formulation. Some would argue that this is too late. The major development work may have been completed before the analysis is begun. It may, for example, be quite difficult to correct imbalances in development uncovered by analysis of objectives. Nevertheless, this may be the best compromise.

Atkin's suggestion implies that there may be ways to achieve the result sought by having some flexibility in approach. This is verified by a recent experience with one of our best instructors. His problem is a common one best approached by analogy. Nearly all English teachers insist that their students outline their compositions. Yet, how many students find they can write quite excellent pieces without first going through this step. Because of their particular cognitive style the "organize first then perform" paradigm is foreign to their way of working. We all know individuals like this and this was a characteristic of this particular instructor. He was using a modern learning facility and to judge how to use it properly and to measure its effect, evaluators needed to know his objectives. He flatly refused to be bothered by specifying them. He was obdurate. He did, however, allow a graduate assistant to visit his classes to try inductively to determine his ob-

jectives. Over the semester the assistant did quite well and at its end showed his work in the form of behavioral objectives to the professor. He included in his report the consequences that flowed from these statements in terms of improved learning methods and measuring devices. The professor was simply delighted. While he has not yet been converted to taking the time to specify these objectives himself, he is now an advocate of their value and has made use of them in developing new instructional devices and the evaluation instruments.

This suggests that there are ways that one can get on with the necessary task of objectives development for evaluation and at the same time show the teacher to whom this cognitive orientation is foreign that he can continue to concentrate where his heart is—on the teaching act and on improving the curriculum, the materials, and the techniques that go toward making teaching most effective.

Another means for identifying objectives involves analyzing already existing test items and evaluation instruments and, by inductive logic, developing objectives from these materials. As noted earlier, test items, being the most specific and concrete level of expression of objectives, become an operational definition of them. If there is agreement that certain measures are relevant and valid, then one has a high specificity of definition and the process of inferring the objectives that match these measures can follow. Thus in some instances, it may be more important to start with test items and work up to formulating objectives if satisfactory measures can be developed or are available. As was noted in the discussion of levels of objectives, the development of objectives is approached in stages, with work at any one level having implications for the others. Similarly, then, it is possible to start at the bottom and work up, at the top and work down, or in the middle and work both ways.

From this exploration, it is apparent that this approach can be used with some flexibility. The behavioral engineer may be doing a project a disfavor if he insists on a lengthy period of specifying behavioral objectives to the considerable discomfort of those with whom he is consulting. More flexibility and some perspective on the process as a whole may suggest that there are wiser courses to follow that may ultimately permit objectives to be derived, as opposed to a "head-on" attack. Popham and Baker (1967) in a series of rules for the development of instructional material stated as a first principle: Don't spend too much time on the initial planning stages. A better principle would suggest that all steps in the process be kept in balance and that, to maintain progress toward the ultimate goal of actual materials production, some steps may need to be tried and then re-attacked later in the developmental process, for example, to return to objectives after measures of them are available as noted above. Furthermore, as anyone who has completed a manuscript draft knows, the first draft is always the hardest. Second and third drafts follow more easily. Furthermore, once ideas are stated, other authors then use and elaborate on them and carry them forward. So any developmental effort is but one stage in a continually ongoing and interactive process of curriculum improvement. Hopefully, each new effort starts where previous efforts have left off. Thus the process must be viewed in its total perspective so that no one step holds up progress on the broad front. Specifically, it would appear that the formulation of objectives need not hold up a project. The problems in using the approach depend in large measure on the way the step of formulation is carried out.

The discussion so far has assumed that there are outcomes to the educational process that can be verbalized or specified. What if the instructor claims there are not?

Common Learning for the Group vs. Unique Learning for the Individual

Perhaps the most serious problem faced by the objectives approach is what to do when there are outcomes of an event that cannot be verbalized or specified, but about which there is certainty that they have value and that the outcomes do occur. This is the position that many humanists find themselves repeatedly

taking. Thus, novice art teachers (and maybe more experienced ones, too) are sure that the creation of some kind of composition is an important part of their curriculum, but it is difficult if not impossible to get them to agree as to what is *good* art work and *why*. Without this consensus it is impossible to help them create a curriculum that leads to the development of "good" work based on a rationale of what kind of work it is, since each curriculum is unique in reflecting the view of art and its creator.

Such a point of view is undoubtedly legitimate at this stage in our understanding of human behavior and of the humanities. Indeed, it may well be a permanent stage, for we may be asking to know the unknowable if all of the arts are idiosyncratic in nature and thus do not lend themselves to any common norm or standard-definition type of approach. Perhaps by definition art must have an element of the inscrutable if it is to be great art. Perhaps the response of the student should always be uniquely his own, and there are severe limits on the extent to which the teacher can "teach" him how to respond.

Though we may have overdrawn the extent to which this concern applies to all or any of the arts, there are no doubt some areas of applicability where the usefulness of the objectives approach is questionable. There well may be instances where the outcomes are completely idiosyncratic, and the important thing is to expose the student to the situation regardless of what results. Difficulty in stating objectives may also result when such a wide range of behaviors may result that they are difficult or impossible to classify and describe in general statements. In these situations our interest in "behavioral products" must yield to specification, as precisely as possible, of an educational process or experience undergone by the student for unspecified effect. While specification and evaluation are still relevant, they now apply to the actions of the teacher and the instructional setting (for example, recording, movie, or museum).

If one grants that these are areas where

idiosyncratic learning is appropriately the major emphasis, one must still decide in how many areas of the educational curriculum one is willing to take on faith the assumption that exposure to certain experiences will have unspecified but real values. To the extent that much of the curriculum comes under such an umbrella, there is no basis for judging the effectiveness of the teacher or the school system. We are harking back to a mystical outlook that seems hardly fitting in a scientific age of rockets and computers.

We would do a distinct disservice to ourselves if we took this point of view with respect to very much of what we now do or hope to do in education. For it is only as we know precisely what we seek that we can know whether we have indeed achieved it and how effective and efficient were the various routes to that achievement. How can the teacher know that he has indeed taught anything unless he can in some way recognize and judge success in that teaching? How efficiently and effectively can students learn if they do not know the directions in which to guide their action and cannot know when they have been successful? Finally, how can a society perpetuate itself, as all do, unless its schools include sizable portions of curriculum that result in normative behavior? It must do this just to maintain communication among its citizens. Clearly much of the curriculum must have common goals, and if this is the case, the objectives approach seems to have considerable value.

SUMMARY

This chapter is based on the premise that education could be improved if, where possible, its decision making were based on careful and deliberate analysis. In this manner, the steps in that decision-making process could be so designed that, from the standpoint of those involved in making the decisions as well as those affected, the resulting decisions included the best orientations, the proper emphases, the necessary variables, as well as providing for contingencies. The previous discussion of the steps for test construction and the explication of the role of objectives formulation in those steps follows this model in the sense that it forces the process to become highly deliberate, careful, and rational. Those who follow this route find themselves giving a conscious and deliberate consideration to a range of variables important to curriculum selection and development (for example, the student, society, demands of subject-matter competence, educational philosophy and psychology, optimal learning sequences). They are forced to plan and sequence in a very concrete way the instructional experiences that might otherwise be used in one of the many possible arrangements—no single one of which is optimal for certain goal-oriented instructional purposes. A set of external reference points and goals provides a clear instructional orientation and permits the development of evidence of success or failure in reaching those goals. Furthermore, student learning is enhanced since, as these goals are shared with students, the students are able to work with the teacher toward the attainment of the goals.

Special attention is focused on a variety of complex objectives that otherwise may be only dimly understood parts of the curriculum. A more concrete means, for example, for handling and achieving affective goals is provided so that objectives may actually be the basis of instruction and thereby achieved, whereas they might otherwise receive only lip service. Because we are more aware of them, effort can be consciously concentrated on achieving complex cognitive and affective goals and the effects of those efforts realized. These and other implications follow from this approach.

Accepting the conclusion, then, that for most of education there are common goals specifiable as behavioral outcomes, we must accord formulation and classification of these objectives central importance in the improvement of instructional procedures. That this objectives approach to curriculum and test construction is not without its problems must be admitted. But many of the problems arise from an improper application of the approach and still others yield to variations in the way the process is applied. The design of tests and other types of evaluation instruments must be shaped and guided by the objectives of the program. Until some better procedure is found, the process by which test maker and curriculum specialist join forces to clarify objectives is one of the most powerful tools available for improving education.

REFERENCES

American Council on Education. *A design for general education.* Washington: ACE, 1944.

Arnstine, D. G. The language and values of programmed instruction: part 2. *The Educational Forum,* 1964, **28,** pp. 337–347.

Atkin, J. M. Behavioral objectives in curriculum design: A cautionary note. *The Science Teacher,* 1968, May, 27–39. (a)

Atkin, J. M. Process in science education. Paper presented at the annual convention of the National Science Teacher Association, Washington, D. C., 31 March 1968. (Reported in *Educational Products Information Forum,* 1968, **8 & 9,** 6–10. (b)

Ausubel, D. P. Crucial psychological issues in the objectives, organization, and evaluation of curriculum movements. *Psychology in the Schools,* 1967, **4,** 111–121.

Ayers, J. D. Justification of Bloom's taxonomy by factor analysis. Paper presented at the annual meeting of the American Educational Research Association, Chicago, February 1966.

Baker, R. L. The educational objectives controversy. Paper presented at the annual meeting of the American Educational Research Association, Chicago, February 1968.

Bernabel, R. *Behavioral objectives: An annotated resource file.* Harrisburg, Pa.: Bureau of Curriculum Development and Evaluation, State Department of Education, 1970.

Bloom, B. S. (Ed.) *Taxonomy of educational objectives.* Handbook I. *The cognitive domain.* New York: David McKay, 1956.

Cardinal principles of secondary education. U. S. Office of Education Bulletin, 1918, No. 35.

Cox, R. C., & Graham, G. T. The development of sequentially scaled achievement tests. *Journal of Educational Measurement,* 1966, **3,** 147–150.

Cox, R. C., & Unks, N. J. *A selected and annotated bibliography of studies concerning the taxonomy of educational objectives: Cognitive domain.* Pittsburgh:Learning Research and Development Center, University of Pittsburgh, 1967.

Dyer, H. S. The discovery and development of educational goals. In *Proceedings of the 1966 Invitational Conference on Testing Problems.* Princeton, N. J.: Educational Testing Service, 1967. Pp. 12–24.

Ebel, R. L. *Measuring educational achievement.* Englewood Cliffs, N. J.: Prentice-Hall, 1965.

Educational Policies Commission. *The purpose of education in American democracy.* Washington: National Education Association and American Association of School Administrators, 1938.

Educational Policies Commission. *The central purpose of American education.* Washington: National Education Association and American Association of School Administrators, 1961.

French, J. W., et al. *Behavioral goals of general education in high school.* New York: Russell Sage Foundation, 1957.

Gagné, R. M. *The conditions of learning.* New York: Holt, Rinehart & Winston, 1965.

Hand, T., Hoppock, R., & Zlatchin, P. J. Job Satisfaction: Researches of 1944 and 1945. *Occupations,* 1948, 26, 425–431.

Havighurst, R. J. *Human development and education.* New York: David McKay, 1953.

Jackson, P. W. *The way teaching is.* Washington: National Education Association, 1966.

Johnson, S. R. Relationships among cognitive and affective outcomes of instruction. Unpublished doctoral dissertation, University of California, Los Angeles, 1966.

Kearney, N. C. *Elementary school objectives.* New York: Russell Sage Foundation, 1953.

Komisar, P. B., & McClellan, J. E. Professor Arnstine and programmed instruction. *The Educational Forum,* 1965, **29,** 467–476.

Krathwohl, D. R. The taxonomy of educational objectives: Its use in curriculum building. In C. M. Lindvall (Ed.), *Defining educational objectives.* Pittsburgh: University of Pittsburgh Press, 1964. Pp. 19–36.

Krathwohl, D. R. Stating objectives appropriately for curriculum and for instructional materials development. *Journal of Teacher Education,* 1965 March, **16,** 83–92.

Krathwohl, D. R., Bloom, B. S., & Masia, B *Taxonomy of educational objectives.* Handbook

II. *The affective domain.* New York: David Mc-Kay, 1964.

Kropp, R. P., Stoker, H. W., & Bashaw, W. L. The validation of the *Taxonomy of educational objectives. Journal of Experimental Education,* 1966, **34,** 69–76.

Lindquist, E. F. Preliminary considerations in objective test construction. In E. F. Lindquist (Ed.), *Educational measurement.* Washington: American Council on Education, 1951. Pp. 119–158.

Lindvall, C. M. The importance of specific objectives in curriculum development. In C. M. Lindvall (Ed.), *Defining educational objectives.* Pittsburgh: University of Pittsburgh Press, 1964. Pp. 10–18.

McGuire, C. A process approach to the construction and analysis of medical examinations. *The Journal of Medical Education,* 1963, **38**(7), pp. 556–563.

Mager, R. P. Preparing objectives for programmed instruction. San Francisco: Fearon, 1962. (Most recent printing under title *Preparing instructional objectives.*)

Metfessel, W. S., Michael, W. B., & Kirsner, D. A. Instrumentation of Bloom's and Krathwohls. taxonomies for the writing of educational objectives. *Psychology in the Schools,* 1969, **6,** 227–231.

Michael, W. B., & Metfessel, N. S. A paradigm for developing measurable objectives in the evaluation of educational programs in colleges and universities. *Educational and Psychological Measurement,* 1967, **27,** 373–383.

Miller, A. T. Levels of cognitive behavior measured in a controlled teaching situation. Unpublished master's thesis, Cornell University, 1965.

Payne, D. A. *The specification and measurement of learning outcomes.* Waltham, Mass.: Ginn & Co., 1968. Reprinted by permission.

Popham, W. J. Probing the validity of arguments against behavioral goals. Symposium presented at the annual meeting of the American Educational Research Association, Chicago, February 1968.

Popham, W. J. *Establishing instructional goals.* Englewood Cliffs, N.J.: Prentice Hall, 1970.

Popham, W. J., & Baker, E. L. *Rules for the development of instructional products.* Los Angeles, Calif.: Southwest Regional Laboratory for Educational Research and Development, 1967.

Raths, J. D. Specificity as a threat to curriculum reform. Paper presented at the annual meeting of the American Educational Research Association, Chicago, February 1968.

Raths, L. E. Evaluating the program of a school. *Educational Research Bulletin,* 1938, **17,** 57–84.

Scannel, D. P., & Stellwagen, W. R. Teaching and testing for degrees of understanding. *California Journal of Instructional Improvement,* 1960, **3**(1), 8–14.

Simpson, E. J. The classification of educational objectives: Psychomotor domain. *Illinois Teacher of Home Economics,* 1966, **10**(4), 110–144.

Smith, E. R., Tyler, R. W., & staff. *Appraising and recording student progress.* New York: Harper & Row, 1942.

Tyler, R. W. Some persistent questions on the defining of objectives. In C. M. Lindvall (Ed.), *Defining educational objectives.* Pittsburgh: University of Pittsburgh Press, 1964. Pp. 77–83.

Walbesser, H. H. *An evaluation model and its application.* Washington: American Association for the Advancement of Science, 1965.

3. Planning the Objective Test

Sherman N. Tinkelman
New York State Education Department

The development of a test, typically, consists of a number of sequential steps, each building upon previous activities and outcomes and each laying a foundation for later decisions and actions. The construction of a standardized test, for example, usually involves these procedures:

1. Developing the test specifications
2. Writing the test items
3. Pretesting the items and analyzing the item statistics
4. Compiling the preliminary test forms
5. Trying out the preliminary test forms to verify time limits, difficulty, reliability, etc.
6. Compiling the final test forms
7. Administering the final test forms for standardization purposes
8. Preparing norms, a test manual, and supplementary test materials
9. Printing and publication.

At each step of this test development process, proper planning is obviously of critical importance if that particular activity is to be completed successfully. In carrying out the step of item pretesting, for example, a variety of problems may arise concerned with designing the pretest forms and administering them under proper conditions to appropriate samples of examinees. Much of this book, therefore, is concerned with planning. Various chapters discuss some special aspect of planning as it relates to some particular phase of test development; for, in the work of test development, planning in the sense of establishing a purposeful design for action, anticipating problems, and giving thoughtful consideration to alternatives is both pervasive and continuous.

While this chapter is concerned primarily with the initial steps in test construction—namely, developing the test specifications—it will be seen, in the discussions to follow, that all subsequent steps in test construction are based directly on this initial planning and, conversely, that the initial planning must take into consideration the demands and the potentialities of all subsequent steps.[1] Hence this chapter serves two important functions. First, it provides specific and concrete hints on how to perform the initial planning that is required before the actual work of writing test items can begin. Second, it is a general introduction, which gives an overall view of the total test development process and the close interrelationships of the various parts, and thus it provides a background for approaching the specific problems discussed in subsequent chapters.

Careful initial planning makes it possible to avoid pitfalls, assures more efficient procedures, and results in a better end product. On the other hand, inadequate initial planning may impair seriously the quality and usefulness of the final test. For example, it may be found that the test items available for use are inappropriate, or that a solid statistical foundation for compiling the final test forms is lacking, or that it is not possible to publish the test with suitable norms or interpretative materials. At the very least, inattention to planning can lead to waste and to delay due to failure to coordinate properly the various phases of test construction.

DEVELOPING THE TEST SPECIFICATIONS

The essence of initial test planning is establishing the test specifications; that is, the sum

[1] The discussion and illustrations for this chapter have been formulated in terms of educational achievement, which is where much of the concern of educational measurement focuses. However, the sequence of decisions and operations is much the same in tests of aptitude and of traits of personality. (See especially chapter 11 for a consideration of problems in the development of aptitude tests.)

total of the qualities and characteristics that the test should possess. Ideally, the test specifications should be so complete and so explicit that two test constructors operating from these specifications independently would produce comparable and interchangeable instruments, differing only in the sampling of questions included.

Planning the test specifications is fundamentally a decision-making process. The test planner is faced with a series of specific questions: What content should the test cover? Shall separate part scores be provided? How many items should the test include? What should be the level of item difficulty? Each decision must be considered on the basis of such factors as the purposes the test planner is attempting to achieve, the manner in which he expects the test to be used, the relative effects that the various alternatives are likely to have on the validity and the reliability of the test, and so forth.

The ensuing discussion in this chapter systematically reviews the various decisions that the test constructor may need to consider. Not every problem discussed may arise in every test situation. Perhaps certain categories of decisions need not be made. However, the test constructor should at least make the deliberate determination that no action is required on a certain point. If some particular specification is overlooked, a decision has been made by default—a decision that may be enormously significant with respect to the effectiveness of the final product. Consideration is given to the following basic steps, which can be considered in the nature of a checklist to guide the development of the test specifications:

1. Define the general purposes and requirements of the test
2. Establish the specific scope and emphasis of the test as expressed by the test outline or blueprint
3. Select appropriate item types
4. Determine the appropriate level and distribution of item difficulties
5. Determine the appropriate number of items in the test and in its parts
6. Establish how the items are to be assembled in the final test
7. Prepare the item-writing and item-review assignments.

Careful attention to these planning steps assures that the subsequent work of test development can proceed on a sound basis. Compare these steps with those proposed in chapter 2 (p. 20), which are more general in their scope.

DEFINING THE GENERAL PURPOSES

When a test construction project is undertaken with only a vague conception of its purposes, the consequences can be unfortunate. The final product, while perhaps a shining example of a high-quality test brilliant in conception and in execution in terms of what the test constructor believed his task to be, may be found to fail utterly to serve the purposes of those who are expected to make use of it. The result may well be stacks of tests lying unused and unmourned in some dark storeroom. The first step in planning any test, therefore, is to clarify the purposes of the test and to obtain general agreement on these purposes among those to whom the final product must be acceptable. It is at this stage that the limits and boundaries are established within which the test constructor works.

To clarify the purposes of the test, the test developer should seek precise answers to the following questions.

1. *What specific areas of achievement are to to be measured?* There should be, of course, little question in the mind of the test constructor as to the general area of achievement with which he is concerned. He is expected to produce a reading test or a French test, or perhaps a general achievement test encompassing a number of areas. The test constructor would be wise, however, to seek an early and full understanding of what *specific* areas of achievement the test is expected to include or to exclude. For example, is it expected that a reading test provide a measure of speed of reading as well as comprehension? Is it sufficient that a French test measure fluency in reading and writing

the language, or is it considered essential that the examinee demonstrate conversational competency as well? Does "American history" for the purposes of this test begin with the first explorers, with the early colonies, or with the Articles of Confederation? Is the purpose of the test primarily to determine the extent of the examinee's information or, rather, his ability to apply this information in solving new problems? The question here is not one of deciding relative emphasis within a defined curriculum area but, rather, one of circumscribing the curricular area within which the test constructor is expected to work. Failure to define this area meticulously at the very outset is to invite confusion and frustration.

2. *Who is to be tested?* For what persons is the test intended, and what backgrounds may these persons be expected to have? Obviously, the task of the test constructor is considerably different depending on whether the test is intended for students who have completed a specific course of study in a single school system, for students in schools that are located over a wide geographic area and that adhere to different curricular philosophies, or for adults who may have had little or no formal educational training.

3. *How are the test scores to be used?* If the test is to be used largely to compare schools or school districts, the test constructor faces a different problem than if the test is to be used for pupil evaluation or guidance. If the test is to be called upon to discriminate as accurately as possible throughout the broad range of pupil achievement, the task is different than if the test is to be used to pass or fail students at the completion of a course of study or to select a small group of scholarship winners. If the test is expected to provide part scores that permit differential diagnosis of certain special skills or competencies, then particular attention needs to be given to the quality of such part scores.

4. *What are to be the time limitations?* Tests vary in length from brief 15-minute surveys to prolonged sessions of 10 or more hours of total testing time. The test constructor's primary concern, of course, is to provide sufficient time for the examinees to demonstrate adequately the type of behavior that the test is designed to measure. However, frequently there are external time requirements imposed upon the test constructor; for example, it may be found that, because of a full testing schedule during a college's orientation week, the test constructor is limited to no more than one hour of testing time. In other testing situations, there may be no limitation on total time, but it may be necessary to have test administration periods conform to classroom periods of 40 or 50 minutes each.

5. *Will there be need for equivalent forms?* Will a single test serve the purpose, or will equivalent forms be needed either immediately or in the future? Equivalent forms may be indicated if students who miss the initial testing have to be provided a second test opportunity promptly, or if the test is to be used to measure pupil status at the beginning and at the end of an experimental program. If ultimately equivalent forms will be needed, the test constructor would do well to plan their simultaneous development.

Illustrative Statement of Test Purposes

The following statement of purposes for a hypothetical test of achievement in French exemplifies the type of general statement that would be helpful:

French, as defined for the purposes of this test, consists of knowledge of French words, ability to translate French prose, knowledge of French grammar, and information about France and French culture. No attempt is to be made to include oral or aural skills except to the extent that these can be measured indirectly in a paper-and-pencil situation. This test is to be administered to high school students throughout the United States who have completed study of three years of French of the level customarily completed in grades 9, 10, and 11. The test must be designed for administration in not more than three class periods, not to exceed 40 minutes each, on separate days over a period of possibly several weeks. The resulting scores are to be used for evaluating total achievement by individual students in terms of relative standing in the norm group.

PREPARING THE TEST BLUEPRINT
Function of the Test Blueprint

The purpose of the test blueprint is to define for the test constructor, in as precise a manner as possible, the scope and emphasis of the test. While the general purpose may be to prepare a test of French, or arithmetic, knowing this seldom supplies the test constructor with an adequate basis on which to begin test preparation. To provide an effective guide for item writing and thus to assure a valid and comprehensive measure of achievement, it is necessary to define the objectives of the test more specifically.

In some cases the purpose of the test is so narrow or so clearly defined that the specific objectives of the test are self-evident. If the purpose of the test is to measure knowledge of the French vocabulary taught during a single semester or ability to solve simple equations in algebra or familiarity with the names of composers and their works, the scope of the test is narrowly circumscribed and the test maker can proceed with a reasonable degree of confidence.

In most situations, however, the scope of the test is defined only broadly by its purposes— a final examination in American history for high school juniors, a test of general high school achievement for use in a research study, a test of current skills in mathematics for placement purposes. Here the test constructor faces a difficult and perplexing problem. What should be the proper scope and emphasis of the test? On what topics should questions be asked? What types of behavior should the examinees be required to demonstrate? What is relatively important and what is relatively unimportant?

It is a frustrating experience for a test constructor to find his test criticized as "lacking balance," "testing the wrong things," or giving an "unfair advantage" to one group or another. It therefore behooves the test constructor to determine at an early stage precisely what the test should include, to establish a defensible basis for his decisions in terms of research findings or expert judgment, and then to obtain general approval of the test blueprint. Often, the blueprint can be accompanied by samples of the various types of items to be included in the test. It is far better to debate the "lack of balance" of a test while it is still at the outline stage when changes can be made easily, than when the test is ready for the printer or after the test has been administered. A clearly established test blueprint by no means eliminates changes at later stages, but it certainly should reduce the probability of misunderstandings and recriminations.

To understand the crucial nature of the blueprint, the basic concept of a test must be kept in mind. A test is a work sample. From the universe of tasks constituting achievement in the area to be tested, a test can only represent a sample. The universe of tasks in certain test situations can be finite and limited—a test of the student's mastery of the particular spelling words taught during the semester, of the 100 spelling "demons," of the chemical symbols of the major elements, or of the names and functions of the parts of a flower. Generally however, even when the area of testing is narrowly defined, the number of tasks is considered infinite for all practical purposes—an English vocabulary test can include any of 500,000 words in a dictionary; a chemistry test can include any of thousands of possible questions on chemicals and their structure, their interactions, and their uses. When the area of testing is fairly broad, samples may be drawn from any of a number of different subdivisions of the area. On the basis of the particular sample of items included in a test, certain inferences concerning the examinees in the domain from which the sample was drawn are to be made. Manifestly, such inferences can be valid only to the extent that the test provides a representative sample of the total area of measurement.

When a test is being used as a selection device, as in the selection of laboratory technicians, it may be possible to get measures of job performance and determine the relationship between test scores and job success. In this case, the general statement of the purpose of the test might be to predict the job or training criterion, and the final check on the test would be its relationship to this criterion. The role of a carefully prepared outline is to make sure that all the relevant abilities, so far as the planner can identify them, are covered in the test.

However, achievement tests generally are not used as prediction devices, and external measures of success to which test performance can be compared generally are not available.

The validity of achievement tests ordinarily can be estimated only by subjective judgments regarding the extent to which the test measures what it is intended to measure—in other words, the extent to which the test content is appropriate, fair, and representative. For a test of American history, for example, innumerable questions can be written. If the first 100 items that come to hand are chosen, there is a danger that the test may have a serious imbalance— perhaps an excess of items concerning colonial history as compared with modern history or items of a factual nature as compared with items measuring understanding of broad trends. It is possible that items dealing with certain important concepts may be ignored entirely. A person who obtains a high score in this test might not necessarily obtain a high score in a test with a significantly different emphasis. To the extent that the test is not a valid sample of the knowledges, skills, and understandings that are important, any inferences concerning an examinee's general achievement in this area are likely to be invalid.

What the test constructor must do, therefore, is to draw up a theoretical outline, or prototype, of what he considers to be high achievement in the area being measured—to be considered to have attained a high level of achievement, a student must be able to demonstrate these specific competencies in these specific areas of the curriculum. This constitutes the test blueprint. The test blueprint is, in effect, the plan of stratification that is then followed in drawing up the test sample. The task of the test constructor is to assure that all these competencies and all these curriculum areas are represented in the test sample with the same degree of emphasis with which they appear in the test blueprint. Tests such as these have sometimes been spoken of as *self-defining*, in the sense that the test itself defines what constitutes desired achievement. There is no external referent to which the test can be compared. Under these circumstances, the wisdom and perceptiveness that go into the test specifications provide the only guarantee of the validity of the test.

Of course, the mere formulation of a test blueprint does not in itself assure valid measurement. If the test maker shows poor judgment in selecting and/or little skill in writing the items, then the performance of examinees on a particular sample of items in, for example, an American history test selected by the test constructor as representative of understanding of, say, American foreign policy may not reflect accurately the examinees' knowledge and understanding of this general topic. To that extent, this sample of items may fail to make a valid contribution to the total test. Hence the blueprint is only the beginning point. Within each area of the blueprint, careful attention must be given to the selection of representative and valid items.

Also, it is possible that the particular construct of competence in American history drawn up by one test constructor may differ from the construct drawn up by another. The test constructor only rarely has a clearly defined picture of the total population of possible items from which a sampling is to be made. To further complicate matters, he usually finds it necessary to establish a hypothetical construct of what competencies a well-educated person *should* have. To the extent that others may not accept his construct, the test is not acceptable. In the case of a test used to predict an external criterion measure, the test constructor is in a position to present objective evidence of the validity of his construct. For self-defining achievement tests, however, subjective judgment remains the ultimate criterion. Hence, it is incumbent upon the test constructor to establish his construct upon as sound and defensible a basis as possible. The following sections offer helpful suggestions towards that end.

Two Aspects of Test Content

The term *test content* has been used rather broadly to cover both the subject matter of the test and the type of ability that it is thought to test. Sometimes these two aspects of test content can be treated together conveniently; for example, if "ability to compute the arithmetic mean from grouped data" is listed as a test topic, both the subject matter and the type of behavior to be tested are at once clear. Usually, however, it helps both the planner and the item writer to separate the subject matter of the test from the type of behavior to be tested and to direct attention specifically to each aspect separately. If, for example, the test outline is confined to subject matter alone, the type of behavior to be tested is left to the judgment of the item writer with quite unpredictable results. The test outline, therefore, should be used to show clearly not only what different areas of subject matter are to be covered but also the types of behavior to be elicited with respect to each area. It also should indicate the relative emphasis to be given the various topics and types of behavior to be tested.

Analysis of behavioral objectives

Since the fundamental objectives of education are ultimately concerned with the modification of human behavior, it is advisable to analyze the objectives of instruction to determine what activities and skills should be appraised in an educational test. Admittedly, there can be practical difficulties that often prevent satisfactory measurement of the ultimate objectives of education by means of a written test. Nevertheless, it is incumbent on the test constructor to define those specific behavioral objectives that reasonably may be expected to be susceptible to such measurement and to provide for those objectives in the test outline.

In this connection, a useful tool for the test constructor is the *Taxonomy of Educational Objectives*, especially the handbook on *The Cognitive Domain* (Bloom, 1956). The details of the *Taxonomy* and its importance for defining intended outcomes of the educational process are given in chapter 2 (pp. 29–30). To review, an outline of the educational objectives identified in Bloom's (1956) *Taxonomy* is given in figure 3.1.

Some test constructors have been hesitant to define educational objectives in words that seemed to them to be more impressionistic than objectively meaningful and that were based on hypothetical mental faculties whose functional independence seemed to them to be seriously open to question. As an alternative, they have argued for describing different test items ob-

I. Knowledge
  A. Specifics
    1. Terminology
    2. Facts
  B. Ways and means of dealing with specifics
    1. Conventions
    2. Trends and sequences
    3. Classifications and categories
    4. Criteria
    5. Methodology
  C. Universals and abstractions
    1. Principles and generalizations
    2. Theories and structures

II. Intellectual abilities and skills
  A. Comprehension
    1. Translation
    2. Interpretation
    3. Extrapolation
  B. Application—use of abstractions in particular situations
  C. Analysis
    1. Elements
    2. Relationships
    3. Organizational principles
  D. Synthesis
    1. Production of a unique communication
    2. Production of a plan or proposed set of operations
    3. Derivation of a set of abstract relations
  E. Evaluation
    1. From internal evidence
    2. From external criteria

FIG. 3.1. A classification of educational objectives. (Adapted from Bloom, *Taxonomy of Educational Objectives*, 1956; see especially pp. 201–207 for elaboration of this outline.)

jectively in terms of the kind of task they present or the kind of overt behavior the examinee demonstrates (Ebel, 1965; Thorndike & Hagen, 1969). On this basis an item would be classified, for example, as one that contributes to the conclusion that the examinee "knows terminology and vocabulary," "knows dates, events, persons, and places," "knows concepts and principles," "can apply generalizations and principles to new situations," "can make valid evaluation judgments," and so forth.

Regardless of what approach he chooses to adopt, the test constructor would be well advised to consider in every test situation the applicability of some type of classification of behavioral objectives. The test constructor often will not wish to establish a classification of behavioral objectives in as great detail as the classification of content, simply because the number of clearly distinguishable and practically useful behavioral objectives are usually quite limited. However, even a limited behavioral classification should help the item writer break from the confining pattern of tests limited solely to knowledge of definitions and facts.

Analysis of subject matter or content

Behavioral objectives do not exist in a vacuum. Content is the vehicle through which behavioral objectives are taught and through which, once learned, they are demonstrated. Therefore, while a test outline devoted to subject matter or curricular content alone would generally constitute an incomplete formulation of the educational objectives which the test should be designed to measure, the importance of careful and accurate analysis of content objectives should not be underestimated. If representativeness is not achieved in the content dimension of the test, the measurement of behavioral objectives will very likely be distorted as well.

The content dimension of the test outline should consist of a detailed analysis of the curricular areas that are to be considered in the test. The detail to which the test planner goes in outlining the subject matter of the test may vary widely from situation to situation according to the purposes of the test. A brief narrow-purpose test may require only a few categories of subject matter. On the other hand, a test designed for comprehensive measurement of a broad field may require a very detailed outline. Thus, a test of achievement in English might first be classified under the general areas of vocabulary, mechanics, reading comprehension, literature, and so forth. Each of these areas might be further subdivided into its major components—for example, literature might be subdivided into the three major areas of English literature, American literature, and world literature. Within English literature, it might be desirable to provide for different chronological periods and, within these periods, for specific important literary movements. Ulti-

mately, if desired, the names of specific authors and works might be listed.

The point to be kept in mind is that the greater the degree of specificity of the outline, the greater is the degree of direction given the test constructor. And thus the greater is the assurance that the final test conforms closely to the expectations of the test planner.

The content outline can have two general functions—prescription and guidance. The test outline is prescriptive to the extent that it is established as a mandate—the test writer *must* supply items in each of the classifications specified. The test outline serves a guidance function to the extent that it is offered as merely a listing of suggested ideas for possible test items. For a particular test, the outline may serve a combination of prescription and guidance functions, but what is mandatory and what is optional must be made clear to the item writers.

How detailed should a content outline be? It must be in at least sufficient detail to establish the minimum degree of prescription that must be imposed on the item writers if the test is to serve its function effectively. It may contain as much additional detail as seems likely to be helpful to item writers in suggesting specific topics on which questions might be based. Thus, if it would be immaterial in terms of the test planner's construct of a person with high achievement in literature whether that person demonstrates such achievement through knowledge of prose writings or of poetry, then no particular balance of weight between prose and poetry need be prescribed in the outline. On the other hand, if the test planner would be reluctant to place the stamp of high achievement on a person with considerable knowledge of prose writings but little or no knowledge of poetry, then some reasonable balance between prose and poetry must be prescribed in the outline. In the area of prose, it may be that the test planner would be little concerned with whether an examinee could demonstrate familiarity with the work of essayists as well as novelists. Then, while the test planner might include essays as a suggested source for items, he would not prescribe any particular balance between essays and other types of prose literature.

Examples of analyses of curricular content are presented in the two illustrative blueprints reproduced as figures 3.2 and 3.3 which follow. In each of these, the total content area of the test has been divided initially into a number of major curricular areas, in the one case chronological and in the other topical. These are the prescriptive areas to which relative weights have been assigned. For item-writing purposes, each major curricular area would be further subdivided, to help assure a better coverage of that area and to suggest ideas for specific questions. For example, Period V in figure 3.2 was expanded by the test constructor as follows:

PERIOD V 1940—PRESENT

Theme: The impact of America's role as a world power on American education

1. Informal Education
   America's international leadership; the "shrinking" world; cold wars; expanding role of foundations; television; change in composition of population; religious revival; UNESCO; propaganda; behavioral engineering; paperback books; new leisure and increased participation in the arts; popular culture

2. Formal Education
   Expansion of junior colleges; adult education in and out of schools; educational TV; explosive growth in college enrollment; development and reform in educational curriculums: programmed instruction, team teaching, ungraded schools; increased bureaucratization; role of philanthropic foundations

3. The Increased Role of the Federal Government
   Research and development; legislation: NDEA, G.I. Bill, NSF; the role of the Supreme Court in education: race, religion and freedom

4. Ideas
   Existentialism, alienation

5. People
   Barzun, Bestor, Black, Bruner, Clark, Conant, Gardner, Hook, Kerr, King, Maritain, Murray, Niebuhr, Riesman, Rogers, Rugg.

	Knowledge	OBJECTIVES Understanding				
CONTENT AREA	Recall of factual information about people, theories and developments	Origins of educational practices	Political relation of education and society	Relationship of the formal educational institutions to informal education	Relationship between American and European educational history	WEIGHT
Period I 1600–1690 Spread of Western culture to the Americas	5	5	4	3	3	20
Period II 1691–1779 Emergence of a distinctive cultural norm in the English speaking colonies	5	5	4	3	3	20
Period III 1780–1875 The popularization of culture	6	6	5	4	4	25
Period IV 1876–1939 The secularization and standardization of education	6	6	5	4	4	25
Period V 1940–present The impact of America's role as a world power on American education	3	3	2	1	1	10
WEIGHT	25	25	20	15	15	100

75

FIG. 3.2. Blueprint of a college proficiency examination in history of American education

| | OBJECTIVES | | | | |
COURSE CONTENT	Knowledge	Comprehension (Translation, Interpretation, Extrapolation)	Application	Analysis	Total
I. Methods of Science; Hypotheses Concerning the Origin of the Solar System	5	2		3	10
II. Minerals and Rocks	5	5			10
III. Changes in Land Features	4	4	2		10
IV. Interpretation of Land Features	2	2	6		10
V. Animal Classification	2	4	4		10
VI. The Plants of the Earth	4	4	2		10
VII. Populations and the Mechanisms of Evolution	3	3		4	10
VIII. Variation and Selection		1	5	4	10
IX. Facts of Evolution and the Theory that Explains Them		2	2	6	10
X. Evolution, Genetics and the Races of Man		3	4	3	10
Total	25	30	25	20	100

FIG. 3.3. Two-axis chart of specifications for a final examination in natural science. (From Nelson, *Let's Build Quality into Our Science Tests*, 1958.)

The two-way classification

A convenient procedure that has been used to present simultaneously both dimensions of a test is the two-way chart as is illustrated in figures 3.2 and 3.3. The *content classification* is placed along the left-hand side of the chart. This classification, whether prescriptive or suggestive, may be in as great detail as desirable; for example, in figure 3.2, it was assumed that it would be sufficient to maintain a balance among five major chronological periods. It is common practice to indicate the relative weight or importance of each content category in terms of percentage weights adding to 100. These weights are entered in the last column at the right; for example, in the test outlined in figure 3.2, apparently it was desired to give somewhat larger weights to Periods III and IV than to Periods I and II and relatively minor weight to Period V.

The *behavioral classification* is placed across the top of the chart, and the percentage weight of each behavior category is placed at the bottom. Thus, it was proposed in figure 3.2, that items that would demonstrate "understanding" by the examinee were given a weight of 75 percent in this test, as compared with 25 percent for "knowledge" items. The "understanding" items, in turn, were further subdivided into four different types of "understanding," each carrying an assigned weight.

If all the behavioral objectives are equally appropriate for each content classification and if it is desired to have all behavioral objectives represented in each content area in proportion to the general importance of these behavioral objectives, then the percentage weight of items in each cell is given by the product of the two marginal totals for the corresponding row and column divided by 100. In figure 3.2 for example, if proportional representation was given to the "knowledge" objective in each content category and if 25 percent of all items were "knowledge" items, then 25 percent of the

Period I items, i.e. 5 percent of the total test, would involve "knowledge" relating to that period. $\{(25\times20)/100=5.\}$ The percentage of weight in each of the other cells can be found in similar fashion. It should be noted that the blueprint indicated the relative weight or importance that was to be assigned to each cell in terms of a total weight of 100 percent and not necessarily the number of items in each cell.

Another example of a test blueprint, this time for a high school final test in natural science, was presented in figure 3.3. In this case, a more detailed prescriptive classification was made of the content objectives, and the behavioral objectives were analyzed somewhat differently.[2]

There is no single scheme of classification that can serve all situations. For each test, it is necessary to develop a unique classification scheme that is appropriate for the special purposes of that test, that describes the achievement of the examinees in a meaningful manner, and that can be helpful to item writers in achieving comprehensive coverage of the domain of that test.

Figure 3.3 illustrates that it is not always convenient or desirable to have all behavioral objectives apply in the same proportion to all content categories. It is clear that the test planner in this instance has made provision for testing the "application" objective with reference to "changes in land features," but not with reference to "methods of science." Moreover, the test planner apparently felt that the "application" objective should have a greater weight in "interpretation of land features" (6 percent) than in "changes in land features" (2 percent).

In the absence of any good reason to the contrary, uniformity of distribution, as in figure 3.2, is a reasonable first assumption. It reduces the possibility of confounding; that is, a type of spurious picture often results when, for example, an examinee achieves a low score in a particular behavioral objective largely

because items measuring that behavior happen to be concentrated in a content area in which he is relatively poorly prepared, while he might have attained a better score if the items measuring this behavioral objective had been spread among other content areas where he would have had an opportunity to demonstrate this behavior to better advantage. The possibility of confounding is particularly serious if part scores are to be reported. On the other hand, it is not wise to force a uniform distribution in a situation where it is not appropriate. Behavioral objectives, such as "knowledge of definitions" or "knowledge of generalizations," often are more appropriate for certain content areas than others. In social studies tests, map-reading skill is a common behavioral objective. Such an objective obviously will be more appropriate to geographical content than to historical content. Similarly, ability to interpret tables, or cartoons, may well be an objective having differential applicability. The test constructor should not hesitate to make adjustments in the blueprint based on logic and reason, while ever mindful of possible confounding effects.

The experience gained in writing test items often contributes to a further clarification of the test objectives, so frequently it becomes desirable to alter the test outline as the item writing proceeds. There are few activities, in fact, that contribute more effectively to the clarification of objectives than the task of translating them into specific test items. In general therefore, it is undesirable to view the original test outline as "frozen"; rather, the test author should deliberately strive to improve the test outline as the test is being built. Probably, the test outline cannot be considered "final" until after the items have been written and tried out, and the final test assembled.

Nevertheless, deviations from the test outline should not be made simply for reasons of expediency. The test constructor may be tempted to make adjustments in the weights as practical problems arise. Ideas for good items in a particular area may be hard to find and even more difficult to work out satisfactorily. However, the assigned weights, even if rough esti-

[2] Other examples of blueprints are given in *Comprehensive Examinations in a Program of General Education* (Dressel, 1949).

mates, constitute the best available estimates of what the weights should be. If the test blueprint rests upon a sound judgmental basis, the test constructor has the professional obligation to obtain items of satisfactory quality and in sufficient numbers to satisfy blueprint specifications. Only as a last resort should significant departures be made from the established outline for reasons of convenience and then only with full realization of the implications for the validity and effectiveness of the test.

Suggestions for Developing the Test Outline

Sometimes the statement of purpose for a test leads at once to the formulation of a test outline; at other times considerable labor is involved. Particularly for educational achievement tests of the self-defining type, the detailed definition of the test objectives may depend upon the analysis of behavior, of jobs, of textbooks, or of curriculums and may entail consultation with subject-matter specialists.

When a teacher is constructing a test for use only in his own classes, perhaps he can be the sole judge of the appropriate weight for each subject-matter topic. When a test is expected to have wide usage, perhaps nationwide, it becomes essential that the judgments of a number of experts in the subject-matter field be solicited. Consequently, it has become standard procedure in the planning of a subject-matter test, especially one for a broad market, to analyze perhaps a dozen of the more widely used textbooks in the field to secure a tentative list of topics to be tested and some indication of the appropriate emphasis to be given to each of them. The median number of pages devoted to a topic is often taken as a rough index of its importance, as judged by textbook writers and editors. This serves also as a crude index of the amount of time given to each topic by classroom teachers. Analysis of syllabi from representative cities and counties scattered throughout the United States provides another method of determining the behavioral objectives and subject-matter content to be measured by objective tests.

In addition, the advice and assistance of authorities with respect to the topics of the test outline and the emphasis on each generally should be sought. The panel of expert consultants should command wide respect, and, in most cases, the panel should constitute an adequate representation of professional thought in the field. For example in the construction of a biology test, it may be unwise to consult only with persons who represent the traditional taxonomic school of biologists; a test that would satisfy this group of experts might be quite unsatisfactory to others in the field who advocate an ecological approach, or a chemical-physical approach, to the study of biology.

Ordinarily, content experts serving as consultants cannot be expected to write test outlines from scratch. The most profitable way to use consultants usually is to submit to them a tentative outline, perhaps one based on analyses of representative syllabi and widely used textbooks. The consultants then are asked to criticize or revise the topics in the outline, to suggest additional topics, and to weight each of the topics finally agreed upon. Sometimes the weights derived from syllabus and textbook analyses and the test constructor's subjective judgment are presented on the outline given to the experts for criticism, but there is the disadvantage that the experts tend to accept such weights and to refrain from suggesting changes in them. In general, therefore, a test outline without any indication of the emphasis to be given the topics is preferable for this purpose. A request to assign weights to the topics is then most likely to stimulate active and thoughtful consideration of the problem.

The following is an illustration of the use of expert judgment in constructing a test outline for a paper-and-pencil mechanical comprehension test. Careful study of handbooks and manuals for mechanics suggested that eight topics for which paper-and-pencil test items could be constructed covered the field rather thoroughly. A list of these eight topics, therefore, was prepared and sent to 16 individuals considered to have a high degree of competence in mechanical comprehension or its measurement. Instructions accompanying the list were, in part:

On the accompanying sheet are brief descriptions of each of eight topics. Please read the descriptions and then estimate what percentage of the total test should be devoted to each topic. Write your estimate in the parentheses given. Your eight estimates should add up to 100 percent. If you think some element of mechanical comprehension other than the eight listed is important in mechanical comprehension as a whole, please write a brief description on the line below the description of topic 8.

The median percentage assigned by the consultants to each topic was used as an indication of the weight to be given each topic in a test of mechanical comprehension (see table 3.1).

TABLE 3.1

Topics for Mechanical Comprehension Test with Their Assigned Weights

Topic	Weight
1. Technical vocabulary	15
2. Tools	10
3. Hydraulics	7
4. Properties of materials and structures	9
5. Uses of mechanical devices	15
6. Mechanics	15
7. Electricity	8
8. Mechanical movements	21
Total	100

PLANNING THE TYPES OF ITEMS

Once the test outline has been established, the next concern for the test planner is to specify the type of item that should be prepared. If no specific directions are given by the test planner, different item writers, faced with the same item-writing assignment and even with the same source materials available, will come up with different item types.[3] In the initial stage, the test planner has two main concerns: (*a*) to achieve a reasonable degree of consistency of format purely for the purpose of producing an editorially coherent test that is pleasing and readable and (*b*) to use any item types that may be peculiarly appropriate, or avoid those that may be inappropriate, to the specific

---

[3] The strengths and weaknesses of different types of items, as well as the principles to be observed in using each item type to its greatest advantage, are discussed in chapter 4.

purposes of this test—from the viewpoint of the objectives to be measured, the procedures for scoring the test, or the manner in which the test is to be administered or printed. If a number of item writers will be involved, it is especially important for the test planner to establish the degree of uniformity in item format that is required and, conversely, the degree of flexibility and discretion that may be allowed the item writers without impairing the effectiveness of the test.

Relation of Item Type to Test Objectives

In general, it is possible to measure the same test objective with a variety of different item types. In certain instances, however, the choice of item type may reflect a deep-seated conviction on the part of the test planner concerning the basic nature of the trait being measured and the appropriate method of getting at that trait.

Though specific test authors have strong convictions, there is far from perfect agreement among different authors on a number of points. For example, in a test of arithmetic problem solving, some test constructors insist that all questions should be of the completion type on the principle that the nature of problem solving dictates that the examinee provide the answer from his own experience rather than by selection from a number of alternatives offered to him. On the other hand, other test constructors, while not concerned with providing the examinee with alternative answers, are disturbed by the possibility that the examinee may be able to work out the correct answer simply by trying out each of the alternatives in turn; hence, they include in every question an option to the effect that the correct answer is none of those listed. Still other workers have so strong a personal conviction that the "none-of-these" option constitutes a serious source of error that they studiously avoid use of this alternative.

Similarly, in testing reading comprehension, a variety of approaches can be used. One can present a reading selection of several hundred words on which a group of from 10 to 15 questions may be based, a series of somewhat shorter reading selections on each of which 3 to 5 questions may be based, or a larger number of very brief reading selections each followed by a single question. Sometimes reading comprehension is measured by omitting key words from reading selections and asking the examinee to provide the word that would best convey the thought of the passage. These different approaches may be thought to reflect somewhat different reading skills, and the type of skill involved may be quite important to the test constructor's conceptualization of the functions he wishes to measure.

An issue that frequently arises with respect to the use of groups of items based on a reading selection, or on a problem situation or on a single theme for matching two sets of concepts, is whether the use of such a group of items would unduly restrict the sampling that can be made from that cell of the blueprint. Perhaps a more representative sampling can be made by using independent questions, each involving a totally different concept or idea. Since comprehensiveness of sampling of each objective is closely related to test validity, a clustering of items might be thought to reduce validity.

In the view of certain test constructors, the particular objective involved may demand that a unique type of behavior be required on the part of the examinee. Whereas ordinarily an examinee may be asked to choose the single best answer in a multiple-choice item, the test planner may feel that in this situation, for example, the objectives of analysis and evaluation are so critical and the content so unstructured in nature, the examinees must be permitted to respond in a situation where more than one answer may be correct or where he may indicate the reasons for choosing a certain answer. Even such an apparently simple issue as to whether an item stem may be stated in negative form (e.g. "Which is the *least* likely result?") may arouse heated discussion, with some test constructors arguing that certain objectives can be measured only by a negative approach and others maintaining that the danger of confusion inherent in negative items outweighs any possible value.

If the test is to have a clearly defined and consistent philosophy of measurement, in close harmony with the objectives of the test, it is incumbent upon the test planner to give careful consideration to the type of test items to be written for each part of the test and to spell out their specifications in precise detail.

Relation of Item Type to Scoring

A major factor affecting item type is the degree of scoring objectivity considered necessary. If tests are intended for extensive use, they are, almost without exception, made relatively objective; and, among the various forms of so-called objective tests, the more objective—such as the multiple choice—are to be preferred in such situations to the less objective—such as the completion. This is true whether hand scoring or machine scoring is contemplated. If the tests are to be scored by machine, however, then selection of the highly objective types of items is clearly mandatory at the present time, although advances in optical scanners may permit more flexibility in this regard in the future.[4]

Furthermore, the nature of the answer sheet or the scoring procedure may well dictate certain item features. Sometimes a school or agency, in order to avoid a variety of answer sheets, will pick a particular answer sheet style as standard. If this answer sheet style only provides for four-option items, the test planner necessarily must forego five-option items or long lists of matching items. If the scoring machine is of a type that only recognizes one best answer, then obviously the test planner must forego items that permit more than one correct answer.

If the test includes items in which there is a significant chance of guessing the correct answer, the test planner should be alert to the fact that correction for chance success becomes an additional issue in planning. Should examinees be instructed to guess or not to guess? Should a greater penalty be applied for wrong answers than for omissions? From the measurement point of view, if all examinees have sufficient time to answer all items, there is little practical difference in the relative rank-

---

[4] A discussion of the use of optical scanners, of their present limitations and future potential in test scoring, is presented in chapter 8; see especially pp. 226–232.

ing of students on corrected scores as compared with uncorrected scores. Hence it is common practice among test constructors to encourage examinees to answer all questions, even if they are not entirely sure of the correct answer, and to make no correction for chance success. On the other hand, many educators argue that to encourage guessing on the part of examinees is poor educational practice, since it fosters undesirable habits.[5]

Relation of Item Type to Administration Features

If the test is likely to be given by different persons, often by persons with little training or experience in test administration, then it behooves the test planner to take precautionary measures to minimize the difficulty of administering the test. Inclusion in the test of items of only one type greatly simplifies the administration of the test, especially when a single overall

---

[5] EDITOR'S NOTE: *The Problem of Guessing.* One topic that tends to creep into a number of chapters, because of its relevance to various aspects of test design, construction, scoring and analysis, is that of guessing and statistical corrections for guessing. Because of its relevance at various points, and in order to reduce repetition and duplication, the issues are discussed briefly by the editor at this point. The issues are identified, but no universal solution is provided. The topic is one upon which opinion of test-makers and theorists appears to remain divided.

"Guessing" is a loose, general term for an array of behaviors that occur when an examinee responds to an alternate choice question to which he does not "know" the answer. The behaviors that may, and probably do, occur are many and varied. They include, among others:

1. Eliminating one or more answer choices judged to be definitely wrong
2. Making use of unintended semantic or syntactic cues available from the wording of the question or the response options
3. Falling into traps set by the ingenious item writer, e.g. cliché-like choices that sound plausible but are wrong
4. Responding on the basis of some element in one of the response choices that attracts him, but at a relatively low level of confidence
5. Using some essentially random fashion of responding —in the extreme, flipping a coin or marking some specific response position or pattern of positions.

Of course, examinees may also omit items on which they do not feel sure of the correct response, and differences appear for different individuals, different schools, and different national cultures in tendency to omit the item when one is not sure of the answer.

Scoring Formulas

Obviously, if individuals respond purely at random, as by rolling a die or using a table of random numbers, they will get some items right. On the average the number right will be k/n, where k is the number on which they guessed, and n is the number of choices per item. The number of items on which random guessing occurred that will be gotten wrong will average $k - k/n$ or

$$\frac{k(n-1)}{n} \quad \text{or} \quad (n-1) \cdot \frac{k}{n}.$$

Since one can never know directly how many were gotten right by guessing, the number is inferred from the

number wrong as being $W/n-1$, where W is the number wrong. Given this estimate of the number gotten right by guessing, it is possible to "correct" or adjust for this effect, using the formula

$$R - \frac{W}{n-1}$$

to provide an estimate of the number of items to which the person "really knew" the answer. Similarly, it is possible to correct statistics on single test items using an expression such as

$$P_c = \frac{R - \dfrac{W}{n-1}}{R + W + O}$$

where

P_c = corrected percent of right answers,
R = number getting item right,
W = number getting item wrong,
O = number omitting item,
n = number of answer choices in an item,

to get an estimate of the percent of examinees who "really knew" the answer to the item.

This logic, however, applies only when the behavior of the examinee is as described in behavior 5 above; that is, he responded as if he were using a table of random numbers. Even then it is applicable only as the *expected average number* of right responses, and values for a single examinee or a single item will show a fairly wide dispersion around the value to be expected on the average. So the adjustment as applied to the score for a specific person or to the proportion succeeding on a specific item is at best a crude and approximate adjustment—because of chance variations in a statistic based on a small sample of data, on the one hand, and because the basic assumption of random choice is rarely met, on the other.

It should be noted that if every examinee answers every item, there will be a simple linear relationship between a score that is simply the number of right answers and one that is calculated by subtracting from the rights a fraction of the wrongs. Since, in this case, $R + W = N$, where N is the number of items, the corrected score becomes

$$\frac{nR - N}{n-1}$$

and depends only upon R, since the other factors are constant over all examinees. Thus, correction for guessing has a significant influence on individual differences

time limit applies. Use of a single item form reduces the amount of time necessary for giving directions and can help to eliminate the possibility that failure to understand directions may invalidate test scores.

Some test constructors have argued that use of several different item types lends interest to a test through its variety. However, the interest value of a test would seem to depend primarily upon the quality of the items rather than upon their external form. If the items are competently constructed even though all of one form, there will usually be no problem of maintaining interest. On the whole, arguments for use of as few item types as possible, and preferably only one, probably outweigh arguments for variety.

Relation of Item Type to Printing Features

Finally, certain aspects of the test items may be dictated by the manner in which the test is to be printed. If the number of pages of the test booklet must be limited, questions based on long reading passages or requiring extensive artwork may be ruled inappropriate. If the type size is large and the size of the page small,

---

in score only when items are omitted and when the number omitted varies appreciably from one examinee to another or from one item to another.

Instruction to Examinees

One can attack the problem of guessing at two points, through adjustments in scoring procedure after the individual has responded on the one hand and through instructions that attempt to control his response before he has responded on the other. Thus, a second aspect of the problem concerns the instructions that should be provided to the examinee. Should he be firmly instructed to answer every item, even if he has no idea which is the correct answer? Should he be instructed to answer only if he is "sure" of the right answer? Should he be given some intermediate instruction, inviting him to respond if he has some idea of what the correct answer is (or some assurance that one or more choices is wrong)?

To instruct the examinee to respond only if he is "sure" of the right answer has received little support among test-makers, though one suspects that this instruction is more prevalent among classroom teachers. On the one hand, there will certainly be individual differences in standards of certainty, so that the instruction will be interpreted differently by different examinees. At the same time, the instruction would seem generally to prevent examinees from displaying knowledge that they actually possess. The timid and insecure would seem to be most severely penalized by such an instruction.

More common has been an intermediate instruction worded somewhat as follows: "You may respond even if you are not sure of the right answer, but do not guess blindly." There is often some such additional instruction as: "A penalty of a fraction of a point will be assessed for wrong answers." This type of instruction is appropriately used only when a penalty *is* in fact assessed for wrong answers, and in that case a wording similar to the one given should presumably be provided. This instruction will not, and does not really try to establish for all examinees a uniform standard of confidence, at which point they will elect to mark an answer. To establish such uniformity is probably impossible, and one criticism of *any* approach that leaves to the examinee the decision of whether he has enough knowledge about a question to hazard a choice is that individuals may deviate by varying degrees from an optimum strategy.

(In general, the deviation seems likely to be in the direction of being too conservative, unless the test-maker is very skilled at making seductive wrong options. In many test items there are cues that permit a person with only limited knowledge to exclude one or more options so that the odds in his favor are improved.) Basically, one has no real alternative to using some such instruction if the correction formula is to be used. The presumption is that when this type of instruction is combined with use of the correction formula, differing individual thresholds of willingness to respond will be of relatively little importance, because the correction formula will compensate for them.

The argument in favor of instructing examinees to answer every item is that if the instruction is followed (and if time is available for all to complete the test), correction of scores for guessing ceases to be of any importance. As was indicated above, corrected and uncorrected scores arrange people in identically the same order and correlate perfectly with one another. Two further arguments are that standards for responding are more uniform for all examinees, and that the scoring of tests is simpler and less subject to clerical error.

Arguments against instructing examinees to answer every question are of three types, which might be designated psychometric, pragmatic and "moral." From the psychometric point of view, it is argued that guessing, to the extent that it approaches random response, introduces variance that is pure error into the final score, and that this variance may be expected to lower the reliability of the score. To the extent that guessing *is* truly random, this argument is unimpeachable. However, when the individual responds with one of the other modes of response listed earlier, it is hard to say just what is the nature of the variance that is introduced. Systematic elimination of options and random selection from among the remainder imply partial knowledge, and such behavior may generate valid variance between individuals. Susceptibility to seductive wrong options certainly does not represent random behavior, but how it relates to the ability that the test is measuring is hard to say. Choices made at a low level of confidence probably represent a mixture of subthreshold knowledge and irrelevant past experience. So it is hard to state with assurance just what mixture of variance is generated by the instruction to answer every item, though there is good reason to be concerned that enough of it may apthen integrated groups of items requiring the examinee to refer back frequently to a single set of directions or to a single code list would be inconvenient. If the test is to be reproduced directly from typed copy, then certain complex item forms requiring interlineations or different styles of type may be impracticable.

Illustrative Specifications of Item Type

On the basis of the total test construction picture, the test planner should develop a precise definition of the types of items desired, indicating both the requirements to be followed strictly and the areas in which flexibility is to be allowed. The following serves to illustrate a hypothetical set of item specifications:

Items should generally be of the four-option best-answer multiple-choice type, with options numbered 1 to 4. True-false or completion items should not be used. No more than one matching item should be used in each of the major content areas, and any such group should involve 3 to 5

---

proach random error so that the reliability of the resulting score will be reduced.

The pragmatic argument is that even though urged to do so, some examinees will fail to answer every item. They may fail to do so because of lack of time; they may fail to do so because they are temperamentally incapable of committing themselves to a choice on a question to which they do not know the answer. Liberal time limits reduce the first problem, and a warning that only two or three minutes remain and that one should quickly mark any unmarked items could eliminate the residue of that problem. However, such marking would clearly generate the type of random error variance referred to in the previous paragraph.

Overcoming the extreme reluctance to guess that seems to characterize some examinees is a more difficult problem. It is especially acute when pupils have been reinforced, as they are in some school systems, for being cautious and not committing themselves until they are sure. One suspects that if a culture were consistent in rewarding the examinee for answering all items, few would fail to respond in that way, but so long as practice remains divided one is likely to encounter some examinees who will resist the instruction to respond to all items.

The argument labeled "moral" would affirm that it is somehow "wrong" to guess at random. One argument offered in support of this wrongness is that in marking a wrong response one is "practicing error" and strengthening the tendency to give this response in the future. Connectionist learning theory of 40 years ago could be interpreted as asserting that occurrence of a connection strengthens that connection, even if no reward or reinforcement is provided. The issue here is what the connection is that is strengthened. If the examinee's mental process is "I think A is the answer, so I will choose it," the connection between the question and answer A appears to be explicit and its strengthening to have some probability. However, this is not random guessing; this is responding in terms of misinformation. When the mental process is "I haven't the foggiest idea what the answer is, so I might as well mark A," there seems to be little connection between the substance of the question and that of answer choice A. So where guessing is most random, the likelihood of any deleterious educational influence seems least.

Beyond that, the moral issue seems to be a vague generalization of disapproval of all types of gambling and games of chance. As such, it is hardly subject to discussion or evaluation in a chapter such as this.

Current Practice

Practice in United States testing organizations and among test publishers with respect to using the correction formula remains divided. The College Entrance Examination Board continues to use such a correction on their Scholastic Aptitude Test, college admissions achievement tests and Advanced Placement Tests. However, the American College Testing Program uses for its tests a score that is simply the number right. Almost without exception, test publishers distributing tests for use by local school systems use a simple "rights" score on their tests.

The fact that among test publishers, as distinct from organizations administering large-scale testing programs, use of simply the number of correct answers as the score is almost universal may be attributable as much to practical convenience as to psychometric conviction. The publishers are selling their tests to many local users, who may do their scoring locally either by hand or by using any of a variety of types of scoring equipment. The requirement to apply a correction formula represents one additional complication and one additional possible source of clerical error. It has probably been as much to simplify the scoring procedure as for any more profound theoretical reason that the simple "rights" score has been adopted by these groups.

With a complex of educational, psychometric and practical issues involved, it is perhaps not surprising that test-makers have failed to reach a consensus on the correction-for-guessing problem. The issues have been recognized and debated throughout the short history of objective testing, but agreement does not seem an immediate prospect. One point on which there does seem to be agreement is that the instructions given the examinee should be consistent with the scoring procedure that is actually used, so that the examinee may have a clear picture of how his errors will be treated.

It has been suggested that the happiest solution to the guessing problem lies not in correcting for guessing but in preventing it. The greater versatility of current optical-scanning equipment permits forms of response that could not be handled in the test-scoring machines of 1950. Some of these formats that permit a great variety of responses are considered in chapter 8. To the extent that the test-maker's ingenuity can adapt them to the varied measurement tasks that he faces, the problem of obtaining credit by guessing may be solved by eliminating it at its source.

R.L.T.

items and 5 to 7 alternatives. Use of problem situations, reading passages, tables, drawings, etc., as the basis for groups of items would be highly desirable. Each such group should contain at least 3 items but not more then 5 items. The introductory material for each group should not exceed the equivalent of 250 words of textual material. The negative stem and the none-of-these option should be avoided. As far as possible, item stems should be of the question type rather than the incomplete statement type. All items should be independent; in no case should the correct answer to one item depend on the answer to a previous item.

PLANNING THE LEVEL AND RANGE OF ITEM DIFFICULTIES

One of the most important responsibilities of the test planner is to define the level and the distribution of the difficulties of the items that are to compose the final test. Obviously, test items can vary widely in difficulty. For any given individual or population, item writers may choose to prepare items that are intended to be relatively easy or relatively hard. The decisions made in this regard may have major implications for the validity and reliability of the final test and for its general suitability for the purpose it is intended to serve.

It is essential, therefore, that the test planner describe the general design of the item difficulties for the guidance of those who are to write the items, perform the item analysis, and compile the final test. To the extent that the design was sound and the subsequent steps in test development conformed with this design, the test is successful in accomplishing its purpose. If the design was faulty, then conformity to this design in the subsequent work of test development only serves to perpetuate the errors made.

Definition of Item Difficulty

When an item is scored as right or wrong, the difficulty of the item is commonly defined as the percentage of examinees answering that item correctly. Thus, if 32 percent of the examinees answer an item correctly, the item is said to have a difficulty index of 32 percent, or .32, usually indicated by the letter p. The difficulty index may vary from 0 for an item answered correctly by no examinee to 1.00, for an item answered correctly by all examinees.

The percentage of examinees answering the item correctly, it will be noted, is the same as the mean item score.

When used in this sense, difficulty has meaning only in terms of a particular reference group. The same item may be easier for college students, for example, than for high school students. Thus, in any discussion of item or test difficulty, or when giving assignments to item writers, it would be well to be sure that the reference group is defined explicitly.

Item difficulty also may be expressed for a particular individual or for individuals of a specified level of ability. If an item is administered once to a single individual and is scored as right or wrong, the difficulty of that item for that individual is 1.00 if he answers it correctly and 0 if he answers it incorrectly. However, it is helpful to think of the difficulty index of an item as the probability of success of individuals of that level of ability on an item of that level of difficulty. That is, to say an item has a difficulty index of p for an individual of ability A is to say that, if an item of difficulty level p were administered to a large number of individuals of ability A, or if an individual of ability A were to answer a large number of items of difficulty level p, then the expectation is that p percent of the answers would be correct.

The difficulty index may be adjusted to eliminate the effect of chance success by the examinees. In a free-response type of item, where there is a large range of possible responses by the examinee, it is commonly assumed that guessing by the candidate plays little or no part. In a multiple-choice item, on the other hand, it is likely that a certain percentage of the examinees who do not know the answer correctly answer the item as a result of guessing. The extent to which guessing is entirely random, rather than based on partial information or on substantial hunches, never can be precisely determined in the case of any specific item. Nevertheless, it is often useful to estimate what percentage of the examinees actually knew the correct answer. For example, if a four-option item is answered correctly by 70 percent of the examinees, then it can be assumed that the 30 percent who failed the item and apparently guessed wrong were distributed, on the average, with 10 percent guessing each of the three wrong alternatives. Most probably, therefore, there were another 10 percent who guessed the correct answer, so that the percentage of candidates who actually knew the correct answer was very likely closer to 60 percent than to 70 percent. Some test makers consider difficulty of items corrected for chance success a matter of interest, especially if items of different types are to be compared.

Optimum Difficulty

Determining the optimum level and distribution of item difficulties in a test is a rather complex problem. The solution depends on such factors as the nature of the trait being measured, the intercorrelations of the items, and the specific purposes of the test planner. It is not the purpose of this chapter to present the statistical and mathematical theory underlying the relationships between item parameters and various test characteristics. However, to provide a better understanding of the test-planning function, it may be helpful to illustrate, in a general way, the kinds of decisions that the test planner might be called upon to make concerning item difficulty.

Where the purpose of the test may be to determine whether the students have mastered certain highly specific skills, such as the spelling words taught last week or 15 new words in Spanish vocabulary, the teacher may expect all items to have a difficulty value close to 1.00. To the extent that students answer any item with less than 100 percent accuracy, the teacher and the students are disappointed.

More commonly, however, achievement tests are designed to differentiate examinees with regard to their competence in the field being tested. The examinees are not expected to obtain perfect or near perfect scores. Rather, the test is deliberately designed to give a broad spread of scores so as to obtain the best possible discrimination among all the persons taking the test. There is no established standard of passing or failing. Usually, the test presents a norm for interpretation of test scores in terms of percentile ranks or other measures of relative standing in the group.

In a situation of this type, and for items having the rather low order of intercorrelation that is typically found in ability tests, it is generally agreed that the best test is one composed of items having a medium level of difficulty and a narrow range of difficulty. The evidence is that this design serves to increase the variance of test scores and to increase the reliability of the test.

What is meant by a medium level of difficulty? Specifically, in a test composed of items in which the chance factor of success may be ignored, as in completion items, an examinee of average ability should be able to answer about one-half of the items correctly—i.e. the average item difficulty for the average examinee should be .50.

Where chance success is a factor in answering the items, as in multiple-choice items, one might expect that the optimal item difficulty level would be such that the proportion of right answers by the average examinee would be .50 after correction for chance; that is, the average item difficulty level *before* correction for chance would be halfway between the chance probability of success and 1.00 (Lord, 1952). However, it has been demonstrated that the test constructor would do well to design the test so that the average item difficulty would be somewhat easier than that level. For example, in a five-option multiple-choice test the chance probability of success is .20. The difficulty level midway between .20 and 1.00 would be .60. However, the optimum average item difficulty is in fact found to be at a level somewhat easier than .60, about .70. In a test composed of items with four options, with chance probability of success at .25, the optimum average item difficulty is at a level somewhat easier than .63, about .75. The explanation for this shift toward relatively easier items lies in the fact that the error variance due to chance tends to be greater for more difficult items where more guessing occurs.

That tests should have a fairly wide spread of item difficulty, from very easy to very difficult, might at first seem to be a plausible assumption. The fact is that items that are very easy or very difficult add little to the effectiveness of a test of this kind. In general, the test reliability and the variance of the test scores increase as the variance of the item difficulty distribution decreases. That is, it is generally preferable that the items in a test have a fairly narrow range of difficulty around the average difficulty level. However, when the test content is very homogeneous (so that item intercorrelations are high) or the group tested is very heterogeneous, a wider spread of difficulty may be called for. In an actual test situation, a very high degree of uniformity of item difficulty is seldom obtainable. Even if item writers strive consciously for uniform difficulty, some degree of spread of item difficulty may be expected.

Not all tests are designed primarily to achieve maximum discrimination among all the examinees. Sometimes a test is designed to serve a *screening* function—perhaps to select a small group of the best examinees, as in the case of a scholarship examination, or perhaps to weed out a relatively small group of examinees, as in selection of persons to be admitted to a training or educational program. In this case, items of medium difficulty for the total group may not be the most appropriate. If a test is to select a small percentage of the best candidates, it may be a fairly difficult test for most examinees; if it is designed to screen out only a small percentage of the weakest candidates, it may be a fairly easy test for most examinees.

If chance is not a factor, it is generally accepted that a screening test should be so designed that the examinee whose ability would place him exactly at the cutting point should have a 50-percent probability of success on the typical item included in the test. Suppose, for example, that a test is designed solely to award scholarships to the top 10 percent of a candidate population. It might be thought, at first, that an appropriate difficulty level would be one such that the average item would be answered correctly by 10 percent of that candidate population, or that the probability of success of the average examinee on the average item would be .10. This is not the case. Rather, it has been demonstrated that the best test for this purpose would be one in which an ex-

aminee whose ability places him at the 90th percentile of the candidate population would have 50-percent probability of success on the average item. What the probability of success would be for the average examinee in the candidate population on such an average item is not immediately apparent. For example, if the candidate population is homogeneous, including many examinees with high ability, the average candidate in that population may have a probability of success on the average item of perhaps .30 to .40. However, if the candidate population is heterogeneous in ability, including many examinees of relatively low ability in comparison with the top 10 percent, the average candidate in that population may perhaps have zero probability of success on items of the difficulty level included in the test. (Of course, if chance success is a factor, as in multiple-choice tests, then the uncorrected item difficulty for the examinee at the cutting point must be correspondingly easier than 50 percent.)

In screening tests, as in tests designed to arrange persons in order of ability, it is found that a narrow range of difficulties is preferable to either a wide range or to uniformity of item difficulties. Such a procedure increases the flexibility of the test. While under one set of circumstances, a 25-percent cutoff might be appropriate, in another situation, because of changes in the demand for or supply of examinees, it may be desirable to cut off 30 or 40 percent. Hence it may be desirable to design the test so that, while it may be less than maximally efficient at the 25-percent cutoff, it would retain a rather high level of efficiency over a range of possible cutoff procedures in the general area of the 25-percent cutoff. The general rule of thumb already advanced for multiple-choice tests—average difficulty at a level a little easier than the 50-percent level for the person at the cutoff score, with some dispersion of difficulty—will serve to enhance such flexibility (Cronbach & Warrington, 1952).

Estimating Mean Test Score

The distribution of the test scores is a function of the items that compose the test. To a considerable extent, the ultimate score characteristics of the test are susceptible to control by careful planning.

There is a direct and invariant relationship between mean test score and mean item difficulty, which can be expressed:

$$M_t = n\bar{p}, \qquad [1]$$

where

$M_t =$ the mean of the test scores of the examinees,

$n =$ the number of test items, and

$\bar{p} =$ the mean of the difficulties of the items.

If the mean item difficulty for a certain group of examinees is p percent, then the mean percentage score of these examinees will be p percent and their mean raw score in the test will be p percent of the number of items in the test. This is a mathematical identity and is true in every case without exception, regardless of the range in individual item difficulties or the intercorrelations among the items. Of course, if item difficulties are estimated from a sample of examinees and not from the total test population, then the relationship holds precisely for the sample but not necessarily for the total test population because of possible sampling errors in estimating the item difficulties.

From the viewpoint of the test planner, this relationship enables him to predict the mean score in the test he is designing. If he is prescribing items averaging 30-percent difficulty and a 120-item test, he may anticipate a mean test score of about 36; whereas, if he is prescribing items averaging 70-percent difficulty, he may anticipate a mean score of 84. If $\bar{p}$ is expressed in uncorrected form, then $n\bar{p}$ is the mean of scores not corrected for chance success; if $\bar{p}$ has been corrected for chance success, $n\bar{p}$ is the mean of scores similarly corrected.

Estimating the Standard Deviation of Test Scores

For effective test planning, the test constructor often needs, in addition to an estimate of the mean level of test scores, an estimate of the probable dispersion of test scores about that mean. There is available a rule-of-thumb procedure for estimating the standard deviation

that, while rough and approximate, often is found to be extremely useful for practical planning purposes. Assuming that the items in a test are generally similar in level of difficulty, the standard deviation of the scores of a test can be estimated by the equation:

$$\sigma_t = n\sigma_{\bar{p}}\bar{r}_{it}, \qquad [2]$$

where

$\sigma_t =$ the standard deviation of the test scores,

$n =$ the number of items in the test,

$\sigma_{\bar{p}} =$ the standard deviation of scores on an item of average level of item difficulty, and

$\bar{r}_{it} =$ the mean point biserial correlation of a single item with total test score.

At this early stage in test planning, the test constructor does not have precise knowledge of all the variables upon which the standard deviation of the test depends. One of these variables, the number of items, he can control positively. The second variable, the standard deviation of the average item, may be approximated from the average item difficulty level that he specifies for the test. The third variable, the item-test correlations, he cannot in a real sense specify. What he can do is predict the level of item-test correlations that competent item writers should be able to achieve. Within these limitations, the test constructor can, even in the planning stage, arrive at a reasonable estimate of the probable standard deviation of the test that he is designing.

Consider the probable value of $\sigma_{\bar{p}}$, the standard deviation of the scores on a typical item. This value will depend directly on the difficulty of the item. If $\bar{p}$ is the percentage of examinees passing an item of average difficulty, then the standard deviation of that average item is $\sqrt{\bar{p}(1-\bar{p})}$. Item difficulties ultimately can be determined fairly accurately by tryout and item analysis. In this planning stage, the test constructor is interested in determining what the item difficulties should be or what the consequences would be if the item writers succeed in framing questions at the difficulty level specified in the test plan. Applying the value of $\bar{p}$ that the test planner projects for the test, he can approximate the value of $\sigma_{\bar{p}}$ in equation 2.

Similarly, while the average item-test correlation, $\bar{r}_{it}$, also can be determined precisely only by empirical item analysis after tryout of the test in its final form, the test planner again can make certain shrewd guesses that enable him to establish a general framework for the test in the planning stages. It should be borne in mind that equation 2 involves the correlation between score on an item and total score on the test as a whole. If the test for which the standard deviation is to be estimated is limited in scope to a single content area or behavioral objective, an estimate can be made of the probable item-test correlation in equation 2 on the basis of previous experience with that particular type of item. Thus, in one battery of high school achievement tests, including items of about 50-percent difficulty for high school seniors, it has been found that average item-test correlations regularly run about: social studies items, .40; science items, .50; mathematics items, .60; vocabulary items, .70. This pattern is not at all uncommon. Vocabulary and mathematics tend to be fairly homogeneous content areas in which relatively high item-test correlations can be obtained by competent item writers. However, in other areas, such as social studies, even competent item writers do well to achieve average item-test correlations of .40 to .50.

However, suppose the test is a broad-scope examination covering a variety of different item types. In general, an item may be expected to correlate higher with score in a test composed of items similar to it than with composite score in a test including many different types of items. With due consideration to the heterogeneity of the parts, it is generally possible to arrive at a reasonable estimate of the probable average item-test correlation for the test as a whole. For example, in a composite examination where the average item correlation with part-test score is about .50, the average correlation of the same items with composite test score perhaps might be reduced to about .30.

For the particular test that the test constructor has on the drafting board, therefore, he

can assume a specific number of items, an average level of item difficulty, and an expected level of item-test correlation. With these estimates, he can apply equation 2 and derive an estimate of the expected test standard deviation. For example, for a 100-item test composed of items of 80-percent difficulty, in which the average item-test correlation may be expected to be about .30, it can be estimated that the total scores would have a standard deviation of about 12 points. It can be observed that as soon as one has estimates of the average item difficulty and the test standard deviation one can immediately estimate reliability using the Kuder-Richardson formula #21, which is expressed

$$r_{11} = \frac{n}{n-1}\left[1 - \frac{n\bar{p}(1-\bar{p})}{\sigma_t^2}\right].$$

It might be noted, in this connection, that the standard deviation of the test scores is much more sensitive to a small change in average item-test correlation than to a small change in average item difficulty. Thus, if even a relatively small increment in average item-test correlation can be obtained by making items somewhat easier, the discriminating power of the total test is improved.

Illustrative Applications

Generally, the test planner strives for as large a standard deviation as possible. Within limits, the greater the variability shown by examinees in the number of items correctly answered, the more accurate is the measure of relative achievement.

Sometimes the novice test planner will be surprised to find the uncomfortable results to which his initial specifications lead him. Suppose that he has specified for a 60-item four-option test that the average uncorrected item difficulty is to be .50. This implies a mean score of 30. Now, if it is reasonable to assume an average item-test correlation of .40, the standard deviation of the test will be about 12 points. Consider, however, that the expected chance score will be 15 and that a set of chance scores will distribute themselves around this mean with a standard deviation of about 3.5.

Thus scores up to perhaps 22 could reasonably represent pure chance. There is now a testing situation in which examinees falling 2/3 of a standard deviation or more below the mean are getting scores within the chance range, so that perhaps 25 percent of the scores in the group will lie in this range of chance scores, and differentiations within this group will have questionable meaning to say the least. On the other hand, if average item difficulty were specified as 70, the mean score would be 35 and the standard deviation 11. Under these circumstances, a perfect score of 60 would be 2.3 standard deviations above the mean, and the range of probable chance scores would end 1.2 standard deviations below the mean. Thus, only 10 percent or so of examinees would be falling within this chance range and only 3 or 4 percent would get a perfect score.

There is a special form of the screening test in which estimation of the score distribution may be of particular concern to the test planner. In this type, the purpose is to determine whether the examinee meets some standard of achievement defined by the test, usually indicated as a "pass mark" such as 65 or 70 percent. Illustrative of this type is the typical school final examination, the civil service test, or the test for professional licensure. Sometimes such tests, while establishing a pass mark, are disguised normative or selection tests in that the raw scores are scaled to percentage grades by means of some arbitrary conversion procedure. However, where test scores are not scaled and the examinee must actually answer 65 or 70 percent of the questions correctly in order to pass, the test planner faces a unique task. The total test must be of such difficulty that a person whose ability just meets the established standard just achieves a passing score.

Ultimately, what the passing score should be can best be determined after test tryout. Where an adequate criterion exists, correlation of test scores with the criterion may be helpful in determining the level of test score that will be predictive of a satisfactory criterion score with reasonable confidence. Lacking a suitable criterion, a substitute procedure would be evaluation by expert judgment of the qualities of persons achieving scores at the critical level. For example, do teachers believe that students who have achieved minimum competence fail the test in excessive numbers or that students lacking such competence pass in excessive numbers?

However, at the stage of test planning, it is incumbent upon the test constructor to reach some preliminary estimate of appropriate difficulty. The most practical procedure is to make some estimate of the percentage of examinees who reasonably may be expected to possess minimum competence among the total group of examinees who normally would be expected to take the test and to gauge the difficulty of the test accordingly.

For any given level of probable average item difficulty and average item-test correlation, the mean test score and the standard deviation of the test scores can be estimated by equations 1 and 2. The distance of the pass mark above or below the mean then can be found in standard deviation units. Assuming the test scores to be normally distributed, reference to a table of the normal curve would indicate the probable percentage of examinees who would attain passing scores. For example, if the mean test score is 60, and the standard deviation is about 15, then a passing score of 70 would be attained by about 25 percent of the examinees. If it is desired that a considerably larger percentage of the examinees pass the test, it would be necessary to pitch the items at a somewhat easier average level of difficulty, so that the mean test score would be higher.

These examples will serve to illustrate how the test planner can analyze a test situation in terms of the purposes of the test and the probable ability of the examinee population and then design the difficulty of his test accordingly. That competent judges can arrive at useful a priori estimates of item difficulty, in terms of both relative difficulty and absolute value of difficulty for a specific population, has been demonstrated by Lorge and Diamond (1954). The usefulness of such estimates is strongly enhanced when judges are provided with items of known difficulty to serve as a standard of comparison to help in evaluating the probable difficulty of new items for the same population of examinees. Nevertheless, it must be kept in mind that subjective judgment is only a preliminary approach to, and not a substitute for, pretesting and item analysis. Because the test planner has requested items of a specified level of difficulty is no assurance that he gets them. Because he believed that items would have a certain degree of homogeneity is no guarantee that they turn out that way. And test score distributions are more often skewed than symmetrical. Only when these assumptions about item parameters have been verified empirically can the test planner be confident that the test functions in the manner desired.

PLANNING THE NUMBER OF TEST ITEMS

An important feature of the test plan is a specification of the number of items to be included in the test as a whole and in the various parts. The test blueprint established merely the relative weights of the various parts and cells; it did not determine the number of items in the test as a whole nor establish the number of items, as opposed to the weights, in each part.

The proper number of items to include in the test as a whole and in each of its parts depends on a number of factors, each of which must be given careful attention by the test constructor. First, the relative weights assigned to the various parts of the test in the blueprint must be assured. Second, the item numbers must be sufficient to achieve the minimum standards of reliability established for the test. Third, both of these objectives must be achieved within reasonable and practical limitations of testing time. Each of these factors—weight, reliability, time—makes certain demands in relation to the number of items. It is the task of the test planner to anticipate these demands, to harmonize them where possible, and to make appropriate compromises and adjustments in the test plan as necessary.

After the desired number of items has been established, the test planner then must determine the number of items that should be prepared by the item writers, making due allowances for anticipated item mortality. Planning concerning numbers of items cannot be rele-

gated entirely to the posttryout period. By that time, it may be discovered that the number of items prepared by the item writers is totally inadequate for the purposes to be accomplished. More seriously, if a test of minimum standards of reliability cannot be produced in conformity with the original specifications, the time to determine whether a test of different specifications will be acceptable is before active test development gets under way, not after.

Relation of Number of Items to Part-Test Weights

In developing the test blueprint, the test constructor assigned certain relative weights to the various parts of the test. These weights were intended to apply whether the test was designed to yield a number of separate part scores for diagnostic purposes or only a single "global" score as a measure of overall achievement. The purpose of the assigned weights was to assure that the various parts would contribute to the composite score in proper relation to their judged importance.

Where a criterion is available and the validity of each part test can be appraised by its correlation with the criterion, it is possible to determine what multiplier should be applied to each part test by multiple regression techniques. These multipliers will generate a score that has the highest correlation with the criterion possible for the existing part tests. A further procedure (Horst, 1949) will indicate how a given amount of testing time should be divided among the several part tests to produce an instrument that has the highest possible validity within the specified limits of testing time.

In the case of a self-defining test, there is no criterion available and no means of establishing weights on that basis. Instead, it is desired to assign weights to the various parts, representing different curricular areas or behavioral traits, on the basis of subjective judgment as to the role that these parts should play in determining the composite score. Theoretically, the role of a part test can be defined in various ways—its relative contribution to total score standard deviation, its relative contribution to total score variance, its relative correlation with total test score, its relative freedom from error variance, and so forth (Gulliksen, 1950).

A common and useful practice in test planning is to consider that the parts of a test will have equal weight in determining total test score if the parts have equal standard deviations. Accordingly, if the test constructor wishes the parts to have *unequal* weight, in accordance with the judged importance of the tests from the viewpoint of content validity, then he can approach that objective by designing the test so that the standard deviations of the various part scores will be in proportion to the desired relative weights as indicated in the blueprint.

The procedure usually followed to achieve such differential weighting of the parts of a test is to assign a number of items to each part in approximate proportion to the desired weight of that part. The standard deviations of the parts of a test, and, therefore, their relative weights, may generally be assumed to be roughly proportional to the numbers of items in these parts. For example, if the "understandings" part of a test should have twice the weight of an "information" part, then the "understandings" part should be allocated twice as many items.[6] This procedure should be quite adequate in most practical situations, even if the actual weight may in fact differ somewhat from the intended weight. After all, the type of judgment involved in establishing the desired weight is usually of a rough and approximate nature, so that complicated procedures designed to achieve with a great degree of precision a set of weights that were only approximate to begin with are not often warranted. Nevertheless, the test constructor should be alert to the possibility that, under certain conditions, gross deviations of effective weights from intended weights may occur and hence be a cause for concern.

In equation 2, it was seen that the standard

[6] This relation of standard deviation to length is only approximate, and, in actual fact, the standard deviation increases somewhat less rapidly than the length. For example, if a 10-item test with reliability of .60 is doubled to 20 items, the standard deviation will be about 1.8 times as great.

deviation of a part test, like the standard deviation of the total test score, is a function of three factors: the number of items, the difficulty of the items, and the item-test correlation (referring here to the correlation of each item with its own part score rather than with total score). It is only when the parts of a test have comparable item difficulties and comparable item intercorrelations that their standard deviations will be approximately proportional to the numbers of items. Such comparability is a reasonable first assumption in many instances. If comparability is not a reasonable assumption, appropriate adjustments in the design of the test may be considered.

In a particular achievement test, for example, it may be desirable to include questions sampling a specified content area, although it is known that the examinees have had little preparation in that area and therefore that the items probably will be quite difficult for them. This practice may be followed perhaps to give the test greater face validity or perhaps to have the test serve specific instructional or supervisory purposes. In other cases, it may be desirable to include items in a certain blueprint area, although the examinees may generally be expected to do very well on such items. An example would be a test that is designed to measure the extent to which the examinees have mastered certain specific objectives of instruction that have been well taught. What will be the probable effect of such item difficulty differences on the standard deviation of the part tests and on their relative weights? Minor differences in average item difficulty, other factors remaining equal, would not affect the relative standard deviations of the parts to any great degree. However, major differences may need to be taken into consideration. If the average item difficulty in the various parts of a test is generally about 50 percent and if the average item difficulty in one particular part is much lower with the same general level of item-test correlations, then equation 2 suggests that the weight of this part would be depressed. Perhaps this would be just as well if this part is included more for appearance than for actual measurement value. On the other hand, if the average item difficulty in the other parts is generally about .80 or .85 and in this one part is closer to .50, then relative weight of this part would be increased. This may be an effect in direct contrast to that desired by the test planner. In that case, he can estimate the probable size of the standard deviations, using appropriate values in equation 2, and can proceed to adjust the number of items in the atypical part so as to attain relative standard deviations in closer proportion to the desired weights.

Similarly, in certain circumstances, the test constructor may wish to take into consideration in his test design departures from the assigned weights that he may expect to result from differences in average item-test correlations in different areas of the test blueprint. (In fact, part-test standard deviation is much more sensitive to a change in average item-test correlation than to a change in average item difficulty.) From equation 2, it is apparent that if two parts of a test have equal numbers of items and equal item difficulties, but one has an $\bar{r}_{it}$ equal to .60 and the other an $\bar{r}_{it}$ equal to .30, the first part would have a standard deviation equal to twice the standard deviation of the second and the first test would have twice the weight in determining the composite score. Should the test planner wish to counteract the greater weight of the first part, he would have to include twice as many items in the second part as in the first part in order to achieve approximately equal standard deviations and weights.

Adjustments of this kind, however, should be made only if the differences in item difficulty and in item homogeneity are likely to be sufficiently great to result in significantly different sets of weights. Thus, it is not general practice to weight the individual items in a test in proportion to their standard deviations because it has been found that when a large number of scores is to be combined it makes relatively little difference what set of positive weights is assigned. When a small number of test scores is to be combined, as when dealing with part scores, differential weighting may make a significant difference in the composite but only if the sets of weights are quite different. For example, the

set of weights 1, 2, and 3 applied to three-part tests is not likely to give a significantly different composite than if the set of weights 1, 2, and 4 were applied. The weights 3, 4, and 5 would give essentially the same results as the weights 2, 4, and 6.

Furthermore, consideration must be given to possible undesirable effects that may result from adjusting the weighting of part tests in relation to their expected standard deviations. It can be argued that the test with higher average item-test correlation is the more reliable test and that it should therefore be allowed to exercise greater weight in the composite. Certainly, if a part test has a very low $\bar{r}_{it}$ and this situation is attributable to poor quality of the items rather than to heterogeneity of content, one should hesitate to weight the score in this part excessively, either by applying a multiplying factor or by adding more items of the same type. The effect may be to blow up the size of small, unreliable score differences, which would then contribute an excessive amount of error variance to the composite score. On the other hand, if the effect of differences in part-test weights is not taken into account, it must be kept in mind that the assigned blueprint weights will not be realized in the final test.

It is not necessary for the test constructor to vary the number of items in the parts of the test in order to achieve differential weighting of these parts. The same result can be achieved by the use of multipliers in the scoring process. If the parts of a test have equal numbers of items and can be expected to have equal standard deviations, the various part scores can each be multiplied by a constant proportional to the desired weight of that part.

Whether the test constructor chooses to control the relative weights of the test parts by using multipliers or by varying the number of items depends on the particular test situation. If items are to be presented in cyclical arrangement, for example, the numbers of items of different types must be equal. Weighting, if desired, can be accomplished only by the use of multipliers applied to each part. On the other hand, if equal numbers of items are not essential to the test design, the use of part multipliers may be found to be a nuisance and a hazard in scoring, even when scoring is done by machine.

Another possible consideration is that the blueprint areas weighted more heavily usually require a larger number of questions in order that all important topics may be sampled adequately. Varying the number of items in proportion to the importance of the blueprint area permits better sampling within blueprint areas at the same time.

In any event, it is clear that the problem of weighting the parts of a test cannot be avoided simply by ignoring it. If weights are not applied consciously and deliberately by the test constructor, he will in effect have weighted the parts by default. If the test constructor merely provides for adding raw part scores, he is in effect weighting the tests in proportion to their standard deviation. Either the test constructor weights the tests, or the tests weight themselves.

Relation of Number of Items to Test Reliability

Reliability, as is developed in chapter 13, may in one sense be considered as the accuracy with which the sample of items represents the universe from which they were drawn. What degree of reliability in the test will be satisfactory depends on the purposes and circumstances of the test. A test designed to compare individuals requires a higher degree of reliability than a test designed to compare groups. Should the test be designed to provide separate part scores, as well as a total score, then the reliability of each part score also must be considered.

The minimum acceptable reliability depends on the seriousness of the decisions to be made about examinees. If the purpose of the test is to place students in broad instructional groups, with ample opportunity for shifting from one group to another as learning progresses, the consequences of faulty measurement may not be critical. If the cutoff score is to be used to award jobs or to grant scholarships, reliable measurement may be critical indeed.

In general, the reliability of a test or test part, as defined above, is a function of the item intercorrelations (or the item-test correlations)

and the number of items. Within limits, the higher the average level of item intercorrelations in a test, the more reliable it will be. For any given level of intercorrelations, the longer the test, the more reliable it will be.

The size of the item intercorrelations depends on the nature of the area being tested and on the skill of the item writers. In any given test situation, there is a practical upper limit for the item intercorrelations that the test planner needs to recognize and to accept. Planning for a test of satisfactory reliability then becomes, for the test planner, a matter of determining the number of items, of the type that he may reasonably expect to be submitted by the item writers, that he needs to include in the test in order to achieve in the total test and in its parts a level of reliability adequate for his purposes.

Certain minimum standards of test reliability should be maintained in accord with the purposes of the test. If the test is designed for individual diagnosis, the test planner may wish to assure a reliability of at least .90, whereas for group survey purposes he may tolerate a reliability of .75 or .80. If the test is designed to provide part scores for individuals, he may wish to establish, for example, a reliability of .85 or .90 for each separate part.

In order to achieve a minimum degree of reliability in a test or test part, assuming a given level of item-test correlation, what is the minimum number of items for which the test constructor must make provision in his test plan? Some clues as to a practical answer to this question can be obtained by application of the following variation of the Spearman-Brown formula, which is developed in chapter 13:

$$r_{tt} = \frac{n\bar{r}_{it}^2}{1 + (n - 1)\bar{r}_{it}^2}, \qquad [3]$$

where

r_{tt} = the reliability of the test (or test part),
n = the number of items in the test (or test part), and
$\bar{r}_{it}$ = the average item-test correlation in the test (or part test).

By use of equation 3, assuming a test (or test

part) of given length and assuming a given value of the corresponding average item-test correlation, a rough and somewhat conservative estimate can be made of the reliability coefficient. Conversely, assuming certain values for the minimum desired level of reliability and for the average item-test correlation, the equation can be solved to provide a rough estimate of the number of items that will be required to achieve that degree of reliability.

For example, suppose that the test blueprint includes a 15-item part test in which it can be expected that the average correlation between items and part-test score will be about .50. If these values are substituted in equation 3, the reliability of this part of the test can be predicted to be about .83. But suppose the test constructor wants a minimum reliability of .90 in this part test. What is the minimum number of items of equal quality that would be required to achieve that level of reliability? If r_{tt} in equation 3 is set equal to .90 and the equation is solved for n, the value of n is found to be equal to 27. In other words, the length of the part test would have to be close to double the original length. Whether it will be possible to have a test with this number of items may well depend on practical limitations of time. Nevertheless, it is of critical importance that the test planner establish the minimum reliabilities demanded by the purposes of the test and determine the related test characteristics that appear necessary to attain such minimum reliabilities.

Relation of Number of Items to Time Limits

After establishing the number of items needed to achieve the desired part weights and minimum test reliability, the test planner must then explore the implications with respect to time requirements. An examinee will require different periods of time to answer different items. An item that one examinee can answer quickly may take another examinee quite a bit of time. Furthermore, the time required by an examinee will not be particularly related to the general difficulty level of an item. It may take only a brief time to answer a difficult item incorrectly; it may take a relatively long time to

work out correctly the answer to an easy item. The time required by an examinee to answer an item is a function, rather, of the mental and manual processes involved. Vocabulary items may require only 10 to 15 seconds each—only as much time as it takes an examinee to read them. The usual multiple-choice question may take 45 to 60 seconds. A complicated mathematics problem or a complex reading selection may take 4 to 5 minutes.

The number of items appropriate for inclusion in a test also depends on the extent to which it is intended to place a premium on speed of performance. A common fault in many tests is inadvertent contamination of the measure of level of performance by the factor of speed. Most tests of comprehension in reading, for example, yield scores that are a mixture of speed and level of comprehension. This matter should be given careful consideration when a test is planned, and the number of items included in the final form of the test should be dependent on a conscious decision either to introduce speed of response or to eliminate it.

In most achievement test situations, assessment of speed of response is not an important measurement objective, and so the test constructor should plan to allow examinees sufficient time to demonstrate their maximum performance level. Even where speed is not a factor, however, it is not usually practical to allow all examinees sufficient time to answer all items. Individual differences in working speed are generally so great that the slowest workers would require an inordinate period of time. Furthermore, no matter how much time is allowed, there are always a number of examinees who seem to be psychologically incapable of relinquishing a test paper voluntarily before time is called. The test constructor usually will wish to plan a time allowance for his test that will be adequate for perhaps from 75 to 90 percent of the examinees to finish.

What the test planner needs to consider, then, is the average time per item that may be required by the examinee who stands at perhaps the 15th percentile in speed of working. If this time should be 45 seconds and if there are 40 items in this part of the test, then obviously a minimum of 30 minutes must be allowed in order to have 85 percent of the examinees finish the test.

One of the purposes of a tryout of the final test is to verify the adequacy of the time allowance. Prior to the test tryout, the test constructor arrives at an estimate of average working time per item on the basis of his judgment and his previous experience. In addition, it is usually instructive to review published standardized tests and note the time allowed by other test constructors for similar items and examinee populations.

Of course, the test constructor is not always at liberty to allow the full time that he may consider necessary. For a school test, he may be limited to a single class period of 45 minutes, or perhaps to two such periods at most. In a civil service test, it may not be practicable to require more than a single examination session of three hours.

Hence the planning of a particular test may become a matter of judicious compromise. Can the length of the test be reduced to fit the allowable time without critical loss of test reliability? Perhaps it will be necessary to sacrifice the reporting of separate part-test scores. Perhaps it will be necessary to use a different type of item, one that can be answered more rapidly. Instead of items measuring the interpretation of complex reading passages, for example, it may be necessary to settle for a type of item that will not provide as satisfactory a measure of this type of reading ability but will provide a more reliable measure of general reading ability in the time available.

From the viewpoint of professional test standards, the reliability of a test is a major consideration. If a minimum degree of reliability is required for a certain purpose and if it appears that it will not be possible to include a sufficient number of items to accomplish that degree of reliability because of externally imposed time restrictions, the professional integrity of the test constructor would demand that he report flatly that the job cannot be done satisfactorily under the conditions imposed. If a college faculty committee wants a 30-minute placement test that provides reliable discrimina-

tions among students in mathematics, social studies, science, and English, they would be well advised that they cannot have it. Either they must provide more testing time, or they had better settle for a more modest objective.

Relation of Number of Items to Test Tryout

It is clear that the number of items to be included finally in the test and in the test parts is established as the end product of a developmental planning procedure. Beginning with the test blueprint and the assigned weights, the test planner makes successive readjustments to the numbers of items in his test plan on the basis of the expected standard deviations of the various parts, their anticipated reliabilities, and the probable time requirements. Obviously, at this point the test plan is an edifice constructed on a foundation of guesswork. If the planning has been done carefully, these are shrewd and intelligent guesses, and they serve to facilitate the work of later test development and to assure a test of high quality. Nevertheless, the point remains that estimates are not a substitute for facts, that planning is only a preparation for tryout and item analysis.

Necessarily, the numbers of items in the various test parts must remain tentative at this stage. After the tryout of the final forms, the test constructor will have actual data on the item difficulties, the part-test standard deviations, the part-test reliabilities, and so forth. These data can be used in modifying the originally specified numbers of items of each type or the number of items in the total test.

Even before the tryout of a form of the final test, however, it is desirable to pretest the individual items submitted by the item writers in order to select items of the specified difficulty level and the optimum level of internal consistency. The number of items that should be requested initially from the item writers should anticipate the mortality rate that is likely to result from the pretesting and review of these items. Some items will be found to be too easy or too hard. Some items almost certainly will be found to lack sufficient internal consistency or to have such serious technical shortcomings as to be beyond salvage. The rate of mortality will vary, of course, with the experience and competence of the item writers. It also will depend upon the type of item. Fewer surplus items commonly are needed, for example, for a test of arithmetic fundamentals or grammatical usage than for a test of creative thinking. Items that are intended to be very hard usually have a higher mortality rate than items designed to be of medium difficulty, simply because so often a low passing rate is a consequence of ambiguity of meaning rather than true complexity of mental process. With some types of items, two or three times as many items should be constructed as will eventually be needed; in other cases the mortality may be only 10–20 percent. Based on these expected mortality rates, the test planner needs to determine the number of items of each type that are to be required from the test writers so that, after pretesting and screening, he has remaining a sufficient number of satisfactory items of the various types demanded by the test specifications.

Some test constructors, in anticipation of item analysis, will ask the item writers to prepare an additional distracter for each item. If the final test is to be made up of four-option items, the item writers are asked to provide a plausible fifth option for each item. After item analysis, the weakest distracter is discarded. In this way it is hoped to reduce item mortality and to improve generally the quality of the items remaining after screening. It is questionable whether this procedure proves economical or productive on an overall basis. It is true that item analysis often reveals a distracter chosen by so few examinees that it can clearly be eliminated without affecting the item difficulty or discrimination. On the other hand, preparation of an additional distracter may well require disproportionate additional effort on the part of the item writers. Furthermore, the probable effect of eliminating any particular distracter is often ambiguous if more than a small proportion of the examinees have chosen that alternative, since it is not possible to predict what choice these examinees would have made in the absence of that distracter.

Ability to judge the tryout needs accurately is a product of experience. However, unless item-writing costs are prohibitively high, it would be well for the beginning test constructor to overestimate the mortality rate. It is a rare pleasure for a test constructor to have an abundance of well-written items from among which to select items for pretesting and to have an abundance of pretested items that have come through the screening process and so constitute good possibilities for the final test. Such an abundance can only serve to improve test quality.

PLANNING ASSIGNMENTS TO ITEM WRITERS AND REVIEWERS

Once the test constructor has determined the number and characteristics of each type of item needed for the test, he is ready to make assignments to the item writers and to the reviewers and editors. Careful attention to the problems involved in this step will assure that the items are received in proper time, in sufficient numbers, and in satisfactory form. The test planner at this stage, again, can avoid countless mishaps by anticipating them.

Item Writing

The question of who is to construct the items needed for a particular test may have important implications for test quality. In some instances, where the subject matter concerned is fairly simple, the most feasible plan is to have the items constructed by an experienced item writer who either knows the subject or can readily acquire the requisite knowledge of the subject. As the subject field becomes more complex and specialized, however, it becomes more and more important that the item constructors have had extensive training and experience in the subject. If test technicians unfamiliar with a complex field of knowledge attempt to construct items in that field, the items are likely to depend to too great an extent on material readily available in books and too little on interpretations that would evidence real understanding. In other words, the resulting tests are likely to be open to the charge of being "textbookish."

In some situations, there may be available

persons who not only know a complex content area thoroughly but who also have had training and experience in the specialized techniques of item writing. More generally, it will be necessary to provide subject-matter specialists with specific training and supervision in item writing. The need to provide such training calls for decisions on such matters as how much training is essential, the proper timing of various aspects of the training, the extent to which training can be conducted in group sessions, the amount of time that can profitably be devoted to discussion and joint revision of individual items, and so on.

The rate of item construction is another matter requiring attention. No single rate of construction applies to all types of items or to all item constructors. Some item forms require more time than others. True-false items, for example, can be written at a more rapid rate than multiple-choice items. There are also wide differences attributable to the subject-matter field. Vocabulary or arithmetic items may be constructed by an experienced item writer at the rate of, say, 50 or more a day, while a rate of from 15 to 20 a day may be entirely acceptable for the production of items for a test of ability to interpret reading materials at an advanced level. For a given item form and subject area, furthermore, some item writers are capable of producing items several times as rapidly as others.

The deadline for completion of the test must be taken into account, together with the expected rate of item production, in deciding how many item writers are needed. Sometimes the deadline is such that a fairly large number of item writers must be used, even though this adds to the problem of training and creates the need for coordination of their work.

How should assignments be made to the available test writers? Again, there are no hard and fast rules. In some cases, it may be desirable to have a single item writer concentrate in a particular cell of the blueprint rather than have this cell included among the assignments of several item writers. The advantage is that if a single item writer is assigned to produce 30 items in a cell, for example, the items are likely to represent a more balanced sampling and to test deeper mastery, with fewer duplications, than if three writers were asked to prepare 10 items each or if five writers were asked to prepare six items each. On the other hand, a set of test items constructed by one person is likely to be influenced by whatever biases he may have in his field of specialization. Use of several item writers with different backgrounds of training and experience is likely to produce a test with a less parochial orientation.

Sometimes, when an item writer has a flair for particular item types, he may be asked to specialize in this type of item across the broad range of the blueprint. For example, developing situational items, which involves setting up a hypothetical situation as a framework for presenting an integrated group of questions, requires a degree of creativity and imagination that some item writers demonstrate more than others. To take advantage of this talent, an item writer might be asked to specialize in this manner.

If a large number of items is to be prepared by an item writer, the problem of staleness needs to be given consideration. After writing a certain number of items in a field, item writers often "run dry," and each additional item is squeezed out only at an excessive price in time, labor, and quality. A fresh item writer in the same area can often turn out items of higher quality much more rapidly.

Rate of payment of item writers who are employed on a consultant basis sometimes can be a perplexing question. Various suggestions have been advanced. A common procedure is to allow a unit price for each item written, with the unit price varying with the time normally required to prepare items of this type. Dissatisfaction with item writers who turn in large numbers of items of relatively poor quality has made it tempting to some test planners to establish a procedure whereby the item writer is paid a unit price per "acceptable" item. Probably the most practical and equitable solution is to pay the item writer on an hourly basis, or daily equivalent, for actual time spent in item writing. While there are individual differences in productivity among item writers, as in all human endeavors, this procedure is most comparable to the compensation practices applying to permanent full-time staff members.

The test planner would do well to make his original assignment on a flexible basis and to ask for a small number of items to be submitted as a first installment within a relatively short period of time. A major advantage here is that the test planner can verify in the very early stages that the item writing is going according to plan and that there is not some fundamental misunderstanding or oversight that will result in serious distortion of the blueprint or violation of the specifications. Perhaps the need for additional training sessions for item writers will be indicated. And if important differences in productivity or quality appear, the test planner will be in a position to make early and appropriate adjustments in his assignments to the item writers.

In large test construction agencies, a test planner sometimes has available a large reservoir of items for which item statistics are known from previous tryouts. In such a situation, though the reservoir of items will need to be replenished and extended periodically, for any specific test the construction of test items may become, to a greater or lesser degree, simply a matter of selecting items from the item bank that conform to the test blueprint and the test specifications.

Item Records

Before item construction is begun, the test planner must decide what records are to be kept on each item. Having each item on an individual card of uniform size facilitates handling and filing. In this connection, each item card should indicate clearly the particular blueprint area for which the item is designed. If reviewers' comments are to be retained, provision for the comments to be recorded in a uniform way is helpful. If a record of any written source used in construction of the item is desired, directions should be given as to how and where such record should be made. The identity of the item writer should be recorded on the initial draft and later transcribed to whatever final record form is maintained for the item. Plans also need to be made for keeping a record of item use and whatever statistical data are desired for each item. It will generally be helpful if the test planner designs and prints a record card that serves his purpose and then distributes the record card for use by all item writers and reviewers.

Item Review

As a general rule, test items should be reviewed, before tryout on any sizable number of subjects, from three points of view: (*a*) the technical, with particular attention to principles of measurement, including those relating to item form; (*b*) the subject matter, with attention to appropriateness of content and to accuracy of the scoring key; and (*c*) the editorial, with attention to appropriate overall format and to editorial consistency from one item to another. Effort spent in intensive review of these three factors will obviate the need to try out unusable items and will improve the general quality of the items tried out.

Sometimes one person has skill in all three areas and thus is able to combine the three types of review. More frequently, different persons are used for the three quite different purposes. No hard and fast rules can be set down as to how many reviewers for each function may be used optimally. The numbers depend to a considerable extent on the type of items and the particular subject-matter area and also on the persons involved. Individuals who earn their livelihood as test constructors, for example, should develop skill in handling such editorial matters as punctuation, spelling, diction, uniformity of style, and so on, so that a review by only one additional person from an editorial standpoint should suffice. Perhaps two test technicians might profitably review the items from the technical point of view. Ordinarily, a larger number of persons should review the subject-matter content intensively—somewhere between, say, 3 and 10, depending on the complexity of the area. Often it is desirable to bring the content reviewers together to discuss points of difference and to attempt to achieve for each item a final version that meets all objections.

All items should be keyed independently by subject-matter experts, and by the test technicians if they have sufficient familiarity with the field, for purposes of verification. A helpful suggestion in this regard is to place the key, and any critical comments, on the reverse side of the item card so as not to influence the item reviewer. It has been found that when the key answer is indicated, for example by an asterisk preceding the option number, the item reviewer tends to accept uncritically the mind set presupposed by the item. He is less likely to find that grain of truth or that element of correctness in a supposedly false option that causes so much difficulty if it goes undetected until after the test has been printed.

Similarly, where the item difficulties are a critical aspect of the test design, each item card might well include on its reverse side an indication of the estimated difficulty level of that item. Item reviewers would be instructed to arrive at their own independent evaluation of item difficulty as a basis for either corroborating or challenging the difficulty estimate of the person who prepared the item.

PLANNING THE COMPILATION OF ITEMS

A group of items is not necessarily a test. The problem remains of selecting and assembling a final test from among the items that have survived the review process and the tryout. The concern, in this section, is to consider problems likely to arise in this connection that should be anticipated in the test plan.

It is the person who compiles the test who will, in the last analysis, determine its scope and emphasis. If the test outline presents only a few broad categories, the scope and emphasis of the assembled test may reflect to a considerable degree the personal judgment of the test compiler. If the test compiler and the test planner are not the same person, the final test may depart significantly from what the test planner had in mind. Hence, the single most important guide to and control over the compilation of items is the test blueprint. This serves to underscore, again, the importance of a detailed blueprint.

In addition, the question of the order in which the items should be assembled must be considered by the test planner. If this order is not designated by the blueprint itself, the test specifications should cover the matter in sufficient detail to make the intent of the test planner entirely clear.

Various ways of arranging or ordering items have been tried. The nature of the items and the character of administrative conditions are usually the determining factors. If the items are homogeneous in content and in difficulty so that they are essentially interchangeable, the order of the items is inconsequential. It is when items are not interchangeable that arrangement becomes an important consideration.

If items measuring different content objectives or different behavioral objectives are included in the same test, then consideration should be given to grouping the items by type, even if they are not formally called part tests or given separate part scores. Usually, the continuity of thought that such grouping allows on the part of the examinee is found to enhance the quality of his performance. Also, if different sets of instructions are involved, grouping has the advantage of economy in presenting instructions.

The order of the groups of items may be based on their relation to a logical organization of the subject—perhaps a chronological order, or perhaps from the simple to the complex, or perhaps from the general to the specific. However, care must be taken that the grouping does not provide an extraneous clue to the correct answer to a particular item. For example, if a question asks the examinee to identify the president who proposed the Fourteen Points, the examinee will be clued to the correct answer if he finds that question included among a group of questions all of which relate to World War I.

If items are not of comparable difficulty, consideration must be given to arranging items in order of difficulty—in the test as a whole where there is no grouping of items by content or within each group where there is such grouping. One purpose is to avoid possible extraneous factors attributable to the psychological effects of early failure, frustration, or blocking. In addition, if speed is at all a factor, the student will have an opportunity to spend most of his time on those questions on which he is more likely to succeed. When time runs out, he is likely to be working at a level at which additional time would result in only minor increments in test score.

Where there is not sufficient time for examinees to answer all questions, then grouping of items introduces the possibility that some examinees may not have been able to complete the last group or groups of items, thus destroying for these examinees the balance established by the test blueprint. Hence, even if separate part scores are not provided, separate time limits must be established for each major group of items so as to insure that each type receives its proper share of attention from the examinees.

If many examinees cannot finish the entire test in the time limit and it is impracticable to make use of a separate time limit for each group of items, it may be desirable to present first the easiest items of type 1, followed by the easiest items of type 2, etc., until the easiest items of all types have been presented. There will then follow a set of moderately easy items of each type, ending with the most difficult items of each type. This is the so-called spiral-omnibus arrangement. Some test planners feel, however, that the spiral-omnibus test may introduce irrelevant variance pertaining to personality characteristics and experience with tests. A sophisticated examinee may skip over the segments he thinks he cannot do quickly or accurately. In addition, the examinee is required to change his mental set rapidly.

If it can be anticipated that several forms of a test are to be needed, plans for their construction should be made when the construction of the first form is being planned. Equivalent forms should not be developed simply by paraphrasing items from Form X to prepare Form Y. Rather, as has been indicated, the test specifications should be so complete and so explicit that independent test forms based on these same specifications, and differing only in the sampling of items selected, should be closely equivalent. The better the job done on the test specifications, the more closely equivalent are multiple forms likely to be.

Another problem that sometimes confronts the test constructor is whether to permit choice upon the part of the examinees. This issue usually arises when the examinees have been exposed to different curricula, so that identical examinations may not be appropriate. In a course in European history, for example, teachers may be allowed some option as to whether they wish to develop certain important principles of the growth of nation states by studying in detail either the unification of Germany or the unification of Italy. In science, one teacher may choose to study genetics in depth; another may choose biochemistry. To make allowances for such differences, tests are sometimes designed so as to allow some degree of choice to the examinees. Generally, this is best accomplished by setting up several homogeneous groups of questions. For example, there may be seven sets of 10 questions each, and the examinee may be permitted to choose any five sets of questions. This procedure is far preferable to asking the examinee to choose, for example, any 50 items out of 70. The examinee may well spend half of his time counting and recounting the questions he has answered.

If choice is allowed, however, it is well to remember that the examinees have not taken the same test. There are, in fact, as many different tests as there are combinations of choices. Comparison of examinees on the same measuring scale is therefore no longer possible, and the scores may lose much of their meaning. This would be true even if the optional parts were truly comparable, which is quite difficult to achieve in tests having different content. Whenever possible, therefore, choice is best avoided.

PLANNING THE PRODUCTION SCHEDULE

The story is told of the test constructor who noticed that his son, who was scheduled to take a statewide high school achievement examination in American history, was spending an unusual amount of time poring over the daily newspapers during the week prior to the examination. The boy explained that he wished to be sure that he would be able to answer any questions that the examiners might decide to include on recent national and international developments. The boy was quite chagrined to learn that the printed question booklets had been lying safely in the school vault for several weeks, that copy had gone to the printer perhaps three months earlier, and that all of the questions had been written at least a year before that. This story serves not only to illustrate that logistics may have an impact on test validity but also to emphasize the point that behind every test administration lies a production schedule.

The planning of an objective test never can be considered complete until the test constructor has established, for the benefit of all those concerned, a realistic schedule indicating the lead time that will be required to carry through the sequence of steps in the developmental program. Such a schedule is invaluable for purposes of making assignments, achieving coordination, and assuring satisfactory progress.

There can, of course, be no precise rules for the preparation of a production schedule. Much will depend on the peculiar circumstances involved—the complexity of the test content, the availability of skilled item writers, the facilities available for statistical analysis, the type of contractual arrangements that need to be made for printing, and so forth. Each of the sequential steps in the test development process must be quantified in terms of probable time requirements so that proper allowance can be made in the total production schedule.

The test planner's first concern is with independent blocks of time. How long should it take to train the item writers? How long will it then take the item writers to complete their assignments? How long will it take to get the items ready for pretesting? When all of these blocks of time are placed end to end, the test planner has an estimate of the very minimum time that is needed to produce a test.

However, the test production schedule is not usually a simple matter of the serial arrangement of independent blocks of time. Generally there are certain critical fixed checkpoints about which the time blocks must be placed. For example, if tryouts are necessary

for purposes of pretesting or standardization, it may be possible to conduct such tryouts only at the end of the school year. It may be that item writers in the number and of the calibre desired are only available during summer months or that the computer or the printing plant are heavily engaged in other work during certain periods of the year. It is when the time blocks for each developmental step have been placed on a calendar with due regard for intervening checkpoints and external controlling circumstances that the test planner has a realistic production schedule.

Schedule planning may be approached on either a *prospective* or a *retrospective* basis. That is, it may be the primary concern of the test planner to estimate, assuming that he were to begin operations immediately, by what date he might be expected to have a printed test ready for administration. On the other hand, it may be that the test date has already been established as part of a regular testing schedule. The problem here is to work backward from the predetermined test date in order to determine how early the work of test development must begin if the test is to be ready for administration as scheduled.

The broad range of test production schedules can be illustrated by a few examples. In a certain civil service examinations unit, which is called upon periodically to produce a new 100-item test of clerical aptitude, without pretesting, the test production schedule allows approximately four weeks for item writing by one test technician. If the test technician is preparing an examination in a technical field that is strange to him, such as real estate management, so that he would need to do extensive fieldwork or library work or need to invite the assistance of consultants, the period allowed for preparation of the examination may be from three to four months. On the other hand, consider the production schedule of the statewide examination for which the above student was preparing so assiduously. These examinations are pretested but not standardized. If the June administration date in any year is to be designated as T, the target date, then the developmental schedule would work backwards as follows:

T	Test administration date
T minus 3 months	Copy must go to printer
T minus 6 months	Compilation of final test form, following item analysis, must begin
T minus 12 months	Items must be ready for pretesting
T minus 20 months	The teacher committees must begin training sessions, prior to item writing, not later than this date.

If a test is to be both pretested and standardized, and these experimental administrations are each to take place at the end of the school year, 12 months apart, the total period of test development could well take as long as three years.

A number of suggestions can be offered concerning the test development schedule. First, it is well to be conservative in estimating production. It should be expected that there will be unforeseen delays. There is a fundamental law of administration that test planners would do well to heed: If something can go wrong, it will. Second, provision should be made for periodic review of progress in ample time *before* critical points in the schedule are reached. In this way, if it appears that the schedule may be in serious danger, there will be an opportunity for proper remedial action. Finally, if the curricular validity of the test is likely to be affected by the exclusion of new developments or trends in content due to the imperatives of the development schedule, then some provision must be made for feeding appropriate items of a current nature into the test before final copy goes to the printer even if the usual pretesting and analysis of such items must be foregone.

REFERENCES

Adkins, D. C., et al. *Construction and analysis of achievement tests*. Washington: U. S. Government Printing Office, 1947.

Ahmann, J. S., & Glock, M. D. *Evaluating pupil growth*. Boston: Allyn & Bacon, 1963.

Bloom, B. S. (Ed.) *Taxonomy of educational objectives*. Handbook I. *The cognitive domain*. New York: David McKay, 1956.

Cronbach, L. J., & Warrington, W. G. Efficiency of multiple-choice tests as a function of spread of item difficulties. *Psychometrika*, 1952, **17**, 127–147.

Dressel, P. L. *Comprehensive examinations in a program of general education*. East Lansing: Michigan State College Press, 1949.

Ebel, R. L. *Measuring educational achievement*. Englewood Cliffs, N. J.: Prentice-Hall, 1965.

Furst, E. J. *Constructing evaluation instruments*. New York: Longmans Green, 1958.

Guilford, J. P. *Psychometric methods*. New York: McGraw-Hill, 1954.

Gulliksen, H. O. *Theory of mental tests*. New York: Wiley, 1950.

Horst, P. Determination of optimal test length to maximize the multiple correlation. *Psychometrika*, 1949, **14**, 79–88.

Lord, F. M. The relation of the reliability of multiple-choice tests to the distribution of item difficulties. *Psychometrika*, 1952, **17**, 181–194.

Lorge, I., & Diamond, L. K. Prediction of absolute item difficulty by ranking and estimating techniques. *Educational and Psychological Measurement*, 1954, **14**, 365–372.

Nelson, C. H. *Let's build quality into our science tests*. Washington: National Science Teachers Association, 1958.

Thorndike, R. L., & Hagen, E. P. *Measurement and evaluation in psychology and education*. (3rd ed.) New York: Wiley, 1969.

4. Writing the Test Item

A. G. Wesman
The Psychological Corporation

Any test consists of a number of tasks to be performed by the examinee. Some of these tasks are scored as indivisible units; others are sub-divided for scoring purposes. Each item in a test yields a unit of information regarding the person who takes the test. The test as a whole is no better than the sum of its parts; a good test is one composed of well-written items.

An *item* may be defined as a scoring unit. An *exercise* may be defined as a collection of items that are related structurally. For example, a matching exercise may consist of five items; a reading passage and the number of items based upon it constitute a test exercise. An *objective* item or exercise is one that can be scored by mechanical devices or by clerks who have no special competence in the field.

The present discussion of item writing is directed primarily toward objective items and exercises used in paper-and-pencil tests of educational achievement. However, many of the suggestions made in this chapter will apply to other types of tests.

Item writing is essentially creative—it is an art. Just as there can be no set of formulas for producing a good story or a good painting, so there can be no set of rules that guarantees the production of good test items. Principles can be established and suggestions offered, but it is the item writer's judgment in the application— and occasional disregard—of these principles and suggestions that determines whether good items or mediocre ones are produced. Each item, as it is being written, presents new problems and new opportunities. Thus item writing requires an uncommon combination of special abilities and is mastered only through extensive and critically supervised practice. Item writing demands and tends to develop high standards of quality and a sense of pride in craftsmanship.

Those who have not tried to write objective test items to meet exacting standards of quality sometimes fail to appreciate how difficult a task it is. The amount of time that competent persons devote to the task provides one indication of its difficulty. Adkins (1947) has pointed out that experienced professional item writers regard an output of 5 to 15 good achievement test items a day as a satisfactory performance. This contrasts sharply with the widely held notion that any good instructor can produce an acceptable test in an evening or two. Further evidence concerning the difficulty of item writing is provided by the amount of money that critical test producers appropriate for the work. It is not uncommon for item writers to receive $3.00 or more for the production of a single good test item or to be paid at the rate of $3.00 to $6.00 an hour. These rates are for items prior to the editing procedures which most professional testing organizations impose. If one takes a realistic accounting approach to the cost of an item up to the point of reproduction for experimental tryout, a value of $5.00 to $15.00 or more is not excessive.

Extensive use of statistical methods for the analysis of responses to test items has seemed to imply that test production can be made a statistical science in which the skill of the item writer is of secondary importance. This notion is based on a misconception of the role of item analysis. Item analysis is evaluative—not creative. Its role is essentially a negative one. It serves to identify clearly bad items; those which are too difficult, too easy, or otherwise nondiscriminating. It does not assure the goodness of an item; it in no way lessens the skill and care requisite in the original item writing. Item analysis data indeed often do call attention to specific weaknesses within what might otherwise be good items and thus provide clues by which an ingenious item writer can make improvements. However, under usual circumstances, the amount of improvement in a poor item that can be effected by editorial revision is slight.

WRITING GOOD ITEMS

The combination of abilities required for successful writing of educational achievement test items can easily be specified in general terms. It is much more difficult to find persons who have these abilities.

First, the item writer must have thorough mastery of the subject matter being tested. The term *mastery of subject matter* as here used has broad connotations. Not only must the item writer be *acquainted* with the facts and principles of the field; he must be fully aware of their implications, which is to say that he must *understand* them. He should be aware of popular fallacies and misconceptions in the field. This is particularly necessary in the construction of multiple-choice items where a portion of the art of item writing is the ability to conceive of distracters which are incorrect by any standard and yet are attractive to those not knowing the correct answer.

In practice, test items sometimes are written through collaboration between test technicians and subject-matter experts. While this procedure is not ordinarily as productive of good items as is the work of a single person who fortunately combines test-making competence and subject-matter expertness, it yields far better items than would be produced by either type of specialist working alone. Collaboration of this sort is very helpful; however, the effectiveness of the collaboration depends not alone on the degree of competence of each specialist but also upon the extent to which each shares a general background in the specialty of his partner.

Second, and of equal importance, the writer who prepares items for use in tests of educational achievement must possess a rational and well-developed set of educational values (aims or objectives) that are not mere pedagogical ornaments but that so permeate and direct his thinking that he tends continually to seek these values in all his educational efforts (see chap. 2, pp. 24–35). It is difficult, if not impossible, for one whose sense of values is inadequate or inoperative to produce good achievement test items consistently. He may have at his disposal detailed syllabi describing course content. He may be well acquainted with what goes on in typical classrooms where certain principles and abilities are being taught. But if he is not clearly aware of the educational values that should be directing the teaching and learning, he is almost certain to emphasize the superficial at the expense of the essential.

Third, the item writer must understand psychologically and educationally the individuals for whom the test is intended. He must be familiar enough with their probable levels of educational development to adjust the complexity and difficulty of his items appropriately and to know what will constitute plausible distracters for multiple-choice items. He must have enough insight into their probable mental processes when confronted with various types of questions to avoid ambiguity, irrelevant clues to correct responses, or the measurement of extraneous abilities.

Fourth, the item writer must be a master of verbal communication. Not only must he know what words mean and insist on using them with precise meanings, but he also must be skilled in arranging them so that they communicate the desired meaning as simply as possible. Always, he must be critically aware of various possible interpretations that the examinee may make of the words and phrases in the item. It is probably true that no sentences are read with more critical attention to meanings, expressed and implied, than those which constitute test items.

Fifth, the item writer must be skilled in handling the special techniques of item writing. Obviously he needs to be familiar with the types and varieties of test items and with their possibilities and limitations. Obviously he needs to know the general characteristics of good items and needs to be aware of the errors commonly made in item writing. But *excellence* in item writing demands more than this. It demands imagination and ingenuity in the invention of situations that require exactly the desired knowledge and abilities. It demands ability to identify the crucial element in each problem situation so that the corresponding item will be as direct and concise as possible. Most of all, it demands the skill and judgment that come only with experience. In test construction, as in other fields, the author usually must learn to write by writing.

Sixth, item writing is not a unitary skill. An item writer may be proficient at writing vocabulary items, yet he may be unable to construct equally good materials for a reading comprehension test. He may be adept in preparing items for a test in formal physics but relatively inept in developing appropriate items for a test of comprehension of principles utilized in simple physical mechanisms. Some kinds of items are easier to write than are other kinds, even for item writers who are generally proficient both in the art of item writing and in various content fields. Experienced constructors of vocabulary tests have remarked that there are more words with satisfactory synonyms than with satisfactory antonyms, but vocabulary items of either type, synonym or antonym, are relatively easy to write. Ten acceptable vocabulary items, whether synonym or antonym type, could probably be written in the time required to produce one satisfactory item intended to measure a complex understanding —even though all are written by a writer with considerable skill in both kinds of item writing.

In consideration of the above requirements, several things should be clear. The process of constructing good test items is not simple. Not all individuals are equipped to master it easily. The abilities needed are too deeply rooted and too slow of growth to be produced in a short period of time. Manuals and rules may provide useful guides and helpful suggestions for item writing, but there are no automatic processes for the construction of good test items. Even an item writer who possesses the needed abilities will find that his success varies with the amount of energy and time that he is willing to devote to the task. Finally, recognition of the skill and painstaking effort that go into the production of a good test is a prerequisite to improvement in item writing.

The high standards for item writing implied by this discussion have not been met often enough in the past. A very large number of educational tests have been produced by non-professional item writers who lack the qualifications suggested and whose tests consequently fall short of the standards set. This situation is likely to continue in some degree for an indefinite future period. Meanwhile, in the interests of better testing, it is desirable that ideal standards as well as present shortcomings and obstacles be recognized. Consistent efforts must be made to overcome the faults and approach the ideals.

No item writer possesses ideal qualifications; rational application of the specific suggestions offered in the remainder of the chapter will, it is hoped, lead to improved testing. It would be unfortunate if the reader reacted to the high standards set and the admonitions expressed in this chapter with the conviction that he might as well not try to write really good items, since the task is so demanding and since outstanding proficiency is so rare. Improvements in teacher-made tests *are* within the ability of the average teacher to achieve; and improved tests can make a significant contribution not only to the field of testing but, through more effective testing, to the learning experience of the examined student as well.

ITEM-WRITING LITERATURE

The literature on item writing is considerably more extensive today than it was when the earlier edition of this volume was published in 1951. In that edition, Ebel observed that even in texts on educational measurement little attention was devoted to the topic. Contemporary textbooks are less guilty of this sin of omission. Although the emphasis varies from one text to another, it is typical rather than exceptional for a book on educational measurement to include a section, if not a full chapter, on item writing. The importance of the topic has been generally recognized.

For the most part however, the sections or chapters place primary emphasis on rules and guidelines for good item writing and on illustrations of varieties of item types. Little of the text content is devoted to reports of research on problems inherent in the writing of items. The absence of such reports is not an oversight on the part of the texts' authors. It merely reflects the fact that relatively little significant research has been published on problems involved in item writing.

There have been useful reports of materials and techniques which one may find helpful; some of these are reported in this section. By and large, such research makes a real contribution but a narrow one. In most instances, the materials and techniques are valuable only in a single subject-matter area: e.g. arithmetic, spelling, or vocabulary. Even when the methodology employed is more generally applicable, the necessary source materials do not exist. Dictionaries and word counts are excellent resource books; parallel sources in the social studies and the physical sciences are not yet available.

That research studies have contributed little to item writing is not very surprising. The inherent difficulties in conducting penetrating and generalizable studies may not be insurmountable, but they are far from easily resolved. It is the sophisticated recognition of these difficulties that is largely responsible for the paucity of attempts at basic research. Early studies suffered from failure to realize that vital variables remained uncontrolled; contemporary measurement specialists have recognized the influence of these variables but have not found the means to control them.

A study may be devised to compare the relative effectiveness of long distracters with short ones; another may investigate the utility of three vs. four vs. five options; a third may compare negatively framed stems with their positive counterparts. Assuming that in each study significant differences are found, what may properly be concluded? If in the first study it was learned that short distracters are more effective can this be generalized to another type of test than the one used? To a writer with lesser or greater language skill than the one who prepared the specific items in the test employed?

It is difficult to anticipate all the significant factors which may determine how an item performs. Some concepts lend themselves more readily to brief distracter statements than do others. The skill of the item writer in imagining attractive misleads may largely account for the differences in effectiveness of three-, four-, and five-choice items. Ingenious matching items may be better than inept multiple-choice items, while well-prepared multiple-choice items are superior to carelessly arranged matching items. Even the mode of presentation of the items may bring about important differences in effectiveness. Short distracters may be essential when a quiz is read to the students rather than being presented in printed form; whether a word is easy to pronounce may be very important in a dictation spelling test but of no importance in a printed recognition test of spelling.

Because these factors are ordinarily uncontrolled in studies of item effectiveness, most research reports what has been done by a single writer with a single test; it does not present recipes that will enable all who follow to obtain similar results. A study may show that one three-choice vocabulary test is just as good without two additional options per item; it will not show that another three-choice vocabulary test with different words and different distracters would not be improved substantially by the addition of well-selected options.

Illustrative Studies Pertaining to Item Writing

Bennett and Doppelt (1956) studied seven verbal item types with respect to the contribution of each type to test reliability and to the speed with which examinees responded. The three most efficient forms were found to be information, synonym, and antonym items.

Frederiksen and Satter (1953) compared difficulty indices of arithmetic computation items in multiple-choice format with those same items in completion form. Difficulty was found to be very similar under the two conditions.

Cook (1958) provided student item writers with data obtained by giving the items in completion form. He compared the discrimination indices of items written with this information and of items written without such information. He found no important differences in item quality; however, he noted that student item writers vary considerably in the effectiveness with which they utilize such information.

Rimland and Zwerski (1962), working with arithmetic reasoning and computation items, compared the frequency with which distracters were selected in a multiple-choice format with the frequency with which they had been given in completion format. They found similar frequencies under the two conditions.

The relationship between the frequency with which words appear in the popular literature and their difficulty as items in verbal tests has been studied by several experimenters. The measure of frequency of occurrence in the literature is ordinarily the rank of the word in the Thorndike-Lorge *The Teachers Word Book of 30,000 Words* (1944). Davis (1944) found correlation coefficients of .05 and .19 between difficulty of items in the *Cooperative Vocabulary Test* and *Word Book* rank. Wesman and Seashore (1949) found correlations of .84 for *Wechsler-Bellevue* Vocabulary and .81 for *Stanford-Binet* Vocabulary with Thorndike-Lorge rank; Cureton (1963) found a similar relationship between item difficulty and converted Thorndike-Lorge *Word Book* rank. Wesman and Seashore (1949) studied the difficulty indices of verbal analogies items from the Verbal Reasoning section of the *Differential Aptitude Tests* in relation to Thorndike-Lorge *Word Book* rank of the stem words. They found that conceptual difficulty in the items had been achieved without recourse to esoteric or specialized vocabulary.[1]

Wesman and Bennett (1946) investigated the use of "none of these" as an option in a vocabulary and in an arithmetic test. Each test was given in two forms to matched groups; one form presented five specific choices, the other form substituted "none of these" for the answer or one of the other options. They found no difference, on the average, in difficulty or in correlation with an external criterion. They concluded that the usefulness of "none of these" as a response depended largely on the specific item in which it was used. Boynton (1950) studied the effects of "none of these" with spelling items; she found that items that employed this option were more difficult than items without it.

Whipple (1957) administered true-false items—some science, some nonscience—with positive and negative phrasing. He found little difference between the two forms of phrasing, with some slight tendency for "true" to be given to positively stated questions. Cramer (1951) applied a similar technique to a current events questionnaire; he reported a tendency to reject statements when they were negatively phrased and to agree with the same statements presented in positive versions.

Wesman (1946) administered two forms of a recognition spelling test; the two forms contained the same spelling words, but those words that were correctly spelled in one form were misspelled in the other and vice versa. He found misspelled words more discriminating than correctly spelled words. He recommended that to build an effective recognition test of spelling, many correctly spelled words should be administered in experimental tryout in order to discover those which would be effective items rather than merely "filler."

Friedman and Fleishman (1956) gave the Rhythm Discrimination test of the *Seashore Measures of Musical Talent* with a third option—"don't know"—in addition to the two usual—"same," "different"—options. The test was slightly more reliable with the third option added. Hughes and Trimble (1956) studied the use of "both 1 and 2 are correct" and "neither 1 nor 2 is correct" as options; they reported "a lack of definitive results." Wesman (1947) examined the effects of having students mark a response only when the item was wrong as against having them record a "right" or "wrong" response for every portion of multipart items. He found students could answer items more quickly when they were asked to identify only the wrong parts; no other significant differences appeared between the two modes.

Marcus (1963) administered four versions of a test to as many groups; the versions differed

---

[1] The contrast in findings by Davis and those of Wesman and Seashore and of Cureton may be attributable to Davis' use of distracters that were very close in meaning to the stem words.

only in that the answer to each item was located in a different response position in each version. No tendency to favor one response position rather than another was revealed. Smith (1958) compared two-choice items with items having larger numbers of choices, and he concluded that the former were preferable in all respects except that of reliability. Dunn and Goldstein (1959) prepared tests in which various rules for item writing were deliberately violated. They reported that the injection of specific determiners, grammatical clues, and extra-long answers made items easier but did not affect the reliability or validity of the instruments.

The studies cited above are intended merely to exemplify some kinds of research that have been, and are being, done. None of them is definitive; none supplies generalizations that may be confidently adopted. In most instances, the authors themselves have perceived the limitations which characterize their research and have been quick to call attention to the dangers of overinterpreting their findings. Item writing continues to be an art to which some scientific procedures and experientially derived judgments make only modest contributions. Accordingly, little of what follows is grounded on solid fundamental research. Rather, it is a presentation of generalizations that proficient item writers have derived from experience, discussion, and contemplation. Perhaps the most widely accepted generalization of all concerns the item writer: his soundness of values, precision of language, imagination, knowledge of subject matter, and familiarity with examinees are essential to the production of good items.

IDEAS FOR TEST ITEMS

The Nature of Item Ideas

Every test item begins with an idea in the mind of the item writer. The production and selection of ideas upon which test items may be based is one of the most difficult problems facing him. While the test plan (see chapter 3) outlines the areas to be covered by the test and indicates the relative emphasis each area should receive, it ordinarily does not specify the content and purpose of each individual test item. The item writer is given the responsibility

of producing ideas and developing them as items that satisfy the specifications of the test plan. The quality of the test produced depends to a considerable extent upon the item writer's success in dealing with this problem.

If expressed formally, the idea for a test item would consist of a statement identifying some knowledge, understanding, ability, or characteristic reaction of the examinee. Item ideas could be, for example:

1. Knowledge of the steps in the enactment of a federal law
2. Understanding of the relation of tides to the position of the moon
3. Ability to add two terms to the first three of a geometric progression
4. Understanding of the effects of picketing by members of a union
5. Ability to infer the meaning of a word from the context in which it is found.

Though in theory it would be sound practice, in actual test construction item ideas seldom are stated formally. Usually ideas exist only temporarily and with no verbal explicitness in the mind of the item writer. An idea occurs to him, he judges its probable contribution to the test, and, if this is satisfactory, he proceeds to translate it into an item in approximately its final form. This procedure is quite adequate; there are few cases in which a useful purpose would be served by preliminary formal statement of the item idea, but in the present discussion it is helpful to consider the essence of an item apart from the phrasing in which it is presented.

The Sources of Item Ideas

There is no automatic process for the production of item ideas. They must be invented or discovered, and in these processes chance thoughts and inspirations are very important. One source that may stimulate the production of item ideas is provided by the written work of the students themselves. Their expressions of ideas on issues and problems may reveal points of difficulty that can be made the basis of discriminating test items. A second source of item ideas is provided by job analysis. This procedure, borrowed from the constructors of selection tests for use in government, business, and industry, also may be applied in the construction of educational achievement tests. In using it, the item writer asks: What is an individual who is proficient in this area expected to be able to do? or In what important ways will the individual who is proficient in this area differ from one who lacks proficiency? The answers to these questions may suggest valuable ideas for test items.

The difficulty of obtaining item ideas depends, of course, upon the nature of the items desired. If the purpose of a test is simply to determine whether or not the examinees possess certain information, the item writer needs only to consult various sources of this information and base items on some of the statements he finds there. The simplicity of this process is probably one of the chief reasons why educational achievement tests so often have been overloaded with informational items. If, on the other hand, a serious effort is being made to measure understanding, ability to interpret and evaluate materials, and similar characteristics of the examinee, the task of obtaining item ideas is much more difficult. In this case, the item writer must acquire a thorough understanding of the subject and must work to invent appropriate novel situations.

The Selection of Item Ideas

The process of selecting item ideas goes on simultaneously with the process of inventing them. Skill in item writing depends not only upon prolific inventiveness but also upon discriminating judgment in the selection. In selecting item ideas the writer must consider their appropriateness, importance, and probable discriminating ability.

Obviously the item ideas should be appropriate—they must be in keeping with the test plan. They should deal *only* with those aspects of achievement the test is intended to cover, but they should deal with *all* of those aspects. The number of items related to each aspect of achievement should reflect the allocation of emphasis specified in the test plan.

Item ideas also should be selected on the basis of importance. While the test plan usually indicates the *general* areas of achievement that are regarded as important, it is the responsibility of the item writer to select important *specific* aspects of achievement as item topics. The term *importance* as used here is almost synonymous with *usefulness* in its broadest sense. The ability to add is important because it is so frequently useful. The ability to apply artificial respiration is important because, once in a lifetime, it may be critically useful. The concepts of atomic structure are important because they are, within a limited area of human activity, fundamentally useful as a basis for understanding physical and chemical phenomena.

In contrast to these fundamental, crucial, or frequently used aspects of achievement are the superficial details, the incidental observations, and the explanatory illustrations and comments that have no enduring significance. For example, it is relatively unimportant that the birth year of Woodrow Wilson coincided with the first Republican presidential campaign. Yet many items dealing with such trivia have found their way into tests of educational achievement.

Finally, in the selection of item ideas it is necessary to consider their probable ability to discriminate between those who possess and those who lack a given understanding or ability. The chief purpose of most tests of educational achievement[2] is to rank examinees as accurately as possible in order of their attainments. Only those items that are answered correctly by the more knowledgeable examinees and missed by those who are less knowledgeable contribute to the effectiveness of such tests. Aspects of achievement that are very easy for all examinees, or those that are very hard, are likely to provide few useful discriminations. Of course, the discriminating ability of an item also depends upon how well it is written, but even the best of writing will not convert some ideas into discriminating test items.

Inclusion of poorly discriminating items is justifiable occasionally because of the contri-

---

[2] The statements in this paragraph do not apply to diagnostic tests or to mastery tests.

bution that the item makes to the apparent validity of the test or because of its probable influence on study and teaching. The decision as to whether or not to include such items, however, is a matter of educational philosophy rather than of psychometric theory. Tests prepared by commercial publishers and by state agencies often are assailed because of their supposed (and sometimes real) influence on the teaching of subject matter in the schools. The argument is that teachers tend to focus on those topics that are included in the tests to the exclusion or disadvantage of perhaps equally important areas with which the test does not deal. To the extent that teachers really do behave in this way, what teachers teach comes to be determined by the tests rather than by what educational authorities over those teachers have prescribed. Regardless of the merits of this criticism when it is addressed at independent standardized tests, the argument has little to commend it when educational authorities thoughtfully decide that they *want* to use the test to influence teaching. Thus, if the director of curriculum in city X deliberately chooses to use a locally made test to impel teachers to attend to certain neglected topics, it is appropriate for the test constructor to include items on those topics even though the items may not have psychometrically desirable characteristics of difficulty level or discrimination power. The plans for tests in American history, for example, usually call for a few items on social history. Because of the widely prevalent emphasis on political and economic history in American schools, good students as a group know little more about social history than do their less-favored classmates. But even though these items may be less discriminating than some others, they may serve a useful purpose. The stated objectives of most history courses include some mention of social history, so that a test that purports to cover the field adequately hardly can avoid including such items despite their lesser contribution to the psychometric characteristics of the test. Furthermore, such items emphasize the importance of social history to students and teachers. In the areas

where teaching practices are somewhat behind the recommendations of leaders in the field, tests can be of some help in leading the way toward improvement.

By the same token, psychometric standards with respect to desired difficulty and discrimination characteristics of items properly may be ignored in mastery tests and in some diagnostic tests. If a teacher's (or superintendent's) purpose is to discover how many pupils have mastered the fundamental skills of simple addition, it is appropriate to include a large number of items that are passed by almost all pupils—items that are accordingly too easy and less discriminating than one might accept for other test purposes. If a test is devised to reveal the specific weaknesses of a student learning to read, items measuring letter-reversal tendencies should be included even though difficulty and discrimination indices do not meet usual test construction standards. As noted above, the educational decision should supersede the psychometric standard. It would be well, of course, for the educator who makes these decisions to recognize that he ordinarily may not ask that the test function as well for ranking purposes as it could if all items met satisfactory standards of psychometric quality. A test differentiates the more able students from the less able only to the degree that the items discriminate.

THE FORMS OF TEST ITEMS AND THEIR APPLICABILITY

The *form* of an objective test item is determined by the arrangement of words, phrases, sentences, or symbols composing it; by the directions to the examinee for response to it; and by the provision made for recording the response. A wide variety of item forms have been suggested and used. One manual on test construction lists 13 major forms with many variations of each. However, it will not be necessary to consider more than a few important types in this chapter; a few popular forms account for the bulk of all items written. Furthermore, most of the problems that arise in using the more common forms also arise in using other forms, and the principles leading to successful use of the forms discussed here apply also to other forms.

It is worth noting that all objective item forms may be divided into two main classes. On the one hand are items to which the student must respond by *supplying* the words, numbers, or other symbols that constitute the response. On the other hand are items to which the student responds by *selecting* a response from among those presented in the item. Between the *supply type* and the *selection type* of items there are real differences, but these differences have frequently been misinterpreted so that various forms have been credited with merits and faults that they do not possess.

The forms that are described here include the short-answer, which represents the supply type, and the true-false, multiple-choice, and matching, which represent the selection type. The item writer needs to be thoroughly familiar with each of these forms, but it is important to note that differences *in form* do not constitute the only or even the most significant differences among test items. Full attention must be given to the pitfalls inherent in each particular form to come to a full understanding of what each particular form can and cannot test and in which test situation that form can and cannot profitably be used. In this connection it should be pointed out that it is now recognized that many earlier studies of the relative merits of different forms lack significance because they failed to consider characteristics and to control variables that are more important than form.

I. The Short-Answer Form

The short-answer form is characterized by the presence of a blank on which the examinee writes the kind of answer called for by the directions. This form is no longer widely used aside from informal classroom testing, and even there it has tended to lose favor. It is included here because misconceptions concerning its value and applicability still persist and because it provides an opportunity to emphasize, by contrast, some of the advantages of other forms.

Three varieties of the short-answer form are:

A. *The question variety*

1. Who invented the cotton gin?
   (Eli Whitney)

2. How many calories will be required to change eight grams of ice at 0° C. to steam at 100° C.?
   (1,440)

B. *The completion variety*

1. *Snowbound* was written by ___*(Whittier)*___ .

2. The body of an insect is divided into three parts: ___*(head)*___ ___*(thorax)*___ . ___*(abdomen)*___ . Insects have ___*(2)*___ antennae and ___*(6)*___ legs. They breathe by means of ___*(spiracles)*___ .

C. *The identification or association variety*

1. After each major city write the state in which it is located.
   Detroit ___*(Michigan)*___
   Chicago ___*(Illinois)*___
   Seattle ___*(Washington)*___
   New Orleans ___*(Louisiana)*___
   San Antonio ___*(Texas)*___
   Atlanta ___*(Georgia)*___

It has often been held that items, such as the short-answer type, that require the examinee to supply an answer are inherently more valid[3] as measures of important educational functions than are items which require "merely" the selection of an answer from among a small number of options (which is the characteristic of such types as the multiple-choice and the matching forms). The argument generally is put forth that by its very essence the ability to *produce* the correct response represents a higher level of competence than does the ability to *recognize* which of several responses offered by

---

[3] An item is valid to the degree it measures what it is intended to measure. Validity depends on proper representation of the idea (i.e. content) to be appraised as well as on the skill with which the item is prepared. (The full discussion of validity forms chapter 14.)

the printed page is best or correct. The argument is sufficiently persuasive so that it is often accepted at its face value, unchallenged and deemed unassailable. The truth of the matter is not, however, quite so simple.

It perhaps is reasonable to assume, at least in theory, that a greater degree of competence is evidenced by production of a correct response than by identification of a correct response from a list of stated options. The examinee who knows a fact and can produce it without clues should also be able to recognize the fact when it is presented in multiple-choice form. The reverse need not be true—a student who could not have produced the free response may be able to select the correct one when faced with it as one of a small number of options. Between the two response modes, then, the superiority of freely produced responses might be acknowledged *if* other considerations were equal. But other considerations are *not* equal—the nature of the function being measured and the skill with which the items are constructed in practice usually swing the advantage from one measurement approach to the other.

Simply put, it is more difficult to write good short-answer free-response items than it is to write good multiple-choice select-response items—especially if one wants to test for something other than simple fact. The essential requirement in preparing free-response items is so to state the problem that the student knows *exactly* what response is expected of him. If the expected response is truly to be short answer, it should be a single word, a name, a symbol, a formula, a sign, or the like. Relatively few areas in which testing is done offer instances in which answers to questions calling for generalizations, principles, or applications can be stated adequately by the examinee with a word or two, a sign, etc. The result is that the large preponderance of short-answer items measure no higher level of mental process than memory for fact.[4]

[4] The temptation to exploit no more than memory for fact is aggravated by the methods used, all too often, to construct short-answer items. It is common, if not typical, practice for teachers to extract from textual

The short-answer free-response type of item suffers from another disadvantage, one of considerable practical importance. Experience has shown that it is nearly impossible to phrase short-answer items on certain essential topics so that the same correct response will be made by all those who know the answer. Item writers are often surprised by the variety of correct responses that appear to questions for which they had conceived only one answer. Most words and phrases have many synonyms and near-equivalents. Also, it is often possible to fill in the blank of a short-answer item with words that are appropriate but that are remote from the intent of the item writer. In the item "Columbus discovered America in _____" the examinee may appropriately respond with either "1492" or "the *Santa Maria*." To ask "When did the War Between the States end? _____" may evoke the desired response "in 1865." It also may elicit "in the 1860s," "when Lee surrendered to Grant," "after five years," "after the South conceded defeat," etc.[5] These responses are figments of this author's imagination, but they are no more farfetched than responses actually given by students. Many of the outlandish responses are wrong and easily can be scored as such. Some, though not the desired and expected responses, are correct and defensible—and should be marked so, even though the teacher considers the student's response to be smart alecky. Achievement items cannot conscientiously be scored on the basis of resentment of the student's attitude or personality; one may resent having to give credit to a smart-alecky response, but if it is a correct

sources a statement which contains a fact, or perhaps a generalization, which the teacher considers significant. This statement, with a key word or words omitted, becomes the short-answer item offered to the student. Such an item is likely to measure whether or not the student remembers the statement as it appears in the text. Even if the original statement dealt with a generalization or a principle, the item still may well be measuring only memory for fact—i.e. the fact that the statement appears in that form in the text. And if memory will serve, the student need not be demonstrating understanding of the principle.

[5] Even mathematical problems which should yield precisely determinable answers cause trouble unless explicit directions have been given concerning the form and precision required in the answer.

response it should be so credited. Furthermore, there are usually degrees of approximation to a precise or accurate answer. The open-minded teacher often finds it difficult to draw a fine line of demarcation between marginally acceptable and marginally unacceptable responses.

As creditable responses to a test item multiply, the scoring key becomes increasingly cumbersome, the scoring procedure more time consuming, and, more importantly, the obtained score less reliable. Scoring cannot be entrusted to clerks or others who lack mastery of the subject matter involved. But even if competent teachers score the test there are significant difficulties. Unless one word or phrase, one number or one symbol is the *only* possible correct response, some exercise of judgment is required of the scorer. One teacher may insist that only the expected answer be credited; another may be more flexible. Additionally, a teacher may credit, because of a favorable attitude toward the student, an alternate response that she might reject from a less well regarded student. To the extent that scoring is affected by subjective factors, objectivity obviously is diminished; and involvement of scorer judgment in the scoring process diminishes item reliability.

For these several reasons, the superiority of short-answer (i.e. supply-type) items over selection-type items is more apparent than real in actual testing situations. It seems appropriate, then, to recommend against the use of the short-answer type of items except in relatively few situations.[6] For routine testing the type may be used where (*a*) the answer called for is clear (to the knowledgeable student), (*b*) the answer can

[6] The item writer (or teacher) who abandons the short-answer form for these practical reasons, but with reluctance to forego the measurement of the higher-level ability to indicate, rather than merely recognize, the desired response may find a degree of consolation. The research that has been done comparing scores achieved on tests composed of short-answer and of multiple-choice items strongly indicates that those who perform best on short-answer tests also are likely to perform best on multiple-choice tests of the same subject matter. It would appear, then, that while good multiple-choice tests may not force the examinee to demonstrate that he can produce the correct response, the tests do identify the students who could produce it.

be given with a single word, sign, symbol, number, or the like (arithmetic problems, spelling dictation, and foreign language vocabulary are prominent examples), and (*c*) the question can be posed simply enough (without extensive qualification necessary to exclude undesired but correct responses) so that the test is not unintentionally a reading test.

II. The Alternate-Choice Form

The alternate-choice form is essentially a two-choice item in which only one of the possible alternatives is explicitly stated. A popular variety is the true-false item which consists of a statement to be judged true or false. Several other varieties are related closely enough to the true-false item to justify considering them as variations of this form. These are the question that is to be answered yes or no and the statement that is to be judged correct or incorrect. Items of the cluster variety and of the correction variety also can be considered variants of this form. Illustrations of the alternate-choice form are:

A. *The true-false variety*

This variety consists of a declarative statement that is true or false.

1. The pressure in a fixed quantity of gas varies directly as its volume if the temperature remains constant. T (F)

B. *The right-wrong variety*

This variety consists of a sentence, equation, or other expression that is to be marked right or wrong depending on whether it is correctly or incorrectly written.

1. Glancing down the famous street, signs of every kind were visible. (Sentence structure) R (W)

C. *The yes-no variety*

This variety consists of a direct question that is to be answered yes or no.

1. Does a ripsaw have straighter teeth than a crosscut saw? (Y) N

D. *The cluster variety*

This variety consists of an incomplete stem with several suggested completions each of which is to be judged true or false.

1. The volume of a mass of gas
   a. tends to increase as the temperature increases.   a. T F
   b. tends to increase as the pressure increases.   b. T F
   c. may be held constant by increasing the pressure and decreasing the temperature.   c. T F
   d. may be reduced to zero by increasing the pressure and decreasing the temperature.   d. T F

E. *The correction variety*

In this variety the examinee is directed to make every false statement true by suggesting a substitute for the underlined word. This variety combines selection of response with the supplying of responses to some items.

1. The use of steam revolutionized transportation in the 17th century.   (*19th*)

An extension of the alternate-choice type presents four or five right-wrong choices unified by inclusion in a single sentence or diagram. The student's task is to decide for each designated part whether that part is correct or incorrect and then to indicate those which are incorrect by blackening the appropriate answer spaces.

1. Ain't we/going to the/office/next week/at all.   A B C D E
   A   B   C   D   E   ■ ‖ ‖ ‖ ■

This kind of item sometimes is perceived as a five-choice item; obviously, it is not. It is five right-wrong items in one structure. This variant has efficiency of space and, often, of reading time to commend it. However, it is also more difficult to write without making sentences that strike the examinee as being contrived or downright silly or sentences that contain ineffective parts included only so that the statement will seem sensible.

In the early days of objective testing, the true-false item was among the most popular. Its attraction was undoubtedly the ease with which it could be prepared. As professional testers became more sophisticated and as teachers became more sensitized by testers' lectures and students' complaints, the popularity of this item form waned. Experience has demonstrated that the simplicity of the form was illusory, and the true-false item has been recognized as one of the least desirable approaches to objective measurement.

Contrary to surface impression, *good* true-false items are among the most difficult to prepare and to defend. The practice of many teachers, and even of early test specialists, was to select isolated sentences from texts and offer them as the test items; the sentence was often reproduced verbatim if the expected response was "true" or with a key word or phrase changed if it was to be keyed "false." The ease of this operation accounted for the item type's popularity. It soon became evident, however, that the procedure incorporated vital weaknesses:

1. A sentence presented out of context frequently loses much of its meaning. Though it may have contributed to an important concept in context, it may fail to represent that concept adequately when isolated from surrounding sentences. As a result, it is likely to be ambiguous.

2. Sentences that can be readily extracted from context without conceptual loss are likely to measure trivia.

3. Few true-false items based on sentences culled from a text measure understandings, generalizations, or principles. Most frequently, they measure memory for fact—either the fact, embodied in the sentence, for which the teacher is testing or the fact that the sentence as quoted in the test does or does not appear in that form in the text.

Attempts to prepare true-false items that measure higher mental processes frequently fail because so few statements one can make are unequivocally true or universally false. It is difficult to compensate by supplying all the modifying conditions that must be taken into account to make "false" or "true" defensible against every conceivable legitimate challenge. Teachers who listen to their students' objections to items open-mindedly are constantly forced to admit reasonableness of interpretations opposite to that called for by the teacher's scoring key.

Specific determiners (irrelevant features that lead the examinee to the correct response) are perhaps more prevalent in true-false items than in any other item form. This occurs in part from the attempt by the teacher to eliminate perceived ambiguities or to make unnecessary an elaborate statement of modifying conditions. For example, the sentence "The boiling point of water is 212° F." may be recognized by the teacher as not necessarily correct if different altitudes are considered. To make this item less disputable and to measure the student's knowledge that the boiling point varies, the sentence is changed to read "The boiling point of water is always 212° F." and the key response is "false." This item statement is now less susceptible to challenge—but it is now an easy item for the test-wise student who may know little about water's boiling point but may know all too well that very few items containing the word *always* are true.

True-false items should be based only on statements that are absolutely and unambiguously true or false. A relatively small proportion of the significant statements that can be made on any subject satisfy this criterion. To meet the standard of absolute truth, a statement must be so precise in phrasing and so universal in application that it requires no additional qualifications and admits of no possible exceptions. If statements that are only approximately true are presented as items in a true-false test, they pose a difficult and unreasonable problem for the examinee. Not only must he know to what extent the statement is true, but he must also guess what degree of untruth will be tolerated by the scorer. Consider the problem of response to these hypothetical true-false statements:

_____?_____ 1a. The numerical value of pi is 3.

_____?_____ 1b. The numerical value of pi is 3.1416.

_____?_____ 1c. The numerical value of pi, correct to four decimal places, is 3.1416.

If presented in separate tests, it is safe to guess that most informed examinees would mark item 1a false and item 1b true. Yet both items are basically alike in being approximations: each is true as far as it goes. Only by further qualification, as in item 1c, can the item be made absolutely true.

The difficulty involved in securing ab-

solutely true statements for use in true-false items may be illustrated by:

2. Calcium chloride attracts a film of moisture to its surface and gradually goes into solution.   _____?_____

This item is true if, and only if, solid calcium chloride is in an atmosphere containing moisture.

This item also is questionable:

3. No satisfactory explanation has ever been given for the migration of birds.   _____?_____

Many explanations have been offered for the migration of birds. It is conceivable that one of them ultimately will prove correct. Furthermore, the item does not specify who must be "satisfied" by the explanation.

Ambiguity is also present in this statement:

4. The nourishment assimilated by the body depends upon the amount of food eaten.   _____?_____

No one would argue that there is a perfect relationship between assimilation and intake over all possible values of intake. It would be equally absurd to claim that there is *no* relationship.

Although changes in wording would improve some of the foregoing items, the basic difficulty is not one of unclear expression. Nor can the difficulty be avoided (although it may be reduced somewhat with some items) by the use of qualified response categories such as "completely true," "mostly true," "mostly false," "completely false." Instead, the ambiguity is an inevitable result of the attempt to apply an abstract standard of absolute truth to statements whose truth is relative, conditional, or approximate.

This requirement of absolute correctness tends to limit the applicability and the validity of items in true-false form. Many important outcomes of instruction are generalizations, explanations, predictions, evaluations, inferences, and characterizations. Since these things often cannot be expressed in statements that are precisely and universally true, they cannot be tested effectively by true-false items. Analyses of responses reveal that it is often the brighter, better-informed students who sense the need for qualifications and the possibility of exceptions to statements presented as true-false items. When this happens, the item loses validity and may even have negative validity.

Some skilled item writers have succeeded in preparing true-false items that, despite the inherent dangers of the type, are reasonably well-constructed and designed to measure complex reasoning processes. An example is:

5. If a square and an equilateral triangle are inscribed in the same circle, the side of the square is longer than the side of the triangle.   _____F_____

Other examples may be found in Ebel (1965). One must consider, however, whether this game is worth the candle. A student guessing haphazardly would have a 50–50 chance of answering these items correctly. How many will exercise the higher mental processes required to arrive at the correct answer—how many will trust to fortune, especially if time limits are pressing?

There are, of course, favorable features of true-false tests. Within given time and space conditions, they permit the presentation of larger numbers of scorable responses than do forms of multiple-choice items. Other considerations being equal, larger numbers of items permit broader sampling of the subject-matter field and make for tests of higher reliability than that which characterizes tests with fewer items.

But, as usual, other considerations are not equal. If the *quality* of an item is poor, it contributes less to valid and reliable measurement than does a better item. On balance, unless there are truly compelling reasons to do otherwise, the test constructor would do well to favor other forms of items.

III. The Multiple-Choice Form

The multiple-choice form consists of the item *stem* (an introductory question or incomplete statement) and two or more *responses* (the suggested answers to the questions or completions of the statement). In this discussion the correct response or responses will be called the *answer*(s) and the incorrect responses, the *distracters* or misleads. The distracters together with the correct answer are called the *options*.

The multiple-choice form is by far the most popular one in current use. It is free from many of the weaknesses inherent in other forms. It is adaptable to a wide variety of item topics. While it has often been used to measure superficial verbal associations and insignificant factual details and while many examples of poor multiple-choice items can be found, it also can be used with great skill and effectiveness to measure complex abilities and fundamental understandings.

Many variations of the multiple-choice form have appeared. It is convenient to discuss these variations as if each constituted a distinct variety of the form. Actually, of course, these variations affect different characteristics of the item and may be combined in various ways. A single multiple-choice item thus may possess the characteristics attributed to several distinct varieties described here.

A. *The correct-answer variety*

This variety of the multiple-choice form consists of an item stem followed by several responses, one of which is absolutely correct while the others are incorrect.

1. Who invented the sewing machine?
   a. Singer
   b. Howe
   c. Whitney
   d. White
   e. Fulton   _____b_____

B. *The best-answer variety*

This variety consists of a stem followed by two or more suggested responses that are correct, appropriate in varying degrees, or downright wrong. The examinee is directed to select the best (most nearly correct) response.

1. What was the basic purpose of the Marshall Plan?
   a. Military defense of Western Europe
   b. Reestablishment of business and industry in Western Europe
   c. Settlement of differences with Russia
   d. Direct help to the hungry and homeless in Europe   _____b_____

The difference between the best-answer and the correct-answer variety is more one of topic than of form. The name of the inventor of the sewing machine is recorded in history beyond question or doubt. The purpose of the Marshall Plan cannot be stated with any such precision. In using the best-answer variety, it is sometimes necessary, in fairness to the examinee, to include in the item stem the specification of the authority or other source that defines "best" in the context of the item. Thus, if the examinee is expected to respond with the opinion of the author of a textbook (and other authorities may differ as to what the "basic cause" or "most influential factor" is), the examinee should be informed of the desired frame of reference. Failure so to specify may penalize the student who has read more extensively on the topic. If, on the other hand, the intent of an item is to assess whether or not the student has thought issues through and reached the conclusion that the examiner considers "best" or "most important," no such qualification of the stem need be made. In that case, of course, the test maker has the responsibility of determining that all competent experts would agree as to what is the *best* answer.

C. *The multiple-response variety*

When the item writer is dealing with questions to which a number of clearly correct answers exist, it is sometimes desirable to include two or more correct answers in the choices offered. When this is done, and the examinee is instructed to mark all correct responses, the item variety is designated as the multiple-response form.

1. What factor or factors are principally responsible for the clotting of the blood?
   a. Oxidation of hemoglobin
   b. Contact of blood with injured tissue
   c. Presence of unchanged prothrombin
   d. Contact of blood with a foreign surface   *b, c*

A multiple-response item is most often a correct-answer item. It may, in some settings, serve for best-answer purposes. Thus, the examinee may be instructed to choose from a list of contributing causes to a social event those that were basic, most influential, or the like. The number of choices to be so identified should ordinarily be specified; if left to the judgment of the examinee, he may be faced with the additional task of judging the threshold of acceptability.

In practice the multiple-response item is not essentially different from the cluster variety of true-false item. This is particularly true if each response is scored as a separate unit, so that the examinee receives one point for each response he does mark that should be marked and one point for each response he does not mark that should not be marked. It is, of course, possible to score multiple-response items on an "all-or-none" basis. In this method of scoring, the examinee does not receive credit for an item unless he marks all the correct or desired responses and only those.

D. *The incomplete-statement variety*

Quite frequently the introductory portion of a multiple-choice item (the item stem) consists of a portion of a statement rather than a direct question.

1. Millions of dollars worth of corn, oats, wheat, and rye are destroyed annually in the United States by
   a. rust
   b. mildews
   c. smuts
   d. molds   *c*

E. *The negative variety*

To handle questions that would normally have several equally good answers, item writers sometimes use a negative approach. The responses include several correct answers together with one that is not correct or that is definitely weaker than the others. The examinee is then instructed to mark the response that does *not* correctly answer the question or that provides the least satisfactory answer.

1. Which of these is *not* true of a virus?
   a. It can live only in plant and animal cells.
   b. It can reproduce itself.
   c. It is composed of very large living cells.
   d. It can cause disease.   *c*

Special care is required in the preparation of items of the negative variety. The stem should be worded with the greatest possible clarity to avoid reading confusion on the part of the examinee. One occasionally finds a stem (or one or more options) phrased in a negative context with instructions to the student to identify the option for which the stem statement is not correct. This may lead students to respond with the wrong answer because they have been tripped up by tricky or careless item writing[7] rather than through lack of knowledge. It is also highly desirable to call the examinee's attention to the fact that an item is of the negative variety by italicising or underlining the negative word (usually "not").

F. *The substitution variety*

The multiple-choice form has been utilized by item writers in testing a student's ability to express himself correctly and effectively. Samples of originally well written prose or poetry are systematically altered to include errors in punctuation, spelling, word usage, and similar conventions. Selected words or phrases in these rewritten passages are underlined and identified by number. Several possible substitutions for each critical phrase are provided. The examinee is directed to select the phrase (original or alternative) that provides the best expression.

Selection

Surely the forces of education should be fully utilized to acquaint youth with the real nature of the dangers to democracy, for no other
1

place offers as good or better opportunities
2

than the school for a rational consideration
3

of the problems involved.

Item

1. a. , for
   b. . For

---

[7] Which of the following was *not* true of George Washington?
a. He was not born in 1708.
b. He did not accept a third term as president.
c. He was never a British subject.
d. He was an experienced military officer before the Revolutionary War.   *c*

c. —for
d. no punctuation   *a*

2. a. As good or better opportunities than
   b. as good opportunities or better than
   c. as good opportunities as or better than
   d. better opportunities than   *d*

3. a. rational
   b. radical
   c. reasonable
   d. realistic   *a*

G. *The incomplete-alternatives variety*

In some cases, an item writer may feel that the suggestion of a correct response would make the answer so obvious that the item would function poorly or not at all. He then may resort to incomplete or coded alternatives; for example, the examinee may be asked to think of a one-word response and to indicate that response on the basis of its first letter:

1. The name of Socrates' most famous disciple began with the letter
   1. A to E
   2. F to J
   3. K to O
   4. P to T
   5. U to Z   *4*

The correct answer is Plato, so response 4 is marked.

The use of incomplete responses makes possible the objective measurement of such traits as active vocabulary. In tests for this purpose it is essential to force the examinee to think of the appropriate response himself. The following item illustrates this application.

2. An apple that has a sharp, pungent, but not disagreeably sour or bitter, taste is said to be *4*[a]
   1. p
   2. q
   3. t
   4. v
   5. w   *3*

[a] The figure indicates the number of letters in the word (in this case "tart"). This restriction serves to rule out many borderline correct responses.

Incomplete responses also may be used in arithmetical problems. The student may be directed to mark a choice on the basis of a certain digit in his answer, such as the third digit from the left. Thus:

3. When one computes the square root of 18, what number should appear in the second decimal place?

A. 3
B. 4
C. 5
D. 6
E. 7

        B

The use of incomplete responses for arithmetic problems prevents a student from using proffered responses as starting points for reverse, short-cut solutions of the problems. (If sophisticated scoring equipment is employed, the student may be instructed to code his answer completely on an appropriate answer sheet. Modern scanners can readily process answers marked in this manner.)

The incomplete-response variety represents a hybrid between the short-answer and multiple-choice form. It has the advantage of perfectly objective scoring. However, like the short-answer form, it is limited to questions for which unique simple correct answers exist. Furthermore, unless the response categories are delimited sharply, credit may be given for wrong answers that happen to fall in the correct response category.

H. *The combined-response variety*

This variety consists of an item stem followed by several responses, one or more of which may be correct. A second set of code letters indicates various possible combinations of correct responses. The examinee is directed to choose the set of code letters which designates the correct responses and to mark his answer accordingly. The following is an example of the combined-response variety. It embodies a weakness that frequently characterizes this variety of item, in that the stem does not really formulate a problem—it merely acts as a base on which to mount the statements that follow. It may also be noted that this item form is much the same as the multiple-response variety described on p. 95.

1. Our present constitution
   a. was the outgrowth of a previous failure.
   b. was drafted in Philadelphia during the summer (May to September) of 1787.
   c. was submitted by the Congress to the states for adoption.
   d. was adopted by the required number of states and put into effect in 1789.

1. a.
2. a, b
3. a, b, c
4. b, c, d
5. a, b, c, d

        5

Another version of the combined-response variety (sometimes referred to as the rearrangement or sequence form) requires that the student rearrange material according to some specified principle. The stem for such an item might read: "Arrange the following historical events in correct chronological order, marking the earliest 1, the next 2, etc.," or "Rank the following chemical elements in order of their atomic weights, marking the heaviest a, the next b, etc."

Still another version of the combined-response variety is represented by the item in which the examinee is required to organize fragments into a desirable whole. An illustration of this version may set the student the task of reassembling a set of scrambled sentences to show the correct order which would constitute a coherent paragraph.

2. A. A sharp distinction must be drawn between table manners and sporting manners.
   B. This kind of handling of a spoon at the table, however, is likely to produce nothing more than an angry protest against squirting grapefruit juice about.
   C. Thus, for example, a fly ball caught by an outfielder in baseball or a completed pass in football is a subject for applause.
   D. Similarly, the dexterous handling of a spoon in golf to release a ball from a sand trap may win a championship match.
   E. But a biscuit or a muffin tossed and caught at the table produces scorn and reproach.

The student is required to indicate the proper position of each sentence. The correct order in this case is *A, C, E, D, B*.

It will be obvious that the combined-response variety is one of the more complex forms of multiple-choice items. It is also one of the more difficult to write well and, sometimes, to score. It permits ready appraisal of mastery of sets of facts or of complex abilities such as organization and comparative evaluation of facts or concepts. Since items of this type are essentially combinations of several true-false items, a single score point for the combination response may obscure as much information as it reveals. The student who answers correctly receives a point of score; the student who is right on all but one of the inherent true-false questions gets no more credit than the student who is wrong on all parts. Whether the advantages of the combined-response item in a particular instance of test construction outweigh the disadvantages is a matter for individual decision; educational philosophy is likely to play a more important role in that decision than do purely psychometric principles.

The multiple-choice form is widely applicable. An idea presented in short-answer, true-false, or matching item form can always be converted into one or more multiple-choice items. Frequently this conversion improves the effectiveness of the item. Since there is only one correct choice that an examinee can make to a well-constructed multiple-choice item in its standard form, the difficulty and subjectivity of scoring which plague most short-answer items readily can be avoided. Since the multiple-choice form is adapted to the best-answer approach, it avoids the ambiguity associated with the application of a standard of absolute truth, which constitutes the chief weakness of the true-false form. Since each multiple-choice item may be independent, the problem of finding a number of parallel relationships, which frequently causes difficulty in the matching form, may be avoided.

IV. The Matching Form

The matching form of objective test exercise consists of a list of premises, a list of responses, and directions for matching one of the responses to each of the premises. Names, dates, terms, phrases, statements, portions of a diagram, and many other things are used as premises. A similar variety of things may be used for responses. The distinction between premise and response is purely formal. In the present discussion the premises are identified as those bearing the item number.

Two chief varieties of the matching form are in common use. One is the simple matching exercise:

Directions: On the blank before each of the following scientific achievements place the letter that precedes the name of the scientist responsible for it.

e	1. Demonstrated the circulation of the blood	a. Louis Pasteur
c	2. Demonstrated the statistical approach to human heredity	b. Gregor Mendel c. Francis Galton d. Robert Koch
b	3. Conducted crucial experiments on the mechanism of heredity	e. William Harvey

In items of this type the basis for matching is almost self-evident. The simple matching exercise is useful chiefly for identification of names, dates, structures, and similar associations.

In the exercise above some of the responses do not match any of the premises. Matching exercises having this characteristic, which is often termed "imperfect matching," are widely used. They do not permit the examinee to determine the correct response to the last premise by elimination. Exercises in which each response matches one and only one premise are termed "perfect matching" exercises. These have a serious limitation in that not all of the premises can function as independent items. In a four-premise exercise, correct response to three of the premises guarantees correct response to the fourth.

Perhaps the best type of matching exercise is that in which a response may match one, more than one, or none of the premises. For example:

Directions: On the line in front of each musical work write the number of the composer who created it.

Composer		Musical Work
1. J. S. Bach	*1*	Brandenburg Concerti
2. Beethoven	*5*	Capriccio Italien
3. Moussorgsky	*2*	Eroica Symphony
4. Rossini	*3*	Night on Bald Mountain

5. Tschaikowsky   _5_   *Nutcracker Suite*

                          _1_   Toccata and
                                   Fugue in D Minor

The other chief variety of the matching form is based on the classification of statements:

Directions: In the following items you are to judge the effects of a particular policy on the distribution of income. In each case assume there are no changes in policy that would counteract the effect of the policy described in the item. For each item print the appropriate letter in the answer space provided:

a. if the policy described would tend to *reduce* the existing degree of inequality in the distribution of income;

b. if the policy described would tend to *increase* the existing degree of inequality in the distribution of income;

c. if the policy described would have no effect, or an indeterminate effect, on the distribution of income.

1. Increasingly progressive income taxes.   _a_

2. Confiscation of rent on unimproved urban land.   _a_

3. Introduction of a national sales tax.   _b_

This variety is well adapted to item topics dealing with explanations, criticisms, and other higher-level learning products.

The matching exercise is poorly adapted to unique topics or test situations. Since each of the responses should have some plausible relationship to each of the premises, both responses and premises must be relatively homogeneous. But many significant topics are unique and cannot be conveniently grouped in homogeneous matching clusters. Consider, for example, the difficulty of incorporating an item like the following in any homogeneous set of premises and responses.

1. Buyers' strikes against higher prices have demonstrated
   a. their effectiveness in the case of foods but not of other products.
   b. their effectiveness in rural areas but not in cities.
   c. their relative ineffectiveness in reducing prices.
   d. their effectiveness in reducing wholesale but not retail prices.   _c_

It may also be pointed out that use of the matching form may exert an undesirable influence on the distribution of emphasis in the test. An item writer may have in mind a particular date-event relationship that is of considerable importance. It occurs to him that there are similar date-event relationships that, though not of similar importance, might be included in a single matching exercise. As a result, the test finally produced may have excessive emphasis in this area, while other important aspects of achievement, which do not lend themselves well to grouping in a matching test, may be neglected.

THE NUMBER OF OPTIONS

What is the optimum number of distracters to use when devising a multiple-choice—or matching—item? Are two distracters better than three? Is a five-option multiple-choice item better than a four-option? There is no clear definitive answer to these questions, but there are considerations involved that are worthy of attention.

Theoretically, the larger the number of distracters, the more reliable is the item. Psychometricians are well agreed on this point of theory. It is analogous to the readily demonstrated fact that a longer test is more reliable than a shorter one if the two tests are composed of equally good items. In theory, the analogy is sound; in practice, however, the theory is not often supported.

When a test is being put together, the universe of relevant, meaningful items is ordinarily broad enough to permit tryout of large quantities of potentially effective items and to select from among them the desired number to make up a test of predetermined length. When an individual item is being written, the number of potentially meaningful, relevant distracters is far more limited; the law of diminishing returns very quickly takes over, even for a highly imaginative item writer. This is not to say that one cannot find additional distracters; more often than not statements can be found to stretch an item to four, five, six, or more distracters. The question is whether the stretching process genuinely contributes to the effective measurement capabilities of the item or whether the additional distracters merely act as filler. Too often the latter is the case. In the usual multiple-choice situation, the item writer who can incorporate two or three really effective distracters may well feel pleased. Items for which as many as four distracters operate effectively are relatively infrequent; the search for additional distracters *after* three or four good ones have already been found is likely to be frustrating and fruitless.

One argument for more options on the original item preparation for tryout is that one does not really know which options will work. If one tries the item out with five or more options, one can drop the distracters that prove to be mere filler (or occasionally a distracter chosen by a larger proportion of able students than of less able) before preparing the final test form. However, when more options are tried than are to be included in the final form, another preliminary item tryout is desirable to ascertain the difficulty and discrimination power of the item in its revised version. Eliminating options changes the task set before the examinee.

To return to the earlier analogy, then, the parallelism may be clarified. A lengthened test is more reliable than the shorter one only if the additional items are of good quality; adding items that are ridiculously difficult, extremely easy, or otherwise nondiscriminating can add little to the value of the original test. So it is with item writing—adding distracters that fail to distract cannot improve the utility of the item.

Examples of the futility of attempting to include large numbers of distracters are not difficult to come by. The reader who wishes to demonstrate the phenomenon to himself needs only to give a set of arithmetic items in short-answer form to an appropriate sample of examinees. He will find that, among the incorrect responses, two or three or perhaps four responses appear with sufficient frequency to indicate their possible utility as distracters for converting the item to multiple-choice form. The remaining incorrect responses will be scattered, with too few examinees agreeing on any further erroneous response to make its employment as an additional distracter worthwhile.

An interesting demonstration from the verbal-information area of measurement was found with the items in the Verbal Reasoning portion of the *Differential Aptitude Tests*. In the original published forms of the test (A and B), each item offered the student 16 choices from which to select a response. The item stem consisted of an analogy from which the first and fourth terms were omitted. An example item was:

X. _____ is to water as eat is to _____

    1. continue   A. drive
    2. drink   B. enemy
    3. foot   C. Food
    4. girl   D. industry

                               2C

The student's task was to select one of the four numbered choices to fill in the blank at the beginning of the stem and one of the four lettered choices to fill in the blank at the end of the stem. The 16 combinations thus available, it was hoped, would make for particularly reliable items, since the likelihood that the correct combination would be chosen by chance was so small. That the total group of 50 items in each form comprised a satisfactorily reliable test was demonstrated by average single-grade single-sex reliability coefficients of approximately .90.

When revised forms (L and M) of the test were undertaken, the authors decided to study the effectiveness of offering all 16 choices per item. A large and representative sample of answer sheets was analyzed with respect to the combinations of incorrect responses which students actually selected. The analysis revealed that for almost every item more than 95 percent of the incorrect responses were encompassed by the four or five most popular pairs of words; the remaining combinations were just filler. In the revised forms, therefore, the student was offered only four distracter word pairs in addition to the correct response. That test reliability suffered not at all from the smaller number of options was shown by the reliability coefficients, similarly computed, for the revised forms: again the average coefficient was about .90. Thus, it is as one might expect—it is not the number of choices but their effectiveness that determines the contribution of the item. Distracters that are not chosen by examinees contribute nothing to an item, except in rare instances: in some items a distracter may be included to enhance the effectiveness of other distracters or to make the set of distracters logically complete. Or "none of the above" may be included in some items in which it is rarely chosen, to make that response more attractive in other items.

A consideration in decisions as to how many distracters to use is that of economy with respect to time. Since most tests are administered with predetermined time limits, the amount of reading matter presented to the student necessarily influences the number of items to which he can respond. Extra distracters mean extra reading time per item; thus fewer items may appropriately be included as the number of distracters per item is increased. Unless the additional distracters appreciably enhance the quality of the item, they are merely depriving the test constructor of the opportunity to include more good items. For reasons such as this, professional test writers ordinarily are asked to write four- or five-choice items.

There are situations in which the nature of the item largely determines how many options are used. More than one or two good distracters are rarely to be found for a recognition test in spelling. Similarly, the *Bennett Mechanical Comprehension Test,* which shows gears, pulleys and the like and appraises understanding of the effects of simple physical forces, is composed entirely of three-choice problems. For most of the items, as they were constructed, a fourth choice would be meaningless.

The age of the intended examinees may influence the optimal number of options especially if the choices involve appreciable amounts of reading or retention. It appears reasonable that six- and seven-year-old children should not be expected to consider as many response possibilities at a time as may be presented to older children. Two- and three-choice items are probably more appropriate for the younger children than are five-choice items.

A practice that has grown up in the test development field, and which probably deserves more consideration than it has generally received, is that of mixing, in a single test or part, items with differing numbers of distracters. The prevalence of tests in which number of options is uniform throughout the test may be largely attributed to two factors: (*a*) the relative inflexibility of early scoring machines often made the scoring of items with differing numbers of options a nuisance, and (*b*) the application of scoring formulas appropriate to items with different numbers of options made hand scoring onerous. A further, but less influential, argument favoring uniformity of number of options was that it made easier the student's task of finding the correct spot on his answer sheet in which to register his response.

That these factors need be granted the importance today which they had in the past is doubtful. Devotion to scoring formulas is less widespread than it was a decade or two ago, and the technology of scoring machines has sped forward so rapidly that slavish adherence to uniform response options is no longer justifiable on this basis alone—certainly not for extensive programs in which test scoring is accomplished by computers.

Thus, the teacher item writer as well as the professional may well consider gaining the flexibility resulting from mixing items with differing numbers of options. As suggested above, the *effectiveness* of distracters is more important to item quality than is the *number* of distracters. Ineffective distracters merely take up reading time that might be more fruitfully employed. The search for additional distracters whose sole function is to complete a predetermined number of options is a waste of time and creative energy for the item writer, who might also be more gainfully occupied. The student might better be reading additional items; the item writer might better be preparing those additional items.

At least some portion of the blame for ineffective and inefficient teacher-made tests may be ascribed to strained attempts to provide additional distracters for purposes of uniformity. In fact, there have been numerous instances in which an otherwise acceptable item has been made defective by inclusion of a distracter that was devised only to give the item the same number of options as other items had. For verification, the reader may inspect the items at the ends of chapters of many textbooks—or go over tests that his fellow teachers have prepared. He should then be convinced that it is better to stop writing distracters when he has run out of good ones than to waste his time and that of his students. (This should not be an excuse for laziness, however.) Item writers should try conscientiously to produce three or four distracters for multiple-choice items. Sometimes good distracters come only after hard searching. Good distracters make good items; some of the best distracters are thought up only after diligent effort.

WRITING THE OBJECTIVE ITEM
General Suggestions

1. *Express the item as clearly as possible—* The production of good test items is one of the most exacting tasks in the field of creative writing. Few other words are read with such critical attention to implied and expressed meaning as those used in test items. The problem of ambiguity in objective test items is particularly acute because each item is usually an isolated unit. Unlike ordinary reading material, in which extensive context helps to clarify the meaning of any particular phrase, the objective test item must be explicitly clear in and of itself. The power of an item to discriminate between the competent and incompetent may be seriously limited by lack of clarity. Except in the case of certain types of vocabulary or reading comprehension test items, the difficulty of an item should arise from the problem involved rather than from the words in which it is expressed. Test items should not be verbal puzzles. They should indicate whether the student can produce the answer, not whether he can understand the question.

Lack of clarity in a test item may arise from

inappropriate choice and/or awkward arrangement of words. It also may arise from lack of clarity in the thinking of the person who wrote it. Many ideas for test items are vague and general at first. Before emerging in final form, they need critical examination and revision. In this process, clarification of ideas goes hand in hand with improvements in wording.

It is difficult to provide a list of specific rules that, if followed, will guarantee clarity. The things that must be done and the things that must be avoided are numerous and varied. Furthermore, their application in specific situations is a matter calling for expert judgment. It is worth noting, however, that many of the suggestions made in the remainder of this section may be considered as elaborations of this first and most important suggestion.

2. *Wherever possible, choose words that have precise meanings—* Lack of clarity in an item frequently arises from inappropriate word choices. Many commonly used words and phrases have no precise meaning. Others have no meaning that applies accurately in the context in which they appear. For example in the following stem, "judicial branch," "government," and "effective" are vague.

1. In recent times, the judicial branch of our government has been more effective than the legislative in which areas?   ?

3. *Avoid complex or awkward word arrangements—* The following item, dealing with the interpretation of the accompanying map of the Northern Hemisphere, was very awkwardly worded on the first attempt:

1. What is the relative length of the shortest path between cities A and C, and the North Pole?
   a. They are approximately equal.
   b. That from *A* is slightly longer than that from *C*.
   c. That from *A* is slightly shorter than that from *C*.
   d. That from *A* is twice as long as that from *C*.   c

When revised, with the addition of two cities among the distracters, the item read as follows:

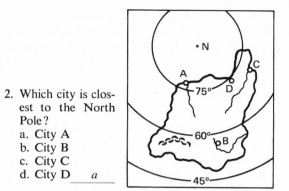

2. Which city is closest to the North Pole?
   a. City A
   b. City B
   c. City C
   d. City D   *a*

While this may not be the place for a discourse on rhetoric, a few suggestions may be made to illustrate the general point involved. The structure of sentences used should be as simple as possible. It is often advantageous to break up a complex sentence into two or more separate sentences. A qualifying phrase should be placed near the term it qualifies. In general, it is desirable to make clear the point of the question early in the sentence and add qualifications or explanations later. Finally, it is often helpful for the item writer to ask himself, Just what is the point of this item? In the answer to this question an item writer may find a simpler, more direct wording for his item; or he may discover that it has little point or one that is not worth testing.

4. *Include all qualifications needed to provide a reasonable basis for response selection*— Frequently an item writer does not state explicitly the qualifications that exist implicitly in his own thinking about a topic. He forgets that a different individual, at another time, needs to have these qualifications specifically stated. Three items will illustrate this point.

1. If a ship is wrecked in very deep water, how far will it sink?
   a. Just under the surface
   b. To the bottom
   c. Until the pressure is equal to its weight
   d. To a depth which depends in part upon the amount of air it contains   *b, d?*

A number of capable students selected response *d*, instead of the intended correct response *b*, because they considered the possibility (which the writer failed to exclude) that a wrecked ship might not sink completely but remain partly submerged. In that case, response *d*, while not good, is the best response available.

2. The greatest loss in hailstorms results from damage to
   a. livestock.
   b. skylights.
   c. growing crops.   *?*

Since the item does not specify loss *to whom* or in *what part* of the country, there is no reasonable basis for response unless the examinee *assumes* that the item refers to the United States as a whole.

3. In a storm, a ship is safer if close to shore.   *T? F?*

The commonly accepted principle is that proximity to shore is associated with safety. The examinee who knows that waves are more violent near shore and that the ship has less room in which to maneuver may mark the item "false." At the same time, if he thinks of "close to shore" as perhaps meaning "in a harbor" he may answer "true" but on a basis other than that which the item writer intended.

5. *Avoid the inclusion of nonfunctional words*— A word or phrase is nonfunctional when it does not contribute to the basis for choice of a response. Unnecessary words and phrases frequently fit easily in the wording of an item but prove on examination to be completely irrelevant to the decisions that must be made in selecting the answer.

Sometimes an item writer may include an introductory statement in an effort to strengthen the apparent appropriateness or significance of the item. This item, from a test of contemporary affairs, includes such a statement.

1. While many in the U.S. fear the inflationary effects of a general tax reduction, there was widespread support for a federal community-property tax under which
   a. husbands and wives could split their combined income and file separate returns.
   b. homesteads would be exempt from local real estate taxes.

c. state income taxes might be deducted from federal returns.

d. farmland taxes would be lower. _____ *a* _____

In order to answer this item, it is necessary to know only in what way the community-property laws affect tax computation. This question can be brought into sharper focus by rewording the item to eliminate reference to "fear of inflation," "general tax reduction," or "widespread support," as follows:

2. Community-property tax laws are designed to permit
a. husbands and wives to split their combined income and file separate returns.
b. homesteads to be exempt from local real estate taxes.
c. state income taxes to be deducted on federal returns.
d. farmland taxes to be lowered. _____ *a* _____

Some introductory statements that are not strictly necessary may occasionally be justified as "window dressing" that helps to clarify the point of an item or to establish its importance. This use is illustrated in:

3. The pollution of streams in the more populous regions of the States is causing considerable concern. What is the effect, if any, of sewage on the fish life of a stream?
a. It destroys fish by robbing them of oxygen.
b. It deprives fish of benevolent bacteria.
c. It fosters development of nonedible game fish that destroy edible fish.
d. Sewage itself has no harmful effect on fish life. _____ *a* _____

If, however, the irrelevant material is put in to make the answer less obvious or to mislead the examinee into choosing an otherwise weak distracter, the result is totally bad. Not only does it tend to destroy the validity of the item for what it is intended to measure, but it weights undesirably the factor of reading comprehension as a determiner of correct response. In general, items should be kept as short as is consistent with clear statement. Examinees vary widely in speed of reading, and the advantage

often given to the rapid reader (especially in tests which provide limited reading time to the examinee) should not be increased unnecessarily.

6. *Avoid unessential specificity in the stem or the responses*— General knowledge is knowledge that may be applied in a variety of specific situations. The superior value of general knowledge over specific knowledge has long been recognized and should be reflected in tests wherever possible. The following item is undesirably specific both in the problem presented and in the options offered.

1. In the 1896 presidential election, William Jennings Bryan received how many electoral votes?
a. 126
b. 176
c. 220
d. 271 _____ *b* _____

A correct response to this item simply indicates that the student remembers what he has read or heard in class. It would be better to test whether he has a general conception of the issues involved in the election campaign. Items aimed at insignificant detail are powerful incentives to rote learning and may unfairly penalize a student whose educational goals are more mature and whose study habits are not aimed at insignificant detail. A better approach is employed in:

2. In the presidential election of 1896, which group favored William Jennings Bryan?
a. Advocates of the gold standard
b. Farmers
c. Eastern industrialists
d. Advocates of a high protective tariff _____ *b* _____

It should not be assumed on the basis of the foregoing discussion that the more general an item is, the better it is. General statements are ordinarily less precise than specific statements. They require more qualifications and admit more exceptions. It is less easy to state an acceptable answer to a general question. Thus, there are disadvantages as well as advantages in the use of general questions. The item writer must strike a careful balance between the two in order to produce the best possible test item.

7. Be as accurate as possible in all parts of an item— Irrelevant inaccuracies are usually unintentional. Even though they may have nothing to do with the selection of the correct response or the elimination of incorrect responses, their inclusion is undesirable. They suggest to the examinee that the item writer is himself poorly informed, thus creating an unfortunate and unfair atmosphere for the test-taking process. The student is entitled to confidence that if he gives a correct answer, it will be recognized by the scoring key as correct—that he will not be penalized by the item writer's misinformation. Consider:

1. Why did Germany want war in 1914?
   a. She was following an imperialistic policy.
   b. She had a long-standing grudge against Serbia.
   c. She wanted to try out new weapons.
   d. France and Russia hemmed her in.   *a?*

In many respects this is a significant and well-constructed item. It does, however, suggest something that has not been established historically. It is unlikely that Germany was actively seeking war in 1914. A more reasonable interpretation is that she was seeking certain goals and would accept war rather than give up those goals. A somewhat similar fault is illustrated by:

2. Studies of general intelligence indicate young people should be first permitted to vote at what age?
   a. 16
   b. 18
   c. 20
   d. 22   *b?*

This item implies that the basic facts about intellectual growth are solid enough to give a basis for answering and that general intelligence is the only factor to be considered in determining minimum voting age. Few sophisticated psychologists, political scientists, or sociologists would accept this view. The intended basis for response in this item is the examinee's information that mental ability, *as defined in many intelligence tests*, does not increase much in the typical individual after the age of 18. But it is in any event undesirable to imply that this factor alone should determine the minimum age for voting. The item also is deficient in the carelessness with which the question is written. Studies of general intelligence do not indicate when young people should be permitted to vote; they may at most permit inference as to when people in general become intellectually mature enough to vote, but the studies are not addressed to this issue directly.

8. *Adapt the level of difficulty of the item to the group and purpose for which it is intended*— Recommendations concerning item difficulty and the statistical basis on which they rest are discussed in chapters 3 and 5. It is sufficient here to point out that the usefulness of a test item depends in no small measure upon the appropriateness of its difficulty for the group of examinees who will take it.

While subjective judgments of item difficulty have been found not highly accurate, an individual who is well acquainted with the general level of ability of the examinees and their typical performance on similar items can do a useful job of estimating item difficulties. In selecting items on the basis of their difficulty, two pitfalls need to be avoided. The first is the application of a "minimum essentials" concept to an achievement test. According to this concept, a test should include only those questions that *all* students should, according to the objectives of instruction, be able to answer correctly. A test composed of items meeting this requirement almost certainly will be too easy to discriminate clearly between different levels of ability. The second mistake is the selection of items from the standpoint of what the ideal student *should* know rather than in terms of what the typical student *does* know. An item writer who is unrealistic about the extent to which typical students appreciate the fine points of a subject is likely to produce unreasonably difficult items.

The above statements assume, of course, that the test is being constructed primarily or exclusively as a device for differentiating students from one another. While this is usually the goal, it need not always be so. There are circumstances in which it is entirely legitimate for the teacher to include items that represent concepts that *all* students should know or that measure skills that *all* students should have. The purpose may be that of diagnosis, to see which students (few though they may be) are likely to be impeded in further progress by inadequate understanding of a basic concept or are in need of special drill on a skill (e.g. in arithmetic processes). Or, recognizing the tendency of students to attribute special importance to items in quizzes and examinations as representing foci for future study, the teacher may include items to take advantage of this tendency and thus direct students' study toward such concepts or skills. It is, of course, necessary for the teacher who includes items such as these to recognize that these items are unlikely to serve simultaneously both psychometric (discrimination) goals and the specific educational purpose. A test composed largely of very easy or very difficult items may serve useful functions, but it will not have good psychometric characteristics—the teacher will need to decide which function he wants to fulfill.

The difficulty of an objective test item is not determined solely by the idea on which it is based. On the same general idea, a writer can often construct several items that differ widely in difficulty. Actually, of course, the items may be testing different abilities, but it is difficult, if not impossible, to define the difference in abilities measured in terms other than the specific differences between the items themselves. Thus, it is a mistake to interpret item analysis data as indicating, for example, that a certain percentage of students in a specified group understand osmosis or the formation of hailstones. All one is justified in saying is that a certain percentage are able to answer correctly a particular item on osmosis or a particular item on the formation of hailstones. Low scores on a test indicate either low achievement or difficult items or both. High scores may reflect the ease of items rather than high achievement.

An item writer can control somewhat the difficulty of multiple-choice and matching items by adjusting the homogeneity of responses or by making use of compound responses. The more homogeneous the responses to a multiple choice item, the greater the difficulty of the item. Where responses are sufficiently heterogeneous, selection of the best is reasonably easy. Two versions of the same vocabulary item illustrate this point.

1. His gaunt companion
   a. beautiful
   b. healthy
   c. scrawny
   d. youthful   *c*

2. His gaunt companion
   a. ugly
   b. ill
   c. scrawny
   d. aged   *c*

Obviously, the responses in the second item are much more nearly alike, so that a more precise and hence, presumably, less widely possessed knowledge is required to select the best. Item writers who have a tendency to look for fine distinctions and thus to produce relatively difficult items may frequently "ease up" the items by substituting distracters that are less like the answer. On the other hand, the item writer should be aware that such changes also may change that which the item is measuring. The hypothetical universe of potential items from which the test constructor draws his sample usually is sufficiently large and representative that it is not necessary to include many items that are inappropriate in difficulty for the group being tested. But if the alteration or elimination of certain items systematically reduces the emphasis on important objectives, the changes are definitely undesirable.

Compound responses may be used to simplify an item which would otherwise be too difficult. This possibility is illustrated by:

3. When the precipitate of ferrous hydroxide is exposed on a filter paper what happens to it? Why?
   a. It turns red due to oxidation.
   b. It turns green due to reduction.
   c. It turns black due to decomposition.
   d. It remains unchanged due to its stability.   *a*

A response to this item may be selected on the basis of knowledge of the outcome of the experiment or on the basis of understanding of the fundamental principles involved.

Compound responses may also be used to increase the difficulty of an item by requiring the examinee to demonstrate two abilities in choosing a response. One common illustration of this possiblity is found in items that require both an answer and an explanation.

4. If a tree is growing in a climate where rainfall is heavy, are large leaves an advantage or a disadvantage?
   a. An advantage, because the area for photosynthesis and transpiration is increased
   b. An advantage, because large leaves protect the tree during heavy rainfall
   c. A disadvantage, because large leaves give too much shade
   d. A disadvantage, because large leaves absorb too much moisture from the air   *a*

9. *Avoid irrelevant clues to the correct response*— Irrelevant clues may make the item easier as a whole or may even change the basis upon which the item discriminates. If all students notice the clue and all respond correctly on the basis of it, the item becomes nondiscriminating and, hence, useless. If only the more capable examinees utilize the clue and all others overlook it (that is, if ability to use the clue is highly related to the ability the test is intended to measure), the item may not be seriously weakened. More commonly, however, a number of examinees who normally would not be able to choose the correct response notice the clue and respond correctly on the basis of it. In this case the presence of the clue definitely weakens the item.

Irrelevant clues may be of several varieties. Clues may sometimes be provided by pat verbal associations:

1. What does an enclosed fluid exert on the walls of its container?
   a. Energy
   b. Friction
   c. Pressure
   d. Work   *c*

It is necessary only to know that "exert" is commonly used with "pressure" to answer the question correctly.

Another type of irrelevant clue is provided by grammatical construction:

2. Among the causes of the Civil War were
   a. Southern jealousy of Northern prosperity.
   b. Southern anger at interference with the foreign slave trade.
   c. Northern opposition to bringing in California as a slave state.
   d. differing views on the tariff and constitution.   *d*

Quite obviously the item stem calls for a plural response, which occurs only in *d.*

An item writer may provide irrelevant clues to the correct responses by consistently stating them more precisely and at greater length than the distracters.

3. Why were the Republicans ready to go to war with England in 1812?
   a. They wished to honor our alliance with France.
   b. They wanted additional territory for agricultural expansion and felt that such a war might afford a good opportunity to annex Canada.
   c. They were opposed to Washington's policy on neutrality.
   d. They represented commercial interests which favored war.   *b*

It should be noted that a single item cannot adequately illustrate this defect. If other items include *incorrect* responses phrased as elaborately and precisely as this correct response, the effect of the clue will be offset. However, there is a natural tendency for an item writer to be more careful in phrasing the correct response than in phrasing the distracters. Precision of phrasing has frequently been used by alert but poorly informed examinees as the basis for choosing the correct response.

Irrelevant clues also may be provided by *any systematic formal differences* between the answer and the distracters. Some item writers tend to place the answer in one favored position among the several alternatives. If, for example, an examinee observes that the third response given is most frequently the answer, or that the first response is seldom correct, he may use such observations as a basis for successful guesses on other items.

One of the most frequently encountered types of irrelevant clue is provided by common elements in the item stem and in the answer. An obvious example of this is:

4. What led to the formation of the States Rights Party?
   a. The level of federal taxation.
   b. The demand of states for the right to make their own laws.
   c. The industrialization of the South.
   d. The corruption of many city governments.   *b*

Common elements in the stem and a response are frequently far less obvious than this, but they may still spoil the effectiveness of an otherwise well-constructed multiple-choice item.

Occasionally an item writer provides clues by inadvertently including interrelated items, so that the statement of one question, or its responses, provides a direct clue to the answer of another. For example:

5. The term *biological warfare* refers to
   a. the struggle of living things to survive.
   b. the use of disease-producing organisms to defeat or weaken an enemy.
   c. the conflict between evolutionists and antievolutionists.
   d. the use of drugs to help save lives in combat.   *b*

6. How far has the use of disease-producing organisms in warfare been developed?
   a. The idea has been suggested but not developed.
   b. Biological warfare has been developed somewhat but it is not yet ready for use.
   c. Techniques of "biological warfare" are developed and ready for use.
   d. Biological warfare was used extensively in World War II, especially by saboteurs.   *c*

The stem and responses of item 6 provide a direct suggestion of the answer to item 5. Interlocking questions are undesirable because they cannot be depended upon to measure what they were intended to measure. The best safeguard against errors of this type is careful rereading of a test as a whole, with particular attention to the relationships among the items.

Words like *all*, *none*, *certainly*, *never*, and *always* have been designated *specific determiners*. They tend to operate as irrelevant clues to the correct response, especially when used in true-false items. Statements including them are predominantly false. These words may be noted by clever examinees and used as a basis for choosing the correct response even when the fundamental knowledge or ability involved is lacking; thus, specific determiners change the basis upon which an item discriminates and often destroy its usefulness. The falsity of the following sample true-false items is obvious because of the specific determiners included:

7. *All* diseases require medicine for their cure.   *F*

8. If water is brought to a boil, *all* bacteria in it will *certainly* be killed.   *F*

9. If drinking water is clear, it is *always* safe for drinking.   *F*

Irrelevant clues provided by pat verbal associations or by common elements in the item stem and one of the responses may be used constructively in multiple-choice items. Deliberately planting clues of this type in the misleads tends to defeat the rote learner or to make the distracters highly attractive to those whose knowledge is superficial. This practice increases the power of the item to discriminate. However, any trick that is used consistently and repeatedly by a test maker, perhaps especially by a teacher, is likely to be identified by some alert test takers and then provide them a cue that they will use to outwit the item writer.

10. *Avoid stereotyped phraseology in the stem or the correct response—* Rote responses are usually based on verbal stereotypes. (A *rote response* is here defined as one in which words are used with no clear conception of their meanings.) These questions (with the intended answers in parentheses) illustrate the opportunities that certain items provide for response by rote:

1. What is the biological theory of recapitulation? (*Ontogeny repeats phylogeny*.)

2. Who was the chief spokesman for the "American System"? (*Henry Clay*)

3. What were the *staple crops* in the colonial South? (*tobacco, rice, indigo*)

In item 1 the verbal stereotype is in the phrase "Ontogeny repeats phylogeny" and its association with the term "recapitulation"; in item 2 "Henry Clay's American System"; in item 3 "staple crops." To demonstrate the stereotyped character of these phrases, the reader is invited to attempt the clarification of "Ontogeny repeats phylogeny," the "American System," and "staple crops." It is true that some examinees may know the meanings of these phrases, but it is also obvious that the items do not *require* this knowledge for successful response.

The emphasis that supply-type items place on some *unique* word or phrase as *the* answer makes them particularly subject to response by rote. When this form is used, it is almost impossible to avoid giving credit to the "lesson learner" who knows the words, whether or not he knows the meaning. Any correct answer supplied, however obviously stereotyped, must be given full credit. With choice-type items, on the other hand, it is possible to avoid such verbal stereotypes among the correct responses, or to work them into the distracters. The extent of rote learning and the harm that it does were discussed by Lindquist at some length in *The Construction and Use of Achievement Examinations* (1936), from which the following is taken.

Consider the following illustrations. The items given below were included in a battery of tests administered to a random sample of 325 physics students in Iowa high schools.

1. What is the heat of fusion of ice in calories? (*80 calories per gram*)
(Answered correctly by 75 percent of the pupils.)

2. How much heat is needed to melt one gram of ice at 0° C.? (*80 calories*)
(Answered correctly by 70 percent of the pupils.)

3. Write a definition of heat of fusion. (*Amount of heat required to change a given quantity of ice at 0° C. to water at 0° C.*)
(Answered correctly by 50 percent of the pupils.)

4. The water in a certain container would give off 800 calories of heat in cooling to 0° C. If 800 grams of ice are placed in the water, the heat from the water will melt
   1. all the ice.
   2. about 10 grams of the ice.
   3. nearly all the ice.
   4. between 1 and 2 grams of the ice.   *2*
(Answered correctly by 35 percent of the pupils.)

5. In which of the following situations has the number of calories exactly equal to the heat of fusion of the substance in question been applied?
   1. Ice at 0° C. is changed to water at 10° C.
   2. Water at 100° C. is changed to steam at 100° C.
   3. Steam at 100° C. is changed to water at 100° C.
   4. Frozen alcohol at −130° C. is changed to liquid alcohol at −130° C.   *4*

(Answered correctly by 34 percent of the pupils.)

It will be noted that these items progressively call for more and more thorough understanding of the heat of fusion of ice. Item 1 requires only a verbal association between "heat of fusion of ice" and "80 calories." This is the sort of association upon which physics pupils are frequently drilled in a more or less mechanical fashion until the association is firmly established. The success with which it has been established in this particular case is evidenced by the fact that 75 percent of the pupils tested gave the correct response to this item.

Item 2 is of essentially the same type as item 1, but employs a different phrasing from the pat form in which the question is usually stated. Even this slight variation in phrasing resulted in a 5 percent decrease in the number of correct responses.

The ability to supply the correct answer to either item 1 or 2 clearly can be of no functional value unless the pupil has some notion of the meaning of "heat of fusion." The data from item 3, however, indicate that there were many students who could make the verbal association called for in item 1 or 2 who had no adequate understanding of the meaning of this term. (It may be noted that item 3 was scored in a very liberal fashion, and that many responses were accepted as correct that were technically imperfect.)

Any student who really understood the definition provided in response to item 3 should have no difficulty in responding to items 4 and 5. It will be noted, however, that only 35 and 34 percent, respectively, of the pupils responded correctly to these latter items. It is clearly apparent from these data that items such as 1, 2, and 3 above can provide only an inadequate basis on which to judge the pupils' understanding of the concept taught. Items of the type of 4 and 5 above are definitely superior. It is significant to observe in this connection that out of the 224 pupils who supplied the correct answer to item 1, only 16 percent succeeded in all of the remaining items; in other words, only one out of every six students who had acquired the verbal association between "heat of fusion of ice" and "80 calories" had acquired even the low level of understanding of these terms called for in items 2, 3, 4, and 5. [91–93]

Several factors probably have contributed to the presence in tests of verbal stereotypes that permit successful response by rote. In the first place, test items tend to reflect the character of the instruction that preceded them. Education has been criticized repeatedly, and with considerable justification, for its preoccupation with verbal symbols and its neglect of the phenomena to which they refer.

In the second place, it is much easier to build items that hold a student responsible for verbal associations than to build items that probe the student's understanding. Many item writers have borrowed statements from texts or references, simply rearranging the words or introducing slight modifications to produce test items. Almost invariably such items can be answered successfully by anyone who has read the texts or references with some care and who possesses a good memory for verbal associations.

The existence of this common fault is not recognized by many item writers, for it is unlikely that they would set out deliberately to test for rote learning. But, apparently, they have failed to appreciate the extreme ease with which a stereotyped phrase, repeated in text or lectures or simply in common speech, is accepted and used by many who have only a vague idea of its original significance.

Items of this type are harmful in two ways. In the first place, they do not provide a valid measure of the desired outcomes of instruction. Such items do not discriminate between those who understand and those who do not. The usefulness of purely verbal associations is strictly limited. Tests emphasizing such associations, if administered at the beginning and end of a course of instruction, may give the impression of striking progress on the part of the student, when, in reality, permanent achievements are negligible. In the second place, such items exert an undesirable influence on teaching and learning. Concentrating the attention of teacher and students on word memory may crowd out efforts to develop understanding.

The solution to this problem is to be found in better phrasing of items. Practical problem situations and fresh wording of essential ideas should be consciously sought. Efforts may be made to penalize the rote learner by including attractive verbal stereotypes among the distracters and by avoiding them as much as possible in the answers.

11. *Avoid irrelevant sources of difficulty*— Just as it is possible to incorporate clues to a correct response inadvertently, it is also possible to place obstacles in the way of the examinee unintentionally. Frequently reasoning problems in mathematics are answered incorrectly by examinees who have reasoned correctly but who have slipped in their computations. This item was designed to measure the principle of price discounts:

1. Mr. Walters was given a 12 1/2% discount when he bought a desk whose list price was $119.75. How much did he have to pay for the desk?   *$104.78*

A number of examinees who understood the principle failed the item because of errors in multiplication and in placement of decimal points. If the item is revised to read:

2. Mr. Walters was given a 10% discount when he bought a desk whose list price was $100. How much did he have to pay for the desk?   *$90*

the computational difficulty is almost entirely removed so that the principle alone can be tested. Test constructors may differ in their opinions concerning the advisability of eliminating computational difficulty from certain mathematics problems, but, when complex or time-consuming calculations are included in the item, the item writer should recognize that he chiefly is testing computational skill rather than understanding of mathematical principles.

It is preferable to decide in advance which skills or understandings are to be assessed and to construct items that will focus on those skills or understandings exclusively. If both problem-solving (reasoning) and computational skills are of interest, separate items or separate tests should be devised to measure the separate abilities.

12. *Expose items to expert editorial scrutiny* — The word *editorial* in this suggestion refers to content even more than to adequacy with respect to grammar, diction, or spelling. No truly professional test construction agency permits items to go out into the field for experimental tryout without first subjecting the items to review by peers or superiors of the item writer. Such a review ordinarily involves:

a. Checking the correctness of the "correct" answer— It is a minor embarrassment for the item writer to have a colleague point out that an item has been keyed incorrectly—that an option designated as incorrect is a better response than the option indicated as correct or that no option is genuinely correct. It is far more embarrassing to have examinees bring such a fact to the item writer's attention. The experienced item writer accordingly makes it a routine practice to submit drafts of items to at least one competent peer. The item is shown without the key response being identified; if the critic selects a different option than the writer intended, the item obviously needs additional attention.

b. Estimating appropriateness of difficulty — While few item critics are able to estimate item difficulty with precision, colleagues who have had experience with examinees similar to those for whom an item is intended often will be able to characterize a proposed item as ridiculously easy or extraordinarily difficult. This kind of characterization may lead the writer to consider whether the task set by the item stem is inappropriate or whether different distracters might better serve the item.

c. Suggestions for better wording— Precision of language and clarity of communication are important to good items. A critic may find it easier to improve the language in which an item is couched than the item writer. Such clarification may improve the stem, the distracters, or both.

d. Suggestions for better distracters— A colleague who is equally familiar with the kinds of misconceptions that prevail among the examinees for whom an item is intended now and again will be able to offer potential distracters that are more alluring and discriminating than one or more of the distracters "dreamed up" by the original writer. No item writer has a monopoly on good distracters; effective contributions should be gratefully received.

e. Appraisal of an item's significance— An item writer will sometimes, under pressure to fulfill a commitment or complete a test for his class, yield to the temptation to write one or more items that are easy to write rather than of true significance. Frequently these will measure inconsequential facts or unimportant relationships. A reviewer can identify these items and thus act as an external conscience for the item writer. The resulting test should be fairer to examinees as well as psychometrically superior.

The Short-Answer Form

1. *Use the short-answer form only for questions that can be answered by a unique word, phrase, number, or symbol*— The need for this restriction was discussed in the previous section. The implication of this restriction is that a test composed exclusively of short-answer items is almost certain to overemphasize vocabulary. It is probably safe to observe that written tests in general, both essay and objective, have always placed too great a premium on vocabulary and too little upon other important aspects of achievement.

2. *Do not borrow statements verbatim from context and attempt to use them as short-answer items*— Ambiguity of the item and perplexing variations in the answers are almost certain to result from this procedure.

3. *Make the question, or the directions, explicit*— Avoid such indefinite questions as:

1. Who was George Washington? *first president of U.S., general, Virginian*, etc.
2. Where did Columbus land? *U.S.A., West Indies, New World, San Salvador*, etc.

4. *Allow sufficient space for students' answers, and arrange the spaces for convenience in scoring*— It is frequently convenient to have all the blanks in a single column at either the left or the right margin of the examination paper.

5. *In computational problems specify the degree of precision expected*— If correctness of a numerical response depends upon stating the unit of measurement, make this fact clear. If not, it is best to include the unit of measurement in the statement of the question; for example:

1. The volume of a cube nine feet on an edge is <u>729</u> cubic feet.

6. *Prepare computational problems so the solution is a whole number except where ability to handle fractions and decimals is one of the points being tested*— As seen in the example in point 11 above (p. 110), a number of examinees who may understand the principle involved in the solution of a problem will answer incorrectly because of errors in arithmetic.

7. *Avoid overmutilation of completion exercises*— An extreme example of this may be observed in this sample item:

1. A hay _____ affords another _____

   of the _____ existing between _____

   and _____.

A student with a good memory who had encountered this statement before might be able to puzzle it out and successfully fill the blanks with the words *infusion, illustration, relationship, animals,* and *plants.* But it is obvious that far too many words have been removed to permit the item to pose a clear-cut problem. Even an expert biologist would find the item troublesome, and he would certainly brand it as trivial (unless he wrote it himself).

The True-False Form

1. *Base true-false items only on statements that are true or false without qualifications*— Item writers frequently have used broad generalizations and other declarative statements as true-false items. While most true-false items are declarative statements, not all such statements make acceptable true-false items, for many of them involve exceptions and hence should be marked false if *truth* is interpreted strictly, although they are true in general.

2. *Avoid the use of long and involved statements with many qualifying phrases*— The difficulty with such statements is that the examinee has trouble identifying the crucial element in the item. If it is necessary to use many words in describing a complex situation for a true-false item, separate sentences should be used. The issue to be judged true or false should be set apart at the end of the item.

3. *Avoid the use of sentences lifted directly from texts or other sources*— Very few textbook statements, when isolated from context, are completely and absolutely true. Moreover, many of them are of value chiefly as supporting or clarifying material and are not in themselves highly significant. Finally, in many cases the meaning of an isolated sentence is not clear.

The difficulties involved in borrowing statements for use as true-false items may be illustrated by:

1. World War II was fought in Europe and the Far East.   *T?*

2. A remarkable transaction occurred toward the end of the reign of Constantine the Great.   *?*

3. Colloids are near-solutions.   *?*

Item 1 is true so far as it goes, but is not completely true for it fails to mention Africa, the Atlantic, and other battle areas. Item 2 is clearly introductory and has no inherent significance. The meaning of item 3 is not clear enough to permit a decision of true or false. It is unfortunate that many similar statements, lacking absolute truth, basic significance, or clear meaning, have found their way into true-false tests.

The Multiple-Choice Form

1. *Use either a direct question or an incomplete statement as the item stem—* There are some item ideas that can be expressed more simply and clearly in the form of incomplete statements than in the form of direct questions.

1. The present Russian government is a
   a. democracy.
   b. constitutional monarchy.
   c. Communist dictatorship.
   d. Fascist dictatorship.   _c_

If this item were written with a direct question as the stem it would require more words and read less smoothly.

2. The present Russian government is of which of the following types?
   a. A democracy
   b. A constitutional monarchy
   c. A Communist dictatorship
   d. A Fascist dictatorship   _c_

On the other hand, some items require direct question stems for most effective expression.

At present there is no adequate experimental evidence on the relative efficiency of the two types of stem. Some experienced item writers exhibit a strong preference for the direct question. Others prefer the incomplete statement. Probably the effect of stem type upon the quality of an item is not large. *There are, however, indications that beginners tend to produce fewer technically weak items when they try to use direct questions than when they use the incomplete statement approach.* Several reasons for this tendency may be suggested:

First, because of its specificity the direct question induces the item writer to produce more specific and homogeneous responses. When an incomplete statement is used as the item stem, the writer's point of view may shift as he writes successive responses. This is evidenced in the frequent tendency on the part of inexperienced item writers to construct incomplete statement items as essentially a series of true-false items with no truly central idea. This tends to confuse the examinee concerning the real point of the item.

Second, it is usually easier for the item writer to express complex ideas (those requiring qualifying statements) in complete question form. The necessity of having the completion come at the end of an incomplete statement restricts the item writer. He is not free to arrange phrases or words to produce the clearest possible statement.

Third and most important of all, the writer of a direct question usually states more explicitly the basis on which the correct response is to be chosen. Contrast these two item stems:

3. In comparing the exports and imports of the United States, we find that: _?_

4. In the United States, how does the value of exports compare with that of imports?
   Exports greater

Item 4 obviously sets up a much more definite basis for choosing a correct response. The difference here is not inherent in the form, since item 3 could be improved without changing it to a direct question. However, there is a greater tendency for item writers to be vague when using incomplete statements than when using direct questions. A reason for the relative absence of vagueness in the direct question form may be that the form itself requires that the complete problem be stated. It has been suggested that whether an incomplete statement is adequately specific might well be checked by attempting to convert the incomplete statement to a direct question; if new material is required for the conversion, the incomplete statement should be reviewed and modified by adding the material necessary to make it equivalent to the question. Some incomplete item stems are altogether too incomplete, as in:

5. Merchants and middlemen
   a. make their living off producers and consumers, and are, therefore, non-producers.
   b. are regulators and determiners of price and, therefore, are producers.
   c. are producers in that they aid in the distribution of goods and bring the producer and the consumer together.

d. are producers in that they assist in the circulation of money.   _a_

Restatement of this item using a direct question increases the number of words but makes it much easier to understand.

6. Should merchants and middlemen be classified as producers or nonproducers? Why?
   a. As nonproducers, because they make their living off producers and consumers
   b. As producers, because they are regulators and determiners of price
   c. As producers, because they aid in the distribution of goods and bring producer and consumer together
   d. As producers, because they assist in the circulation of money   _a_

2. *In general, include in the stem any words that otherwise must be repeated in each response*—These two forms of a test item illustrate this point:

1. The members of the board of directors of a corporation are usually chosen by which of these?
   a. The bondholders of the corporation
   b. The stockholders of the corporation
   c. The president of the corporation
   d. The employees of the corporation   _b_

2. Which persons associated with a corporation usually choose its directors?
   a. Bondholders
   b. Stockholders
   c. Officials
   d. Employees   _b_

It is not always possible, or desirable, however, to eliminate all words common to the responses. In a preceding example (1.6 above), dealing with the activities of merchants and middlemen, it was necessary to introduce each response with the word *as* to make grammatical sense. If the retention of common words in all of the responses makes the item easier to understand, they should be retained. In most cases, however, it will be found that the common words can be transferred to the stem without loss of clarity.

3. *Avoid a negatively stated item stem if possible*— Experience indicates that this approach is likely to confuse the examinee. He is accustomed to selecting a *correct* response and finds it difficult to remember, in a particular isolated instance, to choose an *incorrect* response. The negative approach and the difficulty it frequently causes may be apparent in these sample items:

1. Which of these is *not* one of the purposes of Russia in consolidating the Communist party organization throughout Eastern Europe?
   a. To balance the influence of the Western democracies
   b. To bolster her economic position
   c. To improve Russian-American relations
   d. To improve her political bargaining position   _c_

2. Which of these is *not* true of a virus?
   a. It is composed of very large living cells.
   b. It can reproduce itself.
   c. It can live only in plants and animal cells.
   d. It can cause disease.   _a_

The use of a negative approach can sometimes be avoided by rewording the item, by reducing the number of responses, or both. Where use of negatively stated items appears to constitute the only satisfactory approach, underlining, italicizing, or otherwise emphasizing the "not" is essential.

4. *Provide a response that competent critics can agree on as the best*— The correct response to a multiple-choice item must be determinate. While this requirement is obvious, it is not always easy to fulfill. Sometimes through lack of information but more often through failure to consider all circumstances, writers produce items that confuse and divide even competent authorities. For example, experts disagreed sharply over the best response to each of these questions:

1. What is the chief difference in research work between colleges and industrial firms?

a. Colleges do much research, industrial firms little.
b. Colleges are more concerned with basic research, industrial firms with applications.
c. Colleges lack the well-equipped laboratories that industrial firms maintain.
d. Colleges publish results, while industrial firms keep their findings secret.   *?*

2. What is the chief obstacle to free exchange of scientific information between scientists in different countries?
a. The information is printed in different languages.
b. The scientists wish to keep the information secret for their own use.
c. Scientists do not wish to use secondhand information from other countries.
d. Countries wish to keep some of the information secret for use in time of war.   *?*

The most obvious remedy for this type of weakness is to have the items carefully reviewed by competent authorities. Items on which the experts cannot agree in selecting a best response should be revised or discarded.

Expert reviewers may frequently suggest desirable improvements in the wording of the item, but the item writer should not feel bound to accept these suggestions if they do not affect choice of the answer. Some suggested changes may actually weaken the item. Expert reviewers have a tendency to "split hairs at the PhD level" and to prefer the technical jargon and stereotypes with which they are most familiar. The changes in wording they suggest sometimes may make the item more verbose and confusing to the examinees for whom it is intended or may destroy its ability to discriminate those who understand from those who simply possess verbal facility.

5. *Make all the responses appropriate to the item stem—* Writers sometimes produce items in which no one of the responses is reasonably correct.

1. In which of the following cases is loss

due to hail greatest?
a. To livestock
b. To skylights
c. To growing crops   *?*

2. Why do living organisms need oxygen?
a. Purification of the blood
b. Oxidation of wastes
c. Release of energy
d. Assimilation of foods   *?*

3. What process is exactly the opposite of photosynthesis?
a. Digestion
b. Respiration
c. Assimilation
d. Catabolism   *?*

The responses to item 1 are not "cases." The responses to item 2 are not stated as reasons, as required by the stem. Item 3 illustrates a different type of difficulty. It asks a question that has no possible correct answer, since no process is *exactly* the opposite to photosynthesis. In all three, the items can be improved by rewording.

4. The greatest economic loss in hailstorms for the country as a whole results from damage to
a. livestock.
b. skylights.
c. growing crops.   *c*

5. Why do living organisms need oxygen?
a. To purify the blood
b. To oxidize wastes
c. To release energy
d. To assimilate food   *c*

6. What process is most nearly the opposite of photosynthesis chemically?
a. Digestion
b. Respiration
c. Assimilation
d. Catabolism   *d*

One fairly obvious indication of inappropriate or carelessly written responses is lack of parallelism in grammatical structure. This is illustrated by:

7. Which would do most to advance the application of atomic discoveries to medicine?
a. Standardized techniques for treatment of patients

b. Train the average doctor to apply radioactive treatment
c. Reducing radioactive therapy to a routine procedure
d. Establish hospitals staffed by highly trained radioactive-therapy specialists   *d*

The responses to a multiple-choice item should always be expressed in parallel form. Sometimes this can be achieved by a simple change in wording. In other cases, it requires substitution of a more appropriate response. The revised and improved item is given:

8. Which would do most to advance the application of atomic discoveries to medicine?
    a. Development of standardized techniques for treatment of patients
    b. Training of the average doctor in application of radioactive treatments
    c. Removal of restriction on the use of radioactive substances
    d. Addition of trained radioactive-therapy specialists to hospital staffs   *d*

6. *Make all distracters plausible and attractive to examinees who lack the information or ability tested by the item—* In addition to inappropriate distracters resulting from careless writing, there are others resulting from failure to consider plausibility. Consider:

1. Which element has been most influential in recent textile technology?
    a. Scientific research
    b. Psychological change
    c. Convention attendance
    d. Advertising promotion   *a*

Only the first response is plausible as an answer to question 1. Another example is provided by item 2.

2. Why is physical education a vital part of general education?
    a. It guarantees good health.
    b. It provides good disciplinary training.
    c. It balances mental, social, and physical activities.
    d. It provides needed strenuous physical exercise.   *c*

The alert examinee would reason that nothing can *guarantee* good health, that *disciplinary training* is now in low repute educationally, and that *strenuous* physical exercise is seldom recommended. Such an item might function well as a test of understanding of verbal meaning, but it would not discriminate between those who do and those who do not understand the place of physical education in general education.

Each distracter should be designed specifically to attract those examinees who have certain common misconceptions or who tend to make certain common errors. This mathematics test item illustrates the point:

3. The ratio of 25 cents to 5 dollars is
    a. 1/20
    b. 1/5
    c. 5/1
    d. 20/1
    e. none of these   *a*

The examinee who carelessly overlooks the distinction between cents and dollars, or inverts the ratio, will arrive at one of the distracters rather than at the answer. For some purposes, a very productive procedure for obtaining effective distracters for multiple-choice purposes is to administer the item first in completion form. If the sample of examinees used in this preliminary tryout is representative of the examinees for whom the test is eventually intended, a study of the incorrect responses should reveal the most common errors made and hence the most useful distracters. The item writer who depends solely on his own imagination and experience to guess what mistakes examinees are likely to make rarely will find as good distracters as the examinees' actual errors can provide. The method is especially applicable when factual information is being tested and a single word or number represents the correct response. Solution of arithmetic problems, identification of correctly and incorrectly spelled words, and selection of foreign language vocabulary synonyms are examples of testing situations that lend themselves readily to this method.

Occasionally, one is fortunate enough to find ready-made distracters available through others' researches. In the construction of the *Differential Aptitude Tests*, the selection of potentially effective incorrectly spelled words was considerably facilitated by the availability of Gates' *A List of Spelling Difficulties in 3,876 Words* (1937). The test author who is knowledgeable in a subject-matter field (or seeks the counsel of those who are) will now and again find, in published studies or unpublished dissertations, similarly helpful materials. More often, it will be necessary to do one's own experimenting by giving items in completion format to appropriate samples of examinees.

7. *Avoid highly technical distracters*— Item writers, needing additional distracters, sometimes are tempted to insert a response of which the meaning or applicability is completely beyond the ability of the examinee to understand.

1. Electric shock is most commonly administered in the treatment of
   a. rheumatism.
   b. paralysis.
   c. insanity.
   d. erythema.   c

The first three suggested responses are fairly common terms. The fourth is almost never encountered. It is definitely a "space filler" in this item, but it presents a frustrating problem to the examinee since he is forced to choose a best answer without knowing the meaning of one of the answers. *The level of information or ability required to reject a wrong response should be no higher than the level of ability required to select a correct response.* When this is true, an examinee may sometimes arrive at his choice by successively eliminating incorrect answers. Response by elimination has been criticized, but it has one possible advantage over response by direct selection. The examinee may need more pertinent information to eliminate three plausible distracters than he would need to select one correct verbal stereotype.

8. *Avoid responses that overlap or include each other*— An example of this defect is provided by:

1. The average height of adult U.S. males
   is
   a. less than 5 feet 3 inches.
   b. less than 5 feet 5 inches.
   c. more than 5 feet 7 inches.
   d. more than 5 feet 9 inches.   c

This item is, in effect, a two-response item. The choice lies between *b* and *c*. For if *a* is correct then *b* is also correct, and if *d* is correct then *c* is also correct. More subtle examples of this defect are occasionally encountered in item writing.

9. *Use "none of these" as a response only in items to which an absolutely correct answer can be given. Use it as an obvious answer several times early in the test but use it sparingly thereafter. Avoid using it as the answer to items in which it may cover a large proportion of incorrect responses*— "None of these" is quite appropriate as a response to the correct-answer variety of multiple-choice item. It is inappropriate in best-answer items. An examinee may properly reject all suggested responses if he is working under instructions to choose only completely correct answers. He cannot reasonably be asked to mark "none of these" when his general instruction is to pick the *best* of several admittedly imperfect responses.

"None of these" is a useful response for items in arithmetic, spelling, punctuation, and similar fields where conventions of correctness can be applied rigorously. It provides an easy-to-write fourth or fifth response when one is needed and may be more plausible than any other that can be found. It sometimes enables the item writer to avoid stating an answer that is too obviously correct.

Two dangers are connected with the use of "none of these." The first is that it may not be seriously considered as a possible answer. The second is that the examinee who chooses "none of these" as the correct response may be given credit when he has really arrived at a wrong answer. To avoid the first danger, the examinee must be convinced at the beginning of the test that "none of these" is likely to be the answer to some items. This can be achieved by using it as the correct response to several easy items early in the test.

The second danger can be avoided by sparing use of "none of these" *as the correct answer* after the beginning of the test and by limiting its use as the answer to items in which the distracters encompass most of the probable incorrect responses. "None of these" would be an appropriate answer to:

1. What is the area of a right triangle whose sides adjacent to the right angle are 3 inches and 4 inches long respectively?
   a. 7
   b. 12
   c. None of these _____ c___

Some examinees may miss this item by simply adding 3 and 4. Others might multiply 3 by 4 and forget division by 2. Still others might add 3, 4, and 5. Since the number of possible incorrect responses to this item is limited, they may all be included as distracters, so that only examinees who solve the problem correctly will be likely to choose "none of these."

This situation does not prevail in item 2.

2. What is the sum of
37,859	a. 176,216
46,212	b. 183,127
39,843	c. 186,226
62,312	d. None
?	of these c

It is obviously impossible to anticipate all of the possible errors students might make in responding to this item. Hence, with no further information, it would be undesirable to use "none of these" as the answer with only a few of the possible incorrect responses listed as distracters. It is more appropriate to use it as a distracter. As mentioned earlier, however, it is sometimes possible to anticipate a very large proportion of the incorrect responses for an item if it has previously been administered in completion form. Such items might well be favored for use with "none of these" as the correct response in later portions of the test.

10. *Arrange the responses in logical order, if one exists, but avoid consistent preference for* *any particular response position—* When the responses consist of numbers, they should ordinarily be put in ascending or descending order. If the responses are small numbers such as 1, 2, 3, 4, or 5, the 1 should occur in the first position, 2 in the second position, and so on. If this is not done, there will be a strong tendency for the examinees to confuse the absolute value of the answer with the response position used to indicate it.

If an item contains one or more pairs of responses dealing with the same concept, these should usually be placed together. In the following item, it is preferable to arrange the responses as shown rather than to distribute them at random among the choice positions.

1. Which of these would you expect to be anti-inflationary in the United States?
   a. Increased consumption of goods
   b. Increased exports to Europe
   c. Limitation of credit to consumers
   d. Limitation of the size of savings accounts _____ c___

In many items, however, there is no objection to assigning the responses at random to the response positions. This gives the item writer an opportunity to balance roughly the number of answers occurring in each position.

Some writers have advocated that obvious answers should be placed last so that the examinee will be forced to read and consider the distracters before seeing the correct response. There is no evidence concerning the effectiveness of this procedure, and it appears to be of doubtful value. If the answer is so obvious that the examinee will choose it the moment he sees it, placing it last is not likely to help the item much.

11. *If the item deals with the definition of a term, it is usually preferable to include the term to be defined in the stem and present alternative definitions in the responses—* The reason for this suggestion is that it usually provides more opportunities for attractive distracters and tends to reduce the opportunity for correct response by verbal association. Consider these illustrations:

1. What name is given to the group of complex organic compounds that occur in small quantities in natural foods and are essential to normal nutrition?
   a. Nutrients
   b. Calories
   c. Vitamins
   d. Minerals _____ *c*

2. What is a vitamin?
   a. A complex substance necessary for normal animal development, which is found in small quantities in certain foods
   b. A complex substance prepared in biological laboratories to improve the nutrient qualities of ordinary foods
   c. A substance extracted from ordinary foods, which is useful in destroying disease germs in the body
   d. A highly concentrated form of food energy, which should be used only on a doctor's prescription _____ *a*

In the second item, more of the common misconceptions about the meaning of the term *vitamin* can be suggested and made attractive to the superficial learner.

12. *Do not present a collection of true-false statements as a multiple-choice item—* Such items usually reveal the item writer's failure to identify or specify a single problem. In some cases, the true-false statements are grouped about a single problem and could be easily reworded to make that problem specific. In other cases, the statements are so loosely related that they hardly constitute a single problem at all. This situation is illustrated by:

1. What does physiology teach?
   a. The development of a vital organ is dependent upon muscular activity.
   b. Strength is independent of muscle size.
   c. The mind and body are not influenced by each other.
   d. Work is not exercise. _____ *a*

Here two of the responses show some similarity. The other two are quite diverse. Grouping all in a single item leads the examinee to look for a common principle. It is difficult for

him to arrive at any rational basis for selecting a best response. One beneficial change would be to replace *c* and *d* by others dealing with muscles or muscle activity and to reword the stem to point toward this problem.

The Matching Exercise

1. *Group only homogeneous premises and homogeneous responses in a single matching item—* The premises and responses in this item are not homogeneous.

e	1. A drawing tool used primarily as a guide to draw horizontal lines	a. dividers
		b. arc
d	2. Avoidance of erasures, blots, uneven lines, or poorly shaped letters	c. French curve
		d. neatness
b	3. Any part of the circumference of a circle	e. T-square

Such an item measures only very superficial verbal associations. It is easily solved by those who have only vague concepts.

2. *Use relatively short lists of responses—* Seldom should more than five alternative responses be suggested for a given group of premises. Two reasons for this recommendation concern the item writer. It is difficult to maintain homogeneity in a long list of responses. Furthermore, long lists of responses reflect concentration on one aspect of achievement, thus preventing proper distribution of emphasis. A third reason concerns the examinee. With few responses, little time need be wasted in hunting for a proper response. The examinee may even fix the responses in mind so that his only problem is that of reading each premise and deciding which response best applies to it.

The only necessary limitation to the number of premises is imposed by the requirement that they must all belong with the same homogeneous group of responses. It is often impossible to find a large number of premises to which the same group of responses constitute plausible matchings. Even where it is possible, the item writer should probably use short lists of homogeneous premises of the same kind so that he can sample a larger variety of topical areas.

3. *Arrange premises and responses for maximum clarity and convenience to the examinee—* In general it is desirable to use the longer, more complex statements as premises, to arrange them at the left, and to number them as independent items. The responses should be arranged in order (e.g. alphabetical or chronological), if any logical basis for order exists, to simplify the task of matching.

4. *In the directions explain clearly the intended basis for matching—* In simple matching exercises, the basis may be almost self-evident, but it should be made explicit in the directions. For classification-type items, specific instructions are especially needed. Illustrative items presented in the section on item forms (pp. 98–99) show this detail in directions.

5. *Do not attempt to provide perfect one-to-one matching between premises and responses* — The same response may be used for more than one premise. Occasionally responses that fit none of the premises should be included. Nothing is gained by attempting to provide equal numbers or premises and responses and to assure perfect matching. On the contrary, something is lost because the examinee may be given an irrelevant clue to one correct response.

CONTEXT-DEPENDENT ITEMS

Items in most ability tests have traditionally been independent units; that is, each item presents all the information the examinee is to be offered. There are some test situations, however, in which the item has meaning only in relation to other material presented to the examinee—a graph, a prose passage, etc. This section describes several such test situations and some of the salient characteristics of items prepared where the examinee is referred to context external to the items.

I. The Pictorial Form

The use of items based on pictures and graphic devices has been increasing over the years. For some kinds of testing such devices are particularly effective. Thus, if one wishes to examine the student's ability to read a topographical map, to identify a painting, or to read values on meters, a direct representation of the map, painting, or meter provides a more effective and more realistic basis for item construction than would be provided by verbal descriptions of the objects. There is the additional advantage, for many applications, of requiring less complex language than purely verbal statements would entail. The sought-for knowledge, understanding, or appreciation can consequently be probed with a minimum of contamination from reading comprehension facility.

Items 1, 2, 3, and 4 illustrate the use of a table and of a graph as bases for appraising the examinee's ability to understand devices of this kind. Obviously, a number of meaningful items beyond those shown could be devised.

Item 5 illustrates the use of a picture for measurement of the examinee's ability to apply knowledge of simple physical principles. It would be possible to describe the depicted situation verbally; to do so would impose on the examinee a more complex reading assignment and involve him in creating mentally his own picture of the situation. The pictures permit presentation of the problem with very simple language thereby eliminating possible confusion due to low reading comprehension.

Although it has sometimes been suggested that pictorial and graphic materials be used to enhance the interest value of a test, this is probably of secondary importance at best. Pictorial presentation should be used when it is the most direct or otherwise most appropriate form in which to cast a problem situation. Like other forms, it can be overdone. A problem that can be presented in simple verbal form should not be cast into pictorial form for extraneous reasons. The relevance of the picture, graph, or table for the specific kind of appraisal intended should be the determining consideration.

Preparing the pictorial form

1. *Use pictures, graphs, and similar devices because they are appropriate for the specific measurement purpose, not for interest or entertainment—* The students taking a test for a serious purpose do not need to be entertained; most students faced with an appropriate test of their ability find the task sufficiently

Table for Computation of Gross Estate Tax

(A) Taxable estate equal to or more than—	(B) Taxable estate less than—	(C) Tax on amount in column (A)	(D) Rate of tax on excess over amount in column (A)
			Percent
0	$ 5,000	0	3
$ 5,000	10,000	$ 150	7
10,000	20,000	500	11
20,000	30,000	1,600	14
30,000	40,000	3,000	18
40,000	50,000	4,800	22
50,000	60,000	7,000	25
60,000	100,000	9,500	28
100,000	250,000	20,700	30

Items 1 and 2. The table above is used for computing gross estate tax.

1. How much tax must be paid on a taxable estate of $20,000.00?
   a. $14
   b. $224
   c. $1,600
   d. $2,800   _c_

2. How much tax must be paid on a taxable estate of $35,000.00?
   a. $3,000
   b. $3,900
   c. $6,300
   d. $7,000   _b_

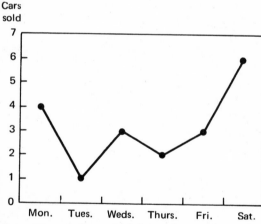

Items 3 and 4 are based on the graph above, which shows the number of cars sold by the Brown Agency in one week.

3. How many more cars were sold on the best day than on the next best day?
   a. 1
   b. 2
   c. 3
   d. 6   _b_

4. On which day were fewest cars sold?
   a. Monday
   b. Tuesday
   c. Thursday
   d. Saturday   _b_

challenging inherently. Decoration as such is unnecessary. A clear presentation of the problem is as much as they ask.

2. *Select or create the device with specific measurement goals in mind*— If a simple principle is the focus of the problem (e.g. item 5), the graphic presentation should be simple; inclusion of irrelevant materials may interfere with good measurement. If the intent is to require the student to abstract from a complex situation those features that are relevant to a solution, more complex presentations may be justified.

3. *Use pictorial representations that are well drawn and easily perceived*— The student should have no doubt about what he is seeing; significant details such as numbers, words, signs, markers, and the like should be large enough and clear enough to avoid misunderstanding due to imperfect viewing or misinterpretation of the artist's or author's intent. Insignificant detail should not be permitted such prominence as to confuse or distract the examinee.

4. *Observe the same care in preparing stems and options based on pictorial devices as is required for other multiple-choice items*— Undue reliance on the pictorial device to carry the burden of meaning of a stem or option may

5. In which picture are the children whirling faster? (If equal, mark C.)   _A_

Item 5 reproduced by permission. Copyright 1947, © 1961, 1962 by The Psychological Corp., N. Y. All rights reserved.

impose an unfair burden on the student and render the item ambiguous.

5. *If it is necessary to prepare text to explain a pictorial device, make the statement as simple to understand as is possible—* It is well to remember that the purpose of the text is to present the problem to the student, not to measure his ability to understand terse or imprecise prose.

II. The Interlinear Exercise

The *interlinear exercise* is an attempt to achieve a happy compromise between the control aspects of multiple-choice testing and the free expression of essay writing. It is an interesting extension of the substitution variety. The examinee is presented with textual material that is poorly written; it may be verbose, show unbalanced structure, contain ineffectual phrases, or be otherwise inadequate as good prose. The examinee's task is to find the defective segments and to substitute for them more effective, more acceptable phrases or organization. An example of a completed interlinear exercise, including the changes made by the examinee, appears in item 1.

1. Never had the fortunes of England ~~dived~~ *fallen* to a

lower ebb than at the moment when Elizabeth *ascended* ~~ascends~~ the throne. The country was humiliated by defeat,ₓ dissension, ~~had torn it,~~ *torn by* and ~~it was being~~ threatened by ~~hosts of~~ danger from without. ~~The English~~ *England's* hope lay in ~~their~~ *her* queen. (Not only) ~~was~~ Elizabethₓ the daughter *was* of Henry but the daughter of Ann Boleyn.

In the text material as it is presented to the examinee, the errors are not identified for him; he must locate and correct or improve the expressions that are faulty. The task is accordingly one which requires *recognition* of defective grammar, awkward construction, and the like and *production* of superior prose in place of the inadequate or incorrect.

Scoring of the interlinear exercise is confined to the specific segments that were originally injected by the passage's author to serve as matter to be improved. Repairs or revisions of other portions of the passage are disregarded. Only the performance on the deliberately implanted segments is scored. Since the exercise is, despite the controls implicit in it, a free-response type of test material, extensive consideration of possible responses is required before scoring can take place. Scorers should have detailed instructions as to the kinds of responses that are acceptable and those that are not. When feasible, it is best to pretest the exercise on appropriate samples of examinees to discover what kinds of corrections or incorrect substitutions are likely to be offered. These responses may then be classified as good, marginally acceptable, or unacceptable, after which appropriate scoring points may be assigned to each response.

Even with detailed instructions, of course, some degree of subjectivity is to be expected in scoring free-response materials. That the effect of this subjectivity can be reduced to a negligible minimum has been demonstrated by the studies performed for the College Entrance Examination Board. By pretesting of passages and intensive training of readers (scorers), it was found that excellent interreader agreement could be obtained; correlation coefficients of .95 and higher were secured in a variety of interreader score comparisons. Thus, a high order of objectivity *can* be achieved; to achieve it, however, the test developer should be prepared to invest as much effort and skill as was devoted in the above program. How formidable such a task may become is demonstrated by the fact that for a typical interlinear exercise in which approximately 50 "errors" had been implanted, the manual of scoring instructions was a 50-page booklet. The interlinear exercise is an interesting approach to measurement but, properly done, it is hardly an easy approach.

III. The Interpretive Test Exercise

The interpretive test exercise represents an approach to objective testing that lends itself particularly well to measurement of understanding rather than memory of significant or insignificant details. Originally used most frequently for the appraisal of reading comprehension or command of such directly taught skills as reading a "pie" chart or using a table in mathematics or social studies, it has in recent years been utilized for measurement of high-level mental processes in virtually all academic areas. The readiness with which it can be addressed to measuring the examinee's ability to *apply* what he has learned is the item type's chief advantage. The difficulty of constructing good interpretive exercises and the inefficiency of the item type per unit of time required are the chief disadvantages.

The interpretive test exercise consists of an introductory selection of material followed by a series of questions calling for various interpretations. The material to be interpreted may be a selection of almost any type of writing (news, fiction, science, poetry, etc.); a table, map, chart, diagram, or illustration; the description of an experiment or of a legal problem; even a baseball box score or a portion of a musical composition. The questions on this material may be based on explicit statements in the material, on inferences, explanations, generalizations, conclusions, criticisms, and on many other interpretations. The interpretive exercise may employ any of several item forms; it includes extensive introductory materials, and hence it has special possibilities for measurement.

The following two illustrations suggest the general form and content of the interpretive test exercise, although they by no means represent all of its possible varieties.

Illustration I.

It has been stated that "like Hellas, the Swiss Land was born divided," and also that "political solidarity had a hard, slow birth in the mountains." Certainly the physical features of the Swiss lands in serving sharply to confine movement and widely to separate settled areas did not facilitate intercourse and thus political cooperation. In mountainous Switzerland, at any rate, village communes tended to occupy the narrow lateral valleys of the Alps, where they engaged in agricultural and pastoral pursuits in a state of almost complete political and economic isolation and self-sufficiency. On the other hand, the geographical position of the Swiss lands was such as to induce a continual current of traffic *en route* for the passes of the Central Alps, whilst the major valleys of the principal rivers formed the main highways of communications. Moreover, the Swiss plateau stretching between Lake Constance and Geneva and cupped between the mountain ranges formed a broad belt of well-watered and relatively low-lying land that was capable of supporting a population much denser than that of the mountains. Actually, it was not the more-favored plateau lands, but certain cantons of the mountains that provided both the leadership in the wars for independence and the nuclear region around which the state grew. The reason seems to be that in the mountain valleys the peasant and shepherd population tenaciously defended its freedom from the encroachment of the feudal powers and largely escaped being reduced to serfdom, as were the inhabitants of the central plateau.

1. What is meant by "the Swiss Land was born divided"?
   1. There were many different religious sects.
   2. Different languages were spoken in different parts of the country.
   3. The mountains isolated the people in different parts of the country.
   4. The people fought among themselves.   *3*

2. With which of the following does the writer compare Switzerland?
   1. Ancient Rome
   2. Ancient Greece
   3. Medieval Italy
   4. Medieval France   *2*

3. Who took the lead in making Switzerland into a united nation?
   1. The traders
   2. The mountain people
   3. The farmers of the plains
   4. The serfs   *2*

4. What does the writer try to do in this paragraph?
   1. To describe the factors in the early commercial development of Switzerland
   2. To point out why Switzerland can never become a united country

3. To explain how trade changed the character of the Swiss nation
4. To show how geographical conditions affected the political unification of Switzerland   *4*

5. Which of the following is the most appropriate heading for this paragraph?
   1. Early Swiss Commerce
   2. Trade Routes and Their Effect on Switzerland
   3. Geography and Swiss Freedom
   4. Agriculture on the Swiss Plateau   *3*

Illustration II.

PRESIDENTIAL ELECTORAL VOTES IN UNITED STATES
BY POLITICAL PARTIES
1904–1944

Year	Republican	Democratic	Progressive
1904	336	140	
1908	321	162	
1912	8	435	88
1916	254	277	
1920	404	127	
1924	382	136	13
1928	444	87	
1932	59	472	
1936	8	523	
1940	82	449	
1944	99	432	

1. Which party held the presidency during 1926?
   1. Republican
   2. Democratic
   3. Progressive
   4. The table does not tell.   *1*

2. In what year was the Republican victory the most decisive?
   1. 1904
   2. 1924
   3. 1928
   4. 1936   *3*

3. Between which two consecutive elections was there the greatest increase in the number of Democratic electoral votes?
   1. 1908 and 1912
   2. 1912 and 1916
   3. 1928 and 1932
   4. 1932 and 1936   *3*

4. The percentage of the electoral votes received by the Democrats was the *largest* in what year?
   1. 1944
   2. 1936
   3. 1928
   4. 1912   *2*

Characteristics of the interpretive exercise

1. *The interpretive exercise provides an opportunity for measuring directly one of the important outcomes of instruction—the ability to interpret and evaluate printed materials—* Throughout this chapter and in preceding chapters the desirability, as well as the difficulty, of measuring directly the important outcomes of instruction has been stressed. Certainly the importance of ability to interpret printed materials is beyond question in modern times. What one needs to know and what one must do are most often presented as printed discussions or directions. These materials must be interpreted and evaluated. Their usefulness depends upon the accuracy and depth of penetration of the interpretations made.

An interesting comparison may be made among essay tests, typical objective tests, and interpretive exercises. The essay test, with which written testing began, asks, in effect, What can you tell about this subject? The prevalent types of objective test ask, in effect, What do you know about this subject? The interpretive exercise asks, in effect, What are you able to find out from this material? or What are you able to do with this material as background? It is not the purpose of this paragraph to compare the merits of these three test devices; rather it is to point out that the interpretive exercise occupies an important place among the various test formats.

2. *The interpretive exercise provides an effective setting in which to ask meaningful questions on relatively complex topics—* In the independent item forms (multiple-choice, true-false, etc.) it is difficult to supply the necessary "raw material" with which an examinee may demonstrate his ability to organize, generalize,

or evaluate. Often several paragraphs of material would be required. To include these in the item stem would make it cumbersome and inefficient. In the interpretive exercise, once the material has been prepared and once the examinee has read it, the material provides the basis for not one, but several items. The group of related items that are part of the interpretive exercise makes more complete use of these background materials than independent items could.

3. *The interpretive exercise requires both a general ability to interpret and a specific background of terms, facts, and principles related to the material presented—* General skill in reading is an important factor in the ability of an examinee to interpret selected materials. Knowledge of the special terms and concepts used and familiarity with the general principles and structure of the specific field with which the material deals likewise are important. Within limits, the relative influence of these two factors is under the control of the item writer. He can include items that call heavily upon general interpretive ability and make almost no demands on specific knowledge; or he can emphasize specific knowledge and minimize general interpretive ability.

It should be noted, however, that the interpretive exercise cannot, and is not intended to, supply a "pure" measure of informational background. Likewise, when it deals with specialized subject matter, it cannot supply a pure measure of general interpretive ability.

4. *The interpretive exercise has wide applications, but its use presents some special problems—* In the description of the interpretive exercise, mention was made of the wide variety of materials that could be presented for interpretation and of the correspondingly wide variety of abilities that could be called for by the questions asked. This wide applicability has not been generally recognized, so that the interpretive exercise has not yet assumed the important role envisioned for it in the field of educational measurement.

On the other hand, some of the difficulties encountered in using interpretive exercises should be clearly recognized. Even skilled experienced item writers find it difficult to construct interpretive exercises of high quality. The selection or construction of suitable materials and the identification of item topics that make maximum use of the inherent possibilities of the material are added problems not encountered in ordinary item writing. The interpretive exercise is relatively time consuming to administer. An hour of testing with interpretive exercises will produce fewer independent scoring units than the same time devoted to independent test items. Partly because of this time factor and also because of the intrusion of general interpretive ability, the interpretive exercise is not an efficient measure of informational background as such.

Writing the interpretive exercise

A. *Reading comprehension in specific subject-matter areas*

1. *Select the type of material to be interpreted for significance and representativeness—* Attention should be given to various types of material, and the most suitable should be selected. In many respects the problem of selecting materials to be interpreted is similar to the problem of identifying topics for independent items. The criteria of significance and the distribution of emphasis necessary to produce a good interpretive exercise vary from field to field. They can be determined only by one who is competent in the field.

2. *Write or rewrite the material to be interpreted so as to provide for the desired interpretations and to eliminate nonfunctional portions—* It is rarely possible to find intact passages of material that are ideally suited for interpretive exercises. Most test passages must either be originally written for the special purpose or developed through thorough revision of existing source materials. It goes without saying that the material should be clearly presented and should conform to the highest standards of form except where deliberate alterations are necessary to provide an opportunity for critical comments or for suggested revisions.

Often the addition or elimination of a word or sentence provides new opportunities for significant questions. The task of producing an interpretive exercise is not simply one of finding suitable material and then writing questions on it. It is rather an integrated task in which preparation of the test exercises and modification of the material go hand in hand.

The first step in constructing a test passage ordinarily consists of searching through materials for a reading selection that seems to contain several promising possibilities for interpretive items. The next step is to construct tentative items that exploit all of the item possibilities which the passage presents. The third step is to *rewrite* the passage so as to eliminate from it anything that does not contribute to the items already built and that is not essential to the continuity of the passage. This condensation may require some modification of the original items or elimination of certain items entirely. A highly condensed version is thus produced that, with reference to the items already constructed, is far more *efficient* than the original passage or that yields far more items "per line of passage" or per unit of total testing time.[8]

The next step is to reconsider the condensed version to determine whether, by further rewriting or additions, the basis for additional good items may be introduced. These changes may again require modification or even deletion of some of the original items. This process of reciprocal revisions and additions to the passages and the set of items continues until the writer feels that he has reached the point beyond which further improvement is not worth the effort. Often the final version has little resemblance to, or contains almost no intact paragraphs or sentences from, the original passage.

The preceding paragraphs describe roughly the manner in which most good interpretive exercises are built. Sometimes, an exceptionally competent test constructor may be able to write from scratch an original selection to satisfy certain predetermined specifications. Even then, the first draft of the passage will ordinarily require many revisions as the items are being constructed.

3. *Decide in advance how much emphasis should be placed upon a student's background information and then construct questions to provide the desired emphasis*— The interpretive exercise provides the opportunity for questions that make much or little demand upon the student's background of special information. This possibility should be clearly recognized, and the items should be written in terms of a definite purpose.

It will be clear that much of what has been said above is little different from the prescriptions one might set forth for a good test of reading comprehension in general. Selection and modification of existing passages, or creation of new passages, calls for similar procedures. The two most significant distinctions between development of interpretive exercises in specific subject-matter fields and development of passages for measuring general ability at reading comprehension are:

a. When measuring reading comprehension as a general ability, it is customary to appraise both speed and level of comprehension; when measuring comprehension in specific subject-matter areas it is usual, and desirable, to minimize the effects of speed of reading and quickness of comprehension.

b. When general reading comprehension tests are constructed, it is important to eliminate insofar as is possible the influence of special knowledge of the subject matter of the passage; ideally, no student should have had prior exposure to the ideas expressed. As indicated above, interpretive exercises in the specific subject-matter areas utilize the examinee's previous learning in the field and may even stress this aspect of his competence deliberately.

B. *Other types of interpretive exercise*

The procedures described for measurement of reading comprehension in specific subject-matter areas may similarly be applied to the

---

[8] Such condensation may be less desirable in a test of reading comprehension, in which one objective is to require the reader to distinguish between relevant and irrelevant material.

development of interpretive exercises to appraise other high-level abilities. Thus, the examinee's ability to understand the meaning of a topographical map and the implications of depicted features may be appraised through adaptation of an existing map or the creation of a map of a mythical geographic site. The latter is ordinarily the preferred device, since it can readily be designed to test for the specific understandings of interest to the test constructor. The ability to read mathematical tables or economic charts may similarly be appraised by adaptation or construction de novo.

The following exercise illustrates the use of a map as a device for appraising the examinee's ability to interpret materials in one aspect of social studies. The exercise and the discussion are reproduced from the pamphlet *Multiple-Choice Questions: A Close Look* (1963).

> In the following questions you are asked to make inferences from the data which are given you on the map of the imaginary country, Serendip. *The answers in most instances must be probabilities rather than certainties.* The relative size of towns and cities is not shown. To assist you in the location of the places mentioned in the questions, the map is divided into squares lettered vertically from A to E and numbered horizontally from 1 to 5.

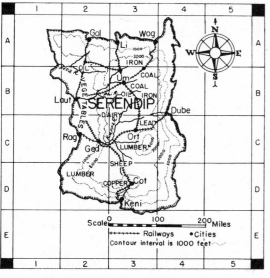

102. Which of the following cities would be the best location for a steel mill?
  a. Li   (3A)
  b. Um   (3B)
  c. Cot   (3D)
  d. Dube (4B)   *b*

A map of an imaginary country, such as that shown above, offers numerous possibilities for questions which measure important understandings. One could ask several questions requiring an understanding of the symbols used on the map. To determine student comprehension of the meaning of contour lines, for example, one might ask which railroad has the steepest grades to climb. Similar questions can be developed which require knowledge of the factors influencing population distribution, economic activities, and so on.

The question reproduced beneath the map requires knowledge of the natural resources used in producing steel and an awareness of the importance of transportation facilities in bringing these resources together. It was part of a general achievement test given to high school seniors.

The student who knows that iron is the basic raw material of steel and that coal commonly provides the necessary source of heat would proceed to locate deposits of these resources in relation to the cities listed in the question. He would be able to eliminate Cot immediately, since there is no iron or coal in its vicinity, although Cot might be an attractive choice to students who mistakenly think that copper is a basic ingredient of steel. Both Li and Dube are located reasonably near supplies of iron, and therefore might be attractive choices. Um, however, is the more clearly "correct" response, because not only are deposits of iron and coal nearby, but they are more readily transportable by direct railroad routes.

The teacher test constructor who is unready, unwilling, or unable to take on the chore of producing graphic materials as ambitious as the above map need not be disheartened. Ready-made maps, cartoons, and other illustrations abound in magazines, newspapers, and other media which can serve as devices on which to base interpretive exercises.[9] Moreover, simpler devices will often serve the purpose. For example, the table on page 121 might be employed to ask questions about the inherent philosophy of taxation, the effects on our national economy, and the like. The item writer's ingenuity is more important than his artistic talents.

As is true for reading comprehension passages, it is highly desirable that exercises employing charts, maps, tables, and the like be so constructed as to permit several significant questions to be based on each figure; to do

---

[9] If copyrighted materials are used, appropriate permission from the copyright owner should be obtained.

otherwise inevitably results in inefficient testing that may, in turn, result in lower reliability in the test when time for test administration is limited. Interpretive exercises should be designed to accomplish efficient, as well as effective, measurement.

CONCLUSION

Throughout this chapter attention has been called to the many subtleties involved in item writing and to the high degree of skill needed by the item writer in dealing with these subtleties. It would be unfortunate if the net effect of these comments were to discourage those who *must* either construct tests or seek some other method—equally valid and equally reliable— of appraising achievement. Recognition of difficulties and complexities and the desire to meet high standards should be balanced by realism. Practical limitations of time and skill will often force the test maker to compromise by preparing tests which fall short of the standards. It is a very poor tester indeed whose tests are so inadequate that it would be better not to test at all. Even tests of modest quality can contribute appreciably to educational and appraisal enterprises.

REFERENCES

Adkins, D. C., with Primoff, E. S. & others. *Construction and analysis of achievement tests.* Washington: U. S. Government Printing Office, 1947.

Bennett, G. K., & Doppelt, J. E. Relative efficiency of seven verbal item types. *Educational and Psychological Measurement*, 1956, **16,** 497–500.
Bennett, G. K., Seashore, H. G., & Wesman, A. G. *A manual for the differential aptitude tests.* (4th ed.) New York: Psychological Corporation, 1966.
Boynton, M. Inclusion of "none of these" makes spelling items more difficult. *Educational and Psychological Measurement*, 1950, **10,** 431–432.

Cook, D. L. The use of free response data in writing choice-type items. *Journal of Experimental Education*, 1958, **27,** 125–133.
Cramer, W. The positive or negative effect of the form of the question upon college students' answers. *Journal of Educational Research*, 1951, **44,** 303–307.
Cureton, E. E. Note on vocabulary test construction. *Educational and Psychological Measurement*, 1963, **23,** 641.
Cureton, E. E. The correction for guessing. *Journal of Experimental Education*, 1966, **34,** 44–47.

Davis, F. B. The interpretation of frequency ratings obtained from "The teachers' word book." *Journal of Educational Psychology*, 1944, **35,** 169–174.
Dressel, P. L., & Nelson, C. H. *Questions and problems in science: Test item folio no. 1.* Princeton, N. J.: Educational Testing Service, 1956.
Dunn, T. F., & Goldstein, L. G. Test difficulty, validity, and reliability as functions of selected multiple-choice item construction principles. *Educational and Psychological Measurement*, 1959, **19,** 171–179.
Durost, W. N., & Prescott, G. A. *Essentials of measurement for teachers.* New York: Harcourt, Brace & World, 1962.

Ebel, R. L. *Measuring educational achievement.* Englewood Cliffs, N. J.: Prentice-Hall, 1965.

Frederiksen, N., & Satter, G. A. The construction and validation of an arithmetic computation test. *Educational and Psychological Measurement*, 1953, **13,** 209–227.
Friedman, M. P., & Fleishman, E. A. A note on the use of a "don't know" alternative in multiple-choice tests. *Journal of Educational Psychology*, 1956, **47,** 344–349.

Gates, A. I. *A list of spelling difficulties in 3,876 words.* New York: Columbia University, Teachers College, Bureau of Publications, 1937.
Gerberich, J. R. *Specimen objective test items: A guide to achievement test construction.* New York: Longmans Green, 1956.
Godshalk, F. I., Swineford, F., & Coffman, W. E. *The measurement of writing ability.* New York: College Entrance Examination Board, 1966.

Hawkes, H. E., Lindquist, E. F., & Mann, C. R. *The construction and use of achievement examinations.* Boston: Houghton Mifflin, 1936.
Hughes, H. H., & Trimble, W. E. The use of complex alternatives in multiple-choice items. *Educational and Psychological Measurement*, 1965, **25,** 117–126.

Lord, F. M., The effect of random guessing on test validity. Educational Testing Service *Research Bulletin*, 1964, No. 9. (a)

Lord, F. M. An empirical comparison of the validity of certain formula scores. *Journal of Educational Measurement*, 1964, **1,** 29–30. (b)

Marcus, A. The effect of correct response location on the difficulty level of multiple-choice questions. *Journal of Applied Psychology*, 1963, **47,** 48–51.

Multiple-choice questions: A close look. Princeton, N. J.: Educational Testing Service, 1963.

Rimland, B., & Zwerski, E. The use of open-end data as an aid in writing multiple-choice distracters: An evaluation with arithmetic reasoning and computation items. *Journal of Applied Psychology*, 1962, **46,** 31–33.

Smith, K. An investigation of the use of "double-choice" items in testing achievement. *Journal of Educational Research*, 1958, **51,** 387–389.

Thorndike, E. L., & Lorge, I. *The teacher's word book of 30,000 words*. New York: Columbia University, Teachers College, Bureau of Publications, 1944.

Thorndike, R. L., & Hagen, E. *Measurement and evaluation in psychology and education*. (3rd ed.) New York: Wiley, 1969.

Travers, R. M. *How to make achievement tests*. New York: Odyssey Press, 1950.

Wesman, A. G., The usefulness of correctly spelled words in a spelling test. *Journal of Educational Psychology*, 1946, **37,** 242–246.

Wesman, A. G., Active vs. blank responses to multiple-choice items. *Journal of Educational Psychology*, 1947, **38,** 89–95.

Wesman, A. G., & Bennett, G. K. The use of "none of these" as an option in test construction. *Journal of Educational Psychology*, 1946, **37,** 541–554.

Wesman, A. G., & Seashore, H. G. Frequency vs. complexity of words in verbal measurement. *Journal of Educational Psychology*, 1949, **40,** 395–404.

Whipple, J. W. A study of the extent to which positive or negative phrasing affects answers in a true-false test. *Journal of Educational Research*, 1957, **51,** 59–63.

Womer, F. B. *Unit VII: Teacher-made tests: Writing the test*. Chicago: Science Research Associates, 1966.

Wood, D. A. *Test construction: Development and interpretation of achievement tests*. Columbus, Ohio: C. E. Merrill, 1960.

5. Gathering, Analyzing, and Using Data on Test Items

Sten Henrysson

Department of Education, University of Umeå, Sweden

The typical steps involved in the gathering, analyzing, and using of data on test items is this chapter's topic. The first sections give a simple and nontechnical presentation of the general principles and concepts involved. In the latter parts, some alternative techniques of item analysis are discussed, along with consideration of other more special problems and methods. In these latter sections, however, it is not intended that a complete account of present theories of item analysis be given.[1] Rather emphasis is placed on those techniques that are practiced and that have been found to be useful in ordinary test construction work. Some studies not mentioned in the text are included in the listing of references at the chapter's end to direct attention to other discussions pertinent to the subject.

The procedures described focus on the construction of objective achievement tests intended to provide valid discriminations among students at all levels of achievement (i.e. so-called norm-referenced tests). Criterion-referenced tests (which are discussed in chapter 17) are not treated here. Most of the principles and techniques discussed in this chapter, however, are applicable to other kinds of tests and have, in many instances, been developed there.

After a large number of test items have been written, following procedures and specifications as discussed in chapters 3 and 4, the next step in test construction is the collection of data as a basis for improving items and selecting the best available items to form the final test. The aim may be to construct a test with one kind of item intended to measure one main

domain or a test containing subtests or items intended to tap different areas of knowledge or behavior. The discussion here focuses on consideration of the construction of a test, or subtest, which measures one main dimension; the problem of selecting items for several subtests is taken up briefly.

TRYOUTS OF TEST ITEMS

The test blueprint, as discussed in chapter 3, defines:

1. The *purpose* of the test—what is to be measured, who is to be tested, what uses will be made of the test scores. One aspect of this step defines which criteria should be used to validate items and the test as a whole.

2. The test *content*—the subject matter to be tested and the type of ability the test will require.

3. The *weights* to be given to the different test categories.

4. The approximate test *length*—at least a rough estimate of the number of items that should be included in the final form as related to the reliability desired and the time available.

5. The *time limit*—to what extent speed of work will be measured.

6. The *item types*—whether multiple-choice, true-false, short-answer, or other types are to be used. For multiple-choice items, the number of distracters should be specified.

7. The *item difficulties*—the number of items on each difficulty level. (Difficulty level should be specified for each category of items.)

8. The test *scoring*—the procedures to be used to assign meaningful and accurate scores to each student's test. Questions such as the following should be considered: Will the scoring be fully objective? Will correction for

---

[1] Such are discussed in the rather theoretical models reported in *Statistical Theories of Mental Test Scores* (Lord & Novick, 1968) and *Studies in Item Analysis and Prediction* (Solomon, 1961).

guessing be applied? Will some system of scoring weights be used?

Fundamental to the whole test construction procedure is the scholarship and ingenuity of the test planners and the item writers in developing the preliminary pool of test items. After the planned pool of items has been written, the next stage involves tryout, analysis, and selection or revision of items. More than one cycle may be required, trying out in a second administration items that have been revised as a result of an initial tryout, until finally a test has been developed that fulfills the requirements set forth in the test blueprint.

As previously discussed (chapter 3), when the items have been written, subject-matter experts and other item writers usually are asked to review and criticize the items to catch factual errors and to try to locate and eliminate at least some of the inadequate items. This review is occasionally supplemented by asking some persons to answer the items and comment; their comments then also can be used in the preliminary screening and revision of the item pool.

Purpose of Tryouts

To help the test constructor select the best items from the available pool and make improvements in weaker items, one or more tryouts are conducted. These tryouts provide data for such purposes as:

1. Identifying weak or defective items—for example, ambiguous or indeterminate items and items with nonfunctioning or implausible distracters
2. Determining the difficulty of each item so that a selection may be made that will have a distribution of item difficulties appropriate to the purpose of the final test
3. Determining for each item its power to discriminate between good and poor students in the achievement variable being measured
4. Determining how many items should constitute the final test
5. Determining appropriate time limits for the final test
6. Discovering weaknesses in the directions to examiner and to examinee, in the sample or practice exercises, in the format, and so forth
7. Determining the intercorrelations among the items to avoid too much overlap or bias in item selection and to check the grouping of items into subtests.

The importance assigned to any one of these purposes and the nature of the tryout will vary with the type of test and the amount of time and resources available. The tryout can be relatively simple (for example, for sets of items designed to provide parallel forms of tests already in use) or involve a series of tryouts (for example, when a new kind of test for an important use is being constructed). The whole tryout procedure can be divided into three stages—pretryout, tryout, and trial administration of the final test.

1. By the pretryout is meant a preliminary administration of test items to a small sample of students from the population on which the test is to be used. This procedure may be highly informal and may involve only the administration of a mimeographed set of items to between 50 and 100 students. In the pretryout, one does not expect to make a complete statistical item analysis of the data collected. Often the test constructor will wish to administer the pretryout himself since much may be learned by direct observation and personal interview.

Sometimes it may not be necessary, or possible, to conduct a pretryout. This may be the case when a parallel form of an existing test is being constructed and/or time is short. However, then one must have a large surplus of items (perhaps twice the number needed for the final test) for use in the tryout so that it is possible simply to discard ineffective items while retaining a workable number for constructing the final test.

2. After a pretryout has been completed and most of the gross deficiencies eliminated, a formal tryout is conducted to obtain more accurate information on each item. This requires a representative sample of students large enough to provide data for a detailed statistical analysis of each item. For this purpose, 300 or more students will be needed. If the final test is to be

constructed for use on several age or grade levels, separate samples are needed for each level.

Occasionally so many deficiencies will be revealed in the tryout and such extensive revision of items made, a second full tryout is needed. This is more often the case when a new kind of test is being constructed.

3. On the basis of the data obtained in the tryouts, the items are improved and selected for the final test. A trial administration then can be made of this test to ascertain exactly how the test will function in actual use and to estimate the norms, validity, reliability, etc., of the final test. Such a trial administration also provides a final check on time limits and on the procedures of administration. No material changes should be made after the trial administration.

Administration of Tryouts

The rules for administering tests as described in chapter 7 are to a very large extent also applicable in the tryout setting. Therefore, this section is restricted to a discussion of some points especially important for tryouts.

Sampling

The tryout sample should be representative of the population to be tested and be selected by an efficient sampling procedure. Ideally, each student in the sample should be individually drawn from the population by simple random or stratified sampling. However, such a procedure is usually not practical, so some procedure of cluster sampling is used. The clusters often consist of whole classes or even whole schools. However, a cluster sample is at best a compromise with practical demands. When there are large variations between schools and classes, especially in certain factors related to success on specific items or the test as a whole, it is important to have a broad sampling of schools as well as individual students. Thus, the sample of 400 or 500 students should be drawn from as broad a range of schools as is administratively possible. (That a sampling method relying on entire schools will be found to be much less efficient than independent sampling of individual students has been demonstrated,

for example, by Lindquist, 1940; Lord, 1959; and Marks, 1947.)

The total sample of tryout items may be divided into several test forms and each form given to a different population sample. The form need not be as long as the final test will be, but, if the total score on the tryout is to be used as the criterion measure of the ability that is to be measured by the items, at least 25 items ought to be included in each form to provide a reasonably stable criterion score.

Testing conditions

Directions for examiners and examinees need to be reviewed and revised on the basis of the tryouts. Provision always should be made to secure complete reports from the examiners on any problems or difficulties that arose during the tryouts. At least some groups of students should be interviewed or asked to write down their comments regarding the directions and the test items.

Teachers or others from the group that will administer the final operational test should administer at least one of the tryouts. For this tryout the directions should be as identical as possible with those that will be used with the final test.

Reporting scores

If possible, scores should be reported to the teachers and administrators who arranged and whose students participated in the tryout. This usually helps to insure their continuing cooperation. If for some reason test scores cannot be reported, an explanation should be provided. When the scores are reported, instructions for their interpretation and use should be supplied.

Students also should be told about the purpose of the tryout and how their teachers will be informed of the results. It has been argued that the students' motivation might be too low if they were told that the results would not influence their school marks. In most cases, however, it is enough to explain the purpose of the tryout and to stress the importance of getting useful results. Then the testing situation itself will give the students the motivation to work as they would in a regular testing situation.

Experience has shown that lack of cooperation can be expected mainly from poorer students, and they would have given very few correct answers even if they had tried harder. Their failure to cooperate will tend to make the items look somewhat more difficult and discriminating than will be found to be true in actual use.

Insuring adequate tryout of all items

To gather accurate data about each individual test item, it is extremely important that all, or nearly all, of the examinees attempt to answer every item on which tryout data are desired. Most tests of educational achievement are not highly speeded but are administered with liberal time limits so as to place the major emphasis on *level* and *power* rather than on *rate* of work. In general, therefore, the best procedure for the tryout is to provide very liberal time limits so that most students have time to consider (not necessarily mark) all items.

When items to be tried out are for a speeded test, one so timed that a considerable proportion of examinees will not have time to finish, a real problem arises concerning the time limits for the tryout. If the tryout is conducted under speeded conditions comparable with the final form, the items toward the end cannot be attempted by a large proportion of the examinees. On the other hand, if the tryout is conducted with generous time limits, the mental set and rate of work of the examinees may be so different from those likely to exist during administration of the final form the tryout data may not be useful. (The fact that test time limit and item placement can have undesirable effects upon the estimates of item parameters for items appearing late in a tryout test has been demonstrated by, for example, Aiken, 1964, and Mollenkopf, 1950.)

Three ways of avoiding this problem have been widely employed. Under one method, the items to be tried out under speeded conditions are followed in the test booklet by a set of "cushion" items, of the same general type as the others, that are to be neither analyzed nor scored. These items should be relatively difficult and time consuming since their only pur-

pose is to keep the faster or abler examinees occupied during the latter part of the test period.

Under a second method, the items to be tried out are placed in different order in two or more booklets; thus if 30 items are to be tried out, items 11–20 in booklet A appear as items 1–10 in booklet B, and items 21–30 in booklet A appear as items 1–10 in booklet C. Thus, every item appears among the first 10 in at least one of the tryout booklets, among the second 10 in one, etc. Item analysis data then is computed for the first 66 2/3 percent (20 items) in each booklet. The second method is essentially the same as the first—in this case, the cushion items in each form are some of the items being tried out. The second method is, of course, the more expensive, since it requires the printing of several tryout forms for the same items and utilizes only a part of the tryout data on each item.

A third method, applicable when items designed for parallel forms of tests are to be tried out, consists of interspersing new items in current final forms. The pool of new items is divided into groups and tried out together with the current test on different samples. Sometimes a whole page or section containing only new test items can be included in the test booklet being used in the regular program. That the scores on the current test can serve as a criterion variable when validating the new items enhances the value of this method. However, since this method involves printing of the extra sections in final form, the procedure is very expensive. When this method is used, a few precautions should be observed:

1. The tryout forms should be included on a rotating basis in order to provide random sampling of the population. Each one of these population samples must be large and representative enough to permit a separate item analysis.

2. Students should be told that tryout materials are included; this should lessen their anxiety later when they discover other students had items they don't recall. However, they need not be told which items are tryout.

3. In a test in which speed plays a role, great care must be taken that tryout items do not waste the examinee's time because of am-

biguity, unusual length, or great difficulty. This problem can be largely avoided by placing the tryout items in a separately timed section.

Surplus of Items for Discard

It is always necessary to try out more items than will be needed for the final test. There is no universal rule defining the margin for discard that must be allowed. In general, the more complex the items or the mental functions tested by them the larger the margin for discard must be. It is safe to say that the margin can be minimized when the items are constructed to provide another form of an existing test, when the items are factual in content or are concerned with narrow and well-defined skills, and when the standard of excellence to be met is not especially high. For example, in a tryout of vocabulary items for parallel forms in a particular testing program, a margin for discard of 20 percent was more than adequate.

The margin for discard likewise depends on the competence and experience of the item writers. Of two writers constructing items for the same test, one may produce a much larger proportion of defective items than the other.

The margin for discard also must be increased as the number of separate categories of items is increased to counterbalance effects of sampling fluctuations in a given category. Suppose that the outline for a history test calls for four items in the category "names in the news." Even if in the long run about two-thirds of items of this kind that are tried out prove acceptable, it would not be prudent to try out only six items in this category. By mere chance it might be that only two or three of them would prove acceptable. A smaller margin for discard is adequate when the test outline calls for a considerably larger number of items in a category because the effect of chance will be correspondingly reduced. A further factor to be considered is the degree of control desired on item difficulty. When rather rigid specifications have been set up for the distribution of item difficulties in the final test, as when parallel forms are being prepared, one must expect some loss of items because they do not match the specifications with respect to difficulty, and the number tried out must be increased to provide for this.

Often, a special provision must be made to try out enough very difficult items, because losses among such items are frequently high. Ordinarily, only a small proportion of the items in the final form are intended to be exceptionally easy or exceptionally difficult. For this reason, only a small proportion of exceptionally easy or difficult items usually are included in the tryout test. But as there are only a few items, margin for discard must anticipate noticeably high mortality. One further reason for high mortality among difficult items is the greater role chance plays in determining responses to very difficult items: there is naturally a greater amount of guessing on such items.

In summary then, the number of items for the tryout must depend to a considerable extent on an individual evaluation of the quality of items by the test developer to decide how many to try out and what allowances to make for item discard.

Organization into Subtests

The criterion variable for an item analysis ordinarily should be rather homogeneous to give results that are easy to interpret. Therefore items constructed for an achievement test are sometimes tried out in separate groups, the total score on each group being used as the criterion for obtaining item analysis data for each item within that group. In constructing a test of college physics, for example, one might try out separate groups of items in mechanics, heat, electricity, and so forth. This is often desirable even though all types of items are later to be intermingled in the final form and all will contribute to a single score. It is obviously important that each group of items be large enough to yield a reliable and valid total score and that all groups be tried out on highly comparable samples. When sufficiently reliable and valid subcriteria are not available, so that a more heterogeneous total score must be used considerations other than item statistics (e.g item content) become more central in the selection of items.

CRITERIA FOR ITEM ANALYSIS

One of the main purposes of the tryout is to ascertain to what extent each item discriminates between good and poor students as defined by a criterion. In selecting the criterion to be used, one wishes to find a good measure of the ability or skill the test is designed to assess. Ideally, the criterion should be independent of the item being evaluated. Such a criterion might be teacher's ratings based on school marks in the germane subjects, or a series of work samples that would provide a greater sampling of the student's ability in the area than is provided by the test itself. However, most often the total score on the test itself is used as the criterion because of difficulties inherent in using an independent criterion. School marks are likely to be influenced by student characteristics; such factors as promptness, neatness, cooperativeness, ability to memorize, etc., may be teaching objectives and hence enter into grades without being relevant to the ability being measured by the test. Any such extraneous factor vitiates the correlation between the item and the criterion and makes it difficult to determine whether low correlations are due to criterion irrelevance or to a weakness in the item. Longer work samples as a criterion have the advantage of enabling a student to show what he can do under a more typical (yet controlled) "work situation" but have the disadvantage of being more difficult to administer because of time requirements and more difficult to evaluate because of greater subjectivity of scoring. The justification for using the total score or the score on a test of similar items is that ambiguities and other weaknesses of individual items are likely to be outweighed by a majority of good valid items and that the total test score is thus a fair overall measure of what the individual items are designed to measure. As weak items are weeded out and the test takes on a final form, this assumption appears to be a reasonable one for most academic tests if item writers are skillful in meeting the test objectives generally. However, use of this criterion can lead to greater homogeneity of content as items unlike the majority of items are eliminated because of lower correlation: the person using the item statistics must keep this danger in mind in selecting items. The danger of restricting content for this reason can be minimized if the content plan is well formulated.

COMPILATION AND USE OF TEST ITEM DATA

There are a number of techniques for analyzing and using data collected in tryouts. At this point attention is focused on one technique for handling data from a pretryout on a small sample and on one more rigorous method for treating tryout data from a large sample of students. Other analysis techniques are discussed in the latter part of the chapter.

Pretryout Data

As noted earlier, it is often useful to conduct a pretryout on a small, informal sample. Though this pretryout is useful primarily for locating gross deficiencies in directions, type of item structure, and level of test difficulty, analysis of the results for individual items is also of some value.

Tabulation of pretryout data

To analyze data from the small pretryout sample (which typically would involve less than 100 students), it is not necessary to use advanced techniques of statistical item analysis; rather it is usually quite sufficient to set up for each test item a simple tabular presentation giving information on:

1. Number choosing the correct answer
2. Number choosing each one of the distracters, omitting the item, and not reaching the item
3. Frequency distribution of criterion scores for the group choosing each of the options (i.e. correct answer or one of the distracters), omitting the item, and not reaching the item.

As an example, these data are given in

table 5.1 for the pretryout of this preliminary version of a vocabulary item:

16. An *esteemed* leader is
    a. feared.
    b. honored.
    c. elected.
    d. valued.
    e. misunderstood.

for which alternative *d* is the correct answer. This item was part of an 18-item pretryout for a 12-item vocabulary subtest intended for final use in a test of English. The pretryout used a sample of 60 students. The total score on the subtest was used as the criterion score.

Table 5.1 details the distribution of responses to the item. The number choosing each response to, omitting, or not reaching the item in each criterion (total score) category is tabulated. The righthand column shows the frequency distribution of total scores on the 18 items for the whole group of 60 students.

The data of table 5.1 can be used to illustrate some basic principles for the analysis of an item. Some words of caution, however, are necessary. Statistical analysis here is based on a small sample; thus all frequencies seen in the table are rather unstable. The number of

items in the test, only 18, is small. With so few items, it is possible that some chance element has played a part in some high scores, and, therefore, one should not attach undue significance to one or two high scores in a distracter column. Besides, even top-scoring examinees are capable of making careless errors either by answering too quickly or by erroneous marking.

It is important to remember also that an item should never be changed for purely statistical reasons. The information supplied by the statistical item analysis is only an aid and a control, which gives the test constructor suggestions about weaknesses in items.

Interpretation of pretryout data

Of the total group of 60, 21 students picked the right answer (*d. valued*); i.e. the proportion of right answers is $p = 21/60 = .35$. This indicates that the item is a fairly difficult one.

Distracters *a*, *b*, and *c* seem reasonably attractive since they were picked by 11, 15 and 8 students respectively. Distracter *e* attracted only two students indicating that *misunderstood* is obviously a wrong answer to almost everyone and thus very implausible

TABLE 5.1

Distribution of Criterion Scores for Students Choosing
Different Answers on Pretryout Item 16

Criterion (Total Score)	Students Choosing Answer Alternative					Students Omitting Item	Students Not Reaching Item	Whole Distribution
	a	b	c	(d)	e			
18				1				1
17		1		1				2
16		1		2				3
15				2				2
14		1	1	1				3
13				3				3
12		2		2				4
11	2		1	2				5
10		2	1	2				5
9	4	1	2	1				8
8	2	3		2				7
7	1	2	2	1				6
6	2	1			1			4
5			1			1		2
4		1		1		1		3
3					1		1	2
Totals	11	15	8	21	2	2	1	60

This distracter probably should be replaced by a more plausible wrong answer.

The next step is to interpret the frequency distributions for the different answer alternatives. The distribution of students choosing the correct answer shows that this answer attracted many students with high total scores but very few with low total scores. This indicates that answer *d* worked well as the correct answer. The distribution of total scores for distracters *a* and *c* show that these tended to attract many students with average or low total scores but few with high scores. This is an important characteristic of a good distracter. Distracter *b* did not seem to work well in this respect since even some students with high total scores chose it. Distracter *b* might therefore be changed if such a change is also indicated by content considerations. Distracter *e* has already been criticized: it should be noted that the two students who did choose it have low total scores.

Another analysis consideration is the number who did not answer the item. Only two omitted the item and only one did not reach it. This indicates that the time limit permitted virtually all students to try the item. The total scores for those who did not answer it are low; thus it is likely that they would not have answered the item correctly even if they had marked an answer. Thus a more liberal time limit would have had very little effect on the number of correct responses on this item.

One can conclude from the data that item 16 is promising, but it could be improved by choosing distracters to replace *b* (*honored*) and *e* (*misunderstood*) to insure that the right answer stands out more clearly as the only correct answer for students with a good vocabulary and therefore is chosen by most of them while at the same time all the distracters seem plausible and attractive to students with a poor vocabulary.

Revision after the Pretryout

After the analysis of pretryout data for item 16, it was decided that distracters *b* and *e* should be replaced by *forceful* and *skillful* which were expected to work as plausible synonyms for *esteemed*. Such changes in an item will have some effect on the proportion of students picking the correct answer. Some who chose distracter *b* (*honored*) in the old version would probably choose the correct answer in the new version. On the other hand, the new distracter *e* (*skillful*) might attract some students who chose the correct answer in the pretryout version. This would tend to decrease the proportion choosing the correct answer. It is difficult to predict which tendency would be stronger.

After items of the pretryout test have been revised thus, and perhaps some of them discarded, a new tryout version should be assembled. If the new version of the test contains many new or markedly revised items, it may be best to conduct a second pretryout on all of the items or at least on the new and revised items. When a large majority (perhaps 80 percent) of the items have remained virtually unchanged following tryout, it is time to try them out on a large sample. As previously indicated this sample ought to contain at least 300 to 400 students picked from the population for which the test is intended by a proper sampling technique.

It should be stressed that all versions for tryout should have a surplus of items. For example, it may be found that too many items are of certain difficulty levels and too few are of others. It therefore may be necessary to exclude some items, though good, and construct some new ones to obtain the desired distribution of items by difficulty level in compiling the final form.

Analysis of Tryout Data

Tabulation of tryout data

The new version of the vocabulary subtest was tried out on a sample of 400 students. Item 16 in the pretryout was placed as number 15 in the new version of 16 items. It read:

15. An *esteemed* leader is
    a. feared.
    b. forceful.
    c. elected.
    d. valued.
    e. skillful.

The data for this item from the tryout are

TABLE 5.2

Distribution of Criterion Scores for Students Choosing
Different Answers on Tryout Item 15

Criterion (Total Score)	Students Choosing Answer Alternative				e	Students Omitting Item	Students Not Reaching Item	Whole Distribution
	a	b	c	(d)				
15				3				3
14	1			3				4
13				8	1			9
12	1	2		16	1			20
11	3	4	1	31	3			42
10	4	4	2	38	6			54
9	6	11	4	24	13			58
8	13	16	11	23	17			80
7	11	12	12	12	14			61
6	9	7	6	5	7	1		35
5	3	2	3	1	4		1	14
4	1	2	2		4	1		10
3					1	1	3	5
2		1					1	2
1					1		2	3
n_i	51	61	42	164	72	3	7	400
p_i	.13	.15	.11	.41	.18	.01	.02	1.00
M_i	7.71	8.08	7.14	9.90	7.65	4.33	2.57	8.48

reported in table 5.2, which follows the format of table 5.1.

Interpretation of tryout data

The data in table 5.2, interpreted in the same manner as the pretryout data in table 5.1, show that 164 of 400 students picked the correct answer; i.e. the proportion of correct answers is $p = 164/400 = .41$.

Analysis shows that all distracters are now reasonably attractive. The least attractive (*c. elected*) was chosen by 42 of 400 students—this seems to be an acceptably high number.

The frequency distributions for the different answer alternatives show that the correct answer has on the whole attracted more of the students with a better vocabulary, as measured by the total score on the test, than the distracters have. The distribution of total scores for the different distracters indicates that they were chosen mainly by students with average or low scores and by few students with high scores. It already has been seen that all four distracters were rather frequently chosen. These facts indicate that this set of distracters is acceptable.

Only three students omitted the item and seven did not reach it; thus the time limit seems

to have been reasonable.

In summary, the data from the tryout of this item show that the item is useful in a test of vocabulary of the given type.

It should be pointed out that full tables such as table 5.2 will be quite a burden to make, especially if many items are tried out. Actually it is not necessary to make these tabulations; this has been done here for instructional purposes. Rather data giving the frequencies and the mean criterion scores for each answer alternative as is done at the bottom of table 5.2 will be sufficient. Another possibility is to calculate the biserial correlations with each of the answer alternatives coded "right" (see p. 140) instead of ascertaining the means.

STATISTICAL ITEM ANALYSIS OF TRYOUT DATA

Different properties of the item can be quantified in a more rigorous fashion by use of statistical indices. Several alternative techniques and indices have been developed for use in an item analysis with this purpose. One set of item analysis techniques commonly employed is described here; alternative methods are discussed in the next section.

Item Difficulty

The desired difficulty level of items for the final test will depend on the purpose of the test. Most classroom tests are intended to provide valid discriminations among students at all levels of achievement. In such instances, a spread in item difficulty is desirable to provide the best students sufficient challenge and yet permit poorer students to demonstrate their capabilities. For tests intended for selection, the bulk of items must be at a difficulty level appropriate for those at the ability level where selection will be made. However, even in selection tests, a few easy items should be included to provide encouragement to the poorer students to attempt the test. (See the discussion of desirable item difficulty distributions on pp. 151–153.)

The simplest and most commonly used measure of item difficulty is p—the proportion of correct answers on the item. (Sometimes percent is used instead of proportion.) Item proportion (or percent) as a measure of item difficulty has two weaknesses: (a) p is actually a measure of item easiness as the larger the item proportion p the easier the item and, more importantly, (b) p is not linearly related to a scale of difficulty with equal intervals and hence cannot be averaged or otherwise treated in a simple statistical manner. It does, however, have a use in estimating total test means and p therefore should be obtained.

A more satisfactory index of item difficulty for some purposes is z, which transforms the item proportions into standard scores of difficulty according to the following rationale. A very common assumption made in test theory is that the ability to answer a particular item varies from very low ability to very high ability in a population of subjects. It is assumed that the subjects are distributed on this item continuum according to the normal distribution as illustrated in figure 5.1. The *item continuum* is a hypothetical construct specific to each item; i.e. a scale measuring the ability to solve the item in question. The different subjects in the population are distributed on this scale or item continuum. However, in practice, the item continuum is dichotomized into only

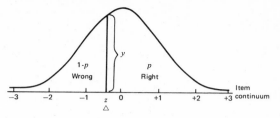

FIG. 5.1. Normal distribution of subjects on the item continuum.

the two categories, right and wrong, in proportion p and $1-p$. This is illustrated in figure 5.1. The value z expresses this point of categorization in standard score form. A table of normal probability curve values is used to find z corresponding to p and gives the level of ability (as measured in standard scores z on the item continuum) necessary to answer the item correctly.

For tryout item 15, analyzed in table 5.2, the item proportion is $p = .41$. As illustrated in figure 5.2, the assumption is made that the best 41 percent on the item continuum for this particular item have answered the item correctly and the poorest 59 percent have given a wrong answer. From a table of normal dis-

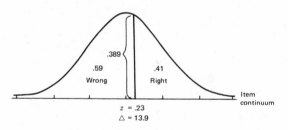

FIG. 5.2. Normal distribution illustrating relation between item proportion and difficulty level for item 15 in the tryout test.

tribution it is found that the standard score that divides this distribution in proportions .59 and .41 is $z = .23$. This is the difficulty index of the item. It says the item discriminates between students below and students above a standard score of z equal to .23 on the underlying item continuum.

Through use of a table of the normal distribution one can obtain the graph in figure 5.3 which shows how the proportion of subjects that can answer an item right decreases when the difficulty index z takes values from -3 to

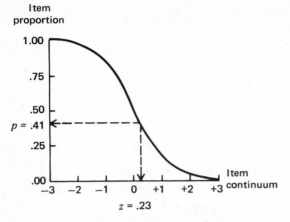

Item
proportion

$p = .41$

$z = .23$

FIG. 5.3. Relation between item difficulty and item proportion, when normality is assumed.

+3. This curve demonstrates that the item proportions p are not linearly related to difficulty level as measured by standard scores z.

It is not always necessary to transform p values into z. Some test technicians prefer to use p, and others prefer z or a linear transformation of z. But the z values are more useful when difficulty indices measured on an interval scale with equal units are needed.

Since z is sometimes negative, some test technicians prefer to transform z to a scale of all positive values. The standard score z with mean equal to zero and standard deviation equal to one can be transformed into scores Δ with mean equal to 13 and standard deviation equal to 4 by the linear transformation equation $\Delta = 13 + 4z$. Δ will in practice take values from about 6 to 20, a high Δ indicating a difficult item. In the example, with z equal to .23, Δ equals 13.9.[2] This indicates the item is of somewhat more than average difficulty. Another commonly used transformation equation is $50 + 10z$, which gives difficulty measures with a mean of 50.

Item Discriminating Power

The biserial correlation coefficient

How does one measure the extent to which an item discriminates? For tryout item 15 the

[2] This standard score scale for item difficulties is generally used in the item analyses of the Educational Testing Service and will frequently be encountered in publications emanating from that organization.

extent the item discriminates between students with high scores and students with low scores is ascertained by using the total vocabulary test score as a criterion. (The tryout vocabulary test is a fairly homogeneous and direct measure of what one is tryout to evaluate; i.e. knowledge of vocabulary.) As a first step, the information of table 5.2 is condensed as in table 5.3 with one column for the right answer and one for all wrong answers. Table 5.3 shows that students with high criterion scores have a much stronger tendency to choose the right answer to item 15 than students with low total scores. This tendency can be quantified by use of the biserial correlation coefficient. This coefficient has the equation

$$r_{\text{bis}} = \frac{M_R - M_W}{S_t} \cdot \frac{p(1-p)}{y}, \qquad [1$$

where

$M_R =$ mean criterion score for student choosing the right answer,

TABLE 5.3

Distribution of Criterion Scores for the Students Choosing Right and Wrong Answers on Item 15

Criterion (Total Scores)	Students Choosing: Wrong Answer	Right Answer	Totals
15		3	3
14	1	3	4
13	1	8	9
12	4	16	20
11	11	31	42
10	16	38	54
9	34	24	58
8	57	23	80
7	49	12	61
6	30	5	35
5	13	1	14
4	10		10
3	5		5
2	2		2
1	3		3
Totals	236	164	400

$M_W = 7.49$ $p = .41$ $M_t = 8.48$
$M_R = 9.90$ $y = .389$ $S_t = 2.36$

$$r_{\text{bis}} = \frac{9.90 - 7.49}{2.36} \cdot \frac{(.41)(.59)}{.389} = .64$$

M_W = mean criterion score for the other students,

S_t = standard deviation of criterion scores for all students,

p = proportion choosing the right answer,

y = ordinate in the unit normal distribution, which divides the area under the curve in the proportions p and $1-p$ (see figure 5.1).

The key part of equation 1 is the difference between the two means relative to the standard deviation. The other values in equation 1 adjust it to take values between -1 and $+1$, like other measures of correlation. An increase in the difference ($M_R - M_W$) for a given p value leads to an increase in biserial correlation and indicates an increase in discriminating power.

The biserial correlation coefficient gives an estimate of the well-known Pearson product-moment correlation between the criterion score and the hypothesized item continuum when the latter is dichotomized into right and wrong. This estimate of the Pearson correlation is based on the assumption that the relation between the two variables follows a normal bivariate distribution in the population of persons from which the sample is drawn. This requires that the criterion scores for the total group have an approximately normal distribution. And it assumes that the distribution of scores on the underlying item continuum (i.e. the dichotomized scale) is in actuality a continuous scale that follows the normal distribution. (This latter assumption also was made when p was transformed into z and Δ.)

The conditions for using the biserial correlation are illustrated in figure 5.4. If the achievement continuum underlying the answers on the item is continuous and the normality assumptions are fulfilled, the correlation surface looks like the one in figure 5.4. In practice only the two categories, right and wrong, on the item scale are available. Using the means for these two categories and the normality assumption, the biserial correlation formula for estimating the Pearson correlation in figure 5.4 can be applied.

The statistics to calculate biserial r for item

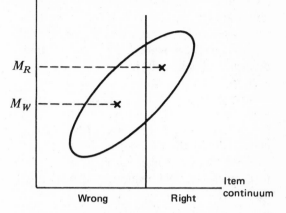

FIG. 5.4. Assumed normal bivariate distribution between item and criterion.

15, from data in table 5.3, are: $M_R = 9.90$; $M_W = 7.49$; $S_t = 2.36$; and $p = .41$. A table of the normal curve shows that the ordinate y equals .389 for p equal to .41. When these data are used in equation 1

$$r_{bis} = \frac{9.90 - 7.49}{2.36} \cdot \frac{(.41)(.59)}{.389} = .64.$$

This relatively high correlation indicates that item 15 is a fairly good measure of vocabulary knowledge.

A somewhat more convenient equation for the biserial correlation is

$$r_{bis} = \frac{M_R - M_T}{S_T} \cdot \frac{p}{y},$$

where M_T is the mean of the total sample. (The rest of the notation is the same as in equation 1.)

As indicated previously, the biserial correlation is an estimate of the Pearson product-moment correlation based on the assumption that the relationship between the criterion scale and the dichotomized item continuum can be represented by a normal bivariate distribution. If the distribution of the criterion scores is bimodal or skewed, the biserial correlation coefficient can yield values higher than 1.00. Examples of this are reported in studies by Adams (1960a) and Richardson (1936b). One way to avoid this difficulty is to transform the criterion scores into a scale giving a normal distribution (e.g. stanines). Another assumption underlying the use of the biserial r is that the subjects can be assumed to be normally distributed on the hypothesized item continuum that is dichotomized into right and wrong answers. If the group of subjects is an unbiased sample from a population like "all pupils in grade 4" or "all pupils of age 14" this assumption usually seems acceptable. One check on the validity of the assumption is to determine whether there is some other related variable that forms a normal bivariate distribution with the criterion.

The point-biserial correlation coefficient

The point-biserial, r_{pbis}, also is used as an item discrimination index; it has the formula

$$r_{pbis} = \frac{M_R - M_W}{S_T} \sqrt{p(1 - p)},$$

in which the notation remains the same as for the biserial correlation. In many situations it is more convenient to use the equivalent formula

$$r_{pbis} = \frac{M_R - M_T}{S_T} \cdot \sqrt{\frac{p}{1 - p}}.$$

The point-biserial correlation also can be calculated by the formula for the product-moment correlation coefficient of which it is a special case.

The point-biserial r is always lower than the biserial correlation coefficient r_{bis} as can be seen from the relationship

$$r_{pbis} = r_{bis} \cdot \frac{y}{\sqrt{p(1 - p)}}.$$

It follows from this formula that $r_{pbis} = 0.8\ r_{bis}$ when $p = .50$, and that r_{pbis} tends to be smaller with respect to r_{bis} the further p gets from .50; for example, when $p = .25$ or $.75$, $r_{pbis} = .73\ r_{bis}$.

When the point-biserial r is used the dichotomized item variable is treated as a true dichotomy; i.e. there are considered to be only two distinct positions on the item continuum, namely right and wrong. This is usually a less plausible assumption about the underlying

item distribution than the assumption of a normal distribution.

An argument put forth in favor of the point-biserial r is that it tells more about the contribution from the particular item to the predictive validity of the total test than does the biserial r (Guilford, 1965, p. 498). This is true in the sense that the point-biserial r will tend to favor items of average difficulty; i.e. with proportion correct around .5. These items tend to make more discriminations between good and poor students than do items with high or low p values. This means that the point-biserial r can be said to be a combined measure of item-criterion relationship and of difficulty level. The point-biserial r therefore is not invariant with change in difficulty level.

Those who prefer indices of discriminating power and difficulty that are independent of each other should use biserial r. When the criterion scores do not follow a normal distribution, an index that can be used instead of the biserial r is

$$\frac{\text{point biserial correlation}}{\text{maximum point biserial correlation}}.$$

This index is reported by Clemans (1958) and in a different form by Brogden (1949) who calls it the *coefficient of selective efficiency* with the notation S. This type of index always has a maximum value of $+1$.

Lord (1963) has pointed out that S is a more efficient estimator of the product-moment correlation than biserial r when the two variables have a normal, bivariate distribution in the population. However, the difference is great only when the correlation is very large—larger than usually found in item analysis data. The biserial r still can be used therefore in item analysis when the assumption of a normal bivariate distribution is applicable.

Correlation with dichotomous criterion

Sometimes the criterion also will be a dichotomy, for example a Pass-Fail criterion in some training courses. When an index comparable to the product-moment correlation is wanted, the *tetrachoric correlation coefficient* should be employed. Like the biserial r, the computation of the tetrachoric r assumes an underlying normal bivariate distribution. The calculation of the tetrachoric correlation coefficient is complicated (Guilford, 1965, p. 327). If an electronic computer is not available, a computing diagram or facilitating table can be used. There are several that are very useful, for example the ones published by Chesire, Saffir, and Thurstone (1933), Davidoff and Goheen (1953), Jenkins (1955), or the U.S. National Bureau of Standards (1959). There are also several approximation formulas available. The correctness of these has been discussed by Castellan (1966) and Cureton (1968), who found that a simple estimate can be obtained that is accurate within the limit of $\pm.01$ in realistic cases.

If the criterion is a dichotomy and both the item and the criterion can be assumed to have distributions of answers that are natural dichotomies, the *phi coefficient*, ϕ, can be used. The assumption of a natural dichotomy is seldom realistic in connection with item analysis. Another difficulty is that the size of the phi coefficient is influenced by the proportions in the marginal frequencies of the fourfold table (Guilford, 1965, pp. 335–336). The phi coefficient is a special case of the product-moment correlation coefficient and can be computed by its formula. Other calculation methods also are available (Guilford, 1965, pp. 333–334).

Correlation with ranked criterion measure

A *rank biserial correlation coefficient* has been suggested by Cureton (1956) and Glass (1965, 1966) for the situation where the criterion scores are reported as ranks in a group. The coefficient proposed by Glass has the formula

$$r_{\text{bis(rank)}} = (2/n)(Y_R - Y_W),$$

where

n = the number of subjects,
Y_R = the average rank of those scoring right,
Y_W = the average rank of those scoring wrong.

This coefficient gives an estimate of the correlation between the two series of ranks as expressed by Spearman's rho. The coefficient does not seem to work as well when there are many tied ranks (Glass, 1965, p. 94).

Efficiency of Distracters

The next step is to calculate measures to judge the efficiency of each distracter. This requires ascertaining proportion p_i of students choosing each distracter and mean criterion score M_i for each of these groups. For item 15, these values are reported in two rows at the bottom of table 5.2. The proportions (.13, .15, .11, and .18) indicate that all distracters are fairly attractive. The means (7.71, 8.08, 7.14, and 7.65) show that all distracters attract groups of students with average and below average criterion scores. The mean scores for the groups choosing wrong answers should be lower than the mean score for those choosing the correct answer. As the students choosing the correct answer had a mean criterion score of 9.90, this requirement is reasonably well fulfilled for this item.

By analogy with the statistical procedure used for the correct answer, some test makers compute the biserial correlation for each wrong answer choice. Such an index quantifies the sharpness with which the option separates low- from high-scoring examinees. For a satisfactory wrong option, the biserial should be negative and of appreciable size. However, the contrast of those who choose a specific wrong option with those who do not has no clear-cut logic in relation to a continuum of ability, since those who do not choose wrong option a may have made some other erroneous choice.

Use of Item Analysis Data for Item Selection

To select items with good discriminating power and of specified difficulty levels for the final subtest, the item analysis data for all items from the tryout are compared. One may plot the items in a coordinate system, with difficulty indices p on one axis and discrimination indices r_{bis} on the other axis, as in figure 5.5. Item 15, for example, has p equal to .41 and r_{bis} equal to .64. This item is plotted as a small circle marked

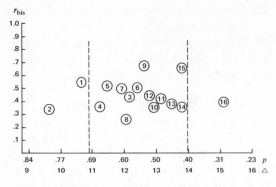

FIG. 5.5. Difficulty and discrimination indices for 16 items in a tryout version of a vocabulary subtest.

"15." Other properties of the item also can be reported. For example, by using different colors for the circles, a black circle might indicate an item rated as acceptable by subject-matter experts, a red circle an item with one or more bad distracters, etc. Here again it must be stressed that items cannot be selected only on the basis of their statistical properties: it should be agreed by all concerned that the item is a good measure of the educational objectives to be tested.

(Since some are more accustomed to item proportions p than to difficulty indices Δ, p values are used in figure 5.5. The Δ values are reported under the respective p values. A comparison between the two rows illustrates that their relation is nonlinear but fairly linear for p values not far from .50.)

The test plan called for a vocabulary subtest of 12 items with difficulty indices p distributed mainly over the interval $p = .7$ to $p = .4$. Which four items among the 16 tried out should be excluded? Item 2 was eliminated as being too easy; item 16 as too difficult. Items 8 and 14 were dropped because of their relatively low discrimination indices: this decision was supported by content criticism of experts. The other 12 items were accepted by experts, have reasonably high biserial r's, and are fairly evenly distributed over the difficulty interval of .7 to .4. Item 1 with p equal to .73 seems a little easy, but it was still accepted for the final test through content considerations.

In the final form, the items usually should be arranged according to difficulty level with the easiest item thus placed first. Thus item 1 could come first, followed by items 4, 5, 7, 3, and so on. In ordering the items in this manner, it should be kept in mind that proportions of success are influenced by errors of sampling and measurement. The sampling error of a proportion p follows the formula $\sqrt{p(1-p)/N}$, where N is the sample size. This means that a proportion of .5 for N equal to 400 has a sampling error of .025. Error of measurement is to a large extent a function of the number of items. A test of 16 items is usually fairly unreliable. For these reasons item difficulties must be used with some caution and the sequence of the items cannot be based only on this information. Content and other editorial considerations should be taken into account.

An Alternative Item Analysis Method

In the past, because the work of tabulation and calculation was less, many test makers preferred to use item analysis methods based on the division of the pupils into a high, middle, and low group on the criterion variable. These methods are of little importance to the worker with access to a computer but are still of some interest to the teacher or other independent worker who does not have access to electronic computing facilities. Much work was done using the top 27 percent and the bottom 27 percent, because this division provided the greatest efficiency in estimating item discrimination under certain reasonable assumptions.

In the upper-lower 27 percent method, the numbers choosing the different answer alternatives are compared for the 27 percent of students with the highest criterion scores and the 27 percent with the lowest. (When the frequencies in the class intervals do not yield exact 27 percent groups, one selects students at random from the critical class interval to obtain groups as close to 27 percent as possible.) When the data of table 5.2. are handled in this manner one gets the frequencies shown in table 5.4. The upper group contains 108 students with criterion scores of 11 to 15 including some of the students with a score of 10; the lower group contains 108 students with criterion scores of 1 to 6 plus some with a score of 7. The frequencies for the total tryout sample are given at the bottom of the table. Table 5.4 indicates that the right answer *d* is much more attractive to the upper group than to the lower—81 of 108 students in the upper group chose *d* compared with 13 in the lower group of 108. The opposite tendency is found in the distracters. The item and its distracters thus are shown to work fairly well.

The distribution in table 5.4 can be made even easier to interpret if the frequencies are reported in terms of percentages. This is done in table 5.5.

A quick guide to the discriminating power of an item is provided by the percentages in table 5.5. Any classroom teacher can prepare such a table and use the information in it to guide the selection and rejection of items for use in future tests with subsequent sections of a course. In general, items are desired in which a substantially larger percentage of the upper group chooses the correct answer and a larger percentage of the lower group chooses each of the wrong options.

On the assumption of a normal bivariate surface, it is possible to estimate the correlation between item and criterion from the percentage passing the item in the high group and in the low group. This correlation is equivalent to the biserial *r*, since it is based on the same assumptions. Fan (1952, 1954) has prepared tables from which this coefficient can be estimated by entering with the proportions of students pass-

TABLE 5.5

Percentage of Examinees from the Upper 27 Percent and Lower 27 Percent Groups Choosing Different Answers on Item 15

Criterion Group	Students Choosing Answer Alternative					Students Omitting Item	Students Not Reaching Item	Total
	a	b	c	(d)	e			
Upper	6	9	2	75	8	0	0	100
Lower	19	17	18	12	24	3	7	100
Total group	13	15	11	41	18	1	2	101

ing the item in the upper and lower 27 percent of the criterion group (e.g. .75 and .12 from table 5.5). Using these values in Fan's tables, a biserial *r* of .63 is obtained, very close to the calculated value of .64. Tables similar to Fan's were prepared by Flanagan (1939). The correlations estimated by these methods have slightly larger sampling errors than the biserial *r* computed in the ordinary way.

Over the years, many other indices of item discrimination have been developed, but they had their basis primarily in computational convenience rather than in statistical or test theory. They are now only of historical interest. Some of them are reviewed and discussed in Anstey (1966), Davis (1946), Ebel (1965), Engelhart (1965), Feldt (1963), and Long and Sandiford (1935).

The Choice among Item Analysis Techniques

Many different techniques of item analysis are available. Most of them provide essentially the same information, and the choice among them is partly a matter of taste and partly of access to data, personnel, or computational facilities. Electronic computers are now very often available and soon all researchers will have access to this equipment. The result probably will be that the need for short-cut methods will decrease and the correlational or the item-test regression approach will become more dominant. Which one of the two will become the more popular is difficult to predict, since, with supplementing data plots, they give essentially similar types of information.

TABLE 5.4

Number of Examinees from the Upper 27 Percent and Lower 27 Percent Groups Choosing Different Answers on Item 15

Criterion Group	Students Choosing Answer Alternative					Students Omitting Item	Students Not Reaching Item	Total
	a	b	c	(d)	e			
Upper 27%	6	10	2	81	9	0	0	108
Lower 27%	21	18	20	13	26	3	7	108
Total group	51	61	42	164	72	3	7	400

ITEM CHARACTERISTIC CURVE

For theoretical analysis of the nature of tests, and for some types of practical problems in item selection, it is useful to think of performance on a test item as dependent in part upon one or more underlying *traits*. A trait, as the term is used here, refers to a construct that is basically statistical, rather than necessarily having any specific psychological meaning or any existence as a distinct entity. It is the latent, underlying attribute that is represented in the pattern of an individual's successes and failures on a set of test items. In this sense, the probability of success on an item g can be considered a function of the individual's position on the underlying trait dimensions. Such a function, $P_g = f(\theta_1, \theta_2, \ldots \theta_k)$, where the θ's represent underlying traits, can be spoken of as the *item characteristic function*. As it stands, it would be represented by some type of surface in a space of k dimensions.

In some types of tests, where the items are quite homogeneous in nature, it will be reasonable to consider that a single trait dimension underlies performance on all the items of a set. This dimension need not be *psychologically* simple, i.e. it could be a composite of verbal fluency, deductive reasoning, and persistence. The dimension is *statistically* unitary in that, to a reasonably close approximation, it operates in the same way as a determiner of success on all the items of the test. When this situation exists, one can think in terms of a single trait dimension—the underlying attribute measured by the test—and can examine the *item characteristic curve*.

TABLE 5.6
Proportion of Right Answers to Item 15 for Each Criterion Score

Criterion Score	Proportion Right Answers
15	1.00
14	.75
13	.89
12	.80
11	.74
10	.70
9	.42
8	.29
7	.20
6	.14
5	.07
4	.00
3	.00
2	.00
1	.00

The item characteristic curve is the function relating probability of success on the item to the examinee's position on the underlying trait dimension; i.e. $P_g = f(\theta)$. Unfortunately, one has no direct measure of the underlying trait θ and can approach it only indirectly through information about performance on all the items of the test (or some other test of the same attribute), or more simply through total score on the test made up of those items. Thus, one can compute the percentage of individuals getting item g correct at each score level on the total test and display these percentages in a table or graph, as shown in table 5.6 and figure 5.6 for the item that is being used for illustration. Such a table or figure shows completely in a pictorial way the manner in which success on the item is related to score on the test as a whole. Its advantage over the summary statistics of difficulty and discrimination that have been discussed in the preceding sections is that it shows the complete picture, including any reversals in the general trend for success on the item to increase as total score on the test increases. Occasionally one may find an item, as illustrated in figure 5.7, on which the apparently ablest students do less well than the students of lower ability. Such a reversal, though it would lower a biserial correlation, would not be clearly identified by a simple statistical index. It

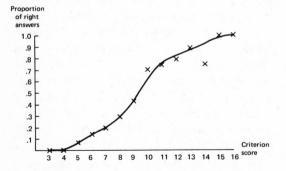

FIG. 5.6. Item-test regression for item 15 in tables 5.3 and 5.4.

Proportion
of right
answers

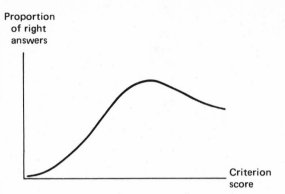

Criterion
score

FIG. 5.7. Item-test regression when the best subjects tend to choose a wrong answer.

serves as a warning to the test maker to examine the item very closely to see whether there is some ambiguity or inaccuracy in it that is misleading the most capable students.

Though a plot such as that shown in figure 5.6 may be of some value for practical work, it has very real limitations even in a practical context and is useless for any theoretical analysis of tests. What is called for is some mathematical expression to relate P_g, the probability of success, to the underlying trait, θ, rather than to raw test score. A function that often seems plausible and promising is the normal ogive[3]

$$P_g(\theta) = \int_{-\infty}^{L_g(\theta)} \phi(t)dt,$$

where $L_g(\theta) = a_g(\theta - b_g)$ is a linear function of θ involving two parameters of the item g, a_g and b_g, and $\phi(t)$ is the normal frequency function. Three representative normal ogives are shown in figure 5.8. The item parameters a and b may be thought of respectively as the "steepness" of the curve and the "difficulty level" or "threshold level" of the item. The more rapidly the percentage of success on the item rises as one moves up the scale of the ability dimension, the more sharply the item discriminates between different levels of ability, so a_g, the measure of the steepness of the curve, is also a measure of item discrimination. For items A and B, the value of a is one. These items are equivalent with respect to steepness and discriminate with

[3] A closely similar function that has certain advantages as a model is the logistic where $P_g(\theta) = e^x/(1 + e^x)$.

equal sharpness though on different segments of the scale of the trait θ. Items B and C differ with respect to steepness but have the same difficulty level, as defined by the point on the scale of θ at which 50 percent of examinees get the item right.

If the underlying trait θ has a normal distribution with mean of zero and σ equal to unity, the parameter a_g bears a simple relationship to the biserial correlation coefficient between the item and the latent trait, a relationship that can be expressed

$$a_g = \frac{r_{bis}}{\sqrt{1 - r_{bis}^2}}.$$

Item C has a smaller value of a, to wit .5, and this shows up in the much flatter profile of the item characteristic curve for item C.

The second parameter of the item characteristic curve, b_g, represents the level on the underlying trait, θ, at which there is a 50 percent probability of success upon the item. It corresponds to the psychophysical concept of the threshold, i.e. the level of intensity at which a stimulus has a 50–50 chance of being perceived. In a population in which the underlying trait θ is normally distributed with mean equal to zero and standard deviation equal to unity, b is given by the expression

$$b_g = \frac{\gamma_g}{r_{bis}},$$

where γ_g is the normal deviate corresponding to P_g, the percentage of success on item g in the total population.

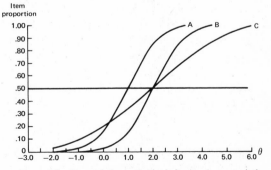

FIG. 5.8. Several hypothetical item characteristic curves of the normal ogive forms. (Adapted from Lord & Novick, 1968, p. 367)

As presented up to this point, both a_g and b_g are population parameters, expressed in terms of a population that shows a normal distribution on the trait θ with mean equal to zero and σ equal to one. It is in relation to this trait θ that the item is assumed to display a normal ogive. But no data are available for the trait θ; data exist only for some test score X. The relationship of the scale of measurement of X to the scale in which θ is expressed is unknown and not necessarily linear. Some procedure is needed for estimating a_g and b_g for a set of items from the observed percentages of success on the several items at different test score levels. Such procedures have been developed (see, for example, Lord & Novick, 1968, pp. 420–422), but they involve the repeated iterative solution of sets of equations until the values converge and become stable. The computational procedures are practical only for the worker who has access to a high-speed computer.

If one does have the computational resources for estimating a_g and b_g, these item parameters appear to have certain practical advantages. Chief of these is the point that they should be independent of the characteristics of the specific group upon which they were determined, given that a common scale for θ is used from group to group. However, a_g and b_g are emphatically *not* independent of the origin and unit of measure in which θ is expressed. Since the metric of θ from one group to another is likely to differ, it would be necessary in practical work to have a certain number of "anchor" items that would be administered to each group. The values of a_g and b_g should show a linear relationship from group to group, and a plot of the values for the anchor items should make it possible to determine values to transform a_g and b_g values in each new group to those for a common anchor or reference group. If item parameters for all items were expressed in this common metric, they would be immediately comparable and immediately translatable into values for any new group, once the mean and standard deviation of the new group on the scale of θ had been determined.

Until now, item characteristic curves have had little practical application in test construction. However, as high-speed computing facilities become more common, their attractive statistical properties may result in their wider use.

SPECIAL PROBLEMS IN ITEM ANALYSIS

Sampling Errors of Discrimination Indices

Discrimination indices are subject to sampling variations. It is important to know the magnitude of these fluctuations in order to determine the sample size necessary to obtain acceptable sampling stability in item indices. Knowledge of sampling errors also is needed to estimate the change in item indices to be expected when the items are tried on a new sample. Formulas for sampling errors of most of the discrimination indices discussed here are available in statistical textbooks. The discussion here is therefore rather short.

The standard error of the *biserial r* is estimated by the formula

$$\sigma_{r_{\text{bis}}} = \frac{\sqrt{\dfrac{p(1 - p)}{u} - r_{\text{bis}}^2}}{\sqrt{N}} .$$

N is used as notation for sample size whereas the other symbols are the same as in the formula for the biserial r (equation 1).

The problem of sampling error and confidence limits of the *point-biserial r* is more complicated (Das Gupta, 1960). Approximate formulas and tables for the standard error of the point-biserial r are given in Perry and Michael (1958) and Iker and Perry (1960).

The formula for the sampling error of *tetrachoric r* is very complicated, especially for the general case. A discussion of this is given by Kelley (1947) and Peters and van Voorhis (1940). Tables of the standard error of tetrachoric r are available in Hayes (1943).

No generally useful formula for the sampling error of the *phi coefficient* seems to be available.

In connection with the *item-test regression*, formulas have been developed for estimates of sampling errors of the discrimination index β and the difficulty index X_{50} (Baker, 1965).

Treatment of Nonattempting Cases

There are different opinions about the choice of a numerator when calculating the proportion of right answers, $p = N_R/N$. One alternative is to divide the number of right answers N_R by N_t, the *total* number of examinees in the tryout sample. Another is to divide N_R by N_a, the number of examinees who *attempted* to answer the item. (An examinee is considered to have "attempted" an item if he has recorded an answer either to this item or any subsequent item in the subtest or test of which the item is a part; this means that the "omitted" are included among the "attempted" while the "not reached" are excluded.)

For power tests, the more closely the value of N_a approaches N_t the better. Thus one should use a liberal time limit or put the item so early in the tryout test version that all or nearly all examinees get a chance to attempt it, or use one of the methods discussed on page 133. In the following discussion it is assumed that one wishes to know the value of p that would be obtained if all students in the sample attempt to answer the item. If one estimates this p value by N_R/N_t, it is assumed that N_R would not be increased if all students attempted to answer; i.e. there is a perfect positive relation between speed and power. If one uses N_R/N_a, it is assumed that the proportion of right answers is N_R/N_a both in the group that has not attempted the item and in the group that attempted the item; i.e. that speed and power are completely uncorrelated. Both assumptions are unrealistic. If the correlation between speed and power is high and/or the time limit is very liberal, the use of N_t is preferred. If the correlation between power and speed is low, it is better to use N_a. To find out about this, one can compare the criterion score for students who have not reached the item with the criterion scores for students who have given the right answer. If the mean criterion score for the "not reached" group is very low, it is likely that very few of them would have answered correctly, if they had attempted the item. Thus when the correlation between speed and power is high, N_t is preferred as the numerator. (This was the case in table 5.2.)

The same argument is relevant for dis-crimination indices such as the biserial correlation. If the "not reached" category is excluded and the computation of the biserial r is made on only the N_a students (those who have attempted the item) there is a tendency for a lower estimate than would be obtained for the total group of N_t students. (This discussion is adapted from Conrad, 1948, who has given a more detailed discussion of the use of N_a when computing p and r_{bis}.)

The Effect of Guessing

When multiple-choice items are used, or any other item type with a limited number of given response possibilities, item statistics are affected to some extent by guessing. Some students will get the item right by a "lucky" guess, and this will raise P, the proportion of correct answers. The effect of guessing upon discrimination indices, such as the biserial correlation, is less predictable. As indicated on pages 59–61, where the issues relating to guessing on objective tests are discussed more generally, the usual correction formula for adjusting for guessing is based upon assumptions that are at best rough approximations to the actual situation, so that an estimate of the "true" difficulty of an item corrected for guessing is at best a fairly crude approximation. As applied to item difficulties, the formula becomes:

$$ P_{RC} = P_R - \frac{P_W}{K - 1} \qquad [2] $$

where

P_{RC} = corrected proportion of correct answers, corrected for guessing,

P_R = observed percent of correct answers,

P_W = observed percent of choice of wrong answers, and

K = number of answer alternatives to the item.

This formula is based upon the assumption that those who do not know the correct answer guess at random. Such an assumption is a great oversimplification. On the one hand, many students have partial knowledge or test sophistication that permits them to rule out one or more choices; on the other, the skillful item writer may have designed one or more item choices so that they capitalize on common misinformation or have a special appeal to the uninformed or only partially informed. Thus, the net effect of guessing on item statistics is always difficult to estimate.

As indicated on pages 59–61, one objective in good test construction is to minimize the tendency to guess blindly. This can be accomplished in part by providing liberal time limits and, in the case of tryout of new items, by following one of the procedures described on page 133 for ensuring that each item appears early enough in the test. Blind guessing can be reduced by providing superficially attractive wrong options. Whether, in addition, a penalty should be introduced for wrong answers and the examinees be informed of this penalty has been and continues to be a matter of controversy.

It probably makes little difference, so far as assembling a test is concerned, whether individual item difficulties are adjusted using formula 2 or whether a somewhat higher average P is set as one's objective in selecting items for the test. One can calculate from formula 2 what the value of P_R would be corresponding to any desired value of P_{RC} and any given value of K. The optimum value of P_{RC} for a restricted-choice test can be expected to be somewhat higher than the .50 that is accepted for free-response items because it can be expected that there will be more guessing on difficult than on easy items and that this guessing will introduce an excess of error variance for those more difficult items. On the assumption of random guessing by all those who do not know the correct answer, an assumption whose reasonableness has already been questioned, Lord (1952) arrived at the following for the optimum mean item difficulty:

NUMBER OF RESPONSE OPTIONS	NOT CORRECTED	CORRECTED
2	.85	.70
3	.77	.65
4	.74	.65
5	.69	.61

Since random guessing seems unlikely, the optimum probably falls somewhere between these values and the 50 percent (for corrected values) that applies to free-response items.

Guessing affects discrimination indices also, and it can be argued that scores corrected for guessing should be used to compute biserial or point-biserial correlations between item and test score. However, the effect of using corrected scores is typically small, at least upon the relative standing of different items (Plumlee 1952, 1954), so that a special effort to produce and use corrected scores is often not worthwhile.

Correction of Item-Total Correlations for Spuriousness

When the total score on a tryout test is used as the criterion variable, the discrimination indices will be spuriously high. This is due to the fact that when a correlation coefficient is computed between an item and the test, the item is also a part of the test and the item score enters in both variables. The smaller the number of items in the total score that is used as a criterion variable, the larger will be the spurious item-criterion relationship. In the extreme case, when the item intercorrelations are all zero and all items are of the same level of difficulty, the spurious item-criterion correlation as calculated by the biserial r will be $1/\sqrt{n}$, where n equals the number of items. For a 25-item test of this type the spurious biserial correlation between the item and the total score will be .20. The spurious effect is reduced when the intercorrelations between items increases but is still enough to be concerned about in practical situations. Consequently items need to be tried out in large groups when discrimination indices are to be obtained without any correction for spuriousness.

The spurious correlation can be eliminated by a correction formula. Such formulas have been developed for the biserial r and point-biserial r. One approach is to use formulas that give the correlation between an item and the total score based upon the sum of the other remaining $n-1$ items in the test of n items. Such formulas of item-remainder correlations have been reported for the point-biserial r by Guilford (1953) and for the biserial r by Henrysson (1963). This approach is not entirely satisfactory since it means that the different items in a test are correlated with slightly different sums of remaining items. Since the total scores based upon these different remainders of items will vary somewhat in content, they will measure slightly different dimensions. It would be more meaningful to estimate the correlations for the various items with the same "true score" for the population of items of which the items in the test are a sample. Such a coefficient also would fulfill the requirement of being invariant as to test length. Formulas of this kind are developed by Henrysson (1963). For the point-biserial r the correction formula is

$$r_{\mathrm{pbisc}} = \sqrt{\frac{n}{n-1}} \cdot \frac{r_{\mathrm{pbis}}S_t - \sqrt{p(1-p)}}{\sqrt{S_t^2 - \sum_i p_i(1-p_i)}}, \quad [3]$$

where

$p_i =$ proportion passing item i, when i takes values from 1 to n. The other notations are the same as in formula 1 above.

For the corrected biserial r, the formula is

$$r_{\mathrm{bisc}} = \sqrt{\frac{n}{n-1}} \cdot \frac{r_{\mathrm{bis}}S_t - \dfrac{p(1-p)}{y}}{\sqrt{S_t^2 - \sum_i p_i(1-p_i)}}. \quad [4]$$

The effect of spuriousness is not very large when the number of items in the test is large and/or the correlations are large .The size of the spurious overlap will, then, be nearly proportional to the size of the uncorrected correlations, and hence a relative comparison can be made without any correction. But if a computer program is routinely used for item analysis, there is good reason to include the correction formula in the program.

Influence of Difficulty and Discrimination Indices on Total Test Characteristics

The influence of item difficulty and discrimination on the properties of the whole test is a rather complicated matter, especially if multiple-choice items and guessing are involved. The mathematical theory of the subject is treated by Cronbach and Warrington (1952), Gulliksen (1950), Lord (1952b, 1953) and Ray, Hundleby, and Goldstein (1962) and will not be discussed here. Rather this discussion will be on a more practical level and refers to free-response items in the beginning, since the conditions are more complicated for multiple-choice items.

Richardson (1936a) has shown that if one wants to construct a test to differentiate examinees above a given level of ability from those below that level of ability (without making any distinctions among examinees within the two groups), all of the items used in the test should be of a difficulty level such that they will be marked correctly by half of the examinees *at the level of ability represented by the line of demarcation*. This is an important consideration in selecting test items because tests are sometimes built for the purpose of separating examinees into two groups. For a test of this kind one should select items at a certain difficulty level so that the maximum discriminating power of the test will be exerted at the passing score used for separating the two groups. However, most tests used in schools are not employed mainly to divide students into two groups at the passing mark; ordinarily discriminations must be made throughout the range of scores to rank students in order of ability.

Consider a group of 10 items to be used with 100 examinees. If all items were perfectly correlated (and thus perfectly reliable), the number of discriminations made by *10* items at 50 percent difficulty level would be identical with the number of discriminations between persons made by *1* item of 50 percent difficulty. This number of discriminations between persons is 2,500, since all the best 50 students are discriminated from the other 50 students $(50 \cdot 50 = 2,500)$. But if the 10 items are spread at difficulty intervals of 9.09 percent from 9.09 percent to 90.90 percent, 4,562 discriminations could be made. The latter arrangement would be optimal for 10 items under the circumstances specified. These data suggest that when the items in a test are uncorrelated maximum discrimination among all the members of a group may be obtained by using items all of 50 percent difficulty, but that when the items are perfectly correlated the items should be spread over the range of difficulty. However, the items in a test are never found to be either wholly uncorrelated or perfectly correlated. Hence, the limiting cases used for illustrations serve merely to guide thinking about the distribution of item difficulties required to obtain maximum discrimination throughout the entire range of scores in a given sample. One can see intuitively however that, since many kinds of test items have low intercorrelations, a distribution of item difficulties clustered around the 50 percent level would often approximate the distribution required to obtain maximum discrimination throughout the range of scores. Cronbach and Warrington (1952) and Lord (1952b) have given theoretical and empirical support for this view. For vocabulary tests and other types of tests that tend to have relatively high item-intercorrelations, the distribution of difficulty indices should be made more platykurtic than usual if equal accuracy of measurement and maximum discrimination are desired throughout the range of scores.

It should be made clear at this point that there is often good reason for avoiding a distribution of item difficulties that will cause a test to yield equal accuracy of measurement throughout the range. The separation of a group of examinees into two subgroups calls for all possible accuracy of measurement at the dividing line; the assignment of marks (which calls for the division of a group into several parts) demands maximum accuracy of measurement at the several dividing points scattered along the range of scores. Even when the members of a group are to be placed in rank order, the purpose for which the rank order is intended usually dictates that a portion of the range deserves greater accuracy of measurement than another. For example, in selecting teachers for a large school system, the qualifying examination should yield greater accuracy in the rank order of the applicants who obtain high scores, since it is unlikely that applicants who obtain low scores will be given serious consideration unless there is a grave shortage of applicants for teaching positions. Selecting a half-dozen high school graduates to be given university scholarships calls for extraordinary accuracy of the rank order at the extreme upper end of the distribution of scores. Consequently a test designed for this purpose should be made up almost entirely of exceptionally difficult items in each of the fields measured.

Brogden (1946) and Cronbach and Warrington (1952) have presented data regarding the effect on test validity of deliberate control of item difficulty and intercorrelation. These confirm the somewhat theoretical formulation presented above. For example, from Brogden's data one finds that, if a test of 45 items (all of 50 percent difficulty and having tetrachoric intercorrelations of .60) has a correlation with a criterion variable of .950, one can increase this correlation to .961 by adding 108 similar items. But one can obtain a correlation of .962 by using only 45 items like the original items except that their difficulty indices form a rectangular instead of a point distribution. Thus, under these unusual conditions, a test of 45 items, fairly well adjusted for difficulty level, may be as useful as a test of 153 items all of 50 percent difficulty.

From the preceding discussion it is apparent that the distribution of difficulty indices should be controlled if maximum efficiency in measurement is to be attained. However, in any systematic control of item difficulty, the test maker also must take into account the discrimination indices of the items, attempting to get good discrimination. Furthermore, the individual items must be satisfactory to subject-matter specialists and the set of items must preserve the balance of content and process called for by the test blueprint. Final selection of items is, therefore, a compromise of these several considerations.

The purpose of most achievement tests is to discriminate equally well among students on all levels of achievement. In such a situation, the average item difficulty for a free-response test should be $p = .5$; i.e. $\Delta = 13$. If the test (this is a purely theoretical example) is of perfect homogeneity (i.e. all interitem tetrachoric correlations are equal to unity), the item difficulties Δ should be distributed with equal intervals over the whole difficulty range from $\Delta = 3.7$ ($p = .99$) to $\Delta = 22.3$ ($p = .01$). If the test is completely heterogeneous (i.e. all interitem correlations are equal to zero), all items should have a difficulty of $\Delta = 13$ ($p = .50$). In practice the degree of homogeneity of tests is somewhere between these extremes. A test that would be considered very homogeneous might have an average biserial r between item and total test of .6 or .7. Such a test should in practice need a range of item difficulties somewhere between $\Delta = 9$ ($p = .84$) and $\Delta = 17$ ($p = .16$) in order to discriminate well on all levels of achievement. A test with an average item-test biserial r of .3 or .4 would be considered rather heterogeneous. In such tests the range of item difficulties should be somewhere from $\Delta = 12$ ($p = .60$) to $\Delta = 14$ ($p = .40$) if the test is to discriminate well at all levels. In theory, the item difficulty variations should be even smaller (Lord, 1955), but variations in item difficulty must be accepted to obtain items with proper content.

These principles refer to items of the free-response type. For multiple-choice items the theory is more complicated, since the item frequencies are increased by the effect of guessing. The values of p should therefore be somewhat higher in multiple-choice tests. Investigations by Cronbach and Warrington (1952), Plumlee (1952), and Lord (1953) on this problem are summarized by Lord (1953): "optimum measurement of a given examinee's ability by means of multiple-choice items requires an item difficulty level somewhat easier than halfway between the chance success level and 1.00 [p. 67]." Thus for multiple-choice items with five alternatives, the average proportion correct, after correcting for guessing, should be somewhere around .60.

Factor Analysis as an Item Analysis Technique

It has often been suggested that factor analysis should be used to analyze the structure of the items in a test more thoroughly than can be done by traditional item analysis. Where computers are not available this is forbidding because of the large amount of computational work involved in the calculation of the matrix of interitem correlations and the factor analysis of this matrix. Where computers are available, this work can be done quickly, and this procedure may be included in programs for item analysis. But even when computers are available, there are still certain difficulties that have decreased applications of factor analysis in this field. Some of these difficulties have to do with the choice of correlation method (Comrey & Levonian, 1958; Carroll, 1945, 1961; Horst, 1964; and McDonald, 1965), while others have to do with the technique of factor analysis itself (e.g. the choice of factor model and of the number of factors).

A factor analysis of the interitem correlations is a further step toward analyzing the test items. It was shown by Richardson (1936b) that the first row of factor loadings obtained by factoring the matrix of phi coefficients between the items in a test by the centroid method are approximately equal to the point-biserial correlations between each of the items and the total test scores. If instead of the phi coefficient matrix, the covariance matrix with item variances in the diagonal is analyzed by the centroid method, a somewhat different set of factor loadings is obtained. The first row of these factor loadings divided by the respective item standard deviations $\sqrt{p_i(1 - p_i)}$ is identical to the row of point-biserial correlations between each item and the total test score. If the loadings are divided instead by the ordinates y_i in the unit normal distribution, the biserial correlations are obtained (Henrysson, 1962). This gives an exact relation between the use of factor analysis and the use of biserial correlations for item analysis purposes.

A factor analysis of the correlations among items will also give more information than the usual biserial or point-biserial correlations or similar methods; for example:

1. It is a check of the dimensionality of the test. If only one large general factor is found, except for some other very small loadings, the

test is measuring only one main dimension.

2. If several substantial factors are found, the factor pattern will indicate that groups of items have something in common not shared by other items.

3. Sometimes the test is constructed to cover different areas of content, and therefore certain patterns of loadings are expected. These hypotheses can be tested by factor analysis.

4. The item structure can be more accurately described by the inclusion of reference tests with known content.

One difficult problem is the choice of factor model or rotational technique. The preliminary factor analysis by principal components, maximum likelihood, or centroid methods usually gives a general factor plus bipolar factors. In most cases this is not a very meaningful solution. A rotation to a more interpretable structure is needed, depending upon the type of test. Often some of these structures are appropriate:

1. A structure with one general factor and group factors. This is often the best model for achievement tests, when one main dimension (e.g. general achievement in social studies) is expected, but some groups of items may have other factors in common.

2. A group factor solution is perhaps applicable if the test is very heterogeneous and actually should be broken down into subtests.

3. The model can be based upon hypotheses about the item structure. It is tested by rotation determining whether a fit to this structure can be obtained.

When the methodological problems are better solved and more experience collected, factor analysis may well become a routine procedure for item analysis.

Item Selection for Maximum Validity

In the construction of achievement tests, the method of eliminating items on the basis of item-criterion correlations or similar techniques is usually very practical and efficient. If the total score on the test or subtest is used as the criterion, this method will emphasize the homogeneity and reliability of the test or subtest. The item–total-score correlation multiplied by the item variance is called the item reliability index. This is different from the item validity index (Gulliksen, 1950, p. 382), which is the correlation with an outside criterion multiplied by the item variance. In most practical situations the selection of items to increase reliability also will tend to increase validity. But it can happen that the test will become too narrow and one-sided in content to have high validity; i.e. emphasis may be placed on one aspect of the desired criterion through selecting those items that correlate with a group of related items predominating in number. It is therefore important to check that the final test agrees with the content specifications drawn up when planning the test.

If the aim is to select from a large pool of items a number of items that in combination maximizes the correlation with an outside criterion, the rational method, at least in theory, would be to use multiple regression analysis. This requires calculation of all the item variances, the interitem phi coefficients, and the point-biserial correlation coefficients between the item and the criterion. It is then possible to obtain all multiple correlations with the criterion for specified groups of items, reject items with negative or zero beta coefficients, and pick the one group of n items that has the maximum correlation with the criterion. This method is impractical in most situations since it requires several conditions that are seldom fulfilled:

1. It is necessary to have a very valid and reliable measure that is a good operational definition of the criterion to be predicted.

2. It is necessary to have a very large sample of subjects (perhaps 10,000 for a test of 30 items) if the results of the regression analysis are to stand up in the cross-validation study.

3. The results have to be cross-validated on a large sample to check that the results are not an effect of sampling errors.

4. The item-criterion correlations ought to be fairly high and the interitem correlations low if each item (or at least each group of items) is to make a unique contribution to the multiple correlation with the criterion.

Furthermore, unless a computer is available, the computational burden of this procedure is impossibly heavy.

To get methods that are more practical and less sensitive to sampling errors, several approximations of the multiple regression approach have been devised. One method, described in more detail by Gulliksen (1950, pp. 380–385) and Magnusson (1966, pp. 212–218), is to try to maximize the ratio between the sum of the item validity indices and the sum of the item reliability indices in the formula

$$ r_{tg} = \frac{\sum\limits_{i=1}^{n} r_{gi} s_i}{\sum\limits_{i=1}^{n} r_{ti} s_i}, \qquad [5] $$

where r_{tg} = Pearson r between total test t and criterion g,

  r_{gi} = point biserial r between criterion g and item i,

  r_{ti} = point biserial r between total test t and item i,

  s_i = standard deviation of item i, i.e. $\sqrt{p_i(1-p_i)}$,

  n = number of items in test t.

If biserial r's are used instead of point biserial r's, s_i should be replaced by y_i, the ordinate in the unit normal distribution that divides the area under the curve in the proportions p_i and $1-p_i$. The item–total-test correlations should be corrected for spurious overlap by formula 3 or 4 to get correlations that are invariant with respect to test length.

One way of using the approach of formula 5 is to plot the item validity and reliability indices in a coordinate system. The reliability index may be plotted as the abscissa and the validity index as the ordinate as in figure 5.9. From this plot, items should be selected that have high validity indices relative to the corresponding reliability indices. Such items should contribute more than other items to the validity of the test, since their ratios between validity and reliability are highest. This increase in test validity is a result obtained by adding valid

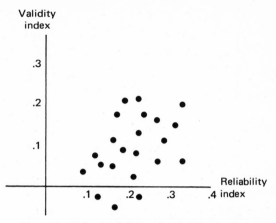

Fig. 5.9. Plot of validity and reliability indices for item selection.

variance not measured by other items to the total test variance. This method is sensitive to sampling errors, and hence a large sample of subjects is needed. The results also should be checked by a cross-validation study.

Several other methods which aim at the same purpose have been developed, for example, by Gleser and Dubois (1951), Horst (1934a, 1936), Richardson and Adkins (1938), and Webster (1956). Where large computers and test-scoring equipment are available, it may become practicable to use more precise multiple regression techniques on very large samples of examinees. However, experience in the matter is rather limited at present. Furthermore, samples available in practical situations will rarely be large enough to justify highly refined techniques.

Computers and Item Analysis

The conditions for statistical treatment of educational research data have improved dramatically through the development of electronic computers and optical scanners. Large masses of data now can be processed and analyzed quickly and with small effort. Many computing centers already have access to a number of programs for item analysis. One can usually acquire an item analysis program fitting his own preferences. A routine program might give the following information:

For each item one might request the relative

frequencies p_i and the mean criterion scores M_i for each answer alternative, the relative frequency of right answers (corrected for guessing, if wanted), the item difficulty Δ, the biserial r with its sampling error, and the biserial r corrected for spuriousness. Some test constructors also will want to inspect a table with the frequency distributions for each answer alternative, as illustrated in table 5.2. The total test and/or an outside criterion could be used as the criterion. Where a computer is available one might wish to include an analysis against score on a subgroup of items as well as on the total test.

For the test as a whole, with scores corrected and/or uncorrected for guessing, one might request the frequency distribution, the mean, the standard deviation, and the Kuder-Richardson formula 20 coefficient.

The computer could also produce a plot of the difficulty and discrimination indices like the one in figure 5.5. It also would be useful if the program allowed the item analysis to be repeated on the same data, some items having been eliminated as a result of the first analysis.

A program of this type will be sufficient in many cases. More special programs might produce such additional information as interitem correlations, factor analysis data, plots of item-test regressions, and results of item selection for maximum validity. For a full discussion of the role of scanners and computers in a system approach to test processing, see chapter 8.

Recording Item Data

It is essential to keep good records of the items with their data in convenient form. This will facilitate the inspection of the items when the selection of items is made. Specially printed 5×8 index cards are quite suitable for this purpose; they are large enough to carry all of the data that are ordinarily required and small enough to be handled easily. These item cards are also very useful to save for the future. Some items not used in the test might be considered in other connections, and some of the items actually used in the test might be considered again for a new test. The item data from earlier tryouts will then be of great help.

The item card should, of course, contain the text of the item either typed or cut out from the test booklet and affixed with rubber cement to the card. Every time that the item is tried out and analyzed one should record the name of the test of which it was a part, the date, the sample of examinees, and the item analysis data. These item data might, for example, be those obtained by the routine item analysis program mentioned in the section on computers. One should also include the key and the principle the item is intended to measure. Space should also be left on the card for notations and comments. It is often desirable to make more than one card for each item, one card to be filed by subject matter and another one by the test of which it is a part. Some computing centers will produce a print out of the data from the computer on a pressure-sensitive label that can be affixed directly to the card, or the computer print out could be recorded directly on a record card. In some very large-scale testing operations, such as those at the Educational Testing Service, the file of test items together with their item analysis data is stored in the memory of the computer, and a selection of items meeting certain specifications with respect to difficulty and discrimination can be called forth by proper instructions to the computer.

REFERENCES

Adams, J. F. The effect of non-normally distributed criterion scores on item analysis techniques. *Educational and Psychological Measurement*, 1960, **20**, 317–320. (a)

Adams, J. F. Test item difficulty and the reliability of item analysis methods. *Journal of Psychology*, 1960, **54**, 255–262. (b)

Adkins, D. C., & Toops, H. A. Simplified formulas for item selection and construction. *Psychometrika*, 1937, **2**, 165–171.

Aiken, L. R. Item context and position effects on multiple-choice tests. *Journal of Psychology*, 1964, **58**, 369–373.

Aiken, L. R. Multiple-answer items and chance

success. *Psychological Reports*, 1965, **16,** 1011–1012.

Anstey, E. *Psychological tests*. London: Nelson, 1966.

Baker, F. B. An intersection of test score interpretation and item analysis. *Journal of Educational Measurement*, 1964, **1,** 23–28.

Baker, F. B. Origins of the item parameters X_{50} and beta as a modern item analysis technique. *Journal of Educational Measurement*, 1965, **2,** 167–180.

Bridgman, C. S. The relation of the upper-lower item discrimination index D to the bivariate normal correlation coefficient. *Educational and Psychological Measurement*, 1954, **14,** 85–90.

Brogden, H. E. An approach to the problem of differential prediction. *Psychometrika*, 1946, **11,** 139–154. (a)

Brogden, H. E. Variation in test validity with variation in the distribution of item difficulties, number of items, and degree of their intercorrelation. *Psychometrika*, 1946, **11,** 197–214. (b)

Brogden, H. E. A new coefficient: Application to biserial correlation and to estimation of selective efficiency. *Psychometrika*, 1949, **14,** 169–182.

Bryan, M. M., Burke, P. J., & Steward, N. Correction for guessing in the scoring of pretests: Effects upon item difficulty and item validity indices. *Educational and Psychological Measurement*, 1952, **12,** 45–56.

Carroll, J. B. The effect of difficulty and chance success on correlations between items or between tests. *Psychometrika*, 1945, **10,** 1–19.

Carroll, J. B. The nature of the data, or how to choose a correlation coefficient. *Psychometrika*, 1961, **26,** 347–372.

Castellon, N. J. On the estimation of the tetrachoric correlation coefficient. *Psychometrika*, 1966, **31,** 67–73.

Chesire, L., Saffir, M., & Thurstone, L. L. *Computing diagrams for the tetrachoric correlation coefficient*. Chicago: University of Chicago Bookstore, 1933.

Clemens, W. V. An index of item criterion relationship. *Educational and Psychological Measurement*, 1958, **18,** 167–172.

Comrey, A. L., & Levonian, E. A comparison of three point coefficients in factor analysis of MMPI items. *Educational and Psychological Measurement*, 1958, **18,** 739–755.

Conrad, H. S. Characteristics and uses of item analysis data. *Psychological Monographs*, 1948, 62(8, Whole No. 295).

Cronbach, L. J., & Warrington, W. G. Efficiency of multiple-choice tests as a function of spread of item difficulties. *Psychometrika*, 1952, **17,** 129–147.

Cureton, E. E. Rank-biserial correlation. *Psychometrika*, 1956, **21,** 287–290.

Cureton, E. E. Note on ϕ/ϕ_{max}. *Psychometrika*, 1959, **24,** 89–91.

Cureton, E. E. Tetrachoric correlation by the camp approximation. *Educational and Psychological Measurement*, 1968, **28,** 239–244.

Das, R. S. Item analysis by probit and fractile graphical methods. *British Journal of Statistical Psychology*, 1964, **17,** 51–64.

Das Gupta, S. Point biserial correlation coefficient and its generalization. *Psychometrika*, 1960, **25,** 393–408.

Davidoff, M. D., & Goheen, H. W. A table for the rapid determination of the tetrachoric correlation coefficient. *Psychometrika*, 1953, **18,** 115–122.

Davis, F. B. *Item analysis data: Their computation, interpretation, and use in test construction*. (Harvard Education Papers, No. 2) Cambridge, Mass.: Harvard University, Graduate School of Education, 1946.

Davis, F. B. Item analysis in relation to educational and psychological testing. *Psychological Bulletin*, 1952, **49,** 97–121.

Ebel, R. L. *Measuring educational achievement*. Englewood Cliffs, N. J.: Prentice-Hall, 1965.

Elfving, G., Sitgreaves, R., & Solomon, H. Item selection procedures for item variables with known factor structure. *Psychometrika*, 1959, **24,** 189–205.

Engelhart, M. D. A comparison of several item discrimination indices. *Journal of Educational Measurement*, 1965, **2,** 69–76.

Fan, C.-t. *Item analysis table*. Princeton, N. J.: Educational Testing Service, 1952.

Fan, C.-t. Note on the construction of an item analysis table for the high-low 27-percent group method. *Psychometrika*, 1954, **19,** 231–237.

Fan, C.-t. On the applications of the method of absolute scaling. *Psychometrika*, 1957, **22,** 175–183.

Feldt, L. S. Note on the use of extreme criterion groups in item discrimination analysis. *Psychometrika*, 1963, **28,** 97–104.

Ferguson, G. A. On the theory of test discrimination. *Psychometrika*, 1949, **14,** 61–68.

Flanagan, J. C. General considerations in the selection of test items and a short method of estimating the product-moment coefficient from the data at the tails of the distributions. *Journal of Educational Psychology*, 1939, **30,** 674–680.

Ghiselli, E. E. *Theory of psychological measurement*. New York: McGraw-Hill, 1964.

Glaser, R. Instructional technology and the measurement of learning outcomes: Some questions. *American Psychologist*, 1963, **18**, 519–521.

Glass, G. V. A ranking variable analogue of biserial correlation: Implications for short-cut item analysis. *Journal of Educational Measurement*, 1965, **2**, 91–95.

Glass, G. V. Note on rank biserial correlation. *Educational and Psychological Measurement*, 1966, **26**, 622–631.

Gleser, G. C., & Dubois, P. H. A successive approximation method of maximizing test validity. *Psychometrika*, 1951, **16**, 129–139.

Goheen, H. W., & Kavruck, S. A worksheet for tetrachoric *r* and standard error of tetrachoric *r* using Hayes' diagrams and tables. *Psychometrika*, 1948, **13**, 279–280.

Green, B. F. A note on item selection for maximum validity. *Educational and Psychological Measurement*, 1954, **14**, 161–164.

Guilford, J. P. The correlation of an item with a composite of the remaining items in a test. *Educational and Psychological Measurement*, 1953, **13**, 87–93.

Guilford, J. P. *Fundamental statistics in psychology and education.* (4th ed.) New York: McGraw-Hill, 1965.

Gulliksen, H. O. The relation of item difficulty and inter-item correlation to test variance and reliability. *Psychometrika*, 1945, **10**, 79–92.

Gulliksen, H. O. *Theory of mental tests.* New York: Wiley, 1950.

Hayes, S. P., Jr. Tables of the standard error of tetrachoric correlation coefficients. *Psychometrika*, 1943, **8**, 193–203.

Hayes, S. P., Jr. Diagrams for computing tetrachoric correlation coefficients from percentage differences. *Psychometrika*, 1946, **11**, 163–172.

Henrysson, S. The relation between factor loadings and biserial correlations in item analysis. *Psychometrika*, 1962, **27**, 419–424.

Henrysson, S. Correction of item-total correlations in item analysis. *Psychometrika*, 1963, **28**, 211–218.

Horst, P. The chance element in the multiple-choice test item. *Journal of General Psychology*, 1932, **6**, 209–211.

Horst, P. The economical collection of data for test validation. *Journal of Experimental Education*, 1934, **2**, 250–252. (a)

Horst, P. Item analysis by the method of successive residuals. *Journal of Experimental Education*, 1934, **2**, 254–263. (b)

Horst, P. Item selection by means of a maximizing function. *Psychometrika*, 1936, **1**, 229–244.

Horst, P. Matrix factoring and test theory. In N. Fredriksen & H. Gulliksen (Eds.), *Contributions to mathematical psychology.* New York: Holt, Rinehart & Winston, 1964.

Iker, H. P., & Perry, N. C. A further note concerning the reliability of the point-biserial correlation. *Educational and Psychological Measurement*, 1960, **20**, 505–507.

Jenkins, W. L. An improved method for tetrachoric *r*. *Psychometrika*, 1955, **20**, 253–258.

Kelley, T. L. *Fundamentals of statistics.* Cambridge, Mass.: Harvard University Press, 1947.

Lawley, D. N. On problems connected with item selection and test construction. *Proceedings of the Royal Society of Edinburgh*, 1942–1943, **61** (Section A, Part III), 273–287.

Levine, R., & Lord, F. M. An index of the discriminating power of a test at different parts of the score range. *Educational and Psychological Measurement*, 1959, **19**, 497–503.

Lindquist, E. F. Sampling in educational research. *Journal of Educational Psychology*, 1940, **31**, 561–574.

Lindquist, E. F. Desirable performance specifications of optical mark scanners to be used in test and questionnaire processing. Proceedings of the International Workshop in Educational Testing, Berlin, May 1968.

Loevinger, J. A systematic approach to the construction and evaluation of tests of ability. *Psychological Monographs*, 1947, **61**(4, Whole No. 285).

Loevinger, J. The attenuation paradox in test theory. *Psychological Bulletin*, 1954, **51**, 493–504.

Long, J. A., Sandiford, P., et al. *The validation of test items.* Toronto, Ont.: University of Toronto, Department of Educational Research, 1935.

Lord, F. M. The relation of the reliability of multiple-choice tests to the distribution of item difficulties. *Psychometrika*, 1952, **17**, 181–193. (a)

Lord, F. M. A theory of test scores. *Psychometric Monographs*, 1952, No. 7. (b)

Lord, F. M. An application of confidence intervals and of maximum likelihood to the estimation of an examinee's ability. *Psychometrika*, 1953, **18**, 57–76.

Lord, F. M. Some perspectives on "The attenuation paradox in test theory." *Psychological Bulletin*, 1955, **52**, 505–510.

Lord, F. M. Test norms and sampling theory. *Journal of Experimental Education*, 1959, **27**, 247–264.

Lord, F. M. Use of true-score theory to predict moments of univariate and bivariate observed score distributions. *Psychometrika*, 1960, **25**, 325–342.

Lord, F. M. Biserial estimates of correlation. *Psychometrika*, 1963, **28**, 81–85.

Lord, F. M. The effect of random guessing on test validity. *Educational and Psychological Measurement*, 1964, **24**, 745–748.

Lord, F. M. An empirical study of item test regression. *Psychometrika*, 1965, **30**, 373–376. (a)

Lord, F. M. A note on the normal ogive or logistic curve in item analysis. *Psychometrika*, 1965, **30**, 371–372. (b)

Lord, F. M., & Novick, M. R. *Statistical theories of mental test scores*. Reading, Mass.: Addison Wesley, 1968.

McDonald, R. P. Difficulty factors and non-linear factor analysis. *British Journal of Mathematical and Statistical Psychology*, 1965, **18**, 11–23.

Magnusson, D. *Test theory*. Reading, Mass.: Addison Wesley, 1966.

Marks, E. Sampling in the revision of the Stanford-Binet scale. *Journal of Educational Psychology*, 1947, **38**, 413–434.

Mollenkopf, W. G. An experimental study of the effect on item analysis data of changing item placement and test time limit. *Psychometrika*, 1950, **15**, 291–316.

Perry, N. C., & Michael, W. B. A tabulation of the fiducial limits for the point-biserial correlation coefficient. *Educational and Psychological Measurement*, 1954, **14**, 715–721.

Perry, N. C., & Michael, W. B. A note concerning the reliability of a point-biserial coefficient for large samples. *Educational and Psychological Measurement*, 1958, **18**, 139–143.

Peters, C. C., & van Voorhis, W. R. *Statistical procedures and their mathematical bases*. New York: McGraw-Hill, 1940.

Plumlee, L. B. The effect of difficulty and chance success on item-test correlation and on test reliability. *Psychometrika*, 1952, **17**, 69–86.

Plumlee, L. B. The predicted and observed effect of chance success on multiple-choice test validity. *Psychometrika*, 1954, **19**, 65–70.

Ray, W. S., Hundleby, J. D., & Goldstein, D. A. Test skewness and kurtosis as functions of item

parameters. *Psychometrika*, 1962, **27**, 39–47.

Richardson, M. W. Notes on the rationale of item analysis. *Psychometrika*, 1936, **1**, 69–76. (a)

Richardson, M. W. The relation between the difficulty and the differential validity of a test. *Psychometrika*, 1936, **1**, 33–49. (b)

Richardson, M. W., & Adkins, D. C. A rapid method of selecting test items. *Journal of Educational Psychology*, 1938, **29**, 547–552.

Siegel, S. *Nonparametric statistics for the behavioral sciences*. New York: McGraw-Hill, 1956.

Solomon, A. (Ed.) *Studies in item analysis and prediction*. Stanford, Calif.: Stanford University Press, 1961.

Stanley, J. C. An important similarity between biserial *r* and the Brogden-Cureton-Glass biserial *r* for ranks. *Educational and Psychological Measurement*, 1968, **28**, 249–253.

Swineford, F., & Miller, P. M. Effects of directions regarding guessing on item statistics on a multiple-choice vocabulary test. *Journal of Educational Psychology*, 1953, **44**, 129–139.

Thurstone, L. L. The calibration of test items. *American Psychologist*, 1947, **2**, 103–104.

Tupes, E. C. Correcting correlation coefficients for group heterogeneity when one variable is a dichotomy. *Psychometrika*, 1963, **28**, 43–48.

Turnbull, W. W. A normalized graphic method of item analysis. *Journal of Educational Psychology*, 1946, **37**, 129–141.

U. S. National Bureau of Standards. *Tables of the bivariate normal distribution function and related functions*. (Applied mathematics series 50) Washington: Government Printing Office, Division of Public Documents, 1959.

Vernon, P. E. Indices of item consistency and validity. *British Journal of Psychology, Statistical Section*, 1948, **1**, 152–166.

Walker, H. M., & Lev, J. *Statistical inference*. New York: Holt, Rinehart & Winston, 1953.

Webster, H. Maximizing test validity by item selection. *Psychometrika*, 1956, **21**, 153–164.

6. Reproducing the Test

Robert L. Thorndike
Teachers College, Columbia University

In the course of its evolution, a test sooner or later comes to a stage where multiple copies are required. Quite a few copies are often needed for purposes of review in the course of construction; a fairly large number of booklets are required for experimental administration; and, when all preparatory work has been completed, the test in its final form must be reproduced in quantity.

KINDS OF REPRODUCTION PROCESSES

Techniques for copying and reproducing materials have developed at a very rapid rate during the 20 years since the first edition of this book appeared. The perfection and widespread use of electrostatic copying machines, of techniques for making masters for any type of duplicating machine from original copy, and of compact and economical offset equipment have made the preparation and reproduction of test materials simpler and more flexible and have made it possible for a school or college duplicating office to produce materials it hardly would have attempted 20 years ago.

In general, reproduction processes can be divided into (*a*) those that are simple and inexpensive enough to be carried on within a school, college, or test-making agency and (*b*) those that one must expect to purchase from a commercial printing establishment. Within the first group are (*a*) procedures for making copies one at a time from an original, (*b*) procedures in which material is drawn or typed directly on a master from which multiple copies are then made, and (*c*) procedures in which a master is produced by a copier from an original and the master is then used for the production of the needed multiple copies. Illustrations of each category, and a consideration of their uses and limitations, are given in the following sections.

Copiers

Almost any adequately equipped office now has, or has access to, one or more document copiers. Copiers are of various types, but the most important for test makers are probably electrostatic copiers, of which those made by Xerox are the best known. With an electrostatic copier, it is quick and easy to make a small number of copies of a black-and-white original document. Typed or printed copy, line drawings, and even artwork with some detail can be satisfactorily reproduced. Prototypes of four-color copiers are available, and continuing development will expand in-house printing capabilities.

Copiers are invaluable when from 1 to 10 copies of draft items are needed for circulation and review by subject-matter specialists or test-construction consultants. When a larger number of copies is required, some other technique usually will be more economical and efficient.

Direct-Master Techniques

There are a number of processes in which copy is typed (and possibly drawn) directly on some type of master from which multiple copies are then made. The final reproduction may be by spirit duplicator, mimeograph, or multilith; and the number and quality of copies depends upon which process is used. The essential common element is that the original master is made directly by the typist or draftsman. The limitations of direct processes are very real and center around the points that (*a*) errors must be corrected directly on the copy, (*b*) original copy is limited to what can be produced by hand or by the typewriter available in the office where the materials are being produced, and (*c*) diagrams and other artwork are limited to those that can be produced by hand in the office directly on the master itself. (It should be pointed out that for all of the forms of final reproduction considered in this section, masters can also be produced on copiers; the various processes are discussed on pp. 161–163.)

Spirit duplicators[1] are useful for producing up to 100 or 150 copies of a document. The equipment is inexpensive and simple to operate in the ordinary office. It is possible to produce copies in several colors. However, there is rather poor resolution of detail, so that one is largely limited to print and to fairly simple line drawings. The ink tends to fade in direct light, so that copies cannot be considered permanent.

Mimeograph has been the workhorse of school and college duplicating offices for many years now and will be familiar to almost any reader of this chapter. A master is produced by typing on a wax stencil. The wax is forced out of the stencil by the impact, leaving a space through which ink can come from the inked pad over which the stencil is placed. Detail is again limited by the fineness of line that it is possible to make on the stencil. Drawings and artwork are especially difficult to produce because they must be drawn on the stencil with a metal stylus; this makes precision work difficult and raises a problem of tearing the stencil. However, once a master has been produced, several hundred copies can usually be made from it. If the typing is firm and uniform (as with an electric typewriter), the resulting copies will be clear and legible. For tryout test booklets that consist entirely of text or that have only a limited number of simple diagrams, this method is quite acceptable. The almost universal availability and the simplicity of operation of mimeograph equipment make it widely useful for teacher-made tests, local testing activities, and the preparation of preliminary tryout forms.

It is possible to prepare master plates for offset reproduction by typing directly on the plate. Much multilith work, which is single-sheet offset printing, is done with plates produced by a direct process. The quality of reproduction is generally clear and crisp—a better quality than can be achieved with the spirit duplicator or mimeograph—and runs of several hundred copies are routine. The equipment is more expensive than a spirit duplicator or mimeograph and requires more special skill for its operation, but where it is available it provides the best quality of reproduction from direct masters.

Preparation of masters for offset calls for a high level of accuracy on the part of a typist because the correction of errors must be carefully made and is thus more troublesome than on masters for the spirit duplicator or mimeograph. By the same token, any drawings on the plates must be carefully planned and accurately carried out, because corrections will show up in the final copy unless carefully made. Given the required skills in preparation of copy, however, the product can be clear, sharp, and of a quality that is acceptable for near-professional test reproduction.

Copier-Produced Masters

For each of the three reproduction techniques described in the previous section it is now possible to produce masters by a copier from a single original document. This possibility removes or eases some of the limitations of the procedures. Thus, by using a copier to produce several masters, one can use any of the reproducing techniques to produce as many copies of the basic document as may be needed. For example, if 500 copies are needed, five masters can be produced for a spirit duplicator and each can be used to make 100 copies. Furthermore, since the master will be produced by the copier from any kind of a basic document, any kind of original material can be reproduced, subject only to those limitations imposed by the degree of sensitivity of the copier to shades of gray and limitations in the resolving power of the copier and the reproducing medium for fine detail in drawings and pictures. Though these limitations are quite real, especially in spirit duplicators and mimeograph, copier-produced masters make it possi-

---

[1] In a spirit duplicator, such as a Ditto, ink is originally transferred to a master from a type of carbon-paper backing. The master is kept moistened with alcohol, and a little of the ink comes off on each sheet of paper as it goes through the rollers and is pressed against the master.

ble to use office-type duplicating machines for a considerably wider range of work than was possible when the master had to be made by a direct process.

Masters for the spirit duplicator can be produced by a thermal-chemical process (Thermofax). The masters are adequate for typing, print, and line drawings, but produce fairly broad lines lacking in precise outline, and so this process cannot be used for fine detail. Photographs (i.e. continuously shaded material) are not reproduced adequately by this procedure. Reproduction is limited to black and white.

Masters for the mimeograph can be produced by a photoelectric spark-discharge process, in which the spark removes the wax from the mimeograph stencil.[2] The spark discharge has high fidelity, and the quality of the black-and-white reproduction is limited primarily by the resolving power of the ink-through mimeograph process. Since an especially high quality of stencil is used in the preparation of these masters, the final results approach the upper limit of mimeograph quality. The process is reported to handle photographs and halftones with a coarse screen, giving quality about like that in a daily newspaper.

There are a number of processes for copying an original and producing a master for use on an offset press. The simplest procedure makes use of an electrostatic copier that has provisions for making its copy on a paper plate that can be directly placed on the offset press.[3] Quality of the final offset printing is limited by the sensitivity of the electrostatic process, and somewhat less fine detail can be reproduced than by other copying processes.

A somewhat more complex and expensive process is a photochemical one in which the master itself has a photosensitive coating and the image of the original document is produced directly on the offset master.[4] Photographic quality of reproduction can be achieved, and,

at this point, it becomes possible to change the size of the original copy through the photographic process. As in all procedures considered up to this point, one is limited to single-sheet-sized masters, suitable for use in a small offset press that reproduces one sheet of a test at a time. The complexity and cost of this equipment is somewhat more than that of the electrostatic copier (which is also useful for the simple document-copying function), but still within the range of what is possible for an in-house duplicating unit.

Finally, masters for offset printing can be made by a complete photographic process. In this case, the original copy is photographed and a photographic negative is produced. Prints are made from the negative on some type of plate, sometimes of paper or papier-mâché but more often of metal. Plates of this sort are used primarily for commercial offset work

2.   **The original of the above is**

    (A) a Roman mosaic
    (B) a medieval cathedral window
    (C) a Turkish carpet
    (D) a Gobelin tapestry
    (E) an illuminated manuscript

FIG. 6.1. Facsimile of test item illustrating photo-offset reproduction of a photograph with copy set by linotype. (Reprinted by permission of the College Entrance Examination Board from *College-Level Examination Program, A Description of the Subject Examinations* [CEEB, 1967], p. 71.)

---

[2] Equipment for copying material onto a mimeograph stencil is produced by Gestettner and by A. B. Dick.

[3] Electrostatic copiers having this provision are produced by the Bruening Company, among others.

[4] The Itek Corporation Platemaker is an example of this type of equipment.

rather than for in-house work. Any type of original document can be reproduced. Plates can be assembled to print 4, 8, or 16 pages at a time. In general, a high quality of professional work is possible. However, few test-making organizations will have the equipment needed for photo-offset printing, and this procedure should be thought of primarily in the context of commercial work by an outside printing company.

Commercial Printing

Reproduction in a commercial printing establishment may be by offset or by letterpress printing. To the test maker, the chief difference between these two processes lies in the form in which copy may be prepared for the printer. Offset work *can* be (but is not necessarily) reproduced without further alteration from copy supplied by the test maker. If copy is prepared in *exactly* the form in which it is finally to be printed, it can be transferred to offset plates photographically, as described in the previous section, and printed without further preparatory work. By contrast, for letterpress printing the test maker supplies the typesetter with copy, marked for typesetting (see fig. 6.2), and the work of composition is carried out in the printing establishment. Proofs must be checked for accuracy and corrected. Material must be arranged in page format and checked again. When the page layout is fully completed and checked, the material is printed. It should be pointed out that copy prepared in this way for letterpress printing—that is, by direct-contact printing in which the type is inked and makes direct contact with the paper—can be printed by the offset process. At the present time the choice between offset and letterpress printing as the final process for transferring the image to paper primarily involves considerations of cost that must be assessed locally in terms of the current price structure and the size of the print run that is required.

GENERAL BOOKLET DESIGN

When the method of reproduction has been decided on, the next problem is the general design of the booklet. It is easy to dispose of this matter if a duplicating machine is to be used. The number of pages is unimportant, since separate sheets are assembled and fastened together; and there is little choice in page size and type size. Legal-size paper ($8\frac{1}{2}'' \times 13''$) takes more material per page and thus may permit the use of fewer pages than $8\frac{1}{2}'' \times 11''$ paper; but the longer sheet has the disadvantage of being somewhat more difficult to handle in filing and packing, since many standard containers and file drawers are designed for the $8\frac{1}{2}'' \times 11''$ size. The choice of type size is usually limited to elite or pica typewriter type, unless special typewriters are available.

However, when booklets are to be printed, there are various factors to be considered in planning the general design that are not involved in the case of duplicated copies.

Page Size

Printed test booklets may be produced in many different sizes. The most economical use of paper limits page size to certain conventional dimensions dictated by the standard sizes of the large paper sheets used by printers. The most common size of page, $8\frac{1}{2}'' \times 11''$, is probably the best size for most purposes. Somewhat smaller sizes, such as $6'' \times 9''$ or $6'' \times 10''$, are occasionally desirable, especially for tests made up of single-line or other very short items; but the $8\frac{1}{2}'' \times 11''$ page is more or less standard, since it provides ample space for pleasing and efficient arrangement of nearly all types of test materials and still is not so large as to make an unwieldy booklet.

Number of Pages

Booklets made by folding and stitching have an even number of leaves or sheets, and therefore, since the leaves are usually printed on both sides, the number of pages is a multiple of four. It is possible to make up booklets with an odd number of leaves by stitching or gluing a single sheet in with the folded set or by using parallel folding without stitching, but any saving in pages is usually canceled by the increased cost caused by the departure from standard procedure. If the number of pages actually required for the test material (including cover page) is not an exact multiple of four, it is almost always best to make the number of

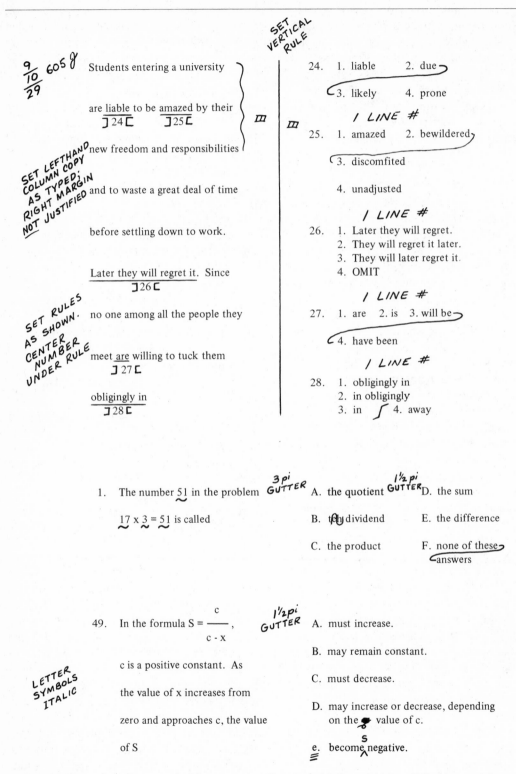

Students entering a university

are liable to be amazed by their
⌐24⌐   ⌐25⌐

new freedom and responsibilities

and to waste a great deal of time

before settling down to work.

Later they will regret it. Since
⌐26⌐

no one among all the people they

meet are willing to tuck them
⌐27⌐

obligingly in
⌐28⌐

24. 1. liable   2. due
     3. likely   4. prone

/ LINE #

25. 1. amazed   2. bewildered
     3. discomfited
     4. unadjusted

/ LINE #

26. 1. Later they will regret.
     2. They will regret it later.
     3. They will later regret it.
     4. OMIT

/ LINE #

27. 1. are   2. is   3. will be
     4. have been

/ LINE #

28. 1. obligingly in
     2. in obligingly
     3. in   4. away

---

1. The number 51 in the problem

    17 x 3 = 51 is called

    A. the quotient   D. the sum
    B. the dividend   E. the difference
    C. the product   F. none of these
                          answers

---

49. In the formula $S = \dfrac{c}{c - x}$,

     c is a positive constant. As

     the value of x increases from

     zero and approaches c, the value

     of S

     A. must increase.
     B. may remain constant.
     C. must decrease.
     D. may increase or decrease, depending
        on the value of c.
     e. become negative.

FIG. 6.2. Illustration of copy marked for typesetting. Compare with figure 6.10 for which this material was prepared

pages equal the next higher multiple of four. The extra space can sometimes be advantageously used in more generous spacing of test materials on the page, or it can be distributed as blank pages at strategic spots. The outside back cover (last page) and the inside front cover (page 2) are good places for blank pages when the extra space is not needed for special purposes within the booklet.

Use of Cover Page

A separate cover page is not essential if the directions to the examinee are short and if strict timing is not important. The title of the test, spaces for the examinee's name and other information (if separate answer sheets are not used), and instructions for taking the test may be placed on the upper part of the first page; the items may then begin on the lower part of that page. However, there is no particular advantage in this arrangement unless such use of the first (cover) page for items makes it possible to bring the total number of pages required down to a lower multiple of four. Suppose, for example, that the items will exactly fill seven pages. If the lower half of the first page is used for items, the only result is that the last page will have blank space at the end, where it serves no purpose. In such a case, it would be better to begin the items on page 2, reserving the cover page entirely for test title, information blanks, directions, sample items, etc. If, however, the space needed amounts to seven and one-half pages, the use of a separate cover page would make the last items fall on page 9. This would necessitate the use of a 12-page booklet instead of an 8-page booklet and involve increased expense for printing. The use of half of the cover page for items would keep such a test down to eight pages.

This use of a part of the first page for items is inadvisable for tests where strict timing is important. The use of a separate cover page is obviously helpful in enforcing a rule that examinees are not to look at the items until the signal to begin is given.

Use of Blank Pages

Similar considerations apply to a test containing more than one part when strict timing

of the separate parts is desired. If a booklet can be arranged so that a part other than the last ends on a right-hand page, the beginning of the next part is not visible until the page is turned. A blank page inserted at the end of a part can be used to force the beginning of the next part over to a left-hand page if such a page arrangement would not otherwise occur. Even when a part does end on a right-hand page, a blank page can be used to advantage (if there are pages to spare in the booklet) by leaving blank the left-hand page following the end of the part and beginning the next part on the right-hand page. Where parts are several pages long, the beginning of a part is somewhat easier to locate on a right-hand page than on a left-hand page.

These paging arrangements are not essential if strictly uniform timing is not especially important. In such a case, the best procedure is to determine first the approximate number of pages required for the items and other essential printed material. If this number is an exact multiple of four, or very slightly less, an arrangement without blank pages or separate cover will keep the printing expense to a minimum. If the number of pages required is not an exact multiple of four, the best use of the extra space will depend on the particular test. Even where strict timing is not important, appearance is somewhat improved by beginning a part on a new page. In some tests, blank pages or parts of pages can be assigned to serve as scratch paper. In tests containing large groups of items referring to the same illustration, passage, or the like, a judicious distribution of blank space helps in arranging the material in such a way that it will not be necessary for the examinee to turn a page in referring back to the data on which the items are based.

Allowance for Directions and Samples

In estimating the number of pages required and planning the paging of the booklet, one should not overlook such material as general and specific instructions, statement of time allotments, and sample items or practice exercises. In a test consisting of only a single type of item, where a single set of directions and one or two sample items are sufficient, the directions and samples can well be placed on the cover. Where different directions, and possibly sample items, are required for different parts, they are placed at the beginning of the part.

Preparation of a Dummy

When a test is being prepared as a booklet, it will almost always pay the test maker to prepare a *dummy*. This is a page-by-page layout of the test showing just where each segment of printed material is to be placed.

Preparation of a dummy assumes that the text for test items has already been typed and that figures and drawings have been roughed out in approximately the size that will be used. It is a help if test items have been typed to the line length (in characters) that is going to be used in the test booklet. Directions, common reference materials, illustrations, and the text of single items can be arranged page by page. The order of items can be rearranged, within limits, to make columns and pages come out even; adjustments possibly may be made in the number of items so as to fit the available space, or conversely plans with respect to the number of pages in the test booklet may be revised so that the required stock of items can be fitted into them.

PAGE LAYOUT

Use of Columns

In planning the layout of individual pages, the first consideration is the length of line to be used for verbal material. Lines of text may run the full width of the page, or the page may be divided into two or even three columns. The best arrangement is that which gives the optimum combination of legibility and economy of space, taking into account the page size, type size, and nature of test materials.

Legibility, insofar as it is affected by length of line, is primarily a matter of avoiding extremes with respect both to actual length in inches and to the relationship between the length and the size of type (that is, the number of characters per line). Very long lines are difficult to read, particularly in such solid, connected material as occurs in reading passages (see fig. 6.3) or in multiple-choice items having lengthy stems and responses. When the eye has too far to travel from the end of one line back to the beginning of the next line, it is easier to lose one's place and reread or skip lines than when the lines are of moderate length. On the other hand, the use of very narrow columns is best limited to items having short elements, such as multiple-choice vocabulary items. If very short lines are used for running text, the division of a great many words at the ends of lines may seriously interfere with legibility (see fig. 6.4).

Economy in the utilization of space is chiefly a matter of selecting a page arrangement that makes due allowance for the foregoing considerations of legibility without leaving too much space unused. Where lines running the full width of the page are used for items having elements that, individually, do not take up most of the line, a good deal of space is wasted (see fig. 6.5). Such waste can be minimized without sacrifice of legibility by the use of a

---

She noticed that there was a button missing from his jacket at once; she always noticed anything amiss with Ernie, because her pride—and she had plenty—was centered upon her boy. But, apart from that, Mrs. Poston was orderly in all her ways. She liked to have everything inside her cottage, from the shining row of neatly labelled tins above the mantel-shelf to the marker in the Bible by her bedside, arranged precisely in its proper place. Pernickety, she called herself—a neat, thin, white-haired, quiet-voiced little woman, the last person in the world to have a murderer for a son.

1. Mrs. Poston's habits of living were

   1 fanatical.
   2 careless.
   3 easygoing.
   4 fastidious.................1( )

2. Mrs. Poston admitted that she was

   1 stern.
   2 fussy.
   3 peculiar.
   4 overly proud...............2( )

FIG. 6.3. Reading passage printed with lines too long for easy legibility

two-column page, provided the number of characters per line is not too small (see fig. 6.6). This condition is more often fulfilled in printed copies than in duplicated copies, since the duplicated characters are the full size of the typewriter type. Material for duplicating-machine copies should not be arranged in two columns if the small number of characters per column line forces an excessive breaking-up of the text. In printed tests (either letterpress or offset), the greater sharpness of the type permits the use of somewhat smaller size type, so that the resulting number of characters per column line is often just right for both legibility and economy.

31. One of the functions of white cells in human blood is to
  31-1 destroy invading germs.
  31-2 break down acid wastes into harmless compounds.
  31-3 liberate energy for the muscle cells.
  31-4 carry oxygen.
  31-5 excrete excess moisture from the body.

FIG. 6.4. Use of very short lines breaks up the text excessively.

1. You are living in a town near a river. In early summer there is a week of heavy rain. The stream rises, overflows its banks, and floods the town. Which of the following factors has probably contributed most to this disaster?

  A. Stream pollution
  B. The drying up of springs
  C. Widespread deforestation
  D. Accumulation of too much topsoil
  E. Fall of the ground water level

2. A single-celled organism is found to have cytoplasm, a nucleus, chloroplasts, vacuoles, and a cell membrane. Which of these indicates that the organism is a plant rather than an animal?

  A. The cytoplasm
  B. The chloroplasts
  C. The nucleus
  D. The cell membrane
  E. The vacuoles

FIG. 6.5. Space wasted on lines containing choices

1. You are living in a town near a river. In early summer there is a week of heavy rain. The stream rises, overflows its banks, and floods the town. Which of the following factors has probably contributed most to this disaster?

  A. Stream pollution
  B. The drying up of springs
  C. Widespread deforestation
  D. Accumulation of too much topsoil
  E. Fall of the ground water level

2. A single-celled organism is found to have cytoplasm, a nucleus, chloroplasts, vacuoles, and a cell membrane. Which of these indicates that the organism is a plant rather than an animal?

  A. The cytoplasm
  B. The chloroplasts
  C. The nucleus
  D. The cell membrane
  E. The vacuoles

FIG. 6.6. Double-column page permits more compact arrangement of same material

Placing of Items on Page

Whatever page arrangement is adopted, all of a given item should appear within a single column or page. It is particularly important that the examinee should not have to turn a page in the midst of any one problem. Items should never be broken at the bottom of a page or column and continued on the next page or column unless some other exceptionally important factor makes such breaking unavoidable. If a test is made up of items of different lengths and if keeping the items in their exact order is not essential, it is often possible to avoid wasting too much space in following this principle by making minor changes in the order of the items. If an item is too long to fit into the remaining space in the column or page, it may be possible to exchange it with a later item that is short enough to fit. Or if the remaining space is insufficient for even the shortest item, the preceding item may be exchanged for a longer item that will take up all or most of the remaining space.

On a two-column page, the columns can be made approximately the same length by similar shifts. Where such shifts are impossible, or fail to make the columns exactly equal, the extra space in the shorter column may be distributed between the items so as to equalize the columns. Care should be taken to keep such shifts in position within appropriate limits, as determined by technical or logical considerations governing the order of items.

Any reference material (passages of text, tables, graphs, etc.) should be on the same page as the items referring to it or at least on a facing page. In dealing with such problems in the arrangement of pages, it should be remembered that even-numbered pages fall on the left and odd-numbered pages on the right of the two-page spread of an open booklet.

Provision for Response

Responses to objective test items may be recorded either (a) in the test booklet or (b) on a separate answer sheet. Whichever way they are recorded, they may be scored either (a) by a clerk or (b) by the use of a scoring machine or an optical scanner. Use of a separate answer

sheet has great advantages so far as economy is concerned. It means that test booklets can be used a number of times and that the scoring process can be carried out much more efficiently. However, a separate answer sheet makes the clerical task for the examinee somewhat more demanding. He must not only determine the answer to the problem that he finds in the test booklet but also identify and carry in memory the number and letter of this answer, find that number and letter on a physically separate piece of paper, and mark in that proper space. This additional task may be too demanding for young children or for persons in cultures in which objective tests are themselves somewhat strange. For groups of this sort, more valid assessment may be achieved if the answer can be marked directly in the test booklet. Thus, some consideration of each of the response scoring patterns is in order.

Any separate answer sheet can readily be adapted for hand scoring. All that is required is an overlay stencil with holes punched corresponding to the right answers. Such a stencil can be very simply and cheaply prepared by punching out the proper spaces on a copy of the answer sheet itself.[5] (It often helps to have two guidemarks on the answer sheet and holes punched at these places on the overlay to check the accuracy of positioning of the stencil over the answer sheet.) A count is made of correct answers marked on the answer sheet and appearing through the holes of the overlay stencil. The answer sheet also must be scanned for double marking of items and, if a formula score is used that treats wrongs differently from omits, for omissions. When tests are commercially produced, the overlay is frequently made of transparent plastic, overprinted with an answer key, so that responses in the correct locations can be easily counted.

Answer sheets to be read by a test-scoring machine or document reader must ordinarily be produced to very fine tolerances so far as spacing is concerned. These forms also are likely to require special guidemarks to control the operation of the optical-scanning equip-

[5] A useful punch for punching out answer stencils is sold by IBM.

ment. The paper must be accurately cut if proper registration is to be obtained. The requirements are almost always beyond the capacity of the in-house duplicating equipment and are often not well understood by the routine commercial printer, so that preparation of such answer sheets is usually best left to the company that produces the scanning equipment or operates the scoring service.

Engineering features of the particular scanner or scoring device often set certain limitations on the arrangement of an answer sheet, especially if a number of part scores are required from a single insertion of the answer sheet. The test maker will need to check these with the maker of the scanning or scoring equipment as he works out the design of the answer sheet and plans the number of items for the different subscores in his test.

Recent developments in optical-scanning equipment have made it possible to scan and score a complete test booklet. Either the test is printed in an accordion-fold format or the bound edge of the booklet is sliced off. In either case, the complete booklet is then fed into an optical scanner page by page. Marks are scanned at predetermined locations on the pages, and a score is computed based upon the number of marks appearing in the correct (and possibly in the incorrect) places. Developments in optical-scanning equipment are proceeding rapidly, so one may anticipate increasing versatility in reading marks on a test booklet. In general, with optical scanning of a booklet it is possible to have the answer marks made in whatever is the most natural location for the examinee. An illustration is given in figure 6.7 of patterns for marking answers directly in a test booklet.

Machine-scorable consumable test booklets, designed for the examinee to mark directly in the booklet, are especially appropriate for tests that will be used in large numbers with young or inexperienced examinees. The test maker who is developing test materials for this type of use will want to consult with the makers of optical scanning and scoring equipment to determine the state of the art and the specifications that must be met for accurate scanning

and scoring. Usually, it will be desirable to have printing done by, or at least supervised by, the maker of the scanner to guarantee that answer marks are appropriately arranged and that printing on the booklet registers within allowable tolerance limits. Machine-scorable booklets are several times as expensive as separate answer sheets for three reasons. In the first place, one multipage booklet is used up for each examinee tested. Secondly, better paper must be used to obtain the needed accuracy of registration. Finally, it is necessary to pass several sheets, rather than only one, through the optical scanner, and thus more time of expensive equipment is required. However, when compared with hand scoring of large-scale testing programs, the procedure becomes very attractive. Increasing resistance on the part of teaching groups to being asked to carry out the clerical chores of test scoring have made the machine-scored booklet a very popular development.

In a minority of cases, tests will still be produced in which answers are to be marked in the booklet, and the booklet is then hand scored. This form of test will be useful when tests are to be given to a relatively small number of examinees and to examinees who cannot be expected to be facile in the use of a separate answer sheet. How shall the answers then be arranged on the page? The decision will represent a compromise between ease of marking for the examinee and ease of scoring for the person who must do the clerical work of scoring the tests. Usually, the convenience of the examinee will be controlling because, if he were mature and experienced enough so that one could ignore his limitations, a separate answer sheet would be used. For this type of test, the test maker should ask himself: What is the simplest, the clearest way to arrange the answer-marking task from the point of view of the examinee? The arrangement of the page should be guided by the answer to this question. Generally speaking, marks should be made close to, and in a consistent spatial relation to, the answer that is being marked—right on it, right under it, or right beside it. The nature of the test task will suggest which is most appropriate.

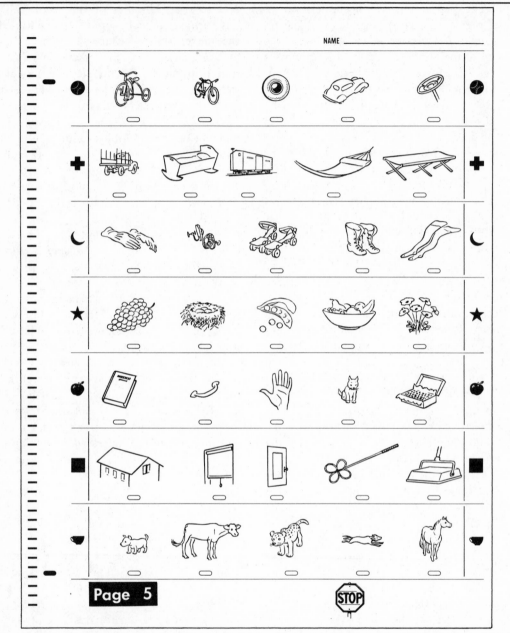

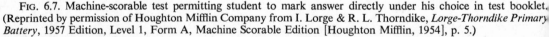

FIG. 6.7. Machine-scorable test permitting student to mark answer directly under his choice in test booklet. (Reprinted by permission of Houghton Mifflin Company from I. Lorge & R. L. Thorndike, *Lorge-Thorndike Primary Battery*, 1957 Edition, Level 1, Form A, Machine Scorable Edition [Houghton Mifflin, 1954], p. 5.)

Identification of Items

All items, of whatever type, should be numbered. Informal tests are sometimes reproduced without item numbers since the test constructor feels no particular need for the numbers at the moment; but some means of identifying individual items is nearly always found desirable afterwards, and it is much simpler and more dependable to number the items as the copy is prepared than to supply identification later. Sometimes both numbers and letters are used to indicate groups and in-

1. The electrical energy that can be obtained from a dry cell is (1) stored in the form of electrical energy, (2) stored in the cell in the form of chemical energy, (3) stored in the cell in the form of mechanical energy, (4) stored in the cell in the form of kinetic energy of molecules, (5) created within the cell...1( )

FIG. 6.8. Item is difficult to read in strung-out form

dividual items respectively. However, serial numbering of individual scorable units seems the simplest and most direct method of identification; groups can be identified in other ways—by marking off with lines or asterisks the separation between groups, by including at the head of the group some such note as "Items 5–9 apply to this diagram," or both. In tests having more than one part, each part may start with item 1, or the items may be numbered consecutively throughout the test. The latter plan is usually necessary if standard answer sheets are used and has the advantage of furnishing positive identification of each item with a single number. For separately timed parts, however, separate numbering of each part provides the examinee with a better idea of his progress relative to the time allowed.

Page Numbers

Page numbers may be placed at the top or bottom of each page, either centered or at the outside edge. (The outside is at the left of even-numbered pages, at the right of odd-numbered pages.) On some tests designed for hand scoring, the page number is placed in the upper *right* corner on both even- and odd-numbered pages, directly above the column of spaces for response in order to facilitate matching the appropriate key strip in scoring.

ARRANGEMENT OF THE INDIVIDUAL MULTIPLE-CHOICE ITEM

Closely related to arrangement of the page, of course, is the arrangement of item elements—reference matter (if any) such as read-

ing passages, diagrams, tables, etc.; question, statement, problem, or, in general, "stimulus"; and suggested answers from which a choice is to be made.

Strung-out Arrangement

The arrangement of multiple-choice items shown in figure 6.8 formerly was used extensively and is still used a good deal in informal tests made for local and limited use. The only advantage of this arrangement is that it permits the use of practically all the space on the page with a minimum of waste, since at most only a part of one line per item is left unused. Among the disadvantages is the fact that the lines of text are likely to be too long for easy legibility. A more serious disadvantage is that, in a long item, the individual choices are not spatially well differentiated. This makes it difficult for the examinee to consider each choice as a whole and to compare and contrast the choices, especially when two or more choices have some words in common. In addition, the association of each label (letter or number) with the choice it identifies is not clear cut and unmistakable when the label is buried within the text.

For these reasons, it is best to have choices strung out in this fashion only for items short enough to fit into a single line and with plenty of space between the choices (see fig. 6.9).

Arrangement in a Uniform Spatial Pattern

For longer items, stem and responses should be arranged in some spatial pattern that will clearly differentiate the choices from the stem and from each other. There are several such

7. Which one of the following gases changes color on exposure to air?
   (1) NO   (2) N$_2$ (3) Cl$_2$ (4) Br$_2$ (5) Ne..................7( )
35. sheen   A. spite   B. luster   C. organ   D. turf   E. plumage.........35( )

FIG. 6.9. Types of items for which horizontal (strung-out) arrangement is suitable

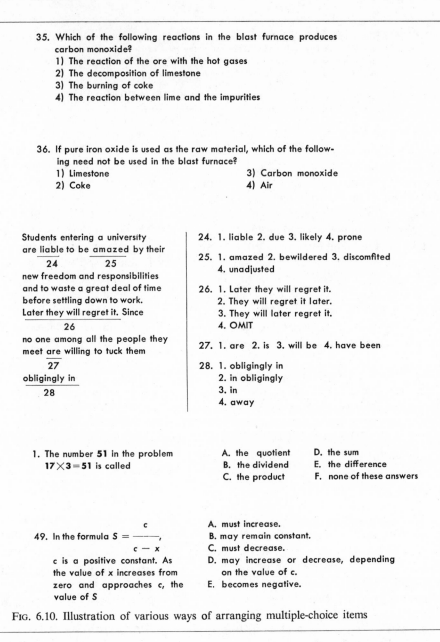

35. Which of the following reactions in the blast furnace produces carbon monoxide?
   1) The reaction of the ore with the hot gases
   2) The decomposition of limestone
   3) The burning of coke
   4) The reaction between lime and the impurities

36. If pure iron oxide is used as the raw material, which of the following need not be used in the blast furnace?
   1) Limestone   3) Carbon monoxide
   2) Coke   4) Air

Students entering a university are liable to be amazed by their
<u>24</u>   <u>25</u>
new freedom and responsibilities and to waste a great deal of time before settling down to work. Later they will regret it. Since
<u>26</u>
no one among all the people they meet are willing to tuck them
<u>27</u>
obligingly in
<u>28</u>

24. 1. liable 2. due 3. likely 4. prone

25. 1. amazed 2. bewildered 3. discomfited
   4. unadjusted

26. 1. Later they will regret it.
   2. They will regret it later.
   3. They will later regret it.
   4. OMIT

27. 1. are 2. is 3. will be 4. have been

28. 1. obligingly in
   2. in obligingly
   3. in
   4. away

1. The number **51** in the problem **17×3=51** is called

   A. the quotient   D. the sum
   B. the dividend   E. the difference
   C. the product   F. none of these answers

49. In the formula $S = \dfrac{c}{c - x}$, c is a positive constant. As the value of x increases from zero and approaches c, the value of S

   A. must increase.
   B. may remain constant.
   C. must decrease.
   D. may increase or decrease, depending on the value of c.
   E. becomes negative.

FIG. 6.10. Illustration of various ways of arranging multiple-choice items

patterns; the selection of the appropriate pattern depends chiefly on the length and nature of the item materials (see fig. 6.10). In tests having items of varying nature and length, it is ordinarily advisable to select the one arrangement that is best suited to the majority of the items and use that same arrangement throughout the test or part, rather than to vary the arrangement from item to item. In most cases, there is more advantage in presenting a uniform spatial pattern for the item elements than in adapting the spatial pattern separately to each individual item.

Where there is a diagram or drawing to which reference is made in the stem, the reference illustration is sometimes placed above and sometimes placed below the stem (see figs. 6.11 and 6.12). In general it seems more

6. The circle in figure 1 has center at O. If PQ and QR are secants and if $x = 40$, what is y?

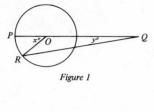

Figure 1

(A) 10
(B) 20
(C) 30
(D) 40
(E) It cannot be determined from the information given.

Fig. 6.11. Diagram interrupts verbal sequence from stem to choices. (Adapted from trial item in *A Description of the College Board Achievement Tests* [CEEB, 1968], p. 89; and reprinted by permission of the College Entrance Examination Board.)

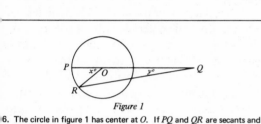

Figure 1

6. The circle in figure 1 has center at O. If PQ and QR are secants and if $x = 40$, what is y?
(A) 10
(B) 20
(C) 30
(D) 40
(E) It cannot be determined from the information given.

FIG. 6.12. Stem and choices kept together

6. The circle in figure 1 has center at O. If PQ and QR are secants and if $x = 40$, what is y?
(A) 10
(B) 20
(C) 30
(D) 40
(E) It cannot be determined from the information given.

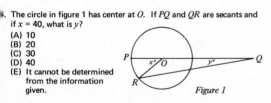

Figure 1

FIG. 6.13. Compact arrangement, especially useful when economy of space is important.

ogical to put the illustration first, followed by the stem or question, in order to avoid separating the choices from the stem (especially when the stem is an incomplete statement).

Differentiation of the Item Elements

Where the choices are rather long, differentiation between item elements is helped by

setting the numbers or letters identifying the items and choices out to the left of the body of text. In addition, stem and choices can be distinguished by the use of a little extra space between stem and first choice and, if there is room to spare, between one choice and the next. Such extra space should, however, be less than the space between separate items in order to preserve the effect of the total item as a unit. (See fig. 6.14.)

1. The legendary founders of Rome were

1   Castor and Pollux.
2   Damon and Pythias.
3   Prometheus and Epimetheus.
4   Romulus and Remus.
5   Baucis and Philemon.......................1( )

2. The river on which the city of Rome is located is the

1   Tiber.
2   Po.
3   Rhone.
4   Rhine.
5   Danube..................................2( )

3. Caesar's partners in the first triumvirate were

1   Pompey and Crassus.
2   Calpurnius and Clodius.
3   Lepidus and Antonius.
4   Cato and Marius.
5   Brutus and Octavian......................3( )

FIG. 6.14. Item elements differentiated by use of varying amounts of space between lines.

When typewritten copy is to be reproduced, the effects produced by variable spacing may be achieved, within limits, by the use of a typewriter having a special line spacer that adds half-line spacing to the conventional single and double spacing. Different amounts of indention may also be used to differentiate item elements.

When tests are set in type, boldface type, italics, or different type styles may be used to set off the stem from the choices or reference material from the item proper. However, it is well to avoid the use of boldface or italic type in large or numerous blocks of material, since such type is harder to read than the ordinary roman type and since its effectiveness for purposes of emphasis is lost by excessive use. Similar effects may be obtained in typewritten copy for offset reproduction by using the Vari-

Typer, the IBM Selectric typewriter with different typeface balls, or by using different typewriters with varying sizes or styles of type for different portions of the copy. In ordinary typewritten copy the means of differentiation are limited to the use of underlining, double underlining, and solid capitals.

When type is set, boldface or other distinctive type faces may be used to emphasize item numbers and to differentiate the identification letters or numbers of choices. In typewritten copy, identifying letters or numbers may be followed by a period, enclosed in parentheses, or separated from the text of the choices by a single parenthesis or a dash (see fig. 6.15).

---

61. Which one of the following states
    grows the most cotton?

    1. Texas
    2. Arizona
    3. New Mexico
    4. California
    5. Florida................................61( )

61. Which one of the following states
    grows the most cotton?

    (1) Texas
    (2) Arizona
    (3) New Mexico
    (4) California
    (5) Florida...............................61( )

61. Which one of the following states
    grows the most cotton?

    1) Texas
    2) Arizona
    3) New Mexico
    4) California
    5) Florida...............................61( )

FIG. 6.15. Illustrations of ways of setting off choice numbers.

Labeling of Choices

There are several ways of labeling the suggested answers. Most commonly used are Arabic numerals and capital letters; lower-case letters are occasionally employed; Roman numerals are rarely used and should be avoided. If responses are to be written by the examinee, either in the booklet or on a separate sheet, Arabic numerals are somewhat more likely to be legible than capital letters and considerably more likely to be legible than small letters or

Roman numerals. If responses are made by marking labeled boxes or spaces on a separate answer sheet, legibility of the examinee's response is not a factor. If numbers are used rather than letters, it may be a trifle easier for the examinee to avoid error in selecting the appropriate space on a separate answer sheet, since the number *4*, for example, is more closely associated with the fourth space than the letter *D*.

A consideration in the labeling of choices that applies regardless of the method by which the examinee indicates responses is the avoidance of confusion between the label identifying the choice and the substance of the choice. If suggested answers to many of the items include Arabic numerals, as in arithmetic tests or other numerical materials, letters will be more distinctive as labels for the choices. If single capital letters appear in many of the answers, as in those involving chemical symbols, numbers will be more clearly differentiated as labels. Lower-case letters are generally to be avoided, since capitals stand out better; but they remain a possibility for labeling in special cases.

Order of Choices

It is more important to use the same system of labeling choices throughout any one test or part than it is to attempt to avoid all duplication between symbols used for labels and symbols used within the choices. Also, the use of standard answer sheets often dictates the way the responses are labeled. In cases where duplication between symbols cannot be avoided, confusion can be minimized if the choices are so ordered that the choice label agrees with the choice itself. Numerical choices are preferably

---

5. If a man spent $3.75 for socks and one pair cost $.75
   how many pairs did he buy?

   1. 1/5
   2. 4
   3. 5
   4. 15
   5. 50

FIG. 6.16. Answers arranged in order of magnitude but likely to cause confusion between the answer proper and the identification number.

5. If a man spent $3.75 for socks and one pair cost $.75, how many pairs did he buy?

1. 50
2. 15
3. 1/5
4. 4
5. 5

FIG. 6.17. A better arrangement, avoiding confusion

listed in order of magnitude, but it is generally considered better to list them out of order if that is necessary for placing, for example, a numerical answer *4* as choice number *4*, rather than as number *2* or *5* (see figs. 6.16 and 6.17).

ARRANGEMENT OF TRUE-FALSE AND COMPLETION ITEMS

True-false and completion items are simpler to arrange than multiple-choice items, since they consist only of statements and simple provisions for response. The chief factors in determining arrangement are legibility and economy of space. The section above on page layout (pp. 166–171) covers these considerations. The illustrations in figure 6.18 show several possible arrangements of true-false items.

29. If a radius of the circle is drawn to the midpoint of an arc, it is perpendicular to the chord of the arc...29(   )

32. Gregor J. Mendel was one of the first scientists to use lenses in the study of small organisms....... —

(   ) 41. Eugenics is the study that seeks to explain the nature of differences and similarities between parent and offspring.

52. The New Testament was originally written in Hebrew................................ T F

65. The English Reform Bill of 1832 was notable chiefly for its reform of the suffrage.......TRUE FALSE

FIG. 6.18. Illustration of ways of arranging true-false items.

ARRANGEMENT OF GROUPED ITEMS

Groups Based on Common Reference Material

Grouped items of any kind present special problems. Where the basis of this grouping is simply the presentation of reference material that is to be used for a series of items, the problem is chiefly a matter of page layout. Where the group consists of material that will fit easily on one page, several arrangements are possible. If the reference material (reading passage, chart, map, etc.) and the items are of such proportions that they will fit within the same margins, the entire group may simply be presented serially, either in a single column or in two columns, with the items following directly after the reference material. If the reference material is wider than the items, it may be centered in the upper portion of the page with the items arranged in two or three columns below. A long narrow diagram may be placed at the left with the items in a single column at the right. Other arrangements may be worked out to accommodate the particular combination of shapes and sizes presented by the materials. The chief factors to keep in mind are ease of reference from the individual items to the common basic material and symmetry, or at least balance, in arrangement (see figs. 6.19 and 6.20).

If the group is too large to fit on a single page, as when a large map or drawing is used or when the number of items in the group is large, the best solution is to put the reference material on a left-hand (even-numbered) page, with the items referring to it on the following right-hand page. Where there are more items than will go on a single page, the reference material and some of the items may be placed on the left-hand page, and the rest of the items on the right-hand page.

If there are several smaller groups, each requiring considerably less than a page, reference material and items may be placed serially, with lines or asterisks to separate groups (see fig. 6.21), or the page may be divided by lines or spaces into horizontal bands, with each group arranged to best advantage within its band.

Groups Based on a Common Set of Choices

A different type of group is that in which the basis of grouping is the use of the same set of choices for a series of items. If the number of items does not differ greatly from the number

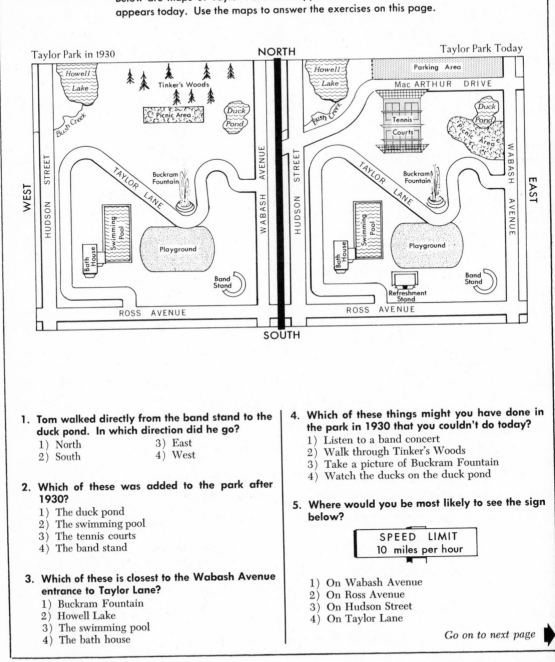

Below are maps of Taylor Park as it appeared in 1930 and as it appears today. Use the maps to answer the exercises on this page.

1. **Tom walked directly from the band stand to the duck pond. In which direction did he go?**
   1) North   3) East
   2) South   4) West

2. **Which of these was added to the park after 1930?**
   1) The duck pond
   2) The swimming pool
   3) The tennis courts
   4) The band stand

3. **Which of these is closest to the Wabash Avenue entrance to Taylor Lane?**
   1) Buckram Fountain
   2) Howell Lake
   3) The swimming pool
   4) The bath house

4. **Which of these things might you have done in the park in 1930 that you couldn't do today?**
   1) Listen to a band concert
   2) Walk through Tinker's Woods
   3) Take a picture of Buckram Fountain
   4) Watch the ducks on the duck pond

5. **Where would you be most likely to see the sign below?**

   SPEED   LIMIT
   10 miles per hour

   1) On Wabash Avenue
   2) On Ross Avenue
   3) On Hudson Street
   4) On Taylor Lane

   Go on to next page ▶

Fig. 6.19. Illustration of page arrangement with reference material. (Reproduced by permission of Houghton Mifflin Company from E. F. Lindquist & A. N. Hieronymus, *Iowa Tests of Basic Skills*, Form 4, Multi-Level Edition for Grades 3–9 [Houghton Mifflin, 1964], p. 51.)

Items 117 through 125 refer to the following experiment. In studying the effect of various salts upon the relative humidity above water solutions of the salts, the following results were obtained.

Percent Relative Humidity above Salt Solutions

Salt Added per 100 g H_2O	Unsaturated Solutions at 68° F.						Saturated Solution at 68° F.	
Formula	Wt. Salt	% Hum.	Wt. Salt	% Hum.	Wt. Salt	% Hum.	Wt. Salt	% Hum.
$CaCl_2$	20 g	80%	40 g	61%	60 g	44%	75 g	32%
$MgCl_2$	29 g	72%	40 g	48%	—	—	55 g	32%
$NaCl$	20 g	89%	—	—	—	—	36 g	78%
$Ca(NO_3)_2$	20 g	98%	40 g	95%	60 g	90%	129 g	59%
$NaNO_3$	20 g	96%	40 g	93%	60 g	86%	88 g	76%
NH_4NO_3	20 g	94%	40 g	88%	60 g	83%	192 g	68%

Using **only** these data, mark the degree of correctness of items 117 through 125 as follows:

1   The statement is **true.**
2   The statement is **probably true;** additional data would be necessary for a final decision.
3   The statement is **impossible to judge;** the experiment provides no evidence upon which to make a prediction of the results to be expected in this case.
4   The statement is **probably false;** additional data would be necessary for a final decision.
5   The statement is **false.**

117.   The relative humidity above a saturated solution of **KCl** is lower than the relative humidity above a saturated solution of **NaCl**

118.   At 68° F. at a concentration of **40 g** salt per **100 g** of H_2O, NH_4NO_3 produces a lower percent humidity than $Ca(NO_3)_2$ does.

119.   These data were collected to explain why saturated solutions absorb moisture from the air.

120.   At 68° F. increasing the concentration of the above solutions of these salts always tends to decrease the relative humidity above the solutions.

121.   At 68° F. the relative humidity above a solution containing **30 g NaNO_3** per **100 g H_2O** is about 94.5%.

122.   At 68° F. the relative humidity above a solution containing **17 g NH_4NO_3** per **100 g H_2O** is 99%.

123.   The relative humidity above a solution containing **80 g $CaCl_2$** per **100g H_2O** is 30%.

124.   On a weight basis, the listed chlorides are more effective than the listed nitrates in reducing the relative humidity at 68° F.

125.   The relative humidity above a salt solution at 68° F. is less than that above pure water at the same temperature because the ions from the dissolved salts take up some of the surface area of the solution.

FIG. 6.20. Illustration of page arrangement with reference material

of choices, the most economical as well as convenient arrangement is to place the items and choices in two adjacent vertical columns. Items so arranged constitute what is usually meant by "matching items."

The three necessary columns (choices, items, and spaces for response) may be arranged in various ways: choices at the left and items at the right, followed by response spaces; or items at the left, with response spaces either before or after the items, and choices at the right. When the responses are to be written in the booklet,

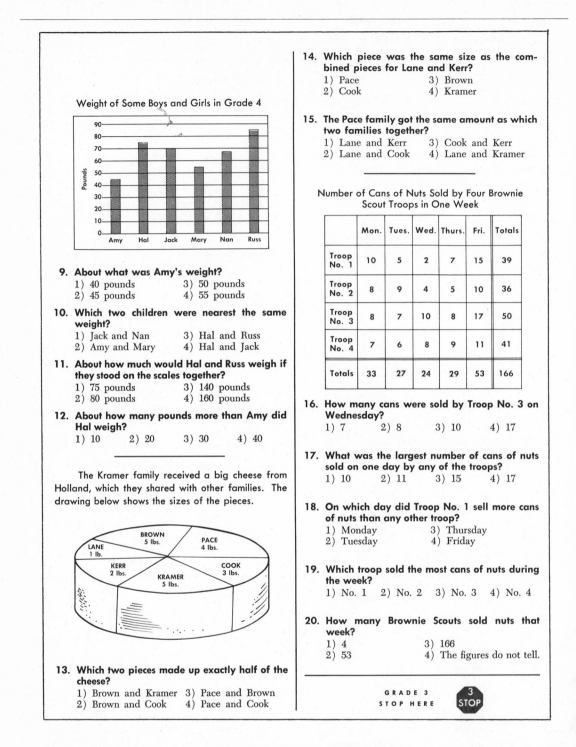

Weight of Some Boys and Girls in Grade 4

9. About what was Amy's weight?
1) 40 pounds   3) 50 pounds
2) 45 pounds   4) 55 pounds

10. Which two children were nearest the same weight?
1) Jack and Nan   3) Hal and Russ
2) Amy and Mary   4) Hal and Jack

11. About how much would Hal and Russ weigh if they stood on the scales together?
1) 75 pounds   3) 140 pounds
2) 80 pounds   4) 160 pounds

12. About how many pounds more than Amy did Hal weigh?
1) 10   2) 20   3) 30   4) 40

The Kramer family received a big cheese from Holland, which they shared with other families. The drawing below shows the sizes of the pieces.

13. Which two pieces made up exactly half of the cheese?
1) Brown and Kramer   3) Pace and Brown
2) Brown and Cook   4) Pace and Cook

14. Which piece was the same size as the combined pieces for Lane and Kerr?
1) Pace   3) Brown
2) Cook   4) Kramer

15. The Pace family got the same amount as which two families together?
1) Lane and Kerr   3) Cook and Kerr
2) Lane and Cook   4) Lane and Kramer

Number of Cans of Nuts Sold by Four Brownie Scout Troops in One Week

	Mon.	Tues.	Wed.	Thurs.	Fri.	Totals
Troop No. 1	10	5	2	7	15	39
Troop No. 2	8	9	4	5	10	36
Troop No. 3	8	7	10	8	17	50
Troop No. 4	7	6	8	9	11	41
Totals	33	27	24	29	53	166

16. How many cans were sold by Troop No. 3 on Wednesday?
1) 7   2) 8   3) 10   4) 17

17. What was the largest number of cans of nuts sold on one day by any of the troops?
1) 10   2) 11   3) 15   4) 17

18. On which day did Troop No. 1 sell more cans of nuts than any other troop?
1) Monday   3) Thursday
2) Tuesday   4) Friday

19. Which troop sold the most cans of nuts during the week?
1) No. 1   2) No. 2   3) No. 3   4) No. 4

20. How many Brownie Scouts sold nuts that week?
1) 4   3) 166
2) 53   4) The figures do not tell.

GRADE 3
STOP HERE   **3 STOP**

FIG. 6.21. Illustration of page arrangement with reference material and grouped items. (Reproduced by permission of Houghton Mifflin Company from E. F. Lindquist & A. N. Hieronymus, *Iowa Tests of Basic Skills*, Form 4, Multi-Level Edition for Grades 3–9 [Houghton Mifflin, 1964], p. 62.)

the first mentioned is usually most convenient. If responses are to be placed on a separate answer sheet, it makes little difference which of the two possible arrangements of item column and choice column is used.

Another kind of group that is essentially a matching set involves a diagram or map with labeled parts that are to be matched with names, descriptions, or other associated phrases. Since the shape and size of the illustration are the controlling factors in the arrangement of such materials, the discussion on page 175 of item groups based on reference material is more pertinent than the considerations applying to purely verbal matching items.

Still another variant of groups of items using the same set of choices is the combination of a small number of choices (usually from two to five) with a relatively large number of items. For such groups, the use of two adjacent vertical columns for choices and items is not economical, since a great deal of space would be wasted in the choice column. Such groups are best arranged by listing the common set of choices at the head of the group—perhaps integrated with the directions for the group— and arranging the items in sequence below (see fig. 6.22). The choices should be distinctly set off from one another and carefully identified with their labels. If the items in the group take up more than a page, the set of choices should be repeated at the head of each page. In many cases, the choices can be repeated in an abbreviated form which will serve as an adequate reminder of the marking code.

PREPARATION OF TEST COPY

The problems involved in preparing test copy will vary depending upon the type of reproduction that is to be used. One set of problems arises when the test is to be typed (and possibly drawn) directly onto a master from which copies are to be made by spirit duplicator, mimeograph, or multilith; a somewhat different set arises when the master is to be produced by a copier; while a still different set arises when the materials are to be turned over to a commercial printer for composition as well as reproduction.

Preparing a Direct Master

Tests that are reproduced, either for tryout or for final use, directly on the stencil or plate from which copies are to be made are usually test forms involving simple layout and small volume. Since these forms of reproduction are limited to text, supplemented only by relatively simple line drawings, and to reproduction of single sheets that are usually stapled together in sequential order, page layout is also relatively simple. Most of the points made on pages 166–178 with respect to page and item layout apply here. The additional consideration that must be borne in mind is that the basic unit is the single page rather than the two-page spread, so that so far as possible each page should be a self-contained unit and reference back and forth between pages should be minimized. The problem cannot always be eliminated—as, for example, in reading tests in which a passage together with its test items may well take up two or three pages; however, a single item should *never* extend from one page to the next, and everything possible should be done to keep any referring back and forth between pages to a minimum.

For effective use of space, it will often be desirable to type the test items out in a preliminary copy, using the line length that will apply in the final typing of the test. The items can then be cut up, shuffled around in different orders (within the limits that may be set by difficulty or common content), and assembled so that the number of lines on each page, or each column of a double-column page, is approximately the same.

Beyond this, the main problem in production of direct masters is obtaining accurate, uniform, firm typing. An electric typewriter can guarantee a firm, uniform stroke, but beyond the skill of the typist, adequate proofreading is the only guarantee of accurate copy. Test items consist of many brief and relatively disconnected parts; errors in transcription are easy to make and can be quite disconcerting to the examinee; so the masters should be proofread with great care and corrected meticulously before they are reproduced. Making corrections on multilith plates calls for somewhat

Directions: Each group of questions below consists of five lettered headings followed by a list of numbered phrases or sentences. For each numbered phrase or sentence select the one heading which is most closely related to it. One heading may be used once, more than once, or not at all in each group.

Questions 2-4

(A) Cambrian period
(B) Devonian period
(C) Jurassic period
(D) Precambrian Era
(E) Tertiary period

2. Trilobites were the dominant creatures.

3. The first calcareous algae appeared.

4. Pantotheria were widespread.

Questions 5-7

(A) Drumlins
(B) Moraines
(C) Natural levees
(D) Till
(E) Topset beds

5. Formed of material dropped by a glacier and shaped by ice which has overridden the deposit

6. Unsorted debris deposited directly by ice but not formed into a stream-lined shape by a glacier

7. Ridges that border rivers through floodplains and that have coarser materials on the side nearer the river

Questions 8-10

(A) Feldspar
(B) Galena
(C) Gypsum
(D) Hematite
(E) Quartz

8. The internal structure consists of tetrahedra which lie in spirals around screw axes.

9. The crystals are hydrates and are tabular with one perfect cleavage that yields thin flexible folia.

10. Crystals are rare; rather, compact granular, fibrous, or earthy masses are found.

FIG. 6.22. Illustration of arrangement of grouped items. (Reproduced by permission of College Entrance Examination Board from *College-Level Examination Program, A Description of the Subject Examinations* [CEEB, 1967], pp. 40–41.)

special skills, and a typist should study one of the manuals supplied by the manufacturer or check with an experienced plate-typist for guidance with respect to the "tricks of the trade."

Preparing an Original for Copying

When an original is to be prepared and then reproduced onto a master before making multiple copies, some new problems are introduced. These problems arise because (a) one is probably interested in producing a more finished and professional-looking product, (b) the methods make possible a somewhat greater range of drawings, diagrams, and (for offset reproduction) photographs, and (c) if reproduction is to be photographic, it may be desirable to change the size of the copy, usually reducing it, in proceeding from original to master.

If one is to produce a good master from an original, it is important that the original be clean and uniformly typed, with corrections carefully made and with any drawings or illustrations accurately inserted in the copy. These problems become especially acute if the master is to be produced photographically. The most uniform quality of typing is obtained with an electric typewriter using a paper or plastic carbon ribbon. This kind of ribbon is typed on only once, so that the blackness of the typing is very uniform. Type on the typewriter should be thoroughly cleaned in advance of typing so that the impression will be as sharp and clear as possible. The choice of paper on which copy is typed is also important. Certain hard-finish papers result in sharper copy and should be used in preference to the standard kinds of paper used for most other office work.

Whether one should attempt to justify lines (that is, make right-hand as well as left-hand margins even) depends upon how professional appearing a product is desired and what equipment is available for preparing the copy. If only a standard office typewriter is available, justifying lines is a burdensome task and the gain is probably not worth the effort. The procedure involves typing out a preliminary copy, using paper on which the right-hand margin is marked, and ending every line short of the margin. A count is made of the blank spaces between the end of the line and the margin. Then when the copy is retyped in final form, enough extra spaces are left between words in the line to bring the last word out to the preset right-hand margin. Certain models of electric typewriter[6] are now being produced with provision for automatic justification of lines. The text is typed by the operator on an electric typewriter that records on a magnetic tape at the same time that it types on paper. The typist types approximately to, but always short of, full-line length. A second machine receives the magnetic tape and, depending upon the specific instructions with which it has been programmed, allocates the extra space in a line in units of about $1/72$ of an inch to the spaces between the words or even to spacing between the letters of a word.

Justifying lines is most important for appearance when sizeable blocks of solid text appear in the test materials, as in reading comprehension passages. Here the even margins represent quite an improvement in appearance. A pretyping will help even when a machine with automatic justification is used because the preliminary draft will permit adjustments in line length by breaking long words or shifting short words up or down a line, so that too much additional white space is not introduced into any one line. The resulting copy will be more uniform and more pleasing in appearance.

Making Corrections

It is usually best not to make erasures on material prepared for copying, as the retyped characters are likely to be smudgy and the change in paper surface where an erasure has been made may produce a "shadow" in the master. On good quality paper, careful erasure of one or two characters need not affect adversely the appearance of the final copies, but the correction methods described in the next few paragraphs usually give better results.

For changes involving material up to several words, one method of correction is the use of

---

[6] Models include the IBM Composer.

opaque white paint. A paint of this type is now supplied by stationery stores under various trade names, such as Snowpak or Wite-out. It is applied over the erroneous words, with the brush that is supplied in the jar, and allowed to dry. When the paint is thoroughly dry, the correct letters can be typed on top of it. Care must be taken to have the white paint of the right consistency and to apply a coat of the proper thickness. If the paint is too watery or spread out in too thin a layer, the original typing will show through. If the paint is too thick, or if too much is applied, it is likely to flake off when dry, particularly when typed upon.

For more extensive corrections, changes are best made by retyping the line or lines involved on a separate piece of paper. The new copy can then either be pasted over the old as a patch or be inserted in place of the old as a cut-out. If the copy is to be photographed, correct alignment of a patch can be insured by guidelines drawn with light blue pencil on both patch and the base paper in precisely the same relative position. A light blue line does not show up in the photographic copy. Adjustment of the patch so that the horizontal and vertical lines are each continuous insures correct placement. A sharp pencil, producing fine guidelines, will give greater accuracy of placement (see fig. 6.23).

Do not use library paste or mucilage for affixing a patch. These adhesives will wrinkle the paper, causing a distortion in the printed copies. Rubber cement, of the variety especially designed for use on paper, should always be used in pasting down correction patches and drawings and in pasting together sections of pages.

To affix a patch permanently, one should apply the cement to both pieces of paper, taking care to spread the cement clear to the edge of the patch and to cover the corresponding area on the base paper. Cement applied only to the patch will hold it temporarily, so that the patch may be removed later if desired. In adjusting the placement of a large patch or a long narrow patch, it is helpful to place between patch and base a piece of clean paper slightly shorter than the patch in one dimension and longer in the other. The ends of the patch can thus be adjusted first, with less danger that the

78.   Which is the most convenient place in which to scrape and stack the dishes and utensils before washing them?

78-1   Space D

78-2   space E
78-3   Space F
78-4   Space g
78-5   Space H

78-1   Space D
78-2   Space E
78-3   Space F
78-4   Space G
78-5   Space H

Fig. 6.23. Illustration of use of guidelines to insure correct placement of patch on typed copy. Upper section represents portion of original page with errors to be corrected; lower section represents patch with corrections. If guidelines in light blue pencil are matched when applying patch, placement will be correct.

patch will become permanently stuck before precise placement is achieved. When the ends are properly aligned, the paper can be slipped out and the rest of the patch pressed down.

Excess cement can be rubbed off with the fingers after the patch is placed. However, in applying cement, care must be taken not to get it on typed material that is not to be covered with a patch, since some of the ink will come off with the cement, leaving a lighter area. Some people prefer to use a brush in applying rubber cement. Others like a small, flexible spatula. An artist's palette knife, in a small size, is a very useful instrument for this purpose. A wooden picnic spoon can also be used. A paper clip, partly unbent, is very handy for applying cement to narrow strips.

An alternate to using patches, either for corrections or for the insertion of drawings, is to use a light table, that is, a ground-glass surface with a light source beneath it. The corrected section that has been typed on a separate piece of paper is superimposed on the uncorrected copy on the light table. The light shining through makes it possible to see both the original and the corrected version at the same time and to line them up precisely. Then the material to be inserted and the material to be replaced are cut out with a razor-sharp knife,[7] both at the same time, while they are held in the perfectly aligned position. This insures that the contour of the part to be inserted matches perfectly the contour of the part to be deleted. The copy can then be turned face down, the correction laid into the hole (which it should fit precisely) and adhesive library tape put over the back of correction and copy to hold the correction in place. As indicated above, this procedure can be used not only for correction but also for the insertion of any type of artwork in typed copy. In this case, what is required are adequate guide or registry marks on the copy with which the artwork can be aligned before the cutting is done.

Minor errors detected by the typist in the course of typing may be corrected at once, by erasing or by using white paint to blot out the error. More extensive corrections involving patching should not be completed until after the proofreading of the test, although the typist may retype the copy for the patch and clip it to the page so that the new copy can be read in the regular process of proofreading.

Proofreading the Copy

Typewritten copy from which a master is to be made should be carefully proofread against the draft from which it was typed, preferably more than once. When the master is to be made photographically, corrections may be marked with a light blue pencil (which will not show in the photograph). For electrostatic and other copying procedures, a very light pencil mark that can be easily erased may be better to cue the existence of an error. Smudges and marks that get on the copy by mistake can be covered with white paint. Page numbers and the numbers and letters identifying items and

choices should be read *as a separate operation,* and they should be read *at least twice,* preferably by different proofreaders. Errors in identification numbers can invalidate whole blocks of responses, and nothing is easier to overlook than errors in such matter if it is not separately checked. Separate checks on spacing, margins, reference notes, parentheses or lines for responses, consistency of punctuation of items, correct answers to samples, and other such features are also desirable.

Particular care should be taken to make sure that patches to be inserted in the material have been proofread and found correct before they are inserted. It is easier to type a new and perfect patch than it is to paste a patch down, find an error in it, and have to put a second (and even a third) patch on top of the original one.

Checking and proofreading should be done with great care because corrections that are not made on the original copy are unlikely to be caught on the master and will not be recognized until reproduction is complete—at which time it is too late to do anything about them.

Determining the Typing Area

Copy for in-house reproduction will ordinarily be typed in the size that it is to be in the duplicated form. Though copy can be reduced in size by making a photostat and using the positive print as the original for making a thermal or electrostatic master, these procedures are involved and not likely to be used. It is primarily in photographic processes for making a master that the issue of changing size from the original to the master, usually through reducing size, is likely to arise. For other processes, determination of the typing area involves simply a decision on the size of the page margins and the subtraction of those margins from the dimensions of the sheet of paper, typically $8\frac{1}{2}'' \times 11''$.

If a master is to be made photographically, which may sometimes be the case for in-house work and will practically always be true if copy is being prepared to be reproduced by a commercial offset printer, it may prove advantageous to type to a larger size and reduce the size of the master photographically. By typing

[7] One such knife is the Exacto.

on a larger page with a larger typeface and then reducing photographically, one gets somewhat sharper outlines for the typed characters. Furthermore, photographic reduction permits complete flexibility in the final type size, and consequently in the amount that can be put on a page. Ordinary typewriters use either a pica (12-point) or elite (10-point) type. If one wishes the final copy to be a size between the two or smaller than either, photographic reduction will be required.

When one knows the dimensions usable for copy on the final printed page and the percentage reduction in size from the original, determination of the dimensions of the space usable for typing on the original is a simple matter of proportion. The desired final dimensions are divided by the percentage that the final is to be of the original to give dimensions of the original. Thus, if an $8\frac{1}{2}'' \times 11''$ page is to have one-inch margins, final copy will occupy a size $6\frac{1}{2}'' \times 9''$. With a 25-percent reduction (i.e. final copy 75 percent of the original), the dimensions of the typing area on the original will be $6\frac{1}{2}/.75 = 8\frac{2}{3}$ by $9/.75 = 12$ inches, thus $8\frac{2}{3}'' \times 12''$.

Providing the Illustrations

The various procedures for producing masters from original copy are capable of handling, with different degrees of fidelity, drawings and illustrations. Limitations, set in part by the process of making the master and in part by the duplicating process, limit spirit duplicators and mimeograph to fairly simple illustrations with a minimum of fine detail and exclude completely the use of photographs and pictures with continuous shading. The offset printing process can handle all kinds of illustrative material, but photographs can be adequately recorded on a master only when that master is produced by a photographic process.

For in-house reproduction, in which no reduction of copy size will occur in making the master, illustrations must be made in the size that they are eventually to appear. Each may be drawn directly on the copy, or inserted as a patch, following the procedures described on pp. 181–183. When an existing drawing or illustration is to be used, it will, of course, be advantageous to insert it as a patch rather than to re-draw it, and the danger of spoiling a page of clean copy by drafting errors always makes the preparation of drawings on separate pages a plausible procedure.

When, as occasionally happens, final copy is being prepared in-house for photo-offset reproduction by a commercial printer, illustrations may originally be of any size. It is convenient and economical if illustrations can be prepared so that they are to be reduced by the same amount as the rest of the page. In that case, they can be inserted in the appropriate space on the page before it is photographed. If the reduction of an illustration is to be by a different amount than the page as a whole, they must be sent to the printer separately, with clear instructions on the back of each illustration showing by how much it is to be reduced and exactly where it is to go in the text. The amount of reduction is determined by the present size of the illustration and the amount of space it is to occupy in the final document. It should be remembered that, whatever the amount of reduction or enlargement, both dimensions of any single piece of copy or blank space will be changed in the same proportion; that is, it is not possible to reduce the width by one percentage and the length by a different percentage.

Halftone illustrations (those showing gradations from black to white) and all illustrations that are not to be reduced in the same proportion as the typed text should *not* be pasted down in the text, but should be sent to the printer in a separate envelope. Each illustration should be identified, with corresponding identification in blue pencil in the space marked off for the illustration on the typed copy.

PROCEDURES FOR LETTERPRESS PRINTING

Preparing the Copy

The preparation of copy for printing by letterpress is a much simpler job than preparation of copy for offset reproduction since the material is to be set in type instead of being photographed. A good legible typescript on

$8\frac{1}{2}'' \times 11''$ paper, using one side only, is used for printer's copy. The typed copy should approximate, if possible, the desired arrangement and spacing of the final printed copy, in order to minimize the markings necessary to indicate to the printer the indention, spacing, and so forth. Copy should be marked to indicate where boldface, italic, or all capitals are to be used. Underlined words will be set in italic type; a wavy line under words indicates boldface type; double underlining indicates small capitals, and triple underlining indicates large capitals.

Copy should also be marked to show the size of type to be used. The unit used in indicating type sizes is the *point*. Figure 6.24 shows several sizes of type. Ten-point type is about the smallest that is easily legible for the body of the text. It is also appropriate to specify the type desired (e.g. Times Roman, Baskerville, Optima, etc.). Figure 6.25 illustrates the four general type styles.

This line is set in 8-point type.

This line is set in 10-point type.

This line is set in 12-point type.

This line is set in 14-point type.

FIG. 6.24. Illustration of different sizes of type

This line is set in an old-style type.

This line is set in a modern-style type.

This line is set in a square-serif type.

This line is set in a sans-serif type.

FIG. 6.25. Illustration of different styles of type faces

Extra space between lines adds to legibility; text set with such extra space is said to be *leaded*. Figure 6.26 shows text set solid (without leading) and figure 6.27 shows text set with 2-point leading.

Headings and titles, such as names of parts, will stand out better if set in larger type than the body. Boldface, italic, or solid capitals can be used for emphasis, either in headings or in single words in the text that are to be stressed.

Some are dinning in our ears that we Americans, and moderns generally, are intellectual dwarfs compared with the ancients, or even the Elizabethan men. But what is that to the purpose? A living dog is better than a dead lion. Shall a man go and hang himself because he belongs to the race of pygmies, and not be the biggest pygmy that he can? Let every one mind his own business, and endeavor to be what he was made.

FIG. 6.26. Illustration of text set solid

Some are dinning in our ears that we Americans, and moderns generally, are intellectual dwarfs compared with the ancients, or even the Elizabethan men. But what is that to the purpose? A living dog is better than a dead lion. Shall a man go and hang himself because he belongs to the race of pygmies, and not be the biggest pygmy that he can? Let every one mind his own business, and endeavor to be what he was made.

FIG. 6.27. Illustration of text set with 2-point leading

The typescript should be carefully proofread; every effort should be made to have it correct in all respects, since *author's alterations* involve needless expense.

Illustrations should not be attached to the copy, but should be placed in a separate envelope and enclosed in the package of copy for sending to the printer. Illustrations should be identified, and the place where they are to be inserted correspondingly identified. It is not necessary to leave on the typed copy the exact amount of space that the illustrations actually require; an inch or two of space can be left at the appropriate place and a note added to identify the illustration that is to be inserted. It is, however, necessary to indicate the final size desired for the illustration. When printing is done by letterpress, separate *cuts* (electrotypes) are made for all drawings or photographs, and these can be made in any desired size. Here, as in the case of offset reproduction, one must consider two factors: How large *must* the picture be to show essential detail clearly? What size will combine best with the material set in type for an economical and yet clear and pleasing arrangement of the page?

Paging the Material

It is usually best not to leave the paging of test materials to the printer but to have the page divisions decided in the test-construction office, since there are so many special considerations in paging a test that the printer cannot be expected to know about.

In the case of homogeneous materials with few or no illustrations, paging can best be done by working with the first set of proofs furnished by the printer. These proofs, called *galley proofs*, are long strips of paper with single columns running continuously. An extra set of galleys may be requested for use in paging. If the test materials divide neatly into columns (if used) and pages without difficulty, it is sufficient to mark in the margins of the proofs the places where columns and pages end. Where several page layouts are possible, it is helpful to cut up the extra set of galley proofs and experiment with different arrangements. When a satisfactory lay-out has been achieved, the pieces of proof can be stapled or pasted to blank sheets of paper (with the item numbers corrected if necessary) and returned to the printer as an indication of the desired final page arrangement. However, if galleys are cut up and rearranged, each piece of printed copy should be labeled with the number of the galley from which it came.

When dealing with material that offers particular difficulty in the arrangement of pages because of numerous illustrations of various sizes or other lack of homogeneity in the test materials, it is helpful to have the printer's copy typed with the same average number of characters per line as the printed copy is to have. This can be done only when the printed copy is to use short lines, as in the case when there are to be two or more columns to the page, since a longer line will contain more characters than will fit on a standard typewriter page. The typed copy is made with a single column on each page. When the width of the typed copy (in terms of characters per line) is approximately the same as that of the printed page, it is much easier to judge the amount of space the printed text will require and to make tentative decisions on the arrange-

ment of the pages. Judgments about lengthwise space requirements can be made by counting the number of lines (in terms of single-spaced material) that the printed page will contain; the number of single-spaced lines on the typescript may be determined by measuring with a ruler, as typewritten lines run six to the inch. The chief reason for making such tentative decisions on page arrangement is that, in order to achieve a satisfactory arrangement, it may be necessary to make changes in the order of items, the size of illustrations, or even the general plan of the page. If such changes are required, it is much cheaper in money and time to make them on the typescript (by cutting and pasting or by changing instructions to the printer) than it is to make them after the text has been set in type and the cuts for the illustrations made.

Correcting the Proofs

The galley proofs should be carefully proofread against the original copy, and all corrections clearly marked in the approved fashion. Some dictionaries contain a page showing proofreader's marks and the proper method of using them; printers usually can furnish a similar sheet.

After the corrections have been made and the pages made up, the printer sends a set of page proofs for checking. These proofs should also be carefully proofread, with particular attention to the arrangement of material on the page and to material not provided for in the galleys, such as page numbers, directions about going on to the next page, etc., in addition to all total *lines* in which corrections were indicated on the galleys. Item and choice identification numbers or letters should be proofread as a separate operation; it is also well to check separately the spacing, provision for response, page numbers, punctuation, samples, etc. If there are extensive changes, a second set of page proofs should be requested for a final check.

It is highly desirable to send a set of the galley and/or the page proofs to the original author of the test and to receive his approval before the final printing. If practicable, he should be asked to key the answers on his copy. This will provide a check on the key and insure his looking at the items carefully.

SUMMARY

This discussion of the procedures involved in reproducing test materials has emphasized the general features of the commonly used duplicating and printing processes and the problems that most directly concern those who are responsible for test construction. Mention has been made of various general considerations in arranging for the reproduction of tests by office-type duplicators, photo-offset printing, and letterpress printing. In addition, more detailed attention has been given to general booklet design, page layout, item arrangement, and the placement and reproduction of illustrations. Practical suggestions regarding the preparation of copy and proofreading have been made.

Whatever the method of reproduction used, the finished test booklet should present an appearance worthy of the care and attention that have gone into the construction of the test. Good format not only is pleasing to the eye, but also helps the test user to secure reliable results from the test. Poor page planning, with overlong lines of text in fine print, blurred or too small illustrations, or confusing arrangement of materials, can seriously impair the efficiency of test performance. If these hazards are removed and the format used to best advantage, the testing materials themselves are free to function.

REFERENCES

Hattery, L. H., & Bush, G. P. Eds. *Reprography and copyright law.* Washington: American Institute of Biological Science, 1964.

Lee, M. *Bookmaking: The illustrated guide to design and production.* New York: R. R. Bowker, 1965.

Skillin, M. E., & Gay, R. M. *Words into type.* (Rev. ed.) New York: Appleton-Century-Crofts, 1964.

United States Government Printing Office. *Style manual.* (Rev. ed.) Washington: GPO, 1967.

University of Chicago Press. *A manual of style.* (12th ed.) Chicago: UCP, 1969.

For information about duplicating machines, consult classified section for the manufacturers' representatives. The following are perhaps the best known:

> Davidson Dual Duplicator
> Ditto
> Gestetner
> Mimeograph
> Multigraph
> Multilith

For information about letterpress and photo-offset printers, consult classified section of city telephone directory.

Many of the larger photo-offset printers issue excellent manuals on the preparation of copy for photo-offset printing.

7. Test Administration

William V. Clemans
Science Research Associates, Inc.

Throughout history, it has been the use of measurement for analysis that has changed the esoteric arts into sciences: alchemy into chemistry, astrology into astronomy, witchcraft into medicine. In each of these instances, analytic measurement was introduced after centuries of little or no progress, and, in each instance, rapid advances in knowledge and technology followed its introduction. This process has been repeated many times over and has resulted in an exponential increase in the total store of information. The vast amount of accumulated knowledge, coupled with the fact that the time available to man for learning is short, means that the efficiency of the educational process must be increased if any sizeable proportion of the total pool of knowledge is to be transmitted to each new generation. This implies that education too must become more of a science and less of an art. However, in education as in medicine, there will always be a place for the highly skilled artisan. To accelerate the transition from art to science, the instruments now available for analytical educational measurement must be used wisely and even more sophisticated instruments must be developed.

Educational measurements are infinitely more complicated than most common physical measurements. The latter are usually made directly with simple tools on relatively stable objects. In contrast, most educational measurements are made indirectly with complex tools on dynamic subjects. An example would be the use of a sample of 100 questions drawn from a universe of millions to evaluate the intelligence of individuals who are changing in relevant ways while the test is in progress and who will continue to change when it is over. The difficulty of the task does not mean that educational measurements should not be attempted. In-stead, it means that for the measurements to be meaningful, the instruments must be selected with care and used with precision.

It is extremely important to control the conditions under which educational measurements are obtained. Even simple physical measurements vary as a function of the environment. For example, a micrometer reading indicating the thickness of a sheet of metal will vary as a function of the temperature. But in physical measurement, environmental factors usually contribute only a very small percentage to the total error variance, whereas in educational measurement, they can easily become the dominant source of error. Three participants in the testing situation can influence the environment in which educational measurements are obtained and can thus affect their meaning. These are the test author, the general administrator, and the examiner. It is the purpose of this chapter to examine the role of each of these, and, as it relates to the others, the role of the examinee. In discussing these roles, ways of improving precision in educational measurement will be suggested.

THE IMPORTANCE OF INSTRUCTIONS FOR ADMINISTRATION

From initial conception to final production, measurement devices go through many developmental stages. During the entire process, a parallel development should be going on that does not evolve from statistical analyses but that can have a vital effect on reliability and validity; namely, the development of instructions for administration. Too frequently, test authors wait until late in the developmental process before attending to the specifications for administration. Such procrastination can significantly reduce the effectiveness of the resulting instruments, since items developed under one set of conditions may yield very different results when administered under another set. Educational measuring instruments must be carefully structured if they are to yield consistent response data, and the specifications for administration are a vital part of that structure.

The precision of a measuring instrument is a function of the clarity of the directions for test administration; these must have exactly the same meaning for the author, the examiner, and the examinee. The principal burden, of course, is the author's, for his directions must be understood by potentially tens of thousands of examiners and millions of examinees. If his language is even slightly imprecise, he can affect the performance of all. Each examiner, on the other hand, must understand the author's directions exactly as they were intended and transmit them without modification to his group of examinees. He must neither add to nor subtract from the author's specifications, for to do so will most certainly affect the performance of his group in reference to others even if it does not affect the relative performance within his group. The examinee's task, of course, is to attend closely to all instructions and follow them carefully. Any break in this communication network will decrease reliability and will tend to invalidate the resulting measurements.

TEST ADMINISTRATION FROM THE TEST AUTHOR'S VIEWPOINT

No matter how fine the basic instrument, if the author does not set the stage for the test administration appropriately, the resulting scores will inevitably lose some of their potential meaning. It is clear, then, that the primary responsibility for test administration lies with the author; the general administrator, examiner, and proctor must follow his lead. It is for this reason that the emphasis in this chapter will be placed on the author's role in test administration, which can be characterized as the attempt to minimize the score variance that results from factors external to the examinees.

Relation between Purpose and Directions

Tests, like all other tools, are developed for a purpose. When the purpose is well understood and defined, the question of how the tool should be used usually has been answered. Therefore, as an initial step in the process of test development, the author should define precisely and completely the need which led to the project—an obvious step but a frequently omitted one.

For his plan for administration to be complete, the author will need to consider such relevant factors as: (a) For whom is the test developed? (b) When will it be used? (c) Where will it be administered? (d) Who will give the examination? (e) Will alternate forms be essential? (f) Will it be administered to individuals or groups and, if to groups, of what size? (g) What response format will be most appropriate? (h) Will any special preparation of the examinee be necessary?

This listing is not comprehensive but does suggest some of the factors that should be considered. The test author must make the list complete for his specific purpose, and, when he has finished it, he will have an outline to guide formulation of the directions for administration. The better the author fulfills this responsibility, the more likely he is to measure what he set out to measure, because what is measured is determined by the examinee's conception of what he is to do and that depends on his understanding of the directions he is given.

Small variations in directions can lead to large variations in what is measured. Consider the differences in the meaning of a score of 10 right out of 20 arithmetic questions with these varying instructions: (a) See how many of these problems you can get right. (b) See how many of these problems you can get right in five minutes. (c) See how many of these problems you can work without making an error. (d) See how fast you can work these problems. The variation in these four suggests that test directions can have a definite effect on the measurements obtained.

All educational measurements are based on responses to a set of stimuli. The test author must keep in mind that the items are only part of the stimulus situation and that the directions are always a critical component of it. It is the combination of the two that provides the total stimulus and the basis for measurement.

General Responsibility of the Test Author

The general charge given to test producers in the *Standards for Educational and Psychological Tests and Manuals* (American Psychological Association, 1966) with respect to test administration is as follows: "The directions for administration should be presented in the test manual with sufficient clarity and emphasis that the test user can duplicate, and will be encouraged to duplicate, the administrative conditions under which the norms and the data on reliability and validity were obtained [p. 32]." The text of the *Standards* emphasizes that the author should try to be very persuasive in carrying out this charge. It points out that persons administering tests may be careless in following instructions simply because they may not understand the need for rigid adherence to them.

In preparing instructions, the test author should assume that the examiner and examinee know nothing about the task that confronts them. Accordingly, the author should set the stage for the examination by presenting clear and simple instructions. Then each examinee's performance should reflect his ability to function with respect to that aspect of behavior for which the instrument was designed rather than his ability to understand the basic directions. Score variations should be due to differences in ability not to different examination conditions.

Relation of Uniform Procedures to Norms

The very concept of a standardized test implies rigid control over the conditions of administration. It is, in fact, this control that permits the instrument to be termed standardized. Norms are an important part of the standardization data, but they will be meaningful only if derived from the administration of the test under the established conditions. The sampling design for determining norms is critical, but, even if it is near perfect, the result-

ing data will be of questionable value unless completely uniform procedures were followed for administering the test. Therefore, it must be emphasized that although tests are not generally released for use or considered finished until norms are established, instructions for administration must be in absolutely final form before norming. For some forms of tests, especially where tasks are being tried out that are novel in format or content, it will be desirable to try out the instructions to make sure they are understood. A critique by administrators or examinees may be helpful in suggesting changes that will improve communications between author, examiner, and examinee and that will serve to eliminate requirements specified by the author that prove unrealistic in an operational setting. All tryouts of this sort, and all revisions resulting from them, must be completed *before* the norming administration. Carelessness in the directions for norming cannot, indeed *must not*, be remedied after norming. For example, if no particular timing device were specified for norming, it would be meaningless to insist on the use of a stop watch for operational use.

In order to insure that norms will be meaningful, all possible steps should be taken to obtain the complete cooperation of the participating groups. During operational use of the test, it is reasonable to assume that the motivation of the general administrator and the examinees is in accord with the purpose of the examination. But this assumption is seldom justified during the norming when, in order to obtain a random sample, administrators who have little desire to administer the test in question are often asked to cooperate. In addition to requesting the complete support of general administrators, examiners, and examinees for the norming, a sample of them should be asked for a critical review of the final draft of the instructions. Their comments may result in modifications that should be introduced before the actual norming. Such a review can improve communication between author, examiner, and examinee and should also serve to eliminate requirements specified by the author that prove to be unrealistic in an operational setting.

Comparable forms of a test must, of course, have precisely the same instructions. The best technique is to have a single manual that applies to all the forms for which comparability is claimed. The instructions in this manual should be the ones used in obtaining reliability and validity statistics as well as in establishing norms. It must constantly be kept in mind that test administration is a critical part of the standardization process.

Some Important Factors in Test Administration

Clarity of instructions

Everyone writing about directions stresses simplicity and clarity. This is obviously important for communication, but, apparently, simplicity and clarity alone are not enough. Marks (1962) stated that he, McGrath (1958), and Myers (1958) have " . . . determined that in general neither college students, high school students, nor junior high school students follow directions [p. 169]." If this generalization is true, it may be that many adults do not follow them either. Marks said that this phenomenon is probably not due to perversity or inability to comprehend but instead may lie " . . . in the poor visual quality of the material presented to them [p. 169]." It is the author's task to find those elements or characteristics of format that will be most effective in causing examiners and examinees to follow directions accurately. Attention should be given to a number of visual factors including the use of such devices as boldface type, underlining, enlargement, contrasting colors, encircling, etc. The test author must do everything he can to get the response he desires. The student must know whether he is to GO ON or to STOP. The examiner must know when he is to follow a direction precisely and when he can paraphrase an instruction, for example in announcing a lunch break. In addition, the examiner should be aided in his verbal presentation by suggestions of where to pause and how slowly to read.

Establishing instructions that can and will be followed is a problem that can be solved empirically and solving it is clearly the responsibility of the test author. Ideally, he should try out his directions in advance on subjects that are comparable to those for whom the test is designed and modify them wherever they present difficulty.

Guessing

Specific instructions for responding to questions to which the examinee does not know the answer (or guessing) must be included for any multiple-choice test. Individual differences in mental set will result in different modes of response to such questions (Cronbach, 1950; Swineford & Miller, 1953). For this reason, standardization will be improved if specific instructions are given. There is good evidence that examinees should be told to respond to every question, whether or not they know the correct answer. Cronbach (1950) recommended this approach because, in his opinion, the random error introduced by this instruction is apt to be less damaging to the meaning of a score than the error introduced by varying tendencies to guess. An additional reason for this instruction is that the psychometric models underlying educational measurement frequently depend on the assumption that all students responded to all questions.

There are those who have opposed directions to guess on the grounds that such an instruction is unsound advice from the educational point of view, promoting undesirable habits or fixation of errors. There is no published evidence to support this thesis.

Mollenkopf (1960) has suggested an interesting alternative to guessing at the end of an examination. He maintains that the examinee not only has a right to know how the test will be scored but also what to do if time runs out. He stated that "directions for many tests either engage in double talk about what to do as the end of the period approaches, or don't say anything at all about the matter [p. 229]." He then stated that his "preference would be for instructing the candidate that he will automatically receive u/k points of credit for items he has not reached, where u represents the number of items not attempted and k is the number of alternatives per item [p. 229]." He suggested that this technique would not only bring the chance element in test scores under some control, but it would also allow the timid to profit equally with the bold.

Time limits

In some instances, such as a typing test, speed is an essential component of the measurement. In others, such as interest inventories, speed is not a factor and everyone is expected to finish. For measurement of many cognitive aspects of behavior, power tests are superior to tests with time limits. However, when such tests are administered to large groups, the usual practice is to set a time limit that allows most examinees to complete the test; for a few individuals, the power test thus becomes speeded. It is difficult to defend this procedure, and yet it is equally difficult to suggest a practical alternative. Nevertheless, the test author must have a better reason than mere convenience for setting limits, because the time allotted can play a fundamental role in defining the nature of the measurement. Several writers (Baxter, 1941; Davidson & Carroll, 1945; Lord, 1956; Myers, 1952) have pointed out that the factors involved in speed of performance may be quite different from those involved in similar tasks under no-time-limit conditions. Myers (1960) also has suggested that time limits may present invisible barriers that block access to the mental functions the test author wishes to measure. The author, of course, must make the decision as to whether it is essential for his test to be timed or not. As Mollenkopf (1960) has suggested, this decision should stem from three considerations: (*a*) the nature of the task itself and the behavior to be predicted; (*b*) comparability of scores; and (*c*) practical administrative convenience.

When time limits are used, the test author must make them clear because the examinee has the right to know precisely what is expected of him. Reading the directions should not be included in the time period because, as Myers (1960) pointed out, when the directions are included in the test period, some examinees will skim or skip them and consequently may respond to an entirely different task from the one the test author intended. The literature on the role of speed in psychological tests is extensive. A good list of relevant publications is given by Morrison (1960).

When time limits are essential, an accurate timing device is required. For any interval of less than an hour, a stop watch or accurate interval timer should be specified. In addition, the instructions should specify that a backup system be used in the form of a second watch or alternate timer, preferably under the observation of a second person. If, in an emergency, a wrist watch must be used, the examiner should be instructed to set the minute hand to twelve and to start the period when the second hand is at zero. The directions also should specify that, wherever possible, examinations should be given in a room with a wall clock. This procedure, if followed, will help to equalize the examinees' access to a timepiece. For any examination more than an hour in length, the directions should also specify that the examiner tell the examinees when one-half hour remains. In some instances, the author may wish to have the examiner announce the time remaining at half hour intervals, or at other specified points during the test.

Environmental factors

Discussions of environmental factors related to administration are usually restricted to obvious elements such as noise, atmospheric conditions, lighting, and physical facilities. But there are a host of other factors that are also important and are often overlooked. Gordon and Alf (1960) made this point clearly in a study on the acclimatization of navy recruits. Their research, based on large samples, showed that those tested during their ninth day at a Naval Training Center scored significantly higher on each of five tests than recruits tested during their third day. Their study did not permit specific identification of the causal factors, but there seemed to be no question that general acclimatization had an effect on performance.

Before preparing instructions related to environment, the test author must know how, when, where, and under what circumstances the tests will be used. For example, group tests designed for use with young children almost certainly will be administered by their own teacher in their own classroom, preferably after they have become acclimated to the school environment. On the other hand, it is not unreasonable to assume that high school students can be tested in large groups in a study hall or cafeteria.

If the test author specifies too much, he may lose his audience. There is little to be gained, and perhaps much to be lost, from going into detailed specifications concerning illumination, temperature, and humidity, since the examiner and examinees, with few exceptions, will have to put up with the conditions that exist. When students can be relocated for testing, some factors can be controlled that otherwise could not, for example the writing surface they will use. A study by Traxler and Hilkert (1942) revealed that students using desks scored higher on the average than those using chairs with desk arms. Noise is another factor that can usually be controlled to some extent. In a recent study, Boggs and Simon (1968) found "that noise produces a significant decrement in performance and that the magnitude of this decrement varies as a function of task complexity [p. 152]."

Motivation and anxiety

Educators are well aware that motivation affects student performance. In fact, some are convinced that the most basic problem confronting them is discovering how to motivate their students. Quereshi (1960) demonstrated that payoff (motivation) significantly influenced the mental performance of individuals. Yamamoto and Dizney (1965) also found a positive relationship between motivation and performance. In their study, a standardized intelligence test was administered to three randomly selected groups of students. The test was introduced to one group as an intelligence test, to the second as an achievement test, and to the third as a "routine" test. Because of the obvious connotations and inherent motivating characteristics of these three sets of instructions, it was predicted that the "intelligence test" group

would do the best, then the "achievement test" group followed by the "routine test" group. The hypothesis was substantiated by this study. The mean IQ for the first group was 116.3, the second 112.1, and the third 109.1.

Although motivation is clearly important, too much stress on achievement can produce anxiety that may decrease an individual's performance. There is a substantial literature on test anxiety; for example, Waite, Sarason, Lighthall, and Davidson (1958) have shown that low anxiety subjects perform better on a simple learning task than high anxiety subjects. Thus the task confronting the test author, general administrator, and examiner is how to motivate students without producing excess anxiety. The general administrator and examiner must assume a major proportion of this responsibility, but the test author must offer guidelines. The general administrator should be advised to notify students, well in advance of the testing date, of the advantages of honestly and sincerely applying themselves to the task. The examiner should be told to conduct himself in a businesslike manner and exhibit an obvious interest in the test and its outcome, both before and during the test administration.

To a very considerable extent, the examinees' attitude toward the test will have been formed before the day it is administered. The announcement of the test and its purpose by the general administrator and the materials available to the examinee before the test date will have helped him formulate his opinion. Nevertheless, instructions just prior to the test can affect the student's attitude. An example of instructions that may help to motivate the examinee are given here in two paragraphs modeled after instructions for the Iowa Tests of Educational Development.

This morning you are going to begin taking a special series of tests. The purpose of these tests is to give both you and your teachers a better picture of your general educational development. The tests will show what background of ideas you have in the social studies and in the natural sciences, how well you can read and interpret different kinds of materials, and how readily you can solve arithmetical problems. This information will help us to discover how well our school as a whole compares with others and in what areas we are strong and in what ones we may need improvement. More important, these tests will help your teachers decide how to adapt their teaching to your individual needs and how to advise you on your future educational plans. The test results can also be of real value in helping you to make decisions about your future.

The results can be valuable in all of these ways only if you do your best on all of the tests. If you do not make a sincere effort, the scores will tell a misleading story about your abilities and your time spent in taking the tests will be worse than wasted. If you look upon these tests as a challenge—as an opportunity to show what you are really capable of doing—then you are bound to enjoy taking them and your time will be well spent.

Preparing the examinee

Familiarity with the examination format can aid the examinee in responding to the test. Experiments with students may not reveal this phenomenon because, in any large sample of American students who are beyond the primary grades, the majority are apt to be fairly sophisticated with regard to multiple-choice tests. However, on an individual basis the consequences of little or no familiarity can be severe. Therefore, it is important that the test author develop procedures designed to eliminate the influence of differential sophistication with multiple-choice tests.

The problem of minimizing the influence of extraneous previous experience as it relates to the examination at hand falls in the category of "response set" behavior. Cronbach (1950) has pointed out that "response sets have the greatest variance in tests which are difficult for the subjects tested, or where the subject is uncertain how to respond [p. 16]." Clearly, one way to reduce such unwanted variance is to have the examinees read and heed the instructions. But Marks (1962) has pointed out that "there is abundant evidence that pupils do not read directions, and therefore cannot follow them, even when the subject matter is of great interest and importance to them [p. 169]." For this reason as well as for pacing purposes, the test author should specify that the examiner is to read the directions aloud as the examinees read them silently. If there is a major change in item

type, the procedure should be repeated. The use of sample questions to further clarify the instructions usually is helpful.

One way of preparing examinees that has been successfully used with a number of examinations is to use a descriptive handbook made available to all examinees in advance of testing. A good example is the booklet produced by the National Board of Medical Examiners for use by medical students. It begins:

For the benefit of those candidates who are not familiar with the objective, multiple-choice form of test, the National Board has prepared samples of the more frequently used types of questions currently included in the Part I and Part II examinations. Candidates will find considerable advantage in studying the instructions accompanying these samples and in becoming familiar with the various types of questions.

Each Part is scheduled for a full two days. Part I consists of a two-hour examination in each of the six basic science subjects listed in the preceding outline. The examination for each subject consists of a large number of questions. Certain questions test the candidate's recognition of the similarity or dissimilarity of diseases, drugs, and physiologic or pathologic processes. Other questions evaluate the candidate's judgment as to whether cause-and-effect relationships exist. Case histories are used to simulate the experience of a physician confronted with a diagnostic problem. Series of questions then determine the candidate's understanding of related aspects of the case, such as associated laboratory findings, treatment, complications and prognosis [p. 2].

This handbook then describes the way the examinations were assembled, how the examinee can best prepare himself for them, what to do on questions for which he does not know the answer, and how the scores will be derived. This is followed by a sample test of 45 questions that thoroughly covers every item type in the test and requires the use of the same kind of answer sheet as the operational test. An answer key is given for the sample test, and a final section, which is updated annually, gives a detailed outline of the topics to be covered in each of the 12 tests.

Although there is no simple answer to the problem of differential sophistication, the

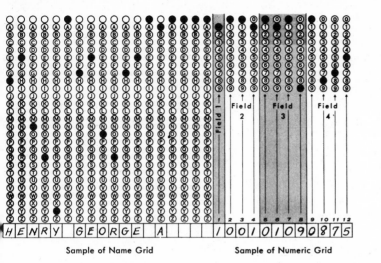

FIG. 7.1. The grid for George Henry. Number 1 in Field 1 (column 1) has been blackened to show the group in which George Henry's averages will appear (for this school the number 1 designates the 11th-grade boys, planning college group). Field 2 (columns 2, 3, and 4) shows the student's homeroom identification number (001); Field 3 (columns 5, 6, 7, and 8) shows his IQ (109); Field 4 (columns 9, 10, 11, and 12) shows his grade-point average (87.5).

author must attempt to minimize the effects on the test score of those personal characteristics of the individual that are not related to the quality the test was designed to measure.

Machine-readable response documents

A variety of optical-scanning devices now are used in the test-scoring process. Each has its own set of unique characteristics and, as a consequence, may require somewhat different instructions for marking. A good practice is to couple the written instructions with a graphic example that shows how the marks should be made. The examinee should be directed to make a readable mark, but the directions should be so phrased that the excessively careful individual does not waste time precisely filling in the circle or space between the lines while the individual on the other end of the continuum is making little more than a dot.

In many instances, the optical scanner is connected directly to a computer. Such a configuration not only allows for great flexibility in scoring but also permits the collection and use of a wide variety of information in addition to the responses to the test items. This additional information is entered on the answer sheet in a special section that is often referred to as a grid A sample grid (Lindquist, 1963) is shown in figure 7.1. It contains sections for both alphabetic and numeric information. Use of the alphabetic grid makes it possible for the com-

puter output device to print each student's name along with his test scores.

Note that the numeric grid section in figure 7.1 is divided into four fields. Imaginative use of these fields will create a variety of ways to use student data for research, interpretation, and analysis. Field 1, for example, can be used to divide the students taking the examination into nine groups for comparative purposes. In this particular example, Field 2 is used for homeroom designation. Quantitative information can be coded into Fields 3 and 4. In this example, intelligence test scores have been entered in Field 3 and grade-point averages in Field 4. These values can be averaged separately and printed out for each group designated in Field 1.

This discussion on the use of grids is intended only to suggest the great variety of potential analyses possible using this approach. Before a testing program is launched, careful study should be given to the way the data will be used. Such study may result in recommendations for data analyses requiring quite different uses of the numeric grid than the example given here.

Some methods of machine scoring require that the optical scanner read special documents (header sheets) in addition to the student response sheets (see discussion of header sheets in chap. 8). Using header sheets increases the flexibility available to the general administrator because they make it feasible to give the computer special instructions for scoring, analyzing, and reporting. For example, they can be used to obtain separate reports by classroom, grade, or building. Of course, it is of critical importance that these sheets be filled out precisely inasmuch as they become an integral part of the computer scoring system. When a program requires their use, the author should provide a graphic example to accompany his written instructions on how to fill them out.

A Check List For Test Authors

As he proceeds with the development of his test, the author should be certain to consider dealing with these topics in his instructions for administration:

I. Introduction
  A. Overview, including such general information as the purpose of the test and the time needed for administration
  B. Discussion of such questions as the relation between testing date and the meaningfulness of norms and the comparability of scores from one year to another
  C. Rationale for the importance of adhering to standard directions
  D. Statement on the physical arrangements necessary to obtain valid results

II. Examiners and proctors
  A. How to select them
  B. Qualifications necessary
  C. Duties and instructions

III. Materials
  A. Receipt and storage of materials, including security measures where appropriate
  B. Provision of supplementary materials needed such as scratch paper and timing devices

IV. Examinees
  A. Notification to examinees prior to testing in an informative and motivating manner
  B. Materials that examinees should bring to the testing session
  C. Procedure for admission of examinees

V. Administration
  A. Instructions that explain the purpose of the test to the examinees and insure their cooperation
  B. Specification of those instructions that must be followed exactly and those that can be paraphrased
  C. Recommendations for answering examinees' questions, including directions for handling defective material
  D. Procedures to be followed in distribution of test materials
  E. Precise instructions for timing
  F. Precise instructions (to examinees) relative to guessing
  G. Instructions on how to mark answer sheet
  H. Specifications for administering additional tests along with the test in question if this situation may arise
  I. Directions, including a graphic example for filling in alphabetic and numeric information on the answer sheet
  J. Specific instructions for responding to each item type
  K. Schedule for administration of the test

VI. Procedures to be carried out after the test
  A. Collection of answer sheets and test booklets (Note: Answer sheets should be collected first and independently of the test booklets as they represent the fruit of the entire examination process.)
  B. Completion of irregularity reports
  C. Completion of special documents or header sheets
  D. Preparation of answer sheets for data processing
  E. Return or disposal of test materials

VII. Test results
  A. Suggestions on how to use the test results (or reference to where such information can be found)
  B. Discussion of how to disseminate the results (or reference to where this information can be found)

TEST ADMINISTRATION FROM THE GENERAL ADMINISTRATOR'S VIEWPOINT

The general administrator is responsible for the selection of tests, supervision of examiners, and use of results. Of course, this role might be shared by three or even more school personnel, but here it is treated as the job of one individual.

Nothing is more fruitless than making educational measurements without a purpose. Scores filed away and not used are a waste of money and valuable time. It should be unnecessary to make such statements, and yet tests are administered and filed away with little use in countless school systems every year. In order to establish a successful and meaningful testing program, the general administrator must work to gain the support and cooperation of all concerned with the educational system. Measurement is the keystone of the educational process; without it, the structure would be weakened and it might even collapse. It is essential for evaluating methods and materials, for the rational assignment of students, for evaluating student progress, for checking on the effectiveness of new technological developments, and for determining the relative efficiency of various subsystems within the total system.

Clearly, a sound testing program consists of a many-faceted continuous process. Although one test can be used for several purposes, many different tests will be necessary for a comprehensive program. As it is the test author's responsibility to carefully describe the purpose of his test, it is the responsibility of the general administrator to determine precisely what information is needed in his school system and to select the tests which have the greatest congruence with those needs. For some purposes, nationally standardized tests will be essential; other needs can be served by carefully constructed local tests. The prescription for test administration given below (modified and augmented from Traxler, 1951) applies to both and assumes that thoughtful selection of tests has already taken place. Some of the recommendations may sound a bit trite, but, for every eventuality planned for in advance, a degree of confidence in the validity of the results is gained.

1. In broad scale achievement testing, match the level of the tests to the level of the students; i.e. do not give tests that are too easy or too difficult.

2. See that the tests are on hand well in advance of the date on which they are to be used. Check quantity of tests immediately upon receipt, and, if more are needed, reorder at once. Store in a secure place.

3. Plan *in detail* for the administration of the tests. Choose examiners and proctors with great care. If possible, use examiners who have had previous experience giving the objective type of test. If inexperienced examiners must be used, they should be carefully rehearsed beforehand. *Remember that some very intelligent people are temperamentally unsuited to the exacting routine of administering a test.* One may use relatively inexperienced persons as proctors for tests being given to larger groups, but they should not be placed in charge of the administration of a test.

4. Prepare an examination schedule and see that every person concerned receives a copy. The schedule should give the time and place of each test, indicate just where students to be tested should report and where those who are not taking the test should be, specify what material the examinees will need when taking the test, and give the name of the individual in charge of each examination. It should usually include provision for a make-up test for those who miss the regular testing.

5. Inform students about the examination and its purposes in a manner that will motivate them and encourage their cooperation without creating undue anxiety.

6. Become intimately acquainted with the test materials and the author's recommendations for standardizing administration.

7. Unless security measures prevent it, provide each examiner with a manual, an answer sheet, and a sample copy of the test several days before the examination. Urge the examiners to study the test materials and to take the test, since there is no better way of learning about it. *Most errors in the administration of tests are caused by failure of the examiners to prepare sufficiently beforehand.*

8. Plan procedures for distributing the test materials to the examiners on the day of the examination, except for the review copies mentioned in point 7.

9. Provide each examiner and proctor with

a written set of instructions outlining his duties at all stages of the examination. If possible, visit each area while the test is in progress.

10. Take precautionary steps to make certain that the physical environment for the examinations is as near the optimum as possible.

11. Make certain that those not participating in the examination do not interfere with it.

12. Eliminate as much noise and external distraction as possible, such as lawn mowing, playground noises, bells signalling the end of periods, etc.

13. See that all materials are collected immediately after the examination.

14. If supplemental information, such as scores on previous tests, are to be incorporated on the student's answer sheet for special analyses, make certain that the data are accurately entered.

15. Prepare specifications for scoring and data analysis.

16. Organize the answer sheets for processing, and see that they are securely packed and sent to data processing.

17. Return all test materials to secure storage.

If these recommendations are followed, the general administrator will have helped significantly to assure that the testing will proceed smoothly and the test results will be meaningful.

TEST ADMINISTRATION FROM THE EXAMINER'S VIEWPOINT

The examiner is a very important person in the measurement process. His job is to carry out precisely the directions of the test author. The meaningfulness of the test scores will depend in no small measure on how seriously he takes his job. In contrast with the general administrator and the test author, in the typical school setting the examiner spends only a small portion of his time on testing. Therefore, he must be informed as to how the information resulting from the tests can be a valuable asset to the educational process. When the examiner fully understands the importance of his assignment, he should be willing to take the time to learn how to perform it well.

Sample of Instructions

The following list of instructions for the examiner has been modified from a list presented by Traxler (1951).

Before the test

1. Read the directions for administration, examine the test booklet and answer sheet, and rehearse the process of giving the test.

2. Clear up any points of potential confusion by discussion with the general administrator.

During the test

1. Make arrangements so that there will be no interruptions or distractions during the testing period. Persons should not come into, or go out of, the room unless absolutely necessary. This is especially important for timed tests.

2. Seat the students as specified in the test instructions.

3. When testing is in large groups and proctors are used, see that each proctor understands what is expected of him before, during, and at the end of the examination. While the test is in progress, circulate among the proctors keeping them alert to their duties.

4. Make announcements slowly and clearly in a voice that is loud enough to be heard throughout the room. Assume a businesslike and efficient attitude that will command attention, but do not be severe. Remember, some students become nervous when faced with an examination.

5. Supply, or have proctors supply, all students with booklets, pencils, and separate answer sheets, if they are to be used. Announce that the students are not to open their booklets until so instructed.

6. Have the students fill in the blanks on the front of the booklets or answer sheets. Be sure to announce the date, specify how names are to be written and/or coded on the answer sheet, and explain other items that may need clarification. Spend sufficient time on this step to see that the students give all the information requested correctly. Ages and birth dates are especially important on tests of academic

aptitude, for these determine what norms will be used.

7. Hold faithfully to the exact wording of the printed directions unless there is a compelling reason for introducing a variation in them, such as a fire in the building. The preparation of directions for a test is an important aspect of test construction and standardization. The wording of the directions has been carefully thought out by the test author. Do not improvise or introduce short cuts. If you do, you may influence the test results significantly.

8. Time the examination with extreme care, using an interval timer or a stop watch. Only in an emergency should a wristwatch be used and only then when it has a second hand and has been checked for accuracy. In many tests, accurate timing is the most important single feature of the entire administration procedure. It is advisable to have one of the proctors check your timing to be sure that no error occurs.

9. Move about the room occasionally or have proctors move about to see that all students are working on the right part of the examination, but do not stand gazing over an examinee's shoulder so long that he becomes self-conscious, and do not move nervously from examinee to examinee. Present a reassuring manner—smile occasionally.

10. Do *not* allow necessary disciplinary actions to disrupt the examinees. The sole purpose of discipline in the testing room is to keep everyone working at his maximum all the time, with a minimum of disturbance from all sources, *including* the examiner and proctors. Use gestures, facial expressions, and whispers in dealing with examinees during the working period. Make it clear that *no* questions will be answered during working periods except in the event of faulty materials. If anyone speaks aloud or makes semiaudible signs of frustration, smile and put your finger to your lips; if this persists, frown. If a serious disturbance seems imminent, *remove* the disruptive examinee from the room quickly and quietly and make an appointment to clear up the trouble later. Any disciplinary measure that disturbs the group can be just as much of a problem as any disturbance caused by an examinee.

11. Stop the examination immediately when the time is up.

After the test has been given

1. Collect the answer sheets and then the booklets.

2. Have the proctors count and turn in all collected materials promptly.

3. Alphabetize and check the papers against the class list, if required.

4. Follow the procedures that have been established to see that any absent examinees make up the examination. This is a bothersome step, but one that is unavoidable, for complete data are essential if the results are to be used successfully in either teaching or guidance.

5. See that the tests are prepared for scoring. Instructions for this step vary and are important, so be certain to follow the directions carefully.

The examiner's role must be a positive one, and he must insure that his proctors also exhibit a positive attitude. Although examinees are not to be allowed to copy from their neighbors, prevention of such activity is only a small part of the examiner's job and should not be emphasized to the examinees. The examiner's task is to make as certain as possible that the scores reflect the true competence of the individual. This objective will be best obtained if he closely follows the author's and general administrator's instructions, and if he creates an atmosphere for the examinees that is conducive to their optimal performance.

REFERENCES

American Psychological Association. *Standards for educational and psychological tests and manuals.* Washington: APA, 1966.

Baxter, B. An experimental analysis of the contributions of speed and level in an intelligence test. *Journal of Educational Psychology*, 1941, **32,** 285–296.

Blommers, P., & Lindquist, E. F. Rate of comprehension of reading: Its measurement and its relation to comprehension. *Journal of Educational Psychology*, 1944, **35**, 449–472.

Boggs, D. H., & Simon, J. R. Differential effect of noise on tasks of varying complexity. *Journal of Applied Psychology*, 1968, **52**, 148–153.

Cronbach, L. J. Further evidence on response sets and test design. *Educational and Psychological Measurement*, 1950, **10**, 3–31.

Davidson, W. M., & Carroll, J. B. Speed and level components in time-limit scores: A factor analysis. *Educational and Psychological Measurement*, 1945, **5**, 411–427.

Feder, D. D. Effect of directions and arrangement of items on student performance in a test. *Journal of Educational Research*, 1936, **30**(September), 28–35.

Fenton, N. An objective study of student honesty during examinations. *School and Society*, 1927, **26**, 341–344.

Gordon, L. V., & Alf, E. F. Acclimatization and aptitude test performance. *Educational and Psychological Measurement*, 1960, **20**, 333–337.

Horst, P. *Psychological measurement and prediction.* Belmont, Calif.: Wadsworth, 1966.

Kelley, T. L. Cumulative significance of a number of independent experiments: Reply to A. E. Traxler and R. N. Hilkert. *School and Society*, 1943, **57**, 482–484.

Kirlin, W. Motivation as a factor in achievement test performance. Unpublished master's thesis, State University of Iowa, August 1938.

Lindquist, E. F. *Iowa Tests of Educational Development, examiner's manual, grades 9–12, Forms X-4 and Y-4.* Chicago: Science Research Associates, 1962.

Lindquist, E. F. *Iowa Tests of Educational Development, manual for the school administrator.* Chicago: Science Research Associates, 1963.

Lord, F. M. A study of speed factors in tests and academic grades. *Psychometrika*, 1956, **21**, 31–50.

McGrath, W. H. Problem solving efficiency as affected by accessary remarks. Unpublished doctoral dissertation, University of Southern California, 1958.

Marks, M. B. Better directions—better response, *Audio-Visual Communication Review*, 1962, **10**(3), 169–175.

Mollenkopf, W. G. Time limits and the behavior of test takers. *Educational and Psychological Measurement*, 1960, **20**, 223–230.

Morrison, E. J. On test variance and the dimensions of the measurement situation. *Educational and Psychological Measurement*, 1960, **20**, 231–250.

Myers, C. T. The factorial composition and validity of differently speeded tests. *Psychometrika*, 1952, **17**, 347–352.

Myers, C. T. Some observations of problem solving in spatial relations tests. Educational Testing Service *Research Bulletin*, 1958, No. 16.

Myers, C. T. Symposium: The effects of time limits on test scores (introduction). *Educational and Psychological Measurement*, 1960, **20**, 221–222.

National Board of Medical Examiners. *Description of examinations, part I and part II.* Philadelphia: NBME, 1967.

Quereshi, M. Y. Mental test performance as a function of payoff conditions, item difficulty, and degree of speeding. *Journal of Applied Psychology*, 1960, **44**, 65–77.

Scates, D. E. Unit costs in the administration of a standardized test. *Educational Research Bulletin*, 1937, **16**(February), 38–45.

Sherriffs, A. C., & Boomer, D. S. Who is penalized by the penalty for guessing? *Journal of Educational Psychology*, 1954, **45**, 81–90.

Swineford, F., & Miller, P. M. Effects of directions regarding guessing on item statistics of a multiple-choice vocabulary test. *Journal of Educational Psychology*, 1953, **44**, 129–139.

Teevan, R. C., & McKeachie, W. J. Effects on performance of different instructions in multiple-choice examinations. *Papers of the Michigan Academy of Science, Arts, and Letters*, 1954, **39**, 467–475.

Tinker, M. A. Speed, power and level in the revised Minnesota paper form board test. *Pedagogical Seminary*, 1944, **64**(March), 93–97.

Traxler, A. E. *Techniques of guidance.* New York: Harper, 1945.

Traxler, A. E. Administering and scoring the objective test. In E. F. Lindquist (Ed.), *Educational measurement.* Washington: American Council on Education, 1951. Pp. 329–416.

Traxler, A. E., & Hilkert, R. N. Effect of type of desk on results of machine-scored tests. *School and Society*, 1942, **56**, 277–279.

Tyler, F. T., & Chalmers, T. M. Effect on scores of warning junior high school pupils of coming tests. *Journal of Educational Research*, 1943, **37**, 290–296.

Waite, R. R., Sarason, S. B., Lighthall, F. F., & Davidson, K. S. A study of anxiety and learning in children. *Journal of Abnormal and Social Psychology*, 1958, **57**, 267–270.

Weidemann, C. C., & Newens, L. F. The effect of directions preceding true-false and indeterminate-statement examinations upon distributions of test scores. *Journal of Educational Psychology*, 1933, **24,** 97–106.

Wevrick, L. Response set in a multiple-choice test. *Educational and Psychological Measurement*, 1962, **22,** 533–538.

Wood, B. D. Studies of achievement tests. *Journal of Educational Psychology*, 1927, **18,** 18–25.

Wood, E. P. Improving the validity of collegiate achievement tests. *Journal of Educational Psychology*, 1927, **18,** 18–25.

Yamamoto, K., & Dizney, H. F. Effects of three sets of test instructions on scores on an intelligence scale. *Educational and Psychological Measurement*, 1965, **25,** 87–94.

Zubin, J. The chance element in matching tests. *Journal of Educational Psychology*, 1936, **27,** 1–17.

8. Automation of Test Scoring, Reporting, and Analysis

Frank B. Baker
University of Wisconsin

One of the major contributions of educational research to educational practice has been in the area of educational measurement. The modest test development projects of individual researchers of the period 1920–1940 have matured into large-scale testing programs involving millions of students at all levels within the educational system. A significant factor in the development of these large-scale testing programs has been the revolutionary developments in electronic technology, which have occurred since the second world war. The application of this technology in the form of optical-scanning equipment and digital computers has made it economically feasible to process the enormous number of tests and questionnaires administered each year. Automated data processing has so pervaded the field of educational measurement that a spectrum of testing programs ranging from local school district programs to nationwide mass testing is dependent upon this technology for success.[1]

It should be noted that, although the technology underlying test-processing equipment was developed outside of the field of education, the "state-of-the-art" in the reading of answer sheets by optical scanners essentially has been defined by persons within the educational testing field. The optical test-scoring equipment developed by E. F. Lindquist of the University of Iowa was operational as early as 1955, and since that time extensive research and development by a number of organizations have brought these machines to their current high level of accuracy and efficiency. Although the initial impact of modern electronic technology has been upon the automation of test scoring and processing, eventually all areas of education

will feel the impact of this technology. Therefore, educational measurement specialists should be prepared to influence the changes in the educative process and the concomitant changes in measurement practices that will be forthcoming as a result of this technology.

Educational measurement encompasses a wide range of techniques and instruments that can be used to measure variables of interest; but, if the results of measurement are to be processed by optical scanners and their associated equipment, the characteristics of this equipment impose a constraint upon the mode of response to these. Because of this underlying constraint, the basic processing and analysis procedures associated with academic testing, questionnaires, personality inventories, and other such instruments are nearly identical. Discussing each separately would be redundant and detract from the presentation; therefore, the present chapter has as its central theme the processing of the results of a testing program such as would be conducted by a school system. The generalization of these procedures to other programs and instruments is left, in large part, to the reader.

The chapter is divided into four major sections. The first deals with the basic principles of optical scanning employed in these test-scoring machines. In the second section, a "systems approach" to the scoring of answer sheets and statistical analysis of the results is presented: the purpose of this section is to demonstrate that one should consider test scoring, reporting, and analysis as an integrated system rather than as separate tasks. The third is devoted to consideration of some of the practical problems associated with operating such a system. The fourth section is an attempt to suggest some ways in which modern technology can be used to improve educational mea-

---

[1] The discussion in this chapter presents an appraisal of the extent of development and use of automation in testing as it has evolved to date in the United States.

surement, and how the resulting improvements, hopefully, will lead to new procedures, new psychometric principles, and new theories of measurement.

OPTICAL SCANNING AND TEST-SCORING EQUIPMENT

In educational testing, the typical test consists of a series of multiple-choice items to which a student responds. The alternative chosen is indicated by using a pencil to mark a small space on the answer sheet that corresponds to that item choice. Thus, the product of a testing session is an answer sheet, such as that shown in figure 8.1, containing a large number of small black marks that are the student's item-response choices. The technological problem is one of developing a device that can detect these marks, compare the response choice with the correct answer, and provide the subject with a test score that is some function of the number of correct responses he has made.

Prior to 1955, this technological problem was solved in one of several ways. The first solution was to provide a human scorer with an answer sheet (stencil) in which holes were punched at the positions of the correct responses. The scorer then laid the stencil over the answer sheet, counted the number of marks appearing in the holes, and recorded this number on the answer sheet: a procedure that was slow and inaccurate. The second solution to the scoring problem was the development in 1935 of an analog machine, the IBM 805 (Downey, 1965, pp. 46–53), that would place the scoring stencil over the answer sheet, count the number of correct responses by summing the electric current passing through the pencil marks, and display the total test score (i.e. total current) on a meter on the machine. The human operator of the machine was responsible for putting each answer sheet into the machine, reading the meter, and writing the score on the answer sheet. Although the human no longer counted the marks on the paper, test scoring was still largely a manual procedure. And again, the solution was a poor one: the accuracy of the machine (specifically, the flow of current) was affected by atmospheric conditions; errors in reading the meter were common; the rate of processing though faster was still relatively slow; and the total procedure was essentially manual (see Traxler, 1953).[2]

Several approaches to test processing based upon the use of Hollerith (punched) cards have been developed. In an early approach the student marked his response choices in spaces provided on the card. A reproducing punch machine with a mark-sense capability then was used to produce a punched card containing the same information. This solution involved the use of electronic accounting machines whose rates of processing are very slow (100 to 200 cards per minute) and not suitable to large-scale test processing. A later approach (Games, 1965) used cards in which the response positions were partially perforated and a small stylus was used to complete the punching of a response choice. These cards then served as input to a digital computer that performed the scoring and reporting.

In 1955 the limitations upon scoring efficiency characteristic of hand scoring or scoring by analog or punched-card procedures were overcome by automated optical test-scoring equipment devised by Lindquist and the staff of the Measurement Research Center.[3] The marks on the answer sheet were detected by special photoelectric sensors, the scoring of the test was done electronically, and the reporting of test scores was by means of punched cards or line printers. Since 1955 considerable research and development effort has gone into producing improved optical-scanning equipment for test-processing purposes. Such equipment currently is available in a wide range of capabilities to meet a variety of needs and has the following advantages: (*a*) flexibility in number and type

---

[2] A special-purpose analog scoring machine for scoring the Strong Vocational Interest Blank was developed by a Mr. Hankes in 1946, but few technical details of this machine are available.

[3] In the interest of historical accuracy, it should be noted that the mid-1950s saw the development of a number of prototype optical scanners and test-scoring machines. Equipment such as the SCRIBE machine built for Educational Testing Service and a special optical machine due to Hankes also were constructed during this period.

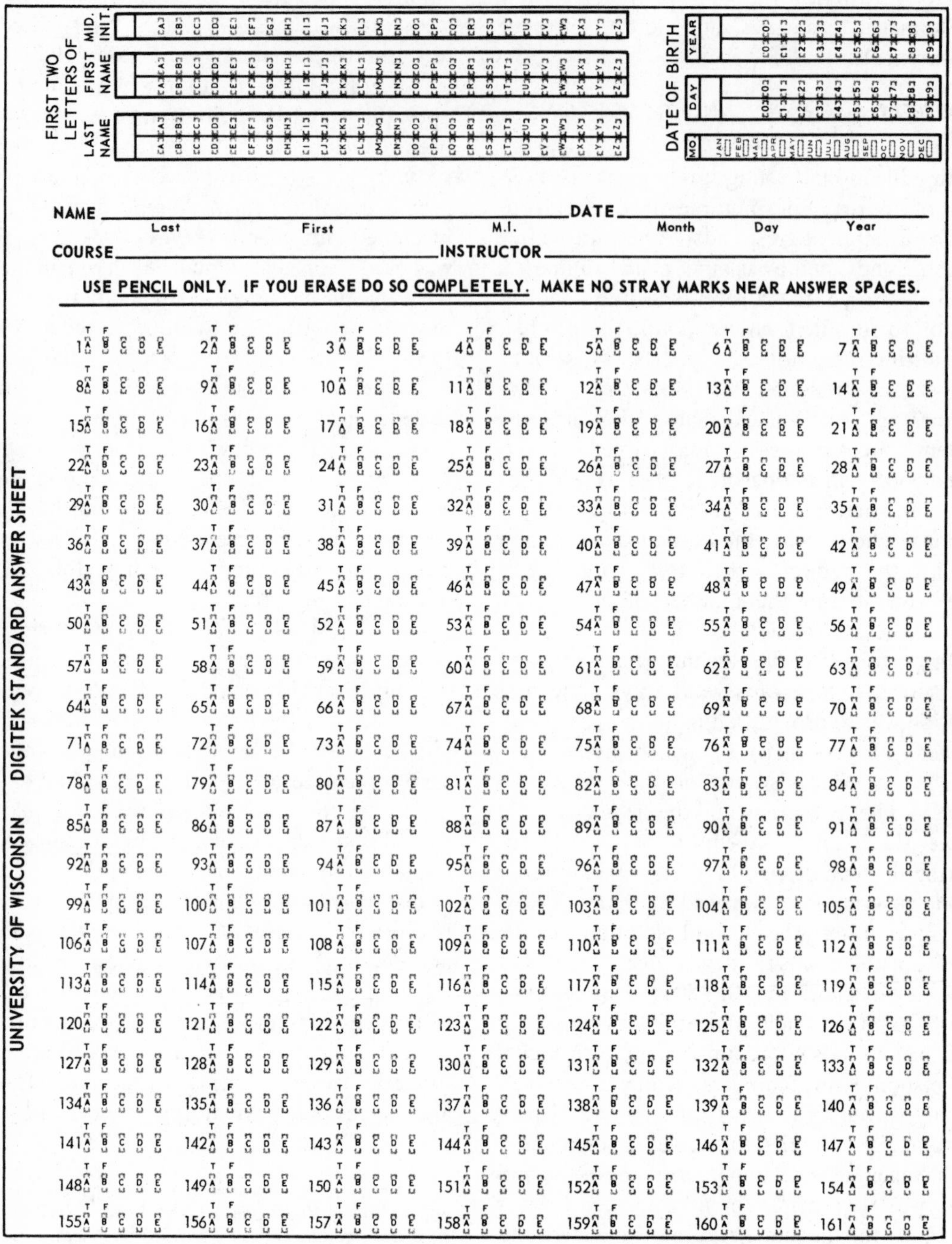

FIG. 8.1. A general-purpose answer sheet for a mark-scan optical scanner

of answer keys that can be applied to the answer sheet, (b) accuracy of results, (c) high rate of processing (on the order of thousands of answer sheets per hour), and (d) elimination of human factors in the scoring process. The optical-scanning test-scoring equipment is so superior in all respects to previous solutions that the analog machine is obsolete and manual scoring should be confined to the scoring of teacher-made classroom tests administered to small samples.[4] Therefore, the remainder of the chapter is devoted to optical scanning and test-scoring equipment and their uses. The reader must be warned that in this age of rapidly changing technology any discussion of the technical details of equipment is outmoded before it can be published; however, it was felt to be desirable to present the basic principles of current (circa 1969) optical scanners to provide the reader with a basis for understanding existing equipment and for placing future developments in better perspective.

Principles of Optical Scanning

There are two basic principles employed within the optical-scanning equipment used in test-scoring systems, one based on transmitted light and one on reflected light. In the first of these a light shines through the answer sheet and is detected by a phototransistor on the opposite side of the sheet. The scanner used in test scoring reads a complete row across the answer sheet at once, thus there are as many phototransistor read positions[5] as there are columns of item-response positions. If a mark has been made on either side of the answer sheet, it will interrupt the light beam between the light source and the phototransistor. The interruption causes the generation of an electrical signal that then is amplified and shaped so that it can be transmitted to a digital computer or electronic-scoring circuitry internal to the scanner. In order that the printed material appearing on the answer sheet does not interfere with the mark sensing, inks are used that are translucent to the infrared light source of the optical scanner. (Fig. 8.2 illustrates a typical transmitted-light read-station in an optical scanner.)

When the light shines through the answer sheet, response choices on both sides of the paper are sensed by the phototransistor. Thus the columns on the front and back of the answer sheet must be in interlaced position. The simultaneous scanning of both sides of an answer sheet is of special value when a battery of related tests is to be given to a group of examinees and a variety of scores for single tests and combinations of tests is desired. When this is the case, items on the front and back of the sheet are likely to be from different tests, and the scoring circuitry, when it reads a given row on the answer sheets, must sort out the positions and assign each one not only to its proper item but also to its proper test.

Optical scanners also can be constructed using reflected light instead of transmitted light. The basic principle underlying this process is that the pencil mark on the paper reflects less light than does the blank paper. Two different styles of read-stations can be based upon the reflected-light principle. In one type of read-station, the light from each mark reflects into a separate bundle of glass fibers (optical fibers); and, at the opposite end of the bundle, a phototransistor detects the presence or absence of the examinee's response choice, or, equivalently, the reflected light is collimated—transmitted to the transistor through a light "tunnel." Thus, there are as many bundles of optical fibers, or light tunnels, as there are marking positions. The second type of reflected-light read-station contains a mirror, which can be positioned, and a series of lenses that aim the reflected light from a small area of the answer sheet onto a matrix of optical fiber bundles. The transistors at the opposite end of the optical fibers generate a matrix of ones and

---

[4] It must be recognized, of course, that at the present time, and for some time to come, there will be schools that do not have ready access to automated test scoring. Furthermore, as developed on pp. 221–226, the installation of a test-scoring and data-processing unit presents a good many problems. Shipment of answer sheets to an outside scoring agency for scoring involves some lapse of time. So hand scoring may continue to play a somewhat larger role than this statement implies.

[5] It is common engineering terminology to refer to most sensing operations as "reading," hence read positions and read-station.

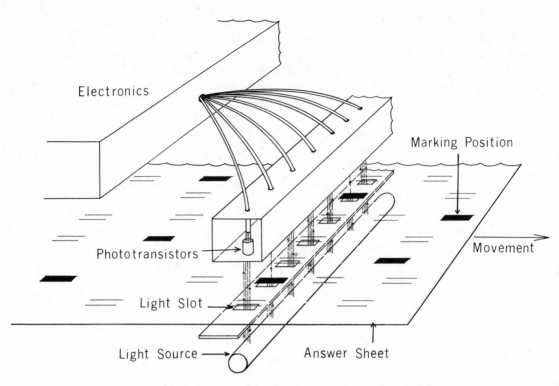

FIG. 8.2. Optical read-station using the transmitted-light principle

zeros that represent the image of the mark on the answer sheet. This type of read-station is commonly used in optical scanners that attempt to read printed information, such as names and addresses from business or government forms. Some test-scoring optical scanners use a similar arrangement except a single phototransistor is used as the sensing element rather than a matrix. In such machines the answer sheet is scanned by rotating the mirror which reflects the light from the answer sheet. (Fig. 8.3 illustrates the read-station of a reflected-light optical scanner of the second type.)

When used in optical test-scoring equipment, the transmitted-light and reflected-light techniques each have their advantages and disadvantages. Equipment employing transmitted light requires a good quality paper that has uniform translucency and is free from scum marks and foreign matter, which could be confused with pencil marks. Less expensive paper can be used with equipment employing reflected light as it need not be of uniform translucency. Thus, in general, fewer spurious signals are received when reflected light is used. The answer sheets used with transmitted-light scanners can be designed so that both sides of the sheet can be read at one time. Such an arrangement is an advantage from a speed-of-processing point of view but a disadvantage in that it places a constraint upon the design of answer-sheet formats. Optical scanners employing the optical-fiber type of reflected-light read-station also can be designed to read both sides of the answer sheet simultaneously; however, those employing the positionable mirror type of reflected-light read-station typically can read only one side of the answer sheet as it passes through the read-station. Because of both technical and practical advantages, the trend appears to be toward greater use of the reflected-light principle in the design of optical test-scoring equipment.

Classes of Optical Scanners

A number of different optical-scanning machines are marketed, and each can be assigned to one of two broad classes—mark scan

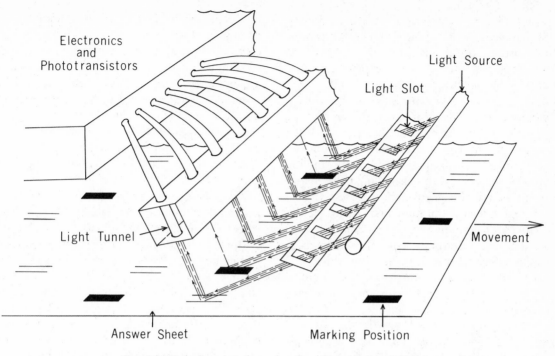

FIG. 8.3. Optical read-station using the reflected-light principle

and character scan. Both types can be used to process test results. These two classes are differentiated by the type of optical scanning they attempt to perform and usually are designated as optical mark readers (OMR) and optical character readers (OCR). The mark-scan equipment, which can be based upon either transmitted- or reflected-light principles, is designed solely to detect (read) marks on an answer sheet. The character-scan class of optical scanners is designed to read alphanumeric characters rather than marks. Information typed on an answer sheet, such as name, address, school, and grade, can be read optically by this type of equipment, which usually is based upon the reflected-light principle. Equipment also exists (Teitelman, 1964) that will read handwritten letters or numbers, and it is anticipated that in the future such machines will be available for a wide range of applications.

Optical Test-Scoring Equipment

The procedures for optical scanning described above provide a means by which an examinee's response to an item can be detected, but this is only an initial step in processing answer sheets. The additional task of applying an answer key and crediting his test score with the proper increment also must be performed. At present there are two types of optical test-scoring equipment in use in processing answer sheets. These may be called "self-contained" mark-scan and "high-capacity" mark-scan. A third type, an optical character reader, also can be used in test scoring; however, its use in scoring is, at present at least, quite limited. Although the three types vary markedly in speed, cost, and design, there is a great deal of similarity in their final products. The real potential of any optical-scoring equipment lies in its ability to translate test-response information into a form acceptable to computers; and all three types can process answer sheets and provide a record for each student that contains identification information, test scores, and item-response choices. These data are stored in a medium that then can serve as input to a general-purpose digital computer. The data-processing and analysis capabilities of digital computers are such that the test data then can be fully exploited.

A prime consideration in the design of mark-scan test-scoring equipment is the work load to be handled. Within educational measurement two distinct work loads can be observed: one is that exemplified by the testing programs conducted by school systems, universities, and other educational institutions where a wide variety of instruments are administered but the volume is low; the other is that typical of the testing programs of the nationwide testing organizations which process several million answer sheets a year. The equipment manufacturers have designed mark-scan test-scoring equipment for each of these markets. Machines of modest capability, which contain an optical scanner and electronic scoring circuitry in a single piece of equipment, have been designed for low-volume applications. The high-volume needs of the large-scale testing programs have been met by special equipment configurations consisting of a high-capacity optical scanner and an associated digital computer, which performs the scoring function. (For lack of more precise terminology, the former are referred to as "self-contained" and the latter as "high-capacity" optical-scoring equipment.)

The self-contained optical-scoring equipment has a modest capability in terms of the number of answer sheets processed per hour (on the order of several thousand), of the maximum number of items on an answer sheet, of the allowable answer-sheet formats, and of the number of different scoring keys that can be applied to an answer sheet as it passes through the machine. Typical examples—circa 1966—of this type of test-scoring machine are the Digitek 100 (Digitek, 1966) and the IBM 1230 series (IBM, 1964). Both of these mark-scan machines are completely self-contained in that they do not require an associated computer to score the tests and record the score on the answer sheet or punch it in a Hollerith card. Recent mark-scan machines record the identification information and the total test and sub-test scores on magnetic tape for use by a computer. These units also can produce a record of each item-response choice of the individual student if this information is desired. Such a record then can be used in what is called an *image mode* with a digital computer. In this mode, the out-

put record of the scanner serves as input to the computer which performs the scoring and creation and storage of data files for further processing and analysis. Although there are some difficulties resulting from the output format of some of these machines (especially the early models that punched Hollerith cards),[6] the self-contained optical test-scoring machine is a capable processor of answer sheets and can be used effectively in a wide range of testing programs.

The test-scoring needs of large-scale testing programs cannot be met economically by the use of the small self-contained machines. Special-purpose machines (such as shown in fig. 8.4) consisting of a high-capacity optical scanner employing mark-scan techniques (OMR) and a small digital computer to process the output of the scanning equipment are used. In this type of scanner, the item-response marks on both sides of the paper are sensed as the answer sheet passes under the read-station, and the item-response choices from a row of an answer sheet are transmitted as binary numbers to a small digital computer. Because the response choices from a row of an answer sheet can be from both sides of the answer sheet and from one or more tests, the small computer has to do a good deal of processing. The response choices must be unscrambled, the proper answer key applied, the particular score incremented, and a series of quality control checks performed. Remarkably, all this is done in the time interval available as the answer sheet moves from one row to the next under the optical read-station in the scanning equipment. The time that it takes for one answer sheet to leave the read-station and the next one to get

---

[6] The IBM model 1230 reads 10 columns from across a row of the answer sheet (typically representing two unrelated items) and punches the 10 responses in a single column of a punched card in what computer engineers call *column binary*. The Digitek 100 punches item responses in the proper column order but introduces other idiosyncracies. Though perhaps annoying to the users, the idiosyncratic card formats of these two machines are of little consequence when the cards are used as input for a digital computer. If these cards are to be used directly by nontechnical personnel, for example to count item responses with a counting sorter, the idiosyncracies are vexing.

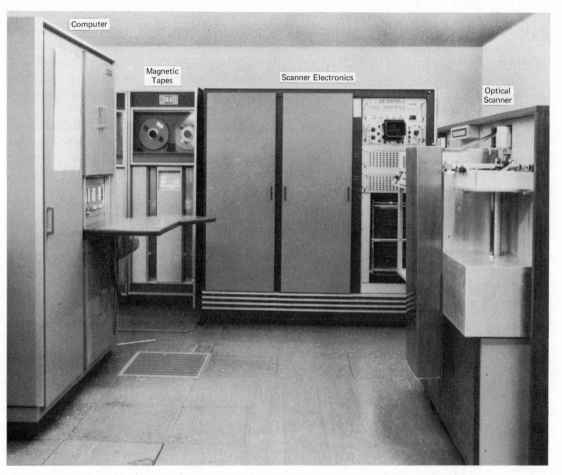

FIG. 8.4. A high-capacity test-processing system at the Measurement Research Center.
(Photo courtesy Westinghouse Learning Corp.)

in position is used by the computer to write the obtained data on some electronic storage medium. Typically, the computer creates a record on magnetic tape or disk file that contains all of the data on the answer sheet as well as the test scores produced by the computer.

Having been designed specifically to meet the needs of large-scale testing programs, this optical-scoring equipment has a speed advantage of about 10 times that of the self-contained machines. The first Measurement Research Center (MRC) equipment processed about 6,000 answer sheets an hour; and later MRC machines process both sides of up to 60,000 sheets an hour, although only a small proportion of the possible marking positions are scored at this rate. In addition to permitting faster processing, the inclusion of a small digital computer in the system also introduces considerable flexibility. The computer can be programmed to accept a wide range of answer-sheet designs and can produce many different scores from a single answer sheet while the sheets are passing through the scanner section.

Optical Character Readers

An additional type of optical scanner, which can be used for test processing, is the optical character reader (OCR) designed to process business forms in the commercial world (Feildelman, 1966; Wilson, 1966). This equipment reads typewritten or, in some cases, hand-printed (Teitelman, 1964) information such as appears on bills, inventory sheets, sales records, government forms, etc. Although it has had limited initial use in test processing, there is a strong likelihood that, because of its wider applicability, this equipment eventually will replace the self-contained optical test-scoring equipment. It is quite unlikely, however, that such equipment readily will replace the high-capacity mark-scan equipment due to the speed, accuracy, and low-per-score cost of that special-purpose equipment.

Optical character readers are character-scan machines that use the reflected-light principle to produce an image of an alphanumeric character in a matrix of optical fiber bundles; this image is then converted by photo-transistor to a matrix of ones and zeros representing presence or absence of light on a given optical fiber bundle. The binary matrix then is compared electronically to matrices of ones and zeros representing the characters the machine is capable of recognizing. If the sensed matrix matches, at an acceptable level, a given matrix in the machine's repertoire, the scanner produces a binary-coded decimal (BCD) representation of the character which is then transmitted to the digital computer. Test scoring readily can be accomplished by including a mark as a character in the reader's repertoire. The optical character reader scans the answer sheet and transmits the BCD representation of the marks to the associated digital computer. The computer then uses this information to perform the scoring function. The results of the scanning and scoring procedures are written by the digital computer as a record on some electronic storage medium. Because of the physical motion involved in positioning the mirror in the optical read-station, the character readers are slower (about 400 to 2,400 characters per second) than optical mark readers, but their ability to read characters rather than just marks allows a wide variety of other applications. For example in a school system, the data processing associated with daily operations—such as pupil accounting, library book inventory, etc.—could easily be performed by character readers. Thus, their relatively slow speed in scoring tests can be compensated for by their use in other areas. It should be noted

that, with properly designed forms, these same tasks could be performed by mark-scan equipment, but the problems associated with the transition from the usual business forms to forms designed for mark scanning inhibits wide use of mark-scan equipment in such applications.

Although the three types of optical-scoring systems—self-contained mark-scan, high-capacity mark-scan, and character reader—differ greatly in speed and design, there is, nonetheless, a great deal of similarity in their final products. Because of this underlying similarity, no further distinctions in the discussion are made among equipments and all three types are referred to as optical test-scoring equipment without identifying a particular type.

Selection of Optical-Scoring Equipment

The choice of a particular machine to perform the test-processing tasks of scanning, scoring, and recording depends upon the volume of answer sheets generated by the testing program and the cost the program is capable of bearing. When the test papers are to be scored and returned directly to the classroom, the processing performed by the self-contained machine alone may be sufficient. However, if the test scores are to be processed in any way, data-processing equipment in addition to the test-scoring machine is required. In an efficient test-processing system, this additional equipment should be at least a small-scale digital computer with its associated input/output devices. Some test-scoring systems have attempted to process test results through the use of electronic accounting machines—such as collators, tabulators, etc.—but such an approach is an exercise in futility! Achieving the full potential of optical-scoring equipment requires a digital computer to process the outputs of the scoring machines. Thus, the optical test-scoring equipment is only a portion of the total investment in hardware, and one must be able to justify the total cost. In many situations, the best solution is not to operate a test-scoring system but to use an existing test-scoring service. Such organizations have the equipment, personnel, and experience to provide good service at a reasonable per-student cost.

Quality control within the optical-scoring equipment is an important consideration in the selection of equipment. Most multiple-choice items require a single response to be marked, but because of the relatively poor quality of marks made by students—e.g. erasures, smudges, etc.—the internal circuitry of an optical scanner must enable the machine to choose the mark most likely to be the response choice made by the examinee. An effective way of achieving this goal is through the use of analog discrimination circuits, which choose the strongest of the multiple signals from a given item. A signal threshold approach also can be used to select signals greater than a given level, but this technique has a disadvantage in that information can be needlessly lost when marks are not consistently above the threshold density. With discrimination circuitry, all marks may be weak but the strongest is chosen. Constructing optical scanners that provide adequate internal quality control is a difficult task and requires expert engineering. Achieving the desired level of quality control depends upon the design of the equipment, so the user must select the best possible design. An additional level of quality control is provided by optical-scoring equipment that includes a small digital computer. The computer can be programmed to perform a number of "validity" checks upon the results of the scanning process. These checks determine whether what the scanner has "seen" is worthy of further processing. It should be noted that when self-contained optical-scoring equipment is used, such checks must be performed separately rather than as an integral part of the scoring process.

The choice of a particular make of optical-scoring equipment also can be influenced by the mechanical characteristics of the equipment. Traditionally, answer sheets have been $8\frac{1}{2}'' \times 11''$, but equipment designed to handle only this paper size would be of limited usefulness. The paper-handling mechanisms should be able to handle a variety of paper lengths and widths at a number of different processing rates. In order to solve certain engineering problems, optical-scoring equipment often requires that the marking positions be located very precisely on the answer sheet. Close tolerances for location of the marking positions on the answer sheet mean that expensive printing processes must be used. In many cases it restricts one to a limited variety of answer sheets available from only a few high-quality printing establishments. A good optical scanner should be such that it will accept answer sheets produced to normal printing tolerances. In addition to accepting normal printing tolerances, the optical scanner should be capable of processing answer sheets that are slightly skewed, or off register, as they pass under the read-station. The best optical test-scoring equipment provides for some latitude with respect to both printing tolerance and register of the answer sheets during processing. The physical layout of the response positions on the answer sheet is another mechanical characteristic of concern. The resolution—the number of marking positions per square inch of answer sheet—of the scanner should be fine enough to provide the user considerable freedom in designing his own answer-sheet layouts. If too few marking positions are available, one must design answer sheets to fit the machine rather than the task, and hence, finer resolution is to be preferred. For example, when responses are made directly in the test booklet, fine resolution enables one to configure the items on a page with only minor concern for the location of marking positions. In those situations where the student responds by underlining, circling, etc., fine resolution simplifies the processing of such results by the computer. Freedom in answer sheet design also should be accompanied by a simple method for adapting the scoring procedure to the answer sheet. In systems involving scoring by digital computers, changing answer-sheet design should not require rewriting of the computer programs that perform the scoring. The worst case is that in which a computer program must be written by a programmer for each answer-sheet design. The best case would be one where the test constructor would specify how to score the instrument in a simple fashion and a general-purpose computer program would generate the scoring procedure.

A test-scoring system whose only function is to provide raw test scores is of limited usefulness. In most cases, the raw test scores are subjected to further processing which yields derived scores, frequency distributions, and summary statistics. Hence, the output of the optical-scoring equipment is merely the input to a separate digital computer. As was mentioned, early self-contained optical-scoring machines produced punched cards containing test scores and/or item-response choices that then were used as input to a computer. The use of punched cards as an intermediary data storage device is an extremely poor practice as cards are the source of many problems. The punching process is prone to error, the cards are handled excessively, problems of damage, loss, and improper card order are common, and storage inevitably becomes a problem. In addition, there are the hidden costs associated with punched cards that make it a very expensive means of communication between the test-scoring equipment and a computer. Thus, if the results of test scoring are to be subjected to further computer processing, the scoring equipment should record the data directly on an electronic storage medium, such as magnetic tape or disk, since this is a more efficient means of communicating with a computer. The attendant increase in efficiency will more than offset the additional cost of optical-scoring equipment that provides this capability.

The above do not exhaust the list of considerations involved in the selection of optical-scoring equipment for a given situation and the reader is referred to Edberg and Peterson (1965) for a more extensive treatment.

A SYSTEMS APPROACH TO AUTOMATED PROCESSING

The modern approach to performing complex tasks falls under the rubric of what is called a "system approach." Under this approach the individual elements of a task are not considered as separate entities but rather as interdependent components of a total process. The present section attempts to look at test scoring, analysis, and reporting as a system rather than as a series of unique operations.

Figure 8.5 provides a flow chart of a hypothetical test-processing system and serves as the thread of continuity for the discussion presented below. The reader should be aware that implementation of such a system can be accomplished in many ways and is not fundamentally dependent upon any given configuration of optical-scoring equipment and computers. The material in chapter 7 brought the testing process up to the entry point of the flow chart given in figure 8.5; namely, that the students have taken the tests, and the answer sheets have been transmitted to a test-scoring facility where they will receive subsequent processing. The paragraphs below discuss in detail the various tasks performed within each of the blocks of the flow chart representing a test-processing system. Most of the following discussion is predicated on the assumption that the test-processing operation is a large-scale one involving an optical scanner whose output is fed into magnetic storage or directly into a digital computer. However, the basic approach that is presented can be employed in situations where many of the tasks are performed manually.

Step 1: Initial Procedures

It is well known that the product of any processing system is no better than the raw materials it receives. This is especially true in education where answer sheets are marked by students who do not generally count neatness among their virtues. Therefore, utmost care must be exercised at all stages of test processing to achieve the maximum possible quality level. No amount of subsequent sophisticated treatment can overcome the difficulties stemming from poor quality of the basic data. It cannot be emphasized enough that continuous quality control throughout *all* phases of a testing program is the essential ingredient in obtaining results in which one can place confidence.

The initial quality control procedures are essentially manual and are designed to assure that the optical-scoring equipment receives answer sheets that it can process. Under these manual procedures the answer sheets are subjected to various checks, such as inspection for

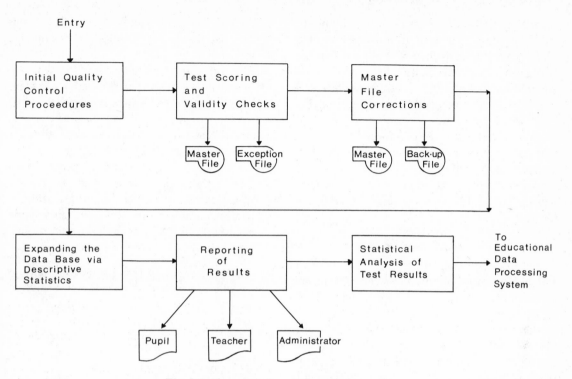

Entry

| Initial Quality Control Proceedures | Test Scoring and Validity Checks | Master File Corrections |

Master File   Exception File   Master File   Back-up File

| Expanding the Data Base via Descriptive Statistics | Reporting of Results | Statistical Analysis of Test Results |

To Educational Data Processing System

Pupil   Teacher   Administrator

FIG. 8.5. Flow chart for a test-processing system

tears, bent papers, light marking, upside-down sheets, excessively smudged sheets, misplaced sheets, etc. If the inspection indicates that the answer sheets are of a quality level acceptable to a given optical scanner, the answer sheets will be processed. If the checks indicate that the papers are of unacceptable quality, the answer sheets will have to be systematically cleaned up, repaired, or subjected to other procedures that will raise their quality level to that acceptable to the optical scanner; this can involve actual re-marking of sheets and erasure of extraneous "doodling," and at considerable cost.

After the initial quality control is completed, the batches of answer sheets can be arranged in an order that will facilitate the remainder of the processing. The arranging of batches at this point will greatly simplify a number of later stages of processing since the structure of the batches can be made to coincide with the way in which data are to be pooled into larger groups. For example, if the papers are structured hierarchically by room, teacher, grade, school, and school district, it is much easier to obtain summary statistics for these units than

it would be if class groups are arranged in order alphabetically by teacher or structured alphabetically by student. The former involves a simple cumulative process, whereas the latter involve considerable sorting and collating to obtain the same results. The identity of the individual batches is maintained through the use of header sheets which precede each batch. The header sheet is optically scanned and contains identification information such as the test, teacher, grade, school, testing date, and date of entry into the test-processing system. The information in the header sheets is treated as a logical unit and accompanies the batch of test results throughout the system. The optical-scoring equipment will place this information in a header record preceding each batch of test results to label them in electronic memory. The header sheet also contains information such as answer-sheet format, the scoring keys to be applied, where multiple responses are permitted, the data to be recorded, etc., that is used by the optical-scoring equipment to establish the tasks it is to perform upon that batch of answer sheets. The header sheet and its corollary, the header record, are invaluable to the accounting system that must maintain a trail of the batches as they proceed through the system. If processing malfunctions occur, it is possible to identify the affected batches and locate back-up files or the source documents from which to reprocess the batch. The end product of the first stage of processing consists of stacks of answer sheets in which each logical grouping is preceded by a header sheet, and there is reasonable assurance that the optical-scoring equipment can process the response forms.

Step 2: Scoring

Upon completion of initial quality control and header sheet insertion, the answer sheets are submitted to the optical-scoring equipment to be scored and the results recorded in a master file. In the scoring process the marks made by the student are detected and the response choice compared with the scoring key. If the student chose the correct response, his raw score is increased by the appropriate amount. The inclusion of a digital computer in the optical-scoring equipment also enables one to record each item response on an electronic storage medium and simultaneously process several subtests or even separate tests from a given answer sheet as it passes through the scanner. Again one must be concerned with quality control. Despite the initial inspection of the answer sheets and application of quality control procedures, there still will be considerable variation in the way students mark the answer sheets so a high quality of output from the scoring stage is dependent upon adequate internal checking mechanisms in the optical scanner itself. Ideally, the majority of the quality control procedures in force during test scoring should be performed by the optical test-scoring equipment. Such equipment should:

1. Recognize and identify unscorable sheets, preferably without removing the defective sheet from the batch, and offset (or otherwise conveniently identify for the edit clerk) each suspect sheet in the output stack
2. Report as much of the information from the defective sheet as can be transcribed accurately so that later corrections have a linkage into the master file
3. Recognize and record instances in which a sheet was not properly registered in the scanner so that the test scores are suspect
4. Recognize and record instances of possible errors, caused for example by double or weak marks, made by the scanner
5. Recognize and record clues to probable errors in the orginal record made by the respondent; for example, in the grid for recording name and other information, a name beginning "AAA" or the like would be suspect and questioned by the equipment.

In general, good optical test-scoring equipment will examine and edit the information transcribed from the document and will draw to the attention of a quality-control clerk all data that are suspect and require hand checking.

The computer programs that process the responses as the answer sheets pass through the optical scanner also have built-in "validity" checks, but the number and type of internal checks performed by the computer is a function of how much time is available between two successive answer sheets as they pass through the optical scanner. The usual checks are for incomplete student names, addresses, etc., excessive number of items with no response, and for exceptionally low test scores which may indicate that an answer sheet is faulty. If the data contained in an answer sheet fail to pass the internal quality control checks of the scanner or the validity checks of the computer programs, its data record is placed in an exception file, on magnetic tape or other electronic storage medium, for subsequent rectification, and the answer sheet in the output stack of the optical scanner is offset or otherwise suitably identified as a reject. The final products of the optical test-scoring equipment are records containing student identification, raw test scores, and item-response choices in a master file and an exception file containing duplicates of those records for which the accuracy or completeness of the data are in doubt. At this point the task of the optical test-scoring equipment is completed and all subsequent processing must be done by other equipment. Typically, the magnetic tapes or disk packs containing the master file and the exception file are removed and transferred to a larger general-purpose digital computer for further processing.

Step 3: Master File Quality Control

The next major task in the processing procedure is to correct the errors indicated by the exception files and to build a master file that has complete and reasonably accurate data. The exception file and all the original answer sheets are transferred to a group of quality control clerks who ascertain from the data in the exception file why the answer sheets were considered exceptions and use the original answer sheets to determine what the information should have been. In most cases, the errors are improper marks made by the students that the scanners were not able to read, missing letters in a name, or discrimination errors that are easily corrected by clerks.

There are a number of ways in which correction of the master file can be performed. The best is to have both the master file and the exception file under control of the digital computer and to display records from the exception file on a cathode ray tube (CRT) display device,[7] such as shown in figure 8.6, which is connected (on-line) to the digital computer (Gruenberger, 1967; Sutherland, 1966). The clerk can see the record, and the computer identifies the errors. The correct data are elicited from the answer sheet, the clerk uses a typewriter-style keyboard connected to the display device to correct the information on the screen, and a push of a button returns the corrected record directly to the computer. A file maintenance computer program then is used to place the corrected student record in its proper place in the master file.

Without an on-line capability, one has to obtain a computer-printed listing of the exception file and provide worksheets for the clerks to use in correcting errors. The clerks locate the errors in the exception file, reconcile them with the aid of the original answer sheets, and indicate the corrections on forms which then are processed by the optical test-scoring equipment. The processing of the correction sheets creates an update file which contains the corrections to be made to the master file. A sub-

[7] Such cathode ray tube devices with their associated typewriter keyboards are known as alphanumeric displays and are easily connected to nearly any digital computer that would be involved in a test-processing system.

FIG. 8.6. An alphanumeric display console which can be connected to a digital computer. (Photo courtesy Computer Communications Inc.)

sequent computer run then must be made to merge the corrections into the master file. Regardless of how the corrections are made, the final output of this stage is a master file in which the *known* errors have been corrected and of a quality felt to be at an acceptable level. It should be noted that one can never be sure of achieving perfect master files because the quality control checks throughout the system are not capable of complete accuracy. However, master files at an acceptable quality control level can be produced.

At this point in the processing of test results, it is advantageous to make duplicates of the master files because, in the next stage of processing, the files will be manipulated and additional information added to the records for each student. The possibility exists that the original information could be destroyed by programming errors or machine malfunctions. Therefore, it is advisable to duplicate the files, or create other suitable backup, and retain one set until subsequent master files containing all of the desired information become available. Bitter experience shows that merely removing the plastic write-enable rings on magnetic tapes is inadequate protection. The only safe practice is to copy the magnetic tape or removable disk file and physically remove it from the machine room. Some installations always maintain backup from two successive stages of processing so that errors that cascade through several stages can be corrected.

If arranging of batches in the initial stages of processing was adequate, the master file organization should be that required by subsequent analyses. In routine school testing programs this is usually the case because results are reported by school system, school, grade, teacher, etc. However, for research use, it may be necessary to form a special arrangement of the data to perform a desired analysis or data reduction. Such a rearrangement can be accomplished by the general file management programs of the computer facility.

Step 4: Expanding the Data Base

The procedures of the first three stages have produced a master file that contains all of the information present in the original answer sheets and the corresponding raw test scores. Because most published tests report derived scores and/or percentiles, the raw test scores require additional processing. A test analysis program for a digital computer is used to compute the desired derived scores and routine summary statistics and thus expand the data base contained in the master file. For illustrative purposes, it will be assumed that the master file has been partitioned through the use of header records into files, each representing a class, teacher, grade, school, school system, or other educational unit. The test analysis program then will proceed from the smallest to largest subdivision and produce summary statistics for all levels. At each level for which the information is of interest, the test analysis program should produce for the raw scores a reliability coefficient, the test score frequency distribution, summary statistics such as the mean and standard deviation of the raw score frequency distribution, and selected percentiles for each test or subtest. This information then is stored in the header records preceding the various subdivisions of the master file. Upon completion of these computations, derived scores based upon local norms for each student record can be produced. The obtaining of derived scores based upon local norms does not occur until this point as the calculation of such derived scores depends upon the summary statistics and frequency distributions computed above. The master file then can be passed through a subroutine of the test analysis program that converts raw scores to derived scores, based upon both local and national norms, and computes frequency distributions and summary statistics based upon the derived scores. In addition, an item analysis that produces item statistics for each possible response choice to all items in the instrument should be performed[8] so that the test itself may be studied. If only national norms were used to compute derived scores, a single pass of the master file through the test analysis program

[8] A detailed discussion of item analysis procedures is given in chapter 5.

would be sufficient. The expansion of the data base in this stage has been confined to rather rudimentary information and in no way represents what could be done. There are no technological reasons to prevent one from applying diagnostic procedures, scaling techniques, item weighting, or other such procedures to expand the data base in a sophisticated manner.

Step 5: Reporting Results

The test constructor, the educational researcher, and the teacher—all have unique uses for the data produced by the preceding four stages and now contained in the expanded master file. To provide these users with the information they desire, a major stage of processing is that of reporting the results in an effective way. The most common mode of data presentation used is that of printed reports arranged by computer programs and produced by high-speed printers under computer control. Although the wide variety of reports produced from test data may not seem to have a common denominator, each is merely a particular configuration of data extracted from the master file. The creation of numerous different reports from a single data base is a common procedure in the commercial world. Generalized report-generation programs exist for most computers which produce such reports on a routine basis.

These programs are able to produce a specific report through control parameters that describe the data base, the report format, and the variables to be reported. The program uses this information to adapt itself to the data base, create procedures to extract the variables from the data base, and establish the necessary print format controls. Once the configuration of the computer program has been accomplished, the data base is processed and the report is printed.

The results of the usual school testing program may be reported to the student, the teacher, the administrator, and other personnel within an educational unit. Each student may receive a listing of the derived scores he has earned on the tests in the program (such as in fig. 8.7), and he may receive a score profile for the subscores of particular tests. The teacher also would receive this information for every student in the class and summary statistics for the class (as shown in fig. 8.8).

The item statistics produced by the test analysis program are of interest to the teacher for diagnostic purposes and to the test constructor for psychometric purposes. These statistics can be used by the teacher to ascertain if the students did not understand certain ideas and to locate common misunderstandings. The test constructor uses these same statistics to study the technical properties of the measuring instrument for a specific group of students.

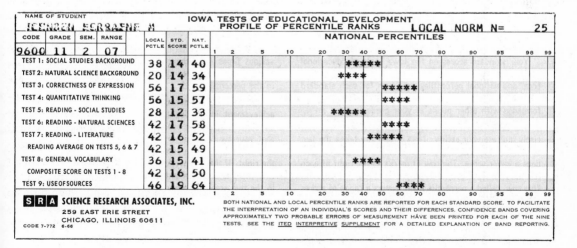

FIG. 8.7. Student report produced by a commercial test scoring service.
(Photo courtesy Measurement Research Center.)

THE IOWA TESTS OF EDUCATIONAL DEVELOPMENT | LIST REPORT OF SCORES | 1   6

SCHOOL   CODE   GRADE   SEM.   DATE TESTED

SAMPLE SCHOOL REPORT   1234567890-051-3596-000   11   2   4-15-67   FORM Y4-FL

IDENTIFICATION		RANGE	1 BACKGROUND SOC. STUD.		2 BACKGROUND NAT. SCI.		3 CORR. OF EXPRESSION		4 QUANT'VE. THINKING		5 READING SOC. STUD.		6 READING NAT. SCI.		7 READING LIT.		READING AVERAGE 5-7		8 GENERAL VOCABULARY		COMP. 1-8		9 USE OF SOURCES		OTHER INFORMATION FIELD 3 FIELD 4	
FIELD 2			S.S. or t	% ile	S.S. or t	% ile	S.S. or t	% ile	S.S. or t	% ile	S.S. or t	% ile	S.S. or t	% ile	S.S. or t	% ile	S.S. or t	% ile	S.S. or t	% ile	S.S. or t	% ile	S.S. or t	% ile		

HD N-CNT=   25,M N-CNT=   25,IMC=00000

FIG. 8.8. Class roster and test scores for a teacher. (Photo courtesy Measurement Research Center.)

Regardless of the group upon which the analysis is based, the report format would be similar to that illustrated in figure 8.9, which was produced by a test analysis program prepared by Baker (1963). Note that descriptive information, such as the frequency distribution, the summary statistics of the test scores, and a reliability coefficient, are reported in addition to the extensive item information for all items and item responses.

The school administrator is not as concerned with individual test scores and item analysis as he is with an overall view of the testing program—the overall performance of groups under his charge, the relative performance of different subgroups, the performance of his groups in relation to groups from similar communities, and the relation of his group to national norms. Therefore, the reports he receives are those which summarize results by grade, school, geographic region, and other subdivisions of interest. Because extensive lists of numbers are difficult to grasp, such reports should be focused upon frequency distributions or histograms of test scores accompanied by summary statistics and a written interpretation of the results. The written interpretation can be prepared manually or could be computer generated by a program that interprets the results. The general format of such a report would be similar to that given in figure 8.10.

Both the test constructor and educational researcher can use the types of reports described above, but each has a need for a more flexible means of observing test results. The test constructor may want to observe distributions of item statistics from special groupings of students and perform other manipulations related to studying the instruments involved in the testing program. The educational researcher may have little interest in psychometric details but may wish to inspect the means, variances, and score distributions for particular groupings within the data base. Neither of these users of the data base may require routine printed reports, but they may want to create specialized reports once they have inspected the data. Such flexibility of reporting can easily be obtained with a cathode ray tube display device, such as shown in figure 8.6,

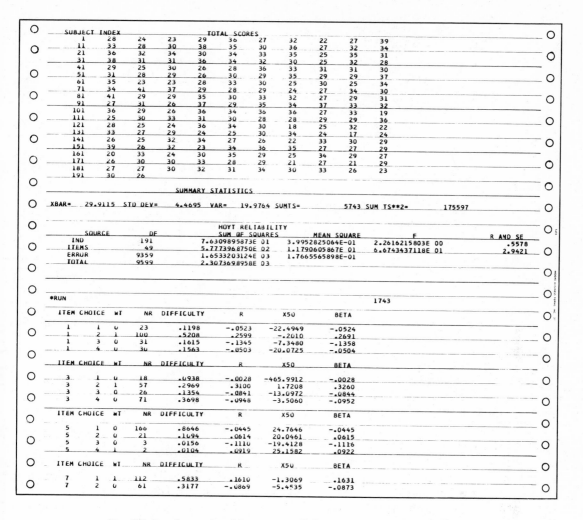

FIG. 8.9. Results produced by a test analysis program for a digital computer

used in conjunction with the file manipulation and report-generation programs of a digital computer. The computer can acquire the appropriate data, and the CRT displays them visually so that they may be studied and serve as the basis for further inquiry by the researcher.

The reports generated during this phase of processing may be the final product for routine school testing programs, but in test development and educational research the generation of reports is usually preliminary to further analysis of the data base.

Step 6: Statistical Analysis Using the Data Base

Just as the test-processing procedures constitute a "system," most computer facilities have taken a system approach (Shannon & Henschke, 1967) to statistical analysis. Such statistical "packages" are designed to accept a data base and perform one or more statistical analyses upon the data. Thus, the test-processing system merges at this point with the statistical analysis system of a computer center, the former providing a well-designed data base and the latter a well-designed analysis system. Procedures for using a given computer program within a statistical analysis system are very similar to those employed by the report-generation programs of the previous section. It is necessary to provide a description of the structure and format of the data base, identify the

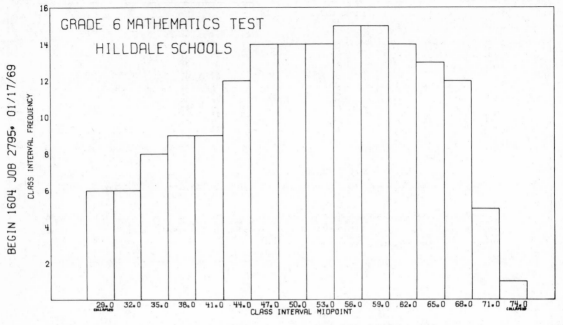

FIG. 8.10. Administrator's summary report as produ▮

variables to be involved in the analysis, indicate the groups to be employed, and specify the analyses. Once the analyses and the data sources have been specified, it is a routine matter to execute the desired analyses. The data base is undisturbed by the statistical analyses, and it is normally possible to perform several different statistical analyses sequentially upon the same data. Alternatively, the data base can be restructured, using the file manipulation programs, and a different type of statistical analysis can be run on each restructuring of the data base; e.g. the structure of the data base required for a chi-square analysis would be different from that for multiple regression.

Most computer centers operate in a mode called *batch processing* where the computing for many persons is done sequentially, and thus this mode does not permit intervention during processing by an investigator as this would require stopping the total operation. A second mode of operation, called *time sharing*, exists in proto-type form at a few computer facilities. In the time-sharing mode, which is an extension of a technique called *multiprogramming*, a number of programs to be processed are all placed in residence in the computer. The computer then

can work on one until a delay—usually an input or output activity from a slower component of the system—occurs. The computer then switches automatically to a second program and continues such switching until all programs have been processed completely. The full potential of time sharing is realized when the investigator has an on-line capability that permits him to interact directly with the machine during the processing of his data. These interruptions do not "waste" computer time, as would be the case in the batch-processing mode, because while one investigator is adjusting his program or adding new data, the computer is busy working on someone else's job (Fano & Corbato, 1966).

Such interactive analysis systems provide the investigator with a very powerful tool. For example, the test constructor could eliminate nondiscriminating items from a test, rescore the tests, and compute a frequency distribution and summary statistics for the new test scores. Both the old and new results then could be displayed on a cathode ray tube for visual comparison. Using the same capability, the educational researcher could factor analyze a set of data, display vector diagrams of the factors, and then

FREQUENCY TABLE				
CLASS INTERVAL	FREQ.	CUMULATIVE FREQUENCY	PERCENT	CUMULATIVE PERCENT
73 – 75	1	167	.60	100.00
70 – 72	5	166	2.99	99.40
67 – 69	12	161	7.19	96.41
64 – 66	13	149	7.78	89.22
61 – 63	14	136	8.38	81.44
58 – 60	15	122	8.98	73.05
55 – 57	15	107	8.98	64.07
52 – 54	14	92	8.38	55.09
49 – 51	14	78	8.38	46.71
46 – 48	14	64	8.38	38.32
43 – 45	12	50	7.19	29.94
40 – 42	9	38	5.39	22.75
37 – 39	9	29	5.39	17.37
34 – 36	8	20	4.79	11.98
31 – 33	6	12	3.59	7.19
28 – 30	6	6	3.59	3.59

		PERCENTAGE	PERCENTILE SCORE
MEAN=	51.9	10	35.26
RANGE=	46.0	20	40.97
VARIANCE=	133.2	30	45.52
STANDARD DEVIATION=	11.5	40	49.10
		50	52.68
SUM SCORES=	3665.0	60	56.14
SUM SQUARED		70	59.48
SCORES=	471713.0	80	62.99
		90	66.83

n X-Y plotter

manipulate the factor structure in various ways in order better to understand the data (Cattell & Foster, 1963). Such interactive analysis systems have great potential for putting the psychometric specialist, the educational researcher, and the administrator in intimate contact with the data base and results of statistical analysis. However, the reader should be advised that, due to technical and economic limitations, such time-sharing systems will be slow in reaching any but major computing installations.

Although the flow chart ends at this point, it is by no means the end of the possible uses of the data base. In the section below, integration of this data base into yet another computer-based system—the educational data-processing system—is described.

Other Uses of the Data Base

The daily operations of an educational unit, such as a school system, also have been affected by the impact of digital computers and their associated technology. Routine student accounting, fiscal data, payroll, inventory, surveys, and other such tasks are highly automated in progressive school systems throughout the country (Goodlad, O'Toole, & Tyler, 1966;

Whitlock, 1964). Viewed within this context, the test-scoring and analysis system described above is only one part of a larger data-processing system operated by the educational unit. The test scores produced by the former are extracted and placed within the cumulative record maintained for each student. The summary statistics, frequency distributions, and results of statistical analyses reported earlier to the administrator become part of the management data base upon which policy decisions are promulgated. Considering the testing program as part of the larger data-processing task of an educational unit also has economic advantages. With proper design of the business forms used in the daily operations of an educational unit, the optical scanners used so effectively in test processing also can be used in the educational data system. Thus, economy of operations can be gained by distributing the cost of the optical-scanning equipment over a number of data-processing activities.

Although the initial consideration was that of a system approach to test processing and analysis, it is clear that this approach to the total data-processing task of an educational unit is advantageous. Not only can optical-scanning equipment, digital computers, and personnel be shared, but the high cost computer programming associated with the various data-processing tasks can be jointly developed at considerable reduction in overall costs. Such an overall system approach also will prevent test processing and analysis from being considered an isolated task with little or no relation to other aspects of education.

PRACTICAL CONSIDERATIONS IN INSTALLING AND OPERATING THE SYSTEM

Installation

An integral part of the sales appeal of anyone selling digital computer systems is that if you choose his brand all your problems are solved. The equipment will do everything promised, and his company will provide you with all the necessary computer programs for your particular needs. Nothing could be farther from the truth. The moment the contract is signed, your problems have begun! A hypothetical scenario for the subsequent events could be:

When processing the first batch of tests, it becomes obvious that a crucial feature of the machine is not present. A quick check with the salesman reveals that this is an optional feature which costs $85 a month. He thought you knew, and you assumed that, because you needed the feature, it was naturally one of the basic capabilities of the equipment. The salesman adds that the minimum delivery time on the item is three months, which is a month after your annual peak load period.

Because the system components have been in production for an extended period, you schedule delivery for two months before the first big testing program of the year believing that all will function properly. Yet six months later the equipment failures and computer-programming errors just now are being reduced to a point that permits some production work.

It becomes apparent that your understanding of how a test-processing system operates and that of the salesman form non-intersecting sets. The computer programs delivered with the equipment are a minor portion of what you believe is necessary to achieve adequate performance.

To compound all these problems, the accountant ascertains that the total cost of operating the system has been four times the salesman's estimate.

If such a total sequence of events actually occurred, the equipment manufacturer, the salesman, and the test processor had better pursue other endeavors, yet individual events such as these have been experienced by many test-processing installations. The events contained in the scenario given above contain several points that are elaborated in the remainder of the present section.

Experience has shown that people tend to underestimate seriously their equipment needs. One tends to think in terms of today's work load and fails to predict realistically the impact of the equipment upon educational practices. In addition, because of long periods of fiscal deprivation, educators "think small" when it comes to purchasing capital goods. Underestimation also is abetted by the salesman who submits a low bid with the expectation that the purchaser will need more capability at a later point in time. He knows that once a purchaser is committed to a given company's product line, he will be reluctant to switch companies to achieve the additional capacity. Due to the tendency to underestimate, it is imperative that data on the present work load be accurate and that the future work load be predicted as well as possible. Prediction can be facilitated by studying the work-load patterns of similar installations that have reached a point in their development that you plan to reach in the future. Such a study can define a baseline for the capabilities of a test-processing system. Once such a baseline has been defined, performance specifications should be written and serve as the basis for equipment bids; failure of the actual equipment to meet these specifications should be considered a serious matter. If the failures are apparent during the bidding process, their implications for total system performance should be determined carefully so that one chooses equipment wisely. In many situations inability to meet performance specifications becomes apparent only after the total system has been established. To protect oneself there should be performance guarantees in the purchase or rental contract. Such guarantees are a standard practice when one industrial concern purchases from another, yet they seem not to appear in contracts between industry and educational organizations. One also should consider purchasing or renting the complete system from a single manufacturer as then the user has some leverage to get deficiencies corrected. If the total system is obtained from a single manufacturer, one company cannot blame others in the system for problems in its equipment. However, acquisition of the complete system from a single manufacturer may involve acquiring certain system components whose performance is less than that of competing manufacturers. One has to balance the advantages of a single company against whatever reduction in performance results. Due to the very rapid rate at which improvements in digital computers and their associated equipment are made, it is usually advantageous to rent. Rented equipment can easily be exchanged and the possibility of substitution of a competitor's device serves as a lever for obtaining better service.

Although it seems obvious that highly technical equipment such as optical scanners and digital computers should be selected by the technical specialists who will be faced with the day-to-day operation of the equipment, one of the unfortunate realities of equipment purchasing or renting is that the decisions are ultimately made by administrators who are not technically competent in the specific area dealt with by the equipment. As a result, a typical ploy used by a salesman is first to try to sell the equipment on technical grounds to those who will use it. Failing here, he then attempts to sell the equipment to administrative personnel on grounds other than the technical merits of the equipment. In a good situation, the administrator who makes the final decision may impose cost and other administrative constraints, but he should rely upon the technical recommendations of his staff and not upon the spurious blandishments of a salesman.

Even though reasonable staff work was performed prior to acquisition of the test-processing system, that staff work may have underestimated the programming support that would be needed and overestimated the support available from the manufacturer. Salesmen of digital computers endeavor to leave the impression that their company will provide all the necessary computer programs (software) either in the form of existing programs or new programs that they will write. The latter is extremely seductive since it leads one to believe they will actually produce such programs; again, experience has shown that satisfactory programs rarely are delivered. The only possible way to make such promises come true is to negotiate for the services of computer programmers at the manufacturer's expense. Personnel then are assigned to your installation by the manufacturer for a specified period, and you determine and supervise their programming efforts. Even though a good initial set of computer programs may be acquired, keeping the programs for the test-processing system up to date is not easily accomplished within a test-processing system; improved test-processing procedures are quickly discovered, new equipment is added to the system, and requests for new types of services are made. Such a dynamic situation means that the computer programs continuously are being modified, new programs being written, and new operating schemes devised and tested. Thus, even a modest test-processing system requires that a long-term computer programming effort be an integral part of the system. Both the staffing and budgeting associated with a test-processing system should take this programming effort into account.

In order to leave the reader with a balanced impression, it must be emphasized that all equipment has its technological limitations. Modern electronic equipment is constructed to meet certain design goals, and the designer must work within constraints imposed by the ultimate cost of the equipment, the technology available, and the tasks to be performed. Therefore, existing equipment embodies many compromises, limitations, etc., which are reflected in a number of ways such as the processing rate of the equipment, the error rates, the mean time between failures, and finally, in the life expectancy of the equipment. Also, because electronic devices such as computers and optical scanners are composed of large numbers of components that are interrelated in complex ways, it is difficult to produce equipment free of defects. Despite the best efforts of the manufacturers, there are few equipment systems or computer programs that will run properly when delivered. Most installations find that there is an initial period (from 3 to 12 months) in which production-line errors, early failure of electronic components, errors in computer programs, etc., are detected with some frequency. One frankly must plan for such a settling-down period and not attempt full-scale production during this time interval. Technical people are used to dealing with such problems and attempt to get the best performance from the equipment within its technological limitations. Nontechnical people tend to believe that electronic data-processing equipment is error free and has no limitations. Thus, a two-way educative process is necessary so that technical personnel do not use equipment limitations or equipment failures as an excuse for inefficient operations and so that those using the results of the test-processing equipment do not expect unrealistic levels of performance.

In the operation of any data-processing system, such as that for test processing, there are both obvious and hidden costs. The obvious costs—such as equipment purchase, maintenance contracts, physical site preparation, and expendable supplies—are easily included in the budget. The hidden costs—such as changes in data collection procedures, retraining of personnel, unanticipated expansion of staff, and in-service training for teachers—can be items of considerable size. Thus, the initial cost figures may be correct for the equipment configuration but fail to take other costs into consideration. A prime example of a hidden cost is the unexpected failure of equipment (unscheduled maintenance) which can be very costly in terms of the service the test-processing system is able to provide its customers and in terms of data-processing tasks that must be repeated. Therefore, it is not unreasonable to insist upon contractual protection covering excessive unscheduled maintenance. Salesmen tend to imply that preventative maintenance contracts will reduce this problem to an insignificant level; if they really do, there should be no objections to such guarantees.

One of the hidden costs included above was that of expanded staff. There are two levels at which this expansion takes place—technical and clerical. Technical personnel, such as computer programmers, are usually well versed in their speciality yet are rarely experienced in the specifics of test processing. Therefore, one must often provide them with the opportunity to learn the techniques of test scoring and processing on the job. This training can be time consuming; hence, rapid turnover among technical personnel can have serious consequences for the effectiveness of the total test-processing system. The best preventatives for such turnover are salaries, advancement possibilities, and working conditions competitive with other organizations employing the same levels of technical skill. The clerical-level personnel present quite a different problem. Clerical workers' pay typically is near the low end of the scale; hence, a high rate of

turnover among clerical personnel is commonplace. Because of this, effective training procedures need to be developed that quickly enable these persons to perform the clerical tasks. In addition, adequate supervision and quality control of their work must be maintained so that personnel turnover does not degrade the quality of test processing.

Operation

The next concern is the practical considerations relating to the operation of a test-processing system. One of the most important aspects of a smoothly operating system is the existence of a clearly conceived overall plan for the operation of the system. From this the authority and responsibility for each aspect of the total process can be assigned, and specific staff members held responsible for proper operation. Despite the existence of an overall plan, there are a host of seemingly trivial operational details that can cause trouble for the best of systems. It is not possible to enumerate them all, but those presented below should provide the reader with some insight into the general class of problems encountered.

Most test-processing equipment is designed to handle a certain range of answer sheets or response forms. The exact range varies from system to system, and, in many cases, those expecting to use a test-scoring service assume that any answer sheet designed for optical scoring can be used. A testing program will be conducted under this assumption and only belatedly is it learned that the given installation cannot process the answer sheets. The charge and countercharge of "Why didn't you tell us?" and "Why didn't you ask?" are issued and ill feelings are generated. The capabilities and limitations of the test-scoring system need to be communicated at frequent intervals to both actual and potential users of its services. The data-processing staff must try to anticipate such problems, and the customer must keep abreast of the situation.

An operational problem that can cause considerable discomfort for the staff of a test-processing system is that of keeping track of batches of tests within the system—the accounting problem. When a batch of response forms is received, they should be logged in and suitably identified. As they or their derived data—on magnetic tape, disk packs, or such—proceed from stage to stage, each step should be recorded and sufficient backup files retained. When the end products are produced and shipped, the batch should be logged out and the final master files saved for a reasonable period. Such a procedure is disarmingly simple when all goes well, but a system malfunction easily can disrupt the usual sequence and play havoc with a poorly designed accounting system. Once such a system is disrupted, considerable effort may be required to realign the batches in the system and regain control of the data flow. The accounting system should be sufficiently flexible to absorb perturbations without disruption of the total test-processing procedure. Such a system would hopefully keep the system supervisor out of the embarrassing situation of having to explain to an irate school principal why he cannot seem to locate the long overdue test results.

A set of problems similar to those deriving from a poor accounting system is associated with inadequate computer-program documentation. As mentioned above, most test-processing systems are quite dynamic and the computer programming reflects this state of flux. Failure to document computer programs adequately at the time they are written can result in a test-processing system whose smooth functioning depends upon the acquired knowledge stored in the memory of a specific computer programmer. If this person departs and if the computer program documentation is inadequate, it becomes nearly impossible to make even minor changes, let alone understand the total program. For some reason, computer programmers traditionally resist documenting their work; however, successful resistance can be very expensive in the long run. Adequate documentation means at a minimum:

1. Flow charts at a sufficiently detailed level to communicate the logical design of the program

2. A narrative description of the program containing the design goals of the program, the analytical or data-processing techniques used to achieve these goals, and a description of how to operate the program; i.e. a user's manual

3. A complete listing of the computer program in which at least every fifth line of code is annotated—such annotations should provide a verbal description of what the code is doing and should be related to the flow chart

4. The date of both the computer program and its documentation.

Such documentation requirements may seem stringent but, if they are not met, one may be faced with the situation of having to rewrite a program rather than go to the expense of attempting to decipher an existing program written by a departed colleague. Numerous governmental agencies now issue computer program documentation requirements to their contractors that are much more stringent than those given above. These agencies are painfully aware of how expensive inadequately documented computer programs can be.

In many test-processing installations, the digital computer used to process the test scores, prepare the printed reports, and perform the statistical analysis is not under administrative control of the test-processing staff. Because of this, difficulties relating to availability of computer time, processing priorities, and programming support will arise. In that many testing programs are conducted at fixed times within the school calendar, test-processing systems experience wide variations in work loads. If a peak-load period occurs when the computer installation also is experiencing a peak load, conflicts can be generated. Therefore, it is necessary for the staffs of both organizations to plan yearly work schedules jointly so that peak-period conflicts can be resolved before they occur. There also is a need for the two staffs to agree upon levels of programming support and the choice of operating procedures for the computer. Areas such as data-transmission formats, control specifications, and file maintenance procedures need to be determined jointly. Cooperation in these and similar matters can result in a significant improvement in overall operating efficiency.

It is clear that the paragraphs above do not consider all of the operational problems which arise, but Schultz's law (what can go wrong—will) easily encompasses the total class of problems. For this reason, operational procedures should be developed that minimize the occurrence of problems and prevent those that do occur from becoming catastrophes.

IMPLICATIONS OF TECHNOLOGY FOR MEASUREMENT

The electronic technology upon which optical-scanning equipment and digital computers depend is very sophisticated and new advances in this field appear in rapid succession. Unfortunately the uses of this technology in education are not equally sophisticated. The technology of optical scanners, digital computers, and electronics has been used in the 1950s and 1960s merely to automate manual procedures in use since the 1920s. Instead of clerks counting marks appearing in holes in a stencil, optical scanners read the marks. Rather than having typists prepare report forms, computer-controlled printers produce these same reports. Thus accuracy, speed, and efficiency have been significantly improved and costs lowered, but the basic conceptualization of how and what to test has been relatively unaffected by advances in technology. A similar phenomenon occurred when digital computers first were applied to scientific computing. Manual computing techniques were transferred from desk calculator procedures to computer programs without change, and the same computing procedures merely were performed faster. In the field of scientific computing such a state of affairs did not persist very long, and technology has had a profound impact upon both what data are collected and how they are analyzed. A corresponding change in the conceptualization of testing and analysis of test results has not been observed.

A classic example of the lack of impact of modern technology is in item analysis techniques. During the 1930s the data processing associated with item analysis was a tedious task

and was a barrier to effective test development. Hence a large number of item analysis techniques were devised to reduce the data-processing and computation procedures to a minimum (Long & Sandiford, 1935). One of the more widely used techniques was the upper-lower 27-percent method (Kelley, 1939). To obtain item indices one computed the proportion of correct responses in the upper and lower 27 percent of the score distribution and entered a table to obtain the values of the item-test correlation, a procedure in which 46 percent of the test papers were not processed. Thus, the technique was designed solely to ease the burden of manual test analysis. Yet, a number of large, highly automated, testing programs employ the upper-lower 27-percent technique for item analysis. The continued use in the form of a digital computer program of a manual technique that was designed solely to circumvent data processing is sheer nonsense in light of the capabilities of digital computers. It is, in fact, more difficult for a computer program to find the upper-lower 27-percent values and obtain the item indices from tables than it is for it compute item difficulty and item-criterion correlation from the total sample. Thus, although item discrimination indices having a much better theoretical basis than the upper-lower 27-percent estimate of the item-criterion correlation exist (Lord & Novick, 1968), they are not being used in many cases because of the carry-over of manual procedures into the automated systems. An example of one of the possibilities in the area of item analysis afforded by the capabilities of digital computers is the curve-fitting approach to item analysis programmed by Baker and Martin (1969). Maximum likelihood procedures are used to obtain estimates of the item parameters X_{50} and β of the item characteristic curve for each of the several response categories. The computational details of this item analysis technique are such that it would be prohibitively expensive in both time and effort to perform such an analysis by hand. Yet, when this item analysis procedure is incorporated into a computer test-analysis program, the estimation of each item parameter takes only a few milliseconds. Thus, the implementation of this procedure in the form of a computer program allows one to use an item analysis technique that has not been feasible in the past. This example is only indicative of the way in which one can use the analysis capabilities of the computer to free one's thinking from the constraints of the past. The first concern should be to develop the best possible conceptualization of an item style and derive its item analysis procedures apart from the computational aspects, because, when computers are available, the computational difficulties are of little concern.

One of the "sacred cows" of educational measurement is the multiple-choice item format. As a result, current testing programs are producing a nation of students whose only mode of test response is to make a small black mark in the appropriate box on an answer sheet. To a considerable extent the invariance in item style and response mode began with the IBM 805 analog scoring devices and has been perpetuated by the use of mark-scan optical test-scoring equipment. There is no technical reason that, even with this equipment, the student could not respond by underlining one of several words in a sentence, by crossing out an appropriate picture, drawing a line in a geometric figure, or even printing a capital letter in the test booklet. All of these response modes and many others are feasible using mark-scan equipment of sufficient resolution. For example, underlining of the verb in a sentence in a booklet can be accomplished by placing marking positions between the rows of print and allowing the underlining mark to pass over several marking boxes. The computer program for scoring can be set to recognize a series of contiguous marked boxes as one line, and the scoring procedures can determine if the correct word was underlined. If the response position is defined as a matrix of several rows and columns, it is possible to respond by circling the correct response, crossing out a figure, or even printing a capital letter. The scanner merely records the presence or absence of a mark in each small box within the matrix. The digital computer program then applies character-recognition techniques to the matrix. When a match is found between what appeared in the matrix and a character in the program's repertoire, the scoring programs can analyze the response. Such techniques have been used in pattern-recognition studies (Selfridge & Neisser, 1960; Uhr & Vossler, 1961) and are easily adaptable to test scoring. Such a mode of response could be especially useful in the early grades of the elementary school where it is difficult for small children to find the correct small box that they want to mark.

The separate answer sheet used with multiple-choice items has evolved as a matter of economics without any real concern over whether such a format is optimum. At the present time, several test-processing services have devised test booklets that allow the student to respond directly in the booklet (see, for example, fig. 6.7). The test booklets are produced in either a fanfold form or as centerbound booklets. The optical test-scoring equipment is programmed to read the marks from the pages of the booklet, thus eliminating the need for separate answer sheets. The Measurement Research Center has developed an interesting mode of response based upon mark-scanned test booklets that permit single free-word response. The response area of the test booklet contains a number of columns, each having 26 marking positions, such as shown in chapter 7, figure 7.1. To spell a word one marks the box corresponding to the appropriate letter in each column. Thus, to spell the word *NOW*, three columns would be used with the box for *N* marked in the first column, *O* in the second, etc. The scanner reads the marks and the digital computer assembles a BCD representation of the word which then is subjected to the scoring procedures. The above examples should suffice to show that with a little thought the mark-scan equipment originally designed to process multiple-choice items can be used to break this mold and facilitate other item types and response modes.

Character-read equipment also has many interesting possibilities with respect to item response. It is possible to let the students respond by typing (at present) or by printing letters (in the future) in a free-response manner.

Computer programs can be written that perform various analyses upon the free responses to ascertain whether the correct choice, or a variation of the correct choice, has been made (Feingold, 1968). Such a free-response capability gives the test constructor considerable latitude in selecting the types of items he is willing to include in a test. One can go beyond single-word free response and permit the student to submit prose to the computer for analysis. Early work by Page (1966) and Daigon (1966) on the grading of essays by computer, though based upon simple word counts, shows considerable promise (see chapter 10 for further details). In this regard it is feasible (circa 1969) to perform a very thorough syntactical analysis of the structure of a student's prose and grade the mechanics of his phrase, sentence, and paragraph construction using whatever rules one pleases. Semantic analysis of the content of such prose is at a much more rudimentary level (Stone, 1966, p. 651) and cannot be automated sufficiently at present for routine testing. It would appear that sophisticated analysis of prose depends upon advances being made in the semantic and syntactical analysis of natural language. (See Bobrow, 1963; Simmons, 1965).

Even if one is not willing to give up the multiple-choice item format, better use can be made of its capabilities. The outcome of scoring the usual multiple-choice instrument is a single numeric test score or perhaps several such scores for various subtests. To obtain such a meager amount of information from a respondent who has been producing as best he can for the testing period is clearly wasteful. This is especially true when a skilled item constructor has employed his knowledge of subject matter and student characteristics to create items that tap many facets of an examinee's knowledge, understanding, attitudes, etc. By reporting only a test score, neither the respondent nor the test constructor gains much information. It is a simple matter to prepare additional scoring keys that produce diagnostic scores related to certain patterns of student performance and obtain a thorough description of the examinee's performance. To illustrate, assume that an arithmetic achievement test for

the sixth grade has been developed. One could readily develop additional scoring keys that would yield scores for, say, understanding of place holders, ability to divide fractions, understanding of mathematical formulas, etc. Such scores could be derived from not just the correct responses but from these and various alternatives that the item writer deliberately constructed to elicit misunderstandings, incorrect concepts, etc. The reader should be aware that considerable psychometric care must be given to the construction of these diagnostic scoring keys so that one may place confidence in the resulting scores and their interpretation.

Under manual procedures, obtaining diagnostic scores was a tedious task; using modern technology, scores can be obtained easily. Inclusion of a comprehensive set of keys producing scores related to achievement, misconceptions, incomplete understandings, etc., paves the way for improved methods of understanding students and for prescription of remedial procedures. The usual numeric test score yielded by such keys is not very informative unless accompanied by the distribution of test scores, test characteristics, and similar information normally unavailable to the student receiving these scores. Numeric scores are necessary for computation of summary statistics and for subsequent statistical analysis, but in their unelaborated form they convey little information to a student or a teacher. If, in addition to the total test score, a large number of diagnostic scores were obtained, one could develop a comprehensive picture of each student in the areas dealt with by the instrument. Given these data, computer programs can be written that produce a verbal paragraph describing the student, his strengths and weaknesses, how he stands in various areas relative to his own past performance and to his peers.

Figure 8.11 is an interpretive report of a test, such as might be prepared by a computer program. The mechanics of having the computer program prepare verbal descriptions depends upon (a) the insight of the test constructor into the area of interest, (b) the relation of levels of test and diagnostic scores to student performance, and (c) the cleverness of the com-

Pupil: Don Dewey
Instrument: Elementary Arithmetic Test

The pupil's achievement level is at the 61 percentile of students in this city and at the 72 percentile of the national norms. The pupil's strengths are in computation and facts where scores were in the upper quarter. The pupil's weaknesses are in the use of formulae and mathematical relationships where scores were in the lower quarter.

Diagnostic keys indicate pupil has good grasp of mechanics of: fractions, place holders, percents, and decimals. Pupil knows number facts.

Diagnostic keys indicate moderate difficulty with items involving a mathematical symbolism. Some difficulty where diagrams are involved.

Compared to last two testings in this subject, he has improved slightly in set theory, decimals, and maintained his own level in other topics.

FIG. 8.11. Test report as might be produced by computer programs

puter programmer in generating connected prose from somewhat disconnected verbal descriptions. The third aspect has been investigated by Finney (1967) in the area of personality testing, and he was able to generate reasonably fluent prose. The reporting of MMPI results as verbal descriptions rather than numeric test scores has been a matter of routine in a medical setting (Rome, 1962) for a number of years and is available commercially from National Computer Systems, Inc. Extension of this capability to other types of instruments would make the results more meaningful to those examined and should facilitate better use of the results of testing.

One word of caution should perhaps be introduced at this point. The capabilities of the computer will make possible very detailed analysis and reporting of test scores, subscores, and even item results. But the computer will not make the data any more reliable. One must be careful that, by reporting elaborate data, users are not encouraged to attach unwarranted confidence to scores with only modest dependability. Verbal reports, especially, can take on a flavor of absolutism. They are rarely expressed tentatively or in probabilistic terms.

The techniques of reporting the results of testing also should take advantage of technological change. A number of devices can be used to prepare reports which convey much more information than is in the usual test report. A class of machines, known as X-Y plotters, can be used to prepare the histograms (see fig. 8.10), profiles, and graphical summaries described in a previous section of the present chapter. Such plotting equipment can be used to a much greater degree, especially in the reporting of results of statistical analyses and of various manipulations the test constructor may perform upon the data base. An additional device used in many computer installations for reporting results is a cathode ray tube that is coupled to an electrostatic printer[9] (Webster, 1963). A digital computer is used to establish the display that appears on the face of the cathode ray tube and the image is printed on a sheet of paper by electrostatic means. Using such a device one can generate three-dimensional perspective displays, showing information such as the fluctuation of local norms with time, and incorporate them into the printed reports. Another interesting application is the area of profile generation and analysis where profiles could easily be displayed and photocopied. Techniques for copying documents and displays are in the midst of great technological change (Hattery & Bush, 1965) and persons in educational measurement should keep abreast of these developments and explore applications of these new techniques to reporting test results.

The existence of well-designed, flexible computer programs for data base manipulation and of modern statistical library programs should have considerable impact upon the techniques of educational measurement. In the system approach described above, only routine derived scores and summary statistics were computed as the tests were processed, but there is no reason why more complex analytical procedures could not be an integral part of such processing. Two areas appear to be fruitful for inclusion of greater analysis sophistication—the scoring procedures and the statistical analysis of the

[9] Technically such an equipment configuration is called a nonimpact printer.

scores. Most present optical-scoring equipment merely scores the items on a 0–1 basis, but, when a computer is part of the scoring equipment, many other scoring procedures are possible. For example, attitude inventories usually have five-point response scales, and a separate weight could be earned at each point so that the total score is a sum of item-response weights. In this same situation it is appropriate to apply scaling techniques such as the method of reciprocal averages which derive a set of scoring weights maximizing the internal consistency of the instrument (Baker & Martin, 1969; Mosier, 1946). Also, certain instruments have been subjected to extensive factor analyses and the underlying structure is reasonably stable. For these instruments it would be possible to obtain factor scores as a part of the scoring process. These few examples are only indicative of extensions of the scoring procedure made possible by optical test-scoring equipment, but which have not, as yet, been made part of the process. Under the previous conceptualization of processing, analyzing, and reporting as unique operations, the information in the data base tends to be underexploited.

The greater part of this chapter has been devoted to the processing and analysis of test results; but there is another side to this coin which also needs to be discussed, namely, the role of the test-processing system in the development of educational measuring instruments. Because the focus of the present book is upon the design, construction, and development of such instruments, these topics need not be restated here; however, it is of interest to show how modern technology can be used to facilitate instrument development. In the early stages of test construction large numbers of items are written, tried out, and item analyzed. Those items that are technically deficient are discarded; the remaining items are studied, modified if necessary, and subjected to the same process again. This iterative procedure is repeated until a satisfactory instrument is obtained. In such a repetitive process, the test-processing system can be of great value to the test constructor in performing the routine mechanics of scoring, analysis, and reporting.

Existing test-analysis programs (Baker & Martin, 1969) provide the test constructor considerable flexibility in this stage of development. The following are a few of the procedures that are routinely accomplished using such programs:

1. Scoring keys can be applied to subsets of items and item analysis procedures applied to all of the items in the test. The item-criterion correlations will reveal items in the subset that do not belong and items not in the subset that should have been included.

2. A series of different scoring schemes can be applied to determine the effect of scoring upon the test score distributions.

3. Item analysis procedures can be performed using an internal, then an external, criterion score and the item characteristics compared.

4. A widely used practice is to employ the method of reciprocal averages to derive a set of item-response weights that maximize the index of internal consistency and then to perform an item analysis using test scores based upon these new weights.

Another useful computer program is that called SEQUIN (Moonan & Pooch, 1966). This program sequentially selects items so that test validity will increase, if possible, as the items are added. For specific criteria it has been found that test validities are substantially higher for shorter tests than if all available items are used to obtain total scores. Such computer programs allow the test constructor to experiment with his existing data over a wide range of possibilities before he must resort to administering the instrument to a new sample.

It is also possible to automate the construction of preliminary forms of an instrument through the use of modern technology when a well-designed item pool exists. A large item pool can be stored in a computer's mass memory and each item described in terms of its content, the nature of its distracters, its item characteristic curve, and characteristics of subjects who have responded to the item. The specifications of the characteristics of the new instrument in terms of its content, test score distribution, reliability, correlation with certain external criteria, etc., can be given to a computer program. The computer program then proceeds to select items from the item pool. As each item is added to the instrument, the program employs heuristics to determine if the item contributes to achieving the design goals. If the item "fits" it is retained and the procedure repeated employing a new item. When the design goals are approximated, additional heuristics are employed to analyze the total instrument and the "weaker" items can be removed and possibly replaced. In this first stage, the test score distributions and other summary statistics could be displayed on an alphanumeric display to enable human test constructors to monitor the final product. Early unpublished work of D. Rock of Educational Testing Service shows that such automated procedures closely approximate human performance on the same test construction tasks.

Individualization and Measurement

One of the major trends within education during the past decade has been toward individualization of education through technology (Bushnell, 1965). Two main approaches have been computer-assisted instruction (CAI) (Coulson & Silberman, 1962) and, more recently, instructional management systems (IMS) (Silberman, 1968). Under the latter the computer is used to handle much of the routine bookkeeping associated with managing a classroom in which each student may be involved in something different. Optical test-scoring equipment and digital computers play a very important role in this approach as the student's daily work sheets and progress tests are designed to be processed by optical test-scoring equipment. The work sheets are scored, diagnostic analysis is performed, and the computer yields a prescription for the next topic the student is to study. Thus, the instructional management system uses the test-processing system as the means by which it collects data on each student, and these data serve as the basis for educational diagnosis and prescription. Data collection in the classroom will be greatly facilitated by small desk-top optical mark scanners that should become available in the

early 1970s. These inexpensive scanners will permit each student to insert his work sheets. tests, etc., into the scanner as the work is completed. This scanner will transmit the item responses over telephone lines to a central computer that will score the items and analyze the performance. The results and the concomitant educational prescriptions then will be printed by a teletypewriter in the classroom for immediate use by the student and his teacher. The capability to submit work sheets, progress tests, etc., from the classroom and immediately to receive the results should greatly enhance the effectiveness of the instructional management systems currently being developed.

Computer-assisted instruction places the student in direct contact with the computer by means of response stations through which the computer and the student conduct a dialog. Although CAI has great intuitive appeal, it will remain a laboratory curiosity until formidable educational and technological problems are solved. Instructional management systems, on the other hand, are both practical and economical due to the use of existing optical test-scoring equipment. Somewhat of a middle ground between these two approaches would be computer-administered tests (Harmon, Helm, & Loye, 1968; Smith, 1963) in which the item sequences are tailored by a computer program to match the examinee's performance as he is being tested, i.e. dynamic testing. Other approaches to individualized testing using special booklets, etc., are possible, but they lack the elegance of computer-administered tests.

Such individualized environments will have a profound effect upon both measurement theory and practice. The situation requires measuring instruments that provide information about the individual, not the group. One would like to measure the level of comprehension of a student at any point in a lesson, not just at an a priori end point. The path through a series of educational experiences must be measured so that one can know not only where a student stands but how he got there. The latter implies that some form of "path analysis" is necessary so that diagnosis and educational prescription can be optimized for the individual.

Given the type of situation envisioned, the classical multiple-choice examination administered to groups of students having a common experience does not appear to be relevant. One would be interested in the psychological processes involved, the patterns of behavior, integration of skills into meaningful behavior, rather than whether the student can select the correct response out of four responses to an item. Traditionally, items have been described by item statistics, but indices of difficulty and discrimination are of limited value in the present context. A scheme will need to be devised that describes the psychological processes involved in responding to an item, the skills and levels of these skills required, and the implications of any response made. Such a descriptive system would enable one to use items and the examinee's responses in a way that is educationally more significant than is presently the case. Even if one were willing to retain the present type of multiple-choice items, considerable problems would be attendant to their use in an individualized environment. Because students are proceeding at their own rate, one would be unable to construct an instrument containing a finite number of items that would ascertain the achievement of all the students in a classroom. The solution to this problem appears to be in some form of dynamic testing, such as described above, but problems of a psychometric nature will still arise. The cherished concepts of reliability, validity, and item characteristics can be translated into practice through only the group, yet under individualized instruction nice neat groups are not available. Thus, one must seek alternative ways of determining the psychometric characteristics of the measuring tools. Elimination of rigidly defined groups and times of testing can be accomplished mechanically, but how this could be reflected in the psychometric characteristics of the measuring instrument is not clear. Comparability of results also will be a problem. If each examinee receives a unique set of items, scores based upon number of items correct would not be meaningful unless the item characteristics were taken into account—perhaps an extension of the item-sampling approaches would be a relevant approach (see Lord & Novick, 1968, chap. 11). Early work by Rasch (1966) and others suggests that it might be possible to estimate underlying ability from an arbitrary set of items, thus bypassing the total test score. If such an analysis capability could be part of a test-analysis program, it would solve the problem of comparability of results in individualized testing. Individualization through computer-assisted instruction, instructional management systems, or by dynamic testing will require some considerable change in measurement theory and practice. Therefore, it is crucial that the field of measurement develop the conceptual framework and psychometric techniques for this new environment.

The few topics considered above do not exhaust the implications of modern technology for test processing, analysis, and reporting. It is clear that what can be accomplished is not constrained by technology since the capabilities of optical-scoring equipment and digital computers far exceed their current level of utilization. The unfortunate lag that exists between actual practice and *easily* attained possibilities can be attributed to economics, a reluctance to change, and perhaps a satisfaction with the status quo. Because of this lag, some exciting possibilities exist for those who would like to explore the implementation of modern technology in the context of educational measurement.

SUMMARY

A technology has existed since the mid-1950s that has enabled persons operating testing programs on either a small or large scale to automate earlier manual procedures for the processing of answer sheets. The processes of test scoring, reporting of test results, and analysis of test data can be very adequately handled by optical-scoring equipment used in conjunction with digital computers. Thus, what previously had been a very tedious, time-consuming, and often expensive task has been reduced to an efficient process with a very nominal per-student cost. As a result, massive testing programs, which a generation ago were considered economically unfeasible, are currently routine practice. It also has become commonplace to expect prompt, accurate reporting of test results from testing programs.

The discussion of test processing in the present chapter treated test scoring, reporting, and analysis as a unified procedure rather than a series of discrete events. Even though one does not have access to the latest, most sophisticated equipment, it is still possible to employ a system approach as it is fundamentally a point of view rather than a specific implementation. In many situations the task must be fractionated and many different pieces of equipment used, yet implementation of the total process can be based upon a system point of view.

When an area such as test-scoring systems is growing rapidly, many persons are receiving their initial exposure to the area and its problems. Because the installation and operation of one's first system can involve many problems, the section on practical considerations was included. Hopefully, the material presented, which distilled the experiences of many persons, will help the reader avoid some of the pitfalls attendant to acquiring such a system. Subsequent systems are always much easier to negotiate and operate as the user is much more knowledgeable than he was the first time.

Despite the impact of modern technology on the mechanical aspects of processing tests and test results, there has not been a corresponding impact of this technology upon either testing practices or upon the theoretical basis of measurement. Essentially, the manual procedures of the 1920s, '30s, and '40s were automated without any serious attempt to investigate what could be done with such a technology. An enormous gap exists between what is possible using existing technology and what is present practice. Many different implications of this technology were suggested in order to motivate the reader to make contributions that will help close this gap.

REFERENCES

Baker, F. B. Generalized item and test analysis program: A program for the Control Data 1604 computer. *Educational and Psychological Measurement*, 1963, **23**, 187–190.

Baker, F. B., & Gurland, J. An extension of item analysis procedure to the case of polychotomous response. *Psychometrika*, 1968, **33**, 259–266.

Baker, F. B., & Martin, T. J. FORTAP: A FORTRAN test analysis package. *Educational and Psychological Measurement*, 1969, **29**, 159–164.

Bobrow, D. G. Syntactical analysis of English by computer: A survey. *Proceedings of the American Federation of Information Processing Sciences*, 1963, **21**, 365–387.

Bushnell, D. Computer-mediated instruction: A survey of new developments. *Computers and Automation*, 1965, **14**(3), 18–20.

Cattell, R. B., & Foster, M. J. The rotoplot program for multiple, single-plane visually-guided rotation. *Behavioral Science*, 1963, **8**, 156–165.

Coulson, J., & Silberman, H. *Programmed learning and computer-based instruction*. New York: Wiley, 1962.

Daigon, A. Computer grading of English composition. *The English Journal*, 1966, **55**, 46–52.

Digitek operating manual. Fairless Hills, Pa.: Digitek Corporation, 1966.

Downey, M. T. *Ben D. Wood: Educational reformer*. Princeton, N. J.: Educational Testing Service, 1965.

Edberg, R. A., & Peterson, J. J. Guide to the selection of scoring machines and optical scanners. *Journal of Educational Data Processing*, 1965, **2**(2, 3), 52–64, 88–98.

Fano, R. M., & Corbato, F. J. Time sharing on computers. *Scientific American*, 1966, **215**, 128–143.

Feildelman, L. A. A survey of the character recognition field. *Datamation*, 1966, **12**, 45–52

Feingold, S. L. PLANIT—A language for CAI. *Datamation*, 1968, **14**, 41–47.

Finney, J. C. Methodological problems in programmed composition of psychological test reports. *Behavioral Science*, 1967, **12**, 142–152.

Functional characteristics, component descriptions, and operating procedures: IBM 1230 optical mark scoring reader. (Form A21-9008-3) New York: International Business Machines Corporation, 1964.

Games, P. A. SCORTIT: A FORTRAN program for scoring and item analysis of Porta-Punch cards. *Educational and Psychological Measurement*, 1965, **25**, 881–884.

Goodlad, J. I., O'Toole, J. F., Jr., & Tyler, L. L. *Computers and information systems in education*. New York: Harcourt, Brace & World, 1966.

Gruenberger, F. (Ed.) *Computer graphics*. Washington: Thompson Books, 1967.

Harmon, H. H., Helm, C. E., & Loye, D. E. Computer assisted teaching. In *Proceedings of a Conference on CAT*. Princeton, N. J.: Educational Testing Service, 1968. P. 35.

Hattery, L. H., & Bush, G. P. (Eds.) *Automation and electronics in publishing*. Washington: Spartan Books, 1965.

Horst, P. Obtaining a composite measure from a number of different measures of the same attribute. *Psychometrika*, 1936, **1**, 53–60.

Kelley, T. L. The selection of upper and lower groups for the validation of test items. *Journal of Educational Psychology*, 1939, **30**, 17–24.

Long, J. A., & Sandiford, P. *The validation of test items*. Toronto: University of Toronto Press, 1935. [Department of Education Research Bulletin No. 3]

Lord, F. M., & Novick, M. R. *Statistical theories of mental test scores*. Reading, Mass.: Addison Wesley, 1968.

Moonan, W. J., & Pooch, U. W. SEQUIN: A computerized item selection procedure. U. S. Naval Personnel Research Activity *Research Memorandum SRM 67–8*, October 1966.

Mosier, C. I. Machine methods in scaling by reciprocal averages. In *Proceedings of the Research Forum, Endicott, New York, August 26–30, 1946*. New York: International Business Machines Corporation, 1947. Pp. 35–39.

Page, E. B. The imminence of grading essays by computer. *Phi Delta Kappan*, 1966, **47**, 238–243.

Rasch, G. An individualistic approach to item analysis. In P. F. Lazersfeld & N. W. Henry (Eds.), *Readings in mathematical social sciences*. Cambridge, Mass.: MIT Press, 1966. Pp. 89–107.

Rome, H. P. Automatic techniques in personality assessment. *Journal of the American Medical Association*, 1962, **182**, 1069–1072.

Selfridge, O. G., & Neisser, U. Pattern recognitions by machines and men. *Scientific American*, 1960, **203**, 60–68.

Shannon, S., & Henschke, C. STAT-PACK: A biostatistical programming package. *Communication of the Association for Computing Machinery*, 1967, **10**, 123–125.

Silberman, H. Design objectives of the instruction management systems (IMS). Paper presented at the annual meeting of the American Educational Research Association, Chicago, February 1968.

Simmons, R. F. Answering English questions by computer: A survey. *Communications of the Association for Computing Machinery*, 1965, **8**, 53–70.

Smith, R. E. Examination by computer. *Behavioral Science*, 1963, **8**, 76–79.

Stone, P. J., Dumphy, P. C., Smith, M. S., & Ogilvie, D. M. *The general inquirer: A computer approach to content analysis*. Cambridge, Mass.: MIT Press, 1966.

Sutherland, I. E. Computer inputs and outputs. *Scientific American*, 1966, **215**, 86–96.

Teitelman, W. Real time recognition of hand-drawn characters. *Proceedings of the American Federation of Information Processing Sciences*, 1964, **22**, 559–575.

Traxler, A. E. The IBM scoring machine: An evaluation. In *Proceedings of the 1953 Invitational Conference on Testing Problems*. Princeton, N. J.: Educational Testing Service, 1953. Pp. 139–150.

Uhr, L., & Vossler, C. A pattern recognition program that generates, evaluates, and adjusts its own operators. *Proceedings of the Western Joint Computer Conference*, 1961, **19**, 555–570.

Users manual. Vol. 4. *Statistical programs for the 1108 computer*. Madison: University of Wisconsin Computing Center, 1969.

Webster, E. The impact of nonimpact printing. *Datamation*, 1963, **9**, 24–30.

Whitlock, J. W. *Automatic data processing in education*. New York: Macmillan, 1964.

Wilson, R. A. *Optical page reading devices*. New York: Reinhold, 1966.

Special Types of Tests | PART TWO

9. Performance and Product Evaluation

Robert Fitzpatrick
American Institutes for Research

Edward J. Morrison
Ohio State University

The usual test presents purely symbolic stimuli and calls for purely symbolic responses to demonstrate the degree to which each examinee possesses certain knowledge or skill. The test constitutes an artificial performance in that the examinee would not be presented these stimuli nor carry out these responses anywhere but in the classroom or some similar place that is remote from the context where the knowledge or skill is to be applied. For example, one reason to teach children arithmetic is so that they can carry out transactions with money in stores, banks, etc. But arithmetic tests are seldom designed to simulate concretely either the stimuli or the responses involved in, say, making change for a purchase of $2.89 out of a $5 bill. Rather, the test is an abstract representation of only those stimuli and responses that are considered to constitute subtraction. Efficiency thereby is served since it would be difficult to test each student in actual financial transactions, not to mention the various other contexts in which subtraction is used. However, this efficiency often may be achieved at the price of applicability. It is a common failing of educational endeavors that the student cannot, or at any rate does not, apply what he has learned when it is appropriate. He may be able to subtract accurately on a paper-and-pencil test but commits errors in making change in the store.

Hence, it is often desirable to increase the "realism" of the test to a degree that permits evaluation of the capability of the student to perform correctly in some class of *criterion situations*. The criterion situations are those in which the learning is to be applied. They are often vocational in nature but may be related to avocations, consumer skills, citizenship behaviors, or any type of performance that is considered important enough to be taught.

Realism may be increased both in the stimuli presented and in the responses required. On the stimulus side, even within a purely verbal context, realism may be varied considerably. For example, the arithmetic problem could be posed as: "Subtract $2.89 from $5.00." Or as: "Sally buys a doll for $2.89 and gives the clerk a $5 bill. How much change should she get?" Alternatively, two children could be asked to role play the situation. Or a filmed depiction of the context leading up to the subtraction problem could be shown. Or, at the extreme, the student could be sent to the store to buy a doll.

In this example, the response does not vary much insofar as it is related to subtraction. However, many other responses may be involved, especially as the situation becomes more realistic. For example, the purchaser of an article should be able to judge value and might sometimes be expected to reject the doll, if it is not worth $2.89, and thereby avoid the subtraction problem. Such a response would be considered irrelevant to the subtraction problem, but the teacher might judge it to be relevant in the overall educational context.

Other examples may be used to illustrate possible variations in test responses. Consider the differences in responses of the student who writes an essay on safe driving practices as contrasted with his actually driving an automobile in traffic. A chemistry student might write the equation representing a chemical process, or he might proceed to mix the substances, apply heat or other treatment, and

237

actually cause the designated chemical reaction to occur. A student cook could be asked to criticize the product of someone else's culinary efforts or to produce his own.

It is apparent that there are many degrees and kinds of artificialities in tests. A test of the class here designated as *performance and product evaluation* is one in which some criterion situation is simulated to a much greater degree than is represented by the usual paper-and-pencil test. This type of test usually is called a *performance test*, and that term will be used here interchangeably with the more complete *performance and product evaluation*. (A discussion of the distinction between *performance* and *product* is presented in a later section.)

The term performance test sometimes is used to mean a trade test—a test used to evaluate vocational capabilities of a skilled or semiskilled worker, such as a machinist, bricklayer, or plumber. However, many trade tests are relatively artificial and verbal. The examinee may be asked, for example, to tell what process he would use for a certain job or to name a tool when shown a picture of it. In this kind of trade test, it is assumed that only those who can *perform* the trade have enough trade *knowledge* to pass the test. This assumption is logically parallel to that made in the case of any other verbal test. Hence, it is not appropriate to consider that all trade tests are performance tests. Nor should the concept of performance test be limited to trades or even to vocations.

Many criterion situations are primarily verbal in nature. The writer, the lecturer, even the teacher are aiming at effective verbal performances as major aspects of their vocations; and all of us write letters, explain tax deductions, and order groceries. The fact that a test is verbal or otherwise symbolic on either the stimulus or response side is not necessarily indicative of artificiality. (Nor, on the other hand, are all artificialities verbal.) Thus, some of the tests described in previous chapters and in the next chapter on essay examinations could appropriately be classified as performance tests.

There is no absolute distinction between performance tests and other classes of tests—the performance test is one that is *relatively* realis-

tic. Since performance tests tend to involve special problems and to require decisions and procedures not usually required for conventional tests, it is useful to distinguish the performance test from other classes of tests and write a separate chapter such as this one. However, it should not be supposed that the distinction is necessarily a helpful one for other than expository purposes.

SIMULATION

The idea of *simulation* has been used in defining performance tests. It may prove useful to explore the concept at some length before using it further. Some writers (e.g. Greenlaw, Herron, & Rawdon, 1962) have traced the genesis of the concept to military war games in which imaginary wars have long been fought by two forces in an agreed-upon situation with some real and some artificial elements. A war game might be carried out by two generals and their staffs sitting at their desks and disposing of imaginary troops and supplies on a map of the agreed-upon scene of battle. Or it might be two squads of infantrymen, each firing at the other with blank ammunition. In either case, an umpire supervises the "play" and judges the outcome; that is, decides who won the war.

It is not really necessary in a game that there be more than one player. The opponents can be represented by actors or merely by a set of artificial responses generated in accordance with predetermined rules. Thus, in military and other contexts, there came to be developed more or less elaborate devices representing certain aspects of an endeavor and requiring an individual to perform his role in the endeavor. "Sand tables," or miniature landscapes, were used by military officers to practice various roles. Gunnery practice was possible through the use of motion pictures correlated with the operation of a simulated gunsight. Link trainers and other representations of aircraft were used to train pilots. Not all the early applications of simulation, however, were military. It has long been common, for example, to use a recorded voice in dictating a standard passage to student stenographers.

All these examples are in training contexts. For the most part, simulations and simulation devices have been developed as training aids. However, a good training aid generally contains a capability for measuring and scoring performance. Thus, most simulations also constitute performance tests; although, as Gagné (1962) has pointed out, there is some degree of incompatibility between the requirements for a training device and those for a performance-measuring device.

It has been common to reserve the term *simulator* for the most realistic and elaborate devices and to call lesser machines *trainers* or *training aids*. It is doubtful that such a distinction is useful, especially with respect to performance measurement. It generally is more useful to conceive of various kinds and degrees of simulation, with a given kind and degree being best for a particular situation. To develop this idea, it is necessary to consider the nature of the reality it is desired to simulate.

Reality and Performance Measurement

Consider a continuing adult activity of some social importance. Associated with this activity are stimuli that influence the performance of a participant. Some of the stimuli are directly and intentionally influential—a red light directs the vehicle operator to stop; a drawing is used to tell a carpenter the intended dimensions of a room; the spoken words of the boss are to be translated into shorthand symbols by the stenographer. These direct stimuli may be designated the *displays*.

Other stimuli influence performance indirectly or unintentionally. These stimuli constitute the *surround*. Included are aspects of the physical environment—light, heat, sound, furniture, etc. Also important is the social environment—the number, varieties, and interdependencies of others engaged in related activities.

The performance is a sequence of responses aimed at modifying the environment in specified ways. The effectiveness of the performance may be judged on a number of bases—primarily the appropriateness or relevance, timeliness, accuracy, on the one hand, and, on the other hand, cost of the responses or of the products thereby produced.

If a performance measure is to be interpreted as relevant to "real-life" performance, it must be taken under conditions representative of the stimuli and responses that occur in real life. But each of these can be analyzed into many aspects, and most aspects (e.g. the task assignment, the ambient humidity, the speed of dictation) vary from occasion to occasion. Hence, it would be desirable for the performance measure to be taken a number of times under a wide variety of conditions. These conditions should be representative of those met in practice. Ideally, one should be able to simulate not just a single set of performance conditions but several representative sets.

Fidelity of Simulation

The fidelity of a simulation, its degree of realism, presumably ranges along some scale from complete artificiality to the actual real-life situation. In many cases, it would be possible to develop a rough-and-ready scale on which to express degree of realism, but such a scale would be deficient in at least two respects. First, since usually there is not a single real-life situation but a large variety of situations, the scale would be ambiguous in its anchor point at the high end. Second, fidelity is unlikely to be unidimensional. Any significant real-life situation involves a number of aspects. It therefore will be difficult to decide whether fidelity is greater when aspect A is simulated well and B poorly than it is when A is simulated poorly and B well (assuming one can measure fidelity for each aspect separately).

An example of a test of typewriting performance illustrates this problem of evaluating different dimensions of fidelity between instruments. Two simulated situations are established, identical in all ways except two. In condition X, the passage to be typed consists of literary quotations; in condition Y, the passage is typical of business letters likely to be encountered in the criterion job situation. The typewriter for condition X is an electric machine of the type used on the job; the typewriter for condition Y, a manual. Which is the better simulation and, hence, the better test? Obviously, opinions could legitimately vary about a question like this. This is so, both because it is difficult to judge precisely the degree of fidelity of each condition and because a judgment must be made about the relative importance of simulating the two types of conditions (typewriter vs. passage).

There are two concepts involved here: *comprehensiveness*, or the range of different aspects of the situation that are simulated, and *fidelity*, the degree to which each aspect approximates a fair representation of that aspect in the criterion situation. Highland (1955) has suggested that the combination of these two concepts be called *representativeness*.

Representativeness, Validity, and Reliability

The *validity of a simulation* means the degree to which it is relevant to its purpose. In the case of a performance test, validity is the degree of correspondence between performance on the test and ability to perform the criterion activity. It is often assumed that the perfectly valid test is the one that has complete fidelity and comprehensiveness. And it is further supposed that any reduction in representativeness will be accompanied by a decrease in validity.

It is tempting to conclude that high representativeness of simulation and high test validity are synonymous. However, there are at least two problems with such a conclusion. First, it must be remembered that fidelity is not a unidimensional quality and that a given amount of change in fidelity of one aspect may not have the same effect as a similar change in another aspect. Second, there may often be interactive effects such that a change toward higher fidelity in one aspect is accompanied by a change toward lesser fidelity in another aspect, or an increase in comprehensiveness may be gained at the cost of lower fidelity of certain aspects.

These matters have not been studied sufficiently to provide any precise indication as to whether these problems are likely to be important in any given case. However, a few studies suggest that there is cause for concern. Negative transfer has been reported on learning tasks in which it was thought that the fidelity was reasonably high (Wilcoxon, Davy, & Webster, 1954). Baldwin and Wright (1962) have described a situation in which simulator

"instability" cancelled out any effects of representativeness and made the simulator useless for their purpose. Ruby, Jocoy, and Pelton (1963) have reported two instructive examples: in one case, a simulation was shown to be insensitive to the effects of two conditions known to be different in real-life situations; in the other case, an increase in fidelity of simulation produced no change in the variable representing performance. It is at least risky to assume a simple and invarying relation between fidelity or comprehensiveness and validity.

One further problem in performance tests is that of reliability. It is characteristic of real-life situations that they are difficult to control. The same circumstances do not recur. The observer who wishes, say, to compare the performances of two teachers must immediately confront the facts that they are teaching different subjects to different students in different classrooms (to enumerate only a few differences). Good measurement is possible only when each examinee can be observed under similar circumstances; that is, when it is possible to control and hence standardize the displays, the surround, and the responses on which evaluation of performance will be based. Such control is characteristic of tests and is reflected in the high reliability of measurement that can be achieved with a good test.

But as the test situation simulates reality more closely, control becomes more difficult. It generally would be agreed by those with experience in the matter that the more closely one tries to simulate a real criterion situation, the less reliable will be one's measurement of the performance. The dilemma of simulation is that increasing fidelity and comprehensiveness appear at least in a general way to be associated, on the one hand, with increasing validity but, on the other hand, with decreasing control and thus reliability.

Cost Factors in Simulation

As a general rule, the more faithful and comprehensive simulation costs more than the less faithful and comprehensive one. Costs include not only direct monetary outlays but also such factors as personnel time, facilities, interruption of normal operations, diversion of resources otherwise usable elsewhere, risk of accidents, and management complexity.

Greater degrees of control and hence (normally) of reliability also may be achieved but at some cost. One resolution of the dilemma of simulation is that, if enough monetary and other resources can be invested, the simulation hypothetically can be made both as valid and as reliable as may be desired.

Since unlimited resources are never available, it is necessary in each case to decide how much to spend and how to distribute expenditures. In some cases, an allocation of resources will have been made in advance, and the only question is that of distribution. In general, however, it should be possible to establish some rational basis for deciding upon a level of expenditure. It is by no means necessarily true that there is a single cost that will represent the best "bargain." However, in just about any case, some combinations of cost vs. effectiveness will be better than others.

The Essentials of Good Simulation

The quality of a simulation is a function jointly of the money and resources that can be committed to the simulation task and of the understanding and ingenuity of the developers. Any simulation involves choices and compromises. Four steps may be identified in making those choices and compromises:

1. Determine through careful analysis the critical aspects of the criterion situation it is desired to simulate in view of the purpose of the simulation.

2. Determine the minimum fidelity needed for each aspect and estimate the worth of increasing fidelity beyond the minimum.

3. Develop a scheme for representing a reasonably comprehensive set of aspects, within the limits of available resources.

4. Adjust comprehensiveness and fidelity, compromising as necessary to achieve a balancing of considerations but with primary attention to the aspects shown by analysis to be most critical for the purpose at hand.

Careful analysis of the aims and conditions of the simulation is essential to proper simulation design. Analysis should lead to identification of those aspects of the displays, surround, and responses that are critical in view of the specific purposes of the simulation. Almost invariably, certain aspects need not be simulated, either because (a) they do not vary enough to have effects that can be detected in the measures of performance or (b) variation in these aspects has little effect on the outcomes that are most important. For example, Wilcoxon and Davy (1954) showed that flight performance of student pilots did not vary measurably when motion simulating the effects of rough air was added to two flight simulators. The students believed the rough air feature to be useful and desirable; hence, it was thought that the feature would contribute to student motivation. However, motivation was considered to be only a secondary aim. The rough air feature was rejected on the grounds that any such expensive embellishment should contribute to the primary objective of performance enhancement as well as to motivation. The primary concern in this study was training effectiveness, but similar considerations would apply in evaluating simulation features as to their effect on the adequacy of performance measurement.

The simulation developer's judgment about the relative importance of features will be influenced by his conceptualization of the problem as a whole. For example, suppose the problem is that of developing a test of competence of a television repair man. One investigator might see the repair job as primarily one of removing and replacing defective tubes, capacitors, etc. He then might emphasize the simulation of the tools and workspace available in the usual work situation and probably would suggest the use of an actual television set chassis. Another investigator might conceive of the job as primarily a logical exercise in identifying the defective part or connection through a series of checks. He might then emphasize the simulation of the procedural steps in the search for the defect and see no need for any but the most rudimentary representation of the television set.

In most cases of practical significance, it

will not be feasible to approach at all closely the theoretical limits of simulation fidelity and comprehensiveness. Some compromise will be necessary. The problem is to achieve a proper balance of factors in the simulation, maintaining costs at a level commensurate with the expected benefit while, at the same time, achieving needed accuracy and reliability of measurement.

A test may be viewed as a type of simulation. We have defined a performance test as one in which some criterion situation is simulated with more fidelity and comprehensiveness than in the usual paper-and-pencil test. In the development of a performance test, it may prove useful to use some of the concepts applicable to the development of simulations generally. At any rate, much of the same kind of careful analysis and balancing of considerations is necessary.

TYPES OF TEST SITUATIONS

General situations, or contexts, in which performance tests may be cast are quite variable. No neat scheme has been proposed for classifying test situations; however, it may be useful to describe some types of situations as a means of illustrating the range of choices available in the development of performance tests.

Situational Tests

The term *situational tests* has come to be applied to tests in which the examinee is told to pretend that he is engaged in some real-life task, the nature and context of which is described to him in some detail before he begins to play his assigned role. Usually, the examinee has little or no specific training for the situation he is to face in the test. In many cases, the roles of other persons are played by confederates of the examiner.

Situational tests appear to have attained their current popularity as a result of the publicity given military applications. According to Kelly (1954), the first attempt to develop standardized situational tests was that of Simoneit and his colleagues in the German Army prior to World War II. During the war,

British and then American espionage agencies used such tests in attempts to select and train effective agents. Typically, the test was intended to induce emotional stress and thus to permit evaluation of the examinee's ability to keep calm and work effectively under stress. Studies of the American tests have been described by the OSS Staff (1948).

Later situational tests have not necessarily emphasized emotional factors but have tended rather to focus on simulation of job-relevant situations and abilities. For example, Glaser, Schwarz, and Flanagan (1956) developed tests to assess ability of candidates for jobs as blue-collar supervisors. In one test, the examinee, playing the role of supervisor, was to deal with a personnel problem brought to him by a "subordinate," who was actually an assistant examiner. Though low in estimated reliability, this test was fairly successful in predicting a criterion measure combining several reports of supervisory effectiveness. Another test was a small job management problem. Each examinee was trained to assemble a small mechanical device. He was then to supervise the assembly of such devices by a crew of four inexperienced "workers." This test was considerably less valid than the role-playing situation. However, a similar test has been found to predict salary progress of young managers fairly well (Bray & Grant, 1966).

An example of the use of situational tests to evaluate the outcomes of training is provided by the work of Sivy, Lange, and Jacobs (1952) with the Leaders Reaction Test. This test was used to evaluate leadership skills of Army noncommissioned officers in a leaders' course. Figure 9.1 is an example of the type of score sheet developed by Sivy, Lange, and Jacobs for this test.

Gordon (1967) has described a series of situational tests used with Peace Corps volunteers:

The first task presented S with the problem of building an infirmary on the South Sea Island of Wabowa. He could ask as many questions as he wished regarding the island and its cultures, and was to present a tentative solution to the problem of getting the natives' approval and cooperation in the project. In the second, S was to describe the

CHECK IN SPACE AT RIGHT POINTS COVERED
BY LEADER IN BRIEFING: ( )

BRIEFING	We are going on a reconnaissance patrol.	_____
	We are to get information on possible enemy positions.	_____
	We are to follow the route shown on this map.	_____
	Spoke clearly and distinctly.	_____
WHEN SHOTS ARE FIRED	Continued on mission.	_____
	Remained calm.	_____
WHEN AGGRESSOR SOLDIER IS MET	Posted security.	_____
	Searched aggressor.	_____
	Sent aggressor back to Hq. under guard.	_____
	Continued on mission.	_____

CHECK ONLY IF PLAIN THAT LEADER:

GENERAL	Kept men under control.	_____
	Reacted quickly to situation.	_____
	Gave clear and distinct orders.	_____

CHECK ONLY IF PLAIN THAT LEADER:

FAILURES OF LEADER	Did not give orders distinctly.	_____
	Became rattled and confused.	_____
	Diverted patrol to investigate shots.	_____
	Did not send aggressor back to Hq.	_____
	Failed to search aggressor.	

Number of checks not in boxes _____.   Number of checks in boxes _____.

Score = _____

(Number of checks not in boxes minus number in boxes)

FIG. 9.1. Type of score sheet utilized in Leaders Reaction Test. (Sivy, Lange, & Jacobs, 1952)

system of checks and balances in American government to a "Venezuelan immigrant" role-player, who during the course of the explanation revealed a lack of comprehension of particular points. In the third, S was to assume that he was conversing with a person from another culture who had strong anti-American attitudes, and was to argue both sides in the imagined discussion. In the fourth task, he was to enlist the aid of an "Indian Government official" in establishing a poultry-raising project, the role-player "official" questioning both S's motives in coming to India and his sensitivity to the Indian culture.

The group activities at the field site consisted of a rabbit cookout and the construction of a wooden privy by each group of Ss. At the laboratory site the movie "Mondo Cane" was shown and discussed and a community development proposal was prepared. The Ss were rated by observers during the course of these activities [p. 113].

As these examples suggest, the range of situations has been limited only by the imagina-

tion of the test developers. On the stimulus side, representativeness varies from elaborate replication of the criterion situation to instructions describing a situation in which the examinee is to play a role. The degree and type of response simulation generally are consistent with comparable aspects of the stimulus simulation.

In-Basket Tests

A type of situational test important enough to be discussed separately is the in-basket test. Much of the work on this type of test has been carried out by Frederiksen and his associates at the Educational Testing Service. As Frederiksen (1966) has described it:

An in-basket test is a rather elaborate, realistic situational test intended to simulate certain aspects of the job of an administrator. It consists of the

	Reliability Estimate	Weight
FACTOR A — EXCHANGING INFORMATION		
Asks subordinates for information or opinion	.79	2
Gives information to subordinates	.35	1
FACTOR B — DISCUSSES WITH OTHERS BEFORE DECIDING		
Discusses with subordinates	.86	1
Communicates face to face	.84	1
Arrives at a procedure before deciding	.71	2
FACTOR C — COMPLYING WITH SUGGESTIONS MADE BY OTHERS		
Concluding decision	.95	1
Follows lead by subordinates	.81	2
Terminal action	.91	1
FACTOR D — ANALYZING THE SITUATION		
Uses program values	.80	1
Conceptual analysis	.72	1
FACTOR E — MAINTAINING ORGANIZATIONAL RELATIONSHIPS		
Number of superiors involved	.87	2
Discusses with supervisors or outsiders	.74	1
Number of outsiders involved as individuals	.73	1
Relates to background material	.90	2
FACTOR F — ORGANIZING WORK		
Work scheduled for same or next day	.67	1
Work scheduled for same or next week	.92	1
FACTOR G — RESPONDING TO OUTSIDERS		
Gives information to outsiders	.77	1
Follows lead by outsiders	.95	2
Courtesy to outsiders	.82	1
FACTOR H — DIRECTING THE WORK OF OTHERS		
Leading action	.78	1
Courtesy to subordinates	.97	1
Gives directions or suggestions	.93	1

FIG. 9.2. Police lieutenant in-basket test-scoring form. (Reprinted by permission of Educational Testing Service from *The In-Basket Technique* [ETS, 1961], p. 75.)

letters, memoranda, records of in-coming telephone calls, and other materials that have supposedly collected in the in-basket of an administrative officer. The examinee is given appropriate background information concerning the administrative unit he is supposed to head and appropriate office materials, such as memo pads, letterheads, paper clips, and pencils. He is told that he is the incumbent of the administrative job and that he is to respond to the materials in his in-basket as though he were actually on the job, by writing letters and memoranda, preparing agenda for meetings, writing notes or reminders to himself, or anything else that he deems appropriate [p. 89].

Later applications of the technique have been made to a wide variety of criterion situations, including jobs which are not considered administrative. Hemphill, Griffiths, and Fred-

eriksen (1962) developed an in-basket exercise for elementary school principals. Lopez (1961) used the technique as an aid in selecting police sergeants for promotion to lieutenant, and, also, a number of industrial applications were described by Lopez (1966).

Figure 9.2 shows a set of scoring factors used by Lopez (1961), along with their reliabilities and weights. The choice of these factors was based on factor analyses conducted in a study of business administrators by Frederiksen (1962) and for the most part confirmed by Hemphill, Griffiths, and Frederiksen (1962).

Frederiksen (1966) has conducted a construct validity study by relating in-basket scores of government administrators in his 1962 study to their scores on a number of tests of cognitive abilities, interests, personality, and biographical information. He concluded:

> The relationships reported in this study are, in general, in directions which one might expect on logical or theoretical grounds, and a variety of types of variables, including biographical, are involved. For example, we may call attention to the following relationships:
>
> Those who take many imaginative courses of action tend to have high ability as measured by the *Vocabulary* test ($r = .41$).
>
> Those who write a great deal tend to get high scores on the *active* scale of the [Thurstone Temperament Schedule] ($r = .40$).
>
> Those who plan to have many discussions with subordinates tend to resemble life insurance salesmen in their responses to the [Strong Vocational Interest Blank] ($r = .37$).
>
> Those who frequently give directions and suggestions tend to be of high GS level ($r = .38$).
>
> Those who tend to prepare for action by becoming informed are likely to resemble presidents of manufacturing concerns (loading = .28) rather than policemen (loading = −.34) in their responses to the [Strong Vocational Interest Blank].
>
> Those who tend to procrastinate are likely to be of low educational level (loading = −.33).
>
> Those who tend to supervise work of subordinates are likely to have supervisory duties in their real jobs (loading = .33).
>
> Although none of these variables could reasonably be considered satisfactory as a final criterion for establishing the validity of any in-basket measure . . . , the findings generally contribute to the validation of in-basket scores in the sense that they reveal that a certain amount of consistency is present both in in-basket performance and in the other variables [pp. 107–108].

Bray and Grant (1966) found a median correlation of .22 between in-basket scores and salary progress in their study of young managers. Lopez (1966) described several studies that suggest that moderately valid results have been achieved with in-baskets in industrial settings. More such studies are needed, but it is clear that the in-basket technique is at least a useful research tool and probably has some validity for many evaluation purposes.

Work-Sample Tests

Perhaps the most common, if least commonly standardized, type of test is the work sample. The "boss" tells the examinee to perform a job-relevant task and assesses performance by observing either process or product. Thus are many semiskilled workers selected and evaluated, especially in less literate cultures.

The work sample could be considered a type of situational test. However in contrast to the usual situational test, the work-sample test normally employs an actual job situation for which the examinee is expected to have had the necessary training and experience.

Though relatively few work-sample tests are standardized, some of the earliest performance tests grew out of attempts to standardize work samples. Not as early as some, but typical in many ways, were the studies of Tiffin and Greenly (1939). In attempting to identify competent punch-press operators, employers often had used informal work samples. Tiffin and Greenly set out to design a standard simulated situation and uniform scoring procedures. Their approach to simulation was the use of a miniature punch press, which was much more convenient for testing than an actual press but required many of the same skills to operate. One indication of the adequacy of the simulation was that their tests could distinguish between groups of operators with and without prior experience operating a punch press.

A more recent and perhaps more typical example of a work-sample test is found in the work of McNamara and Hughes (1955). As a criterion measure of proficiency of card-punch operators, they used a numerical grade based on speed and accuracy scores in four half-hour sessions of actual operation of the card-punch machine.

It is frequently appropriate in a work-sample test to introduce certain difficulties or defects that the examinee is to overcome or repair. For example, Wilson and Mackie (1952) inserted open and short circuits at various points in sets of sound-powered telephones. The examinees, who were Navy electrician's mates, were to find the defects and choose proper repair methods.

Many tests in commercial education, industrial arts, vehicle operator training, and similar settings are of the work-sample type. Several of these are discussed in later sections.

Games

The history of games as tests is a long one. Pennington (1961) has described the evolution of the modern war game:

In 1811 Von Reisswitz transferred the War Game from a chess board to a sandtable. The terrain was modeled in sand with blocks of wood representing troops. Later an "improved" model substituted a plaster model and included woods, trees, villages, etc. . . . . .

Further modifications on the Von Reisswitz game were made by his son including using a map instead of a sandtable and writing a set of rules for playing the game. Kaiser Wilhelm II ordered the game be adopted by the German Army. One can now predict what would happen. As time progressed more elaborate rules for the conduct of the game were written, intricate calculations were required and umpires to run the game as well as "improvement," i.e., more detail in the representation of terrain and gathering statistics from past wars to predict the outcome of an engagement [p. 3].

Other than war games, the only common games in education are related to business management. Many management games are of such comprehensiveness and fidelity that electronic computers are required to provide information about the consequences of the actions of the players. Figure 9.3 illustrates some of this complexity in a relatively simple game, played by means of a computer called ASCOT (Analogue Simulation of Competitive Operational Tactics). Some excerpts from the manual for this game, as quoted by Robinson (1961), are:

This business exercise is designed to portray the operation of up to five competing neighborhood service stations in a local trading area. They are located relatively close to each other so that the operation of each station affects all the others. Certain important assumptions and relationships are built into this competitive business exercise. How-

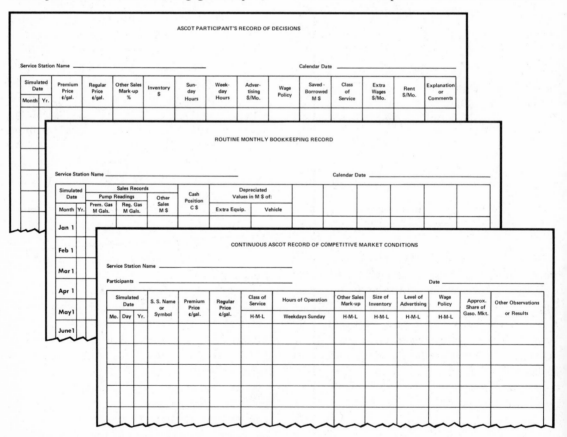

FIG. 9.3. Forms used in the ASCOT game. (From *Management Games* by Joel M. Kibbee, Clifford J. Craft, and Burt Nanus. Copyright © 1961 by Reinhold Publishing Corporation, by permission of Van Nostrand Reinhold Company.)

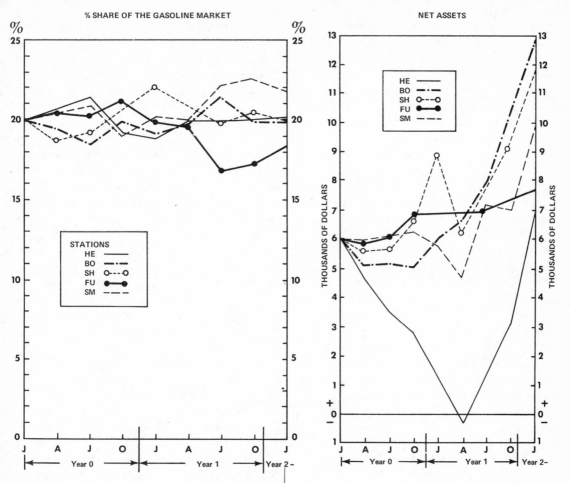

% SHARE OF THE GASOLINE MARKET

NET ASSETS

STATIONS
HE ———
BO —·—·
SH O---O
FU ●—●
SM — — —

Fɪɢ. 9.4. Sample ASCOT game outcomes. (From *Management Games* by Joel M. Kibbee, Clifford J. Craft, and Burt Nanus. Copyright © 1961 by Reinhold Publishing Corporation, by permission of Van Nostrand Reinhold Company.)

ever these are only relatively simple, natural effects and are not as important to participants' success or failure as are the moves and counter-moves of their competitors versus their own tactics. To illustrate this: a method of operation which is highly successful on one occasion might later (under different conditions) prove only fair. This could be a result of different tactics influenced by competition, not of any change in the rules of the game.

ASCOT is a special-purpose computer, consisting of five station units and a master console, which continuously calculates and displays the sales and profits resulting from all the participants' decisions. Participants set their decisions on their station consoles and read the results on dials (like actual gasoline-pump or cash-register readings). The master console is under the control of the umpires who may introduce periodic changes in operating and business conditions for added realism [p. 260].

In this game, competition from other players is important. However, as has been pointed out, there is no reason in principle that the other players could not be simulated by the computer. In order for the game to be effective as a performance test, this would be highly desirable. Figure 9.4 shows sample results of play by five players. Note that, although the player representing station HE maintained a reasonable share of the market, his assets underwent a severe decline. This decline was overcome through liberal financial support and an umpire role-playing the part of a company sales representative working with him.

A problem in the design of games is whether the outcome of a specified action by the examinee should be fully determined in advance or should have a probabilistic component. A purely deterministic approach would mean that a particular choice of action by a player—say, spending $1,000 to advertise his gas station in the local newspaper—would result each time in a specified increment of sales. In a probabilistic approach, on the other hand, the outcome would vary on a random basis according to some predetermined distribution of likely outcomes. Sometimes, advertising might bring in a lot of business and on other occasions it would result in little or no extra sales. The probabilistic approach is more faithful to real life, but it introduces an element of luck that is incompatible with the objectives of most tests. Hence, it seems undesirable. However, without the probabilistic aspect, many games would be highly limited as simulations. The authors of MATRIX, an interesting combination of in-basket and primarily nonprobabilistic game, point out that this game is not suitable for administration to the same examinee twice, since he will have become aware of many of the contingent outcomes that constitute the point of the game (Plattner & Herron, 1963).

Projects, Contests, and Rehearsed Performances

Special projects often are assigned by teachers for students to complete, usually out of class. Many such projects can be conceived as performance tests, and it may often be useful if the teacher so conceives them.

Science fairs and art contests are project-type activities that are frequently well organized and carefully judged. However, the evaluation of a project is made difficult by the fact that each student is usually doing a quite different project. Not only is it hard to compare the relative merits of the projects in general, but it is difficult to decide what the general bases for evaluation should be. For example, what relative weight should be assigned to the matter of originality and appropriateness in the selection of a project topic? Should neatness and sturdiness of the project presentation or exhibit be considered important? Both the students and the judges should be told about these matters in advance. An example of in-

structions to the student competitors in a science fair is shown in figure 9.5. It would be desirable to state the criteria for judging projects in even more detail than this.

In music, drama, and related disciplines, it is common for the student to be evaluated on the basis of his rendition of a specified work, normally one that is not original with the student and one that he has rehearsed specifically with the performance in view. The rehearsals may or may not have been supervised, and preliminary evaluations may or may not have been carried out in the course of rehearsals. In drama or an ensemble work in music, it is often necessary that more than one student perform at the same time. Sometimes, it is possible for faculty members or other polished performers to act as the other members of the ensemble, so that distracting errors by the student's fellow players are less likely.

Diagnostic Problem-Solving Tests

There is a type of test, which is not entirely comparable with the other types enumerated here, that deserves mention because it simulates certain contingent aspects of the criterion situation that are not usually thought amenable to controlled simulation. In any work sample that involves a problem to be solved, it is necessary to decide what information is needed to help solve the problem. If obtaining the information is time consuming or otherwise costly, it becomes important to obtain only the information really needed. Performance tests have frequently been designed to provide superfluous information and thus to test the examinee's ability to reject irrelevant information, but they have not often tested skill in choosing the necessary items of information.

An innovative approach to this problem was proposed in the Tab Item by Glaser, Damrin, and Gardner (1952). The Tab Item contains descriptions of checks a repairman might wish to make in diagnosis of a specified malfunction, along with a simulated indication of the result of each check. Figure 9.6 shows a sample set of items. In the original Tab test, the material shown in boxes was covered by perforated tabs that could be pulled out or torn off the page. In later versions,

STANDARDS FOR JUDGING

The following four criteria receive equal consideration from the judges:

Scientific Method of Thinking: Ideas logically organized, well-planned, complete and concise story, thorough and accurate research, evidence that student knows the subject thoroughly.

Effective, Dramatic Presentation of Scientific Truths: Idea of exhibit should be clearly and dramatically conveyed. Explanatory lettering should be large, neat, brief.

Creative Ability: Exhibit should be original in plan and execution. Clever use of salvage materials is important. New applications of scientific ideas are best of all.

Technical Skills: Workmanship, craftsmanship, rugged construction, neatness, safety, lettering, etc.

Hints For Winning

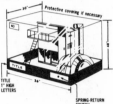

SAMPLE EXHIBIT: (Note: All exhibits will not look like this, of course. This is just to illustrate and emphasize maximum size and title placement. Don't build your exhibit larger!)

These are just a few of the specific things the judges will be looking for in your Fair exhibit:

1. TELL A STORY and keep it brief! Plan your labels carefully, make lettering neat and large.

2. NEATNESS is essential. A sloppy, shoddy exhibit will be disqualified.

3. STURDINESS: The judges will take into account the fact that your exhibit must stand up for four weeks of rugged use by visitors. Use heavy-duty materials like wire, metals, screws—not balsa wood, tape, glue. **The Planetarium is positively not responsible for loss or damage to exhibits.** *Protect your property with glass, screen, or plexiglas.*

4. COMMERCIAL EXHIBITS, or exhibits *predominantly* using man-ufactured parts, are almost never winners. Don't assemble kits!

5. INGENUITY: Use a creative approach! This is *most* important! It means two things: clever use of salvage materials—and new ways of ex-pressing, dramatizing or applying scientific principles. Be original!

6. RULES: Above all, keep your own copy of this Handbook nearby for frequent reference. Read it carefully. Don't spend months on a fine ex-hibit only to find it disqualified at the last minute because of an avoidable infraction of the rules.

FIG. 9.5. Extract from the instructions to students in a science fair. (Buhl Planetarium and Institute of Popular Science, 1968, p. 8.)

chemical coatings that can be removed by rubbing with a pencil eraser have been used. Thus, the examinee can get the results of as many or as few of the checks as he thinks necessary, but he has been told that his score will be diminished if he pulls more tabs than necessary.

This ingenious idea has been adapted and expanded upon in other contexts, particularly by McGuire and her co-workers in measuring the diagnostic skills of physicians and medical students (as reported in McGuire & Babbott, 1967). Included in what these investigators called *simulation exercises* were various highly realistic results of blood tests, X rays, and other diagnostic measures, along with indica-

tions of the responses of the patient to the treatment prescribed by the examinee. In describing requirements for a useful test of this nature, McGuire and Babbott (1967) noted:

A clinical problem which purports to simulate the physician-patient encounter must have the following characteristics: First, it must be initiated by information of the type a patient gives a physician, not by a predigested summary of the salient features of the case, and if it is to be realistic it must be couched in terms the patient or a referring physician would use. Second, the exercise must require a series of sequential, interdependent decisions representing the various stages in the diagnostic work-up and management of the patient. Third, the examinee must be able to obtain in realistic form information about the results of each decision, as a basis for subsequent action. Fourth,

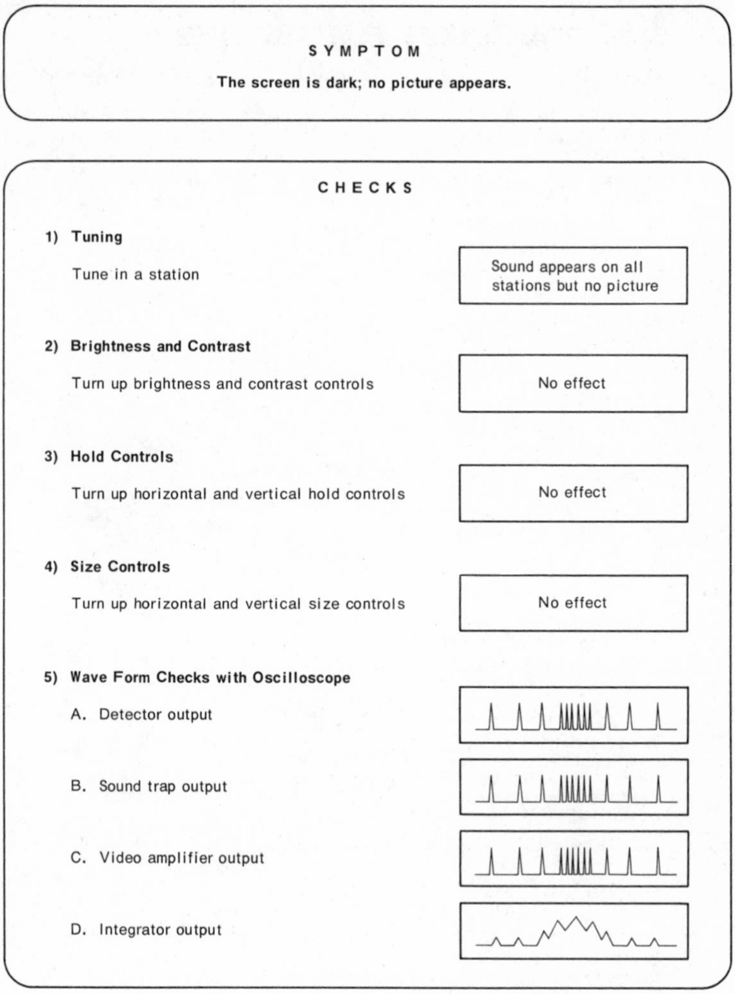

```
┌──────────────────────────────────────────────────────────┐
│                         SYMPTOM                            │
│              The screen is dark; no picture appears.       │
└──────────────────────────────────────────────────────────┘
```

```
┌──────────────────────────────────────────────────────────┐
│                          CHECKS                            │
│                                                            │
│  1)  Tuning                                                │
│                                          ┌──────────────┐  │
│       Tune in a station                  │Sound appears on all│
│                                          │stations but no picture│
│                                          └──────────────┘  │
│                                                            │
│  2)  Brightness and Contrast                               │
│                                          ┌──────────────┐  │
│       Turn up brightness and contrast controls │ No effect │  │
│                                          └──────────────┘  │
│                                                            │
│  3)  Hold Controls                                         │
│                                          ┌──────────────┐  │
│       Turn up horizontal and vertical hold controls │No effect│ │
│                                          └──────────────┘  │
│                                                            │
│  4)  Size Controls                                         │
│                                          ┌──────────────┐  │
│       Turn up horizontal and vertical size controls │No effect│ │
│                                          └──────────────┘  │
│                                                            │
│  5)  Wave Form Checks with Oscilloscope                    │
│                                                            │
│       A.  Detector output                                  │
│                                                            │
│       B.  Sound trap output                                │
│                                                            │
│       C.  Video amplifier output                           │
│                                                            │
│       D.  Integrator output                                │
└──────────────────────────────────────────────────────────┘
```

FIG. 9.6. Example of tab items in television repair. (Glaser, Damrin, & Gardner, 1952, p. 10.)

once these data are obtained, it must be impossible for the examinee to retract a decision that is revealed to be ineffectual or harmful. Fifth, the problem must be constructed so as to allow both for different medical approaches and for variation in patient responses appropriate to these several approaches. Hence, provision must be made for modifications in the problem as the patient responds to the specific interventions chosen by each examinee. Finally these modifications must differ among examinees, according to the unique configuration of prior decisions each has made [pp. 1–2].

With a test of this sort, there are so many alternatives branching out at each step that it is rare for two examinees to be faced with exactly the same set of contingencies. However, McGuire and Babbott have obtained adequate reliabilities in scoring such tests and have shown that experienced physicians perform better on them than do senior medical students.

APPLICATIONS OF PERFORMANCE TESTING

In principle, a performance test could be developed for any criterion situation. In practice, the use of performance tests has tended to be limited to evaluation of skills related to certain occupations. The following sections list some of the occupations and other activities for which performance tests have been developed.

Secretarial

Tests in Print (Buros, 1961) lists 18 published tests in stenography and 14 in type-

THE SEASHORE-BENNETT STENOGRAPHIC PROFICIENCY TEST

SUMMARY CHART

NAME_____ DATE_____

Tested with Form B-1_____   Total Score_____
           Form B-2_____

PENALTIES FOR EACH LETTER

	LETTERS				
	1	2	3	4	5
TYPING 1. Neatness and cleanness					
2. Arrangement					
3. Quality of stroke					
4. Errors					
ENGLISH 5. Errors					
SHORTHAND 6. Errors					
Maximum Score	20	20	20	20	20
Sum of penalties					
LETTER SCORE (20 minus sum of penalties)					

MAKE A CHECK IN THE PROPER BOX IF ANY OF THE POINTS BELOW APPLIES

A. Scoring stopped — over 20 penalties					
B. Incomplete — not scored					
C. Too mixed up to score					
D. Letter not attempted					

SUMMARY

Signed_____

FIG. 9.7. Summary scoring chart for the Seashore-Bennett test. (Reprinted by permission of The Psychological Corporation from *The Seashore-Bennett Stenographic Proficiency Tests* [Copyright by Psychological Corporation, 1956], p. 7. All rights reserved.)

writing. Of these, it appears that 13 of each are work samples. Several of these tests are arranged in series, each incorporating several levels of skill. One of the better tests is the Seashore-Bennett Stenographic Proficiency Test (Seashore & Bennett, 1948). A "typical business voice" dictates five commercial letters—two short and slow, one long and rapid, two intermediate in length and speed—on a tape or record. The dictation lasts 15 minutes and examinees are then given half an hour to transcribe their shorthand notes. (Scoring procedures are summarized in figure 9.7.) Of course, it is possible (in fact, it is common practice) for each company or office to develop its own stenographic test. The advantages would be those associated with closer simulation of the actual work context. But the Sea-shore-Bennett has advantages in careful standardization and extensive norms. And the Seashore-Bennett has been shown to be related to other measures of secretarial ability. For example, one study showed it to be related (correlations ranged from .59 to .85) to supervisory judgments of job performance a year later (Bender & Loveless, 1958).

Language

Proficiency in speaking, writing, or understanding a foreign language often is assessed informally by eliciting a performance or product sample. For example, the examiner may simply ask some more or less complex questions in the language. The examinee may be required to answer in the language or may be allowed to use his native language.

Standardized tests usually have been of the multiple-choice type, but recently there have been developments in the direction of improved simulation of criterion situations related to educational objectives. An example is the series of tests called the MLA Foreign Language Proficiency Tests for Teachers and Advanced Students, developed by the Modern Language Association of America and the Educational Testing Service. For each language (French, German, Italian, Russian, and Spanish), there are six tests. Listening Comprehension is presented first by tape recording of questions or statements in the language, then by multiple-choice questions (also in the language) about the passage. In the Speaking test the examinee speaks into a tape recorder and his productions are scored by judges on the basis of detailed instructions; reliability of scoring is reported to be .89. The Writing test calls for insertion of appropriate words in blank spaces of text and editing of poorly written passages in the language. Other tests of Reading Comprehension, Applied Linguistics, and Civilization and Culture are relatively conventional.

Vehicle Operation

Road tests are used in most jurisdictions as part of the examinations for automobile driver's licenses. These have been reviewed by McGlade (1960). The course to be driven may be a standardized, but relatively artificial, layout or an actual route through streets carrying normal, but varying, traffic. The former type of course is probably preferable, unless it can be shown that in actual traffic examinees perform in ways more representative of their normal driving habits. Performance in driving tests usually is evaluated by means of a check list. Part of one such check list is reproduced in figure 9.8.

Art

Drawings or paintings are, of course, frequently evaluated informally. A few standardized tests, such as the Knauber Art Ability Test, have been developed with aims of providing both standard stimuli or instructions to elicit the drawing and standard procedures for evaluating the product. In one study (Skager,

Klein, & Schultz, 1967), students were assigned drawing problems and discussed the implications of each problem during a class period. A typical problem involved a drawing of outdoor subject matter, such as buildings or natural terrain, with selection of specific content left up to the student. Each of several judges, working alone, then rated each drawing for esthetic quality in one of seven categories. The reliabilities of these ratings ranged from .62 to .81 with three to six judges. There was little correlation between these ratings and other indices of success in art, such as grade point average at the school of design where the study was carried out. The authors (Skager et al., 1967) reported that better results have been achieved elsewhere; nevertheless, there is doubtless much room for improvement in testing for artistic performance.

Music

It is common practice in music education for experts to judge the quality of musical production in auditions, contests, and more informal settings. Most standardized tests of musical achievement are not aimed at the ultimate criterion performance but at certain intermediate skills and knowledges. The Aliferis-Stecklein Music Achievement Tests (published by the University of Minnesota Press), for example, provide subscores on melody, harmony, and rhythm at the college-entrance level and on melodic interval, chord, and rhythm at the college-midpoint level. The task of the examinee is to listen to a number of short piano renditions and match each one with the appropriate musical notation in the test booklet. Thus, the simulation is generally faithful but representative of only criterion situations involving listening to music (as would a conductor or composer) rather than producing it (as would a performing artist).

Industrial Arts

Industrial arts instruction typically makes extensive use of assigned projects, the results of which are evaluated. A well-designed project of this sort is described in figure 9.9. Note that the instructions are explicit and fairly complete. If

ROAD TEST CHECK LIST

FOR

TESTING, SELECTING, RATING AND TRAINING TRUCK DRIVERS

by Amos E. Neyhart

Consultant on Driver Education, American Automobile Association, and
Administrative Head, Institute of Public Safety, University Park, Pa.

**Copyright, 1955, by and available from the American Automobile Association,
Washington, D. C., and Institute of Public Safety, University Park, Pa.**

Name_____ Age_____ Checked By_____

Street and Number_____

City and State_____ Date_____

Time of Test - Beginning_____ Ending_____ Elapsed Time_____

Odometer Reading - Start_____ Finish_____ Miles Traveled_____

FINAL SCORE (Sum of Parts I and II)_____ Final Letter Grade_____

PART I - SPECIFIC

ITEM	DEDUCT	CHECK (√) ITEMS MISSED BY DRIVER	DEDUCTIONS
I. CHECKING THE DRIVER			
A. Fails to enter vehicle from curb side — when practical	2	☐	
B. Fails to check doors to see if closed properly	2	☐	
C. Fails to adjust windows for ventilation	2	☐	
D. Fails to adjust rear-view mirrors	3	☐	
E. Fails to adjust seat properly	1	☐	
F. Fails to assume erect and alert driving position	1	☐	
II. STARTING ENGINE			
A. Fails to depress clutch pedal	1	☐☐☐☐☐☐☐	
B. Does not check gearshift lever for neutral position	2	☐☐☐☐☐☐☐	
C. Fails to turn on ignition switch before pressing starter button	1	☐☐☐☐☐☐☐	
D. Does not release starter button as soon as engine starts to operate on its own power	2	☐☐☐☐☐☐☐	
E. Spends too much time trying to get engine to run, fails to use choke properly	1	☐☐☐☐☐☐☐	
F. Does not allow engine to warm up	5	☐☐☐☐☐☐☐	
G. Races engine during warm-up period	5	☐☐☐☐☐☐☐	
H. Fails to check air pressure	5	☐☐☐☐☐☐☐	
III. STARTING THE VEHICLE IN LOW			
A. Fails to check traffic conditions	5	☐☐☐☐☐☐☐	
B. Selects wrong gear (does not start in low)	3	☐☐☐☐☐☐☐	

FIG. 9.8. A check list for evaluation of vehicle operators. (Reprinted by permission of the American Automobile Association from A. E. Neyhart, *Road Test Check List for Testing, Selecting, Rating and Training Truck Drivers.* Copyright 1955 by AAA.)

this test were to be used in more than one classroom, it would be desirable to include information telling the examinees how it is scored.

Agriculture

Many agricultural products are readily measured. It is common in agricultural education to use product measures in evaluation of student progress. A typical listing of such measures is (adapted from Phipps, 1952, p. 322):

1. Average no. of animals
2. Lbs. beef per cow
3. Lbs. milk per cow
4. Height and weight of heifer at 6 mos.
5. Height and weight of heifer at 12 mos.
6. Height and weight of heifer at 18 mos.
7. Lbs. feed to produce 100 lbs. milk
8. Lbs. feed to raise a heifer to 12 mos.
9. Returns per $100 feed fed
10. Cost of producing 100 lbs. milk
11. Hours of labor per cow
12. Hours of labor per heifer
13. Labor and management earnings.

The measures are highly objective and reliable. However, often there may be questions about the degree to which they reflect factors other than the skill of the student, such as the initial quality of the animals and plants involved and the general hospitality of the soil and climate to the type of farming involved.

Sports and Physical Fitness

Physical educators have used performance tests extensively. Many swimming and track and field events are directly performance tests.

SAMPLE PRACTICAL TEST-WROUGHT METAL

Name _____   Class _____   Date _____

1. Compute the material necessary for the Shelf Bracket below. Complete the Bill of Materials by filling in the blank spaces.

2. Select the proper stock from the rack and cut to length. File the rough ends smooth and square.

3. Using the drawing below as the pattern, form and fit the parts of the shelf bracket together.

4. Spot weld all the parts together.

5. Locate and drill two 1/8 inch diameter holes in the center of the back brace as indicated on the drawing.

6. Clean and present for marking.

7. Time started _____ Time completed _____ Total time _____

Tools and Materials: _____

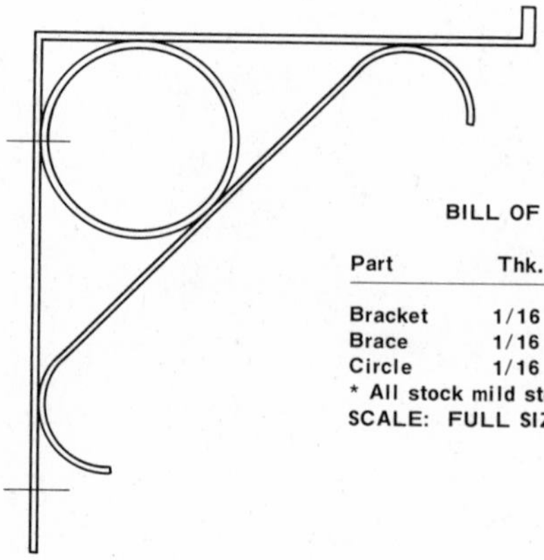

_____

_____

BILL OF MATERIALS

Part	Thk.	Wdth.	Lngth.
Bracket	1/16	3/8	_____
Brace	1/16	3/8	_____
Circle	1/16	3/8	_____

* All stock mild steel.
SCALE: FULL SIZE

FIG. 9.9. Instructions for a performance test in metalworking. (Reprinted by permission of the Board of Education of the City of New York from *Industrial Arts Metalworking in the Secondary Schools: First Year* [the Board, 1967], p. 158.)

The nature of the competition cannot be sufficiently controlled in most other sports to permit easy interpretation of individual performance. Hence, a number of tests have been developed to evaluate skill in specific aspects of various sports. An example is a badminton test in which the examinee attempts to volley the shuttlecock against a specified area of a wall as many times as he can in a specified time (F. A. Miller, 1951). Wilson (1966) found this test to correlate .63 with a test of badminton knowledge and .43 with a judgment of ability based on an interview.

A related area of evaluation is that of physical fitness. A problem in this area has been one of achieving comprehensiveness with a minimum number of different tests and with facilities likely to be generally available. Fleishman (1964) attacked this problem through a series of factor analytic studies. He identified nine relatively independent aspects of physical fitness and has proposed 10 tests to measure them. He was able to show that certain traditional tests are not helpful in assessing physical fitness, either because they are unreliable or because they are only weakly associated with any major factor of fitness. He also found that it is important to describe each test and its scoring in detail, since many unwanted variations otherwise will appear. An example of his test descriptions is shown in figure 9.10.

Test Instructions

PULL-UPS

Testing Arrangements:

All that is needed is a horizontal metal or wooden bar, approximately 1½ inches in diameter, and high enough so the student can hang off the floor with his arms and legs fully extended.

Instructions:

The student jumps up and grips the bar with his palms facing his body (the *underhand* grip). From his hanging position, at the signal "Start," he pulls himself up by his arms until he can place his own chin over the bar. He then lowers his body to a fully extended position.

The student is told to do as many pull-ups as possible and not to stop until he is no longer able to pull himself up. He is told not to pause more than two seconds, either at the top or bottom of each cycle, otherwise he will be told to stop. He is cautioned that if his arms are not fully extended or his chin not over the bar, he will be penalized.

The examiner counts the number of pull-ups aloud to the student each time he lowers himself fully. If he is to be penalized the examiner indicates credit for only "one half" to let the student know this.

Demonstrate, one correct pull-up. Kicking, twisting, or raising of legs should not be allowed. If the student starts swaying, the examiner should put his palm or forearm against the student's legs to stop the swaying.

Scoring:

Record the number of times the student has pulled himself up correctly.

FIG. 9.10. Instructions for a test of physical fitness. (Reprinted by permission of Prentice-Hall, Inc. from E. A. Fleishman, *The Structure and Measurement of Physical Fitness* [Prentice-Hall, 1964], p. 167.)

DEVELOPING PERFORMANCE TESTS

Since performance and product evaluation is essentially the same as any other type of evaluation, the same principles and concepts apply to the development of these tests as to any other type of test; that is, much of what is discussed in the other chapters of this book is applicable. The following sections are devoted to discussing certain problems which become more severe in performance test development.

Studying Objectives

In the development of any test, it is of first importance to define carefully the objectives of measurement. In most cases, these follow directly from the educational objectives. Educational objectives specify the attainment of a given level of capability in certain criterion performances. (These matters are discussed in chapters 2 and 3.) When performance testing is appropriate, it is often necessary to have more than the usual amount of information about the criterion performances. This is so because it is necessary, in a performance test simulation of even moderately high fidelity and comprehensiveness, to know quite specifically what is to be simulated. For example, in a conventional

Step No.	Initiating Condition	Response Description	Terminating Condition	Conditional Referral	Probable Deficiencies	Critical Criteria	Contributing Requisites
1.	thermometer in holder	removes thermometer from holder	thermometer in hand	—	—	—	—
2.	thermometer in hand	wipes thermometer with fresh wipe	thermometer dry	—	—	—	—
3.	thermometer dry	grasps thermometer at non-bulb end	thermometer between thumb and fingers	—	—	—	—
4.	thermometer between thumb and fingers	shakes down thermometer by flicking wrist	completion of several shakes	—	drops thermometer	does not continue step overly long	—
5.	completion of several shakes	reads position of mercury in thermometer	confidence in reading	a. if less than 35°C, go on to step 6. b. if 35°C or higher, return to step 3.	inaccurate reading	—	—
6.	confident reading is less than 35°C	inserts bulb end of thermometer in patient's mouth under tongue	thermometer correctly positioned	—	causes patient discomfort	—	—
7.	thermometer correctly positioned	waits three minutes	end of three minutes	—	—	—	—
8.	end of three minutes	removes thermometer from patient's mouth	thermometer in hand	—	—	—	—
9.	thermometer in hand	reads position of mercury in thermometer	confidence in reading	—	inaccurate reading	reads to accuracy of .1°C	knowledge of appropriate expected temperature
10.	confidence in reading	replaces thermometer in holder	thermometer in holder	—	—	—	—
11.	thermometer in holder	records patient's temperature on reminder sheet	patient's temperature recorded	—	inaccurate recording	—	—

FIG. 9.11. Task analysis worksheet for taking oral temperature. (Klaus, Gosnell, Chowla, & Reilly, 1968, pp. 8–9.)

test of electronic troubleshooting, it would normally be sufficient to specify that a particular voltage is to be, say, 125. But suppose that in a performance test this voltage is to be displayed on an actual meter and it is found that the meter reading varies from 124 to 126 when a voltage of 125 is applied. Then it is necessary to consider whether the displayed voltage can be allowed to vary this much without invalidating the problem.

The more closely the criterion performance is to be simulated, the more information is needed. Information is needed about the actions or performances required, about the cues or appropriate stimuli for each action, about the environmental and social conditions under which various situations occur, and about the appearance and functioning of equipment that is met within the course of the activity.

The techniques of task analysis (R.B. Miller, 1962, 1963) are frequently useful. An excerpt from a task analysis is shown in figure 9.11. The exact format and content of task analyses vary widely according to the specific purposes of the analyst (Snyder, 1960). It is essential, however, that three aspects of each task and subtask be specified: (a) the stimuli (both displays and surround) or initiating condition, (b) the action or response, and (c) the terminating condition or indication by which the performer may know that his action has been completed properly.

The level of specificity of analysis may be made as fine as desired and may, but usually does not, approach the elemental analysis of time and motion studies.

The task analysis should pay particular attention to contingencies; that is, circumstances under which the individual must or should deviate from the "normal" procedures. If the job is at all complex, the possible varieties of contingencies will be infinite. Hence, it is necessary to deal with classes of contingencies. One method of contingency analysis begins with identification of the display indications that may signal an abnormal condition. The analyst then identifies other displays that may or should be observed in order to verify the condition, to diagnose the cause of the condition, and to identify related conditions (as, for example, when an overheated apparatus catches fire). Actions that the performer may take are identified separately. A summary matrix is used to show which actions may ensue from each observation and which observations may lead to each action. Finally, the analyst attempts to specify the conditions under which each action task should be carried out (Fitzpatrick, 1964).

It is necessary also to specify the relative importance of the various aspects of the activity. Certain tasks are likely to be judged more important than others; for example, it is usually considered more important for a secretary to be able to type than to file, though both skills may be of considerable importance. Certain criteria of task achievement may be more important than others; for example, typing speed may in certain situations be considered less important than typing accuracy. In many cases, minimum necessary standards can rationally be set, and these may combine more than one criterion dimension; for example, at least 60 words per minute with no more than an average of two errors.

There are various means of collecting the information necessary for detailed and comprehensive task description. These are generally the same as those that are appropriate for job analysis (see, for example, Tiffin & McCormick, 1965, pp. 60 ff.). Most methods involve either observing the activity, reading about it, or interviewing people who have experience with it. A technique that in many cases may be useful is the critical incident technique (Flanagan, 1954). In this technique, people with appropriate experience in the activity are asked to describe specific occasions when individuals have done something that was either especially effective or especially ineffective in achieving the aims of the activity. For example, Fine, Malfetti, and Shoben (1965) collected more than 2,000 incidents of "good" and "bad" driver behavior as a basis for developing the Columbia Driver Judgment Test.

The results of task analysis (or whatever alternative means of analysis is used) provide the test developer with a comprehensive description of the overall criterion situation. However, the measurement objectives are not necessarily so comprehensive. A particular course of training may not have been designed to cover the whole criterion situation. For example, a course in drafting might be designed to develop skill only in drawing two-dimensional projections and not in depicting objects in proper three-dimensional perspective as might be required in some jobs. Or, the test may be given before the students have completed the entire course of study. Hence, the measurement objectives must be made appropriate to the context in which the test will be applied.

A properly stated objective defines a class of performances of which the student-examinee is to be capable after the prescribed study and practice. It also specifies the conditions under which the performance is to be demonstrated and defines the criteria for success. Thus, in order to prepare objectives, it is necessary to consider both the conditions for testing and the aspects of performance that will be taken into account in evaluating the performance.

Finally, of course, the measurement objectives must depend upon the purposes of testing; that is, upon the uses to which the test results may be put. Measurement objectives associated with a given criterion situation might be considerably different if the purpose is prediction of educational outcomes (chapter 11), improvement of learning and instruction (chapter 17), student planning and guidance (chapter 18), selection and placement (chapter 19), or assessment and evaluation of educational programs (chapter 20).

Formulating the Test Concept

Given that the study of objectives has shown that the measuring instrument should have some of the characteristics of a performance test, many questions about the nature of the test still remain. It is important that systematic means be used to guide the decisions made in developing the test. A general description of all important characteristics of the proposed test should first be prepared; that is, an overall blueprint of the test. The matters to be covered in this description are those covered in the remaining sections of this chapter. Since these matters are interdependent, some integrative concept must be formulated to coordinate the effort. As was pointed out in the discussion of simulation, the test developer's concept of the test will affect all the decisions he makes in developing it.

Test Content

The study of objectives should have identified the relevant subject matter about which the test is to be concerned. If the criterion performance is at all complex, however, it will not be feasible to include all of it in the test.

If the criterion performance reasonably can be viewed as consisting of an aggregation of a large number of task or skill elements, one could simply enumerate the elements and choose at random for the test as many elements as necessary or feasible. However, the elements normally are not easy to specify in comparable form. For example, one might say that the elements of the job of a piano student are the productions of certain notes and chords; but the music teacher would object that what is really essential is the sequential production with due concern for rhythm, emphasis, and other qualities, the proper values of which are dependent on each selection or arrangement to be played. Hence, the usual solution is to have the student demonstrate his skill by playing a selection considered appropriate to his level of training. Thus, Brahms's *Lullaby* might afford

the beginner an opportunity to apply all the skills he has learned but would perhaps not be sufficiently representative of the range of skills of a concert pianist.

The sampling problem, then, is often one of finding a few tasks or other definable units of activity that will require display of a reasonable variety of the abilities in question. This problem has been analyzed in a slightly different context by Lennon (1956), who has suggested that its solution rests on the reasonableness of at least three assumptions:

1. The area of concern to the tester can be conceived as a meaningful, definable universe of responses.

2. A sample can be drawn from this universe in some purposive, meaningful fashion.

3. The sample and the sampling process can be defined with sufficient precision to enable the test user to judge how adequately performance on the sample typifies performance on the universe [p. 298].

It is generally the best practice to include in the test several short tasks rather than one or two relatively long ones. Better comprehensiveness of coverage usually will be achieved in this way. Reliability of measurement also may be enhanced. Furthermore, this practice minimizes the likelihood that some examinees will have undue advantages in that they practiced a test task beforehand, either coincidentally or as a result of prior knowledge of the test content. However, the tasks chosen must be substantial enough to cover the important skills and to permit adequate simulation. Also, consideration should be given to efficiency in the use of testing time. If too much time is devoted to starting, stopping, and explaining the next part of the test, many of the advantages of using multiple tasks will be lost.

In choosing or developing test tasks, it is desirable to achieve variety of content and context, within the classes of tasks relevant to the objectives. Unless reliability of measurement is unusually low, there is no point in having the examinee repeat the same task performance. However, it should be recognized that tasks that seem on superficial analysis to be similar may require quite different skills. For example, in the Typing Test for Business (Doppelt,

Hartman, & Krawchick, 1968) the Numbers subtest, requiring the typing of numbers exactly as printed, correlates only .26 with the Tables subtest, in which the examinee must plan the spacing as well as type the largely numerical content.

A frequent problem is whether to tell the student in advance the tasks or other units on which he will be examined. In general, he should be told only if the units contain essentially all the elements of the objectives. For example, if in the process of making a birdhouse, the woodworking student must demonstrate all the important skills desired (measuring, sawing, planing, nailing, etc.), then it is proper to tell him in advance that he will be called upon to make a birdhouse, and that his overall evaluation will be based on this product. On the other hand, suppose that a nursing student is to be examined on her (simulated) management of a patient with a particular disease. The disease should probably not be announced in advance, since some of the desired skills are specific to certain diseases and all would not be represented in the management of one or even a few diseases.

Stimulus Aspects

The stimulus aspects of the test situation may conveniently be described under three headings.

Instructions

It may often be possible through written or oral instructions to influence not only the examinee's specific responses to other test stimuli but also his attitudes and approaches to the test situation. Instructions have not always been explicit; that is, the examinee has sometimes had to infer or assume that he is expected to act in certain ways without his having been told so. In many types of performance tests, it is especially important to plan the instructions in considerable detail, since examinees may vary substantially in their assumptions about implicit instructions.

For the most part, instructions should be explicit. The only general circumstance that calls for leaving the instructions implicit is one in which it is desired to test whether the examinee knows that certain things should be done regardless of instructions. For example, in a driving test, the examinee might simply be told, at the end of a series of maneuvers: "Park the car just past the next intersection, get out, and wait on the sidewalk." Presumably, the student should, without further instructions, perform such actions as turning off the ignition and applying the hand brake. It would be appropriate to penalize the examinee if he fails to do so.

However, even under very realistic conditions, the examinee may perceive the test as an artificial situation in which he does not, or at least need not, do things as he would in real life. Hence, it may often be desirable to emphasize in the initial instructions what aspects of the performance are to be carried out with high fidelity; i.e. as they would be in real life.

The instructions also should make clear the bases upon which performance will be scored. The relative importance of speed and accuracy should be discussed when it is relevant. It is often desirable to show the examinee the scoring procedures and the instructions to the judges, so that he can know exactly how good and poor performance will be defined. Time limits should also be specified (Mollenkopf, 1960).

The instructions should teach each examinee how to take the test. In general, the test is not meant to be a measure of ability to take tests or to comprehend difficult instructions, but rather it is intended to get at the ability to perform in a certain way after that way is clearly understood. It may be necessary to devote a substantial portion of the testing time to this instructional function. If the instructions are complex, it is desirable to incorporate a way of assuring the examiner that every examinee knows the task; i.e. a performance test of grasp of instructions.

Displays

The displays present the stimuli to which the examinee is to respond. In a paper-and-pencil test, the displays are the test items. They are static and generally use relatively abstract symbols to represent or describe the real world.

In a performance test, in contrast, the displays need not be static and may be quite concretely realistic. The displays may be presented in writing, through speech, by diagrams, as numbers or formulas, or by any of a variety of other symbolic or physical means. Physical objects or equipment may serve as, or include, displays. The keyboard of a piano, for example, acts as a display as well as the means of response. The odometer of an automobile, on the other hand, is a pure display with no response aspects for the driver. The displays may change their values and even be replaced by other displays in the course of a performance test; for example, in a test of automobile driving, the roadway and competing traffic are likely to change continually. All these and other characteristics of the displays should be planned and justified.

When the initial concept of the performance test has been established, it is often helpful to search out and catalog the differences in the test displays and those representative of the criterion situation. Not all such differences are undesirable; but it is well to know exactly what the differences are, so that proper simulation compromises can be made. Three types of such differences may be distinguished:

1. Failure to include a display aspect. For example, in most in-basket tests, there is no telephone on the desk of the examinee-administrator. He is therefore deprived of many typical stimuli (as well as of a response channel).

2. Inclusion of superfluous displays that provide undesired cues. For example, in gunnery simulators designed to present surprise targets, the equipment may emit a characteristic click or other noise just before a target is presented. In such a case, the test may measure an entirely different function than the one intended.

3. Low fidelity of displays. For example, the examiner who is assigned to play the role of an Indian government official may not have enough information to play the role properly. If so, the examinee would be dealing with a different problem than the one intended.

Surround

In any test situation, the surround should be arranged so that unwanted distractions are excluded and good performance is encouraged. Lighting, ventilation, heat, humidity, noise, and other conditions should be such as to facilitate performance, unless there is a reason to simulate conditions with which it is necessary to cope in the criterion situation. For example, it might be desirable to test ability to receive Morse Code not just in a classroom, but in a busy and noisy message center, if that is the expected context of performance on the job. Other aspects of the surround are sometimes simulated merely as a means of helping the examinee to perceive the situation as a real one. Thus, in sophisticated aircraft simulators, the characteristic squeak of the tires upon meeting the runway is usually reproduced, even though there is no evidence to show that this has any relation to performance of the pilot. If such features are inexpensive, there is likely to be no harm in them and they may sometimes do some good.

In general, a given aspect of the surround is not simulated unless there is some justification for doing so. However, it should be recognized that there is a certain amount of ambiguity between displays and surround. For a vehicle operator, for example, a tree would normally be just a part of the passing scenery; but, in an emergency requiring him to steer his vehicle off the roadway, the same tree might be an important display. Careful analysis often is necessary to identify the important displays and to evaluate the influence of the surround under various conditions of performance.

Response Aspects

Examinee responses presumably are controlled by the test stimuli, including the instructions, which are determined in part by the test content. Yet, there is still some freedom to vary certain characteristics of the responses or, to put the matter the other way around, it is necessary to plan response aspects of the test in at least three respects.

Response fidelity

The examinee may be required, or afforded opportunity, to make responses which are more or less similar to those he would make in the criterion situation. If the response simulation is to be at high fidelity, it normally would be necessary for the examinee actually to respond in whatever ways are normal in the activity. At low fidelity, he typically would describe how he would respond, given particular stimuli. For example, the student of television repair might be asked to respond by describing the tests he would perform to localize difficulties in a malfunctioning set.

Low stimulus fidelity implies low response fidelity in at least some respects. If no television set has been presented, the repairman cannot conduct actual (high fidelity response) tests on it. However, he could manipulate an actual voltmeter, which could be connected to an electrical simulation of relevant aspects of a television set; that is, lack of stimulus fidelity need not restrict response fidelity in all respects.

Many tasks have repetitive response aspects that are relatively unimportant and therefore need not be simulated at high fidelity. For example, a technician usually must disassemble a piece of equipment before he can repair it. But the disassembly process is often very easy and yet time-consuming, involving the repetitive use of screwdrivers and wrenches. In such a case, the performance test might start with the equipment already disassembled.

Use of equipment

Many criterion performances require or allow the use of equipment through which the responses of the performer are mediated. Uniform policies about use of equipment should be established for all examinees. Variations in equipment quality or state of repair may affect the quality of the product; a balky sewing machine may produce a faulty stitch even though the student has fed the material in straight. (A later section is devoted to equipment calibration and maintenance.) A related problem is that some items of equipment must or may be fitted to the individual. Hence, in these situations, it may be necessary to allow or require each examinee to provide his own equipment.

Performance aids

Some kinds of equipment or materials are not directly involved in the performance but are such as to assist the performer. Some support performance by guiding the performer; e.g. a metronome or accompanist for a musical performer. Other aids are used only at certain stages in the learning process and are not used in the final criterion performance; e.g. a harness used by a gymnast to prevent falls. Strictly speaking, some such performance aids are stimuli, but they are perhaps planned for best in conjunction with response aspects. The primary decision of the test planner is what performance aids to allow or require.

Performance vs. Product

A fundamental question is whether to evaluate performance or product or both. Three issues need to be considered before some answers are suggested.

Nature of performance

The required performance may be such as to dictate or make academic the question of product vs. performance evaluation. Some performances have no product or, at any rate, performance and product are indistinguishable: examples of such performances are dancing and public speaking. In some cases, the process may be judged irrelevant, or there may be so many acceptable variations in performance that product alone is important; for example, a teacher of creative writing is unlikely to care how the student arrived at his product, short of plagiarism. In less extreme cases, experts in the subject matter may be able to agree about the relative importance of process and product and thus specify an appropriate combination.

Feasibility of measurement

Sometimes, it is clear that the product is what ought to be measured, but it cannot be measured well enough. Or, the product could be measured adequately, but to do so would cost more than can be afforded. For example, suppose a student of welding is tested on his ability to join two parts of a structure. The adequacy of his weld might most properly be evaluated by elaborate tests of the strength of the structure or X-ray examination of the integrity of the weld. But such tests are expensive if performed properly. Hence, it might be best to evaluate the student's welding ability by observing the degree to which he follows proper procedures.

Importance of side effects

The term *side effects* is used here to indicate outcomes that are not observable in the product. Many side effects are unwanted outcomes. An example is accidents. A lathe operator, say, may be evaluated primarily on the quantity and quality of his work. But it is also desirable that he avoid injury to himself and others. Hence, it may be necessary not only to evaluate the number and kind of products he makes but also to observe his procedures to make sure that he is using proper safety equipment and precautions.

Weighting performance and product

The final decision about the relative weights to be given performance and product should depend upon the specific measurement objectives and circumstances. However, some general advice can be given about the conditions, other than those already mentioned, that favor one or the other type of evaluation. The summary by Highland (1955) is a good one:

The following conditions will make it more likely that the test constructor will wish to score performance in terms of the *process*—that is, in terms of how something is done.

1. The steps in a procedure can be specified and have been explicitly taught.

2. The extent to which an individual deviates from accepted procedure can be accurately and objectively measured.

3. Much or all of the evidence needed to evaluate performance is to be found in the way that performance is carried out and/or little or none of the evidence needed to evaluate performance is present at the end of performance.

4. An ample number of persons are available to observe, record, and score the procedures used during performance.

The following conditions will make it more likely that the test constructor will wish to score performance in terms of *products* evident after performance has been completed, and available even though the performance itself has not been observed.

1. The product of performance can be measured accurately and objectively.

2. Much or all of the evidence needed to evaluate performance is to be found in the product

available at the end of performance and/or little or none of the evidence needed to evaluate performance is to be found in the way that performance is carried out.

3. The proper sequence of steps to be followed in attaining the goal is indeterminate, or has not been taught during training or when, though everyone knows the steps, they are hard to perform and skill is ascertainable only in the product.

4. The evaluation of the procedures used during performance is not practicable because persons are not available to observe, record, and score these procedures [p. 34].

Maintaining Good Testing Conditions

As pointed out more fully in chapters 3 and 7, it is important that the testing conditions be favorable and uniform for all examinees. For most printed tests, such uniformity readily can be arranged. For performance tests, it is usually more difficult to achieve and maintain standard conditions.

Training examiners

The examiner may play any or all of three major roles: (*a*) the test administrator, who explains the rules (instructions), keeps order, and answers questions, (*b*) the actor, who plays a role to help simulate the criterion situation, and (*c*) the observer, who records and usually evaluates the performance. Training is needed for each role. The administrator must know the rules and the permissible answers to questions. The actor must understand and be able to project his assigned role, must follow his instructions closely and consistently, and often must be able to improvise when he is confronted with an examinee whose approach is unorthodox. The observer must understand the performance criteria and scoring rules and should perhaps have a general appreciation of the mechanisms of human bias and selective perception. If there is to be more than one examiner of any type, the training should be explicitly planned and formally carried out. Each examiner should be tested, preferably with a performance type of test, at intervals to make sure that he can perform in a manner resembling that specified.

Maintaining and calibrating equipment

As the human examiners must be trained, so must the machine components be adjusted frequently to assure their consistent and proper functioning. General care and maintenance of mechanical and electrical equipment is necessary to preclude breakdowns and incomplete operation. More subtle variations in machine function also must be monitored and adjusted. Two main types of error usually are identified. Constant errors are those in which the signal or other characteristic is consistently improper; e.g. an odometer always reads 5 miles per hour faster than actual speed. A constant error, if substantial in relation to the likely accuracy of examinee performance, must be compensated for in some way, preferably by adjusting the machine so that the error disappears. Variable errors are those which fluctuate in all directions, theoretically at random. If variable errors are unduly large, they may mask the effects of the examinee's performance. For example, if a power saw vibrates a quarter inch from side to side as it operates, it is impossible to determine whether the operator is able to cut with accuracy within an eighth of an inch. Hence, the equipment must be calibrated and made more precise if the test is to reflect examinee performance.

Equipment error may vary from time to time in the same piece of equipment and from one copy of the equipment to another at the same time. Some standard of frequency and accuracy of calibration must be established and continuously adhered to if test scores are to be compared across machines and across time.

Test security

A serious problem with some performance tests is that of security. Occasionally with intent but more often inadvertently, examinees may gain advance knowledge about a test and thereby obtain an unfair advantage over others. The fewer the number of items, the more likely it is that some examinees will get advance knowledge and the more important is information about any given item. In an extreme case, a performance test in cooking, say, might consist of the preparation of a meal. If the menu for the meal were known to some examinees and not to others, it is obvious that those examinees with advance information would be able to practice the specific actions required in the test rather than the general skills that were the learning objectives.

If it is possible for all examinees to have advance knowledge of the test procedures and content, then no examinee would have an unfair advantage. The best solution to the problem of test security is to keep no secrets. This solution may often have educational advantages, also, since it tells students in advance exactly what will constitute evidence of sufficient learning. However, this solution is feasible only when the test developer can find or develop a set of performances that comprehensively cover all the learning objectives. In most cases, this is not possible; it is usually necessary to sample from many possible performances and hence impossible to avoid the test security problem.

Some specific advice on test security is given by Highland (1955):

1. Give as many tasks or units of activity to each individual as the available supply and practical considerations permit . . . .
2. If possible, devise and administer equivalent forms of the test so that a student never knows on which form he is to be tested . . . .
3. Arrange the situation so that those tested have no opportunity to talk to other class members not yet tested.
4. Emphasize that helping other class members will tend to lower the individual's own score.
5. If the test consists of several tasks or units of activity, change the order of administering these as frequently as possible.
6. Make frequent changes in the place within the testing room where a particular task or problem is given so that it isn't possible for examinees to pass along information to others not yet tested . . .
7. Deny the examinee information concerning the rightness or wrongness of his response. This operates against the usefulness of the test as a learning device, but usually performance tests are administered because of their measurement rather than their teaching characteristics [pp. 54–55].

Guiding examinee performance

It may sometimes be desirable to provide for special guidance of some examinees. Such guidance would, in effect, constitute a supplementary set of instructions, to be provided only in specified circumstances. The usual circumstance would be that the examinee either shows clearly that he is unable to proceed or shows that he has made an error that will preclude his performing succeeding steps correctly. The guidance should be designed to be the minimum to enable him to undertake the next step properly. It should, of course, be recorded and taken into account in evaluating the examinee's performance.

Rules and procedures for guidance should be established in advance. The aim should be to leave as little as possible to the discretion of the examiner or proctor at the time of testing.

If it appears that there will be extensive need for guidance, consideration should be given to revising the test concept. Different tasks might be chosen, in which performance of later steps is less dependent on successful completion of early steps. Or the test might be halted briefly at the end of each critical step and guidance given to *all* examinees.

Administrative considerations

The administration of many performance tests is a complex matter for which careful advance planning is necessary. Often, it is not feasible to have enough copies of equipment and tools so that all examinees can be tested on the same task at once. Then it is necessary to establish multiple testing stations, develop schedules for rotation of examinees among stations, and provide examiners and proctors to manage the administration. Consumable supplies must be made available as needed. Activities should be planned for examinees who are waiting to be tested, and communication among examinees should be controlled. Careful records should be kept on matters relevant to later administration or interpretation, such as equipment malfunctions, examiner errors, confusion on the part of examinees, or other disturbances of the planned testing routine.

Observing and Recording Performance

If there is a more or less permanent product to be evaluated, it is normally not necessary to observe it until after it has been completed. For example, in the in-basket type of test, the examinee writes memos and letters as his test responses; these are then available for evaluation.

On the other hand, if the evaluation is of a performance or if the product is evanescent (e.g. writing on a blackboard), then it is necessary to observe and record relevant aspects of the performance as it occurs. It would in principle be possible to transform almost all performances into products by recording them on audio and video tapes or other media, and for some purposes it is desirable to do so. However the expense of such a transformation would often be difficult to justify.

In either case, it is necessary that the performance be at some time observed. In a few unusual cases, the observation can be purely mechanical or electronic, without human involvement after the planning stage except in case of equipment breakdown. In most practical situations, one or more human observers must perform the function.

The observer first of all must be told what to observe. Even though he may be an expert in the subject matter of the test, he is likely to be unsystematic and erratic in his observations unless he is directed to note specific aspects of the situation. Also, different observers are likely to observe different aspects, unless directed and trained to observe the same things.

The observer must be in a position to see and hear the things he has been directed to observe. If he cannot observe all that is wanted, then steps should be taken to: (*a*) use more than one observer, each instructed to attend to certain aspects of the situation (e.g. 3 or 4 umpires in a baseball game); (*b*) constrict the test situation so that it is more manageable for observation (e.g. reduce the number of examinees to be tested simultaneously); or (*c*) have the observer attend to different aspects of the situation in succession and lengthen the period of observation if necessary to permit an adequate sample of each aspect (e.g. in a simulated business conference, the observer might attend to participant A for 5 minutes, then to participant B for 5 minutes, etc.).

The observer must be told how to classify and record his observations. His judgments should, when it is feasible, be of the most simple ort: item A is or is not of type X; the medical student did or did not ask whether the patient had a history of allergy to a proposed medication. Then he can record his observations easily and reliably. Such a circumstance implies that the various possible occurrences have been anticipated and precodified. With good analysis, this is normally possible. When it is not possible (or, at any rate, has not been done), it is necessary to demand more complex judgments of the observer. In most cases, these demands amount to implicitly combining the observation process with that of evaluation. Such a combination generally is undesirable. Much mischief has been associated with failure to disentangle observation from evaluation. It is frequently found, for example, when judges disagree in rating a performance that there is no way to determine whether the judges (a) were attending to different aspects of the performance, (b) had different implicit standards against which to compare the performance, or (c) having agreed in their judgments of the elements or subparts of the performance, arrived at an overall evaluation in different ways. Since the difficulty cannot then be accurately diagnosed, it is impossible to prescribe a specific remedy. Some type of checklist or other form should be used to record observations. A checklist should be carefully designed so that there is little or no room for disagreement about the meaning of any word or statement or about the judgment that the action did or did not occur. For example, consider the item:

Checked voltage: Yes____ No____

There may be more than one voltage, and it may not be clear what it means to check it. A more precise statement might be:

Recorded grid voltage in log: Yes__ No__

If accuracy of the action is important, the item must somehow indicate the allowable tolerance for error, preferably in quantitative terms; e.g.:

Recorded grid voltage in log accurately within ±2 volts: Yes____ No____

It may sometimes be helpful to draw a diagram or other pictorial aid to specify tolerances. The use of such aids is illustrated in figure 9.12. An-

other type of aid is the template or the model; the observer compares the product with a correct version or with a pattern reflecting correct shape and dimensions (i.e. with a physically realized standard).

It is not always possible to reduce observations to checklist (yes—no) form. Multiple-category items and continuous measures are frequently appropriate when dealing with physical characteristics such as time, distance, weight, etc.

Scoring Performance Tests

The purpose of a score is to represent performance concisely. A score is usually a number but may be another kind of symbol or verbal statement such as Pass or Fail.

It is not always desirable to have only one score. Subscores are useful whenever they may lead to valid inferences that would not ensue from consideration of the overall score. Such occasions are likely to arise when the test has tapped more than one relatively independent aspect of the total performance. Each such aspect might be considered to be the appropriate subject of a separate score. On the other hand, if the subparts of the test do not measure different things but are essentially operating as samples of the same performance, then subscores serve no purpose and may be misleading.

Scores are normally evaluative in nature and are intended to be measures of some quality such as a skill. Smode, Gruber, and Ely (1962) have identified seven major classes of scores or measures:

1. *Time:* Measures dealing with time periods in production or performance.
2. *Accuracy:* Measures dealing with the correctness and adequacy of production or performance.
3. *Frequency of occurrence:* Measures dealing with the rate of repetition of behavior.
4. *Amount achieved or accomplished:* Measures dealing with the amount of output or accomplishment in performance.
5. *Consumption or quantity used:* Measures dealing with resources expended in performance in terms of standard references.
6. *Behavior categorization by observers:* Measures dealing with classifying more complex behaviors into operationally defined subjective cate-

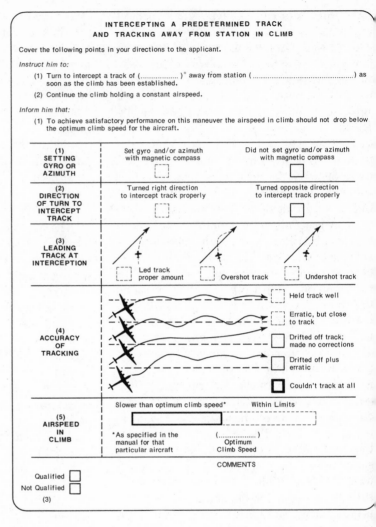

FIG. 9.12. A sample task in a pilot flight test. (United States Department of Commerce, Civil Aeronautics Administration, 1950, p. 9.)

gories. Observations are placed into discrete classes on a continuum for the event observed.

7. *Condition or state of the individual in relation to the task:* Measures dealing directly with the state of the individual which describe the behaviors and/or results of acts that have occurred [p. 46].

Most conventional tests are scored by counting the number of items performed correctly. Many performance tests may be scored in just this way. This type of scoring is acceptable when the record of test performance consists of a large number of items (say, more than 20), for each of which "correct" performance can be unambiguously recognized. If the record of performance presents the item in more than

two categories, these must be reduced to two.

A more complex method of scoring must be adopted when (*a*) the number of items is small or (*b*) more than two categories of performance per item are retained. In most cases, it is possible to avoid these conditions. If the number of items is small, it is usually possible to add more items, either by identifying additional aspects of a single performance that can and should be evaluated or by requiring additional performance samples of the examinee. If an item includes more than two categories of performance, it usually is easy to dichotomize it. For example, a continuous record of performance time might be reduced to two categories such as: (a) less than 2 minutes, (b) 2 minutes or more. However, there are situations in which it is not feasible or appropriate to avoid one or the other or both of the above conditions. Then a more complex scoring scheme is used.

The essential problem in developing a scoring scheme is to attach the appropriate weight to each constituent item. In a composite score the effective weight of any item is proportional to the product of its nominal weight and its standard deviation. It is, of course, the effective weight that is of interest.

Two fundamentally different approaches to this problem may be identified. One approach is primarily statistical, the aim being either to maximize the correlation of the composite with some external criterion or to satisfy some internal statistical criterion. The other approach is rational and attempts to maximize the content or construct validity of the measure.

The correlation of a linear composite with a criterion is maximized by the methods of multiple regression; the beta weights are the weights to apply to the elements. Two major difficulties with such weights must be recognized. First, they tend to be unreliable; that is, they are likely to fluctuate from sample to sample, so that results in practice may be disappointingly less impressive than the results of an initial study. Second, the criterion is typically imperfect, both in its reliability and, more importantly, in its relevance and comprehensiveness. Especially in the case of the performance test, it is difficult to find a criterion that truly represents, better than does the test itself, the performance it is intended to measure or predict. When a relevant, comprehensive, and reliable criterion can be developed, it is, of course, desirable to use it as the primary means of establishing weights for the test elements. Even if a criterion is somewhat imperfect, it can still be an important source of information as a partial basis for determining weights.

A number of statistical methods have been proposed for selecting test element weights so as to maximize reliability, minimize measure-ment error, or satisfy some other internal statistical condition. Several of these methods are discussed by Gulliksen (1950). None of them has an entirely persuasive rationale. In certain specific situations, one or another such method may make sense. In the usual conditions under which performance tests are constructed, it seems unlikely that any such method would be appropriate. However, some statistical considerations might well have an influence on weighting decisions. Given two test elements of about equal importance, for example, it might be appropriate to give more weight to the more reliable one.

Normally, it is not appropriate to depend primarily on a statistical approach, but rather it is necessary to establish the weights of the test elements by nonstatistical rational means. In general, such means involve the use of expert judges to estimate the relative importance of each element in relation to the overall aims of the test. These judgments should be based primarily on the task analysis or other study of the activity that was carried out in planning the test. It may often be the case that weights for the subtests or items will have been set in the planning stage and that no further explicit step is necessary. However, there are secondary considerations that may have to be taken into account. The number of scored items may not have been predicted accurately in the original planning, for example. Adjustments are often necessary in many detailed aspects of the test, even though the overall test concept is retained. Hence, a new set of judgments may be desirable or even necessary. (The weighting of subtests is discussed in detail in chapter 3.)

The recommended procedure is to have the judges first study the objectives, the test content, and any preliminary data that may help in understanding how the test may function. Then they may judge directly the relative weight to give each test element (assuming that the element variances have been made equal) in order that its relative importance may be accurately reflected in the composite. If the number of elements is small, it may be best to ask each judge to distribute some constant number of weighting points—say 20—among the elements. If the number of elements is greater than perhaps 10, such a procedure would become unwieldy and should perhaps be replaced by a simple rating procedure on a 3- or 5-point scale. Much more elaborate procedures may, of course, be used, but the precision to be gained is not usually sufficient to justify the extra effort.

A special problem of weighting arises when there is the possibility of a catastrophic event that would be judged almost infinitely more important than any other item on the test. For example, suppose a student during an automobile driving test loses control and allows the vehicle to be wrapped around a tree. He would undoubtedly receive the lowest score on any item concerning ability to control the vehicle. It can be argued that any such component should be very highly weighted, so that no examinee who has an accident can pass the test. But the high weights would influence the scores of others who do not have accidents, most likely in ways not intended by the test developer. The best solution in such a case is to treat the accident or other extreme incident as a disqualifying condition; that is, as soon as the examinee's performance becomes so bad as to suggest to the examiner that it is unsafe or useless to continue, the test is simply discontinued.

USE OF PERFORMANCE TESTS

A performance test (performance or product evaluation) has been defined here as a test in which a criterion situation, such as a job, is simulated to a relatively high degree. The essence of good simulation lies, first, in careful analysis of the measurement objectives and the criterion situation and, second, in judicious balancing of comprehensiveness of coverage and fidelity of simulation within the limits of available resources. Careful planning of all aspects of a performance test is necessary if it is to achieve its aims.

The potential value of the performance test lies in its closer approach to reality—its greater relevance in determining the degree to which the examinee can actually perform the tasks of the criterion job or other situation. This value generally is achieved at some cost, not only in money and other resources but in reliability of measurement. If the loss of reliability becomes extreme, the relevance is illusory since it cannot be measured. The test developer must weigh the factors of relevance, reliability, and cost in deciding how far in the direction of faithful simulation his test plans should go. The test user has a similar problem. There is no formula to help make these calculations.

The relatively low reliability of performance tests is not an entirely universal or necessary characteristic. Many of the suggestions made in this chapter have been aimed at improving reliability. It must be admitted, however, that much of our advice is based on experience and hunch rather than on scientific evidence and hypothesis. Both empirical and theoretical studies of the problems of performance tests are acutely needed.

If an adequately relevant and otherwise suitable paper-and-pencil test is available or can readily be developed, there is no point in using or developing a performance test. However, the ready availability of paper-and-pencil tests has often blinded us to considerations of relevance. It is an exercise in futility to measure accurately something one does not want to know. Relevance is the primary consideration, and good measurement is only a means to the end of appropriate evaluation.

It appears that the importance of measurement and evaluation has been increasingly recognized in recent years. At least some of the dissenters to this trend have been arguing not against measurement but against irrelevant measurement. As more experience is gained with and more evidence accumulated about performance tests, it is likely that more such tests will become available and more efficient means for their development and use will be found. In certain fields of education, performance tests have been widely used. They can and probably will be used widely in many other areas in the future.

REFERENCES

Baldwin, R. D., & Wright, A. D. *An attempt to develop a radar operator screening test: A report of simulator instability.* Washington: Human Resources Research Office, 1962. [Technical Report 79]

Bender, W. R. G., & Loveless, H. E. Validation studies involving successive classes of trainee stenographers. *Personnel Psychology*, 1958, **11**, 491–508.

Board of Education of the City of New York. *Industrial arts metalworking in the secondary schools: First year.* New York: Board of Education, 1967.

Bray, D. W., & Grant, D. L. The assessment center in the measurement of potential for business management. *Psychological Monographs*, 1966, **80**(17, Whole No. 625).

Buhl Planetarium and Institute of Popular Science. *Handbook of rules and instructions, Twenty-Ninth Annual Pittsburgh Regional School Science Fair.* Pittsburgh: Buhl Planetarium, 1968.

Buros, O. K. *Tests in print.* Highland Park, N. J.: Gryphon Press, 1961.

Doppelt, J. E., Hartman, A. D., & Krawchick, F. B. *Typing test for business: Manual.* New York: Psychological Corporation, 1968.

Fine, J. L., Malfetti, J. L., & Shoben, E. J., Jr. *The development of a criterion for driver behavior.* New York: Columbia University, Teachers College, 1965.

Fitzpatrick, R. *A method for analysis of crew tasks associated with equipment malfunctions and other contingencies.* Pittsburgh: American Institutes for Research, 1964.

Flanagan, J. C. The critical incident technique. *Psychological Bulletin*, 1954, **51**, 327–358.

Fleishman, E. A. *The structure and measurement of physical fitness.* Englewood Cliffs, N. J.: Prentice-Hall, 1964.

Frederiksen, N. Factors in in-basket performance. *Psychological Monographs*, 1962, **76**(22, Whole No. 541).

Frederiksen, N. Validation of a simulation technique. *Organizational Behavior and Human Performance*, 1966, **1**, 87–109.

Gagné, R. M. Simulators. In R. Glaser (Ed.), *Training research and education.* Pittsburgh: University of Pittsburgh Press, 1962. Pp. 223–246.

Glaser, R., Damrin, D. E., & Gardner, F. M. *The tab item: A technique for the measurement of proficiency in diagnostic problem-solving tasks.* Urbana: University of Illinois, College of Educa-

tion, Bureau of Research and Service, 1952.

Glaser, R., Schwarz, P. A., & Flanagan, J. C. *Development of interview and performance tests for the selection of Wage Board supervisors.* Washington: The Adjutant General's Office, Personnel Research Branch, 1956. [PRB Technical Research Note 53]

Gordon, L. V. Clinical, psychometric, and work-sample approaches in the prediction of success in Peace Corps training. *Journal of Applied Psychology*, 1967, **51**, 111–119.

Greenlaw, P. S., Herron, L. W., & Rawdon, R. H. *Business simulation in industrial and university education.* Englewood Cliffs, N. J.: Prentice-Hall, 1962.

Gulliksen, H. *Theory of mental tests.* New York: Wiley, 1950.

Hemphill, J. K., Griffiths, D. E., & Frederiksen, N. *Administrative performance and personality: A study of the principal in a simulated elementary school.* New York: Columbia University, Teachers College, Bureau of Publications, 1962.

Highland, R. W. *A guide for use in performance testing in Air Force technical schools.* Lowry Air Force Base, Colo.: Armament Systems Personnel Research Laboratory, 1955. [ASPRL-TM-55-1]

Kelly, E. L. The place of situation tests in evaluating clinical psychologists. *Personnel Psychology*, 1954, **7**, 484–492.

Klaus, D. J., Gosnell, D. E., Chowla, M. J., & Reilly, P. A. *Controlling experience to improve nursing proficiency: Determining proficient performance.* Pittsburgh: American Institutes for Research, 1968. [U. S. Public Health Service Research Grant No. NU 00158]

Lennon, R. T. Assumptions underlying the use of content validity. *Educational and Psychological Measurement*, 1956, **16**, 294–304.

Lopez, F. M., Jr. The in-basket technique as applied in a selection situation. In *The in-basket technique.* Princeton, N. J.: Educational Testing Service, The Conference on the Executive Study, 1961. Pp. 66–83.

Lopez, F. M., Jr. *Evaluating executive decision making: The in-basket technique.* New York: American Management Association, 1966. [AMA Research Study 75]

McGlade, F. S. An evaluation of the road test phase of the driver licensing examinations of the various states: An investigation of current road tests and testing procedures and the development of a valid and reliable road test based on derived implications. Unpublished doctoral dissertation, New York University, 1960.

McGuire, C. H., & Babbott, D. Simulation technique in the measurement of problem-solving skills. *Journal of Educational Measurement*, 1967, **4**, 1–10.

McNamara, W. J., & Hughes, J. L. The selection of card punch operators. *Personnel Psychology*, 1955, **8**, 417–427.

Miller, F. A. A badminton wall volley test. *Research Quarterly*, 1951, **22**, 208–213.

Miller, R. B. Analysis and specification of behavior for training. In R. Glaser (Ed.), *Training research and education*. Pittsburgh: University of Pittsburgh Press, 1962. Pp. 31–62.

Miller, R. B. Task description and analysis. In R. M. Gagné (Ed.), *Psychological principles in system development*. New York: Holt, Rinehart & Winston, 1963. Pp. 187–228.

Mollenkopf, W. G. Time limits and the behavior of test takers. *Educational and Psychological Measurement*, 1960, **20**, 223–230.

Neyhart, A. E. *Road test check list for testing, selecting, rating and training truck drivers*. Washington: American Automobile Association, 1955.

U. S. Office of Strategic Services. *Assessment of men*. New York: Holt, Rinehart & Winston, 1948.

Pennington, A. W. History and classification of war games. In J. Overholt (Ed.), *First war gaming symposium proceedings*. Washington: Washington Operations Research Council, 1961. Pp. 2–5.

Phipps, L. J. *Handbook on teaching vocational agriculture*. (6th ed.) Danville, Ill.: Interstate, 1952.

Plattner, J. W., & Herron, L. W. *Simulation: Its use in employee selection and training*. New York: American Management Association, 1963.

Robinson, P. J. The use of analogue computers in operational games. In J. M. Kibbee, C. J. Kraft, & B. Nanus, *Management games*. New York: Reinhold, 1961. Pp. 255–273.

Ruby, W. J., Jocoy, E. H., & Pelton, F. M. Simulation for experimentation: A position paper. In American Institute of Aeronautics and Astronautics, *AIAA simulation for aerospace flight conference*. New York: AIAA, 1963. Pp. 350–355.

Seashore, H. G., & Bennett, G. K. A test of stenography: Some preliminary results. *Personnel Psychology*, 1948, **1**, 197–209.

Seashore, H., & Bennett, G. K. *The Seashore-Bennett stenographic proficiency tests: A standard recorded stenographic work sample*. New York: Psychological Corporation, 1956.

Sivy, J., Lange, C. J., & Jacobs, O. *Development of an objective form of the leaders reaction test*. Pittsburgh: American Institute for Research, 1952.

Skager, R. W., Klein, S. P., & Schultz, C. B. The prediction of academic and artistic achievement at a school of design. *Journal of Educational Measurement*, 1967, **4**, 105–117.

Smode, A. F., Gruber, A., & Ely, J. H. *The measurement of advanced flight vehicle crew proficiency in synthetic ground environments*. Wright-Patterson Air Force Base, Ohio: Aerospace Medical Division, 1962. [Report MRL-TDR-62-2]

Snyder, M. B. Methods of recording and reporting task analysis information. In U. S. Air Force, Wright Air Development Division, *Uses of task analysis in deriving training and training equipment requirements*. Wright-Patterson Air Force Base, Ohio: WADD, 1960. Pp. 11–31. [WADD Technical Report 60-593]

Tiffin, J., & Greenly, R. J. Experiments in the operation of a punch press. *Journal of Applied Psychology*, 1939, **23**, 450–460.

Tiffin, J., & McCormick, E. J. *Industrial psychology*. Englewood Cliffs, N. J.: Prentice-Hall, 1965.

United States Department of Commerce, Civil Aeronautics Administration. *Pilot flight test report for the Airline Transport Rating flight examination*. Washington: USDC, CAA, 1950.

Wilcoxon, H. C., & Davy, E. *Fidelity of simulation in operational flight trainers: Part I. Effectiveness of rough air simulation*. New York: Psychological Corporation, 1954. [Technical Report SPEC-DEVCEN 999-2-3a]

Wilcoxon, H. C., Davy, E., & Webster, J. C. *Evaluation of the SNJ operational flight trainer*. Port Washington, N. Y.: U. S. Navy Special Devices Center, 1954. [SPECDEVCEN 999-2-1]

Wilson, C. L., & Mackie, R. R. *Research on the development of shipboard performance measures*. Los Angeles: Management and Marketing Research Corporation, 1952. [Office of Naval Research Contract N8onr70001]

Wilson, R. M. *Assessing competency in physical education activities*. Springfield, Ill.: Charles C Thomas, 1966.

10. Essay Examinations

William E. Coffman
The University of Iowa

In view of the extensive development of new procedures for measuring educational achievement and the extensive criticisms aimed at the traditional methods by experts in the field of measurement and evaluation, one might have expected a dramatic reduction in the uses of essay examinations. Apparently nobody has made a systematic survey, but it seems clear, even to the casual observer, that essay examinations still are widely used in spite of more than half a century of criticism by specialists in educational measurement. Teachers at all levels of the educational system ask students to explain, discuss, compare and contrast, translate, analyze, evaluate, calculate, relate, or undertake some other intellectual operation with respect to some aspect of the content of the educational program. Essay questions often are used in classroom quizzes to determine whether the students have studied the assignment or to provide the teacher with feedback regarding the effectiveness of an immediately preceding lecture or discussion period. They also are used widely in examinations on which students' educational or professional futures depend. For some teachers, the essay questions may be only a useful but relatively small element in examinations consisting primarily of objective questions. For many teachers, however, the essay examination continues to be the only "respectable" method of collecting evidence of student achievement. Even in the United States, where the growth of objective testing methods has been vigorous and widespread, essay examinations continue to flourish. In many parts of the world, they never have been seriously challenged as the proper method of assessing the output of the educational system.

DEFINITION

According to Stalnaker (1951)

the essay question is defined as a test item which requires a response composed by the examinee, usually in the form of one or more sentences, of a nature that no single response or pattern of responses can be listed as correct, and the accuracy and quality of which can be judged subjectively only by one skilled or informed in the subject. The most significant features of the essay question are the freedom of response allowed the examinee and the fact that not only can no single answer be listed as correct and complete, and given to clerks to check, but even an expert cannot usually classify a response as categorically right or wrong. Rather, there are different degrees of quality or merit which can be recognized [p. 495].

As a brief summary of the concept, Stalnaker's definition appears acceptable, although it may be necessary to elaborate at a number of points if the definition is to encompass the different types discussed in this chapter. For example, the essay question may encompass such widely differing tasks as development of a familiar essay demonstrating the ability of the examinee to express effectively his own thoughts on some topic of wide human interest, translation into English of a passage presented in another language, outlining of a research design for investigating a sociological question, derivation of a mathematical proof, or explanation of the nature of some scientific phenomenon. It may require only a brief response, or it may demand an extensive exposition.

The essay examination may be defined as one or more essay questions administered to a group of students under standard conditions for the primary purpose of collecting evaluation data. It is differentiated from the short-answer examination discussed in chapter 4 by the fact that expert judgment rather than the application of a clerical key is required in assigning grades or scores. It is differentiated from the term paper or term project by its focus on evaluation, its administration under standard conditions, and its attempt to sample the outcomes of instruction. Generally, the term paper or project is designed, at least in part, to facilitate learning as well as to evaluate learning. Furthermore, the only time limits are likely to be those of the course, and the student usually has some flexibility in the content and focus of the project.

It is necessary to recognize that any brief definition is necessarily inadequate and that the underlying concept is an evolving one, not only in relation to the discussion of this particular chapter but also over time as new ideas are incorporated into the concept. One may conceive of relatively short essay questions for which most of the acceptable answers could be anticipated, a key prepared, and the grading reduced largely to a clerical task. One also can conceive of a general problem requiring extended effort over a period of several weeks that might be designed primarily for the collection of evaluation data and the administration of which might be considered to be standard for all members of a class. Furthermore, the question of how to differentiate simple clerical counting from complex analytical procedures becomes a difficult one as computers are developed and programmed to carry out analyses of verbal content and structure (Page, 1966). If it becomes as routine a task to count and combine complex aspects of verbal responses as it is now to count marks on an answer sheet, it may be necessary to reformulate the definition of the essay question in terms of the complexity of the task of programming a computer to evaluate the answers. For the present, however, it seems acceptable to focus the definition on the freedom of responses allowed the examinee and on the evaluative judgments required of the graders.

A definition in these terms leaves considerable scope for variation in the nature of essay questions. One cannot formulate an exhaustive list of kinds of essay questions; creative teachers will continue to invent new kinds. One cannot anticipate all of the kinds of answers students may compose; creative students will continue to confound unimaginative examiners. One can, however, examine approaches that creative teachers have used in selecting questions to ask and in reaching sound judgments about the values of answers created by students. Such examples can help to indicate the scope and flexibility of the essay for evaluating the outcomes of instruction.

CONSIDERATIONS FAVORING USE OF ESSAY EXAMINATIONS

To some extent, the persistence of the essay examination may be only a reflection of the typical tendency of any large enterprise to resist change. New approaches to testing originally were developed by specialists in the fields of education and psychology and did not spread rapidly to other areas within the educational community. Students preparing for careers in teaching were exposed to the new ideas, but they found that instructors in fields other than psychology or education continued to use essay examinations. Furthermore, many of these instructors were not reluctant to register their beliefs that the new methods hardly deserved scholarly status. Moving into the school system following the completion of the training program, the neophyte teacher, particularly at the secondary school level, was likely to encounter a strong cadre of experienced teachers who had no skill in constructing objective tests. Good objective test questions are difficult to prepare, and horrible examples are readily available to the critic who looks for them. It is not surprising, then, to find the new school teacher adopting, not the new practices he had been taught in his courses in education, but rather those to which he had been exposed more generally as a student. The old establishment usually absorbs the revolutionary trickle; it is only in exceptional cases that the new idea survives and prospers.

On the other hand, superior practices may be expected to prevail in the long run. Here and there, with each new wave of enthusiastic innovators, there will be some who will resist the establishment and even undertake a missionary function. The critics of essay examinations had built what appeared to be a strong case. They had pointed out that teachers differed greatly in their judgments of the quality of a particular paper, that often a student's grade depended more on who happened to read the paper than on what was written on it. They had demonstrated that if teachers put aside a group of examination papers and then reread them some months later without reference to the grade given originally, there were significant discrepancies in the two sets of grades. They had called attention to the fact that only a few questions could be asked on any essay examination and that, if a second examination were given in a day or so, there would be large shifts in the order of merit of the papers. There seemed to be a strong case against the essay examination.

The fact that, after more than half a century of efforts to introduce objective testing, essay testing continues to exhibit an obvious vigor suggests that the early diagnosis may have been more pessimistic than it should have been. Perhaps there is some need to review the case for the essay examination. What is it about the procedure that continues to attract thousands of teachers who have been exposed to newer methods of testing?

The Essay Examination as a Performance Test

In the first place, a case can be made for the essay examination as a special form of the performance test discussed in detail in chapter 9. The argument would go something like: A major purpose of education is to prepare individuals to interact effectively with other individuals in the realm of ideas. The basic tool of interaction is language (including the mathematical symbol system), and the educated man is one who can react appropriately to questions or problems in his field as he encounters them. It is not enough to be able to recognize a correct fact when it is presented or to discriminate among alternatives posed by others; the educated man is the master of his collection of ideas. He is able to marshal

evidence to support a position, and, hopefully, he is able to extend his range of understanding and to contribute to the advancement of ideas and constructs within his field. The only way to assess the extent to which a student has mastered a field is to present him with questions or problems in the field and see how he performs. The scholar performs by speaking or writing. The essay examination constitutes a sample of scholarly performance; hence, it provides a direct measure of educational achievement.

As will be pointed out later in this chapter, this argument is not supported by available evidence; however, the fact that it persists among teachers suggests that it should not be discarded without careful study. Too often in the past, the scientific fact has given way before new evidence and the common-sense viewpoint has been supported by that same evidence.

Difficulty of Constructing
Good Objective Tests

The persistence of essay examinations, in the second place, appears to be a reflection of the judgment of teachers and other examiners that no effective alternatives are available. The typical teacher has grown up with essay examinations; he has encountered a wide variety of them in his own experience as a student; and, so far as he can tell from his own experience, the essay examinations he has prepared seem to have done a satisfactory job. This does not necessarily mean that he is correct in his judgment. As Stalnaker (1951) noted:

The grades assigned to the papers are usually based in part on what the student has written and in part on what the teacher, from other knowledge of the candidate, believes he meant by what he wrote. Norms, correlations, reader or test reliability, and validity do not worry the teacher. If he knows what they are, he ignores them in dealing with his own classroom situation. The popularity of the essay question should not, therefore, be misinterpreted to indicate that it is the most suitable test form for many purposes, that it is in a "healthy" condition, or that improvements are not needed [p. 497].

It should be recognized, however, that the classroom teacher, at least the typical elementary or secondary school teacher, seldom is interested in pure measurement. Rather, he is engaged in a constant process of interacting with students and making tentative value judgments on the basis of such interactions. The examination he administers is simply one source of information about the progress of the student. As Jackson (1968) pointed out, the teacher is making thousands of judgments every day. If some of them are faulty, they can be corrected later on as the actions he takes on the basis of the judgments stimulate in students reactions that provide additional feedback. It is natural for the teacher to modify his judgments on the basis of an accumulation of evidence. He is always judging the meaning of one bit of information in the context of a pattern of accumulated evidence. He is not likely to be impressed by findings that show that teachers reach different conclusions about the quality of a paper when they know who wrote it from the one they reach if they mark the paper without knowing who wrote it. He will probably conclude that even though a single isolated judgment may be faulty, the product of cumulated judgments over a full semester or year is a valid one. Furthermore, the teacher who has undertaken to construct an objective test has probably found it a frustrating experience. In theory—and in practice under the special conditions obtaining in many of the large-scale test development centers—it is possible to present almost any scholarly problem in objective machine-scorable form. In practice, for the classroom teacher, it is a demanding, time-consuming task likely to be completed successfully only by the teacher with a creative flair, extensive training and experience, and time to concentrate for extended periods on the task. Even the professional test builder sometimes fails in his attempts to construct objective test questions for measuring complex analytical skills (Serling, 1967); the typical classroom teacher or college instructor is likely to find his reach in this area greatly exceeding his grasp. After a few attempts at building objective tests to measure complex skills and understandings, the typical teacher is likely to return to the familiar essay

examination whenever he wishes to do more than measure the student's knowledge of facts.

This is not to say that it is easy to construct effective essay examinations. It is not. But the teacher confronted with an essay question that has gone sour can at least have the satisfaction of having tried to elicit a profound response, and he can take his own failure into account at the point of reading the paper. His amateurish efforts at constructing objective questions are likely to produce questions firmly anchored to the factual surface of the subject. Thus, the classroom teacher, faced with the alternative of using essay questions, which he finds easy to prepare and not too demanding to read, or objective questions, which he finds difficult to prepare and essentially superficial in what they appear to measure, decides to use essay questions.

There have been many research studies designed to assess the relative effectiveness of essay and objective tests. The results tend to favor objective tests. Generally, however, carefully constructed objective tests have been compared with run-of-the-mill essay tests. It would be desirable to have a large-scale study comparing the general effectiveness of essay examinations prepared and read by typical classroom teachers for use in their own classes with objective examinations prepared by classroom teachers for the same purpose. In the classroom setting, the cumulative effect over a period of a semester or a year might well favor the essay examination. Such a study would be difficult to design and expensive to carry out, but it would help to clarify many issues that at present remain in the area of opinion.

The popularity of essay examinations is not limited to the classroom teacher. Essay examination questions also are used by external examiners. In many parts of the world students earn the right to certificates of achievement, the opportunity to enter the next higher level of the educational system, or access to a profession by passing essay examinations set by official examining bodies. The secondary school student in France, and in many other countries that have adopted a French system of education, sits for the baccalauréat. His counterpart in schools operating under the British system sits for *O-Level* and *A-Level* examinations. The candidate for civil service status in India achieves eligibility by passing essay examinations. Even in the United States one still observes the use of essay examinations for determining such diverse qualifications as eligibility for advanced standing on entering college and admission to the bar.

To a considerable extent, tradition and lack of information about suitable alternatives may be responsible for the continuation of external essay examinations. The examiners responsible for setting external examinations, in many cases, have no reason to question the procedure. As classroom teachers, they have grown up with it; they have used essay questions in their classes with their own students and are seldom aware of the extent to which they depend on information other than the examination responses in deciding what grade a student should receive. Furthermore, they have had only limited experience with well-constructed objective examinations. As a result, seldom has the impetus for change arisen because of a dissatisfaction with the examinations themselves. Rather, it has been the increasing magnitude of the task of processing the examination papers that has encouraged examination boards to seek alternative procedures. As the numbers of candidates have increased and as the cost of hiring readers has mounted, those responsible for setting a variety of external examinations have begun to explore the possibility that some of the newer methods might offer relief.

Effects on Teaching and Learning

The elimination of essay questions from external examinations does not follow immediately the awareness that alternatives exist, however. There continues to be a concern on the part of examiners that multiple-choice or short-answer objective tests may not be suitable alternatives. Even if the measurement provided by objective tests is satisfactory, there is concern about the effects of these on teaching and learning. In Britain one hears educators discussing the possibility of "backwash." In

the United States teachers inquire how one can expect students to learn to write if they do not have to write on examinations. How can teachers be expected to take the time to assign writing exercises and to read them critically when the payoff is of a different kind? To a considerable extent, resistance to the use of objective test items is a reflection of sincere and real questions regarding their appropriateness, not only on the part of external examiners but on the part of the classroom teacher as well.

Such questions are not without foundation. In many cases, the student obtains his ideas about the things he is expected to learn from the kinds of questions he encounters on examinations and governs his study procedures accordingly. Furthermore, teaching practices may depend on the kinds of external examinations. If the critical examinations for determining eligibility for higher education call for the student to recognize the correct synonyms for a series of vocabulary words, teachers will devote class time to exercises in vocabulary building and students will buy sets of practice exercises and spend time working with them. If the examinations that determine a course grade require only that the student recall or recognize the content of textbooks or lectures, the student will concentrate on learning factual details or memorizing explanations given by the teacher regardless of what is said about the importance of other outcomes of the course. Many years ago, Meyer (1934, 1935) reported that the form of the examination expected by students determined the nature of the studying that the students carried out. Furthermore, he found that greater achievement on any type of examination followed study in anticipation of an essay examination. It is doubtful, however, if Meyer's findings may be applied today without reservation. Since he completed the studies, there have been major advances in the art of objective item writing. The stereotype of the objective test item as a true-false question testing recall of superficial information cannot be applied to the types of questions found in good objective tests published in the 1960s, although they still appear to apply to typical classroom tests (Gustav, 1964). At least two studies (French, 1956; Vallance, 1947) call into question the superiority of essay questions as stimulators of good study procedures. There is need for much more research on the question, research that recognizes the complexity of the problem and provides for an assessment of the relative effects of different types of essay and objective questions, with different types of subject matter and in a variety of different educational settings.

It appears, then, that the essay examination is still a popular—and often preferred—procedure throughout the educational systems of the world, including those of the United States. There is no evidence that the procedure is on its way out; in fact, there is some evidence, as in the reintroduction of an essay question into the College Board English Composition Test (College Entrance Examination Board, 1966), that a modest expansion of use of essay questions may be under way. It therefore behooves the measurement specialist to assess clearly the advantages and limitations of the procedure and to take such steps as he can to insure that sound practices are encouraged and unsound ones discouraged.

LIMITATIONS OF ESSAY EXAMINATIONS

The person who proposes to defend essay testing needs to understand fully the limitations of the procedure; otherwise, he will fare poorly in discussions with the advocates of objective testing procedures. It is not without reason that much essay testing has been called into question. The essay examination undoubtedly is inefficient in comparison with objective tests in terms of testing time and scoring costs. Basically, the problem is one of unreliability; a significant portion of the variance of scores on essay examinations consists of systematic or variable error unrelated to the underlying ability one wishes to assess.

The theoretical aspects of test reliability are discussed in detail in chapter 13; however, it seems desirable in this chapter to analyze the problem of reliability with specific reference to essay examinations since there has been considerable confusion in applying theory to the special context of the essay examination. A cursory examination of the research literature, for example, would suggest that the major problem with essay examinations is that, when different raters are asked to judge the same paper, they disagree in their judgments. A majority of the published studies have been concerned with one or another aspect of this source of error. Lack of consistency in grading, however, is not the only, or necessarily the most serious, source of error in scores on essay examinations. Even if it were possible to achieve high consistency in grading, there would still be the problem of variability in individual performance from sample to sample. There also would be the problem of systematic and variable error inherent in the fact that, in the typical essay examination, the examinee is required to write out answers in a limited amount of time; what an examinee can produce in a limited time differs from what he can produce given a longer time, and the differences vary from examinee to examinee.

The ideal model for conceptualizing the problem of reliability of essay examinations is a multifaceted one of the type described by Gleser, Cronbach, and Rajaratnam (1965). It is seldom possible, however, to obtain in a single experiment the data required to develop estimates of the magnitude of each of the various components of error. Besides, the estimates are likely to vary depending on the content of the examination, the level at which the examination is administered, the variability of the examinee group, the extent of training of both those who prepare the questions and those who rate the answers, and the context in which the test scores are to be used. Thus, in any particular situation, the tester is likely to have to depend to a considerable extent on his background of experience and his rational analysis of likenesses and differences between the situation in which he is working and situations of one sort or another reported in the literature. It is from such a point of view that each of the limitations of essay examinations is discussed in the sections that follow.

Error Associated with Rating of Essays

There is extensive evidence that it is difficult

to achieve consistency in grading essay responses. The problem is a complex one, and appropriate procedures for analyzing it are difficult to design. The accumulated evidence leads, however, to three inescapable conclusions: (*a*) different raters tend to assign different grades to the same paper; (*b*) a single rater tends to assign different grades to the same paper on different occasions; and (*c*) the differences tend to increase as the essay question permits greater freedom of response (Finlayson, 1951; Hartog & Rhodes, 1936; Noyes, 1963; Pearson, 1955; Vernon & Millican, 1954).

Each of these conclusions is more complex than the simple statement indicates. For example, the grades assigned by different raters may differ as a result of various influences. First, raters may differ in their severity. One characteristically may assign relatively high grades while another may tend to assign generally low grades; for example, in an experiment involving the Advanced Placement Examination in American History, one rater assigned a total of 499 points to a group of 60 papers while a second assigned only 357 points to the same papers (Coffman & Kurfman, 1968). The significance of such variability differs with the testing situation. If scores determine only relative position in the group of examinees rather than who passes and who fails and if every reader rates every paper and the ratings are summed, the fact that raters have different standards is of no particular significance. If, however, some readers rate some papers while other readers rate other papers, the mark an examinee receives will depend on which rater happens to read his paper; and, if a particular level of rating is required to achieve a passing grade on the examination, examinees may pass or fail depending on which rater happens to rate which papers.

Not only do raters differ in their standards, they also differ in the extent to which they distribute grades throughout the score scale. Some tend to distribute scores closely around their average; others will spread scores much more widely. If some papers are read by a rater who distributes scores widely while other papers are read by one who tends to pile scores up at some point on the scale, it makes considerable difference which rater assigns the scores to a paper that is relatively good or relatively poor. The good student hopes his paper will be read by the first rater; the poor student that he will be lucky enough to draw the second rater.

Finally, raters may differ in the relative values they assign to different papers. A paper judged by one rater to warrant a high grade may be judged inferior by another. To some extent, such differences may be reflecting only the random differences that accompany any human response; if so, they are inescapable. On the other hand, some of the differences may be reflecting real differences in the criteria that raters are applying. If so, it should be possible to identify subgroups of raters who are applying common criteria. In a study involving the reading of English composition papers, Diederich, French, and Carlton (Diederich & Link, 1967, pp. 197 ff.; French, 1962) were able to identify five different characteristics of the papers that contributed to variability in the grades assigned by raters. The five characteristics were labeled *ideas, form, flavor, mechanics*, and *wording*. Subgroups of readers who emphasized the same factors in rating the papers were less variable in their judgments than those from different subgroups. To the extent that such "schools of thought" exist among readers of essay examinations, the rating assigned to a particular paper will depend on which type of reader happens to assign the rating.

Much of the literature on rating reliability of essay examinations is difficult to assess because of the great variety of procedures that have been used to estimate reliability. In many cases, reliability is estimated by obtaining the product-moment correlation between two sets of ratings. It should be recognized that this procedure is likely to overestimate the reliability, because, in the process of computation, the means and standard deviations of the two sets of scores are equated and only the difference in relative value assigned to the same paper is treated as error. If sets of ratings by a single pair of raters are involved, the overestimate may be extensive since differences in mean ratings and in variability of ratings of the two raters have been ignored. On the other hand, if the two sets of scores have been assigned by a large number of different raters, each of whom has assigned some scores to the first reading and some to the second, then most of the differences among raters in standards and in tendencies to distribute scores widely or narrowly will be incorporated in the estimate of error. There may still be differences in the means and standard deviations attributable to order effects—that is, the tendency of groups of raters to shift their standards as the reading proceeds.

Ebel (1951) has pointed out that an analysis-of-variance approach to the estimating of reliability will permit one to estimate different components of error and to incorporate the relevant ones into the estimate depending on the situation. Stanley (1962) has suggested an analysis-of-variance design appropriate for studying the reliability of essay scores. Gleser et al. (1965) have presented a general model that may be modified to fit particular experimental situations. Gosling (1966) has reported on the applications of similar procedures in Australia. If such methods were more generally adopted, it would become easier to make comparisons among the findings of different studies.

It sometimes has been argued that while the demonstrated differences in ratings assigned by different raters may be relevant to the grading of large-scale essay examinations, they are irrelevant to the grading of the classroom examination. The classroom examination is designed to assess the extent to which a particular teacher's goals of instruction have been achieved. The students who have been in close association with the teacher from day to day have had an opportunity to learn his value system, and he has had an opportunity to teach the students the kinds of essay responses he values. The fact that other teachers in other settings may assign different scores to the essay responses of his students is no cause for concern. The important point is that the classroom teacher has made his judgment.

This line of argument should be given serious consideration. There is a fundamental difference between the typical classroom situation and the typical large-scale testing situation so far as essay examinations are concerned. It is possible to achieve a level of communication between teacher and students in a single class that is difficult, if not impossible, to match between examiners and candidates in a large-scale program; and the classroom teacher can relate a particular test score to a larger context and discount extreme discrepancies. In evaluating the argument, however, one needs to be aware of the fact that there is a source of error in essay rating attributable to variations in the judgments of raters from time to time—when teachers are asked to grade a set of papers, to put them aside for a period of weeks, and then grade them a second time, the agreement between the two sets of papers is far from perfect.

The magnitude of the error in such cases varies widely from rater to rater. Finlayson (1951) reported, for example, reliability coefficients ranging from .636 to .957 with a mean of .810 for four raters who reread two sets of essays. These coefficients may be compared with those between the first ratings for an examinee's two essays by the same raters, which ranged between .601 and .798 with a mean of .687, and the intercorrelations among pairs of raters, which ranged from .591 to .770 with a mean of .703. The intrarater variability, like the interrater variability, consists of three components—one related to the general grading standard, one to the variability of assigned grades, and one to the relative standard for different papers. The typical research report based on a product-moment coefficient takes into account only the third of these components. The teacher who proposes to use essay examinations for evaluating his students would be well advised to consider the advantages of cooperative plans of the type described by Diederich (1967) and by Diederich and Link (1967). The individual teacher working alone without feedback inadvertently may be making many errors of judgment.

It is difficult to make precise statements about the level of reliability that can be achieved in grading essay examinations. The level will tend to be lower if the examination is administered to a large group with heterogeneous backgrounds rather than to a small group whose background of instruction is homogeneous. It will tend to be lower if many different raters have to be trained to apply a common standard of evaluation in reading the papers. It will tend to be lower for less exact and more discursive subject matters, so that responses to a set of mathematical problems, to a set of questions in chemistry involving relationships in chemical equations, to a set of questions on generally accepted historical concepts, and to a general composition topic form a sequence of descending order with respect to the level of reading reliability that can be achieved. A search of the literature reveals coefficients of rating reliability varying from .98 to .35 depending on the context, the content, and the number of raters involved. Discussions of reliability in any particular context should be guided by experimental data obtained in that or a similar context.

Discussion of rating reliability would not be complete without some reference to the high reliability reported for certain experienced examiners in situations where essay examinations have key positions in the educational setting. For example, Gosling (1966) has reported that the correlations between the marks of the chief examiner and the average of the marks of 10 other examiners on a sample of papers on three essays in an English composition examination administered in Australia were .98, .96, and .97. The experiment in which these correlations were obtained took place after a group of 100 raters had finished marking the papers of some 30,000 candidates, each of whom had written three compositions. Marks were assigned on a 15-point scale ranging from a high of A+ to a low of E−, and the raters were guided by a list of criteria and a set of 10 reference compositions chosen from a trial run sample to represent selected points on the scale. The experiment was described by Gosling (1966):

1. After scripts had passed through the marking system in the normal way, a random sample of sixty of the scripts of male candidates and a random sample of sixty of the scripts of female candidates was taken. Thus, for each of these 120 scripts, the system mark was known for each composition and for the total composition section of the Written Expression paper.

2. The 120 scripts were divided into eight sub-samples of fifteen scripts—each containing eight scripts from male and seven from female candidates, or seven from male and eight from female. Allocation to the sub-samples was random apart from the necessity for balancing the sexes of candidates.

3. Eight teams of ten essay markers (five male and five female) were selected randomly. One of the sub-samples of scripts was assigned to each team and each member of the team marked Test 4 on each of the fifteen scripts, in ignorance of the system mark and of the ratings of other members of the team.

4. Eight teams were again selected randomly, subject only to the provision that a marker did not have as a member of his or her team a marker who had previously been a fellow team member. Sub-samples were again assigned to teams and Test 5 marked the same way.

5. A further eight teams were selected, sub-samples assigned and Test 6 was marked in the same way.

6. The Chief Examiner marked first all of the Test 4s, then all of the Test 5s, and finally all the Test 6s in the sample scripts [pp. 44–45].

The experimental design appears to have insured that all ratings were assigned independently and that assignment of raters to papers was appropriately randomized. On the other hand, the raters had all had extensive experience in applying the scale to essays on these particular topics. It is doubtful that such consistency would have been observed had the experiment been conducted at the beginning of the period of rating.

Error Associated with the Sampling of Questions

Even if it were possible to achieve a high degree of rating reliability, there would still be the problem of sampling reliability to consider. As Ebel (1965) pointed out, "Students spend most of their time in thinking and writing when taking an essay test. They spend most of their time reading and thinking when taking an objective test [p. 90]." Since writing is inherently a slower process than thinking and reading, the time required for recording answers sets the limit on the amount of information that can be obtained in any given period of time. The more complicated the question, the more time required to compose and record an answer.

Basic to the concept of sampling reliability is the notion that each sampling unit should be independent and equally likely to be chosen in the sample. In this sense, the basic sampling unit for an essay examination is the question; the size of the sample is determined by the number of different questions in the examination. If the examinee is asked to deal with a number of different aspects of a single topic, the different aspects cannot be considered strictly independent; rather, it is likely that the ability to deal with one aspect is more closely related to the ability to deal with another aspect of a single question than it is with the ability to deal with a question on another topic.

There is some evidence that there is an increment in reliability per question if questions are "longer" rather than "shorter," but the increment is not proportional to the time required for longer answers. For example, Godshalk, Swineford, and Coffman (1966) reported the reliability of a score based on five independent ratings of a 20-minute essay as .485 and of a score based on the sum of two such scores as .653. In contrast, the reliability of a score based on five independent ratings of a 40-minute essay was only .592. In general, the greater the number of different questions included in the examination, the higher the reliability of the score for an examination of a given time limit. A major problem facing the teacher who is preparing an essay examination is to effect a satisfactory compromise between the desire to increase the adequacy of the sample by asking many different questions and the desire to ask questions that probe deeply the understanding the student has developed.

It should be recognized that the problem of how large a sample of questions to include is more critical in some situations than in others. The importance of test reliability is directly related to the nature of the decisions to be made on the basis of the test scores. If, for example, a test is administered by a teacher as a basis for making tentative decisions regarding progress to date and next steps to be taken in instruction and if it is only one in a sequence of tests which together will provide the basis for evaluating the student's progress, relatively low reliability can be tolerated. If, however, the examination is to constitute the sole basis for determining access to the next level of the educational system or entrance into a profession, the test had better be highly reliable. The teacher who is associated daily with a group of students is not likely to be misled by a particularly aberrant performance; the external examiner is in no position to temper his judgment if a student has encountered a particularly unlucky sample of questions.

Illustration of Relationship of Components of Error

Additional light may be obtained on the relationship among various components of error in essay examinations by examining the data presented in table 10.1. The data were obtained from a special study based on 200 papers from the Advanced Placement Examination in American History administered in May 1964 (Swineford, 1964a). The examination consisted of a 45-minute section containing 75 multiple-choice questions and a 135-minute section consisting of 3 essay questions. During the operational scoring session, each essay question was rated once following a procedure that insured that each question would be rated by a different rater. Since there were a number of different raters assigned to each of the three questions, variability among the scores on a question reflected not only true differences in the quality of the answers but also all three of the components of error in rating that have been discussed in the preceding section of this chapter. The scores reported on the examination were the sums of the ratings on the three questions. Following the completion of the operational scoring session, a sample of 200 papers was rated a second time with the distribution of papers controlled so that no paper was rated twice by the same rater. The scores on this experimental rating then were compared with those from the operational rating.

TABLE 10.1

Intercorrelations of Objective Score, Operational Essay Scores, and Experimental Essay Scores

$(N = 200)$

Variable	Obj. Score	First Question		Second Question		Third Question		Total Essay	
		Op.	Ex.	Op.	Ex.	Op.	Ex.	Op.	Ex.
Objective score		.519	.354	.444	.575	.603	.526	.664	.636
First question:									
Operational	.519		.541	.409	.448	.483	.382	.793	.599
Experimental	.354	.541		.314	.369	.280	.316	.476	.738
Second question:									
Operational	.444	.409	.314		.620	.403	.357	.764	.559
Experimental	.575	.448	.369	.620		.393	.424	.616	.772
Third question:									
Operational	.603	.483	.280	.403	.393		.669	.807	.593
Experimental	.526	.382	.316	.357	.424	.669		.600	.774
Total essay:									
Operational	.664	.793	.476	.764	.616	.807	.600		.740
Experimental	.636	.599	.738	.559	.772	.593	.774	.740	
Mean	31.96	5.92	5.74	5.58	5.32	5.94	5.76	17.44	16.82
Standard deviation	12.59	2.36	2.58	2.42	2.44	2.54	2.69	5.77	5.87

Source: Swineford, 1964a, table 4, p. 10.

The correlations between the first (operational) and second (experimental) ratings provided estimates of the reliability of the ratings. For the first essay question, the reliability estimate was .541; for the second, .620; for the third, .669. The corresponding coefficient for the two total essay scores was .740. It must be recognized, however, that these estimates were based on product-moment coefficients and did not take into account any difference in standard between the first and the second rating. There was such a difference. In every case, the mean score on the experimental rating was lower than that for the operational rating. This is not an isolated phenomenon. It has been observed that, when essay examinations are read over a period of several days, there is a tendency for grades assigned later in the period to be lower than those assigned earlier in the period (Godshalk et al., 1966). These estimates of rating reliability, then, are overestimates of the consistency of rating to be expected from time to time unless some procedure is available to control for differences in standards. If the Spearman-Brown prophecy formula is applied to the coefficient .740, it is estimated that the rating reliability of total essay scores based on two or three independent ratings of each question would have been approximately .85 and .90 respectively. It is possible to achieve high rating reliability, but it requires large amounts of professional time to obtain the required number of independent ratings.

High reliability of rating, of course, does not insure that score reliability also will be high. Notice, for example, that the correlations between ratings of different questions tended to be lower than those between different ratings of the same question. The several coefficients relating scores on one question with scores on a different question range from a low of .280 (experimental rating of questions one and three) to a high of .483 (operational reading of same two questions). Fluctuations of this magnitude are common for data of these kinds and reflect the composite effects of variability among raters and variability among students in their responses to different questions. Examiners usually insist that in choosing questions for a particular examination there be a conscious effort to choose questions that relate to different aspects of the area being measured. In other words, the questions for a particular form of a test are chosen systematically and cannot, therefore, be considered a random sample from a population of questions. Nevertheless, the intercorrelations among questions often appear to belie such claims, and it is instructive to see what conclusions follow if the assumption is made that the questions have been chosen at random. Such an assumption is a conservative one and can lead to pessimistic conclusions regarding the score reliability of an essay examination, but, in the absence of data permitting the exploration of alternative hypotheses, it provides some useful insights.

The data in table 10.1 may be analyzed in more detail. For example, the average of the 12 coefficients relating independent ratings of different questions was .3815. If it is assumed that the three questions have been chosen at random from among the population of possible questions for the examination, this average coefficient may be taken as an estimate of the average reliability of a single question of this kind rated by one rater. An estimate of the reliability of the total score based on the sum of the ratings of three questions may be obtained by applying the Spearman-Brown formula. The resulting estimate of the reliability of the operational total essay score is .649. This may be compared with the estimate of .650 as the correlation between the objective score and the essay score obtained by averaging the two empirical coefficients, .664 and .636. In spite of the fact that the examiners were not attempting to make the two sections equivalent, the correlation between the score on the 45-minute objective section and the score on the 135-minute essay portion is as high as the estimate of the correlation of a score on a parallel 135-minute essay test with the original essay test score. (In passing, it is instructive to note that under the assumption of random sampling of items it would require a 675-minute essay test of 15 questions, each graded by a different rater, in order to obtain a score reliability of .90.)

The reliability estimate for the objective score, based on the Kuder-Richardson formula #20 (KR20), was .864. If the figure of .649 is taken as the estimate of reliability for the essay score, the correlation between essay and objective scores, corrected for attenuation, is .868— i.e. $.650/\sqrt{(.649)(.864)}$. The two sections of the test are not measuring exactly the same things, and it would be appropriate to combine the two scores to obtain a composite total assuming there is agreement that the unique contribution of the objective section score is relevant to the purpose of the test. Suppose, however, that one doubts the validity of the unique part of the objective score, feeling that performance on the essay questions is the only relevant evidence of achievement in American history. Even then the combined score can be defended. The correlation between a perfectly reliable essay examination and the operational essay score is estimated by taking the square root of the estimated reliability—i.e. $\sqrt{.649} = .806$. The correlation of the objective score with a perfectly reliable essay score is obtained by dividing the correlation between objective and essay by the square root of the estimated reliability of the essay score—i.e. $.650/\sqrt{.649} = .807$. The 45-minute objective score appears to provide as much information about performance on the ideal essay examination as is provided by the 135-minute essay examination when the essay score consists of three different topics each read once by a different reader.

Before concluding, however, that these data may be used to sound the knell for essay testing, it is appropriate to recall that the data cannot be generalized without qualification. The particular objective test used in the Advanced Placement Examination in American History rests on a solid foundation of 20 years' experience in constructing such questions for the College Board and other examinations. It is doubtful that the quality of these questions could be duplicated in many places, certainly not by the typical classroom teacher. Then too, the estimate of reliability for the essay score is more likely to be a minimum than a maximum.

To the extent that the questions do tap different strata of the achievement domain and that parallel questions might be constructed, the correlation between this test and a parallel test should be somewhat higher than the estimate of .649. Any such increase would signal unique measurement for the essay score; however, it is unlikely that the increase would be large relative to the variance common to the objective section and the variance attributable to scoring error. After all, a liberal interpretation of reading reliability provides an estimated coefficient of only .740.

It is important also to recognize that the students who took this examination had been prepared to expect an examination consisting of both essay and objective questions and that their classes were taught by teachers judged to be highly qualified. One possible interpretation of the correlation between essay and objective sections of the test is that the two sections measure distinct kinds of achievement both of which had received emphasis in the courses that the students had taken. (See chapter 14, esp. pp. 457-58 and 496-99 for additional discussion.) There is no guarantee that these results would be duplicated if some of the students included in a new sample had been exposed to widely different types of expectations; that is, if some had been exposed only to essay examinations and some had been exposed only to objective examinations in their classes. Finally, one needs to consider the possibility that differences in subject-matter content might lead to differences in the relationships between essay and objective test scores. Certainly, one may expect differences in the magnitudes of the coefficients depending not only on the variabilities of the samples of students but also on the kinds of questions that are asked. Typically, examinations in mathematics tend to be more reliable than those in history whether the questions are essay or objective. In contrast, questions in literature tend to be less reliable than those in history. However, the evidence is spotty. There is need for studies that control the various sources of error and provide the basis for comparisons of the type presented here for a wide variety of testing contexts.

How about Validity?

The defender of essay examinations admits that there is a problem of reliability, both in the sense of adequacy of sample and in the sense of consistency of scoring; but he argues that, if the essay questions require the student to demonstrate skills and knowledge that cannot be demonstrated through the use of objective questions, then the lower reliability of essay examinations can be tolerated. After all, the real concern is with validity. What good does it do to measure the wrong things with high reliability? There is something to be said for such a position. To the extent that a relatively unreliable essay examination is measuring relevant factors and a highly reliable objective test is measuring irrelevant factors, the former is more acceptable. Unfortunately, this argument is not always supported by the available evidence. It may turn out that an essay examination is measuring the same factors as those measured by a competing objective test. Furthermore, irrelevant factors may be reflected in essay test scores as well as in objective test scores.

Lack of unique measurement for an essay examination is illustrated by the data from the Advanced Placement Examination in Mathematics administered in May 1964 (Swineford, 1964b). The test consisted of a multiple-choice section of 45 questions administered in 90 minutes and a free-response section of 7 questions also requiring 90 minutes. The KR20 estimates of reliability for the two sections were .850 and .701 respectively, the lower reliability reflecting primarily the smaller number of questions in the free-response section; the reliability of rating for free-response (essay) problems in mathematics is generally high. The correlation between the two sections was .764. The coefficient of correlation, corrected for attenuation, was $.764/\sqrt{(.850)(.701)} = .990$. Clearly, in this case, the use of free-response questions resulted in a loss of reliability without any corresponding gain in validity even if the score on the free-response problems is taken as the criterion. It would have been more efficient to use the whole 180 minutes for an extended 90-item objective test. One reason for the lack of uniqueness in the free-response questions in the Advanced Placement Examination in Mathematics may be simply that the objective questions were unusually well constructed. One should not overlook, however, the danger that in attempting to achieve high reliability for an essay examination one may be led into giving up the very uniqueness that is claimed for it. It generally is true that the shorter and more straightforward the essay question, the more consistently answers can be marked and the larger the sample of questions that can be presented. On the other hand, the more limited the question, the more probable it is that the question can be translated into multiple-choice form without loss of validity. One needs to guard against eliminating the special values of essay questions by reducing them to short-answer questions measuring primarily factual recall. One also should keep in mind the possibility that the common factor structure of the test was a result of the type of preparation the candidates had undergone. Not all mathematics students would necessarily be equally well prepared for objective and free-response questions.

Even when questions are kept relatively complex and call for the formulation of complex responses, the uniqueness of the response may be ignored in the grading. One may, for example, in an effort to increase the reliability of rating, develop a checklist of specific points to be counted by the raters. To the extent that the list is limited to points on which it is easy to reach agreement, the consistency of grading will be increased; however, the increased reliability may be achieved at the cost of eliminating from consideration the very factors that the essay question was designed to elicit.

It also should be noted that the essay prepared under the conditions of everyday life and the essay written under examination conditions are seldom equivalent products. There is an element of artificiality in the essay examination as well as in the objective examination. Ordinarily the essay examination is administered under a definite time limit. In order to obtain as large a sample as possible, the examination typically will include a number of questions, and ability to create and record answers rapidly is required for a high level of performance. To the extent that speed of handwriting or speed of formulating ideas or selecting words is relevant to the test performance but not to the underlying abilities one is trying to measure, the test scores may include irrelevant factors. The budding journalist may need to cultivate speed in his composition; the budding poet may expect to be able to proceed with his composition at a more leisurely pace. To the scientific librarian required to respond rapidly to a succession of requests for information, the ability to call up information rapidly may be a valuable asset; the theoretical physicist is unlikely to find verbal fluency a particularly crucial factor.

Unfortunately, there is little experimental evidence relating performance in essay examinations to various ability factors. One might hypothesize, however, that differences in one or more of the manual dexterity and verbal fluency factors identified by Carroll (1941), Taylor (1947), or Wittenborn (1945) would account for some of the variance in essay examination scores. To the extent that these factors are related to the test performance but unrelated to the particular underlying ability one wishes to assess, the validity of the test is reduced.

Of course, essay responses do not have to be collected under strict time limits nor do they have to be limited to handwritten format. Under certain conditions it is possible to offer a "take home" examination or even to lock the examinee in a small room for days at a time as was the practice in Imperial China (DuBois, 1965). One might permit examinees to dictate responses; however, this might simply increase the weight on verbal fluency factors and reduce the weight on manual dexterity factors. In some cases, the use of typewriters might be appropriate but probably only at the risk of shifting the loading of irrelevant factors from poor handwriters to poor typists. It is difficult, in the examination, to simulate the everyday situations in which people apply their knowledge and skills, whether essay or objective questions are used.

It seems clear from the analysis to this point that it is possible to construct and grade essay examinations that are as reliable and as valid as examinations of the more objective type, but that there are costs involved. Students will have to spend more time thinking and writing than they would spend thinking and reading—and marking answer sheets—if they had been given a comparable objective examination. Examiners will have to spend much more time reading and evaluating the essay examinations than they would spend in grading the objective examinations. In fact, the objective examinations are typically graded by machines. Evidence is accumulating that it may soon become feasible to replicate by electronic computer, at a cost considerably below that of professional raters, the grading of some types of essays (Page, 1966); however, computer grading still will be significantly more costly than the grading of objective tests, primarily because of the greater cost of transcribing essay responses to computer tapes. The time when the typical student can be expected to operate the teletype machines used in providing verbal input to computers or when machines can read and transcribe ordinary handwriting is still some distance in the future.

It should be remembered, however, that there is a cost inherent in objective examinations also. They are expensive to construct. It takes time to write questions that measure important educational outcomes and not simply recall of isolated facts. It takes time to review the questions in order to insure that ambiguities are removed and that the intended meaning will be clear to the informed reader. It requires considerable effort to obtain an appropriate pretest sample and to collect and analyze the data for an item analysis. If the number of individuals to be examined is small, it may require less effort to collect and process reliably an adequate sample of essay responses than to construct, administer, and process an objective examination of comparable validity. Often, the decision to use one or the other procedure will depend on judgments regarding their relative values for purposes other than measurement, particularly if it is estimated that relative costs are not too disparate. Which, for example, will provide the better definition, for the student, of the objectives toward which he ought to be working? Or, which will provide the teacher better detailed information about misconceptions students may have?

IMPROVING ESSAY EXAMINATIONS

Since there are definite advantages and recognized limitations in the use of essay questions in examinations, it behooves the knowledgeable test constructor to do all that he can to maximize the advantages and to minimize the limitations if his use of essay questions is to result in sound evaluation. He should limit the use of essay questions to appropriate test situations, adopt sound techniques for constructing questions, recognize the importance of obtaining an adequate sample and act accordingly, and adopt scoring procedures designed to reduce scoring error. He must at the same time be aware that current knowledge about essay testing is not necessarily final and remain open to new ideas that may be developed. Each of these points requires elaboration.

Limit Use to Appropriate Situations

There are special problems whenever essay questions are used in large-scale testing programs. The costs both in the time required for students to write answers to a representative sample of questions and in the time of readers to develop reliable ratings is often prohibitive. At the same time, for many contexts, the essay examination remains the preferred method of obtaining evidence of the candidate's ability to perform effectively. For example, many would insist that the only truly convincing way of demonstrating that students have learned to write effectively is to have them undertake writing assignments on a number of topics and see how they perform.

Use as criterion measures for validating objective tests

Faced with such a dilemma, evaluation specialists have turned their attention to inventing more efficient ways of obtaining evaluation evidence. There remains, however, the problem of demonstrating that new ways are valid. It has been suggested that one way of validating new procedures would be to administer the new type test to a sample of students along with a criterion essay examination long enough to provide a reliable measure and realistic enough to be considered a work sample of performance. It may not be feasible to administer a 20-hour performance test in, say, biology to all students who elect to take an examination in biology for admission to college, but it might be feasible to administer it to a sample of 1,000 students for the purpose of validating a shorter multiple-choice test. The long examination would define the achievement to be measured. If a machine-scorable examination produced scores that correlated highly with the long essay examination, then the machine-scorable test might be accepted as a feasible alternative for large-scale testing purposes.

This was the approach taken by Godshalk et al. (1966) in validating objective measures of English composition skill. They found that 1-hour objective examinations could be assembled that produced scores that correlated between .72 and .76 with a 2 1/3-hour criterion essay measure having a score reliability of .84. It must be recognized, however, that really comprehensive criterion tests are difficult to construct and that samples of students willing to undertake the writing of essay examinations that may require several days or panels of raters willing to spend the time developing reliable scores for such examinations are difficult to come by. It is likely that the task of establishing relationships between criterion measures and efficient operational tests will seldom be accomplished by single crucial experiments. Rather, it probably will be necessary to carry out a succession of studies the findings of which will permit the establishment of a network of relationships. The task of validating objective tests of achievement is one of establishing construct validity rather than predictive validity (see chapter 14). In establishing such a network, essay examinations will have a critical function to perform.

Use as parts of essay-objective examinations

Even when the validity of objective tests of achievement has been established, there will remain the concern about possible "backwash" effects discussed above. It therefore may be desirable and appropriate to supplement large-scale objective testing with some limited number of essay questions. By concentrating such questions on complex integrative tasks that are relatively difficult to present in objective form and by adopting one of the more efficient grading methods (to be described below), a large-scale testing program may retain the values of the essay question without incurring prohibitive costs.

Use in classroom tests

It is in classroom tests of educational achievement, however, that essay questions will continue to have their widest use. Here, the number of students to be examined is relatively small so that the ratio of time required for constructing a good objective examination is high relative to the time required for rating a good essay examination. In a large-scale testing program, it is almost impossible to design a question that requires all students to construct an answer by applying what they have learned to an unfamiliar situation. Some of the candidates may have encountered the same question as part of their regular instruction. In the individual class, however, the teacher is aware of what has been used as instructional materials and can choose familiar or unfamiliar materials for testing, depending on the purpose to be served by the questions. Even for groups of classes within a school, it is possible to develop appropriate essay questions if teachers are willing to share their knowledge of what students have been taught. For example, Diederich and Link (1967, p. 190) suggested that a school might assign one or two literary works of appropriate difficulty per year that are to be read for examination only—which means that all teachers are forbidden to discuss them. An examination that might constitute a widely variable task for different students in a large-scale testing situation might represent a common and clearly defined task for the members of a single class.

Adopt Sound Construction Techniques

The preparation of a good essay examination is not simply a matter of thinking up a series of apparently representative questions. It is not possible in the space available here to discuss in detail the many specific guidelines that have been developed for preparing questions in particular subject-matter areas. These may be found in more specialized texts (Jewett & Bish, 1965; Kruglak, 1965; Solomon, 1965). It is appropriate, however, to outline general procedures that are appropriate regardless of the area in which the test is to be constructed.

Define objectives carefully

The first step in constructing any test, essay or objective, is to define clearly the objectives to be covered by the examination and to relate the questions to the objectives. If, for example, one expects students to apply what has been learned to the solution of new problems, it is not appropriate to ask them, on an examination, only to recall and record a problem solution that has been presented in detail in class. Too often questions are presented that appear on the surface to require the application of knowledge when they are actually requiring only the remembering of what the teacher told the class some days before. By setting forth in systematic form the objectives to be covered by the examination and relating the questions to the framework of objectives, it is possible to insure that the questions making up the test are not restricted to a limited aspect of the total. Many of the principles of test planning discussed in chapter 3 apply to essay examinations as much as they do to objective tests.

Formulate well-focused questions

After the objectives to be measured have been specified, the next step is to determine the amount of freedom of response to be allowed and to construct questions accordingly. It may appear that an appropriate way to capitalize on the freedom of response possible with essay questions would be to present students with some such task as: "Show how your thinking about the field of physics has been changed by your experiences in this class," or "Discuss Modern Art." However, such questions provide freedom not only to the student but also to the reader, and attempts to rate answers to such questions do not produce reliable scores. There

must be some structure, or the student may readily miss the intent of the examiner—or be free to bluff if he understands the intent of the question but is not prepared to deal with it. Stalnaker (1951) presented the case very effectively:

Essay questions which can be read with some consistency by the methods commonly used are almost always restrictive in the sense that they are questions so worded that all candidates will interpret in the same way the task to be done. Some indication is usually desirable concerning the length of the answer expected. An example of a restricted essay question, but one which still allows an extended answer is: "Explain the principal doctrines and practices of mercantilism and show how they affected international relations in the eighteenth century." The restriction may be even greater, as in the following questions:

Answer briefly each of the following questions. The essential points in each case can be covered in a few sentences. Be as definite and concise as possible.
a. What is meant by the statement that France, before 1789, was centralized but not unified?
b. Why did the Dreyfus affair become an issue of national significance?
c. Who said the following and to what end? "If happiness is present, we have everything, and when it is absent, we do everything with a view to possessing it."

The answer to this last question is in part objective and in part essay. It might be answered, but not without careful thought, somewhat as follows:

Epicurus. It is a formulation of his well-known hedonism and an indication of the way intelligence facilitates the good life.

Such essay questions requiring relatively short answers give the candidate freedom to select from his background of knowledge pertinent information bearing on a particular problem, to decide how best to present this information or reasoning, and to compose and write down the answer. There are several advantages in forcing the candidate to address himself to a particular narrow problem. It is a real situation. The task is defined. The examinee knows what is required, and is not put into the situation where he must guess what some particular examiner had in mind. All examination questions have some restrictions, even the broadest projective type of question; the questions requiring a brief response merely restrict the field to a somewhat greater extent, while still allowing the candidate ample freedom. Such questions have all the fundamental characteristics of the essay question, and they can be read with reliability. They should be used more widely [pp. 519–520].

Construct model answers

The task is not finished when the questions are formulated with such restrictions as the examiner thinks appropriate. It is desirable that the examiner attempt to construct a model answer for each question, or better still, that questions formulated by one examiner be answered by another. In preparing the model answers, the examiners should pay attention to the writing time that will be allowed in the examination. Often examination questions are approved, and incorporated into examinations, that cannot be answered adequately even by the examiner in the time available. Since it is expected that the examiner probably knows as much as even the best student, no question should be permitted in an examination unless an examiner can compose a top-rated answer in the time available. If the examiner preparing the answer also has written the question, he probably should be able to prepare an ideal answer in less than the allowed time. After all, he has the advantage of coming to the question with a special background of thought. It is likely that if this practice were common, many questions that now find places in essay examinations would end up in the waste basket or undergo drastic revision.

Have questions reviewed

Even if the examiner can compose a satisfactory answer, there is no assurance that his intent will be communicated to the examinee by the wording he has used. Statements that are perfectly clear to the speaker or writer are often misinterpreted by the listener or reader. In the preparation of large-scale examinations, it is unlikely that a question will be approved until it has been reviewed by somebody other than the writer. This is not so likely to be the case if the examination is intended for classroom use. More often than desirable, teaching is a profession that is practiced on one's own. Each teacher practices his profession in the company of students but seldom in the presence of colleagues. Such a context is conducive to the development of exaggerated impressions regarding one's ability. If students fail to answer examination questions, the most natural interpretation for a teacher to make is that they have not exerted the effort necessary to learn the subject. It requires unusual insight on the part of a teacher to entertain the hypothesis that the teaching may have been inadequate or that the test questions may have been ambiguous. There is an occupational hazard here to be avoided. One way of doing so is to subject one's products to the criticism of one's colleagues. When teachers have asked colleagues to criticize test questions and to suggest revisions, they have been rewarded by useful suggestions.

Pretest, if possible

Experience indicates that even when essay questions have been carefully formulated and reviewed, it is possible for them to produce unsatisfactory results when they are actually used. Ideally, every question should be tried out under field conditions to see how it functions. Just as the construction of good choice-type questions requires that they be pretested, so the development of good essay questions is facilitated by field trials. Even if it proves possible to obtain essays from only a few students for a pretest, it is usually desirable to do so.

There are three questions that can be answered by studying pretest results: (a) Do examinees appear to understand the intent of the question, or do they appear to interpret it in ways that were not intended? (b) Is the question of appropriate difficulty for the examinees who will take it? (c) Is it possible to grade the answers reliably? These are interrelated questions, and the only way to obtain conclusive answers is to obtain a representative sample of responses and conduct an experimental scoring session leading to the generation of score distributions and estimates of reliability. The ideal experiment would be one in which parallel questions were tried out, each question being read independently by at least two readers following a design that permitted estimates of the various components of variance (see chapter 13). Usually, it will be necessary to follow something less than the ideal procedure. Even an informal pretesting based on a small number of responses from students in no way representative is likely to be better than no pretesting at all. The contrast between the type of response anticipated by the examiner and the type actually written by examinees, particularly if the examiner is inexperienced in setting essay examinations for other than his own students, can be dramatic. In general, examiners tend to ask questions that are too difficult, and pretesting can help to eliminate the more impossible questions and to encourage revision of others.

Recognize the importance of adequate sample of questions

Studies designed to examine the interaction between students and questions have generally demonstrated a significant interaction (Godshalk et al., 1966; Gosling, 1966; Young, 1962); in other words, some students do better on some questions while other students do better on others. To some extent, the grade a student obtains depends on which questions appear on an examination. The more questions there are, the less likely it is that a particular student will be too greatly penalized because he happens not to know how to answer a particular question. Thus, other things being equal, the more questions there are on an examination, the more reliable the examination will be. The wise examiner will think carefully before limiting his examination to a single essay question or even to a small number. He will recognize that in most situations a number of short answers are preferable to a few long ones.

The appropriate definition of *short* and *long* will differ, however, depending on the achievement to be assessed. For certain purposes, it may be appropriate to limit responses to single sentences. To determine an individual's skill in varying sentence structure, it would be more appropriate to have him construct 10 sentences, each to a different set of specifications, than to have him write a single 10-sentence composition. On the other hand, to determine his ability to construct a unified paragraph, 10 short independent sentences would be of little use while a single 10-sentence paragraph would be appropriate although it might provide relatively unreliable scores. The first consideration is always whether or not the proposed question form is one that will provide valid evidence.

One should recognize, however, that judgments may be faulty; what may look like the appropriate question length may in practice turn out to be inappropriate. The long question may provide so many opportunities for bluffing or otherwise distorting the picture of the underlying ability of the examinee that the supposed advantage of the long answer is not attained. Carefully constructed questions designed to elicit short but relevant answers have often proved to be superior as estimates of what the examinees have learned.

The extended composition that permits the student to assemble and integrate a large body of material is probably more appropriately used as a learning exercise rather than as an examination task, although extended composition may be elicited in a take-home examination in certain cases. There are some evaluative judgments that will always have to be made on the basis of observing the students over a period of time rather than on the basis of written responses in test situations. To the extent that students may be placed in more or less standardized situations and that the observations are systematic, the judgments are likely to be valid—probably more valid than judgments based on extensive answers to questions presented under the restrictions common to examination settings.

Some examiners, aware of the dangers of limited samplings, offer a number of alternate questions from which the examinee is to choose. This procedure is widely followed when the test is designed to assess a skill such as English composition rather than understanding of the content of a field. The rationale for the practice is that since it is the student's underlying ability to express ideas in written form one wishes to assess, it is only fair to permit him to demonstrate the ability with a subject for which he has an affinity. The argument is an attractive one. Students approve of the practice for it seems to offer them an advantage, particularly if they are not outstanding students who are able to deal with all kinds of questions. Teachers find the practice satisfying, for it removes some of the stigma of basing grades on only a limited sample of the student's work.

There is a little evidence that under certain conditions the practice of offering alternate questions may be justified, particularly in large-scale testing programs where the examiners have reason to believe that students come to the

TABLE 10.2

Frequency Distributions of Scores on Twelve Questions

Score	Group I					Group II						
	1	2	3	4	5	6	7	8	9	10	11	12
14		1	1									3
13	1	—	1							1		9
12	1	—	—	3	1	3				1	1	4
11	3	2	1	1	—	3				1	—	9
10	5	1	7	3	2	3	2	3	2	4	—	12
9	7	7	13	3	7	6	3	5	1	4	3	18
8	11	8	9	5	7	15	6	14	3	7	—	19
7	27	8	13	1	6	17	11	15	6	10	1	21
6	49	14	28	9	5	19	13	17	6	9	1	29
5	36	22	29	7	9	12	12	20	3	16	3	24
4	34	19	29	8	15	7	3	9	5	13	3	15
3	7	11	18	6	8	4	1	10	1	8	3	5
2	1	11	8	1	6	3		6	2	2	—	9
1	1	1	2	1	3	—		1			1	3
0						1						1
Total	183	105	159	48	69	93	51	100	29	76	16	181
Mean	5.91	5.29	5.59	6.10	5.32	6.58	6.37	5.73	5.97	5.95	5.56	7.06
S.D.	1.88	2.35	2.35	2.75	2.54	2.30	1.53	2.06	2.06	2.35	2.83	3.01
Sect I Mean	31.7	32.8	35.3	40.0	36.6	34.2	38.6	31.9	37.2	31.2	33.0	35.5

Source: Swineford, 1964a, table 1, p. 5.

examination after exposure to different curricula and where they are likely to represent widely different backgrounds. For example, Wiseman and Wrigley (1958) reported that when children taking the 11+ examinations in England were offered a choice among five topics, the brighter children tended to choose three of them while the less able children tended to choose the other two. There were significant differences between the average scores for the several topics even after an adjustment for differences in the ability of the children, but the remaining differences were small (less than one point of mark on the 0–20 mark scale). The authors argued that when testing composition ability within a population of widely differing ability, it is fairer to offer a variety of topics, some of which are more appropriate for the less able students, than to offer a single topic.

Such a practice, however, is defensible only if it can be demonstrated that the grading procedure adequately adjusts for differences in the difficulties of the questions. The danger is that the better students may choose the more

difficult questions and then receive lower scores because of the difficulty of writing outstanding answers. The problem is demonstrated in the data of table 10.2 based on a sample of 370 students who wrote the Advanced Placement Examination in American History in 1964 (Swineford, 1964a). The essay section of the examination consisted of two groups of questions. There were five questions in the first group and seven questions in the second group. Each student was to select three of the questions, including one from each group.

Frequency distributions of the scores on the 12 questions are presented in table 10.2, which also includes their means and standard deviations and the mean scores on the 75-item 45-minute objective section (sect. I) of the test for the candidates selecting each question. The mean essay question scores range from 5.29 to 7.06, a difference that represents about 12 percent of the possible score range. There is a comparable range in the mean objective scores. The two sets of means, however, do not vary together, for the correlation between them is but

.26. This low correlation may simply reflect the fact that the variation among mean scores is not great; however, it does seem difficult to account for the fact that the 159 students who chose question 3 received an average score of only 5.59 on the question while the 181 students who chose question 12 received an average score of 7.06. The two groups of students had essentially the same mean score on Section I of the test. The data strongly suggest that a student who chose to write on questions 1, 6, and 12 would have a clear advantage over one who chose questions 3, 4, and 11. It is not clear, however, whether the differences are a reflection of variations in the reading standards or variations in the quality of instruction received by students selecting the several questions. A variety of questions was included in the examination because it was known that considerable latitude was given to teachers of advanced placement courses to select different foci for courses and for individual students to concentrate their study on particular aspects of American history. Students might logically be expected to choose those questions most appropriate to the course they had studied.

On the other hand, there is some evidence that, when they are given a choice, many students are unable to select the question on which they will make the highest score (Educational Testing Service, unpublished data; Meyer, 1939). If alternate questions appear necessary in order to take account of differences in curricula, it seems desirable to require students to choose groups of questions on the basis of the curricula they have studied rather than to select them on the basis of their general impression of their ability to write appropriate answers. To the student without systematic training in a particular area, a demanding question may appear to be relatively easy.

Adopt Sound Scoring Procedures

No matter how much care has been given to the construction of an essay examination, without procedures that insure reliability of scoring the examination will not function effectively. The individual teacher who approaches the task of scoring a classroom test should be aware of the ways in which he may introduce biases into his ratings and adopt procedures designed to minimize them. The director of large-scale testing programs has an even more challenging problem; for the scores from such programs often are of critical significance, and there is no opportunity to modify judgments on the basis of day-to-day interaction with the examinee. In both cases, it is critical that the attention of the reader of the examination be focussed on the significant aspects of the examination paper, that the personal idiosyncrasy of the reader be minimized, and that the same standards of judgment be applied to each of the papers.

Two common approaches to the problem of obtaining reliability in the ratings of essays have been used. One attempts to reduce scoring variability by providing detailed guides to the rating; the other concentrates on global ratings and reduces the error by including a number of independent ratings in the total score. Both have their advocates. To some extent, the appropriateness of the method will depend on the type of examination.

To the extent that different aspects of the ideal answer to a question can be specified and set forth in check-list form, the process of grading can be transformed into one of identifying and checking off the several aspects. The extent to which the analysis should be carried will depend on the complexity of the question, the importance of the examination, and the time available for making the ratings.

The analytical procedure of rating essays is especially appropriate for examinations dealing with content subjects, such as history. An illustration is provided by the guide prepared some years ago at Educational Testing Service for rating answers to an essay question in an examination in American history. The question was:

American foreign policy during the period 1789–1826 and during the 1930's is often characterized as "isolationist." Compare the "policies of isolation" of these two periods. How appropriately does the term "isolation" characterize these policies?

Raters were asked to consider seven different aspects of the answer:

A. Rationale of Isolation, 1789–1826
B. Specific Isolationist Practices, 1789–1826

C. Rationale of Isolation in 1930's
D. Specific Isolationist Practices 1930's
E. Comparison of Policies of Isolation of Both Periods
F. Appropriateness of Term
G. Quality of English

For each of the seven aspects, detailed guides were provided to the reader, who was required to indicate his judgment by checking one of several judgment categories. For example, the guide for aspect B, "Specific Isolationist Practices, 1789–1826," took the following form:

B. Specific Isolationist Practices, 1789–1826
   1. Neutrality Proclamation 1793
   2. Jay's Treaty 1794 (To avoid League of Armed Neutrality)
   3. Pinckney's Treaty 1795 (To avoid Franco-Spanish U. S. Alliance)
   4. Washington's Farewell Address 1796
   5. Jefferson's First Inaugural Address 1800 ("Entangling Alliances")
   6. "Neutrality" Legislation—Embargo Act 1807
   7. "Neutrality" Legislation—Non-Intercourse Acts 1809–10
   8. "Neutrality" Legislation—Macon's Bill #2 1810
   9. The Monroe Doctrine

---

a. Discusses four of the above, describes each accurately, and connects each with the "rationale" in A; or mentions six.
b. Discusses three of the above, describes each accurately and connects each with the "rationale"; or mentions four.
c. Discusses two of the above, describes each accurately, and connects each with the "rationale" or mentions three.
d. Discusses one of the above, describes each accurately, and connects each with the "rationale" or mentions two.
e. No credit.

In recording his judgment, the rater simply checked the letter corresponding to his judgment for each of the seven aspects. For example, he might have checked c for aspect B above, indicating that the examinee had discussed two specific isolationist practices, describing each accurately, and connecting each with the "rationale."

The seven check marks indicating the rater's

judgments would not automatically provide a score for the essay. This was a reflection of the fact that it has been found desirable to separate the task of judging from the task of scoring. This permits the rater to concentrate on making the judgments and increases the reliability of the rating. At the same time, it permits the scoring to be handled by clerks or by computer. Even if a classroom teacher is both judge and scorer, it is desirable to separate the functions if an analytical procedure is followed.

The scoring process consists of assigning weights to each of the scoring categories and adding the weights for each of the checked categories. There is no need to spend a lot of time developing a complex set of weights: research has indicated that there is little to be gained by such a procedure. The simplest system of weights that differentiates the several levels of judgment is usually as good as a more elaborate one. For example, one might assign weights of 4, 3, 2, 1, and 0 to categories a, b, c, d, and e respectively, in the example above. If the rater then checked c, two points would be recorded for the judgment.

An analytical procedure of this sort is expensive to administer because of the necessity of recording and summarizing a number of different judgments. For large-scale testing programs, the cost may be prohibitive. For the classroom teacher, the time required to prepare the guide and to apply it will be considerably more than for a procedure requiring only a judgment based on general impression. The ratings almost surely will be more reliable; one needs to be sure that they also will be more valid.

Diederich (1967) has pointed to the danger that, in the attempt to identify elements that can be counted, one may give attention to superficial aspects of an answer:

Another way to reach high agreement may be illustrated by an essay question I remember from an examination on Homer's *Odyssey:* "Write a unified essay on the women in the *Odyssey*." This is the "unstructured" type of question that literature teachers love. It is supposed to get at the ability to organize material, independent thinking, critical insight, originality, imagination, and other fine qualities. But the specifications used in grading the answers were quite different. First, the staff made a list of about 12 women in the *Odyssey* that they thought students should remember and gave five points for each one that a student mentioned. But they subtracted one point for misspelling the name, another for omitting or mistaking the place where she lived, and a third for mentioning her out of order. Then they put down three things about each woman that they thought students should remember and gave either one, two, or three points for each one, depending on the accuracy of the statement. At the end, they allowed each reader to give from one to five points for what they called "good writing." Each paper was graded independently by two readers, and they boasted that the average agreement or correlation between pairs of readers was .80. I did not doubt it, but what about all those fine objectives? All that they really measured was total recall of what happened plus ability to spell some rather difficult Greek names [pp. 582–583].

The danger of focussing on elements of a response and missing the essential value also may be present when one is rating composition skills. Wiseman (1949) reported having frequently had the experience of marking school essays by analytical methods and finding that the obviously "best" essay is not at the top of the list. The problem is that a composition often achieves its effect by a unique combination of elements. The effective weights of the elements vary depending on the nature of the communication, and it is impossible to assign weights appropriately independent of some judgment about the nature of the overall communication.

In analytical rating, there is another danger that must be guarded against—the danger of overlooking particular elements of a composition because of a previously formed general impression. This is the well-known *halo* effect. It is more likely to be a problem if the analytical rating requires value judgments of quality than if it involves judgments regarding the presence or absence of particular elements. Scannell and Marshall (1966), for example, reported that teachers in training were unable to rate essay responses to social studies questions on content independent of errors in spelling, punctuation, and grammar. Marshall (1967) replicated the finding with experienced teachers. Page (1967a) was able to obtain statistically significant differential judgments of

different aspects of English compositions, but he used the sum of eight different ratings for each trait.

It is possible, of course, that halo is simply another name for the essential unity of any effective essay response. To the extent that a unique communication has been created, the elements are related to the whole in a fashion that makes a high interrelationship of the parts inevitable. The evaluation of the part cannot be made apart from its relationship to the whole. On the other hand, when different raters assess the parts in different ways depending on the way they assess the whole, one suspects that this is reflecting an irrelevant halo rather than a creative unity.

When applied to appropriate types of essay examinations, analytical reading methods have proved effective in improving the reliability of rating. In the test analysis for the 1956 Advanced Placement Examinations, for example, Swineford (1956) reported coefficients of rater reliability of .951 for American History, .945 for European History, .849 for French, .909 for Biology, .980 for Chemistry, and .978 for Physics. These were long essay examinations (French, 2 1/2 hours; Chemistry, 1 1/2 hours; American History, European History, Biology, and Physics, 2 hours each), and each question had been rated twice; however, even for individual questions within examinations, the reliabilities were relatively high. For the chemistry examination, the rating reliabilities of scores for individual questions based on the sum of two ratings ranged between .811 and .976.

In an effort to avoid some of the problems associated with analytical reading, many examiners have turned to a procedure that calls for the rater to read a question rapidly, form a general impression, and then record a rating. This procedure rests on the proposition that the halo effect noted when several analytical ratings of a product are compared may actually be reflecting a vital quality of the paper. Individual raters will differ in their general impressions of the paper, and these differences will be present to some extent in analytical as well as in global ratings. Since global ratings may be obtained in less time than analytical ratings, why not obtain several global ratings by different raters in preference to a single analytical rating? Coward (1950) investigated the problem and concluded that, if the time devoted to reading is constant, it is possible to get two global ratings of an English composition test in the same time as a single analytical rating and that the reading reliabilities obtained for the two procedures are essentially equivalent. Following a succession of failures to obtain efficient and reliable ratings of English compositions by analytical methods, Godshalk et al. (1966) turned to a global method. Instead of providing raters with a detailed guide of qualities to consider in reaching a judgment, they adopted a simple training method that encouraged consensus by having raters rate a sample of papers and compare their ratings with those of other raters. They (Godshalk et al., 1966) described the procedure:

The readers were asked to make global or holistic, not analytical, judgments of each paper, reading rapidly for a total impression. There were only three ratings: a score of "3" for a superior paper, "2" for an average paper, and "1" for an inferior paper. The readers were told to judge each paper on its merits without regard to other papers on the same topic; that is, they were not to be concerned with any ideas of a normal distribution of the three scores. They were advised that scores of "3" were possible and that the "safe" procedure of awarding almost all "2's" was to be avoided. Standards for the ratings were established in two ways: by furnishing each reader with copies of sample essays for inspection and discussion, and by explaining the conditions of administration and the nature of the testing population; and by having all readers score reproduced sets of carefully selected sample answers to all five questions and report the results. The scores were then tabulated and announced. No effort was made to identify any reader whose standards were out of line, because the fact would be assumed to have a correcting effect. The procedure was repeated several times during the first two days of scoring to assist readers in maintaining standards [p. 10].

In a large field test conducted at a later time a 4-point scale was used, the categories being described as *demonstrates competence, suggests competence, suggests incompetence, demonstrates incompetence*. A detailed study of this

procedure under operational conditions indicated that the sum of three such ratings, which could be obtained in approximately 5 minutes of reading time, produced scores that had a reading reliability of .672 (Myers, McConville, & Coffman, 1966).

More recently, Godshalk (personal communication) has suggested a modification of the 4-point scale, which appears to be even more effective. The reader is told to make a preliminary judgment on the basis of the 4-point scale and then to use the margins on each side of the four points for papers that seem clearly better than average or poorer than the average for a category. Experience suggests that the reading rate is at least as high using this 9-point scale as the 4-point. The procedure was used in reading one of the questions in the 1966 Advanced Placement Examination in English. Each paper was read twice by 2 different readers in a group of 56 readers. The distribution of scores for the two readings, the means, the standard deviations, and the intercorrelation are reported in table 10.3. The product-moment correlation between the two sets of readings, which is .700, is a good estimate of the reliability of a single reading since the two

---

TABLE 10.3

Frequency Distributions of Essay Subscore for One Question of the 1966 Advanced Placement Examination in English

(56 readers were involved)

Score	First Reading	Second Reading
9	1	1
8	8	6
7	12	15
6	29	33
5	40	44
4	66	64
3	101	91
2	176	180
1	61	60
0	1	1
Mean	3.05	3.09
Standard Deviation	1.65	1.67
r_{12}	.700	

Source: adapted from table 2, p. 5, of "The Test Analysis of the Advanced Placement Examination in English," Form OBP, Educational Testing Service *Statistical Report*, 1966, No. 66-90.

TABLE 10.4

Estimates of Components of Variance and Reliability Coefficients for Scores Based on the Sum of Two Ratings for Questions in Advanced Placement Examinations, 1967

Examination	Question	Rating Scale	Source of Variation[1]					Reliability[2]
			σ_p^2	σ_r^2	σ_d^2	σ_{rxd}^2	$\sigma_{rxp(d)}^2$	
American History	1	15-point	57.07	1.70	4.74	3.17	12.17	.840
		9-point	46.06	2.98	0.97	3.03	28.67	.721
	2	15-point	52.80	0.00	0.00	0.07	16.76	.862
		9-point	50.58	10.62	0.00	0.00	31.75	.705
German	1	15-point	56.97	0.79	0.00	0.00	26.76	.805
		6-point	59.06	0.00	0.00	0.42	34.27	.773

Source: prepared by author from data collected for a study not yet reported elsewhere.

[1] Sources of variation:

p = papers
r = ratings
d = days
rxd = ratings by days
$rxp(d)$ = ratings by papers within days.

[2] The formula used in estimating the reliability was

$$r_{ii} = \frac{\sigma_p^2}{\sigma_p^2 + \dfrac{\sigma_r^2 + \sigma_d^2 + \sigma_{rxd}^2 + \sigma_{rxp(d)}^2}{2}}$$

means and standard deviations are essentially the same. The reliability of the sum of the two readings is estimated to be approximately .82, even though the distributions of scores are highly skewed.

The question might be raised regarding the optimum number of categories for a global rating scale. It is desirable to maximize the reliability of the rating by using a scale that is fine enough to reflect whatever differentiations the raters are able to make. At the same time, it is desirable to minimize the amount of time required for making the judgments. It is likely that no definitive answer can be given to the question; each set of circumstances is likely to produce its own answer within relatively broad limits. There is some evidence, for example, that for content examinations raters are able to distinguish more than nine quality levels without an appreciable increase in the time required for making the ratings. For a number of years, readers of Advanced Placement Examinations in such content fields as history, science, and foreign languages have been making ratings of essay questions on a 15-point scale. At the reading session in June 1967 two studies were carried out, one comparing the 15-point rating of American History papers with a 9-point rating, the other comparing the 15-point rating of German papers with a 6-point rating. All

papers were rated twice using each scale, and scores were transformed to a common scale prior to the analysis. (A detailed report of the study is being prepared for publication.) In both cases, the 15-point rating proved to be more reliable, and there was no evidence of a difference in reading rate. The results are summarized in table 10.4. It may be that the superiority of the 15-point scale is attributable to the greater experience of the readers with that particular scale. In any case, it would appear that the sum of two ratings of an essay can provide scores of acceptable rater reliability for examinations of these kinds.

It is important to recognize that, whether the method of rating is analytical or global, an increase in reliability will be achieved as the number of independent ratings is increased. The principle is the same as that operating to increase score reliability by increasing the number of questions in an examination. In general, the pooled judgment of several readers will be more reliable than the judgment of a single reader. It is not always feasible, however, to have each question read by several different readers. Whenever this is not possible, it is desirable that each question on an examination be rated by a different reader.

The classroom teacher may well ask how this principle applies to him. Ordinarily, he is on his own and must make all the ratings for the examinations he administers. Two possibilities ought to be considered. First, he can at least minimize the probability of halo by rating question by question rather than paper by paper. This will reduce the danger that a student's answer to one question will influence the rating on another. Second, he might consider a suggestion, proposed by Diederich and Link (1967), that common examinations, at least in English composition, be administered to all students in a secondary school. Since the skills being measured are those that develop gradually over a period of time, it is possible to have all students write on the same topics and to have all members of the staff participate in the grading. It might be profitable to explore the possibility that the procedure be adapted to other areas, particularly in large schools where a number of different individuals teach the same subject.

This discussion of methods of rating essay responses would not be complete without some reference to the potential impact of the research on computer grading of essays being carried out by Ellis Page and his associates at the University of Connecticut (Page, 1966, 1967a, 1967b). The computer is a tireless, accurate, and rapid scanner of strings of symbols. To the extent that it can be programmed to scan and summarize significant elements and combinations of elements in those strings, it can overcome some of the limitations of human raters.

It probably will be a long time before the computer can be programmed to deal directly with the intrinsic variables of interest in essay responses; that is, to operate on the responses in the same manner as the trained human rater. Already, however, it has proved possible for the computer to identify and deal with correlates of those variables so as to produce scores that are indistinguishable from those produced by human raters. If one must depend on human raters, it will probably be prohibitively expensive to obtain, on a routine basis, reliable subscores for such aspects of English compositions as ideas, organization, style, mechanics, and creativity. It is possible, however, to ob-

TABLE 10.5

Computer Simulation of Human Judgments for Five Essay Traits

(30 predictors, 256 cases)

A Essay Traits	B Hum.-Gp. Reliab.	C Mult. R	D Shrunk. Mult. R	E Corr. (Atten.)
I. Ideas or Content	.75	.72	.68	.78
II. Organization	.75	.62	.55	.64
III. Style	.79	.73	.69	.77
IV. Mechanics	.85	.69	.64	.69
V. Creativity	.72	.71	.66	.78

Source: Page, 1967a. © E.T.S. 1967. Reprinted with permission of the author and publisher.

Note: Column B represents the reliability of the human judgments of each trait, based upon the sum of eight independent ratings, August 1966.

Column C represents the multiple-regression coefficients found in predicting the pooled human ratings with 30 independent variables found in the essays by the computer program.

Column D presents these same coefficients, shrunken to eliminate capitalization on chance from the number of predictor variables (cf. McNemar, 1962, p. 184).

Column E presents these coefficients, both shrunken and corrected for the unreliability of the human groups (cf. McNemar, 1962, p. 153).

tain such scores on a sample of papers for the purpose of establishing a criterion measure and then to attempt to approximate the criterion scores by computer simulation. In table 10.5 are reproduced data reported by Page (1967b). They suggest that actuarial simulation of rating of stylistic aspects of writing is already possible. Research efforts now are being turned to deeper dimensions of stylistic analysis and to subject-matter content as in essay questions in history, philosophy, or science. Hopefully, such efforts will not only provide economical methods for approximating human judgments; but, more importantly, they may throw light on the processes by which the human judgments are generated.

Be Aware of Limitations of Current Knowledge about Essay Testing

It should be recognized that in the area of essay testing, as in most areas of human endeavor, few of the important questions have been answered in any final way. Research has demonstrated that essay tests are unreliable in many cases; that is, that when an attempt is made to replicate the testing procedure using different questions and different raters, the results disagree so that the ordering of the inlividuals and even the judgment of general level of a group may change. What is often not recognized is that the term *errors of measurement* often reflects ignorance of "what goes on" when students write essay answers and teachers rate those answers. Further research may permit the incorporation into the systematic variance of much of what is now labeled error.

The fact, for example, that global judgments of writing ability are often superior to the sum of analytical ratings may simply reflect the fact that not enough is known to permit one to vary the weights of the several analytical ratings depending on some still unidentified characteristic of the total communication. It may be that for "Communication Situation A" short sentences are superior to long ones, while for "Communication Situation B" the opposite is the case; and that it has not yet been learned how to prepare "questions" that require that responses be limited to one communication situation only. To date, attempts to develop models of the communication process have been relatively primitive. Perhaps as electronic data-processing tools become more widely understood by those concerned with research on English composition, it will become possible both to identify the critical elements and to examine their interrelationships using equations more complex than the linear multiple regression model now in common use.

Even today, however, it is possible to identify certain critical aspects of the examination process and to insure that each is given its proper weight. It does not do much good to achieve high rating reliability (usually at considerable expense), for example, if the sample is so inadequate that the test reliability remains low. In this context, it would be well to keep in mind the fact that the scoring reliability of a single objective test item is likely to be in excess of .99, yet nobody would confuse this coefficient with the reliability of a test made up of two or three such items. One needs always to develop some estimate of the consistency to be expected between the test one is administering and one of the many possible alternate tests that might be substituted for it.

Overconcern with either rating reliability or score reliability, however, may lead one to forget that the typical test is designed to provide information, on the basis of a particular behavior sample, about some underlying quality that is the real concern of the evaluator. The test behavior inevitably will provide a limited picture. In many cases, the test is clearly an indirect way of obtaining evidence, and one cannot estimate how closely the indirect measure reflects the underlying criterion unless one can obtain a more direct sample and make a comparison. In such cases, there is a need for formal validity studies in which the more direct evidence is collected and compared with the indirect. In other cases, however, the test is a sample, though often a very small sample, of the underlying quality. In those cases, it needs to be recognized that as the test sample becomes closely representative of the underlying quality, the correlation of the test with fundamental underlying quality will tend to become higher than its correlation with a parallel test, which would also be but a small sample (Coffman, 1966). To reject a test of relatively low reliability that was really a sample of the underlying quality in favor of a more indirect measure of higher reliability might be to settle for lower validity for the measure. This danger should always be weighed and experimental evidence sought when competing methods of testing are being evaluated.

NEEDED RESEARCH

In 1951, Stalnaker could write that the essay question "is a test form which, in spite of its widespread use, has been subjected to almost no exacting experimental study [p. 528]." Such a statement can no longer be made. Since Stalnaker wrote, there have been many studies reported, some of which can certainly be characterized as exacting experimental studies. However, in relation to the variety and complexity of the questions one may ask about essay examinations, the research evidence is still fragmentary.

This is not surprising. The researcher who attempts to study essay testing is faced with formidable problems. Essay questions are used for examinations in many different subject fields, and within any field the essay questions may differ greatly in what they require the student to do; it is not wise to try to generalize across fields or across question types within a field on the basis of research on a single field or a single question type. An essay examination of adequate length to sample achievement in even a single field requires half a day of testing time; one does not lightly undertake to double the testing time in order to estimate the parallel-form reliability of the examination. The rating of a single large-scale essay examination involves hundreds of raters and may require a week or more of rating time; one does not routinely complicate the procedure by introducing experimental procedures to isolate the various components of error variance. The pretesting of essay questions involves asking students to take time to write answers and employing teachers to rate what has been written; few essay questions are subjected to the extensive pretesting and statistical analysis commonly applied to objective test questions. If research findings are unfavorable to essay testing, one often suspects that the problem is inadequacy of execution rather than basic flaws in the method; to carry out a comprehensive study of essay testing often requires more time of researchers, students, and teachers than they are willing to spend.

One possible way out of the dilemma is to continue conducting studies of limited scope, giving careful attention to how each new study will contribute to a tight network of related evidence. Eventually, however, it will be necessary to conduct some comprehensive studies; the answers to some critical questions depend on understanding complex relationships that cannot be answered without large amounts of data on the same individuals. Some way must be found to enlist the cooperation of students and teachers in research if decisions regarding examination practices are to be based on evidence rather than opinion.

Most of the research on essay testing already completed has dealt in one way or another with the question of reliability. The research of the future must devote more attention to the question of validity. Is it true that essay questions can elicit more valid information about the achievement of examinees than other types of questions? If so, what are the kinds of questions and what are the content areas in which they are appropriately used? In what contexts are essay questions more valid than other types? Are the claims for desirable side effects from the use of essay examinations and undesirable side effects of the use of other types of examinations legitimate? Are essay examinations really "work samples" as some claim, or is the essay examination, in its own way, as artificial as the objective question? From time to time in this chapter, reference has been made to the need for further research on one or another of these questions. The questions tend to merge with one another in complex ways when one begins to study them, however. It is the purpose of this section of the chapter to call attention to problems likely to be encountered in future research in the area. The points to be made are suggestive rather than exhaustive. The individual researcher will undoubtedly discover many others.

Problem of Uniqueness

It has been argued that essay examinations are more valid than other types of examinations, such as multiple choice, because they require the examinee to do what he must do in the real world—i.e. to organize and communicate his thoughts in relation to a problem, some aspects of which are new to him. Generally, however, even in the most intensively studied area, English composition, the evidence for this position is inadequate. The typical research study has taken the form of:

1. Constructing (or locating) essay and objective tests covering the same content.

2. Administering both to the same sample in a design that permits an estimate of test reliability for both types of questions.

3. Calculating the essay-objective correlation and the two reliability coefficients.

4. If the correlation between essay and objective tests, corrected for attenuation, is very high, concluding that the two test forms are measuring essentially the same thing; if the cor-

rected coefficient is low, concluding that the essay test is measuring some unique factor or factors.

This type of research can be faulted on a number of counts. In most cases, the investigator or his associates have constructed (or selected) both types of tests and consciously or unconsciously one type is favored over the other. (One might ask what the effect would be if competing teams were assigned the task of constructing the experimental tests—a team favoring the essay examination and a team favoring the multiple-choice examination.) If uniqueness is demonstrated, there is no guarantee that the uniqueness is related to the criterion because no criterion measure was included in the design. If uniqueness is not demonstrated, it is not clear whether the finding is generalizable beyond the particular sample used in the study because no information is given on the background of the individuals in the sample. It may be that individuals in the sample have been taught to answer essay questions and objective questions to the same relative level of performance. One is left with the feeling that perhaps another group of subjects with different training might have performed quite differently.

Future research on the uniqueness problem should meet these standards:

1. There should be a clearly specified criterion, preferably one more representative of the "real world" than the essay examination itself. The criterion might consist of simulated problems permitting the student greater freedom than the examination situation—to consult source material, to think deeply, to draft and revise. Or, it might consist of the accumulation of products and/or ratings over a period of time.

2. Essay and objective tests to be compared should be equally well constructed. If objective items are pretested, essay questions should be pretested also. If essay questions are constructed by classroom teachers, objective questions also should be constructed by classroom teachers.

3. Attention should be given to the possible interaction of teaching method and test performance. It will probably be impossible to introduce experimental teaching methods judged to be inferior, but it should be possible to locate situations where such methods are being used and to compare students from these situations with students from more favorable situations.

4. The studies should be conducted using different examination content. There is need to know whether findings in history are the same as those in physics. Or whether essay examinations in engineering have characteristics similar to those in law. It is not sufficient to investigate essay testing in general; one needs to understand the nature of variations from content field to content field.

The Context Problem

It has already been noted that there is need for more information about the extent to which essay questions are relevant to particular subject areas. There is also need for more information on the relation between essay and objective testing in different contexts. Most authorities seem to believe that essay questions are likely to be particularly useful in classroom tests where the number of examinees is limited and the examiner has had limited experience in writing objective tests. In contrast, most of the research has been carried out in large-scale examination situations. There is need for research comparing the information obtained from teacher-made essay examinations with that obtained from teacher-made objective examinations. Attention needs to be given to teacher-by-method interactions, and studies should be carried out in various subject fields.

Research on this problem will be difficult to design. Any attempt to develop a common criterion appropriate to different teaching contexts introduces the risk of imposing an artificial context and destroying the very situations one wishes to investigate. It may be that one should not approach this problem on the basis of an experimental design. Rather, the approach might better be one of observing practices and attempting to abstract common and contrasting elements. In practice, what kinds of examinations do teachers at a given educational level and in a particular content field write? What kinds of information do they abstract? What relationship exists between the training of the teacher in formal testing procedures and the examination procedures used by the teacher? If teachers who use essay examinations are asked to prepare parallel objective examinations (or objective examinations to supplement the essay examinations) and if teachers who use objective examinations are asked to prepare essay examinations, how will the resulting examinations be judged by experts in evaluation? How will they function when administered to students?

Problem of Side Effects

Much has been written about the undesirable side effects of discontinuing the use of essay examinations, but there have actually been few studies of the problem. The few reported studies have followed a relatively simple design. Experimental subjects have been informed that they will be examined in essay format or objective format and then they have been examined using both formats. No information has been provided on the backgrounds of experience of examinees with either format prior to the experiment, nor has there been any attempt to relate the outcomes to variations in teaching techniques. It may be that the extent of the side effects in either direction are more closely related to the expectations of students regarding the meaning of examination scores than to any objective concept regarding examination format.

Again, it is unlikely that a researcher will be permitted to conduct long-term modifications in either teaching practices or examination practices on a random-sampling basis. It will be necessary to search for schools or classes within schools that constitute natural experimental variations. If, for example, a change in test format is introduced into a national testing program, what changes can be observed in the study practices of students in what kinds of classes in what kinds of schools? It may be that no differences can be detected. What about changes in teaching practices? Is it possible that well-informed teachers do not change their teaching practices but that poorly informed teachers do?

The questions about essay examinations that need to be studied are not simple ones, and they will not be answered on the basis of simple, limited experimental research. Rather, they are complicated questions requiring persistent effort using whatever methods will break through the curtain surrounding much teaching and learning. It is likely that much of the research will require painstaking observation and systematic classification of records rather than the application of classical experimental designs.

SUMMARY

Despite widespread evidence of limitations inherent in the essay examination, the procedure continues to be widely used, not only by classroom teachers but also by external examiners responsible for appraising status at critical points in educational or professional careers. In some contexts, there is reason to believe that essay examinations are the only suitable methods available either because examiners lack the skills to develop objective tests of high quality or because the essays constitute direct measurement of the criterion performance and therefore provide more valid measurement than alternative approaches.

There is little doubt that for many purposes, particularly when large numbers of candidates are to be examined and when the measurement involves subject-matter knowledge, objective testing is more efficient than essay testing. On the other hand, when questions are carefully constructed and focussed on performances involving the communication of complex relationships among ideas and when carefully planned scoring procedures designed to minimize systematic and variable scoring error are applied, essay examinations can provide reliable and valid evidence of achievement.

The variables involved in the determination of essay examination scores are complex, and their relationships may differ from situation to situation in many ways. Thus, research data are seldom definitive or applicable over a wide span of situations. The task of building a framework of research findings to guide decisions of users of essay examinations is far from finished. Even where the guidelines seem clearly established, it is usually desirable to conduct periodic quality-control studies.

REFERENCES

Carroll, J. A. A factor analysis of verbal ability. *Psychometrika*, 1941, **6,** 279–307.

Coffman, W. E. On the validity of essay tests of achievement. *Journal of Educational Measurement*, 1966, **3,** 151–156.

Coffman, W. E., & Kurfman, D. A. A comparison of two methods of reading essay examinations. *American Educational Research Journal*, 1968, **5,** 99–107.

College Entrance Examination Board. *Annual report of the College Board* 1965–66. New York: CEEB, 1966. Pp. 32–33.

Coward, A. F. The method of reading the Foreign Service Examination in English Composition. Educational Testing Service *Research Bulletin*, 1950, No. 57.

Diederich, P. B. Cooperative preparation and rating of essay tests. *English Journal*, 1967, **56,** 573–584.

Diederich, P. B., & Link, F. R. Cooperative evaluation in English. In F. T. Wilhelms (Ed.), *Evaluation as feedback and guide*. Washington: Association for Supervision and Curriculum Development, National Education Association, 1967. Pp. 181–232.

DuBois, P. H. A test-dominated society: China, 1115 B.C.–1905 A.D. In *Proceedings of the 1964 Invitational Conference on Testing Problems*. Princeton, N. J.: Educational Testing Service, 1965. Pp. 3–11.

Ebel, R. L. Estimation of the reliability of ratings. *Psychometrika*, 1951, **16,** 407–424.

Ebel, R. L. *Measuring educational achievement*. New York: Prentice-Hall, 1965.

Finlayson, D. S. The reliability of the marking of essays. *British Journal of Educational Psychology*, 1951, **21,** 126–134.

French, J. W. The effects of essay tests on student motivation. Educational Testing Service *Research Bulletin*, 1956, No. 4.

French, J. W. Schools of thought in judging excellence of English themes. In *Proceedings of the 1961 Invitational Conference on Testing Problems*. Princeton, N. J.: Educational Testing Service, 1962. Pp. 19–28.

Gleser, G. C., Cronbach, L. J., & Rajaratnam, N. Generalizability of scores influenced by multiple sources of variance. *Psychometrika*, 1965, **30,** 395–418.

Godshalk, F. I., Swineford, F., & Coffman, W. E. *The measurement of writing ability*. New York: College Entrance Examination Board, 1966.

Gosling, G. W. H. *Marking English compositions*. Victoria: Australian Council for Educational Research, 1966.

Gustav, A. Student's preferences for test format in relation to their test scores. *Journal of Psychology*, 1964, **57,** 159–164.

Hartog, P., & Rhodes, E. C. *The marks of examiners*. New York: Macmillan, 1936.

Jackson, P. W. *Life in classrooms*. New York: Holt, Rinehart & Winston, 1968.

Jewett, A., & Bish, C. E. (Eds.) *Improving English composition*. Washington: National Education Association, 1965.

Kruglak, H. Resource letter AT-1 on achievement testing. *American Journal of Physics*, 1965, **33,** 255–263.

Marshall, J. C. Composition errors and essay examination grades reexamined. *American Educational Research Journal*, 1967, **4,** 375–386.

McNemar, Q. *Psychological statistics*. (3rd ed.) New York: Wiley, 1962.

Meyer, G. An experimental study of the old and new types of examination: I. The effect of the examination set on memory. *Journal of Educational Psychology*, 1934, **25,** 641–661.

Meyer, G. An experimental study of the old and new types of examination: II. Methods of study. *Journal of Educational Psychology*, 1935, **26,** 30–40.

Meyer, G. The choice of questions on essay examinations. *Journal of Educational Psychology*, 1939, **30,** 161–171.

Myers, A. E., McConville, C. B., & Coffman, W. E. Simplex structure in the grading of essay tests. *Educational and Psychological Measurement*, 1966, **26,** 41–54.

Noyes, E. S. Essay and objective tests in English. *College Board Review*, 1963, **49,** 7–10.

Page, E. B. The imminence of grading essays by computer. *Phi Delta Kappan*, 1966, **47,** 238–243.

Page, E. B. Grading essays by computer: Progress report. In *Proceedings of the 1966 Invitational Conference on Testing Problems*. Princeton, N. J.: Educational Testing Service, 1967. Pp. 87–100. (a)

Page, E. B. Statistical and linguistic strategies in the computer grading of essays. *2eme Conference Internationale Sur Le Traitement Automatique Des Langues* (Proceedings), August 23–25, 1967, No. 34. (b)

Pearson, R. The test fails as an entrance examination. In Should the general composition test be continued? *College Board Review*, 1955, No. 25, 2–9.

Scannell, D. P., & Marshall, J. C. The effect of selected composition errors on grades assigned to essay examinations. *American Educational Research Journal*, 1966, **3**, 125–130.

Serling, A. M. Three methods of testing literary comprehension at the advanced placement level. *College Board Research and Development Reports 66–7, No. 4*. Princeton, N. J.: Educational Testing Service, 1967.

Solomon, R. J. Improving the essay test in the social studies. *National Council Social Studies Yearbook*, 1965, **35**, 137–153.

Stalnaker, J. M. The essay type of examination. In E. F. Lindquist (Ed.), *Educational measurement*. Washington: American Council on Education, 1951. Pp. 495–530.

Stanley, J. C. Analysis of variance principles applied to the grading of essay tests. *Journal of Experimental Education*, 1962, **30**, 279–283.

Starch, D., & Elliott, E. C. Reliability of grading of high school work in English. *School Review*, 1912 **20**, 442–457.

Swineford, F. Test analysis, Advanced Placement Tests, Form EBP. *Statistical Report* No. 28 Princeton, N. J.: Educational Testing Service, 1956.

Swineford, F. Test analysis, Advanced Placement Examination in American History, Form MBP. Educational Testing Service *Statistical Report*, 1964, No. 53. (a)

Swineford, F. Test analysis, Advanced Placement Examination in Mathematics, Form MBP. Educational Testing Service *Statistical Report*, 1964, No. 52. (b)

Taylor, C. W. A factorial study of fluency in writing. *Psychometrika*, 1947, **12**, 239–262.

Vallance, T. R. A comparison of essay and objective examinations as learning experiences. *Journal of Educational Research*, 1947, **41**, 279–288.

Vernon, P. E., & Millican, G. D. A further study of the reliability of English essays. *British Journal of Statistical Psychology*, 1954, **7**, 65–74.

Wiseman, S. The marking of English composition in grammar school selection. *British Journal of Educational Psychology*, 1949, **19**, 200–209.

Wiseman, S., & Wrigley, S. Essay-reliability: The effect of choice of essay-title. *Educational and Psychological Measurement*, 1958, **18**, 129–138.

Wittenborn, J. R. Manual ability, its nature and measurement. *Educational and Psychological Measurement*, 1945, **5**, 241–260; 395–409.

Young, D. Examining essays for eleven plus classification. *British Journal of Educational Psychology*, 1962, **32**, 267–274.

11. Prediction Instruments for Educational Outcomes

Paul A. Schwarz
American Institutes for Research

The discussion in preceding chapters considered the construction of tests to measure the progress students who had already completed a course had made toward the course objectives. In this chapter, the discussion turns to the development of tests to forecast the progress students who have not even begun the course are likely to make if they are admitted. How does one proceed?

The first step is to determine the exact skills and attributes the course is supposed to develop. These are the specific outcomes to be predicted, and they are identical to those that were assessed with achievement and proficiency tests discussed in the earlier chapters. But for prediction instruments, test exercises that directly measure these outcomes cannot be written: applicants to the course as yet have not achieved them. Thus the second step is to develop a list of skills and attributes the applicants have had a chance to acquire, through earlier experiences and courses, and that are related to the to-be-predicted set in such a manner that the applicants who have achieved the one tend later to achieve the other. Test exercises that measure these skills and attributes then are written. The result is an "achievement" test that measures the outcomes of earlier courses and earlier experiences rather than the outcomes attributable to the course itself. And to the extent that achievement of these earlier outcomes is in fact correlated with achievement of the target outcomes, the test serves as an effective predictor.

It follows that the development of a prediction instrument differs from the methodology described in the preceding chapters only in the manner in which the outcomes to be measured by the test are selected. To extend the methodology to include prediction, the procedures used for identifying the outcomes of past experiences that are likely to predict achievement of a given set of instructional objectives must be added to the methodology.

SELECTING THE SKILLS AND ATTRIBUTES TO BE MEASURED

When content for a prediction test is selected, the test constructor is free to include any skill or characteristic that the applicants have had a chance to develop. He need not limit himself to the outcomes of the formal education that they have completed but can draw also on all the jobs, hobbies, readings, travels, social activities, and other developmental experiences to which the applicants have been exposed. The trick is to find among these hundreds or thousands of item possibilities the ones that are most closely related to the future outcomes to be predicted.

To do this, there is no other choice but to use an enlightened trial-and-error approach. As a first step, the test constructor selects from the huge pool of potentially predictive applicant characteristics a manageable subset that he considers relevant on the basis of his knowledge of human behavior and that actually can be measured within the practical constraints (on time or cost or examiners) that the intended user of the test has imposed. Then, he writes items to measure the subset that he has selected. These items are administered to individuals who have had the developmental experiences characteristic of the applicant group and whose performance on the target outcomes can be measured. He might test a sample of individuals who have already completed the course to obtain comparison data on the target outcomes immediately, but this procedure is subject to errors that may be introduced by generalizing from course graduates to the less-experienced applicant group. He might test, and later follow up, a sample of applicants, but this sacrifices speed for the sake of results more representative of the population for which the test actually is intended. Either method, however, does enable him to compare the examinee's performance on the precourse and postcourse measures and, thereby, to determine empirically which of the characteristics included in the trial test do seem to be predictive. These characteristics are retained. The rejected types of items are replaced by selecting other characteristics from the large pool with which he began. This process of tryout, evaluation, and replacement is repeated as often as necessary to produce a testing program ready for operational use. A test may be considered ready for use when the cost of administering it is justified by the gain in accuracy that it affords in the administrative decisions (selection, guidance, etc.) it is supposed to upgrade; and its development is completed when further cycles of revision do not result in useful additional gains.

The empirical aspects of this process are described more fully in other chapters. Here the concern is with the rational process of selection of the initial subset of the many potentially predictive characteristics to be subjected to empirical evaluation. The effectiveness of the instrument produced and the efficiency in producing it clearly depend on the adequacy of this initial selection, since the empirical data can do no more than to confirm or reject the specific hypotheses with which one decides to begin actual test construction.

One common approach to this step is to begin with those characteristics of the applicant group on which data can be collected most easily. In the student files of most colleges, for example, there are application blanks, transcripts, test scores, and other historical information dating back to the day the students were themselves applicants for admission. The test constructor readily can compare these data with subsequent performance to determine which elements seem predictive. Among his positive findings will be some elements that are not in fact effective predictors but that happened to fit certain idiosyncrasies of the particular tryout group he happened to use and

therefore showed a positive relationship not generalizeable to future applicant groups. To eliminate these spurious elements, he repeats the study with a second tryout group and accepts only those items that also pass this separate cross-validation. If more items are needed, he tries to deduce from his empirical findings the additional categories of information that might be effective and continues the trial-and-error procedure until he obtains an adequate predictor instrument.

The objectivity of this "shotgun" approach is intuitively appealing, as is the economy of using information already on file. But the approach does have two serious limitations. The first is that the test constructor does not apply his knowledge of the course requirements or of the dynamics of human behavior and thus will almost certainly fail to include predictive elements that analysis and deduction would have suggested. This is one instance in which a purely statistical approach is less effective and less efficient than one based on professional judgment. The second limitation is that he will usually not be able to make adjustments in the instrument after it has been developed, to adapt it for a slightly different use or to reflect changes in the applicant population being recruited, without repeating the developmental procedure. An instrument based solely on empirical data provides no evidence on the important question of *why* it is effective and therefore is not readily generalized to groups that differ from those on whom the initial data were collected.

For these reasons, it is preferable to select the items to be included in the first tryout on rational grounds. Using this approach, the test constructor begins by analyzing the target outcomes and generating one or more hypotheses about the types of prior outcomes that should be predictive. He then writes a set of trial test items on the basis of these hypotheses and uses the empirical results of the initial tryout to confirm or reject the hypotheses with which he began. In this way, he generates not only a specific set of predictive test items but also a set of rational *principles* for item construction. And the availability of such principles greatly simplifies the task of developing alternate forms, adjusting the instrument for different applicant groups, or extending it to new applications.

The initial set of hypotheses is called the test *rationale*. It is generally useful to prepare a written rationale before the test is constructed, using the format that Flanagan (1951) has suggested. This format consists of a precise description of the outcomes to be predicted, an analysis of these outcomes in terms of their psychological implications, and detailed specifications for the trial items to be prepared. Flanagan (1951) cited the following example, taken from an Air Force testing project, for predicting a candidate's skill in "defining a difficult problem correctly":

Description of the Behavior. This behavior consists of identifying and defining the nature and extent of a problem. The fact that a problem exists has already been recognized, and the task is now one of defining the exact nature of the problem so that its solution can be directly and systematically attempted. Ineffective behavior in this respect is illustrated by an airplane commander who recognizes that the morale of his crew is bad, and proceeds to institute new policies and take miscellaneous actions without determining first what the specific nature of the problem is. Effective behavior, on the other hand, is illustrated by a navigator who recognizes that he is not determining his positions accurately and sets out systematically to find where the difficulty lies so that he can take the necessary steps to correct the situation.

Analysis of the Behavior. The basis of the behavior identified as defining a difficult problem seems to lie in the ability to crystallize and order a conglomeration of diverse factors. This includes recognizing the relationship among factors and evaluating their relative importance. It involves sorting out and organizing the relevant aspects in such a way that the most direct and efficient attack on the problem is clearly discernible. The characteristic might be termed "clear and orderly thinking," and is probably uniquely important in determining effectiveness in this category of behavior.

Item Specifications. For measuring the ability to define difficult problems a printed test would be used. The examinee would be presented with a paragraph, as brief as possible, containing a conglomeration of factors dealing with a problem situation. Some factors would be relevant and others irrelevant. The examinee would be required to select the statement which most concisely and directly summarizes the essential aspects of the problem [pp. 153–155].

The formulation of a comprehensive rationale is in itself a useful exercise in that it forces the test constructor to think through his assumptions. The completed rationale also provides a convenient vehicle as well for a critical review by item editors and consultants.

Most of the widely used prediction instruments are based on a small set of tried and true rationales developed during the past 60 years. This chapter reviews these rationales, indicating their major advantages and limitations, and then suggests a number of opportunities for advancing the state of the art through innovation.

COMMON PREDICTOR RATIONALES

Adequacy of Preparation

No instructional program begins at an "absolute zero" of student sophistication. To profit from the instruction, the entering student must have already acquired certain knowledge and skills that the course takes for granted— basic skills such as the ability to read, or specialized skills such as the ability to solve differential equations. One of the most straightforward of admission procedures is to measure the applicants' achievement of these entry skills and to screen out the individuals who have not attained the minimum level the course of study requires.

Such screening is most useful in situations in which the applicants are known to vary widely with respect to one or more of the necessary entry skills. The admission of foreign students to an American university is one clearcut example. Many foreign students have not the command of English necessary to keep up with the pace of instruction and advance verification of their competency in English is an indicated screening procedure.

Assumptions

The rationale for screening applicants on the basis of course prerequisites is largely self-evident, but it does entail one implicit assumption. When an applicant who has not acquired a needed skill by the time of admission is rejected, it is assumed that he will not be able to develop this skill through remedial work while the course proceeds. It is important to review this assumption periodically because of the continuing effort that is being made to expand opportunities for remedial study throughout the educational system.

Application

The basic problem in developing an appropriate screening procedure is that it is in practice surprisingly difficult to specify the exact types and levels of entry skills that are truly essential. In the above example, the screening of foreign students on the basis of their language skills may seem at first glance to be an obvious and entirely straightforward procedure. But further analysis will suggest that most of the standard criteria of English competency—such as correct grammatical usage—are probably irrelevant to the fundamental communication skills that the student must have to profit from courses in which English is the medium of instruction. And even for skills that seem clearly relevant to effective communication—such as reading speed—there is no easy way to establish a fixed cut-off point below which students should be rejected. At what rate *does* a student have to be able to read to keep up with American instruction? The construction of an accurate screening test can itself be a research task of substantial proportions.

Care also must be exercised in the interpretation of the scores obtained from tests based on this rationale. Unless one is prepared to make a number of additional assumptions (discussed in subsequent rationales), one should not combine the scores on a screening test with other selection criteria and thereby permit a high score on this test to compensate for deficiencies in other respects. For example, a top score on an English competency test *may* be predictive of the success of a foreign student entering an engineering curriculum, but there is nothing in the basic rationale for screening tests to suggest that this should be so; the rationale indicates only that students with low scores should be rejected. The admissions pro-

cedure of the institutions that give extra credit for a high mark on a screening test without recognizing or checking the additional assumptions that this implies is clearly without rational basis. However, it may well be the case that the same test that functions at one level as a screening test functions at a higher level as a measure of scholastic attainment and is justified by the rationale elaborated in the next section.

History of Scholastic Attainment

Going beyond the screening of unqualified applicants to the question of which of the remaining applicants are likely to be most successful, reliance is placed in part on a measure of the applicants' achievement in the preparatory institutions they attended before. An instrument to evaluate their attainment in these institutions is constructed and their future performance is predicted directly from the results. Those who achieved the most then, it is predicted, will achieve the most now.

Assumptions

The rationale for using academic attainment as a predictor involves three major assumptions. It is reasoned that

1. *if* the educational experiences provided by the preparatory institutions that the applicants attended were approximately the same, and
2. *if* the applicants' differential accomplishment in response to these equivalent experiences was the result of fairly stable differences in their individual performance characteristics, and
3. *if* accomplishment in the new institution is a function of the same types of performance characteristics,

then the applicants should continue to achieve differentially in the same way as before. The extent to which these three assumptions are valid in the particular situation in which they are applied determines the accuracy of the predictions that are obtained.

Experience has shown that the first of the above assumptions—i.e. the equivalence of past educational experiences—is the least valid in most practical situations. Typically, the applicants have attended different preparatory institutions and have received instruction of varying degrees of effectiveness. The inputs that helped to shape their respective achievements have *not* been the same. And, if the quality of the preparatory institutions is sufficiently heterogeneous, it may be found that indices of prior attainment measure differences not so much in the performance characteristics of the applicants as in the excellence of the institutions they attended before.

Such inequities in the quality of prior instruction should be expected to reduce but not to obliterate the accuracy of predictions based on scholastic attainment. A certain proportion of the applicants who attended poor preparatory institutions may as a result have failed to acquire the prerequisite skills discussed in the preceding rationale and be unable to succeed in the more advanced institution, irrespective of their theoretical performance potential. For this group, an index of academic attainment serves the same function as a screening test and affords corresponding accuracy for purposes of prediction. For other applicants, the quality of the institutions they attended before may well be correlated with their individual performance capabilities, as a result of the selection practices of these institutions. The better institutions might set higher admission standards or might draw students from higher socioeconomic levels, and either of these factors could contribute to the predictive accuracy of attainment measures. But these fringe benefits are incidental to the main thrust of the rationale for using indices of scholastic attainment; and considerably greater accuracy may be obtained by adjusting the applicants' scores in accordance with the quality of their prior schooling, especially when the differences among the schools they attended are large. Some appropriate methods for adjusting scores are described later in this section.

Deviations from the second assumption—i.e. that each applicant's attainment is a reflection of fairly stable performance characteristics with which he was born or which he has developed—have somewhat different implications.

Inevitably, past accomplishments of some applicants will have been shaped to a disproportionate extent by incidental events and will not accurately reflect their current potential. Family crises, difficult social adjustments, uncorrected vision problems, personality clashes with one or more teachers, and many other factors extraneous to the above rationale can and do attenuate the value of school achievement as a predictor. But the hope of making adjustments to compensate for these kinds of discrepancies (which are a source of error in all prediction instruments) is unrealistic. Tests that are equally "fair" to every applicant do not exist. The overall effect of such errors can be minimized, however, by using attainment measures in combination with other types of instruments and thereby reducing the net impact of the extraneous fluctuations that affect each test.

The third assumption—i.e. that the same performance characteristics that shaped the applicant's attainment in the past will continue to do so in future—is generally reasonably well fulfilled. Institutions at different levels of the educational pyramid do tend to require the same kinds of performance, and it is only when students apply to highly specialized institutions or decide to break away from the curriculum they have been pursuing that the requirements are likely to differ qualitatively from those they encountered before. The accuracy of prediction can frequently be sharpened, however, by narrowing the focus of measurement from overall attainment to attainment in the particular courses that are most closely related to the new curriculum and, as is elaborated below, by narrowing the focus still further to the specific outcomes of these courses that are the most closely related to the new outcomes to be achieved.

Overall, the rationale for academic attainment as a predictor is one of the least demanding of those commonly used. It does not require the test constructor to determine the specific performance characteristics that are important to success in the new institution but lets him proceed on the much simpler assumption that they are the same as the ones that shaped the applicant's performance in the educational experiences he encountered before. Individual differences in ability, interest, motivation, or any other important determinant of student attainment are all encompassed in this one rationale.

Application

Academic attainment can be measured by the use of achievement tests or by performance records such as school grades. Each method has certain advantages and limitations. The major advantage of tests is that all applicants are evaluated on precisely the same set of criteria, insuring comparable scores for applicants from different institutions. The main advantages of school records are that they are based on performance over a period of time rather than on a "one-shot" evaluation and they are generally cheaper to obtain than test scores.

Achievement tests—Tests of attainment in the major school subjects are readily available and may be used singly or in combination to predict performance at the next higher educational level. The manuals provided with the major published tests typically indicate the level predictive accuracy that can be expected, and these data as well as numerous independent studies (e.g. Travers, 1949) show that standardized achievement tests as a class are effective predictors.

They may not be maximally *efficient* predictors, however. As noted in preceding chapters, the content of an achievement test is a representative sample of all of the outcomes at which the student's past courses have been directed, which is entirely appropriate for purposes of a comprehensive assessment. But from the point of view of prediction, a representative sample of course objectives is likely to include certain items that are not closely related to the requirements of future courses and that as a result contribute little to the predictive accuracy of the test. An achievement test in high school mathematics, for example, should properly include both geometry and trigonometry problems, if it is to serve its intended role of assessment. But it may be that geometry problems are in fact much more predictive of college success. If this is really the case, the efficiency of the test for predictive purposes will be increased by expanding the elements that offer the greatest validity and ignoring the rest; and this can often be accomplished with a minimum of additional research. Beginning with a standard achievement test, the test constructor determines the predictive accuracy of the items related to each of the separate outcomes the test is intended to measure and then uses these empirical data to select content for an improved custom-made version.

The same distinction between assessment and prediction is pertinent also to the perennial arguments about the relative merits of objective and essay tests. To many educators it seems self-evident that comprehensive achievement tests in such courses as English must include composition exercises if they are to appraise adequately the attainment of outcomes related to self-expression. This is a reasonable view in the case of assessment, where comprehensiveness is itself an important objective and where failure to incorporate certain outcomes may lead the teachers to deemphasize these aspects of the instruction. But for prediction, the same line of reasoning does not apply. In any given situation, it may be found that objective tests yield as accurate a basis for prediction as is available from any combination of attainment measures: that the seemingly different information provided by essay tests does not increase the accuracy of the predictions at all. This would be the case, for example, if the outcomes best suited to objective measurement are also the ones that are the most predictive elements of the course, or if the students who have attained these outcomes are the same ones who have attained those represented in essay tests. It follows that not only the selection of outcomes to be included in a prediction instrument but also the decisions pertaining to the format of the test items are best made on the basis of empirical validity findings.

An empirical approach also is indicated in attempting to compensate for differences in the quality of the preparatory schools the applicants have attended; i.e. for deviations from the first assumption of the above rationale. In theory, the ideal solution would be for each higher-level institution to carry out separate validity studies for the applicant groups drawn from different preparatory schools, to develop a separate regression equation for predicting the future attainment of the applicants in each of these groups, and then to use the predicted attainment score of each applicant rather than his raw achievement test scores as the basis for admission. This procedure would eliminate the nonpredictive differences in the achievement of applicants from higher- and lower-quality schools (since these would not appear in the predicted attainment scores), yet retain all of the predictive differences, such as those resulting from systematic differences in the ability of the students who typically enter the various preparatory institutions.

The practical difficulties of implementing this theoretically ideal solution are, however, enormous. Few institutions accept a large enough sample of students from every preparatory school that generates applicants to permit separate validity studies; and, even if the process were carried out by a centralized testing service that has access to sufficiently large samples, the computational requirements would almost certainly prove too cumbersome for regular use. The application of this method to the American College Testing Program, for example, would require at least 175,000 different regression equations (Lindquist, 1963). The most reasonable compromise is to try to find dimensions along which preparatory institutions can be classified and to use such "moderator" variables to adjust the general regression equation. Either student-based variables, such as the school mean on a scholastic aptitude test, or environment-based variables, such as the amount of school expenditures per student, could be tried; but the research in this area is too sparse to provide guidance as to what procedures for grouping are likely to permit improved prediction. It is not even known whether scaling objective achievement tests on the basis of the quality of prior instruction will

in fact increase their accuracy in prediction. Most of the scaling efforts to date have been applied to school grades, as described in the following discussion, not to standardized tests.

School grades— When school grades are used as the index of achievement, the above problems are compounded by variations in the grading standards applied by different schools and different instructors. Here the concern is not only with the predictive validity of student achievement per se but also with the reliability of the indices with which achievement is being appraised. Unlike scores on a standard achievement test, the letter grades awarded by different institutions seldom reflect comparable levels of student attainment.

This difficulty has been widely recognized, and numerous adjustment techniques have been developed. The simplest of these is to use the applicant's rank in his graduating class rather than an index based on his grades directly; e.g. to consider the 50th ranking student in a class of 100 at institution A equivalent to the 75th ranking student in a class of 150 at institution B, irrespective of the absolute values of the grade-point averages they achieved. This procedure assumes that the academic potential of the graduating classes of institutions A and B is the same, which is hazardous, and that these institutions have computed rank-in-class on the same basis, which is known to be false. Yet, reducing the unreliability of letter grades in this manner is worthwhile. In most studies, rank-in-class is found to yield consistently better results than grade-point averages or other absolute scores.

A second approach is to scale the grades given by each school in accordance with the level of future performance they actually predict, as determined through empirical studies. Bloom and Peters (1961) applied this approach to both the predictor (high school grades) and the criterion (freshman grades in college) so as to correct for variations in the grading standards of both types of institutions and reported substantial gains in the accuracy of prediction. But Lindquist (1963) repeated this study with a larger and more representative sample and con-cluded that the very slight gains obtained do not justify the computational labor involved. His suggestion was to use grades as they are as one component of a multiple predictor and to count on the other instruments to compensate for the inequities uncorrected grades may in-troduce. It should be noted, however, that both of these studies were carried out on students in the reasonably homogeneous high schools of the United States and that quite different results might be obtained in countries in which there are considerably larger interschool variations. Differences between schools would be expected to be large especially in educational systems in which the crucial admission decisions are made at the point of transition from the elementary to the secondary school level, where it would be the differences among primary schools that would be the important consideration.

A third approach is to scale grades on the basis of independent measures of institutional differences, along the lines earlier suggested for the adjustment of achievement test scores. This has been done mainly through the use of student-based data, such as scores on intel-ligence tests (Toops, 1933), scholastic aptitude tests (Reitz, 1934), and tests of academic achievement (McClelland, 1942). But Chauncey and Fredericksen (1951) reported that it was found adequate at Harvard to use the simple institution-based variable of public school versus private school as the sole basis for cor-rection. In light of the rapidly rising educational aspirations in this country and elsewhere, re-search leading to the more effective use of scholastic performance data would seem worth-while.

Intelligence

It was noted in the preceding discussion that, although the rationale for attainment measures does depend on the equivalence of the performance requirements of lower-level and higher-level educational institutions, the test constructor need not try to identify the specific requirements that are important. The remaining rationales each posit a certain requirement that is thought to be related to scholastic success and

attempt to measure directly the applicant's capability for meeting this requirement.

Historically, the major effort of this type has been directed at the measurement of "intel-ligence," usually defined as the applicant's basic ability to learn. It was thought that indi-viduals differ greatly, and to a large extent genetically, in the facility with which they acquire new information and skills; and the intelligence test was one early attempt to quantify this difference as a basis for educa-tional prediction. More recently it has been re-placed to a considerable extent by the scholastic aptitude test, which is based on an analysis of the skills required in school rather than on the presumed indicators of genetic endowment; but the term still enjoys wide popular usage, and, for this reason, the original rationale and its subsequent evolution are reviewed here.

Assumptions

The basic assumption underlying the classic intelligence test is that the learning of any given skill is a function of *motivation*, *oppor-tunity*, and an innate *ability to learn* and that individual differences in the mastery of skills for which motivation and opportunity are equal therefore reflect differences in the ability factor alone. Operationally, the constructors of the early intelligence tests reasoned that

1. *if* gross differences in motivation are avoided by selecting skills that all individuals are ex-pected to develop as a matter of course in the particular culture in which they live, and
2. *if* gross differences in opportunity are avoided by selecting from these skills a subset that can be mastered on the basis of only those experiences that are uniformly available to all of the individuals to be com-pared,

then individual differences in proficiency in this subset of skills will constitute a reasonably pure measure of the individuals' relative ability to learn. And so basic a measure, it was thought, would be predictive not only of academic per-formance but also of success in most other prob-lem-solving situations.

Tests based on this rationale were criticized

virtually from the time of their inception. But most of these criticisms were addressed to fringe issues such as the stability of scores expressed in the form of an intelligence quotient, and the basic difficulties inherent in the above assumptions (though pointed out regularly by a number of investigators) were not until recently understood and accepted by the professional community at large.

The crucial deficiency of the classic intelligence test is that the skills specified in the rationale—i.e. skills that all of the examinees have had equal motivation and opportunity to acquire—probably do not exist. At least, no satisfactory set of skills has as yet been discovered. Such factors as sex, rural or urban location, and especially socioeconomic status are related to performance on the standard test items; and the differences are often substantial. In the Otis Beta test, for example, Davis and Havighurst (1948) found that 73 of the 80 items resulted in significant differences for children at high and low socioeconomic levels. Part of this difference could be a valid one in that the abilities of the children of parents in the upper socioeconomic strata could be innately superior, but the available evidence suggests that a sizeable factor of opportunity to learn also is involved. Studies of identical twins reared under different socioeconomic conditions, for example, have shown that the less advantaged twin generally obtains the lower intelligence test scores. Anastasi (1965) reported a correlation of .79 between discrepancy in educational advantage and discrepancy in IQ for 20 pairs of twins reared apart.

Efforts to produce items that will satisfy the above requirements have continued, however, notably in the construction of "culture-free" or "culture-fair" tests. Typically, the approach to these types of tests has been to write test exercises that are not taught explicitly in any culture, so that the opportunity (or lack of opportunity) for mastering them as a function of prior experience would be more nearly equal in different cultural settings. This would tend better to satisfy the second of the above assumptions, concerned with the opportunity factor alone. But it also rules out the use of the skills

that are the most emphasized in each culture, in direct contradiction to the parallel assumption that has to be made about the motivational factor; and is thereby counterproductive. As Anastasi (1949) has noted, the "minute residue" left after eliminating content that differentiates among cultures or subcultures is so trivial to all cultures that it can hardly yield appreciable validity for any practical criterion one may wish to predict.

Thus, measures of innate learning ability have not (and probably will not) be developed. But this is a largely theoretical issue that does not greatly affect the predictive utility of the so-called intelligence tests. As shall be seen in the next section, the items that have been used in these tests are essentially equivalent to the items generated by the rationale for scholastic aptitude tests; and quite accurate predictions of academic performance can be obtained in many practical situations. It is only the historical interpretation of the scores as indices purely of innate learning ability that must be avoided.

Application

The methodological problems of preparing an intelligence test are fundamentally the same as those encountered in the construction of aptitude tests and will be discussed in the following section. It should be noted, however, that most of these problems were initially studied in the context of intelligence testing and that it is the literature on intelligence that contains the most detailed methodological information.

Specific Aptitudes

Early in the development of the intelligence test, Spearman (1904) concluded that the mastery of a given skill depends not only on a general ability common to all skills but also on a specific ability that varies in accordance with the particular type of skill being learned. The suggestion was that a test of the common ability factor could serve as only a partial predictor. Some years later, Thurstone (1946) went one step further to suggest that the ability to learn is made up of a number of quite independent factors that should be measured by separate tests. He saw the classic intelligence test as an amalgam of separable entities that confounded the accuracy of predictions that could otherwise be obtained. And, eventually, the Thurstone view was accepted by many test specialists.

To identify the specific abilities into which "intelligence" can usefully be divided, two major kinds of approaches have been applied. They rely on different analytic techniques and proceed from fundamentally different assumptions.

Factor analysis has been the more common of these approaches. The standard technique is to administer a variety of test tasks to a reasonably large sample and to deduce from the intercorrelations among these tasks the number of separate dimensions along which they must differ from each other in order to produce the obtained pattern of intertest variation. Each of these dimensions may then be regarded as a qualitatively different skill that is represented in the total collection of tasks and that, in conjunction with the other skills or "factors," fully accounts for the examinees' overall test performance. In his pioneer work, Thurstone (1938) concluded that there was a minimum of eight factors to be considered; using additional kinds of tests and different analysis methods, Guilford (1957) has since extended the number to 120. And further explorations of this type are still being actively pursued.

The principal objective of these studies is to develop a detailed "map" of the cognitive domain, which is a logical follow-up to the original concept of innate ability factors. A considerable body of theory about the structure of human abilities underlies the research, especially in the selection of the kinds of test exercises to use in collecting the data. But the relevance of the resulting classification scheme to *operational* selection and guidance decisions is not one of the criteria for task selection. The entirely reasonable assumption is that once all of the different kinds of abilities have been inventoried, the determination of which are predictive of which kinds of attainments will be a simple problem of matching.

The alternative approach is to begin with an analysis of the outcomes to be predicted and to construct tests in accordance with the specific skills that attainment of these outcomes seems to require. The test constructor assembles data on the performance requirements of the various courses and/or occupations for which the applicant group will be considered, deduces (on rational grounds) the major types of skills necessary to meet these requirements, and designs test exercises that call for the same types of skills; thereby obtaining a "preview" of the applicants' performance in activities directly related to the content of the course as a basis for prediction. Flanagan (1959) used the term *job elements* to describe skills identified in this manner and concluded that a total of 21 separate job elements are involved in the major occupations and careers for which American high school students typically are considered. In this scheme, prediction for any one job or curriculum is based on measures of the four to six most relevant job elements included in the overall list.

The term *aptitude test* has been used variously by different authors. It has been used to designate the discrete tests that result from the factor analysis of cognitive test items, to differentiate these from the more global intelligence test. It has been used to refer primarily to the tests of noncognitive skills, such as eye-hand coordination, that were developed alongside the intelligence test for specialized applications in training and vocational education. And it has been used, most generally, in the job-element sense to refer to any test that simulates a specific skill important to the attainment of a certain instructional objective. The rationale for instruments that fit this last all-inclusive definition will be described.

Assumptions

The link between the items of an aptitude test and the skill in which the applicant's eventual proficiency is to be predicted lies in the similarity of the mental, perceptual, and/or physical operations that they require. The test constructor reasons that

1. *if* the level of proficiency an individual can

attain in the skills he is to develop as a result of a course depends in part on the nature of the operations that these skills require, and

2. *if* there are skills he can perform in advance of the course that require essentially the same types of operations, and

3. *if* he has had sufficient practice in these latter skills to have attained a fairly stable proficiency level,

then this level should be indicative of the level he will attain in the new skills taught in the course. A job-element aptitude test measures the applicant's current level of proficiency in a specific skill that has been selected as relevant in accordance with these assumptions.

There is little question about the general validity of the first assumption. Proficiency levels do vary, in a group of individuals or within a single individual, as a function of the task and its component operations. But, since prediction instruments can seldom be prepared to encompass all of the component operations, the assumption's validity in practice depends on the degree to which the operations selected by the test constructor are in fact important. The upper limit of the predictive accuracy he can obtain is fixed by the proportion of the variance in student achievement that is accounted for by this particular sample of task operations, and an adequate analysis of the target skills is therefore the first critical step in the construction of aptitude tests. A number of practical guidelines pertinent to this analysis are suggested later in this section.

The validity of the second assumption depends on the fidelity with which the operations involved in the target skill can be represented in tasks that the applicants can perform in advance of the course. In principle, this is seldom a problem. When the target skill is stripped of the specialized knowledge and applications taught in the course, the reduced task is nearly always one that the applicants have encountered before if they have had the formal and extra-curricular preparation normal in the culture. Reasonably exact test exercises usually can be prepared. The problem that frequently does arise, however, is the practical one of deciding

whether to try for the maximum fidelity possible, which would give the best results for this particular course or occupation but limits the utility of the instrument for other similar applications; or whether to use more basic tasks generalizeable (with some loss in fidelity) to an entire class of skilled operations. For the user of tests, this issue often reduces to the choice between inexpensive published instruments and costly custom-made procedures.

The importance of the third assumption—i.e. that the applicants have had adequate practice in the specific tasks included in the test exercises—derives from the characteristics of the learning curve for most skilled operations. In the early stages of learning, proficiency levels change rapidly and relatively minor differences in the backgrounds of the applicants can exert a disproportionate effect on the measurements obtained. With increased practice, each applicant's performance begins to approach an asymptote that may be interpreted as his maximum "capacity" for this type of operation and that affords the reasonably stable index necessary for prediction. The test constructor can and should provide opportunities for practice at the beginning of the test, but normally must select tasks with which (or with analogies of which) the applicants have already had considerable experience if he is to obtain meaningful scores. This may require certain compromises with the second assumption of fidelity in the representation of the target operations, since the tasks that afford the closest approximation to the target skills are usually among those the applicants learned recently, while the tasks in which they have had the most practice are the more basic ones that they have been able to perform for some time.

The tasks that best satisfy all three assumptions clearly depend as much on the background of the applicants as on the outcome to be predicted. To obtain equally accurate predictions of the identical skill for such different groups as boys and girls or Asians and Europeans, different test exercises, consistent with their different experiences, may have to be used. But, unless these different groups are to be compared with each other, this poses no special problems. The test constructor is free to use an item on oil lamps in measuring mechanical aptitude in one culture and an item on automobile engines to obtain the same information in another; and it is obviously to his advantage to do so by identifying the tasks most consistent with the background of the particular group with which he is working. International organizations that use a standard set of aptitude tests everywhere simply because the *target* skills are identical at all locations are not taking full advantage of the flexibility afforded by this rationale.

Overall, the aptitude test differs from the achievement test in that the items may be based on skills not explicitly taught in school and from the intelligence test in that the content is derived from the characteristics of the specific outcome to be predicted. But the assumptions of the three rationales are entirely compatible, and, under certain circumstances, the identical test item can logically appear in all three types of tests. It has already been noted that the items that best meet the equal-motivation and equal-opportunity assumptions of the intelligence test involve the same verbal and symbolic operations that are also essential to successful performance in school and therefore converge to the items of the scholastic aptitude test generated by the above rationale.

Application

The procedures described in earlier chapters for the construction of achievement test items apply also to the development of an aptitude test. But there are certain differences in approach or at least emphasis to be considered. These arise in the determination of the specific operations to be measured, in the formulation of an index of proficiency in these operations, in the design of test exercises consistent with the rationale, and in the special provisions that may be necessary to insure examinee motivation.

Content selection— The selection of content appropriate to an aptitude test involves two major steps. The first is to enumerate the operations that the students will be expected to per-

form at the end of the course—the behavioral outcomes that constitute the key course objectives. The second is to identify the specific skills that underlie the effective performance of these operations, so that test exercises dependent on similar skills can be constructed. Goodness of fit to the actual skill requirements is the criterion for content selection.

For the first step, the test constructor profitably can employ one or more of the techniques of "job analysis," which are as useful in analyzing educational outcomes as they are in establishing the requirements of a certain occupation. But, for prediction purposes, he should focus these techniques more narrowly than is the rule in most other applications. Instead of obtaining a complete inventory of all pertinent outcomes, he should try to identify the subset of operations in which significant variations in individual performance actually occur and which are, therefore, appropriate targets for improved selection procedures. An analysis of the extremes of performance—errors and outstanding achievements—is frequently the indicated approach.

For the second step of identifying the specific skills that underlie effective performance, there are no systematic methods of analysis he can apply. A review of past findings is helpful, but accuracy in picking out the characteristics of a task that account for most of the observed variability in its performance continues to depend largely on the experience and insight of the test constructor. At this crucial stage, test development is as much of an art as a science. Some general guidelines, however, can be suggested.

To develop a sufficiently precise statement of the operation to be performed, it is useful to think of the *criterion* according to which its effectiveness will be assessed. If the criterion is not implicit in the statement, the definition is insufficiently precise. "Effective use of English," for example, is clearly too vague. Is the important outcome the breadth of vocabulary the student has at his command? Is it his knowledge of the mechanics? Is it his effectiveness of expression? Each of these criteria is related to a different set of operations, which may require different types of test exercises for the most accurate prediction.

Another important characteristic to be considered in defining a skill is the *object* to which the operation will be applied. That performance in *reasoning* operations may vary for tasks involving words, symbols, and numbers is one reasonably clear-cut example. Perhaps less obvious is the importance of the object associated with such skills as *memory*, which are usually thought of as unitary operations. Yet, memory for materials organized within a meaningful framework, as is required in most courses and occupations, may be quite different from the more abstract memory typically measured in laboratory experiments; and the classic memory tasks (e.g. learning of nonsense syllables) may therefore be quite inappropriate as predictors.

In addition to defining each of the major operations as precisely as possible, the test constructor should also consider them as a group, in terms of their probable *interrelations*. Since he will be able to develop tests for only a sample of the component skills and since the overall accuracy of the battery will depend on the unique variance each instrument measures, a minimum of overlap among the separate test scores is another important criterion for content selection. The findings of factor analytic studies are a helpful guide to the major kinds of activities for which separate tests should be constructed, as is the content of the various multifactor aptitude batteries that have been developed. In the standard published batteries, tasks that require verbal reasoning, mathematical reasoning, abstract reasoning, mechanical reasoning, computation, visualization, perceptual discrimination, and physical dexterity are the ones most frequently represented.

The test constructor should not limit himself to these standard categories of aptitude in analyzing the target performance, however. The activity may include a highly specific skill that does not neatly fit any of these categories and that he cannot adequately describe with the standard terminology of aptitude testing but

that can nevertheless be predicted by replicating its basic characteristics directly in ad hoc test items. An example is the skill of typewriting, which involves quite different motor operations than standard dexterity tasks and is not adequately predicted by broad-spectrum dexterity tests. By devising a new test format that was specifically addressed to the operations performed by a typist in that it required the selective use of each finger, Flanagan (1964) was able to obtain considerably more accurate predictions. When the analysis of an activity according to the standard dimensions of aptitude proves unproductive, the feasibility of direct replication should be explored.

Power and speed— A second important decision concerns the index to be used in evaluating the applicant's present proficiency level. The issue under consideration is the relative emphasis to be given to difficulty and to speed in the design of the test items, and this cannot be resolved in quite the same manner for aptitude tests as was suggested for achievement tests in an earlier chapter. Though it is often desirable to emphasize speed in the test exercises only to the extent that it is also required in the target outcomes, this is not necessarily true when the purpose is prediction, and it may in fact be quite inefficient.

Specifically, the test constructor may hypothesize that speed in the performance of a highly practiced skill is an index of the applicant's *overall facility* in this type of operation and therefore generalizeable to more advanced skills that require similar operations whether or not speed is involved. To predict success in an engineering curriculum, for example, he may use a test of speed in simple arithmetic computations, reasoning that the applicants' relative levels of accomplishment in elementary numerical operations will serve as at least a partial indicator of their achievement in advanced operations that also involve numbers. Many such hypotheses, of course, may not survive empirical validation. But any that do have merit will result in considerable savings in test development and testing time, and the opportunities for predicting nonspeeded skills from simple speeded test exercises should for this reason be considered explicitly in the design of aptitude tests.

Extraneous operations— Ideally, test exercises would require those and only those operations that the test constructor has decided to measure as the basis for prediction. But in practice they require a variety of extraneous knowledge and skills that the student also must have to display the skill presumably being measured. These represent potential sources of error that are introduced into the test in three major ways during the process of test construction.

The first is in meeting the purely mechanical requirements of mass administration or objective scoring or automated data-processing routines. Studies of groups who have had no prior experience in taking tests, such as those of Biesheuvel (1952) in South Africa, have shown that mastery of the normal testing routine requires substantial specific learning and may account for more of the variance in the scores of naive examinees than the test task itself. Such extreme problems are highly unlikely in the test-wise American culture, but the competitive advantage of individuals who have had greater practice in taking tests has probably been underestimated; and the test constructor should try to insure that all examinees— whether or not they are capable of earning high scores—at least understand the mechanics of the testing procedure. Demonstrations by the examiner are a useful adjunct to oral or printed directions, as is an adequate number of practice exercises especially if proctors can be provided to check the results of the practice trials and thereby confirm each examinee's comprehension. When several tests are to be used, casting them into the same general format also will reduce the variety of mechanical operations the examinee has to learn.

The second source of extraneous errors derives from the inclusion of specific content materials that are incidental to the problem but essential to its solution. In one type of nonverbal reasoning test, for example, the task is to group objects in accordance with a property they have in common. The emphasis is on proficiency in concept formation, but the examinee clearly must be able also to recognize each object from the line drawing by which it is represented and have certain factual information about its functions and characteristics. Individual differences in either of these extraneous elements can distort the test scores. Similarly, a test of mathematical reasoning based on word problems may produce irrelevant differences in the scores of applicants who have unequal skills in reading comprehension. Errors of this type are more common in aptitude than in achievement tests because the former include a greater number of exercises that the examinees have not encountered before. A preliminary tryout in which examinees are observed individually while they "talk through" each test item is often a useful precaution.

The third source of such measurement errors is in the (deliberate or inadvertent) formulation of the strategy that will yield the highest test score. In most time-limit tests, there is an optimum mix of accuracy and speed, and the typical instruction to "work as quickly as you can without making mistakes" does not result in a uniform approach on the part of the entire applicant group. Certain applicants will be more reckless or more conservative than the average examinee and as a result obtain higher or lower scores. Various mathematical corrections can be applied. The most satisfactory is to validate both the raw score and the error score against the criterion to be predicted and to determine the weighting of errors that maximizes the validity coefficient. The result is a scoring formula that is analogous to the correction for guessing sometimes applied to achievement tests.

Motivation— Central to the rationale of the aptitude test is the assumption that all applicants are exhibiting the maximum performance of which they are capable in performing this type of operation. If the test is being taken for purposes of admission or selection, adequate motivation usually can be taken for granted, at least at the beginning of the testing session. The main task of the test constructor is to try to insure that the examinee will not become discouraged as a result of ambiguous instructions, low quality reproduction, or other deficiencies that may suggest a maximum effort is not worthwhile. If the time limits are set so that it is impossible to complete all of the items this should be explained in advance of the test.

Interest

Because even the most accurate aptitude tests account for less than half of the variance in individual attainment, there has been a continuing effort to devise supplementary instruments to predict portions of the variance remaining. The interest test has been the most popular of these instruments, particularly for differential prediction in classification or guidance applications. It attempts to measure the relative reinforcement an individual derives from various types of activities, assuming, on the basis of considerable evidence, that satisfaction can be an important determinant of attainment.

The problem in assessing interest has been that simply asking the individual about his interests in various curricula or occupations seldom results in the information desired. One reason is that most individuals have not enough knowledge about the specific activities that are involved in each of the course or job options to report their probable reactions. A second is that they cannot readily separate the reinforcement value inherent in the performance of these activities from the overall connotations of each career in terms of income, prestige, and other attractions. The answers to direct questions necessarily are generalized responses based in part on erroneous or irrelevant impressions, and the major interest tests that have been developed rely on more indirect approaches. The discussion considers the four approaches that have been most widely used.

Assumptions

The rationales for the four types of interest tests to be considered are discussed separately, but certain similarities and differences will be noted. The first three are similar in that they are all based on the specific operations that comprise the target outcomes and begin with an identical assumption. The differences among the tests in this group lie only in the nature of the data the student is asked to provide. The fourth rationale is based on characteristics typical of individuals who have already achieved the target outcomes and therefore differs in all respects from the other three.

Expressed preferences— The first type of test lists a wide variety of specific activities, and the student indicates which of these he most enjoys or would most enjoy doing. The assumptions are that

1. *if* an individual's success in learning and performing a certain operation depends in part on the kinds of reinforcement this operation affords, and
2. *if* he has already performed other operations that have the same reinforcement characteristics, and
3. *if* he can assess the relative reinforcement he derived from performing these other operations, and
4. *if* he reports these assessments correctly,

then his stated preferences will provide a partial index of his success in achieving the outcomes to be predicted.

The first two assumptions are analogous to those made in the rationale for aptitude tests. The test constructor has again to postulate that certain characteristics of the criterion behavior are important determinants of the students' eventual performance and then to find activities in which they have already engaged that have the same characteristics. But this is considerably more difficult in the case of interest tests because much less is known about the characteristics of an activity that are associated with individual differences in reinforcement than about the characteristics that are associated with individual differences in skill. And what is known suggests that an individual's affective responses to a past activity probably were shaped to a considerable degree by many quite specific situational factors and that he may therefore respond quite differently when he engages in a similar activity in a new situation. As a result, the feasibility of meeting these assumptions in the interest domain is and will probably continue to be limited to contrasts between broad categories of widely different activities, such as between "those dependent mainly on persuasiveness in interpersonal relationships" and "those dependent mainly on accuracy in repetitive clerical operations."

The third and fourth assumptions, pertaining to the accuracy of the students' assessments and to their honesty in reporting them on a test, represent both the greatest strengths and the most serious weaknesses of this rationale. On the positive side, it is clear that every individual has access to infinitely more data about his reactions than can possibly be obtained from other sources and that the potential accuracy of the assessments he makes himself is therefore substantially greater than the potential accuracy of alternative approaches. But, on the negative side, it has been apparent that the accuracy actually obtained from self-assessments falls far short of this high potential, even when the honesty and conscientiousness of the respondents is not in doubt. To scale his preferences accurately, each respondent would have to be able to isolate the one characteristic of a task that the test constructor is trying to portray when he uses a specific illustration (e.g. building a boat) that in fact has numerous characteristics, to separate the processes involved in each activity from the products to which they lead, to compare reactions that may have occurred at widely disparate times and locations, and to report what these reactions were without considering what he believes they should have been or what new responses he hopes to develop. These requirements can be met only partly and approximately at best. As a result, the difficulty of the judgmental task imposed on the respondents tends also to limit preference tests to broad categories of interests among which reasonably accurate discriminations can be expected.

Biographical data— The second type of interest test also lists a large number of activities but the student is asked to provide only factual data

about the nature and extent of his participation—a statement of his preferences is not required. The assumptions are that

1. *if* an individual's success in learning and performing a certain operation depends in part on the kinds of reinforcement this operation affords, and
2. *if* the activities in which he has had opportunities to participate in the past include a number of activities that have the same reinforcement characteristics, and
3. *if* he has taken advantage of these opportunities selectively, by participating more extensively in the activities that he found the most reinforcing,

then a record of his current and prior activities should provide a partial index of his success in achieving the outcomes to be predicted.

The first two assumptions are comparable to those made for the preference test, and the test constructor's ability to satisfy them is subject to the same limitations. The third assumption—that an individual's interests are reflected in what he actually does with his time—avoids the difficult judgments required of the respondent in the preceding rationale but raises other issues that can be equally complex. Because the respondent does not indicate the extent to which his decision to participate in a given activity was based on interest rather than on the many other factors that normally influence an individual's allocation of time, interests can be inferred only when he makes the same type of decision repeatedly in a variety of situations; and an interest test based on this rationale must encompass a sufficiently broad range of activities to permit these trends to emerge. The problem is to find a sample of activities that will afford such breadth for all respondents, given the considerable variability that can be expected in the kinds of opportunities to which they individually have been exposed. By eliminating the subjective assessments of the preference test, the test constructor also eliminated the flexibility that the respondent had in adapting the test items to fit his individual experiences; e.g. to respond to the item "work as a clerk in a drugstore," even though he has never done this, on the basis of experience in other but similar occupations. In a factual biographic report, the respondent provides only the information explicitly requested (i.e. he cannot use his experience in a shoe store to answer the drugstore question); and the task of formulating an adequate sample of test items is correspondingly more demanding.

It follows that the difficult task imposed on the respondents in the preference test is not resolved by the biographic report but is simply shifted to the test constructor. Choosing between the two types of instruments reduces to the choice between subjectivity-flexibility and objectivity-rigidity, which is one of the classic trade-off decisions in the measurement field. The issues are fundamentally the same as those that underlie the use of observational check lists or structured interviews rather than open-ended procedures, and there are equally sharp differences in the various practitioners' points of view. To date, the relative excellence of the instruments that have been produced has seemed to be less a function of type than of the care with which each has been constructed. Combination approaches in which the respondent provides subjective data to amplify personal history items also have been tried.

Incidental information— The third type of interest test is based on the same assumptions as the biographic data report but does not determine the student's history of participation in various activities through items that request this information directly. Instead, the items measure the specialized knowledge that an individual who has participated in these activities would as a result have acquired; and his extent of participation (and hence his interest) is inferred from his test score.

There are two major advantages to determining participation through this indirect approach. The first is that it automatically verifies and to some extent quantifies such information as might alternatively have been obtained from a biographic report. In responding to biographic questions, the student can indicate directly whether or not he has participated in a certain activity and, within limits, the extent of

his participation. But he cannot readily gauge the intensity of his involvement relative to other participants, and this is an additional index of interest that a knowledge test can provide.

The second advantage is that a knowledge test can encompass an important category of activities that is too diffuse to be reduced to biographic reports. This is the category of "incidental" learning experiences to which the individual has been exposed through casual reading, listening, and observation that are part of everyday life. It may be assumed that individuals also learn selectively from these sources of knowledge and that their interests are therefore reflected in the kinds of incidental information they have picked up and remember. A particularly appropriate index can be obtained from items that measure the advance knowledge the examinees have acquired about the specific career in which their future performance is to be predicted. There is much reasonably sophisticated information the budding scientist can pick up from the popular science magazines, for example, long before he studies the same topics formally in advanced courses.

Tests of incidental information also are less susceptible to differences in the backgrounds of the examinees than the biographic reports, since they do not measure participation in a specified sample of activities directly. Individuals who have acquired the requisite knowledge as a result of different experiences get the same score. This latitude is a mixed blessing, however. The new problem that arises is that certain individuals will have acquired the requisite knowledge without participating in activities even remotely related to the target behavior, and for these individuals interests will be inferred incorrectly. If the performance to be predicted involves working outdoors, for example, it would be reasonable to measure knowledge of outdoor sports as an indication of prior participation in activities similar to the target behavior in this respect. But many individuals acquire a reasonably detailed knowledge of sports from reading the newspaper or watching television in the comfort of their own homes without having ever participated in these activities directly. The high test scores they might obtain would be misleading. More generally, it has been found that the individuals highest in scholastic aptitude or "intelligence" have acquired greater amounts of incidental information of all types than individuals with lesser cognitive skills and will exceed the norm on a test of specialized knowledge irrespective of their interests and inclinations. Two techniques useful in compensating for such discrepancies are described later in this section.

Similarity to occupational groups— The fourth type of interest test may contain items similar in format to those in any of the above instruments but differs in content and in the procedures used for content selection. The assumptions are that

1. *if* individuals successful in a given career consistently report similar degrees of interest in certain activities, and
2. *if* these reports differ from those of individuals pursuing other careers, and
3. *if* comparable results would have been obtained from these individuals before they entered their respective careers,

then an applicant's interest profile should be predictive of success in accordance with its similarity to the profile characteristic of the group already successful in that career.

The activities that discriminate in this manner, it will be noted, need *not* have any logical relationship to the operations the career actually requires. If a strong interest in fishing tends to differentiate architects from the general population, items on fishing are entirely appropriate to tests constructed in accordance with this rationale. This in effect routinizes the selection of test content, which was the single most difficult step in the instruments described above.

Also, in developing instruments of this type, the test constructor need be much less concerned about the degree to which respondents can provide accurate reports of their actual reactions to the activities described. Because prediction is based on the similarity between the statements made by the applicant and the statements made by the criterion group, the accuracy of these statements is not so crucial an issue as it was before. The fact that architects say they enjoy fishing more consistently than do other groups is sufficient for purposes of this rationale. As a consequence, instruments of this type usually follow the simple format of the expressed preferences test, though biographic or information tests that discriminate among occupational groups also could be developed.

The test constructor's chief concern, having discovered a set of activities that discriminates among occupational groups, is the stability of these interests over time, as required by the third assumption. Any interest that the individual develops as a result of his occupational experiences is clearly inappropriate as a basis for prediction with applicant groups. The stability of each trial item should be checked explicitly through follow-up studies of samples typical of the applicant population. Strong (1955) has done the most extensive research of this type and has found that a wide variety of expressed preferences does remain constant over fairly long periods of time.

The limitations of this approach are those characteristic of all instruments based solely on empirical data. As pointed out in the introductory remarks, the test constructor cannot tell why a certain item is an effective predictor and, as a result, cannot determine the kinds of changes in environment or in applicant groups that will render the test ineffective. He must continue to monitor the results; and, when changes occur, must in effect repeat the entire developmental procedure.

Application

The two interest tests that are used most widely are the *Kuder Preference Record—Vocational* (Kuder, 1960), developed in 1934, and the *Strong Vocational Interest Blank* (Strong, 1959), developed in 1927. These are examples of tests that were initially developed, respectively, by the use of expressed preferences and of comparisons with successful vocational groups. Tests of biographic data and of incidental information have been constructed chiefly for specialized applications, notably by the military for purposes of classification. The research carried out by the Army Air Force Aviation Psychology Program, as summarized by Guilford and Lacey (1947), was particularly significant in the development of these types of interest measures.

Certain of the technical problems that arise in the construction of interest tests deserve special mention. These pertain to the selection of content, scoring, and public relations.

Content selection— The items to be included in an interest test may be selected in accordance with either internal or external criteria. The internal approach assumes that every individual's interests may be described along a small set of reasonably independent dimensions and that the items to be included are therefore those that best determine the examinees' relative positions on these dimensions. The test constructor obtains responses to a large pool of trial items, representative of a broad range of activities and experiences, and groups them on the basis of their intercorrelations into major factors or clusters. These factors then are defined as the important dimensions of the interest domain, and the items that best discriminate among them are the ones selected. The final test yields a profile of factor scores that presumably account for the variance attributable to interest in any curriculum or occupation, but the nature of these relationships remains to be determined through separate validity studies. This approach is analogous to the development of the factored aptitude tests described above.

In the second approach, items are selected in accordance with the external criterion to be predicted. This criterion may be a measure of actual attainment or a related index such as the measure of discrimination among occupational groups used in the Strong type of test. For biographic reports and tests of incidental information, it is good practice to write item rationales in advance of the empirical tryout, explaining the chain of reasoning that produced each of the items included in the initial version. For, unlike the typical aptitude test in which each item is a replication of the same task or operation, these instruments consist of heterogeneous items each of which is in effect a miniature test based on a different assumption. When an information item on chess is grouped with an information item on cryptography as a part of a measure of analytic interests, for example, clearly two separate hypotheses that require separate confirmation have been made.

The selection of items for information tests also should take account of the typically high correlation between general knowledge and cognitive ability noted in the discussion of the test rationale. Often, this correlation can be reduced by selecting items that are much more likely to be learned through active participation in the activity than by passive means. To test participation in outdoor sports, for example, items concerning special clothing or equipment are usually superior to items on rules or procedures that a spectator can readily observe. Also, such tests may include a subset of items irrelevant to the interests to be assessed, so as to obtain an independent index of the individual's general level of knowledge, which may then be used to make a statistical adjustment of his raw interest score. Subtracting the examinees' scores on a test of literature from their outdoor activities scores is typical of this type of correction. Its chief limitation is the generally low reliability of the resulting difference-scores.

Scoring— Many interest tests use a forced-choice format in which several activities are put together in a set, and the respondent indicates his relative preferences, in effect, by distributing a fixed number of "points" among the activities in each set. As a result, the scores he obtains on the various interest factors are interdependent—each depends on the number of available points that he has expended on the others. This makes it hazardous to compare two individuals on any one interest dimension out of the context of their other scores, which limits the utility of the test for certain applications. Clemans (1966) has reviewed the problems posed by *ipsative* scores of this type in detail.

Mechanical-scoring problems arise in the interest tests that assign varying weights to individual items to reflect their unequal excellence as predictors. This is frequently the case in tests in which each item is based on a separate rationale, such as the biographic report. Much of the cumbersomeness of these types of tests has been eliminated by the expanded use of automated scoring equipment, however. Such equipment makes it more practical also for the user of standard tests to devise his own system of weights to achieve a better fit to the particular applications with which he is concerned.

Public relations— Interest tests of the expressed preferences type have considerable face validity and tend to be popular with the respondents. But biographic reports and information tests sometimes lead to adverse reactions. The biographic report may be regarded as objectionable on the grounds of invasion of privacy, which has been the cause of increasing concern in recent years. Questions on family income, household conditions, and other sensitive issues therefore should be avoided—if socioeconomic status is important, more subtle indices can be devised. The information test may be criticized as being irrelevant, particularly if a set of nonpredictive items has been included to permit statistical adjustment of the test scores. This problem can be reduced by incorporating as much face validity as practicable in the items that are to serve as controls.

Other Nonintellective Predictors

A variety of instruments that were developed primarily as diagnostic instruments for clinical applications are sometimes used in conjunction with aptitude and interest tests to predict certain differences in individual performance that are not adequately explained by the above rationales. These differences include the variations in level of effort, persistence, and perseverance under adverse conditions that commonly are ascribed to differences in *motivation;* the entire gamut of differences in the social behaviors that are described with such terms as *character, attitude,* and *adjustment;* and the overlapping but ill-defined behaviors that determine the *reaction of others* in interpersonal relations. Depending on the nature of the outcomes

to be predicted, such nonintellective characteristics of performance can be as important to success as proficiency in skilled operations.

The following discussion is concerned with the use of nonintellective measures as predictors of these kinds of behavior. It does not consider their utility in screening out applicants with emotional disturbances, except to note that such medical applications also can contribute to admission or selection decisions.

Assumptions

The general rubric of "personality measures" encompasses a broad range of instruments that can be classified in a variety of ways. For purposes of the present discussion, it seems adequate to group them into only two categories, in accordance with the two major kinds of information that are used as the basis for prediction in the nonintellective domain. First the discussion considers the procedures that focus on the applicant's typical *responses* to certain situations and then considers those that focus not on his responses but on the *results* he typically obtains.

Response-oriented procedures— Measuring the examinee's response tendencies is by far the more common procedure. The test constructor reasons that

1. *if* the target performance requires that a certain response be made (or not made) in a specified stimulus situation, and
2. *if* this future response will be a function in part of experiences that the applicant already has had, so that these experiences also affect his present response to related stimulus situations, and
3. *if* the nature of his present response in these related situations can be determined,

then his probable response to the target situation can be inferred. These assumptions are parallel to those that underlie the various aptitude tests, but they are much more difficult to satisfy in the nonintellective domain.

The basic premise of the first assumption— that nonintellective responses are crucial to many kinds of performance—can be accepted without reservation. The problem arises in trying to specify the exact set of "desirable" responses that are necessary for effective performance and that therefore should be the ones predicted. For in many of the careers that are most dependent on nonintellective responses, fixed stereotypes of effective behavior may not exist. One familiar example is afforded by the teaching profession, in which comparable results are routinely being achieved by individuals whose classroom behaviors reflect widely discrepant or even contradictory personality characteristics. In these situations, an admissions procedure that accepts or rejects applicants on the basis of a fixed set of presumably necessary characteristics is inherently unrealistic. Better results might be obtained by trying to identify the perhaps numerous *combinations* of characteristics that are equally effective in the target situation and then admitting applicants who exhibit any one of these functionally equivalent combinations.

Identifying the responses that are uniformly "undesirable" is simpler, and a list of clearly negative characteristics usually can be developed. But these are likely to consist of such extreme behaviors that even highly accurate measures would accomplish little more than to screen out the grossly unfit. And, unless the applicant pool is unusually heterogeneous in basic qualifications, only slight increments in the accuracy of selection can be expected.

The premise of the second assumption—that certain of the applicant's present responses are determined in part by factors that will later play a similar role in the target situation—is supported by most of the research on the dynamics of learned behavior. But the crucial consideration is how significant a role this actually will turn out to be; i.e. how much of the variance in the target responses will in fact be attributable to these common factors. And here the prospects are poor. For the same body of research also has suggested that responses as complex as those in the nonintellective domain are controlled by a surprisingly large number and variety of specific situational characteristics, many of which would seem on rational grounds to be quite irrelevant to the response in question. Until techniques for identifying more of these characteristics and for incorporating more of them into test exercises are developed, only modest validity can be expected.

Still, there would seem to be improvements that even now could be made. The traditional approach to personality measurement has concentrated almost entirely on the similarity of the responses built into the testing situation and those relevant to the target performance, ignoring the similarities or differences in the associated stimulus factors. The assumption has been that an applicant who exhibits an aggressive response in one situation is, other things being equal, likely to react similarly in a second situation that also calls for an aggressive or a passive response. Recognizing that other things usually are not equal in the nonintellective domain and trying for a closer match of the situational specifics might yield better results.

As will be seen in the discussion of the specific testing procedures used in the nonintellective domain, the methodological problems posed by the third assumption—that the applicant's present response characteristics can be determined—are also more difficult than those encountered in developing aptitude tests. One basic reason for this is that an aptitude test tries to measure the maximum level at which the examinee *can* perform, which is a reasonable index to obtain during the course of a testing session, while a nonintellective test tries to determine the way in which he *typically does* perform, which is a considerably more challenging testing objective. If measurement is based on the examinee's responses during a controlled testing session, one can usually arrange to have him exhibit the fairly large sample of relevant responses that an index of "typicality" requires; but, having collected all of the data in a situation that is decidedly atypical, one cannot expect to have obtained truly typical responses. If instead one arranges to observe him in less tightly structured situations so as to avoid the artificiality of a more formal test, one may have to wait a long time indeed to collect a sufficient sample of the particular responses with which one is concerned.

Assembling relevant historical data is one useful compromise, but the basic dilemma of structure versus spontaneity has not yet been adequately resolved for measures of typical performance.

Result-oriented measures— The second approach is to try to predict the individual's performance on the basis of the outcomes he has achieved in situations that presumably require adequate nonintellective responses, without trying to specify what these responses should be. The assumptions here are that

1. *if* an individual carrying out a given activity will encounter certain situations that require appropriate nonintellective responses, and
2. *if* an applicant for admission to this activity has already encountered a number of similar situations, and
3. *if* his effectiveness in these situations can be determined,

then his probable effectiveness in the target situations can be inferred. The emphasis is not on his actions but on the result.

· This shift in emphasis does not eliminate the difficulties noted in the rationale based on responses but does afford appreciable simplifications. By ignoring the process by which the applicant is to achieve the desired results, the test constructor is much less dependent on an a priori stereotype of appropriate behavior and can accommodate such functionally equivalent approaches as were noted in the teacher example. He has still to be able to specify the desired outcomes that depend on nonintellective approaches (e.g. "students voluntarily seek the teacher's help with personal problems"), and this is no doubt a formidable undertaking. But it is likely to be more productive than the search for uniformly desirable teacher behavior.

In satisfying the second assumption—i.e. in finding situations the applicant has encountered that are similar to the target situations—the test constructor again is faced with the problem of matching stimuli that he cannot identify as important. And this problem remains as difficult as before. But the very process of writing test exercises on the basis of situational characteristics should result in the inclusion of a larger proportion of these unknown stimuli than would be expected in items based chiefly on similarities in responses.

The major disadvantage of this approach is implicit in the third assumption—that the results of the applicant's nonintellective inputs into these earlier situations can be determined. For outcomes normally are the joint product of knowledge and aptitude factors as well as nonintellective characteristics, and there is no way to differentiate these components in the interpretation of the applicant's score. If the test is to increase the accuracy of prediction already available from cognitive measures, the test constructor should try to reduce such overlap by selecting situations that require minimal knowledge and skill; but this can increase significantly the difficulty of finding a sufficient number of suitable test items.

Application

As in the ability and interest domains, considerable effort has been devoted to the identification of the major factors of personality, which are usually called *traits*. The initial formulations were based largely on clinical findings; since the development of the methods of factor analysis, this has become the standard approach. And because the clinical and empirical findings have been generally congruent, the concept of traits has dominated the techniques of measurement in the nonintellective domain. The construction of response-oriented instruments has consisted largely of writing test exercises addressed to behaviors classified within the same trait grouping as the target behaviors; and even in the more pragmatic result-oriented procedures, the selection of similar situations is frequently based on those likely to be affected by the same trait characteristics. On balance, the contribution of the concept of traits in generating the many separate hypotheses necessary for producing a sufficient number of items for these kinds of measures can hardly be questioned. But in light of the preceding discussion, one might wish that the tidiness of the formulation had not detracted quite so much from the importance of the associated situational characteristics.

In this section, the four major categories of instruments that have been developed in accordance with the above specifications are briefly described.

Self-reports— Most of the response-oriented instruments have been based on the applicant's own reports of his own typical behavior. He may be given a minimum of direction concerning the situational specifics, as in the tests that ask him to mark the one adjective in each set of five that is most descriptive of his usual behavior; or provided with considerably more situational structure, as in the test exercises that ask: What would you probably do if . . . ? Or, instead of focusing on discrete behaviors, the test might ask him to indicate the extent to which he agrees with each of a set of opinions or generalizations, assuming that such attitudes will be predictive of a whole class of specific responses. And there are many more variations.

The major concern of the authors of these kinds of tests has been the ease with which applicants can deliberately distort their answers so as to project the personality image they think is desired. To control these effects, some authors have incorporated parallel questions into the test so as to be able to check the consistency of the applicant's answers; some have carefully pretested the options presented in each item to insure that they are equally attractive to the general applicant population; some have even constructed special subtests to measure the degree to which each applicant has slanted his answers as a basis for a statistical correction. The most satisfactory approach perhaps is to try to write test exercises that are less transparent, but this also can boomerang if the applicants still attempt to outguess the test constructor and, because of the subtlety of his items, guess incorrectly.

A second concern has been the difficulty of providing the examinees with explicit criteria for scaling their responses to self-report items, the lack of which may lead them to make decisions in borderline cases on the basis of response characteristics irrelevant to the aims of the test. Certain individuals, for example, will tend more than others to avoid such options as "uncertain" or "don't know," irrespective of the content of the items; or to choose "true" rather than "false" when the statement lends itself to different interpretations. Such *response sets* may be a significant source of variance in the self-report test and should be controlled. Their effects can be resolved either in the design of the test items—e.g. by not permitting "don't know" responses—or in the scoring of the test, by tabulating such responses and developing an appropriate statistical correction.

Even if the effects of distortion and irrelevant response sets could be adequately controlled, however, these instruments would probably remain marginally effective predictors. For the self-report requires respondent judgments at least as complex as those earlier noted in the discussion of the expressed-preferences interest test. And the basic problem of providing adequate structure with respect to specific situational characteristics is exceptionally difficult in a pencil-and-paper procedure. On the other hand, as the test constructor incorporates more and more details into the test exercises, the resulting scores are likely to turn more and more into measures of reading comprehension.

Projective techniques— To avoid certain of these measurement problems, some use also has been made of projective techniques, in which the examinee responds to ambiguous stimulus situations and presumably reveals his response characteristics by the interpretation he gives to the fragmentary or meaningless stimuli that are presented. But the characteristics that can be identified from the responses generated by these techniques are even further removed from the stimuli that determine performance in the target situation than are the data provided by self-reports, and this severely curtails the validity of projective tests as predictors. They appear more serviceable in eliciting the bizarre kinds of responses of concern in a clinical setting than in predicting the "normal" responses of interest in most educational and occupational applications.

Biographical information— A third popular approach has been to predict on the basis of selected historical data thought to be relevant to the applicants' nonintellective characteristics. Most frequently, this type of information has been obtained from the applicants themselves, through personal history forms or biographic data blanks filled out as part of the selection procedure. The applicants' honesty in completing such forms appears to be high, especially when the answers requested are of a type that *can be* verified on objective grounds (though actual verification is in fact not intended).

Biographic data blanks can accommodate either the response-oriented or the result-oriented approach or a combination of both. To obtain an index of the applicant's "sense of responsibility," for example, one might focus on his own actions, such as the reasons he cites for giving up the part-time jobs he held in the past, or on the apparent judgment of others, such as the number of times he was elected secretary of a club or other organization. Or one might stretch the chain of hypotheses even further by assuming that certain family characteristics (e.g. having younger siblings) create situations conducive to the distribution of responsibility, and that these situations in turn reinforce responsibility-taking behavior; and ask simply for factual data on family composition.

Whatever the approach, however, it should be clear that each item of a biographic test is based on one or more separate hypotheses that require empirical confirmation. This raises the same issues discussed with respect to the biographic interest test, and the same difficulties of finding a sufficient number of viable hypotheses usually are encountered.

Situational tests— To provide greater opportunities for matching specific situational characteristics than are afforded by pencil-and-paper measures, a number of instruments based on the applicant's performance in a live situation have been developed. Group discussions, role-playing problems, and simulated job exercises are examples of this type of test. The applicant carries out one or more specified tasks that have been designed to elicit behaviors related to the target performance and is evaluated by an examiner who is present throughout the test as an observer. In the early development of these tests, the basis for evaluation was usually the examiner's professional insight and judgment. More recently, detailed check lists have been introduced, and the examiner serves chiefly as a recorder.

The check lists most commonly used combine the response-oriented and the result-oriented approaches. A group discussion exercise that is to measure the applicants' potential leadership qualities, for example, may be scored in part on the basis of each participant's own contributions—who takes the lead in defining the issues, in encouraging others to comment, etc.—and in part on the basis of the group's apparent orientation—to whom do the participants address most of their questions. Items of this latter type have given quite promising results in the limited and mainly exploratory studies in which they so far have been applied.

The major disadvantage of these tests is that they are too costly and time consuming for many practical applications. They are expensive to construct, they can be administered to only a few applicants at a time, and they require the presence of a trained observer throughout each session. Also, their reliability has tended to be quite low, suggesting that even longer sessions (and therefore even higher costs) may be required. But despite their high absolute cost, their cost-effectiveness may in fact be greater than that of alternative approaches.

These then are the standard rationales available to the test constructor. If he applies them diligently, he can expect to match the levels of accuracy typical of current selection and guidance procedures. What are his chances of doing better? In theory, his chances are high. Since the validity of existing instruments is probably much lower than the potential validity of their underlying rationales, the test constructor should be able to increase accuracy by devising new versions that correspond more closely to the assumptions enumerated in the above section. And to the extent that the standard rationales do not accommodate all of the pertinent aspects of student behavior, he should be able to develop supplementary rationales to tap variance not now being predicted. But, in practice, ingenious tests and unique rationales seldom turn out to be more effective than available procedures; and the accuracy of educational prediction has not been raised appreciably for 20 to 30 years. Associated with each type of selection and guidance problem there seems to be a certain level of accuracy that cannot be exceeded.

This suggests that the crucial limitations may lie not so much in the test constructor's proposed solutions as in the formulation of the problem itself. And it may be that a sharper articulation of selection and guidance objectives will advance the state of the art in prediction more surely and rapidly than will the development of yet another generation of new testing procedures. The present discussion is concluded with a description of four categories of constraints inherent in the standard prediction model and the suggestion that herein may be found the most attractive opportunities for innovation.

OPPORTUNITIES FOR INNOVATION
Definition of the Target Performance

One of the practical constraints imposed on the test constructor is that he is seldom called on to predict attainment in a specific activity, as assumed in the above rationales. More typically, he has to predict attainment in a cluster of related activities that have been subsumed under a single label, even though somewhat different kinds of performance are involved. This is the case in college admission tests, since the field in which each student will major is not normally fixed in advance and since there is considerable latitude even within fields with respect to specific course options. This is also

the case in vocational testing, since it is quite impractical to develop separate prediction formulas for the thousands of available job positions.

Accordingly, the attainment of applicants who are given the same tests for presumably the same purpose may in fact consist of a variety of separate attainments, reflecting the requirements unique to the various subspecialties they entered after admission. And it may be quite impossible for the test constructor to forecast these attainments with equal accuracy on the basis of predictors applied uniformly to the entire applicant group. The heterogeneity of the activities encompassed by the cluster of courses or jobs with which the test constructor is working imposes an upper bound on the accuracy that can be achieved, irrespective of the excellence of his predictors.

One way of increasing accuracy, therefore, is to restructure the current admission practices to permit separate selection into a larger number of more narrowly defined clusters. This can be done either by using different instruments for the various subclusters or by combining the same instruments with different weights and can at least in principle result in substantial gains in overall student attainment. Whether these gains justify changing the established admissions procedures is a more complex issue, however. The objectives of most educational institutions are not limited to maximum productivity but include also a sizeable component of community service, and more narrow specialization at the time of admission may be considered quite undesirable from this point of view. Still, the test constructor should try to assess the limitations imposed by the definition of the target performance and, if restructuring the problem is not feasible, scale the investment in test construction to the levels of accuracy that realistically can be expected.

In guidance or classification, where the objective of the test constructor is differential prediction, this constraint is compounded by the degree to which the clusters to be differentiated in fact represent different kinds of performance. If attainment in one cluster depends on substantially different requirements than attainment in another, the test constructor can devise instruments addressed to these separate requirements and can hope to obtain reasonably independent predictions. But if there are many elements common to the requirements of the two clusters, his search for independent predictors will be in vain. Here, it is the overlap among the clusters with which he is working that imposes an upper bound on the accuracy of differential prediction that he can attain.

Trying to differentiate clusters that are in actuality similar can greatly reduce the efficiency of test construction. Because of the substantial portions of variance that remain unpredicted even under the best of circumstances, the test constructor will seldom be able to compute the degree of criterion overlap from tryout results with predictor tests and will not know whether to attribute his inability to differentiate certain clusters to the inherent nature of the activities or to the quality of the predictors. And he may continue to invest in the development of additional predictors, reaching for levels of discrimination that cannot be attained.

Analytic techniques, such as task analysis, are helpful in estimating the degree of overlap between two activities before test construction begins. Yet, it follows from the above rationales that descriptive analyses can provide only partial and tentative information. For, properly speaking, overlap in prediction is a function not of the similarity of the tasks but of the similarity (or within-individual correlation) of the performance characteristics that mastering these tasks requires. Such jobs as pastry cook and watchmaker, for example, though dissimilar in descriptive terms, could in fact be different applications of highly similar attributes and skills and might therefore not be suited to differential prediction. But the test constructor cannot readily identify this overlap from an analysis of the component operations.

The need is for a sort of factor analysis of the domain of target performance, leading to a taxonomy of reasonably homogeneous activity clusters. The problem has been that any one individual does not normally enter a variety of curricula and occupations, which makes it impractical to try to assemble a sufficient sample of individuals whose performance in different activities can be compared. But there are certain opportunities of this type, such as rotational training programs; and there is certain relevant information to be obtained also from laboratory studies and from the intercorrelation matrices of classification programs. A synthesis of such data followed by systematic exploration of the gaps thereby identified might be productive. Certainly, the development of sharper guidelines for deciding *what* to predict should be an early step in the improvement of prediction procedures.

Criterion Measures

Though the test constructor may know in a general way what the target performance is that he is trying to predict, for example in an undergraduate elementary education program aimed at acquiring the understandings and techniques of an effective teacher, he has a good deal of difficulty in analyzing that totality into manageable specifics. He has still further difficulty in devising procedures for appraising those specifics of target performance. The concern for this analysis and development must be central to the improvement of prediction procedures. For instruments to appraise target performance will constitute the only means at his disposal for determining the relative effectiveness of his trial predictors; and will, to the extent that he relies on an empirical basis for item selection, shape the content of the predictors as well. The accuracy of prediction he can achieve (or at least the accuracy he can determine he has achieved) is highly dependent on the adequacy of the criterion measures.

Dissatisfaction with criterion instruments is endemic in the field of prediction. And, although the frequently expressed conviction that current predictors are more accurate than the available criteria reveal is clearly gratuitous, the need for improved criterion measures is real. The lack of accurate assessments of target performance is without doubt the most severe of the constraints imposed on the test constructor.

The methodological difficulties of assessment have been described in detail in preceding chapters and need not be reiterated here. But it should be noted that any of these difficulties may become a double problem in the case of prediction. Because the above rationales depend on the assessment of past behavior as a basis for inferring future performance, a predictor is in a sense itself a criterion measure (i.e. of past attainment); and one may therefore encounter the methodological difficulties of assessment in both the criterion and the predictor. This has been especially debilitating in the affective domain, where the basic problems of assessing personality-tied responses apply equally to past behavior and to the target performance and thereby impose a dual constraint on the predictive accuracy that can be obtained.

Implicit in a dual constraint, of course, is the opportunity for dual gains. A resolution of any of the major assessment problems (whether through the improvement of tests or the discovery of other indicators of effective performance) will not only improve the accuracy of criterion measures but also make possible the design of predictors more consistent with the assumptions of the above rationales. For the test constructor, the criterion problem remains the single most important target for innovation.

Background of the Examinees

As has been pointed out, many of the prediction rationales assume that the examinees have had comparable opportunities to acquire the skill being measured throughout their past lives. Systematic differences in background can distort seriously the test scores. The extent to which such differences exist in the applicant population is therefore another external constraint imposed on the test constructor.

Easing this constraint by changing the nature of the applicant group is seldom realistic. But the same effect sometimes can be achieved by postponing the time at which the decision has to be made. As students progress through the educational system they are exposed to increasing numbers of common experiences, both in the classroom and extracurricularly; and this growing pool of shared experiences enables the test constructor to design more uni-formly applicable predictors. If it is feasible to defer early decisions, such as those made in Europe on the basis of "eleven-plus" or similar examinations, more accurate instruments can be developed. The greater maturity of the students and their increased capacity for enlightened self-selection are additional advantages of postponed placement decisions.

Two other approaches to heterogeneous applicant groups have already been suggested. The first was to administer the same tests to all applicants but to use separate regression equations to predict the performance of the distinct subgroups that comprise the total applicant population. This approach has serious practical limitations and raises also the as yet unanswered question of which characteristics make subgroups distinct. The second was to try to limit the content of the tests to the core of knowledge and skills appropriate to the entire group. This has the disadvantage of eliminating from consideration many of the elements that for one or more subgroups are the most predictive.

There is little doubt, however, that compromise solutions more effective than current practice can be developed. The need is for more complete information about the similarities and diversities of experience typical of applicant groups at various educational levels—for preliminary research that can guide item selection. Not enough is known, for example, about the differences in English usage among the American subcultures to evaluate their possible implications for the design of verbal aptitude tests. Nor is sufficient data available to evaluate more specific suggestions, such as Krug's (1964) notion that biographical inventories offer greater promise than aptitude or achievement tests for selection from racially mixed groups, at least at the upper levels. These and related possibilities should be actively explored.

Characteristics of the Instruction to Be Provided

It follows from the preceding remarks that prediction problems cannot be isolated from the total "system" in which they occur. The target performance and the examinee population are two of the major components of this system; the instruction the students are to receive is a third. Any characteristic of the instructional program—beginning level, content, methods, duration—may influence directly the establishment of appropriate requirements for admission.

The most common difficulty that the instructional program causes the test constructor is that mastering the instruction usually requires certain skills extraneous to those required by the target performance; and that these additional skills must somehow be reflected in the predictors. The course may require tool skills such as memory, for example, that are introduced by the nature of the instructional materials, or entirely superfluous skills that are taught as the result of an inadequate analysis of the target performance; e.g. the undue emphasis on theory characteristic of much vocational training. The student may never again have to use these skills once he is graduated but without them he may not be able to reach graduation, and they are for this reason functional determinants of success. The wider the disparity between the target performance and the performance required in training, the lower the accuracy with which the former can be predicted. Revisions in the instructional program are the only effective solution.

The recent changes in the philosophy of instruction have even more serious implications. Traditionally, a fixed curriculum was developed on the basis of the educational objectives, and it was the task of the test constructor to predict the differential attainment of a group of individuals following this standard sequence of instruction. Tests were used, in effect, to fit the students to the curriculum; and poor performance was regarded as an error in selection. But, increasingly, instruction is being adapted to the students on an individual basis through a variety of new instructional techniques. And poor performance is being regarded as an error in instructional methods, leading to program modifications.

It seems clear that the standard predictors can have at best limited utility for the kinds of decisions these new approaches require. But the kinds of predictors that will be useful—or, in fact, the appropriate role of prediction in adaptive instructional systems—has not yet been determined. As the new methods of education expand, this could become the single most crucial issue in educational testing. These issues are considered more fully in chapter 17.

REFERENCES

Anastasi, A. Some implications of cultural factors for test construction. In *Proceedings of the 1949 Invitational Conference on Testing Problems*. Princeton, N. J.: Educational Testing Service, 1949. Pp. 13–17.

Anastasi, A. *Differential psychology*. New York: Macmillan, 1965.

Biesheuvel, S. The study of African ability. *African Studies*, 1952, **10,** 105–117.

Bloom, B. S., & Peters, F. R. *Use of academic prediction scales for counseling and selecting college entrants*. New York: Macmillan, 1961.

Chauncey, H., & Fredericksen, N. The functions of measurement in educational placement. In E. F. Lindquist (Ed.), *Educational measurement*. Washington: American Council on Education, 1951. Pp. 85–116.

Clemans, W. V. An analytical and empirical examination of some properties of ipsative measures. *Psychometric Monograph*, 1966, No. 14.

Davis, W. A., & Havighurst, R. J. The measurement of mental systems. *Science Monthly*, 1948, **66,** 301–316.

Flanagan, J. C. The use of comprehensive rationales in test development. *Educational and Psychological Measurement*, 1951, **11,** 151–155.

Flanagan, J. C. *Technical report, Flanagan Aptitude Classification Tests*. Chicago: Science Research Associates, 1959.

Flanagan, J. C., & Fivars, G. The Tapping Test— a new tool to predict aptitude for typing. *Delta Pi Epsilon Journal*, 1964, **6,** 33–39.

Guilford, J. P. A revised structure of intellect. *Reports from the Psychological Laboratory of the University of Southern California*, 1957, No. 19.

Guilford, J. P., & Lacey, J. I. *Printed Classification Tests*. (Report No. 5 of the Army Air Force Aviation Psychology Program.) Washington: U. S. Government Printing Office, 1947.

Krug, R. E. Possible solutions to the problem of cultural bias in tests. In *Selecting and training Negroes for managerial positions*. Princeton, N. J.: Educational Testing Service, 1964. Pp. 77–90.

Kuder, G. F. *Manual for the Kuder Preference Record—Vocational*. Chicago: Science Research Associates, 1960.

Lindquist, E. F. An evaluation of a technique for scaling high school grades to improve prediction of college success. *Educational and Psychological Measurement*, 1963, **23,** 623–646.

McClelland, W. *Selection for secondary education*. London: University of London Press, 1942.

Reitz, W. Predicting college achievement with marks and ranks adjusted for inter-high school variability. *Bulletin of the American Association of College Registrars*, April 1934, 162–181.

Spearman, C. The proof and measurement of association between two things. *American Journal of Psychology*, 1904, **15,** 72–101.

Strong, E. K. *Vocational interests eighteen years after college*. Minneapolis: University of Minnesota Press, 1955.

Strong, E. K. *Manual for the Strong Vocational Interest Blank*. Palo Alto, Calif.: Consulting Psychologists Press, 1959.

Thurstone, L. L. Primary mental abilities. *Psychometric Monograph*, 1938, No. 1.

Thurstone, L. L. *Multiple factor analysis*. Chicago: University of Chicago Press, 1947.

Toops, H. A. Transmutation of marks. *Ohio College Association Bulletin*, No. 125(June 1933), 1093–2000.

Travers, R. The prediction of academic achievement. In W. T. Donahue et al., *Measurement of student adjustment and achievement*. Ann Arbor: University of Michigan Press, 1949. Pp. 147–190.

Measurement Theory | PART THREE

12. The Nature of Measurement

Lyle V. Jones
University of North Carolina at Chapel Hill

Measure is one of the thousand most common words in printed English (Thorndike & Lorge, 1944). As is usual with words that have had a long history and wide currency, measure has many different meanings and applications. In a count of its occurrence in a sample of 2,500,000 words, measure occurred more than 400 times and was used in 40 different ways.

In a basic study of usage, the primary senses of measure as a noun referred to all of these: the process of, the result of, the instrument for, and the units used in measuring. Not only did measure mean the act or the process of determining the extent, duration, and dimensions of a thing, but it also meant the instrument by which the process is done, the units in which the instruments are graduated, and the results of the act itself.

Measure, in addition, refers to less exact instruments, processes, and units. Among its 40 meanings, the word also referred to any instrument used as a basis for comparison even when that comparison involved the processes of estimation or judgment. As used popularly, measure refers not only to procedures that have precision but also to acts of subjective estimation. Measure refers to the determination of the charge on the electron and also to the estimation of beauty; it refers to the determination of the weight of an automobile and also to the estimation of an individual's tolerance for frustration. Such a range of meanings for a scientific term is unfortunate. To avoid misunderstanding here, the noun *measure* shall refer to a particular result obtained by measurement procedures; the verb *to measure* shall refer to the act of measurement.

What, then, is *measurement?* Much of this chapter represents an effort toward developing an answer to this question. In the first section, the approach is discursive and somewhat intuitive. The final section of the chapter includes a more rigorous discussion of the term.

Unanimity concerning the meaning of measurement may appear unlikely. One may measure the length of a table, the weight of a diamond, the duration of a horse's run around a track, the resistance of an electric circuit, the achievement of a student, the visual acuity of a clam, or the extent of expressed pain of a patient. Each of these different measurements involves not only different attributes of different objects or events but also different purposes. But each measurement is purposive. In every case, measurement provides information about an attribute of the entity measured. Frequently, the information provided is relevant to predictions about related phenomena. For instance, the length of a table may be needed to judge whether it will fit in a recess. The respective purposes for the other measurements may be setting a price upon a jewel, determining whether to enter a horse in a competitive race, passing on the safety of a radio, evaluating the performance of a teacher, relating behavior to neurological data for an infrahuman organism, or selecting an anesthetic for an operation.

The purpose of measurement always, then, is to acquire information about attributes of objects, organisms, or events. The information always is relevant to the description of the phenomena measured. In most cases, interpretation of the measures allows some kind of prediction.

Note that what is measured is not an *object* but a *property* or *attribute* of an object. One does not measure a table, but one may measure a table's length (or width, height, weight, light-reflecting property, etc.). One does not measure a student, but one may measure his weight or his achievement in arithmetic. By attribute or property, one refers to a recognized characteristic on which the objects of a set can vary. Each object in the set may be assigned a specific *value* of the attribute. The term attribute, as used here, is synonymous with the term *variable* in common scientific usage. Weight in pounds is an attribute of students. This *variable* takes on different *values* for different students—for Tom, 137; for Jeffrey, 154; for Kathleen, 118.

Not only is it the case that the subjects of measurement consist of attributes of objects rather than objects themselves, but also the attributes that can be measured are of a restricted kind. *To be measurable an attribute must fit the specifications of a quantitative variable.* A quantitative variable is one for which meaningful interpretation may be given to the magnitude comparison of any two attribute values; that is, the difference in magnitude between two values must be interpretable in the sense that it honestly represents a corresponding quantitative difference in the attribute. Now it is generally accepted that the *results* of measurement will be expressed quantitatively, i.e. in the form of numbers. It is also the case that the attribute measured must be capable of being conceived of in quantitative terms.

Whether or not it is sensible to speak of the measurement of other than quantifiable attributes has remained a source of confusion about the nature of measurement. Consider the assessment of attributes of a person. Clearly, it is sensible to measure a person's height, weight, income, or number of siblings. All of these are quantifiable attributes. A large class of attributes of a person are not so clearly quantifiable: his achievement in algebra, his knowledge of world history, his skill in carpentry, his aptitude for scholastic endeavor, his interest in science, or his attitude concerning extrasensory perception. Yet in each of these cases, one may define the attribute in such a way that a quantitative statement about it is sensible. One may conceive of the magnitude of a student's algebra achievement relative to that of other students or conceive of the extent of his knowledge of world history, of the amount of his skill in carpentry, etc. To the degree that one is successful in *defining* the attributes quantitatively, it becomes meaningful to try to devise procedures for measuring these attributes. (It is easy

to forget that only in recent decades has it become reasonable to consider measurement of such attributes. Considerable controversy attended the appearance of L. L. Thurstone's [1929] paper that bore the title "Attitudes Can Be Measured," which in present times seems overdefensive.)

Other attributes (a person's name, his place of birth, or his choice of college major) are not amenable to quantitative definition and to attempt measurement of them does not seem sensible. While a "value" for such attributes might be ascertained and while a numeral could be used, for convenience, to code that value, the numeral assigned would constitute a classificatory index rather than a measure. Magnitude comparisons between these assigned values do not convey relevant information about differences between corresponding attributes. The reason that no unit of measurement is established for these attributes is that they do not lend themselves to interpretation in terms of magnitude. Thus one would not speak of "measuring" these attributes.

The definition of an attribute in quantitative terms is a necessary but not a sufficient requisite to measuring the attribute. *A measurement procedure also demands that a unit of measurement be established,* and the measurement procedure must be consonant with the established unit. The unit may be quite arbitrary: e.g. a pound, a foot, a minute, a degree Fahrenheit, or an error on an examination item. Measurement may be further refined by defining as a unit the smallest difference in magnitude that can be detected by available instrumentation: e.g. a tenth of an ounce, a millimeter, a microsecond. Or a unit may be derived from a combination of arbitrary units: e.g. pounds per square foot, dollars per school district, errors per minute, nanoseconds per cycle. A measurement of an attribute consists of determining, for a given object, the number of units of the attribute. More will be said later concerning the importance of selecting the unit to assure interpretability and generality of measurement.

Measurement, then, is a purposive acquisition of information about the object, organism, or event measured by the person doing the measuring. It is a determination of the magnitude of a specified attribute of the object, organism, or event in terms of a unit of measurement. The result of the measurement is expressed by a numeral. The classification of attributes, either qualitative or quantitative, is distinguished from the measurement of attributes, which must be quantitative.

THE CONCEPTION AND PERCEPTION OF ATTRIBUTES

Measurement in differing areas of science tends to involve different kinds of objects, organisms, and events or, at least, different sets of attributes. The physicist, for instance, studies gases, liquids, and solids and is interested in attributes such as volume, velocity, or amounts of energy. The psychologist and the educator, on the other hand, deal with organisms, frequently with human individuals or groups. They are interested in attributes such as aptitudes, interests, or achievement. Such differences among classes of attributes to be measured necessarily involve differences in the procedures employed for measurement.

Some measurements can be made quite simply and directly; for instance, the length of an object can be measured by counting the number of unit-length standard rulers that, when laid end to end, traverse the object. The weight of an object can be measured by balancing it against a number of unit-weight standards. The time between two events also can be measured by comparison of that duration with known standard intervals, e.g. seconds on a stopwatch. Other attributes, however, can be estimated only from their effects. In temperature, the variations in height of a column of alcohol or of mercury are known to be related to variations in temperature. In scholastic achievement, the differences in level of performance on tests are presumed to be related to differences in knowledge of the material. The estimate of achievement in school, just as of temperature in a room, can be observed only by its effects. The inference about an attribute from its effects involves either an assumption or a demonstration of a relation between effect and attribute. In the case of temperature, an established relation has been

discovered between thermal dynamics and the height of a mercury column. Similarly, for human achievement it has proven possible to establish relations between the mastery of skills and proficiency of performance, on the one hand, and the adequacy of responses to questions demanding specific items of information, on the other. These two examples of measurement, then, are logically similar. However, the former enjoys advantages of greater precision, primarily as a consequence of the greater degree of specification and control of the conditions of observation.

In scientific observations, whether direct or indirect, the conditions for observation are carefully specified in terms of time, place, and circumstance. In physics and chemistry, observations at sea level at 25° centigrade may differ markedly from observations of the same attribute at 0° centigrade at 5,000 feet above sea level. In psychology, the behavior of an individual at 2 A.M. at his desk in his own home may differ markedly from his behavior at 10 A.M. at his desk in his classroom. The statement about an observation, necessarily, must contain specification of the conditions under which it is performed. It is in this respect that precision of psychological measurement suffers in comparison with that of physical measurement. Many relevant features of the conditions remain beyond the control of the observer; indeed, many such features may not even be recognized by the observer as having relevance. That component of the outcome of measurement attributable to unspecified conditions becomes classed as *error of measurement*.

What is to be observed is, of course, crucial. No attribute can be observed unless man has arrived at some concept of it. Every object has as many different attributes or properties as there are different ways one can conceive of it. Physical objects have properties such as height, weight, color, shape, function, etc. Humans have not only the properties of physical objects but also such other characteristics as intelligence, health, education, and personality. In science, the attempt is made to specify completely in advance the particular properties, characteristics, aspects, or traits that are to be observed. For ages, man disregarded certain properties or attributes of phenomena because he did not know of them or their behavior. He did not notice ultraviolet radiation nor the fact that quartz reacted differently from glass to ultraviolet light. Nor did he notice electrical currents in the brain or that some people taste phenylthiocarbonate. What is observed depends upon man's conceptual equipment to translate sensory experience into the notion of a property or an attribute. The notion of attribute involves recognizing common elements within subsets of observations as sensed by the observer.

This conceptual definition of an attribute is an important step towards its systematic observation, but it is only a first step. Also necessary is an operational definition in terms of the conditions under which the observation is made and of the method used to measure the attribute. In the observation of the tensile strength of steel, the specification of the operations of preparing the sample, of fastening it in the instrument, and of the instrument itself are necessary to the precise definition of the measured attribute, tensile strength. Similarly, in the observation of the aptitude of students for graduate study, the specification of the operations for giving the test and for motivating the students, as well as a description of the items in the test and the method of scoring responses, may be necessary to the definition of the attribute.

The property observed, then, is dependent both upon man's ability to conceive of it and upon his ability to observe it. The adequacy of observation is a primary antecedent to the adequacy of measurement. In this sense, it is true, as Protagoras announced, "Man is the measure of all things." It is man who studies gases and solids, who studies behavior and culture, and all measurement ultimately depends on the occurrence of sensory data and upon its perception by observers. The need to adopt a suitable unit for measurement, however, has fostered reliance on tools as aids to perception. The greater the need for precision, the more sophisticated have become the tools. Some tools for measurement (rulers, balance scales, thermometers, and containers for measuring volume) serve primarily to define a standard unit and to promote agreement among observers. Other tools (microscopes or telescopes) magnify effects so that they become more amenable to observation and measurement. Still other tools or machines (radiation counters and linear accelerators) enable observers to perceive specified classes of phenomena by transforming effects so that they become susceptible to human sensation. Many instruments not only detect but also record attribute values, thus preserving a permanent record of the measured phenomenon.

In the absence of instruments for extension of the senses or in the absence of devices for the recording of more precise estimates, human observations are liable to greater variability. Instruments are a means for reducing measurement error and promoting agreement among observers. Instruments are steadily improved upon, so that the newer instruments tend to make possible greater reduction in the magnitude of measurement error. The phenomenon observed produces a variation in the instrument that provides observers a recorded representation of the estimated value of the attribute.

Statements about an attribute are empirical to the extent that they depend upon what is experienced. For such statements to be incorporated into the body of scientific knowledge, the relevant experiences of different observers must be in agreement. If only one observer and no one else could make the observation, there could be no demonstration of its wider acceptability. In general, science demands a *reproducibility* of observations. Whenever conditions and methods are identical, the observations should be identical (within the range of measurement error) unless the object underwent some changes during the observation or subsequent to it. The development of apparatus as an aid to measurement has promoted commonality of perceptual judgments among observers and has enhanced opportunities for agreement and reproducibility.

MEASURING DISTANCE: A CASE HISTORY OF EVOLUTION OF MEASUREMENT

In the twentieth century, one is apt to take for granted that direct physical measurement always has been marked by precision, standardization, and objectivity. It is instructive to be reminded how fallacious is this view. Consider, for example, the historical development of procedures for measuring linear distance.

A basic unit of length, widely used from earliest recorded history until the nineteenth century, was the cubit (later called elbow or ell)—the length of the forearm from the point of the elbow to the tip of the outstretched middle finger. Subsidiary units, thought to be in use from 7000 B.C., include the digit (the breadth of a finger), the palm, the little span (tip of outstretched forefinger to tip of little finger), the great span (tip of outstretched thumb to tip of little finger), the foot, and the pace. In view of the prominence of individual and subgroup differences in bodily stature, it is hardly surprising that efforts to standardize units within and across cultures remained unsuccessful until recent times. Yet efforts within cultures were made as early as 2300 B.C.; from Babylonian ruins have been discovered knotted cords, in bas-relief on stone, with knots at 5-cubit intervals. Cubit rods, of wood, date from about 1500 B.C. An Egyptian cubit rod of that period, with subsidiary measures marked upon it, still resides in the Louvre.

Throughout much of recorded history, civil authority has been vested in kings. In Egypt, the royal cubit consisted of 7 palms, or 28 digits (in contrast to the Assyrian cubit of 6 palms). In England, Edward I in 1305 decreed: "Three grains of barley dry and round make an inch; twelve inches make a foot; three feet make an ulna; five and a half ulnae make a rod; and forty rods in length and four in breadth make an acre." (The reference length, happily, was not the barley grain "dry and round," but rather "the iron ulna of our lord the King." Yet, the barleycorn is a unit that remains in use today. It is the unit of shoe size. A shoe of size 9 is one barleycorn longer than a shoe of size 8.) The fourteenth-century statute of Edward I was confirmed by Henry VII in 1497 (at which time a bronze rod replaced the iron ulna), then by Elizabeth I in 1588 (replacing the earlier bronze rod with another). In 1835, a gunmetal bar became "the imperial yard." It remains so today, defined as correct at 62° Fahrenheit with barometer at 30 inches of mercury.

In France, the official standard of linear measurement for a thousand years, from the time of Charlemagne, was the Arabic hashimi cubit, containing 2 feet, or 24 inches (but equal to 25.56 present-day inches). Yet in 1800, variability of conventions within France was so great that three distinct standards of length are said to have been in use within the single city of Bordeaux. In 1791, the French Académie des Sciences proposed a metric standard for distance measurement, defining the meter as one ten-millionth of the earth's polar quadrant passing through Dunkirk and Barcelona. Gradually, over the following 50 years, the metric system was ruled compulsory in parts of France and Italy, in Austria, and in Germany. Later, its optional use was legalized in Great Britain and in the United States. In 1875, a 17-nation treaty, known as the Convention of the Meter, stipulated adoption of a standard platinum-iridium meter bar, stored in a vault at the International Bureau of Weights and Measures in Sèvres, France.

Efforts to further standardize distance measures have continued in recent years. Between 1958 and 1960, several conventions were established. The U.S. inch (2.54005 cm) and the British inch (2.5399956 cm) were revised to conform to Canadian and Australian standards (2.54 cm). The adjustment was motivated largely by needs associated with the manufacture of precision tools. In 1960, the Eleventh General Conference of Weights and Measures, with 38 countries represented, sanctioned an international meter at 1,650,763.73 vacuum wavelengths of monochromatic orange light emitted by a krypton atom of mass 86. This has become the international standard for all distance measurement in those fields of science and technology where precision and standardization are required.

It seems apparent that only as needs for precision mounted did conventions for the measurement of distance become firmly established. Local community standards were sufficient for a world in which barter and trade was largely constrained within communities. But today stringent international standards are needed, particularly for the standardization of precision tools required in science and industry.

CLASSIFICATION

Perhaps the simplest form of systematic observation is to perceive that two objects are similar or dissimilar in some respect. Eventually the observer notes that he is recognizing the same likeness or difference for a great many object pairs, and, at this point, he abstracts the similarity as a conceived property. He then may group objects that are similar in this property into classes. In the simplest case, a dichotomous classification may be used: short versus not short, heavy versus not heavy, intelligent versus not intelligent, male versus female. Finer distinctions then may be recognized, and a larger number of classes may be generated: extremely short, short, medium, tall, extremely tall; or boy, man, girl, woman. The definition of each class becomes the basis for classifying. The definition requires specifying the basic distinguishing signs for judging inclusion within the class. Objects or persons then can be sorted into each class by a "go–no-go" criterion. Whenever observers can agree on the criterion for class inclusion, they then can communicate to each other by using some class name to designate objects within the class. In this way, there may be agreement on the class: e.g. heavy objects, or extremely tall persons, or baseball players.

All objects that go into the class are considered the same or equal under the convention that all differences other than that of the defined property are disregarded. Of course within such a class as defined, further subclasses may be recognized on the basis of some characteristic common to the members of the subgroup but not to all the members of the class. Thus the subclasses of pitchers, catchers, and outfielders may be found within the class of baseball players. Note that the formation of such subclasses may rest upon the definition of a new attribute. The attribute of experience playing baseball was sufficient for the first classification. The attribute of position played must be recognized before establishing the subclasses

within the class of baseball players. Class membership, therefore, first rests upon an observer's recognition of an attribute, then upon defining classes in terms of likenesses and differences. With respect to the attribute(s) considered, each class is considered to be homogeneous. Yet members of a class may differ in terms of finer distinctions of that attribute or in terms of other attributes that, when recognized, may promote additional classification.

The classification of objects need not constitute measurement, since (a) the property, which serves as the basis for classification, need not be interpretable in terms of magnitude and (b) class membership, the consequence of observation, need not be represented by a numeral. Classification is, however, an essential prelude to measurement. The first steps toward progress in any science thus involve qualitative rather than quantitative distinctions. Properties must be recognized and classificatory procedures must be developed prior to the establishment of techniques for measurement. After a property has been successfully abstracted and similarity classes for that property have been defined, it may be discovered that successive classes lend themselves to quantitative interpretation; that is, the attribute-values of objects assigned to different classes may exhibit systematic differences in magnitude. If so, the quantitative definition of the attribute becomes possible, and measurement procedures may be devised. Measurement of an attribute, then, may evolve following successful efforts to generate a classification system.

RANKING

Following the classification of a set of objects, it may be possible to make a further judgment indicating the relative order of the subclasses. By *order* is meant a complete ranking of subclasses that is asymmetric and transitive. It is asymmetric in the sense that if subclass C is ranked higher than B, then B cannot be higher than C. It is transitive in the sense that if C is ranked higher than B and B is ranked higher than A, then C is ranked higher than A. Whether or not such ordering of subclasses yields a meaningful result would seem to depend upon whether the relevant attribute can be considered quantitative, that is, whether subclasses can be compared in magnitude. The attribute in baseball of position played is qualitative rather than quantitative, and the subclasses, pitcher, catcher, shortstop, center fielder, etc., are not amenable to meaningful ranking. (However, with a subtle change in definition of the attribute—e.g. salary associated with position played, importance to the team of position played—rank orders might be meaningfully established.) For any one position, say pitcher, one can conceive of an attribute such as effectiveness or success as a pitcher. If coaches could agree upon the sorting, several successive subclasses of pitchers could be formed, such as superior, average, and below average. Indeed, depending upon the perceptual ability of the judges, there may be as many subclasses as there are players. In either case, the subclasses would be ordered in terms of the defined attribute, success as a pitcher.

Observers can recognize differences in the relative amount of many properties. Shades of blue can be distinguished in the range from the pure hue to a nearly washed-out white; apples can be graded on the basis of discriminable marks; and the scholastic success of children is judged by their teachers. It is not unusual for a teacher to rank one student ahead of another in scholastic success. As a matter of fact, some teachers can arrange the students in a class in a complete rank order, so that Robert stands ahead of Jane who stands ahead of Elizabeth, etc.

Ranking may be based on a judgment of some observed property, as when contestants are arranged according to beauty. Sometimes the ranking is based on direct comparison, as may be the case in a ladder tournament where one determines the order of tennis players by permitting them to play against each other, pair by pair. A good example of ranking based on direct comparison is the replacement series of metals. When zinc is dropped in a copper solution, copper plates out and the zinc dissolves. But copper will not replace zinc in a zinc solution. By successive experiments, it is found that a replacement order exists, beginning with gold,

the easiest to replace: gold, mercury, copper, zinc, sodium. Such an order can be established without a more complete understanding of the property associated with that order. All that is necessary is to observe a hierarchical relation. For metals, a hierarchy exists since sodium replaces all the metals listed before it, zinc replaces all those listed before it, and so on. Never is the order reversed, as it would be if copper could replace sodium.

For some properties, establishing order by direct comparison leads to ambiguity. Often this is a consequence of measurement error. Occasionally, when the property being investigated is a complex resultant of several simpler properties, that composite property resists unambiguous ordering by a method of direct comparison. In a tennis ladder, it may be that Davis always wins when playing Thomson, and Thomson always defeats Rhine. Perfect ordering by a method of direct comparison would demand that Davis be victorious when matched against Rhine. But success at tennis depends upon a complex set of factors. It is entirely possible that, while Davis beats Thomson and Thomson beats Rhine, Rhine always wins over Davis. Such a "circular triad" violates the transitivity condition of perfect order. A method of direct comparison, in this case, is inadequate to establish an order. Note, however, that by using other criteria it may still be possible to rank the players on success at tennis. One criterion suitable for this purpose would be proportion of matches won against common opponents. In this case, a unit of relative number of matches won is available, so that more information than order of success could be recorded. Specification of such a unit and utilization of the added information that it provides converts rank ordering into measurement.

The value of developing procedures to establish order among classes of observations is great. In the nineteenth century, a standard set of ordered classes useful to captains of sailing ships was the Beaufort scale of wind velocity. Lacking an instrument for measuring wind velocity, judgments were made about it. On the Beaufort scale, 13 different ordered subclasses are recognized, from calm to hurricane. Intermediate steps are light air, various intensities of breezes and gales, and storm. For purposes of reporting, however, all wind velocities that experts called calm are symbolized by the numeral 0; light air is coded 1, slight breeze is 2, and so on up to numeral 12 for hurricane. The numerals are labels in an arbitrary, hierarchical order. As a matter of fact, the numerals 6, 7, 8, . . . 18 or 4, 8, 13, 15, . . . 47 could have been used to label the subclasses from calm to hurricane. From these labels, one cannot say that two hours of light air (1) would move a ship as far as one hour of slight breeze (2).

Two objects may have adjacent ranks on some attribute, yet the difference in attribute values may be either very small or very large. Suppose a teacher were to rank the heights of the members of a class of 33 youngsters. It is reasonable to expect substantial reliability in such ranks. Pupils in ranks 15, 16, and 17 would probably differ little in height, but pupils in ranks 1 and 2, as likewise those in ranks 32 and 33, would be likely to differ much more in their measured heights. The numerals assigned to the rank orders give useful information about relative position, or direction of differences, but they do not allow inferences concerning the amount of the difference between one object and another.

Ranks are not fixed. If 33 pupils were ranked in height, the set of numerals 1, 2, 3, . . . 33 could be put into one-to-one correspondence with Robert, Jane, Elizabeth, and so on, to John who is, say, 33. If some independent observer arranged the 33 pupils in the same order, there would be a feeling of confidence about the rank assigned to each pupil. In a larger group, the additional pupils might possess amounts of height that would require some of them to be placed ahead of Robert, or between Jane and Elizabeth. These new pupils would change the rank order and the sequence of numerals assigned. The ordinal numerals merely mean that 1 (for first) has a rank higher than 2 (for second) and that, since 2 has a rank higher than 3, 1 must rank higher than 3.

Do procedures that lead to ordering of objects on an attribute qualify as measurement of that attribute? The more general answer is no, in terms of the definition of measurement adopted here. Measurement requires not only an ordered assessment of magnitude of a property but also that the magnitude be expressed in *number of units*. And when objects or events are placed only in rank order with respect to an attribute, resulting data are not amenable to interpretation based upon unit differences on the attribute. However, ordered data may sometimes be transformed to an equal-unit scale by the imposition of a *measurement model*. Such a model is that introduced by Roger Shepard (1962) and discussed later in this chapter. Given a sufficient number of replications of a set of ordered data, those data may be analyzed under this measurement model to provide a metric scale. Thus, while the establishment of order does not constitute measurement, it nevertheless may be the first part of a two-part procedure that does.

In addition, there is a special sense in which the specification of rank always may be interpreted as a statement involving units. One may define, as an arbitrary unit for a given property, position within an ordered set of objects ranked on that property. Then the object ranked 1 is in the first position; the object ranked 2 is $2-1=1$ position below the first object; the object ranked 3 is $3-1=2$ positions below the first; the object ranked 10 is $10-3=7$ positions below the third object. *Position* is a perfectly legitimate unit, and, in terms of that unit, a procedure for ranking is also a procedure for measurement.

There is an important difference, however, between a "legitimate" measurement unit for a property and one that is adequate for the purposes at hand. Recall that measurement is purposive. Typically, the results of measurement are to be used to predict related phenomena. But the unit of position within an ordered set of objects is confined in meaning to that particular set of objects. It may have some use as a unit so long as interest is restricted only to that set of objects. But it lacks predictive generality when objects are added or deleted from the set or when new objects are substituted for those in the observed set. Furthermore, position often is a conceptually weak unit, since equal differences in position may be associated with grossly unequal differences in magnitude of the attribute being considered. Again, this feature restricts the predictive generality of a simple ordering of observations.

Consider again the unit suggested earlier for measuring success at tennis—relative number of matches won against common opponents. It represents a meaningful magnitude and meets these conditions for measurement. Yet it suffers from some of the same weaknesses as position within an ordered set. While such a measurement for a given tennis player would not change as more players are measured, it would be likely to change with changing composition of the common opponents. Such lack of stability clearly limits the predictive value of the measure.

This apparent defect in stability, however, may more reasonably characterize the attribute than the measure of it. Magnitudes of success at tennis, like magnitudes of ability at arithmetic, skill in woodworking, or degree of extroversion, are "rubbery" magnitudes as a consequence of lack of complete definition. Magnitudes of these attributes are likely to shift with changes in time and context more dramatically than, say, the magnitude of length of an iron bar shifts with changing temperature. To expect invariance of any measure, it is essential that all relevant features of the attribute be specified (i.e. controlled). To the extent that the attribute is vaguely defined or is subject to change in values over time and varying conditions, its measurement *should* yield different results at different times and under different conditions. This is not a fault of inadequate measurement so much as a fault in the definition of the attribute.

THE UNIT OF MEASUREMENT

Ordinal arrangement can be developed into measurement if it is possible to specify a suitable unit so that one may determine how near to each other the measured objects are in the attribute of interest. If a subset of objects can be said to be equally spaced on the attribute in question, then the difference between any two of them may be assigned unit magnitude; that difference (or distance in a spatial analog) is a suitable unit for expressing the magnitude of the attribute for all objects in the parent set.

The unit chosen must have relation to the perceived property and should represent a fixed and equal increment of that property regardless of the total magnitude of the property. In measuring income, the dollar is a suitable unit if the property under study is the money each person receives. In those terms appropriate in an accounting office, the gap between $3,000 and $5,000 is the same as the gap between $13,000 and $15,000. But if the income is conceived in terms of goodness of living permitted, the count of dollars earned does not linearly represent the increase in reward. The increase from $3,000 to $5,000 may represent a gigantic change from penury and misery to a modestly comfortable state in which it is possible to obtain necessities; the increase from $13,000 to $15,000 may represent an almost negligible increase in the means for enjoying a comfortable life. The designation of an appropriate unit for measuring income conceived as reward remains a problem of considerable interest in the behavioral sciences. (Various sources of evidence converge to suggest that the logarithm of dollars may provide a suitable unit.)

In some fields, an increased understanding of the relation of the perceived property to other important properties has led to increasingly satisfactory units. Recognition of relations between heat and expansion of mercury or alcohol led to development of the thermometer, calibrated in degree units. Discovery of the relation between blood volume in a person's finger and consequent impedance to the passage of light led to design of the photoelectric plethysmograph for measuring amount of blood flow. Appreciation of the relation between the development of aptitudes and the age of a child led to the definition of mental age units for assessing a child's "intelligence age."

In estimating hearing, a primitive measure was the distance at which a child could hear a sound. In the watch test, a ticking watch was brought closer and closer to the child until he could just hear it. This is a simple experimental device for arranging children in order in terms of keenness of hearing. The score on the test (distance) could be taken as a measure of hearing acuity if observers accept the convention that children who hear at 20 feet, 15 feet, and 10 feet, say, differ from each other by equal degrees of keenness. For measuring hearing, such a convention might be adopted provisionally, to provide numbers that might be related to alternate measures of hearing acuity. If the numbers are found to be functionally related in other than a linear way to other measures, redefinition of this measure of hearing as a nonlinear function of distance of hearing might follow.

Another method that might be used to measure hearing is to produce varying sounds at a standard distance. A primitive scientist might have dropped increasing weights on a drumhead and noted the smallest weight that would produce a sound the child could hear. In modern times, these crude methods can be replaced with electronic techniques. The intensity of the stimulus might be measured by the pressure of the sound waves emitted by the resonator, the unit of pressure being the dyne, which is a unit abstracted from the falling of weights. Then hearing might be scored in terms of the number of dynes per square centimeter. But as a unit of hearing, a dyne per square centimeter is not perceived as being equal over varying magnitudes of sound. If a sound of 20 dynes per square centimeter force is compared with another of 40 dynes, an observer asked to locate the sound halfway between the two in loudness will set the resonator not at 30 dynes but at about 28, near the geometric mean. Experimentation has shown that the intervals of the hearing scale as developed from listeners' judgments are related logarithmically rather than linearly to units of force. Similarly, it can be shown that, since the force of the sound decreases proportionately as the square of the distance from the source, the distance measured in the watch test is not a linear measure of hearing as defined by listeners' judgments.

From many studies of the nature of hearing, of what it means to say that one sound is twice as loud as another, has come a unit of measurement known as the *bel*. The bel is a logarithmic function of the power of the sound; the sound that is 1 bel louder than another is 10 times as strong in terms of dynes/cm^2 and a 2-bel difference corresponds to a ratio of 100 to 1 in sound energy. (Since the bel is inconveniently large, a *decibel*, one-tenth as large, is more frequently used; 1 bel equals 10 decibels, and 2 bels equals 20 db.) The bel or decibel is a unit on a scale having equal-appearing intervals; that is, the scale is linear with relation to loudness as judged by observers. The establishment of equal-appearing intervals rests on the agreement of judges; for example, in setting a tone halfway between two standard tones.

Linearity of a scale, it should be noted, is with relation to some judgment or operation. A scale that increases linearly, in this sense, has a fixed unit, a unit that is equal with reference to that judgment or operation. A householder shopping for an air conditioner cannot safely accept as a unit of its efficiency its rating in horsepower, for horsepower is not linearly related to the amount of cooling he will purchase. He can judge the wisdom of his purchase more adequately in terms of a unit such as a Btu., a fixed unit of thermal energy.

Because measurement always deals with a property that has been previously perceived and is to some degree familiar, there is a danger of believing that the "obvious" unit is in some way peculiarly right for measuring the property. There is a compatibility between the notions of the height of persons and the length of a measuring stick that makes the inch an appealing unit for measuring growth. In fact, common sense rejects as absurd any suggestion that the foot rule does not provide a scale of equal intervals for height. Yet height can be redefined as "height age" and measured in years rather than inches. All that is required is the median height of six-year-olds, seven-year-olds, etc. Then, with a record of these data, one may compare a given child with the standards and report that he has seven-year-old height; or, perhaps even more precisely, that his height age is 7.2 years. The only justification for this seemingly roundabout and "unnatural" measuring scale is that in some studies one year of growth is a more useful unit for a scale of equal intervals than is the inch. Once, the largest (or thickest) tree of a species was thought to be oldest. Now, one relies on a count of the annular rings as a measure of age, even though the rings are unequally spaced on a foot rule. The more obvious measure of size does not maintain a linear relation to age, while a count of the number of rings does.

If one has a measuring device on which successive equal intervals are in some way marked or recorded, one may compare an object with the standard. The observer reads the number of units needed to "equal" the test object. The comparing and reading are visual in the case of length, but a calibrated series of pitch pipes can be used as a standard for tone and a comparison then is made by the appropriate operation of listening and comparing. When comparing and matching is supplemented by counting, the full power of measurement procedures becomes realized. The importance of counting in the historical evolution of the number concept is stressed by Dantzig (1956) in his engrossing book on the development of mathematics.

THE SCALE ORIGIN

Some attributes may be characterized as exhibiting a particular value that indicates complete absence of the attribute. It is usual to assign the numeral 0 to that value, where zero refers to the origin on the measurement scale. A primitive example of an attribute with a meaningful zero point is *number*. Counting is the measurement procedure for determining number. When assessing the number of objects in a set, a count of zero indicates absence of any number of objects, a count of one represents occurrence of one object, etc. Length and weight also constitute attributes for which a measurement of zero may be taken to imply total absence of any magnitude of the attribute. All such attributes are amenable to analysis in terms of a counting operation—counting the number of units of the attribute present in a given object or event. For many other properties, a measured value of zero signifies other than absence of the attribute. A measure of zero temperature, on either a centigrade or Fahrenheit scale, does not imply absence of heat. Nor does a score of zero on an intelligence scale necessarily imply absence of all intelligence on the part of the person being tested. The usefulness of measurement does not always demand a conception of the property such that the associated scale exhibits an *absolute origin*. So long as the unit remains fixed at all levels of magnitude, *differences* may be determined and meaningfully compared. Often this comparison is of major interest.

On any scale with a meaningful absolute zero point, ratios of pairs of measures are capable of meaningful interpretation. An object of weight 6 oz. is twice as heavy as an object of weight 3 oz. A jar with volume 50 cc has five times the capacity of a vial with volume 10 cc. But a temperature of 50° C. does not represent five times the heat of a temperature of 10° C. (although temperature can be conceived of and measured on an absolute scale so that such ratio statements become meaningful). Nor does a score of 600 on the Graduate Record Examination represent twice the level of achievement of a score of 300 (and, at present, the conception of achievement is such that agreement on the definition of an absolute zero level of achievement is not likely). On a scale for which ratios have no meaning with respect to the attribute measured, it also is the case that the simple sums of measures do not lend themselves to adequate interpretation. For, without an absolute zero, the numerical value of a measurement represents a distance from some arbitrary point on the scale; that value includes a constant, usually of unknown size, that specifies the distance from the arbitrary origin to the absolute zero. The sum of two such measures includes an amount equal to twice the unknown constant.

While the sum of measures is not readily interpretable on other than an absolute scale, the mean of two (or more) measures is directly interpretable in the same way that each individual measure is. Let X_i be a value on a scale with unknown origin, where A_i is the corresponding value on a scale with absolute zero.

Then

$$A_i = X_i + C,$$

where C is unknown. Summing a set of n such values,

$$\sum_{i=1}^{n} A_i = \sum_{i=1}^{n} X_i + nC.$$

Dividing both sides of this equation by n yields

$$\frac{\sum_{i=1}^{n} A_i}{n} = \frac{\sum_{i=1}^{n} X_i}{n} + C,$$

or

$$\overline{A} = \overline{X} + C.$$

Related to this feature, note that the difference between any measure and the mean of n measures always is on a scale with an absolute origin, whether or not the zero point for initial measures is absolute.

$$A_i - \overline{A} = (X_i + C) - (\overline{X} + C) = X_i - \overline{X}.$$

Also, differences between any two values, X_i and X_j, are on a scale with an absolute origin, since

$$A_i - A_j = (X_i + C) - (X_j + C) = X_i - X_j.$$

Ratio statements, then, are always applicable to measurement differences.

While most measurement in psychology and education is made on scales without absolute zero points, some efforts to develop absolute scales of preference or value have met with success (e.g. Jones, 1967). The methods used in these investigations demand that data be gathered pertinent to people's preferences for pairs of objects as well as for individual objects. The question then is whether a method can be found for converting the data such that the sum of the two measures for single objects will equal the measure for the corresponding pair of objects. If there can be discovered a transformation so that this summation criterion is met for all object pairs, then that transformation provides an absolute measurement scale. First, of course, it was essential to define conceptually an interpretation for total

absence of preference, for only then is it meaningful to consider devising an absolute scale for its measurement.

DISCRETE AND CONTINUOUS VARIABLES

Quantitative attributes of objects, events, or organisms may be either discrete or continuous. A *discrete* attribute is one that exists only in a number of indivisible units. Examples of discrete properties are number of students in a classroom, number of items correctly answered on a test, or a person's annual earned income (number of cents). For *continuous* attributes, such as length, temperature, attitude, or esthetic value, the attribute is free to vary continuously; two adjacent magnitudes of the attribute may differ by an indefinitely small amount.

When one actually comes to measure attributes, however, the distinction between discrete and continuous variables loses much of its importance. For, as noted earlier, precision of measurement is limited by the smallest resolution magnitude that can be detected by the instrumentation used and perceived by observers. The familiar illuminated sign displaying time and temperature at the street corner measures the continuous variable time only to the minute and measures the continuous variable temperature only to the degree Fahrenheit. A stopwatch provides much greater precision for the measure of time yet provides results only to the tenth of a second. Electronic clocks are capable of still more precise measurement of time but only to the millisecond, microsecond, or nanosecond. Always there is a "smallest" interval beyond which further precision cannot be found with existing instruments. *Measurement of continuous variables, then, always is discrete* in terms of a unit equal to that smallest interval. By this interpretation, fractional measures may be viewed as multiples of the smallest fractional part; a measure such as 3.261 seconds is interpreted as 3,261 milliseconds.

Consider the measurement of a continuous variable in terms of the smallest resolution magnitude of the instrument. Call that magnitude, to be taken as the unit of measurement, a number a. Measuring an object then must yield a result $n \cdot a$, where n is a whole number. Since the variable is continuous, the same result should be recorded for every object where the attribute in question has magnitude within the interval between $n \cdot a - a/2$ and $n \cdot a + a/2$. This represents *rounding* of the magnitude to the nearest integral value of its unit. (For some measurements, such as those displayed by the time-and-temperature clock, a different convention is used. Here the result recorded is $n \cdot a$ for all magnitudes between $n \cdot a$ and $(n+1) \cdot a$; that is, magnitudes are *truncated* rather than rounded. Truncated measures are slightly biased, tending to be uniformly too small. When a number of such measures are cumulated, the bias may become appreciable. For this reason, rounded measures generally are preferred.)

It is clear from the above that even if measurement were totally free from errors of observation and errors of recording, the measure $n \cdot a$ would characterize a range of magnitudes rather than a single magnitude point. This particular feature is absent from measures of discrete properties, since each such measure represents not a range of values but the precise whole-number outcome of a counting operation.

DISTRIBUTIONS IN MEASUREMENT

Even in the most precise problem areas of science, successive measurements of the same continuous attribute of a given object or event will fail to agree. Despite all efforts to control factors incidental to the observation, such factors still will vary a little. The additive resultant of these variations in many factors is likely to affect the outcome of the measurement. Also, even with highly refined instrumentation, one must anticipate variation in the accuracy of scale reading, particularly in interpolation within small intervals on the scale. These composite sources of variability contribute to a *distribution* of results when the measurement process is employed repeatedly.

Consider an example of careful efforts to make a physical measurement, the aim of which is to estimate the gravitational constant, g. A steel bar is dropped from a known height, and the speed with which it falls is measured using a

beam of light and a column of photoelectric cells. As the bar falls, light is reflected from mirrors precisely mounted on the bar, and the reflected light activates the photoelectric cells. This precise determination of the speed of fall, measured at many points, allows calculation of the acceleration of the bar.

A set of 32 such determinations was made in a Canadian laboratory in August 1958.[1] Results appear in the form of the histogram in figure 12.1. Measurement was made to the nearest ten-thousandth of a centimeter per second; then results were grouped in units of 0.0005 cm/sec² to provide data for the histogram. The histogram serves to display graphically the distribution of results; that is, the set of measures obtained for the 32 observations. This distribution resembles others that portray variability due to error of measurement. A smooth normal curve superimposed on the histogram fits the data satisfactorily (i.e. about as well as could be expected for 32 numbers randomly selected from a normally distributed population).

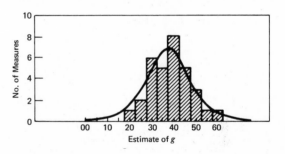

FIG. 12.1. Distribution of estimates of the gravitational constant using steel bar no. 1, August 1958. Note: for estimate of g, third- and fourth-place decimals to be added to 980.6100 cm/sec². (Data from Youden, 1962.)

Frequently, the normal distribution is found to provide a good fit to empirical distributions of measurement errors. Indeed, the normal distribution function discovered by DeMoivre in 1733 was introduced as the *curve of error*. The widespread finding of good fit of the normal distribution to measurement errors may be justified statistically by the central limit theorem—that any variable that is an additive resultant of a large number of relatively inde-

[1] Data for this example were found in Youden, 1962.

pendent causal influences will be distributed normally. The measurement error associated with a given observation may be considered to be such a variable. It may be thought of as the additive resultant of a large number of relatively independent variables attributable to effects of unspecified conditions of measurement. Then, by the central limit theorem, whatever the form of the distributions of these component variables, as their number increases, the distribution of the composite measurement error approaches the normal distribution.

Given the data of figure 12.1, how might one determine a single best estimate for the constant of gravitation? A reasonable solution, and one recommended by considerations of statistical inference, is to take the mean of the observed measures as the best estimate. This number has as its expected value the mean of the normal distribution from which these 32 observations are assumed to have been sampled. In this case, the mean is 980.6139 cm/sec^2 (or 32.17199 ft/sec^2).

Is it also true that the expected value of the mean of the sample observations is the "true value" of the attribute in which one is interested, in this case g, the gravitational constant? The answer is no. One is impotent to know the true value of g but must rely on fallible empirical observations. Always those observations *as a set* are made under specified conditions. The height above sea level affects g, as does the latitude at which observations are made. Also, the instrument used is not free from systematic error. Any set of observations, no matter how carefully controlled, will yield an estimate of g that not only is uncertain but is likely to be *biased;* that is, to have an expected value that differs systematically from the value of g as abstractly conceived.

Consider a second experiment, conducted at the same Canadian laboratory in December 1959. Once again, 32 observations of acceleration were made using the same measurement apparatus as before, except for replacement of the steel bar with another that had been constructed to the same stringent standards as the first. The histogram of resulting measures appears as figure 12.2. The two sample distribu-

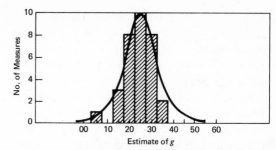

FIG. 12.2. Distribution of estimates of the gravitational constant using steel bar no. 2, December 1959. Note: for estimate of g, third- and fourth-place decimals to be added to 980.6100 cm/sec^2. (Data from Youden, 1962.)

tions, figures 12.1 and 12.2, show considerable overlap. Figure 12.2 again shows the typical normal distribution form. The mean determination from figure 12.2 is 980.6124 cm/sec^2 (32.17194 ft/sec^2), agreeing with the mean of figure 12.1 within two parts in a million. Yet, there is strong statistical evidence of a reliable difference between the means of the two distributions. Given that the same controls were exercised in the two experiments, the conclusion would be that there is a difference between the two bars—an inference drawn from the strong statistical evidence that the expected values of the means from the two experiments are different. Under such conditions, clearly, the expected value of neither mean should be accepted as the value of "true g." The first sample mean is a good estimate of a population parameter, the mean of a *sampling distribution* of results that might be obtained under the conditions of Experiment 1. The second sample mean estimates a mean of a sampling distribution of results that might be found under conditions of Experiment 2. The population means that are estimated, then, are different to the extent that different conditions are employed in the replicated experiments.

The mean of sample distributions is often a useful statistic, as has been seen above. Also useful is a statistic sensitive to spread or variability of the distribution. Especially appropriate for samples randomly drawn from a normally distributed population of values is the *standard deviation*. For the distributions of figures 12.1 and 12.2, not only are the means different, but also the standard deviation for figure 12.2 is smaller than that for figure 12.1. The distribution of figure 12.2 portrays less spread, less variability of measures. Knowledge of the variability of distributions is essential in inferential statistics in order to make decisions concerning whether a difference between two means, say, exceeds the range expected in view of the variability of the distribution of each.

When a problem involves physical measurement, it is typical that one can choose an instrument guaranteed to provide equal units of measurement, in terms of the property measured, at all magnitudes of that property. Often this feature is operationally verifiable, particularly with direct measurement of such properties as length, weight, or time. An object A might be found to be 2 inches long. Object B may be 10 inches long and object C may be 12 inches long. When objects A and B are placed end to end, the resultant will be found to be just as long as object C. Thus it is demonstrated that the 2-inch difference from 12 inches to 10 inches represents the same length as the 2-inch difference from 2 inches to 0 inches.

For problems involving educational and psychological measurement, there often is less assurance concerning the fixedness of the unit over the whole range of the property being assessed. In a test of vocabulary knowledge, the number of correct answers to a 50-item test might constitute a person's "score." Here there is no assurance that a difference of 2 units reflects the same vocabulary difference regardless of the range in which the difference appears. Scores of 36 and 34 differ in terms of number of items correct neither more nor less than scores of 17 and 15. But it does not necessarily follow that equal differences in number of items correct may be interpreted as equal differences in vocabulary knowledge.

Were one to know the form of the population distribution of aptitude, it would be possible to define a unit of measurement using known features of that distribution. In particular, assume that the population distribution is normal; that is, that vocabulary knowledge, as conceived of for a given study, is normally distributed in a population of students. Then

the distribution of test scores could be "normalized" for that population by performing a suitable transformation; the standard deviation of the normalized distribution then would serve as a suitable fixed unit. It would be linearly related to the unit magnitude of vocabulary knowledge to the extent that (a) the transformed scores on the administered test have validity for assessing vocabulary knowledge (see chapter 14) and (b) the assumption of normally distributed vocabulary knowledge is justified.

This procedure for defining a unit of measurement has been widely used in psychological measurement ever since its enthusiastic advocacy by Francis Galton in the latter part of the nineteenth century. A common unit for nationally adopted aptitude and achievement examinations is one-hundredth of a standard deviation, as defined by a large normative sample of scores. The scores are transformed to yield a normal distribution with mean 500 and standard deviation 100. Then a score of 700 differs from a score of 650 by the same amount (in standard deviation units) as a score of 600 differs from a score of 550. Further discussion of this method and other methods for establishing equal units on educational and psychological tests may be found in chapter 15.

To define a stable unit of measurement as a standard deviation of a normalized distribution is defensible only to the extent that in the population the attribute being measured may be conceived as being normally distributed. Restricting attention to distribution of *errors* of measurement, such as those of figures 12.1 and 12.2, the normality assumption is often at least approximately justified. Even though the distribution of measures taken over the population of objects is markedly nonnormal, the sampling distribution of measurement error will be expected to approximate closely the normal form. Establishing a unit of measurement based upon the standard deviation of error distributions is the basis for Thurstone's methods of psychological scaling (see Bock & Jones, 1968; Thurstone, 1959). Often, however, as in the case of nationally administered aptitude examinations, it is not the error distribution but the distribution of the attribute measures that is assumed to be normal. Galton discovered that anthropometric measures, when taken over large groups of subjects, did tend to distribute normally. From this evidence concerning bodily characteristics he proposed to extend the same principles to mental traits. Alternatively, one might assume that a mental trait is the additive resultant of a large number of independent influences. Then the central limit theorem of statistics would lead to an expectation of a normal distribution of that trait in the population. In either case, the data reported by E. L. Thorndike (1927, App. III) supports the adequacy of the normal distribution for fitting distributions of individual differences in intellective traits. Thorndike assembled data from a variety of distinct intelligence tests and distinct samples of children at several age levels. The resulting empirical distributions of scores are well described by the normal distribution function.

Assume, then, that from the definition of a mental trait it is sensible to expect a normally distributed population. Then a normalizing transformation of arbitrary scores (e.g. number of questions answered correctly or time taken to complete a task) does serve to provide a fixed scale unit, namely the standard deviation of the resulting normal distribution. The transformed scores would be considered in establishing the validity of the test. To the degree that validity is established by the methods of chapter 14, the unit of measurement may be interpreted as a unit on the trait dimension rather than only on the test-performance dimension. (This argument was quite effectively made by Thorndike, 1927, ch. 7.)

DIMENSIONALITY OF ATTRIBUTES

In physical measurement, properties such as distance and time generally are conceived to be unidimensional attributes. A property such as the volume of containers, however, may be conceived either along a single dimension or may be considered a multidimensional function of several more primitive measurement dimensions.

For each of a given set of solid containers, volume can be determined empirically as a uni-dimensional measure. Each container might be filled with a specific gas (to a specified pressure). Then, using a hydraulic device as an instrument to record the volume required for a given amount of gas at the standard pressure, the volume of each container can be ascertained. The consequence of this measurement procedure is a set of numbers representing the volumes of the containers in, say, cubic centimeters. The numbers are arrayed along the single real-number dimension. Alternatively, indirect measure of volume might be determined if the shapes of the containers could be sufficiently specified. For any solid, if it is possible to express the height as a joint analytic function of breadth and depth, then the volume may be analytically expressed by methods of integral calculus, integrating height with respect to breadth and depth. Knowledge of the component dimensions allows an analytic determination of the volume of a solid.

Clearly, it would be instructive, for some purposes, to know not only the volume for each of a set of containers but also the values of the component spatial dimensions. For other purposes, knowledge of the volume alone might be sufficient. One takes for granted, for measures such as volume, that the units of measurement along the component dimensions are compatible with the unit of measure for volume as directly ascertained; for, only under these conditions can it be expected that empirical measures and analytic determinations will agree. Should depth of a rectangular solid be measured in centimeters, length be measured in inches, and height be estimated in terms of the number of *variably sized* matchsticks that may be placed end to end between top and bottom of the solid, the resulting product would not conform to empirical results in cubic centimeters, nor would it be characterized by equal measurement units, nor would its meaning as a measure of volume be comparable from one container to another.

Analogous problems arise in psychological and educational assessment of multidimensional attributes. Typically, tests of intelligence, scholastic aptitude, or achievement include items that sample a variety of distinct abilities.

Two identical total test scores may result from very different profiles of abilities. If test items vary in difficulty level and if differing difficulty is found for items tapping different abilities then the total score will lack interpretability in the same way that the volume measure determined from haphazardly assigned "units" lacks interpretability. This is a consequence of using number of items correct as a unit of measurement (at least at an intermediate stage, even if later normalizing transformations are invoked).

Since interpretation of "total score" measures in multidimensional tests with varying item difficulties is fraught with difficulties, efforts in test construction often are directed toward defining subtests homogeneous in content or in item difficulty or both. Factor analytic methods, applied to test items, have proven useful for this purpose. To the degree that such efforts meet success, the determination of subtest scores will meet the requisites of measurement. Construct validity of subtests then may be established, and prediction of criteria (e.g. scholastic success) can be attempted using a composite of the subtest scores. The methods of multiple linear regression have proven widely serviceable to specify the particular weighted composite that most efficiently predicts a criterion. That particular composite then may be considered a measurement of a complex of attributes, known to be linearly predictive of the criterion.

Another promising set of methods for multidimensional measurement stems from the contributions of Shepard (1962), Kruskal (1964), and others. By these methods, it is possible to analyze nonmetric multidimensional data so as to generate measures for a number of objects. The data represent the similarities between pairs of objects, as judged by one or more judges. These similarities are assumed to be in the correct rank order, but they do not constitute measures since the metric distances between objects are not known directly from the data. In fact, it is these metric distances that are produced by the analytic methods. They provide for a representation of n objects geometrically by n points. The resulting interpoint distances are consistent with the similarities

data. From the distances may be derived a set of measures for the objects. These methods resemble factor analytic methods in that they provide coordinates of n points in a space of several dimensions. The dramatic promise of the methods resides in their power to transform ranked data into distance measures.

UNCERTAINTY AND STATISTICS

The uncertainty of observations once was held to be at least theoretically avoidable. Were it not for the fallibility of observers and for the technical inadequacy of apparatus, it was said, phenomena could be measured without error. All that is required would be complete control of the conditions of observation, then repeated measurements would yield identical results. With general acceptance in physics of Heisenberg's Uncertainty Principle, these assumptions of deterministic, unchanging results of measurement had to be rejected. In terms of the Uncertainty Principle, absolute accuracy is impossible not only in practice but also in theory. At a subatomic level, to measure a phenomenon is not merely to observe it but to act upon it (by the vehicle of measurement operations) and thereby to modify its course. This conclusion, fundamental to quantum theory in physics, leads inescapably to a statistical basis for all measurement, no matter how precisely controlled.

Since one must anticipate less than perfect agreement in successive measurements of the same thing, any one measurement or a subset of measurements may be considered a sample from an indefinitely large population. The population is defined conceptually in terms of all the measurements that might be obtained on a property of a given object under specified conditions. To the extent that the property, the object, and the specified conditions remain unchanged, a given measurement may be considered to be *randomly sampled* from this population; for each element in the population then will have an equal probability of appearing in a given observation.

When phrased this way, it is clear that the entire body of methods developed for statistical inference are appropriate tools for making predictions from measurement. Hypothesis-testing procedures provide the means for deciding whether observed differences in measurement are reliable or, alternatively, whether it is tenable that they are a consequence of measurement error. Confidence estimation methods provide the means for predicting *parameters* of the sampling distribution of measures; more precisely, they are used for establishing an interval that, with specified high probability, will include the value of the parameter.

It is well to remember, however, that statistical reasoning, like logical reasoning, is a *formal* method, devoid of content. The methods of statistical reasoning are convenient and efficient methods capable of yielding rational decisions about groups of numbers, where numbers form an abstract representation of the data supplied to the statistical model. It is the responsibility of the research user of this model to inject the content that gives the conclusions meaning in terms of the aims of his research. He must precisely specify the aims of his investigation—just what is the nature of the question to be answered? Then he must select an attribute to be measured—one that allows quantitative definition, and one that clearly is relevant to the specified experimental question. Finally, the investigator must adopt measurement procedures chosen so that conclusions based upon the measures safely may be interpreted as conclusions about the attribute measured.

ALTERNATIVE PERSPECTIVES ON MEASUREMENT

The view concerning the nature of measurement expressed in this chapter differs from other views in the literature on the topic. Some writers have defined measurement more stringently, demanding that the term be restricted to the assignment of numbers to events only where there exist operations *upon the events* similar to the arithmetic operations upon the numbers. The operation most often singled out for testing is that of summation—addition in arithmetic. By this view, unless concatenation of events is possible and leads to results that conform to those obtained by addition of the numbers correspondingly assigned to those events, some-

thing less than measurement has been achieved. Other writers have defined measurement less stringently, as the assignment of numbers to events by any set of rules. By this view, even the assignment of social security numbers constitutes measurement. There is no one right definition of measurement. As with definitions of other concepts, one simply is faced with the need for establishing a semantic convention for purposes of communication.

Campbell's (1920, 1921, 1928) treatment of measurement, while prepared with obvious concern for physical science applications, nevertheless was important to social scientists since it established a framework for discussing the nature of measurement. Campbell defined measurement as the assignment of numerals to represent properties by a fundamental process that involves establishing methods for judging equality and for adding objects with respect to the property. Whether a property is measurable then rests entirely upon experimental inquiry. The crucial test, according to this view, is whether an experimental analog to addition of the property can be discovered and whether the axioms of addition in arithmetic can be demonstrated to conform to results of physical summation. Once fundamental measurement is established (e.g. for the properties weight and volume), useful measurements of other properties may be *derived*. Thus density of an object is defined as a ratio of weight to volume of the object (with units for each agreed to in advance). A derived measurement rests squarely upon earlier establishment of fundamental measurement. The property lending itself to derived measurement actually is defined as a function of two or more fundamental measures.

No one would suggest that the procedures recommended by Campbell to produce fundamental or derived measures are inadequate ones. Many behavioral scientists, however, consider Campbell's definition overly narrow. For many attributes of interest in the behavioral sciences, there exists no natural operation of concatenation of attributes. Acceptance of the stringent requirements proposed by Campbell would seem to disallow most (if not all) efforts of measurement in psychology and education.

It is, then, not surprising that alternative views have arisen within the behavioral sciences.

Luce and Tukey (1964) adopted the aims of Campbell's fundamental measurement to provide an additive measurement scale but suggested alternatives to concatenation as a test of additivity. They noted that, by *simultaneous conjoint measurement*, it may be possible to arrive at an additive scale characterized by equal intervals along the attribute continuum. Conjoint measurement demands simultaneous observation of objects or events on two quantitative attribute dimensions. Each observation must be recorded as a triplet of numerals. There is a value on dimension 1, a value on dimension 2, and a response value for the event, perhaps generated by a person's judgment. Analysis is most easily thought of in terms of two-way analysis of variance. The problem is to find some monotonic transformation of the response variable such that it may be considered an additive composite of the values on dimensions 1 and 2. If such a transformation is found, it constitutes a fundamental measurement scale. The Luce and Tukey approach is related to the scaling methods by *factorial decomposition* studied by Shepard (1962), Kruskal (1964), and others, mentioned earlier. This field of development has proven to be one rich in theoretical implications and practical import for the establishment of measurement (in the equal-unit sense) by transforming data that submit only to ordinal interpretation.

The concept of measurement introduced by Stevens (1946, 1951, 1957) has greatly influenced subsequent thinking about measurement in the behavioral sciences. Stevens modified only slightly the definition proposed earlier by Campbell by asserting that measurement is the assignment of numerals to aspects of objects or events according to rules. However, the impact of this slight change of wording is considerable. The critical distinction, of course, resides in the difference between demanding of properties that they adhere to the additive rules of arithmetic (Campbell) and asking only that some rule be used in assigning numerals (Stevens). The only procedure by which assignment of numerals to events fails to quality as

measurement, according to Stevens, is random assignment.

Within this broadened concept of measurement, Stevens conceived of four major scale types—nominal, ordinal, interval, and ratio—naturally ordered by "strength of scale." The scale type associated with a given measurement depends upon which properties of the real number system serve as a useful model. An additional fifth scale type, a logarithmic interval scale, also has been proposed by Stevens (1957). Coombs, Raiffa, and Thrall (1954) and Luce (1956) have proposed others, involving partial orders and ordered intervals.

A detailed theory of scale types is presented by Suppes and Zinnes (1963). When numbers are assigned to objects, the objects may be said to be mapped into an abstract numerical space of some known structure. The mapping must assure one-to-one correspondence between objects and points in the numerical space. Furthermore, the formal properties of the empirical operations and *relations among objects* must correspond to the operations and *relations among numbers* in the appropriately chosen numerical space. The scale type is then determined by noting the *admissible transformations* of numbers in the abstract numerical space that leave invariant the correspondence between empirical operations and relations and numerical operations and relations. If the only such admissible transformation is the identity transformation, the scale type is *absolute* (or *ratio*). If a positive linear transformation is admissible, the scale type is *interval*. If any monotone transformation is admissible, the scale type is *ordinal*. If any arbitrary substitution of numbers is admissible, the scale type is *nominal*.

As noted by Suppes and Zinnes, there then are "a nondenumerable infinity of types of scales which are characterized by various groups of numerical transformations [p. 14]." This point also is emphasized by Kaplan (1964), who suggests that "the range of possibilities [of scale types] is basically limited only by our imagination and ingenuity in constructing [abstract] spaces. . . . As has happened over and over again in the history of science, the most abstract and even bizarre mathematics has afterwards turned out to have a homely and concrete application [p. 197]."

The general approach of Suppes and Zinnes is considerably amplified and extended in an important book by Pfanzagl (1968). Of particular interest is Pfanzagl's detailed treatment of the meaningfulness of statistical summaries of data as a function of the scale type established for the measurement procedures that give rise to those data.

Rozeboom (1966) challenged the usefulness of emphasizing scale type as defined by "admissible scale transformations." Rozeboom argued that the scale-type perspective "disastrously inverts the proper order of inquiry by seeking to answer questions about scale-property meaningfulness in terms of the scale's type rather than by judging a scale's type in terms of what on it is meaningful [p. 196]." Furthermore, preoccupation with scale type "stultifies concern for scale content" by confusing the question of *whether* a measurement scale is meaningful with the questions of *what* it means. "At all times, the proper question to ask about a given scale property is not whether it means anything, but *what* [p. 197]."

The thesis of the present chapter is consonant with Rozeboom's concerns that one focus attention on *how* one may interpret a scale. Interpretation involves the translation of propositions about scaled variables into propositions about their empirical counterparts. Then the scale type is always relative to a particular interpretation and is not a fixed property of that set of numbers that result from given measuring operations. For example, the number of dollars received as a measure of monthly wage conforms to a ratio scale type. Yet that same number of dollars, if interpreted as an index of utility of income, may meet only the criteria of an ordered scale (since utility of dollars may be a nonlinear transformation of number of dollars). The scale type of "dollars per month" is different, depending upon the meaning assigned to dollars per month, i.e. depending upon the conception of the attribute for which dollars is a measure.

In the present chapter, measurement has been defined in such a way that some scale types fail to qualify as instances of measurement. This is not to deny the usefulness of ordered scales or even of nominal scales but simply reflects the view that measurement is an assessment of *magnitude* and that a measure represents an *amount*. One may measure either from an absolute or arbitrary origin and in terms of any carefully defined standard unit. But differences between measures must be interpretable as *quantitative differences in the property measured* in order that the process be one of measurement.

REFERENCES

Bock, R. D., & Jones, L. V. *The measurement and prediction of judgment and choice.* San Francisco: Holden-Day, 1968.

Campbell, R. N. *Physics: The elements.* Cambridge: Cambridge University Press, 1920. (Reprinted: *Foundations of science,* New York, Dover, 1967.)

Campbell, R. N. *What is science?* London: Methuen, 1921.

Campbell, R. N. *An account of the principles of measurement and calculations.* London: Longmans, Green, 1928.

Coombs, C. H. *A theory of data.* New York: Wiley, 1964.

Coombs, C. H., Raiffa, H., & Thrall, R. M. Some views on mathematical models and measurement theory. *Psychological Review,* 1954, **61**, 132–144.

Dantzig, T. *Number: The language of science.* (4th ed.) New York: Doubleday Anchor, 1956.

Jones, L. V. Invariance of zero-point scaling over changes in stimulus context. *Psychological Bulletin,* 1967, **67**, 153–164.

Kaplan, A. *The conduct of inquiry.* San Francisco: Chandler, 1964.

Kruskal, J. Nonmetric scaling by optimizing goodness-of-fit to a nonmetric hypothesis. *Psychometrika,* 1964, **29**, 1–28.

Luce, R. D. Semi-orders and a theory of utility discrimination. *Econometrica,* 1956, **24**, 178–191.

Luce, R. D., & Tukey, J. W. Simultaneous conjoint measurement: A new type of fundamental measurement. *Journal of Mathematical Psychology*, 1964, **1,** 1–27.

Pfanzagl, J. *Theory of measurement*. New York: Wiley, 1968.

Rozeboom, W. W. Scaling theory and the nature of measurement. *Synthese*, 1966, **16,** 170–233.

Shepard, R. N. The analysis of proximities: Multidimensional scaling with an unknown distance function. *Psychometrika*, 1962, **27,** 125–139 & 219–246.

Stevens, S. S. On the theory of scales of measurement. *Science*, 1946, **103,** 667–680.

Stevens, S. S. Mathematics, measurement and psychophysics. In S. S. Stevens (Ed.), *Handbook of experimental psychology*. New York: Wiley, 1951. Pp. 1–49.

Stevens, S. S. On the psychophysical law. *Psychological Review*, 1957, **64,** 153–181.

Suppes, R., & Zinnes, J. L. Basic measurement theory. In R. D. Luce, R. R. Bush, & E. Galanter (Eds.), *Handbook of mathematical psychology*. Vol. 1. New York: Wiley, 1963. Pp. 1–76.

Thorndike, E. L. *The measurement of intelligence*. New York: Columbia University, Teachers College, 1927.

Thorndike, E. L., & Lorge, I. *The teacher's word book of 30,000 words*. New York: Columbia University, Teachers College, 1944.

Thurstone, L. L. Attitudes can be measured. *American Journal of Sociology*, 1928, **33,** 529–554.

Thurstone, L. L. *The measurement of values*. Chicago: University of Chicago Press, 1959.

Youden, W. J. *Experimentation and measurement*. New York: Scholastic Book Services, 1962.

13. Reliability

Julian C. Stanley
The Johns Hopkins University

When a feature or an attribute of anything, whether in the physical, the biological, or the social sciences, is measured, that measurement contains a certain amount of chance error. The amount of chance error may be large or small, but it is universally present to some extent. Two sets of measurements of the same features of the same individuals will never exactly duplicate each other. In some cases, the discrepancies between two sets of measurements may be expressed in miles and, in other cases, in millionths of a millimeter; but, if the unit of measurement is fine enough in relation to the accuracy of the measurements, discrepancies always will appear. The fact that repeated sets of measurements never exactly duplicate one another is what is meant by *unreliability*. At the same time, however, repeated measurements of a series of objects or individuals will ordinarily show *some* consistency. The block of wood that was the heaviest the first time the set of blocks was weighed will tend to be among the heaviest blocks the second time, and consistency will be the rule among all the blocks of the set. The same, to a degree, will be the case for the weights of the boys in a classroom or for their performance on a test of reading comprehension. This tendency toward consistency from one set of measurements to another is called *reliability*.

PRELIMINARY CONSIDERATIONS

The consistency of a set of measurements may be approached from the two somewhat different viewpoints of *intraindividual* and *interindividual variability*. In the former, one is concerned with the actual magnitude of errors of measurement expressed in the same units as individual scores. One thinks of a series of repeated measurements of some characteristic of a particular object and of the distribution of scores that would result from this repeated measurement. Thus, if a number of independent chemical analyses were carried out on a single batch of steel to determine the percentage of carbon in the steel, the percentage would vary somewhat from analysis to analysis. If the analysis were repeated 100 times, 100 *estimates* of the *true* percentage would result. These estimates would have a frequency distribution for which measures of central tendency and variability could be computed. The variability of the values in the frequency distribution of repeated measurements, typically expressed as the variance of the distribution, indicates the variability (and hence the magnitude) of the errors of measurement. This statistic is called the *variance error of measurement*. Its positive square root is called the *standard error of measurement*. A similar series of repeated measurements could be obtained for anatomical measures such as height or weight. Theoretically, such a series also could be obtained for measurements of reading comprehension, number facility, or any other behavior. In practice, however, a long series of independent repetitions of the *same* measurement process is almost impossible in the case of human behavior because the individual does not remain the same under the impact of repeated measurements. Consequently, in educational and psychological testing the variance error of measurement for an individual (intraindividual variability) always must be estimated indirectly.

A second approach to consistency in measurement may be made in terms of the consistency with which the individual maintains his position in the total group on repetition of a measurement procedure. This leads to the study of interindividual variability. If two *parallel* measures[1] are obtained for each individual within a group, a more or less direct index of the consistency of the measurements is available in the correlation between the two sets of scores. This is one type of *reliability coefficient*. For many purposes, this reliability coefficient lends itself to direct and simple interpretation, since under certain conditions it estimates directly the proportion of the variance of any test-score distribution that may be attributed to systematic differences among individuals, not to chance errors. The virtues of these two approaches, and others, to the concept of reliability are compared later in the chapter.

In one situation, the consistency of the measurements from one instance to another may be very marked and the variations quite minor, e.g. simple measurements of a common physical property of a group of persons who differ markedly from each other on that property. In another situation, the consistency may be almost vanishingly small so there is practically no relationship between the rank of an individual in the group on one set of measurements and his rank on another parallel set of measurements. Theoretically, either consistency or inconsistency may be thought of as approaching zero as a limit, but in practice both are usually present to some degree in any measurement procedure. For example, at the extremes, the reliability of coin-flipping scores made by several tossers (e.g. number of heads in n fair tosses of a coin) is theoretically zero, whereas the reliability of ages carefully ascertained from the same birth certificates at two different times should approach 1.00.

The degree of reliability of a set of measurements is a very important consideration, both in the practical day-to-day use of tests and in empirical research. Some consideration will be given to the importance of reliability, and of data concerning reliability of a particular measuring instrument, in each of these two contexts.

In practical work in measurement and evaluation, a score for an individual on some test is obtained to make some judgment about him and, usually, to take some practical action based on this judgment. For example, a boy is given a reading test to determine whether he is making satisfactory progress or whether he needs special attention and, possibly, remedial work. Sometime later, he may take a series of examinations so that a college may decide whether he is to be admitted. Still later, he may be given an interest inventory to provide some supplementary indication whether he should be encouraged to specialize in law, medicine, engineering, or some other field. In selecting a test to be used for a practical testing project, and in interpreting the test results for several different purposes, the educator or guidance worker must always give first attention to the *validity* of his instrument for the decision or characterization that he proposes to make. Evaluation of this validity will depend in part on rational analysis and in part on empirical evidence, as discussed more fully in chapter 14. He then will be concerned about the accuracy of the

---

[1] *Parallel measures* will be defined later in this chapter.

instrument. If the validity of several instruments for his purpose appears sub-stantially equal, he usually will choose the most reliable test, the one which will pro-vide the most precise estimate of the variable being studied, from among those available. In interpreting the results from administration of a test, it is always desir-able to know how much the obtained score is likely to vary from a true evaluation of the individual's ability on the variable.

Clearly, any degree of unreliability in the score resulting from the application of a measuring device is distressing to the person who must use that score as a basis for a practical decision about an individual. Unreliability places a question mark after the score and causes any judgment based on it to be tentative to some extent. The lower the reliability of the score, the more tentative the judgment or decision must be, until, in the extreme case, as the reliability approaches zero, the score provides no basis at all for any judgment or decision about individual differences. The question of the relevance of the score to the decision, though crucial, falls outside the scope of this chapter; it is discussed in chapter 14.

Reliability becomes of critical importance in research studies at a number of points. In any study of prediction, and in any study of improvement resulting from training, *some* degree of reliability in the measure of the criterion being predicted, or in the ability being trained, is imperative, if one is to achieve better than chance any prediction of individual differences on the one hand or any evidence of improvement on the other. One can make no worthwhile prediction of a completely unreliable criterion, or of a perfectly reliable criterion with quite unreliable predictors; and in an experiment one can demonstrate no improvement with a measure of performance which depends entirely upon chance factors. The accuracy of prediction that it is possible to achieve is limited by the reliability of the measure through which the per-formance is manifested. Data on reliability of predictors and criteria are necessary if the research worker is to be able to interpret the extent to which imperfect correla-tion between predictors and criteria is due to lack of overlapping function (or common variance) and the extent to which it is due to lack of precision in the mea-sures.

In the analytical study of the relationships among groups of tests, information concerning reliability is again crucial. Low correlation among tests arises to some extent because the measures cover unrelated aspects of behavior and to some extent because the test scores themselves are not completely reliable. If two instruments predict a certain criterion equally well, and in that sense are equally valid, their reliability is an irrelevant consideration for that purpose. Reliability would enter the discussion only because the less reliable measure would become the more valid one correlationally (see chapter 14) if lengthened and the more reliable measure would become the less valid one if shortened. (Dependence of reliability on test length will be considered more fully later in this chapter.)

Considerations in Evaluating Reliability

Studying the reliability of a measuring instrument for a particular group of examinees involves three types of operations: *logical*, *statistical*, and *empirical*. One must first identify the conditions under which accuracy of performance needs to be estimated, that is, the type of inference that is to be made from the evidence. Then the procedures for data collection and statistical analysis must be chosen so that they are logically consistent with the inference that is to be made. One may be inter-ested in consistency in performing one specific task or set of tasks, or in consistency with which performance on a specific sample represents performance on a much larger universe of possible tasks; one may be interested in consistency at a point in time or consistency over a span of time. Each of these variations calls for a corresponding variation in the data that are collected or in the manner in which the data are analyzed.

In many discussions of reliability determination, the lion's share of attention is devoted to the statistical techniques involved. Much attention also needs to be given to the logical and empirical aspects. The empirical procedures are very closely bound up with the logical aspects of the problem, so that one must first determine what is to be accomplished and what purposes are to be served by a measure of reliability. The empirical operations must be planned with these purposes in view and evaluated in the light of them. For that reason, the next several sections of this chapter are devoted chiefly to the logical and empirical aspects of reliability. Consideration of all but a few basic statistical procedures comes later. The discussion begins with an overview and becomes more specific and detailed.

Reliability and Analysis of Variation

Whenever an adequately differentiating measuring device is applied to a group of individuals of differing ability and a score is obtained for each individual in the group, the resulting distribution of scores will spread out over a range of two or more score values. The variation in any set of scores arises from a number of different sources. Consider measurements of weights of each of the children in a particular school classroom. These differ due to variations in the age of the children, their sex, their parentage, the nourishment they have received during the years of their life, whether or not they have been sick recently, whether or not they took a drink of water just before coming to be weighed, the exact angle from which the nurse happened to be looking at the scales, and a host of other factors, minor and major, short-term and lasting.

The variation in a set of scores arises, in part, because of systematic differences in the quality being measured among the individuals in the group; and, in part, it arises from unpredictable inaccuracies in the measurement of the separate individuals. Thus in the example above, certain variations among children could be thought of as inaccuracies in the observation of the variable, i.e. as errors of measurement for different children. (Of course, many such factors *could* be controlled experimentally.) These variations would account for some part, though possibly a small one, of the variations in weight recorded for the different children in the class. The evaluation of the reliability of any measure reduces to a determination of how much of the variation in the set of scores is due to certain systematic differences among the individuals in the group and how much to other sources of variation that are considered, for particular purposes, errors of measurement.

There are a number of different statistics that have been developed as summary values to describe the variability in a set of scores. These include the range, various interpercentile ranges, average deviation, and variance (or its square root, the standard deviation). Of these statistics, the most suitable for describing the variability of a set of scores is usually the variance, σ^2.[2] A particular advantage of the variance is that it can be broken down into separate parts when these parts combine

---

[2] In symbolism for the variance of a distribution, σ^2 is used to represent the theoretical population value, while s^2 usually designates the unbiased estimator of σ^2. (See any standard statistics textbook for further explanation.)

additively to give a total. Thus, if the variance of weight of children in a class were 150 pounds, this might break up into a variance of 125 associated with the individuals and a variance of 25 associated with the errors of that particular set of measurements. These parts constitute the total variance of 150 for the set of scores. Whenever a number of *uncorrelated* factors[3] combine *additively* to produce a score, it is possible to analyze the total variation into components of variation that are associated with particular factors, and these components will sum up to give the total variance.[4] That is, $\sigma^2 = \sigma_1^2 + \sigma_2^2 + \ldots + \sigma_k^2$, where σ^2 is the total variance of the distribution of scores and σ_1^2, σ_2^2, $\ldots$, σ_k^2 are the parts of the variance associated with uncorrelated, additive factors $1, 2, \ldots, k$ respectively.

For example, the variance in weight of children in a classroom might be broken down into variance associated with age, variance associated with sex, variance associated with family, and other variances associated with every other definable stable characteristic of the individuals in the group. (Some of these variables might not be uncorrelated with others of them, however.) There also will be variance that is associated only with the one particular set of measurements, that is, variation that will not be reproduced another time. This may be designated *error variance*. The existence of this error variance corresponds to the fact of unreliability, and its size relative to the total of all variance is a measure of the degree of unreliability of a measurement procedure.

However, what will appear as error variance in a set of observations will depend on how the measure is defined and how the measurement is carried out. If half the children in the class had been weighed on one scale and half on another that was adjusted to read a pound heavier, the scale on which a child had been weighed would be a source of error variance; if all had been weighed on the same scale no variance would have arisen from this source. If some children were weighed just before lunch and some just after, this could have been a source of variation that would be considered to be error.

Also, two different weighings of the same person may be done on the same or different days, by the same or different weighers, on the same or different scales, etc.

It is well to pause briefly at this point and see with just what general type of error one is concerned when speaking of error variance. Not every type of error, not every discrepancy from the value which an omniscient recording angel would register for the specimen in question, qualifies as a part of the error variance. Suppose children were weighed on scales that were adjusted incorrectly in such a way that every one of the children was given a weight two pounds above his "true" weight. This adjustment error is uniform and systematic and results in a *constant error*. As described, it actually does not contribute at all to variance among individuals, though it does make every observation incorrect. Again, suppose that the scales on which children were weighed were in error in such a way that they credited each child with two pounds for each pound he weighed in excess of 50 pounds. This would not be a constant error, but it would be *systematic*—that is, it can be stated in definite terms. Furthermore, each child's actual weight can be determined if one knows the simple

---

[3] These are not the factors of psychometric "factor analysis" (see Harman, 1967), but instead are any identifiable sources of variation within a set of data in the analysis-of-variance sense (see Fisher, 1925 et seq.), as the subsequent discussion indicates.

[4] When factors are not uncorrelated, it becomes necessary to analyze covariances or interaction components as well as variances. For example, fat boys may irritate the tester, or actual weight may affect the angle at which the scale is observed.

conversion formula. In the present discussion, the concern is not with such constant or systematic errors, disastrous though they may be to scientific accuracy.

The type of errors considered when one speaks of chance errors of measurement are errors that are unrelated to the future performance of the individual to which one wants to make inference. What is meant is that the type of measurement error with which one is most concerned is *random error*, uncorrelated with the individual's true score or with his error of measurement on another form of the test. For an excellent discussion of such errors, see Cochran (1968).

Repeatedly throughout this chapter, the expression *true score* will be used. The term is convenient but apt to be a little misleading. As used, true score is not the ultimate fact in the book of the recording angel. Rather, it is *the score resulting from all systematic factors one chooses to aggregate*, including any systematic biasing factors that may produce systematic incorrectness in the scores. This larger expression should be understood whenever the term true score is used. Let $C_1, \ldots, C_n$ be a denumerable set of circumstances influencing X, the observed score. It should be clear, therefore, that there may be different true scores for an individual if the set of circumstances is differently defined. A *particular* true score for a *particular* set of circumstances is the score which would be obtained *on the average* if the particular set of circumstances remained constant. The concept of true score will be treated more mathematically later in this discussion.

The heart of any treatment of reliability involves recognition that true variance is *wanted* variance and that what is wanted will depend on the interpretation proposed by the investigator. For example, instrument effects may be considered *chance* effects whenever the instrument is allowed to vary from one individual to another, as when each child is weighed on a different scale and the reliability of the set of weights is in question. Or consider an oral examination—the series of questions may be entirely different for different subjects, and this difference may contribute to chance error. However, the same questions could be used for each subject, so that chance variation from subject to subject would not include examination differences.

Some Basic Formulas

In this brief section, several basic formulas are stated but not derived in order to introduce certain fundamental relationships somewhat intuitively early in the chapter. Fuller, more rigorous development will come later.

Designate the variance of true scores of a group on a trait by σ_T^2 and the variance of errors of measurement by σ_e^2. If the magnitude of the error of measurement covaries zero with the magnitude of the true score, then

$$\sigma_X^2 = \sigma_T^2 + \sigma_e^2; \qquad [1]$$

that is, the variance of the obtained scores (σ_X^2) equals the variance of true scores (σ_T^2) plus the variance arising from errors of measurement (σ_e^2). As will be explained in detail later, this occurs because of the definition for the pth person (i.e. examinee) on the fth form of the test, namely

$$X_{pf} = T_p + e_{pf}, \qquad [2]$$

where X_{pf} is the obtained score of the pth person on the fth form, T_p is the true score of that person, and e_{pf} is his error of measurement on that form.

It is also possible to relate the components of variance in equation 1 to the reliability coefficient mentioned earlier in this chapter. One has two parallel forms of a test, f and f', such that $T_{pf} = T_{pf'}$ and certain other conditions to be discussed later hold. Then one can state (without proof here but to be proved later) that

$$\rho_{ff'} = \frac{\sigma_T^2}{\sigma_T^2 + \sigma_e^2} = \frac{\sigma_T^2}{\sigma_X^2}, \qquad [3]$$

and, therefore,

$$\rho_{ff'} = \frac{\sigma_X^2 - \sigma_e^2}{\sigma_X^2} = 1 - \frac{\sigma_e^2}{\sigma_X^2}, \qquad [4]$$

where $\rho_{ff'}$ is the population coefficient of correlation between scores on parallel forms f and f' and σ_X^2 is the population variance of obtained scores on either form. Also,

$$\sigma_e^2 = \sigma_X^2(1 - \rho_{ff'}). \qquad [5]$$

Formula 3 shows that *the numerical value of the reliability coefficient of a test corresponds exactly to the proportion of the variance in test scores that is due to true differences within that particular population of individuals* on the variable being evaluated by the test. A test is *un*reliable for a given group of examinees in proportion to the magnitude of its error variance relative to its observed-score variance, because, as formula 4 shows, $\sigma_e^2/\sigma_X^2 = 1 - \rho_{ff'}$.

Restriction of Range Lowers Reliability

σ_e^2, the variance of errors of measurement, does not usually differ greatly from group to group unless the groups of persons are quite different. Therefore, the magnitude of $\rho_{ff'}$, the coefficient of correlation between scores on parallel forms of a test, is heavily influenced by the magnitude of σ_T^2, the variance of true scores. Suppose that, for a heterogeneous group such as all students in grades 9 through 12, σ_e^2 for a certain vocabulary test is 20 points and σ_T^2 equals 180. Then via formula 3, $\rho_{ff'} = 180/(180+20) = .90$. For tenth graders, however, σ_e^2 may still be approximately 20, but σ_T^2 may be just 80, yielding a reliability coefficient of only .80 for that grade. *The magnitude of reliability coefficients is dependent on the dispersion of true ability in the group tested.* The more heterogeneous the group, the higher $\rho_{ff'}$ is likely to be for a given test.

Defining Sources of Variation

The basic problem in determining the reliability of a testing procedure relative to a particular group of individuals becomes that of *defining* what shall be thought of as true variance among individuals and what shall be thought of as error variance, in relation to the type of inference one wishes to make from the test scores. When this definition has been made, the next step is to devise those series of empirical and statistical operations that will provide the best estimates of the defined fractions of variance. In the next section, therefore, the analysis of types and sources of variance in test scores is considered. Much later in the chapter, various experimental operations that have been proposed to provide data for estimating reliability will be considered.

Sources of Variation in Test Scores

As noted above, variance in a set of scores from any measuring device arises from a great variety of specific sources. However, these may profitably be grouped, for purposes of discussion, into a few major categories. A classification of sources of variance for test scores, based on Thorndike (1951), is presented in table 13.1.[5] Although a discussion of likely sources of variation should be illuminating, their allocation to true or error variance could rightly be considered to be dependent upon the conditions and purposes of testing. For example, it may not be desirable to equate trait persistence with trueness in every situation. *There is no single, universal, and absolute reliability coefficient for a test.* Determination of reliability is as much a logical as a statistical problem. The appropriate allocation of variance from different sources calls for practical judgment of what use is to be made of the resulting statistical value. This point will become increasingly apparent as the discussion of table 13.1 progresses.

What is "general" and what is "specific," what "lasting" and what "temporary," and what is intraorganismic and what due to administrative conditions, formats, etc., seem to depend largely on what domain of content one is dealing with, what meta-theoretic commitments one has about that content and how to assess it, and the uses to which observations are put. One investigator's "general traits" may be another's "response sets" or "error." And clearly, as usually defined, general versus specific is a function of the battery of tests used. Despite these important reservations, however, table 13.1 can help the test constructor and user to understand better what he is doing when he assesses reliability.

The categories given in table 13.1 do not exhaust the possible range of categories. Certainly, many more subcategories could be listed under most of the major headings, so those which are presented should be thought of as illustrative rather than exhaustive. A consideration of each of the categories will help one decide which fractions of variance should be thought of as true systematic variance in the quality being measured and which should be thought of as error variance.

Category I of table 13.1: Lasting and general characteristics of the individual

Variance within a set of scores usually arises principally because different individuals manifest different amounts of certain persistent traits. Thus, in a series of intellectual tests, some type of ability to reason deductively might be a general quality which enters into a number of the tests and which, for each of the tests, accounts for part of the individual differences in performance. Or several arithmetic tests might have a common factor of facility with numbers. Verbal comprehension is likely to enter into a wide range of tests requiring reading. Almost any test performance will depend in part upon general abilities that also are involved in a number of other types of test performance. The type of variance which is now under discussion represents a persistent, lasting characteristic of each individual, causing stable individual differences in test performance. Since it arises from a persisting feature of each individual, this variance is clearly systematic variance and should be so treated in any sequence of operations set up to provide an estimate of reliability.

Two rather special types of persisting general factors deserve particular mention. These are the general ability to comprehend instructions and what may be termed

[5] The table is specific to tests but highly suggestive for other measurements. The reader is invited to develop for himself a parallel table appropriate for nontest variables such as ratings of children as to their conduct.

TABLE 13.1

Possible Sources of Variance of Scores on a Particular Test

I. *Lasting and general characteristics of the individual*
   A. Level of ability on one or more general traits, which operate in a number of tests
   B. General skills and techniques of taking tests ("test wiseness" or "test naiveté")
   C. General ability to comprehend instructions

II. *Lasting but specific characteristics of the individual*
   A. Specific to the test as a whole (and to parallel forms of it)
      1. Individual level of ability on traits required in this test but not in others
      2. Knowledges and skills specific to particular form of test items
      3. Stable response sets (e.g. to mark A options more frequently than other options of multiple-choice items, to mark true-false items "true" when undecided, or to choose socially desirable options)
   B. Specific to particular test items
      1. The "chance" element determining whether the individual does or does not know a particular fact (sampling variance in a finite number of items, not the probability of his guessing the answer)
      2. Item types, such as the data-sufficiency items of the Scholastic Aptitude Test, with which various examinees are unequally familiar (cf. II. A. 2)

III. *Temporary but general characteristics of the individual*
   (Factors affecting performance on many or all tests at a particular time)
   A. Health
   B. Fatigue
   C. Motivation
   D. Emotional strain
   E. Test-wiseness (partly lasting; cf. I. B)
   F. Understanding of mechanics of testing
   G. External conditions of heat, light, ventilation, etc.

IV. *Temporary and specific characteristics of the individual*
   A. Specific to a test as a whole
      1. Comprehension of the specific test task (insofar as this is distinct from I. B)
      2. Specific tricks or techniques of dealing with the particular test materials (insofar as distinct from II. A. 2)
      3. Level of practice on the specific skills involved (especially in psychomotor tests)
      4. Momentary "set" for a particular test
   B. Specific to particular test items
      1. Fluctuations and idiosyncrasies of human memory
      2. Unpredictable fluctuations in attention or accuracy, superimposed upon the general level of performance characteristic of the individual

V. *Systematic or chance factors affecting the administration of the test or the appraisal of test performance*
   A. Conditions of testing—adherence to time limits, freedom from distractions, clarity of instructions, etc.
   B. Interaction of personality, sex, or race of examiner with that of examinee to facilitate or inhibit performance
   C. Unreliability or bias in grading or rating performance

VI. *Variance not otherwise accounted for* (*chance*)
   A. Luck in selection of answers by sheer guessing
   B. Momentary distraction

---

test-wiseness (see Millman, Bishop, & Ebel, 1965). These factors are mentioned because they are likely to enter into any test score, whether they are wanted or not. That is, performance on many types of tests is likely to be in some measure a function of the individual's ability to understand what he is supposed to do on the test. Particularly as the test is novel or the instructions complex, this factor is likely to enter in. In addition, test score is likely to be in some measure a function of the extent to which the individual is acclimated to tests, both cognitively and emotionally, and has a certain amount of sagacity in taking them. Freedom from emotional tension, shrewdness in guessing, and a keen eye for secondary and extraneous cues are likely to be useful in a wide range of tests. The presence of variance in scores due to variation in comprehension of test instructions and in test-wiseness is usually undesirable from the point of view of the purposes of the test in question. Typically, it represents variance that is systematic but, if unrelated to the criterion of interest, will reduce the validity of the test.

These influences must be recognized. They present a challenge to the author of the test to minimize them, except where their presence is specifically desired, by providing the clearest possible instructions and a minimum of secondary cues. These factors may present more a problem of validity than of reliability; as far as the present analysis is concerned, they represent a general, somewhat lasting quality of the individual and, treated as such, contribute "true" variance. Preferably, however, instructions can be improved and test-wiseness variance reduced by training as much as possible. Insofar as comprehending instructions and test-wiseness are closely related to basic intellectual ability, their variance will be difficult to eliminate.

Category II of table 13.1: Lasting but specific characteristics of the individual

In addition to variance that is common to a range of tests, each test will have some variance that arises from persistent characteristics of the individuals being studied but is *specific to the particular area* being tested. That is, there is some variance that will be present in spelling tests, for example, but in no other kinds of tests. There are, of course, degrees of specificity of knowledge or skill, so that further narrowing down may take place even within a given field. In addition to variance that characterizes the whole field of performance, such as spelling or numerical computation, there may be *variance associated with the specific format and manner of testing* (see, for example, Sax & Collet, 1968). In the case of spelling this might relate to oral presentation as in a spelling bee versus writing words from dictation or recognition of errors in words presented in a printed test. A numerical operations test might be presented in free-response or in multiple-choice format, and variance might be associated with that feature. Finally, in any test there is likely to be *variance associated with the particular sample of test items*. There will be a certain amount of variation in specific bits of knowledge or skill, so that even the individual who has high overall ability in the area in question will lack certain specific items of knowledge or skill and the individual low in general performance will succeed on isolated items not known by his generally more proficient fellow examinee. The sampling of items—words to be comprehended, formulas to be known, generalizations to be applied, and the like—will be a source of variation in the resulting test scores. Given two tests made up of samples independently chosen from the same universe of items, individuals will fail to receive identical scores on the two tests because of variation in the particular items that each individual happens to have the skill or information to answer. Yet both tests may be equally appropriate.

At this point, some difficulty in logically determining what shall be allocated to systematic variance and what to error variance begins to be encountered. Variance specific to the area covered by the test (category II. A. 1) is certainly systematic variance, and any operation for determining reliability should be so planned that this type of variance is treated as systematic. The problems arise in connection with variance associated with the particular test format and with the particular sampling of test items. The question is one of finding the most useful definition of the universe to be sampled. How broadly shall one define what is being measured? Shall it be defined (*a*) in terms of an area of content only? (*b*) in terms of an area of content and test format? (*c*) in terms of an area of content, test format, and particular set of test items?

The first definition above leads to experimental procedures that appear to come closer to evaluating test validity than test reliability. That is, if format is considered a source of error variance, one is led to correlate tests with different types of items and manner of presentation (see Campbell & Fiske, 1959). One then begins to inquire whether the test is consistent with other measures rather than whether that particular test measures consistently. The third definition is, of course, the narrowest but has practical meaning in some cases where one is interested in performance on a limited set of test items for their own sake. More usually, test performance is viewed as an indication of ability to perform on the whole universe of items of which the test represents a limited (actually or hypothetically random) sample. Sources of variation due to differing characteristics of the various samples of items may, therefore, in an entirely correct sense be part of the error of measurement. Whether or not a certain circumstance or source of variability should be controlled in assessing reliability depends on the construct the tester thinks he is measuring. At this point, the discussion will forego trying further to associate the categories of table 13.1 with either systematic or error variance without regard to a specific test for a specific use.

Category III of table 13.1: Temporary but general characteristics of the individual

A third group of factors making for variation in test scores is certain general but temporary characteristics of the individual or of the testing situation—such factors as state of health, amount of sleep the previous night, presence or absence of worries or other distracting influences, and a host of other internal factors that may have bearing upon the efficiency of the individual's work. Different test performances will be susceptible to these factors in varying degrees, but all will probably be influenced by them in some measure. The factors vary both in their permanence and their generality. Some may change from day to day, some from hour to hour. There may even be very short-time fluctuations in efficiency that represent a change from minute to minute. In general, however, one may think of these factors as ones that characterize an individual at a particular testing session but not at another session.

Here again, a problem arises as to what allocation is to be made of variance of this type. Once again, the problem becomes that of determining the type of consistency that it seems significant to measure. Is it important to determine how consistent a measure one has of the individual as he exists at a particular moment? Or is it important to determine how consistent his performance is from day to day and week to week? For some purposes the former may be the significant information, for some purposes the latter. If interest lies in studying the intercorrelations among a battery of tests given at one time, the appropriate measure of reliability for use in conjunction with those correlations would seem to be a measure of consistency at that moment in time. However, if the test results are to be used for predicting something about the individual at some later date or evaluating the result of training over some extended period, the more meaningful definition of reliability would appear to be that of consistency over a comparable period of time. There are other specific purposes for which tests might be used, and, in each case, it will be necessary to decide whether it is more meaningful for the temporary characteristics of the individual (category III) to be thought of as a source of systematic variance or as a source of error variance.

The general discussion so far has provided no indication whether this or any other *possible* influence does in fact yield practically significant amounts of variance. That is, it has not been shown whether what is done with variance in the above category makes any *practical* difference. That cannot be a matter of general theoretical discussion but must depend on specific empirical evidence in each case. The answer probably will vary widely in different areas of measurement. It might be guessed, for example, that in a simple unspeeded test of general vocabulary less of the variance would be accounted for by temporary characteristics of the individual than in a test of mood or feeling tone, for which substantial within-day and day-to-day swings might be expected. By carefully planning the testing procedures one can estimate the magnitude of the variability arising from different sources. Some will be more difficult to estimate empirically than others. Near the end of this chapter, consideration is given an analysis-of-variance (anova) scheme for estimating variance components (Cronbach, Gleser, Nanda & Rajaratnam, 1970).

Category IV of table 13.1: Temporary and specific characteristics of the individual

A further group of certain relatively temporary and specific factors make for variation in test performance. In this category are included influences that tend to be more limited both in time and in scope than those discussed in the immediately preceding section. Certain of these factors characterize performance on a test as a whole. If the test is novel and the instructions difficult, individuals may vary in the extent to which they "catch on" to the nature of the task. In part this will probably represent general ability to understand instructions (category I. C), but in part it may represent temporary or "chance" variations superimposed on that general ability. Again, a test may call for certain specific tricks or techniques of which the individual does or does not "get the hang," such as solving an algebra problem by using the "back solution," i.e. inserting each proposed answer in turn to see whether it fits. Furthermore, performance on many tests, particularly measures of complex coordination or skill, is susceptible to considerable improvement with practice. A temporary feature of some importance may be the individual's practice level at the moment of testing. Finally, there are certain factors which, for the lack of any better term, may be grouped together under the heading of "mental-set" at the time of taking the test. Was the subject emphasizing speed or accuracy if it was a speeded test? To what cues was he particularly alert if it was a perceptual task? What was his momentary mood if it was an attitude or interest inventory? (See Glass, 1964.)

In addition, the subject's set brought about by his understanding or hypothesis about the *use* to be made of the scores can be critical for personality, interest, and attitude assessment. Such sets are not only abundant sources of variance in selection and evaluation contexts, but also their response effects apparently are diverse, depending on the kinds of settings.

For many types of simple and standard tests, the sources of variation grouped in category IV.A can perhaps be ignored. However, in novel types of tests, highly speeded tests, measures into which introspective interpretation enters heavily, and for performances that are in the formative stage (unconsolidated knowledge comes and goes, quite apart from any inadequacy in the test), the possibility of encountering variance from such sources as have just been discussed must be given serious consideration. The rationale for allocation of this type of variance would appear to follow much the same lines as that for variance attributable to general temporary conditions (category III) discussed above.

In addition to factors specific to a particular test and date of testing, there may be even more specific and temporary factors. These are factors that are specific to an item, or a few items, and a minute or a few minutes of time. Such factors appear as short-time fluctuations of memory or attention, momentary blockings of performance, cyclic variations in effort, and a variety of other fluctuations superimposed upon the general level of performance. These factors (category IV.B), insofar as they affect scores, introduce variable and unpredictable error into the score, and the resulting variance usually should be allocated to error variance.

Category V of table 13.1: Systematic or chance factors affecting the administration of the test or the appraisal of test performance

For some situations, sources of variance not only in the subject being tested but in the conditions of giving and appraising the test must be recognized. Factors of timing of a test, test instructions, amount of noise and distraction, electric light failures, broken pencil points, and the like may vary from person to person or subgroup to subgroup. One can see that this type of variation is especially likely to arise with tests that are individually administered by a number of examiners, tests that are closely timed, or tests that have very complex instructions. Also, variance may be introduced in appraising the test performance or other behavior that is to yield a score. This is true in proportion as the appraisal depends on the judgment of another human being. In essay examinations, rating scales of all sorts, projective tests, or in fact anything that calls for interpretation or evaluation by an observer or scorer, variance due to the scorer will enter in. There will be variance associated with different scorers, variance associated with changes in each scorer from time to time, and variance representing unpredictable within-scorer inconsistency. These types of variance (category V) become important in certain particular measurement situations; where they occur they ordinarily constitute error variance, and procedures should be planned to identify them and treat them as error.

Category VI of table 13.1: Variance not otherwise accounted for (chance)

Finally, the concept of chance to take care of variance not otherwise accounted for must be considered. One can never find identifiable factors that will account for all the variance in a set of test scores. Some variance arises from guessing at answers, some from other obscure variable influences that cannot be defined or specified. The variance of this type (category VI) is error variance in its purest form, and the operations that define reliability must allocate it to that category.

Some readers may have sensed that the distinction between reliability, discussed in this chapter, and validity, discussed in the next chapter, is somewhat blurred. What is usually wanted is a decomposition of test and criterial scores into their components of variation and covariation. Once there are sufficiently precise estimates of those components, for whatever purposes intended, then the distinction between the concepts of reliability and validity becomes less useful. A synthesis of the Cronbach,

Gleser, Nanda, and Rajaratnam (1970) approach to reliability, discussed later in this chapter, with Cronbach's approach to validity in the next chapter seems likely in the years ahead.

Procedures for Estimating the Reliability of Measurements

Studying the reliability of a measuring instrument requires estimating the consistency of repeated measurements of the same object or group of objects. In the physical sciences, many repetitions of a measurement of a single object or phenomenon sometimes will provide a reasonable method for estimating the precision of the measurement procedure. In dealing with humans, however, the individual's behavior is likely to be changed as a result of the operation of measurement, and so it is often practicable to measure a single individual only a few times. In practice, therefore, all procedures of reliability estimation generally useful for the behavioral sciences are based upon getting a small number of measurements, typically only one or two, for each individual in a representative group. These measurements provide scores, again usually only one or two for each individual, for analysis. The typical analysis includes computation of the coefficient of correlation between two sets of scores.

One cannot compute a reliability coefficient directly unless there are at least two test scores per examinee. Where the score being obtained is a composite, one can, however, examine the consistency among the several parts of the measure and thereby get a reliability estimate when only a single test has been given. For example, in the very simple situation of a two-item test, one can study how scores on one item covary with scores on the other, as will be seen later in the discussion of one-form methods for computing reliability coefficients.

In formula 3, it was stated that the reliability coefficient of a test is the ratio of the variance of true scores to the variance of obtained scores (made up of true measure and error). Where two parallel forms of a test are available, the definition of parallel forms insures that this reliability coefficient is in fact the product-moment correlation between the two forms. *Parallel forms* in this situation are defined as tests that overlap completely in their true-score distributions, and that have for each form the same proportion of true-score variance to total-score variance. (This implies that the variance of errors of measurement on one form is the same as that on the other form, that true scores covary zero with errors of measurement, and that errors of measurement covary zero from one form to the other.)

The perceptive reader may sense, correctly, that the requirement that examinees' true scores do not change differentially from one examinee to another over the time interval between tests means perfect stability for the ability being tested over the time interval between tests. In practice, this is highly unlikely, unless the time interval is brief. Many of the formulations of classical test-score theory as explained in this chapter apply mainly to the one-form or the zero-instability-between-forms reliability coefficient, where the second form is a hypothetical "instantaneously administered" one. (For the full rationale, see Tryon, 1957; for a more empirically based approach, see Cronbach et al., 1970.)

It must now be determined how parallel measures may be set up so that the correlation between them may be obtained and how the true-score variance of a set of scores may be estimated so that its ratio to the total variance may be calculated. These are, in fact, one and the same problem. Parallel forms of a test will be defined as forms on which the pth person has identical true scores and zero-covarying errors of measurement, with identical variance of errors of measurement on the two forms, over persons. More formal definitions will come later in this chapter. Next, what actual testing operations will correspond satisfactorily to the logical requirements for parallel forms must be considered. Some logical requirements were considered in the previous section in connection with the desired allocation of different fractions of variance.

A number of different testing and statistical procedures have been proposed to provide the necessary coefficient of correlation between obtained scores on parallel forms of a test. Many of these represent efforts to develop shortcuts to the preparation and administration of two separate forms built to the same set of specifications and, therefore, assumed to be parallel. Others have been defended as preferable procedures. Later in the chapter, several sets of experimental and statistical procedures are considered in turn, and each is described and evaluated in terms of its treatment of different categories of variance. The major procedures are:

1. Administration of two parallel forms under specified conditions, and correlation of the resulting scores.

2. Repeated administration of the same test form or testing procedure, and correlation of the resulting scores.

3. Subdivision of a single test into two presumably parallel groups of items (half-forms a and b), each scored separately, and correlation of the resulting two scores. This yields an estimate of the reliability coefficient of the half-test, say r_{ab}. The reliability coefficient of the whole test is estimated to be $2r_{ab}/(1+r_{ab})$.

4. Analysis of the covariance among individual items, and determination of the true-score and error variance therefrom, which encompasses several seemingly diverse procedures.

Each of the four types of procedures and the mathematical models underlying them will be discussed in subsequent sections. First, though, a bit of test-theory history.

A Little History

The formula for the normal distribution of random errors was derived more than two centuries ago (DeMoivre, 1733; also see Pearson, 1924; Walker, 1929). Karl Pearson published his derivation of the formula for the product-moment coefficient of correlation, r_{xy}, in 1896. A special case of r, the reliability coefficient, was derived early in this century. The British psychologist Charles Spearman (1904) introduced the concept of the reliability coefficient defined as "$r_{p'p}$ = the average correlation between one and another of . . . several independently obtained series of values for p [p. 90]." Six years later, Spearman (1910) introduced into the English language the term *reliability coefficient* defined as "the coefficient between one half and the other half of several measures of the same thing [p. 281]." Most of the intervening years have been spent explicating and at times obfuscating the meaning of the key phrases "one half," "other half," and "same thing." Fortunately, Spearman and his successors, with their semantic intuitions and elementary mathematical formulations, produced a test theory that held up very well under subsequent formal mathematical analysis (see Novick, 1966).

In the first edition of his *Introduction to the Theory of Mental and Social Measurements* (published by the measurement pioneer J. McKeen Cattell's Science Press)

Edward L. Thorndike (1904, p. 129) cited Spearman's famed article entitled "The Proof and Measurement of Association Between Two Things," which appeared in the January 1904 issue of the *American Journal of Psychology*. (Ah, for the brief publication lag of yesteryear!)[6] With this book Thorndike launched educational and psychological measurement in the United States on a systematic basis that even today one can envy. He provided no proofs (indeed, Spearman himself gave few proofs until mathematicians prodded him) but spelled out clearly such matters as correcting an obtained coefficient of correlation for attenuation—i.e. lessened magnitude—due to errors of measurement, estimating the coefficient of correlation when there are *m* independent measures of Trait A and *n* independent measures of Trait B, and using probable errors of measurement. (A probable error is .6745 times the corresponding standard error. If errors of measurement are normally distributed, half of them will be within plus and minus one probable error of measurement of their mean.)

By 1913, most of the basic test theory, except that unique to factor analysis, had been set forth by Spearman (1913). Numerous details and procedures remained to be worked out, and many applications were yet to be made; but, a dozen years before Fisher's (1925) *Statistical Methods for Research Workers* introduced the framework of modern experimental design, educational and psychological measurement was headed firmly down the correlational road so well constructed by Francis Galton, Karl Pearson, and Charles Spearman. Several Americans, such as Truman L. Kelley (1927) and Edward E. Cureton (1931), gave it further impetus. Kelley's (1924) major work, *Statistical Method*, appeared just a year before Fisher's and therefore did not reflect the statistical revolution being fomented in England.[7] The history of test theory after World War I might have been substantially different had Fisher's book preceded Kelley's by several years.

Prior to 1937, the reliability of a single form of a test was ascertained either by retesting the same students with that form (called the test-retest method) or by dividing the items of the form longitudinally into two sets of presumably parallel items (thus creating two half-forms of the test), computing the coefficient of correlation between the half-form scores from a single testing session, and adjusting that *r* with a statistical formula to estimate the reliability of scores on the whole form. As will be seen later, both of these procedures, test-retest and split-half, were objectionable in certain specific respects. Finally, 33 years after Spearman's basic article appeared, Kuder and Richardson (1937) used the variance-covariance structure of the items of a single form to compute several new reliability coefficients. Two of these, based on their formulas 20 and 21, are used widely today in lieu of test-retest or split-half methods, though they have certain limitations, also, as are described later.

Not until Kenneth H. Baker (1939) in the United States and Robert W. B. Jackson (1939) in England applied analysis-of-variance (anova) procedures to test items was there the beginning of rapprochement of the Pearsonian correlational approach

---

[6] If the *British Journal of Psychology* had commenced publication by 1904, instead of 1907, Spearman would probably have published his first articles in it rather than in the *American Journal of Psychology*—and would they have influenced U.S. psychometrics so quickly and profoundly?

[7] R. A. Fisher's name does not appear in the index to Kelley's book, nor does the term *variance* occur in the index or table of contents, even though Fisher published several important statistical papers prior to 1924—but, unlike Spearman, entirely in British journals, and not psychological ones.

with Fisherian experimental design and analysis. Two years later, Cyril Hoyt's (1941) article in the prestigious United States professional journal *Psychometrika* caught the attention of quantitatively oriented measurement specialists and ushered in a new means of assessing the reliability of one-form test scores.

Hoyt was a student of Palmer O. Johnson at the University of Minnesota. In 1935, Johnson had studied at the University of London with Ronald A. Fisher, Cyril Burt, Jerzy Neyman, and Robert W. B. Jackson, who was completing his doctorate under Burt. Much of the credit for the introduction of anova principles into test theory and practice seems due to Burt, even though his major published work in this area did not appear until 1955 (see Burt, 1955). Hoyt's arithmetical procedure for computing one-form reliability coefficients caught on fairly quickly, though his difficult derivation seems not to have been well understood by most readers. Fisher himself was not concerned with test theory per se, but his data layout and analysis procedures paved the way for Hoyt (1941), Lindquist (1953), Burt (1955), and especially the Cronbach and associates (1970) approach.

A few of the other influential publications in test theory were Brown (1911), Brown and Thomson (1921), Brigham (1932), Thurstone (1932), Deming and Birge (1934a, 1934b), Goodenough (1936, 1949), Jackson and Ferguson (1941), Loevinger (1947), Thorndike (1949), Gulliksen (1950), Cronbach (1951), Lord (1952), Cattell (1964), Cureton (1965), Gleser and associates (1965), Lord and Novick (1968), and Winer (1968). Unpublished material by Buros (1963, 1966) seems to have had some impact on certain measurement specialists. This short list by no means does justice to the authors of many important, specific contributions, usually reported in journal articles. Some of these will be mentioned later. For an excellent history of the first quarter of a century, see Walker (1929). Later reviews by Scates (1947), Goodenough (1949), and Linden and Linden (1968) add breadth and perspective.

CLASSICAL TEST-SCORE THEORY

From Spearman's 1904 article onward, psychometrics has operated largely with concepts of true score and error of measurement. Numerous attempts (perhaps most notably by Guttman, 1945, 1953; Gulliksen, 1950; Tryon, 1957; Cureton, 1958; Koutsopoulos, 1962, 1964; Novick, 1966; Rozeboom, 1966; Lord & Novick, 1968; Kristof, 1969; and Jöreskog, 1969) have been made to extend the semantic and syntactical meanings of these terms. Spearman's original formulations have held up rather well, so that much of the voluminous literature on these topics over the years is still valid. Some essentials will be sketched here; this leaves many of the details for the reader to seek in the above references and elsewhere.[8]

It is hypothesized that forms of a particular test exist in infinite number, each of these forms measuring the same ability, trait, or characteristic in the following manner. Let X_{pf} designate the observation of variable X for the pth person ($p = 1, 2, \ldots, P, \ldots, \infty$) on the fth form ($f = 1, 2, \ldots, F, \ldots, \infty$) of the test, each form being composed of I items. (In actuality the scores of a sample of P persons on F forms, where both P and F are finite, are observed.) For the simplest case it is considered that the pth person has the same true score, T_p, on every form of the test, and that the rest of his obtained score on the fth form, i.e. $X_{pf} - T_p$, is entirely a ran-

---

[8] For short, elementary treatments of reliability, see American Psychological Association (1966, pp. 25–32), Brown (1970), Cronbach (1970, pp. 151–182), Stanley (1964, pp. 150–160), Stanley (1971, in press), Thorndike (1964), and Thorndike and Hagen (1969, pp. 177–199).

dom error of measurement, e_{pf}, specific to his performance on that form on that occasion. That is,

$$T_p = \lim_{F \to \infty} \frac{\sum_{f=1}^{F} X_{pf}}{F} = E_f(X_{pf}) = \mu_{X_p},$$ [6]

where $E_f(\ )$ is the expectation operator, indicating computation of the population mean of the one person's infinite number of obtained scores, and μ_{X_p} is the population mean of the X_{pf}'s, taken over forms for the pth examinee. In symbols this relationship is written

$$X_{pf} = T_p + e_{pf}.$$ [7]

The errors are random from form to form. They have a population mean of zero for *each* person. They covary across forms zero with a given person's true score and also zero with each other from form to form for a given person. The true score, T_p, of the pth person is merely the expectation (i.e. the population mean) of all that person's X_{pf}'s; that is, $E_f(X_{pf})=E_f(T_p+e_{pf})=E_f(T_p)+E_f(e_{pf})=T_p+0=T_p$.

The variance of the X_{pf}'s of the pth person—that is, the variance across forms of a person's infinite number of obtained scores—is $E_f[X_{pf}-E_f(X_{pf})]^2=E_f(X_{pf}-T_p)^2= E_f(e_{pf}^2)=\sigma_{e_{p*}}^2$. $\sigma_{e_{p*}}^2$ is the variance of measurement errors for the pth person; its positive square root, $\sigma_{e_{p*}}$, is called the standard error of measurement for the pth person.[9]

One can estimate $\sigma_{e_{p*}}^2$ from as few as two scores, X_{pf} and $X_{pf'}$, one on form f and the other on form f', where $f \neq f'$, *provided* that the forms are chosen independently and randomly. In practice, no infinite population of forms from which to choose exists, so that independence and random selection are assumed rather than operationally assured. One generalizes to an infinite number of forms "like these two."

An unbiased estimator of $\sigma_{e_{p*}}^2$ is $\widehat{\sigma_{e_{p*}}^2}=\Sigma_{f=1}^{F}(X_{pf}-\overline{X}_{p.})^2/(F-1)$, where the circumflex sign ($\frown$) means "unbiased estimator of" the parameter beneath it. Note that $\overline{X}_{p.}$ is the mean for one person over several forms. If there are just two forms (i.e. $F=2$), the formula simplifies to $(X_{pf}-X_{pf'})^2/2$. This will tend to be quite an unstable estimator, because it is based on only two observations.

The concept *reliability coefficient* is not applicable to a single individual but only to a group of persons, because that coefficient of correlation involves variation among the scores of different examinees. That is, reliability coefficients are measures of *inter*individual differentiation, whereas the variance error of measurement characterizes *intra*individual variability for a particular trait, ability, or characteristic.

One can ask meaningfully, What is the reliability coefficient of this test for my seventh-graders? but not, What is the reliability *coefficient* of this test for a particular student? One might, however, ask how reliable a certain procedure for measuring height is for a single student, meaning how variable are the successive measurements *he* receives. *The variance error of measurement is descriptive of intraperson variability;*

---

[9] Please note carefully how the subscript asterisk is used here and later. $\sigma_{e_{p*}}^2$ denotes the variance (σ^2) of the errors of measurement (e) for the pth person across the infinite number of *forms* of the test. That the variance is taken across forms rather than persons (as will be done later in the chapter) is indicated by the asterisk (*) in the position formerly occupied by the f. $\sigma_{e_{*f}}^2$ would denote the variance of errors of measurement across the infinite number of persons, one error of measurement per person for just *one* form of the test, the fth. Definitionally, $\sigma_{e_{p*}}^2 = E_f(e_{pf}^2)$, whereas $\sigma_{e_{*f}}^2 = E_p(e_{pf}^2)$.

the reliability coefficient involves the relationship of intraperson variability to interperson variability.

Reliability Coefficient for a Single Form

Returning to the model of formula 7, it is found that the product-moment coefficient of correlation between true scores, T, and obtained scores, X, for a single form (the fth) over the entire infinite population of persons is

$$\rho_{T_* X_{*f}} = \rho_{(T, T + e_f)} = \frac{\text{Cov}\ (T, T + e_f)}{\sigma_T \sigma_{X_f}}$$

$$= \frac{\text{Cov}\ (T, T) + \text{Cov}\ (T, e_f)}{\sigma_T \sigma_{X_f}} = \frac{\sigma_T^2 + 0}{\sigma_T \sigma_{X_f}} = \frac{\sigma_T}{\sigma_{X_f}}. \qquad [8]$$

Thus the correlation of the true scores of persons with their obtained scores on the fth form is the standard deviation of their true scores divided by the standard deviation of their obtained scores on that form. This ratio can vary from 0 to 1, inclusive.

Interpreting reliability coefficients

What does a reliability coefficient of, say, .91 on the 90-item Scholastic Aptitude Test, Verbal, mean? It indicates the percentage of the variance of obtained scores on the test, 91 percent, that is due to true-score variation; hence only 9 percent of the variance of obtained scores is due to errors of measurement. This is easily shown (cf. formulas 1, 3, and 4):

$$\frac{\sigma_X^2}{\sigma_X^2} = \frac{\sigma_T^2}{\sigma_X^2} + \frac{\sigma_e^2}{\sigma_X^2},$$

so

$$\frac{\sigma_T^2}{\sigma_X^2} = 1 - \frac{\sigma_e^2}{\sigma_X^2} = \rho_{TX}^2 = \rho_{X_f X_{f'}}, \qquad [9]$$

where σ_e^2 / σ_X^2 is the proportion of variance due to errors of measurement rather than to true scores.

The standard error of measurement for obtained scores on the SAT-V will be $\sigma_e = \sigma_{(X-T)} = \sigma_X \sqrt{1 - \rho_{XT}^2} = \sigma_X \sqrt{1 - .91} = \sigma_X \sqrt{.09} = .3 \sigma_X$, i.e. 30 percent of the standard deviation of the obtained scores. For a reliability coefficient of .84 the error percentage of the standard deviation becomes 40; for .75, it is 50 because $(1 - .75) = .25$ of the obtained-score *variance* is due to errors of measurement.

$\sigma_{TX}^2 / \sigma_{eX}^2$ is like signal-to-noise ratio

The information-theory concepts of signal and noise (see Pollack, 1968) can be helpful in understanding how the reliability of a test operates. Each somewhat parallel test item represents an attempt to communicate information about a certain ability of each examinee tested. For a single item the ratio of signal to noise is low, so usually one cannot tell much about an examinee's true ability from his answer to one item. With two items the situation improves—how much depending on the signal-to-noise ratio of each item. As the number of items measuring a common attribute increases, so does the signal-to-noise ratio, because the item true scores covary quite positively with each other, whereas the item error scores covary little or not at all. True scores (signals) cumulate more rapidly than errors of measurement (noise) do. This is a very rough picture of the relationship between the true-score variance to error-of-measurement variance ratio, $\sigma^2_{T_X}/\sigma^2_{e_X}$, and the signal (analogous to $\sigma^2_{T_X}$)-to-noise (analogous to $\sigma^2_{e_X}$) ratio. The ratio may also be written, equivalently, as $\rho^2_{TX}/(1-\rho^2_{TX})$ or as $\rho_{X_fX_f'}/(1-\rho_{X_fX_f'})$.

This ratio seems to be coming into much wider use, and properly so. Differences in test reliability among several tests or different ways of scoring tests frequently appear negligible unless expressed in signal-to-noise ratios. An improvement of only .01 in a high reliability coefficient is equivalent to the increase in reliability obtained by lengthening the test 10 percent or more. One can readily appreciate the practical significance of the improvement in these terms. The chief value of the signal-to-noise ratio is that an increase of p percent in this ratio corresponds to an increase of p percent in the length of the test. For further discussion, see Cronbach and Gleser (1964), Garner (1962), Jackson (1939), and Lord and Novick (1968, pp. 118–119 & 198).

Estimated True Scores

Assuming linear regression of the T_p's on the X_{pf}'s (not quite true but probably close enough to be useful most of the time; see Lord & Novick, 1968), the least-square equation for estimating the pth person's true score, T_p, from his obtained score, X_{pf}, is

$$\hat{T}_p = \beta_{TX_f}X_{pf} + \alpha_{TX_f} = \mu_{X_f} + \rho^2_{TX_f}(X_{pf} - \mu_{X_f}),\qquad [10]$$

where $\hat{T}_p$ is the estimated true score, β_{TX_f} is T-on-X slope coefficient, α_{TX_f} is the T-on-X intercept, μ_{X_f} is the population mean of the persons' obtained scores, and $\rho^2_{TX_f}$ is the squared population correlation coefficient between true scores and obtained scores.

The true score corresponding to X_{pf} is T_p. What is the true score corresponding in scale of measurement to $\hat{T}_p$? It is $T_p' = E_f[\mu_{X_f} + \rho^2_{TX_f}(X_{pf} - \mu_{X_f})] = \mu_T + \rho^2_{TX}(T_p - \mu_T)$.

What is the error of *measurement* made when one uses the known $\hat{T}_p$ in lieu of the unknown T_p'? It is, in simplified notation (i.e. dropping the form subscript),

$$\hat{T}_p - T_p' = \mu_X + \rho^2_{TX}(X_p - \mu_X) - [\mu_T + \rho^2_{TX}(T_p - \mu_T)]$$

$$= \rho^2_{TX}(X_p - T_p) = \rho^2_{TX}e_p,\qquad [11]$$

whose expected value, over persons, is 0, and which covaries 0 with the T_p''s.

Therefore, as the linear model analogous to formula 7, one has $\hat{T}_p = T_p' + e_{\hat{T}_p}$ $= [\mu_T + \rho^2_{TX}(T_p - \mu_T)] + [\rho^2_{TX}(X_{pf} - T_p)]$. This is merely the linear transformation $\beta_{TX}(\ ) + \alpha_{TX}$ of $X_{pf} = T_p + e_{pf}$.

In words, the linearly estimated true score of the pth examinee, $\hat{T}_p$, is an "obtained" score composed of the analogous true score, T_p', and the analogous error of measurement, $\hat{T}_p - T_p'$. When one uses the $\beta_{TX}(\ ) + \alpha_{TX}$ transformation of X_{pf}, as in formula 10, to estimate T_p, one must apply the same transformation to $T_p + e_{pf}$ to get the true score and error of measurement appropriate for $\hat{T}_p$.

What is the variance of the $(\hat{T}_p - T'_p)$'s—that is, the variance error of measurement of the $\hat{T}_p$'s? From formula 11, it is found to be

$$\sigma^2_{\rho^2_{TX}e_*} = \rho^4_{TX}\sigma^2_{e_*} = \rho^4_{TX}\left[\sigma^2_X(1 - \rho^2_{TX})\right].$$ [12]

Also,

$$\rho_{\hat{T}_*T'_*} = \rho_{[\mu_X + \rho^2_{TX}(X-\mu_X),\ \mu_T + \rho^2_{TX}(T-\mu_T)]} = \frac{\rho^4_{TX}\sigma^2_T}{\rho^2_{TX}\sigma_X\rho^2_{TX}\sigma_T} = \frac{\sigma_T}{\sigma_X},$$

which agrees with formula 8.

Therefore, $\rho_{\hat{T}T'} = \rho_{XT}$, because the $\hat{T}_p$ scores, obtained by a linear transformation of X_p's, cannot be more or less reliable than the X_p's themselves are. For further details see Stanley (1970) and pp. 432–34.

How does one use formula 10 to estimate the true score of the pth person when one knows X_{pf}, that person's obtained score on the fth form? If $P > 1$ persons have been tested, one can substitute for $\mu_{X_{*f}}$ in the formula its unbiased estimator, $\overline{X}_{.f}$, but what can one use for $\rho^2_{T_*X_{*f}}$? Discussion of this enters, in a later section, when methods for estimating reliability coefficients from a single form of a test are considered. If one defines $\rho^2_{T_*X_{*f}}$ as the reliability coefficient of the fth form (call this ρ_f), then the computing version of formula 10 becomes

$$\hat{T}_p = \overline{X}_{.f} + r_f(X_{pf} - \overline{X}_{.f}).$$ [13]

It is obvious from formula 13 that a person's estimated true score will be closer to the mean of the group with which he was tested than is his obtained score, unless the test is perfectly reliable. This is known as *regression toward the mean due to errors of measurement*. From formula 8, it can be shown that $\sigma^2_{T_*} = \rho^2_{T_*X_{*f}}\sigma^2_{X_{*f}} = \rho_f\sigma^2_{X_{*f}}$; so, since the reliability coefficient can vary only from 0 to 1, inclusive, the variance of true scores is always a percentage of the variance of obtained scores on the form, from 0 percent when the reliability coefficient is 0 to 100 percent when it is 1.

Because a person's obtained score is likely to be larger than his true score if above the mean and smaller than his true score if below the mean of the group in which he is tested, $\hat{T}_p$ is a score useful for constructing a symmetrical confidence interval on T'_p, as will be seen later. Also, for matching individuals from two different groups, it is better to match on estimated true scores than on obtained scores if the group means are different and/or the two sets of scores are unequally reliable. Estimated true scores are especially important when X is measured on a ratio scale (e.g. linear distance or weight) or an absolute scale (e.g. number of sperm cells). Estimated true scores might, for example, be useful in deciding whether a man is fertile or not.

F. M. Lord (in a private communication) has pointed out that, while matching on the basis of observed scores usually does not give satisfactory results, matching on $\hat{T}_p$'s may not be much better—or even feasible—when the group means differ considerably and the reliability coefficients are low. Lord suggested that the following rather extreme, but convincing, hypothetical example be considered. Each of two groups has normally distributed obtained scores with standard deviation of 1 and reliability coefficient of $\rho^2_{TX} = .50$. The group means of the obtained scores are 0 and .75, respectively—i.e. they are $.75\sigma$ apart.

The standard deviation of the true scores in each of the two groups is $\sigma_T = \rho_{TX} = .717$. Because $\mu_X = \mu_T$, the *means* of the true scores remain 0 and .75; now, however, the means are $.75/.717 = 1.05$ standard deviations apart, rather than the .75 for obtained scores.

The standard deviation of the estimated true scores in each group is $\sigma_{\hat{T}} = \rho_{TX}^2 = .50$. Because $\mu_X = \mu_{\hat{T}}$, the group means of the $\hat{T}$'s remain 0 and .75. Now, however, the means are $.75/.50 = 1.5$ standard deviations apart, which is twice as far apart as the obtained scores are. Persons $.75\sigma_{\hat{T}}$ above the mean of the lower group must be matched with persons $.75\sigma_{\hat{T}}$ below the mean of the upper group, for example. There simply may not be enough subjects available from whom to secure the desired number of pairs matched on $\hat{T}$. Of course, T's are not known, so they cannot be used for matching, and X's have the undesirable regressive property. Matching has this and other pitfalls (see Lord, 1967; Stanley, 1967a; and Thorndike, 1963).

Several forms

Formulas 8 and 10 are specific to the fth form, because both contain f subscripts. It has been required, however, that each person's true score be identical from form to form, and this insures that the variances of true scores over persons will be the same from form to form. The variance of obtained scores on the fth form in the infinite population of persons is the variance of a sum, $\sigma_{X_{*f}}^2 = \sigma_{(T_* + e_{*f})}^2 = \sigma_{T_*}^2 + \sigma_{e_{*f}}^2 + 2\sigma_{T_* e_{*f}}$, where $\sigma_{T_* e_{*f}}$ is the covariance, across persons, of true scores with errors of measurement on the fth form. This becomes $\sigma_{X_{*f}}^2 = \sigma_{T_*}^2 + \sigma_{e_{*f}}^2$, if $\sigma_{T_* e_{*f}} = 0$.

In this formula it is noted that the variance of true scores, $\sigma_{T_*}^2$, is the same for every parallel form of the test. The variance of obtained scores, $\sigma_{X_{*f}}^2$, can vary from form to form only as does $\sigma_{e_{*f}}^2$, the variance of the errors of measurement. If every form has the same number of items, say I, the same item format (e.g. five-option multiple-choice items), and of course the same type of content, as would all seem necessary in order for the true score of the pth person to be constant from form to form, one can probably assume without substantial error that the variance errors of measurement, over persons, are constant from form to form: $\sigma_{e_{*1}}^2 = \sigma_{e_{*2}}^2 = \cdots = \sigma_{e_{*\infty}}^2 = \sigma_e^2$. This makes the variance of obtained scores, over persons, constant from form to form: $\sigma_{X_{*1}}^2 = \sigma_{X_{*2}}^2 = \cdots = \sigma_{X_{*\infty}}^2 = \sigma_X^2$.

From this, one can rewrite formula 8 as $\rho_{TX}^2 = \sigma_T^2/\sigma_X^2$, meaning that the squared correlation between the true scores and obtained scores of persons on any form can be expressed as the ratio of the true-score variance, over persons, to the obtained-score variance, over persons, on that form or any other.

Similarly, formula 10 may be rewritten as $\hat{T}_p = \mu_X + \rho_{TX}^2(X_{pf} - \mu_X)$, if it is assumed that the population mean of obtained scores, over persons, is the same for every form. Is this a reasonable assumption? Yes, it follows from the previous assumptions that the mean error of measurement for each form is zero and the true score of an examinee remains the same from form to form.

Reliability Coefficient from Two Forms

For two forms, the two scores of the pth person tested may be written, in the simple model for classical true-score theory, as $X_{pf} = T_p + e_{pf}$, and $X_{pf'} = T_p + e_{pf'}$, where the subscript f designates the fth form of the test, and the subscript f' designates another form of the test, $f \neq f'$.

If the reliability coefficient is defined as the coefficient of correlation, for the entire infinite population of persons, of the obtained scores on the fth form with those on the f'^{th} form, one secures

$$\rho_{X_{*f}X_{*f'}} = \frac{\text{Cov}\,(T + e_f, T + e_{f'})}{\sigma_{X_f}\sigma_{X_{f'}}}$$

$$= \frac{\text{Cov}\,(T, T) + \text{Cov}\,(T, e_{f'}) + \text{Cov}\,(e_f, T) + \text{Cov}\,(e_f, e_{f'})}{\sigma_{X_f}\sigma_{X_{f'}}}$$

$$= \frac{\sigma_T^2}{\sigma_{X_f}\sigma_{X_{f'}}} = \frac{\sigma_T^2}{\sqrt{(\sigma_T^2 + \sigma_{e_f}^2)(\sigma_T^2 + \sigma_{e_{f'}}^2)}}, \qquad [14]$$

because the errors of measurement are assumed to correlate zero with the true scores and with each other.

It is noted that, if the variance of errors of measurement is the same for the fth and the f'^{th} forms, the denominator of the reliability formula in formula 14 becomes simply σ_X^2, thereby yielding the result of formula 3, which stated in words is: *The reliability coefficient of a test is the ratio of the variance of true scores to the variance of obtained scores.* In simplified notation, this is $\rho_{XX'} = \sigma_T^2/\sigma_X^2$.

Thus to estimate the reliability coefficient from two forms of a test that have the same true score for the pth person, one simply computes $r_{X_{*f}X_{*f'}}$, the coefficient of correlation between the obtained scores of the P persons who have taken both forms. This will tend to vary from about zero to as much as one, depending on the reliability of the measurements, though it could be negative due to sampling error or a violation of assumptions. Like other computed Pearson product-moment r's, it is not an unbiased estimator of the corresponding parameter, $\rho_{X_{*f}X_{*f'}}$ (see Olkin & Pratt, 1958), but for samples large enough to provide a reasonably stable estimate of the coefficient of correlation for the population, the bias is negligible; for $P \geq 30$, the bias can be disregarded.

Variance Errors of Measurement from Two Forms

The variance of the errors of measurement, over the infinite population of persons, on the fth form is $\sigma_{e_{*f}}^2$, the unbiased estimator of which is $s_{e_{*f}}^2$, computed with $(P-1)$ degrees of freedom.[10] How does one compute $s_{e_{*f}}^2$? Consider the variance of the difference between the obtained scores of each person in the infinite population on forms f and f'. Noting that $X_{pf} - X_{pf'} = (T_p + e_{pf}) - (T_p + e_{pf'}) = e_{pf} - e_{pf'}$, it is seen that this variance is $\sigma_{(X_{*f} - X_{*f'})}^2 = \sigma_{(e_{*f} - e_{*f'})}^2 = \sigma_{e_{*f}}^2 + \sigma_{e_{*f'}}^2$, the covariance term having vanished because the errors from form to form are assumed to covary zero. The mean variance error of measurement of the two forms is given by

$$\overline{\sigma_{e_*}^2} = \frac{\sigma_{(X_{*f} - X_{*f'})}^2}{2}. \qquad [15]$$

$\overline{\sigma_{e_*}^2}$ involves the traditional bar-and-dot notation for a mean. The over-bar designates a mean, here a mean variance. The dot indicates that the mean was taken over forms—in this case, over just two forms, f and f'. The position of the asterisk indicates that the variances are over persons. The computing formula is as in formula 15, with σ^2 replaced by the analogous s^2: $\overline{s_{e_*}^2} = s_{(X_{*f} - X_{*f'})}^2/2$.

It is interesting to note further that the variance of the differences between obtained scores on two forms may be written as

---

[10] As noted, s^2 indicates the unbiased estimator of the corresponding σ^2.

$$\sigma^2_{(X_{*f}-X_{*f'})} = \sigma^2_{X_{*f}} + \sigma^2_{X_{*f'}} - 2\rho_{X_{*f}X_{*f'}}\sigma_{X_{*f}}\sigma_{X_{*f'}}, \qquad [16]$$

revealing clearly that here the two-form variances are not assumed to be equal and that the subtractive term involves the two-form reliability coefficient. If the two forms are parallel, their obtained-score variances will be equal; then formula 16 reduces to formula 5 for the variance error of measurement, i.e. $\sigma^2_e = \sigma^2_X(1 - \rho_{X_{*f}X_{*f'}})$.

Note carefully how $\sigma^2_{e_{*f}}$ differs from $\sigma^2_{e_{p*}}$. The latter is the variance of the errors of measurement for *one* person (the pth) over an infinite number of forms; the former, as in formula 5, is based on the errors of measurement—one error per person—for an infinite number of persons tested on one form, the fth. $\sigma^2_{e_{p*}}$ is mainly of theoretical interest, because it is usually not possible to test one person repeatedly with various forms of a test without his true score changing in the process. On the other hand $\sigma^2_{e_{*f}}$ is applicable only to the average person if $\sigma^2_{e_{p*}}$ does in fact vary from person to person, as it probably does because of differing degrees of carefulness, differing guessing tendencies, different ability levels, and the like. Because when P, the number of persons tested, is fairly large, σ^2_e is estimated readily and reasonably accurately from the scores of P persons on two parallel forms of the test—or even from their scores on just one form, as will be seen shortly—it is used frequently, whereas the variance of the obtained scores of just one person on several forms rarely is.

One usually works with the *standard* error of measurement, which is the positive square root of the variance error of measurement. What does this show? Errors of measurement, e_{pf}, vary randomly from form to form around a person's true score, T_p, with mean, $\mu_{e_{p*}}$, equal to zero, and standard deviation, $\sigma_{e_{p*}}$. If the errors of measurement are distributed normally around the pth person's true score, it is known that about 16 percent of the time his obtained score will exceed his true score by at least $1\sigma_{e_{p*}}$, and about 16 percent of the time it will be at least $1\sigma_{e_{p*}}$ below his true score. (His true score itself, however, cannot be known.)

Computing Estimated True Scores

Formula 10 showed how to estimate a person's true score from his obtained score on one form. Given a person's obtained score, X_{pf}, and a suitable two-form reliability coefficient, one can estimate his true score as follows:

$$\hat{T}_p = \overline{X}_{.f} + r_X(X_{pf} - \overline{X}_{.f}), \qquad [17]$$

where $\overline{X}_{.f}$ is the mean, over persons, of the fth-form scores of his group, and r_X is the reliability coefficient appropriate for the X_{pf}'s of that group.

Knowing the variance error of measurement for a comparable group, one can use the variance of obtained scores of one's own group on form f to secure an estimate of the reliability coefficient appropriate for one's group, because variance errors of measurement for a given test fluctuate less from group to group than do variances of obtained scores. Test manuals usually list enough information, typically one or more reliability coefficients and the variance of obtained scores, to permit estimating the variance error of measurement from this relationship: reliability coefficient equals one minus the ratio of the variance error of measurement to the variance of obtained scores. One should be *sure*, though, that the norm group on which the variance error of measurement is based is really approximately like the present group, at the same grade and ability level, of the same sex, etc. Also, if scores on two parallel forms were correlated to obtain the reliability coefficient, one should be sure that the time intervening between the administration of the two forms was slight, because otherwise the true scores on the two forms might not correlate perfectly.

If one actually has the two scores X_{p1} and X_{p2} available for each examinee, formula 17 becomes

$$\hat{T}'_p = \frac{\overline{X}_{.1} + \overline{X}_{.2}}{2} + \frac{2r_{X_{*1}X_{*2}}}{1 + r_{X_{*1}X_{*2}}}\left(\frac{X_{p1} + X_{p2}}{2} - \frac{\overline{X}_{.1} + \overline{X}_{.2}}{2}\right).$$

$$r_{(X_{*1}+X_{*2})(X_{*1}'+X_{*2}')} = \frac{2r_{X_{*1}X_{*2}}}{1 + r_{X_{*1}X_{*2}}} \qquad [18]$$

is the estimated reliability coefficient for the $(X_{p1}+X_{p2})/2$ scores, or the $(X_{p1}+X_{p2})$'s —i.e. the reliability coefficient of the mean or the sum of obtained scores based on *two* parallel forms of the test; each X_{p1} is parallel to corresponding $X_{p1'}$, and each X_{p2} is parallel to the corresponding $X_{p2'}$. As will be seen later, formula 18 is a simple version of the Spearman-Brown Prophecy (or Step-Up) formula. When the test has any estimated reliability at all (i.e. $r_{X_{*1}X_{*2}} > 0$), the step-up formula will increase the reliability coefficient, because the mean (or total) score on two forms is more reliable than the score on just one form.

Alternately, the estimated reliability coefficient based on two forms is

$$r_{(X_1+X_2)(X_1'+X_2')} = 1 - \frac{s^2_{(X_1-X_2)}}{s^2_{(X_1+X_2)}} = \frac{4r_{12}s_1s_2}{s_1^2 + s_2^2 + 2r_{12}s_1s_2},$$

which reduces to formula 18 when $s_1 = s_2$.

Practice effects from form 1 to form 2 affect $\overline{X}_{.2}$ and X_{p2}'s but not $r_{X_{*1}X_{*2}}$ unless the effects vary from examinee to examinee. Even constant practice effects complicate the theory, because $\hat{T}'_p$ becomes an estimate of a somewhat different quantity for two forms than $\hat{T}_p$ was for one.

The variance error of *measurement* of a form across persons is the variance of $(X_{pf}-T_p)$, i.e. $\sigma^2_{(X_{*f}-T_*)}$. What is the variance of $(\hat{T}_p-T_p)$ across persons? It is $\sigma^2_{(\hat{T}_*-T_*)} = \rho^2_{TX}\sigma_X^2(1-\rho^2_{TX}) = \rho^2_{TX}\sigma^2_{eX}$, which differs from the $\sigma^2_{(\hat{T}-T')}$ of formula 12 by the factor ρ^2_{TX}. $(T'_p = \beta_{TX}T_p + \alpha_{TX}$, the true score appropriate for $\hat{T}'_p$.) $\sigma^2_{(\hat{T}-T')} \leq \sigma^2_{(\hat{T}-T)}$. It can be shown that $\sigma^2_{(T-\hat{T})}$ is the variance error of *estimate* for linearly estimating T from $\hat{T}$—that is $\sigma^2_{[T-(\beta_{T\hat{T}}\hat{T}+\alpha_{T\hat{T}})]}$, which is algebraically equivalent to $\sigma^2_{[T-(\beta_{TX}X+\alpha_{TX})]}$. Thus, the variance of T's around a given $\hat{T}$ is $\rho^2_{TX}\sigma^2_{eX}$, whereas the variance of $\hat{T}$'s around a given T' is $\rho^4_{TX}\sigma^2_{eX}$, which is the variance error of *measurement* for the $\hat{T}$'s (see Stanley, 1970).

The $1-\alpha$ "confidence interval"[11] for T'_p is

[11] Only in a loose sense is this a confidence interval, though as a practical matter it should probably be used frequently in place of the more commonly employed $\overline{X}_{pf} \pm z_{(1-\alpha/2)}s_{eX}$, which is a confidence interval whenever the errors of measurement are normally distributed. As usually treated in the statistical literature, the $1-\alpha$ confidence interval yields the correct conclusion $1-\alpha$ of the time in the long run, regardless of the frequency distribution of the parameter estimated (in this case, regardless of the frequency distribution of true score in the groups tested). The trouble with formula 19 is that it assumes a linear regression of true score on observed score. As pointed out in Lord and Novick (1968), if this regression happens to be linear for some particular group of examinees, it is highly unlikely that the regression will still be linear in a selected subgroup. All in all, there is no reason to expect linear regression and every reason not to expect it. Never-

$$\hat{T}_p - {}_{(1-\alpha/2)}t_{(P-1)}r_{XX'}s_X\sqrt{(1 - r_{XX'})} < T'_p$$

$$< \hat{T}_p + {}_{(1-\alpha/2)}t_{(P-1)}r_{XX'}s_X\sqrt{(1 - r_{XX'})}, \qquad [19]$$

where $\hat{T}_p = \beta_{TX}X_p + \alpha_{TX}$; $T'_p = \beta_{TX}T_p + \alpha_{TX}$; ${}_{(1-\alpha/2)}t_{(P-1)}$ is the tabled "Student" t at the $(1-\alpha/2)$ percentile point with $(P-1)$ degrees of freedom; and $r_{XX'} = r_X$, the one-form reliability coefficient or its equivalent.

There is some confusion in the literature regarding the use of s_{e_X}, $\sqrt{r_{XX'}}s_{e_X}$, and $r_{XX'}s_{e_X}$ with $\hat{T}$ (cf. Davis, 1964, p. 50; Gulliksen, 1950, p. 43; Kelley, 1947, eq. 11:22 & 11:27; Nunnally, 1967, pp. 220–221; and Stanley, 1964, p. 159). $s_{e_X} = s_X\sqrt{1-r_{XX'}}$ is the estimated standard deviation of the $(X-T)$'s, which is the standard error of *measurement* for the X's. $\sqrt{r_{XX'}}s_{e_X}$ is the estimated standard deviation of the $(\hat{T}-T)$'s, which is the standard error of *estimate* for estimating T from X (or from $\hat{T}$). $r_{XX'}s_{e_X}$ is the estimated standard deviation of the $(\hat{T}-T')$'s—i.e. the standard error of *measurement* for the $\hat{T}$'s. For further discussion, see McHugh (1957), Lord and Novick (1968, pp. 66–69), Stanley (1970), and pp. 432–434.

Thus the variance of the errors of measurement in the predicted true scores is smaller than the variance error of measurement of the obtained scores (due to the reduced scale of the former), unless the reliability coefficient is one (that is, there are no errors of measurement), because in estimating true scores by formula 13 one moves each obtained score one-minus-the-reliability-coefficient distance toward the mean of the obtained scores.

A numerical example will show how formula 19 is used. The pth examinee earned a score of 56 on one form of a test for which the mean of his class of 31 students was 45.00. The reliability coefficient for his class is estimated to be .81. The variance of the obtained scores on a form for his class is computed to be 131.58. Therefore, the standard error of measurement is $\sqrt{131.58(1-.81)} = 5.00$. His estimated true score is $\hat{T}_p = 45 + .81(56-45) = 53.91$.

The .90 confidence interval for his T' is $53.91 \pm 1.697(.81)(5.00) = 47.04$ to 60.78, a range of nearly 14 points. The best estimate of his (one and only) T' is 53.91, but there are 5 chances in 100 that it is lower than 47.04 and 5 chances in 100 that it is higher than 60.78. There is little chance that his T' is as low as the class mean, however, because that figure (45) is not included within the 90 percent confidence interval, whose lower bound is 2.04 points above 45.00.

A far more common method is setting up a confidence interval for T_p to take into account errors of measurement, e.g. $X_{pf} \pm (z_{.95})s_{e_X} = 56 \pm 1.645(5.00)$, i.e. 47.775 to 64.225, a range of more than 16 points. This technique centers the interval on the student's obtained score rather than on his estimated true score. It is correct only for examinees scoring at the mean of the group, because there $\hat{T}_p = X_p = \overline{X}..$ [Also, this procedure typically involves z of the unit-normal distribution instead of t, although, of course, t could be employed. $z_{(1-\alpha/2)} \leq t_{(1-\alpha/2)}$, the z being smaller unless t is based on an infinite number of degrees of freedom. Note here that for 30 df and α equal to $.05+.05$ (i.e. equal to .10), t is 1.697 versus the z of 1.645].

One may consider α equal to 10 percent too stringent and prefer, say, 20 percent, in which event one would compute the 80 percent confidence interval by substitut-

theless, formula 19 may still be preferable, because its reduction of error-of-measurement bias will probably exceed its inefficiency due to varying curvilinearity from subgroup to subgroup. Still, $X_{pf} \pm z_{(1-\alpha/2)}s_{e_X}$ yields a genuine confidence interval that is applicable even when the examinee in question is not a member of any group—a circumstance that makes formula 19 impossible to use.

ing for the t of 1.697 a t of 1.310, thereby shortening the confidence interval appreciably. A common practice is to use $z=1$, thereby setting up the 68 percent confidence interval. At least one test publisher reports graphically (though inappropriately) the *percentile-rank* band that extends from $X-s_e$ to $X+s_e$ to emphasize the fallibility of obtained test scores. It is incorrect to look up the end points of this confidence interval in a norms table showing percentile ranks for X_p's, the *obtained* scores. For example, a certain number such as 107 might have a percentile rank of, say, 90 in the obtained-score distribution but 94 in the true-score distribution.

The percentile rank of $\hat{T}_p$ in a given group is the same as the percentile rank of X_p, so no conversion table is required to determine the percentile rank of the point score. The standard score is not affected either: $z_{X_p}=z_{\hat{T}_p}$.

Understandably, it might be confusing to many test users to suggest converting X_p's into $\hat{T}_p$'s; also, this requires knowing the reliability coefficient appropriate for the particular group tested or, at least, s_X^2 for that group and s_{eX}^2 for a similar group. One could "program" an approximate procedure in a test manual, but the lessened bias might not be worth the trouble, especially if the reliability coefficient of the test for a typical group is high. Furthermore, one may not be sure to which group a given examinee "really" belongs. For example, how much regression on a vocabulary test would be expected for a bright twelfth grader who happened to be tested along with ninth graders?

Error Difference in Obtained Scores
of Two Persons on the Same Test

A numerical example may facilitate understanding at this point. The obtained score of one examinee (say, Bill) was 56, whereas that of another (Dave) was 50 on the same test. Is Bill's true score on the test higher than Dave's true score? That is, in subsequent testing with comparable forms of this test, will Bill continue to score higher than Dave most of the time? It is known from above that Bill's estimated true score is 53.91. Dave's is $\hat{T}_{\text{Dave}}=45+.81(50-45)=49.05$.

The standard error of measurement for $\hat{T}$ on this test for the average examinee is $r_X s_e=.81(5.00)=4.05$. Assuming that this 4.05 characterizes the form-to-form vacillation of both Bill and Dave and that Bill's errors of measurement are independent of Dave's, it is seen that the variance error of measurement for the difference between $(\hat{T}_{\text{Bill}}-T'_{\text{Bill}})$ and $(\hat{T}_{\text{Dave}}-T'_{\text{Dave}})$ is given by $s^2_{(\hat{T}_B-T'_B)-(\hat{T}_D-T'_D)}$ $=s^2_{(\hat{T}_B-T'_B)}+s^2_{(\hat{T}_D-T'_D)}=(4.05)^2+(4.05)^2=32.805$, so the estimated standard error of measurement is taken to be $\sqrt{32.805}$, or 5.727.

Obviously, this standard error of the estimated difference due to errors of measurement is larger than the difference between the estimated true scores of the two boys, $53.91-49.05=4.86$, so the difference is not statistically significant (because the ratio of 4.86 to 5.724 is a t of only .85, with 30 df, whereas even at the .20 level of statistical significance for a two-tailed test a t of 1.31 is required). The 50 percent confidence interval for the difference is $4.86\pm0.683(5.727)=.95$ to 8.77. Thus it is known that, although one estimates the difference between their estimated true scores to be 4.86 points, there are 25 chances in 100 that it is less than .95 points and 25 chances in 100 that it is more than 8.77 points. (It is, of course, no accident that half the sum of .95 and 8.77 is 4.86, because the confidence interval is symmetrical around the estimated difference.) Therefore, by this rather lax 50 percent confidence interval criterion Bill has a slight edge over Dave, but one certainly would not give high odds in a bet that Bill's true score is higher than Dave's.

Note that the same conclusion would have been reached with obtained scores; e.g. $(56-50)/\sqrt{5^2+5^2}=.85$. One must not make the mistake of concluding that interval estimates of true scores or of differences between true scores by least-squares methods are somehow generally superior to interval estimates with obtained scores only. When the criterion is probability of correct decision, then least-squares estimates are no better than obtained scores if the scale of measurement is determined only within a linear transformation. For ratio scales (e.g. linear distance) or absolute (e.g. counting numbers 0, 1, 2, $\cdots$) scales, however, the estimated true-score interval is preferable. Also, for matching groups with respect to a variable or for pooling unequally reliable scores, appropriate point estimates of true scores are preferable to obtained scores.[12] Overall, it seems better to work with estimated true scores rather than with obtained scores, if the reliability coefficient(s) and mean(s) used to get the former are suitable for the particular group(s) involved.

Error Difference in z Scores of Same Person on Two Different Tests

If the pth examinee has an obtained z score of $+1$ on an arithmetic test (X) and -1 on a reading test (Y) in his group, how reasonable is it to suppose that his true standard score is the same on both? Let $X_{pf}=T_{X_p}+e_{X_{pf}}$ and $Y_{pf}=T_{Y_p}+e_{Y_{pf}}$, with the usual zero expectations, over persons, for errors of measurement, for covariances of true scores with errors of measurement, and for the covariance of errors of measurement with each other.

The variance error of measurement of $\rho_{TX}^2 \zeta_{X_p} - \rho_{TY}^2 \zeta_{Y_p}$, the difference between the two estimated true scores in standard-score form (ζ denotes the population z score), is

$$\sigma^2_{e_{(\rho_{TX}^2 \zeta_X - \rho_{TY}^2 \zeta_Y)}} = \rho_{TX}^4(1 - \rho_{TX}^2) + \rho_{TY}^4(1 - \rho_{TY}^2).$$

The α confidence interval for

$$T_{\rho_{TX}^2 \zeta_{X_p}} - T_{\rho_{TY}^2 \zeta_{Y_p}}$$

is

$$(r_X z_{X_p} - r_Y z_{Y_p}) \pm {}_{(1-\alpha/2)} t_{(P-1)} \sqrt{r_X^2(1 - r_X) + r_Y^2(1 - r_Y)}, \qquad [20]$$

where r_X and r_Y are one-form reliability coefficients computed from the data or estimated from test manuals, and ${}_{(1-\alpha/2)} t_{(P-1)}$ is the tabled Student t at the $(1-\alpha/2)^{\text{th}}$ percentile of the t distribution with $(P-1)$ degrees of freedom.

The more usual version (for $T_{\zeta_{X_p}} - T_{\zeta_{Y_p}}$), employing obtained scores rather than estimated true scores, is

$$(z_{X_p} - z_{Y_p}) \pm {}_{(1-\alpha/2)} t_{(P-1)} \sqrt{2 - r_X - r_Y}. \qquad [21]$$

The confidence interval of formula 21 is centered differently from the confidence

---

[12] If possible, matching should be done a priori, as randomized blocking, on the basis of pretest scores and not by selection of cases from groups that were preformed in some systematic way (see Lord, 1967; Stanley, 1967a; Thorndike, 1963).

interval found via formula 20, but both types of z scores are equally reliable, because $r_{XZ}z_{X_p}$ is merely a simple linear transformation of z_{X_p}. The reliability coefficient of X, z_X, or $r_{XZ}z_X$ is r_X, which is the ratio of true-score variance to obtained-score variance.

A practical example

To set up the confidence interval shown in formula 20 one needs the two z scores and estimates of the two reliability coefficients. At the beginning, this discussion set the $z_{x_{pf}}$ for a given person at $+1$ and his $z_{y_{pf}}$ at -1. Are his true scores in arithmetic versus reading probably different? If the two computed reliability coefficients are .70 and .80, respectively, and based on 51 examinees, the 90 percent confidence interval is $[.70(+1)-.80(-1)] \pm 1.676\sqrt{(.70)^2(.30)+(.80)^2(.20)} = 1.50 \pm 0.88 = 0.62 - 2.38$.

This person definitely seems to have a higher true standard score for arithmetic than for reading. His superiority in arithmetic relative to reading is estimated to be 1.50 standard deviations, which is half a standard deviation less than the difference between his two obtained z scores. There is 90 percent confidence that the difference between his semistandard true scores is not less than .62 nor more than 2.38 standard deviations.

Had the obtained z scores themselves been used, rather than the estimated semistandard true scores, the .90 confidence interval would have been $[+1-(-1)] \pm 1.676\sqrt{2-.70-.80} = 2.00 \pm 1.18 = 0.82 - 3.18$. The ratio of interval width to mean difference is the same for both methods; e.g. $(2.38-.62)/1.5 = (3.18-.82)/2$, within the limits of rounding-off error.

Which method is preferable? The estimated true-score procedure centers the confidence interval around an estimate of the long-run difference between semistandard true scores on the two tests (here, 1.50), whereas by taking the raw difference (here, 2.00) between obtained standard scores the nonregressing procedure uses a difference likely to be affected systematically by errors of measurement on the next testing. For example, the above person scored one standard deviation above the mean on a test whose parallel-forms reliability coefficient for the group with which he was tested is estimated to be .70. The best estimate of his z score on a parallel form of the arithmetic test, assuming no intervening change in his true score, is not 1.00, but instead $(.70)(1) = .70$, because it is expected that persons who have scored above the mean on this test in this group will regress 30 percent of the way downward towards the mean. (For a full set of z scores, the mean is zero, of course.) Likewise, it is expected that examinees on the reading test will regress $(1-.80) = 20$ percent of the way towards the mean of zero. This gives the person whose scores are being discussed a regressed z score of $(.80)(-1) = -.80$ on the reading test. The difference between his semistandard true scores on the two tests is estimated to be $(.70)-(-.80) = 1.50$. This, in fact, is the difference that would be predicted between obtained z scores for this person when he takes a new set of parallel forms of these two tests.

Such use of reliability coefficients does not improve the reliability of the scores themselves, of course, but it should help one interpret obtained scores better. Estimated true scores become especially important when one is trying to match individuals from groups whose means (and perhaps reliability coefficients, too) are not the same. To match on obtained scores under these circumstances will mean that the individuals are not matched on expected true scores and therefore will probably differ on obtained scores the next time they are tested with a parallel form. Also, for pooling data from different groups, estimated true scores are preferable to obtained scores. For further discussion, see Campbell and Stanley (1966), Lord and Novick (1968), and Thorndike (1963).

Reliability Coefficients for Differences

How reliable are the individual differences between the arithmetic and reading scores of a group of examinees, and under what conditions do the reliability coefficients for such differences increase or decrease? Given two comparable forms a and a' for the arithmetic test and two comparable forms r and r' for the reading test, where a and r are administered at one testing session and a' and r' at a subsequent one, it can be ascertained that the reliability coefficient for the raw-score difference $(X_{pa} - X_{pr})$ is (dropping most of the subscript X's and asterisks to simplify the notation)

$$\rho_{(X_{*a}-X_{*r})(X_{*a'}-X_{*r'})} = \frac{\rho_{aa'}\sigma_a\sigma_{a'} + \rho_{rr'}\sigma_r\sigma_{r'} - \rho_{ar'}\sigma_a\sigma_{r'} - \rho_{a'r}\sigma_{a'}\sigma_r}{\sqrt{\sigma_a^2 + \sigma_r^2 - 2\rho_{ar}\sigma_a\sigma_r}\sqrt{\sigma_{a'}^2 + \sigma_{r'}^2 - 2\rho_{a'r'}\sigma_{a'}\sigma_{r'}}} . \quad [22]$$

This can be estimated from data for P persons tested with two forms of each test, if r's are substituted for the ρ's and s's for the σ's. More simply, if two tests have been administered and then comparable forms of them have been given later, one would correlate the differences directly. (For an example, see Stanley, 1967b.) σ's for comparable forms were not assumed equal in formula 22. If one does assume that $\sigma_a = \sigma_{a'}$, $\sigma_r = \sigma_{r'}$, and $\rho_{ar'} = \rho_{a'r}$, then formula 22 simplifies to

$$\rho_{(X_{*a}-X_{*r})(X_{*a'}-X_{*r'})} = \frac{\rho_{aa'}\sigma_a^2 + \rho_{rr'}\sigma_r^2 - 2\rho_{ar'}\sigma_a\sigma_r}{\sigma_a^2 + \sigma_r^2 - 2\rho_{ar}\sigma_a\sigma_r} . \quad [23]$$

Either formula 22 or 23 is the one to use if the reliability coefficient for obtained-score differences is desired. From formula 23 one can see that the coefficient will be one if both tests are perfectly reliable and if $\rho_{ar'} = \rho_{ar}$ (i.e. if no decrement caused by $\rho_{ar'} < \rho_{ar}$ occurs during the time interval between a and r'). If the reliability coefficients are both zero, the coefficient will also be zero, because in this situation $\rho_{ar'}$ and ρ_{ar} also will be zero.

Usually in comparing an examinee's score on, for example, an arithmetic test with his score on a reading test, standard scores with fixed mean (e.g. zero), and fixed variance (e.g. one) for the group tested are used. For example, $z_{pa} = (X_{pa} - \overline{X}_a)/s_{X_a}$; then $\bar{z}_a = 0$, and $s_{z_a}^2 = 1$. This would be done separately for the arithmetic test and the reading test, to remove the possibly unequal influence of a versus r resulting from different variances for the two tests in formulas 22 and 23. If one works with the differences $(z_{pa} - z_{pr})$, all the σ's in formula 23 become ones, and it simplifies to

$$\rho_{(z_{*a}-z_{*r})(z_{*a'}-z_{*r'})} = \frac{\dfrac{\rho_{aa'} + \rho_{rr'}}{2} - \rho_{ar'}}{1 - \rho_{ar}} . \quad [24]$$

Formula 24 makes clear the dependence of the reliability coefficient for differences on the reliability coefficients of the two tests and the intercorrelations of the obtained scores on the two tests both across and within time intervals. Again, if the two test reliability coefficients are each unity, the reliability of the differences equals 1.00 if temporal stability is perfect.[13] If each of the two reliability coefficients is zero, then $\rho_{ar'}$ also becomes zero and the expression reduces to zero.

When the two tests are equally reliable (i.e. $\rho_{aa'} = \rho_{rr'} = \rho$), formula 24 assumes an even simpler form:

$$\rho_{(z_{*a}-z_{*r})(z_{*a'}-z_{*r'})} = \frac{\rho - \rho_{ar'}}{1 - \rho_{ar}}. \qquad [25]$$

For tests that correlate zero this becomes simply the reliability coefficient of either test, whereas for formula 24 the reliability coefficient for the differences becomes the average of the two different test reliabilities. The moral seems clear: *to secure reliable differences within or between individuals, use tests with high reliabilities but low intercorrelations.* (Of course, one's choice of tests must be governed by other con· siderations, especially validity.) High test reliability is crucial, for, as seen from formula 24, when the reliability coefficient of both tests is one, the reliability of the differences will be one, no matter how well (but less than 1.00) or poorly the tests correlate, provided that there is no change in the correlation between a and r across the time interval. On the other hand, if the tests correlate as highly as the reliability coefficient of each test (i.e. both tests measure the same thing), then the reliability of the differences will be zero. Two intermediate cases may be worth considering. Suppose that each test has a reliability coefficient of .75 and that the tests correlate .25. Then the reliability of the differences between z scores is $(.75-.25)/(1-.25)$ $=.50/.75=.67$, not a great deal lower than .75. If the test reliability coefficients were .75 and the intercorrelation .50, the ensuing reliability coefficient for the differences would be $(.75-.50)/(1-.50)=.25/.50=.50$. The value .75 may be somewhat low for use with the scores of an individual, and the .50 for differences may be definitely unsafe for that purpose.

The more highly two tests correlate positively, the greater is the overlap between the true scores of examinees, and the higher is the proportion of their obtained-score differences which is error. This leads to low reliability of differences within or between examinees. Table 13.2, adapted from Thorndike and Hagen (1969, p. 197), shows how the reliability of a difference score based on z's depends on the coefficient of correlation between the two tests and the average reliability coefficient of the two tests, assuming that $\rho_{ar'} = \rho_{ar}$ for formula 24. For instance, if the row entry is .40 and the column entry is .70, the tabled value is $(.70-.40)/(1-.40)=.50$.

The Reliability of Simple Change Scores

When one, however, is considering a pretest and a posttest based on the *same* type of test (rather than on two different tests, such as arithmetic and reading) and wishes to know the reliability coefficient of such differences (posttest score of an examinee minus his pretest score), an interpretative problem may arise. Suppose that, initially, parallel forms X_f and $X_{f'}$ of the arithmetic test are given. Then, after several weeks of instruction in arithmetic, two more arithmetic tests, Y_f and $Y_{f'}$,

---

[13] More generally, the reliability coefficient of the differences is unity if $1-(\rho_{aa'}+\rho_{rr'})/2$ $=\rho_{ar}-\rho_{a_1'}$, i.e. the unreliable component equals the unstable component.

TABLE 13.2

Reliability of a Difference Score

Coefficient of Correlation between the Two Tests (r_{fg})	Mean Reliability Coefficient of the Two Tests $[(r_{ff'}+r_{gg'})/2]$					
	.50	.60	.70	.80	.90	.95
.95						.00
.90					.00	.50
.80				.00	.50	.75
.70			.00	.33	.67	.83
.60		.00	.25	.50	.75	.88
.50	.00	.20	.40	.60	.80	.90
.40	.17	.33	.50	.67	.83	.92
.30	.29	.43	.57	.71	.86	.93
.20	.38	.50	.62	.75	.88	.94
.10	.44	.56	.67	.78	.89	.94
.00	.50	.60	.70	.80	.90	.95

parallel with each other but perhaps not with forms X_f and $X_{f'}$, are administered. How reliable, for example, are the individual differences, $(X_{pf}-X_{pf'})$? One would expect them to have zero reliability because differences between obtained scores on parallel forms should reflect only errors of measurement.

What about the reliability coefficient, however, of the $(Y_{pf}-X_{pf})$ difference scores? The usual identity, obtained difference score equals true difference score plus error-of-measurement difference, is written out $Y_p-X_p=[(T_{Y_p}+e_{Y_p})-(T_{X_p}+e_{X_p})]=(T_{Y_p}-T_{X_p})+(e_{Y_p}-e_{X_p})$.

The reliability coefficient of the (Y_p-X_p)'s is

$$\rho^2_{(T_Y-T_X)(Y-X)} = \frac{\sigma^2_{(T_Y-T_X)}}{\sigma^2_{(Y-X)}} \qquad [26]$$

$$= \frac{\sigma^2_{T_X}+\sigma^2_{T_Y}-2\rho_{T_XT_Y}\sigma_{T_X}\sigma_{T_Y}}{\sigma^2_X+\sigma^2_Y-2\rho_{XY}\sigma_X\sigma_Y} = \frac{\rho^2_{T_XX}\sigma^2_X+\rho^2_{T_YY}\sigma^2_Y-2\rho_{XY}\sigma_X\sigma_Y}{\sigma^2_X+\sigma^2_Y-2\rho_{XY}\sigma_X\sigma_Y},$$

where $\rho^2_{T_XX}$ and $\rho^2_{T_YY}$ are the reliability coefficients of X and Y, respectively. Formula 26 is identical with formula 23, which was secured through the comparable-forms reliability coefficient, $\rho_{(Y_f-X_f)(Y_{f'}-X_{f'})}$, when $\rho_{ar'}=\rho_{ar}$, so statistically it does not matter whether one talks about differences, change, growth, or gains. Logically and empirically, though, it does.

When $\rho_{T_XX}=\rho_{T_YY}$ and $\sigma_X=\sigma_Y$, formula 26 reduces to

$$\rho^2_{(T_Y-T_X)(Y-X)} = \frac{\rho^2_{T_XX}-\rho_{XY}}{1-\rho_{XY}}, \qquad [27]$$

where $\rho^2_{T_XX}$ is the reliability coefficient of X (or of Y), and ρ_{XY} is the coefficient of correlation between X and Y, which reflects any nonconstant true-score difference between X and Y, plus any instability of scores caused by time and other experiences that occur between X and Y. If $\rho^2_{T_XX}=\rho_{XY}$, the reliability of the $(Y-X)$'s is zero. Compare formula 27 with 25; except for the prime in formula 25 they are identical.

There may be a dilemma implied here, however, for the measurement of change. The lower the correlation between pretest and posttest scores, the higher the reliability of the measure of change (here, $Y_p - X_p$), but the less confident is one that the same thing is being measured on each occasion—and if the same thing is not being measured, what does change mean? However, the very fact of *change* implies that one is not repeating the *same* observation. Whether or not one is assessing the same attribute (in the Stanford-Binet Intelligence Scale at ages 6 and 8, for example) would depend on empirical study of the correlation of the tasks when administered concurrently (see Bereiter, 1963).

Covariance of X with Y—X

A raw-change measure such as $Y_p - X_p$ is not "base free." That is, the correlation between initial status, X_p, and the change scores, $Y_p - X_p$, is likely to be negative because

$$\rho_{X, Y-X} = - \frac{\sigma_X - \rho_{XY}\sigma_Y}{\sqrt{\sigma_X^2 + \sigma_Y^2 - 2\rho_{XY}\sigma_X\sigma_Y}} \, .$$

If $\sigma_X = \sigma_Y$ and $\rho_{XY} \neq 1$, $\rho_{X, Y-X} = -\sqrt{(1-\rho_{XY})/2}$, which can take values from minus one (for $\rho_{XY} = -1$) to almost zero, including the value $-.707$ when $\rho_{XY} = 0$. Some researchers, unaware of this mathematical restriction on the positive values of the correlation coefficient between initial status and gain, have reported a negative r as an important *empirical* finding. It may or may not be, as explained in the next paragraph. Positive $\rho_{X, Y-X}$ can occur only when $\rho_{XY}\sigma_Y > \sigma_X$, or $\rho_{XY} > \sigma_X/\sigma_Y$. What will $\rho_{X, X-Y}$ be when the two standard deviations are equal? If $\sigma_X = \sigma_Y$, then $\rho_{X, X-Y} = \sqrt{(1-\rho_{XY})/2} \geq 0$. Thus the sign of the r between initial status and change is heavily dependent on the direction in which the change is considered to have taken place, $Y - X$ versus $X - Y$.

A spurious tendency to negative correlation occurs because e_X appears with a positive sign in X and with a negative sign in the difference $Y - X$. This can be seen analytically: $\sigma_{X, Y-X} = \sigma_{T_X}(\rho_{T_X T_Y}\sigma_{T_Y} - \sigma_{T_X}) - \sigma_{e_X}^2$. The (subtractive) error variance is due to the identity of the e_X's in X and $Y - X$. The rest of the covariance will tend to be negative, also, unless $\rho_{T_X T_Y}\sigma_{T_Y} \geq \sigma_{T_X}$, which occurs when $\rho_{T_X T_Y} \geq \sigma_{T_X}/\sigma_{T_Y}$. Such a negative covariance of initial status with gain expressed as final status minus initial status may well be meaningful when it occurs; for example, over a certain time period heavier people may actually tend to lose weight, and lighter ones tend to gain it.

Other Measures of Change, Growth, or Difference

Though $Y_p - X_p$ seems intuitively to be the "natural" way to measure change, it is not the best estimator of $T_{Y_p} - T_{X_p}$, the true change. Errors of measurement in X and Y can affect this difference between obtained scores seriously.

Lord (1956, 1958, 1963) and McNemar (1958) proposed and discussed estimating $T_{Y_p} - T_{X_p}$ via its multiple regression on the most predictive linear composite of X_p and Y_p. Cronbach and Furby (1970) extended the Lord and McNemar procedure. They also questioned the value of change scores for most purposes, particularly the residual-change procedures of DuBois (1957) and Tucker, Damarin, and Messick (1966). The DuBois procedure merely involves using errors of estimate, as explained in the following section. (Errors of estimate are widely employed for another purpose that is discussed there.)

No further attention will be given in this chapter to the Tucker-Damarin-Messick residual-gains technique, but persons who contemplate using it or a similar procedure, including DuBois', should first study the Cronbach and Furby review and critique.

The Reliability of Residual Scores

Knowing the X_{pf}'s and Y_{pf}'s for a group of examinees, one can estimate the Y's linearly from the X's via the least-squares procedure

$$\hat{Y}_{pf} = \beta_{Y_{*f}X_{*f}} X_{pf} + \alpha_{Y_{*f}X_{*f}} = \mu_{Y_f} + \rho_{X_f Y_f} \frac{\sigma_{Y_f}}{\sigma_{X_f}} (X_{pf} - \mu_{X_f}).$$

Then for the pth person on the fth form the difference between the observed Y and the estimated Y will be a residual or error of estimate, ϵ:

$$\epsilon_{pf} = Y_{pf} - \hat{Y}_{pf} = (Y_{pf} - \mu_{Y_f}) - \rho_{X_f Y_f} \frac{\sigma_{Y_f}}{\sigma_{X_f}} (X_{pf} - \mu_{X_f}).$$

This is an *obtained* residual score. What is the analogous *true* residual score? It is the expectation, over *forms*, of the errors of estimate for the pth examinee:

$$T_{\epsilon_p} = E_f \left[(Y_{pf} - \mu_{Y_f}) - \rho_{X_f Y_f} \frac{\sigma_{Y_f}}{\sigma_{X_f}} (X_{pf} - \mu_{X_f}) \right]$$

$$= (T_{Y_p} - \mu_{Y.}) - \rho_{XY} \frac{\sigma_Y}{\sigma_X} (T_{X_p} - \mu_{X.})$$

if $\rho_{X_f Y_f}(\sigma_{Y_f}/\sigma_{X_f})$ is a constant, $\rho_{XY}(\sigma_Y/\sigma_X)$, for all forms.

The analogous error of *measurement* of the residual score is

$$e_{\epsilon_{pf}} = (Y_{pf} - \hat{Y}_{pf}) - E_f(Y_{pf} - \hat{Y}_{pf}) = (Y_{pf} - T_{Y_p}) - \rho_{XY} \frac{\sigma_Y}{\sigma_X} (X_{pf} - T_{X_p})$$

$$= e_{Y_{pf}} - \rho_{XY} \frac{\sigma_Y}{\sigma_X} e_{X_{pf}}$$

if $\mu_{Y_f} = \mu_{Y.}$ and $\mu_{X_f} = \mu_X$ for every f—i.e. if $\mu_{Y_1} = \mu_{Y_2} = \cdots = \mu_{Y_F} = \mu_Y$, and similarly for μ_{X_f}. Over persons or forms, this error has an expectation of zero.

These true scores covary zero with these errors of measurement, so the usual equation of classical test theory (obtained score equals true score plus error of measurement) holds: $\epsilon_{pf} = T_{\epsilon_p} + e_{\epsilon_{pf}}$.

What is the reliability coefficient of the ϵ_{pf}'s? It is the ratio of the variance of true residual scores of persons to the variance of their obtained residual scores,

$$\rho_{T_{\epsilon\epsilon}}^2 = \frac{\sigma_{T_\epsilon}^2}{\sigma_\epsilon^2} = \frac{\rho_{T_Y Y}^2 - \rho_{XY}^2 (2 - \rho_{T_X X}^2)}{1 - \rho_{XY}^2}. \qquad (\rho_{XY}^2 \neq 1)$$

If both tests are perfectly reliable (i.e. $\rho_{T_Y Y} = \rho_{T_X X} = 1$), then the reliability of the residual scores, or errors of estimate, also will be perfect. If $\rho_{T_Y Y} = \rho_{T_X X} = 0$, the reliability coefficient of the errors of estimate also will be zero, because then $\rho_{XY}^2 = 0$.

If the reliability coefficients are $\rho_{T_Y Y}^2 = \rho_{T_X X}^2 = k$, then the reliability coefficient for the errors of estimate becomes

$$\rho_{T_{\epsilon\epsilon}}^2 = \frac{k - \rho_{XY}^2(2 - k)}{1 - \rho_{XY}^2} .$$

For example, when $k = .80$ and $\rho_{XY} = .40$, $\rho_{T_{\epsilon\epsilon}}^2 = .724$. The reduction in reliability, from .80 to .724, is small because .80 is large relative to $(.40)^2 = .16$.[14]

$Y - \hat{Y}$ covaries zero with X, so it is a base-free measure (as $Y - X$ is not). However, Cronbach and Furby (1970) have pointed out that this quality has been overvalued.

The chief use of errors of estimate as scores is in searching for "overachievers" and "underachievers"—persons whose actual Y scores are much greater or much less, respectively, than their estimated scores $\hat{Y}_p = \beta_{YX} X_p + \alpha_{YX}$. (Of course, one can predict Y from two or more predictor variables, rather than just from X, if he desires.) The concepts of over- and underachievement are usually poorly defined and misleadingly handled, as Thorndike (1963) has shown clearly. Nevertheless, the search for variables that "explain" marked deviations from prediction of subsequent academic success, where the predictors are prior grades and test scores, is likely to continue. Those searchers who use $Y_p - \hat{Y}_p$ to choose their subjects for study should at least consider how reliable such "scores" are.

How Reliable Should Differences Be?

Reliability coefficients for difference measures will be rather small unless two reliable variables that intercorrelate poorly are involved. Reliability-of-differences procedures may be especially useful when one is trying to infer whether a certain person's arithmetic-reasoning ability as measured in a certain way exceeds his general-vocabulary knowledge as measured in a certain way. Errors of both kinds are possible when one is trying to determine whether the person's true score on one variable exceeds his true score on the other. One may conclude that it does when in fact it does not, or that it does not when in fact it does. Wide confidence intervals, such as .95 or .99, bias the decision strongly in the direction of concluding that no difference between the person's two true scores exists when in fact it does. On the other hand, narrow confidence intervals, such as .67 or .50, will increase the percentage of false true-score-difference decisions as compared with the wider intervals. For a discussion of this problem, see Feldt (1967).

Difference and gain scores that are too unreliable for use with individuals may nevertheless be adequately reliable for use with groups, because the variance error of measurement of a mean difference or gain is $1/P^{th}$ that of a single difference or gain. Also, where a small reliability coefficient is due to restricted range of talent in a homogeneous group rather than to large variance error of measurement, as might happen in an experiment where true-score within-treatment variability is kept at a minimum (even at zero), one can use the measures without the concern that would be felt if comparisons of individuals per se were the object.[15]

---

[14] Note that the formula yields seemingly peculiar results when $0 < (\rho_{XY} = k) < 1$. E.g. when $\rho_{XY} = k = .5$, $\rho_{T_{\epsilon\epsilon}}^2 = .17$, instead of the 0 one might intuitively expect when the two instruments are parallel forms of the same test. This apparent paradox arises because the true-score component of $\hat{Y}_{pf}$ is $\beta_{YX} T_{X_p} + \alpha_{YX}$, rather than $\beta_{T_Y T_X} T_{X_p} + \alpha_{T_Y T_X}$.

[15] A word of caution seems in order. If in an experiment one restricts the true-score variability

Because the reliability coefficient of test scores increases as the number of items increases and the variance error of measurement of a mean decreases as the number of examinees used in computing it increases, there can be a certain trade-off between number of items and number of observations. Determining the number of items and the number of examinees required to secure the desired variance error of measurement of means is a straightforward statistical operation. This is somewhat different from the usual advice that the reliability coefficients of the instrument itself should be high.

G. V. Glass (in a private communication) suggested the following approach to studying the effects of increasing the number of items versus the number of examinees. Let X_{pif} be the score of the pth person ($p=1, 2, \cdots, P$) on the ith item ($i=1, 2, \cdots, I$) of the fth parallel form ($f=1, 2, \cdots, F$) of a test. For the fth form, the random-sampling variance of the mean,

$$\overline{X}_f = \sum_{p=1}^{P}\left(\sum_{i=1}^{I} X_{pif}\right)\Big/ P,$$

is

$$\sigma^2_{\overline{X}_f} = \frac{\sigma^2_{X_f}}{P} = \frac{\sigma^2_{T_X} + \sigma^2_{e_X}}{P}.$$

If the examinees take F parallel forms of the test, the sampling variance of their mean form scores,

$$\overline{X}. = \sum_{f=1}^{F}\sum_{p=1}^{P}\left(\sum_{i=1}^{I} X_{pif}\right)\Big/ FP = \sum_{f=1}^{F} \overline{X}_f/F,$$

is

$$\sigma^2_{\overline{X}.} = \sigma^2\left(\frac{\sum_{f=1}^{F} \overline{X}_f}{F}\right) = \sigma_2\left(\frac{\overline{X}_1 + \overline{X}_2 + \cdots + \overline{X}_f}{F}\right)$$

$$= \frac{1}{F^2}\left(\sum_{f=1}^{F}\sigma^2_{\overline{X}_f} + \sum_{f=1}^{F}\sum_{f'=1}^{F}\sigma_{\overline{X}_f \overline{X}_{f'}}\right) \qquad (f\neq f')$$

$$= \frac{1}{F^2}\left[F\sigma^2_{(\overline{T}_X+\overline{e}_{X_f})} + F(F-1)\sigma_{(\overline{T}_X+\overline{e}_{X_f},\, \overline{T}_X+\overline{e}_{X_{f'}})}\right]$$

$$= \frac{1}{F^2}\left[F(\sigma^2_{\overline{T}_X} + \sigma^2_{\overline{e}_X}) + F(F-1)\sigma^2_{\overline{T}_X}\right]$$

$$= \sigma^2_{\overline{T}_X} + \frac{\sigma^2_{\overline{e}_X}}{F} = \frac{\sigma^2_{T_X}}{P} + \frac{\sigma^2_{e_X}}{FP} = \frac{\sigma^2_{T_X} + (\sigma^2_{e_X}/F)}{P}.$$

It is evident that administering $F>1$ parallel forms to each examinee (i.e. increasing the number of items) reduces the sampling variance of the errors of measurement,

---

within treatments by having as experimental subjects persons homogeneous with respect to one or more characteristics, as for example by using persons whose obtained IQ scores fall within the interval 95–105, he cannot generalize from the experimental findings beyond that restricted range. "Blocking" or covarying techniques can, however, be used to reduce within-treatment variability without restricting generalizability (see Campbell & Stanley, 1966).

whereas testing more persons reduces the sampling variance of both true scores and errors. For fixed $\sigma^2_{T_X}$ and $\sigma^2_{e_X}$ one can readily study the change in $\sigma^2_{\bar{X}}$. as F and P are varied (see Cleary & Linn, 1969b).

Of increasing importance is the design where scores for individuals are not desired, but reliable estimates of mean knowledge are. For example, how well can the average seventh grader in the Northeast read a typical newspaper item? What percentage of such students can spell *separate* correctly? The investigator may wish to use a large number of items but have no need for asking any one examinee to answer all, or even many, of them. He can employ a balanced incomplete-block design (see Cox, 1958) or a similar plan and thereby get unbiased estimates of the desired item parameters (e.g. item means, variances, and covariances) from which estimates of test parameters can be made. This can readily be made an efficient procedure for a given amount of time and money. Its increased use can be anticipated (see Cahen, Romberg, & Zwirner, 1970; and Lord & Novick, 1968).

The Statistical Significance of Differences between Means

A low level of reliability that would make scores, especially difference scores, largely meaningless for individuals can be tolerated when one is interested in comparing mean differences. Here, the emphasis should be on the standard (or the variance) error of measurement of the mean, not on the reliability coefficient. The variance error of a mean due to errors of measurement is $1/n^{\text{th}}$ the variance error of measurement of the single scores. That is, $\sigma^2_{(\bar{X}-\bar{T})} = \sigma^2_{(X-T)}/n$, where n is the number of examinees.

Therefore the formula for testing the significance of the difference between $(\overline{SAT\text{-}V}_{\text{females}} - \overline{SAT\text{-}M}_{\text{females}})$ and $(\overline{SAT\text{-}V}_{\text{males}} - \overline{SAT\text{-}M}_{\text{males}})$ due to errors of measurement only (i.e. *not* to sampling fluctuations) is

$$t_{(n_{\text{males}}+n_{\text{females}}-2)} = \frac{(\overline{V}_f - \overline{M}_f) - (\overline{V}_m - \overline{M}_m)}{s_d \sqrt{\dfrac{1}{n_f} + \dfrac{1}{n_m}}},$$

where

$$s_d = \sqrt{\frac{(n_f-1)[s^2_{V_f}(1-r_{V_f V'_f})+s^2_{M_f}(1-r_{M_f M'_f})]+(n_m-1)[s^2_{V_m}(1-r_{V_m V'_m})+s^2_{M_m}(1-r_{M_m M'_m})]}{n_f + n_m - 2}},$$

the standard error of measurement of $[(V_f-M_f)-(V_m-M_m)]$. Here, $r_{V_f V'_f}$, for example, is $r^2_{T_{V_f} V_f}$, the one-form reliability coefficient or its two-form equivalent.

When Does $\rho^2_{T_X X} = \rho_{X_f X_{f'}}$?

It may be well at this point to stress the conditions under which $\rho^2_{T_X X} = \rho_{X_f X_{f'}}$ so that the one-form reliability coefficient can be estimated from the coefficient of correlation between scores on two parallel forms. As usual, begin with

$$X_{pf} = T_p + e_{pf} \quad \text{and} \quad X_{pf'} = T_p + e_{pf'}. \tag{28}$$

Then

$$\rho_{T_* X_{*f}} = \frac{\sigma_{TX_f}}{\sigma_T \sigma_{X_f}} = \frac{\sigma_{T(T+e_f)}}{\sigma_T \sigma_{X_f}} = \frac{\sigma^2_T}{\sigma_T \sigma_{X_f}} = \frac{\sigma_T}{\sigma_{X_f}},$$

so

$$\rho_{TX_f}^2 = \frac{\sigma_T^2}{\sigma_{X_f}^2} \cdot$$

Also,

$$\rho_{X_{*f}X_{*f'}} = \rho_{XX'} = \frac{\sigma_{XX'}}{\sigma_X\sigma_{X'}} = \frac{\sigma_{(T+e_X)(T+e_{X'})}}{\sigma_X\sigma_{X'}} = \frac{\sigma_T^2}{\sigma_X\sigma_{X'}} \cdot$$

This simplifies if $\sigma_X = \sigma_{X'}$, which it does because the definition of parallel forms requires that $\sigma_{e_f}^2 = \sigma_{e_{f'}}^2$, and that fact, in conjunction with $\sigma_{T_*}^2 = \sigma_{T_*}^2$, is sufficient to make $\sigma_X^2 = \sigma_{X'}^2$. Therefore, $\rho_{XX'} = \sigma_T^2/\sigma_X^2 = \rho_{TX}^2$. For this to hold, it is crucial that T_p not change from form f to form f'—i.e. that there be no instability of the ability or characteristic measured on the two occasions. The difference between X_{pf} and $X_{pf'}$ must be due entirely to $e_{pf} - e_{pf'}$. (A milder restriction would be that $T_{pf'} = T_{pf} + c_{ff'}$, as when $c_{ff'}$ is the practice effect, $\mu_{\cdot f'} - \mu_{\cdot f}$, uniform for all examinees, but even that creates some logical and statistical problems [see Novick, 1966]. However, ρ_{TX} and $\rho_{XX'}$ themselves are unaffected by linear transformations of true scores.)

The requirement, essentially, is that forms f and f' be taken in such a manner that they are effectively simultaneous, so that scores from one to the other do not vary systematically. Thus, it is inappropriate to replace ρ_{TX}^2 by $\rho_{XX'}$ if fluctuations in T that differ from examinee to examinee—i.e. not $c_{ff'}$, but instead $c_{(ff')_p}$—occur from form f to f'. This is likely to happen if much time or learning intervenes. Later, how to secure estimates of ρ_{TX}^2 from responses to the items of just one form will be considered. Using ρ_{TX}^2 rather than $\rho_{XX'}$ in formulas may be a desirable precaution to keep one from carelessly "plugging in" an $r_{XX'}$ that inappropriately represents r_{TX}^2.

Understanding may be clarified further by recalling that $T_p = E_f(X_{pf})$, and $e_{pf} = X_{pf} - T_p$. The true score is a construct for a person, being the mean of his obtained scores on an infinite number of hypothetical parallel forms. In this sense, his true score *cannot* vary from form to form. It is only when one is confronted with the obtained scores of more than one person on more than one form that practical considerations of differential instability from form to form become evident. There is no need to *define* "parallel forms" for a single person, but there is this need for groups of examinees.

The formulation in equation 28 is of course not the only possible specification. As Lord and Novick (1968) explained in detail, one may under some circumstances prefer setting up "randomly parallel" forms by item sampling, such as drawing I items randomly from a pool of items to constitute one form, a different set of I items for the second form, etc. For randomly parallel forms it is inappropriate to assume that $T_{pf} = T_{pf'}$, because the items in one set may be more (or less) difficult than the items in another set; the two sets of items are not interchangeable.

Even with the formulation of equation 28, forms f and f' are not quite interchangeable, because for errors of measurement of parallel forms it was required only that $\sigma_{e_f} = \sigma_{e_{f'}}$ and, of course, that $E_p(e_{pf}) = E_p(e_{pf'}) = 0$. That $E_p(e_{pf}^n) = E_p(e_{pf'}^n)$ was specified only for $n = 1$ and $n = 2$. Therefore, errors of measurement may have different distributions for forms f and f'—e.g. different skewness and kurtosis. Thus, one is dealing here with "weak" (assumptions) test-score theory. Lord has developed "strong" test-score theory, particularly to estimate the distribution of true scores from that of obtained scores (see Lord & Novick, 1968).

The Spearman-Brown Prophecy Formula Derived
from Parallel Composites

It was stated in formula 18, without proof, that the reliability coefficient for the sum or the mean of two scores on parallel forms of a test, $X_{pf}+X_{pf'}$ or $(X_{pf}+X_{pf'})/2$, is twice the reliability coefficient for either form, divided by one plus the reliability coefficient of either form, and that this is a special case of the Spearman-Brown prophecy formula (see Brown, 1910, Spearman, 1910). Specifically, it is the case for two forms—i.e. for $F=2$. What is the general formula for F forms, where $f=1, 2, \cdots, F$? Consider that for the pth person one has the sum of F scores $X_{p1}+X_{p2}+ \cdots +X_{pF}$ and also the sum of G scores $X_{pI}+X_{pII}+ \cdots +X_{pG}$, where F and G are not necessarily equal. How do the two sets of sums correlate? For typographical simplicity below, let Cov(X, Y) represent σ_{XY}.

$$\rho_{FG} = \rho_{(X_{*1}+X_{*2}+\cdots+X_{*F})(X_{*I} + X_{*II}+ \cdots+X_{*G})}$$

$$= \frac{\text{Cov}(X_{*1} + \cdots + X_{*F}, X_{*I} + \cdots + X_{*G})}{\sigma_{(X_{*1}+\cdots+X_{*F})}\sigma_{(X_{*I}+\cdots+X_{*G})}}$$

$$= \frac{\sum\limits_{f=1}^{F} \sum\limits_{g=1}^{G} \text{Cov}(X_f, X_g)}{\sqrt{\sum\limits_{f=1}^{F} \sigma_{X_f}^2 + \sum\limits_{f=1}^{F}\sum\limits_{f'=1}^{F} \text{Cov}(X_f, X_{f'})} \sqrt{\sum\limits_{g=1}^{G} \sigma_{X_g}^2 + \sum\limits_{g=1}^{G}\sum\limits_{g'=1}^{G} \text{Cov}(X_g, X_{g'})}}$$

$$= \frac{FG \left[\dfrac{\sum\limits_{f=1}^{F} \sum\limits_{g=1}^{G} \text{Cov}(X_f, X_g)}{FG} \right]}{\sqrt{F\left[\dfrac{\sum\limits_{f=1}^{F}\sigma_{X_f}^2}{F}\right] + F(F-1)\left[\dfrac{\sum\limits_{f=1}^{F}\sum\limits_{f'=1}^{F}\text{Cov}(X_f, X_{f'})}{F(F-1)}\right]} \cdot \sqrt{G\left[\dfrac{\sum\limits_{g=1}^{G}\sigma_{X_g}^2}{G}\right] + G(G-1)\left[\dfrac{\sum\limits_{g=1}^{G}\sum\limits_{g'=1}^{G}\text{Cov}(X_g, X_{g'})}{G(G-1)}\right]}}, \qquad [29]$$

where $f \neq f'$ and $g \neq g'$.

Without any simplifying assumptions thus far, the correlation of sums can be expressed as the ratio of FG times the mean covariance of the F tests in one battery with the G tests in the other battery divided by the product of two expressions, each of which contains the number of tests in the battery (F or G) times the mean of the variances of the tests in the battery, plus $F(F-1)$ or $G(G-1)$ times the mean of the within-battery test covariances.

If the standard deviation of the sum of the scores for one battery is the same as that for the other battery, the denominator of formula 29 simplifies and the formula becomes

$$\rho_{FG} = \frac{FG \, \overline{\text{Cov}}(X_f, X_g)}{F\sigma_{X_.}^2 + F(F-1)\overline{\text{Cov}}(X_f, X_{f'})} = \frac{G \, \overline{\text{Cov}}(X_f, X_g)}{\sigma_{X_.}^2 + (F-1)\overline{\text{Cov}}(X_f, X_{f'})},$$

where the overbars designate the aforementioned means.

If on the average the tests covary across batteries to the same extent that they covary within batteries, the formula becomes

$$\rho_{FG} = \frac{G \overline{\text{Cov} (X_f, X_{f'})}}{\sigma_{X.}^2 + (F - 1) \overline{\text{Cov} (X_f, X_{f'})}} = \frac{G\rho_{X_f X_{f'}} \sigma_{X_f} \sigma_{X_{f'}}}{\sigma_{X.}^2 + (F - 1)\rho_{X_f X_{f'}} \sigma_{X_f} \sigma_{X_{f'}}}.$$

If one can take the covariance of one test with a second test and the mean of the variances of the two tests in lieu of the mean covariance and the mean variance, respectively, of all the tests, the formula becomes

$$\rho_{FG} = \frac{G\rho_{X_f X_{f'}} \sigma_{X_f} \sigma_{X_{f'}}}{\dfrac{\sigma_{X_f}^2 + \sigma_{X_{f'}}^2}{2} + (F - 1)\rho_{X_f X_{f'}} \sigma_{X_f} \sigma_{X_{f'}}}.$$

By substituting r for ρ and s for σ, one can use this formula to estimate the correlation of sums under the assumptions made in the derivation of the formula. Further simplification can be made, however, when $F=G$ and $\sigma_{X*_f} = \sigma_{X*_{f'}}$. The formula becomes the well-known Spearman-Brown prophecy formula,

$$\rho_{FF'} = \frac{F\rho_{X_f X_{f'}} \sigma_{X_f}^2}{\sigma_{X_f}^2 + (F - 1)\rho_{X_f X_{f'}} \sigma_{X_f}^2} = \frac{F\rho_{X_f X_{f'}}}{1 + (F - 1)\rho_{X_f X_{f'}}}. \qquad [30]$$

Formula 30 can be applied either to a battery of tests or a set of test items (actually, often a test is a "battery" of shorter tests—the items themselves). Thus, knowing only $r_{X*_f X*_{f'}}$, the estimated reliability coefficient for a test form containing $I \geq 1$ items, one can estimate the reliability coefficient of a test consisting of FI items, the $I(F-1)$ added items being comparable to the first I items in the ways assumed in the derivation. Essentially, it is assumed that the first I items do not correlate better (or worse) with each other, on the average, than they correlate with the added items or than the added items correlate with each other, and that no increased fatigue, lowered motivation, or other deterring (or facilitating) influences occur because of the increased length of the test. For tests of useful length administered under well-controlled conditions these assumptions often will be met closely enough for the estimate to be serviceable.

Of course, formula 30 also can yield an estimate of the reliability coefficient of the shorter test when one has an estimate of the reliability coefficient of the longer test, because F can be less than one as well as greater.

Several illustrations may help to clarify use of the formulas. If a 5-item test has a reliability coefficient of .22, what reliability coefficient would be expected for a test four times that long (i.e. having 20 items) created by adding 15 items like the first 5? From the computing version of formula 30, one calculates, using $F=4$, $\hat{\rho}_{4,IV} = 4(.22)/[1+(4-1)(.22)] = .88/1.66 = .53$, where the Roman numeral subscript IV designates the parallel form of the lengthened test. This means that, if one form of a test composed of 5 items correlates .22 with a parallel form of that test that also has 5 items, then a form composed of 20 items similar to the initial 5 should correlate .53 with a parallel form containing 20 items.

One also can ask, theoretically, how many items like these five would the test have to contain in order to yield a reliability coefficient of .90? Solving formula 30 for $\hat{F}$ (the multiple needed), the following is secured: $.90 = \hat{F}(.22)/[1+(\hat{F}-1)(.22)]$, so $\hat{F}=31.91$. Therefore, theoretically one would need 31.91(5) (equals 160) items to attain the desired reliability coefficient, .90. Unless the items are especially pleasant and nonfatiguing, the formula is likely to overestimate reliability, however, so it might take more than 160 items, or even be virtually impossible to reach the .90 reliability coefficient with one form of the test in a single sitting.

If the estimated reliability coefficient of a single item is .13, what is the predicted reliability coefficient of a test composed of 60 such items? Here $F=60$, so using formula 30, it is found that $\hat{\rho}_{60,LX}=60(.13)/[1+(60-1)(.13)]=.90$.

Conversely, if a 60-item test has a reliability coefficient of .90, the average reliability coefficient of its items is estimated to be .13, using formula 30 and F equal to $1/60$:

$$\widehat{\rho_{ii'}} = \frac{\dfrac{1}{60}\,(.90)}{1 + \left(\dfrac{1}{60}-1\right)(.90)} = \frac{.90}{.60-59(.90)} = .13.$$

This .13 is approximately the mean intercorrelation of the 60 items—that is, approximately

$$\bar{r} = \frac{\displaystyle\sum_{i=1}^{60}\sum_{j=1}^{60} r_{ij}}{60(59)},$$

where $i \neq j$ (see Stanley, 1957a). A reliability coefficient of .90 for 60 items whose average intercorrelation is .13 characterizes a number of well-made tests, such as the Mathematical portion of the Scholastic Aptitude Test of the College Entrance Examination Board. The Verbal section of this test usually has 90 items that yield a reliability coefficient (computed somewhat differently from the comparable-form method) of approximately .90, so these items have an average reliability coefficient of about .09.

The Spearman-Brown Formula Derived from One Composite

The Spearman-Brown formula was derived via parallel composites. It can be secured readily from just one battery, and the process illuminates its derivation further. Consider the sum, S, of the F test (or item) scores of the pth examinee:

$$S_p = \sum_{f=1}^{F} X_{pf} = X_{p1} + X_{p2} + \cdots + X_{pF}.$$

Write the usual identity (obtained score equals true score plus error of measurement) for this sum: $S_p = T_{S_p} + e_{S_p}$. Therefore,

$$S_p = \sum_{f=1}^{F} X_{pf} = (T_{p1} + T_{p2} + \cdots + T_{pF}) + (e_{p1} + e_{p2} + \cdots + e_{pF}).$$

Then the desired reliability coefficient is

$$\rho^2_{T_S S} = \frac{\sigma^2_{(T_1+T_2+\cdots+T_F)}}{\sigma^2_{(X_1+X_2+\cdots+X_F)}}$$

$$= \frac{\sum\limits_{f=1}^{F} \sigma_{T_f}^2 + \sum\limits_{f=1}^{F} \sum\limits_{f'=1}^{F} \rho_{T_f T_{f'}} \sigma_{T_f} \sigma_{T_{f'}}}{\sum\limits_{f=1}^{F} \sigma_{X_f}^2 + \sum\limits_{f=1}^{F} \sum\limits_{f'=1}^{F} \rho_{X_f X_{f'}} \sigma_{X_f} \sigma_{X_{f'}}}. \qquad (f \neq f') \qquad$$

Using two relationships from test-score theory, that $\sigma_{T_f}^2 = \rho_{T_f X_f}^2 \sigma_{X_f}^2$ and $\sigma_{T_f T_{f'}}$ $= \rho_{T_f T_{f'}} \sigma_{T_f} \sigma_{T_{f'}} = \sigma_{X_f X_{f'}} = \rho_{X_f X_{f'}} \sigma_{X_f} \sigma_{X_{f'}}$, one can convert this formula to the form

$$\rho_{T_S S}^2 = \frac{\sum\limits_{f=1}^{F} \rho_{T_f X_f}^2 \sigma_{X_f}^2 + \sum\limits_{f=1}^{F} \sum\limits_{f'=1}^{F} \rho_{X_f X_{f'}} \sigma_{X_f} \sigma_{X_{f'}}}{\sum\limits_{f=1}^{F} \sigma_{X_f}^2 + \sum\limits_{f=1}^{F} \sum\limits_{f'=1}^{F} \rho_{X_f X_{f'}} \sigma_{X_f} \sigma_{X_{f'}}} \qquad (f \neq f')$$

$$= \frac{F \overline{\rho_{T_f X_f}^2 \sigma_{X_f}^2} + F(F-1) \overline{\rho_{X_f X_{f'}} \sigma_{X_f} \sigma_{X_{f'}}}}{F \overline{\sigma_{X_f}^2} + F(F-1) \overline{\rho_{X_f X_{f'}} \sigma_{X_f} \sigma_{X_{f'}}}}$$

$$= \frac{\overline{\rho_{T_f X_f}^2 \sigma_{X_f}^2} + (F-1) \overline{\rho_{X_f X_{f'}} \sigma_{X_f} \sigma_{X_{f'}}}}{\overline{\sigma_{X_f}^2} + (F-1) \overline{\rho_{X_f X_{f'}} \sigma_{X_f} \sigma_{X_{f'}}}}. \qquad [31]$$

This can be simplified if $\overline{\rho_{T_f X_f}^2 \sigma_{X_f}^2} = \overline{\rho_{X_f X_{f'}} \sigma_{X_f} \sigma_{X_{f'}}}$. Then formula 31 becomes (the subscript X's are dropped to simplify notation)

$$\rho_{SS'} = \frac{F \overline{\rho_{ff'} \sigma_f \sigma_{f'}}}{\overline{\sigma_f^2} + (F-1) \overline{\rho_{ff'} \sigma_f \sigma_{f'}}} = \frac{F \left(\dfrac{\overline{\rho_{ff'} \sigma_f \sigma_{f'}}}{\overline{\sigma_f \sigma_f}} \right)}{1 + (F-1) \left(\dfrac{\overline{\rho_{ff'} \sigma_f \sigma_{f'}}}{\overline{\sigma_f \sigma_f}} \right)}. \qquad [32]$$

It can be shown (see Stanley, 1957a) that $\overline{\rho_{ff'} \sigma_f \sigma_{f'}} / \overline{\sigma_f^2}$ is the *intra*class coefficient of correlation among the forms. If instead of $f = 1, 2, \cdots, F$ forms of a test one has $i = 1, 2, \cdots, I$ test items, formula 32 is equivalent to the well-known Hoyt (1941) or Cronbach (1951) coefficients of equivalence (i.e. reliability coefficient based on the internal consistency of the items in a single form); a special case of these coefficients, when the items are scored dichotomously (zero if answered incorrectly or omitted, one if answered correctly), is the Kuder and Richardson (1937) Formula No. 20 (KR20) coefficient.

If one assumes that $\overline{\rho_{ff'} \sigma_f \sigma_{f'}} = \overline{\rho_{ff'}} \ \overline{\sigma_f \sigma_f}$, formula 32 simplifies to

$$\rho_{SS'} = \frac{F \overline{\rho_{ff'}}}{1 + (F-1) \overline{\rho_{ff'}}}.$$

This assumption is most likely to hold when σ is constant for all f, f'.

In practice, one often assumes that $\overline{\rho_{ff'}}$ can be approximated by ρ_{TX}^2, using the items of a single test, or via $\rho_{X_1 X_2}$ when scores on two parallel forms of the test administered close together are available. These lead to

$$\widehat{\rho}^2_{T_SS} = \frac{F\widehat{\rho}^2_{TX}}{1 + (F-1)\widehat{\rho}^2_{TX}} \qquad [33]$$

or

$$\rho_{SS'} = \frac{Fr_{X_1X_2}}{1 + (F-1)r_{X_1X_2}}, \qquad [34]$$

which is the Spearman-Brown prophecy formula in its familiar form as seen earlier in formula 30.

The assumptions above that $\overline{\rho^2_{T_fX_f}\sigma^2_{X_f}} = \overline{\rho_{X_fX_{f'}}\sigma_{X_f}\sigma_{X_{f'}}}$ and that $\overline{\rho_{X_fX_{f'}}\sigma_{X_f}\sigma_{X_{f'}}}$ $= \overline{\rho_{X_fX_{f'}}}\,\sigma_{X_f}\sigma_{X_f}$ strongly imply that $\rho^2_{T_fX_f} = \rho_{X_fX_{f'}}$ and $\sigma^2_{X_1} = \sigma^2_{X_2} = \cdots = \sigma^2_{X_F}$ for every f, f'—i.e. that the forms are parallel. However, the averaging procedure probably lessens the effect of violation of those assumptions. As F becomes large, $\overline{\rho_{X_fX_{f'}}\sigma_{X_f}\sigma_{X_{f'}}}$ tends to dominate $\overline{\rho^2_{T_fX_f}\sigma^2_{X_f}}$ in formula 31, which suggests use of formula 33 or 34 in this case.

If the various forms of which the battery consists were administered with time intervals or in such other ways as to make $\rho^2_{T_XX} > \rho_{X_fX_{f'}}$, it will be preferable to use battery-reliability formula 29, rather than one of the formulas in this section. Unless the relationship $\rho^2_{T_XX} = \rho_{X_fX_{f'}}$ holds at least approximately, one is in the more general battery-reliability situation, of which the Spearman-Brown procedure is a very special case. Of course, one can instead use formula 31, which does not involve assumptions about forms being parallel.

For expected reliability as a function of the number of choices per item, see Ebel (1969).

Reliability as stepped-up mean item intercorrelation

If the units of the battery are scores X_{pi} on I single test items, rather than scores on longer tests, it seems hardly sensible to assume that $\sigma_{X_1} = \sigma_{X_2} = \cdots = \sigma_{X_T}$, so one employs formula 32 directly. The usual procedure, mentioned above, is to take as the reliability coefficient of the "typical" item in the test the *intra*class coefficient of correlation,

$$\rho_i = \frac{\overline{\rho_{ij}\sigma_i\sigma_j}}{\overline{\sigma_i\sigma_i}}, \qquad [35]$$

$(i \neq j)$, which is the ratio of the mean item covariance to the mean item variance. (If $\sigma_1 = \sigma_2 = \cdots = \sigma_I$, this reduces to $\overline{\rho_{ij}}$, the mean item intercorrelation.) Usually there will be little difference between this $\rho_{\text{intraclass}}$ and $\overline{\rho_{ij}}$, but the former is preferable because it does not involve the assumption of equal σ_i.

By stepping up ρ_i via the customary Spearman-Brown formula, one secures a lower bound to the one-form reliability coefficient:

$$\rho^2_{T_XX} \geq \frac{F\rho_i}{1 + (F-1)\rho_i}.$$

This can be estimated in several equivalent ways, three of which are the following formula and formulas 36 and 37:

$$\widehat{\rho^2_{T_X X}} = \frac{I \overline{r_{ij}s_i s_j}}{\overline{s_i^2} + (I-1)\overline{r_{ij}s_i s_j}} \cdot$$

$$\widehat{\rho^2_{T_X X}} = \frac{I \left[\dfrac{\sum\limits_{i=1}^{I} \sum\limits_{j=1}^{I} r_{ij}s_i s_j}{I(I-1)} \right]}{\dfrac{\sum\limits_{i=1}^{I} s_i^2}{I} + (I-1)\left[\dfrac{\sum\limits_{i=1}^{I} \sum\limits_{j=1}^{I} r_{ij}s_i s_j}{I(I-1)} \right]}$$

$$= \left(\frac{I}{I-1} \right) \frac{\sum\limits_{i=1}^{I} \sum\limits_{j=1}^{I} r_{ij}s_i s_j}{s^2 \left(\sum\limits_{i=1}^{I} X_i \right)} = \frac{I}{I-1} \left[1 - \frac{\sum\limits_{i=1}^{I} s_i^2}{s^2 \left(\sum\limits_{i=1}^{I} X_i \right)} \right] \qquad [36]$$

(where $i \neq j$), which is *coefficient alpha* (Cronbach, 1951). The s^2 whose subscript is in parentheses is the variance of the examinees' total scores on the test—i.e. of the $(X_{p1}+X_{p2}+ \cdots +X_{pI})$'s. s_i^2 is the variance of scores on the ith item.

If the items are scored just 0 or 1, substitute $p_i q_i$ for s_i^2, where p_i is the proportion of persons who marked the ith item correctly, and $q_i = 1 - p_i$.

In terms of analysis-of-variance (anova) mean squares, the estimated intra-class coefficient of correlation among items, ρ_i, can be written from formula 35 as (see Stanley, 1957a)

$$\hat{\rho}_i = \frac{MS_{\text{persons}} - MS_{(\text{persons}\times\text{items})}}{MS_{\text{persons}} + (I-1)MS_{(\text{persons}\times\text{items})}},$$

because $MS_{\text{persons}} = \overline{s_i^2} + (I-1)\overline{r_{ij}s_i s_j}$, and $MS_{(\text{persons}\times\text{items})} = \overline{s_i^2} - \overline{r_{ij}s_i s_j}$.

Stepping up this $\hat{\rho}_i$ with the Spearman-Brown formula (see formula 33), one secures

$$\widehat{\rho^2_{T_X X}} = \frac{MS_{\text{persons}} - MS_{(\text{persons}\times\text{items})}}{MS_{\text{persons}}} = 1 - \frac{MS_{(\text{persons}\times\text{items})}}{MS_{\text{persons}}} \cdot \qquad [37]$$

This is Hoyt's (1941) formula. $MS_{(\text{persons}\times\text{items})}$ estimates σ_{ex}^2/I, and MS_{persons} estimates σ_X^2/I. $MS_{\text{persons}} - MS_{(\text{persons}\times\text{items})}$ estimates σ_T^2/I. Strictly speaking, the derivation of Hoyt's formula via the intraclass-correlation anova model requires that the I test items of which the test is composed be selected *randomly* from a huge number of such items, which means that successive forms of the test are *randomly* parallel.

It can also be derived, as above, from the non-anova framework, so this condition does not restrict use of formula 37. Unless the items were indeed sampled randomly, however, one is *assuming* that persons do not interact with items, so that $E_I(MS_{\text{persons}\times\text{items}}) = \sigma_{ex}^2/I$. Otherwise, I times this mean square will overestimate the variance of measurement errors unless the items were obtained by random sampling, actual or at least hypothetical. (But see Loevinger, 1965, who objects strongly to the concept of a population of test items.)

Correlation Coefficients Attenuated by Errors of Measurement

Errors of measurement tend to make coefficients of correlation smaller than they would be if the measures correlated were error free. If each person has two scores, X_{pf} and Y_{pg}, obtained from form f of the X measure and form g of the Y measure, what will be the correlation, over persons, of *true* scores on X with true scores on Y? It turns out that this can be expressed in terms of the actual correlation of fallible measures on X with fallible measures on Y and the reliability coefficient for each of the two tests. It is *not* assumed that X and Y measure the same thing; the correlation between true scores on the two tests may vary from -1 to $+1$, inclusive, depending on what X and Y are. As before, analysis begins with the classical true-score model $X_p = T_{Xp} + e_X$ and $Y_p = T_{Yp} + e_X$. Then

$$\rho_{T_X T_Y} = \rho_{(X-e_X)(Y-e_Y)} = \frac{\text{Cov}\,(X - e_X,\ Y - e_Y)}{\sigma_{T_X}\sigma_{T_Y}} = \frac{\text{Cov}\,(X, Y) - 0 - 0 + 0}{\sigma_{T_X}\sigma_{T_Y}}$$

$$= \frac{\rho_{XY}\sigma_X\sigma_Y}{\sigma_{T_X}\sigma_{T_Y}} = \frac{\rho_{XY}}{(\sigma_{T_X}/\sigma_X)(\sigma_{T_Y}/\sigma_Y)} = \frac{\rho_{XY}}{\rho_{T_X X}\rho_{T_Y Y}}$$

$$= \frac{\rho_{XY}}{\sqrt{\rho_{XX'}}\,\sqrt{\rho_{YY'}}}. \qquad\qquad [38]$$

Formula 38 is Spearman's well-known and venerable correction for attenuation (i.e lessening) of correlation coefficients by errors of measurement in one or both of the correlated variables.

Note from formula 38 that, for

$$\rho_{T_X T_Y} \geq 0, \qquad \rho_{XY} = \rho_{T_X T_Y}\rho_{T_X X}\rho_{T_Y Y} = \rho_{T_X T_Y}\sqrt{\rho_{XX'}}\,\sqrt{\rho_{YY'}} \leq \rho_{T_X T_Y}.$$

The reliability coefficients used to estimate $\rho_{T_X T_Y}$ from ρ_{XY} via formula 38 must be suitable estimates of the one-form $\rho_{T_X X}$ and $\rho_{T_Y Y}$, *not* of $\sqrt{\rho_{XX'}}$ and $\sqrt{\rho_{YY'}}$ with instability of true scores between X and X' or Y and Y', because there is no such instability in $\rho_{T_X X} = \rho_{T_X(T_X+e_X)}$ or in $\rho_{T_Y Y} = \rho_{T_Y(T_Y+e_Y)}$. For example, if true scores on X change differentially over time, then $\rho_{T_X X} > \sqrt{\rho_{XX'}}$, and hence then $\sqrt{\rho_{XX'}}$ is not appropriate in formula 38. A concession to practice effect that changes all true scores alike by an added constant $c \lessgtr 0$ can be made, however, because $\rho_{T_X X} = \sqrt{\rho_{X(X'+c)}} = \sqrt{\rho_{T_X+e_X,\ (T_X+c)+e_X'}} = \sigma_{T_X}/\sigma_X$.

The correction for attenuation has been computed with inappropriate reliability-coefficient estimates in the denominator so often that researchers have become suspicious of "corrected" r's. However, if appropriate care is taken, formula 38 can provide crucially important estimates of the maximum correlation that can be obtained between X and Y, no matter how error free each is made. For specific uses of the correction for attenuation see chapter 14; there Cronbach argues that correction for attenuation is essential in arriving at scientifically valid statements of relationship (also see Cureton, 1970; Lord, 1957; Porter, 1967; Stanley, 1961; Livingston & Stanley, 1970; Norman, 1967).

How an Increase in Reliability Affects Validity

From formula 33 it was clear that lengthening a test by adding comparable items increases its reliability. How does this affect its correlation with other variables? Because $\rho_{T_X T_Y} = \rho_{(cT_X)(dT_Y)}$ (where c and d are positive constants), the correlation between true scores on two variables is the same for the shorter and the longer versions of the tests. Therefore, via formula 38 one can write $\rho_{XY} = \rho_{T_X T_Y} \rho_{T_X X} \rho_{T_Y Y}$ and $\rho_{xy} = \rho_{T_X T_Y} \rho_{T_x x} \rho_{T_y y}$, where the lower-case subscripts designate the less reliable tests. Divide the first equation by the second, obtaining $\rho_{XY}/\rho_{xy} = \rho_{T_X X} \rho_{T_Y Y}/\rho_{T_x x} \rho_{T_y y}$, which can be written as $\rho_{XY} = \rho_{xy}(\rho_{T_X X} \rho_{T_Y Y}/\rho_{T_x x} \rho_{T_y y})$.

For instance, if $\rho_{xy} = .50$, $\rho_{T_X X} = .80$, $\rho_{T_Y Y} = .90$, $\rho_{T_x x} = .70$, and $\rho_{T_y y} = .80$, then $\rho_{XY} = .50[(.80)(.90)/(.70)(.80)] = .50(1.286) = .64$. But this is a rather extreme example, because the reliability coefficient of one measure jumped from $(.70)^2 = .49$ to $(.80)^2 = .64$, and of the other from .64 to .81. To go from .64 to .81 requires an increase in test length of 140 percent, because via the Spearman-Brown formula $.81 = F(.64)/[1+(F-1).64]$, and therefore $F = 2.40$. Moderate changes in the reliability of a variable affect its correlation with another variable only slightly.

β_{YX} Corrected for Attenuation

It is simple to show how the slope coefficient β_{YX} is affected by random errors of measurement: $\beta_{T_Y T_X} = \sigma_{T_X T_Y}/\sigma_{T_X}^2 = \sigma_{(X-e_X)(Y-e_Y)}/\sigma_{T_X}^2 = \sigma_{XY}/\rho_{T_X X}^2 \sigma_X^2 = \beta_{YX}/\rho_{T_X X}^2$. Because $0 \leq \rho_{T_X X}^2 \leq 1$, β_{YX} will be closer to zero than will $\beta_{T_Y T_X}$ unless the X-measures are error-free. β_{YX} is not affected by errors of measurement in the Y variable.

Other statistics such as η_{YX}^2, the correlation ratio, can also be corrected for the influence of errors of measurement. See Cochran (1968 and 1970).

Battery Reliability for Weighted Subtests

A test battery is composed of several subtests, each of which measures an ability, trait, or characteristic somewhat different from that measured by the other subtests. When a total score for the battery is secured by computing a weighted sum of the subtest scores of an examinee, it is desirable to estimate the reliability coefficient of the composite scores to ascertain how they would fluctuate on a second testing. This coefficient can be derived by a slight extension of the correlation-of-sums approach utilized in formula 29. In fact, from the formula for the reliability coefficient of a weighted composite, a number of the formulas already derived can be deduced readily as special cases.

Let X_{ps} be the score (X) of the pth person $(p = 1, 2, \cdots, P, \cdots, \infty)$ on the sth subtest $(s = 1, 2, \cdots, S)$. Let w_s be the multiplicative weight for scores on the sth subtest, and c_s be the additive constant for that subtest, so that the pth person has the composite score $B_p = (w_1 X_{p1} + c_1) + (w_2 X_{p2} + c_2) + \cdots + (w_S X_{pS} + c_S)$. All S of the additive constants can be summed into a single constant, $c_1 + c_2 + \cdots + c_S$. which does not affect the covariance or the correlation of the composite scores with any other set of scores and can therefore be ignored. The w's may be regression coefficients yielding the best-weighted composite of the X's for predicting a criterion, or they may be other weights such as the variance-equating z score transformation

$$\xi_{X_{ps}} = \frac{X_{ps} - \mu_{X_{*s}}}{\sigma_{X_{*s}}} = \frac{1}{\sigma_{X_{*s}}} X_{ps} - \frac{\mu_{X_{*s}}}{\sigma_{X_{*s}}},$$

where $1/\sigma_{X_{*s}} = w_s$, and $-(\mu_{X_{*s}}/\sigma_{X_{*s}}) = c_s$. More commonly, of course, all the weights are unity.

Now consider that for the sth subtest there is a *parallel* subtest taken at another time in a battery that is parallel, subtest by subtest, with the initial battery, with $s = 1, 2, \cdots, S$ matched, subtest by subtest, with $s' = 1', 2', \cdots, S'$, where $S = S'$. Subtest 1 has, in the other battery, a parallel subtest $1'$, subtest 2 has a parallel subtest $2'$, etc.; $w_s = w_{s'}$ for all $s = s'$. Then by the usual formula for the correlation of sums the following formula is secured:[16]

$$\rho_{BB'} = \rho_{(w_1 X_{*_1} + w_2 X_{*_2} + \ldots + w_S X_{*_S})(w_{1'} X_{*_{1'}} + w_{2'} X_{*_{2'}} + \ldots + w_{S'} X_{*_{S'}})}$$

$$= \frac{\displaystyle\sum_{s=1}^{S} \sum_{s'=1'}^{S'} w_s w_{s'} \, \mathrm{Cov}(X_s, X_{s'})}{\displaystyle\sum_{s=1}^{S} w_s^2 \sigma_{X_s}^2 + \sum_{s=1}^{S} \sum_{t=1}^{S} w_s w_t \, \mathrm{Cov}(X_s, X_t)}$$

(where $s \neq t$, the tth subtest in a battery being any subtest other than the sth)

$$= \frac{\displaystyle\sum_{s=1}^{S} w_s w_{(s'=s)} \, \mathrm{Cov}[X_s, X_{(s'=s)}] + \sum_{s=1}^{S} \sum_{(s' \neq s)=1}^{S} w_s w_{(s' \neq s)} \, \mathrm{Cov}[X_s, X_{(s' \neq s)}]}{\displaystyle\sum_{s=1}^{S} w_s^2 \sigma_{X_s}^2 + \sum_{s=1}^{S} \sum_{t=1}^{S} w_s w_t \, \mathrm{Cov}(X_s, X_t)}$$

$$= \frac{\displaystyle\sum_{s=1}^{S} w_s^2 \rho_{X_s, X_{(s'=s)}} \sigma_{X_s}^2 + \sum_{s=1}^{S} \sum_{(s' \neq s)=1}^{S} w_s w_{(s' \neq s)} \rho_{X_s X_{(s' \neq s)}} \sigma_{X_s} \sigma_{X_{(s' \neq s)}}}{\displaystyle\sum_{s=1}^{S} w_s^2 \sigma_{X_s}^2 + \sum_{s=1}^{S} \sum_{t=1}^{S} w_s w_t \rho_{X_s X_t} \sigma_{X_s} \sigma_{X_t}} . \qquad [39]$$

When each weight is the reciprocal of the corresponding standard deviation (i.e. $w_s = 1/\sigma_{X_s}$), as when the X's are standard scores, each weight cancels out the corresponding σ, and so formula 39 simplifies to

$$\rho_{BB'} = \rho_{\left(\dfrac{X_{*_1}}{\sigma_{X_{*_1}}} + \cdots + \dfrac{X_{*_S}}{\sigma_{X_{*_S}}}\right)\left(\dfrac{X_{*_{1'}}}{\sigma_{X_{*_{1'}}}} + \cdots + \dfrac{X_{*_{S'}}}{\sigma_{X_{*_{S'}}}}\right)} \qquad [40]$$

$$= \frac{\displaystyle\sum_{s=1}^{S} \rho_{X_s X_{(s'=s)}} + \sum_{s=1}^{S} \sum_{(s' \neq s)=1}^{S} \rho_{X_s X_{(s' \neq s)}}}{S + \displaystyle\sum_{s=1}^{S} \sum_{t=1}^{S} \rho_{X_s X_t}} .$$

Formula 40 indicates that the reliability coefficient of a battery of S subtests, *for each of which the variance is one*, consists of the sum of the reliability coefficients of the S subtests, plus the sum of the $S(S-1)$ correlation coefficients between noncomparable subtests across batteries, divided by the number of subtests in the battery plus twice the sum of the $S(S-1)/2$ possibly different within-battery correlation

---

[16] The procedure can be facilitated and mistakes avoided by using three pooling squares. As row headings for the first square write $w_1 X_{p1}, w_2 X_{p2}, \cdots, w_S X_{pS}$. As column headings for the first square write $w_{1'} X_{p1'}, w_{2'} X_{p2'}, \cdots, w_{S'} X_{pS'}$. Then fill in the S times S' cells of the square. Those entries will indicate the cross-battery covariances. For within-battery covariances, label the rows and the columns of one table $w_1 X_{p1}, w_2 X_{p2}, \cdots, w_S X_{pS}$, and the rows and columns of another table $w_{1'} X_{p1'}, w_{2'} X_{p2'}, \cdots, w_{S'} X_{pS'}$. In the present case the two batteries are parallel, subtest by subtest, so only one of the *within*-battery pooling squares is needed.

coefficients. Clearly, this battery reliability coefficient will be one if every subtest is perfectly reliable and the sum of the across-battery correlation coefficients equals the sum of the within-battery correlation coefficients. Usually, across-battery r's will be smaller, on the average, than within-battery r's, particularly if an appreciable time interval separates the administration of the two batteries, because of instability of the measured characteristics across time.

If the S subtests intercorrelate zero, both across and within batteries, formula 40 reduces to the mean of the reliability coefficients, which can take values from zero through one. This situation occurs when there are S orthogonal factor scores for each examinee and each set of factor scores has unit variance.

When the weights do not disappear, as they do in formula 40, one works with formula 39 to take them (and the variances) into account. Of course, it is not appropriate to use formula 40 unless the weights actually are reciprocals of the corresponding standard deviations.

Note closely that formulas 39 and 40 both require an actual measurement "experiment" involving the administration of two strictly comparable batteries under comparable conditions with the desired time interval between the administrations. Rarely is this done, except during the standardization of test batteries by commercial publishers, and yet it is quite important. For example, how reliable is a Wechsler full-scale IQ over a two-week interval? This full-scale IQ is based on standard scores from about a dozen subtests, approximately half of which are summed to yield a verbal IQ and the other half to yield a performance IQ. Given the data required by formula 39, based on the group of persons and the time interval to which one wishes to generalize, computing three battery reliability coefficients—for verbal IQ, performance IQ, and total IQ—becomes straightforward.

Of course, *it is unnecessary to use formulas 39 or 40 when one actually has two comparable sets of composite scores*, because then one merely correlates them directly to secure the desired reliability coefficient. Formulas 39 and 40 are useful primarily for estimating the reliability coefficient of a weighted composite *at one point in time*, knowing the one-form reliabilities and the intercorrelations of the components at that one time.

These procedures also are useful for multiple-regression prediction purposes, where the predictor weights are secured statistically to minimize the squared errors of estimate in the sample. Typically, such weights will differ systematically from one group, such as freshman women at routine colleges, to another, such as freshman women in highly selective colleges, so the battery-reliability-coefficient formulas are needed. The tests used for predictive purposes may be so different from each other that no one would term them a "battery" except in the optimally-weighted-for-best-prediction sense. With the advent of fast, easy computation by electronic computer, there will probably be less a priori weighting of tests in a battery henceforth, and more statistical weighting for predictive purposes. The sampling stability of multiple-regression weights and of the multiple-correlation coefficient, topics discussed in many intermediate statistics textbooks, are not considered here.

Weighting also affects variance errors of measurement, of course, but the usual formula, $\sigma^2_{\text{meas}} = (\text{variance of obtained scores})(1 - \text{reliability coefficient})$, holds for batteries if one uses the variance and reliability coefficient for the composite scores. In a simple case, multiplying every score in a distribution by a constant multiplies both the true scores and the errors of measurement by that constant: $w_f X_{pf} = w_f(T_p + e_{pf}) = w_f T_p + w_f e_{pf}$. Then one has

$$\sigma^2_{w_f X_{*f}} = w_f^2 \sigma^2_{X_{*f}} = w_f^2 \sigma^2_{T_*} + w_f^2 \sigma^2_{e_{*f}} + w_f^2 [\text{Cov}(T_*, e_{*f}) = 0]$$

$$= w_f^2 \sigma^2_{T_*} + w_f^2 \sigma^2_{e_{*f}}.$$

Because obtained scores, true scores, and errors of measurement are kept on the same multiplicative scale by the common weight, the reliability coefficient of the form is not affected. Additive constants make no difference even in the variances. However, because multiplicative constants differing from test to test affect the variances differently from test to test, their influence on the reliability of composite scores cannot be ignored, as was seen in formula 39.

For a thorough review of weighting, see Darlington (1968). Stanley and Wang (1970) and Wang and Stanley (1970) review studies which show that differential weighting of test-*item* scores is quite unlikely to improve the reliability or validity of resulting test scores. However, they indicate several ways in which differential weighting of the *options* will probably improve the reliability of the test somewhat and perhaps its validity also. See Hendrickson (1970), who weighted the options of items on the Scholastic Aptitude Test differentially. For cross validation of mul-tiple-regression weights, see Herzberg (1969). Cronbach and Gleser (1965) discuss work, especially by Horst and MacEwan (1956, 1957) and Horst (1956), on optimal test length for several predictive purposes.

Ways to Estimate Reliability Coefficients

During most of the preceding discussion, reliability coefficients based on two comparable forms of a test were used. Where the basic one-form reliability coefficient was defined (see formula 9) as $\rho^2_{T_* X_{*f}} = \sigma^2_{T_*} / \sigma^2_{X_{*f}}$, no methods for actually computing it were offered. Such methods are of three main types: (*a*) test-retest with the same form, (*b*) splitting of one form into two forms, and (*c*) utilizing the variances and intercorrelations of the items of the form. (Method *c* was mentioned above; see formulas 36 and 37.) Each of these is considered in turn. First, however, it is helpful to relate briefly *two*-form reliability determination to the sources of variance of table 13.1.

Reliability via parallel test forms

Since the formal definition of reliability has been phrased in terms of the correlation between parallel sets of measures, it seems obvious that the procedure for reliability determination which makes use of parallel forms will measure up to logical requirements. This is in fact true, provided satisfactory procedures for preparing parallel tests can be established. This is a problem in the logic and practice of test construction and in the definition of the universe of items, testers, occasions, etc., that is to be sampled. (This latter "universe" consideration for actual testing situations will be discussed later. See Cronbach et al., 1970, in press.)

In preparing parallel test forms, there is danger, on the one hand, that the two tests will vary so much in content and format that each will have substantial specific variance (category II.A) distinct from the other, in which case the correlation between the two will underestimate the desired reliability. There is the reverse danger that the two forms may overlap to such an extent in specific details of content that variance due to specific sampling of content (category II.B) may be common to the two tests. In that case, this variance will be treated as systematic rather than chance variance, and the obtained correlation will over-estimate the independent-forms reliability.

The best guarantee of parallelism for two test forms would seem to be that a complete and detailed set of specifications for the test be prepared in advance of any final test construction. The set of specifications should indicate item types, difficulty level of items, procedures and standards for item selection and refinement, and distribution of items with regard to the content to be covered, specified in as much detail as seems feasible. If each test form is then built to conform to the outline, while at the same time care is taken to avoid identity or detailed overlapping of content, the two resulting test forms should be truly comparable. That is, each test must be built to the specifications, but within the limits set by complete specifications each test should present a random sampling of items. In terms of the practical operations of test construction, it will often be efficient to assemble two parallel test forms from a single pool of items that have been given preliminary tryout. Within the total test if the test is homogeneous in the character of its content, or within parallel homogeneous sections of a heterogeneous test, items from the pool should be assigned to the two forms in such a way as to give the same distribution of item difficulties and the same distribution of item-test correlations in each form. Random sampling within defined strata seems a desirable way to create the forms.

Two tests constructed in the above way will treat as systematic variance that variance in categories I and II.A of table 13.1. They will treat as error variance that in categories II.B, IV.B, and VI. The allocation of variance in categories III and IV.A will depend upon the time interval between the administration of the two forms. If they are given in immediate sequence, this last variance will be treated as systematic variance; if some time intervenes between the testings, this variance will be allocated to error. For many uses of the resulting statistic, it will probably be more meaningful to let some time elapse between the two testings, thus treating temporary day-to-day fluctuations as errors of measurement. The question arises as to how long an interval should elapse. For most purposes, the answer to this lies in the thought that it is day-to-day fluctuations that it is desirable to allocate to error. An interval of a few days or weeks usually would appear sufficient. With longer intervals the problem of genuine growth and change in the individual is encountered, and the coefficient may be lowered because of these changes. Of course, for some purposes interest may be in consistency of performance over an extended period of time, but consistency of this type represents a rather different concept of reliability.

In most of the usual types of tests of ability or achievement, preparing parallel forms should not present undue difficulty. There are some situations, however, in which parallelism will be difficult to achieve. This is true when either (a) the test task is quite unusual or (b) a single exposure to the test changes the individual to such an extent that he is really a different individual at the second exposure. The former case may occasionally arise in connection with unusual problem-type tasks, particularly of the "gestalt" variety. The second case is the more common source of difficulty. In any task that is sufficiently novel so that the experience of being tested adds a significant increment to the individual's practice with the task, he is a somewhat different individual at the time of a subsequent test. In novel or insight tasks, or in tasks that present essentially a learning situation, the changes may be quite marked. The problem of defining reliability for such a changing function is a difficult one, and no completely satisfactory solution seems available.

In an operational sense, the reliability of tests constructed with any degree of care whatsoever can be assessed. No one is debarred from investigating test reliability just because the tests were prepared without elaborate specifications. It is true that the closer one comes to complete specifications the higher the reliability will be, but by specifying more narrowly one constrains the universe, perhaps unduly for the extent of generalizability desired.

Reliability via repetition of the identical test form

In some cases, obtaining two parallel measures will reduce to repetition of identically the same measuring instrument, the only difference being the time at which it is administered and perhaps the person by whom it is administered. For instance, two parallel measures of weight could be obtained by weighing the members of the group being studied on the same scales at two times a day apart. The same situation would hold for almost any physiological or anatomical measurement. In these cases, the problem of sampling items from a larger universe of behavior is not encountered, and so distinct equivalent test forms are neither meaningful nor possible. Parallelism in this case results from identity of measuring instrument and procedure.

There are also certain behavioral measures in which the situation of sampling from a large universe of different tasks does not arise. This is the case in simple repetitive tasks of motor speed and skill or of perceptual judgment. Thus, in a test of simple reaction time, in which a measurement of the individual is obtained by timing repeatedly his simple reaction to some stimulus, the test task is so defined that no varied sampling from a more extensive universe of behavior is involved. (One is, of course, sampling from the examinee's stream of consciousness, internal mental sets, electrical noise, minute aspects of the physical equipment, etc.) Here, again, repetition of the same test provides the meaningful definition of *parallel measures*. The same would tend to be true of the type of perceptual judgment that is involved in the simple psychophysical experiment, as with judgments of brightness, length, weight, and so forth. In all these cases, repetition of the test appears to provide an acceptable procedure for reliability determination.

Very likely, these cases are not different in principle from psychological measurement. What makes them *seem* qualitatively different is the present more thorough understanding of, for example, the theory of gravitation and the related technologies. In measuring weight, there is a well-developed theory that explicitly specifies the "domain" of parallel indicators and delineates which parameters and boundary conditions are germane and which are irrelevant. Consider, for instance, using a bathroom scale to weigh astronauts on the moon as well as on earth, or a pan balance to weigh feathers in a drafty room, or a butcher's scale to weigh fluid masses that overlap the pan, or the effects of rusty springs, tilted pans, or blunt knife edges on various "scales." Apparently, it is simply that theory of mass and gravitation and physical technologies are sufficiently explicit and complete to permit "weighing" most *ordinary* objects to whatever degree of precision one is willing to pay for in money and effort. This seems simply a matter of degree, not of kind, and becomes obvious when one considers weighing a star, subatomic particle, or cloud.

In most measures of intellect, temperament, or achievement, however, repetition of the same test form and correlation of the two sets of scores is at present less defensible as an operation for determining reliability than it is for physical measurement. In these cases, a particular test consists of a limited sample from a much larger universe of rather diverse possible items. The test score has practical significance insofar as it is representative of the individual's ability to respond to all of the tasks in the universe which it undertakes to sample. Reliability is a matter of the adequacy of the sampling of items as well as the consistency of behavior of each individual.

In other words, in this case sampling of items (category II.B) is an appreciable source of variance. Practical usefulness for the result dictates that this variance be treated as error variance in determining the reliability of the test. Repeating the same test form holds the sampling of items constant so that this factor is treated as systematic rather than error variance. Reliability coefficients calculated from a repetition of the same test may be expected to be higher than those based upon different forms to the extent that variance associated with sampling of items is a factor. This type of consideration is related to content and construct validity—see chapter 14.

A second possible difficulty with repetition of the same test, which may or may not be important in any given case, is actual memory of particular items and of the previous response to them. Insofar as this memory is effective in leading the individual to repeat the same response he made the time before, the results on two test administrations tend to be abnormally alike. The same answers may be repeated not because the individual is consistent in his behavior and arrives at the same conclusion in the same way, but because he happens to remember his previous response. In effect, some of the variance associated with momentary memories and chance choices (categories IV.B and VI.) becomes common to the two testings and is treated as systematic variance. Memory of previous responses is likely to be a factor in proportion as (a) the test is short, (b) the test items are distinctive and easily remembered, and (c) the interval between testings is short.

Another element that should be considered in deciding whether a repeated test is parallel to the original test is the attitude of the person tested. Especially where a test is quite long, as is the case with some interest and personality inventories, for example, repetition may be tedious for the subject, and he therefore may give more haphazard responses. This would, of course, operate to lower the correlation between the two testings. If a test score is likely to be greatly affected by motivation, as when the test requires very rapid or very concentrated work, it is especially important that the subject should feel that both testings will have equal significance for him. If one were to retest a group of men who had been accepted for training as computer programmers, for example, and correlate these scores with scores earned during the initial selection period, before the men were sure of being accepted, the changed motivational conditions might well reduce the correlation and yield an underestimate of reliability. This matter of changed attitude and motivation also could affect a retest with a presumably parallel form of the test but is probably likely to be most acute when the same test form is repeated.

Sometimes it is possible to rearrange the order of the items and/or the item options in order to break memory sets when the form is readministered. One device might be to randomize the order of the options for each item each time the test is administered and also to randomize the order of the items if there is no sharp difficulty gradient. Randomizing the order of options would often be feasible for both ability and self-report tests (e.g. intelligence and personality), whereas randomizing the order of items would tend to be more justifiable for self-report devices than for ability tests. Item order would be randomized separately within each sub-test. Computer techniques give promise of making such randomizing operationally feasible.

In summary, for those types of tests in which sampling of items and memory of previous responses are not an issue and for which reasonable comparability of motivation seems likely, a second application of the same test at a later date and correlation of the two sets of scores provide an adequate set of operations for reliability estimation. In the many other cases, however, in which the factors of sampling and memory are significant sources of variance, repetition of the same test form will yield an estimate of reliability which tends to be systematically too high. In these latter cases the procedure is to be avoided. The correlation also will be unrepresentative, and probably too low, if the attitude of the subject changes from one testing to the other.

Reliability via subdivision of single total test

The preparation and administration of two equivalent test forms, though often satisfactory as a procedure for estimating reliability, present certain practical difficulties. These center around the problems of the time and labor involved both in the construction and the administration of two complete test forms. If only a single form of a test is needed for the research or practical use to which the test is to be put, it often seems unduly burdensome to prepare two separate tests merely in order to obtain an estimate of reliability. Furthermore, when a test is developed and administered as part of a research project, time for the administration of an equivalent form of the test is often not conveniently available. In the interests of economy it becomes desirable to set up procedures for extracting an estimate of reliability from a single administration of a single test. One group of such procedures subdivides the total test artificially into two half-length tests and correlates the scores on those. This coefficient of correlation estimates the reliability, say r_{ab}, not of the full test, but of a test only half as long. The reliability of the full test must be estimated by the use of the Spearman-Brown formula $2r_{ab}/(1+r_{ab})$. The second group of procedures is based essentially on the analysis of variance of the examinee-by-item scores. The procedures for subdividing the test will be considered in this section, and the next section will be devoted to procedures based upon analysis of the item variances and covariances.

Constructing half-tests

If a test is composed of $2n$ separate items or parts, there are $(2n)!/2(n!)^2$ ways in which two subtests, each composed of n items, can be assembled from it.[17] Certain procedures have been proposed for selection from among these possible sets of sub-tests, either on logical grounds or on grounds of convenience. The more usual procedures include: (a) selecting for the two half-tests sets of items that appear equivalent in content and difficulty, (b) putting alternate items or trials into each half-test, such as odd-numbered items into one half-test and even-numbered items into the other, or (c) putting alternate groups of items or trials into each half-test.

---

[17] For example, a two-item test can be subdivided into two half-tests of one item each in just one way: $(2 \cdot 1)/(2 \cdot 1 \cdot 1) = 1$. If there are the four items $a, b, c,$ and d, they can be divided in three ways as follows: a and b vs. c and d; a and c vs. b and d; a and d vs. b and c. Check: $4!/2(2!)(2!)$ $=(4 \cdot 3 \cdot 2 \cdot 1)/2(2 \cdot 1)(2 \cdot 1) = 3$. The number of possible ways rises rapidly. For a ten-item test it is 126.

The specific merits of each of these three procedures were considered in detail by Thorndike (1951, pp. 580–586) in the previous edition of this book, which should be consulted by those readers interested in specific applications of "split-half" reliability. Because such procedures have, in many instances, been superseded by uses of item variances and covariances that do not involve splitting (for the background and rationale, see Cronbach, 1951), in this edition most of the details of split-half reliability, interesting though they are, are omitted.

A cautionary note is in order, however. Where several items refer to the *same* unit (e.g. reading passage, graph, or table), the group of items in this unit rather than the individual items should be the basis for split-halving or other internal-consistency determination. Experimental independence is critical for such analysis. For example, if a 40-item test consists of 10 paragraphs and 4 items refer to each paragraph, there are just 10 (not 40) units to be split-halved or analyzed by the Hoyt (1941) or coefficient alpha (Cronbach, 1951) procedure. The test is composed of 10 experimentally independent strata, within each of which 4 items are "nested." Correlation among items within strata will probably be higher than among items across strata.

Errors of Measurement and Reliability of Split-Halved Tests

It was seen on pages 370 and 380 that the half-test correlation, r_{ab}, can be multiplied by 2 and divided by (1+itself) to yield an estimate of $\rho_{ff'}$, the reliability coefficient of the whole test. This is the simplest version of the Spearman-Brown prophecy formula, with $F=2$; see formula 30. One can consider the matter somewhat more fundamentally through an extension of the classical test-theory model, modifying formula 2 ($X_{pf}=T_p+e_{pf}$) as follows:

$$X_{pa} = T_{pa} + e_{pa} \quad \text{and} \quad X_{pb} = (T_{pa} + c) + e_{pb}, \qquad [41]$$

X_{pa} and X_{pb} being the obtained scores on halves a and b of the test. The true score on half b is assumed to differ from the true score on half a by a constant, c, the same for all persons tested. That is, the difficulty of the halves may not be identical, but they measure the same thing such that $2T_{pa}+c=T_p$. The half-test errors of measurement are assumed uncorrelated with each other and with the true scores. Also, $e_{pa}+e_{pb}=e_{pf}$, and $X_{pa}+X_{pb}=X_{pf}$.

Now consider the variance of the differences between each person's obtained half-scores, over all persons:

$$\sigma^2_{(X_{*a}-X_{*b})} = \sigma^2_{[(T_a+e_a)-(T_a+c+e_b)]} = \sigma^2_{(e_a-e_b-c)}$$
$$= \sigma^2_{(e_a-e_b)} = \sigma^2_{(e_a+e_b)} = \sigma^2_{e_{*f}},$$

because the constant, c, does not affect the variance, and the variance of the difference between uncorrelated measures is equal to the variance of their sum. Thus, with the model shown in formula 41, the variance of the difference between obtained half-test scores is directly the error variance for the *whole*-sum scores, with no assumption that the variance of the X_{pa}'s in the population of persons is equal to the variance of the X_{pb}'s. In other words, although the variance of the T_{pa}'s must equal that of the $(T_{pa}+c)$'s, there is no assumption made that $\sigma^2_{e_a}=\sigma^2_{e_b}$. Compare this procedure with the similar one which led to formula 15 for whole forms.

Note that $\sigma^2_{X_{*f}}=\sigma^2_{(X_{*a}+X_{*b})}$, the variance of the sum of the half-test scores. Thus the reliability coefficient for the whole-test scores may be written as

$$\rho^2_{T_*X_{*f}} = \frac{\sigma^2_T}{\sigma^2_{X_f}} = 1 - \frac{\sigma^2_{ef}}{\sigma^2_{X_f}} = 1 - \frac{\sigma^2_{(X_a-X_b)}}{\sigma^2_{(X_a+X_b)}}$$

$$= 1 - \frac{\sigma^2_a + \sigma^2_b - 2\rho_{ab}\sigma_a\sigma_b}{\sigma^2_a + \sigma^2_b + 2\rho_{ab}\sigma_a\sigma_b} = \frac{4\rho_{ab}\sigma_a\sigma_b}{\sigma^2_f}, \qquad [42]$$

for which a convenient computing version is $1 - s^2_{(X_a - X_b)}/s^2_X$. The simple Spearman-Brown formula was *not* used in this derivation, but one can generate it quickly from the next-to-last step in the derivation by assuming that $\sigma^2_{X_a} = \sigma^2_{X_b}$.

One obtains the correlation coefficient between the two sets of half-test scores, the two standard deviations, and the one variance needed to enter formula 42, works directly with half-test-score differences and sums, or obtains the correlation coefficient and uses it in the Spearman-Brown formula, formula 30, with $F = 2$. Unless the half-test-score variances are substantially different, which they probably will not be if a reasonably long test was split longitudinally (i.e by taking items for each half all through it, instead of, say, the first half versus the second half), the formulas tend to yield nearly the same result.

Devising algebraically equivalent versions of formula 42 has been a favorite office game of psychometricians. See Thorndike (1951, p. 581) for three others. The last three formulas in 42 were presented by Rulon and Flanagan (see Rulon, 1939).

One-Form Reliability, without Repeating or Splitting

Any procedure for subdividing a total test into a particular two halves must be chosen somewhat arbitrarily from among the very large number of possible ways of making that subdivision. With this problem of choice in mind, several psychometricians have developed procedures to make use of all the variance and covariance information about consistency of performance from item to item within a single form of a test and thus provide a unique estimate of internal equivalence. The first such published development was by Kuder and Richardson (1937; also see Richardson & Kuder, 1939). Other, but equivalent, derivations of the most generally useful formula, KR20, were carried out subsequently by Jackson and Ferguson (1941) and others. A version not confined to 0, 1 scoring was devised via the analysis of variance by Hoyt (1941). See Cronbach (1951), Novick and Lewis (1967), and Stanley (1957a) for later developments.

This approach yields a type of reliability estimate analogous to those obtained from subdividing a test into half-tests and has many of the same characteristics and limitations. Implicit in the method and in the split-half approach is *the assumption that the examinee had an opportunity to consider each item.* Item characteristics such as item difficulty, item variance, and item intercorrelations may have their meanings distorted when an appreciable percentage of the group has not had time to attempt the item. Though there may be deliberately omitted (i.e. intentionally not marked) items, there should not be many "not reached" items. Consistency of performance cannot be evaluated unless the subject had an opportunity to perform. More generally, experimental independence of the various items is required.

Analysis of the consistency between items or trials of a test provides an estimate of consistency *at a specific time*. The temporary factors that were grouped in categories III and IV.A of table 13.1 remain relatively constant for each individual during a single test period and are, therefore, considered as systematic rather than error variance. No estimate of the day-to-day consistency of the individual is possible with these procedures.

This type of one-form reliability coefficient can be derived via the correlation of sums, as in formula 29, with the modification that items rather than test forms are the elements of the test "battery" (i.e. of the test form itself). Let X_{pif} be the score (X) of the pth person $(p = 1, 2, \ldots, P, \ldots, \infty)$ on the ith item $(i = 1, 2, \ldots, I)$ of the fth form of the test (here, just two forms, the fth and g^{th} are considered). Thus for each person there are two sets of item scores, $X_{pf} = X_{p1f} + X_{p2f} + \ldots + X_{pIf}$ and $X_{pg} = X_{p1g} + X_{p2g} + \ldots + X_{pIg}$, where X_{pif}'s are actual and the X_{pig}'s are hypothetical. Then the desired coefficient is obtained via correlation of the X_{pf}'s with the X_{pg}'s, together with assumptions to define forms f and g as being parallel:

$$\rho_{X_{*f}X_{*g}} = \rho_{(X_{1f} + \cdots + X_{If}, X_{1g} + \cdots + X_{Ig})}$$

$$= \frac{\text{Cov}(X_{1f} + \cdots + X_{If}, X_{1g} + \cdots + X_{Ig})}{\sigma_{(X_{1f} + \cdots + X_{If})}\sigma_{(X_{1g} + \cdots + X_{Ig})}}$$

$$= \frac{\displaystyle\sum_{i=1}^{I}\sum_{i'=1}^{I}\text{Cov}(X_{if}, X_{i'g})}{\sqrt{\displaystyle\sum_{i=1}^{I}\sigma_{X_{if}}^2 + \sum_{i=1}^{I}\sum_{j=1}^{I}\text{Cov}(X_{if}, X_{jf})}\sqrt{\displaystyle\sum_{i=1}^{I}\sigma_{X_{ig}}^2 + \sum_{i=1}^{I}\sum_{j=1}^{I}\text{Cov}(X_{ig}, X_{jg})}} \quad (i \neq j)$$

$$= \frac{I^2\overline{\text{Cov}(X_{if}, X_{i'g})}}{\sqrt{I\sigma_{X_{.f}}^2 + I(I-1)\overline{\text{Cov}(X_{if}, X_{jf})}}\sqrt{I\sigma_{X_{.g}}^2 + I(I-1)\overline{\text{Cov}(X_{ig}, X_{jg})}}}. \qquad [43]$$

$\rho_{X_{*f}X_{*g}}$ via formula 43 is estimable from the data for two forms of a test, but it is not yet a reliability coefficient, because nothing has been done to make forms f and g parallel. By *parallel* is meant that $X_{pf} = T_p + e_{pf}$, $X_{pg} = T_p + e_{pg}$, and $\sigma_{e_{*f}}^2 = \sigma_{e_{*g}}^2$, so that automatically $\sigma_{X_{*f}}^2 = \sigma_{X_{*g}}^2$. (It could have been required merely that $X_{pg} = (T_p + c_g) + e_{pg}$, where c_g is constant for each person on form g, but this would permit the mean of one form to differ from that of another and cause difficulties in estimating true scores. In the randomly parallel-form case, which Lord & Novick, 1968, treat, the $\mu_{X_{*f}}$'s do differ from form to form.)

Coefficient alpha

Making the obtained-score variances equal for the two forms simplifies the denominator of formula 43. If it is assumed further that the mean covariance across forms in the numerator of the formula equals the mean within-form covariance in the denominator of the formula,[18] the following version emerges:

$$\rho_{X_{*f}X_{*g}} = \frac{I^2\overline{\text{Cov}(X_{if}, X_{jf})}}{\sigma_{X_f}^2} = \frac{I^2\dfrac{\displaystyle\sum_{i=1}^{I}\sum_{j=1}^{I}\text{Cov}(X_{if}, X_{jf})}{I(I-1)}}{\sigma_{X_f}^2}$$

---

[18] This assumption is reasonable *if* the items within the test are factorially homogeneous, a rather important "if." Thus, the formula is not appropriate if single items (or small groups of items) have appreciable unique variance that is reproduced in the parallel items of the other form. When the test is "lumpy" and the item clusters are identifiable, the test should be treated as stratified or as a battery of subtests in order to ascertain reliability. See Cronbach (1951) and the section on battery reliability in this chapter.

$$= \frac{I}{I-1}\left[\frac{\sum_{i=1}^{I}\sum_{j=1}^{I}\mathrm{Cov}(X_{if}, X_{jf})}{\sigma^2_{X_f}}\right]. \qquad (i \neq j) \qquad [44]$$

Formula 44 is more general than the corresponding KR20 coefficient (Kuder & Richardson, 1937), which applies only to items scored one if correct and zero otherwise (whether marked incorrectly, omitted, or not reached), because it permits any kind of scoring, including the dichotomous zero-or-one item scores. As will be seen later, it is equivalent to Hoyt's (1941) coefficient, of which KR20 is also a special case for dichotomous scoring of items, and to coefficient α (Cronbach, 1951). Formula 44 would be tedious to use, however, because it involves the $I(I-1)/2$ possibly different item covariances, which number, for a 25-item test, $25(24)/2 = 300$. An electronic computer could provide the sum of the covariances quickly and perhaps inexpensively, but it is possible to require instead simply the sum of the I item variances by noting that

$$\sigma^2_{X_f} = \sum_{i=1}^{I}\sigma^2_{X_{if}} + \sum_{i=1}^{I}\sum_{j=1}^{I}\mathrm{Cov}(X_{if}, X_{jf}), \qquad (i \neq j)$$

and that therefore

$$\sum_{i=1}^{I}\sum_{j=1}^{I}\mathrm{Cov}(X_{if}, X_{jf}) = \sigma^2_{X_f} - \sum_{i=1}^{I}\sigma^2_{X_{if}}.$$

Applying this equivalency to formula 44 a simplified version is obtained,

$$\rho_{X_{*f}X_{*g}} = \frac{I}{I-1}\left(\frac{\sigma^2_{X_f} - \sum_{i=1}^{I}\sigma^2_{X_{if}}}{\sigma^2_{X_f}}\right) = \frac{I}{I-1}\left(1 - \frac{\sum_{i=1}^{I}\sigma^2_{X_{if}}}{\sigma^2_{X_f}}\right). \qquad [45]$$

By replacing the σ's of formula 45 with s's, one can estimate the internal-consistency reliability coefficient of a test composed of I parts and administered to P persons. In this estimating form, for unit-weighted items or subtests, the formula is a special case of coefficient alpha (Cronbach, 1951) and yields exactly the same results as Hoyt's (1941) coefficient (see Stanley, 1957a).[19] The Hoyt procedure is perhaps simpler to use, because it employs the standard anova procedure applied to a persons-by-items matrix of raw scores and therefore is couched in the now familiar anova terminology. It is derived in a quite different form from that for formula 45, however, as will be seen later.

When items are scored dichotomously, zero or one, the variance of an item is simply its difficulty (i.e. the proportion of examinees marking it correctly) times one minus that difficulty (i.e. the proportion of examinees marking it incorrectly or omitting it). This can be shown readily:

$$\sigma^2_{X_{*if}} = E_p(X^2_{pif}) - [E_p(X_{pif})]^2 = \phi_{.if} - \phi^2_{.if} = \phi_{.if}(1 - \phi_{.if}), \qquad [46]$$

[19] If differential weights of any sort are used, whether they involve giving a wider range of credits for some items than for others, or actually multiplying item or subtest scores by weights to obtain the weighted-composite total score for each person, simply enter the sample version of formula (45) with the scores so multiplied.

where, as before, $E_p(\ )$ is the expectation operator indicating the mean over all persons in the population, and the ϕ's are the item-difficulty parameters. $\phi_{.if}$ is the population mean of the ith dichotomously scored item of the fth form.

Kuder-Richardson 20

By substituting the right-hand portion of formula 46 into formula 45, one obtains the parametric form of the KR20 formula:

$$\rho'_{X_{*f}X_{*g}} = \frac{I}{I-1}\left[1 - \frac{\sum\limits_{i=1}^{I} \phi_{.if}(1 - \phi_{.if})}{\sigma^2_{X_{*f}}}\right], \qquad [47]$$

where the prime on the ρ indicates that this is a special case of the more general formula 45. For actual computing purposes, one substitutes every sample $p_{.if} = \sum_{p=1}^{P} X_{pif}/P$ for the ϕ's,[20] and the sample $s^2_{X_{*f}}$ for $\sigma^2_{X_{*f}}$.

If all items are of equal difficulty, ϕ, and if all item intercorrelations are one, then formula 47 reduces to the form:

$$\rho'_{X_{*f}X_{*g}} = \frac{I}{I-1}\left[1 - \frac{I\phi(1-\phi)}{I\phi(1-\phi) + I(I-1)\phi(1-\phi)}\right]$$

$$= \frac{I}{I-1}\left[1 - \frac{I\phi(1-\phi)}{I^2\phi(1-\phi)}\right] = \frac{I}{I-1}\left(1 - \frac{1}{I}\right)$$

$$= \frac{I}{I-1}\left(\frac{I-1}{I}\right) = 1.$$

When this occurs there is, in effect, a one-*perfect*-item test, because an examinee's total score will be either zero or one and will be predictable with 100 percent accuracy from his response to any one item.

Thus KR20 can have the maximum value 1 when (and only when) all the items are of equal difficulty, because only then can dichotomously scored items intercorrelate perfectly. If two dichotomously scored items i and j have difficulties of, say, .2 and .6, their covariance cannot exceed $.2(1-.6)=.08$—that is, the product of the smaller proportion correct (.2 is smaller than .6) and the smaller proportion incorrect $(1-.6$ is smaller than $1-.2)$; the greatest coefficient of correlation between scores on these two items is $.08/\sqrt{.2(.8)(.6)(.4)}=.41$, not 1.

Effect of variability of item difficulties

What is the maximum possible value of KR20 when the dichotomously scored items have quite varied difficulties? For example, consider a discrete, rectangular distribution of item difficulties $1/(I+1)$, $2/(I+1)$, $\cdots$, $I/(I+1)$. If, for instance, there were 19 items, they would have difficulties .05, .10, $\cdots$, .95, symmetrically spaced with respect to 0 and 1 and .05 apart. This is rather extreme diversity of item difficulty and represents a case where some of the item intercorrelations would be

---

[20] Two types of p's clash here: the by-now familiar subscript p, which designates the pth person (i.e. examinee), and p as a widely used indicator of the difficulty of a test item (the larger p, the *easier* the item, so that a p of one indicates an item that all P examinees marked correctly, whereas a p of zero indicates an item that all P examinees omitted or marked incorrectly). We shall use the subscript p for persons throughout the chapter but the difficulty nonsubscript p infrequently.

quite small. The highest possible correlation for the .05 item with the .95 item would be $(.05)(.05)/\sqrt{.05(.95)(.05)(.95)} = .0526$. Thus even if every person who passed the hard item also passed the easier item, and every person who failed the easy item also failed the hard item, the correlation between the scores on the two items will be just .0526. No more agreement than 5 percent at top and 5 percent at bottom is possible for these two items, and that leaves 90 percent in the middle with 0, 1 scores.

The answer to the question posed at the beginning of the preceding paragraph is that the highest possible KR20 for such rectangularly dispersed items is obtained by substituting in the KR20 formula the sum of item variances and the variance of total scores that result under the conditions of rectangularized item difficulties and maximum possible item intercorrelations. These are, respectively, $I(I+2)/6(I+1)$ and $I(I+2)/12$ (see Stanley, 1968). When these are substituted into formula 47 the formula for the maximum KR20 obtainable with such varied-difficulty items is $I/(I+1)$, which converges on 1 as I becomes large.

One can get exactly the same result by stepping up with the Spearman-Brown formula the ratio of the mean interitem covariance to the mean of the item variances, which ratio for the situation described is $1/2$: Max $KR20 = I(1/2)/[1+(I-1)(1/2)] = I/(I+1)$. Thus, even though the varied-difficulty items can intercorrelate at most only about .50, on the average, just nine maximally intercorrelating items are needed to produce a KR20 of .90. Therefore, at the upper extreme of item intercorrelation, heterogeneous difficulty of items does not keep KR20 much below 1.00 if the number of items is appreciable. For further discussion, see Brogden (1946) and Carroll (1961).

Kuder-Richardson 21

In a following section, "Maximum Variability of Test Scores," a discussion of situations where dispersing item difficulties may be desirable is given. First, though, consider a formula, KR21, proposed by Kuder and Richardson (1937), that is even simpler than KR20; KR21 is used rather widely because it is computed easily. KR21 is obtained from formula 47 by substituting for the product of the I different ϕ's and their complements I times the product of a single difficulty that is the grand mean of all the item scores, over both persons and items, and its complement:

$$E_p\left[\sum_{i=1}^{I} X_{pif}/I\right] = E_p\left[\sum_{i=1}^{I} X_{pif}\right]\bigg/ I = \mu_{.f}/I,$$

so formula 47 becomes

$$\rho''_{X*_f X*_g} = \frac{I}{I-1}\left[1 - \frac{I(\mu_{.f}/I)(1 - \mu_{.f}/I)}{\sigma^2_{X_f}}\right] = \frac{I}{I-1}\left[1 - \frac{\mu_{.f}(I - \mu_{.f})}{I\sigma^2_{X_f}}\right]$$

$$= \frac{1}{I-1}\left[I - \frac{\mu_{.f}(I - \mu_{.f})}{\sigma^2_{X_f}}\right].$$

The computing version,

$$KR21 = \frac{1}{I-1}\left[I - \frac{\overline{X}_{.f}(I - \overline{X}_{.f})}{s^2_X}\right],$$

requires only the number of items in the form (I), the mean of the total scores of persons on the form ($\overline{X}_{.f}$), and the standard deviation of the total scores (s_X^2). No individual-item statistics are needed. Of course, as derived above, KR21 is a simplification of KR20 on the assumption that all I items are equally difficult. Following Tucker (1949), Horst (1966, p. 290) shows that the magnitude of KR20 exceeds that of KR21 for the same set of item scores to the following extent:

$$ \text{KR20} = \text{KR21} + \frac{I^2}{I-1}\left(\frac{s_p^2}{s_X^2}\right), \qquad [48] $$

where s_p^2 is the variance of the item difficulties—i.e. of the p_i's.

The discrepancy term in formula 48 cannot be negative. It will be zero only when the variance of the item difficulties is zero—that is, when all I items are equally difficult, which is seldom the case, especially for ability tests. When the items are spaced rectangularly, with item difficulties $1/(I+1)$, $2/(I+1)$, $\cdots$, $I/(I+1)$, their variance, s_p^2, is $(I-1)/12(I+1)$; when the variance of total scores, s_X^2, is as high as attainable by maximally intercorrelated, dichotomously scored items of these difficulties, it is $I(I+2)/12$. Then the discrepancy in formula 48 becomes

$$ \text{KR20} - \text{KR21} = \left(\frac{I^2}{I-1}\right)\left[\frac{\dfrac{I-1}{12(I+1)}}{\dfrac{I(I+2)}{12}}\right] = \frac{I}{(I+1)(I+2)}, $$

which decreases in magnitude as I increases. For $I=50$, it is less than .02, partially because, as has already been seen, the maximum attainable value of KR20 itself is less than one when item difficulties vary. This result holds only for *maximally intercorrelated* items, but one can readily explore other possibilities. In actual practice, KR21 may be considerably smaller than KR20. For further discussion, see Webster (1960).

For tests composed of dichotomously scored items, Lord (1959) has shown that, under certain reasonable circumstances, the one-form standard error of measurement is approximated rather well by $0.432\sqrt{I}$. This leads to $r_{T_XX} = 1 - 0.187I/s_X^2$; if the items are not too easy or too difficult, the coefficient estimates KR20 about as well as KR21 does.

The reliability of speeded tests

As noted earlier, one-form methods for computing reliability coefficients must not be used with speeded tests, because such methods tend to produce spuriously high estimates of $\rho_{XX'}$. A *speeded* test is one on which the examinees would earn higher scores if they were given more time. A *power* test is one on which the examinees would not tend to earn higher scores, even if the time allowance were increased; though they may not have had time to mark all items, the items are scaled in difficulty from easy to hard so that by the end of the time limit nearly all the examinees are working on items so difficult that they mark only a chance percentage of them correctly. They have "run out of ability."

It is simple to show why split-halving the items from a very easy test that was administered with a single time limit into odd versus even items will produce a very high reliability coefficient. Suppose that a test has I items, each so easy that no examinee marks any one incorrectly, but that the time limit is so short that virtually no examinee can mark all items. A person's total score will be I_m, the number of items he marked. His half-scores will each be $I_m/2$. The computed reliability coefficient of the half-test will then be $r_{I_m/2,\ I_m/2} = 1$ if all examinees mark an even number of items, and not much less than 1 when odd I_m's occur. Of course, this type of test measures no ability other than speed of marking. The usual test with a time limit that prevents most examinees from marking all items is a measure of both ability and speed, frequently more of the former than the latter if the test was carefully devised.

One-form intraclass coefficients are spuriously high for tests that measure speed of responding; they will almost always be higher than coefficients derived from separate forms. This occurs because the items marked by some examinees but not reached by others tend to increase the mean interitem correlation. Consider two very easy items near the end of a speeded test. Examinee p works fast and marks both of them, correctly (because they are quite easy). He gets item scores of one and one. Examinee p' is slower and does not reach either item, so his scores on these two items are zero and zero. This perfect agreement would produce a coefficient of correlation of one between scores of examinees on the two items. Of course, the covariance of item i with item j, both of which were reached and marked correctly by all examinees (or incorrectly by all of them), would be zero; a pure speed test administered with ample time allowance would produce a score of I for every examinee and no variation of obtained (or true) scores.

If sheer speed is an important element in the taking of a particular test, it is essential that reliability coefficients be obtained by correlating scores from two *separately timed* tests or half-tests, rather than on scores from a test with a single time limit. Various efforts to estimate speed and other-ability components from scores on a single form have been made, but the practical tester or the researcher using tests will be well advised to choose the two-form route unless he has the time and facilities to study speed versus power carefully. A simple solution for ability tests where speed of responding is not meant to influence scores much is to arrange the items in order of difficulty from easy to hard and then to allow enough time for nearly all examinees to consider every item up to the point where they are merely guessing.

Stated in other words, reliability estimates for speeded tests can be obtained by splitting the test in half *time-wise* rather than *item-wise*—e.g. giving 15 minutes for each of two (content-wise) parallel halves. The identification of test length with time rather than with number of items and a design such as the above permit classical theory to be used validly. For further discussion of speededness, see Lord and Novick (1968, pp. 131–133 & 384).

Maximum Variability of Test Scores

This may be a good place to determine how variable a set of test scores can possibly be. Consider item scores from a test composed of I dichotomously scored items, for which each examinee's total score is

$$X_p = \sum_{i=1}^{I} X_{pi}.$$

The variance of such scores is

$$\sigma^2_{X_*} = \sigma^2_{(X_{*1}+X_{*2}+\cdots+X_{*I})} = \sum_{i=1}^{I} \sigma^2_{X_{*i}} + \sum_{i=1}^{I}\sum_{j=1}^{I} \rho_{X_{*i}X_{*j}}\sigma_{X_{*i}}\sigma_{X_{*j}}. \quad (i \neq j)$$

This will be maximal when every item variance, $\sigma^2_{X_{*i}} = \phi_{.i}(1-\phi_{.i})$, has its greatest possible value, $.5(1-.5)=.25$, and every $\rho_{X_{*i}X_{*j}}=1$. (That is, each examinee who marks any item correctly marks them all correctly, and all other examinees get none correct.) Then this formula becomes $\sigma^2_{X_*}=.25I+I(I-1)(1)(.25)=.25I[1+(I-1)]$ $=I^2/4$. The standard deviation of the test scores will be the square root of this, $I/2$. Such a variance or standard deviation occurs only when half (i.e. $P/2$) of the examinees earn the maximum possible score, I, and the other half earn the minimum possible score, zero, with no scores at all between zero and I.

Contrast this with the situation where every one of the $I+1$ scores from 0 through I is earned by $1/(I+1)^{th}$ of the examinees—the so-called discrete rectangular distribution. Then the variance is $I(I+2)/12$, which is the same as $I^2/4$ only when $I=1$, when both variances become $1/4$. Otherwise, the variance of the two-point distribution of scores will always be greater than that of the rectangular distribution—three times as great as I approaches infinity. It is twice as great for $I=4$, i.e. for a four-item test.

By setting $\rho_{X_{*i}X_{*j}}=1/3$ for the correlation of each item in the test with every other item, above, one sees that (for a test composed entirely of dichotomously scored items of .5 difficulty) one obtains $I(I+2)/12$, the variance of the discrete rectangular distribution of the scores $0, 1, 2, \cdots, I$, so it must be *necessary* to have this degree of item intercorrelation if one wishes to obtain a rectangular distribution from 50 percent difficulty items. (Obviously, such intercorrelation is not *sufficient* to produce a rectangular distribution, for the variance $I(I+2)/12$ might also be found for a number of other-shaped distributions.) Above the item intercorrelation of $1/3$ the total scores tend to become more frequent at the extremes and less frequent in the middle, until for the perfect intercorrelation (i.e. one) situation only the extreme two scores have any frequencies. Test constructors prevent this by varying the item difficulty from easy to difficult, rather than setting it at approximately .5 for each item, so that even with high intercorrelations thinning out in the middle does not occur. This will usually be unnecessary, however, and poor strategy, because for most ability, aptitude, and achievement tests in many situations it will be best if all items are of equal (and middle) difficulty. Such a test is likely to be better than other-difficulty tests of the same content for discriminating among all except 1 or 2 percent of the examinees in each tail, unless the group is exceptionally heterogeneous. But see Fiske (1966) who for psychological tests in the personality domain argues "for constructing tests with rectangular distributions of item means rather than with means clustering near .5 [p. 87]." Also, see Cronbach and Gleser (1965), who discuss the effect of item difficulty on the efficiency with which certain decisions are made.

Actually, few if any ability tests have average item intercorrelations approaching .33, because of errors of measurement and content specificities that affect such items. Earlier it was pointed out that the SAT-M regularly has reliability coefficients near .90 for 60 items intercorrelating about .13 on the average when administered to rather heterogeneous groups, and the SAT-V produces reliability coefficients of .90 or more with 90 items intercorrelating about .09. Self-report devices may have items intercorrelating in the .33 range or higher, however, because of examinees' striving to be consistent or to make a good impression.

Random errors of measurement are normally distributed for examinees whose true scores are not too near the floor or the ceiling of the test and therefore tend to fill up the middle of the distribution. Two-point distributions of actual test scores based on more than one item are rare, and so are rectangular distributions. The former can be created by testing some persons for whom the test is ridiculously easy along with others for whom it is woefully difficult, as for example if one gave a tenth-grade vocabulary test to Harvard Phi Beta Kappas and to mentally retarded 10-year-olds. For related discussion, see Humphreys (1956), Stanley (1968), and Tucker (1946).

Randomly Parallel Forms

Suppose that there exists a huge number of test items measuring a particular ability, trait, or characteristic such as knowledge of general vocabulary or arithmetic-computation skill. Define a person's true score conceptually as I times the expected item score he would receive when tested with all of these items, without systematic changes in him. Call the difference between this true score and any of his obtained scores on a random set of I items his error of measurement on that form of the test. To facilitate further discussion it will be helpful to set up the following notation.

Let X_{pi} be the score of the pth person on the ith item. Let the number of persons in the population of examinees and the number of items in the population of items both be infinite. Draw a sample of $p = 1, 2, \cdots, P$ persons randomly from the infinite population of persons, and a sample of $i = 1, 2, \cdots, I$ items randomly from the infinite population of items. The resulting matrix of item scores could be depicted as in table 13.3.

Define the pth person's total score on the I items of the fth randomly parallel form of this test as the sum of his I item scores, where scoring of an item need not be just zero and one; i.e.

$$X_{pf} = \sum_{i=1}^{I} X_{pif} = I \overline{X}_{p.f}.$$

Thus, X_{pf} is the total score of the pth person on the fth form.

Then the required identity is

$$X_{pf} = IE_i(X_{pi}) + [X_{pf} - IE_i(X_{pi})] = T_{p*} + e'_{pf}, \qquad [49]$$

where $E_i(X_{pi})$ is the expectation (i.e. the mean) of the infinite number of item scores of the pth person, T_{p*} is the true score of the pth person, and e'_{pf} is the obtained-score minus true-score discrepancy of the pth person on the fth form. Here, error of "measurement" also includes random differences among forms in difficulty, because a person's true score *on a given form* is not necessarily the same as his true score on another form. That is, $T_{p*} = E_f(T_{pf})$, but T_{pf} does not necessarily equal $T_{pf'}$. This means that $\sigma_{e_{*f}e_{*f'}}$, the covariance of errors of measurement between forms, tends not to be zero. That correlation of errors produces complexities beyond the scope of this chapter. See Lord and Novick (1968, especially chap. 11) for further discussion.

Finite Sampling of Items

Usually, one does not have an existent large pool of test items from which to create forms randomly. Instead, one has at hand perhaps $2I$ items that he can stratify

TABLE 13.3

Schema for a Persons-by-Items Matrix of Item Scores

Persons	Items					
	1	2	$\cdots$	I	$\cdots$	∞
1	X_{11}	X_{12}	$\cdots$	X_{1I}	$\cdots$	$X_{1\infty}$
2	X_{21}	X_{22}	$\cdots$	X_{2I}	$\cdots$	$X_{2\infty}$
.	.	.	$\cdots$	.	$\cdots$	.
.	.	.	$\cdots$	.	$\cdots$	.
P	X_{P1}	X_{P2}	$\cdots$	X_{PI}	$\cdots$	$X_{P\infty}$
.	.	.	$\cdots$	.	$\cdots$	.
.	.	.	$\cdots$	.	$\cdots$	.
∞	$X_{\infty 1}$	$X_{\infty 2}$	$\cdots$	$X_{\infty I}$	$\cdots$	$X_{\infty\infty}$

into I blocks of 2 items each on the basis of characteristics such as content, difficulty, and correlation with the other items. For the latter situation, stratified-random parallel forms can be created by flipping a coin, rolling a die (e.g. dichotomized as odd numbers versus even numbers), or using a table of random numbers to assign one item from each block randomly to form f and the other to form f'.

More generally, if one has FI items, he can put them into I blocks of F items each and choose one item randomly from each block (sampling without replacement) to construct a form; in this way F different stratified-random parallel forms can be created. The more homogeneous the blocks and the larger the number of items, I, in a form, the more nearly equal the means and the variances of the $F \geq 2$ forms will be.

Most generally, one may group the pool of items into any number of strata that seems reasonable on the basis of a content outline and/or statistical characteristics. Correlated errors from form to form may be accentuated if the items within a block are too alike in content, as for example "The opposite of love is _____" and "The opposite of hate is _____." This gets one back to what is to be treated as error. In the straight test-retest situation between-form differences in content do not occur. For stratified parallel forms such differences will usually be small.

Often in practice $F = 1$, so that only a "grab group" of $FI = I$ items is available. Inferences cannot be made probabilistically to any randomly sampled population of items but instead can be made to a hypothetical population of items "like these." A little later, when the anova approach to reliability is considered, several models for retesting with the same or with different items are examined.

For the moment, however, note that the model for sampling randomly from an infinite population of items takes into account just sampling fluctuations in the drawing of the I items for each randomly parallel form, not changes in the testing conditions and persons (e.g. practice effects) from one form to the next. Only the actual administration of two or more forms of a test on two or more occasions can provide evidence about such changes in conditions and persons.

For randomly parallel forms, the error of measurement defined in formula 49 includes systematic form differences that arise in random sampling of items, whereas for parallel forms each X_{pf} is considered to consist of a true score (the same from form to form) plus a random error of measurement that does not include between-form differences. Thus for randomly parallel forms the variance error of measurement for the pth person is

$$\sigma^2_{e'_{p*}} = E_f(e'^2_{pf}) = E_f[(X_{pf} - T_{p*})^2],$$

where E_f is the "expectation" operator that indicates taking the mean over all the infinite number of forms, $f = 1, 2, \cdots, \infty$. This will be larger than the variance error of measurement that does not include between-form differences as error.

Also, the definition of the pth person's true score for randomly parallel forms as

$$E_f\left(\sum_{i=1}^{I} X_{pif} \right) = E_f(X_{pf}),$$

equivalent to that in formula 49, reveals that true between-form differences are averaged to yield the overall "true" score, whereas for parallel forms they are not, because in the latter case all μ_f's are assumed to be identical. The population means over persons for the various randomly parallel forms will differ, depending on the range of difficulty of the items in the population of items and the number of items per form—the greater the range and the smaller the number, the greater the variation of the form means. Analogous fluctuation in the variance of obtained scores will occur from form to form. For greater detail, see Lord and Novick (1968, chap. 11).

Though random sampling of items provides a satisfactory conceptual scheme for estimating sampling fluctuations, it has limitations (some of which are discussed in detail by Loevinger, 1965) when just one or two forms are at hand and they were not constructed by simple- or stratified-random sampling from a large population of items. Situations where just I items are available will be treated in the next section.

SOME RECENT APPROACHES TO TEST-SCORE THEORY

Anova and Variance Components

It is becoming increasingly obvious that when one tests he is conducting a study and that, therefore, testing should be treated as controlled investigation. The simplest such study occurs when each of P persons is tested with I items, yielding a P times I matrix of the item scores (X_{pi}'s). What can one learn statistically about such scores? One can, of course, sum the I item scores for each individual and determine how variable the total scores ($X_p = \sum_{i=1}^{I} X_{pi}$) of the examinees are, over persons:

$$s^2_{X*} = s^2_{(X_{*1}+X_{*2}+\cdots+X_{*I})} = I\left[\overline{s^2_{.}} + (I - 1)\overline{r_{ij}s_is_j} \right]. \ (i \neq j) \qquad [50]$$

Thus the variance of the total raw scores of the P persons equals I times the mean of the I item variances plus $I(I-1)$ times the mean of the $I(I-1)$ item covariances. The more variable the scores on the various items are and the more the items covary with each other, the larger the total-score variance will be. Thus it is seen again that the variation among persons is related rather closely to the mean intercorrelation of the items, though the number of items, I, is quite influential. If the mean intercorrelation of the I items is zero, then the variance of the total scores reduces to $I\overline{s^2}$.

One also might look at the covariances of the item-score profiles of persons in a similar way. A more systematic procedure, however, is to use the two-factor (i.e.

persons and items) anova framework, applicable when both P and I are greater than one. One draws I items randomly from a population of $\mathcal{I}$ items ($I \leq \mathcal{I} \leq \infty$). One draws P persons randomly from a population of $\mathcal{P}$ persons ($P \leq \mathcal{P} \leq \infty$). Ideally, each of the P persons tested should receive the I items in random order, independently of the order for any other person, and should have plenty of time to consider all items. The items need not be equally difficult, but their content should be homogeneous enough that it is not considered desirable to separate them into two or more subtests.

Let $X_{pi(r)}$ represent the obtained score of the pth person ($p = 1, 2, \cdots, P, \cdots,$ $\mathcal{P}$) on the ith item ($i = 1, 2, \cdots, I, \cdots, \mathcal{I}$) on the rth replication of that item ($r = 1,$ $2, \cdots, R \leq \infty$). Then the anova model is $X_{pi(r)} = \mu + a_p + b_i + [(ab)_{pi} + e_{pi(r)}]$, where a_p is the main effect of the pth person, b_i is the main effect of the ith item, $(ab)_{pi}$ is the interaction effect of the pth person on the ith item, and $e_{pi(r)}$ is the replication effect for the pth person on the ith item (nonidentifiable here, because there is no replication within the pi factor-level combinations—i.e. $r = 1$—hence the parentheses around the r).

The a's are distributed with mean zero over all persons and variance σ_a^2; the b's are distributed with mean zero over all items and variance σ_b^2; the ab's are distributed with mean zero over all persons, mean zero over all items, and variance σ_{ab}^2; and the replication errors are distributed with mean zero and variance σ_e^2 for each pi. These σ's are called variance components, because $\sigma_X^2 = \sigma_a^2 + \sigma_b^2 + \sigma_{ab}^2 + \sigma_e^2$ for the random-effects model (see Glass & Stanley, 1970).

In this situation the expectations of the anova mean squares (i.e. the average of the mean squares over all hypothetical replications of the testing) are (following Cornfield & Tukey, 1956):

$$E(MS_a) = \sigma_e^2 + (1 - I/\mathcal{I})\sigma_{ab}^2 + I\sigma_a^2$$

$$E(MS_b) = \sigma_e^2 + (1 - P/\mathcal{P})\sigma_{ab}^2 + P\sigma_b^2$$

$$E(MS_{ab}) = \sigma_e^2 + \sigma_{ab}^2. \qquad [51]$$

One can estimate σ_a^2, the variance of the population means of the persons, by the formula

$$\widehat{\sigma_a^2} = (MS_a - MS_{ab})/I \qquad [52]$$

with little negative bias, provided that $\sigma_{ab}^2/\mathcal{I}$ is small relative to σ_a^2, because

$$E[MS_a - MS_{ab}]/I = \{E[MS_a] - E[MS_{ab}]\}/I$$
$$= \{[\sigma_e^2 + (1 - I/\mathcal{I})\sigma_{ab}^2 + I\sigma_a^2] - (\sigma_e^2 + \sigma_{ab}^2)\}/I$$
$$= \sigma_a^2 - \sigma_{ab}^2/\mathcal{I}.$$

Even when $I = \mathcal{I}$ (i.e. one uses for a single form all the available items) the bias will usually be small if I is fairly large, as often it is. Some interaction of persons with items is to be expected, but probably it will tend to be small relative to the magnitude of σ_a^2 if the population of persons is heterogeneous with respect to the ability or trait being measured. Thus, though theoretically it is desirable for the popuation of items to be huge in order that the $-\sigma_{ab}^2/\mathcal{I}$ term will have negligible influence, one gets little bias unless σ_{ab}^2 is rather large and $\mathcal{I}$ rather small.

When $I/\mathcal{I}$ approaches zero, the $(1-I/\mathcal{I})$ coefficient of σ_{ab}^2 in $E(MS_a)$ approaches one, thereby making $E(MS_a)$ differ from $E(MS_{ab})$ only in that the former has the term $+I\sigma_a^2$, not present in the latter, so the estimate of σ_a^2 by formula 52 becomes unbiased, no matter how large σ_{ab}^2 happens to be. Then it is said that the items constitute a random-effects factor. If $(1-P/\mathcal{P})$ approaches one, so that persons also constitute a random-effects factor, too, one has a components-of-variance model, sometimes called a random model or Model II. Then the expected mean squares are as in formula 51, but with the two coefficients in parentheses changed to ones. The (now unbiased) estimator of σ_a^2 for the random model is still as shown in formula 52.

Gulliksen (1950, p. 154) and Stanley (1957a, pp. 90–91) have shown that MS_{ab} equals the mean of the I item variances s_i^2 minus the mean of the $I(I-1)$ covariances of i with j, where $i\neq j$. Call the mean of the variances, $\bar{s}^2$, A and the mean of the covariances, $\overline{r_{ij}s_is_j}$, B. Then $MS_{ab}=A-B$. It is easy to prove (Stanley, 1957a, pp. 90–91) that $MS_a=A+(I-1)B$. (Compare this with the result of formula 50, divided by I.) Substituting in formula 52,

$$\hat{\sigma_a^2} = \frac{[A + (I - 1)B] - (A - B)}{I} = \frac{A - A + B(I - 1 + 1)}{I} = B \quad [53]$$

is obtained. This shows that *the estimated variance component for persons in the random-effects persons-by-items model is simply the mean of the covariances among the I items sampled.* In this context the so-called *intra*class coefficient of correlation is $\rho_{\text{intraclass}}=\sigma_a^2/[\sigma_a^2+(\sigma_e^2+\sigma_{ab}^2)]$, which is estimated (not without a little bias; see Olkin & Pratt, 1958) by

$$\hat{\rho}_{\text{intraclass}} = \frac{\dfrac{MS_a - MS_{ab}}{I}}{\dfrac{MS_a - MS_{ab}}{I} + MS_{ab}} = \frac{MS_a - MS_{ab}}{MS_a + (I - 1)MS_{ab}} \cdot \quad [54]$$

Substituting in formula 54 the relationships $MS_a=A+(I-1)B$ and $MS_{ab}=A-B$,

$$\hat{\rho}_{\text{intraclass}} = \frac{B}{A} = \frac{\overline{r_{ij}s_is_j}}{\overline{s_is_i}} \qquad (i \neq j) \quad [55]$$

is obtained, so the *estimated* intraclass coefficient of correlation from the variance of the means of persons (i.e. examinees) is simply the ratio of the mean covariance among items to the mean of the item variances. *If* the items are equally variable in the population of persons, $\rho_{\text{intraclass}}$ reduces to the mean Pearson product-moment ρ among items, revealing that *this* intraclass coefficient of correlation is closely related to the mean *inter*class correlation of the I items in the form (see Stanley, 1957a, 1961).

For dichotomously scored items the variance of an item over persons is the product of the proportion of persons marking the item correctly and the proportion marking it incorrectly, and this cannot be constant from item to item unless the various items are of equal difficulty. Thus for dichotomously scored tests where the items vary in difficulty the estimated intraclass ρ of formula 55 will differ from the mean of the item intercorrelations, though probably not by much unless the item variances are quite heterogeneous. The relationship $\overline{r_{ij}s_is_j}/\overline{s_is_i} \neq \overline{r_{ij}}$ usually obtains even when items are not scored dichotomously.[21]

Reliability Coefficient via Intraclass ρ

Consider the situation when an infinite number of examinees has been tested with an infinite number of items. Then formula 55 may be written

$$\rho_{\text{intraclass}} = \frac{E_{ij}[\rho_{ij}\sigma_i\sigma_j]}{E_i[\sigma_i\sigma_i]} \cdot \qquad (i \neq j) \qquad [56]$$

If the obtained score of the pth person on the ith item, X_{pi}, is considered to consist of a true score for that item (i.e. the mean of the scores earned by the pth person on an infinite number of comparable forms of that item) plus a random error of measurement which is the difference between his obtained score for that item and his true score for the item,

$$X_{pi} = T_{pi} + e_{pi}, \qquad [57]$$

and if the errors of measurement covary zero across items with each other and with the true scores on the items, then using formulas 56 and 57 one may write

$$\rho_{\text{intraclass}} = \frac{E_{ij}[\text{Cov}(T_i + e_i, T_j + e_j)]}{E_i[\text{Var}(T_i + e_i)]} = \frac{E_{ij}[\text{Cov}(T_i, T_j)]}{E_i[\text{Var}(T_i)] + E_i[\text{Var}(e_i)]}, \qquad [58]$$

where $i \neq j$.

What are the weakest conditions under which formula 58 might reduce to the conventional form for the reliability coefficient of the ith item, $\sigma^2_{T_i}/\sigma^2_{X_i}$, the ratio of the variance of true scores on the item to the variance of obtained scores on the item? For the numerator it is sufficient that $T_{pj} = T_{pi} + c_{ij}$, where c_{ij} is a constant difference between the true scores of all persons on the i, j^{th} pair of items (see Novick & Lewis, 1967, p. 6). This suffices for the $\text{Var}(T_i)$'s of the denominator, too. The numerator may then be written σ^2_T for any item, and $E_i[\text{Var}(T_i)]$ may also be written σ^2_T for any item. However, $E_i[\text{Var}(e_i)]$ remains the mean of the infinite number of $\text{Var}(e_i)$'s instead of the desired constant $\text{Var}(e)$ for every item. Then formula 58 becomes $\rho_{\text{intraclass}} = \sigma^2_T/(\sigma^2_T + \overline{\sigma^2_e})$; σ^2_T designates the true-score variance over persons for any *item*, and

$$\overline{\sigma^2_e} = \sigma^2\left(\sum_{i=1}^{I} e_i\right)\Big/ I$$

is the mean of the item variance errors of measurement or, equivalently, $1/I^{\text{th}}$ times the variance error of measurement of total scores on the form. It is not generally true that

$$\sigma^2_T + \sigma^2\left(\sum_{i=1}^{I} e_i\right)\Big/ I$$

will equal the actual σ^2_X for each item, so even when the items differ in true score pair-wise by a constant, formula 56 does not quite yield the mean of identical reli-

---

[21] For two empirical checks on this relationship, see Stanley (1961, p. 215).

ability coefficients for the items, though the discrepancy may usually be small. This arises because for any $\sigma_{e_i}^2$ the value

$$\sigma^2 \left(\sum_{i=1}^{I} e_i \right)^{/I}$$

is substituted.

Far more serious, however, is the probable invalidity of the assumption that $T_{pj} = T_{pi} + c_{ij}$ for every ij. Thus $\rho_{\text{intraclass}}$ may appreciably underestimate the mean of the $\rho_{T_{X_i}X_i}^2$'s.

Formula 54 is the basis for a number of related procedures for securing one-form reliability coefficients, including the KR20 coefficient (Kuder and Richardson, 1937), Hoyt's (1941) anova coefficient, and coefficient alpha (Cronbach, 1951). Formulas for these three are all identical with the formula that results when one considers formula 54 to provide an estimate of the reliability of the average item in the form and "steps this up" with the Spearman-Brown formula (Spearman, 1910; Brown, 1910) to estimate the reliability coefficient of a test composed of I items, each that reliable. In words, it is: reliability coefficient of a test I items long equals I times the reliability coefficient of the typical item in the test divided by the expression $1 + [(I-1)$ times the reliability coefficient of this typical item]. In symbols the formula becomes $\hat{\rho}_{II'} = I\hat{\rho}_{\text{intraclass}} / [1 + (I-1)\hat{\rho}_{\text{intraclass}}]$.

Applying this to formula 54 yields

$$\hat{\rho}_{II'} = \frac{MS_a - MS_{ab}}{MS_a} = 1 - \frac{MS_{ab}}{MS_a} = 1 - \frac{s_e^2/I}{s_X^2/I} = \frac{\widehat{\sigma_T^2}}{\widehat{\sigma_X^2}}. \qquad [59]$$

$MS_a - MS_{ab}$ may be recognized as I times the $\widehat{\sigma_a^2}$ of formula 52, so $(MS_a - MS_{ab})/MS_a$ is the form for estimating the familiar variance ratio: variance of true scores divided by variance of obtained scores. (If the actual variance of the obtained scores,

$$X_p = \sum_{i=1}^{I} X_{pi},$$

of the P persons is desired, multiply MS_a by I to change it from the scale of item means, $\overline{X}_{p.}$, to that of sums.)

The coefficient alpha (Cronbach, 1951) version of formula 59 is

$$\hat{\rho}_{II'} = \frac{I}{I-1} \left[1 - \frac{\sum_{i=1}^{I} s_i^2}{s_X^2} \right]. \qquad [60]$$

Formula 60 is algebraically equivalent to formula 59, as Stanley (1957a, pp. 86–87) and others have shown. Also, compare formula 60 with formulas 44 and 45.

A special case of formula 60, which was derived earlier than formulas 59 and 60 by Kuder and Richardson (1937), occurs when all the I items are scored dichotomously. If R_i is the number of the P persons taking the test who marked item i correctly (i.e. right), and W_i is the number of persons who marked the ith item incorrectly (i.e. wrong) or omitted it ($R_i+W_i=P$ for every item), then formula 60 may be rewritten

$$\hat{\rho}_{II'} = \frac{I}{I-1}\left[1 - \frac{\left(\sum_{i=1}^{I} R_i W_i\right)\bigg/ P^2}{s_X^2}\right],\qquad [61]$$

because the variance of the ith dichotomously-scored item is $(R_i/P)(W_i/P)$.

In this era of electronic computers, the most useful of the formulas is likely to be the first part of formula 59, unless item variances are needed for other purposes.[22] A by-product of the anova leading to formula 59 will be estimated variance components.

Rather than use intraclass coefficients of correlation, one may prefer to set up approximate confidence intervals for σ_a^2 or exact ones for $\sigma_a^2/(\sigma_e^2+\sigma_{ab}^2)$, in which case it is necessary to introduce normality assumptions (see Brownlee, 1965, p. 481; Cronbach et al., 1970, in press; Lindquist, 1953, pp. 357–382; and Scheffé, 1959). Because of their strong reliance on coefficients of correlation in the past, educational researchers may not feel as confident with point estimates of variance components and confidence intervals for them as they feel with r's, but the former are straightforward and useful. Compare Cleary and Linn (1969a), Feldt (1965, 1969) Mendro and Glass (1969), Nitko and Feldt (1969a, 1969b), and Payne and Anderson (1968) for significance levels and sampling distributions of certain reliability coefficients.

Choosing Persons and Items Non-Randomly

In practice, one usually has neither chosen randomly from any population the P persons to be tested nor has one chosen I items at random from a pool of items. Probably P available persons were tested with an existent set of I items. Clearly, operational conditions for the random-effects model are not met when a "grab group" of P persons is tested with a "grab set" of I items; for, from a probabilistic standpoint, no generalization can be made to other persons and other items. Yet the tester probably would not repeat his testing with the same persons and the same items. He wants to generalize to a population of persons "like these" tested with a population of items "like these," which implies the random-effects model for two hypothetical populations. Cornfield and Tukey (1956, pp. 913–914) encourage this type of generalizing when actual random sampling cannot be done. Note that this model does *not* apply to sampling clusters from populations of clusters (of "grab groups" of persons and "grab sets" of items) but instead to simple random sampling conceptually from the two hypothetical target populations of persons and of items. For determining the internal consistency of a test this is perhaps the most appropriate model, though whenever feasible both persons and items should actually be sampled randomly so that the tester will know for which specific populations he is estimating variance components.

When Examinees Are Presented Different Items

Suppose that there exists a huge pool of items testing a certain trait or characteristic, such as knowledge of general vocabulary, and a huge population of poten-

---

[22] In using formula 61, which is KR20, employ P rather than $P-1$ for obtaining the s^2 in the denominator. For formula 60 it makes no difference, provided that either P or $P-1$ is used in both numerator and denominator. Derive the $R_i W_i/P^2$ formula to see why.

tial examinees. Draw an examinee randomly, and then for him draw I_1 items randomly from the population of items. Select a second examinee, and for him draw I_2 items randomly, independently of those for the first examinee. Continue with a third examinee, etc., until P examinees have been drawn randomly and each has been assigned a random set of $I_p \geq 1$ items.[23] Let the pth person's mean score on his I_p items be

$$\overline{X}_{p.} = \frac{\sum_{i_p=1}^{I_p} X_{pi_p}}{I_p}.$$

Because the item pool being sampled randomly, *independently for each examinee*, is huge (strictly speaking, infinite), the probability that any two examinees will have any item in common approaches zero. Also, each examinee may have a different number of items from another examinee, depending on how many are needed to secure from him the information needed to make some contemplated decision.

The model for this situation is simply that of the one-factor random-effects anova, where here each person is considered a "level" of the persons factor and the within-persons variation among items is anova-type "error": $X_{pi_p} = \mu + a_p + e_{pi_p}$, μ is the grand mean of all persons on all items, a_p is the deviation from μ of the mean of the pth person on all items (i.e. $\mu_p - \mu$), and $e_{pi_p} = X_{pi_p} - \mu_p \cdot \sigma_a^2$ is the variance component for persons, analogous to the variance of true scores of persons, and σ^2 is the pooled within-persons variance, analogous to the variance error of measurement. Expected mean squares are:

$$E[MS_a] = \sigma^2 + \left(\frac{\sum_{p=1}^{P} I_p - \frac{\sum_{p=1}^{P} I_p^2}{\sum_{p=1}^{P} I_p}}{P - 1} \right) \sigma_a^2;$$

$$E[MS_e] = \sigma^2.$$

Call the coefficient in parentheses, above, c. (It reduces to I when the number of items is the same for each person.) Then the unbiased estimator of the component of variance among persons, σ_a^2, is $\widehat{\sigma_a^2} = (MS_a - MS_e)/c$.

The definitional formula for the intraclass coefficient of correlation (Fisher, 1925, sect. 40) is $\rho_{\text{intraclass}} = \sigma_a^2/(\sigma_a^2 + \sigma^2)$, with limits $-[1/(c-1)]$ to 1. This is estimated by

$$\hat{\rho}_{\text{intraclass}} = \frac{\dfrac{MS_a - MS_e}{c}}{\dfrac{MS_a - MS_e}{c} + MS_e} = \frac{MS_a - MS_e}{MS_a + (c-1)MS_e}. \qquad [62]$$

$\rho_{\text{intraclass}}$ is a lower bound to the reliability coefficient of the average item, so the estimated reliability coefficient of the total scores, X_p, *of persons receiving I_p*

---

[23] Some examinees must get more than one item each, or else within-person variability cannot be estimated.

items may be obtained by stepping up $\hat{\rho}_{\text{intraclass}}$ with the Spearman-Brown formula by a factor of I_p. Thus,

$$\hat{\rho}^2_{T_*X_*} = \frac{I_p\hat{\rho}_{\text{intraclass}}}{1 + (I_p - 1)\hat{\rho}_{\text{intraclass}}} = 1 - \frac{MS_e}{MS_a}, \qquad [63]$$

where $T_p = I_p E_i(X_{pi})$, the pth person's true score for I_p items. Note carefully that this one-form reliability coefficient applies only to examinees who received I_p items, where that is a certain definite number such as 6, even though $\rho_{\text{intraclass}}$ itself is estimated via formula 62 from data for all the P examinees.

$$MS_e = \sum_{p=1}^{P}\left[\sum_{i_p=1}^{I_p}(X_{pi} - \overline{X}_{p.})^2\right]\bigg/\sum_{p=1}^{P}(I_p - 1),$$

and therefore reflects differences in item difficulties within persons, as well as actual errors of measurement in responding to the items.

$$MS_a = \sum_{p=1}^{P} I_p(\overline{X}_{p.} - \overline{X}..)^2/(P - 1).$$

When $I_p = I$ for all p (that is, each examinee answers the same number of items),

$$I^2(MS_a) = \frac{I\sum_{p=1}^{P}\left(\dfrac{\sum_{i=1}^{I} X_{pi}}{I} - \dfrac{\sum_{p=1}^{P}\sum_{i=1}^{I} X_{pi}}{PI}\right)^2}{P - 1}$$

$$= \frac{\sum_{p=1}^{P}\left(\sum_{i=1}^{I} X_{pi} - \dfrac{\sum_{p=1}^{P}\sum_{i=1}^{I} X_{pi}}{P}\right)^2}{P - 1}$$

$$= s^2\left(\sum_{i=1}^{I} X_{pi}\right),$$

the variance of the P total scores of the examinees. Thus, from formula 63 and this result one may write

$$\hat{\rho}^2\left(T_*\sum_{i=1}^{I} X_{*i}\right) = \hat{\rho}^2_{TX} = 1 - \frac{I(MS_e)}{I(MS_a)} = 1 - \frac{I(MS_e)}{s^2_X} = \frac{s^2_X - I(MS_e)}{s^2_X} = \frac{s^2_T}{s^2_X},$$

a familiar relationship. $I(MS_e)$ is the estimated variance error of measurement for the total scores—i.e. for the $X_p = \sum_{i=1}^{I} X_{pi}$. This formula holds only for $I_1 = I_2 = \cdots = I_p = I$, i.e. when all persons have the same number of items.

What factors cause the $\overline{X}_p.$'s to differ from person to person? Errors of measurement, sampling fluctuations in item difficulties, and luck of persons in drawing items all contribute to making $\overline{X}_p.$ differ from $\overline{X}_{p'}.$, where $p \neq p'$. For example, person p may happen to draw several quite easy items and/or several items with which he is particularly familiar. The analysis takes all three sources of variation into account, so it is appropriate for the sampling plan described.[24] In the next section, the consequences when all persons answer the same items are examined.

One-Way-Anova Coefficient Computed from Two-Way Data

On page 422 it was shown that for the random-effects model with P persons drawn at random from an infinitely large population of persons and all administered the same I items drawn at random from an infinitely large pool of items the expected mean squares are: $E(MS_a) = \sigma^2 + \sigma_{ab}^2 + I\sigma_a^2$; $E(MS_b) = \sigma^2 + \sigma_{ab}^2 + P\sigma_b^2$; $E(MS_{ab}) = \sigma^2 + \sigma_{ab}^2$. One can collapse this into a between-persons versus within-persons analysis by pooling the sums of squared deviations for b (items) and ab:

$$MS_{(\text{within persons})} = MS_{(b+ab)} = \frac{(I-1)MS_b + (P-1)(I-1)MS_{ab}}{(I-1) + (P-1)(I-1)}.$$

The average value of this new mean square is

$$E[MS_{(b+ab)}] = \frac{(I-1)E[MS_b] + (P-1)(I-1)E[MS_{ab}]}{P(I-1)}$$

$$= \sigma^2 + \sigma_{ab}^2 + \sigma_b^2.$$

One can estimate σ_a^2 as $\widehat{\sigma_a^2} = [MS_a - MS_{(b+ab)}]/I$, but

$$E\left[\frac{MS_a - MS_{(b+ab)}}{I}\right] = \sigma_a^2 - \frac{\sigma_b^2}{I} \leq \sigma_a^2,$$

so it is important that σ_b^2/I be negligible. If the items vary little in difficulty and I is fairly large, σ_a^2 will be estimated without much negative bias.

How does the bias affect the estimation of intraclass ρ, which has σ_a^2 in both numerator and denominator?

$$E[\hat{\rho}_{\text{intraclass}}] = E\left[\frac{MS_a - MS_{(b+ab)}}{MS_a + (I-1)MS_{(b+ab)}}\right]$$

$$\doteq \frac{E[MS_a - MS_{(b+ab)}]}{E[MS_a + (I-1)MS_{(b+ab)}]}$$

$$= \frac{I\sigma_a^2 - \sigma_b^2}{I\sigma_a^2 + I(\sigma^2 + \sigma_{ab}^2) + (I-1)\sigma_b^2}, \qquad [64]$$

where $\doteq$ means "is approximately equal to," because the expectation of a ratio is not in general exactly equal to the ratio of the expectations of its numerator and denominator (see Stanley, 1957b).

Formula 64 assumes the familiar form for a two-factor intraclass ρ if $\sigma_b^2 = 0$. Also, for I large enough so that the distinction between I and $(I-1)$ can be ignored it becomes $(\sigma_a^2 - \sigma_b^2/I)/(\sigma_a^2 + \sigma^2 + \sigma_{ab}^2 + \sigma_b^2)$, revealing that though the bias disappears

---

[24] The *order* of administration of I_p items to the pth person was not specified. If it were random, differential residual effects might occur, as when one person's first items are so difficult that they discourage him for subsequent items, whereas another person's first items are easy. In practice, each examinee's items would probably be arranged in ascending order of difficulty for a previous tryout group.

from the numerator as I becomes large, it remains essentially constant in the denominator.

Perhaps most important is the bias in the reliability coefficient itself:

$$E[\widehat{\rho^2_{T_*X_*}}] = E\left[\frac{MS_a - MS_{(b+ab)}}{MS_a}\right] \doteq \frac{E[MS_a - MS_{(b+ab)}]}{E[MS_a]}$$

$$= \frac{I\sigma^2_a - \sigma^2_b}{I\sigma^2_a + \sigma^2 + \sigma^2_{ab}}, \qquad [65]$$

which, if $\sigma^2_b = 0$, becomes

$$\frac{\sigma^2_a}{\sigma^2_a + \dfrac{\sigma^2 + \sigma^2_{ab}}{I}}. \qquad [66]$$

The biasing term, $-\sigma^2_b$, in formula 65 occurs only in the numerator; if $\sigma^2_a \neq 0$, the bias decreases as I increases.[25]

The moral seems clear: Unless the number of items is large (and an "item" can be any unit of data) and the variation of the item difficulties is small, the ratio of mean squares shown in brackets for the first step of formula 65, above, should not be used when all persons answer the same items, whereas the equivalent procedure of formula 63 is proper when items are assigned to the examinees randomly and independently from a huge item pool. Cronbach and associates (1970, in press) discuss in depth the use of reliability estimates based on persons-by-items data (i.e. all examinees answer the same items) for generalizing to situations where each examinee has a different random set of items (or of raters, tests, judges, etc.). If the I items administered to all P persons were drawn at random from a huge pool of items, the pooling of between-items and interaction sources of variation in the above manner will provide the basis for estimating the reliability of data conforming to the model used to obtain formula 63. For further details, see Cronbach and associates (1970, in press); Cronbach and Azuma (1962); Cronbach, Rajaratnam, and Gleser (1963); Cronbach, Schönemann, and McKie (1965); Gleser and associates (1965); Hunter (1968); Rajaratnam (1960); Rajaratnam, Cronbach, and Gleser (1965).

One must keep firmly in mind the typical differences between psychometric theory and measurement practice. When one actually conducts a rating study, for example, he rarely assigns raters at random to ratees, but instead has the raters rate those examinees whom they know best, and under conditions where a great deal of variation in the rating procedures may occur. One cannot properly "assume" that the raters were assigned at random to ratees when in fact they clearly were not. In such a situation variability and fluctuations must be assessed empirically, as well as theoretically, and appropriate limitations should be placed on conclusions of the study.

[25] Formula 66 is the Spearman-Brown step-up, with factor I, of the intraclass ρ for the random-effects persons-by-items two-factor anova model, $\rho_{\text{intraclass}} = \sigma^2_a/(\sigma^2_a + \sigma^2 + \sigma^2_{ab})$. Note how formula 66 differs from this in a way that reduces the denominator of formula 66 linearly as I, the number of items, increases. Theoretically, as $I \to \infty$, this estimate of $\rho_{T_*X_*} \to 1$, if $\sigma_a > 0$. Actually, if the number of items in the test becomes quite large, examinees may get fatigued or bored, causing σ^2_a, σ^2, and σ^2_{ab} to change. This limitation applies to most uses of the Spearman-Brown prophecy formula, which, however, usually works well over a considerable range of I.

ANOVA VS. CLASSICAL TEST THEORY

There are two chief competing points of view about the determination of the reliability of measures. One of these, featured in this chapter, stems from the work of Charles Spearman, principally from 1904–1913, as extended by Cureton (1931, 1958), Gulliksen (1950), Jackson and Ferguson (1941), Kelley (1921, 1942), Lord and Novick (1968), and many more. The other approach, developed by Cronbach and associates (1970), uses Fisher's (1925 et seq.) analysis-of-variance framework—as amplified by Burt (1955), Cornfield and Tukey (1956), Lindquist (1953), Stanley (1962), and others—to estimate variance components for designs involving a number of classificatory factors such as testing occasion and examiner. This important overarching anova schema requires the testing conditions to match the "real world" to which the tester plans to generalize by having in the design itself those factors that determine the generalizability of measurement findings.

It was shown above how one can pool sources of variation. This is a chief principle in the Cronbach-Gleser approach. If one has gathered the multifactor data in the initial standardization of a test, he can pool sources of variation in order to estimate components of variance appropriate for later testing. For example, if initially all examinees have the same items, but subsequently items are assigned at random to examinees, the persons $\times$ items anova can be collapsed into the between-persons analysis. A more comprehensive example beginning in the next paragraph should make this moving from the standardization situation to the field use of a measurement procedure clearer. Those students who understand complex analyses of variance well, including nested designs and repeated measurements, can learn the Cronbach-Gleser methods readily. It is not possible in this chapter to do justice to them; instead, see the Cronbach and associates (1970) volume, which provides the details. However, the following brief treatment may be suggestive.

Suppose that in standardizing a test one uses a design involving two sexes and T testers, each administering the same I items to each of T sets of n males and n females (there being $2nT$ persons tested). Suppose further that an infinite population of items is stratified on difficulty at $L \geq 1$ levels and that the items for the test are drawn, m items for each level, in stratified-random fashion from that population. The basic matrix of item scores for only the tth tester will be as shown in table 13.4.

This is a mixed-model design for the "generalizability" sample. Persons within sex, items within levels, and testers are considered to have been drawn randomly from their respective infinite populations. Persons are "nested" within sex, persons are nested within testers, and items are nested within levels. Also, each person is measured repeatedly by the same I items.

The sources of variation for the ensuing data (i.e. item scores) can be found by considering how many ways the factors can occur (given the three nesting restrictions) individually, two at a time, three at a time, four at a time, and five at a time. Write down $s\ p\ l\ i\ t$ (sex, person, level, item, tester). Note that nesting prevents the following combinations from occurring: sp, pt, and li. Taking the five letters one at a time yields s, p(within st), l, i(within l), and t. Taking two letters at a time yields the following seven sources: sl, si, st, pl, pi, lt, and it. Three at a time permits only slt and sit. Four at a time permits no combinations at all, nor does five at a time.

Thus, there are 14 computable sources of variation, for each of which an expected mean square can be written. These indicate how to estimate variance components from computed mean squares. For rules of thumb useful in determining $E(MS)$'s, see Millman and Glass (1967).

With the analysis of the table 13.4 data in hand one could estimate the variance

TABLE 13.4

**Test Consisting of $mL = I$ Stratified-Random Items Administered
to n Males and n Females by the tth Tester; X_{split} Notation**

Sex	Person	1				2					L		
		1	2	$\cdots$	m	$m+1$	$m+2$	$\cdots$	$2m$	$\cdots$	$I-m+1$	$I-m+2$	$\cdots$ I
	1	X_{1111t}	X_{1112t}	$\cdots$	X_{111mt}								
Male (1)	2	X_{1211t}	X_{1212t}	$\cdots$	X_{121mt}		etc.						
	.	.	.	.	.								
	.	.	.	.	.								
	n	X_{1n11t}	X_{1n12t}	$\cdots$	X_{1n1mt}								
	$n+1$			$\cdots$									
Female (2)	$n+2$			$\cdots$									
	.			.									
	.			.									
	$2n$			$\cdots$									

component among persons who had been tested, say, by different testers with items randomly assigned without stratification, a different set to each person, and with no record of the person's sex available. This would collapse the five-factor design into a one-factor design involving only two sources of variation, between persons versus within persons.

Less reductively, one might wish to estimate the variance component among persons tested by various testers (a person having been assigned *randomly* to one tester *or* another) but still "blocked" on sex and all answering a common stratified set of test items. That can be done from the matched generalizability data. This brief verbal explanation will probably be fairly intelligible to readers who understand expected mean squares well but vague and esoteric to others. The best way to master this approach, which is worth much effort, is to learn fundamentals of the analysis of variance thoroughly and then study the Cronbach and associates (1970, in press) book carefully.

Reliability estimates reported in test manuals or journal articles are often based on special studies (e.g. involving excellent test administrators, or where the examiners *know* they are participating in a reliability study). Therefore, they may be imperfectly applicable to workaday, routine applications of the measuring instrument. Careful planning of the generalizability study within the Cronbach-Gleser-Nanda-Rajaratnam framework can allow for this. For example, several levels of tester excellence and of tester awareness could be used explicitly in the standardization design.

OTHER CONSIDERATIONS IN TEST THEORY
The Reliability of Factor Scores

Factor analysts have begun to develop methods for maximizing the internal-consistency reliability coefficients of their factor scores (see Bentler, 1968; Glass,

1966; Horn, 1969; Kaiser & Caffrey, 1965). Earlier workers had done something similar when they divided a set of test items into several subtests so that items within a subtest correlated highly with each other but less well with the items in other subtests. For example, see Loevinger, Gleser, and DuBois (1953); also see Elashoff (1969) and Elashoff and Spiegel (1969). The principal thing that determines the Hoyt, alpha, or Kuder-Richardson coefficient of a test or subtest is the mean intercorrelation of its items, so any procedure such as factor or cluster analysis of test items that affects the mean item intercorrelation within subtests will affect the magnitude of this coefficient. Homogeneous tests or subtests have higher internal consistency than heterogeneous ones do.

Test Theory for "Tailored" Testing

Administering exactly the same test to each of a number of examinees who differ considerably in the ability, trait, or characteristic being measured seems wasteful of time and effort, because some examinees will answer most of the items incorrectly, and others will answer most of them correctly. For almost every examinee the effective length of the test is less than I, the number of items, and considerably less than that for an appreciable percentage of the examinees. Group testing is often less expensive and troublesome for the examiners than tailoring of the items to each examinee would be, however, and for that reason it has persisted even in the face of the computer revolution.

There are signs, however, that more individualized testing may be in the offing. Already, computer-assisted instruction incorporates continual testing as an integral didactic aspect of the programmed instruction. Also, determining an examinee's ability by testing him with items of difficulty optimal for him should gradually replace the cumbersome paper-and-pencil testing programs of many sorts that cover the country.

It is intuitively obvious that an examinee should be given items at his 50 percent point on the ability continuum, such that he can just barely answer about half of the items correctly and just barely miss the other half. If he misses an item, he is given a slightly easier one. If he answers an item correctly, he is given a slightly more difficult one. This up-and-down method is continued until his ability parameter is estimated with the desired confidence. Though the process can be carried out without computerization, quite likely the speed, flexibility, accuracy, and storage capacity of high-speed digital computers will make them ideal examiners of individuals. Probably, too, computers will be programmed to yield decisions about an individual, e.g. to determine on the basis of sufficient but not excessive testing into which reading group or algebra section he should be placed.

The theory of tailored testing has not yet been worked out fully, but Lord (1970; 1971, in press) has made a good beginning by drawing heavily on developments in bioassay (see also Cleary, Linn, & Rock, 1968; Owen, 1969). Undoubtedly, test specialists will find individualized testing of increasing importance. There will be many opportunities to explore theoretical and practical aspects of it.

Error of Measurement, or Error of Estimate?

In most parts of this chapter, errors of measurement have been considered according to the classical test-theory model $e_p = X_p - T_p$. Are errors of *estimate* of the form $(Y_p - \hat{Y}_p) = Y_p - (\beta_{YX} X_p + \alpha_{YX})$ useful in test theory? In other words, how do errors of measurement differ from errors of estimate? It seems desirable to expand a bit here on earlier coverage in this chapter.

Take the simplest situation first. $X_p = T_p + e_p$ *defines* e_p directly, without explicit regression parameters. $\sigma^2_{(X-T)} = \sigma^2_e = \sigma^2_X(1 - \rho^2_{TX})$ is the variance error of measurement, as was seen earlier. What is $\hat{X}_p = \beta_{XT}T_p + \alpha_{XT}$? It is

$$\hat{X}_p = \left(\frac{\sigma_{XT}}{\sigma^2_T}\right)T_p + \left[\mu_X - \left(\frac{\sigma_{XT}}{\sigma^2_T}\right)\mu_T\right] = \frac{\sigma_{(T+e,T)}}{\sigma^2_T}T_p + \mu_X - \frac{\sigma_{(T+e,T)}}{\sigma^2_T}\mu_X$$

$$= \left(\frac{\sigma^2_T}{\sigma^2_T}\right)T_p + \mu_X - \left(\frac{\sigma^2_T}{\sigma^2_T}\right)\mu_X = T_p.$$

Figure 13.1 shows this relationship. The errors in *estimating* X_p's from the corresponding T_p's are $X_p - T_p$. Their variance error of estimate is $\sigma^2_X(1 - \rho^2_{XT})$, which is the same as the variance error of measurement. Of course, true scores are not known, so actually the X_p is taken to estimate T_p, rather than the reverse, so the error-of-measurement viewpoint seems more appropriate.

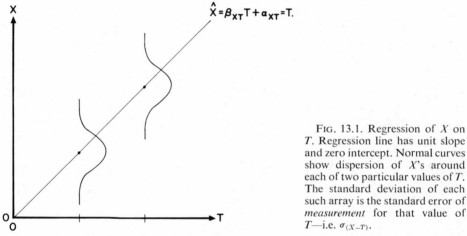

FIG. 13.1. Regression of X on T. Regression line has unit slope and zero intercept. Normal curves show dispersion of X's around each of two particular values of T. The standard deviation of each such array is the standard error of *measurement* for that value of T—i.e. $\sigma_{(X-T)}$.

What happens if T is estimated from X? Earlier it was shown that

$$\hat{T}_p = \beta_{TX}X_p + \alpha_{TX} = \rho^2_{TX}(X_p - \mu_X) + \mu_X. \qquad [67]$$

The error of *estimate* for this is $T_p - \hat{T}_p = (T_p - \mu_T) - \rho^2_{TX}(X_p - \mu_X)$. See figure 13.2 for the relationship; linear regression of T on X is assumed, and probably holds closely enough in many situations.

The variance error of estimate is $\sigma^2_{(T-\hat{T})} = \sigma^2_T(1 - \rho^2_{TX})$, which is the usual form for a variance error of estimate. This can also be written

$$\sigma^2_{(T-\hat{T})} = \rho^2_{TX}\sigma^2_X(1 - \rho^2_{TX}) = \rho^2_{TX}\sigma^2_e. \qquad [68]$$

$\rho^2_{TX}\sigma^2_e$ is the variance of any one of the vertical arrays in figure 13.2, if the arrays are assumed to be homoscedastic (i.e. have equal variance) for every value of X.

The variance error of *measurement* of the $\hat{T}_p$'s is

$$\sigma^2_{e\hat{T}} = \sigma^2_{[(\beta_{TX}X+\alpha_{TX})-(\beta_{TX}T+\alpha_{TX})]} = \rho^4_{TX}\sigma^2_e. \qquad [69]$$

This is the variance to use in setting up a confidence interval for $E_f[\beta_{TX}X_{pf}+\alpha_{TX}]=\beta_{TX}T_p+\alpha_{TX}$, which is the true score corresponding to $\hat{T}_p$. It will be shorter than the confidence interval for T_p, using $\rho^2_{TX}\sigma^2_e$.

In regression language, the error of *measurement* corresponds to the error made when estimating $\hat{T}_p$ from T_p: $\hat{T}_p-\hat{T}_p=\hat{T}_p-\beta_{\hat{T}T}T_p+\alpha_{\hat{T}T}=\rho^2_{TX}e_p$, whose variance is $\sigma^2_{(\hat{T}-\hat{T})}=\rho^4_{TX}\sigma^2_e$, as in formula 69. This seems rather strange, however, because $\hat{T}$ actually is estimated from X, in formula 67, and not $\hat{T}$ from (unknown) T. Thus in these regression terms the variance error of measurement makes no sense, but fortunately it enables us legitimately to avoid the impossible estimating from T and yet get the same precision. Error of measurement arises from the *definition* of obtained scores and true scores, rather than from regression procedures.

The discrepancy between formulas 68 and 69 arises because $\beta_{TX}X_p+\alpha_{TX}$, $\beta_{TX}T_p+\alpha_{TX}$, and $\beta_{TX}e_p$ are on the same linearly transformed $X_p=T_p+e_p$ scale, whereas $\beta_{TX}X_p+\alpha_{TX}$, T_p, and $(\beta_{TX}X_p+\alpha_{TX})-T_p$ are not. Thus, if one works with $\hat{T}_p$'s, precision is increased by using the variance error of *measurement*.

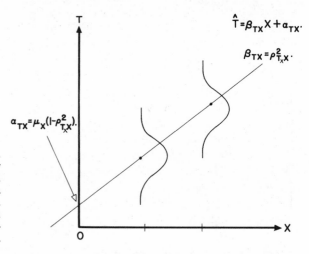

Fig. 13.2. Regression of T on X. Curves show dispersion of T's for each of two particular values of X. The mean squared error for a given array is $E_p[(T_p-\hat{T})^2\,|\,X]$. For all arrays combined, the mean square of the $(T-\hat{T})$'s is the variance error of *estimate*—i.e. $\sigma^2_{(T-\hat{T})}$.

The standard literature on this point is mixed and not explicitly comparative, Compare Davis (1964, p. 50), Glass (1968), Gulliksen (1950, p. 43), Kelley (1947, formulas 11:14, 11:22, and 11:27), and Nunnally (1967, p. 220). Also see Stanley (1970) and Livingston (1970a).

The Effect of Correlated Errors

Throughout this chapter it has been assumed that $\sigma_{Te}=\sigma_{e_fe_{f'}}=0$; i.e. true scores covary zero with errors of measurement, and errors of measurement on one form covary zero with errors of measurement on another form. These are two fundamental assumptions of classical test-score theory. They are crucial to the one-form and two-form reliability coefficients. The derivation of the former was:

$$\rho^2_{TX}=\left(\frac{\sigma_{TX}}{\sigma_T\sigma_X}\right)^2=\left(\frac{\sigma_{T,T+e}}{\sigma_T\sigma_X}\right)^2=\left(\frac{\sigma^2_T+\sigma_{Te}}{\sigma_T\sigma_X}\right)^2=\frac{\sigma^2_T}{\sigma^2_X}.$$

If $\sigma_{Te}\neq0$, $\rho^2_{TX}\neq\sigma^2_T/\sigma^2_X$. Positive covariation of true scores with errors of measurement increases the ratio, whereas negative covariation reduces it.

For two forms,

$$\rho_{X_f X_{f'}} = \frac{\sigma_{X_f, X_{f'}}}{\sigma_{X_f}\sigma_{X_{f'}}} = \frac{\sigma_{T+e_f, T+e_{f'}}}{\sigma_{X_f}\sigma_{X_{f'}}} = \frac{\sigma_{TT} + \sigma_{Te_{f'}} + \sigma_{e_f T} + \sigma_{e_f e_{f'}}}{\sigma_{X_f X_{f'}}} = \frac{\sigma_T^2}{\sigma_X^2},$$

if $\sigma_{Te_{f'}} = \sigma_{e_f T} = \sigma_{e_f e_{f'}} = 0$ and $\sigma_{e_f}^2 = \sigma_{e_{f'}}^2$. In particular, positive covariation of errors of measurement, which often occurs (e.g. in test-retest situations), increases the ratio.

As, for example, Traub (1968) pointed out, test-theory models that do not assume zero covarying of true scores and errors of measurement, or of errors of measurement with each other on different occasions, can be constructed; they may reflect the real world more accurately than the zero-covarying model does. For further discussion see Box (1954), Maxwell (1968), Rozeboom (1966), and Werts and Linn (1970, in press).

Criterion-referenced Reliability

"Criterion-referenced" measurement—measurement with respect to a fixed standard, rather than with respect to the mean of a norm group—poses some special problems for reliability theory. Criterion-referenced measures are meant to be used in situations in which there may be no variation among the true scores of the examinees; these measures are intended not to discriminate among persons, but to discriminate each person's score from a fixed criterion score. Therefore, a criterion-referenced test can give reliable information even though its classically defined reliability coefficient equals zero. However, Livingston (1970b) has shown that the classical concepts of reliability can be redefined in a more general form which will apply to criterion-referenced measures.

The key is to redefine variance, covariance, and correlation in terms of the deviation of scores from the criterion, rather than from the mean. The important relationships of test theory can then be derived in this more general form. The derivations parallel those of classical test theory. Livingston's formula for the criterion-referenced reliability coefficient is

$$\rho_C^2(T_X, X) = \frac{\sigma_T^2 + (\mu_X - C_X)^2}{\sigma^2 x + (\mu_X - C_X)^2},$$

where μ_X is the mean score and C_X is the criterion score. An interesting characteristic of criterion-referenced reliability theory is that classical reliability theory appears as a special case—i.e., the case in which the mean equals the criterion. Livingston also shows that other standard concepts of classical norm-referenced test-score theory, such as correction for attenuation and the Spearman-Brown formula, apply to criterion-referenced measurement.

CONCLUDING REMARKS

The reliability of tests is a vast topic. In this chapter it has been possible just to touch, often too briefly, on some of its more important aspects in order to provide useful formulas and introduce the reader to a number of concepts that he may wish to pursue further. Probably the most advanced, systematic treatment of classical test theory, with many modern additions, is Lord and Novick (1968). A number of other books offer at an intermediate level, beyond elementary-textbook content, various approaches to test theory. These include Cronbach and associates (1970, in press), Davis (1964), Horst (1966), Nunnally (1967), and Rozeboom (1966). Most test-theory research published in the United States appears chiefly in monographs, textbooks, and three journals: *Psychometrika, Educational and Psychological Measurement*, and the *Journal of Educational Measurement.*

Most of test theory is applicable not only to aptitude and achievement measures but also to other types of psychological instruments such as interest, attitude, and personality inventories or devices. Perhaps projective techniques require the most care in assessing reliability. For a systematic treatment of this topic see Jensen (1959).

Bayesian methods are beginning to be applied to psychological testing, notably by Lord (1969) and Novick (1970); also see Novick and Jackson, 1970. The alert researcher will keep abreast of new developments based on this approach.

As was noted several times in this chapter, reliability is closely related to validity. In the next chapter Cronbach explains the basic concepts of validity and extends them in original ways. His presentation will shed further light on the reliability of tests.

REFERENCES

American Psychological Association. *Standards for educational and psychological tests and manuals.* Washington: APA, 1966.

Baker, K. H. Item validity by the analysis of variance: An outline of method. *Psychological Record*, 1939, **3**, 242–248.

Bentler, P. M. Alpha-maximized factor analysis (alphamax): Its relation to alpha and canonical factor analysis. *Psychometrika*, 1968, **33**, 335–345.

Bereiter, C. E. Some persistent dilemmas in the measurement of change. In C. W. Harris (Ed.), *Problems in measuring change.* Madison: University of Wisconsin Press, 1963. Pp. 3–20.

Box, G. E. P. Some theorems on quadratic forms applied in the study of analysis of variance problems II. Effects of inequality of variance and of correlation between errors in the two-way classification. *Annals of Mathematical Statistics*, 1954, **25**, 484–498.

Brigham, C. C. *A study of error.* New York: College Entrance Examination Board, 1932.

Brogden, H. E. The effect of bias due to difficulty factors in product-moment item intercorrelations on the accuracy of estimation of reliability by the Kuder-Richardson formula number 20. *Educational and Psychological Measurement*, 1946, **6**, 517–520.

Brown, F. G. *Principles of educational and psychological testing.* Hinsdale, Ill.: Dryden Press, 1970.

Brown, W. Some experimental results in the correlation of mental abilities. *British Journal of Psychology*, 1910, **3**, 296–322.

Brown, W. *The essentials of mental measurement.* Cambridge: Cambridge University Press, 1911. (& Thomson, G. H., 2nd ed., 1921.)

Brownlee, K. A. *Statistical theory and methodology in science and engineering.* (2nd ed.) New York: Wiley, 1965.

Buros, O. K. Summary of definitions, basic concepts, and formulas in the schematization of test reliability. Unpublished paper, 5 February 1963.

Buros, O. K. Schematization of old and new concepts of test reliability based upon parametric models. Unpublished paper, 11 February 1963 & 22 December 1966.

Burt, C. Test reliability estimated by analysis of variance. *British Journal of Statistical Psychology*, 1955, **8**, 103–118.

Cahen, L. S., Romberg, T. A., & Zwirner, W. The estimation of mean achievement scores for schools by the item-sampling technique. *Educational and Psychological Measurement*, 1970, **30**, 41–60.

Campbell, D. T., & Fiske, D. W. Convergent and divergent validation by the multitrait-multimethod matrix. *Psychological Bulletin*, 1959, **56**, 81–105.

Campbell, D. T., & Stanley, J. C. *Experimental and quasi-experimental designs for research.*

Chicago: Rand McNally, 1966. [Originally published as chap. 5 (pp. 171–246) in N. L. Gage (Ed.), *Handbook of research on teaching*, 1963.]

Carroll, J. B. The nature of the data, or how to choose a correlation coefficient. *Psychometrika*, 1961, **26**, 347–372.

Cattell, Raymond B. Validity and reliability: A proposed more basic set of concepts. *Journal of Educational Psychology*, 1964, **55**, 1–22.

Cleary, T. A., & Linn, R. L. A note on the relative sizes of the standard errors of two reliability estimates. *Journal of Educational Measurement*, 1969, **6**, 25–27. (a)

Cleary, T. A., & Linn, R. L. Error of measurement and the power of a statistical test. *British Journal of Mathematical and Statistical Psychology*, 1969, **22**, 49–55. (b)

Cleary, T. A., Linn, R. L., & Rock, D. A. Reproduction of total test score through the use of sequential programmed tests. *Journal of Educational Measurement*, 1968, **5**, 183–187.

Cochran, W. G. Errors of measurement in statistics. *Technometrics*, 1968, **10**, 637–666.

Cochran, W. G. Some effects of errors of measurement on multiple correlation. *Journal of the American Statistical Association*, 1970, **65**, 22–34.

Cornfield, J., & Tukey, J. W. Average values of mean squares in factorials. *Annals of Mathematical Statistics*, 1956, **27**, 907–949.

Cox, D. R. *Planning of experiments*. New York: Wiley, 1958.

Cronbach, L. J. Coefficient alpha and the internal structure of tests. *Psychometrika*, 1951, **16**, 297–334.

Cronbach, L. J. *Essentials of psychological testing*. (3rd ed.) New York: Harper & Row, 1970.

Cronbach, L. J., & Azuma, H. Internal-consistency reliability formulas applied to randomly sampled single-factor tests: An empirical comparison. *Educational and Psychological Measurement*, 1962, **22**, 645–665.

Cronbach, L. J., & Furby, L. How we should measure "change"—or should we? *Psychological Bulletin*, 1971. **74,**

Cronbach, L. J., & Gleser, G. C. The signal/noise ratio in the comparison of reliability coefficients. *Educational and Psychological Measurement*, 1964, **24**, 467–480.

Cronbach, L. J., & Gleser, G. C. *Psychological tests and personnel decisions*. (2nd ed.) Urbana: University of Illinois Press, 1965.

Cronbach, L. J., Gleser, G. C., Nanda, H., & Rajaratnam, N. *The dependability of behavioral measurements*. New York: Wiley, 1971.

Cronbach, L. J., Rajaratnam, N., & Gleser, G. C. Theory of generalizability: A liberalization of reliability theory. *British Journal of Statistical Psychology*, 1963, **16**, 137–163.

Cronbach, L. J., Schönemann, P., & McKie, D. Alpha coefficients for stratified-parallel tests. *Educational and Psychological Measurement*, 1965, **25**, 291–312.

Cureton, E. E. Errors of measurement and correlation. *Archives of Psychology*, 1931, May (Whole No. 125).

Cureton, E. E. The definition and estimation of test reliability. *Educational and Psychological Measurement*, 1958, **18**, 715–738.

Cureton, E. E. Reliability and validity: Basic assumptions and experimental designs. *Educational and Psychological Measurement*, 1965, **25**, 327–346.

Cureton, E. E. The stability coefficient. *Educational and Psychological Measurement*, 1970, **30**, in press.

Darlington, R. B. Multiple regression in psychological research and practice. *Psychological Bulletin*, 1968, **69**, 161–182.

Davis, F. B. *Educational measurements and their interpretation*. Belmont, Calif.: Wadsworth, 1964.

Deming, W. E., & Birge, R. T. On the statistical theory of errors. *Reviews of Modern Physics*, 1934, **6**, 119–161. (a)

Deming, W. E., & Birge, R. T. Comment concerning "On the statistical theory of errors." *Physical Review*, 1934, **46**, 1027. (b)

DeMoivre, A. *Approximatio ad summam terminorum binomii* $(a+b)^n$ *in seriem expansi*, 1733. See Walker (1929, pp. 13–14).

DuBois, P. H. *Multivariate correlational analysis*. New York: Harper & Row, 1957.

Ebel, R. L. Expected reliability as a function of choices per item. *Educational and Psychological Measurement*, 1969, **29**, 565–570.

Elashoff, J. D. Optimal choice of rater teams. I: Theory. *Psychometrika*, 1969, **34**, 21–32.

Elashoff, J. D., & Spiegel, D. E. Optimal choice of rater teams. II: Applications. *Psychometrika*, 1969, **34**, 33–44.

Feldt, L. S. The approximate sampling distribution of Kuder-Richardson reliability coefficient twenty. *Psychometrika*, 1965, **30**, 357–370.

Feldt, L. S. A note on the use of confidence bands to evaluate the reliability of a difference between two scores. *American Educational Research Journal*, 1967, **4**, 139–145.

Feldt, L. S. A test of the hypothesis that Cronbach's α or Kuder-Richardson coefficient twenty is the same for two tests. *Psychometrika*, 1969, **34**, 363–373.

Fisher, R. A. *Statistical methods for research workers*. Edinburgh: Oliver & Boyd, 1925 et seq.

Fiske, D. W. Some hypotheses concerning test adequacy. *Educational and Psychological Measurement*, 1966, **26**, 69–88.

Garner, W. R. *Uncertainty and structure as psychological concepts*. New York: Wiley, 1962.

Glass, G. V. How may salience of a membership group be increased? *Journal of Educational Measurement*, 1964, **1**, 125–129.

Glass, G. V. Alpha factor analysis of infallible variables. *Psychometrika*, 1966, **31**, 545–561.

Glass, G. V. Response to Traub's "Note on the reliability of residual change scores." *Journal of Educational Measurement*, 1968, **5**, 265–267.

Glass, G. V. & Stanley, J. C. *Statistical methods in education and psychology*. Englewood Cliffs, N. J.: Prentice-Hall, 1970.

Gleser, G. C., Cronbach, L. J., & Rajaratnam, N. Generalizability of scores influenced by multiple sources of variance. *Psychometrika*, 1965, **30**, 395–418.

Goodenough, F. L. A critical note on the use of the term "reliability" in mental measurement. *Journal of Educational Psychology*, 1936, **27**, 173–178.

Goodenough, F. L. *Mental testing; its history, principles, and applications*. New York: Rinehart, 1949.

Gulliksen, H. O. *Theory of mental tests*. New York: Wiley, 1950.

Guttman, L. A basis for analyzing test-retest reliability. *Psychometrika*, 1945, **10**, 255–282.

Guttman, L. Reliability formulas that do not assume experimental independence. *Psychometrika*, 1953, **18**, 225–239.

Harman, H. H. *Modern factor analysis*. (2nd ed.) Chicago: University of Chicago Press, 1967.

Hendrickson, G. F. An assessment of the effect of differentially weighting options within items of a multiple-choice objective test using a Guttman-type weighting scheme. Unpublished PhD dissertation, Johns Hopkins University, 1970.

Herzberg, P. A. The parameters of cross-validation. *Psychometrika Monograph Supplement*, 1969, **34**(2, Pt. 2, Whole No. 16).

Horn, J. L. On the internal consistency reliability of factors. *Multivariate Behavioral Research*, 1969, **4**, 115–125.

Horst, P. Optimal test length for maximum differential prediction. *Psychometrika*, 1956, **21**, 51–66.

Horst, P. *Psychological measurement and prediction*. Belmont, Calif.: Wadsworth, 1966.

Horst, P., & MacEwan, C. Optimal test length for maximum absolute prediction. *Psychometrika*, 1956, **21**, 111–124.

Horst, P., & MacEwan, C. Optimal test length for multiple prediction: The general case. *Psychometrika*, 1957, **22**, 311–324.

Hoyt, C. Test reliability estimated by analysis of variance. *Psychometrika*, 1941, **6**, 153–160.

Humphreys, L. G. The normal curve and the attenuation paradox in test theory. *Psychological Bulletin*, 1956, **53**, 472–476.

Hunter, J. E. Probabilistic foundations for coefficients of generalizability. *Psychometrika*, 1968, **33**, 1–18.

Jackson, R. W. B. Reliability of mental tests. *British Journal of Psychology*, General Section, 1939, **29**, 267–287.

Jackson, R. W. B., & Ferguson, G. A. Studies on the reliability of tests. University of Toronto, *Department of Educational Research Bulletin*, 1941, No. 12.

Jensen, A. R. The reliability of projective techniques. I. Review of the literature. II. Methodology. *Acta Psychologica*, 1959, **16**, 3–31 & 32–67.

Jöreskog, K. G. Statistical analysis of sets of congeneric tests. Educational Testing Service *Research Bulletin*, 1969, No. 97.

Kaiser, H. F., & Caffrey, J. Alpha factor analysis. *Psychometrika*, 1965, **30**, 1–14.

Kelley, T. L. The reliability of test scores. *Journal of Educational Research*, 1921, **3**, 370–379.

Kelley, T. L. *Statistical method*. New York: Macmillan, 1924.

Kelley, T. L. *Interpretation of educational measurements*. Yonkers-on-Hudson, N. Y.: World Book, 1927.

Kelley, T. L. The reliability coefficient. *Psychometrika*, 1942, **7**, 75–83.

Kelley, T. L. *Fundamentals of statistics*. Cambridge, Mass.: Harvard University Press, 1947.

Koutsopoulos, C. J. The mathematical foundations of classical test theory: an axiomatic approach. Educational Testing Service *Research Bulletin*, 1962, No. 17; ETS *Research Bulletin*, 1964, No. 3.

Kristof, W. Estimation of true score and error variance for tests under various equivalence assumptions. *Psychometrika*, 1969, **34**, 489–507.

Kuder, G. F., & Richardson, M. W. The theory of the estimation of test reliability. *Psychometrika*, 1937, **2**, 151–160.

Linden, K. W., & Linden, J. D. *Modern mental measurement: A historical perspective* Boston: Houghton Mifflin, 1968.

Lindquist, E. F. *Design and analysis of experiments in psychology and education*. Boston: Houghton Mifflin, 1953.

Livingston, S. A. Some observations on the estimation of true scores. Center for Social Organization of Schools *Technical Report*, The Johns Hopkins Univ., June 1970, No. 69. (a)

Livingston, S. A. The reliability of criterion-referenced measures. *Ibid.*, July 1970, No. 73. (b)

Livingston, S. A., & Stanley, J. C. What is the "true" coefficient of partial correlation? Baltimore: Prof. Stanley, The Johns Hopkins Univ., June 1970.

Loevinger, J. A systematic approach to the construction and evaluation of tests of ability. *Psychological Monograph*, 1947, **61**(4, Whole No. 285).

Loevinger, J. Person and population as psychometric concepts. *Psychological Review*, 1965, **72**, 143–155.

Loevinger, J., Gleser, G. C., & DuBois, P. H. Maximizing the discriminating power of a multiple-score test. *Psychometrika*, 1953, **18**, 309–317.

Lord, F. M. A theory of test scores. *Psychometric Monograph*, 1952, No. 7.

Lord, F. M. The measurement of growth. *Educational and Psychological Measurement*, 1956, **16**, 421–437.

Lord, F. M. A significance test for the hypothesis that two variables measure the same trait except for errors of measurement. *Psychometrika*, 1957, **22**, 207–220.

Lord, F. M. Further problems in the measurement of growth. *Educational and Psychological Measurement*, 1958, **18**, 437–451.

Lord, F. M. Tests of the same length do have the same standard error of measurement. *Educational and Psychological Measurement*, 1959, **19**, 233–239.

Lord, F. M. Elementary models for measuring change. In C. W. Harris (Ed.), *Problems in measuring change*. Madison: University of Wisconsin Press, 1963. Pp. 21–38.

Lord, F. M. A paradox in the interpretation of group comparisons. *Psychological Bulletin*, 1967, **68**, 304–305.

Lord, F. M. Estimating true-score distributions in psychological testing (an empirical Bayes estimation problem). *Psychometrika*, 1969, **34**, 259–299.

Lord, F. M. Some test theory for tailored testing. In W. H. Holtzman (Ed.), *Computer assisted instruction, testing, and guidance*. New York: Harper & Row, 1970, in press.

Lord, F. M. Robbins-Monro procedures for tailored testing. *Educational and Psychological Measurement*, 1971, **31**, in press.
Lord, F. M., & Novick, M. R. *Statistical theories of mental test scores*. Reading, Mass.: Addison-Wesley, 1968.

McHugh, R. B. The interval estimation of a true score. *Psychological Bulletin*, 1957, **54**, 73–74.
McNemar, Q. On growth measurement. *Educational and Psychological Measurement*, 1958, **18**, 47–55.
Maxwell, A. E. The effect of correlated errors on estimates of reliability coefficients. *Educational and Psychological Measurement*, 1968, **28**, 803–811.
Mendro, R. L., & Glass, G. V. The approximate sampling distribution of the stratified-alpha generalizability coefficient. University of Colorado, Laboratory of Educational Research, Research Paper No. 26, 1969.
Millman, J., Bishop, C. H., & Ebel, R. L. An analysis of test-wiseness. *Educational and Psychological Measurement*, 1965, **25**, 707–726.
Millman, J., & Glass, G. V. Rules of thumb for writing the anova table. *Journal of Educational Measurement*, 1967, **4**, 41–51.

Nitko, A. J., & Feldt, L. S. The power functions of some proposed tests for the significance of coefficient alpha. Paper presented at American Educational Research Association convention, Los Angeles, 1969. For abstract see V. Crockenberg (Ed.), *AERA paper abstracts, 1969*. Washington: AERA, 1969. (a)
Nitko, A. J., & Feldt, L. S. A note on the effect of item difficulty distributions on the sampling distribution of KR20. *American Educational Research Journal*, 1969, **6**, 433–437. (b)
Norman, W. T. On estimating psychological relationships: Social desirability and self-report. *Psychological Bulletin*, 1967, **67**, 273–293.
Novick, M. R. The axioms and principal results of classical test theory. *Journal of Mathematical Psychology*, 1966, **3**, 1–18.
Novick, M. R. Bayesian inference and the classical test-theory model. Educational Testing Service *Research Bulletin*, 1970, No. 6, in press.
Novick, M. R., & Jackson, P. H. Bayesian guidance technology. *Review of Educational Research*, 1970, **40**, in press.
Novick, M. R., & Lewis, C. Coefficient alpha and the reliability of composite measurements. *Psychometrika*, 1967, **32**, 1–13.
Nunnally, J. C. *Psychometric theory*. New York: McGraw-Hill, 1967.

Olkin, I., & Pratt, J. W. Unbiased estimation of certain correlation coefficients. *Annals of Mathematical Statistics*, 1958, **29**, 201–211.
Owen, R. J. A Bayesian approach to tailored testing. Educational Testing Service *Research Bulletin*, 1969, No. 92.

Payne, W. H., & Anderson, D. E. Significance levels for the Kuder-Richardson twenty: An automated sampling experiment approach. *Educational and Psychological Measurement*, 1968, **28**, 23–39.
Pearson, K. Mathematical contributions to the theory of evolution: III. Regression, heredity and panmixia. *Philosophical Transactions*, A, 1896, **187**, 253–318.
Pearson, K. Historical note on the origin of the normal curve of errors. *Biometrika*, 1924, **16**, 402–404.
Pollack, I. Information theory. In D. L. Sills (Ed.), *International encyclopedia of the social sciences*, 1968, Vol. 7, pp. 331–337.
Porter, A. C. The effects of using fallible variables in the analysis of covariance. Unpublished Ph.D. dissertation, University of Wisconsin (Madison 53706), 1967.

Rajaratnam, N. Reliability formulas for independent decision data when reliability data are matched. *Psychometrika*, 1960, **25**, 261–271.
Rajaratnam, N., Cronbach, L. J., & Gleser, G. C. Generalizability of stratified-parallel tests. *Psychometrika*, 1965, **30**, 39–56.

Richardson, M. W., & Kuder, G. F. The calculation of test reliability coefficients based on the method of rational equivalence. *Journal of Educational Psychology*, 1939, **30**, 681–687.

Rozeboom, W. W. *Foundations of the theory of prediction.* Homewood, Ill.: Dorsey, 1966.

Rulon, P. J. A simplified procedure for determining the reliability of a test by split halves. *Harvard Educational Review*, 1939, **9**, 99–103.

Sax, G., & Collet, LeV. S. An empirical comparison of the effects of recall and multiple-choice tests on student achievement. *Journal of Educational Measurement*, 1968, **5**, 169–173.

Scates, D. E. Fifty years of objective measurement and research in education. *Journal of Educational Research*, 1947, **41**, 241–264.

Scheffé, H. *The analysis of variance.* New York: Wiley, 1959.

Spearman, C. The proof and measurement of association between two things. *American Journal of Psychology*, 1904, **15**, 72–101.

Spearman, C. Correlation calculated from faulty data. *British Journal of Psychology*, 1910, **3**, 271–295.

Spearman, C. Correlations of sums or differences. *British Journal of Psychology*, 1913, **5**, 417–426.

Stanley, J. C. K-R 20 as the stepped-up mean item intercorrelation. *14th Yearbook of the National Council on Measurement in Education*, 1957, pp. 78–92. (a)

Stanley, J. C. Index of means vs. mean of indices. *American Journal of Psychology*, 1957, **70**, 467–468. (b)

Stanley, J. C. Analysis of unreplicated three-way classifications, with applications to rater bias and trait independence. *Psychometrika*, 1961, **26**, 205–219.

Stanley, J. C. Analysis-of-variance principles applied to the grading of essay tests. *Journal of Experimental Education*, 1962, **30**, 279–283.

Stanley, J. C. *Measurement in today's schools.* (4th ed.) Englewood Cliffs, N. J.: Prentice-Hall, 1964.

Stanley, J. C. Problems in equating groups in mental-retardation research. *Journal of Special Education*, 1967, **1**, 241–256. (a)

Stanley, J. C. General and special formulas for reliability of differences. *Journal of Educational Measurement*, 1967, **4**, 249–252. (b) Errata, *Ibid.*, 1968, **5**, 181.

Stanley, J. C. Maximum possible Kuder-Richardson Formula 20 coefficients for test scores from constant, rectangular, and rectangular-normal distributions of difficulties of dichotomously scored zero-chance-success items. In *Proceedings, 76th Annual Convention, American Psychological Association*, 1968. Pp. 185–186.

Stanley, J. C. Definition of true score appropriate for estimated true scores. *Educational and Psychological Measurement*, 1970, **30**, 523–531.

Stanley, J. C. Reliability of test scores and other measurements. In L. C. Deighton (Ed.), *Encyclopedia of education.* New York: Macmillan, 1971, in press.

Stanley, J. C., & Wang, M. D. Weighting test items and test-item options, an overview of the analytical and empirical literature. *Educational and Psychological Measurement*, 1970, **30**, 21–35.

Thorndike, E. L. *An introduction to the theory of mental and social measurements.* New York: Science Press, 1904.

Thorndike, R. L. *Personnel selection; test and measurement techniques.* New York: Wiley, 1949.

Thorndike, R. L. Reliability. In E. F. Lindquist (Ed.), *Educational measurement.* Washington: American Council on Education, 1951. Pp. 560–620.

Thorndike, R. L. *The concepts of over- and underachievement.* New York: Columbia University, Teachers College, Bureau of Publications, 1963.

Thorndike, R. L. Reliability. In *Proceedings of the 1963 Invitational Conference on Testing Problems.* Princeton, N. J.: Educational Testing Service, 1964. Pp. 23–32.

Thorndike, R. L., & Hagen, E. *Measurement and evaluation in psychology and education.* (3rd ed.) New York: Wiley, 1969.

Thurstone, L. L. *The reliability and validity of tests.* Ann Arbor, Mich.: Edwards Brothers, 1932.

Traub, R. E. Comment on Glass' response. *Journal of Educational Measurement*, 1968, **5,** 343–345.

Tryon, R. C. Reliability and behavior domain validity: Reformulation and historical critique. *Psychological Bulletin*, 1957, **54,** 229–249.

Tucker, L. R. Maximum validity of a test with equivalent items. *Psychometrika*, 1946, **11,** 1–13.

Tucker, L. R. A note on the estimation of test reliability by the Kuder-Richardson formula (20). *Psychometrika*, 1949, **14,** 117–119.

Tucker, L. R., Damarin, F., & Messick, S. A base-free measure of change. *Psychometrika*, 1966, **31,** 457–473.

Walker, H. M. *Studies in the history of statistical method.* Baltimore: Williams & Wilkins, 1929.

Wang, M. D., & Stanley, J. C. Differential weighting, a survey of methods and empirical studies. *Review of Educational Research*, 1970, **40.**

Webster, H. A generalization of Kuder-Richardson reliability formula 21. *Educational and Psychological Measurement*, 1960, **20,** 131–138.

Werts, C. E., & Linn, R. L. Path analysis: Psychological examples. *Psychological Bulletin*, 1970, **74,** 193–212.

Winer, B. J. The error. *Psychometrika*, 1968, **33,** 391–403.

14. Test Validation

Lee J. Cronbach
Stanford University

Narrowly considered, *validation* is the process of examining the accuracy of a specific prediction or inference made from a test score.[1] Suppose, for example, that a "readiness test" ranks first graders according to their anticipated progress under a given school's program of instruction in reading. The accuracy of such forecasts is investigated by comparing each pupil's actual progress during the year with what the test had predicted. More broadly, validation examines the soundness of *all* the interpretations of a test—descriptive and explanatory interpretations as well as situation-bound predictions.

To explain a test score, one must bring to bear some sort of theory about the causes of the test performance and about its implications. Validation of test interpretations is similar, therefore, to the evaluation of any scientific theory. Physical scientists, one notes, speak not of validating a measuring procedure but of validation of scientific theories, as in the title of Frank's (1956) symposium volume. Since each experiment checking upon a theory is an opportunity to modify or extend the theory, validation is more than corroboration; it is a process for developing sounder interpretations of observations. Construction of a test itself starts from a theory about behavior or mental organization, derived from prior research, that suggests the ground plan for the test. Studies of the new test show how to improve it and some-

times lead to a change in the very conception of the variable to be measured.

A case in point is the *California F Scale* (Adorno et al., 1950), which asks the examinee whether he agrees or disagrees with a list of statements. Since the statements imply respect for power and distrust of human inclinations, the scale originally was thought to measure adherence to authoritarian beliefs. Validation studies led to the counterinterpretation that the agree-disagree format accounts for many (or even most) high scores. In this view, high scorers are habitual "yea sayers" who agree with just about any assertion, whereas low scorers are more likely to be independent and critical. The framing of this hypothesis led to studies of acquiescence as a personality trait and to the creation of instruments expressly designed to appraise acquiescence (e.g. Hundleby, 1966); findings from studies on acquiescence are summarized by Wiggins (1968, esp. p. 308). These studies have implications reaching far beyond the *F* Scale itself: the acquiescence hypothesis is now considered in any research that uses questionnaires to study personality, to assess the effectiveness of some procedure for citizenship education, etc.

In the narrow view, validation consists of checking the test score against some other observation that serves as *criterion*. The aim of testing is to predict this criterion, and the merit of the test is judged simply by the accuracy of prediction. The theory of prediction was very nearly the whole of validity theory until about 1950; in the last two decades, testers have given increasing attention to descriptive and explanatory interpretations and have relegated prediction theory to a secondary position. All validations rely on mathematical formulations developed for prediction studies: basic sources

---

[1] For simplicity, I refer to tests and test scores throughout the chapter. The statements, however, apply to all procedures for collecting data, including observations, questionnaires, ratings of artistic products, etc. Most statements apply to protocols and qualitative summaries as well as to numerical scores. For some writers, *to validate* means to demonstrate the worth of, but I intend to stress the openness of the process—i.e. *to validate* is *to investigate*.

on these formulations are *The Prediction of Personal Adjustment* (Horst et al., 1941), *Personnel Selection* (Thorndike, 1949), *Theory of Mental Tests* (Gulliksen, 1950), and *Statistical Theories of Mental Test Scores* (Lord & Novick, 1968).

Whereas most theoretical papers on prediction develop algorithms for processing validation data, one recent development—statistical decision theory—is primarily conceptual. This set of ideas can be brought to bear whenever decision makers employ tests to obtain better practical results—e.g. in assignment of students to different instructional paths. While decision theory is mathematical, the formulas it offers (Cronbach & Gleser, 1965) are significant more because they cause the decision maker or test designer to view his work in a new light than because of any assistance they offer in the processing of data. (This viewpoint, introduced briefly in the present chapter for the help it gives in planning and interpreting validity studies, reappears in chapter 19, which is devoted to decision making in education.) The formal conclusions reached by applying prediction theory or decision theory are literally true only when the test will be used in a situation just like that in which validation was carried out and when the criterion in the validation study is accepted as complete and free from bias. The modern specialist in industrial psychology (Dunnette, 1967) sees the formal theories not as giving the decision maker a rule for action but as aiding him to think about the meaning of the test in his situation. Undoubtedly educators will swing to this same conception.

Much of the writing on validation since 1950 has been concerned with validating descriptive or theoretical interpretations and with the logical and procedural requirements for such validation. The lead in this direction was taken by the Cureton (1951) chapter of the first edition of this book and by Peak's (1953) paper on social-psychological observations. (See also a very early paper on sociological measures by Bowers, 1936.)

The broader view of validity was given formal recognition in *Technical Recommendations*, prepared in two companion versions by a joint committee of professional organizations (American Psychological Association, 1954, for psychology, and American Educational Research Association, 1955, for education) and later reissued with some extensions and revisions in a single version, *Standards for Educational and Psychological Tests* (American Psychological Association, 1966). The committee was charged with setting forth quality standards for commercially published tests. To carry out the charge the committee stated, as explicitly as it could, what validating research should be completed before a test is widely distributed. To develop recommendations applicable to the varied types and uses of tests, the committee distinguished three types of validity—criterion-related, content, and construct (American Psychological Association, 1966—wording slightly altered here):

Criterion-related [predictive] validation compares test scores, or predictions made from them, with an external variable [criterion] considered to provide a direct measure of the characteristic or behavior in question.

Content validity is evaluated by showing how well the content of the test samples the class of situations or subject matter about which conclusions are to be drawn.

Construct validity is evaluated by investigating what psychological qualities a test measures; i.e. by determining the degree to which certain explanatory concepts or constructs account for performance on the test [pp. 12–13].

This terminology has been generally accepted but not without objection; in particular, several authorities on educational testing consider the treatment of achievement test validation in the *Standards* inadequate (personal communications). Preparation of the initial *Technical Recommendations* was sponsored by educational research organizations, but it received its impetus from the American Psychological Association. The critical issues at the time were those arising from the spurt in diagnostic testing of mental patients by clinical psychologists. The investigations and theoretical writings that stimulated the committee were those dealing primarily with personality measures, which attracted much attention between 1945 and 1955. Even Cureton, writing in the first edition of this book on educational measurement, developed as his principal example of a validation problem the measurement of generosity. In the present chapter it appears desirable to attempt a new statement centered on educational uses and interpretations of tests. Though this alters the emphasis and some details of the formulation, it is a direct evolution from the *Standards* rather than a contradiction of them.

Validation of an instrument calls for an integration of many types of evidence. The varieties of investigation are not alternatives any one of which would be adequate. The investigations supplement one another. The person validating a test should give thought to all questions suggested under the three rubrics listed by the committee, though the relative importance of the questions varies from test to test. For purposes of exposition, it is necessary to subdivide *what in the end must be a comprehensive, integrated evaluation of the test.*

Any description of how tests can and should be validated emphasizes ideals that are somewhat remote from practice.

1. The models employ logical and mathematical concepts (e.g. random sampling) that only rarely correspond to what can be achieved in practice. The rigorous argument such models permit clarifies what validation studies mean, even though the studies fit the model only loosely.

2. To conduct all the studies that may be relevant to a given test is far beyond the resources of a test developer. The scale of the validation effort will be determined by the circumstances of test development. At one extreme, a classroom teacher may make no systematic study of a quiz he gives his students. At the other, a publisher of an aptitude measure for extensive use in guidance may devote two years to research before the test is published and then periodically conduct additional studies as long as the test remains in print. Even in the former case, it is valuable for the teacher to know what types of questions about validity

may arise, if only to recognize the limitations of his quiz.

3. The developer's validation study ordinarily reports how well the test can perform in the hands of qualified observers and interpreters. Test administration and interpretation are likely to decline in quality when the test is released from the developer's control

In the end, the responsibility for valid use of a test rests on the person who interprets it. The published research merely provides the interpreter with some facts and concepts. He has to combine these with his other knowledge about the persons he tests and the assignments or adjustment problems that confront them, to decide what interpretations are warranted.

It is useful to distinguish two uses of tests: (*a*) for making decisions about the person tested and (*b*) for describing him. Decisions generally are intended to optimize some later "criterion" performance of the individual or group, hence the decision maker is particularly concerned with criterion-oriented validation. Descriptive use relies on content validity or construct validity. But the correspondence among categories is not so neat as this. The decision maker very often applies a test in a situation other than the one in which the validation was conducted; to defend such an extrapolation, he must use descriptive interpretations. And, on the other hand, where a test is to be used descriptively, studies relating it to a practical outcome may shed light on its interpretation. Table 14.1 summarizes the structure of the argument to be developed. Though table 14.1 will undoubtedly serve better as review than as preview, it is introduced here to serve as a road map. The wording is by no means the only way to state such concepts. The reader may consult papers by Loevinger (1957), de-Groot (1961), and Cattell (1964) for other arrangements of much the same ideas.

The order of this discussion, unlike that of the *Standards*, will come to the analysis of decision making last. Because construct validation is complex and of crucial importance, it is given a long section separate from the aspects of validation that rely primarily on judgments

TABLE 14.1
Summary of Types of Validation

FOCUS OF INVESTIGATION	QUESTION ASKED	USE MADE OF STUDENT RESPONSE DATA	USE MADE OF JUDGMENT
Soundness of Descriptive Interpretations:			
Content validity	Do the observations truly sample the universe of tasks the developer intended to measure or the universe of situations in which he would like to observe?	Scores on test forms constructed independently may be compared.	To decide whether the tasks (situations) fit the content categories stated in the test specifications. To evaluate the process for content selection, as described in the manual.
Educational importance	Does the test measure an important educational outcome? Does the battery of measures neglect to observe any important outcome?	None.	To compare the test tasks with the educational objectives stated by responsible persons.
Construct validity	Does the test measure the attribute it is said to measure? More specifically: the description of the person in terms of the construct, together with other information about him and in various situations; are these implications true?	Scores are compared with measures of behavior in certain other situations. Or the test is modified experimentally and changes in score are noted.	To select hypotheses for testing. To integrate findings so as to decide whether the differences between persons with high and low scores are consistent with the proposed interpretation. To suggest alternative interpretations of the data.
Usefulness for Decision Making (Criterion-Oriented):			
Validity for selection	Do students selected by the test perform better than unscreened students?	Regression of outcome measure on test score is examined.	To decide whether the criterion fully represents the outcomes desired, including outcomes more distant in time. To decide whether a new situation is enough like the validation situation for the results to generalize.
Validity for placement	Is performance improved when students are allocated to treatments according to their test scores?	Regression slope relating outcome measure to test score for one treatment is compared with that for another treatment.	Same as above.

about the test operations.

It is important to distinguish between absolute and comparative (differential) interpretations.[2] The testing movement in psychology started with the Darwinian emphasis on differences among individuals, and all the theoretical work behind test scores has attempted to conceptualize differences in abilities or traits. Practical psychological testing has been directed largely toward selection of students or employees or classification of psychiatric patients; in such decisions emphasis also has been on differences. Psychological test theory, therefore, has concentrated on comparative interpretations. For the psychologist, what the test measures has been defined as whatever causes some persons to get high scores and others to

[2] My use of the terms *absolute* and *differential* is unfortunately not the same as Horst's usage, which Hills adopts in chapter 19 to discuss another problem.

get low scores. If everyone scores the same except for variation due to errors of observation, the psychologist is likely to say unthinkingly that the test measures nothing. The preoccupation of psychometric theory with comparative measurement is reflected in the *Standards* and in the various "coefficients" used to appraise tests.

To locate an individual on a scale without reference to the distribution of test scores of his classmates or of a norm group is to make an absolute statement. (Such a scale need not have equal units or a "true zero point.") Educators frequently interpret absolute standings. If an end-of-course test shows that every mechanic in a training program has reached a required standard of proficiency, the educator is satisfied with the training program. The test, though reporting no individual differences, answers his question. In curriculum evaluation one always wishes to know the extent to which certain important kinds of behavior have been acquired; individual differences are of secondary concern. In student selection, test interpretation is absolute if there are places enough for all qualified applicants. A U.S. college considering an applicant from a foreign country needs to know whether he understands English well enough to succeed. Once it knows that he does, nothing is added to the interpretation by reporting where he ranks in relation to some reference group. Similarly in planning instruction, the decision to send the learner on to a more advanced unit of work or to provide further review depends on what *he* can do. The performance of his classmates has no bearing on the decision.

(The statement that the score of the individual can be interpreted by itself is likely to puzzle those who realize that any inference is based on past observations of other students. This is not to be denied. In a decision about the foreign student in the example above, it would be helpful to know how well previous foreign students with his test score succeeded. But information about his expected criterion performance is not information about his relative standing on the test [i.e. is not norm information; Glaser, 1963].)

Absolute measurement is well illustrated by the historic Ayres handwriting scale (Ayres, 1912). To create his scale, Ayres had judges arrange specimens of pupil handwriting according to quality. Then suitably spaced specimens were selected to represent different levels of proficiency. These standard specimens were reproduced to be used as a guide in assigning scores in the future. A teacher, looking at successive Ayres scores in a pupil's cumulative record, can judge how the pupil's handwriting has progressed simply by referring to the chart of specimens representing those score levels.

Recently there has been a revival of interest in the design of instruments for absolute measurement of educational outcomes (see Ebel, 1962; Glaser, 1963; Tyler, 1966). At the same time, absolute performance on mental test tasks has become a topic of general psychological theory. The logical theory of Piaget (Flavell, 1963) and the computer-based models of Simon and others (Hunt, 1968) attempt to account for a person's passing some tasks and failing others, not for his standing among his peers.

AIMS OF VALIDATION

The phrase *validation of a test* is a source of much misunderstanding. One validates, not a test, but an *interpretation of data arising from a specified procedure*. A single instrument is used in many different ways—Smith's reading test may be used to screen applicants for professional training, to plan remedial instruction in reading, to measure the effectiveness of an instructional program, etc. Since each application is based on a different interpretation, the evidence that justifies one application may have little relevance to the next. Because every interpretation has its own degree of validity, one can never reach the simple conclusion that a particular test "is valid."

An ancient view of the relation between tests and the "real world" still colors statements about tests. Once it was usual to design a test for a specific practical function—for example, to predict success in routine clerical work. Since one phenomenon of practical importance, differences in clerical success, was the raison d'être of the test, validation of the test reduced to one simple question. Today it is rare that one criterion is truly primary. Today's test is made to serve dozens of purposes. Indeed, most testing would be impracticable if one needed a different test for each decision. Even a test with a narrow purpose has many validities—the College Board Scholastic Aptitude Test is intended to forecast college success, but it does not predict equally well in all colleges and the relative importance of its Verbal and Quantitative subscores depends on the curriculum.

The asymmetric conception of the test as a predictor of a certain performance has been discarded in favor of a symmetric view. According to this symmetric view, persons are observed in situations. Some are artificial occasions for observations, which are called tests, and some are situations arising in the natural course of the person's work or schooling. Relating these observations to each other tells one about the situational demands and about the resources individuals bring to bear. To study the validity of a test interpretation is to study how behavior in one situation is related to behavior in another. Both observations reveal characteristics of the individual, and both types of behavior should be understood.

Decisions and Descriptive Interpretations

A decision is a choice between courses of action. The college admits or rejects a prospective student. The high school allocates an algebra student to a fast, average, or slow section. The primary school decides that one child should be taught to read immediately, and that another should first practice on auditory and visual discriminations. The justification for any such decision is a prediction that the outcome will be more satisfactory under one course of action than another. Testing is intended to reduce the number of incorrect predictions and hence the number of decisions that will be regretted later. When validating a decision-making process, the concern is with the question: What is the payoff when decisions are made in the proposed way, and how does this compare with the payoff resulting when decisions are made without these data?

This discussion proposes to contrast deci-

sion making with descriptive uses of tests (see Tukey, 1960). Whereas a decision dictates what will be done at an immediate juncture in a specific situation, a description can be used many times for many purposes. These are descriptive statements: Frank is mentally retarded; Marjorie can converse fluently in French; Sam has strong technical and mathematical interests; Tom knows statistical formulas but has difficulty in judging where to apply each one. In evaluation of instruction one makes somewhat similar descriptive statements about the class as a whole. Likewise, a scientific study—say, of the antecedents or consequents of political beliefs—leads to propositions describing citizens who have a certain set of beliefs. A description is more than an adjectival phrase; it pulls behind it a whole train of implications. To say that a child is mentally retarded is to call up a great number of expectations about what he will do in response to various demands. These expectations will bear on future decisions, but few if any of those choice-points can be definitely foreseen at the time of testing. To validate a description is to answer the question: When persons are described in this way on the basis of these data, *how much confidence can be placed in each of the implications of the description?*

While the distinction between decisions and descriptions clarifies the logic of validation, nearly every test leads to both types of interpretation. The Strong Vocational Interest Blank was conceived strictly in a predictive context, on the hypothesis that job success and satisfaction will be greater if young men enter careers consistent with their Strong scores. Today, however, the experienced counselor uses the test descriptively, to increase the client's understanding of himself. Per contra, a test originally descriptive in intent (e.g. a reading test) may be weighted into a decision rule. The decision maker asks only whether the test predicts outcome and need not stop to examine which reading skills the test covers, as he would for a descriptive interpretation. Abstract concepts apply to decisions, but they apply indirectly through sentences that conjoin many concepts to arrive at a prediction. The principal difference between decision making and description is that in the former the report on the test includes a specific practical recommendation, and in the latter the report stores information that can be used to reach recommendations about diverse concerns as they arise.

What Procedure Is Validated

The casual phrase *test validation* seems to imply that the score one interprets comes from a naked instrument. The instrument, however, is only one element in a procedure, and a validation study examines the procedure as a whole. Every aspect of the setting in which the test is given and every detail of the procedure may have an influence on performance and hence on what is measured. Are the examiner's sex, status, and ethnic group the same as those of the examinee? Does he put the examinee at ease? Does he suggest that the test will affect the examinee's future, or does he explain that he is merely checking out the effectiveness of the instructional method? Changes in procedure such as these lead to substantial changes in ability- and personality-test performance, and hence in the appropriate interpretation of scores. Such social-psychological effects are discussed at length by I. Katz (1964), Masling (1960), and Yamamoto and Dizney (1965). Schwarz's (1963) observations on how details of testing procedure affect scores also are pertinent.

The measurement procedure being validated needs to be described with such clarity that other investigators could reproduce the significant aspects of the procedure for themselves. Published tests have an explicit format that controls the procedure to a substantial degree. The wording of the items, the rules for scoring, the instructions given the person tested, the time limits, the amount of coaching or encouragement allowed, and the like, are specified. Even these controls leave room for variation in the age and sex of the examiner, the examinee's immediately preceding exertions or frustrations, and other significant influences. Techniques such as ratings, interviews, and observations of performance usually are controlled even less completely.

Operational definition of the universe of procedures

A report of validation research contains, explicitly or implicitly, an operational definition of the procedure under study. This definition indicates the class of stimuli to which the person is exposed, the instructions he is given, and the rules by which his responses are evaluated. The set of conditions that obtained in the validation study is only one among many sets of conditions that fit the definition. For the research to be maximally useful, all such sets of conditions should be equivalent; that is, they should have the same relationships with other variables and, consequently, the same significance. The person planning a validation study must make a judgment as to which aspects of the procedure can be altered without substantially altering a person's score and which cannot (see N. E. Miller, 1959, p. 215). Aspects considered likely to affect the score should be controlled and should be included in the operational definition. The many combinations of conditions that conform to this definition constitute a *universe of admissible operations* (Cronbach, Rajaratnam, & Gleser, 1963; Cronbach et al., in press). The average of the scores the person would receive if he were (hypothetically) observed under all admissible sets of conditions is referred to as his *universe score*. This is an extension of the concept of *true score* (see chapter 13).

There are many reasons for not specifying every detail of the procedure, the most obvious being that the next investigator cannot fully reproduce the procedure originally used. Date of testing, room, examiner, and so on are sure to change. If Form A of the test is used in the validation study, strict operationism might seem to demand mentioning Form A in the definition. But an investigator will ordinarily have constructed the several forms of his test to be equivalent; and, if he has confidence that every form would generate similar validity data, he will not restrict the universe to one form. The universe definition amounts to a working hypothesis that all operations admissible under it are equivalent and open to much the same interpretation. This implies that all facets of the procedure that affect its meaning have been specified.

An investigator sometimes neglects to mention a significant aspect of his procedure. If so, another investigator whose procedure differs in this respect is measuring a different variable. The findings of the original validation do not apply to his score. The investigator validating a measure of personality may fail to include, as part of his definition of admissible procedures, the events preceding administration of the test. But Atkinson and his colleagues, studying a certain projective technique, found that its correlations and hence the meaning of the test score changed when subjects were in an "aroused" state, i.e. were tested at the time of a course examination (Atkinson & Feather, 1966, pp. 89–90, 289, 341). These investigators therefore specify a "neutral" occasion as part of the procedure for their test.

The universe definition may be so restrictive that later users of the instrument cannot adhere to the procedure called for; for example, the pupils in the validation study may be told that no one but the investigator at a distant university will see their scores, yet the test cannot be given this way when used for practical purposes by a school. If there is doubt as to whether a present tester's procedure is the same in all significant respects as the original, then the original validation data do not provide a solid justification for the interpretation of the present scores.

Two sets of admissible observations will not agree perfectly. This might seem to imply that a study of the validity of scores from one observation would not apply to observations under other admissible conditions. The validity study does apply, however, if one can regard the departures from equivalence as random errors that do not *systematically* alter the meanings of scores. For example, readers of essays are likely to assign rather different marks to the same papers. If this results from variations in mood and attention, the readers are giving different approximations to the same information. But if some readers are emphasizing logic, some grammatical form, and some literary style, then the marks they assign differ in meaning. The

procedure will have to be brought under greater control if validation based on one set of readers is to pertain to marks assigned by other readers. One control would be to give firm instructions to graders. A weaker control would be to ascertain the viewpoints of the original graders. Then the user of the method could determine that his graders, taken as a group, have preferences like those who provided data for the validation study.

Sequential procedures

Traditional test theory deals with an instrument of fixed length and content. This is unduly restrictive, as it often makes sense to modify the test to fit the individual. A sequential procedure is divided into stages; after each stage of testing one decides whether to terminate the test or to collect further data, and, if the latter, what data to collect. Individual tests always have been sequential to some degree. Complex sequential procedures now are possible in tests administered by computer. Though the sequential procedure branches in so many ways that no two subjects "take the same test," it is still necessary to inquire into the soundness of decisions or descriptions reached. To specify the procedure being validated is to specify the rules governing it: the items available, the contingencies that determine the sequence of items for the individual, and the scoring rules, together with all the other information required to define a more conventional test.

Clinical interpretations

The transformation of test performance into a report on the individual is a part of the procedure being validated, and therefore the transformation procedure has to be included in the universe definition. The transformation may be objective—an encoding operation that could be carried out by machine; or it may be subjective —an integration of the tester's impressions. A mechanical rule is obviously a part of the procedure. It is perhaps not so obvious that an informal method of drawing inferences is likewise part of the procedure being validated. The universe definition should specify the class of interpreters to be used and the instructions given to them. Only in some local and transitory context would one be satisfied to study the validity of judgments made by a particular Admissions Officer X for their own sake; the usual question is how well the procedure works in the hands of persons *like* X.

USES OF JUDGMENT IN VALIDATING DESCRIPTIVE INTERPRETATIONS

Descriptive interpretations take many forms. What the test measures may be described in a phrase; there may be a formal specification for the universe of tasks the test claims to represent; there may be an elaborate theory to account for the scores. Thus for the Remote Associates Test (Mednick & Mednick, 1967) the manual gives a fairly explicit definition of the content, an associated claim that the test reflects "the forming of associative elements into new [and useful] combinations," and a reference to a theoretical paper that advances numerous propositions about the origins of this trait and the behavior expected to accompany high and low degrees of the trait.

Several aspects of the validation of descriptions may be distinguished:

1. The universe specification defines a class of procedures. In most instances the test developer exhibits or describes one procedure and points to a broader universe that, in his opinion, it represents. An achievement test is said to represent a body of content outlined in the test manual. That outline constitutes the universe definition. To ask, Are the tasks used in collecting data truly representative of the specified universe? is to examine *content validity*.

2. An evaluative interpretation is made in deciding whether a curriculum is producing satisfactory results or whether a student is doing satisfactory work. To justify this, the test must measure the important outcomes. The question is: Was the right universe selected for measurement?

3. Where the description implies what is to be expected of a person, the validator asks: Is this expectation sound? Validation of the implications of the description is *construct valida-*

tion. A description that refers to the person's internal processes (anxiety, insight) invariably requires construct validation.

(There is a fourth question, about the interpretation suggested to the untrained person by the label attached to test scores. This question is discussed on pp. 460–62.)

As illustration, consider the Thurstone-Chave (1929) scale for measuring attitude toward the church:

1. This scale is accompanied by an unusually complete account of the process of construction; one who studies the report is reasonably sure what universe of opinions the test represents and why certain scores are interpreted as "neutral." Content validity therefore was satisfactory as a measure of 1929 opinions; the test does fit the specified universe, though a similar universe of opinions today would not be identical.

2. Religious educators presumably regard a favorable attitude toward the church as an important potential outcome of their youth programs. The Thurstone-Chave scale, then, measures something useful in their evaluations. But it surely does not collect all the attitudinal information desired. Dealing with the church in general, it does not tell the religious educator how students feel about their own particular denomination; consequently, it is not by itself an adequate evaluation instrument.

3. Construct validation calls for evidence on such questions as: Does the Thurstone-Chave score really indicate what the person believes, or can he fake so as to make a good impression? Does a strongly positive score imply more active participation in church programs? Does a high score imply the same feelings in a highly educated person as in an uneducated person? The first question might require an experiment in which a random half of the subjects are directed to try to present a church-favoring image of themselves. For the second question, one would have to devise an index of participation based on actual behavior and compare this with test scores. For the third, a depth interview would perhaps be required to get at inarticulate beliefs.

Construct validation asks the broad question: Can one explain the test behavior and what it implies for behavior in other situations? The content consideration is one of sampling, of whether the test operations conform to the specification. The consideration in evaluation is importance—is the universe selected an important one? Content validation asks whether the test fits the developer's blueprint, and the question about importance asks whether the test user would have chosen the same blueprint. Since users have different aims, no general answer to that question can be offered.

It might seem that educational importance is the critical aspect of an achievement test. But it is equally essential to show that the items are soundly selected to represent the objective. And construct validation is needed to give meaning to the results—to explain a poor performance, to forecast how it will handicap the student, to suggest how to teach more effectively in the future, etc.

A test score has an endless list of implications, and one cannot validate the entire list. Construct validation is therefore never complete. Construct validation is best seen as an ever-extending inquiry into the processes that produce a high or low test score and into the other effects of those processes. Many of the implications suggested for a score will prove unwarranted; ordinarily, this leads one to correct the theory used in interpreting the test rather than to reject the test.

Validity of the Test as a Content Sample

Whether the operations that finally constitute the test correspond to the specified universe is the question of content validity. It is so common in education to identify "content" with the subject matter of the curriculum that the broader application of the word here must be stressed. For observations of sociability, the universe specification presumably will define a category of "social acts" to be tallied and a list of situations in which observations are to be made. Each observation ought to have validity as a sample of this universe. Within the subject-matter conception of content, it may be wrong to restrict the universe to the content of

texts or lessons. The universe of content for a certain published test of skill in map reading, for example, was derived from textbooks and from recommendations by authorities. In the end, seven skills and various subskills, along with a classification of types of maps, formed the universe definition. The plan called for using several road maps even though these are rather uncommon in textbooks. Road maps, it is said, permit effective testing of skills that curriculum authorities propose be taught. Moreover, reading of road maps is important outside of school. Indeed, the authors recommend that the teacher enrich the instructional program by bringing in such maps, which amounts to saying that the universe specification for the test is more significant educationally than the universe on which the textbooks are based (Lindquist & Hieronymus, 1964, pp. 34–35; see also pp. 459–60 below).

Absolute character of content interpretations

Content validity has to do with the test as a set of stimuli and as a set of observing operations. The measuring procedure is specified in terms of a class of stimuli, an injunction to the subject that defines his task (i.e. what he is to try to do with the stimuli), and a set of rules for observing the performance and reducing it to a score. One may for the present think primarily of the achievement test that presents verbal items, tells the student to select the right answer, and applies a predetermined scoring key. But the argument is general, applying to a proficiency test in which the subject repairs an electronic apparatus and to an observation of how a child spends his time in the preschool. (To be sure, in the latter case the "injunction" may be no more than "It's time to go outside now, children.")

As Melton (1966) implied in discussing task taxonomies and process taxonomies in the analysis of learning, judgments about content validity should be restricted to the operational, externally observable side of testing. Judgments about the subject's internal processes state hypotheses, and these require empirical *construct* validation. With regard to the Watson-

Glaser Test of Critical Thinking, for example, it is a matter of content validation to have a qualified person judge whether the authors did indeed assemble a set of problems of the sort they called for in their specifications. To ask the judge whether scores reflect critical thinking is to solicit his speculations about construct validity.

Content validation as defined here looks on the test as an instrument for absolute measurement, though a test validated in this way may have differential uses also. From an absolute point of view the score on a task indicates that the person does or does not possess, in conjunction, *all* the abilities required to perform it successfully. A dictated spelling test is a measure of hearing *and* spelling vocabulary *and* ability to write. In terms of content, the spelling test tests ability to spell from dictation whether the pupil is deaf or has normal hearing.

In principle, validity of the selection of content is to be judged without considering at all the persons to be tested; attention is restricted to the test materials and the universe description. If the content is validly selected, the test is content-valid for persons of all kinds. Perhaps a student fails a test in chemistry because he works slowly, or his anxiety level is high, or his understanding of English is defective, or he makes computational errors. But he *has* failed to perform satisfactorily on a set of chemical problems, and the report of failure is valid. To protest the examination because too little time was allowed is to protest the definition, not the fit of the test to the definition. Very often such a protest rests on values, the objector regarding unspeeded performance as a more worthy educational aim than performance under time pressure. Another protest might be that the directions are inadequate, and hence the subject did not have a fair chance to show his knowledge of chemistry. But the directions are a part of the universe, and so it is the universe definition that is under criticism.

Response specifications

The universe specification often gives attention exclusively to the selection of topics, ignoring the form of stimulus and the response required. This can produce a bad test. For example, to decide when a gunner was sufficiently trained, the Navy tested his performance in gun operation. To reduce testing cost, a verbal pencil-and-paper examination covering gun operation was prepared, but it correlated only .62 with the performance test. Then a test in pictorial form was made to cover the same "content"; it correlated .90 with the performance test. The two pencil-and-paper tests proved to be far from interchangeable, the verbal test depending heavily on reading ability (Ninth Naval District Headquarters, Training Aids Section, 1945). A second example concerns the selection of file clerks. Two tests of "ability to alphabetize" were prepared. One gave five names in haphazard order and asked the applicant which name would come third after alphabetization. The other test gave four names in alphabetic order and asked where in the list a fifth name should go. Despite the superficial similarity, there was zero correlation between the tests (Mosier, 1947). Probably the second test is closer to the responses actually required of clerks who alphabetize.

Professional constructors of achievement tests cross a content outline with a set of response-process categories, expressing the latter in such terms as recall, reasoning, and application of principles. Such a specification has value in broadening the test. But, since task operations controlled by the tester are not to be confused with processes used by the subject, it is evident that the usual content-by-process grid is not a universe specification. An item qua item cannot be matched with a single behavioral process. Finding the answer calls for dozens of processes, from hearing the directions to complex integration of ideas. The shorthand description in terms of a single process is justified when one is certain that every person can and will carry out all the required processes save one. Even to speak of "required processes," however, is misleading, since the task can perhaps be performed successfully by alternative processes (French, 1965). A task that arouses analytic thinking in one student may require nothing but recall in a student who has previously encountered the problem (McGuire, 1963).

A proper response specification deals with the result a person is asked to produce, not the process(es) by which he succeeds or fails. "Reads printed words aloud" is a description of an observable response; it says nothing about whether the reader is to look and say or to sound the word out. A person who insisted on separating these two response processes would have to devise a new task specification, perhaps requiring the reading of nonsense constructions that no subject has seen before. If a category of the form, say, "ability to evaluate arguments" is to mean anything as a task specification, the designation must be fleshed out to describe something about the stimulus, the accompanying injunction to the subject, and the aspect of behavior to which the scorer is directed to attend.

The classification of objectives attempted in the *Taxonomy of Educational Objectives* (Bloom, 1956) does not adhere to the standard herein proposed. The authors stated that that classification is primarily educational and logical, with psychological considerations subordinate. Yet the *Taxonomy* deals with "the intended behavior of students . . . the ways in which individuals are to act, think or feel [p. 12]." Statements on response specifications in this chapter follow traditional psychological behaviorism. Kendler (1965), for example, equated "behavior" with "publicly observable acts and movements ranging from responses that are defined in terms of their achievements to specific muscular contractions and glandular secretions [p. 1]." Kendler clearly was willing to make inferences about internal processes but insisted on a sharp distinction between observations and inferences. It was the need for this very distinction that led educators originally to elaborate objectives in terms of behavioral indicators. The headings of the *Taxonomy* may be taken as working hypotheses for the psychological interpretation of test behavior. What processes a test measures can be established only by construct validation; even then, the conclusion applies only to a certain population of persons. (The investigator who uses the *Taxonomy* as a source of psychological constructs for interpreting tests will profit from the discussion of validation by Kropp, Stoker, & Bashaw, 1966.)

For a multiple-choice test, the specifications should go beyond a statement of topical categories to state the general characteristics of misleading alternatives (distractors). For some skill tests, it will even be possible to list half-a-dozen categories of errors that are to be systematically represented among the distractors. The content of an item can be altered radically by changing the distractors, while keeping the correct response the same. An arithmetic test may offer numerical distractors all of which are close to the correct answer, or it may offer a choice among widely scattered numbers. This changes what the test measures, as Messick and Kogan showed (1965).

Content validity necessarily is limited by the adequacy of the universe specification, which is usually couched in imprecise everyday terms and can rarely mention every pertinent aspect of the task. R. B. Miller (1962, esp. pp. 193–215) has provided a valuable discussion of task description, in the ideal case and as currently practiced. He noted that one must fall back upon a theory of task performance in deciding which cues or actions are relevant and therefore need to be specified. Hence, though psychological processes are not properly part of the task description, whatever one knows or suspects about them determines the way he specifies the universe. This is well illustrated in Hively's (1968) development of specifications for a "universe-defined" mathematics test.

The very model of sampling from a universe requires some defense, since even a sympathetic reviewer has called it "puzzling," "confusing," and "fuzzy" (Thorndike, 1966). Loevinger (1965) made a sharper attack; she accepted sampling from a population of persons but argued that to speak of sampling situations or items is an illegitimate extension of the model. Loevinger's recommendation—that claims of content validity be dropped and attention confined to construct validation—is sound in some contexts but much too sweeping (see p. 486).

The issues are too complex to treat adequately here, but a few comments may be clarifying. First, let it be agreed that true random sampling is rarely practiced.[3] Despite this, it is customary to apply statistics derived from a random-sampling model to groups of persons who were not truly drawn at random and are only loosely representative of the population of persons to which the investigator generalizes. Sometimes the mismatch between model and reality is serious, sometimes not, but the problem is not peculiar to content sampling. It is, rather, an outcropping of the age-old philosophical issue of how to justify inductive inference.

A more directly pertinent argument is that persons are discrete elements and that the population is in principle countable, whereas content is an ill-shaped and undifferentiated mass. Hence there is a danger of vagueness in any reference to a content universe. Moreover, while there may be a definable domain of content there is no existing universe of items. The only items in existence are those that constitute the so-called sample. Though it must be acknowledged that writing items to fit a content domain matches the drawing of beans from an urn much less neatly than does sampling of persons, at least two points in defense still can be made.

1. The requirement is that universe boundaries be well defined; this is the requirement of operational definition. It is a requirement equally in thinking about populations. Even to arrive at the presently accepted limits of the human species was a cultural achievement, and some population concepts in current use (e.g. "middle-class males in Western countries") are quite loose in definition. For a statement about a population to be rigorous, the population

must be defined well enough that qualified readers can agree as to whether any particular person is included by the definition or ruled out by it. So also for universes of items.

2. It is not essential that a universe be denumerable (helpful though that would be). Sampling the atmosphere to measure the presence of fission products must, like content sampling, dip a bucket into an ill-defined and inhomogeneous flow. The sample may not be representative. In preparing test items to represent topics there is a similar risk, which is discussed in the following section.

A duplicate-construction experiment

What, now, would constitute a rigorous validation of the fit between the operational definition of the universe and the actual test operations? To stimulate thought one can suggest an experimental validation through duplicate construction. The construction would involve judgment, but the validation would employ completely hard data. No study such as is outlined here has ever been carried out, though Ebel (1962) has approximated it. While studies of this sort will surely provide disturbing results, they have much to teach regarding the preparation of instructions for item writers.

In principle, the rules for selecting test content can be described so fully that there is virtually no uncertainty as to what domain of tasks is sampled. The would-be driver in California must demonstrate "knowledge of the State Motor Vehicle Code." The responsible officials have set a passing standard, say, 85 percent. The content to be covered appears in a finite set of paragraphs. The test constructor may write one or more multiple-choice questions on each paragraph of the code. He will next ask competent judges to review the questions, rating a question acceptable if a person who understands the relevant paragraph will select the right answer and the person who has a false idea on that point will not. Some form of tryout followed by item analysis is the likely next step. Finally, the test maker will choose, say, 40 questions to constitute one form of the test.

[3] Even in purely scientific work with animals, while subjects are randomly *assigned* to experiments, they are not randomly chosen from their class. Yet the investigator generalizes to the class: a species, a strain, an age group within the strain, etc. (Bakan, 1968, pp. 19 ff.)

The experimental verification would call for a second team of equally competent writers and reviewers to work independently of the first, according to the same plan. They would be aided by the same definition of relevant content, sampling rules, instructions to reviewers, and specifications for tryout and interpretation of the data as were provided to the first team—they would work from the same operational definition of admissible procedures. If the universe description and the sampling are ideally refined, the first and second tests will be entirely equivalent. Any person's score will be the same on both tests, within the limits of sampling error.[4] To be precise, if the scores are X_1 and X_2 and the corresponding standard errors of measurement are σ_{e_1} and σ_{e_2}, then the mean of $(X_1 - X_2)^2$ should be no larger than $\sigma_{e_1}^2 + \sigma_{e_2}^2$. For this purpose σ_{e_1} and σ_{e_2} can be derived from split-half analyses of X_1 and X_2 respectively.

A favorable result, on a suitable broad sample of persons, would strongly suggest that the test content is fully defined by the written statement of the construction rules. The evidence would provide a compelling answer to the rejected applicant who complains that the licensing test was unfair to him because a different set of examiners would have posed other questions. An unfavorable result would indicate that the universe definition is too vague or too incomplete to provide a content interpretation for the test.

To be sure, test construction is no better than the writers and reviewers of items. If there is a tacit assumption, on the part of everyone who participates in the test construction, that a certain topic is of negligible importance, items on that topic will not appear in the test even though it falls within the universe definition. A common blind spot is almost impossible to detect.

As Lennon (1956) has put it, "a 'representative' sample is one that *re-presents* the universe—that is, one that duplicates or reproduces the essential characteristics of the universe in their proper proportion and balance [p. 301]." To get representativeness one must specify the logical subdivisions of the universe as well as its boundaries. The constructor may sample randomly, but he does better to sample systematically within subdivisions, drawing a certain proportion of the items or observations from each subdivision. There are various ways to fix the proportions. One possibility is ecological representativeness, such that each task category is weighted by its frequency of occurrence. One could define the ecology of the driver by considering any 10-minute period behind the wheel as a unit and, in principle, could sample such units systematically for a representative sample of drivers and observe whether each legal rule did or did not apply during each unit sampled. Rules having to do with turn signals and right-of-way would be checked with high frequency, while certain others such as the speed limits when towing a trailer would be checked infrequently. The number of test items on each topic would be made proportional to the frequency observed, or weights would be applied to produce a comparable effect. Another sampling rule, which would define a different universe of tests, would call for weighting traffic laws according to the frequency with which violations of them appear in accident reports.

Test construction is never so logical as this. Ambiguity remains in many definitions of universes; the importance of subtopics more often is established by judgments than by tallies; and reviewing of draft items is an art not reducible to rules. No one has ever carried out the two-team study. It is not at all uncommon, however, for the test developer to claim validity by construction, bolstering the claim with a detailed account of the construction process. The test manual may list the textbooks from which content for items was chosen or may display the specifications given to the item writers. The reader is left to judge for himself whether this definition is explicit enough to allow two inde-

---

[4] The term *sampling error* ordinarily is encountered in discussions of the accuracy of the mean score for a group of persons, sampled from a population, on a fixed test. Here, and at several other places in this presentation, the reference is to the accuracy of a mean score on a group of items or observations, sampled from a universe of admissable observations, for a fixed person. A more general treatment of these kinds of sampling variation is given in Cronbach et al., in press.

pendent teams to arrive at approximately interchangeable tests.

The experienced writer of test items will consider the whole idea of interchangeable tests unrealistic, because the difficulty of an item is determined by innumerable details of format and wording, not just by the sampling of content. It is unlikely that such details can be specified well enough in the universe description that two teams will write items of equal average difficulty even for the identical content. Yet this ideal should be approached if an absolute interpretation is to be made.

Accuracy of content

Judgment is required in establishing the accuracy of items as well as their relevance to the universe specifications. Test items should stand up under criticism from experts in the subject matter tested. Mathematicians should agree that the keyed answer in a mathematics test does indeed follow from the premises offered. In a Japanese test, specialists should agree that the form of the verb in the keyed answer is indeed the one normal in Japanese usage. An item in a biology test inquiring about identical twins should be consistent with the latest literature on the subject known to geneticists, not just with some out-of-date or superficial conclusion presented in a textbook. The tape-recorded national test in English for Japanese students should feature the voices of natives of English-speaking countries, not the accented speech of Japanese teachers of English.[5] (The authorities have at times deliberately selected the latter, to make the test easier.) Items that meet criteria like these are perhaps no longer representative of the content studied by the student, but it will rarely be argued that the validity of an educational test suffers because

[5] Even in this matter, however, there is room for subtlety. It seems obvious that a valid test of listening comprehension in English will present stimulus passages in the voice of a native speaker of English. But in Sarawak, where English is the official language and the subject is important in the curriculum, ability to understand the English spoken by teachers and officials of Malay or Chinese origin is what is needed. The student will rarely, or never, encounter a native speaker of English.

the key calls for the answers the student *should* have learned rather than those he was taught!

Content validity is impermanent. The items or tasks in the test reflect social events, job descriptions, accepted beliefs about the world, decisions about what the curriculum should cover, etc. These change with the passage of time, so that sooner or later the test becomes unrepresentative. The prospective user must be satisfied that a second team following the specified procedure *today* would arrive at a test reasonably like the original.

One cannot hope to perfect items to the point where a hypercritical reviewer cannot quibble over conceivable ambiguities or exceptions to the keyed answer. Statements dealing with complex subject matter are invariably open to some misinterpretation, as any textbook writer can testify. Test items (whether essay or objective) are especially difficult to write because they must be so brief. The function of the critical review is to eliminate likely misconceptions and particularly any misconception running through several items. Technical errors and ambiguities are not likely to impair test validity seriously unless they are sufficiently numerous to make a difference of several points in a person's score or unless items are to be interpreted one at a time. It is no answer to a critic, however, to point to high correlations between technically sound and technically unsound items. Such evidence suggests only that skill in test taking is a more important component of the score than mastery of the relevant content.

Irrelevance of correlational evidence

Correlations have nothing to do with content validation. Test constructors with a smattering of statistical training sometimes mistakenly use data from an item analysis to reduce the pool of items to a set of "homogeneous" items having consistently positive intercorrelations. *But nothing in the logic of content validation requires that the universe or the test be homogeneous in content.* The topics in the motor vehicle code are diverse: hand signals, right of way, reporting an accident, and so on. To make a decision about an applicant for a license, it is necessary to know whether he would pass a certain proportion of the items in the universe. If the items have low correlations (or if they vary in difficulty), it will take a larger sample of items for one to be confident that the examinee's universe score reaches the required level. No matter how heterogeneous the universe is, if given enough items one can estimate a universe score as precisely as wished. Low item intercorrelations do not necessarily imply failure of the test content to fit the definition. Indeed, if the universe is heterogeneous, consistently *high* item intercorrelations imply inadequate sampling. If one item stands apart from the others, having a low correlation with the test as a whole or with the other items in its subcategory, the test constructor ought of course to inspect the item. The low correlation may be a sign of ambiguity. Or it may be a sign of validity—the driver who doesn't pass the speed limit questions may be the one who does have first-hand knowledge of the penalties for speeding! When the test constructor routinely discards the item whose correlation with the total score for the item pool is low, he risks making the test less representative of the defined universe (Cox, 1965). It is improper to report high item-test correlations as evidence of content validity.

The correlation of items with a criterion is likewise irrelevant to content validity. No one seriously expects the scores of drivers to correlate well with a miles-without-accident criterion. If a study *were* to show a correlation of zero between the two, the legislature would not repeal the requirement that drivers study the code and pass a test. Legislators would argue that knowledge of the law has utility and that limiting the test to items that predict the criterion would be unsound. The law, for example, requires the driver to report a change of address to the state; an item testing knowledge of this would not correlate with the accident criterion, and yet it is of manifest importance.

Correlations between tests are irrelevant to content validity (except in the construction experiment). Some critics are inclined to object to the creation of separate tests or scores for per-formances that correlate highly. But even if there is a large correlation between, say, a measure of comprehension of chemical-bond theory and a measure of ability to apply chemical-bond principles, there is justification for keeping the measures separate. First, the absolute level of attainment of one objective might be much higher than that of the other; and this could suggest a need to modify the curriculum. Second, though the items correlate at the end of the instruction currently being given, some new instructional procedure might develop one competence while neglecting to develop the other. Keeping the categories separate in the list of objectives at least reminds all concerned to entertain such a possibility when evaluating the new program. This matter is discussed further in connection with construct validation, where correlations *are* relevant.

Improving content validity

Most of the worthwile suggestions for improving content validity have been made in earlier chapters on planning and writing the test, but the logic of content validation has some implications for the test constructor that deserve emphasis here.

A good test is not guaranteed merely by the assembly of "good" items. It is the ensemble of items that must be considered, and, if one is to judge whether the ensemble samples the right kinds of behavior, there must be clear specifications. The test constructor who takes content validity seriously will begin, not by jotting down items as they occur to him or by soberly preparing one item regarding each page of the textbook, but by translating each of his educational objectives into task specifications. He usually will be most successful if he subdivides his gross objective rather finely. Within each subdivision he will need to go beyond listing topics that might be tested, to state the forms in which behavior relevant to each topic appears. He needs to clarify whether the student is to be presented with technical words, descriptions of situations in everyday words, pictures of situations, or concrete objects. Response specifications are equally important. All too often, the multiple-choice format has been taken for granted. If the constructor thinks about his aims with an open mind he will often decide that the task should call for a response constructed by the student—written open-end responses or, if inhibitions are to be minimized, oral responses. Nor are the directions to the subject and the social setting of the test to be neglected in defining the task.

The test constructor, after thinking about the aspects of stimulus and response that affect success, must choose one of the many possible universe definitions, with the aid of whatever advice he can get. For one purpose, a listening test should perhaps measure children's ability to comprehend standard Middle-Atlantic middle-class enunciation; for another, a test of ability to understand the local dialect is wanted. One could construct a test that is content-valid for either purpose but not a test valid for both.

The universe definition, once completed, goes a long way toward generating the items to be used or the observations to be made. According to the rationale for content validity, substituting other types of tasks for those the specifications call for cannot be justified by the argument that the substitutes correlate highly with the specified items. This evidence is pertinent enough when one is to measure individual differences; but substituting recognition items for recall items or verbal items for pictorial items probably alters the absolute score, and thus does not report level of mastery of the specified universe. On the other hand, the test constructor is warned against making items uniform in any respect not called for by the task definition. To do so is to narrow the range of tasks and to obtain a relatively poor sample of the universe. The test of ability to comprehend spoken French should have passages read by as many qualified narrators as possible. This requires more effort than recording a single voice, but the benefit to validity is obvious. To test map reading one should employ maps with varying conventions—even including one or two maps where north is not at the top—unless the universe specification has ruled out such variations.

Educational Importance of What Is Measured

When observations at the end of instruction are used to determine how successful some educational activity has been, the interpretation embodies value judgments. If the values are not acceptable, the conclusion is not acceptable. An evaluation battery is a collection of procedures used to decide whether a given educational program is satisfactory, whether the individual student has made satisfactory progress, etc. The conclusion that posttest performance is satisfactory (or unsatisfactory) is warranted only if there is a match between the test content and educational aims. Hence the validity of an evaluative conclusion depends on the value question: Did the tests appraise the qualities I consider it most important to teach? That question might elicit a positive answer from one educator and a negative one from another looking at the same tests (Tucker, 1966).

A person deciding whether instruction has had satisfactory results must have some conception of acceptable performance (e.g. a score of 80 percent or better on a certain universe of words to be spelled). Suppose, now, that the content of every scale in the battery is unambiguously labelled and that the precision of each measure is adequate. A claim that the battery enables one to judge how satisfactory student performance is can then be challenged on any of three grounds: (a) on at least one of the scales, the proposed standard of performance is not accepted; or (b) at least one of the scales measures something of no importance; or (c) there is at least one outcome desired from the treatment that the battery does not assess. The third objection is the critical one. The first objection is easily met by applying a new standard to the data. Each educator ought to apply the standard appropriate to *his* institution, not the standard put forward by a remote arbiter. The second objection reduces to the first, for the educator who "attaches no importance" to variable Z is saying that any score along the range of Z is acceptable to him. He may, on grounds of efficiency, prefer not to spend time in measuring Z, but he cannot argue that measuring Z generates misinformation. So long as *some* persons reaching decisions about the course in question consider Z important—whether they are citizens in his community or educators in another community who will read his report—it would be well to measure that outcome. Otherwise the battery does not serve the purpose of those decision makers.

If the original test or battery is a composite covering various types of content or various objectives, it implicitly weights those elements, either by the number of items allocated to each or by the way the score is calculated. Such a weighting cannot satisfy decision makers who hold values unlike those of the test developer. *Consequently, an ideally suitable battery for evaluation purposes will include separate measures of all outcomes the users of the information consider important.* Admittedly, there is a practical limit to the number of outcomes that can be measured. Where an evaluation program leaves important outcomes unmeasured, these omissions ought at least to be pointed out to users of the information. Reporting separate scores allows for the application of various systems of values. It also enables the investigator to examine the nature of any weaknesses in the program. In his own studies of the data, the evaluator should look at each response in turn to extract fine grain information, and, in his reports, he very likely should give the frequency for each category of error separately.

The recommendation that the evaluation battery be comprehensive seems to run counter to the concept that an educational test should measure what has been taught. And students think a test "unfair" when it asks about topics not covered in the course. One can agree that it is unjust to let the fate of an individual be determine by a test for which, through no fault of his own, he is ill-prepared. But this only illustrates once more how a test valid for one decision can be invalid for another. Though it is unfair to judge the quality of a teacher's work by a test that does not fit the course of study he was directed to follow, that test may be a fair basis for judging the curriculum. If teacher plus course-of-study have left the pupil ignorant of contemporary literature, this is a significant fact about the adequacy of his education.

Sometimes a test can "fit the curriculum" entirely too well. If the key to a test in literary comprehension gives credit only for an "authorized" interpretation that the teacher has handed down to the students, it tells nothing about their ability to interpret literature. Far better is the plan of putting into an assigned reading list certain works marked "for examination only" which the teacher is forbidden to discuss. Paul Diederich, who proposed this, goes on to suggest having several teachers participate in the grading so that the student is not tempted to tailor his response to the tastes of his own teacher (see chap. 10, pp. 291–96). Glaser and Klaus (1962, p. 436) pointed out that it would be fundamentally wrong for a proficiency test to be restricted to the universe defined by the content of lessons; such a test could never disclose whether the course is covering a wide enough range of content and so would be failing to fulfill its purpose. The universe pertinent in summative evaluation is the universe of tasks graduates are expected to perform. To be sure, a curriculum developer who has a restricted objective can use a restricted test to determine how well he achieved *his* end. But if other educators considering adoption of the course desire outcomes that go beyond his aims, they will find his studies inadequate.

The primary reason for examining the whole range of outcomes that interest responsible educators is to maximize the soundness of evaluative conclusions. The effect of such measurement upon teachers and students is a further advantage. Teachers who honestly intend to cover a whole long list of objectives find that class time is insufficient to pursue them all with equal zeal. They are most likely to sacrifice those objectives for which no evaluation data will be collected. Similarly, the student, in deciding what to study and how, is strongly influenced by his perception of what "counts." Any broadening of the evaluation procedures is therefore likely to have a healthy educational effect.

Semantic Adequacy of the Test Title

A matter that is peripheral and yet of great importance concerns the choice of test title. A test may be highly valid in the content, construct, or predictive sense when properly interpreted with the aid of the full information provided in the test manual. In communications to teachers, employers, and the examinees themselves, however, a brief title or descriptive phrase states what the test is about. If this phrase is a poor summary of the sophisticated professional interpretation, it promotes possibly serious misconceptions.

A test of ability to discriminate pitch differences between pure tones can be made to have unassailable content validity. It is less safe to call the test a measure of pitch discrimination without further qualification. (In musical sounds overtones modify the task.) And the construction process gives no warrant at all for calling it a "measure of musical talent." Likewise, a test that predicts first-year grades in several technical institutes is probably a good test for certain academic decisions. But to call it a test of "engineering and physical science aptitude" suggests quite the wrong connotations to an employer or the admissions committee of a graduate school.

The user assumes that he knows what is meant by "musical talent," "engineering aptitude," "creativity," and "fundamentals of statistics." The sophisticated user will check whether his conception applies to the test by studying the instrument and the manual, but the unsophisticated one will not. It is therefore desirable that the labels communicate adequately. At worst, they should not suggest outright misconceptions.

Labels cannot be proof against misinterpretation. A label that communicates satisfactorily to psychiatrists will not be semantically appropriate for school personnel. The best strategy for the test developer is to devise a neutral label that does not attempt to suggest in a few words what the test score means. Labels that describe the tasks rather than the processes supposed to underlie successful performance are generally satisfactory; e.g. Porteus Maze Test, Outdoor Interests, Interpretation of Reading Materials in the Natural Sciences. Some tests have names deliberately chosen to mask from the subjects the purpose of the inquiry; it

is certainly legitimate to call an instrument "Inventory of Opinions" rather than "The Conformity Scale," though the use of disguised tests must be constrained by regard for the examinee's right to privacy.

Many criticisms made by test users arise from unacceptable labels. Consider the language teacher who says, "That test doesn't properly measure *my* students' 'mastery of Spanish.' I teach by the audiolingual method, and that test calls entirely for written responses to printed questions." The critic is comparing *his* definition of "mastery of Spanish" with the test content and protesting the mismatch. He is objecting to the test author's choice of universe, not to his selection of items. Similarly, in this objection: "This so-called test of achievement in elementary science covers only miscellaneous bits of knowledge such as the meaning of *centigrade* and *lever* and *spore*; it collects no evidence on the child's competence in scientific reasoning." Or: "This measure of 'attitude toward the Negro' collects reactions to statements about the Negro's legal rights but does not touch on willingness to associate with blacks."

These objections have two elements. One is an accusation of ambiguity, which can often be reduced or eliminated by a change in the label. If the Spanish test were labeled "ability to comprehend Spanish text," there would be little ground for semantic complaint. The second complaint, that what the test measures is educationally unimportant, does not challenge its interpretability. If the label makes clear what is measured, one is free to accept or reject the test for his own purpose. The claim that a test measures "knowledge of the names and locations of the bones of the human skeleton" may be completely valid even if no educator considers that knowledge important. To call the test a measure of "anatomical knowledge" or of "knowledge of health facts" is to imply a broader claim, objectionable on the grounds of truth-in-advertising. Whenever a prospective test user scans test items and concludes that they do or do not fit the label, he is informally examining semantic appropriateness.

Judgments by test users are rarely summarized in a statistical manner, but one could develop formal evidence of semantic appropriateness. One procedure would be for the investigator, having constructed his test, to mix his items into a collection of miscellaneous items from tangential domains. Then he would ask each judge to place check marks beside the items that, in his opinion, fall within the area denoted by the test label. Ideally, every item from the actual test would be checked as appropriate, and items supposed to measure something else would be checked rarely. The procedure could be extended to check the semantic appropriateness of subscore labels.

To claim validity on the basis of judgment is very often special pleading. An example is the following contention regarding an attitude measure for college applicants.

> The majority of the items . . . about a student's aspirations, attitudes, expectations, and personal needs (housing, financial aid, and the like) are valid in the sense that the student's response is the best single criterion; it is inconceivable that another person (a parent, teacher, or friend) or a special assessment device could provide more accurate information about a student's aspirations and expectations. The student himself is the best authority for responses to structured questions like: "What is the highest level of education you expect to complete?"

This argument is disingenuous. To be sure, the student knows his own hopes and fears, but will he express them candidly on a report to a college that is deciding whether to admit him, how much financial aid to offer him, etc.? Judgments about test items are worthless unless the judge maintains a skeptical attitude, remaining alert to ways in which an undeserving subject can earn a good score and vice versa. And no judge can give a dependable answer to the questions that require empirical validation, to which the discussion now turns.

INTERPRETATIONS EMPLOYING CONSTRUCTS

Whenever one classifies situations, persons, or responses, he uses *constructs*. The term *concepts* might be used rather than *constructs*, but the latter term emphasizes that categories are deliberate creations chosen to organize experience into general law-like statements. Some constructs are very close to the stuff of ordinary experience—red, for example, or human being. But even these concepts are cultural products. Different cultures distinguish different colors in the spectrum. Nor is it obvious to the untutored mind whether an African pygmy is a member of "our" species. Some constructs that start as works of imagination eventually are isolated and observed directly with the aid of suitable instrumentation (e.g. monochromatic light). Some constructs are little more than ecological categories embracing events that occur in the same context (e.g. the gross national product or facts about American literature). For some constructs there are only hazy and contradictory findings (as of this writing several constructs related to "cognitive style" fit that description). Some constructs (e.g. red-green color blindness) are embedded in well-articulated, well-substantiated theories.

Constructs for interpreting tests usually have been identified with a class of responses, particularly in the personality domain. A person is said to be extrovert, or emotionally stable, or persistent, for example. Another important class of constructs describes situations. There are, for example, the categories used to group occupations for such purposes as compiling employment trends, conducting sociological inquiries, and helping young people make vocational choices. One would scarcely say that a construct appears in the sentence, "This test indicates that you will do well as an assembler in this camera factory," but a situational construct is evident in "You will do well at fine manual work." The following references are pertinent to the formulation and validation of situational constructs: Sells, 1963; Pace and Stern, 1958.

The rationale for construct validation (Cronbach & Meehl, 1955) developed out of personality testing. For a measure of, for example, ego strength, there is no uniquely pertinent criterion to predict, nor is there a domain of content to sample. Rather, there is a theory that sketches out the presumed nature of the trait. If the test score is a valid manifestation of ego strength, so conceived, its relations to other variables conform to the theoretical expectations.

Constructs are important in educational measurement. Every time an educator asks, "But what does the instrument really measure?", he is calling for information on construct validity. Constructs help to interpret both measures used to appraise educational outcomes and measures used to forecast response to instruction. The relevance to education of personality constructs such as authoritarianism may be granted readily. It is perhaps less obvious that construct validation is relevant for tests of subject-matter learning. Many phrases used to characterize commonplace educational tests appear to describe mental processes: scientific reasoning, reading comprehension, etc. If such a term is amplified to specify a class of tasks, the interpretation can be limited to content interpretation. Interpreters, however, usually consider processes behind the score.

How process interpretations may go beneath the surface of a test is demonstrated by the recent research on simulation of intellectual processes such as playing chess, learning, and the solution of letter-series and analogies problems (Hunt, 1968; Reitman, 1965, esp. pp. 28–31, 203–240; Simon & Kotovsky, 1963). The investigator attempts to write a computer program that will respond to the problem in the same way that a human being does, making similar false starts and errors as well as correct responses. The program may be designed to fit people in general or one particular person. When and if simulation succeeds, it can describe the strategies the person uses, his techniques of self-regulation, and the like, and can display a computer program whose output matches his task performance. The program for, say, letter-series performance constitutes a theory to account for the person's behavior. Validation of this theory (an interpretation through constructs) is entirely separate from the validation of the test as a sample of letter-series problems.

Consider further reading comprehension as a trait construct. Suppose that the test presents paragraphs each followed by multiple-choice questions. The paragraphs obviously call for reading and presumably contain the information needed to answer the questions. Can a question about what the test measures arise? It can, if any counterinterpretation may reasonably be advanced. Here are a few counterhypotheses (Vernon, 1962):

1. The test is given with a time limit. *Speed* of reading may contribute appreciably to the score. The publisher claims that the time limit is generous. But is it?

2. These paragraphs seem abstract and dull. Perhaps able readers who have little *motivation* for academic work make little effort and therefore earn low scores.

3. The questions seem to call only for recall of facts presented in simple sentences. One wants to measure ability to comprehend at a higher level than word *recognition and recall.*

4. Uncommon words appear in the paragraphs. Is the score more a measure of *vocabulary* than of reading comprehension?

5. Do the students who earn good scores really demonstrate superior reading or only a superior *test-taking strategy?* Perhaps the way to earn a good score is to read the questions first and look up the answers in the paragraph.

6. Perhaps this is a test of *information* in which a well-informed student can give good responses without reading the paragraphs at all.

These miscellaneous challenges express fragments of a definition or theoretical conception of reading comprehension that, if stated explicitly, might begin: "The student considered superior in reading comprehension is one who, if acquainted with the words in a paragraph, will be able to derive from the paragraph the same conclusions that other educated readers, previously uninformed on the subject of the paragraph, derive." Just this one sentence separates superior vocabulary, reading speed, information, and other counterhypotheses from the construct, reading comprehension. The construct is not identified with the whole complex practical task of reading, where information and vocabulary surely contribute to success. A distinctive, separate skill is hypothesized. One can easily imagine a simulator asking: What do we have to provide for in the computer program, in addition to a word-recognition-and-interpretation mechanism, before the computer would answer these questions as this person does? If it can be established that there is an information-processing skill of comprehension distinguishable from speed, vocabulary, general knowledge, etc., then the school would try to invent methods of improving comprehension as such, and it would need an unconfounded measure of comprehension to judge how successful the instruction is.

Validating an interpretation using a construct investigates the effect of each disturbing influence pointed out by the counterhypotheses. Construct validation of the reading comprehension test is a step toward the design of a superior test, since corrections and controls can reduce some of the unwanted effects.

Educators are puzzled when a *content* category such as "ability to spell words ending in *-gn*" is referred to as a *construct*. But content categories almost always *are* constructs. A construct is an intellectual device by means of which one *construes* events. It is a means of organizing experience into categories. A culture forms a category when it is observed that certain things have similar causes, consequences, or correlates. Attention is paid to similarities that are useful in explaining and forecasting; other similarities are ignored. The *-gn* category of spelling words is a useful construct, because children who have trouble with some words in that category have trouble with most of them and because remedial teaching overcomes the entire difficulty without teaching every word in turn. The spelling teacher does not find *-gr* words (*agree, aggravate, angry*) a useful construct. Even though the category is logically defensible, it is not used because it does not correspond to the organization of spelling performance. While the content type of construct does lead to interpretations about what the high scorer can do in other situations and about the processes that enable him to earn the high score, the interpretative theories are usually thin and primitive. The Gagné "hierarchies" of achievement are networks offering empirical hypotheses about the content a person has mastered or might master (Gagné & Paradise, 1961).

Although a performance is always complexly determined by many characteristics of the test and its setting, interacting with many characteristics of the person, interpretation in terms of just one construct is often intended. If so, items or tasks should be simplified to the greatest degree consistent with the conception of the target variable. If one wants to know, for example, whether the applicant driver understands the significance of the various stripings of the center line of a highway, one must design the item so that even an illiterate can pass it. This will mean using pictorial materials or miniature objects and simple oral directions (in a language other than English if necessary). Otherwise, an applicant's failure on the item is open to counterinterpretations. Likewise for reading comprehension: To measure it as a distinctive process, one must reduce to a minimum the demands for vocabulary or other knowledge, must use large clear type, must make the directions easy to grasp, and must elicit the examinee's best efforts. If one is convinced that no person can fail on the basis of poor vision, poor motivation, poor vocabulary, etc., then the test does measure the intended variable.

Data Relevant to Construct Validation

Construct validation is difficult to explain because so many diverse techniques are required to examine diverse hypotheses and counterhypotheses. Construct validation requires the integration of many studies. There is no such thing as a coefficient of construct validity nor does the series of studies permit a simple summary. To summarize the evidence on the validity of the Stanford-Binet scale as a measure of the construct *general intelligence*, for example, is to summarize all that is known from 60-odd years of research, on populations ranging from school children to adult criminals, and from the United States and France to the most primitive communities.

Construct validation begins with the claim that a given test measures a certain construct. This claim is meaningless until the construct is amplified from a label into a set of sentences.

When the test interpreter says, "John Jones is high on trait X," he implies many things about Jones. The sentences that generate those implications spell out the meaning of the construct. A conveniently brief example of the elaboration of a construct is the following paragraph in which Grimes and Allinsmith (1961) summed up the meaning of *compulsivity* as it related to a study of reading instruction.

In summary, the compulsive person appears to have exaggerated conceptions about exactness and order, and is oriented motivationally and perceptually by these concerns. Compulsives are described as relatively rigid, preoccupied with small details, inhibited in spontaneity, conforming, perfectionistic, seeking certainty, and intolerant of the ambiguous or incongruous situation. Of course these adjectives apply in marked degree only to disordered personalities (or to some fairly well-adjusted people in periods of stress). But obsessive-compulsive *tendencies* can be observed in . . . many children who are clinically within the normal range. . . . It seems logical to predict that [a] structured phonics program would facilitate school progress for children who show evidence of "high" compulsivity compared with similar children exposed to an unstructured whole-word reading program. The latter approach would probably be perceived by such children as disorganized and unsystematic, and they could be expected to have difficulty in complying with the requirement to guess in ambiguous situations [p. 252].

In principle there is a complete theory surrounding the construct, every link of which is systematically tested in construct validation. While something like this does happen as theory evolves through an endless succession of studies, investigations are far less systematic than this. The test developer (or some later writer) proposes a certain interpretative construct, explains at greater or less length what the construct means, and offers *some* evidence that persons scoring high on the test also exhibit other behavior associated with the construct. The intial report is usually far from convincing; the sophisticated reader will think of alternative ways to account for the test behavior.

If the construct interpretation is taken seriously by the profession, its validity is challenged over and over again. The challenge consists of proposing a counterhypothesis; that is, an alternative construct to account for the test behavior in whole or part. While one could carry out construct validation by a plodding verification of every sentence written about the construct, the work would be interminable. It is the plausible counterinterpretation that directs research toward a possibly vulnerable part of the theory (Webb et al., 1966, pp. 8–9).

It might sound as if construct validity is either present or absent, but most studies lead to an intermediate conclusion. The reading test may truly require comprehension, but it also makes demands on vocabulary. The spelling test is indeed a spelling test, but some fraction of the individual differences are due to hearing acuity. The emphasis in construct validation should be on the strength of each relation rather than merely on its statistical significance. Construct validation aims more at comprehension than at a numerical result. The statistics describing a relation pertain only to the population represented in a study. In a normal group one would find only a slight relation between hearing ability and standings in the spelling test, but the relation would be strong when there are many students with defective hearing.

There will be alternative explanations for the same test, all of which may be tenable. Sometimes the first person earns a good score by one process while the next person substitutes some other process to reach the same score. There will be fine-grain and coarse-grain explanations that serve different purposes. And there will be alternatives, such as the wave and particle models for light, each of which accounts neatly for only a part of the evidence.

Procedures used to examine trait interpretations fall into three broad categories: correlational, experimental, and logical. Correlational studies determine how persons high (and low) on the test differ in everyday life or in the laboratory. Many types of correlational studies will be discussed below. The experimental study attempts to alter the person's test performance by some controlled procedure. If it can be shown, for example, that procedures designed to increase a child's confidence raise his score on an information test, this challenges the interpretation of the test as a measure of knowledge alone. A logical analysis of the test content or the scoring rules may disclose disturbing influences in the score. A simple example is the observation that a certain outcome measure is invalid because the test has a low ceiling, so that pupils who do well on the pretest can gain only a few points at most.

Correlational Studies

Convergence of indicators

Persons who score high on the test ought to score high on other indicators of the same construct. These indicators may be other tests, ratings of everyday behavior, or reports regarding the social groups to which the person belongs. One would expect persons who contribute money regularly to a church to score higher on the Thurstone-Chave scale measuring attitude toward the church than others in the same income bracket. One would expect experienced carpenters to score higher on a Test of Carpentry Knowledge than apprentices or handymen. On an achievement test in mathematics one would normally expect persons who have taken more math courses to score higher, on the average. Each of the foregoing statements relates the test to a measure presumed to be an indicator, though perhaps a weak and indirect one, of the same construct. Such a study looks for *convergence* of indicators (Campbell & Fiske, 1959). In examining convergence, the relation between the universe scores for the two procedures should be considered, not the relation between the observed scores; the latter may be much weaker (Block, 1963). A formal correction for attenuation (see p. 498) may be used, but it usually suffices to take unreliability into account informally.

In a convergence study, no one of the indicators is taken as a criterion or standard. Suppose that students have taken a group test of reading comprehension and that their comprehension has been rated on the basis of an individual questioning procedure also. A high correlation tends to confirm that both measures reflect reading comprehension. A low correlation casts doubt on both measures, presumably equally; they evidently do not reflect the same individual differences. At this point one has no basis for saying that either of them has superior validity as a measure of reading comprehension—the only recourse is to bring in further indicators and find out which procedure, if either, behaves as a reading comprehension measure should.

Some indicators come from everyday observations. On-the-job ratings (e.g. in engineering) might be seen solely as criteria in a study concerned with hiring decisions. They also can be seen as observations to be accounted for by constructs. An analysis of the job performance, preferably one that leads to the development of several distinct indices, sheds light on the tests (by showing what each one predicts), clarifies what it means to be, say, a "good" engineer, and perhaps suggests still better prediction methods (Astin, 1964; Wallace, 1965).

A special indicator may be designed. For example, consider the counterhypothesis that the reading comprehension test is highly dependent on speed of reading. To evaluate this challenge the investigator needs an indicator of comprehension for which this counterinterpretation is unreasonable. He could prepare four forms of the test, administering forms A and B with the standard time limit and forms X and Y with a very liberal time allowance. He could give all four tests to the same persons or could give them in pairs to randomly formed subgroups. Then if the cross-correlations AX, AY, BX, and BY are about the same as correlations AB and XY, the time limit evidently has no effect on the ranking of individuals. The investigator can conclude that the test is unspeeded (unless some critic insists that speed and power are perfectly correlated). If the cross-correlations are lower, this is evidence that the time limit tests measure some aspect of individual differences other than what the tests given with plentiful time measure. A comparison of test means is also called for if absolute interpretations are likely to be made.

Although indicators of the same construct are expected to converge, high correlations are not necessarily expected. The score on an observation is determined in part by social-psychological elements in the situation, specific qualities of the stimuli, characteristics of the observer, and other variables. An indicator different in these respects could not correlate perfectly with the first indicator, even if both contain much information relevant to the construct. Whenever practical, it is desirable to base conclusions about an individual on data from several indicators of the construct, as Cook and Selltiz (1964) have explained in connection with attitude scales (see also Webb et al., 1966).

The finding that two indicators converge in one population does not imply that they would necessarily converge in another. One reason for a drop in correlation is restriction of range; correlations tend to be smaller in a group where scores have a narrow range. This will be discussed further in connection with criterion-oriented validation. The degree of association between two variables may depend on the treatment to which persons have been exposed. (See "Convergence of variables across groups" p. 473.)

More generally, the association may depend on a third variable. Consider two tests of arithmetic reasoning, one using simple words and short sentences and one using complex paragraphs. In a group of superior readers these are likely to be strongly correlated; in a group of poor readers they will have a weak relation because students who do well on the first test cannot cope with the second. When the slope of the X-on-Y or Y-on-X regression depends on the level of some variable Z, Z is said to be a moderator variable (see Cronbach, 1970, pp. 438 ff.). A finding of agreement between two proposed indicators of a construct is not necessarily the last word. The interpretation must be modified if some later investigator finds a lack of agreement for persons of another type.

Discriminability from other constructs

Campbell and Fiske (1959) pointed out that it is not sufficient to demonstrate convergence of indicators (i.e. to give evidence of strong

positive correlations among them). They asked also for evidence that one construct can be distinguished from another; this requires that indicators of one construct have relatively low correlations with measures interpreted in terms of other constructs. This is an echo of the general methodological principle of parsimony, which states that different scientific names should not be applied to the same thing or the same construct. If two tests are very similar in what they measure, it complicates theory to retain two trait names for them.

The rule of parsimony cannot be applied universally or thoughtlessly (Cronbach, 1954). Sometimes correlated constructs need to be kept separate; this is true of "weight" and "mass," "atomic weight" and "atomic number." This point will be elaborated with educational examples in the presentation of the topics of factor analysis and correlations across treatment groups.

Gagné (1969) elaborated the idea of discriminability into a proposed strategy for educational measurement. As noted before, a task requires many abilities in conjunction, and failure on any of them will probably lead to failure on the task. Hence a single task is bound to give equivocal evidence. If, however, one can modify the task so that every component ability of the original, save one, is required, the fact that the modified task is (or is not) easier than the complete task becomes quite illuminating. Tasks so closely related may tend to influence each other if given in succession. Consequently, it may be good practice in an evaluation study to distribute the two tasks at random among the persons treated. Percentages of success on the two tasks should indicate whether the instruction the group received has developed the one extra competence the more complex item requires. One might, for example, pose an abstract question to half the students to measure their knowledge of the relation of gravitational force to distance, and to the others pose a concrete question on application of this knowledge. Or one might compare critical thinking on an emotionally neutral syllogism with thinking about a logically equivalent but emotionally loaded syllogism. (Indeed, one might employ counterbalanced syllogisms, loaded with opposing biases.)

Consistency across methods of observation

McClelland (1951) has said, "To a very considerable extent, the disagreement among theoretical psychologists in the field of personality arises from the fact that they are dealing with different data to start with and cannot use each other's concepts [p. 53]." Much the same thing could be said about research on higher mental processes including those that are objectives of instruction. The only remedy is to seek constructs each of which accounts for a range of data, i.e. that transcends any particular method of observation (Webb et al., 1966, p. 3). Measures of the same trait derived from dissimilar data ought to converge. Hence Campbell and Fiske (1959) suggested that a correlational study of validity encompass measures of several traits, each measured by two or more methods.

Suppose, for example, two traits of teachers, Clarity and Warmth, are to be considered. Three measuring procedures could be used—a supervisor could report his general impressions of the teachers, students could check a list of teacher descriptions to indicate which ones fit their teacher, and a sample of discussions in the classroom could be recorded on tape and carefully rated. Getting two scores by each method gives six measures for each teacher. Hypothetical correlations are presented for purposes of discussion in table 14.2.

Such intercorrelations form a multitrait-multimethod matrix. The hypothesis is that the correlations will be fairly substantial in the triangular sections of the layout and that the remaining correlations, each of which pairs supposedly distinctive traits, will be low. The measures of *Warmth* converge reasonably well, having intercorrelations of .50. While each could be an acceptable measure of warmth, the correlations are low enough to suggest that the methods are not interchangeable and that they give better information in combination. It would be wise to correct the coefficients for attenuation; if the corrected values are well below 1.00, further studies to shed light on the differences between methods would be desirable.

In the *Clarity* triangle at the upper left, supervisor and observer measures agree well enough ($r = .50$). But the student measure is inconsistent with the hypothesis ($r = .20$); whatever it measures, it is not clarity as perceived by

---

TABLE 14.2

Hypothetical Correlations of Clarity and Warmth
Scores Obtained in Three Different Ways

	CLARITY OF TEACHER AS SCORED FROM			WARMTH OF TEACHER AS SCORED FROM		
	Supervisor Rating A	Student Data B	Recording C	Supervisor Rating D	Student Data E	Recording F
Clarity as scored from						
A. Supervisor rating		.20	.50	**.30**	.20	.20
B. Student data	.20		.20	.35	**.65**	.35
C. Recording	.50	.20		.30	.20	**.30**
Warmth as scored from						
D. Supervisor rating	**.30**	.35	.30		.50	.50
E. Student data	.20	**.65**	.20	.50		.50
F. Recording	.20	.35	**.30**	.50	.50	

the professional observer. There are three within-method across-trait correlations, A with D, B with E, and C with F, which prove to be .30, .65, and .30 respectively. The first and third values, considered alongside the within-trait r's of .50, indicate that the supervisors and the observers are discriminating warmth from clarity. The students, however, tend to rate a teacher high or low on both scales; hence warmth and clarity are not discriminated in the student data. The fact that the student rating does agree with the other data on warmth suggests that if students like a teacher they tend to give him credit for clarity.

The convergence of the supervisors' ratings of clarity with those taken from recordings tends to support the proposed interpretation; the divergence of the student measure does not. In this case, one would be inclined to discard the student measure rather than the construct of clarity. If the correlation of B with E had been .10 instead of .65, one would still say that B is measuring something different from A and C, but one might retain B, distinguishing clarity as perceived by students from clarity as perceived by professional observers. This breaks the original construct into two parts and leads one to investigate what cues students consider in rating clarity.

Factor analysis

A great deal of the correlational research on test validity employs factor analysis. The mathematics behind this technique of summarizing correlation matrices is described in chapter 16. The interpretation proceeds along the same lines as in the analyses above. Tests that by hypothesis are indicators of a certain construct are expected to show substantial loadings on the same factor. When one of them loads on a second factor, this shows that the indicator is impure. A similar anomaly occurs if a test *not* supposed to represent the construct loads on the factor linking its indicators. Each anomaly challenges the hypotheses. If a factor analysis of table 14.2 were carried out, one could extract a strong factor linking D, E, and F—as hypothesized—together with B, this loading being contrary to the hypothesis. There would be a

second factor linking A and C, again *per* hypothesis; the failure of B to load on this factor has the same implication as the low AB and BC correlations already interpreted. Factor analysis reorganizes a table of correlations to emphasize convergences. Dozens of measures may enter a study of ability or personality, producing hundreds of intercorrelations. Reducing the central core of this information to a compact table of factor loadings often has a clarifying effect.

In construct validation one wishes to know how much of the test variance is attributable to each of a number of constructs, including both the intended construct and the impurities. Factor analysis leads directly to such a statement, since, if the factors are uncorrelated, the squared loadings can be interpreted directly as percentages of the test variance.

It oversimplifies to describe a test score in terms of a few factor loadings. Variables not worth distinguishing for one purpose may need to be separated in another context. When factor analysis shows that most of the variance in a large set of items can be described in terms of a single Mathematical Reasoning factor, this suggests using a single score. For occupational guidance, however, one might want a separate Computation score, even though it correlates perhaps .70 with Reasoning. So long as the correlation of Computation with Reasoning is appreciably less than 1.00 after correction for attenuation, two separate constructs may be worth retaining. This argument can be carried further. Reasoning about probability may correlate highly with reasoning about maxima, series, and loci and yet be worth separating from them—this would enable one to tell a statistics student that, although his general mathematical ability is good, he needs a course on probability. And, within a course, there is a place for telling the student, that despite his A grade, he does not understand DeMoivre's theorem.

Too energetic a wielding of the scrub brush of parsimony scrapes away significant information. A baby leopard with his spots scrubbed off is no doubt a kitten, but saying that leopards have a high loading on the cat factor does not imply that one should discard the concept of *leopard* and take the kitten home for a pet.

Traditionally, *specific* factors are neglected because they rarely interest the psychological researcher. Variation that appears in only one measure is ignored when the aim is to characterize the person by means of a minimum number of pervasive traits. The psychologist hopes to reach a general scientific account or a broadly significant prediction formula by employing just a few variables.

But there is value in detailed information on educational outcomes. To make day-to-day decisions about instruction the teacher wants to know what particular ideas and particular subskills the student has mastered. What instruction a student should have today can be judged only from a microanalysis of his performance. This may be an informal inference from the questions he puts to the teacher and from his errors on assigned problems, or it may be a systematic diagnosis. While the inference may be too specific to deserve the designation of "construct" (e.g. "Mary does not know what *eclipse* means"), the diagnosis usually employs categories broader than this. Moderately restricted and hence diagnostically useful constructs, such as "mastery of scientific vocabulary," are likely to disappear if testers unthinkingly lump in a single score whatever outcomes tend to correlate. A gap between the subscore "communality" and its retest reliability coefficient indicates a subscore with a specific factor that may be important in educational diagnosis. Similar narrow factors are considered by many contemporary psychotherapists.

Factor analysts often speak as if they were discovering natural dimensions that reflect the nature of the nervous system. Correlations and factors, however, merely express the way performances covary in the culture from which the sample is drawn. The usual high correlation between verbal and numerical abilities is due in part to the fact that persons who remain in school are trained on both types of content. If a culture were to treat map making as a fundamental subject, then map-making proficiency, it is suspected, would correlate highly with verbal and numerical attainments. It is likely that some arithmetic curricula generate a high correlation between computational speed and arithmetic reasoning, and that some others generate a low one. While it may be convenient to give the same name to superficially different performances when a person who can do one task is also likely to be able to do the other, it is a mistake to assume that this covariation implies any inherent unity of process between the tasks. (See also pp. 457–58.)

Construct validation may examine item intercorrelations. (Current opinion would favor alpha factor analysis of product-moment correlations or covariances for this purpose [Kaiser & Caffrey, 1965].) If a test is alleged to measure scientific reasoning, for example, a factor analysis of the items may disclose that one large subset of items, which hang together in the factor analysis, refers to the solar system. Since the construct of scientific reasoning is a general one, the test maker would not want the test score to be determined to any great degree by knowledge about this particular topic. He would therefore replace some of these items. For construct validity, one would ordinarily desire sufficient coherence among items contributing to a score so that one factor would account for most of the intercorrelation of items. But many constructs are exceptions. If the construct is conceived as a conglomerate, one would expect the items to fall into clusters. An example of such a construct might be understanding of the fine arts within which items on painting and ballet could form coherent clusters. In such a case, subscores very likely would be a useful supplement to the total score. Another exception is the measuring device that deliberately uses disparate items to offset each other, for example, a reasoning test that includes fallacious arguments of both liberal and conservative varieties.

Factor analysis is a treacherous technique, largely because it can rearrange the same data in many ways. Expecting a certain network of relations, a factor analyst adapts his methods so as to confirm those relations if he possibly can. This is done without dishonesty, just as the fashionable photographer can always find an angle from which a young lady's face appears glamorous. The photograph is recognizable—it "follows from the data." So does the factor analysis. But the interests of scientific inquiry would very likely be better served if factor analysis (or any other method of assembling evidence on convergence and divergence of indicators) were habitually designed to *disconfirm* the initial hypotheses. If an attempt to fit the data to the conceivable *counterhypotheses* gets nowhere, then one would properly accept the original hypotheses (Chamberlain, 1965). Unfortunately, the flood of factor-analytic research is too great for other investigators to reexamine much of it critically. Criticism displaying conflicting interpretations is illustrated in Humphrey's (1967) discussion of Cattell's (1963) conclusions regarding "fluid intelligence" and in a reanalysis of Hofstaetter's (1954) data by Cronbach (1967). The following extended example based on Guilford's work may be illuminating.

Guilford (1967) hypothesized a complex "structure of intellect" in which mental tests are classified according to three facets: operations (e.g. divergent production of ideas), content (e.g. figural), and products (e.g. classes). A test titled Figural Similarities was hypothesized to represent Divergent production, using Figural materials to produce Classes: thus, a DFC test. The structure may be thought of as a box or egg crate, with each operation-content-product combination identifying one cell. Guilford devised tests to represent many of the cells and performed a factor analysis. If a rotation of the results can bring the tests labeled DFC together, with loadings on the same factor, he reports that the tests have been shown to measure the hypothesized DFC factor. The accumulation of such evidence is said to demonstrate the validity of the whole structure. Each study builds on its predecessors and the conceptualization of categories and tests is continually revised as the data require; each later set of data then constitutes a further check on the evolving system.

In a representative study (Hoepfner & Guilford, 1965), ninth graders were given 57 tests, mostly of the divergent sort in which a problem has more than one acceptable answer

and the person is asked to give as many answers as he can. The authors interpreted their factor analysis as strongly confirming the structure. Hypotheses identifying a test with one or another operation were confirmed by the test's loading on a factor identified with that operation 74 times out of 81 opportunities. (Some tests appeared on more than one factor.) The content assignments fitted 71 times out of 81 and the product assignments, 52 times. Considering the three-way combinations, "Of the 57 test variables . . . , 48 exhibited their largest significant loadings on the factors upon which they were hypothesized to cohere, 7 exhibited their largest loadings on factors other than those for which they were hypothesized, and 2 exhibited no loadings over .30, but their highest loadings were on their hypothesized factors [p. 19]." This is consistent with the predicted clustering, despite some anomalous results. The finding is fairly representative of the long series from which the validity of Guilford's system has been argued.

These results are introduced to document the point that a factor analysis that seems to substantiate a theory does not necessarily dispose of counterhypotheses. It is proposed here to test structural hypotheses simply by examining the raw correlations between tests, though this would not meet the approval of factor analysts (Cattell, 1957, pp. 20 ff.). The following example uses tests that are all presumed to measure one operation, divergent production. Regarding this set, the following hypotheses[6] may be stated:

1. Divergent tests having both content and product in common will tend to have higher correlations than those having one of these, or neither, in common.

2. Divergent tests having the same product

[6] These hypotheses are not being tested as Guilford would formulate them. He prefers to identify factors only at the level of the cell and refrains from speaking of a figural or a classes factor. Guilford (1964) designed tests in "a frank effort to achieve minimal correlation between every pair of tests of two different factors [p. 402]." This would lead to hypothesis 1 but not to 2 and 3. The logic here, however, is very close to that of tables 6 and 7 of the Hoepfner-Guilford report. The counts cited above for content and product separately come from those tables.

designation will tend to have higher correlations with each other than tests having different product designations.

3. Divergent tests having the same content designation will tend to have higher correlations with each other than tests having different content.

The hypotheses were arrived at by considering the possibility of content factors such as divergent-figural and divergent-semantic and product factors such as divergent-classes and divergent-relations, along with the operation-content-product factors implied at the cell level by the Guilford structure. This study amounts to a simple and incomplete test of the hypothesis that classifying divergent tests by content or by process *alone* accounts for correlations as well as the three-way structure does. For each divergent test, the correlations in the Hoepfner-Guilford study have been tallied in four groups, according to the designation of the second test entering the correlation, as follows:

CP—same content, same product;
Cx—same content, different product;
xP—same product, different content;
xx—different product, different content.

Hypothesis 1 predicts that the greatest correlations will be for CP. Hypotheses 2 and 3 predict that the lowest correlations will be for xx. While the correlations would be altered by correction for the unreliability of the tests, there appears to be no systematic variation in reliability coefficients that would affect these conclusions.

The number of correlations greater than the arbitrary but not unreasonable value of .40 are counted; and the count is compared with the total number of correlations of that type. The results for the DMC (divergent, semantic, classes) tests are:

CP :   2 out of 6 or 33%;
Cx : 19 out of 48 or 40%;
xP :   2 out of 28 or 7%;
xx :   7 out of 96 or 7%.

The relations $CP>xP$, $CP>xx$, and $Cx>xx$ are confirmed for DMC, but the hypotheses

TABLE 14.3

Number of Categories for Which a Hypothesized Difference in Correlations Appears in Hoepfner-Guilford Data for Divergent Tests

RELATION	NUMBER OF CATEGORIES (OUT OF 14)[a]		HYPOTHESIS
	Supporting	Contradicting	
$CP>xx$	$10\frac{1}{2}$	$3\frac{1}{2}$	Confirmed
$CP>Cx$	7	7	Denied
$CP>xP$	9	5	
$Cx>xx$	$10\frac{1}{2}$	$3\frac{1}{2}$	Confirmed
$xP>xx$	9	5	

[a] If percentages are equal, category is counted as $\frac{1}{2}$ in each column.

that $CP>Cx$ and $xP>xx$ are not. Every category of divergent task represented in the study by at least two tests was analyzed similarly, leading to the results summarized in table 14.3. That $CP>xx$ and $Cx>xx$ is confirmed, but there is no support for $CP>Cx$ and the other two relations are only weakly confirmed.

These results seem to support classifying divergent tests with respect to content; content similarities do account for correlations among tests. Once tests are sorted by content, the additional classification with respect to product seems to add little or nothing. This analysis is inconsistent with the summary of the factor analysis quoted above and leaves one discontented with the three-facet description. It seems that a simpler large-factor model captures most of the information. This illustrative analysis is not offered as a definitive criticism of the Guilford system; far more painstaking reanalyses using data from many studies would be required to evaluate the system against various alternatives and to identify which of the cell classifications are important to retain.

Disagreement among analysts is not a fatal flaw in factor analysis, but it is a warrant for caution in using the results. Factor analysis is so intricate that the general reader cannot expect to reanalyze the data for himself, and, unfortunately, it is rare that a second specialist reexamines a given body of factor analytic data to decide whether alternative hypotheses are tenable. Probably the general reader interested in the validity of a particular test should pay chief attention to the zero-order correlations of that test rather than to the highly processed factorial results.

Convergence of variables across groups

A factor analysis of even a large number of measures of educational outcomes is likely to identify only a few factors. This is too often interpreted as implying that the several outcomes "are not really different." Comprehension of physical laws will certainly be correlated with ability to reason scientifically because, in a general population, those who have studied science will do better on both types of test. Even if the study is confined to persons who have studied physics, the correlation will remain high because the ablest students will have made greatest progress along both directions. If the high correlation means that there is no distinction between comprehension and reasoning, one could not criticize a curriculum for emphasizing the laws and making no effort to promote reasoning.

At first glance there appears to be a head-on conflict. The curriculum reformer argues that comprehension and reasoning are distinct attainments, and the correlational study proves that whoever is best in one respect is best in the other. The contradiction is resolved by a distinction between a within-group correlation and an across-groups correlation. Within a group completing the same course of study, the two variables correlate. But suppose the class averages for 50 classes are determined and a correlation across groups is computed from these 50 pairs of values. The curriculum reformer who contends that some teachers neglect to develop reasoning is predicting that this across-groups correlation will be fairly low, that some groups will rank high on comprehension but not on reasoning. Even if the correlation across groups turns out to be high, the reformer has a tenable position to which to retreat. If he can design a curriculum that concentrates on scientific reasoning, whose graduates score exceptionally well on the reasoning test while scoring at the average on the comprehension test, he has proved his point. The high correlation meant only that present curricula are holding the balance between reasoning and comprehension so nearly constant that the best programs (or those drawing the ablest students) get the best results on both dimensions.

One source that illustrates correlation across groups is the International Study of Achievement in Mathematics (Husén, 1967, esp. Vol. II, pp. 48, 50, 129, 156). The same tests were given in many countries, each of which follows a different curriculum. Correlations across countries do not resemble the within-country correlations in magnitude; they answer a different question.

A correlation across groups is typically a good deal higher than that within groups. For this reason, an interpretation of a relationship across groups, or a comparison of that relation with the within-group relation, should be based on the regression slope rather than the correlation.

Between-group correlations only recently have come to prominence in social science and their interpretation is only beginning to be discussed in the technical literature. Such correlations have long been used in sociological research but, as Robinson (1950) pointed out, they have been wrongly interpreted as having the same meaning as correlations based on individuals. Grice (1966) recommended their use in the experimental validation of constructs in learning theory. He stressed the importance of the across-treatments regression because "the question reduces to whether or not the measures yield similar S-R laws when experimental variables are manipulated. . . . For in the long run, the conditions under which measures are not related in a simple fashion are of as much significance as those in which they are [pp. 494, 497]." A paper by Bowles and Levin (1968) cuts across the sociological and economic literature, giving technical recommendations and a bibliography.

Analysis of variance components

Analysis of variance of the type employed in studies of reliability (see chap. 13) is often useful in construct validation (Endler & Hunt, 1966; Cronbach et al., in press). In the study of ratings of teachers described above, it was suggested that a construct of warmth, general over observers, could be applied; this was supported by the intercorrelations among three types of observers. The same conclusion could have been established by analysis of variance, if assuming that scores share a common metric. Generality would be shown in a large component of variance for teachers—large, that is, in comparison with the interaction between teacher and type of observer.

To consider a fresh example, components of variance can be extracted from marks assigned to compositions. The usual single testing does not provide the required data. A special experiment is required in which two and often more compositions are obtained from each examinee and these are scored by two or more graders. The analysis separates out the effects on the student score of the topic assigned, the date of testing, the grader, and various interaction effects. It thus indicates the magnitude of each "impurity" in the score and tells how closely the score corresponds to the hypothesized general stable composition ability (Coffman & Kurfman, 1968).

Studies of process

Observing how persons respond to the test, then contrasting the observations made on high and low scorers, usually adds insights that amplify the meaning of the construct. A good example of research on process is French's study (1965) showing that the factor loadings of aptitude tests change as a function of the student's style of work.

In a performance test, such as the Porteus Maze, it is relatively simple to observe the process, noting whether, for example, the subject proceeds impulsively to try a path without first surveying the problem and whether he becomes disorganized when a trial response is blocked. The usual multiple-choice test, on the other hand, is unrevealing even if administered individually for purposes of the study. To get more complete data one often asks the student to work the problems aloud. If he is sufficiently articulate, the observer learns where he is blocked, what irrelevant cues affect his answer,

how alert he is to detect his errors, etc. Sometimes it is proper to go over a completed multiple-choice test orally, asking the student to give his reasons for accepting one of the alternative answers and his reason for rejecting each of the others. This may bring to light a number of cues that lead students to the right answer by an unacceptable process or vice versa.

While the literature on testing frequently recommends devices such as these, there are few reported examples of such validation. Bloom and Broder (1950) reported strikingly useful results with University of Chicago students as subjects, and, in opinion polling, Schuman (1966) found open-end questioning a profitable way to clarify the significance of responses to multiple-choice questions. Connolly and Wantman (1964), however, were able to get only inarticulate responses from college students they interviewed; Kropp (1956) and McGuire (1963) also have pointed to difficulties in using the oral-response technique.

Experimental Attempts to Alter the Test Score

Experimental interventions in which something is deliberately done to change student scores, as a means of identifying influences to which the test performance is sensitive, have been mentioned several times. The treatment may be a change in time limit, a special instruction, etc. The investigator, knowing of what his treatment consists, can predict its effect on the tests; the results confirm or challenge some part of his interpretation of the measuring instrument. Only a few further examples are needed.

Does the reading comprehension test of the earlier example depend primarily on the strategy with which students attack the task? Give the test normally. Then coach a group to use some strategy that is expected to be superior and administer a parallel test. If scores improve, the test is sensitive to the strategy. (For a study of this general type, see Jacobs, 1966.) The experiment would be improved by using a control group who are given some form of pseudo-coaching believed not to have an effect on performance.

Does the reading test depend on motivation to an important degree? Design a way of improving motivation, perhaps by providing a friendly examiner who takes the role of a colleague in a game, perhaps by rewarding persistent effort with trinkets, candy, or coin. Check the effect on scores (I. Katz, 1964; McCoy, 1965).

Does an art appreciation test obtain information on the student's true beliefs, or is it subject to faking? Divide the group and administer the test to half the group with the usual directions; request the other half to fill it out so as to make a good impression (or, perhaps, to give the answers their teacher would). A significant difference in the means would show successful faking. An example is Parker's (1966) demonstration that students' self-reports on personality depend on whom they expect to see the information.

The studies listed above all represent short-term interventions at the time of measurement, altering the test performance rather than any more fundamental characteristics of the person. Long-term treatments of an educational or therapeutic nature also may be used in validation research, as was illustrated above in discussing an attempt to produce exceptional improvement in students' scientific reasoning.

Judgment and Logical Analysis

One of the best sources of counterhypotheses is a scrutiny of the test. A judge who knows a great deal about the faults discovered in past tests is likely to detect impurities unsuspected by the developer. The reader is reminded of impurities previously discussed, such as the spelling test that depends on hearing acuity and the gunnery test that depends on reading. Criticisms on such counts as these are objections to the universe definition employed in constructing the test and thus go beyond the sampling considerations of content validity.

Strictly speaking, logical analysis of content cannot disprove a validity claim. The analysis puts forth a counterhypothesis whose pertinence can be verified only empirically. Where readers are able to bring relevant experience to bear, however, they are often willing to accept the criticism at once. When it is pointed out that hearing acuity makes the usual interpretation of the spelling test inappropriate for the hard-of-hearing child, no one is so pedantic as to insist on "proof."

Criticisms of a proposed interpretation may be generated also by psychometric analysis. Again, the successful critic is likely to be one aware of the faults such analyses have turned up in the past. A test developer may attempt to measure a construct by a complicated index that combines two or more observations. A critical study of the mathematical properties of the index may give one reason to think that the proposed interpretation is unsound. The best-known example is the undermining of the so-called accomplishment quotient, the "age" score on an achievement test divided by the same child's mental age. This quotient turns out to be automatically biased against the brighter student (Thorndike, 1963, pp. 6–15). Somewhat related is the demonstration that a score representing "gain in accomplishment," formed by subtracting one achievement score from a later one, is grossly misleading. Indeed, it is possible for this type of gain score to be negative even though the pupil has actually increased the universe score the test performance represents (Lord, 1963; Cronbach & Furby, 1970). Still another example is an attempt to measure teachers' "insight" into students. The teacher forecasts the responses the student will give to a questionnaire, and the students' responses form a scoring key for evaluating the forecast. Purely mathematical analysis shows that this kind of score is influenced by the teacher's response biases and stereotypes, so that it is probably wrong to interpret it as a measure of the teacher's diagnostic sensitivity (Cronbach, 1958; Gage & Cronbach, 1955).

The Formal Testing of Nomological Networks

Construct validation is described formally in philosophy of science. (For an excellent introduction, see Hempel, 1966; for a more complete account, see Hempel, 1965, esp. pp. 3–46, 173–228.) Although the process the educator or behavioral scientist uses to integrate evidence has far more of the intuitive in it than the philosopher's account would suggest, it is instructive to review the idealized process.

A theory consists of constructs and observables, interconnected by statements. A theory may include the statement, for example, that a solid metal rod expands in length as a linear function of any increase in its temperature. This employs the constructs *solid, metal, length,* and *temperature.* For this statement to be meaningful, each construct must be connected with an indicator—one must have ways of knowing whether the rod is solid, whether it is metal, and what its length and temperature are at any point in time. Another statement in the network may be that the coefficient of linear expansion for copper is $16.42 \cdot 10^{-6}$; this coefficient allows one to replace the ambiguous "expands as a linear function" with a definite equation. Introducing the construct *copper* means that one or more further indicators are required; thus one may suppose it is agreed that procedures P, Q, and R all identify specimens of copper. The statements connecting constructs with each other, and observable indicators with constructs, constitute a nomological network (*nomological* meaning law-like).

Given information about several of the observables, one can use the network to infer the values of other observables. For example, if a rod is identified by procedure P as copper, and one knows an initial length and temperature, one can infer the length expected at some new temperature. Now if the temperature is increased to that value, and the new length agrees with the inferred value, one is entitled to greater confidence in *every proposition from which the inference was derived.* The experiment increases confidence in the law of expansion, in the stated coefficient, in the procedure for measuring temperature, etc. Most significant, the study has to some extent validated the claim that procedure P identifies copper, that is, has validated P as an indicator.

If, on the other hand, the new length is not what was expected, every statement used in the chain of inference is thrown into question. With a well-established theory such as this, one is likely to challenge some superficial aspects of the experiment (e.g. is the thermocouple working properly?). Only after the investigator has eliminated such possibilities will he acknowledge the presence of a challenge to the theory. Once he takes the challenge seriously, he will devise further experiments to determine just which link of the network is weak.

Suppose he concludes that the rod "does not behave like copper." Yet it was classified as copper by the hitherto accepted procedure P. A reasonable next step would be to try procedures Q and R, also recognized ways of identifying copper. If the rod meets these criteria also, the scientist must reexamine propositions connecting copper to other parts of the network. Could it be that copper does not obey the law of expansion? The obvious test is to try a number of samples of copper (verified as such by tests P, Q, and R jointly). Suppose it is found that some give the predicted results and some are anomalous. Now the scientist would most likely introduce a new construct—Type II copper. For the present, the only indicator that distinguishes the two types of copper is the expansion test. Over a period of time, other differences between Type I and Type II copper will be discovered and these will make new indicators available. The continuing research will eventually explain why the two types differ.

This is the process by which science advances (though this statement of it is overly simple). There is, at any time, a network linking constructs and observables. Figure 14.1 schematically displays a well-developed network in biology: each arrow stands for a relationship that could be developed into a formal proposition. (Another example is N. E. Miller's discussion [1959, pp. 276 ff.] of a network representing thirst as a factor in animal behavior.) The statements in a network may be precise equations or they may be quite vague, but they should lead to inferences definite enough to be capable of contradiction by observations.

A construct validation checks on the validity of the network as a whole, or at least of the propositions from which the inference derives.

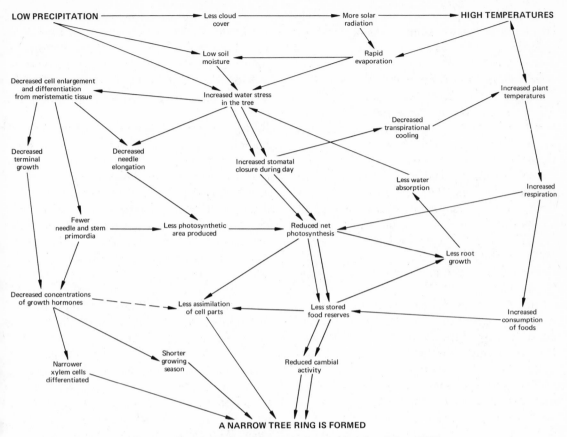

FIG. 14.1. A well-developed theoretical network (after Fritts, 1966)

When a contradiction of expectation occurs, one challenges parts of the network by suitable further studies until he "locates the trouble." The resolution may take many forms, of which these are the most significant for this discussion:

1. The interpretation of a supposed indicator may be declared invalid—e.g. the magnetic compass is an invalid indicator of the location of the North Pole.

2. A construct may be abandoned or two constructs may collapse into one—e.g. the abandonment of "instincts."

3. The construct may be subdivided and new indicators developed to distinguish between the new constructs—e.g. the tests for identifying monozygotic and dizygotic twins.

4. The network may be modified to account for the anomaly. Most often, the construct name and the indicators remain, but the set of

sentences that outline associated characteristics is modified. Such a modification recently occurred in the discovery that argon and other "noble gases" can form compounds.

After many such modifications, contradictions become increasingly rare. The subsequent piling up of confirmations can establish enormous confidence in the usefulness of a construct and its indicators. Note the reference to *usefulness*, not to *truth*. For topics near the frontier of science there are competing interpretative systems. And even the long-established network remains vulnerable to challenge from a Planck or an Einstein.

The logic of confirmation and disconfirmation is the same for constructs in education and social science as in the natural sciences. The greater difficulty of controlled experimentation with persons makes causal hypotheses about them hard to defend, but this probelm is encountered also in astronomy, paleontology, and other natural sciences.

A network interpreting "need for achievement"

The research of J. W. Atkinson and his coworkers, including particularly David C. McClelland, Norman T. Feather, and George Litwin, produces a suitable example of construct validation. The construct studied, *need for achievement*, should be of considerable interest to educators. There was a formal network from which testable hypotheses were derived, and the sequence of papers (presented or cited in Atkinson & Feather, 1966, and Feather, 1968) exhibit the evolution of a construct through successive confirmations and disconfirmations.

Murray (1938) had employed the Thematic Apperception Test and other subtle measures of personality to measure what he called "needs." Each need is a separate construct, and it has taken some 30 years of effort to substantially validate just one construct and its measure. McClelland, and later Atkinson, concentrated on the single need "for achievement" (*n* Achievement), starting with exploratory studies (McClelland et al., 1953). The theory that

emerged (Atkinson & Feather, 1966, chap. 20; Heckhausen, 1967) is so complex that it is possible here to cover only some major features, omitting the rationale that generated these hypotheses and omitting several hypotheses, some of which have practical significance for education.

Figure 14.2 diagrams a fraction of the nomological network. The horizontal lines are boundaries separating observables from theoretical constructs; the observables (which are underlined) appear at the top and bottom of the diagram. Certain liberties with Atkinson's terminology and notation have been taken in the interests of brevity and ease of recall. Atkinson was, in this section of network, interested in *n* Achievement and Anxiety. He hypothesized that high *n* Achievement is to be understood as equivalent to being motivated to seek opportunities to succeed (M_S). Anxiety, he hypothesized, implies a disposition to avoid the risk of failure (M_{AF}). Some theorists might prefer to eliminate one of the two constructs, but Atkinson did not consider the terms to be mere opposites. M_S is thought of as involving the enjoyment of challenge and accomplishment; M_{AF} as involving a sense of shame or embarrassment when one fails. A person might

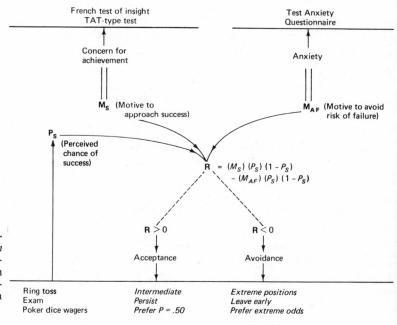

FIG. 14.2. A portion of the interpretative network for *n* Achievement. (Reprinted by permission of Harper & Row from L. J. Cronbach, *Essentials of Psychological Testing*, 3rd edition [Harper & Row, 1970], p. 661.)

combine strong M_S with strong M_{AF} (ambivalence), and a person with little M_{AF} might also have little of the effort-inducing M_S (indifference). The next construct is perceived probability of success (P_S), the apparent difficulty of the task. R, the resultant, is the hypothesized motivational state of the subject who, having a certain level of M_S and M_{AF}, is confronted with a task in which he thinks he has chance P_S of success. As figure 14.2 shows, Atkinson has offered an equation linking measures of these constructs. A more detailed network would show subordinate assumptions from which the equation is derived. There are two things to note about the equation. If M_S is greater than M_{AF}, R will be positive; if less, R will be negative. If R is positive there is a tendency to accept the task, and if negative, a tendency to shun it. Second, since P_S ranges between .00 and 1.00, the product $P_S(1-P_S)$ is at its maximum when $P_S = .50$ and drops to zero as P_S approaches zero or one. Hence, whether R is positive or negative, the tendency it implies is weak if the task is extremely easy or difficult, and is at its strongest when the difficulty is intermediate.

Now still at the construct level, there are various implications. First, M_{AF} and M_S are distinct constructs, not different names for the same thing. Second, persons with strong M_S tend to approach most strongly (i.e. to prefer) tasks of intermediate difficulty. Third, persons with strong M_{AF} tend to avoid most strongly tasks of intermediate difficulty. There is a further implication regarding the combined effect of the M_S and M_{AF} tendencies.

At the operational level, Atkinson was interested in the claim that n Achievement is measured by two projective tests, a picture-interpretation test derived from the Thematic Apperception Test and a story-completion test developed by E. G. French. Each of these has been used in some of the studies validating the network; for the present purpose, the symbol *Proj* is used to represent whichever of the tests is involved. To ask whether the tests differ in any important way leads beyond the research being discussed. Atkinson accepted, as a measure of the construct Anxiety, the Test Anxiety

Questionnaire (TAQ) of Mandler and Sarason. To find out whether persons with various score combinations behave as the network predicted, he needed operations to represent "acceptance" and "avoidance" of tasks of specified difficulty. He used various experimental indicators of which only three are discussed here:

Ring-toss distance. The subject is allowed to select the distance (1 ft. to 15 ft.) from which he will throw rings at a peg, thereby adjusting probability of success.

Persistence. In a moderately difficult three-hour course examination, how long does the student work before he turns in his paper?

Gambling preference in a poker-dice game. The person has a chance to choose between high, low, and medium risks.

TABLE 14.4

Subjects, Classified on Proj and TAQ, Compared to Median for All Subjects on Experimental Measures

Experimental Measure	All Ss	High-Proj– Low-TAQ	High-Proj– High-TAQ	Low-Proj– Low-TAQ	Low-Proj– High-TAQ
Preference for intermediate ring-toss distances					
Above median	22	10	4	4	4
Below median	23	3	6	5	9
Persistence on examination					
Above median	21	11	4	3	3
Below median	23	4	6	4	9

Source: adapted from Atkinson & Litwin, 1960.

The data from various studies may now be brought to bear on the predictions:

1. Correlations between Proj and TAQ ranged from .11 to −.15 for different samples when Proj was given to subjects not specially aroused. This tends to support the implied separation of the constructs, though correction for attenuation would make the interpretation clearer.

2. On the ring-toss measure, there was a clear confirmation of the prediction (table 14.4). Intermediate distances were often chosen by the

high-Proj–low-TAQ subjects, rarely by the low-Proj–high-TAQ subjects.

3. On examination persistence, there was a similar confirmation. (The reader is warned that different statistical analyses gave somewhat different impressions; if he is interested in the research for its own sake he should consult the original papers.)

4. On the study of preference for wagers, the high-Proj–low-TAQ subjects tended to prefer bets with a large probability of winning, not the intermediate risks as predicted.

At this point Atkinson modified his network by suggesting that the motivation M_S does not affect response in a gambling situation where the person's own efforts cannot improve his chances for success. This was stated as a hypothesis awaiting investigation. (For recent work on this question, see Feather, 1968.) On the whole, these and other studies indicate considerable justification for the interpretation set forth in the network. The central equation is not finally established, as other equations also could predict the results. But the system of relations is shown to be plausible.

Incidental to Atkinson's main work was his finding on the construct validity of the Need for Achievement score of the Edwards Personal Preference Schedule, a self-report questionnaire. The conclusion was that this does not measure the construct indicated by the network. In the first place, it has a negligible correlation with Proj and with a rating of need for achievement by acquaintances (with which Proj does correlate). Secondly, in the ring-toss game, subjects with high Edwards *Ach* scores showed *less* preference for intermediate distances. On examination persistence they did not differ from the low-Proj group. The suggestion from this and other research is that the questionnaire measure represents a cultural stereotype rather than a personal motivational commitment (McClelland, 1958). But there are indications that special questionnaire procedures can measure *n* Achievement as well as the projective test does (Carney, 1966; Sherwood, 1966; Vukovich, Heckhausen, & von Hatzfeld, 1964). This leads toward a much more elaborate net-

work and an extension of the interpretations for both types of tests.

In presenting this summary, reliance necessarily has been placed on the review by Atkinson and Feather. Other personality theorists might suggest alternative networks and might cite studies done in other laboratories that call parts of the Atkinson theory into question. (Useful sources on these other studies are Heckhausen, 1967, and Wiggins, 1968.) Acceptance of a construct interpretation, in the end, requires the concurrence of the persons who have thought deeply about the problem and have given due weight to research from laboratories with other orientations.

Controversial Aspects of Construct Validation

The rationale for construct validation has been generally accepted by psychological testers. Writers on educational testing also have adopted the terminology even though its application to educational tests has not been discussed in any detail hitherto. A minority of writers, however, object to the whole line of reasoning. The objectors adhere to an ultra-operationalism, arguing that a construct has scientific status only when it is equated with one particular measuring operation (Bechtoldt, 1959; Brodbeck, 1957; Brodbeck, 1963, esp. pp. 59–72). Then, since no construct has more than one indicator, the nomological net is no more than a list of the empirical relationships of the defining indicator. There is a new list—a new network—for each indicator.

These critics, who wish to associate a new interpretation with each operational definition, are obviously advocating a reliance on content validity and a prohibition on construct interpretations. This is diametrically opposed to Loevinger's (1965) prescription alluded to earlier. The position expressed here is that the choice of interpretation is the prerogative of the investigator; a type of interpretation productive in one context may be sterile in another.

The writers on curriculum and evaluation who insist that objectives must be "defined in terms of behavior" are taking an ultraoperationalist position, though they have not offered a scholarly philosophical analysis of the issue. The person who insists on "behavioral" objectives is denying the appropriateness and usefulness of constructs. The educator who states objectives in terms of constructs (e.g. self-confidence, scientific attitude, the habit of suiting one's writing style to his purpose) regards observables as indicators from which the presence of the characteristics described by the construct can be inferred. But he will not, for example, *substitute* "volunteers ideas and answers in class" for "self-confidence." From the construct point of view, behavior such as this is an indicator of confidence but not a definer. Indeed no list of specific responses-to-situations, however lengthy, can define the construct, since the construct is intended to apply to situations that will arise in the future and cannot be specified now.

The arguments regarding the legitimacy of construct interpretations of tests reflect issues long-argued among philosophers of science. Nagel (1961, chap. 6) classifies views as descriptive, realist, or instrumentalist. In the instrumentalist view, "Theories are intellectual tools . . . conceptual frameworks deliberately devised for effectively directing experimental inquiry, and for exhibiting connections between matters of observation that would otherwise be regarded as unrelated [p. 131]." This is essentially the position taken by Cronbach and Meehl (1955) in advocating construct validation of tests. The critics of construct validation of educational measurements seem generally to prefer the descriptive view, that theoretical terms, in Nagel's words, "are simply a shorthand notation for a complex of observable events and traits [p. 118]," though some of the critics may be "realists" at heart.

A strict operationalism is used in the more advanced areas of physical measurement, where each key property, such as mass and length, is identified with a particular operation (Huntoon, 1965). The basic operation for measuring length, for example, involves comparison with the wave length of a certain line in the spectrum of the gas krypton. While the investigator in the physics laboratory uses meter sticks and other handy devices, he has agreed that these measures are to be considered only approximations to the standard measure, and each of the everyday procedures is calibrated against the standard. The use of a standard operation is possible when a construct is mature and part of a well-confirmed network. Among the many operations that relate to the construct, the standard is the one that performs best; i.e. the data from it conform most precisely to the laws in the network. It was on just such a basis that the physicists decided in 1960 to employ the krypton line as the standard of length in place of the former standard, a platinum meter bar kept in a vault in Paris. When Huntoon wrote in 1965, he foresaw that the krypton standard was ready to be pushed aside in favor of still newer operations based on the laser. Having a standard does not prevent investigators from using different measures of length and interpreting them all in terms of the same construct. But when the measuring procedures lead to discrepant results, the common way to resolve the issue is to repeat the experiment with the standard procedure or with a procedure closely coordinated to the standard. Even though the standard "defines" the concept, it can be overthrown by an anomalous result. The concept of weight, for example, was greatly altered when Huygens and Newton concluded that an object would give different spring-balance readings at different points on the earth's surface. From these statements it is clear that even the strict operationist position makes use of constructs embedded in a network (see Bridgman, 1927, esp. pp. 52 ff.).

Some modern operationists, however, consider it an unsound strategy to think of the construct apart from one specified measure. Perhaps the strongest statement in the educational literature is Ebel's (1961): "If the test we propose to use provides in itself the best available operational definition, the concept of validity does not apply [p. 643]. But this language gives the game away, for the "best available" definition is presumably not the best conceivable, and How good is the operation? remains a meaningful question. If an investigator says, "French's test is a pretty good measure of need for achievement, but it is not a pure measure of it," he is saying that he thinks of a person with high need for achievement as having certain characteristics in addition to a high universe score on French's test. If so, the construct has surplus meaning for him. A particularly striking example of surplus meaning is contained in the charge that mental tests are biased against certain cultural groups and therefore are not definers of *mental ability*. The contention is that the tests systematically give lower scores to these disadvantaged persons than their *true ability* warrants. To investigate this, one must somehow find indicators of *true ability* independent of the test. The operationists object to surplus meanings, because, as in this example, they are vague and difficult to pin down in observed relationships.

Surplus meaning is an advantage, insofar as it sends out shadowy lines connecting the systematic observations with situations and variables that have not been systematically studied. These lines constitute an interim basis for judgments that would otherwise have to be made without any scientific guidance, and they constitute hypotheses whose testing will extend or correct the network. McClelland (1951) commented in this connection that "historically the most rapid advance in theory would seem to occur when someone hits on a lucky hypothetical construct which has a number of implications which can be tested [p. 84]." The disadvantage in surplus meaning comes when the tentative, speculative nature of the surplus is forgotten, as it has been in some past interpretations of the mental test score as a measure of "learning ability" or "capacity."

The gambit of arbitrarily naming one measure as *the* operational definition is not helpful (Hempel, 1966, pp. 91 ff.). Surplus meanings were not removed from the minds of educators and psychologists by the attempt once made to insist that "intelligence is just what the Stanford-Binet Scale measures." Similarly with *n* Achievement: neither the French test, nor the modified Thematic Apperception Test, nor the Edwards questionnaire score can serve as a standard for *n* Achievement; none is a suffi-

ciently excellent measure. Someone might propose to identify the construct with a composite score extracted from all three tests (or, rather, the corresponding universe scores). But to combine three tests of uncertain validity is only to arrive at another unsatisfactory standard. Kaplan (1964) put it well: "The closure that strict definition consists in is not a precondition of scientific inquiry but its culmination. To start with we do not know just what we mean by our terms, much as we do not know what we think about our subject matter. We can, indeed, begin with precise meanings, as we choose; but so long as we are in ignorance we cannot choose wisely [p. 77]." In discussions among physical scientists and philosophers of science, most participants including Bridgman himself recognize that a literal adherence to the "one concept, one operation" position is impractical and, if adhered to, stifles thought (Frank, 1956). Hempel (1965) ended a lengthy examination of the issue with the statement: "[If it is] the sole purpose of a theory to establish deductive connections among observation sentences . . . theoretical terms would indeed be unnecessary. But if it is recognized that a scientific theory should provide possibilities also for inductive[,] explanatory[,] and predictive use and that it should achieve systematic economy and heuristic fertility, then it is clear that theoretical formulations cannot be replaced by expressions in terms of observables only [p. 222]."

The issue raised by the ultraoperationalists is possibly just a terminological one, since there seem to be few differences of opinion about how tests and test interpretations can and must be used (Hochberg, 1961). There is universal agreement that general propositions embodying descriptive concepts must in the end be verified by means of systematic observation and that the procedures used to gather these observations must be given a full operational description in order to make the report useful.

In the verification of networks the argument is inductive. One shows that the construct is consistent with the evidence; one does not show that the construct represents something that exists concretely. Almost certainly other networks could be devised that would be equally consistent with the evidence, and those networks would employ different constructs. A network, then, is *a* representation of present knowledge, not the only possible representation.

The fact that construct validation can always accept negative evidence by reshaping the network is both its strength and its weakness. One can dispose of an anomaly by adding a conditional clause or an auxiliary construct, as Atkinson did when preference among wagers did not conform to his expectation. This is objectionable only when the a posteriori addition to the network is believed. So long as it is recognized as a statement awaiting validation, it serves a useful purpose. To be sure, one can encumber the network to the point of unmanageability as the Ptolemaic astronomers did with epicycles and equants, but the cure is to invent a cleaner network not to banish constructs.

The educational planner, the teacher, the counselor, and the student learning to direct his own life all have to think in terms of concepts that describe behavior in a broad class of situations. One of the tasks of social science is to seek the right breadth for its concepts (Nagel, 1961, pp. 505–508). *Citizenship* is no doubt too broad; *ego-strength* is a good deal better, since it leads one to anticipate different behavior in situations all of which might be thought of as calling for citizenship. One cannot expect, at least in this century, to disentangle ego-strength from interacting traits and situational variables, and so long as each measure is subject to interactive effects, no one measure can be accepted as a standard. One can retreat to very narrow concepts; citizenship could be broken down at least to the level of "participation in elections" and "obedience to speed laws." This would increase the number of variables beyond the point where they could be investigated and would leave out of the discussion whatever behavior citizens exhibit in the less standardized aspects of their lives.

The social scientist will conduct investigations with the aid of clearly defined observations and will record precisely what he did; at this level, he can be as rigorous and as opera-tional as any critic could demand. In deciding what the findings mean for any circumstance that has not yet been the focus of an investigation, however, he must invoke broader constructs.

It is not important to argue whether these looser inferences shall be considered "science" or not. It is important for testers to recognize that they use such inferences and for them to scrutinize dispassionately the underlying evidence and reasoning.

"The crucial point is that the logical canons employed by responsible social scientists in assessing the objective evidence for the imputation of psychological states do not appear to differ essentially (though they may often be applied less rigorously) from the canons employed for analogous purposes by responsible students in other areas of inquiry [Nagel, 1961, p. 484]." The proponents of construct validation insist that the person who puts forward test interpretations must be one of Nagel's "responsible social scientists."

Now it is true that the test developer can simply say, "If you want to know what my test means, look at the items or the operations." But this thrusts the burden of construct validation onto the consumer, who will inevitably make inferences beyond the universe of situations representatively sampled by the test.

The most serious criticism to be made of programs of construct validation is that some of them are haphazard accumulations of data rather than genuine efforts at scientific reasoning. Merely to catalog relations between the test under study and a variety of other variables is to provide a do-it-yourself kit for the reader, who is left to work out his own interpretative theory. Construct validation should start with a reasonably definite statement of the proposed interpretation. That interpretation will suggest what evidence is most worth collecting to demonstrate convergence of indicators. A critical review in the light of competing theories will suggest important counterhypotheses, and these also will suggest data to collect. Investigations to be used for construct validation, then, should be purposeful rather than haphazard (Campbell, 1960). After collecting his data, the investigator is expected to integrate the hypotheses and findings with each other and to offer a final conclusion as to the soundness of the construct interpretation and the influence of impurities that have been identified. The 1966 *Standards* discussed some requirements of construct validation, but the procedures cannot be cataloged exhaustively and no guide can tell just how to meet the requirement of hard-headed reasoning from data to conclusions.

PREDICTIONS AND DECISIONS

Basic Concepts

Decision making in education is best illustrated in the selection of applicants for advanced training and in the allocation of students to curricula or to different instructional schemes (see chap. 19). Any decision is a choice among treatments. *Treatment*, as used here, is an abstract term that applies to any training program, occupational assignment, counseling procedure, etc. In *classification*, there are two or more paths along which the person may proceed—for example, into a science curriculum or an arts curriculum. Where the alternative treatments lie on a continuum (elementary, intermediate, and advanced levels in French, for example), one may speak of a *placement* decision. In *selection* the decision maker has the option of rejecting the person altogether, so that the institution has no further concern with him. Selection is often combined with classification. To make a decision, one predicts the person's success under each treatment and uses a rule to translate the prediction into an assignment. The appropriate rule is obvious when there is a single basis for judging success and there is no constraint on the number of persons assigned to any treatment; in such a case validity depends on the accuracy of the predictions. When one validates a proposed rule for more complex cases, additional considerations enter.

Validation of a decision rule logically requires an experiment in which, after being tested, persons are allocated to the alternative treatments *without regard to the scores* whose usefulness is being validated. In selection research, the design calls for accepting persons without regard to their test scores. Indeed,

logic requires strictly random assignments.[7] Subsequent outcomes for each person are observed. The outcomes observed represent the objectives of the institution or the person; they may include proficiency at the end of instruction, persistence in the treatment, satisfaction, etc. The more comprehensive the list of outcomes investigated, the more adequately the predictions are evaluated.

Giving the test before the start of a course, before hiring, or, to speak generally, before treatment is said to provide for *predictive* validation. The outcome measure follows some months of treatment. Sometimes, however, test data and outcome data are collected at about the same time—concurrently—by testing students or workers for whom outcomes are already known. Such concurrent validation must not be confused with a true follow-up study. Testing workers already on the job is a sensible first step in research; one can apply various aptitude tests to workers whose proficiency on the job is known and retain for further investigation the tests that correlate concurrently with proficiency. But validity for decision making is not established by the concurrent study. If the speaking ability of teachers correlates with their success as teachers, this fact is suggestive. This evidence as it stands does not warrant using a speech test to select persons for training as teachers, since it may be that superior speech was developed *during* the training by certain responsive students who entered with inferior speech and who would have been eliminated by a speech test at the start.

The joint distribution of outcomes and test scores is examined to determine what decision rule produces the most satisfactory distribution of outcomes. Suppose it is found, for example, that persons who score 75 on test 1 and 60 on test 2, assigned to treatment A, do better on the average than similar persons assigned to treatment B. Then the decision rule will direct that

---

[7] To be sure, if there is some basis for classification that figures in the decision rule along with the test and to whose use the institution is committed, it may be used in allocating persons for the validation study. Then the research examines only what benefit the test adds.

in the future such persons be sent into or counseled into treatment A (subject to any limit on the number of persons who can be accommodated in treatment A). If the rule so derived is at all complicated (e.g. calling for weighted combination of scores), further data must be collected to *cross-validate* the decision rule.

The decision rule, instead of being extracted from a follow-up study, may be suggested independently. A classification rule may be suggested a priori, or the proposal may be to make decisions in a clinical manner. Again, validation requires allocation of persons to treatments without regard to test scores. At the time of testing, a paper decision about each person must be made according to the proposed rule and sealed up so that it does not affect the disposition actually made of him. Ultimately, one can decide which of the assignments worked out well and which badly; if the decision rule is sound, the paper decision disagreed with the actual assignment more often for cases who failed than for the successful cases.

Local Validation vs. Extrapolation to Other Times and Places

The necessity of defining the testing procedure was discussed earlier. It is equally necessary, in a decision-oriented validation, to describe carefully the treatments applied and the outcome data collected.

Extrapolation is involved in using any validity study, no matter how limited the interpretation. The proposition that the Smith test predicts grade average in Law School A is tested on a particular sample of students entering in year t. The study is completed in year $t+3$, and the findings are used to justify admission decisions made in years $t+4$ and beyond. Meanwhile the faculty, the curriculum, and the supply of students have been changing. Hence the situation in which the test is used differs from the one in which data were collected. Empirical validation is inevitably retrospective, yet the use of the test is always prospective. The logic of decision making requires extrapolation from the past and therefore calls for a judgment about the similarity between the new

conditions and the old. This judgment takes advantage of whatever situational constructs one can bring to bear.

A formal criterion-oriented study builds a strong bridge of statistical inference from the data to a generalization, but, at the end of the bridge, the test interpreter has reached only an intermediate conclusion. To act, he must extrapolate with the aid of constructs and plausible inference; as it were, he must swim from the well-anchored conclusion to the point of decision (Cornfield & Tukey, 1956, p. 913). The extrapolation may involve much or little hazard. As an example where the hazard is considerable, consider a vocational-interest measure keyed according to the responses of middle-aged men well established in a particular career. It is applied to advise an adolescent that he will enjoy the work of, say, an aviator "because his interests are like those of aviators." A generation ago (when the original key for the Strong Vocational Interest Blank was established), the aviator was a leather-helmeted daredevil; today he is a junior executive whose armchair happens to move about the sky while he directs subordinates. Can the old key be applied? If a new key is made now, what data can forecast psychological requirements for being a pilot when today's adolescent in turn is in midcareer? No matter what data are collected today, the formal bridge can carry one only a short way toward predicting the job satisfaction of tomorrow's pilot.

A study that predicts success by a statistical formula has clearest significance when the formula is developed in the locale of the proposed application and the situation is sufficiently stable that the findings are representative of what will happen in succeeding years. Only if the supply of applicants and the curriculum remain much the same in character are the findings likely to remain directly applicable.

In the manual for the Differential Aptitude Tests (Bennett, Seashore, & Wesman, 1966), for example, the eight subtest scores are correlated with subsequent grades in school courses. The correlations fluctuate considerably from school to school, though this is to some extent attributable simply to the instability of correlations from small samples. The data for boys taking introductory (grade 10) geometry are representative. Stated here are the highest and lowest of the correlations reported in seven schools, for a one-year interval between test and grading (the number of cases for each correlation appears in parenthesis):

Verbal reasoning	.61 (31 cases) to .32 (56 cases)
Numerical reasoning	.64 (31 cases) to .18 (28 cases)
Abstract reasoning	.73 (34 cases) to .18 (28 cases)
Clerical speed and accuracy	.34 (56 cases) to − .06 (28 cases)
Mechanical reasoning	.50 (38 cases) to − .07 (28 cases)
Spatial reasoning	.57 (38 cases) to .20 (56 cases)
Spelling	.70 (28 cases) to .16 (37 cases)
Grammar	.64 (31 cases) to .29 (37 cases)

The most obvious implication of such confusing findings is that validation studies should be based on samples of 100 cases or more, even if this requires combining several years' data (where the treatment can be assumed to remain much the same). Second, it is true that the mixture of abilities represented in the battery as a whole predicts geometry marks; a simple unweighted composite score will predict with validity .50 or better in each school. The remarkable variation in the size of correlations and in the pattern of correlations could be better understood if the standard deviation of test scores in each sample were reported; as explained below, correlations are smaller in a group whose range is restricted. Even acknowledging such effects, one cannot dismiss the fact that in one school (38 cases), the spatial test has a higher correlation than any other test, and in another school (31 cases) it has the lowest correlation save for the clerical test. Obviously, a weighting formula fitted to the data for the former school would have emphasized just the wrong tests for predicting in the latter. Different schools may emphasize different abilities in teaching and grading.

These data, incidentally, illustrate the importance of an empirical check on hypotheses that seem reasonable a priori. One would expect success in geometry to depend on spatial and abstract reasoning and not to have much in common with spelling and grammar. But the median correlations for the four tests are much the same (.39 to .43).

Direct practical guidance is derived from a published validity study only if (*a*) the relationships are so low as to warrant abandoning a test or (*b*) the relationships are so consistent over a number of institutions that one can generalize to a whole class of institutions with confidence. Where neither statement is true, local validation would appear to be the answer. To establish a decision rule locally requires a healthy sample size and a defensible criterion—requirements that may be hard to meet.

The classical theory of prediction gives no attention to problems of extrapolation. The theory recognizes that the students are a sample from a population of students and that the criterion score is a sample of a universe of criterion observations; but the population and the criterion universe are taken to be fixed and the treatment is tacitly assumed to be fixed in all its details. The legitimacy of an extrapolation to new conditions cannot be judged by purely statistical means. To be sure, if studies in a dozen law schools report similar regressions of grade average onto the Smith test, one can confidently form a generalization though it is still confined to the population of law schools these dozen represent.

Loevinger (1957) correctly emphasized that predictive validations are ad hoc, answering a narrowly defined question as of a certain locale at a certain time. On the other hand, the practical decision maker often can reasonably hope for validity generalization (Mosier, 1951). If law schools require much the same courses, teach the courses similarly, and admit similar populations of students, a battery ought to have similar validity in every law school. It is fanciful to suggest that this holds for all law schools, but it may well be true for a large subset of them. Suppose it is found, in a cooperative study, that a battery gives similar results in schools *A*, *B*, *C*, . . . and *G*, but that schools *H* and *I* do not fit the pattern. Then law schools

$J, K, L, \ldots$ not in the original study can profit from its findings if it is clear what A to G have in common and how they differ from H and I. That is, one uses constructs about the varying nature of law schools to describe the class of law schools over which the generalization appears to hold.

Test-outcome relationships, wherever found, generalizable or not generalizable, open the way to important substantive inquiries. The variation in coefficients for the spatial test discussed above makes one intensely curious about the underlying instructional differences. Research that isolates the features of text and class activity that capitalize on spatial ability and the features that minimize its importance would move the investigator away from sheer prediction and toward understanding. Such research, however, must go much deeper than the validity coefficient itself and examine the instructional processes in all their qualitative complexity (Wallace, 1965).

Possible Invalidity of the Criterion

In the classical decision-oriented study, the outcome measure, or criterion, is central. The whole weight of predictive validation rests on the criterion score and leads to retention of that predictor information and that decision rule most likely to produce high scores on the criterion. As Bechtoldt has said (1951), the formal model of a criterion-oriented study accepts a set of operations for measuring outcome "as an adequate *definition* [italics added] of whatever is to be measured [p. 1245]." If the investigator uses a criterion that he does not regard as entirely adequate, he cannot accept the calculated test-criterion relationship as fully justifying a rule for action even in his local situation.

In a competent study lasting eight years, the Educational Testing Service collected data on thousands of engineers in industry (Hemphill, 1963). Its best testing program could predict only 5 percent of the variance among supervisor's ratings of young engineers. The ratings, it was found, had little to do with technical skill or knowledge and a lot to do with the personal relation that developed between engineer and supervisor. Consequently, the team wound up its criterion-oriented study with the conclusion that the ability tests should play an important part in the company's selection program *just because* they do not agree with the rating criterion! (Hemphill, 1963, p. 236.)

The critical role of the criterion is illustrated repeatedly in Ghiselli's (1966) compilation of findings from the validation of tests used in employee selection (see also Brogden & Taylor, 1950). Some studies use end-of-training measures as outcomes while others take performance on the job as the outcome measure. For personal service occupations, for example, intellectual tests have coefficients of about .50 for predicting training criteria, while the coefficients against on-the-job criteria are near zero. Reading a report that a certain test has a validity of .50 for selecting, say, switchboard operators, an employer might think that test useful in deciding whom to hire. But if the result comes from a training criterion, the test perhaps only selects employees who will complete training faster; some of the rejected employees might, after a longer-than-average training, be superior as operators. Unless training costs are substantial, the employer cannot justify using the test to select prospective operators. One reason for the better prediction of training criteria is that they often depend on verbal performance in the classroom and in examinations, which is readily predicted, whereas success on the job depends on nonverbal qualities that are hard to assess. All too often a training criterion is systematically biased against persons from disadvantaged subcultures; and a test that "validly" predicts the criterion seems likely to be an unjust basis for decisions.

There is a paradox here. The machinery of validation rests on acceptance of the criterion measure as being perfectly valid (save for random error), yet common sense tells one that it is not. One solution might be to abandon all thought of comparing the test to a criterion when the premise of criterion validity is so dubious. This is not appealing, because the methods of analyzing test-to-criterion relations are precise and sophisticated. The tester has preferred to retain this advanced analytic machinery, though he must interpret with caution the results he gets from it. Every report of validation against a criterion has to be thought of as carrying the warning clause, "Insofar as the criterion is truly representative of the outcome we wish to maximize, . . . " The report has to contain a clear description of the criterion and should contain a critique of it by the investigator. The reader must school himself to examine criteria with a hard eye, to convince himself that a test that predicts the stated criterion will also predict the outcome *he* is seeking (Astin, 1964). In effect, he will ask about the criterion measure all the questions asked about descriptive interpretations of a test. Does it fit the declared universe of relevant outcomes? Are these the educationally important outcomes? What constructs account for the criterion performance? In fact, a test-criterion study may be seen as simply another examination of convergence of indicators, and its interpretation must be as careful as that of any study of convergence.

The time dimension is important in thinking about criteria. An investigator usually collects criterion data at one point in time, ordinarily within a year of the predictive measurement. But a short-run criterion cannot tell the whole story, as is illustrated by the finding that superiority during training need not imply superiority on the job. The pressures and opportunities of later life differ from those in school, and success is judged on different bases; discrepancies between short-run and long-run criteria are the rule rather than the exception (Ghiselli, 1960). Where resources permit, the investigator should extend his validation study in time, though he may have to produce an interim report based on an early criterion so that decision making can proceed. Eventually, the accumulation of long-term follow-up studies will indicate the extent to which various types of early criteria are related to long-run outcomes of importance to educators. One must remember, however, that a study completed in 1970 refers to events of the 1960s and may or may not indicate the shape of events in the 1970s.

Cureton (1951) illustrated the way investigators reason from intermediate and imperfect criteria:

> Suppose we are unable to make direct observations of "success in engineering," or even to define it accurately and unambiguously, but still wish to construct an engineering aptitude test for use in counseling high school seniors and college freshmen. First we may predict success in mathematics, if only because failure in mathematics bars the student from further professional study in engineering colleges. Then we may predict graduation or nongraduation, or final grade-point average in the engineering college. We know that success in the engineering profession is not the same thing as our "criterion" (grade-point average) of success in the engineering college, but we have reason to believe that there is some fairly substantial relation between these two types of success. We should not rest content at this point, however. We should correlate both the test scores and the grade-point averages with, say, salaries at age thirty-three (or ten years after graduation), election to honorary engineering societies, and any other partial indices of engineering success that may become available. If either or both of our early scores (test score or grade-point average) correlates substantially with *several different* biased indicators of ultimate success, we shall believe we have increasing evidence that it would also correlate substantially with an unbiased indicator if such could be found [p. 635].

That is to say, the criterion is an indicator of a construct that, like most powerful constructs, should transcend any particular method of observation (see p. 466). Brogden and Taylor (1950) noted that criterion bias due to the omission of relevant elements or the inclusion of irrelevant elements is much less serious if these elements do not correlate with the predictors. The biases that enhance the apparent validity of one predictor while lowering the apparent validity of another are the ones that introduce systematic injustice into decisions.

Nowadays, a decision-oriented validation is likely to examine many separate, relatively pure criteria. The several outcome measures for a particular job or educational experience may have low intercorrelations and may depend on different predictors (e.g. Holland & Nichols, 1964). Kelly (1966), in a mammoth study with more than 50 measures of medical-student performance, found that most of them could be predicted. A surprising number of them were predicted better by interests and other noncognitive variables than by ability measures. The outcomes had low intercorrelations; within the same medical specialty, intercorrelations below .20 were found for three successive measures of knowledge—fourth-year course grades, National Board examination score, and State Board examination score. The tests that predict one outcome will often not be those that predict another, and a prediction formula that maximizes one outcome may reject persons who would be outstanding by another criterion. Further studies illustrating this important point are summarized elsewhere (Cronbach, 1970, pp. 363, 387, 401, 414, 672). The use of multiple-outcome measures has been increasingly prominent in validation of tests for employment (Dunnette, 1967). A job title does not itself define a job; what is important to success of one bookkeeper may be relatively unimportant for the bookkeeper in another office. While a single criterion of success might be used in selecting bookkeepers for one particular office, or for a well-standardized job in a single firm, this cannot be the correct approach for an investigator who wants to develop information useful to every firm selecting bookkeepers. Industrial psychologists therefore recommend the use of partial criteria, each representing an element in the overall job (Guion, 1965).

Specific criteria will often have to be artificially constructed. For instance, one might measure proficiency in routine bookkeeping operations by giving the worker a "kit" of invoices, credit slips, etc., and measuring his speed and accuracy in working out a balance. Such a narrowly defined criterion is probably more predictable and certainly more interpretable than the supervisor's global rating or a measure of duration of employment; but it is obviously partial and needs to be accompanied by measures of the other skills of bookkeeping. A similar breakdown of educational outcomes is likely to be useful (Anastasi, 1966, p. 313). Attention is drawn particularly to Ryans' (1957) discussion of the analysis of teacher performance and the construction of multiple criterion measures of it.

Using multiple criteria

A statistical analysis relating each outcome to each of the initial tests says a great deal, but it stops short of a decision rule. The industrial psychologists who have given most attention to the problem recommend that the full array of test and outcome relationships be reported by the original investigator so that each institution can work out its own decision rule. A firm wanting to hire bookkeepers would be advised to study just what its bookkeepers have to do and to judge the relative importance of the various outcomes in terms of its requirements. These judgments can be used in combining the several criteria into a composite that represents the desires of that firm (Primoff, 1959). Then the predictors are combined so as to predict the composite criterion for that firm. A firm that weights the criterion elements differently will also weight the predictors differently. A procedure of this sort has been used with some success in hiring (Guion, 1965), and perhaps it can serve in educational selection.

The choice of combining rule depends on the decision maker's purposes or values (i.e. those of the institution he represents). To borrow Cureton's (1951) illustration of the combination of speed and accuracy scores for typing performance: If typescript is to be prepared for photo-offset publication, accuracy is all important and speed distinctly secondary. In rough-draft typing, on the other hand, speed takes on great weight and accuracy becomes secondary. A weighting of these two outcomes satisfactory for the selection of workers who have to prepare perfect copy will be unsatisfactory for selecting rough-draft typists—unless, of course, speed and accuracy are highly correlated [p. 628].

Statistical devices such as canonical correlation, for handling several predictors and several criteria simultaneously, are not appropriate for the decision-oriented study. The aim of such a study is to develop a decision rule that will maximize the utility of the work force or the educational system. Utility depends upon values, not upon the statistical connections of scores. A canonical analysis will rearrange the criterion dimensions into a new set of uncorrelated measures, and the first of these measures (to which greatest attention is ordinarily paid) is whatever combination of outcomes is best predicted by the test data. An aspect of performance that is relatively easy to predict (e.g. likeability) will receive heavy weight in the canonical variate even though it interests the decision maker much less than, say, the ability to solve problems creatively. In selection research, one must continually resist the temptation to focus on criteria that are easy to predict. Attention should go to those that are most important.

It is not only the values of institutions and employers that need to be reflected in criteria. In vocational choice and many other decisions the purpose is to maximize the satisfaction of the person counseled, and his values may be quite different from those of the institutional decision maker. The counseling process has to help the client bring his values to the fore and use them in arriving at a course of action (M. Katz, 1963). There is no possibility of a universal decision rule. Each individual brings to bear his own values and his own willingness to take risks (Cronbach & Gleser, 1965, pp. 130 ff.). Moreover, there is no fixed set of alternative treatments.

Consider further the prediction of success in bookkeeping. The young man considering bookkeeping as a career cannot know which firms he might work for, and there is no way to forecast which elements will count most heavily in his success. The only alternative is to forecast which job elements he will handle well and which poorly. If the forecasts are generally favorable, he can prepare himself for a bookkeeping career and subsequently seek work that emphasizes the job elements he handles best and enjoys most. But this is to use the test battery descriptively to give him a full picture of himself rather than to predict his level of success.

Outcome Measures in Education

The outcomes of education against which tests are most often compared fall into three classes: achievement tests, judgments, and career data. A typical use of an achievement test would be the application of a reading test to verify forecasts made by a reading-readiness test. The most common judgmental criterion is the course mark or the grade average, but use is also made of ratings by teachers on performance or personal qualities. Ratings may also be collected from job supervisors or acquaintances of the subject or derived from carefully controlled observations. The third category, career facts, is a broad one, represented by such questions as: Does the person complete the training? What occupation does he enter? How well satisfied is he with his career? Or to give examples in the context of citizenship education: Does he have a police record? Does he vote in local elections? Does he read magazines dealing with public affairs?

When a test is to be the outcome measure in a validation study, it is often worthwhile to develop a far more elaborate measuring procedure than would be employed for routine measurement of individuals. A procedure too expensive for large-scale use may give excellent criterion data in an intensive study. For example, one might observe the student physician as he conducts a medical examination or require the student architect to spend three weeks developing a design for a preschool or present the student mechanic with a series of malfunctioning engines that he is to diagnose and repair.

It is possible that the same achievement test, given at different times, will rank students in different orders. This is not a matter of sampling error alone. When a test is given as an end-of-course examination, students are presumably at the peak of their preparation. If it is given several months later, without special opportunity to review, some students will have lost a great deal of their proficiency whereas others will have retained or even improved their knowledge. This statement is supported by many experimental studies showing that retention depends on understanding and on overlearning. These studies, unfortunately, have been concerned with the learning of small units of material under experimental conditions. Rarely does a study ask the question most important from the viewpoint of predictive research: How does the correlation of a predictor test with an achievement test given at the end of a regular school course compare with the correlation between the predictor and a delayed achievement test that measures more permanent gains?

The criterion provided by course marks is notoriously unsatisfactory, but the ease of obtaining such data makes them the most common of all outcome measures. The difficulties are least serious when all the grades were assigned by a single teacher in a single class, since, then, the students are likely to have been located on the same scale. But there is no guarantee that this scale truly represents mastery of the course. One notable instance is some data for the Differential Aptitude Tests (DAT), reported in the 1959 manual, where for 70 geometry students in a certain school the tests had unexpectedly low correlations with marks. One of the test authors, out of curiosity, made inquiries and discovered that in this school the course marks reflected classroom conduct as much as they did achievement. The typical teacher's preference for docile students also may account for the frequent finding that girls receive higher grades than boys. Carter (1952) correlated an objective test of algebra achievement with marks given by six experienced teachers in the same schools. The boys were given lower grades, though they were a trifle ahead of the girls on the achievement test. The correlations were .35 for girls taught by women, .57 for girls taught by men, .37 for boys taught by women, and .78 for boys taught by men.

If teachers use different bases for judgment and some are more generous than others, throwing grades from several algebra teachers into a single distribution merely piles one source of error on another. If an investigator is so unwise as to pool classes taught from different materials and by different methods, it becomes even harder to determine what if anything the pretests predict. In a grade average, matters are further confounded by the fact that some students choose harder courses and carry heavier loads than others and by the fact that factors considered in grading differ from field to field (Terwilliger, 1966). The grade-average criterion may be justified practically, as no school wants to admit students who are likely to be dropped for poor grades. There are few educators, however, who would want to defend a high grade average as fully representing the outcomes toward which they aim.

Much has been written regarding the deficiencies of ratings and marks. It is not practical here to review the research and the recommendations that have been made; the reader is directed to the following sources: Cronbach, 1970, chapter 17; Thorndike & Hagen, 1969, chapter 13; Guilford et al., 1962.

With regard to career data as criteria, the best examples are probably the long-term follow-up studies of Strong and Terman. The former, having devised his Vocational Interest Blank, rested the initial claim to validity on the fact that men in an occupation earned higher scores on the key for that occupation than did other men. But the test was intended for students, and one could not be sure that interests measured in late adolescence would forecast adult job satisfaction. Strong traced the students to determine what careers they entered, whether they persisted in those careers, and what degree of success they achieved. Thus, 20 years after the tests were given in college, he was able to report that the life histories of the majority of the men had been consistent with the test scores (Strong, 1955). Terman administered tests of mental ability to a large number of exceptional children. In a follow-up study that has continued more than 40 years (Oden, 1968), he and his associates related the tests to an enormous variety of indices of success and adjustment: school marks, years of school completed, degrees earned, occupational level attained, income, marital happiness, patents credited, books and articles published, honors, mental health (judged from self-report on feelings of anxiety, psychiatric treatment, etc.), etc. Another criterion based on career data is the inventory of extracurricular achievement of high school students, which takes into account published writings, scientific apparatus designed, prizes won, business experience, etc. (Holland & Nichols, 1964).

The Test-Criterion Relationship in Selection

Only two of the formal models for processing validation data will be examined. The first is the selection decision where there is a single predictor, a specified instructional treatment for persons admitted, a single criterion scale, and a rule specifying the proportion of applicants to be admitted. The second is a placement decision, like the first model except that persons are divided between two instructional treatments, none being rejected. These cases are less limited than they might appear to be; one can treat each of several criteria in turn or combine them, and multiple observations can be combined into a composite predictor by techniques discussed in chapter 16. Furthermore, the rationale and most of the conclusions introduced here apply to more complex classification decisions (see Cronbach & Gleser, 1965). The models are formal and lead the investigator to definite numerical results; these results are always to be a point of departure for thinking, not a substitute for it.

Sampling of subjects

The data for research on selection consist of paired predictor and outcome scores for persons who have been through the specified treatment. These persons generally have been screened. A college will have rejected the applicant who has not finished high school and may have ruled out any applicant whose high school marks or test scores fell below a certain level. The persons in the study may be a sample of (a) the entire population of applicants, (b) the population of screened applicants, or (c) the population of persons who presently enter *and remain in* the treatment.

There is no general rule as to which population should be studied. If data can be collected for a representative fraction of the unscreened population a, the correlation of predictor with outcome will almost certainly be higher than in a study of population b. The former correlation credits the test for predictive information that overlaps what other screening data already provide. Since population c is severely curtailed by the elimination of poor performers in the course of treatment, the correlation will be lower in that population than in a or b. In population a, one learns about the predictive validity of the test considered by itself, and that information may be significant when one is publishing a report for the benefit of all possible users of the test. In population b, one learns what the test adds to the other information in use. That is what is significant for the local decision maker. If the prescreening is changed, the analysis of the original population b is no longer relevant. The one clear conclusion is that any screening affecting the sample must be taken into account in interpreting the result.

One design for validating educational predictors is to test applicants, use the test results in selection along with other data, and ultimately collect criterion information on the persons who survive the selection and several months of instruction. This is a study of population c and fails to give the test credit for the failures it eliminated. Sometimes (see below) a correction formula can estimate results for population b. A better procedure is to administer the test, set the scores aside during selection, and collect criterion data on all the cases that survive selection on other bases. Some criterion information—if no more than the fact of withdrawal—should be recorded for everyone selected. This study bears directly on population b. A third possibility is to admit a random sample of applicants without screening of any sort. Multiple-correlation techniques can be used to show how much the test score adds to the prediction from other screening information. An advantage of this approach is that it permits one to evaluate the contribution of all the pieces of information.

It is good practice, where the sample size is sufficient, to treat separately the data for boys and girls, whites and blacks, and for subgroups differing markedly in previous preparation. Not infrequently, the predictive significance of a score differs from subgroup to subgroup (Krug, 1966; Seashore, 1961). The final summary should pool subgroups for which regression lines are not significantly different. Complex policy problems arise in using subgroup statistics. If it were statistically valid to use different tests or different cutting scores for boys than for girls (for example), the decision maker would have difficulty convincing applicants that he was not discriminating unfairly against one sex or the other.

Expectancy tables, regression slopes, and correlations

A particularly satisfactory way of organizing input-output data is the *expectancy table*, which reports the distribution of outcomes for persons having any particular pretest score. Such tables, or charts, may be arranged in various ways. Table 14.5, for example, displays cumulative proportions—the odds that for a person with a certain predictor score, the outcome will be at or above each level. This presentation makes evident the association of higher predictor scores with better outcomes; at the same time it calls attention to the uncertainty of any prediction. The expectancy chart, being a direct tabulation of data, can be understood by persons who have no statistical training and can be constructed by anyone who accumulates follow-up data. The expectancy table can be used when outcome data are categorical—e.g. completes course of study, withdraws voluntarily, is dropped—rather than numerical. The reader is warned that different impressions can be given by categorizing the outcome data in different ways. For example, results are altered if students who are placed on probation but ultimately survive are classed with the failures rather than with the successes.

Three types of summary statistics may be derived from an expectancy table: a trend line, a measure of dispersion or uncertainty, and a coefficient that compares the uncertainty after testing with the uncertainty before testing. Here consideration is given to only the common methods of analysis which assume that the variables are continuous, the trend is linear, and the dispersion is the same in every column.

The relation of outcome Y to predictor X is stated by a trend line. This could be established by locating the average outcome for each X category and connecting these points, but sampling fluctuations make such a line jagged. The straight line that best fits the points is described by a regression equation of the form:

$$\hat{Y} = \beta(X - \mu_X) + \mu_Y,$$

where $\hat{Y}$ is the estimate or prediction of Y, and μ_X and μ_Y are means. The parameter β, describing the slope of the line, equals the covariance of X with Y, divided by the variance of X (see McNemar, 1969, p. 136). This β is not what educational statisticians know as a "beta weight." This is an unstandardized weight (often denoted by b).

For each person there is an estimate $\hat{Y}$ and an error of estimate $\hat{Y} - Y$. The uncertainty of prediction is described by the standard deviation of $\hat{Y} - Y$; this is represented by $\sigma_{Y \cdot X}$. It is called the standard error of estimate.

Although the straight-line model fits most tests and most continuous criteria, it cannot be trusted blindly. In studies of employees a curved regression line is sometimes found, such that differences in test scores have no predictive significance so long as the score is above a certain minimum; sometimes, indeed, outcomes are best for persons with an intermediate test score, and persons with very high or very low test scores tend to do poorly on the job (Kahne-

---

TABLE 14.5

A Specimen Expectancy Table

Chances in 100 that a freshman will reach a certain grade average in College C if his predictor score X is

	50–54	55–59	60–64	65–69	70–74	75–79	80–84	85–89
A− or better	1−	1−	1	3	6	13	23	37
B− or better	4	8	16	28	41	57	72	84
C− or better	32	47	62	76	86	92	96	99
D− or better	80	89	95	98	99	99+	99+	99+

Note: This table is based on the report for a particular college. Results were obtained by an indirect method assuming a bivariate normal distribution rather than by simple tabulation. (From *Indiana Prediction Study*, 1965, p. 46.)

man & Ghiselli, 1962). Sometimes at the college level, it is found that an aptitude test predicts whose grades will be above average better than it identifies those who will fail. Hypotheses that motivational variables have curvilinear relations are common; thus, some intermediate level of aspiration or degree of compulsiveness very likely promises better achievement than a score at either extreme. Unfortunately, adequate, repeated demonstrations of such relations are nonexistent.

The third summary statistic is the correlation coefficient ρ_{XY}. While it may be calculated directly from the series of X and Y scores, another equation is more illuminating:

$$\rho_{XY}^2 = 1 - \frac{\sigma_{Y \cdot X}^2}{\sigma_Y^2} .$$

(This equation is stated in terms of population parameters. In general, in this chapter, statements refer to the population, but the remarks and equations apply with little or no change to sample statistics. For a treatment that gives meticulous attention to the sample-population distinction, see Lord & Novick, 1968.) The error variance $\sigma_{Y \cdot X}^2$ is one index of uncertainty about the location of Y after the individual has been tested, and σ_Y^2 is a comparable index of uncertainty before testing. Therefore, ρ_{XY}^2 describes the proportion by which uncertainty has been reduced. To put it another way, the squared correlation indicates what proportion of the variation in the criterion is forecast by the prediction equation. Under the usual linear assumption, a complementary statement also holds; ρ_{XY}^2 is the proportion of the test variance that is relevant to the outcome.

The correlation of X with Y is traditionally called "the validity coefficient for test X." More precisely, one would speak of the validity of linear predictions, from the test scores obtained under certain specified conditions, of individual differences on the outcome measure Y, among persons representative of a certain population, who are subjected to a certain treatment. Any alteration in treatment, population, or outcome measure will alter the coefficient.

The predictor score is only one of the many admissible observations of that variable. Marks on student essays, say, are to be correlated with an objective test of ability to choose among alternative wordings of an idea. One reader applies a highly traditional standard to the essays and penalizes for contractions and colloquialisms; a second applies a more liberal standard. If the objective test is keyed according to a traditional standard, the first reader can be expected to agree with it better than the second. Their regression slopes and errors of estimate will also differ. The two readers are samples from the universe of admissible readers; the universe is evidently not homogeneous. Where it is suspected that conditions within the universe are not equivalent in what they measure, this should be checked by determining separate validity coefficients for conditions separately.

It is to be regretted that testers, preoccupied with differences among individuals, have placed more emphasis on the correlation coefficient than the regression function and the error of estimate. Any preselection of subjects is likely to have a strong effect on σ_Y and ρ_{XY}. The standard error and the regression coefficient β are much less sensitive to restriction of range, and therefore provide a more general description of the X, Y relation. The difficulty in using β and $\sigma_{Y \cdot X}$ is that they are expressed in terms of a particular set of Y units and are hard to interpret unless the Y scale has a clear practical significance. If the criterion scale shows the salaries a company pays engineers with 10 years of service, the regression function is meaningful; if it is only a ranking by supervisors, the units reveal nothing. Criterion-referenced scales for educational outcomes (see pp. 652–55) will make regression functions more useful in educational prediction.

An equation that relates ρ_{XY} to σ_X is sometimes used to estimate ρ in a population of wider or narrower range. Suppose that one has data from one population, say f. Let $\sigma_{X(f)}^2$ represent the variance in that population, $\rho_{XY(f)}$ the corresponding correlation of X with Y, etc. For some other population g, one defines $\sigma_{X(g)}^2$ and $\rho_{XY(g)}$, etc. Let m equal $\sigma_{X(g)}^2 / \sigma_{X(f)}^2$. Assume that β and $\sigma_{Y \cdot X}$ are the same whether X is large or small. Then it can be shown (Gulliksen, 1950, p. 137) that

$$\rho^2_{XY(g)} = \frac{m\rho^2_{XY(f)}}{1 + (m-1)\rho^2_{XY(f)}}.$$

Compare this equation with the Spearman-Brown formula (p. 395). While this formula gives some indication of the effect of selection on coefficients, it is almost never strictly appropriate because the underlying assumption is a strong one. The estimated coefficient will be in error if any variable correlated with Y (other than X itself) is used to screen one population and not the other. (For more complicated cases, see Gulliksen, 1950, pp. 128–172; Wiseman, 1967; Lord & Novick, 1968, pp. 140–148.)

Instead of taking an intact sample of persons, a validator sometimes traces cases from the high and low ends of the test-score distribution. This reduces the cost of a follow-up study, especially when criterion measures are costly to obtain. A comparison of the criterion means of the two groups gives a good test of the null hypothesis and tells whether the test and criterion are related, but it does not tell how strong the relation is in the parent population. The correlation for such a sample greatly overestimates the correlation in the intact population. Fortunately, the slope of the regression line and the value of $\sigma_{Y \cdot X}$ computed from the sample with extreme X scores can be taken as unbiased estimates of the slope and standard error for the entire population. From these and σ_X for the population, the population correlation can be estimated by the equation

$$\rho^2_{XY} = \frac{\beta^2 \sigma^2_X}{\beta^2 \sigma^2_X + \sigma^2_{Y \cdot X}}.$$

A validation study might instead select cases from the extremes of the criterion-score distribution; then the Y-on-X regression slope and standard error are uninterpretable, but a correlation can be calculated.

Interpretation in terms of utility

How useful a test is for selection depends on the importance of the decision, the cost of testing, and the proportion of applicants who will be accepted, as well as on the validity coefficient. Where more than one outcome of a treatment is measured one can develop an expectancy table, a regression equation, and a correlation for each measure. But to appraise formally the usefulness of the test for selection decisions, one must represent profiles of possible outcomes on a single scale: a *utility* scale that tells how much each profile is worth to the institution. This utility measure serves as a composite criterion that reflects the values of the decision maker.

Assume that the treatment given accepted persons is fixed in advance and that Y is expressed in units of utility or value. Then the gain in utility due to use of the test for selection is

$$\Delta U = (\mu_Y - \mu_{Y_o}) - C/\phi; \qquad [1]$$

where

$\Delta U =$ gain per man accepted, as a consequence of basing selection decisions on the test, expressed on a utility scale;

$C =$ the cost of testing, per man tested, in utility units;

$\phi =$ the selection ratio, the proportion of persons in population b who are accepted;

$\mu_Y =$ average outcome for the men selected on the basis of the test;

$\mu_{Y_o} =$ average outcome for all men in population b.

To relate this to test validity, additional assumptions must be introduced. Again writing β for the regression slope and defining μ_X and μ_{X_o} as the average scores of selected and unselected men, equation 1 becomes

$$\Delta U = \beta(\mu_X - \mu_{X_o}) - C/\phi. \qquad [2]$$

If, further, it is specified that X is normally distributed, one can write ξ for the ordinate of the unit normal curve corresponding to ϕ. The equation then takes the form

$$\Delta U = \beta \sigma_X \xi/\phi - C/\phi, \qquad [3]$$

and these values from the normal-curve table suggest how utility depends on the selection ratio:

Selection ratio ϕ 0.01 0.10 0.30 0.50 0.80
$\quad\quad\quad\quad\quad$ ξ/ϕ 3.00 1.80 0.93 0.80 0.35

$\quad\quad\quad\quad$ ϕ 0.90 0.99
$\quad\quad\quad\quad$ ξ/ϕ 0.20 0.03

Because it is difficult to assign utility values to outcomes, these equations are not likely to be applied formally by test developers. Nonetheless they are instructive. Other things being equal, the value of a test is proportional to the regression slope β and consequently to ρ_{XY}. Thus the coefficient expresses the benefit from testing as a percentage of the benefit one could get from perfect prediction of outcomes (Brogden, 1949).

This statement assumes that the treatment is fixed in advance. Perhaps, however, treatment can be adapted. If a new selection device provides a higher quality of student, the pace of instruction can very likely be increased or perhaps a greater amount of independent study can be used with profit. When such adaptation is possible, the value of a test is more nearly proportional to ρ_{XY}^2 than to ρ_{XY} (Cronbach & Gleser, 1965, pp. 44 ff.). Another point to be noted from equation 2 is that even a strong test-criterion relation (β large) offers little benefit if nearly everyone is accepted (ϕ large); conversely, a modest test-criterion relation can produce a large benefit if ϕ is rather small. As ϕ approaches one or zero, however, the cost of testing outweighs the benefit.

What is an acceptable level of validity?

No rule of thumb can be given regarding the strength of relationship required to make a test useful. For a selection decision, the question is answered by equation 2 or 3. If the regression slope is great enough for improved outcomes to offset the cost of testing, testing is beneficial. This depends not just on the correlation between test and criterion, but also on the importance of the decision, which is reflected in the standard deviation of Y_∞ and indirectly in β. A test of modest validity that provides information not otherwise available is worth using, when it is important to minimize errors in decision making. Errors in decision making

are likely to be most serious when they cannot be reversed or can be reversed only at a great price.

While the foregoing argument is stated as if the test were to be used for just one decision, in educational testing the information is usually placed in the student's file and used for many later decisions: admission, choice of major, selection of courses, career planning, etc. A test with multiple uses can repay a cost that would be unreasonable if a test were to be used once and forgotten. Even greater value is obtained from a test that offers scores that combine in different ways to bear on a wide range of decisions. In the descriptive uses of tests also, it may be wiser to spread one's testing so as to obtain many scores of moderate validity than to concentrate the same expenditure on measuring a single variable with great validity. Sometimes it is better to pin down one fact and remain in ignorance of all the others, and at other times it is better to obtain partial information on all the dimensions. The purposes of testing determine just how one should compromise between "fidelity" and "bandwidth." (See Cronbach & Gleser, 1965, esp. pp. 65–68, 97–107.)

Relations involving universe scores

The observed X and Y are samples, respectively, from universes of test and criterion measures. The universe score X_∞ might be considered the ideal representation of X-type behavior, and the universe score Y_∞ the ideal representation of the defined class of criterion measures. The relation between the two universe scores is of more fundamental interest than the relation between observed variables. Assuming that X and Y are observed independently, the observed test-criterion relation depends on three things: the relevance of the X information (i.e. the X_∞-to-Y_∞ relation); the generalizability of X (i.e. the X-to-X_∞ relation); and the generalizability of Y (the Y-to-Y_∞ relation). The observed X has a strong relation to the observed Y only when all three of these component relationships are strong. No matter how relevant the predictor behavior may be to the outcome, the observed relation will be weak if either variable is thinly sampled. Hence, when the X-to-Y relation is weak, X_∞ lacks relevance to Y_∞, or too small a sample of X or Y information has been taken.

If the criterion score Y comes from one observer's report on a student's attentiveness based on 20 minutes' observation, the investigator could strengthen the X-to-Y relation by using more observers or a larger time span or both. To estimate the effect of such changes one employs a mathematical model that speaks of averaging j observations of X_∞ and k of Y_∞ to form new scores, X_j and Y_k. The limiting values X_∞ and Y_∞ are approached as j and k become indefinitely large. Ignore, for the moment, the fact that there are two or more distinct ways of extending the sample of criterion behavior. For theoretical purposes, j or k may be regarded as continuous and, possibly, as fractional (e.g. consider cutting the original 20 minutes down to 10, in which case $k = .5$). With these symbols, meaning can be given to the general validity coefficient $\rho_{X_j Y_k}$; special cases of it include $\rho_{XY} = \rho_{X_1 Y_1}, \rho_{X_\infty Y}, \rho_{X_\infty Y_\infty}$, etc. (The coefficients $\rho_{X_k X'_k}, \rho_{XX_\infty}$, etc., have been discussed under the heading of reliability [see pp. 400–01]. Here X and X' represent two measures of X; equivalence among the X measures and among the Y measures is assumed to simplify the discussion.)

To explain these correlations, one starts with $\rho_{X_\infty Y_\infty}$, which indicates the relevance of X_∞ to Y_∞. Now $\rho^2_{X_\infty Y_\infty}$ is the fraction of the variance of Y_∞ predictable from X_∞ (see shaded portion of Panel A in figure 14.3). The residual variance equals $\sigma^2_{Y_\infty}(1 - \rho^2_{X_\infty Y_\infty})$. This residual variance reflects genuine differences among persons that affect Y but are not detected by an accurate measurement of X.

When a single observation Y is made, the score differs from Y_∞. This difference, a sampling error, is not predictable. Panel C shows the variance of the single observation Y, as the sum of the two variances of Panel A plus a variance arising from this sampling error. Panel B takes into account the law that the variance of an average of k similar, uncorrelated observations equals $1/k$ times the variance of a single observation; this applies to the k errors of observation that are averaged to form the error component of Y_k. The other two components are unchanged in averaging.

The error variance in Y_1 equals $\sigma^2_{Y_1}(1 - \rho_{Y_1 Y'_1})$, or, in a simple notation, $\sigma^2_Y(1 - \rho_{YY'})$. Therefore

$$\sigma^2_{Y_k} = \rho^2_{X_\infty Y_\infty}\sigma^2_{Y_\infty} + (1 - \rho^2_{X_\infty Y_\infty})\sigma^2_{Y_\infty}$$
$$+ \frac{1}{k}(1 - \rho_{YY'})\sigma^2_Y. \qquad [4]$$

But it is also known that $\rho^2_{X_\infty Y_\infty}\sigma^2_{Y_\infty}$ is the part

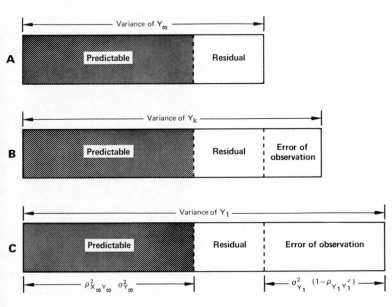

FIG. 14.3. Components of criterion variance as a function of number of observations k. Length of bar represents total variance of the average of k observations on Y. Shaded portion represents variance predictable from X_∞.

of $\sigma^2_{Y_k}$ predictable from X_∞, i.e. the shaded portion of Panel B. Now the fraction that represents the proportion of predictable variance is formed:

$$\rho^2_{X_\infty Y_k} = \frac{\rho^2_{X_\infty Y_\infty}\sigma^2_{Y_\infty}}{\sigma^2_{Y_k}} = \frac{\rho^2_{X_\infty Y_\infty}\rho_{YY'}\sigma^2_Y}{\sigma_{Y_k}}, \quad [5]$$

or, substituting from equation 4 and simplifying,

$$\rho^2_{X_\infty Y_k} = \frac{\rho^2_{X_\infty Y_\infty}\rho_{YY'}\sigma^2_Y}{\rho_{YY'}\sigma^2_Y + \dfrac{1}{k}(1 - \rho_{YY'})\sigma^2_Y}$$

$$= \frac{k\rho^2_{X_\infty Y_\infty}\rho_{YY'}}{(k-1)\rho_{YY'} + 1}. \quad [6]$$

Using the Spearman-Brown formula of p. 395, one may rewrite this as

$$\rho^2_{X_\infty Y_k} = \rho^2_{X_\infty Y_\infty}\rho_{Y_k Y'_k}. \quad [7]$$

Since the multiplier $\rho_{Y_k Y'_k}$ is less than 1.00 (equal, in the limiting case where $\rho_{YY'}$ equals 1.00), this equation indicates the degree to which the correlation between X_∞ and an incomplete measure of Y is reduced (attenuated) by the errors of measurement. The greater these sampling errors, the smaller the fraction of the Y variance that is predictable.

The attenuating effect of imperfect observation of X is similar; reasoning like that above leads to two further equations:

$$\rho^2_{X_j Y_\infty} = \rho^2_{X_\infty Y_\infty}\rho_{X_j X'_j} \quad [8]$$

and

$$\rho^2_{X_j Y_k} = \rho^2_{X_\infty Y_\infty}\rho_{X_j X'_j}\rho_{Y_k Y'_k}. \quad [9]$$

Each of the equations 7–9 has a special case where $j = k = 1$. The special case of equation 9 may be written

$$\rho^2_{X_\infty Y_\infty} = \rho^2_{XY}/\rho_{XX'}\rho_{YY'}. \quad [10]$$

Knowing ρ_{XY}, $\rho_{XX'}$, and $\rho_{YY'}$, one may calculate $\rho^2_{X_\infty Y_\infty}$ from equation 10 and then may derive the correlations for any j and k with the aid of equation 9.

It can also be shown that the regression

slope describing the dependence of Y_k on X_j is given by

$$\beta_j = j\beta_1/[(j-1)\rho_{XX'} + 1]. \quad [11]$$

Equations 5–10 were valid whether X_j was defined as the sum or average of j observations; likewise for Y_k. But equation 11 applies only to the average, as it is written. For sums, the value given by equation 11 would have to be multiplied by k/j. As j increases, the regression function becomes steeper. The slope (and, in consequence, the utility of testing) does not depend on the accuracy with which the criterion Y is observed. For this reason, k does not enter the formula.

One perplexing problem may be noted in passing. Sometimes one has no way of estimating criterion reliability. Consider the student's grade in a history course. One can readily investigate the accuracy with which performance is assessed—but what about the reliability of the performance itself? One can take the position that an event is an event, reliable because it occurred (Cureton, 1965, p. 336), but one also may detach himself and recognize that many fortuitous elements enter the criterion performance. One student is ill for two critical weeks before the midterm. Another falls in love and neglects his work. Another clashes with his instructor. Surely their grades in history would be different if they had a chance to start fresh with all conditions set back to what they were at the start of the term. The illness and the love affair would strike different students or at other times. The student who drew an incompatible instructor might this time draw a congenial one. Much of the criterion variance arose out of happenstance and could not possibly have been predicted.

Equation 10 is said to "correct for attenuation," and the phrase "ρ_{XY} corrected for attenuation," when not otherwise qualified, refers to $\rho_{X_\infty Y_\infty}$. This measure of relevance is more pertinent in construct validation than the observed correlation. The practical decision maker, however, must be concerned with β_j or $\rho_{X_j Y_\infty}$ for various values of j, as these indicate how much prediction would be improved by taking a fuller sample of X, or how much impaired by measuring X less thoroughly. Little practical interest attaches to correlations of the hypothetical X_∞, save as these indicate the highest value correlations of X_j could possibly reach. Four warnings regarding the use of these equations are called for:

1. The assumption of equivalence is not trustworthy. If observations within the universe are not equivalent, a corrected coefficient may be much too high or too low. It was noted earlier that marks from two readers of an essay might not have equal correlations with an objective test; the two sets of data would produce different estimates of $\rho^2_{XY_\infty}$, etc.

2. The analysis assumes that the X and Y measures are independent random samples of their universes. If each X is paired with one of the Ys, the correlation for such linked observations will perhaps be higher than the correlation that takes X and Y from different pairs. The latter value must be used in the equation. An example of pairing would be a study of the correlation between two variables, both judged by the same observer. The equation requires that an X score from one observer be correlated with a Y score from a second, independent observer.

3. A sample correlation is an estimate of the correlation in the population. Sampling errors in the estimate, which cause little trouble in directly calculated slopes or correlations, sometimes have a much magnified effect on ratios into which they enter. If $\rho_{XX'}$ or $\rho_{YY'}$ is underestimated, or ρ_{XY} is overestimated, the corrected coefficient (with j or $k > 1$) will be too large and sometimes greater than 1.00. If $\rho_{XX'}$ is underestimated, β_j will be overestimated. Hence coefficients used in such estimates should be based on large samples of persons. The sample size must be particularly large if the estimated reliability coefficient is low. Preferably, the *same* large sample will be used to obtain the estimates of $\rho_{XX'}$ and $\rho_{YY'}$ and the four intercorrelations ρ_{XY}, $\rho_{XY'}$, $\rho_{X'Y}$, and $\rho_{X'Y'}$, which together estimate the expected value of $\rho_{X_1 Y_1}$. Sampling theory for corrected coefficients is given by Forsyth and Feldt (1969).

4. A given observation can be regarded as belonging to more than one universe. In the example suggested at the start of this section, Y belongs to a universe of observers with period of observation fixed, to a universe of observation periods with observer fixed, and to a universe encompassing both observers and observation periods. Each universe definition implies a different universe score Y_∞, a different ρ_{YY_∞}, etc. It is important to qualify any statement about a corrected coefficient or slope to make clear from what universe the hypothesized additional observations are drawn.

The mark given an essay and the score on an objective test of writing ability, for example, will not correlate perfectly, but one might wish to know if, apart from errors of measurement, they measure the same individual differences. Consider only the errors in the essay measure. To use as $\rho_{XX'}$ in the correction formula a correlation between two scorings of the same essay is only to ask whether that particular essay, scored repeatedly, would give a good estimate of the objective measure. To use a correlation between two essays scored by the same scorer as $\rho_{XX'}$ is to ask whether a large number of such samples of behavior could provide a good estimate of the objective measure. But one is probably interested in a universe that covers both essays and scorers and to get an estimate for that universe requires that $\rho_{XX'}$ be determined from two essays, each scored by a different scorer, or from some more complex design (Cronbach et al., 1971, in press).

Despite the hazards and possible ambiguities attending them, corrected slopes and coefficients are well worth examining. The industry and resources of the investigator determined how thorough a criterion measure was taken, hence any reported ρ_{XY} is to some degree adventitious; it is ρ_{XY_∞} or β_1 that answers the significant question about the value of X_1 as a predictor. When the next tester has the option of extending or curtailing the measurement of X, the functions relating $\rho_{X_j Y_\infty}$ and β_j to j guide him in planning his test.

The Test-Treatment Interaction in Placement

The discussion now turns to the second basic case, the classification decision. Only the simplest case, two-category placement, is considered, the case where every subject will be assigned or advised into whichever of two predetermined treatments promises to be the better for him. It can easily be argued that placement decisions are more significant in education than selection decisions. In evaluating selection decisions, one ignores what happens to the persons screened out of the institution; only the production of the workers actually hired affects the balance sheet of a firm. But a school system that uses tests to "select" students who may take algebra is not rejecting the students who fall below the cutting score. These are sent into an alternative program—a simpler mathematics course or a program that does not include mathematics. Whatever the school does with them, their mathematical competence at the end of the year is as much a part of the school's balance sheet as the competence of those who take algebra. The placement model, then, is the pertinent one when the school is concerned with the consequences of its policies for all the students under consideration.

Let treatments be labeled A and B, and the respective outcomes Y_A and Y_B be expressed on a common utility scale, since rational examination of a placement decision is not possible until the outcomes have been expressed in the same units. Again, let X be the predictor. There will be two expectancy tables, one for A and one for B, and two corresponding regression functions. The regression lines may align in various ways, as illustrated in figure 14.4. In the first two examples, treatment A gives better average results than B at all levels of X studied. Hence all persons in this range should be assigned to A and the test has no value even though it validly predicts outcome. In the third panel the regression lines cross at the point labeled X^*. The

decision rule is to assign all persons for whom $X > X^*$ to B and all others to A. The utility of the test is to be judged by comparing the average outcome when persons are so assigned with the average outcome when all persons are assigned to whichever treatment is best for the average subject. It is assumed for the sake of simplicity that whatever course of action maximizes the average outcome is preferred, that the regressions of outcome on test score are linear, and that X is normally distributed.

Let β_A and β_B represent the regression slopes. The crossover point X^* is identified with a certain ordinate ξ^* and an area ϕ^* of the normal distribution, where ϕ^* is the proportion of cases assigned to treatment B. The gain in utility per man is

$$\Delta U = (\beta_B - \beta_A)\sigma_X \xi^*/\phi^* - C.$$

Compare this with equation 3 which applies to selection. It is seen that the utility of a test for placement depends on the difference in regression slopes—not on the slopes or the correlations directly. Moreover, the utility depends on where within the X distribution the lines cross, as this affects ξ^* and ϕ^*. A "validity coefficient" indicating that test X predicts success within a treatment *tells nothing about its usefulness for placement*. Such has been the overemphasis on validity coefficients, however, that there is no published test, even among those recommended for placement decisions, whose manual reports regression equations for alternative treatments that lead to comparable outcomes.

The relations exhibited in figure 14.4 (ii) and 14.4 (iii) are known as interactions (Lubin, 1961). The word *interaction* is used as in the analysis of variance, implying that the advantage of treatment A over B varies according to the level of the predictor X. Assume that X is

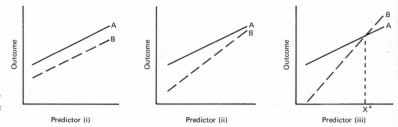

FIG. 14.4. Possible predictor-criterion relations when there are two treatments.

Predictor (i)   Predictor (ii)   Predictor (iii) positively correlated with success under treatment A; then the interaction is very strong if the slope for treatment B is negative or is much steeper in a positive direction than that for A. But if the dependence of outcome on test score is about the same for both treatments, the interaction is slight. This implies that the usual aptitude variables that correlate with success under all sorts of educational treatments have little value for placement decisions. An important line of current research is attempting to identify relatively specific predictors that forecast success in one kind of treatment and not another. (See chap. 19 for examples of this.)

One almost never obtains ideal data for studying the usefulness of tests for career guidance or for placement into curricula, because one can follow only the students who enter each career or program. Even if the tests applied prior to entrance are sealed up so that they cannot influence the decision, the persons entering one treatment differ from those entering another, due to self-selection and counseling based on data other than these tests. While the obtained regression functions are meaningful if similar self-selection and counseling on similar grounds are expected to continue in the future, one should not conclude from such a study that "persons at level 70 on this test do better in A than in B," because the persons with score 70 who entered the A group in the validation study are probably not, on the average, like those with score 70 who entered the B group.

Dunn (1966) reported an ingenious validation of a placement test in college mathematics. Freshmen were assigned to courses at various levels on the basis of the test and later questioned as to their satisfaction with the difficulty level of the course. The study suffers, inevitably, from the fact that students at any score level tended to be assigned to just one course, but nonetheless it is likely to be suggestive to persons validating tests for placement use.

Whereas the usual concept of a formal experiment calls for assigning all cases at random, a much more limited application of randomization will give considerable information and be more acceptable to educational administrators and students. Suppose that the best a priori opinion is that high-scoring students will profit most from treatment A and low-scoring students from B. Then there is an intermediate region, embracing perhaps a quarter of the students, where the treatments are equally suitable so far as one can judge in advance. It should be practicable enough to assign students with scores in this region of indifference on a truly random basis and to focus the statistical analysis on those cases.

In selection studies, attenuation formulas are used to demonstrate the effect on correlations of measuring X or Y more thoroughly. In placement studies, attention centers on regression functions and only these need to be corrected. One may apply equation 11, entering $\beta_B - \beta_A$ in place of β_1 and calculating $(\beta_B - \beta_A)_j$.

The preceding development has shown that regression functions are primary and correlation coefficients secondary in the evaluation of tests for practical purposes. The regression function is expressed in Y units, and if those are no more than arbitrary scoring units devised for a particular study the equation has little value. To make regression functions most useful, outcomes need to be reported in meaningful units. After validating a proposed placement test against the Ayres handwriting scale one could say to a school administrator: "If you do not use a predictor test, you can expect that six months later 10 percent of your pupils will write with this quality (pointing to samples of excellent writing), 40 percent with this quality (good), etc. If you apply test X and assign those who score below level X^* to this experimental teaching method, you can expect that six months later 13 percent of the total group will write with this quality (pointing), 57 percent with this quality, etc." Such a communication—and only such a communication—puts the administrator in a position to decide whether the gains in outcome justify the labor of testing and of introducing a second method of instruction for part of the class.

This discussion of placement and classification is rather different from that in chapter 16, where attention focuses on the discriminant function and the closely related "centour" method. There the model assumes that persons

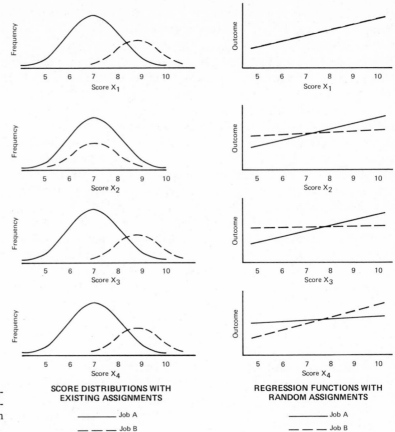

FIG. 14.5. Artificial data contrasting analyses under the discriminant-function and regression models.

SCORE DISTRIBUTIONS WITH
EXISTING ASSIGNMENTS

——————— Job A

— — — — Job B

REGRESSION FUNCTIONS WITH
RANDOM ASSIGNMENTS

——————— Job A

— — — — Job B

fall into types and that the task of the tester is to find out to which type each of the persons now under consideration belongs. Thus one might sort out Navy recruits into those who are most like present rangefinders, those most like present aircraft machinists, and so on. Some writers on high school guidance employ a similar concept. The formulation from a utility standpoint, on the other hand, assumes a continuous criterion and emphasizes regressions.

For the sake of argument, consider a highly artificial case. There are four aptitude dimensions, X_1 to X_4. There are two job classifications, A and B. The outcomes in job A and job B have been reduced to a common scale, labeled Y. Figure 14.5 presents the data that would be of interest. On the left side are the data used for a centour analysis; namely the frequency of each score among men now in job

A or B. (It is assumed that there are twice as many men employed in A as in B.) On the right side are the results from an experimental validation in which some men at each score level are assigned to each job; as in figure 14.4, the average outcome at each score determines the regression line for the treatment.

By the centour system of interpretation, X_1, X_3, and X_4 are relevant to classification. Persons with lower scores on these will tend to be assigned to job A. X_2 is considered irrelevant by this system of interpretation. According to the regression lines, however, X_1 is irrelevant because it does not forecast which tasks the men will perform best. A high score on X_2 and/or X_3 favors assignment of the man to job A. The two systems thus disagree radically in their interpretation of scores X_1, X_2, and X_3. Only with regard to X_4 do the two systems essentially agree. The regression model is pertinent when classification is to obtain the greatest possible outcome (whether in terms of grades, production, or personal satisfaction).

This discussion of the limitations of criteria, of the imperfect experimental designs commonly used to study the validity of tests for decision making, and of the assumptions involved in the customary mathematical analysis should lead the reader to a cautious and critical attitude. It should not, however, so discourage him that he fails to appreciate the past and present contributions of tests to educational decision making, and the greater contribution that can be expected as future research, using better designs and collecting more diversified outcome information, gives a better understanding of the relation between test performances and the requirements of various educational treatments.

Everything said in this chapter has returned to a concern with understanding. The evidence from a single criterion-oriented validation pins down a fact about a particular local situation. That study, like every other study involving the test, helps to amplify the picture of what the test means and how it relates to the demands of nontest situations. The study, properly examined, also helps one to understand the nature of educational treatments and their psychological requirements. As they accumulate, therefore, criterion-oriented studies play the same role as do other studies pertinent to construct validation. They generate a theory of individual differences and a theory of tasks and situations. On the strength of such understanding one can make reasonable judgments about the design of new educational situations and the design of new measuring instruments. Since these judgments in turn need to be validated, the process of investigation, and therefore the growth of knowledge, never ends.

REFERENCES

Adorno, T. W., Frenkel-Brunswik, E., Lenison, D. J., & Sanford, R. N. *The authoritarian personality.* New York: Harper, 1950.

American Educational Research Association. *Technical recommendations for achievement tests.* Washington: AERA, 1955.

American Psychological Association. *Standards for educational and psychological tests and manuals.* Washington: APA, 1966.

American Psychological Association, American Educational Research Association, & National Council on Measurements Used in Education. Technical recommendations for psychological tests and diagnostic techniques. *Psychological Bulletin*, 1954, **51** (Suppl.)

Anastasi, A. Some current developments in the measurement and interpretation of test validity. In A. Anastasi (Ed.), *Testing problems in perspective.* Washington: American Council on Education, 1966. Pp. 307–317.

Astin, A. Criterion-centered research. *Educational and Psychological Measurement*, 1964, **24**, 807–822.

Atkinson, J. W., & Feather, N. T. (Eds.) *A theory of achievement motivation.* New York: Wiley, 1966.

Atkinson, J. W., & Litwin, G. H. Achievement motive and test anxiety conceived as motive to approach success and motive to avoid failure. *Journal of Abnormal and Social Psychology*, 1960, **60**, 52–63.

Ayres, L. P. *A scale for measuring the quality of handwriting of school children.* New York: Russell Sage Foundation, 1912.

Bakan, D. *On method.* San Francisco: Jossey-Bass, 1968.

Bechtoldt, H. P. Selection. In S. S. Stevens (Ed.), *Handbook of experimental psychology.* New York: Wiley, 1951. Pp. 1237–1267.

Bechtoldt, H. P. Construct validity: A critique. *American Psychologist*, 1959, **14**, 619–629.

Bennett, G. K., Seashore, H. G., & Wesman, A. G. *Differential aptitude tests, manual.* (3rd ed.) New York: Psychological Corporation, 1959.

Bennett, G. K., Seashore, H. G., & Wesman, A. G. *Differential aptitude tests, manual.* (4th ed.) New York: Psychological Corporation, 1966.

Block, J. The equivalence of measures and the correction for attenuation. *Psychological Bulletin*, 1963, **60**, 152–156.

Bloom, B. S. (Ed.) *Taxonomy of educational objectives.* Handbook I. *Cognitive domain.* New York: David McKay, 1956.

Bloom, B. S., & Broder, L. J. *Problem-solving processes of college students.* Chicago: University of Chicago Press, 1950.

Bowers, R. Discussion of "A critical study of the criterion of internal consistency in personality scale construction": An analysis of the problem of validity. *American Sociological Review*, 1936, **1**, 69–74.

Bowles, S., & Levin, H. M. The determinants of scholastic achievement: An appraisal of some recent evidence. *Journal of Human Resources*, 1968, **3**, 3–24.

Bridgman, P. W. *The logic of modern physics*. New York: Macmillan, 1927.

Brodbeck, M. The philosophy of science and educational research. *Review of Educational Research*, 1957, **27**, 427–440.

Brodbeck, M. Logic and scientific method in research on teaching. In N. L. Gage (Ed.), *Handbook of research in teaching*. Chicago: Rand McNally, 1963. Pp. 44–93.

Brogden, H. E. A new coefficient: Application to biserial correlation and to estimation of selective efficiency. *Psychometrika*, 1949, **14**, 169–182.

Brogden, H. E., & Taylor, E. K. The theory and classification of criterion bias. *Educational and Psychological Measurement*, 1950, **10**, 159–186.

Campbell, D. T. Recommendations for APA test standards regarding construct, trait, or discriminant validity. *American Psychologist*, 1960, **15**, 546–553.

Campbell, D. T., & Fiske, D. W. Convergent and discriminant validation by the multitrait-multimethod matrix. *Psychological Bulletin*, 1959, **56**, 81–105.

Carney, R. E. The effect of situational variables on the measurement of achievement motivation. *Educational and Psychological Measurement*, 1966, **26**, 675–690.

Carter, R. S. How invalid are marks assigned by teachers? *Journal of Educational Psychology*, 1952, **43**, 218–228.

Cattell, R. B. *Personality and motivation structure and measurement*. Yonkers, N. Y.: World Book, 1957.

Cattell, R. B. Theory of fluid and crystallized intelligence: A critical experiment. *Journal of Educational Psychology*, 1963, **54**, 1–22.

Cattell, R. B. Validity and reliability: A proposed more basic set of concepts. *Journal of Educational Psychology*, 1964, **55**, 1–22.

Chamberlain, T. C. The method of multiple working hypotheses. *Science*, 1965, **148**, 754–759.

Coffman, W. E., & Kurfman, D. A comparison of two methods of reading essay examinations. *American Educational Research Journal*, 1968, **5**(1), 99–107.

Connolly, J. A., & Wantman, M. J. An exploration of oral reasoning processes in responding to objective test items. *Journal of Educational Measurement*, 1964, **1**, 59–64.

Cook, S. W., & Selltiz, C. A multiple-indicator approach to attitude measurements. *Psychological Bulletin*, 1964, **62**, 36–55.

Cornfield, J., & Tukey, J. W. Average values of mean squares in factorials. *Annals of Mathematical Statistics*, 1956, **27**, 907–949.

Cox, R. C. Item selection techniques and evaluation of instructional objectives. *Journal of Educational Measurement*, 1965, **2**, 181–186.

Cronbach, L. J. Report on a psychometric mission to Clinicia. *Psychometrika*, 1954, **19**, 263–270.

Cronbach, L. J. Proposals leading to analytic treatment of social perception scores. In R. Tagiuri & L. Petrullo (Eds.), *Person perception and interpersonal behavior*. Stanford, Calif.: Stanford University Press, 1958. Pp. 353–379.

Cronbach, L. J. Year-to-year correlations of mental tests: A review of the Hofstaetter analysis. *Child Development*, 1967, **38**, 284–289.

Cronbach, L. J. *Essentials of psychological testing*. (3rd ed.) New York: Harper & Row, 1970.

Cronbach, L. J., & Furby, L. How we should measure change—or should we? *Psychological Bulletin*, 1970, **74**, 68–80.

Cronbach, L. J., & Gleser, G. C. *Psychological tests and personnel decisions*. (2nd ed.) Urbana: University of Illinois Press, 1965.

Cronbach, L. J., & Meehl, P. E. Construct validity in psychological tests. *Psychological Bulletin*, 1955, **52**, 281–302.

Cronbach, L. J., Rajaratnam, N., & Gleser, G. C. Theory of generalizability: A liberalization of reliability theory. *British Journal of Statistical Psychology*, 1963, **16**, 137–163.

Cronbach, L. J., Gleser, G. C., Nanda, H., & Rajaratnam, N. *The dependability of behavioral measurements: Multifacet studies of generalizability*. New York: Wiley, 1971, in press.

Cureton, E. E. Validity. In E. F. Lindquist (Ed.), *Educational measurement*. Washington: American Council on Education, 1951. Pp. 621–694.

Cureton, E. E. Reliability and validity: Basic assumptions and experimental designs. *Educational and Psychological Measurement*, 1965, **25**, 327–346.

deGroot, A. D. *Methodologie*. den Haag: Mouton, 1961. (English language version, 1969.)

Dunn, J. E. A study of the University of Arkansas mathematics entrance exam as a placement device. *Journal of Experimental Education*, 1966, **34**, 62–66.

Dunnette, M. D. *Personnel selection and placement*. Belmont, Calif.: Wadsworth, 1967.

Ebel, R. L. Must all tests be valid? *American Psychologist*, 1961, **16**, 640–647.

Ebel, R. L. Content standard test scores. *Educational and Psychological Measurement*, 1962, **22**, 15–25.

Endler, N. S., & Hunt, J. McV. Sources of behavioral variance as measured by the S-R Inventory of Anxiousness. *Psychological Bulletin*, 1966, **65**, 336–346.

Feather, N. T. Valence of success and failure in relation to task difficulty: Task research and recent progress. *Australian Journal of Psychology*, 1968, **20**, 111–122.

Flavell, J. H. *The developmental psychology of Jean Piaget.* Princeton, N. J.: Van Nostrand, 1963.

Forsyth, R. A., & Feldt, L. S. An investigation of empirical sampling distributions of correlation coefficients corrected for attenuation. *Educational and Psychological Measurement*, 1969, **29**, 61–71.

Frank, P. (Ed.) *The validation of scientific theories.* Boston: Beacon, 1956.

French, J. W. The relationship of problem-solving styles to the factor composition of tests. *Educational and Psychological Measurement*, 1965, **25**, 9–28.

Fritts, H. C. Growth-rings of trees: Their correlation with climate. *Science*, 1966, **154**, 973–979.

Gage, N. L., & Cronbach, L. J. Conceptual and methodological problems in interpersonal perception. *Psychological Review*, 1955, **62**, 411–423.

Gagné, R. M. Instructional variables and learning outcomes. In M. C. Wittrock & D. Wiley (Eds.), *Evaluation of instruction.* New York: Holt, Rinehart & Winston, 1970, in press.

Gagné, R. M., & Paradise, N. E. Abilities and learning sets in knowledge acquisition. *Psychological Monographs*, 1961, **75**(14, Whole No. 518).

Ghiselli, E. E. The validation of selection tests in the light of the dynamic character of criteria. *Personnel Psychology*, 1960, **13**, 225–231.

Ghiselli, E. E. *The validity of occupational aptitude tests.* New York: Wiley, 1966.

Glaser, R. Instructional technology and the measurement of learning outcomes. *American Psychologist*, 1963, **18**, 519–521.

Glaser, R., & Klaus, D. J. Proficiency measurement: Assessing human performance. In R. M. Gagné (Ed.), *Psychological principles in system development.* New York: Holt, Rinehart & Winston, 1962. Pp. 419–476.

Grice, G. R. Dependence of empirical laws on the source of experimental variation. *Psychological Bulletin*, 1966, **66**, 488–498.

Grimes, J. W., & Allinsmith, W. Compulsivity, anxiety, and school achievement. *Merrill-Palmer Quarterly*, 1961, **7**, 247–271.

Guilford, J. P. Zero correlations among tests of intellectual abilities. *Psychological Bulletin*, 1964, **61**, 401–404.

Guilford, J. P. *The nature of human intelligence.* New York: McGraw-Hill, 1967.

Guilford, J. P., Christensen, P. R., Taaffe, G., &

Wilson, R. C. Ratings should be scrutinized. *Educational and Psychological Measurement*, 1962, **22**, 439–447.

Guion, R. M. Synthetic validity in a small company: A demonstration. *Personnel Psychology*, 1965, **18**, 49–65.

Gulliksen, H. *Theory of mental tests.* New York: Wiley, 1950.

Heckhausen, H. *The anatomy of achievement motivation.* New York: Academic Press, 1967.

Hempel, C. G. *Aspects of scientific explanation and other essays.* New York: Free Press, 1965.

Hempel, C. G. *Philosophy of the natural sciences.* Englewood Cliffs, N. J.: Prentice-Hall, 1966.

Hemphill, J. K. *The engineering study.* Princeton, N. J.: Educational Testing Service, 1963.

Hively, W., II, Patterson, H. L., & Page, S. H. A "universe-defined" system of arithmetic achievement tests. *Journal of Educational Measurement*, 1968, **5**, 275–290.

Hochberg, H. Intervening variables, hypothetical constructs, and metaphysics. In H. Feigl & G. Maxwell (Eds.), *Current issues in philosophy of science.* New York: Holt, Rinehart & Winston, 1961. Pp. 448–456.

Hoepfner, R., & Guilford, J. P. Figural, symbolic, and semantic factors of creative potential in ninth-grade students. Reports from the Psychological Laboratory of the University of Southern California, 1965, No. 35.

Hoffman, B. *The tyranny of testing.* New York: Crowell-Collier, 1962.

Hofstaetter, P. R. The changing composition of "intelligence": A study in *T*-technique. *Journal of Genetic Psychology*, 1954, **85**, 159–164.

Holland, J. L., & Nichols, R. Prediction of academic and extracurricular achievement in college. *Journal of Educational Psychology*, 1964, **55**, 55–65.

Horst, P. *Psychological measurement and prediction.* Belmont, Calif.: Wadsworth, 1966.

Horst, P., Wallin, P., & Guttman, L. *The prediction of personal adjustment.* (SSRC Bulletin No. 48) New York: SSRC, 1941.

Humphreys, L. G. Critique of Cattell's "Theory of fluid and crystallized intelligence." *Journal of Educational Psychology*, 1967, **58**, 129–136.

Hundleby, J. D. The construct validity of a scale of acquiescence. *British Journal of Social and Clinical Psychology*, 1966, **5**, 290–298.

Hunt, E. B. Computer simulation: Artificial intelligence studies and their relevance to psychology. *Annual Review of Psychology*, 1968, **19**, 273–350.

Huntoon, R. D. Status of the national standards for physical measurement. *Science*, 1965, **150**, 169–178.

Husén, T. (Ed.) *International study of achievement*

in mathematics: A comparison of twelve countries. New York: Wiley, 1967.

Indiana Prediction Study. Manual of freshman class profiles in Indiana colleges. New York: College Entrance Examination Board, 1965.

Jacobs, P. I. Effects of coaching on College Board achievement test scores. Educational Testing Service Research Bulletin, 1964, No. 24.

Jacobs, P. I. Effects of coaching on the college-board English-composition test. Educational and Psychological Measurement, 1966, 26, 55–67.

Kahneman, D., & Ghiselli, E. E. Validity and non-linear heteroscedastic models. Personnel Psychology, 1962, 15, 1–11.

Kaiser, H. F., & Caffrey, J. Alpha factor analysis. Psychometrika, 1965, 30, 1–14.

Kaplan, A. The conduct of inquiry. San Francisco: Chandler, 1964.

Katz, I. Review of evidence relating to effects of desegregation on the intellectual performance of Negroes. American Psychologist, 1964, 19, 381–399.

Katz, M. Decisions and values: A rationale for secondary school guidance. New York: College Entrance Examination Board, 1963.

Kelly, E. L. Alternate criteria in medical education and their correlates. In A. Anastasi (Ed.), Testing problems in perspective. Washington: American Council on Education, 1966. Pp. 176–194.

Kendler, H. H. Motivation and behavior. In D. Levine (Ed.), Nebraska symposium on motivation. Lincoln: University of Nebraska Press, 1965. Pp. 1–23.

Kropp, R. P. The relationship between process and correct item-response. Journal of Educational Research, 1956, 49, 385–388.

Kropp, R. P., Stoker, H. W., & Bashaw, W. L. Validation of the Taxonomy of educational objectives. Journal of Experimental Education, 1966, 34, 69–76.

Krug, R. E. Some suggested approaches for test development and measurement. Personnel Psychology, 1966, 19, 24–35.

Lennon, R. T. Assumptions underlying the use of content validity. Educational and Psychological Measurement, 1956, 16, 294–304.

Lindquist, E. F., & Hieronymus, A. (Eds.) Manual, Iowa Test of Basic Skills. Boston: Houghton Mifflin, 1964.

Loevinger, J. Objective tests as instruments of psychological theory. Psychological Reports, 1957, 3, 635–694.

Loevinger, J. Person and population as psychometric concepts. Psychological Review, 1965, 72, 143–155.

Lord, F. M. Elementary models for measuring change. In C. W. Harris (Ed.), Problems in measuring change. Madison: University of Wisconsin Press, 1963. Pp. 21–38.

Lord, F. M., & Novick, M. R. Statistical theories of mental test scores. Reading, Mass: Addison Wesley, 1968.

Lubin, A. The interpretation of significant interaction. Educational and Psychological Measurement, 1961, 21, 807–819.

McClelland, D. C. Personality. New York: William Sloane Associates (Dryden Press), 1951.

McClelland, D. C. Methods of measuring human motivation. In J. W. Atkinson (Ed.), Motives in fantasy, action and society. Princeton, N. J.: Van Nostrand, 1958. Pp. 7–42.

McClelland, D. C., Atkinson, J. W., Clark, R. A., & Lowell, E. L. The achievement motive. New York: Appleton-Century-Crofts, 1953.

McCoy, N. Effect of test anxiety on children's performance as a function of type of instructions and type of test. Journal of Personality and Social Psychology, 1965, 2, 634–641.

McGuire, C. Research in the process approach to the construction and analysis of medical exams. In National Council on Measurements in Education, 20th yearbook, 1963. Pp. 7–16.

McNemar, Q. Psychological statistics. (4th ed.) New York: Wiley, 1969.

Masling, J. M. The influence of situational and interpersonal variables in projective testing. Psychological Bulletin, 1960, 57, 65–85.

Mednick, S. A., & Mednick, M. Remote Associates Test. Boston: Houghton Mifflin, 1967.

Melton, A. W. Individual differences and theoretical process variables. In R. M. Gagné (Ed.), Learning and individual differences. Cleveland: Charles E. Merrill, 1966. Pp. 238–252.

Messick, S., & Kogan, N. Category width and quantitative aptitude. Perceptual and Motor Skills, 1965, 20, 493–497.

Miller, N. E. Liberalization of basic S-R concepts: Extensions to conflict behavior, motivation, and social learning. In S. Koch (Ed.), Psychology as a science. Vol. 2. New York: McGraw-Hill, 1959. Pp. 196–292.

Miller, R. B. Task description and analysis. In R. M. Gagné, Psychological principles in system development. New York: Holt, Rinehart & Winston, 1962. Pp. 187–230.

Mosier, C. I. A critical examination of the concepts of face validity. Educational and Psychological Measurement, 1947, 7, 191–206.

Mosier, C. I. Problems and designs of cross-validation. Educational and Psychological Measurement, 1951, 11, 5–11.

Murray, H. A. Explorations in personality. New York: Oxford University Press, 1938.

Nagel, E. *The structure of science.* New York: Harcourt, Brace & World, 1961.

Ninth Naval District Headquarters (Great Lakes, Ill.), Training Aids Section. A comparative study of verbalized and projected pictorial tests in gunnery. Unpublished manuscript, 1945.

Oden, M. The fulfillment of promise: Forty-year follow-up of the Terman gifted group. *Genetic Psychology Monographs,* 1968, **77**(1), 3–93.

Pace, C. R., & Stern, G. G. An approach to the measurement of psychological characteristics of college environments. *Journal of Educational Psychology,* 1958, **49**, 269–277.

Parker, J. The relationship of self-report to inferred self-concept. *Educational and Psychological Measurement,* 1966, **26**, 691–700.

Peak, H. Problems of objective observation. In L. Festinger & D. Katz (Eds.), *Research methods in the behavioral sciences.* New York: Dryden Press, 1953. Pp. 243–300.

Primoff, E. J. Empirical validation of the J coefficient. *Personnel Psychology,* 1959, **12**, 413–418.

Reitman, W. R. *Cognition and thought.* New York: Wiley, 1965.

Robinson, W. S. Ecological correlations and the behavior of individuals. *American Sociological Review,* 1950, **15**, 351–357.

Ryans, D. G. Notes on the criterion problem in research, with special reference to the study of teacher characteristics. *Journal of Genetic Psychology,* 1957, **91**, 33–61.

Schuman, H. The random probe: A technique for evaluation of the validity of closed questions. *American Sociological Review,* 1966, **31**, 218–222.

Schwarz, P. A. Adapting tests to the cultural setting. *Educational and Psychological Measurement,* 1963, **23**, 672–686.

Seashore, H. G. Women are more predictable than men. Presidential address, Division 17, American Psychological Association, New York, 1961.

Sells, S. B. (Ed.) *Stimulus determinants of behavior.* New York: Ronald Press, 1963.

Sherwood, J. J. Self-report and projective measures of achievement and affiliation. *Journal of Consulting Psychology,* 1966, **30**, 329–337.

Simon, H. A., & Kotovsky, K. Human acquisition of concepts for sequential patterns. *Psychological Review,* 1963, **70**, 534–546.

Strong, E. K., Jr. *Vocational interests 18 years after college.* Minneapolis: University of Minnesota Press, 1955.

Terwilliger, J. S. Self-reported marking practices and policies in public secondary schools. *Bulletin of the National Association of Secondary School Principals,* 1966, **50**, 5–37.

Thorndike, R. L. *Personnel selection.* New York: Wiley, 1949.

Thorndike, R. L. *The concepts of over- and underachievement.* New York: Columbia University, Teachers College, Bureau of Publications, 1963.

Thorndike, R. L. Reliability. In A. Anastasi (ed.), *Testing problems in perspective.* Washington: American Council on Education, 1966. Pp. 284–291.

Thorndike, R. L., & Hagen, E. *Measurement and evaluation in psychology and education.* (3rd. ed.) New York: Wiley, 1969.

Thurstone, L. L., & Chave, E. J. *The measurement of attitudes.* Chicago: University of Chicago Press, 1929.

Tucker, L. R. Experiments in multimode factor analysis. In A. Anastasi (Ed.), *Testing problems in perspective.* Washington: American Council on Education, 1966. Pp. 369–379.

Tukey, J. W. Conclusions vs. decisions. *Technometrics,* 1960, **2**, 423–433.

Tyler, R. W. The objectives and plans for a national assessment of educational progress. *Journal of Educational Measurement,* 1966, **3**, 1–4.

Vernon, P. E. The determinants of reading comprehension. *Educational and Psychological Measurement,* 1962, **22**, 269–286.

Vukovich, A., Heckhausen, H., von Hatzfeld, H. F. *Konstruktion eines Fragebogens zur Leistungmotivation.* Unpublished manuscript, University of Münster, 1964.

Wallace, S. R. Criteria for what? *American Psychologist,* 1965, **20**, 411–417.

Webb, E. J., Campbell, D. T., Schwartz, R. D., & Sechrest, L. *Unobtrusive measures: Nonreactive research in the social sciences.* Chicago: Rand McNally, 1966.

Wiggins, J. S. Personality structure. *Annual Review of Psychology,* 1968, **19**, 293–350.

Wiseman, S. The effect of restriction of range upon correlation coefficients. *British Journal of Educational Psychology,* 1967, **37**, 248–252.

Yamamoto, K., & Dizney, H. F. Effects of three sets of test instructions on scores on an intelligence scale. *Educational and Psychological Measurement,* 1965, **25**, 87–110.

15. Scales, Norms, and Equivalent Scores

William H. Angoff
Educational Testing Service

One of the principal difficulties encountered in the interpretation of test scores is that the varieties of scales on which they are expressed and the varieties of groups on which the scales are defined are almost as numerous as the tests themselves. The result is that it is virtually impossible for the test user to develop a practical familiarity with all the scales that he would have occasion to use. By way of contrast, the problems of interpretation of physical measurement that the typical man in the street uses every day—height, weight, temperature, and time, for example—are quite different and considerably simpler. For him, the number of types of scales that he encounters and uses frequently is much more limited. He therefore has the opportunity to develop a skill and ease with the units of his scales and does not need to make frequent reference to manuals that describe their characteristics. He has no need to familiarize himself with the definitions and descriptions of the scales, nor does he need to familiarize himself with details about the precision of the scales. A glance at the measuring instrument itself or, at most, a trial application of the measuring instrument is sufficient to give him the information he needs. Similarly, he has little need for "tables of norms" or for detailed descriptions of the appropriate uses of his "tests." His direct and frequent experience with them provides sufficient guidance for him in the large majority of instances.

The problems of measurement in psychology and education, however, are quite different. Unlike the user of the common physical measurements, the test user does require detailed information and guidance if he is to avoid the kinds of errors that are typically made in using test scores. In part, the need for detailed information is attributable to the very nature of educational and psychological measurement. In part, also, it arises from the multiplicity of characteristics for which measurement is sought and from the multiplicity of tests that are designed and available to measure these characteristics. The test user must recognize that measurement in education is extremely imprecise in comparison with the more common types of physical measurement and that the various kinds of instruments used in education differ markedly in precision; he also must know how to evaluate this precision. He needs to know what kinds of uses of tests are appropriate for his purpose, what kinds are inappropriate, and how to get maximum information from his measurements. To do this he needs to understand the meaning of the score itself and what it represents, how it relates to other measurements of the same dimension made for the same individual at other points in time, how it relates to the measurement of the same dimension for other individuals, how it relates to and how it can be used with measurements of different dimensions, and what the nature of the evaluative information is that he himself needs to guide his decisions. All of this, and more, is needed to give the score the meaning it must have in order to be useful. And, clearly, meaning is essential, for without meaning the score itself is useless; and, without a meaningful score to transmit the value of the test performance, the test ceases to be a measuring instrument and becomes merely a practice exercise for the student on a collection of items.

The present chapter is devoted to a discussion of some of the devices that aid in giving test scores the kind of meaning they need in order to be useful as instruments of measurement. For the purpose of this discussion it may be helpful to consider a complex testing program or a system of test offerings, part or all of which are administered at various times to heterogeneous groups of examinees. A first requirement for the transmission of the scores is that an appropriate scale structure be defined. This process of definition will be denoted by the term *scaling*. Also, since test scores, even when appropriately scaled, have limited meaning and since it will be necessary for the test users to interpret these scores in order to use them for assessment and possible later action, a second requirement is that special *norms* or other interpretive guides be prepared that will give meaning to the scores, sometimes as an inherent characteristic of the scale. Finally, since it may be necessary to have available several forms of each of the tests, a third requirement is that provision be made for the maintenance and perpetuation of the scale on which scores on the first form are reported, even as new forms are introduced and old ones withdrawn from active use. The operation involved in maintaining the scale is carried out by *equating* or *calibrating* each new form to one or more of the existing forms for which conversions to the reference scale (i.e. the reporting scale) are already available. Since all three concepts— scaling, norming, and equating—are separable, in this discussion the matter of *norms* is treated separately from that of *scales*, and the latter in turn is treated separately from the matter of *equating* and *calibration*. The problems of *comparable scores* are given separate treatment but within the context of the equating of nonparallel tests.

SCALING

Unlike the more common physical dimensions, for which well-established and generally satisfactory scales exist, the educational and psychological attributes for which it is wished to produce scales bring with them special problems that are not only complex but apparently unyielding as well. The concepts underlying some of the physical scales—those, for example, that are used to measure length and weight—have a direct counterpart in one's daily experience and seem to offer relatively obvious definition. The notion that one bar of steel is twice as long as a second bar is a meaningful one, easy to transmit

and understand, even without the definition or the original derivation of the system of units for measuring them. The fact that this notion is implied when one says that the first bar measures six feet and the second only three derives from a willingness to accept the concept of zero length and a willingness to agree on an operation that defines the distance denoted as one inch, for example, at one part of the yardstick as equal to the distance denoted as one inch at any other part of the yardstick.

Mental measurement enjoys no such advantages. The zero point is by no means as obvious here as it is in physical measurement. Indeed it is difficult to imagine what might be meant by the absence of a mental ability, and one may even question whether the very concept of "amount" of mental ability has any meaning. In any case, a zero raw score on a mental test would certainly not signify "zero ability," since the raw score is necessarily a function of those items that appear in the test. Similarly, there is no assurance that equal differences between scores in different regions on the scale of a psychological test represent equal differences in units of ability. Suppose, for example (to adapt from an illustration suggested informally by F. M. Lord), Mary can type 20 words a minute; Margaret can type 30 words a minute; Jean, 50; and Julia, 60. Margaret's score exceeds Mary's by 10 units and Julia's score exceeds Jean's by 10 units. In the obvious sense, perhaps, the units are equal, and, therefore, it can be concluded that Julia's typing ability exceeds Jean's by the same amount that Margaret's typing ability exceeds Mary's. However, there may be other ways to define the units of typing ability besides the direct count of the number of words typed per unit of time. Suppose Mary can increase her typing speed from 20 to 30 words a minute after a week's practice while it takes Jean four weeks of practice to increase her speed from 50 to 60. In this sense, the difference between Mary's and Margaret's abilities is only one-fourth the size of the difference between Jean's and Julia's abilities. Then again suppose 99 percent of the girls who have completed a semester's course in typing can do 20 words a minute or better and

97 percent can do 30 words or better; while only 40 percent can do 50 words and only 20 percent, 60. Perhaps, then, the difference (40 minus 20) between Jean and Julia should be taken to be 10 times greater than the difference (99 minus 97) between Mary and Margaret or, perhaps, taken to be some indirect function of the differences in percentages that have just been observed.

The fact that the scales used in psychological measurement are not known to be characterized by equal units and a real zero point (i.e. that they are not ratio scales), or by equal units alone (i.e. that they are not interval scales), has led some writers (e.g. Stevens, 1951) to maintain that the usual kinds of statistical treatments that are meaningful with ratio and interval scales are not meaningful in the case of psychological measurement. Lord (1953), on the other hand, has argued that statistical operations and the conduct of significance tests could be carried out appropriately and meaningfully even if the system of numbers were only nominal in character; that is even if they represented identification numbers like those on the backs of football players—numbers that could not, by any stretch of the imagination, be considered to represent a scale.

Some consideration also should be given to the contention that the problem of inequality of units is not as unique to psychological measurement as it may appear. The same problem may be found in physical measurement. For example, it was just pointed out that the difference in typing speeds of 40 and 50 words a minute could be taken to be 4 times as great as the difference between 20 and 30 words a minute, if it were found that an improvement in speed from 40 to 50 takes 4 times as long as an improvement from 20 to 30. In the same sense it could be argued that in a certain context the distance from 30 to 68 inches should be taken as 15 times the distance from 18 to 30 inches, instead of about 3 times the distance, because people take about 15 times as long to achieve the former growth as the latter. The significant point here is that there is nothing "natural" in the equality of physical units; "equal" units are equal in psychological *or* in

physical measurement only because there is an arbitrarily agreed on definition and convention that is both convenient and useful to us and also one that satisfies certain empirical tests that are implied by the model.

Accordingly, score scales for various psychological tests have been defined to have approximately equal units in some special sense. For example, they have been defined in terms of the performance of a particular group of individuals, either with or without a transformation of the distribution shape. However, in such instances, as Lord[1] pointed out:

> ... the claim for equality of score units can no longer be justified on an external operational basis. Such score scales can be said to have equal units of ability only if we are willing arbitrarily to define the ability in terms of the scale itself. However, such a definition of ability, while not indefensible, cannot hope to be generally accepted since the units of ability would vary with the group tested as well as with the choice of the measuring instrument.

The group for which the test is intended may easily change in the course of time and will not necessarily—indeed, it is not likely to—continue to be as appropriate a fundamental reference point as it may have appeared to be initially. If the transformation of raw to scaled scores is not linear—that is to say, if the intent is not to retain the original distribution shape—but is so designed as to yield, for example, a normal distribution for the reference group, there are additional considerations. There is some question that the assumption of a normal distribution in particular is appropriate, especially when selective processes have been active on the population, as they so often are. Also, the transformation to a normal shape, or to any other shape, can mask many of the indications of poor (or good) test construction. It is an elementary fact that no amount of stretching and compressing the score scale will improve the differentiating power of the test in a range of the scale where the test itself fails to differentiate adequately. On the other hand, this consideration, arguing as it appears to do for the retention of the raw score scale, or some linear

---

[1] Informal communication, October 1950.

transformation of it, also argues that the scale separations between successive raw scores are all equal. This is, of course, true, but only in the most literal and specific sense. In the more general sense, the notion of the equality of raw score units clearly violates one's sense of an underlying scale since the raw score scale separations are only the result of the interaction of the particular items that happen to have been put in the test and therefore have no generality.

The arbitrary nature of psychological scales becomes clearer when one considers the nature of the scales of measurement of physical objects:

Physical measurement scales, such as that for weight, possess unambiguous equality of units because such equality has been operationally clearly defined for them: two weights are said to be equal if they balance when placed on a suitable weighing device; one weight is said to be twice another if one of the former will balance two of the latter. [Typing ability] can be measured on a scale that has the same properties as the scale of weights, if we are willing to accept the requisite operational definition of this ability [for example, the number of words correctly typed per minute]. Problems arise in mental measurements either because (a) experts cannot agree on a clear operational definition of the ability to be measured or (b) the ability is defined in terms of operations for which the symbolic processes of addition or multiplication can be given no useful operational meaning. Any set of measurements can be expressed in terms of a scale with equal units, in some sense, if only we can agree on a definition in operational terms of what is meant by equality.[2]

Much of the work of the experimentalists in psychology during the latter nineteenth and early twentieth centuries was directed at the problem of defining equal psychological units and studying the relationship between those units and the corresponding units of physical measurement. Much of Thurstone's work in the scaling of judgments and attitudes also was concerned with testing out the notion that psychological scales, if properly derived, might achieve some of the characteristics of the more advanced physical scales. His work on the law of comparative judgment (Thurstone, 1927) and his work on the method of equal-appearing

intervals (Thurstone, 1928b; Thurstone & Chave, 1929) are attempts to develop such scales. The applications of his method of absolute scaling (Thurstone, 1925) led him to estimate the zero point of intelligence (Thurstone, 1928a) in the hope that the essential characteristic of the ratio scale could be found to apply to psychological measurement. Later developments in the concepts of scaling include the work of Guttman (1950) whose work with attitude statements led him to define a scale as a system of units in which knowledge of the score would reproduce, within a limited margin of error, the actual responses to the attitude statements. As has been pointed out above, a variety of score scales have been proposed for use with psychological tests. Some of these are defined to have approximately equal units in some particular sense. Others lay claim to value because they possess special qualities— meaning in terms of the performance of defined and well-known groups of people or meaning in terms of the judged quality of the performance tested. Still others have been proposed which lay claim to value because they are "unencumbered" by meaning. The most commonly known scales of these various types are described below.

Raw Score Scale

In the operational sense the number of items answered correctly, with or without a correction for guessing, may be considered a scale in its own right; that is, it may be asserted that one point of score will be considered to represent the same amount of ability wherever it occurs on the score scale. Therefore, a score difference of a given number of points is by definition the same at whatever score level it occurs. This is clearly an arbitrary definition, but then all other definitions are similarly arbitrary. Nevertheless, it is important to recognize that raw scores as such have little if any generality, since they are a product of the items contained in the test. On the one hand, this characteristic of the raw score scale is considered by some to be useful, because the flaws in the test—e.g. its inappropriate difficulty for the groups for which

[2] *Ibid.*

it is intended—will be immediately apparent and will serve to motivate the press for a more appropriate test. On the other hand, it is considered by others to be a disadvantage for the very reason that it has no generality. Moreover, unless there is and will continue to be only one form of the test, the use of raw score scales can prove to be a source of confusion to the test user. Because of the natural and expected variation in difficulty from form to form, a raw score of given value will not always have the same meaning or represent the same level of ability. The form of the test would have to be specified and its characteristics known and kept in mind by the test user. The need to keep track of this additional information can prove to be cumbersome. The solution here is to adopt a reliable system of equating test forms that will make it possible to translate all forms into a common score scale. But since, in this case, all but one of the forms would require some adjustment of the raw scores, it would seem less confusing to convert raw scores on *all* forms to an arbitrary scale that is different from any of the raw score scales.

The raw score scale is perhaps the most obvious example of a scale that has no inherent meaning and cannot be interpreted without some kind of supporting data. Such data may be normative in the sense that they describe the performance of groups of individuals whose characteristics are known to the test user, or they may be functional in the sense that they indicate minimum score levels that are considered acceptable for entering or completing some activity or for receiving special recognition. Ideally, of course, both kinds of data should be made available whenever applicable.

Percentage-Mastery Scale

The scores reported on this scale are taken to represent an absolute kind of judgment that the student has mastered some percentage of the subject matter under consideration. Thus, if for example the student earned a percentage grade of 85, it is said that his examination paper gives evidence that he has mastered 85 percent of the material covered by the examination. If he earns a grade of 63, then this is taken to mean that he has mastered 63 percent of the material. And so on. In addition, it is sometimes the custom to specify some percentage as one that would represent a minimum degree of mastery to be called "passing" and perhaps another one to be called "honors." Although this type of percentage scale is still widely used in schools and colleges, there is general agreement among test specialists that it is one of the poorest ways in which to express test performance. One of the principal objections to it is that the "absolute" character of the scale is illusory. Since it is impossible to set finite limits on knowledge, it is logically false to think that a student has mastered some percentage of that knowledge. On the other hand, if, for the purpose of the test, certain defined limits of knowledge are agreed upon, then it is possible that the percentage-mastery scale may be useful. However, careful thought would have to be given to the appropriateness of the scale of numbers to the particular universe of knowledge sampled by the test, and the percentage-mastery figures for different levels of acceptability would have to be worked out, keeping in mind the particular purpose of the test and the nature and quality of the group. Certainly what is known about the variety of the types of uses and the variety of standards for a test that is widely used would argue that one set of standards of acceptability for all purposes may not be realistic. Therefore, either the percentage-mastery scale would have to be considered appropriate only for tests with highly specific purposes, or there would have to be a different specific scale (derived from a different definition of "pass") for each purpose for which the test is to be used— a solution which is almost certain to invite confusion.

There are additional hazards in the use of a general percentage-mastery scale that could lead to misinterpretation and misuse if they are not anticipated. For example, the use of a common set of percentages for more than one test fails to take into consideration the relative difficulty of the group of items comprised by the test. There will naturally be variation in difficulty from test to test, and what appears to be 85 percent competence in one test may, for example, actually represent only 69 percent competence on another more difficult test. Finally, the use of an "absolute standard" implies a unanimity among standard setters that most certainly does not exist. Again depending on the use to which the test and the mastery scale is put, it may be advisable to set the percentage values based on the results of a controlled poll of experts. In general, however, because of its extremely unrealistic and misleading character, the percentage-mastery scale would best be avoided entirely in choosing a system for transmitting and reporting scores.

It is interesting to note that the percentage-mastery scale is one of the few scales used in educational measurement that makes reference to a norm in the sense of a standard or goal of achievement. Most of the educational test scales are defined in terms of a statistical norm, that is to say, in terms of the performance of a defined "norms group." Some scales, like the percentile-derived linear scale described below, are dependent *both* on goals and standards of performance as well as on statistical data. This simultaneous use of two apparently unrelated types of reference points for defining scales of measurement is not unique. The conventional mode of expressing visual acuity, for example, makes use of letters of such size and shape that they can be read without error by the average person with clinically normal eyesight (after correction to his optimum level of acuity). In this example, the "average person" represents the statistical norm, a referent in terms of *performance as it exists;* the notion, "clinically normal eyesight," represents the desired standard of performance, a referent in terms of *performance as it should be.*

Linear Transformation (Standard Scores)

The unadjusted linear transformation, apparently first used by Hull (1922), is one of the simplest of all the formal scaling methods. The test is administered to a group of individuals who are considered in some sense to be a standard reference group. Sometimes they are drawn at random from a defined population with certain specified characteristics; sometimes they represent a readily and conveniently available group of individuals who are considered to be similar in most important respects to the population for which the test is intended.

Once the scale-defining, or standardization, group has been agreed on and the choice of the system of units has been made, the method of scaling is a simple one involving only a relocation of the raw score mean at the desired scaled score value and a uniform change in the size of the units to yield the desired scaled score standard deviation. Since the transformation to scaled scores represents a change only in the first two moments of the distribution, it exerts no effect on the shape of the raw score distribution. If the raw score distribution is normal, then it remains so after conversion. Similarly, if it is skewed either positively or negatively, or if it is platykurtic, leptokurtic, multimodal, etc., it remains so even after conversion. The method does not seek to transform the units of the raw score scale to some other system in which the units are taken in some sense to be equal. In the linear transformation the separation between successive raw score units, or between scaled score units corresponding to successive raw scores, is considered equal only in the operational sense that each score represents one more item answered correctly than the preceding score.

Once the scale-defining group has been tested, its raw score mean and standard deviation are entered into the fundamental linear scaling equation which states that the standard-score deviate for any given scaled score equals the standard-score deviate for its corresponding raw score for the group (ω) chosen as the standardization group. Thus, $z_{c_\omega} = z_{x_\omega}$, or

$$\frac{C - M_{c_\omega}}{s_{c_\omega}} = \frac{X - M_{x_\omega}}{s_{x_\omega}}.$$

Then $C = AX + B$, converting raw scores on Form X to the scale (C), in which $A = s_{c_\omega}/s_{x_\omega}$ and $B = M_{c_\omega} - AM_{x_\omega}$. The values of M_{c_ω} and s_{c_ω} are arbitrarily chosen and assigned. The conversion equation is the equation of a straight line in which A represents its slope and B its intercept— i.e. the point on the ordinate at $X = 0$ where it is intersected by the line.

A few of the tests for which scores are reported on a linear derived scale with mean and standard deviation preassigned and defined in terms of a basic standardization group are: the Scholastic Aptitude Test and the Achievement Tests of the College Board ($M_{c_\omega} = 500$, $s_{c_\omega} = 100$), the Army General Classification Test ($M_{c_\omega} = 100$, $s_{c_\omega} = 20$), and the Cooperative Achievement Tests that were developed in the 1960s ($M_{c_\omega} = 150$, $s_{c_\omega} = 10$).

Percentile-Derived Linear Scale

Occasionally it is desired to report scores on a scale in which specified scores have preassigned normative meaning—normative in the sense of performance as it exists *as well as* normative in the sense of what is set as a standard. For example, it may be decided that the minimum passing score on a qualifying test be fixed at 70—a number that is often taken by the public to represent minimum acceptable performance—*and* that some percentage, say 65 percent, will pass. It also may be decided that the scaled score 95 will represent honors performance and that only 10 percent will receive honors grades. In order to produce a scale that will represent these characteristics, a distribution is formed of the raw scores on the test and the 65th and 90th percentiles are determined. Say that the test consists of 150 items and that the 65th and 90th percentiles are found to be 89 and 129 respectively. Two equations are written representing the transformation of the raw scores to the scale, again following the linear form $C = AX + B$: $95 = A(129) + B$ and $70 = A(89) + B$. Solving the equations for A and B, it is found that $A = .625$ and $B = 14.375$. By definition, the scale of scores resulting from this transformation will assign passing scores of 70 and above to the upper 65 percent of the group tested and honors scores of 95 and above to the upper 10 percent of the group tested. It should be understood, however, that the scale satisfies only those points that were fixed and no others. For example, a raw score of zero, it is noted, earns the examinee a scaled score of 14; a perfect raw score earns the examinee a scaled score of 108. If it is desired to fix these values also—

for example, if it is desired that a raw score of zero convert to a scaled score of zero and that the maximum raw score of 150 convert to a scaled score no higher than, say, 99 or 100 [3] — then to impose these additional restrictions will mean that the conversion will no longer be linear throughout. (A linear conversion results from the imposition of no more than two constraints.) There will be one conversion equation operating between scaled scores of zero and 70, another, as already calculated, operating between 70 and 95, and a third between 95 and the agreed-upon scaled score maximum.

In the procedure just described the values of 70 and 95 were—or could have been—defined in the sense of a standard, as scores that should, in some sense, be reached by no more, or no less, than certain fixed percentages of individuals. The determination of the raw scores *attaching* to those percentages, however, was normative in the sense of performance as it exists, since it was made from data resulting from the actual administration of the test. But the scale need not have been dependent on such data at all. It could have been decided on the basis of a careful review and scrutiny of the items themselves, leading to the judgment that the lowest acceptable, or passing, raw score should be set at some agreed-upon value and that the lowest raw score to be designated honors should be set at some other agreed-upon value. These two raw score values corresponding to the desired scaled score values then would be used to form the simultaneous equations, $C_1 = AX_1 + B$ and $C_2 = AX_2 + B$, and solved to determine the values of A and B of the line transforming raw scores to scaled scores.

A systematic procedure for deciding on the minimum raw scores for passing and honors might be developed as follows: keeping the hypothetical "minimally acceptable person" in mind, one could go through the test item by item and decide whether such a person could answer correctly each item under consideration. If a score of one is given for each item

---

[3] The value of 100 is sometimes avoided because of the connotation it carries of perfect performance which could be confused with perfect knowledge.

answered correctly by the hypothetical person and a score of zero is given for each item answered incorrectly by that person, the sum of the item scores will equal the raw score earned by the "minimally acceptable person." A similar procedure could be followed for the hypothetical "lowest honors person."[4]

With a number of judges independently making these judgments it would be possible to decide by consensus on the nature of the scaled score conversion without actually administering the test. If desired, the results of this consensus could later be compared with the number and percentage of examinees who actually earned passing and honors grades.

Percentile Rank Scale

Very likely the most familiar scale for reporting test scores is the percentile rank scale, which gives the percentage of individuals in a particular group scoring below the midpoint of each score or score interval. The precise percentile rank is obtained by totaling the frequencies for all the scores below the particular score plus half the frequencies at the score and dividing by the total number of cases. Sometimes the group on which the percentile ranks are based is assumed to be a random sample of a more general population; sometimes it is a more specialized group chosen for its possession of characteristics similar to those of the individuals to be evaluated. Percentile ranks are essentially self-interpreting and are used for making relative (i.e. normative) types of evaluations of the individual's performance. Distributions of percentile ranks for the groups on which the ranks are based are necessarily rectangular. The percentile rank scale itself is clearly ordinal and, according to most points of

[4] A slight variation of this procedure is to ask each judge to state the *probability* that the "minimally acceptable person" would answer each item correctly. In effect, the judges would think of a number of minimally acceptable persons, instead of only one such person, and would estimate the proportion of minimally acceptable persons who would answer each item correctly. The sum of these probabilities, or proportions, would then represent the minimally acceptable score. A parallel procedure, of course, would be followed for the lowest honors score.

view, its units are unequal since they are intended to provide equal proportions of a group, not equal intervals on a scale of ability.

Normalized Scale (Normalized Standard Scores)

It was pointed out earlier that since the properties of the raw score scale, or a linear transformation of the raw score scale, are dependent on the characteristics (e.g. difficulties and intercorrelations) of the particular items that happen to have been chosen for the test, it is frequently considered to be advantageous to transform the scale to some other system of units that would be independent of the characteristics of the particular test and, in the sense of a particular operational definition, equally spaced. The assumption underlying the search for equal units was that mental ability is fundamentally normally distributed and that equal segments on the base line of a normal curve would pace off equal units of mental ability. McCall (1939) seems to be the one who is principally associated with this kind of scale, although others including Flanagan (1939, 1951), Kelley (1947, pp. 277–284), Pearson (1906), E. L. Thorndike (Thorndike, Bregman, Cob, & Woodyard, 1927, pp. 270–293), and Thurstone (1925) also have argued for it or used it in their research. Operating on the assumption that the normal curve is characteristic of homogeneous groups that have not undergone prior selection, McCall proposed that a group of 12-year-olds be chosen at random from the population and defined as the standard group. The members of this group are tested, a distribution is formed of their scores, and mid-percentile ranks are attached to their scores, which are then transformed to normal deviate scores corresponding to those percentile ranks but with a preassigned mean of 50 and standard deviation of 10. The resulting scale is the well known *T-scale*. The numbers 50 and 10 are arbitrarily assigned, of course; any other reasonable pair of numbers, such as 500 and 100, 100 and 20, 25 and 5, etc., would do as well. In general, however the standardization group is defined and whatever the system of numbers for the scale may be, the method is essentially as just described and the result essentially the same; that is, a normalized score corresponding to any given raw score is the normal deviate (or a linear transformation of the normal deviate) that has the same percentile rank as does the given raw score.

The procedure for normalizing a frequency distribution is generally: mid-percentile ranks, or relative cumulative frequencies (i.e. percentages of cases falling below the lower limits of successive score intervals) if that is more convenient, are computed (as in table 15.1) and plotted and smoothed. If the distribution is plotted on arithmetic graph paper (ordinary graph paper), the points will fall in an S-shaped pattern. It is preferable, therefore, to plot the points (as in figure 15.1) on normal probability paper, which tends to rectify all bell-shaped distributions (it is designed to yield a straight line for all distributions that are strictly normal) and thereby to simplify the smoothing. Smoothing is usually done by hand with the aid of an appropriate French curve or spline. There are very few guidelines available to achieve the desired results of smoothing except to say that the smoothed curve should in general sweep through the points in such a way as to equalize the divergences of the points on either side of the line. (Ideally, the smoothed distribution should preserve all the moments of the observed distribution.) Beyond this general rule the judgment of the person working with the data will determine the degree to which irregularities in the data are defined as such and smoothed out.

Distributions may also be smoothed analytically before they are plotted. Analytical methods may be preferred to hand smoothing because they *are* analytical and do not depend on the subjective judgment of the test specialist. One such method, developed by Cureton and Tukey (1951), which preserves parabolic and cubic trends within successive sets of points, involves a rolling weighted average of frequencies. In order to determine a new smoothed frequency f'_i, in interval i, the method involves multiplying the weights, $-3/35$, $12/35$, $17/35$, $12/35$, and $-3/35$ respectively, by the frequencies, f_{i-2}, f_{i-1}, f_i, f_{i+1}, and f_{i+2}, and summing the products. (Tukey suggested smoothing

the square roots of frequencies and then squaring the smoothed values.) Another method, which is at present appropriate only to rights-scored tests, is derived from the negative hypergeometric distribution (Keats, 1951; Keats & Lord, 1962). Keats has pointed out that "whereas all other methods will tend not to give more stable estimates of percentiles, this method, when appropriate, will reduce the standard error of the estimates obtained below that for either smoothed or unsmoothed distributions."[5]

Difficulties in smoothing, and therefore with the normalizing procedures in general, are frequently encountered near the ends of the distribution where data are relatively scant; and thus percentile rank values, and consequently normalized scores, must be estimated, tempering meager data by judgment or, in extreme instances, extrapolating without the benefit of any supporting data.

Once the smoothed ogive is available, new percentile-rank values are read from the curve at the midpoint of each score interval and recorded. Finally, normal deviate values (z_n) corresponding to the new percentile ranks are read from the table of the normal curve and transformed to the scale (C_n) having the desired mean, M_c, and standard deviation, s_c, by the formula, $C_n = s_c z_n + M_c$. The procedure is illustrated in table 15.1 and figure 15.1.

The transformation to a normal distribution is *not* considered advantageous when there is reason to believe that the peculiarities in the shape of the raw score distribution reflect actual peculiarities in the distribution of ability of the group tested. For example, if the group is a heterogeneous one, composed of separate subgroups of different levels and dispersions, the distribution will very likely be platykurtic even though the subgroups may individually be normally distributed. Also, if the group has been subjected to prior selection, the group tested may appear to be skewed, even though the population from which it came may originally have been normal. Moreover, there is some reason to question the assumption that

---

[5] Personal communication, November 1967.

TABLE 15.1

Normalization of Scores on Form 4a of the STEP Mathematics Test

Raw Score	Frequency	Cumulative Frequency	Percent Below	Percentile Rank (Figure 15.1)	Normal Deviate	Scaled Score $M=50; s=10$
50	1	680	99.9	99.82	2.91	79
49	5	679	99.1	99.5	2.58	76
48	6	674	98.2	98.8	2.26	73
47	6	668	97.4	97.8	2.01	70
46	12	662	95.6	96.4	1.80	68
45	17	650	93.1	94.6	1.61	66
44	11	633	91.5	92.5	1.44	64
43	17	622	89.0	90.0	1.28	63
42	24	605	85.4	87.2	1.14	61
41	26	581	81.6	84.1	1.00	60
40	23	555	78.2	80.9	.87	59
39	20	532	75.3	77.8	.77	58
38	30	512	70.9	73.9	.64	56
37	22	482	67.6	70.0	.52	55
36	28	460	63.5	66.0	.41	54
35	23	432	60.1	62.0	.31	53
34	28	409	56.0	58.0	.20	52
33	25	381	52.4	54.1	.10	51
32	26	356	48.5	50.1	.00	50
31	25	330	44.9	46.1	−.10	49
30	30	305	40.4	43.0	−.18	48
29	20	275	37.5	39.8	−.26	47
28	26	255	33.7	36.0	−.36	46
27	22	229	30.4	32.7	−.45	45
26	22	207	27.2	29.8	−.53	45
25	12	185	25.4	26.5	−.63	44
24	25	173	21.8	24.0	−.71	43
23	18	148	19.1	21.2	−.80	42
22	13	130	17.2	18.9	−.88	41
21	13	117	15.3	16.5	−.97	40
20	13	104	13.4	14.2	−1.07	39
19	13	91	11.5	12.2	−1.17	38
18	12	78	9.7	10.3	−1.26	37
17	9	66	8.4	8.8	−1.35	36
16	9	57	7.1	7.0	−1.48	35
15	11	48	5.4	5.7	−1.58	34
14	13	37	3.5	4.4	−1.71	33
13	7	24	2.5	3.3	−1.84	32
12	4	17	1.9	2.4	−1.98	30
11	3	13	1.5	1.7	−2.12	29
10	5	10	0.7	1.2	−2.26	27
9	1	5	0.6	0.8	−2.41	26
8	2	4	0.3	0.5	−2.58	24
7	1	2	0.1	0.28	−2.75	22
6	0	1	0.1	0.15	−2.97	20
5	0	1	0.1	0.08	−3.16	18
4	0	1	0.1	0.04	−3.35	16
3	1	1				
2						
1						

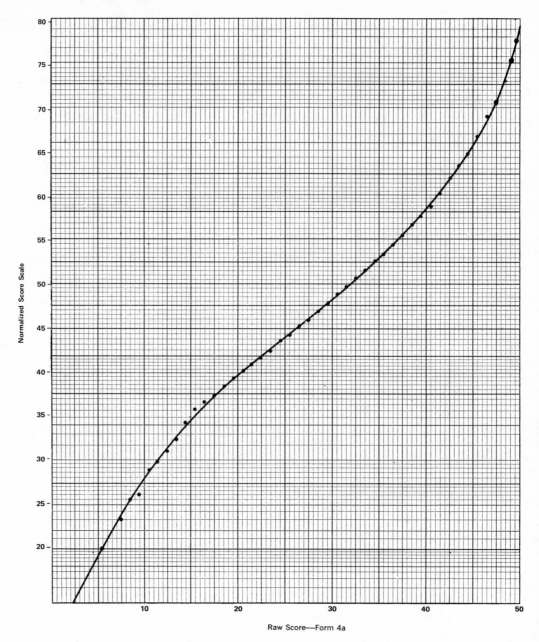

FIG. 15.1. Ogive for Form 4a of the STEP Mathematics Test

the normal distribution is necessarily preferable to other distribution shapes as a basis for the definition of equality of units. Whether the distribution of ability is "basically" normal or nonnormal will never be known of course, but from an empirical analysis carried out by Keats (1951) and another analysis by Lord (1955c) it would appear that the distributions of raw scores on tests are actually more often found to be platykurtic than normal, quite possibly because of ceiling and floor effects.

There have been some well-known normalized scales in use that bear special mention here. One was the original scale for the Profile and Advanced Tests of the Graduate Record Examinations ($M = 500$, $s = 100$)[6], and another is the scale for the Iowa Tests of Educational Development ($M = 15$, $s = 5$). Still another such scale is the *stanine scale* (Flanagan, 1948, 1951), which was first used in the Air Force Aviation Psychology Program during World War II. The *stanine scale* is a single-digit scale extending from 1 to 9 (it derives its name from "standard nine") with preassigned percentages falling in each of the nine scores. The highest- and lowest-scoring 4 percent are assigned scores of 9 and 1, respectively; the next higher and lower 7 percent are assigned scores of 8 and 2; the next 12, 7 and 3; the next 17, 6 and 4; and the remaining 20 percent are assigned the stanine value of 5. The resulting distribution has a mean of 5 and standard deviation of about 2. These values come from the table of the normal curve and, except for the end intervals 1 and 9 which are open ended, they correspond to intervals half a standard deviation in width. Because it was expressed in a single digit and did not require more than one column of an IBM card, the stanine scale was especially useful during World War II at a time when data-processing equipment was still in its early stages of development and could not cope as flexibly as the later versions of electronic machines with data for an individual that could not all be expressed in the 80 columns of a single card. The stanine was then, and is now, especially useful in situations where more precise determinations are not required. Indeed, because it compresses finer distributions into a nine-point scale, it tends to discourage capitalization on small differences that are not meaningful, in view of the possible unreliability and large error of measurement of the test.

The stanine scale has not been universally endorsed. Lindquist and Hieronymus (1964) have pointed out that for all their apparent simplicity, stanine scores are more difficult to interpret than percentile ranks, because the percentages of the distribution that fall into

[6] At the present time the scaled scores for the tests of the Graduate Record Examinations are converted from raw scores by linear transformation.

each stanine score category must be kept clearly in mind. Secondly, the stanine is regarded as unnecessarily coarse, particularly for reliable tests. Third, by definition, stanine distributions are equally variable from test to test and from group to group; and therefore, when for example, they are separately derived for a test for each of a succession of grade groups as is sometimes done with stanines, they mask differences between groups with respect to variability. (It could be added that in the same sense they also mask differences in level since by definition all stanine distributions have a mean of 5.) It is pointed out that differences in rates of growth between subjects like reading, in which students have opportunities to advance on their own, and subjects like arithmetic, in which student progress is more likely to be controlled through the curriculum, are not observable when stanine scores are defined subject by subject and grade by grade. This third limitation applies, of course, to any scale that is defined separately by test and grade group. Moreover, these reservations are more properly directed at the *use* of stanines and other group-referent scales than at the scales themselves.

Another well-known system of scaled scores that is based on the area transformation is the *scaled score* system for the Cooperative Test Service, developed during the 1930s by Flanagan (1939, 1951). Operating on the premise that raw score units, or a linear transformation of raw score units cannot in general be expected to represent equal units of ability, and on the assumption that mental ability is normally distributed in an unselected group, Flanagan proposed to transform the raw score distribution to a normal shape. This was also the position and the approach taken by McCall (1939). However, Flanagan recognized that one of the problems associated with the McCall procedure was the selection of the particular group for which the scores were to be normalized, especially where the distribution on which the scale is based contains the scores of several subgroups with different means and standard deviations. A second difficulty was that the units at the extremes of a scale based on only one distribution will tend to be unreliably scaled, since the cases on which reliable observations can be based are so scant in those regions of the scale.

It was first pointed out by Thurstone (1938) that a simple test could be made to determine whether a scale could be constructed that would simultaneously normalize the distributions of two different intact homogeneous groups. For each score the percentile rank is taken in each group and converted to its normal deviate value. If the two groups can be normalized on the same scale, then a plot of the pairs of normal deviates would fall on a straight line. This result would indicate that it might be possible to construct a scale so that other unselected homogeneous groups also would be normal on the same scale. The process of scaling the Cooperative Tests involved a procedure of adjusting the sizes of the raw score units of the tests to yield simultaneously normal distributions for each of a succession of grade levels. The Flanagan method is in principle quite similar to the method of absolute scaling, which was originally developed by Thurstone (1925) and illustrated for test items (rather than scores) in which the ability was assumed to be normally distributed. However, the principles of Thurstone's procedure are equally applicable to the scaling of test scores. A point of emphasis in the Flanagan scaling is that the groups for which the scale produces normal distributions must be homogeneous groups that have not been subjected to prior selection. If, for example, they were composed of two or more separate subpopulations with different means, it would not be reasonable to expect that the total combined distribution would be normally distributed. If, also, the group had undergone prior selection, it would be expected that the distribution for the remaining cases might well be skewed.

The specific procedures followed in deriving Flanagan's system of scaled scores are already described elsewhere in detail (Flanagan, 1939). Therefore, only a very brief summary of the principles and procedure of the system is attempted here. It is observed that if two overlapping normal distributions with different means and also with different standard devia-

tions are plotted on the same scale, the (non-directional) distance between their means (or medians) may be expressed as:

$$\frac{M_\alpha - M_\beta}{s_\alpha} = z_\alpha$$

and

$$\frac{M_\alpha - M_\beta}{s_\beta} = z_\beta,$$

where α and β refer to two groups of individuals, z_α represents the normal deviate in distribution α for the value of M_β, and z_β represents the normal deviate in distribution β for the value of M_α. From these two equations it follows that $z_\alpha s_\alpha = z_\beta s_\beta$ and $s_\alpha / s_\beta = z_\beta / z_\alpha$. That is to say, the ratio of standard deviations for α and β is the reciprocal of the ratio of their normal deviates. Therefore, in order to derive a scale that will simultaneously normalize two distributions, the percentile rank of each median is found *in the other distribution* and converted to a normal deviate, from which the relative sizes of the two standard deviations, in terms of the scaled score units, may be determined.

When a scale is sought that will simultaneously normalize *more* than two overlapping distributions, one of the groups (preferably a large, centrally located group with large variability) is chosen as the *basic* group. Then, by means of the procedure just described, a first approximation to the ratio of the scaled score standard deviations for each of the other (normalized) distributions, relative to the basic distribution, is calculated and the scale units adjusted to yield these ratios. This approximation is tested out, and the entire procedure iterated until it is judged that the newly derived values of the scaled units are in good agreement with the values just previously determined.

For the test in each subject (in the Cooperative Test series) the numerical values assigned to the scale were defined in terms of an estimate of the performance of the nation's high school students, assuming that they had attended a typical high school and had had the typical amount and kind of instruction in the subject at the usual time in their high school career. The

"50-point" was the score estimated to be that of the average student so defined, but who *also:* (a) had an IQ between 98 and 102 on the Otis Self-Administering Test of Mental Ability, Form A (administered in grade 7); (b) earned a total score of 92 on the Stanford Achievement Test, Form V, at grade 8.4; and (c) was between 14.25 and 14.75 years old at the beginning of grade 9. The value of 10 was taken to represent the standard deviation of scores for the nation's population of students who were 14.5 years old at the beginning of grade 9, but who were otherwise unselected.

The Flanagan scaling procedure makes it clear that the process of scaling may involve two separate steps: (a) the determination of the interpoint distances, which Flanagan accomplished by extending the scale over a range of grade groups in such a way that each group would be normalized on that scale; and (b) the assignment of a set of reference numbers to the units of the scale, which he accomplished by defining the "standard group" and assigning particular values for the mean and standard deviation.

Inasmuch as the scales for all the various achievement tests of the Cooperative Test Service were constructed with the same normative meaning attaching to the means (50) and standard deviations (10), the score scales for the various tests are considered *comparable*. The *norms* for the various tests, however, are not comparable, of course, nor were they intended to be, since different types of students choose to study the various subjects represented by the tests. For example, although the score of 50 on the Intermediate Algebra Test is comparable to the score of 50 on the Trigonometry Test, since they have the same meaning in reference to the same underlying group, it would not be expected that the same proportion of students who actually choose to study intermediate algebra and trigonometry would earn scores of 50 on their respective tests. Since the group studying trigonometry is very likely a more highly selected and more able group than the group studying intermediate algebra, the mean scaled score for the trigonometry norms group would be higher and the percentile rank of a scale score of 50 would be lower than the corresponding values for the norms group for intermediate algebra.

Even though the scaling distributions may be restricted to students who are homogeneous in all the important respects, it is possible that in the actual situation there will be some effects—natural effects of selection for example—operating on a distribution to cause it to skew in one direction or the other as well as to differ in mean and standard deviation. In order to allow skewness to vary, Gardner (1947) developed his system of K units, following in many respects the model of the Flanagan system but assuming the more general Pearson Type III curve instead of restricting himself, as Flanagan did, to the normal curve (which is a Pearson Type III with zero skewness).

It will be helpful to quote Gardner's (1950) own summary of the intent of his procedure: "The initial criterion under which the curves were fitted was that *the proportion of cases in each grade falling below any specific score shall remain invariant after the appropriate Type III curves have been fitted to the overlapping grade frequency distributions* [p. 42]."

By way of contrast with the foregoing curvilinear scaling methods, corresponding *linear* scaling operations retain the interpoint distances as reflected by the raw scores. In such instances the process of scaling involves merely the selection of a suitable number system to which raw scores are transformed in linear fashion. Occasionally the number system is defined in terms of the performance of a selected norms group (e.g. as was done in defining McCall's T-scale), but sometimes it is defined nonnormatively (as in the case of the College Board scale) on the basis of a conveniently available group of individuals but not necessarily one with clear normative properties.

Age Equivalent Scale

Unlike other systems of scale unit construction which seek to transform the raw score scales to a system that will reflect equal units in some sense or to approximate a desired distribution form, age equivalent scales are intended to convey the meaning of test performance in terms of what is typical of a child at a given age and are used principally at those ages where the function measured increases rapidly with age. The method of scaling tests to produce age equivalents generally has been carried out as follows:

1. Representative samples of children over a range of ages are administered the test to be scaled. Children falling within six months of a particular birthday are often grouped together as representing a given year group. The test should include items that are easy even for very young and dull children and extend in difficulty to items that are difficult even for much older children of advanced intelligence.

2. The mean (or median) test score of the children at each age interval is found and plotted on arithmetic graph paper against the midpoint of the age interval.

3. A smooth curve is drawn through the points in such a way as to minimize insofar as possible the distances from the points to the curve and at the same time to represent what appears to be the lawful relationship among the points. As is true of all hand smoothing operations, the accomplishment of these two objectives simultaneously will require the test specialist to exercise some compromise between them.

4. The smoothed value of each of the mean scores is assigned the age designation of the group for which it is the mean. These designations are the age equivalents; they are, in summary, the chronological ages for which the given test performances are average.

5. Finally, year-and-month values are obtained by interpolating on the curve.

Age equivalents had considerable appeal during the early history of psychological testing. Their disadvantages, however, are quite serious. There are four types of issues to consider.

In the first place, there is a basic ambiguity about age equivalents. It is an elementary fact that in any scatter diagram which represents a correlation less than unity, there are two regression lines that do not coincide. As Thurstone (1926), and later, Gulliksen (1950) pointed out, mental age may be defined in terms of either of these two lines and produce quite different results. In correlating age with test performance there is the regression of test performance on age and there is also the regression of age on test performance. Consider intelligence test scores as an example. Although the practice has been to use the former regression, mental age norms could just as logically be developed by finding the mean age of children who reach specified levels of performance and assigning those mean ages to the specified levels of performance. The mental age units corresponding to the different levels of performance would be different for the two regressions, and the interpretations attaching to these mental ages also would be different. For if the regression of performance on age is used, as it usually is, the individual who scores above the mean, for example, would be judged to be more outstanding than if the regression of age on performance were used. Depending on which regression one used, the mental age interpretation given to the *same test score* would be different. Moreover, the lower the correlation between age and test performance (as a consequence, for example, of the unreliability of the test), the greater will be the discrepancy between the two types of interpretation.

Second, the use of the age curve fails to take into account the variation about that curve. If the correlation between age and test is high and the variation about the regression line small, than a child who stands at, say, the 95th percentile in his age group may appear, for example, to be two years advanced beyond his age. If, on the other hand, the correlation between age and test score is low and the variation about the regression line large, then the same child who stands at the 95th percentile in his age group will appear to be *more* than two years advanced beyond his age. If one computes an IQ as ratio of mental to chronological age he will, as a result, earn a higher IQ. In general, when the correlation between age and test score is low, children are perceived to be more extreme—more advanced *or* retarded—than when the correlation is high. The difficulty is that the age equivalent can give a distorted and exaggerated impression of a child's level of advancement or retardation, the more so if the test is unreliable, or for other reasons relatively uncorrelated with age. Moreover, although the age equivalent is purportedly a normative measure of an individual's performance, it fails to tell one, as percentile-rank-within-age tables would, how rare his performance is.

There is still a third problem in the interpretation of age equivalents, such as mental ages. An age equivalent is meaningful only if there exists an age for which the given test performance, denoted by the age equivalent, is average. To say that an intelligence test performance of a six-year-old child represents a mental age of nine may seem reasonable, because the average nine-year-old does indeed perform at that level on the test. But what shall be used as the age equivalent for a comparably superior sixteen-year-old? Since performance on intelligence tests flattens out during adolescence and shows little further gain associated with age, there probably exists *no age* at which the average performance equals his. This limitation in age equivalents is made clear by Terman and Merrill (1937, p. 30) and also by Thurstone (1926).

Finally, it should be pointed out that the very notion of a "mental age" that conveys the meaning of the same intellectual performance irrespective of chronological age is at variance with what is known about the psychology of the individual. While it is true, for example, that some six-year-old children can perform as well as the average for nine-year-olds on tests of general intelligence, a six-year-old child is nevertheless not like a nine-year-old, nor does he have the mental equipment of a nine-year-old, regardless of his score. Indeed, all that can be said about the bright six-year-old is that he is a bright six-year-old or, in statistical terms, that he stands, say, above the 99th percentile in comparison with other children of his age. A (normative) statement of this sort is more appropriate, since it involves a comparison within the child's own age group rather than an expression of performance in terms of what is typical of other age groups.

Grade Equivalent Scale

Another scale, similar in many of the important respects to the mental age scale, is the scale of grade equivalents. Grade equivalents are derived very much like age equivalents.

First, representative samples of children in each grade for which a grade equivalent is desired are given the test in question, usually an achievement test. The test is designed to include items ranging in difficulty from those that are easy for children even in the lowest grade to those that are hard for children even in the highest grade. Ordinarily, only tests containing items of appropriate difficulty are given at each grade level, and an anchor test is used to calibrate the separate tests in terms of a single reference scale (see pp. 587–90; also, Lindquist & Hieronymus, 1964). Then the mean test score for children at each grade level is found and plotted on ordinary graph paper against the numerical designation of the grade. Next, the plot is smoothed, and the smoothed value of each of the mean test scores is assigned the grade designation of the group for which it is the mean. Paralleling the development of the age equivalents, these designations are the grade equivalents, i.e. the grades for which these test performances are average. Finally, grade-and-month (or tenth-of-grade) values are obtained by interpolating on the curve.

The disadvantages of the grade equivalent parallel those of the age equivalent. Here too, the equivocacy of the regression is a problem; depending on which regression line between grade and test performance one uses, the interpretation of the grade equivalent given to the *same test score* could be quite different. The more unreliable the test and the lower the correlation between grade and test performance, the greater will be the difference between these two interpretations. Moreover, since the grade equivalent fails to take into consideration the variation in test score about the curve relating grade and test score, the significance of the grade equivalent is not uniquely interpretable. For some tests, for example in arithmetic where the correlation between grade and test score is high, the finding that a child is two grades advanced in terms of his test performance may indicate that he stands quite high (say, at the 95th percentile) relative to his grade group. For other tests, for example in reading or in social studies where the correlations are lower, the same finding that he is two years advanced beyond his grade will indicate that he stands only moderately above his grade group. Thus, like age equivalents, grade equivalents are highly affected by the correlation between grade level and test performance, and the information that would be required to interpret an individual's relative standing in a group is simply not available in the grade equivalent as it is in the usual percentile rank distribution.

But beyond the statistics, there is a still more serious problem of interpretation from an educational point of view. To say that a sixth-grader's performance has a grade equivalent of eight is to say that he performs at the level of a student in the eighth grade. Clearly, in any subject-matter area that is closely tied to the grade level this cannot be, for the fact is that the sixth-grader has necessarily been taught *and tested* with the type of material that is appropriate to *his* grade; he has not been exposed to the kind of educational material in school that is normally given to an eighth-grader, nor has he in general had the opportunity to demonstrate his proficiency with eighth-grade material (Angoff, 1960).

There are additional problems with the grade equivalent, most of which Flanagan already has pointed out (1951):

1. It assumes that growth is uniform throughout the school year and that either no growth takes place during the summer or that growth during the summer is equal to one month of growth during the school year. There is certainly reason to doubt that these assumptions are universally justified in all subject-matter areas, or, indeed, whether they are even generally true (see Beggs & Hieronymus, 1968).

2. Grade equivalents for the low and high grades are often impossible to establish from available data and have to be obtained by extrapolation from existing observations. This is an extremely unreliable procedure and represents at best little more than educated guesses.

3. In parallel with the development of age equivalents, the grade equivalent, as mentioned above, can only be calculated where there is a grade for which the given test performance is average. Therefore, a grade equivalent for grades beyond, say, the ninth grade is meaningless for those subject-matter areas that are not taught in school beyond the ninth grade.

4. Because of the differences in correlation between age and performance from one subject-matter area to another and because of differences in the extent to which the teaching practices in the different areas are geared to particular grade levels, it is easy to come to the erroneous and meaningless conclusion that exceptional talent in arithmetic, for example, is less common than exceptional talent in reading or that growth in arithmetic is more rapid than growth in reading. As Flanagan (1951) pointed out, "the crux of the situation is that all of these methods are of necessity based on some characteristics of the distributions of obtained scores for the populations involved, and that none of these characteristics is in any sense 'fundamental,' but all are influenced by, or are a function of, arbitrary practices in instruction and curriculum organization [p. 711]." These are the factors that cause differences among the various subjects taught in school with respect to overlap from grade to grade. And it is these differences in overlap—the differences in the between-grade variability relative to the within-grade variability—that are reflected in the differences among the correlations between test scores in each of the various subjects and grade level and invalidate any statements regarding comparability across subject-matter areas.

5. The grade equivalent scale is necessarily dependent on, indeed an artifact of, the particular way in which the subject-matter area in question is introduced and the way in which it is emphasized in the curriculum throughout the grades. Differences from one school and community to another in this regard will have a profound effect on grade equivalents. Gulliksen (1950) pointed out too that

the relationship between age and grade norms is affected by changes in the educational customs regarding promotion from grade to grade. In the early 1900's promotion was based primarily on achievement. The pupil who did not learn as rapidly as the average was not promoted. Such an educational system would give rise to a marked difference between age and grade norms, and also lead to a smaller dispersion of scores within each grade, accompanied by less overlap in the scores of adjacent grades. The present custom of promoting a pupil primarily on the basis of age will increase the resemblance between age and grade norms (or between age and grade equivalents), increase the dispersion of scores within a given grade, and produce a marked overlap in the scores of adjacent grades. Norms (or grade equivalents) that were determined under the former system of promotion (primarily on the basis of achievement) cannot be compared with norms (or grade equivalents) established under the present system of promotion primarily based on age. Similarly, norms that have been established under limited educational opportunities, and when the illiteracy rate is high, cannot be expected to resemble norms established when the educational level of the population is increased, and the illiteracy rate is low [p. 291].

6. In general, the use of grade equivalents tends to exaggerate the significance of small differences, and in this way, as well as in other ways described above, to encourage the improper use of test scores. Because of the large within-grade variability it is entirely possible, for example, for a child who is only moderately above the median for his grade to appear on the grade equivalent scale to be as much as a year or even two years advanced. A comparison of the grade equivalents with percentile ranks would make this fact clear.

7. Some teachers tend to confuse the grade equivalent norm with a desired or ideal standard of performance and make the judgment that their class is doing satisfactory work if they are performing up to the "norm," without regard to other important and relevant factors such as the general level of intelligence of their children or other factors related to differences in curriculum emphasis. Although this kind of misinterpretation can occur with all kinds of normative data, it is probably most likely to be made when the interpretive data for the test call for the translation of test performance into a *single* grade equivalent value.

Contrary to the claims that sometimes are made for them, grade and educational (or mental) age equivalents do not provide a good basis for comparability among tests, nor do they represent a uniquely better metric than other scales, such as the normalized or linear scales, for measuring growth. There is indeed general agreement that they are inferior to percentile rank tables when it comes to the interpretation of an individual student's test scores or in comparing his standing on several tests. The principal claim that can be made for the grade and age equivalents is that they have a simplicity and directness of meaning in terms of the test user's everyday experience that are not shared by other scales. However, the difficulties and confusions that are attendant on the use of these equivalents would indicate that their simplicity is far more apparent than real and that the truly simple scales may well be those for which there has been no attempt to capitalize on the use of direct meaning. Moreover, while it is possible that direct meaning may be a highly desirable feature in a system of derived scores, the trouble is, as has frequently been pointed out, that users read into such scores more or different meanings than they actually possess.

The IQ Scale

Although the IQ as a ratio of mental age to chronological age is seldom, if at all, in use today, it will be valuable to examine its psychometric properties. The determination of the IQ for an individual, as the IQ was originally conceived, was accomplished by finding the mental age (i.e. the age equivalent) for his performance, dividing that number by his chronological age, and multiplying by 100. By definition, then, an individual is of average intelligence if his mental age equals his chronological age, giving him an IQ index of 100. To the extent that his performance is higher than would be expected for his age his IQ is higher than 100, and to the extent that his performance is lower than would be expected for his age his IQ is lower than 100.

The primary value of the IQ lies in the apparent simplicity with which it can be interpreted and explained and, also, in its built-in comparability from one age to the next. To the extent that the sampling has been adequate and comparable from one age to another in the construction of the mental age norms and to the extent that the growth pattern of intelligence, or rather of performance on the items comprised by the test, is reasonably similar from one child to the next, and, finally, to the extent that the regression of score on age is homoscedastic, the IQ remains fairly constant from age to age.

In reviewing the data for the 1937 revision of the Stanford-Binet, Terman and Merrill observed (1937, p. 40) that there was more than a chance fluctuation in the standard deviations of IQs from age to age. Five years later, McNemar (1942, p. 85) pointed out that this fluctuation was an inverse function of the differences in the variability of the difficulties of the items appropriate at the different ages. (It also may have been a function of the differences in item-test correlations at different age levels.) This fluctuation in variability means in effect that ratio IQs are *not* comparable from age to age, but that an IQ at one age may be equivalent in relative position to a somewhat higher or lower IQ at a different age. In other words, the fluctuation in variability undermined the assumption or claim of the constancy of the IQ. An individual's IQ could shift from one age to the next, not because of any change in intelligence relative to other individuals of his age, but merely because of changes in the variability of test performance from one year to the next. In order to eliminate these types of fluctuations, the IQs that were developed for the 1960 L-M Revision are *deviation IQs*, rather than ratios as originally defined. Deviation IQs are essentially standard scores and as such they yield the kind of normative interpretation that is not available in the age and grade equivalents. In this respect and also in the respect that they avoid some of the statistical and educational-psychological confusions of the age equivalents, they represent a decided improvement over the ratio IQs.

The development of the deviation IQs is a fairly simple matter, conceptually. For each age group a random sample of individuals was selected and tested, and a conversion system developed to yield a mean of 100 and standard deviation of 16 for those individuals (Terman & Merrill, 1960). Assuming that a child's rank-order position in intelligence test scores remains constant from age to age, the method of reporting scores as deviation IQs, standardized with the same mean and standard deviation at each age, ensures that that child's IQ also will remain constant from one age to the next.

Except for minor procedural differences which may involve a normalization of the score distributions, the same general approach to the standardization of means and standard deviations has been followed in the development of IQ scales for virtually all of the intelligence tests that provide IQ equivalents, including the Wechsler Adult Intelligence Scale (WAIS), the Wechsler Intelligence Scale for Children (WISC), the Lorge-Thorndike Intelligence Tests, the Kuhlmann-Anderson Test, the Pintner General Ability Tests, the Otis Tests, and the California Test of Mental Maturity. Indeed, the Stanford-Binet is one of the tests that has relatively recently adopted the deviation IQ. The Wechsler-Bellevue Intelligence Scale used it as early as 1939. It is interesting that the tests do not all adopt the same value for the standard deviation of IQ within age. The WISC, for example, uses 15, instead of the value 16 that was adopted in the 1960 revision of the Stanford-Binet (Seashore, Wesman, & Doppelt, 1950). The implication of this difference is that—aside from differences in the standardization groups resulting from sampling errors, and possibly other factors—the Stanford-Binet and WISC IQs are not comparable. That is to say, high or low IQ values are rarer on the WISC than on the Stanford-Binet.

The EQ and AQ Scales

The ease of interpretation to which the ratio IQ *apparently* lent itself was quite likely influential in the development of similar indices, such as the educational quotient (EQ), which is the ratio of educational age (similar to mental age in conception but calculated for achievement in subject-matter areas) to chronological age and even the achievement quotient (AQ), which is the ratio of the EQ to the IQ, that is to say the ratio of the educational age to the mental age. The AQ appeared to represent an attempt to measure over- and underachievement in terms of a ratio of "actual achievement" to "potential ability." Flanagan pointed out (1951, p. 716) that the AQ has been discredited principally because: (*a*) it is sensitive to random errors of measurement, norming, and scaling—the error in the AQ is larger than the error in a simple quotient like the IQ, for example, since it is the result of the combined errors in both the EQ *and* the IQ; (*b*) it is subject to errors resulting from the *differences* in the norms samples used in the standardization of the tests from which the age equivalents are obtained; (*c*) the different growth curves used to establish educational age and mental age cause difficulties, especially at the extreme ages where extrapolated values are used and where unselected age groups are hard to obtain; (*d*) other factors, such as the high correlation between intelligence and achievement tests and the variability in age at the particular grade levels at which the different subjects are taught, affect the practical value of the AQ adversely. Furthermore, the *expected* AQ differs for different values of the IQ. Because of regression effects, the expected AQ is less than 100 for IQ values above the group mean and over 100 for IQ values below the group mean. The amount of this effect is proportional to the size of the IQ deviations. As a result, AQ values are characterized by a systematic bias.

Normative vs. Nonnormative Derived Scales

In general, if one were to examine the various reasons for preferring systems of derived score scales for standardized tests rather than the original raw score scales, one would find that the reasons fall into about four principal categories (Angoff, 1962):

1. For the sake of convenience in handling test score data, it is frequently desirable to convert raw score data to scales with preassigned characteristics in round numbers that are easy to recall and easy to use. The stanine scale is a good example of a scale that possesses this characteristic, as is the IQ scale, the 50–10 scale, and others.

2. As has already been pointed out, the raw score scale of a test is considered by some to be no more than an ordinal scale. Some doubt has been expressed that it should be used, for example, to compare changes in different regions of the scale. In an effort to make comparisons of this sort possible, raw score scales are converted to derived scales in which the unit separations between scores are in some operational sense equal. Tucker's proficiency scale, Flanagan's scaled score system, and Gardner's K scores are derived scales of this type.

3. Derived scales are used when more than one form of a test is available and the forms are used interchangeably. In such instances, it is desirable to equate the scores reported for the forms in order to make them independent of the difficulty characteristics of the form on which they were earned. It also is considered desirable to report scores on a scale that is clearly different from, and therefore cannot be confused with, the raw score scale of any form. The derived scale, then, exists as a referent for all test forms on which scores are made interchangeable as a result of a process of equating. The College Board scale is one of a number of scale systems that purport to relate test forms in this way.

4. It usually is maintained that the raw score scale yields little or no immediate meaning of its own. For that reason, derived score scales are established in which normative meaning is directly incorporated. The scales described in the preceding discussion are scales of this type, those that derive their systems of units from the administration of the test to a *standardization group* (a group drawn as a representative or random sample of a defined population). In the sense that the knowledge of any derived score yields *inherent evaluative* knowledge of a test performance in comparison with the test performance of members of a known population, the scale is taken to be a *normative scale*. McCall's T scores represent a scale of this type, as do all the others that have been described so far.

There is little argument that a derived score scale is useful in a situation where there is a system of interrelated test forms. To refer to ability measures in terms of the unadjusted raw score scales of the forms when the forms are not precisely equivalent in difficulty would only invite confusion. Similarly, there is little argument that it is convenient to use a scale system that is based on a set of numbers that are easy to recall. It would be difficult to imagine why one would choose to assign a number like, for example, 81.27 as the mean of a distribution of derived scores rather than a round number like 50 or 100. Finally, there is little question that educational and psychological measurement would be vastly improved if its scales could be expressed in terms that everyone would agree represent equal units of ability. Such a scale, with units equally spaced throughout, would permit the direct comparison of score differences in one region of the continuum with score differences in any other region of the continuum.

With regard to the *normative* characteristic of the scale there has been some dispute. Generally speaking, it has been taken for granted that it is at least desirable, if not even necessary, that the system of numbers for a scale have inherent normative meaning; i.e. that it be defined in terms of the performance of a representative group of individuals. The argument is that, since such a scale gives the user immediate normative information, it is therefore more useful than one that is not normatively derived. This view has been expressed by many writers, including especially Flanagan (1939, 1951, 1953, 1962) and Gardner (1947, 1949, 1950, 1962, 1966). On the other hand, Tucker (1953) has described the usefulness of a scale that is independent of the characteristics of reference groups, one in which meanings attaching to a test score depend on the test itself and the items it comprises. Lindquist (1953) has argued too that "the best type of scale is one that is divorced as much as possible from any normative meaning [p. 38]." Such a scale, he pointed out,

has the very distinct advantage that if the norms change after the scale has been established . . . then there is no need to abandon the scale on that account, or to rescale the test. Instead, all one need do in that case is to leave the reference scale as it was before, because it does not depend on normative meanings, and make whatever changes in the normative scales associated with it [that] happen to be appropriate [p. 38–39].

Angoff (1962) has made essentially the same point, that the commitment to a particular norms group in the definition of a scale is not only unnecessary but unnecessarily restrictive as well, since it imposes a particular kind of normative interpretation on the scores that may not always be appropriate. Angoff maintained, as Lindquist had, that any built-in normative meaning was likely to become obsolete with time and, consequently, to lead to the misinterpretation of test scores. Moreover, since only one meaning could be built into a score scale, this meaning could serve only one purpose of the test to the exclusion of all others. In general, he pointed out, scales of measurement are quite useful even when they have no inherent or definitional meaning. By way of illustration he showed that in spite of the fact that the original definition (i.e. the "meaning") of most of the commonly employed units of measurement (like inches, pounds, degrees Fahrenheit, etc.) is totally unknown—indeed, lost—to the large majority of the public, their usefulness is by no means impaired by this loss. What makes these units truly meaningful to the user is their *familiarity;* and what allows these units to become familiar and otherwise useful is the *constancy* of their meaning—the fact that an inch, for example, represents the same length on any ruler, and that it also represents the same length this year as last. Similarly, in the case of test scales the more permanent and useful meaning is the meaning that comes with familiarity. Here too, familiarity comes as a result of the successful maintenance of a constant scale—which, in the case of a multiple-form testing program, is achieved by rigorous form-to-form equating—and through the provision of *supplementary normative data* to aid in interpretation and in the formation of specific decisions, data which would be revised from time to time as conditions warrant.

Whatever the merits of normative versus nonnormative scales may be, there is little question that it is not *necessary* to derive a score scale normatively. For example, the scale may be defined in a nonnormative fashion as Guttman did (1950). The *Guttman scale*, unlike the methods of scaling described above, was developed in the context of attitude and opinion measurement and was intended primarily to determine whether a universe of attitude statements is unidimensional; that is, whether there is a singleness of meaning in an area of opinion or attitude. Unlike the methods of scaling previously described, which are primarily intended to assign a system of numerical values to raw test scores, Guttman's method is intended to determine whether a scale, as he defines it, exists. The assignment of numerical values is secondary.

A perfect scale in Guttman's sense is one in which an individual who agrees with a strong statement of attitude also will agree with a milder statement of that attitude; similarly, an individual who disagrees with a mild statement of attitude will disagree also with a stronger statement of that attitude. For example, if an individual indicates on a social-distance questionnaire that he is unwilling to have as a neighbor a member of nationality group X, he would similarly be expected to say that he would be unwilling for his child to marry a member of that nationality group. As mentioned earlier in the context of mental tests, a perfect scale is one in which a person who passes an item of given difficulty also will pass any other item of lesser difficulty; an individual who fails an item of given difficulty will fail also any other item of greater difficulty.

Knowledge of a person's score on a questionnaire (or a test) that forms a Guttman scale permits perfect reproduction of his actual responses. To the extent that the item responses are reproducible, the questionnaire is said to be homogeneous, unidimensional, and reliable in the sense that the items have high tetrachoric intercorrelations.

One of the difficulties of the Guttman approach lies in the fact that it is *deterministic* in the sense that the subject's response to each item is completely determined by his position on the scale. However, this characteristic of the Guttman model is not likely to be realized in practice, even approximately, because of the relatively large errors of measurement. An alternative approach is to assume that the *probability* of the subject giving a particular response is completely determined by (a) his position on a scale and (b) one or more constants associated with the item. In the case of ability tests the assumption is made that the probability of a correct response P is completely determined by: (a) the ability a of the subject as measured on some scale; (b) the difficulty d of the item; and (c) its discriminating power v. In other words, P is determined by, or is a function of, a, d, and v only; i.e. $P = f(a, d, v)$.

The particular functional relationship to be used between the items and the ability continuum is a matter of assumption. Various suggestions for this relationship have been made, including polynomials (Lazarsfeld, 1950), the cumulative normal ogive (Lawley, 1943; Lord, 1952a, 1952b; Tucker, 1951, 1953), the logistic curve (Birnbaum in Lord & Novick, 1968), and a simpler form (Rasch, 1960). All of these models are special cases of the general latent structure model and carry with them the assumption that all the items in the test are measuring the same ability, but that chance factors affect the response pattern. Furthermore, in all of them, ability a is a property of the individual that is constant over all the items in an item domain, and d and v are properties of items which are independent of other items administered. A major hope of those using this approach is that item constants such as d and v will in fact prove to be relatively invariant over populations and that inferred ability a will be relatively invariant over different sets of items. That this hope may be realized is indicated in a study by Wright (1968). Conceivably, the flexibility afforded in scaling, norming, and equating by these invariances could well lead to some major innovations in mental measurement.

The probabilistic model chosen as an example to be given below was developed by Rasch and is algebraically the simplest. This model contains the assumption that all items are of equal discriminating power. With this assumption the parameter v may be omitted; i.e. $P = f(a, d)$. The Rasch assumption for the form of the functional relationship is: $P = a/(a+d)$, where a and d are zero or positive and, therefore, P takes on values from zero to one.

With this relationship assumed and with complete data for all subjects, it can be shown that, for estimation purposes, equal numbers of correctly answered questions imply equal ability a for the individuals tested. Hence, one could construct a two-way table to check the assumptions of the model. Rows in this table would correspond to items, and columns would correspond to raw scores. An entry in the table would be the proportion of people with a raw score corresponding to the column who correctly answered the item corresponding to the row. This proportion would be an estimate of P which is a function of the ability a of all individuals with that raw score and of the difficulty d of the item. By taking logarithms and manipulating the equation relating a and d, it can be shown that $\log\{P/(1-P)\} = \log a - \log d$. Thus if the two-way table of P's just described undergoes the transformation $\log\{P/(1-P)\}$, the resulting entries should fit a two-way analysis-of-variance model without interaction and with item and raw score level as the main effects. Furthermore, since the coefficients of $\log a$ and $\log d$ are unity, a plot of cell entries for any row against the means of the columns should produce a straight line with a slope of 45 degrees. Slopes that depart radically from 45 degrees indicate that the items are not equally discriminating. The test constructor who uses this model may wish to make such tests on his data as did Rasch (1960) in his empirical study of the model.

For data that fit the model, it is possible to estimate the ability level, a, associated with a raw score on a scale with an origin, which is simply to say that division of one ability level by another is a permissible numerical operation under the model. This is so because column averages of the table that are used to check the model are estimates of $\log a$ plus an arbitrary constant and hence may be written as $\log ka$. Hence by taking antilogs of the column averages an estimate of ka may be obtained. The choice of k would not affect ratios of a's and hence a is estimated on a ratio scale (Stevens, 1951). The choice of k may be governed by numerical (or other) convenience.

Theory development in this area has taken a direction towards greater complexity to account for the varieties of tests found in practice. However, test constructors might well consider the advantages of preparing tests according to the more restrictive requirements that are necessary if the raw score, or some simple transformation of it, is to have an unambiguous and useful meaning.[7]

Another scale that follows the general probabilistic model is Tucker's proficiency scale, (Tucker, 1951, 1953; Lord, 1952a). In constructing this scale, the items of the test are first ranked in order of difficulty, and the rank order is examined for invariance with respect to different populations. This invariance, once verified, establishes the homogeneity of the domain of the test. Then for each item or homogeneous group of items, an item characteristic curve (a curve of percentage passing at each score level) is drawn against the raw score on the test, and different parts of the scale are expanded and contracted, so to speak, in order to normalize all item characteristic curves simultaneously. The score corresponding to an agreed-upon percentage-pass (e.g. 70 percent) on the item is taken to describe the scale difficulty of the item. The individual's score is the place on the scale corresponding to the group of items that he was able to respond to just barely satisfactorily.

The intent of the Tucker procedure is to establish a system of scale unit separations which, unlike the McCall T-scale for example, will be independent of the performance of any particular group of examinees. The assignment of numerical values to the scale units then could be made by any one of a number of ways, so long as the relative distances between units remain unchanged. This latter restriction implies a linear transformation, which could be derived in a normative fashion as described earlier in this section by testing some defined group of individuals to whom an agreed-upon scaled-score mean and standard deviation would be assigned, or by one of the nonnormative methods described below.

A nonnormative linear conversion to scaled scores also may be established by arbitrary

---

[7] The preceding paragraphs on the probabilistic models of scaling has been contributed by J. A Keats and R. F. Boldt.

decision or by agreement among judges as a result of detailed study, as described in connection with percentile-derived linear scales (pp. 514–15). In this method two raw scores are arrived at: one, for example, corresponding to the hypothetical minimally acceptable person and the other corresponding to the hypothetical lowest honors person. Corresponding to these two scores a pair of scaled scores are arbitrarily chosen, such as 70 and 95, to represent passing and honors. Two simultaneous linear equations are then written, expressing the relationship between these particular raw and scaled scores, and solved for the slope and intercept values of the linear equation relating the raw scores to the scale.

The foregoing technique of setting minimum scores is applicable in many other situations, including those where scale definition is not under consideration. For example, in those situations where a single general ability test is administered to all the members of a heterogeneous group, say army recruits, and some guidelines need to be established at the outset for assignment to occupational specialties for which different levels of ability are required, judgments may be made of the probability that the minimally acceptable individual in each of the specialties will pass each item. The sum of the probabilities for each specialty then defines the minimally acceptable score for that specialty. Similar kinds of judgments also may be used to set minimum standards of ability for admission to officer candidate school or to other training programs. Later validity studies will help to verify the appropriateness of the initial cutting scores or to correct them if necessary.

There is, finally, a very simple and obvious type of nonnormative scale that is derived solely from the scores of the test itself and is useful when there are multiple forms of the test. The scale may be defined as the test score scale of the first form or, preferably, by means of a convenient but arbitrary translation of the test score units into scaled scores without normative properties. For example, the mean chance score on the first form may be assigned a scaled score of 50 (or any other number) and the maximum score assigned a scaled score of 150 (or any other number). These two points define the general range of scaled scores for the first form and therefore the general range of scaled scores for all other forms that may directly or indirectly be equated to that form. The equation for converting the test scores to the defined scale is found by solving a pair of simultaneous equations in much the same way shown for the percentile-derived linear scale or for the scale derived from the judgment of minimum standards. For example, if the test in question has 200 items and the mean chance score is zero (that is, if the test scores are corrected for guessing), then the simultaneous equations will be: $150 = A(200) + B$ and $50 = A(0) + B$, from which it is found that $A = .500$ and $B = 50.00$. If the test scores are not corrected for guessing, then, assuming that the test consists of five-choice items only, the equations will be: $150 = A(200) + B$ and $50 = A(40) + B$ (the score of 40 representing the mean chance score for a test of five-choice items), from which it is found that $A = .625$ and $B = 25.00$. It should be understood that, just as the scale values are arbitrarily chosen, the test scores corresponding to those scale values are also arbitrarily chosen. For example, the raw scores corresponding to scaled scores 50 and 150 on this form might have been 0 and 200 or, indeed, *any* pair of usable values, no matter what the scoring formula may have been. Except for the changes in the numerical values of the units, this converted score scale has the very same properties that are characteristic of the raw score scale. Its advantage over the raw score scale lies in the fact that it *is* a converted score scale, clearly different from the raw scores and, by design and choice, not likely to be confused with the raw scores—a scale in terms of which raw scores from different forms have already been calibrated and are now expressed. Given such a converted score scale, the question, On what form of the test was this score of 43 earned? becomes unnecessary and, moreover, irrelevant.

There is much to be said for the point of view that the score scale should have a normative referent and yield automatic normative interpretation, particularly in the case of tests that have a highly specific purpose and for which the target population is clearly defined. However, where the test is intended for use in a variety of circumstances and for a variety of subgroups and it is desired to make the supplementary norms and validity data the vehicle for score interpretation, then it may be desirable to define the scale in terms of a set of numbers that are themselves as much divorced from normative interpretations as possible. In such instances, it will be sufficient that the important benchmarks for the scale be chosen to satisfy the criterion of convenience. In the case of the preceding illustration the scale centers about 100. It might just as well, of course, have centered about 50, or 500, or 5, or 25, or any other convenient number. The choice of the specific set of numbers for this method of scaling—or any other method of scaling—would depend on the particular purposes of the program, the need to avoid confusion with other test scales already in existence, and the reliabilities of the tests in the system.

The process of defining a scale has been observed here to be conceptually and also practically separable into at least two parts: (a) the definition or determination of the relative interpoint distances on the scale; and (b) the assignment of a system of numerical values to the benchmarks on the scale. Some of the methods that have been described here accomplish both of these purposes at once. These include, among others, the linear scale with preassigned mean and standard deviation, the percentile-derived linear scale, and the area transformation to the McCall T-scale or to stanines. In the case of the linear conversions to the scale, the assumption is implicit that the psychological distances between successive raw scores are equal, since the linear transformation does nothing to change the relative sizes of these distances; distances between scaled scores corresponding to successive raw scores are always equal in a linear transformation of raw scores. The process of transforming scores is intended only to change the number system. In the case of the area transformations—i.e. the transformation of the distribution to a normal curve or to a distribution of some other desired shape—

not only does the scaling procedure change the number system, but at the same time it also redefines the unit separations (except, of course, in those instances where the raw score distribution already conforms to the desired shape). However, these two processes can be carried out separately and independently. It is possible in a *first step* to define the scale separations in accordance, for example, with the procedure followed by Tucker or with the procedure followed by Flanagan, and in a *separate step* to define the system of numbers in which the test scores are to be expressed. Since it would be desired to retain the scale separations that were determined in the first step, the transformation to scaled score numbers necessarily would have to be linear, either normative (by defining the values of the mean and standard deviations or by defining the values of two percentiles) or non-normative (by defining the values of two "absolute" standards of performance or by otherwise defining arbitrarily the values of two benchmarks on the scale).

It may be useful to observe that additional distinctions may be made between the various types of scales that have been described here. For example, there are *distributive* and *nondistributive* scales, that is to say, scales based on the performance of groups of individuals and scales otherwise defined. Some of the distributive scales are *normative*, in the sense that they are based on samples of examinees systematically drawn from clearly defined populations. Others are *arbitrary*, in the sense that they are based on conveniently available groups of examinees for whom the test is appropriate but not on the results of a systematic sampling effort. By way of illustration, the College Board scale, based on the performance of the 10,654 examinees who took the Scholastic Aptitude Test in April 1941, is just such an *arbitrary distributive scale*. It is derived from a linear transformation of the raw score mean and standard deviation of an available and appropriate, and reasonably typical, group of examinees. These examinees represent a homogeneous group in the sense that they chose to take the Scholastic Aptitude Test for admission to one or more of the colleges requiring the test of their applicants. However, beyond that restricted definition, the group has no normative meaning and little if any normative usefulness. Normative comparisons are made, as they are required, against specific norms groups for whom data are collected to answer specific questions. *Nondistributive scales* are scales that are independent of the characteristics of any group of individuals. Examples of such scales are the linear derived scale, which depends on the definition of a set of standards for honors and passing, the Tucker proficiency scale, the Guttman scale, and the scale resulting from the linear transformation of a pair of arbitrarily chosen raw scores to a pair of arbitrarily chosen scaled scores.

The point also should be made, as it was earlier in this section, that the term *normative* itself has at least two separate meanings. In the sense in which it is used in this chapter, it has a statistical meaning; it refers to the actual performance of well-defined and understood groups of individuals who are used for reference, comparison, and evaluation of test scores. In this sense it refers to *performance as it exists*. In another sense the term normative refers to *standards* or *goals* of performance. The method of scaling that depends on the judgment of passing or honors is normative in that sense.

In general, it would appear that the long-term value of a test and the scale on which its scores are expressed will depend more on the measurement qualities built into the test (and consequently into the scale) and on the nature of the psychological domain from which the test items are sampled, than on any normative properties which might be embodied in the scale and be appropriate in the short term. To define the interpoint distances for a test scale after the fact, in terms of a defined group and distribution form but without regard for the psychometric properties of the test, cannot help but appear to be insufficient and, moreover, to depend on arbitrary and adventitious choice. Although it may be convenient at first to have normative information inherent in the scale, the obsolescent nature of normative data, resulting from changes in the composition of the population and/or from changes in the educational

programs, soon reflects itself in a disagreement between the current norms and the existing scale (i.e. the old norms) and dramatizes the lack of fundamental and lasting significance in the original scale. Application of the Tucker-Rasch type of model, on the other hand, would permit the specification of test construction methods in order to satisfy certain desirable psychometric properties and would make possible a more general system of scale separations that would be invariant with respect to any norms population.

NORMS: INTERPRETIVE DATA

As was pointed out earlier in this chapter, it is frequently the practice to incorporate normative meaning into the definition of a scale. In the preceding section, scales of this type (as well as scales not based on normative groups and therefore without normative meaning) were discussed, but only as they related directly to the matters of scale definition. In the present section, the issue of norms is central; matters relating to scales are introduced only as they bear on the problem of norms.

By now it has become almost axiomatic that raw scores on a test yield no meaning unless they are accompanied by relevant supplementary data that will place the score in an appropriate interpretive context. These data take a number of forms. Some of them are solely descriptive of the test itself and include such matters as the number of items in the test, its timing and consequent speededness, its reliability and standard error of measurement, its statistical validity, the intercorrelations among its parts, and, if the scores are not raw scores but are reported on a derived scale, the nature of that scale. Such information makes it possible to evaluate the general usefulness of the test. Other kinds of interpretive data permit the evaluation of the level of score earned by a student. These data also take a number of forms. When they represent descriptive statistics that are compiled to permit the comparison of a particular score (or mean) with the scores (or means) earned by the members (or groups of members) of some defined population, the data are referred to as *norms*. Typically, norms take the form of a percentile rank distribution that makes it possible to determine an individual's *relative standing* within the defined population so that an interpretive statement such as the following may be made: Douglas is at the 98th percentile in verbal ability and at the 92nd percentile in mathematical ability in comparison with all high school seniors. Other kinds of norms, also descriptive of relative standing, are those that are reported in a manner intended to convey more concrete meaning, e.g. those that equate test score to age or to grade level. Norms of this type permit statements such as: Carolyn has a mental age of 11 years and 3 months on the Stanford-Binet and a grade equivalent of 6.7 on the Vocabulary Test of the Iowa Tests of Basic Skills.

In general, there are two kinds of meaning that have been attached to the term *norms*. One of these is associated with notions of acceptable, desired, or required *standards* or *clinical ideals*. Thus it may be said that Mr. Jones is 15 pounds overweight, meaning that he is 15 pounds heavier than *he should be*. The determination of what he should be may have been made previously on some independent basis, related to medical or athletic considerations, to the work that Mr. Jones does or is applying to do, or to some other consideration. The other kind of meaning of the term *norms*, which may lead to quite different interpretations of the same performance, is the *statistical* meaning and is the one in terms of which educational and psychological measurements are most often interpreted. Thus a test performance is said to be high or low nearly always in relation to a defined group of other individuals and only rarely in terms of a previously set standard. The fact that the two kinds of "normative" interpretations can be quite different may be illustrated by noting that the same Mr. Jones who may be clinically overweight by 15 pounds may be 10 pounds underweight when compared with other men of the same age, height, and morphological structure. Clearly, then, the comparison group is also clinically overweight, even more so than Mr. Jones. The possibility of confusion between norms as representing *achievement as it exists* and norms as representing *standards to be*

achieved has already been noted. It is possible for example, as Lindquist and Hieronymus (1964) have observed, that an elementary school may give more adequate attention to the study of arithmetic than to map-reading skills and that the development of skill in map reading may be generally neglected in all schools, even in those schools where the students earn relatively high scores in map reading. In a school, then, whose average is below the norm in arithmetic and above the norm in map reading, the need for better instruction may, nevertheless, be greater in map reading than in arithmetic. Clearly, what constitutes satisfactory performance, or what is an acceptable standard, can only be determined subjectively by the school in terms of its own objectives and emphases and in terms of what may reasonably be expected of its students.

Statistical normative data may be said to satisfy more than one function. By presenting frequency distributions and other associated descriptive statistics for samples of well-defined and well-known populations of individuals, the publisher of the test makes it possible to develop a familiarity with the scale for the test. Normative data also make it possible to acquire an understanding of the dimensions in which major subgroups of the population differ and the degree to which the variables of the test are associated with classifications of the population. Finally, norms make it possible to assess the level of performance of an individual or a group and to use that assessment as a basis for decision and action.

Conrad (1950) and Schrader (1960) have both outlined certain generalizations that are appropriate to the construction of norms. The following are essentially restatements of their generalizations:

1. The characteristic measured by the test must permit the ordering of individuals along a transitive asymmetric continuum from low to high, i.e. the scale must be ordinal, at least.

2. The test must represent a reasonable operational definition of the characteristic under consideration, so that all tests that are intended to measure that characteristic will yield similar orderings of the same individuals.

3. The test must provide an evaluation of the same psychological characteristic throughout its range of scores.

4. The group (or groups) on which descriptive statistics are based should be appropriate to the test and to the purpose for which the test was designed and intended. This is a matter that will bear particular emphasis, since a norms population is meaningful and therefore useful *only* to the extent that it has been defined carefully. In some instances, as in the case of achievement tests in specific subject areas which are not uniformly offered or taught in precisely the same way, the problem of defining the norms population is not easy. A population must be chosen for which not only the subject of the test but the test itself is appropriate; and *appropriateness* is itself a concept that is frequently hard to define and keep distinct from the concept of *difficulty*.

5. Finally, data should be made available for as many distinct norms populations as there are populations with which it is useful for an individual or a group to be compared. One might add to these a sixth point, namely that the items for the test itself should have been selected on the basis of data for samples drawn from the population for which the test is intended, that is the group or groups for which norms will be given.

In addition, the population (or populations) defined and chosen as the basis for a set of norms should be homogeneous, in the sense that the individuals are all clearly members of it, and, in the case of educational tests, logical or even actual competitors for the same goals or rewards (e.g. accepted and enrolled freshmen in colleges of engineering). Similar considerations, incidentally, apply to the *use* of norms. The choice of the appropriate group with which to compare an individual should be made on the basis that it is useful and reasonable for the individual to be compared with its members. Obviously, because of differences that exist from group to group, a given individual may have as many different percentile ranks as there are groups with which he is compared. Thus, while his score on a test may be regarded as the *measurement* of his level of talent and is represented by a single fixed number (except, of course, for errors of measurement), his percentile rank is not fixed but represents an *evaluation* of his talent and will naturally vary depending on the normative group with which he is being compared. Therefore, it behooves the user, when he wishes to evaluate an individual's performance, to choose the normative groups with care and with an awareness and understanding of the differences among them.

Also, it is plain that the size of the norms group, in terms of both the number of schools and the number of students, and the design of the sampling procedure must be carefully worked out in order to maximize the precision of the norms and to minimize their bias.

Finally, the manner in which norms are presented should follow from the purpose or use for which the norms are intended. A number o different types of normative data are discussed later in this section of the present chapter; for the present it will be sufficient to say that norms are most commonly presented in the form of percentile (sometimes referred to as mid-percentile) ranks. The percentile rank for each score is calculated quite simply by counting up the total number of examinees scoring below the score interval in question, adding to that number half the number in the interval, and dividing by the total number of examinees.

Types of Norms

National norms

The most general and most commonly used type of norms is the *national norms*, appropriate to the educational and age level (or levels) for which the test is constructed. One of the problems in defining the national norms group arises from the large number, variety, and complexity of the characteristics of students, as well as of schools and communities, that are correlated with and relevant to test scores. The variables that are associated with the characteristics of students include educational level, age, sex, race, present or intended field of study, socioeconomic level of parents (educational, occupational, and economic determinations), and sometimes, for achievement test norms, the aptitude test scores of the students. The variables that are associated with the school may include size of school, type of support (public, independent, and religious), pupil-teacher ratio, per pupil expenditure, curricular emphasis, and proportion of students who are college bound. Beyond this, the significant variables include region (for example South versus non-South), type of community (i.e. rural-urban-suburban, or size of geographical area served by the school, or population density), socioeconomic level of the community, presence or absence of—or size of—a community library, etc. Davenport and Remmers (1950) made a study of sociological and economic characteristics by state and found a multiple correlation of about .96 with mean scores on qualifying tests for World War II A-12 and V-12 college training programs. R. L. Thorndike (1951) and Mollenkopf (1956) conducted similar studies at the community level and found much lower multiple correlations, ranging from about .45 to about .65. Thorndike offered some hypotheses to explain the differences between his results and those found by Remmers and Davenport, but in any case it is clear that community variables represent an important set of factors to consider in the construction of norms. To a limited extent it is possible to stratify on these variables, that is to say, to define homogeneous categories or strata on the variables and to sample appropriately within the categories. Occasionally, when the categories are sufficiently distinct and also meaningful to the user it may be helpful to provide *differentiated norms* separately by category. Thus norms are sometimes available separately by region, by sex, by type of school support, by type of community (urban-rural), and, of course, by educational level.

Schrader (1960) has pointed out that national norms have the distinct advantage of being simple, definite, and unique. National norms also have the advantage that, to the extent that publishers succeed in providing truly precise and unbiased national norms, it is possible to achieve score comparability across the tests of different publishers. On the other hand, the availability of a single norms table tends to obscure the fact that a percentile rank

is not unique but represents only one of many possible evaluations of a test score. Furthermore, national norms may frequently be too general to permit specific action. Clearly, the more specific and, of course, the more relevant the norms group, the easier it is to make appropriate decisions based on test scores. Ideally, there should be as many norms tables as there are types of decisions to be made. However, as valuable as they may be for detailed decisions, one of the problems of providing many sets of differentiated norms (in addition to the substantial costs involved) is that the user is frequently confused by the wealth of information available to him and yearns for the simplicity of a single norms table.

Local norms

Although it is unquestionably the responsibility of the test publisher to make available the kinds of norms that are appropriate for the uses he claims for his test, in many instances the most useful kind of norms are the *local norms* collected by the user himself and based on students enrolled in his own institution. These norms have the advantage of homogeneity, since the students included in the norms all come from the same educational and social milieu and constitute a group with which the test user has first-hand knowledge and familiarity. Further homogeneity may be effected by separating the total group into finer subgroups that differ from one another in important and relevant respects.

Local norms are especially valuable when they are collected in a way that will permit the formation of particular decisions, for example, in the identification of students who would benefit from special instruction or in separating a total class into homogeneous subgroups for whom the instructional pace can be more clearly defined. The data that help to make such decisions are those that relate one set of scores to another, as in local studies of growth; or those that relate aptitude test scores to achievement, as in the construction of expectancy tables (described below); or those that relate test scores to individual or group characteristics, as in the preparation of *differentiated local norms*, for example by sex, by curriculum, or by intended major field of study.

Age and grade equivalents

In general, there are two kinds of normative, or reference group, comparisons (Lindquist & Hieronymus, 1964). One kind of comparison makes use of a *single* reference group and describes the standing of an individual's score in relation to the distribution of scores for that group. This type of reference is exemplified by the percentile distributions mentioned above and also by the normative scales described in the previous section on scaling. The second kind of comparison makes use of the mean scores on a *series* of reference groups and essentially identifies the group whose mean score is most nearly like the score under consideration. This approach is exemplified by *grade equivalents*, which are appropriate for subject-matter achievement tests highly dependent on the curriculum and on the grade in which the subject is taught. It is also exemplified by *age equivalents*, which appear to be more appropriate for such measures as general aptitude and intelligence which are less highly dependent on the curriculum.

The principal limitations of age and grade equivalents are those that have already been discussed in the previous section on scaling (pp. 521–22). Most of these limitations result from: (*a*) the fact that the equivalents are intended to represent an "equating" of age or grade level with performance on a test with which the age or grade level is imperfectly correlated; and (*b*) the fact that age or grade level is *differently* correlated with different subject-matter tests. The imperfect correlation between age or grade and test performance leads to a number of anomalies, ambiguities, and inconsistencies that impair the usefulness of the age or grade equivalents. This is unfortunate because, except for these defects, "equivalents" (which, it should now be clear, are *not* equivalents at all) appear otherwise to have the ideal characteristics of interpretive data— clarity, definiteness, and direct meaning. Additional difficulties with these equivalents arise from the fact that they can lead to absurd con-

clusions, for example: John has a grade equivalent of 6.3 in arithmetic skills when, in fact, John is only in third grade and has never been exposed to the arithmetic skills normally taught in sixth grade. Somewhat related to this kind of absurdity is the problem of assigning a mental age to a child for a level of performance that—because the curve of age versus performance flattens out in midadolescence—is not average at *any* age.

Another factor that contributes to the confusion surrounding these equivalents, particularly grade equivalents, is the variation from one community to another and even more, from one period of time to another, in the customs regarding the promotion of children through the grades. When promotion is based primarily on achievement, as it was in the earlier part of the twentieth century, the correlation between performance and grade level tends to be higher. When promotion is based primarily on age, the correlation between performance and grade level is lower. Grade equivalents derived under these two sets of conditions are not comparable (Gulliksen, 1950, p. 291).

Norms by age and grade

A kind of normative data that makes use of the relationship between test performance and age (or grade), but avoids many of the problems associated with the equivalents, is the *age* or *grade norms*. These data are essentially nationally representative percentile rank distributions, differentiated by age or grade. Instead of age or grade *equivalents*, they yield the usual kind of percentile rank that describes the person's relative standing in relation to other individuals who are of the same age or in the same grade. Unlike the equivalents, they make clear to the user just what the dispersion is within each age or grade group (that is, error of estimate in the bivariate plot of performance vs. age or grade), what the variation in dispersion is from age to age or grade to grade, and how the test score changes as a function of age or grade. Moreover, they do not permit the logically impossible statement that an individual stands at a level of development for which he has had no actual experiences. At the same time it should be pointed out that, like all norms for educational and psychological tests, changes in educational philosophies and customs will render norms obsolete. Norms, including age and grade norms, collected at some prior time when the curricular emphases and methods of instruction were different from what they are today are simply not comparable with norms collected under present-day conditions.

It is interesting to note that the substitution of age and grade *norms* for age and grade *equivalents* effectively separates the function of norms from that of scales. Thus it is possible to develop a metric for a system of test forms and, entirely independently, to develop a collection of different kinds of norms—differentiated, for example, by grade, by region, by sex, by type of community, etc.—without committing the scale to any one of these sets of norms. The scale remains constant so long as the test is appropriate and relevant to the times. The norms, on the other hand, are free to develop and change as necessary to provide the particular interpretive information required at the time.

As has been pointed out, policies and practices regarding promotion have a direct bearing on the manner in which norms are prepared. Because of the custom, prevalent in the early 1900s, of promoting children to a higher grade only if their achievement warranted, it was typical for achievement test scores to show a higher correlation with grade level than they do today. It was also typical for the distribution of age for children in the same grade to be highly dispersed and positively skewed. In order to standardize the population within grade and at the same time to make it more homogeneous, some test constructors suggested the development of *modal age norms*, that is to say, grade norms for children of approximately the same age. While this procedure certainly helped to clarify and standardize the norms considerably, one of the problems associated with it was that the actual modal age group varied from one community to another, depending on local practice with respect to age at school entrance and also depending on local policies with respect to promotion. However, this problem, it is

fair to say, was equally characteristic of norms to which the modal age concept and technique were not applied at all. Thus, while it may have been possible to collect data nationally on which to develop a system of modal ages in grades, it was quite possible that the modal age in grade for a given community would differ from the national norm to a degree that would affect the usefulness of the test norms in that community.[8] One method of developing modal-age-in-grade norms was the system of *ridge route norms* developed by Kelley (1940), which involved taking the 12-month range in each grade that showed the heaviest concentration of ages and considering this age range as the modal age group for that grade.

The effect of basing grade norms on such modal age groups was to free them to some extent of the influence of the local practices of retardation and acceleration, to move in the direction of greater homogeneity and precision, and to produce a modal age group for each successive grade level that was usually one year older than for the previous grade. An additional effect, as would be expected in view of the typical positive skew in the distribution of ages within grade, was to produce a modal age population slightly above average in intelligence, since it included only those students who started at the modal age and were regularly promoted. In contrast, at most elementary grade levels, the unselected grade group was below average in intelligence because it included a number of older students who had been held back (Flanagan, 1951).

In general, the practice of constructing modal age norms is not as common today as it was 30 to 40 years ago. Because of the current philosophy (and practice) that elementary school children should, in general, be advanced

[8] This state of affairs, it is noted, applies to norms for educational tests generally, since such norms necessarily reflect educational practices. Therefore, to the extent that educational practices vary throughout the country, the problem remains that no single set of national norms would be entirely appropriate and applicable in a particular community. This condition would argue for the superiority of local norms that are assembled by the test user himself, who is familiar with and understands the local educational customs and can control his data accordingly.

to the next higher grade along with others of their own age, the distribution of age within grade is now more homogeneous and further selection is less necessary.

Some of the difficulties with *age norms* (as distinguished from grade norms) appear to arise from the fact that they are often developed for tests in specific curriculum, or subject-matter, areas for which grade norms are probably more appropriate. As a result, they present special difficulties. Flanagan (1951) has pointed out four problems that are associated with age norms. For one thing, they ignore grade level and implicitly assume that it is the chronological age, not the grade level in which instruction was received, that is more relevant to performance. This is an assumption that is probably not warranted for tests that measure specific educational outcomes, although it may be for tests of general intellectual functions that are not explicitly taken up in the classroom. Secondly, it is often difficult to select a reasonably representative age group, even by testing in several successive grades. Thirdly, age norms assume that growth is even and regular throughout the year and the same during the summer months as during the school year. This, too, is very likely unwarranted for tests that are based on explicit educational outcomes. Finally, they do not apply very well for subjects that are not taught on a continuing basis, since this would mean combining into one distribution data for students who *have* had and students who *have not* had instruction in a given subject-matter area.

Item norms

Sometimes a teacher who has administered a standardized test to her class will want to prepare an item analysis, essentially a percent-pass figure for each item, based on the responses of his students in order to determine the particular areas in the curriculum that need additional emphasis or elaboration. The identification and evaluation of the items or item areas that present difficulties have to be made, however, on the twin bases of *norms as a standard of performance* and *norms as existing performance*. For the first of these bases, the teacher (or, more generally, the community school system) must have in mind the inherent difficulty of the concepts tapped by the items, their relative importance in the total context of the subject, and some realistic conception of how easily these concepts can be grasped within the limitations of the abilities of the students in his class. For the second of the two bases, the norms as existing performance, he needs to have a similar set of item analysis data for a large group of students whose educational goals and whose personal and social characteristics match those of his own students, ideally a group of students assembled in the local community or in his own classes over a period of time. The use of the subjective *and* the statistical evaluation will enable him to identify the sources of weakness in his students that require additional attention.

School-mean norms

The norms that test publishers customarily have made available to test users are norms based on the performance of individuals for use in the evaluation of individuals. Although this kind of use is the purpose for which they are likely to be used most frequently, norms data based on the performance of individuals sometimes also are used by teachers and principals in evaluating *mean* performance of their students, as though the norms represented relative standing among other means. However, norms based on individuals are simply not appropriate for this purpose. The variability of scores for individuals is far greater than the variability of school means, in the ratio of about 2.0 or 2.5 to 1 (Lindquist, 1930; Lord, 1959). Therefore, a school whose students average higher than the mean of the norms will be underevaluated, since the average performance of those students will appear to be less superior than it actually is. Similarly, a school whose students average lower than the mean of the norms will be overevaluated, since their performance will appear to be less inferior than it actually is. In recent years, test publishers have taken to publishing *school-mean norms* to serve the purposes of the schools who want to compare their own means with the means of other schools (Cooperative SCAT Series II Handbook, 1967; Lindquist &

Hieronymus, 1964). Since the school is typically the unit of sampling in preparing test norms, it is a fairly simple matter for the publisher to construct a distribution and, from it, a table of percentile ranks based on the means themselves. An additional advantage of these school-mean norms is that they make clear to the user how large a sample of schools was actually used in the preparation of the norms, a piece of information which is particularly significant and informative in view of the manner in which norms samples are typically selected. Since the school is the unit of sampling, the stability of the norms depends heavily on the number of schools sampled as well as on the number of students. Like general norms, the value of school-mean norms can be greatly enhanced if they are further differentiated in terms of school and community variables. However, differentiated school-mean norms will be possible only when the total norms program is large enough, as in the case of a program of the size of Project Talent (Flanagan et al., 1962) in which 1,353 schools were sampled, to permit the presentation of sufficiently large subsamples of schools to be meaningful.

User-selected norms

Sometimes the norms that are provided by the publisher, differentiated by region, type of control, type of student body, etc., do not satisfy the various purposes for which a school or college wishes to examine data. Occasionally a college will wish to compare itself with other colleges which it regards as its competitors for the same applicants. For example, a college located near a metropolitan area where there are, say, six or seven colleges, all different in curriculum, type of control, selectivity, etc., may nevertheless be interested in knowing how its students compare with the other five or six. One highly selective liberal arts institution may wish to compare the scores of its applicants with the scores of applicants to another highly selective, but *technical*, institution in the same city or in the same state, perhaps because it feels that they are both drawing from essentially the same applicant pool. Sometimes these institutions manage to exchange their data individ-

ually and directly. Sometimes the test publisher can make available to the test user who requests it a combined distribution for the students enrolled at certain institutions specified by the user. It would be customary under these circumstances for the publisher to specify some minimum number of institutions for such a norms group in order to protect the anonymity of the individual institutions as well as to guard against excessive sampling errors, and also to specify the manner in which the students were selected to represent each institution. In general, since normative comparisons can have highly specific purposes, it also may be desirable to develop some systems of norms, in addition to those that are conventionally prepared today, that are based on sociometric clusters of institutions, i.e. institutions whose officials feel that they have something in common apart from the groupings that may be imposed on them by virtue of their formal characteristics.

Special-study norms

In general, norms are useful to the extent that the reference group is meaningful to the user. The national norms group is an obvious example of one such group. Differentiated norms, which further specify the strata within the national norms group, are also useful, perhaps more so than the national norm, for the same reason—they describe the behavior of homogeneous groups of individuals who have characteristics that are known and meaningful to the user. Local norms have the same characteristic; they are particularly well known and familiar to the user and are most useful to him for that reason. Similarly, a valid case can be made for norms that are *not* based on a random or representative sample of some defined population, but are based on *all*, or virtually all, the students in a well-known segment of the total population: e.g. all enrolled freshmen at the "Seven Sister" colleges; all ninth-grade students in the particular communities of Grosse Pointe, Shaker Heights, and Newton; all third-graders in the disadvantaged areas of Philadelphia. The special-study norms capitalize on the familiarity to test users of certain well-known groups of students and, in a manner of speaking, yield as much information about the sensitivity of the test and its ability to differentiate within both high- and low-scoring groups of students as it does about the groups themselves.

Norms that yield "direct meaning"

In order to make test scores meaningful various techniques have been sought, either to describe the scores in terms of the performance of general groups (as in the case of national norms), in terms of the performance of more specific groups (as in the case of differentiated norms), and in terms of highly familiar groups (as in the case of local, user-selected, and special-study norms). All of these types of norms, however, are statistical and provide meaning only through the definition or familiarity with the group used as a basis for the norms. Ebel (1962) has maintained that the essential meaning of a student's performance is lost when it is said that he performs better than some particular percentage of his peers, unless it also can be specified precisely just what it is that he can do better than they. Ebel therefore suggested that the test in question be given "content meaning." He proposed that the test be illustrated by a short—say, a 10-item—test of highly discriminating items representative of the test to be normed. The items in the short test would be reproduced in detail for the test user to examine, so he could become familiar with their content, and therefore—since they would be a miniature representation of the full test—indirectly familiar with the content of the full test. Then, for students earning each of certain selected scores on the full test, a distribution of scores would be made on the short test. The user would then observe the modal score on the short test for each of the selected scores on the full test, and with the knowledge he would then have of the content of the short representative test, he would have a better idea of the meaning of the different scores on the full test.

Another type of content meaning, suggested by Ebel, derives from the ability to reproduce the universe of content from which the test items are drawn. Thus, the meaning of a raw score on a vocabulary test is derived from the fact that the items of the test are drawn in a specified random fashion from a specified source.

A third type of normative data that yield direct meaning is one that is described under the heading *expectancy tables* (p. 547). For each of a series of specified scores on the test (say, here, an achievement test), a distribution of course grades is given. Then, just as they are able to do with the content norms just described, the test users can observe the modal course grade and the dispersion of grades corresponding to each of the available scores on the test. In this way, the test scores acquire meaning in terms that are already available and familiar to the test users—on the scale of course grades that they themselves customarily assign to students. If the grades are assigned independently of the test, these data, which would normally emerge from a validity study, can later serve as guidelines in defining ranges of scores that would be equivalent to, or would merit, a grade of A, B, C, etc. Thus validity data can be made useful in two ways: first, the data on grades lend meaning to the scores on the test; and second, after meaning is established and after the user develops familiarity with the test as an independent instrument, the process is frequently reversed and the data on the test can be used to help objectify and standardize the assignment of course grades.

Functional interpretations

Test scores can also be made meaningful in terms of the student's ability to perform tasks of known difficulty. This kind of score interpretation is one which would permit statements like: A student who earns a score of x on the French test can read a French newspaper with comprehension. A student who earns a score of y on the mathematics test can solve problems in differential equations. A student who earns a score of z on the economics test understands the principle of marginal utility. The value of this kind of interpretation is that it appears to describe test performance in *absolute* and familiar terms that are easily transmitted and understood. However, like other types of score interpretation that appear to yield direct and immediate meaning, these functional descriptions are not quite so simple and clear-cut as they may seem. These descriptions imply, for example, that knowledge and understanding (e.g. of marginal utility), or ability and proficiency (to read French with comprehension or to solve differential equations), can be complete and absolute and can be described at a single standard or level of excellence. The use of these functional descriptions in the manner described fails to recognize that there are many degrees of ability to perform a real-life task. (The principle of marginal utility, for example, can be "understood" at many levels of sophistication.) These descriptions also fail to recognize the differences in difficulty that are inherent even in a task that appears as common and familiar as the task of "reading a newspaper." Clearly, there are many kinds of newspapers with many kinds of literary styles, each one representing a different kind and level of difficulty. There are also differences in difficulty between one type of written material and another, even within the same newspaper.

Although the interpretation of test scores by means of functional descriptions is by no means a straightforward, uncomplicated task, it is a way that merits additional study. Very likely it would involve a psychophysical scaling of various levels of accomplishment of tasks that are *apparently* familiar to the test user and the formation of a distribution of scale values for these tasks for selected scores on the test—much in the way that has already been described for the miniature test proposed by Ebel and for the course grades described in the preceding section.

Quality ratings

In a manner similar to that described for the short test, the course grades, and the functional descriptions, distributions of test scores can be made for each of a series of quality ratings that are customarily given to the students by the test users, ratings such as outstanding, excellent, good, fair, and poor or for a series of administrative judgments and courses of action like those implied by the descriptions high honors,

honors, pass, and fail. As before, the value of referring the test scores to these ratings lies in the assumption that the ratings are familiar and meaningful to the user, and reasonably reliable. If these conditions do not hold, then the test scores will fail to acquire the desired meaning, or will fail to acquire stable meaning, or both.

It may bear repetition that while the various kinds of ratings described here will help initially to bestow meaning on the scores, it is almost inevitable that as the test in its various alternate forms continues to be used, the metric for the system will gradually acquire its own meaning to a point where the role of the test and the role of the ratings are reversed and the *test* becomes the instrument to bestow meaning and stability on the *ratings*.

In each of the "direct meaning" types of score interpretation there is necessarily a *bivariate distribution* or *scatterplot* of the test score versus the rating (or versus the miniature test). Therefore, as would be true of any scatterplot, and as was also true of age versus performance and grade level versus performance, there is not *one* regression but *two*. In the preceding discussions the test score was uniformly taken as the independent variable, and the evaluations that resulted were the average scores on the "meaningful" variable (the miniature test, or the course grades, functional descriptions, or judgments and ratings) for selected scores on the test to be normed. But as in the case of age and grade versus test score, the regression could just as easily have gone in the other direction. The evaluations might have resulted in the average *test score* for each score on the "meaningful" variable. The fact that the interpretations are not unique would argue for presenting them in more than one way. For example, the fact that two regressions exist is evidence, of course, that the correlation between the "meaningful" variable and the test score is not a perfect one. This is so largely because the "meanings" themselves are likely to be highly unreliable and variable. The same consideration applies to the miniature test which, it is noted, would very likely be much less reliable than the very test for which it is being used as a criterion of meaning. This is not to say that such evaluations are not useful. However, as Ebel himself has suggested (1962), they are most informative if, in addition to the modal values on the "meaningful" variable for each array of test score, the entire scatterplot is given. In this way, the user can see directly what the degree of relationship is between the test score and the criterion.

One way out of the dilemma of the regression lines is to develop a line of comparability[9] between the two variables by the equipercentile method, or by an explicitly linear method if the results of the equipercentile equating turned out to be essentially linear. This type of procedure would yield ranges of scores corresponding to course grades of A, B, C, etc., to quality designations of outstanding, excellent, good, etc., for example, or to scores on a short test. These ranges would have the advantage of not depending on the direction of regression. However, as described in the paragraph that follows, these ranges of scores will not necessarily be unique with respect to the set of data and might therefore have to be determined anew for each set of data.

It would be expected, particularly in the case of the course grades and in the case of the judgments of quality and administrative action, that there would be some real and systematic differences in the regression system between one group and another, say, between one college and another. Obviously, the demands of quality and the criteria by which quality is judged will be quite different at a highly selective institution than at a community college whose purpose it is to provide educational opportunities for all secondary school graduates who apply, irrespective of ability level. For that reason, the "meaning" that emerges from a study of the relationship of test scores and judgments will not be general but will differ, depending on the group of individuals who make the judgments of quality and also depending on the group for whom the judgments are made. For this reason determinations of "meaning" have to be made locally and applied locally.

[9] Described in the section on equating and calibration and in the section on comparable scores.

Additional ways of making scores meaningful could include procedures for constructing some of the nonnormative scales described in the scaling section of this chapter. Scores on the test could be attached to various levels of accomplishment by means of the judgment of experts who would be asked for their estimate of the minimum score that they feel would permit the designation of passing, honors, or high honors, or the designation of outstanding, excellent, good, etc. As indicated above, these techniques might well serve initially to give the test meaning but might later come to serve the opposite role, of giving the judgments themselves more rigor and precision.

Score differences

Although the most common types of norms are those that have already been discussed, there are other types of norms or, more generally, other types of interpretive data for tests. Some of the particularly interesting, and at the same time, troubling and difficult kinds of interpretive data are those that deal with score differences. Two such kinds of data—*growth* data and *over- and underachievement* data—are discussed here, not necessarily because they have originated in the same psychological context, but because they have many of the same methodological problems in common.

Growth— Although the measurement of status is indispensable for most of the purposes for which tests are used, it is also frequently important to make an assessment of growth. Considered in their simplest terms, growth measures involve the determination of status at the beginning and again at the end of the period of time in question. However, certain fundamental requirements must be satisfied before a determination of growth can be made. First of all, it is self-evident that the tests given at the beginning and end of the period must clearly be measures of the same function; otherwise, growth measurement is not possible. Secondly, the two tests (or better, the two test forms) must be expressed in the same units; that is to say, the test scores must be equated before the observation can be made that change has taken place.

If not, then it will be possible to make the rather awkward observation that an individual, or indeed the average for an entire group of individuals, has dropped from the first to the second occasion when, in fact, everyone has improved his performance. This can easily happen if the second form is noticeably more difficult than the first. Even if the forms appear to have been equated, the careful investigator will do well to protect his data from the sampling errors of equating—which exist, of course, as they do in any statistical process—by dividing his total group into two random halves and administering the forms in the order X-Y to one half and in the order Y-X to the other half. There is an additional problem. Unlike physical measurement, where the effect is frequently either negligible or nonexistent, the very act of administering an educational or psychological test often produces a measurable change in the individual. Therefore a third requirement is that some careful controls need to be instituted to distinguish *growth*—which would be defined as an increment in score associated with the passage of time—from *practice*—which may be defined as an increment resulting solely from previous exposure to the test (that is, when little or no time has elapsed since the first testing, except as necessary to overcome the possible effects of, say, fatigue or boredom).[10]

One highly disturbing characteristic of score changes is their extremely low reliability (see pp. 383–92). This may be explained by saying that the error of measurement of a score difference is essentially the *sum* of the errors of measurement of the two scores that go to make up that difference. (More precisely stated, the variance error of a difference between two independent scores is the sum of the variance errors of the component scores.) Since the

[10] There are many other problems involved in the measurement of educational growth, some of them clearly beyond the scope of the present chapter but thoroughly treated in a rapidly growing literature dealing with the theory and methodology of score change, for example, in articles written by Lord (1956; 1958), McNemar (1958), Manning and DuBois (1962), Thorndike (1966), Tucker et al. (1966), and in a series of articles edited by Harris (1963), where there is also an extensive bibliography on the problems of score change.

errors on two independent tests are uncorrelated, there is no third subtractive term in the variance error of the difference to attenuate it. On the other hand, the variance of a difference score is not twice the variance of the component scores but something considerably less. If the two component standard deviations are equal, then the variance of the difference equals $2s_x^2(1 - r_{xy})$, where x and y are the component (pretest and posttest) scores. Indeed, the higher the correlation between pretest and posttest scores, the smaller is the variance of the difference. Finally, when the reliability of the difference score is computed, the proportion of score variance attributable to error is quite substantial. For example, if the average reliability for the two tests is .90 and the correlation between them is .85, then, applying the formula given by Gulliksen (1950) for the reliability of the difference in scores on tests X and Y, when $s_x = s_y$,

$$r_{dd} = \frac{\bar{r}_{xx} - r_{xy}}{1 - r_{xy}},$$

the reliability of the difference score is .33. Clearly, it would be very unusual for the reliabilities of score differences between two parallel measures to be high, since the test-retest (alternate-form) correlation, r_{xy}, will generally be almost as high as the average reliability, $\bar{r}_{xx}$. In general, low reliabilities will occur unless, as Lord (1956) has pointed out, a very long period has intervened between the two testings or unless the trait measured is subject to rapid changes over time. Because of the highly unreliable nature of score differences, it is extremely easy to get a distorted picture of gain scores for individual score interpretation. (*Mean* score differences for groups of individuals, however, would be expected to be much more reliable, the more so for larger groups.) A preferred interpretation would involve making an estimate of the *true* gain, as derived by Lord, for example, rather than interpreting the observed gain literally.

Although the assessment of growth data is vital to the successful conduct of educational research, the problems of interpreting those data are sufficiently numerous and complex that investigations in this area should not be undertaken casually. Anyone seriously interested in conducting studies involving score changes would be well advised to make a thorough examination of the methodological literature first.

Over- and underachievement— It has always been hoped that the use of appropriate measures in education would make it possible to identify those students whose potentially good performance was being adversely affected by other factors not related to ability. Once these students were identified, it would be a logical next step to determine the nature of these other factors and to take steps to correct them.

In order to carry out this type of educational diagnosis and cure, it was thought necessary to administer two kinds of tests—a test of intelligence, or "innate" ability, and a test of achievement. The difference between an individual's scores on these two tests would then be taken as an indication of the extent to which his achievement in school was falling short of his ability. Today, educators are far less certain that there is a clear distinction between ability and achievement, just as they are less certain today of the distinction between nature and nurture, concepts that very likely led to the formulation of *ability* (or *aptitude*) and *achievement* as separate and separable entities. In any case, it has become clear that the conceptual distinction between measures of aptitude and measures of achievement is not always a sharp one, and so the distinction is often made operationally—for example achievement tests consist of items that are closely dependent on the material explicit in the curriculum (e.g. geography, trigonometry, American history, etc.); aptitude tests do not.

At the time when the distinction between ability (or aptitude or intelligence) and achievement was thought to be a real distinction—also at the time when test scores were more frequently expressed in the form of quotients than they are today—the degree of over- or underachievement exhibited by a student was sometimes described in terms of the AQ. However, this index is subject to all the problems already discussed in connection with age norms and age equivalents in addition to which is the fact that it is highly sensitive to methodological and sampling differences in the development of the educational age and mental age indexes. A variation of the AQ, suggested by Cureton (1937), was the ratio of the observed educational age to the educational age expected of that individual on the basis of his mental age. The expected educational age was defined as the average educational age for all individuals with a given mental age.

Often the concepts of over- and underachievement become semantically troublesome. While it was reasonable to conceive of an individual who was, so to speak, working below his potential, the question was sometimes asked, how is it possible to achieve *beyond* one's potential? The term *potential* seems to imply a physiological limit that, by definition, cannot be exceeded. Without attempting to resolve these logical difficulties, the research in this area more recently has simply addressed itself to the question of accounting for the discrepancy between *actual* and *predicted* achievement. In a review of the problems of design of studies of over- and underachievement, R. L. Thorndike (1963) observed that the whole problem of over- and underachievement may be thought of as essentially the problem of errors of prediction, and he offered these reasons for those errors:

1. Errors of measurement, or unreliability, both in the predictor and in the criterion.

2. Heterogeneity in the criterion variable; i.e. errors of prediction result from the intermingling of two or more subgroups, each evaluated on a continuum that is *ostensibly* the same for all subgroups but actually different. (Thorndike gave as an example of criterion heterogeneity the case of two groups of students, one coming from a college where the marking system is strict, the other coming from a college where the marking system is lenient. Errors of prediction arise from the fact that the As, Bs, Cs, etc., from the two colleges have been combined as though they have the same meaning. Either the criterion variable should be adjusted for its different meaning in the two

groups or the groups should be analyzed separately.)

3. Limited scope in the predictors, i.e. not all of the relevant determiners of the criterion variable have been studied. Thus, a person's performance may differ from expectation only because of the investigator's failure to establish the expectation appropriately.

4. The unpredictability of the events that intervene between prediction and outcome—uncontrollable variations in the quality and type of instruction, exposure to different kinds and amounts of remedial teaching, and patterns of educational, vocational, and personal guidance. Moreover, "chance" events occur in an individual's life that cannot be predicted and cannot be assessed even if they could be predicted.

5. Unmodifiable characteristics in the individual's nature or background—e.g. sex, race, socioeconomic status, parents' educational level; and the customs, attitudes, and opportunities for intellectual stimulation both at home and in the community.

6. Personal and educational factors that *are* subject to modification and manipulation. (As Thorndike has pointed out, these are the areas that represent the main focus of research concern in the work on over- and underachievement. These are the areas in which it is wished to identify the relevant factors and their interrelationships, if a modification in these factors will produce desired changes in the criterion.)

7. Finally, a source of error, which Thorndike discussed in a separate context, is "criterion contamination." Examples of criterion contamination are: (*a*) the "Hawthorne effect"—the improvement (or impairment) in the criterion measure simply as a result of the individual's awareness that he is a subject in the experiment; (*b*) direct "coaching" on the criterion test, or more generally, an effect on the specific criterion score, positive or negative, that is not a reflection of a general effect in the individual; (*c*) a bias in the subjective judgment of the individual who assigns a rating on the criterion measure. (*d*) An additional type of criterion contamination, distinct from the above three and not discussed by Thorndike, comes about when the criterion rating has been affected, consciously or unconsciously, by the rater's prior knowledge of the individual's score on the predictor. Sometimes, only the rater's evaluation of the criterion performance is influenced. Sometimes, when, for example, the rater is also the instructor, his knowledge of the predictor score may influence his *treatment* of the individual, and this in turn may influence the individual's actual criterion performance (an effect which has been referred to as the "self-fulfilling prophecy"). Both types of contamination nearly always will have the effect of producing a high correlation between predictor and criterion.

The methodological problems involved in the study of over- and underachievement are similar in many ways to the interpretation of score gains, since, like score gains, the discrepancy between criterion and predictor also represents a *difference score*. For example, like the score gain, the discrepancy between actual and predicted achievement is extremely unreliable. Also, the biasing effects of regression are just as prominent in studies of over- and underachievement as they are in studies of score gains. The selection of high and low groups on the predictor will *necessarily* result in the (fallacious) identification of "underachievers" and "overachievers," since individuals who are high scoring on the predictor are likely to be lower scoring on the criterion and since individuals who are low scoring on the predictor are likely to be higher scoring on the criterion. That is, the method of the study *coerces* the result of the study. For the same reason, the definition of over- and underachievement in terms of the difference between comparable scores on predictor and criterion will not work; high-scoring individuals on the predictor are generally lower scoring on the criterion and will therefore show small or negative differences; and low-scoring individuals on the predictor are generally higher scoring on the criterion and will therefore show large differences. The *only* kind of discrepancy score that is unbiased in this respect is the difference between the actual achievement for an individual and the achievement that is estimated for him on the basis of his standing on the predictor.

Sometimes the study of the relationship between predictor and criterion reveals the fact that there are different kinds of relationships for different subpopulations and that a moderator variable is required to account for the differences. For example, it is possible that while scores on the various scholastic aptitude tests that are currently in use are highly predictive of college success for white students, they are not so highly predictive for black students, or that the slope and intercept of the regression line are different for black and white students. Generally, however, when the same regression system applies equally well for all subgroups, it is common practice to operate on the discrepancy between actual and predicted achievement in an effort to reduce it.

Aside from the possible confusions that may result from the use of the terms overachievement and underachievement, it may be quite useful to examine the possibility that a student is performing as well, or perhaps better, than he would be expected to do on the basis of his performance on some predictor variable. For this purpose the discrepancy score between actual and expected performance is the score to use. However, because of the unreliability of such differences it would be advisable to consider as significantly over- or underachieving only those individuals whose discrepancies are clearly extreme. Similarly, also because of the unreliability of differences, it would be advisable to consider as those who have gained or lost significantly from pretest to posttest only students whose *true score* gains or losses are extreme.

Expectancy tables

A highly effective way to examine a student's record for the discrepancy between aptitude and achievement scores—indeed, between any two scores or evaluations—is to prepare expectancy tables of criterion scores for fixed values on the predictor variable. These tables are essentially scatterplots of predictor versus criterion, or, from another point of view, norms on the criterion variable, differentiated by score on the predictor variable. For each score or score interval on the predictor, a percentile rank distribution of scores on the criterion variable is formed, showing the percentage of cases

scoring at and below each chosen score on the criterion variable. Thus, as in all sets of differentiated norms, criterion performance is evaluated, but only among individuals who are homogeneous with respect to their performance on the predictor. Frequently the percentages given in expectancy tables are the proportions of individuals earning the same score on the predictor who earn a criterion score *as high or higher* than the score indicated.

Sometimes expectancy tables are prepared by generating, as an approximation, idealized normal distributions, one for each score interval on the predictor variable X, using actual data only to calculate the predicted criterion scores Y and the standard error of estimate. These values are taken, respectively, to be the means ($M_{y \cdot x}$) and the standard deviation ($s_{y \cdot x}$) of the Y arrays and are used in conjunction with tables of the normal ogive to determine the percentage of cases falling at and below (or at and above) each criterion score in each of the Y arrays of the table.

The construction of expectancy tables is very simple, constituting merely an extension of the usual norms distribution. However, their very simplicity makes them especially effective in displaying validity data and in making evaluations of over- and underachievement. Nevertheless, care should be exercised in these evaluations that the distinction between prediction and criterion is a clear one, separated either by an intervening period of time between the two determinations or by an unmistakable difference between the functions measured in the two determinations. If this condition is not met, if it is not clear which measure makes the promise and which yields the fulfillment, then the notion of achievement-relative-to-a-baseline is necessarily confused and meaningless.

Profile charts

Some of the comparisons that are made in the interpretations of an individual's (or a group's) test scores are the comparisons with an arbitrary but relevant *standard* of performance. Others, very likely the most common types of comparisons, are the normative or the *interindividual* comparisons, those that are made against the existing performance of a relevant reference group. Still others, like studies of growth and studies of over- and underachievement, involving the comparison of two or more scores obtained by a single individual, are the *ipsative* or *intraindividual* comparisons. Unlike *normative* comparisons, which are taken from a series of measurements, each administered to a member of a group and evaluated in terms of their departure from mean of the group, *ipsative* comparisons are taken from a series of measurements, all administered to one individual and evaluated in terms of their departure from the mean of the individual. Ipsative measurements—a term apparently originated by Cattell (1944)—are of value in the field of counseling and guidance where it is considered important to know, for example, which of various occupational careers an individual is most interested in pursuing or in which of various aptitude and achievement areas he shows relative strengths and weaknesses. Ipsative measurements also would be important in identifying those areas in which the individual needs special additional instruction or remedial help.

The device that is most often used for intraindividual comparisons is the *profile chart*. This is essentially a graphic representation of a system of comparable scores on a series of tests on which an individual's various scores are plotted. The construction of the comparable score scales requires that the series of tests be normed in advance, all on the basis of a single well-defined and *relevant* group of individuals, and converted to a scale with the same system of numbers and yielding the same distribution shape (frequently normal) for all tests. The evaluation of performance itself is in fact *both* normative *as well as* ipsative, since it involves a determination of the configuration of the individual's scores and a comparison of the scores relative to one another and, also, a comparison of the individual scores and the configuration of scores against those of the norms group.

One of the principal difficulties with the individual profile chart is the fact that it depends on the evaluation of differences among scores for an individual. Since the reliability of such score differences is ordinarily low, the usefulness of generalizations based on such differences is frequently questionable.

A second difficulty is that interpretations of profile charts depend on the particular method of scaling employed. If the tests are scaled in terms of grade equivalents, for example, an individual whose scores are equally high relative to the reference group in social studies and arithmetic may nevertheless have two different grade equivalents in this group—say, 8.4 in social studies but only 6.2 in arithmetic. This difference in grade equivalents is largely the result of the difference in the correlations of the two tests with grade level; the within-grade dispersion in social studies is likely to be larger than the within-grade dispersion in arithmetic.

The comparison of an individual's profile chart with the flat profile of a group on a series of tests is a normative comparison, analogous, in some sense, to the comparison of an individual's score with the distribution of scores for a norms group. There is, however, an important difference. A norms distribution displays the dispersion in the group and permits the placement of the individual in a particular rank position relative to that group. The profile chart, on the other hand, permits only the simple observation that the individual's profile is different from the group's profile (which is, by definition, a straight line connecting the 50th percentile points across all the tests). It does not permit an evaluation of the *degree* of departure of the individual's profile chart from the aggregation of profile charts for the members of the reference group. The flat profile of the reference group may indeed represent the profile of not a single member of the group and may be quite different even from the modal profile in the group. A more defensible approach to the problem of comparing profiles than the use of the profile chart would involve the definition of the individual's position as a point in *n*-dimensional space and the determination of the relative departure of that point from the *n*-dimensional centroid (see chapter 16).

Technical Problems in the Development of Norms

There are at least two principal sources of inaccuracy in a normative evaluation, say a percentile or percentile rank. One of these, the error of measurement, arises from the imprecision of the test and the testing process. The other arises from the inaccuracies of the sampling procedures and in the data used in developing the norms themselves. (Still other inaccuracies are inherent in the statistical procedures and in the data used in scaling and equating the scores.) Lord (1955b) has pointed out that the two sources of error may be considered to be additive, in the sense that the variance error in the determination of an individual's percentile rank involves the sum of the variance errors corresponding to the two sources of inaccuracy. However, the two kinds of error operate differently. Errors of measurement for individuals are a function of the testing process and may be thought of as independent of one another. As such they tend to cancel out for individuals when considered in the aggregate and vanish as the size of the group increases for which a normative evaluation is sought. The error in the norms, however, is a different matter. While this error also depends on the size of the group, it is the group used in *developing the norms* that determines the error, *not* the group for whom the evaluation is sought. Thus once the norms are determined, the error, which may have been considered random at the time of sample selection, now remains in the norms in the form of a bias and is transmitted *equally* to all evaluations of a given score, whether it is an individual's score or the mean score for a group even of a thousand individuals or more. In this sense, it behaves like the error of equating, discussed later in this chapter, which depends in part on the size of the sample *used* for determining the conversion equation. But once the error becomes part of the conversion equation, it remains fixed and permanent and independent of the size of the group for whom the mean score is converted to the scale for the other test. If the group used for developing the conversion is separate from the group used for norming, then the variance error of the normative evaluation of a converted score is the sum of the *three* sources of variances—the test, the norms, and the equating. The error in the evaluation is also, of course, a function of the *level* of the score, since each of the three types of error varies with score level.

Sampling

Cornell (1960)[11] has pointed out that sample statistics lack precision when: (*a*) the errors of random sampling are large, i.e. when there is a wide dispersion of the distribution of the sample statistic about the population parameter; (*b*) when there is a bias, e.g. when the mean of all such sample statistics and the parameter are not the same; and (*c*) when the observations themselves are inaccurate or incomplete. Although the sampling frame in general should be so designed as to minimize random errors and to avoid entirely systematic errors (bias), it is sometimes the better strategy to accept a small bias if by doing so it also is possible to reduce the random errors substantially. The essential measure of error is the sum of squared deviations about the parameter, and whichever procedure yields the smallest value for that sum is the procedure to follow.

Since the usefulness of decisions that are based on statistical data depends heavily on an accurate assessment of the error in the data, it is extremely important to develop a plan for the collection of the data for which the error is known or at least can be approximated. There are a number of samples for which the error is unknown:

1. A sample of convenience—one that happens to be easily available. Samples of convenience will almost certainly be biased. They will more often be taken from schools that are easily accessible by conventional modes of transportation, larger and therefore helpful in building up the size of the norms sample, better known and therefore more likely to be brought to mind, more innovative and progressive, more willing to try out new ideas (as in testing), more cooperative and willing to be known as "forward-looking" institutions that have participated in a "national survey" or "study" and therefore more easily available, and less likely to be embarrassed by the performance of their students. These characteris-

[11] The author wishes to acknowledge the valuable assistance provided by the outline and, in many instances, the particular phrasing used in Cornell's excellent overview of sampling. The following pages describing the various types of samples and sampling procedures borrow heavily from his treatment of this topic.

tics, needless to say, are associated with higher test scores.

2. A sample based on an outdated list or on a list that does not adequately cover the target population, for example, a list of secondary schools that includes only those under public control and not private and parochial schools.

3. A sample with a high proportion of non-response or nonparticipation.

4. A "pinpoint" or "representative-area" sample, for example, the purposive selection of individuals or groups or clusters of individuals (e.g. classes, schools, or communities) that are thought to be "typical."

5. A "quota" sample, in which the primary sampling unit—e.g. the state or region—is selected by an appropriate sampling plan, but in which the choice of the specific community or school is made by the test publisher's regional representative or salesman according to general guidelines that are defined for him in advance. For example, he may be instructed to choose two large urban schools, one suburban school, and one rural regional school in a defined region but will be permitted to choose the specific schools himself. The problem here, of course, is that, within the limits of his authority, he will very likely choose a sample of convenience.

6. A sample that is selected on the basis of expert opinion. For example, a number of educators, presumably knowledgeable in their field, assemble a list of schools that in their judgment represent the target population.

In all of these procedures there is likely to be a bias, either because the sampling frame itself is biased, because the participants are self-selected and by definition biased, or because conscious nonautomatic choices are likely to be made on the basis of insufficient knowledge or on the basis of conscious or unconscious predilection. Nor does the danger of bias exist only with respect to the mean. It is frequently overlooked that bias can and does exist with respect to variability. "Typical" samples, for example, are likely to have less variability than random samples.

Finally, there are samples that have subtle biases, sometimes because the sampling procedure itself is biased and therefore inappropriate, sometimes because the samples are drawn from biased populations. Samples that contain such biases are those that are dependent on occasionally implicit (and incorrect) assumptions, for example, that surname initials are uncorrelated with ability, that birthdates are equally frequent and also uncorrelated with ability, that telephone subscribers or owners of television sets are a random segment of the population, and so on.

Unlike the foregoing methods of selecting samples, there is a class of sampling procedures called *probability sampling*, which, if carried out properly, does permit the objective evaluation of error. The characteristics of probability sampling are: (*a*) the process of selecting the individuals or elements in the sample is not left to the judgment or convenience of the investigator but is automatic; (*b*) each individual (or primary element) in the sample has an equal, or at least *known*, probability of being selected in the sample; and (*c*) the weights used to compensate for disproportionate representation in the sample are derived from these probabilities and are used in the estimation of the population parameters.

There are various methods of selecting random samples. Most often, in large norms or sample survey projects, these methods are used not singly but in combination. The simplest method is the *unrestricted* or *simple random* sampling method, which involves the selection of a group of individuals of size N in such a way that each individual has the same probability of being selected, and every possible combination of N individuals has the same probability of being selected. One way to accomplish this is to assign to each of the individuals in the population a unique serial identification number and to select the individuals for the sample from a table of random numbers. When the population is much larger than the sample, as would be true of most norms projects, the individuals may be drawn from the population pool without replacement. Otherwise, either replacement is necessary—which would mean that the same individual could appear in the sample more than once—or care should be taken to use standard error formulas that are appropriate to selection from finite populations. While the unrestricted random sampling procedure is simplest conceptually, it is nearly always extremely difficult administratively and much more costly to execute than its precision warrants. In most instances, equivalent precision can be achieved much more economically by other methods of sampling.

Stratified random sample— A modification of the unrestricted random method which effectively introduces greater precision into the results is one that first divides the total population into relatively homogeneous *strata* on the basis of one or more variables that are correlated with the variable in question (i.e. test score). For example, it is not uncommon, in sampling for norms, to stratify on the basis of region, type of school (public, private, religious), and size of school. Once the strata are established, the sampling within strata is conducted by the method of simple random sampling. The allocation of sample sizes to the strata leads to a more stable estimate if the sampling units are allocated among strata in proportion to the total number of units in the strata. If the allocation of sampling units is far from optimum, then it is possible for the stratified sample to have a sampling variance even greater than that of a simple random sample of the same size. Generally speaking, efficiency in stratified sampling is achieved by taking proportionately larger samples in strata that are larger, more variable, and cheaper to sample.

Stratified sampling, which capitalizes on the relationship between certain variables and test score, tends to enhance the reliability or the precision of the norms. If the multiple correlation (R) of the stratification variables with test score is known for the unit of sampling— e.g. the school—then the variance error, $SE_{\bar{x}}^2$, of the mean of the norms group is approximately:

$$SE_{\bar{x}}^2 = \frac{s_{\bar{x}}^2}{k}(1 - R^2),$$

where k equals the number of schools in the norms sample and $s_{\bar{x}}^2$ is the variance of observed school means. Thus, if a particular level of precision is achieved by simple random sampling of k schools, then that same level of precision can be achieved with only $(1 - R^2)k$ schools if the stratified sampling method is employed. If R is about .55, as R. L. Thorndike (1951) and Mollenkopf (1956) found for community variables, then only 70 percent as many communities would have to be used with stratified sampling methods as would be necessary if the communities were sampled entirely at random from the population.

Systematic sampling— The first step in drawing a *systematic*, or *spaced*, *sample* of size m from a population of M elements is to divide the list of M elements into m successive blocks or subgroups of size c (where $c = M/m$) and, starting at a random element in the first block to select every c^{th} element. If the listing of the M elements in the population is random, then systematic sampling is essentially equivalent to simple random sampling. However, if the blocks are sufficiently homogeneous, i.e. if the variance within blocks is smaller than the variance between blocks, then systematic sampling is more precise than random sampling and resembles stratified sampling. For example, if the elements of the list are students and the students are arranged in order of test score, then a systematic sample automatically stratifies by test score. If the elements of the list are schools and the schools are grouped by geographical region, then a systematic sample automatically stratifies by region.

The principal advantage of the systematic sample is its simplicity, and, of course, the fact that, if the list is arranged in homogeneous categories with respect to a variable that correlates with test score, it will be a stratified sample. The danger in a systematic sample is that it may have unwittingly been drawn in phase with an unsuspected periodicity in the ordering of the population. To take an obvious example, if the population were a population of children and were ordered: boy, girl, boy, girl, etc., then a systematic sample of every c^{th} individual, where c were an even number, would result in a sample of individuals all of the same sex. To guard against this possibility it is advisable to construct a list of m random numbers and to select according to a *different* random number in each of the m blocks. If the blocks previously have been arranged in a stratified fashion, then this procedure will yield a strict stratified-random sample.

Cluster sampling— Very seldom, if ever, are norms samples selected with the individual student as the unit of sampling. To carry out such a selection, e.g. at one grade level in a city, it would be necessary to assemble a list of all the students at that grade level in the entire city and draw a random sample without regard to the school or the class within the school. The result of such a sampling effort would be that perhaps two students would be drawn from one class in a school, three from another class in that school, one perhaps from a class in a second school, none from other classes in that school, etc. Clearly, for reasons of administrative convenience and economy alone, it is far better to take a "natural" group, or *cluster*, of individuals, such as the school or the class within the school, as the unit of sampling. In addition, such selection would be less disruptive of the school's program and undoubtedly less disturbing to the students who are selected. Moreover, data collected for entire classes and schools would be more useful at a later time to both the students and the schools and would form a better basis for research.

For these reasons norms samples nearly always have been chosen with the school as the unit of sampling, a procedure that is quite proper and certainly reasonable under the circumstances. However, probably because of their failure to appreciate fully the significance of the fact that sampling error is a function of the method of random sampling, test publishers in the past have tended erroneously to estimate the standard error of their norms samples as though the students in their samples had been drawn individually and at random from the total student pool. It happened also, that by choosing the school as the unit and testing exhaustively in the school, as would be the preference of the school officials, it was easy for test publishers to build up the total sample size to what appeared to be quite respectable proportions. The result was that their assessment of the precision of their norms was deceptively high, and this encouraged them to continue to use an insufficient number of schools for norms in the belief that the reliability of the norms depended solely on the number of individuals tested.

The distinction between the two kinds of variance errors—based on students and based on schools—may be described as follows: As a general principle the variance error of the mean of the entire distribution of a norms sample is a function of the variance of the scores (or means of scores) earned by the units of sampling divided by the number of such units. Thus, when the individual student is used as the unit of sampling, the appropriate variance error of the overall mean is given as:

$$\text{SE}^2_{\bar{x}} = \frac{s^2_x}{\sum_i^k n_i} = \frac{s^2_x}{N}, \qquad [1]$$

where s^2_x is the variance of all the individual scores in the sample, k is the number of schools in the sample, and $\sum_i^k (n_i) = N$ is the sum of the number of individuals tested in each of the schools in the sample, i.e. the total number of individuals in the entire sample. On the other hand, when the school is used as the unit of sampling and there is no sampling of students within school, the appropriate variance error of the overall sample mean, assuming that all schools are of equal size, is given as:

$$\text{SE}^2_{\bar{x}} = \frac{s^2_{\bar{x}}}{k}, \qquad [2]$$

where, as before, $s^2_{\bar{x}}$ is the variance of observed school means. Now if the students in each school represented merely a random sample drawn from the entire pool of students, then (leaving aside the variations in school size) equations 1 and 2 would be equivalent. The fact is, however, that the students in each school do *not* represent a random sample of all students. There are marked individual differences among schools. Lord (1959) estimated that the standard deviation of school means is about four-tenths the size of the standard deviation of individual scores. This would represent a significant intraclass correlation and indicate that the school does indeed represent a homogeneous "cluster." Earlier Lindquist (1930) called attention to the same fact and argued strongly that because of the great variation in *school* achievement relative to the variability in achievement of individual students, the practice of emphasizing mere *size* of the norms sample was fallacious. When the school is used as the sampling unit, it is the number of *schools* as well as the number of *students* that determines the reliability of the norms. Lindquist (1966) also pointed out that the ratio of the variability among schools relative to the variability among students appears to be a function of the subject matter, with greater ratios associated with subject-matter areas in which the opportunity to learn what is tested is relatively restricted to the classroom.

To illustrate the fact that equations 1 and 2 give quite different results, it may be helpful to consider some fictitious but reasonable data and to observe the results of applying the two equations. Say that a norms administration has been conducted in a random sample of 256 schools ($k=256$) tested at the 12th-grade level, where the number of students (N_i) averages about 100. Assume that the test has been standardized on all 25,600 students and that the scores have been converted to a scale on which the standard deviation for all students combined is 10. Say further that Lord's estimate holds here and the standard deviation of school means is 4. According to equation 2, then, the appropriate standard error of the mean of the norms sample (ignoring the variation in school size) is $4/\sqrt{256}=.25$. If equation 1 had been used (inappropriately) here, the standard error of the mean would have been calculated as $10/\sqrt{25,600}$, or .0625, a standard error one-fourth as large as it should be. In order to achieve a standard error of .25 by random sampling of students, only $(10)^2/(0.25)^2$, or 1,600, students would have had to be tested instead of 25,600—one-sixteenth the actual number. The ratio of the numbers of students that

are required under the two methods of sampling to reach the same level of precision is known as the *efficiency* of simple random sampling of students relative to cluster sampling of schools. (It is understood, of course, that this is only *statistical* efficiency. In spite of the greater statistical efficiency of simple random sampling, it is generally more efficient from an administrative point of view to use cluster sampling for norms.)

There are additional distinctions and refinements, not only in the design of the sampling procedures but also in the assessment of the reliability of the norms. Equation 2, for example, is appropriate for cluster sampling when testing is exhaustive in each cluster and when all clusters (or schools) are of the same size. When the schools vary in size, as they inevitably do, then according to Lord (1959), the variance error of the mean of the norms, as given in equation 2 should be modified, as follows:

$$\mathrm{SE}_{\bar{x}}^2 = \frac{s_{\bar{x}}^2}{k}(1 + C_N^2).\qquad[3]$$

Equation 3 is a convenient approximation to the desired variance error in which $C_N = s_N/\bar{N}$ is the coefficient of variation of school size. Therefore, to use, for illustration, data collected by Mollenkopf (1956) in a sample of 426 10th grades: if s_N, the standard deviation of school size (i.e. the size of the 10th grade in a school) is 91 and $\bar{N}$, the mean of the school sizes, is 108, then $1+C_N^2=1.71$, adding 71 percent to the size of the variance error represented by equation 2. As a result of this modification it should be clear that if the variation in school sizes relative to mean size given in the illustration is typical, then *about 25 times as many cases would be necessary in exhaustive cluster sampling to achieve the same reliability of norms as would be achieved by simple random sampling.* One can then judge the extent to which the reliability of norms can be misrepresented by the simple but inappropriate use of the size of the total norms sample as a measure of the reliability.

Frequently it is convenient and desirable to do successive sampling, for example to sample schools as the primary unit and, once the schools have been selected, to sample students *within* schools. Such a plan would be called *two-stage* sampling. The variance error appropriate to two-stage sampling would contain two separate additive terms, each appropriate respectively to the two separate types of sampling. Sometimes the sampling is a multi-stage process. For example, the principal unit of sampling may be the community. Then schools may be sampled within community, classes within schools, and finally students within classes. Just as for two-stage sampling, there would be a separate additive error term in the formula for the variance error of the overall mean, each term identified with the variance error for the corresponding stage in the sampling process.

In general, two-stage sampling *at least* is required for most norming projects. It is appropriate, in fact highly useful, in reducing the excessive sampling errors that are characteristic of cluster sampling, when, for example, two or more tests are to be normed simultaneously for the same population. Under these circumstances, the appropriate procedure is to select the schools first and then, assuming that the time limits and oral instructions permit, to administer each of the tests to a random fraction of each class. The best practical procedure for accomplishing this is to package the test books for each of the, say five, tests in the order a, b, c, d, e, a, b, c, d, e, a, b, etc., and to distribute them in this way in each classroom, thus automatically drawing simultaneously five systematic random samples. (As cautioned above, care should be taken to avoid the possibility that the method of drawing this sample will be in phase with a periodicity in the seating arrangement in the classrooms.) The great advantage of this procedure over the procedure of selecting a different set of schools for norming each test is that it maximizes the number of schools—the significant factor in the error of cluster sampling—in each of the five norms samples. Moreover, since all five tests are normed on random samples, all drawn in the same way and all in precisely the same schools, the variation among samples attributable to differences among schools is eliminated. It should be pointed out, however, that this greater comparability highlights the need for taking special care that the sampling of schools be planned and conducted in such a way as to avoid bias; for any errors in the sampling here will be reflected in the norms for all the tests.

It is probably advisable for tests that are normed in two or more grades to be administered to the students (or to random samples of the students) in all such grades in all schools in the norms sample. Otherwise, if the sample of schools selected for each grade is independently drawn, then the progression of means in the population from each grade to the next will not be reflected in the sample data. Although rare, it will even be possible for students in the norms sample at a higher grade to earn a lower mean score than the students in the norms sample at a lower grade—purely as a result of random fluctuation—and this is more likely to happen if the grade-to-grade differences are small. While it is true, of course, that random selection of schools tends to give protection against such inversions, it often happens that the characteristics of the sample are so disturbed by the refusal of some schools to participate in the norms program that when the norms data finally are assembled the sample is no longer random as originally intended. In these circumstances, score inversions between grades can be the result. The procedure of testing the students in all the grades in all the schools sampled for norms will introduce a grade-to-grade correlation across schools, thereby reducing the standard error of the difference between grade means and consequently reducing the likelihood of an inversion in the relative order of the means in successive grades. For the same reason—to reduce the standard error of the difference between means of successive grades—it is advisable, in constructing norms for successive grades that necessarily cut across schools—norms for grades 4–12 for example—to test the entire succession of grades in each of the communities sampled, taking care to provide continuity by finding the feeder schools whenever possible for each of the schools at the higher grade levels.

In general, the purpose of the sampling procedure is to ensure that each individual in the population stands an equal chance of being selected for the norms sample. Three two-stage sampling procedures will be described to accomplish this. In each procedure the first stage will involve the selection of schools, and the second will involve the selection of students.

1. In the first method, schools are drawn at random from the total pool of schools, each school standing the same chance with each other school of being drawn for the sample. With this kind of sampling arrangement the distribution of school sizes, for example, will approximate the distribution of sizes in the population, and it is appropriate therefore to test the same fixed *proportion* of students in each school. If that proportion is 100 percent, then, of course, there is no error for sampling within schools and the variance error of this sampling procedure is the same as that given in equation 3. If the proportion drawn in each school is less that 100 percent (but the same in each school), then the variance error of the entire two-stage sampling process is given by the equation:

$$SE_{\bar{x}}^2 = \frac{1-f}{kf\overline{N}}\,\overline{S_x^2} + \frac{1}{k}\,(1 + C_N^2)s_{\bar{x}}^2, \quad [4]$$

where

$\overline{N}$ is the average school size,

f is the proportion of the students tested in each school, and

$\overline{S_x^2}$ is the arithmetic mean of the within-school variances for the norms population (Lord, 1959). Table 15.2, from Lord (1959) and based on Mollenkopf's (1956) data collected at grade 6 and, also, at grade 10, demonstrates how sampling within schools can produce economies in the numbers of students required for testing. For example, given a standard deviation of individual scores of 10, a standard deviation of school means of 4, a mean school size ($\overline{N}$) of 58, and a value of C_N (the coefficient of variation of school size) equal to .55, only *nine* percent of the number of students that would be required for exhaustive (100 percent) sampling within schools would be needed if a random sample of only *two* percent in each school were actually chosen for testing (grade 6 data). If $\overline{N} = 108$ and $C_N = .84$ and if only a random *one*

TABLE 15.2

Efficiency of Two-Stage Sampling Procedures for Sixth-Grade Data and for Tenth-Grade Data

	Subsampling Proportion* (f)	Number of Schools Needed in Sample (k)	Portion of Error Variance Attributable to First Stage of Sampling $\frac{1}{k}(1 + C_N^2)s_{\bar{x}}^2$	Portion of Error Variance Attributable to Second Stage of Sampling $\frac{1-f}{kf\overline{N}}\overline{S_x^2}$	Standard Error of Mean of Norms Distribution (Equation 4)	Expected Number of Examinees Tested ($kf\overline{N}$)	Ratio of Number of Examinees ($kf\overline{N}$) to Number Required with Usual Cluster-Sampling Method
6th Grade Data	1.00**	36.0	.579	.000	.76	2088	1.00
	.50	38.5	.541	.038	.76	1116	.53
	.25	43.5	.479	.100	.76	632	.30
	.10	58.5	.356	.223	.76	339	.16
	.05	83.5	.250	.329	.76	242	.12
	.02	158.5	.131	.448	.76	184	.09
10th Grade Data	1.00**	36.0	.758	.000	.87	3888	1.00
	.50	37.0	.738	.021	.87	1998	.51
	.25	39.1	.698	.060	.87	1056	.27
	.10	45.2	.604	.155	.87	488	.13
	.05	55.5	.492	.266	.87	300	.08
	.02	86.3	.316	.442	.87	186	.05
	.01	137.6	.198	.560	.87	149	.04

* The impossibility of fractional students is ignored.
** This row represents the usual type of simple cluster sampling.
Note: Reprinted from Lord, 1959, with permission of *Journal of Experimental Education*.

percent of the students in each school were tested, then the total number of students would need to be only *four* percent as many as would be required by norming procedures in which all the students are tested in each of the schools chosen for the norms (grade 10 data). It should be added, however, that while the numbers of students required for norms are shown in both illustrations to be dramatically reduced as a result of the sampling within schools, this saving is achieved at the expense of increasing the number of schools from which the students are drawn—in the first illustration by a factor of 4.4; in the second illustration by a factor of 3.8.

2. In the second procedure, schools are again drawn at random from the total population of schools, with each school standing the same chance of being selected. If a *fixed number* of students are selected from each school, instead of a fixed proportion, it would be necessary to weight the frequencies for the larger schools proportionately more heavily than for the smaller schools. The variance error of the mean of the norms for this norming procedure is given in the equation:

$$\mathrm{SE}_{\bar{x}}^2 = \frac{1}{nk}\left(1 + C_N^2 - \frac{n}{\overline{N}}\right)\overline{S}_x^2$$
$$+ \frac{1}{k}(1 + C_N^2)s_{\bar{x}}^2,$$

[5]

where *n* equals the fixed number of students tested in each school (Lord, 1959). Here too the economies of sampling within school are dramatic but not quite as dramatic as if the number tested within each school were proportionate to the size of the school.

3. In the two procedures discussed thus far each school has the same probability of being selected for the norms sample. In the third, the likelihood that a school would be chosen is proportional to the size of the school. Once the school is chosen, the number of students is held fixed; the same number of students is tested in each school, irrespective of its size. That this method of selection gives each student in the population the same probability

of being selected for the sample as every other student may be demonstrated by considering the joint probability of the two selection procedures. Under this plan of selecting schools each school has the probability N_i/N_t of being selected, where N_i is the number of students in the school and N_t is the number of students in the population. With a fixed number of students to be tested from each school, the probability that an individual student from a school will be tested is n/N_i. The product of these two probabilities, n/N_t, indicates that the likelihood that a particular student will be chosen is independent of the school he is attending and is the same for all students.

A practical and effective way of sampling schools in proportion to size may be described thus:

1. List the schools in the population (or if stratified sampling is being conducted, in the particular stratum of the population) in any convenient order and indicate the number of students in each school.

2. For each school determine a range of numbers: the lower of the two numbers in the range is obtained by summing the numbers of students in all the schools that precede it in the list and adding one; the higher of the two numbers is obtained by summing the numbers of students in all the schools that precede it in the list and adding the number of students in that school. That is, determine the cumulative enrollment figure for all schools preceding and including each listed school.

3. Choose *k* numbers (*k* equaling the number of schools to be selected) from a table of random numbers, no random number to be larger than the total number of students in the population.

4. For each random number identify the school with the range of numbers within which that random number falls. (If, in this process the school is identified twice, it should be drawn twice and appear twice in the sample of schools. For the second stage of sampling, then, it would be appropriate to draw two subsamples of students independently—i.e. with replacement—from the school.)

The variance error of the two-stage sampling

plan in which the probability that each school is selected for the sample is proportional to its size and in which the number of students selected from each school is fixed is given in the equation:

$$SE_{\bar{x}}^2 = \frac{1}{nk}\left(1 - \frac{n}{N}\right)\bar{S}_x^2 + \frac{1}{k}s_{\bar{x}}^2, \qquad [6]$$

in which it is assumed that school size is unrelated to school achievement and to within-school variance (Lord, 1959). If these assumptions can be satisfied, then the sampling error given by equation 6 is seen to be clearly smaller than that given by equation 5. However, if the assumptions underlying equation 6 are *not* satisfied—if the large schools generally have larger within-school variances or larger between-school variances than the small schools—then the sampling variance of equation 6 may turn out to be larger than that of either equation 4 or 5.

As was pointed out earlier in this section, it is advantageous, from the point of view of improving the precision of the sample, to stratify on the basis of variables that are related to test score. However, upon examination of equations 3, 4, and 5, it is clear that the variance error of the norms also can be reduced by reducing the variation in school size (that is by reducing the value of C_N). In other words, the error in the norms can be reduced by stratifying on school size, even though school size may be unrelated to test score. Once the schools are grouped into strata that are relatively homogeneous by size, sampling can be carried out independently in each stratum by any one of the three procedures already described, after which the frequencies for each of the strata would be appropriately weighted to approximate their representation in the population. From a purely intuitive point of view this procedure is eminently reasonable since it ensures that the relatively rare large schools will be adequately sampled. No such result is assured without stratification on size.

The variance error of the mean of a norms sample, drawn by stratifying the norms population on one or more dimensions, is given as:

$$SE_{\bar{x}}^2 = \frac{1}{\left(\sum_h K_h N_{i_h}\right)^2} \sum_h K_h^2 N_{i_h}^2$$

$$\cdot \left[\frac{1 - f_h}{k_h f_h N_{i_h}}\bar{S}_{x_h}^2 + \frac{1}{k_h}s_{\bar{x}_h}^2\right],$$

where K_h is the number of schools in stratum h in the population; k_h, N_{i_h}, f_h, S_{x_h}, and $s_{\bar{x}_h}$ are, respectively, the values of k, N_i, f, S_x, and $s_{\bar{x}}$ for stratum h. It is assumed in this equation that school size is constant within stratum and that the proportion of schools in each stratum used in the sample is small.

Although the present discussion of sampling procedures has been written as though the second stage of sampling normally involves the selection of students at random from each school, the practicalities of the real situation often militate against this. Administrative constraints in the schools below the college level may permit the random selection of *whole classes* within schools but not ordinarily the random selection of individual students. In schools that operate under the educational philosophy of homogeneous grouping, these classes represent *clusters* of students in the accustomed sense of the term; they should not be regarded as representing random samples of individuals drawn at large from the school.

School-mean norms

The use of school-mean norms was considered on page 539. A major disadvantage of the procedure of sampling within schools is that it does not provide the mean score for all the students in each school but only for a sample of them. Moreover, since the obtained means are derived from subsamples of the students in each school, they necessarily will be more dispersed than would be the means based on all students in each school. In order to make it possible to provide school-mean norms, an estimate is therefore needed of the variance of the means of the k schools assuming *all* the students in each school had been tested. Such an estimate is provided by the equation (Lord, 1959):

$$\hat{s}_{\bar{X}}^2 = s_{\bar{x}}^2 - \frac{1}{k} \sum_i^k \frac{N_i - n_i}{n_i N_i} S_{x_i}^2,$$

where

$s_{\bar{X}}^2$ = the estimate of the variance of the means for *all* the students in the schools in the norms sample,

$s_{\bar{x}}^2$ = as before, the variance of the observed means,

k = the number of schools,

N_i and n_i = respectively, the total number of students in school i and the number of students tested in school i, and

$S_{x_i}^2$ = the observed variance of scores in school i.

With the value of $\hat{s}_{\bar{X}}^2$ available, it remains to use the ratio $\hat{s}_{\bar{X}}/s_{\bar{x}}$ as a scaling factor and to construct a frequency distribution of the means, $\overline{X}_i$, having the same general shape and overall mean as that observed for the distribution of $\bar{x}_i$ but with a standard deviation equal to $\hat{s}_{\bar{X}}$.

Size of tolerable error in norms

Once the mathematical relationships between the types and numbers of sampling units and the size of the resulting sampling error are clarified, the practical questions normally arise: How small should the error be? How many schools and students are needed for the norms? Unfortunately, these questions cannot be answered in the abstract. They obviously depend on a number of factors: the purpose for which the norms are intended; the importance of the decisions that would be based on the norms and their dependence on precision; the opportunities that would be available to reverse those decisions, once they are found to require correction; and the cost, in any sense of the word, of making the wrong decision as against the cost of increasing the precision. It should be remembered that the error of norms cannot be regarded in the same way as one would regard the error of measurement; it does not depend on the number of cases being evaluated and does not tend to vanish as that number increases. As indicated earlier in this section once the norms are determined the error stays on in the manner of a bias and is just as prom-

inent whether the score that is being evaluated is the score of an individual or the mean score for a large group.

Although definitive answers cannot be given to the question of maximum tolerable error in norms, some guidelines may be developed to aid in the consideration of sample size, based, as Lord (1959) has done, on expected differences between major subgroups in the population. Consider an example similar to the one he discusses, and say that one has separate norms for northern and southern schools. Suppose also that the true difference in means for the two subgroups is about 2.5 points in favor of the northern schools on a scale for which the standard deviation of scores for all students in the country is 10 points. Finally, suppose that $s_{\bar{x}}$, the standard deviation of school means, is 4, that C_N equals .8, and, also, that there are about three times as many schools in the north as in the south. One might then ask: How many schools should be chosen from each region, with 100 percent sampling in each school, to give near certainty—say, at a confidence level of 99.5 percent—that the difference in means will not be reversed, with southern schools scoring higher than northern schools? According to equation 3 the variance error of the mean of the norms for the southern schools would be $(16)(1.64)/k$; the variance error of the mean of the norms for the northern schools would be $(16)(1.64)/3k$; and the variance error of the difference in those means (the sum of those two variances) would be $(4)(16)(1.64)/3k$. With the variance error of the difference fixed at 6.66 (the square of 2.58, which would correspond to the 99.5 percent level for one-tailed confidence) and the difference between means fixed at 2.5, 6.66 equals $[(2.5)^2(3)k]/[(4)(16)(1.64)]$ and k equals 37 (approximately). Therefore, 37 schools would be needed for the southern norms and 111 schools for the northern norms. Naturally, with different levels of confidence specified for the reversal in the means or with mean differences other than the one considered here, the number of schools required for the norms would be different. It should not be overlooked too that the error that was assessed here is the error in the mean. If instead one were to consider the error in the median, the standard error would be 25 percent greater than the standard error of the mean, implying that at the level of confidence specified one would need 56 percent more schools than one had counted on—about 58 schools in the south and 173 in the north. Moreover, the error in the norms would increase as one moves out to the tails of the distribution. At the 1st and 3rd quartiles the standard error is 1.36 times the error at the mean; at the 10th and 90th percentiles the error is 1.71 times the error at the mean; at the 5th and 95th the ratio of standard errors is 2.11; and at the 1st and 99th the ratio is 3.74.

In view of the size of the error in norms distributions, it is clearly advisable to take advantage of the techniques of multistage and stratified sampling in an effort to reduce the error. In order to prevent reversals in score of the kind just discussed it is advisable to test successive grades in each school, if grade norms are to be prepared. It is similarly advisable to test the same students at both times in the year, if spring and fall norms are to be prepared. In general, longitudinal norms, or a logical approximation to the notion of longitudinal norms—as, for example, testing in successive grades in the same schools, if the same students cannot be followed through the grades—are far preferable to cross-sectional norms, for which the standard error of the difference between grades is so much greater.

Beyond the general considerations that norms should be as precise as their intended use demands and the cost permits, there is very little else that can be said regarding minimum standards for norms reliability. Lindquist (1930) once suggested that the standard error of the mean of a norms distribution should be no greater than one-eighth of the standard deviation of school averages ($s_{\bar{x}}$). If $s_{\bar{x}} = .5s_x$, as he estimated, then the standard error of the norms (at the mean) would be one-sixteenth the standard deviation of individual scores. Then, 64 schools drawn at random from the population of schools, or 256 students each drawn at random from the population of students, would be needed to satisfy his suggested standard of norms reliability. When regarded in this light, it would not seem that such a standard is excessively high, especially in view of the fact that, with appropriate attention to the more sophisticated techniques of sampling, it is possible to increase the precision of norms without appreciably increasing costs.

Another rule for deciding on the maximum tolerable error in norms might be derived from the purpose of the test itself and its need for precision, which, in turn, should be reflected in the standard error of measurement of the test scores. A general consideration, suggested by R. S. Levine,[12] might be that the combined error at the mean due to error of measurement *plus* error in the norms should not be appreciably greater than the error of measurement alone (see also Cooperative School and College Ability Tests, 1967). Say, specifically, that the standard error arising from both sources of error combined should be no more than one percent larger than the standard error of measurement alone. Since the combined variance error is (approximately) equal to the sum of the variance errors in the components ($SE^2_{combined\ error} = SE^2_{meas} + SE^2_{norms}$), the standard error of the norms alone is found to be $(SE_{meas})\sqrt{(1.01)^2 - (1.00)^2}$, or $.14SE_{meas}$. By this rule, then, the standard error of the norms (at the mean) should be no more than 14 percent of the standard error of measurement. If, for example, the standard deviation of the distribution of scores is taken to be 10 and the standard error of measurement is 3.0 (test reliability equaling .91), and if Lindquist's rule, that the standard deviation of school means is $.5s_x$, is used, then by equation 2 the number of schools required for simple cluster sampling is about 142. If, instead, the standard deviation of school means is taken to be $.4s_x$, then the number of schools required is only about 91. It is clear that for less reliable tests the error of norms by the rule suggested here would be relaxed and the number of schools required for the norms sample would be correspondingly reduced. If the reliability of the test is .84 and the standard error of measure-

[12] Personal communication, April 1967.

ment $.4s_x$ and if the standard deviation of school means is taken at $.5s_x$, then the number of schools required for norms drops from 142 to about 80. With the same test reliability (.84) and a standard deviation of school means of $.4s_x$, the number of schools drops from 91 to about 51.

General Considerations in the Development of Norms

More fundamental than the numbers of students or the numbers of schools that are used for the norms is the consideration that the population be clearly specified in advance and that the sample be drawn with strict adherence to the rules for automatic and random selection. Otherwise, there is no guarantee that the norms will represent any particular population, and the considerations of error that have been discussed here—i.e. the considerations of random departures from a population parameter—will not apply. This is not to say that norms data that fail to meet these ideal conditions are not useful. They may, in spite of their bias, represent a close enough approximation to the ideal for most practical purposes. It is only that, in the absence of these conditions, it may not be possible to make an accurate assessment of the degree of bias in the norms or the size of their error.

One major problem in the development of norms (alluded to earlier) is the fact that many schools that are invited to participate in a norms administration will decline the invitation. If willingness to participate is correlated with score level, as may well be the case, then obviously the failure of a substantial proportion of the sample of schools to participate in the testing will bias the results.

There are various ways to help counteract this bias. One is to choose two or three times as many schools for the norms as are needed for each category of size, region, type, etc., and to resort to a random second or third choice within that category if repeated efforts to persuade a school to test are unsuccessful. Another, of course, is to try to make the testing as attractive and profitable to the schools as possible, by providing them with data on the performance of their students and relating those data to standard measures already in use. Finally, every attempt should be made to confine the lengths of the testing periods to the lengths of the class periods and, of course, to keep the amount of testing to a minimum. One way of accomplishing this, if more than one test is to be normed (and all tests require the same amount of testing time), is to follow the procedure suggested above, of randomizing the tests within each classroom so that each student takes only one test.

Another way of reducing testing time is to follow a procedure suggested by Lord (1962) for unspeeded tests that are scored simply for number right. In this procedure the total test is divided into random sets of items drawn at large from the total test. Each set of items is then administered to a random fraction of the total group. Lord reported in his study of this procedure that, from the data for each of the subgroups, he made separate estimates of the mean and variance for the full-length test and averaged them to yield a single estimate of the mean and a single estimate of the variance. These estimates then were applied to the formula for the negative hypergeometric distribution (Keats & Lord, 1962) to generate frequencies for the entire range of scores. The results of Lord's study indicate that high norms reliability can be achieved by administering fewer items to many examinees just as it can be achieved by administering many items to fewer examinees. Therefore, the procedure is especially useful in those situations where the cost of administration time, or the difficulty in obtaining it, is greater than the cost or difficulty in obtaining examinee groups. However, it should be cautioned that the procedure offered by Lord is not universally appropriate—for example when performance on an item is not independent of the context in which it occurs. This means among other things that it cannot be applied when there are items near the end of the test that are omitted because the examinees do not have enough time to attempt them. Also, although it is possible that this procedure of estimating norms can be extended to tests that are scored by other methods, at the present time it is appropriate only to those tests that are scored number right.

One of the persistent difficulties with norms, made most apparent in the concept of the national norm, is the fact that the samples chosen by the different publishers for their tests probably differ so that the norms are not directly comparable, despite the fact that they may all purport to be national norms. There are a number of reasons for this. One is that the test publishers may define the norms population somewhat differently, possibly with respect to the decision to include or not to include atypical subgroups (e.g. schools for retarded or disturbed children, schools for the physically disabled, schools for children in bilingual and bicultural areas, schools for delinquent children, etc.). Another is that different publishers will treat special problems of sampling in different ways (e.g. the problem of the nonparticipating school) with the inevitable result that various elements of bias will creep into the norms. And a third, of course, is the fact that norms will differ as a result of sampling error alone. Lennon (1964, 1966) has called attention to the problem of differences in the norms groups of different publishers and has urged that an anchor test be administered to norms groups in order to estimate the parameters of a single standard norms group for all tests. Two procedures for accomplishing this purpose suggest themselves, both involving the administration of an anchor test, say Test U, to the "standard" norms group (Group t) as well as to the norms group (Group α) of an individual publisher who is administering his test, say Test X, for norming. If it is assumed that the regression system of X on U is the same for Group t as for Group α—that is, that the standard error of estimate, the slope, and the intercept of X on U are the same for Group t as for Group α—then the following equations,[13] attributed to L. R Tucker (Gulliksen, 1950, chap. 19; Angoff, 1961a), can be used for estimating the mean and variance on Test X for Group t, the "standard" norms group:

$$\hat{M}_{xt} = M_{x\alpha} + b_{xu\alpha}(M_{ut} - M_{u\alpha}),$$

and

$$\hat{s}_{xt}^2 = s_{x\alpha}^2 + b_{xu\alpha}^2(s_{ut}^2 - s_{u\alpha}^2).$$

Once these estimates are made, the frequencies for the entire distribution of Test X may be generated by means of the negative hypergeometric distribution (Keats & Lord, 1962) *if* Test X is scored for number right. Otherwise a normal distribution with the estimated mean and variance may frequently be taken to be a reasonably close approximation for most practical purposes.

Another procedure for estimating the frequencies of the distribution for the "standard" norms group is one that was suggested by Lord[14] and used by Levine (1958) in estimating the national norms for the College Board Scholastic Aptitude Test. This procedure is analogous to the procedure described in the preceding paragraph and derives from the same assumptions but deals with the frequencies of the distribution of scores instead of the mean and variance. Working with the scatterplot of scores on Test U versus Test X for the publisher's norms group, Group α, and dealing one at a time with each interval of score U_i on the distribution of Test U for Group t (the "standard" norms group), the ratio of frequencies, $f_{it}/f_{i\alpha}$, is calculated and then multiplied by each of the observed frequencies in the array for score U_i. When this is completed for the arrays for all values of U_i, there will be a new scatterplot of scores on Test U versus Test X estimated for Group t. At this point the frequencies are added across all values of scores on U to yield a total frequency for each score X_j. These frequencies, one for each level of score X_j, represent the estimated distribution on Test X for the "standard" norms group, Group t. Finally, this distribution may be smoothed by any one of the methods already described—with the aid of a French curve or spline, by the analytical method of a rolling weighted average of frequencies such as that described by Cureton and Tukey (1951), or, if

---

[13] The derivation of these equations is given in the section of this chapter on equating and calibration.

[14] Personal communication, c. 1957.

Test X is scored number right, by the negative hypergeometric distribution developed by Keats and Lord (1962).

Within the past decade or two, there have been some noticeable improvements in the manner in which norms have been developed and reported. Probably the most significant developments have been noted in a fast-growing literature on the theory of sampling, especially as applied to norms development, and an accompanying awareness on the part of test publishers and investigators in general of the practical significance of these advances. For example, the painstaking efforts and care with which the sampling plan for Project Talent (Flanagan et al., 1962) was developed and executed is evidence of a sophistication in these matters that had not existed as little as 10 years previously. The development of the recent norms for the Lorge-Thorndike Intelligence Tests (Lorge et al., 1966) and for the Iowa Tests of Educational Development (Lindquist et al., 1966) also shows an attention to technical detail that has not been observed until recently. Lennon (1966) has pointed out too that the definitions and descriptions of the characteristics of the norms populations and the descriptions of the methods of sampling from those norms populations that are currently found in test manuals are more detailed, comprehensive, and technically advanced than they had been before. However, Lennon also pointed out, as had Cureton (1941) and Schrader (1960), that because of differences among test publishers in their definitions of the norms populations and in their methods of sampling from those populations, the percentile ranks for the "national" norms groups reported by various publishers were not directly comparable. Both Lennon and Cureton suggested as a solution to this problem the use of an anchor test that would permit establishing the comparability of different tests in terms of the same estimated national norms group. (Methods of estimating distributions with the use of an anchor test were described above.) Cureton also had suggested, as a solution to the problem of comparability of norms, the use

of the concept of a standard group such as Toops' "Standard Million" (c. 1939). Toops had suggested that the characteristics of norms populations for the Ohio College Entrance Tests could be standardized and thus made comparable from test to test and, at the same time, made relatively homogeneous, by applying a series of restrictive or stratifying criteria whenever a norms sample was to be collected. However, it should be pointed out here that, although the use of restrictive criteria, such as those that Toops had recommended, would tend to make norms comparable over a period of time, they would not be equally representative of the population taking the test if the population changed. For example, Toops restricted his population to white students. While this restriction would not have excluded many black students from the norms populations 30 years ago, it would very likely exclude many more, even proportionately, today and very likely still more in years to come, as the proportion of black students enrolled in institutions of higher education increases.

EQUATING AND CALIBRATION

In most testing programs or test offerings it is manifestly advisable, for various reasons, to have multiple and interchangeable forms of the same test. However, since two forms of a test can rarely if ever be made to be precisely equivalent in level and range of difficulty, it becomes necessary to *equate* the forms—to convert the system of units of one form to the system of units of the other—so that scores derived from the two forms *after conversion* will be directly equivalent. If this is properly done, then, and only then, is it possible to say—after appropriate controls are considered—that there has been a change in a group's mean, say, from 20 to 25 points, after a period of special instruction (and perhaps as a consequence of it), even though the test forms administered on the two occasions were different forms. With equating properly executed it becomes possible to measure growth, to chart trends, and to merge data even when the separate pieces of data derive from different forms of a test with somewhat different item characteristics. It also becomes possible to compare directly the performances of two individuals who have taken different forms of a test. In a high-premium selection program, for example for college admissions or for scholarship awards, it is especially important for reasons of equity alone that no applicant be given special advantage or disadvantage because of the fortuitous administration of a relatively easy or difficult form of the test.

In adhering strictly to the concept of equating, a special point should be made of the notion that what is being sought is a conversion from the units of one form of a test to the units of another form of the *same* test, much in the sense that one thinks of a conversion from inches to centimeters, from pounds to grams, from Fahrenheit to centigrade, and so on. This notion implies two restrictions. The *first* is that the two instruments in question be measures of the same characteristic, in the same sense that degrees of Fahrenheit and centigrade, for example, are both units of temperature, inches and centimeters are both units of length, etc. In the case of the more common types of physical measurement this requirement is obvious. It makes no sense to ask for a conversion from, say, grams to degrees of Fahrenheit or from inches to pounds. Similarly, it makes little sense to ask for a conversion from a test of, say, verbal ability to a test of mathematical ability, or indeed across any two tests of differenct functions. This is not to say that it is inappropriate to draw a regression line relating two tests of different function, any more than it is inappropriate to regress, for example, weight on height. However, the problem of regression and prediction and the problem of transforming units are different problems. The latter is highly restrictive with respect to the types of characteristics under consideration; the former is not. The *second* restriction implied by the notion of equating is that, in order to be truly a transformation of only systems of units, the conversion must be unique, except for the random error associated with the unreliability of the data and the method used for determining the transformation; the resulting conversion should be independent of the individuals from whom the data were drawn to develop the conversion and should be freely applicable to all situations. Indeed, these two restrictions that are imposed on the concept of equating—that the characteristics measured by the tests be identical and that the transformation be independent of the groups of individuals used to develop the conversion—go hand in hand. For if the two tests were measures of different abilities, then the conversions would not be unique but would very likely be different for different types of groups. A conversion table relating scores on a verbal test to scores on a mathematical test developed from data on males, for example, would be noticeably and predictably different from a similar conversion table developed from data on females—owing to the fact that in our society men and women perform much more similarly on verbal material than on mathematical material. This issue of the nonuniqueness of conversion tables across different tests has been discussed in greater detail by Angoff (1966). However, suffice it to say here that equating, or the derivation of *equivalent scores*, concerns itself with the problem of unique conversions which may be derived only across test forms that are *parallel*, that is forms that measure, within acceptable limits, the same psychological function. (The operational definition of parallelism that may be adopted here is essentially the one offered by Wilks, 1946, and extended by Votaw, 1948: two tests may be considered parallel forms if, after conversion to the same scale, their means, standard deviations, and correlations with any and all outside criteria are equal [Gulliksen, 1950].) The problem of *nonunique* conversions of scores across *nonparallel* forms will be reserved for fuller consideration later in the discussion of *comparable scores*.

A commonly accepted definition of equivalent scores is: *Two scores, one on Form X and the other on Form Y (where X and Y measure the same function with the same degree of reliability), may be considered equivalent if their corresponding percentile ranks in any given group are equal* (Flanagan, 1951; Lord, 1950). Thus, if the two forms were sufficiently different in difficulty that the shapes of the distributions of raw scores for the same group of examinees were markedly different, the method of equating that would yield equivalent scores is one that would stretch and compress the scale of one form (say Form X) so that its distribution would coincide with the distribution of the other form (Form Y). As a consequence of this method of equating, an individual would earn the same converted score regardless of the form he took.

In general, the conversion of X scores to their equivalent Y scores will be curvilinear. If, for a given group of examinees, Form X is the easier form and Form Y the more difficult form, the equating of scores on X to scores on Y (X on the abscissa; Y on the ordinate) will yield a curvilinear conversion following the general shape of the scatterplot relating the two forms, i.e. concave toward the upper left. If Form X is the more difficult form and Form Y the easier form, then the conversion will similarly be curvilinear but concave toward the lower right. As another example, if Form Y gives a more platykurtic distribution of scores for a group of individuals than does Form X, the conversion, again following the general shape of the scatterplot, will be generally S-shaped. Finally, if the two distributions are of the same shape, differing in none of their moments beyond the second, the conversion will be linear.

By definition, successive forms of a test are constructed to be very nearly equivalent in all the important respects. Therefore, it is reasonable to assume that the shapes of the raw score distributions will be the same and that the conversion of X scores to Y scores can be accomplished simply by changing the origin and unit of measurement; that is, by adjusting only the first two moments. As was just indicated, this type of conversion is expressed in the form of a straight line. To correspond with the earlier definition of equating, the *equipercentile* definition, which stated that scores on two tests are equivalent if they correspond to equal percentile ranks, the definition for *linear* equating would state that scores on two tests are equiva-

lent if they correspond to equal standard-score deviates,

$$\frac{Y - M_y}{s_y} = \frac{X - M_x}{s_x}, \qquad [7]$$

which has precisely the same form as the equations for linear scaling $\{z_{S_\omega} = z_{X_\omega}$ or $(C - M_{c_\omega})/s_{c_\omega} = (X - M_{X_\omega})/s_{x_\omega}\}$ discussed on page 513. When the terms are appropriately rearranged, equation 7 takes the form, $Y = AX + B$, where $A = s_y/s_x$ and $B = M_y - AM_x$, A being the slope of the conversion line, and B the intercept (the point on the Y axis where it is intersected by the conversion line). It is important to emphasize that linear equating is a very close approximation to equipercentile equating when the shapes of the raw score distributions are similar. If one is prepared to assume that differences in the shapes of the distributions of raw scores on the two forms are sufficiently trivial so they may be disregarded, linear equating is to be preferred. Unlike equipercentile equating, it is entirely analytical and verifiable and is free from any errors of smoothing, which can produce serious errors in the score range in which data are scant and/or erratic.

There is little doubt that the only way to ensure equivalent scores when the distribution shapes are different is to equate by curvilinear (equipercentile) methods. Under such circumstances the equivalency is established by stretching and compressing the raw score scale of one of the forms so that its distribution will conform to the shape given by the other form. In some extreme instances the stretching and compressing is so dramatic that a difference between two adjacent converted scores in one part of the raw score scale may be seen to be as much as two or three times the difference between two adjacent converted scores in another part of the raw score scale. This is the expected result of equating two tests that differ greatly in their difficulty characteristics and is indeed inevitable if a system of equivalent scores is being sought that is independent of the characteristics of the particular test forms.

If, on the other hand, it is recognized that the raw score scale for a test reflects the inherent characteristics of that test—its level of difficulty, the dispersion of its item difficulties, and the intercorrelations among its items—and one wants the converted score scale for the test to reflect these characteristics, a model that permits a different kind of transformation of the raw scores may have to be erected. Suppose, for example, one is operating a testing program that is administered annually and is addressed to the same general level and range of examinee ability year after year. Suppose also that, as a result of administrative action, the purposes of the testing program are extended; say that the tests are now also to serve in the selection of scholarship winners. Because of this additional function it is now desired to make a variety of discriminations in the upper ranges of ability, even at the expense of some discrimination in the lower ranges. To accomplish this, harder tests are introduced and administered to the new groups of examinees. If the new forms are equated to the old ones by means of equipercentile equating, their scaled scores will be forced to conform with the scaled scores of earlier forms, and the fact that they have a higher ceiling than the earlier forms will not be reflected in their scaled scores. As a result of the equipercentile equating, then, the scaled scores for the very high-scoring examinees will tend to underrepresent their levels of ability; that is to say, such examinees will earn lower scaled scores than their abilities warrant, at a level approximating those of the less able examinees.

It therefore may be well to examine another model for the equating—or better, the *calibration*—of test scores, one that permits test forms to reflect their characteristics on the scale. For this purpose a convenient analogy may be found in the measurement of degrees of heat. On the one hand, there is the scale of temperature as one that extends from about $-460°$ Fahrenheit ($-273°$C.) upwards; on the other hand, there is a specific measuring instrument—thermometer—designed to measure degrees of heat in a certain region on the scale of temperature. Each type of thermometer is explicitly constructed for a separate and different purpose.

There is the thermometer that is designed to measure the temperature in the householder's bedroom, a thermometer which is constructed and calibrated to yield reasonably accurate measurements of temperature ranging from, say, 40° Fahrenheit to 100° Fahrenheit; measurement beyond those limits is seldom necessary. There is also the thermometer that is constructed and calibrated to yield highly accurate measurements of body temperature, this over the relatively narrow range from about 94° Fahrenheit to 108° Fahrenheit. And there is the thermometer that is constructed and calibrated to yield measurement in the higher ranges of temperature for the purpose of measuring the heat of molten steel. Thus, each thermometer measures appropriately for its purpose but in a different range on the temperature scale.

The parallel between the scale of temperature and the scale of the ability measured by a system of tests is not an unreasonable one. Ideally this situation can be described by imagining that a long and reliable test of the ability under consideration has been constructed and it has been scaled in any one of the ways that have been discussed above. This test and the scale that is defined for it become the basic reference for the entire system of forms to follow. Later forms, when they are introduced, will be calibrated to that reference form and, consequently, to the scale. Thus, as in figure 15.2, the result of calibrating Form A to the reference scale is that the 60-item test, Form A, yields a range of scaled scores running from about 40 to 160. (The raw score scales of the five forms in figure 15.2 are drawn to exhibit a linear relationship with the scale that is defined for the reference form. This need not be the case, of course. The linear relationship is used here for the sake of simplicity in the illustration.) The result of calibrating Form B (also 60 items) to the scale is that that form yields a range of scaled scores from about 50 to 170. From the comparison of these two ranges it would appear that Form B is generally a harder test than Form A. Given a group of individuals whose mean ability

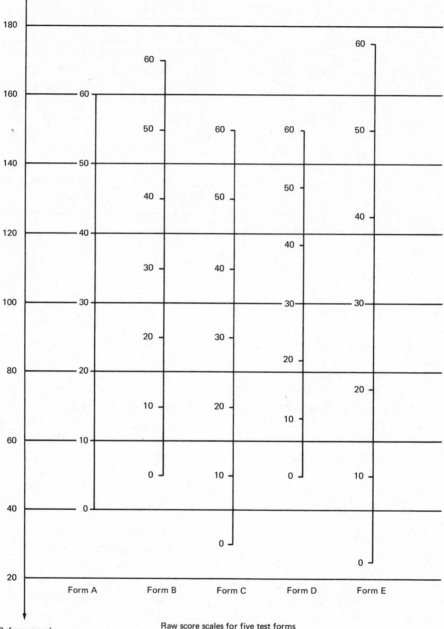

Reference scale

Raw score scales for five test forms

FIG. 15.2. Relation between the raw score scales of five test forms and scores on the reference scale

would best be represented by a score of, say, 120 on the reference scale, their mean *raw* score on Form A would be about 40, but their mean raw score on Form B would be lower, only about 35. Another way of saying this is to observe that the mean item difficulty for such

a group on these 60-item tests would be .67 for Form A and .58 for Form B. It also is observed that both 60-item forms appear to measure the same range of scaled scores, about 120 points, and are therefore about equally precise. Form C, on the other hand, appears to be a very easy form; the mean p value for the group of individuals with mean ability score of 120 would be as high as .75. Of these three forms, Form C has the lowest ceiling and would therefore be expected to provide the poorest differentiation among the higher ability individuals. It also has the lowest floor and therefore may be expected to provide the best differentiation among lower ability individuals. Form D appears to measure the narrowest range of talent; it gives poor discrimination at both the lower and the higher levels of ability. However, within the limits of its range it appears to measure more accurately than do the other forms, an observation that may be verified from an examination of the standard deviation of raw scores on this form for some appropriate group of examinees in comparison with the standard deviation of raw scores on other forms for the same group of examinees. This observation will be discussed in more detail below. However, for the moment it may suffice to say that one is dealing with a test in which the same number (60) of items are operating within a narrow range of scores (from about 50 to about 150 on the scale, about 100 points) and which is, therefore, making finer discriminations within the scale than Form E, for example, which operates within a range of about 150 points on the scale. Similar kinds of judgments regarding the relative difficulties of the various forms in the system, the ranges of talent over which they differentiate among individuals, and the degree to which they differentiate accurately can be made from a study of the results of the calibration.

Although the model just described for the calibration of test forms provides a convenient and familiar backdrop for consideration of the issues, it is a model that obviously assumes more than is warranted by the facts. It implies, for example, that calibration need not involve an equation of any higher order than the linear equation—that no moments beyond the second need be considered in calibrating one form to another. This is not necessarily so, of course. The restriction to a linear equation has no fundamental theoretical justification and is probably little more than a reflection of the early

state of the art. Secondly, the model obviously implies far greater precision in the methods of calibration and also in the tests themselves than is the case. The precision of the techniques of educational measurement rarely, if ever, warrants the degree of precision implied by the results shown in figure 15.2.

Throughout the course of this description of the calibration model, the analogy has been drawn, and will continue to be drawn, between the calibration of test scores and the calibration of physical measuring instruments. It needs little elaboration to make the point that, while this analogy is a useful one, it is, like all analogies, limited and incomplete, grossly so here because of the vast difference in precision between the two kinds of measurements. In the case of the temperature scale, for example, the distinction between equating and calibration is essentially nonexistent. The result of a measurement of temperature will be the same, whatever thermometer is used to make that measurement—so long as it is appropriately constructed and calibrated to yield that result. This is not so in educational measurement. Two tests that are designed to discriminate over different but overlapping ranges of ability and calibrated accordingly will not necessarily, even in the long run, yield the same score for an individual of given ability. If properly *equated*, however, they *will* yield the same score. Thus, the thermometer analogy may be useful here *for the very reason* that it is incomplete and for the reason that it points to the need for the two separate models in the consideration of score conversions.

The model just described also permits one to consider the calibration of test forms that are not only unequally difficult but unequally reliable as well. Procedures for dealing with the problem of unequal reliabilities will be outlined later on in this chapter. However, the model bears on the distinction between equating and calibration and is relevant here. If one insists on the interchangeability of scores on alternate forms as a prerequisite for the equating model, then there is some serious question about the appropriateness of attempting to equate unequally reliable tests, however the equating is accomplished. Lord[15] has pointed out that there is no single transformation of units for unequally reliable tests that will render the scores interchangeable, since no such transformation will make the true score distributions (standard deviation equaling $s_1\sqrt{r_{11}}$) equal *and at the same time* make the distributions of estimated true scores (standard deviation equaling $s_1 r_{11}$) equal. This condition is necessary for scores to be considered equivalent and interchangeable. The author is inclined to agree and would add the point that scores earned on two tests that are unequally reliable are *for that very reason* not interchangeable; nor is there any equating procedure or transformation of units possible that will make the scores earned on those tests equally reliable and therefore interchangeable. If, however, one considers the calibration model, for which the criterion of interchangeability throughout the range of scores is not intended to apply, then it may be quite reasonable to think of tests of different reliability as being "referred" to the same psychological scale, in the same sense that thermometers of different precision may be referred to the same scale of temperature. Here too, it is noted, the thermometers are not interchangeable for the very reason that they are not equally precise.

Thus it is found that the five forms of the 60-item test illustrated in figure 15.2, while all equally long in terms of numbers of items, do not all discriminate over the same number of scale units. That this is evidence of their different reliabilities is not only intuitively reasonable but is observed, as it will be below, when their standard errors of measurement, expressed in terms of the reference scale, are shown to be different and in a predictable way.

There are thus two models of scale adjustment to account for differences in difficulty and range of measured ability. One is the linear, or z-score, model of score *calibration*, a way by which the level and range of ability over which the test is intended to discriminate are reflected in the scores on the reference scale. The other is the curvilinear or equipercentile

[15] Personal communication, February 1967.

model (and method) of *equating*, to which the linear method is sometimes a good approximation. Indeed, the linear method is equivalent to the equipercentile method when the shapes of the distributions are the same, that is when, except for the first two, all standardized moments of the distributions of raw scores on the two tests for any given group of examinees are the same. When the raw scores for each of two unequally difficult tests are converted by both methods to a scale that is separate and different from each of the two original raw score scales, it becomes clear that the two models are necessarily different, indeed antithetical. Within the error of the system the linear method reflects its characteristics in the scaled scores it produces; and if the tests differ in difficulty, it will yield scaled scores for one form that cannot be achieved by examinees who take the other form. The equipercentile method, on the other hand, adjusts for these differences, thus ensuring that, within the error of equating, the scaled score for an individual will be the same *regardless* of the characteristics of the form he took.

Methods for Equating Test Forms

In the last 15 or 20 years, with the appearance of new testing programs and offerings, and with the growth and further development of old ones, all requiring the administration of interchangeable test forms, many new designs and methods have been developed and refined for the equating of test scores. These various methods differ in a number of respects. Some require the administration of a single test, others require more than one; some deal with analytical statistics (means, variances, correlations), others deal with the graphical treatment of percentiles; finally, some—indeed, most—deal with score data, others with item data. The discussion that follows attempts to make a classification of the various methods. In the case of each method in which score data are used, two procedures will be offered where possible, a linear and analytical procedure and also its curvilinear or equipercentile analog. Also, in each case, the linear method may be taken to be an approximation to the equipercentile method when the distributions are similar. It also may be taken as a method of calibration in its own right, whether the distributions are similar or not.

Design I: Random groups—one test administered to each group

In this method a large group of examinees is selected who are sufficiently heterogeneous to sample adequately all levels of score on both forms (X and Y) of the test. (Since, in this method as in all other methods, it is assumed that Forms X and Y are parallel in function at least, it is not necessary to draw the group from some defined population. It is sufficient to say that the population must be one whose level and range of ability are adequately represented by the general level and range of difficulty of the items on the two forms. If the tests *are* parallel, then the resulting conversion of scores from X to Y should be unique, except for random errors of equating, and not associated with the particular kind of group used in the equating.) The group is divided into two random halves, one half (α) taking Form X, the other half (β) taking Form Y. A simple and effective way to form random halves of the group is to package the test books in alternating sequence and to pass them out to the examinees as they are removed one by one from the top of the package. This procedure will fail to yield randomly equivalent subgroups only when the examinees themselves are seated in a sequence (e.g. boy, girl, boy, girl, etc.) that may be correlated with test score.

    A. *Equally reliable tests*

      1. *Linear procedure*

Following equation 7, the means and standard deviations—on Form X for Group α and on Form Y for Group β—are calculated. The standard-score deviates (z_{x_α} and z_{y_β}) for the two groups are then set equal,

$$\frac{Y - M_{y_\beta}}{s_{y_\beta}} = \frac{X - M_{x_\alpha}}{s_{x_\alpha}}. \qquad [8]$$

When the terms of equation 8 are rearranged they yield the linear equation,

$$Y = \frac{s_{y_\beta}}{s_{x_\alpha}} X + M_{y_\beta} - \frac{s_{y_\beta}}{s_{x_\alpha}} M_{x_\alpha}, \qquad [9]$$

which is of the form, $Y = AX + B$, where A (the slope of the conversion line) $= s_{y_\beta}/s_{x_\alpha}$, and B (the intercept of the conversion line) $= M_{y_\beta} - AM_{x_\alpha}$. This conversion equation, like all score conversions, is symmetrical; unlike regression equations, the same equation may be used for converting scores from the scale of Form X to the scale of Form Y, or from the scale of Y to the scale of X.

If Form Y is an earlier form of the test for which there already exists a conversion to the reference scale, C—let us say, in the form of the equation, $C = A'Y + B'$—then the substitution in it of the equation, $Y = AX + B$, will yield a new equation, $C = A''X + B''$, relating raw scores on Form X directly to the scale, where $A'' = A'A$ and $B'' = A'B + B'$.

The foregoing linear *equating* (preferably *calibration*) will make it possible to illustrate some of the observations made about figure 15.2. Say that there are five 60-item forms of a test on which scaled scores are to be reported. Also say that each of the five forms was administered to a random fifth of a large group (a testing plan which represents a simple extension of the random-halves administration just described). Finally, say that there already exists an equation relating Form A, the first of the five forms, to the reference scale: $C = 2.0X_a + 40$. When projected on the scale, this form yields a minimum scaled score of 40 [$C = (2.0)(0) + 40$], a maximum scaled score of 160 [$C = (2.0)(60) + 40$], and a range of scaled scores of 120 (160 − 40).

Now equate Form B to Form A. Using the data from the administration, shown in table 15.3, and substituting in equation 8, it is found that $(X_a - 30)/10 = (X_b - 25)/10$, or $X_a = X_b + 5$. Substituting into the equation relating Form A to the scale, $C = 2.0X_a + 40$, the equation relating Form B to the scale, $C = 2.0X_b + 50$ is found. Form B is clearly a more difficult test than Form A, since it yields a mean of only 25 for a group of individuals who are essentially equivalent in ability to a group who earned a mean of 30 on Form A. This greater difficulty of

TABLE 15.3

Scaled Score Values for Five Forms of a 60-Item Test

FORM	RAW SCORE STATISTICS M_x	s_x	CONVERSION EQUATION	SCALE VALUES Minimum	Maximum	Range
A	30	10	$C = 2.00X_a + 40$	40	160	120
B	25	10	$C = 2.00X_b + 50$	50	170	120
C	35	10	$C = 2.00X_c + 30$	30	150	120
D	30	12	$C = 1.67X_d + 50$	50	150	100
E	30	8	$C = 2.50X_e + 25$	25	175	150

Form B is reflected in the minimum and maximum scaled scores, 50 and 170, which, of course, are determined by the scaled score conversion equation for Form B. The more difficult the form, the higher is the "location" of that form on the reference scale. Similarly, the easier the form, the lower is the "location" of that form on the reference scale, as may be seen by examining the statistics for Form C. Form C has a higher raw score mean than either Form A or Form B, and as a result appears lower on the scale, with a minimum scaled score of 30 and a maximum of 150. However, since the raw score standard deviations for Forms A, B, and C are the same, their ranges of measurement, as reflected on the scale, are also the same. Form D, on the other hand, has a large raw score standard deviation and therefore discriminates over a narrow range on the scale; Form E has a small raw score standard deviation and therefore discriminates over a wide range on the scale. It appears to be intuitively reasonable that difficult forms should appear higher on the scale than easy forms. A raw score of 40 on a generally difficult form *should* represent a higher level of talent than a raw score of 40 on an easier form. Similarly, it is intuitively reasonable that forms with larger raw score standard deviations should encompass a narrower range of scaled scores since large standard deviations of raw scores are characteristic of more reliable tests. It also would be expected that of two equally long forms the form that discriminates over a narrower range of talent would be the more reliable form. This general observation is further confirmed by an examination of the standard errors of measurement for tests that have different standard deviations, say, Forms D and E, as expressed on the reference scale. The raw score standard errors of measurement at score 30 are both about 3.9, as calculated by a formula developed by Lord (1957). However, when the standard errors of measurement are expressed in comparable terms, that is to say on the reference scale, it turns out that Form D is much more precise than Form E. The scaled score standard error of measurement is about 6.5 (3.9 times 1.67, the slope of the conversion line) for Form D but as much as 9.8 (3.9 times 2.50) for Form E, consistent with what one would expect from the relative sizes of their standard deviations. It is in this way that the linear transformation makes it possible to observe fairly directly the properties of difficulty and discrimination for the various forms.

Like all statistical procedures, equating is, of course, also subject to random error, arising here from the sampling fluctuations of the means and standard deviations of scores on Forms X and Y. The standard error of equating (Lord, 1950) is described as the standard deviation of converted scores on the scale of Y, corresponding to a fixed value of X, in which each converted Y score is taken from a conversion line that results from an independent sampling of Groups α and β from a basic group that is normally distributed in both X and Y. The standard error of equating by the method just described is given in the equation:

$$\mathrm{SE}_{y*}^2 = \frac{2s_y^2}{N_t}(z_x^2 + 2), \qquad [10]$$

where $SE_{y*}^2 =$ the variance error of equated Y scores,

$N_t = N_\alpha + N_\beta$, and

$z_x = (X - M_x)/s_x$.

From equation 10 it can be seen that the variance error of equating by equation 9 is 1.5 times as large at 1 standard deviation away from the mean of X as it is at the mean, 3 times as large at 2 standard deviations from the mean, and more than 4 times as large at 2.5 standard deviations from the mean.

2. *Curvilinear analog*

Two distributions are formed, one on Form X for Group α and another on Form Y for Group β. Mid-percentile ranks, or relative cumulative frequencies (i.e. percentage of cases falling below each interval) if that is more convenient, are then computed for each distribution, as in table 15.4, and plotted and smoothed, as in figure 15.3. The general principles of hand smoothing have been described in the section on scaling, in which it was pointed out that the experience and judgment of the person working with the data will determine the degree to which irregularities in the data are defined as such and smoothed out. Indeed, it is this subjectivity, necessarily part of the hand smoothing process in equipercentile equating, that has helped to cause some test constructors to avoid it and to prefer analytic linear methods of equating instead.

Distributions also may be smoothed analytically before they are plotted. Two such procedures were mentioned in this chapter in connection with normalized scales and also in the section of this chapter on norms. One is a rolling weighted average method developed by Cureton and Tukey (1951). Another method, which is at present appropriate only to rights-scored tests, is derived from the negative hypergeometric distribution (Keats & Lord, 1962).

Difficulties in smoothing by hand are frequently encountered near the ends of the distributions where data are relatively scant. Sometimes data run out before the minimum and maximum scores on the test are reached, with the result that the ogives (and, later in the equating process, the conversion curve itself) have to be extrapolated without the benefit of supporting data. Obviously, such a procedure can lead to intolerably large errors. It is for this reason, to give adequate representation in data to all score levels on the tests, that it is desirable to use relatively heterogeneous groups for equating, sampling the cases particularly heavily at the ends of the raw score range.

When the ogives for both Forms X and Y have been plotted and smoothed, corresponding percentiles are read from each smoothed ogive, recorded as in table 15.5, and plotted, one against the other, on arithmetic graph paper, as in figure 15.4. Generally, 30 points or so are adequate to describe the relationship between the two tests. The curve connecting these points is similarly smoothed and also extrapolated to the end-points on the test in order to cover the full range of possible scores. The resulting smoothed curve is used to record the conversion from Form X to Form Y and vice versa (table 15.6). Additional smoothing can be done in the recorded values by computing differences between the successive values and adjusting them to yield a smooth progression of numbers. The values in table 15.6 are ordinarily rounded and reported in the test manuals to the nearest whole numbers.

B. *Unequally reliable tests (linear calibration)*

It has already been pointed out that when the two forms are not interchangeable, for example when their reliabilities are unequal, their scores cannot be "equated" in any meaningful way. Therefore, there will be no attempt made here to discuss the "equating" of unequally reliable tests (i.e. by equipercentile methods). However, the calibration of unequally reliable tests *can* be discussed, because in that model there is no issue of interchangeability. Each test form discriminates within a region of the ability continuum and at a level of precision peculiar to the test form itself. For forms known to differ significantly in reliability it is not only appropriate but preferable that the calibration involve true scores rather than observed scores, as in the equation:

$$\frac{Y - M_{y_\beta}}{s_{\hat{y}_\beta}} = \frac{X - M_{x_\alpha}}{s_{\hat{x}_\alpha}},$$

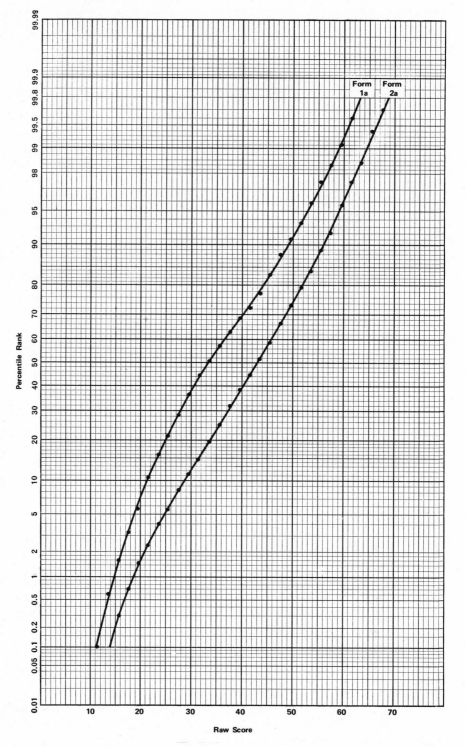

Fig. 15.3. Ogives for two forms of the STEP Social Studies Test (plotted on arithmetic probability paper)

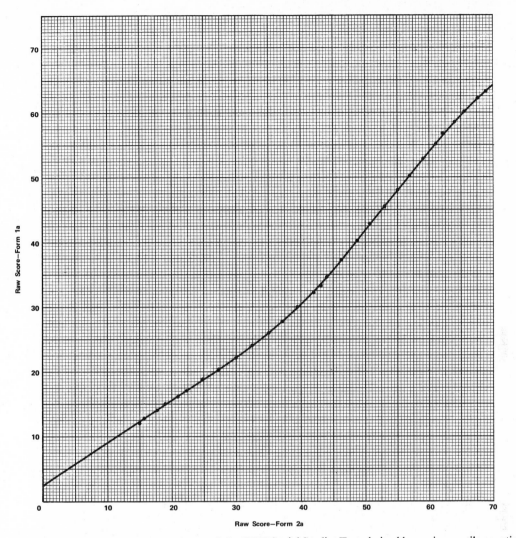

FIG. 15.4. Equivalent raw scores on two forms of the STEP Social Studies Test, derived by equipercentile equating

where $s_{\tilde{x}} = s_x \sqrt{r_{xx}}$ and $s_{\tilde{y}} = s_y \sqrt{r_{yy}}$. The equation for converting scores from the scale of Form X to the scale of Form Y becomes:

$$Y = \frac{s_{\tilde{y}_\beta}}{s_{\tilde{x}_\alpha}} X + M_{y_\beta} - \frac{s_{\tilde{y}_\beta}}{s_{\tilde{x}_\alpha}} M_{x_\alpha},$$

also of the form $Y = AX + B$, where $A = s_{\tilde{y}_\beta} / s_{\tilde{x}_\alpha}$ and $B = M_{y_\beta} - AM_{x_\alpha}$.

Design II: Random groups—both tests administered to each group, counterbalanced

As in design I a large group of individuals is

selected and divided into two random halves, one half (α) taking Form X followed by Form Y, the other half (β) taking Form Y followed by Form X. In order to guard against errors in administration it is advisable, especially when Forms X and Y are administered in one extended testing session (as is desirable if communication among examinees is to be controlled), to bind the pairs of test books together, half with Form X on top and half with Form Y on top. The booklet sets would then be packaged in alternating sequence (XY, YX, XY, YX, etc.) and distributed in that order to the examinees.

TABLE 15.4
Distributions of Raw Scores on Two Forms of the STEP Social Studies Test

Raw Scores	Form 1a					Form 2a				
	Frequency Grade 12	Frequency Grade 13	Combined Frequency	Cumulative Frequency	Percentage Below	Frequency Grade 12	Frequency Grade 13	Combined Frequency	Cumulative Frequency	Percentage Below
68–69							2	2	677	99.7
66–67							2	2	675	99.4
64–65							6	6	673	98.5
62–63	1	2	3	689	99.6	2	5	7	667	97.5
60–61	0	3	3	686	99.1	3	9	12	660	95.7
58–59	0	5	5	683	98.4	4	21	25	648	92.0
56–57	0	6	6	678	97.5	4	17	21	623	88.9
54–55	4	7	11	672	95.9	6	28	34	602	83.9
52–53	2	14	16	661	93.6	15	14	29	568	79.6
50–51	4	14	18	645	91.0	16	28	44	539	73.1
48–49	5	16	21	627	88.0	20	26	46	495	66.3
46–47	10	24	34	606	83.0	23	30	53	449	58.5
44–45	13	25	38	572	77.5	23	23	46	396	51.7
42–43	11	24	35	534	72.4	28	18	46	350	44.9
40–41	10	18	28	499	68.4	19	24	43	304	38.6
38–39	18	19	37	471	63.0	25	19	44	261	32.1
36–37	17	23	40	434	57.2	31	16	47	217	25.1
34–35	27	18	45	394	50.7	23	13	36	170	19.8
32–33	21	21	42	349	44.6	22	12	34	134	14.8
30–31	26	31	57	307	36.3	16	8	24	100	11.2
28–29	29	26	55	250	28.3	15	5	20	76	8.3
26–27	32	15	47	195	21.5	12	6	18	56	5.6
24–25	24	14	38	148	16.0	7	4	11	38	4.0
22–23	27	9	36	110	10.7	7	4	11	27	2.4
20–21	23	11	34	74	5.8	3	3	6	16	1.5
18–19	14	3	17	40	3.3	4	1	5	10	0.7
16–17	8	4	12	23	1.6	2	1	3	5	0.3
14–15	6	1	7	11	0.6	2		2	2	
12–13	3	0	3	4	0.1					
10–11		1	1	1						

A. *Equally reliable tests*

1. *Linear procedure*

In this method, given by Lord (1950), it is assumed that the practice effect on Form Y as a result of having taken Form X first and the practice effect on Form X as a result of having taken Form Y first are proportional to the standard deviations of the two tests: $K_x/s_x = K_y/s_y = H$. Also, the best estimate of H is taken to be the average of the differences between the means on Form X and the means on Form Y when each is expressed in standard deviation units:

$$H = \frac{1}{2}\left(\frac{M_{x_\beta} - M_{x_\alpha}}{s_x} + \frac{M_{y_\alpha} - M_{y_\beta}}{s_y}\right).$$

It is recalled that the prototype of the equation for the linear equating of test scores is given by equation 7, $(Y - M_y)/s_y = (X - M_x)/s_x$. The formulas to use for obtaining the values to be substituted in equation 7 are given as follows:

$$M_x = \tfrac{1}{2}(M_{x_\alpha} + M_{x_\beta} - K_x), \qquad [11]$$

$$M_y = \tfrac{1}{2}(M_{y_\alpha} + M_{y_\beta} - K_y), \qquad [12]$$

$$s_x^2 = \tfrac{1}{2}(s_{x_\alpha}^2 + s_{x_\beta}^2), \qquad [13]$$

and

$$s_y^2 = \tfrac{1}{2}(s_{y_\alpha}^2 + s_{y_\beta}^2). \qquad [14]$$

When equations 11 to 14 are substituted in equation 7, a linear equation of the form $Y = AX + B$ is found, where

$$A = \sqrt{\frac{s_{y_\alpha}^2 + s_{y_\beta}^2}{s_{x_\alpha}^2 + s_{x_\beta}^2}},$$

and

$$B = \tfrac{1}{2}(M_{y_\alpha} + M_{y_\beta}) - \frac{A}{2}(M_{x_\alpha} + M_{x_\beta}).$$

If it may be assumed that the bivariate surface of X versus Y is normal for the population of which the two half-groups are samples, and if it may also be assumed that the standard deviations for each form and the correlation between forms are the same in the population, then the variance error of scores converted to the scale of Y (Lord, 1950) is found to be:

$$SE_{y*}^2 = s_y^2(1 - r_{xy})\frac{z_x^2(1 + r_{xy}) + 2}{N_t} \quad [15]$$

in which z_x is defined as before: $z_x = (X - M_x)/s_x$. That the counterbalanced method of

TABLE 15.5
Equipercentile Points on Two Forms of the STEP Social Studies Test

PERCENTILE RANK	RAW SCORE ON FORM 1a	2a
0.2	12.0	15.0
0.3	12.7	15.7
0.7	14.0	17.6
1.2	15.1	19.0
2	16.1	20.9
3	17.1	22.3
5	18.8	24.8
8	20.4	27.3
12	22.1	30.0
17	24.0	32.4
23	25.9	35.0
30	27.9	37.2
38	30.0	39.5
46	32.3	42.0
50	33.3	43.0
54	34.6	44.0
62	37.2	46.1
70	40.1	48.6
77	42.9	50.6
83	45.4	53.0
88	48.0	55.0
92	50.2	57.0
95	53.0	59.0
97	55.1	61.0
98	56.9	62.1
98.8	58.6	64.0
99.3	60.0	65.4
99.7	62.1	67.5
99.8	63.1	68.9

TABLE 15.6
Equivalent Raw Scores on Two Forms of the STEP Social Studies Test

FORM 2a	FORM 1a	FORM 2a	FORM 1a
0	2.5	36	26.8
1	3.1	37	27.7
2	3.8	38	28.6
3	4.4	39	29.5
4	5.0	40	30.4
5	5.7	41	31.3
6	6.4	42	32.3
7	7.0	43	33.3
8	7.7	44	34.4
9	8.4	45	35.6
10	9.1	46	36.8
11	9.7	47	38.0
12	10.4	48	39.3
13	11.0	49	40.6
14	11.7	50	41.8
15	12.3	51	43.0
16	13.0	52	44.3
17	13.6	53	45.5
18	14.3	54	46.7
19	15.0	55	47.9
20	15.6	56	49.1
21	16.3	57	50.3
22	16.9	58	51.5
23	17.6	59	52.7
24	18.2	60	53.9
25	18.9	61	55.1
26	19.5	62	56.3
27	20.2	63	57.4
28	20.8	64	58.5
29	21.5	65	59.5
30	22.2	66	60.5
31	23.0	67	61.5
32	23.7	68	62.5
33	24.5	69	63.4
34	25.2	70	64.2
35	26.0		

equating is highly precise may be observed by comparing its variance error, given in equation 15, with the variance error in equation 10 for the linear equating method in design I. For two forms that correlate .80, for example, the variance error of converted Y scores at $z_x = 0$ is one-tenth the size of the error of design I; that is to say, one would need *10 times* the number of cases for equating by design I in order to achieve the precision provided by design II.

A variant of this procedure is to combine the data on Form X of the two half-groups, combine the data on Form Y for the two half-groups, and equate by the method described in design I.

2. *Curvilinear analog*

The curvilinear analog of the counter-balanced method is one that corresponds to the procedure described briefly in the preceding paragraph, in which data on Form X and also on Form Y are combined for the two half-groups, and the equipercentile procedure described in design I is applied.

B. *Unequally reliable tests (linear calibration)*

When Forms X and Y are unequally reliable, the average within-group variance should be calculated not on the basis of observed scores, as shown in equations 13 and 14, but on the basis of true scores. The appropriate values, corresponding to those in equations 13 and 14, are given in equations 16 and 17:

$$s_{\tilde{x}}^{2} = \tfrac{1}{2}(s_{x_\alpha}^{2} r_{xx_\alpha} + s_{x_\beta}^{2} r_{xx_\beta}),   [16]$$

and

$$s_{\tilde{y}}^{2} = \tfrac{1}{2}(s_{y_\alpha}^{2} r_{yy_\alpha} + s_{y_\beta}^{2} r_{yy_\beta}).   [17]$$

In addition to its greater reliability—which is to be expected in view of the fact that it makes use of so much more data than the methods of design I—design II enjoys the additional advantage that it makes it possible to obtain two independent determinations of the parallel-forms reliability coefficient. On the other hand, it does require twice as much administration time as does design I and therefore imposes an administrative burden on participating schools, which occasionally makes it difficult to obtain subjects. Another disadvantage of the method is that it is sensitive to clerical errors. Since the method does depend on the separation of examinees taking the tests in the two orders, special pains must be taken that the candidates do take the tests in the order designated for them and that the answer sheets be accurately identified not only as to the form of the test but also as to its ordinal position in the administration.

Design III: Random groups—one test administered to each group, common equating test administered to both groups

A. *Equally reliable tests (linear calibration)*
The methods described under designs I and II are appropriate only in those situations which permit the assignment of examinees to *random groups*. (This is particularly true of design I, which is likely to be much more sensitive than design II to the demand for random assignment.) The significance of this point may become clearer if the purpose of equating is reconsidered: Any raw score, or any statistic that is taken over raw scores, is a function of *both* the ability (abilities) of the individual(s) *and* the characteristics of the test. In order to compare the performances of individuals (or groups) who have taken different tests, it is necessary to make prior adjustments in the test scores—i.e. to equate the tests—so that differences in the scores (or in the statistics) will insofar as possible be solely the result of differences in the individuals (or groups). The adjustment that is sought in the test scores must therefore be a function *only* of the differences in the tests, uncontaminated by the characteristics of the groups that were originally used to determine the adjustment. (To draw on the temperature-thermometer analogy again: the equation, $F = 1.8C + 32$, is useful because it is independent of the method used to derive it and *also* independent of the substances used in the derivation—in addition to the fact that it is universally applicable.) Reference to equations 8 and 9 makes it clear that if Groups α and β are not drawn at random from the same population, differences between them can represent a very significant factor in altering the A and B values and introducing major sources of bias into the equation. However, even where the groups *are* chosen at random, there will inevitably be small differences between them which, if disregarded, will appear in the conversion equation as precisely the kind of bias that has just been discussed, a persistent and ineradicable source of error that will affect all individual and group comparisons that depend on it. Clearly, greater control over the equivalence of the groups used in the equating cannot help but enhance the precision of the equating.

In order to effect this control, the methods of equating and calibration to be described in this section and all others to follow make use of a test score, U, based on a set of items in addition to (or common to) those represented by Forms X and Y, that is used to adjust for the differences that may be found to exist between Groups α and β. In the administration of the tests, Form U is given with Form X to Group α. The identical Form U is also given with Form Y to Group β. Equations appropriate to a random administration of X and Y, with U administered to all examinees, have been developed by Lord (1955a) in a derivation in which he makes maximum likelihood estimates of the population means and variances on Forms X and Y. These equations are:

$$\hat{\mu}_x = M_{x_\alpha} + b_{xu_\alpha}(\hat{\mu}_u - M_{u_\alpha}), \quad [18]$$

$$\hat{\mu}_y = M_{y_\beta} + b_{yu_\beta}(\hat{\mu}_u - M_{u_\beta}), \quad [19]$$

$$\hat{\sigma}_x^2 = s_{x_\alpha}^2 + b_{xu_\alpha}^2(\hat{\sigma}_u^2 - s_{u_\alpha}^2), \quad [20]$$

$$\hat{\sigma}_y^2 = s_{y_\beta}^2 + b_{yu_\beta}^2(\hat{\sigma}_u^2 - s_{u_\beta}^2), \quad [21]$$

where $\hat{\mu}_u = M_{u_t}$ and $\hat{\sigma}_u^2 = s_{u_t}^2$, and $t = \alpha + \beta$. These estimates are applied as before to equation 7, to form the conversion equation, $Y = AX + B$, where $A = \hat{\sigma}_y / \hat{\sigma}_x$ and $B = \hat{\mu}_y - A\hat{\mu}_x$.

The error variance for this method of equating is given by Lord (1950) as:

$$SE_{y*}^2 = 2\hat{\sigma}_y^2(1 - \hat{r}^2)\frac{(1 + \hat{r}^2)z_x^2 + 2}{N_t}, \quad [22]$$

in which it is assumed that

$$\hat{r} = \frac{b_{xu_\alpha}\hat{\sigma}_u}{\hat{\sigma}_x} = \frac{b_{yu_\beta}\hat{\sigma}_u}{\hat{\sigma}_y}.$$

From this it is seen that when $\hat{r} = 0$, this error variance is the same as that for the linear method of design I. When $\hat{r} = .70$, it is one-half as large at the mean ($z_x = 0$) as that for design I. When $\hat{r} = .87$ it is one-fourth as large at the mean as that for design I.

It may be helpful to examine equations 18 to 21 in a little detail. If Groups α and β are identical in their mean performance on Form U, then the values of the parenthetical terms in equations 18 and 19 are found to be zero. That is to say, group adjustments are un-

necessary, and the best population estimate of mean scores on Forms X and Y is the mean that was actually observed for Groups α and β. Similar kinds of considerations, of course, apply to equations 20 and 21.

It is also noted in these equations that no restrictions are placed on the nature of Form U. It is clear, however, that the usefulness of Form U for equating depends on the extent to which it is correlated with the tests being equated. If, for example, $r_{xu} = 0$ (and, presumably, $r_{yu} = 0$, since X and Y are parallel forms), this would indicate that observations made on Form U are irrelevant to the psychological functions measured by Form X or Form Y and are therefore not useful in making adjustments in these measures. This might be true if Forms X and Y were measures of mathematical aptitude for college freshmen and Form U, to take an extreme example, were a measure of height. Obviously, observations made on a variable like height are useless in determining the extent of the adjustments that should be made in a variable like mathematical aptitude. In a manner of speaking, then, the correlation, r_{xu}, which is part of the regression coefficient, b_{xu}, and expresses the degree of relevance that Form U bears to Form X, determines the extent to which the amount of the difference in the parenthetical term may be utilized in making the adjustments for the differences in the groups. The ratio, s_x / s_u, which is the other part of the regression coefficient, may be regarded as a scaling factor used to convert the parenthetical expression from the scale of Form U to the scale of Form X.

The great advantage of this method of equating is its flexibility and adaptability to varying conditions. Form U may be administered in addition to and separate from Form X and/or Form Y. The expression *and/or* is to be noted especially. There is no need for Form U to play precisely the same role in both Forms X and Y. It may be an integral part of Form X, for example, but entirely separate from Form Y. It may be a separately timed section of Forms X and Y. Indeed—and this characteristic endows it with a wide range of administrative power—it may be included within Forms X and/or Y as a set of discrete items interspersed throughout the tests but capable of yielding a total score. In any case, the fundamental restriction is that, however it is used, Form U must represent *the same kind of task* to Group α as it does to Group β. For example, it must be equally subject to contextual and ordinal effects when taken by the two groups; it must be equally subject to the effects of speededness; and it must be equally subject to the effects of motivation, practice, boredom, or fatigue. Within these obvious, commonsense restrictions, the degrees of flexibility indicated above are quite real. Nevertheless, there are certain practices that are recommended: The equating test (or anchor test, or link test, or common test, as it is variously called), Form U, should be long enough and reliable enough to yield data that can be used effectively for making the fine adjustments for differences between the groups that are required. A recommended rule of thumb is that it consist of no fewer than 20 items or no fewer than 20 percent of the number of items in each of Forms X and Y, whichever number of items is larger. It also has been considered advisable, when Form U is defined as a score based on a set of items interspersed through the operational tests, X and Y, to avoid taking such items from the latter part of the test where the effects of speededness are likely to be pronounced.

The same general principle, that Form U represent the same psychological task to both groups, should be adhered to when it is a separately timed test. For example, it either follows the administration of both X and Y or it precedes them both; it is equally affected by practice (or boredom or fatigue) on X and Y; and it does not repeat any items that already appear in X and Y.

The method of equating described here has other dimensions of flexibility. For example, it allows an economical use of its data for the equating of three or more forms as well as two forms. Say there are three parallel forms to equate: X, Y, and Z. These are administered to groups α, β, and γ, respectively, and the performance (mean and variance) for the combined group $(\alpha+\beta+\gamma)$ is estimated using the same

assumptions in the case of the three forms as were made in the equating of two forms. Once these estimates are available they can be entered into the fundamental conversion equation, equation 7, to derive a conversion relating any two of the tests in question.

The method permits other variations. The equating test, Form U, need not be treated as though it were a single variable. It may indeed yield not only one, but two, three, four, or as many scores as are required for making the adjustments between groups. Say that Forms X and Y are alternate forms of a test consisting of *both* verbal and mathematical items. In order to make adjustments for the differences between the groups of individuals taking those forms it would be desirable to use an equating test, Form U, that similarly contains both verbal and mathematical items. The scores on these two kinds of items may be combined to yield a total score, *U*, and applied as has been described above; on the other hand, they may be *kept separate*, as scores *V* and *M*, and used in *multiple combination*. The equations used for estimating the mean and variance for the combined group *t* on Forms X and Y with the use of a multiple predictor are extensions of equations 18 to 21:

$$\hat{\mu}_x = M_{x_\alpha} \cdot b_{xv.m_\alpha}(\hat{\mu}_v - M_{v_\alpha})$$
$$+ b_{xm.v_\alpha}(\hat{\mu}_m - M_{m_\alpha}), \tag{23}$$

$$\hat{\mu}_y = M_{y_\beta} + b_{yv.m_\beta}(\hat{\mu}_v - M_{v_\beta})$$
$$+ b_{ym.v_\beta}(\hat{\mu}_m - M_{m_\beta}), \tag{24}$$

$$\hat{\sigma}_x^2 = s_{x_\alpha}^2 + b_{xv.m_\alpha}^2(\hat{\sigma}_v^2 - s_{v_\alpha}^2) + b_{xm.v_\alpha}^2(\hat{\sigma}_m^2 - s_{m_\alpha}^2)$$
$$+ 2b_{xv.m_\alpha}b_{xm.v_\alpha}(\hat{\sigma}_{vm} - s_{vm_\alpha}), \tag{25}$$

$$\hat{\sigma}_y^2 = s_{y_\beta}^2 + b_{yv.m_\beta}^2(\hat{\sigma}_v^2 - s_{v_\beta}^2) + b_{ym.v_\beta}^2(\hat{\sigma}_m^2 - s_{m_\beta}^2)$$
$$+ 2b_{yv.m_\beta}b_{ym.v_\beta}(\sigma_{vm} - s_{vm_\beta}), \tag{26}$$

where $b_{xv.m_\alpha}$, for example, is the raw-score regression weight for predicting *X* from *V*, with *M* held constant, and $s_{vm_\alpha} = r_{vm_\alpha}s_{v_\alpha}s_{m_\alpha}$. Also, consistent with the notation used in equations 18 to 21, $\hat{\mu}_v = M_{v_t}$, $\hat{\mu}_m = M_{m_t}$, $\hat{\sigma}_v^2 = s_{v_t}^2$, $\hat{\sigma}_m^2 = s_{m_t}^2$, and

$\hat{\sigma}_{vm} = s_{vm_t}$. That is to say, the estimates of the population parameters for the common variables, V and M, are taken directly from the corresponding observed statistics for the combined group, t ($t = \alpha + \beta$).

There is still another variation possible. The equating test, Form U, that is administered to Group α need not be precisely the same test as the Form U administered to Group β. It may be a *quasi-common* test. That is to say, it may actually be *two different forms* of the same test (say U and W), so long as they are both expressed in the same units—that is, so long as the W scores have been converted to the scale of U, or vice versa, or both converted to some other single scale. Any of these variations is possible, the only requirement being that scores on the two forms must be directly and universally comparable. It is understood, of course, that this variation may be introduced not only when the equating test represents a single predictor, but also when it represents multiple predictors, as in equations 23 to 26. Under these circumstances, the two V forms must be expressed on the same scale, as must the two M forms. V and M, however, need not be expressed on similar-appearing scales.

B. *Unequally reliable tests (linear calibration)*

Levine (1955) has shown that, for a random-groups administration, when Forms X and Y are unequally reliable, it is appropriate to base the conversion on *true*, rather than observed, scores. Under this set of conditions, and when Form U is separate and exclusive of X and Y, the slope and intercept of the conversion equation, $Y = AX + B$, are found to be: $A = b_{xu_\beta}/b_{xu_\alpha}$, and $B = \hat{\mu}_y - A\hat{\mu}_x$, where b_{xu_α} and b_{yu_β} are the usual regression coefficients, as observed in Groups α and β, respectively, for predicting X from U and Y from U, and where $\hat{\mu}_x$ and $\hat{\mu}_y$ are calculated as in equations 18 and 19. The additional assumption required in Levine's derivation is that Form U be parallel in function to both Forms X and Y.

When Form U is an included part of X and Y, $A = (b_{xu_\alpha}\hat{\sigma}_y^2)/(b_{yu_\beta}\hat{\sigma}_x^2)$ and $B = \hat{\mu}_y - A\mu_x$. The values of $\hat{\mu}_x$, $\hat{\mu}_y$, σ_x^2, and σ_y^2 are calculated as in equations 18 to 21 respectively.

Design IV: Nonrandom groups—one test to each group, common equating test administered to both groups

A. *Basic linear method for groups not widely different in ability*

The methods described under designs I, II, and III are appropriate in situations which permit the assignment of examinees to random groups. However, there are frequently situations, as in the operation of a highly secure testing program, where it is considered inadvisable to introduce new forms prior to their first operational use, even in an experimental equating administration, and where the demands of the program do not permit the presentation of more than one form at an operational administration of the test. Under these circumstances equating based on the random administration of test forms is not possible. The methods of all three of the foregoing designs are ruled out, and the data used for equating have to be drawn from the operational administrations themselves, where little control, if any, can be exercised over the choice of equating samples. If, for example, a new form of a test is introduced at, say, the regular September administration in a testing program and it is desired to equate that form to an older form, even one given at a previous September administration where the examinees are similar to these in many respects, there would still be no assurance that the groups taking the two forms were drawn from the same population. Therefore, even when care has been taken, as it was in the present example, to choose the α and β groups in such a way as to minimize their differences, some means must be found to observe the differences that do exist between the two groups and to make adjustments for them.

The methods to be described in the present section derive their data from the same design as that previously described in connection with the maximum likelihood method developed by Lord (1955a) and the true-score adaptation of that method by Levine (1955). It may be helpful to recapitulate the essentials of the design: Form X is administered to Group α; Form Y is administered to Group β. Form U, a test which is based on a set of items in addition to (or included among) those represented by Forms X and Y, is administered to both Groups α and β and is used to adjust for differences that may be found to exist between them. Estimates of the mean and variance on both Forms X and Y are made for the combined group, Group t (t representing $\alpha+\beta$), and are applied in equation 7 to yield a linear equation relating raw scores on Form X to raw scores on Form Y. Because the equations that provide these estimates of mean and variance are so basic to the problem of equating, their derivation, attributed to L. R Tucker (Gulliksen, 1950, chap. 19; also Angoff, 1961a), is repeated here. The equations are based on the three principal assumptions of univariate selection theory: that the intercept of X on U is the same for Group t and Group α, i.e.

$$M_{x_t} - b_{xu_t}M_{u_t} = M_{x\alpha} - b_{xu\alpha}M_{u\alpha}; \quad [27]$$

that the regression coefficient of X on U is the same for Group t and Group α, i.e.

$$b_{xu_t} = b_{xu\alpha}; \quad [28]$$

and that the variance error of estimate of X from U is the same for Group t and Group α, i.e.

$$s_{x_t}^2(1 - r_{xu_t}^2) = s_{x\alpha}^2(1 - r_{xu\alpha}^2). \quad [29]$$

Substituting equation 28 in 27 and solving for $\hat{M}_{x_t}$,

$$\hat{M}_{x_t} = M_{x\alpha} + b_{xu\alpha}(M_{u_t} - M_{u\alpha}), \quad [30]$$

the symbol (⌃) here, as before, designating an estimated value. Substituting, in equation 29, $b_{xu_t}s_{u_t}$ for its equivalent, $r_{xu_t}s_{x_t}$, and also $b_{xu\alpha}s_{u\alpha}$ for its equivalent, $r_{xu\alpha}s_{x\alpha}$, and solving for $\hat{s}_{x_t}^2$,

$$\hat{s}_{x_t}^2 = s_{x\alpha}^2 + b_{xu\alpha}^2(s_{u_t}^2 - s_{u\alpha}^2). \quad [31]$$

Parallel assumptions and development are made for the relationship between Forms Y and U and Groups β and t, resulting in the following two equations which parallel, respectively, equations 30 and 31.

$$\hat{M}_{y_t} = M_{y\beta} + b_{yu\beta}(M_{u_t} - M_{u\beta}), \quad [32]$$

and

$$\hat{s}_{y_t}^2 = s_{y\beta}^2 + b_{yu\beta}^2(s_{u_t}^2 - s_{u\beta}^2). \quad [33]$$

(The symbols $\hat{M}_{x_t}$, $\hat{s}_{x_t}^2$, $\hat{M}_{y_t}$, and $\hat{s}_{y_t}^2$ are used in equations 30 to 33 instead of $\hat{\mu}_x$, $\hat{\sigma}_x^2$, $\hat{\mu}_y$, and $\hat{\sigma}_y^2$, respectively, because here simply an estimate for a combined group is being discussed, not an estimate for a population.) Equations 30 to 33 are then substituted in the prototype equation 7, $(Y-M_y)/s_y=(X-M_x)/s_x$ to yield the conversion equation, $Y=AX+B$, where $A=\hat{s}_{y_t}/\hat{s}_{x_t}$ and $B=\hat{M}_{y_t}-A\hat{M}_{x_t}$.

It is noted that the computational procedures for arriving at the estimates in equations 30 to 33 are precisely the same as for equations 18 to 21 respectively, although the derivations of the two sets of equations are entirely different.

The same kinds of flexibility are appropriate in the present method of equating as in the maximum likelihood method. Form U may be administered in addition to and separate from Form X *and* Form Y, or as part of Form X *and* part of Form Y, or, finally, separate from Form X *but* as part of Form Y. It may be a separately timed section for Forms X and Y, or it may be a set of discrete items interspersed through the two forms but capable of yielding a total score. However, except for the requirement of strict random assignment of Forms X and Y, the basic precautions of administrative design that have been described in connection with the maximum likelihood method are observed here—in sum, that Form U is constructed and administered to represent psychologically the same task to both groups.

The general caution that statistical methods should not be used unless the assumptions that are basic to their derivation can be fulfilled is seldom as clear as it is here. Formulas 30 to 33 are applicable only when it may be assumed that the regression systems for Groups α and β would have been the same had the groups taken precisely the same tests. This is not an unreasonable assumption when the groups are similar in all relevant respects, even if Forms X, Y, and U are not parallel measures. (Lord, 1960, pointed out that, if the groups are very much different in ability, the intercepts of scores on one test on scores on another will differ significantly for the two groups, even if the two tests in question *are* parallel measures.) However, if Form U is *not* parallel to X and Y,[16] then Groups α and β must be drawn at random from the same population. The importance of this requirement can be made clear if one considers as an example the problem of equating two forms (Form X and Form Y) of a test in elementary French grammar at the secondary school level, using performance on a test of verbal aptitude (Form U) to adjust for differences in the groups taking X and Y. Clearly, growth in the function measured by X and Y is much more rapid than growth in the function measured by U. Therefore, if Group α is a group of students who have completed only three months of elementary French while Group β has completed five months of elementary French, one would expect that their scores on the French test would be substantially different even though there were no observable difference in their verbal aptitude. That is to say, under these circumstances, the assumption basic to this equating design, that the regression of scores on X on scores on U (or Y on U) is the same for the two groups, is one that cannot be supported, with the result that the data would be inapplicable to the equating problem.

Like the maximum likelihood method, the method derived from selection theory need not be restricted to the equating of *two* forms of a test but can be used to equate three and more forms. In the administration, each of these forms would be administered to a separate group; but Form U, the equating test, would be given to all groups. Estimates would then be made of the mean and variance on each of the test forms to be equated for the total group taking Form U, in accordance with equations 30 and 31, and carried out as many times as there are forms to be equated. Also, as in the maximum likelihood method, Form U need not be restricted to yielding a single score but may yield a number of scores used in multiple combination in a manner parallel to that described in equations 23 to 26.

Finally, Form U may be a *quasi-common* test. That is to say, it may actually be two different forms of a test, one administered to Group α and the other to Group β. The only restriction is that the two forms be expressed on the same scale, so that appropriate comparisons and adjustments may be made for differences between the two groups in the process of equating the tests.

These variations, it should be pointed out, need not be introduced singly into the basic procedure but may be used in combination. It is entirely possible, for example, to equate four tests simultaneously, using four different forms of Form U (so long as they are all expressed on the same scale) and, in addition, providing for two separate subscores of each Form U to be used in multiple combination, as in equations 23 to 26.

B. *Curvilinear method for groups not widely different in ability*

An appropriate curvilinear, or equipercentile, analog (suggested by Lord[17] and described by Levine, 1958) to the basic linear equating method described in the preceding section can be derived from the fundamental assumptions stated in equations 27, 28, and 29. If, again, there are two groups of individuals, α and β, one (α) having taken Form X and an equating test U and the other (β) having taken Form Y and the same equating test U, the first step in the equating process is to estimate the frequencies in the distributions of both Form X scores and Form Y scores for the combined group t ($t = \alpha + \beta$), in a manner precisely the same as was described in the section of this chapter on norms. This is done by: (*a*) combining the two distributions of Form U scores to form a distribution of Form U scores for Group t; (*b*) working with the scatterplot of U scores versus X scores, multiplying, for each interval of score (*i*) on Form U, the ratio of frequencies, f_{i_t}/f_{i_α}, by each of the frequencies in the array for score interval U_i. (By varying the size of U_i appropriately it is possible to keep the ratio, f_{i_t}/f_{i_α}, from being excessively large. This is particularly important when the fre-

[16] The assumption is still made that Forms X and Y are parallel. This assumption is never relinquished in considering the problems of equating and calibration.

[17] Personal communication, c. 1957.

quencies, f_{i_t} and f_{i_α}, are relatively small.) When this is completed for the arrays for all values of U_i, there will be a new scatterplot of U versus X estimated for Group t. The next steps in the procedure involve: (c) making a similar estimate of the frequencies in the scatterplot of U versus Y for Group t; and (d) determining the frequencies for each of the scores on Form X (and also on Form Y) simply by adding the frequencies in the cells across the values of U. These frequencies represent the estimated distribution on Form X for the entire Group t, and, correspondingly, the estimated distribution on Form Y for the entire Group t. With these distributions in hand Form X scores can be equated to Form Y scores by the usual equipercentile method. (It should be mentioned that this method, like other "nonrandom-group" methods, is also appropriate under the more restrictive condition in which individuals are assigned to groups at random.)

C. *Linear methods for samples of different ability*

1. *Equally reliable tests*

Levine (1955) has shown that when Groups α and β are widely different in ability the assumptions that are basic to classical selection theory are not appropriate. Instead, other assumptions are made but *under the restriction that Form U is parallel in function to both Forms X and Y:* (a) that the intercept of the regression line relating true scores on Form X to true scores on Form U (a relationship expressed by a correlation of unity) is the same for Group t as for Group α:

$$M_{x_t} - \frac{s_{\tilde{x}_t}}{s_{\tilde{u}_t}} M_{ut} = M_{x\alpha} - \frac{s_{\tilde{x}\alpha}}{s_{\tilde{u}\alpha}} M_{u\alpha}, \quad [34]$$

where $s_{\tilde{x}} = s_x\sqrt{r_{xx}}$ and $s_{\tilde{u}} = s_u\sqrt{r_{uu}}$; (b) that the slope of the line of relationship is the same for Group t as for Group α:

$$\frac{s_{\tilde{x}_t}}{s_{\tilde{u}_t}} = \frac{s_{\tilde{x}\alpha}}{s_{\tilde{u}\alpha}}; \quad [35]$$

and (c) that the variance errors of measurement for Form X are the same for Group t as for Group α:

$$s_{x_t}^2(1 - r_{xx_t}) = s_{x\alpha}^2(1 - r_{xx\alpha}). \quad [36]$$

From equations 34, 35, and 36, it can be shown that

$$\hat{M}_{x_t} = M_{x\alpha} + \frac{s_{\tilde{x}\alpha}}{s_{\tilde{u}\alpha}}(M_{u_t} - M_{u\alpha}), \quad [37]$$

and that

$$\hat{s}_{x_t}^2 = s_{x\alpha}^2 + \frac{s_{\tilde{x}\alpha}^2}{s_{\tilde{u}\alpha}^2}(s_{u_t}^2 - s_{u\alpha}^2). \quad [38]$$

Equations parallel to equations 37 and 38 may be derived by making the same assumptions for the relationship between Form Y and Form U as administered to Groups t and β, to yield the equations,

$$\hat{M}_{y_t} = M_{y\beta} + \frac{s_{\tilde{y}\beta}}{s_{\tilde{u}\beta}}(M_{u_t} - M_{u\beta}), \quad [39]$$

and

$$\hat{s}_{y_t}^2 = s_{y\beta}^2 + \frac{s_{\tilde{y}\beta}^2}{s_{\tilde{u}\beta}^2}(s_{u_t}^2 - s_{u\beta}^2). \quad [40]$$

Finally, as before, the conversion equation relating Form X scores to Form Y scores is written $Y = AX + B$, where $A = \hat{s}_{y_t}/\hat{s}_{x_t}$ and $B = \hat{M}_{y_t} - A\hat{M}_{x_t}$. Some simplifications can be introduced into the computation of equations 37 to 40. Angoff (1953) has shown that the data of the equating experiment itself may be used to estimate the ratios of the standard deviations of true scores. In the development of his equations, $s_{\tilde{x}}/s_{\tilde{u}} = n$, the ratio of effective test lengths of Form X to Form U. When Form U is included in Form X, the test of parallel function, $n = s_x/r_{xu}s_u = 1/b_{ux}$; when Form U is separate and exclusive of Form X, then $n = (s_x^2 + s_{ux})/(s_u^2 + s_{ux})$. Similar applications of formulas may, of course, be adopted for the data involving Form Y and Form U.

2. *Unequally reliable test (linear calibration)*

When Forms X and Y are unequally reliable, modifications in the equations are required. When Form U is exclusive of X and Y $Y = AX + B$, where $A = (b_{yu_\beta}r_{uu\alpha})/(b_{xu_\alpha}r_{uu\beta})$, and

$$B = M_{y_\beta} - AM_{x_\alpha} + \frac{b_{yu_\beta}}{r_{uu_\beta}}(M_{u_\alpha} - M_{u_\beta}).$$

When Form U is included in X and Y, $A = b_{ux_\alpha}/b_{uy_\beta}$, and $B = M_{y_\beta} - AM_{x_\alpha} + [(M_{u_\alpha} - M_{u_\beta})/b_{uy_\beta}]$.

Design V: Other methods involving score data

A. *Forms X and Y equated to a common test*

1. *Linear procedure*

A method of equating Forms X and Y that is intuitively reasonable is one that, like others just described, also involves the administration of an additional test, U, either following the administration of both X and Y or preceding them both. If X and Y are parallel forms of the same test it is reasonable to assume that each of them has the same practice effect on U when U is administered second, or that U exerts the same practice effect on X and Y, if U is administered first. Form X is equated directly to U; Form Y is equated to U; and scores on X and Y equivalent to the same score on U are themselves taken to be equivalent. Thus, if $X = A_{xu}U + B_{xu}$,[18] where $A_{xu} = s_{x_\alpha}/s_{u_\alpha}$ and $B_{xu} = M_{x_\alpha} - A_{xu}M_{u_\alpha}$, and if $Y = A_{yu}U + B_{yu}$, where $A_{yu} = s_{y_\beta}/s_{u_\beta}$ and $B_{yu} = M_{y_\beta} - A_{yu}M_{u_\beta}$, then $Y = A_{yx}X + B_{yx}$, where $A_{yx} = A_{yu}/A_{xu}$, and $B_{yx} = B_{yu} - A_{yx}B_{xu}$. In order to insure that the conversion equation, $Y = A_{yx}X + B_{yx}$, has the appropriate generality, Form U must be a parallel form of X and Y if there is to be freedom in the choice of Groups α and β. If Form U is not parallel to X and Y, then Groups α and β must be drawn at random from the same population. Under conditions of random sampling, Lord (1950) has shown that the variance error of equating by this method is given by:

$$SE_{y^*}^2 = 4s_{y_\beta}^2(1 - r)\frac{z_x^2(1+r)+2}{N_t} \quad [41]$$

where it is assumed that $r = r_{xu_\alpha} = r_{yu_\beta}$. Comparison of equation 41 with equation 15 shows

---

[18] A variant in the notation for the A and B values is introduced from this point on wherever necessary to avoid ambiguity. In general, A_{gh} and B_{gh} are the slope and intercept parameters, respectively, of the linear equation for converting scores from the scale of H to the scale of G, as follows: $G = A_{gh}H + B_{gh}$.

that this method of equating has four times the error variance of the counterbalanced method described as design II. Lord pointed out that half of this increase in error variance is attributable to the fact that in this method only half the examinees take each test, X or Y, whereas in design II all examinees take both tests. The other half of the increase in error variance arises from the fact that this method really involves two equatings instead of only one. Lord then pointed out that at the mean ($z_x = 0$) the error variance for this method is even larger than that for design I (administration of Forms X and Y to random halves of a total group; no additional equating test administered), unless r is at least .50. If r is zero, the error variance of this method is exactly twice that for design I. Even if r is somewhat greater than .50, the error variance in equation 41 will be larger than that in equation 10 if z_x is sufficiently large. This would indicate that if r is less than .50, it would be better to ignore all data relating to Form U and use the method of design I (assuming, of course, that Groups α and β are randomly chosen; this is essential) than to use the present method. Undoubtedly the added advantage of the data from Form U is more than offset by the fact that there are two equatings here instead of just one and therefore two sources of error.

2. *Curvilinear analog*

The curvilinear analog to the method described in the preceding section is clear. Forms X and U are equated by an equipercentile method, as are Forms Y and U. Then for each score on Form U the equivalent scores on X and Y are found, plotted, and smoothed to yield a conversion from X to Y.

B. *Forms X and Y predicted by a common test*

1. *Linear procedure*

If the same design of administration is carried out—Form X administered to Group α, Form Y administered to Group β, and Form U administered to both groups—it is possible to define as equivalent those scores on X and Y that are predicted by the same score on U. Thus if $\hat{X} = b_{xu}U + D_{xu}$, where $b_{xu} = r_{xu_\alpha}(s_{x_\alpha}/s_{u_\alpha})$ and $D_{xu} = M_{x_\alpha} - b_{xu}M_{u_\alpha}$, and if $\hat{Y}=b_{yu}U+D_{yu}$, where $b_{yu}=r_{yu\beta}(s_{y\beta}/s_{u\beta})$ and $D_{yu}=M_{y\beta}-b_{yu}M_{u\beta}$, then $Y=AX+B$, where

$$A = b_{yu}/b_{xu} \qquad [42]$$

and

$$B = D_{yu} - AD_{xu}. \qquad [43]$$

The same considerations regarding the generality of results apply to this method as to the method just previously described. The administration of Form U must either precede the administration of both X and Y or it must follow them both. Form U must be parallel in function to X and Y if there is to be freedom in the choice of Groups α and β. However, if there is to be freedom in the choice of Form U, then Groups α and β must be randomly drawn from the same population.

2. Curvilinear analog

In the curvilinear adaptation, scatterplots of X on U and Y on U are drawn up. Means of the X arrays and means of the Y arrays are calculated for corresponding fixed values of U, plotted and smoothed. The resulting curve relating the points $M_{x.u}$ versus $M_{y.u}$ describes the relationship between Form X and Form Y.

C. Forms X and Y predicting a common test

1. Linear procedure

Again using the same design of administration—Form X administered to Group α, Form Y administered to Group β, and Form U administered to both groups—scores on X and Y are defined as equivalent if they predict, instead of being predicted by (as in the preceding definition) the same score on U. Thus if $\hat{U}=b_{ux}X+D_{ux}$, where $b_{ux}=r_{ux\alpha}(s_{u\alpha}/s_{x\alpha})$ and $D_{ux}=M_{u\alpha}-b_{ux}M_{x\alpha}$, and if $\hat{U}=b_{uy}Y+D_{uy}$, where $b_{uy}=r_{uy\beta}(s_{u\beta}/s_{y\beta})$ and $D_{uy}=M_{u\beta}-b_{uy\beta}M_{y\beta}$, then $Y=AX+B$, where

$$A=b_{ux}/b_{uy} \qquad [44]$$

and

$$B=(D_{ux}-D_{uy})/b_{uy}. \qquad [45]$$

The same considerations regarding the choice of tests and groups and the same considerations regarding administrative procedure apply here

as in the method just described where scores on Forms X and Y are predicted by scores on U

2. Curvilinear analog

Here, too, scatterplots are drawn up, but this time of U on X and U on Y. Means of the U arrays are calculated and plotted for fixed values of X and also for fixed values of Y yielding two curves which are then smoothed. Finally, values of X and values of Y are read from their corresponding graphs for the same values of U, plotted against each other, and smoothed.

There are undoubtedly many other variations in ways of dealing with the basic set of data described here. It would be expected, of course, that the most reliable and most generally applicable results would be those obtained from the maximum use of the available data, collected under appropriate and rigorous conditions.

Design VI: Methods of score equating based on item data

A. Thurstone's absolute scaling method (Thurstone, 1925; also Fan, 1957)

The method described here applies to the following situation: Group α takes Form X and Group β takes Form Y. Forms X and Y have a set of items in common for which difficulty values, p, have been obtained and converted to their corresponding normal deviates z', which, unlike the p values, are expressed on a linear scale. Like all methods of score equating, this method assumes that Forms X and Y are parallel forms and therefore can be converted to a unique common scale. It also assumes that the distributions for Groups α and β would both be normal on this scale. For the present purpose the common scale is taken to be the scale of Y.

The purpose of the method is to find relationships between the sets of item difficulties for the two groups that will lead to a conversion from raw scores on Form X to raw scores on Form Y, as in the equation, $Y=AX+B$, where $A=s_{y\alpha}/s_{x\alpha}(=s_{y\beta}/s_{x\beta})$ and $B=M_{y\alpha}-AM_{x\alpha}$ $(=M_{y\beta}-AM_{x\beta})$. If it is assumed that the distribution of ability scores is normal within the Groups α and β, then the following statements can be written describing the scale value, Y_i, of any item, i, on the scale of the ability represented by Y, assuming perfect correlation between item and ability:

$$z_{i_\alpha} = \frac{Y_i - M_{y_\alpha}}{s_{y_\alpha}}, \qquad [46]$$

and

$$z_{i_\beta} = \frac{Y_i - M_{y_\beta}}{s_{y_\beta}}, \qquad [47]$$

where M_{y_α}, M_{y_β}, s_{y_α}, and s_{y_β} are the ability score means and standard deviations for Groups α and β, and z_{i_α} and z_{i_β} are the standard-score values of the scale position of item i for Groups α and β, respectively. Setting 46 and 47 equal,

$$z_{i_\beta} = (s_{y_\alpha}/s_{y_\beta})z_{i_\alpha} + \frac{M_{y_\alpha} - M_{y_\beta}}{s_{y_\beta}}. \qquad [48]$$

If also a bivariate plot of the normal deviates, z'_{i_β} versus z'_{i_α}, is constructed, the relationship between them can be expressed as:

$$z'_{i_\beta} = (s'_\beta/s'_\alpha)z'_{i_\alpha} + M'_\beta - (s'_\beta/s'_\alpha)M'_\alpha, \qquad [49]$$

where M'_α, M'_β, s'_α, and s'_β are the means and standard deviations of the normal deviates for the two groups.

Assuming that 48 and 49 are alternative expressions of the same relationship, it is concluded that the slopes are equal, or that

$$s_{y_\alpha}/s_{y_\beta} = s'_\beta/s'_\alpha, \qquad [50]$$

and that the intercepts are equal, or that

$$(M_{y_\alpha} - M_{y_\beta})/s_{y_\beta} = M'_\beta - (s'_\beta/s'_\alpha)M'_\alpha. \qquad [51]$$

From equations 50 and 51 the estimated values, $\hat{s}_{y_\alpha}$ and $\hat{M}_{y_\alpha}$, may be obtained for the calculation of the values of the slope, $A = \hat{s}_{y_\alpha}/s_{x_\alpha}$, and the intercept, $B = \hat{M}_{y_\alpha} - AM_{x_\alpha}$, of the conversion equation relating raw scores on Form X to raw scores on Form Y: $\hat{s}_{y_\alpha} = s_{y_\beta}(s'_\beta/s'_\alpha)$ and, $\hat{M}_{y_\alpha} = s_{y_\beta}[M'_\beta - (s'_\beta/s'_\alpha)M'_\alpha] + M_{y_\beta}$.

Ordinarily, the plot of points for z'_{i_α} versus z'_β will form a narrow linear elliptical pattern, verifying (by the fact that it is linear) that the distributions of Groups α and β can be normalized on the same scale and indicating, by the high correlation represented by the tight swarm of points, that the items have the same "meaning" or represent the same "task" for the two groups of individuals. Indeed, the pattern of these points, represented analytically as the item-group interaction, will reveal the presence of items that may be "biased" toward one of the two groups. The technique of examining the bivariate plot of item difficulties, either graphically or analytically, has proved to be an extremely useful tool in the search for cultural bias in test items (Cleary & Hilton, 1966), in the investigation of curricular differences in achievement test items (Angoff, 1970, in press), and in item calibration (Thurstone, 1947).

The principal test of the validity of the Thurstone method of absolute scaling is the extent to which equations 48 and 49 are indeed representations of the same line. With the use of actual data taken from the administration of a power test to widely different subgroups of examinees, and also with fictitious but perfectly consistent item and score data for groups of different ability, Fan (1957) compared the results that would be obtained from score data appropriate to equation 48 and from item data, based on the same examinees, appropriate to equation 49 and found that the results were indeed quite different. These differences, he pointed out, could not be attributed to sampling error in the data but necessarily resulted from the attempt to equate test forms that are administered to groups of different ability.

It is possible that the failure of the Thurstone method (of calibrating tests through item statistics) to deal adequately with groups that are substantially different is due to the obviously untenable assumption that the item-ability (or item-test) correlations are unity. On the other hand, Torgerson (1958, p. 395) points out that the requirement of perfectly discriminating items is unnecessarily restrictive. The model, he goes on to say, will fit the data, assuming only that the item characteristic curves are normal ogives and that the correlations of the items with the underlying ability are all equal. Clearly, this latter assumption especially, like the assumption of perfect item-test correlations, is also rarely, if ever, met in practice. As a result, the absolute scaling method as applied to item data, although important from a theoretical and historical point of view, is not useful in practice except when the distributions of the groups are very nearly alike, at least in the first two moments.

B. *Swineford-Fan method of equating*

Like the Thurstone method of absolute scaling (i.e. equating) the Swineford-Fan procedure (Swineford & Fan, 1957) is based on estimations made from a set of items common to two forms of the same test, Form X and Form Y, where Form X is administered to Group α and Form Y is administered to Group β. In order to calculate the slope, $A = s_{y_\alpha}/s_{x_\alpha}$, and intercept, $B = M_{y_\alpha} - AM_{x_\alpha}$, of the equation, $Y = AX + B$, relating Form X to Form Y, it is necessary first to estimate M_{y_α} and s_{y_α}.

The estimation process derives from the fact that for a test, W of n items the raw (rights) score mean and standard deviation can be expressed in terms of item statistics as follows:

$$M_w = \sum_{i=1}^{n} p_i, \qquad [52]$$

and

$$s_w = \sum_{i=1}^{n} p_i d_i, \qquad [53]$$

where

p_i = proportion of correct responses for item i,

$d_i = (M_i - M_w)/s_w$, and

M_i = mean raw test score of those answering item i correctly.

Equation 53 comes from Gulliksen (1950, chap. 21) in which it is shown (eq. 20, p. 377) that $s_w = \sum_{i=1}^{n} r_{iw}\sqrt{p_i q_i}$, where r_{iw} is the point-biserial item-test correlation, and (eq. 32, p. 387) $r_{iw}\sqrt{p_i q_i} = p_i(M_i - M_w)/s_w$.

If, for the set of common items, a bivariate plot is made of the normal deviate values, z_i', corresponding to the values, p_i, as observed in the two groups, a line may be drawn relating

the z' values for the two groups, as follows:

$$z_\alpha' = (s_\alpha'/s_\beta')z_\beta' + M_\alpha' - (s_\alpha'/s_\beta')M_\beta', \qquad [54]$$

where, as before, M' and s' are the mean and standard deviation, respectively, of the z values. Using this line the z_α' values may be estimated from the z_β' values for the *noncommon* items in Form Y. Converting the values of z to values of p for all the items in Form Y— those estimated for Group α as well as those observed—and summing for all items in Form Y, an estimated value of M_{y_α} may be generated as shown in equation 52.

Making a similar plot of the values d_i for the set of common items, it is similarly possible to develop a line relating the d values (which it is noted, are independent of the metrics of the tests) for the two groups, as follows:

$$d_\alpha = (s_\alpha''/s_\beta'')d_\beta + M_\alpha'' - (s_\alpha''/s_\beta'')M_\beta'', \qquad [55]$$

where M'' and s'' are the mean and standard deviation, respectively, of the d values. Corresponding to the procedure followed with equation 54, equation 55 can be used to estimate the d values for the noncommon items in Form Y for Group α. Multiplying the observed values of d_i and p_i for the common items and the estimated values of d_i and p_i for all noncommon items in Form Y, and summing the products, it is possible, as shown in equation 53, to generate an estimated value of s_{y_α}. With the estimated values, $\hat{M}_{y_\alpha}$ and $\hat{s}_{y_\alpha}$, and the corresponding observed values, M_{x_α} and s_{x_α}, the conversion parameters are calculated for the equation, $Y = AX + B$.

Equating and Calibration Systems

Ordinarily, the standard error of equating as shown in equations 10, 15, 22, and 41, is quite small in comparison with the standard error of measurement. However, as has already been pointed out, the error of equating appears in the conversion equation itself, and so it is transmitted to every score to which the equation is applied and affects the summary statistics of all scores very much in the manner of a bias. In this respect it is like the error in norms distribution but *unlike* other kinds of statistical error, as, for example, the error of measurement in a mean, which tends to vanish as the sample size is increased. Thus, while the error of equating is small in relation to the error of a single test score, it can loom quite large in relation to the error in a mean and can seriously affect comparisons of group performance. Moreover, in any large testing program where many forms of the same test are produced and equated, the error of equating can become quite considerable, if left unchecked. If, for example, successive forms were each equated to their immediate predecessors in chain fashion, then the variance of equated scores for the most recent form in relation to the original form would be $n\mathrm{SE}_y^2$ (where SE_y^2 is the average variance error of any one equating process and n is the number of equating links in the chain). That is to say, the variance error in the entire system would increase directly as a function of the number of links, or equatings involved, and could become competitive in size even with the variance error of measurement in a single score. On the other hand, if the equating system were allowed to develop, not as a simple chain but without any plan, then it is entirely possible that separate "strains" or "families" of scales could develop, with the very likely result that two forms, contiguous with respect to the order of their appearance, could be quite distantly related in terms of the number of equating links between them, and as a result of equating error alone, could yield two scaled scores for a given ability level that differed much more than they would have if the forms had been schematically closer together.

In order to reduce the form-to-form equating errors and to work toward the development of a cohesive and internally consistent system, it is advisable to equate each new form, not to one, but to *two* previous forms, and to average the results. Say that Y is an old form for which there already exists an equation, $C=A_{cy}Y+B_{cy}$, permitting the conversion of raw scores to the reporting scale. If scores on the new form (X) are equated to raw scores on Form Y, resulting in the equation $Y=A_{yx}X+B_{yx}$, it becomes possible to develop the conversion,

$C=A_{cx}'X+B_{cx}'$, relating Form X raw scores to the scale, simply by substituting one equation into the other: $A_{cx}'=A_{cy}A_{yx}$ and $B_{cx}'=A_{cy}B_{yx}+B_{cy}$. If Form X also is equated to a second old form, Z (for which there already exists the equation, $C=A_{cz}Z+B_{cz}$), resulting in the equation, $Z=A_{zx}X+B_{zx}$, it becomes possible to develop a second conversion, $C=A_{cx}''X+B_{cx}''$, also by substituting one equation into the other: $A_{cx}''=A_{cz}A_{zx}$ and $B_{cx}''=A_{cz}B_{zx}+B_{cz}$. If it is assumed that the characteristics of Form X will dictate its conversion parameters (the slope and intercept of the equation converting raw scores to scaled scores), then it also may be hypothesized there will be a unique "true" line relating Form X to the scale. The two conversion lines, $C=A_{cx}'X+B_{cx}'$ and $C=A_{cx}''X+B_{cx}''$, may then be regarded as two estimates of the true line and averaged if it appears that the differences between them are only random. (An "average" line may be determined by bisecting the angle between the lines or by averaging the A values and averaging the B values.) In a large-scale testing program, like the College Board's Scholastic Aptitude Tests (SAT) used for admissions, where new forms of a test are introduced at frequent intervals, it is possible to erect a systematic network of equating linkages among the test forms by specifying the ways in which the pair of old forms would be chosen for the equating of each of the new forms. Such a plan was indeed worked out for the College Board program (McGee, 1961), designed to organize the linkages among the test forms in a "braiding" fashion, by which it was hoped to shorten the "equating distance" between every form and every other form and to knit the system more tightly together. If properly executed, such a plan tends to enhance the reliability of the conversion for any new form, and, in consequence of this greater reliability, it tends to enhance the equivalence or calibration of scores among forms.

Calibration of Tests at Different Levels of Ability

Some systems of tests are designed to permit the measurement of a set of abilities over a wide range of talent, as would be found over a series of age levels—for example from early childhood to adolescence—or over a series of grade levels—from the elementary grades to college level. There are a number of systems of tests of this type, both tests that yield an IQ or grade equivalent—for example the Stanford-Binet, the Kuhlmann-Anderson, the Lorge-Thorndike, and the Iowa Tests of Basic Skills—and tests that do not—for example the Cooperative School and College Ability Test and Sequential Tests of Educational Progress.

If there were one very long test, appropriately constructed for the entire expanse of talent, then each examinee in the standardization group would take the same long test, and raw scores on that test could be scaled in one of the ways described earlier in this chapter (see section on scaling). However, to give each examinee the same long test is clearly uneconomical; since there would be so many items that would be clearly too easy for him and (or) so many items that would be clearly too difficult for him, it would be a waste of his time and effort for him to take them all. In some tests, like the Stanford-Binet (Terman & Merrill, 1960), each examinee takes only those items that differentiate for him, plus enough additional easy and difficult items to verify that he has truly exhausted the band of item difficulty that would provide adequate measurement of his ability. Once the "basal" and "empty" years have been established, it is assumed that the examinee would have passed all items below the basal year and would have failed all the items above the empty year, had he taken them. In other tests, like the Lorge-Thorndike Multi-Level Edition (Lorge et al., 1966), there is a series of eight tests, one test for each of eight levels. Each test consists of a group of modular units, or subtests, also graded in difficulty but more finely. As one proceeds from one test level to the next higher level, the easiest modular unit is dropped from the beginning of the test and a more difficult modular unit is added at the upper end. Thus, every one of the eight available test levels has a considerable proportion (80 percent) of items in common with the test level just below it and also with the test level just above it. (The exceptions to this,

of course, are the lowest test level, which has items in common only with the levels above it, and the highest test level, which has items in common only with the levels below it.) In still other tests, like the Cooperative School and College Ability Test (SCAT) (1956), five mutually exclusive tests are available pitched at five spans of grade level.

Particularly in the case of tests like the Lorge-Thorndike and the SCAT, procedures have been developed for calibrating each test level with the other tests in the series in order to yield scores on one underlying scale. The different procedures have much in common, but there are many variations in approach. One such approach may be described as:

1. One test in the center of the series (say, V, W, X, Y, and Z) is chosen as the anchor, and the tests just above and just below it are calibrated to it. Scores on this test (Level X) are put on an arbitrary *interim scale* for the purposes of the calibration operations, simply by defining one score (say, 450) to correspond to the minimum raw score on the anchor form and another score (say, 550) to correspond to the maximum raw score on the anchor form, taking care to provide no less than one scaled score unit for each raw score unit on the anchor form. This operation yields the equation, $C = A_{cx}X + B_{cx}$, using the notation adopted earlier, where A_{cx} and B_{cx} are the slope and intercept, respectively, of the linear equation relating scores on Level X to the Interim Scale.

2. A set of common test material is constructed for purposes of the calibration. In the case of the Lorge-Thorndike Multi-Level Edition the common material appears as an integral part of the tests; in the case of other tests like SCAT, common test material was prepared explicitly for the calibration and administered along with the operational forms of SCAT, but not as an integral part of those forms. Preferably, the common material should contain items that will be sufficiently discriminating for the two groups for which the two adjacent test levels are appropriate.

3. A sample of students is chosen representing the group for whom the anchor test (Level X) is appropriate, and another sample is

chosen representing the group for which the next level of test (say, Level Y, the level below it) is appropriate. The Level X test and the Level Y test are administered to random halves of both groups. (This is most easily accomplished by packaging the Level X test and the Level Y test in alternating order and distributing them to both groups.) If the common test material is separate, then it should be administered as an integral test to everyone in both groups and, of course, in the same order (preceding *or* following the operational test, X or Y).

4. Using equations 30 to 33, estimates of mean and variance are made for both levels for the combined group taking both levels. These estimates are then applied to equation 7, resulting in the equation, $X = A_{xy}Y + B_{xy}$. Substituting into the equation for converting raw scores on Level X to the interim scale results in the equation, $C = A_{cy}Y + B_{cy}$.

5. The process in steps 2 to 4 is repeated in order to calibrate Level Z to Level Y and, through Level Y, to the interim scale. In the same way, Level W is calibrated to Level X and, through it, to the scale; and Level V is calibrated to Level W and, through it, to the scale. The result of this process is a series of conversions to the interim scale, one conversion for each test level. If, for example, each of the series of five tests described here were to occupy 100 scaled score points on the interim scale and had 50 percent overlap with its neighbor, then the entire length of the interim scale would extend from 350 to 650—with Level Z extending from 350 to 450, Level Y from 400 to 500, Level X from 450 to 550, Level W from 500 to 600, and, finally, Level V from 550 to 650.

Once the articulation of these tests is accomplished, the attention of the test constructor can be turned to the questions of defining the final scale and providing norms. It is entirely possible that the scale adopted here for interim purposes would be satisfactory for permanent use. The advantages characteristic of such a scale already have been discussed in the section of this chapter on scaling—especially that a scale defined nonnormatively gives maximum flexibility for providing a variety of normative

data and for updating the norms at regular intervals. However, the same advantages, and more, would be characteristic of the scales developed by Lazarsfeld, Lord, Tucker, Birnbaum, and Rasch (also discussed in the section on scaling), which are highly superior to the interim scale discussed here, since they are based on the inherent psychometric properties of the tests themselves.

If an IQ scale is to be developed, then distributions of the interim scaled scores are prepared for a random sample of individuals at each age level. Normal deviates corresponding to the mid-percentile ranks are determined, multiplied by 16 (to give an IQ scale with a standard deviation of 16 at each age; they would be multiplied by 15 to give the scale a standard deviation of 15 at each age) and 100 is added to result in a scale with a mean of 100. This process provides a conversion from the interim scale to a normalized deviation IQ at each age level. Since the conversion from raw scores to the interim scale is already established for each level, it is possible to express the relationship between raw scores and deviation IQs directly, bypassing the interim scale.

Procedures similar to these can be applied to the computation of grade equivalents. The conversion to the interim scale is precisely the same as described, but the computation beyond that point is different. After the norms are collected separately by grade, the mean or median interim scaled score is computed at each grade level, and a smooth curve is drawn relating grade and score, and scores are recorded to tenths of a grade. Here too, since the conversion from raw scores to the interim scale is already established for each test level, it is possible to express the relationship between raw scores and grade equivalents directly, bypassing the interim scale.

There are numerous detailed variations possible in this calibration. Linear equations other than those following the Tucker derivation are possible. Also, the various test levels can be equated by one of the equipercentile methods. Or, raw scores on the adjacent test levels can be normalized, and the normalized scores equated by any one of the appropriate linear procedures described in this section. As a result of either of these two latter classes of methods there will be a curvilinear transformation from raw to interim scores. As is often true with procedures that depend on locally determined statistics (e.g. percentiles), extrapolation may be necessary at the extremes of each of the raw score scales where there are insufficient data to define the transformation in detail. One group of procedures that shows promise of overcoming the difficulties at the extremes of the distribution are those in the process of development by Wright (1968).

A principal concern in this calibration across tests of different level is that the psychological function measured may change from level to level, in which case the notion of a single reference scale, equally appropriate throughout the series of levels, tends to lose its meaning. Generally speaking, this problem is more serious for tests which are highly dependent on the curriculum and on school subjects that may be introduced at different points in time as a function of local custom and decisions and developed through the grades at different rates and sequences. It is probably not as serious for tests of general intellectual abilities that are acquired and developed outside the classroom.

COMPARABLE SCORES

Unlike the problem of *equivalent* scores, which is restricted to the case of parallel forms of a test, that is to tests of the same psychological function, the problem of *comparable* scores may be thought of quite simply as the problem of "equating" tests of *different* psychological function. Ordinarily, two tests are considered to have been made comparable *with respect to a particular group of examinees* if their distributions of scores are identical. (Frequently, comparable scores are defined, not in terms of the shapes of the distributions—i.e. all standardized moments—but in terms of the mean and standard deviation alone.) As the definition indicates, score scales are comparable only with respect to a specific group tested under specific conditions. Comparability will also hold reasonably well with respect to other groups, but only if those other groups are drawn

from the same population as the group on which comparability was originally established. Thus, comparable scores for two tests will differ, depending on at least three considerations:

1. *The nature of the group.* Different reference groups will yield different relationships between the two tests. This consideration is basic and will be discussed in more detail.

2. *The definition of comparability.* Different definitions of comparability will yield different relationships. For example, it was just mentioned above that two tests could be considered comparable if their distributions of scores are identical. This is one definition. Another definition is that two tests are considered comparable if the distributions of their *true scores* are identical. If the two tests are unequally reliable, then these two definitions will yield different types of comparability.

3. *The method of deriving the comparability.* Different methods of deriving comparable scores may yield quite different results.

Sometimes the distinction between *definition* of comparability and *method* of deriving comparable scores is unclear, and the two may be considered as essentially equivalent. Whatever the definition or method of comparability, the relationship is meaningful *only* with respect to a *single* particular group or population of individuals or to random samples drawn from a single population.

The methods of establishing tables of comparable scores between tests are almost as numerous as the methods of equating scores and include both linear and curvilinear procedures. Although the methods discussed here are principally the linear methods, it should be understood that whenever a linear method is appropriate, the curvilinear analog, if there is one, is similarly appropriate. In fact, in some instances, when the shapes of the raw score distributions differ substantially, the curvilinear approach may be preferable.

Probably the most common procedure of defining comparability is simply to administer the two or more tests (frequently a battery of tests) to a common basic reference group and to scale the tests in such a way that the mean and standard deviation have the same numerical values, respectively, on each of the various tests. Sometimes, in addition, the distributions are normalized. Scores on the various tests of the battery then are used to plot profiles for purposes of differential diagnosis, remediation, and placement.

Some of the methods of equating (equivalent scores) are not appropriate for defining comparability because they call for some basic assumptions that are necessarily excluded in the problem of comparable scores. These include the methods of equating and calibration attributable to Levine (1955), since they all assume not only that Forms X and Y are parallel (as do all methods of equating) but also that the equating test, Form U, is parallel in function to both X and Y. Clearly, if X and Y are not parallel, U cannot be parallel to both of them.

In general, the methods that make use of an equating test, or those that make use of a set of common items that are interspersed throughout the tests, have their limitations for deriving systems of comparable scores for the very reason that X and Y are tests of different function. For example, the method of absolute scaling (Thurstone, 1925) assumes that the correlations between the common items and the total test are perfect. Even if this assumption could be defended for Tests X and Y that are parallel, it could not be defended for tests of different function. Items that correlate perfectly with X cannot correlate perfectly with Y if X and Y themselves do not correlate perfectly.

Very likely the most defensible procedure for deriving comparable scores is that described under design I, in which Tests (note: *here* they are *not* test forms) X and Y are administered to random halves of a group that is drawn, also at random, from a defined population. The methods of design III (Lord, 1955a) and design IV derived by Tucker (Gulliksen, 1950; Angoff, 1961a), and probably the methods described under design V (other methods involving score data) are also appropriate, but with some reservations that may be regarded as further restrictions on the generality with which a table of comparable scores may be applied and used. Specifically, if Tests X and Y are tests that measure distinctly different characteristics, then in all likelihood Test U, the anchor or equating test, will not correlate equally with them. Con-

sequently, the second terms in equations 18 to 21, and also in equations 30 to 33 will be unequally regressed. This will not ordinarily pose a problem except for the fact that the estimations of mean and variance for the test with the lower correlation with Test U will be relatively unreliable and biased with respect to the estimations for the other test. In the equating model, on the other hand, where $r_{xu} = r_{yu}$, the estimations for both tests are equally regressed.

Some of the variations of the procedure involving the use of common tests may be appropriate here too, for example: establishing the comparability of three or more tests simultaneously, using multiple predictors, and using a *quasi-common* equating test (see pp. 576–79; also p. 581).

By way of illustration, it may be useful to describe the method of equating that makes use of all three of the foregoing variations but as applied to the problem of comparable scores. Consider a testing battery, like the one used in the College Board Admissions Testing Program (also the Graduate Record Examinations Program), in which all examinees take a common core of tests, say both the Verbal and the Mathematical sections of the SAT, and in addition, one or more of the various Achievement Tests of their own choosing in specific subject-matter areas. One procedure that is sometimes thought appropriate for making the scales on the various tests comparable is to define the mean and standard deviation at some convenient pair of numbers (in the case of the College Board program, at 500 and 100, respectively) for the particular group of people taking each test. (Other types of comparability involve the definition of *all* the moments of the distribution, not only the first two.) However, assuming—as is often the case—that the groups of people taking the various tests are drawn from different populations, such a procedure would fail to satisfy the fundamental definition of comparability, which is that certain agreed-upon moments of the distributions of scores on the two tests be identical *with respect to a particular (single) group of examinees.* The choice of the same system of numbers for all the tests would only ensure that the scales *appear* to be comparable. But since they would not be comparable in the accepted sense, their apparent comparability would necessarily be false and misleading.

The example of the College Board Admissions Testing Program is helpful in this context because it possesses the characteristics that make for a relatively complex system of comparable scores. The procedure that has been followed there has two basic components, the comparability of the two sections of the SAT and the comparability of the various Achievement Tests with one another and with the SAT. In the case of the SAT all candidates, or virtually all candidates, take both the Verbal and the Mathematical sections. The exceptions are extremely rare and can easily be identified and removed from the standardization group. Thus it was a reasonable thing to define the mean and standard deviation for both the Verbal and Mathematical sections as 500 and 100 respectively for a particular standardization group. The group taken for this purpose consisted of those tested at the April 1941 administration of the SAT. As a result of this procedure comparability is established between Verbal and Mathematical in the linear sense (since only the first two moments are so defined) and without approximation, since both tests are taken by the same group of examinees.[19]

The problem of the Achievement Tests is another matter, however. Here, the choice of test is left to the examinee and to the college of application, which, of course, also represents a matter of choice for the examinee. Since the tests chosen by the examinees are those on which they feel they are most likely to do well, it is expected that, because of this self-selection, there would be differences in the abilities of the groups that elect to take the various tests, differences that are likely to be evident in the scores on the SAT. Since, also, the scores that are reported on the various tests of the Achievement Test battery are used more or less inter-

changeably by many of the colleges in evaluating the abilities of their applicants, it becomes necessary to introduce as precise a comparability among the test scales as possible, that is to say, to adjust the scales for the various tests in order to reflect the levels and dispersions of the groups of candidates who choose to take them. In another, but closely related, sense, it is important to insure that the principal requirement of the definition of comparability be satisfied, that the moments of the distributions of scores be defined in terms of the *same reference group*. Since, in this situation, the tests are not all taken by all the members of the reference group, it becomes necessary to make estimations. The appropriate equations for these estimations are similar to those described briefly above for the situation where more than two forms (say X, Y, and Z) of a test are being equated and where estimates of raw score mean and variance are made for the combined group, all of whom take the equating test. Additional variations are: (*a*) that not one equating test but two, are used in multiple combination; and (*b*) that the students do not necessarily all take precisely the same form of SAT-Verbal or the same form of SAT-Mathematical. Thus, the SAT is used in the sense of a *quasi-common* test. Following the form given in equations 23 to 26 which may be extended to as many tests and corresponding test groups as necessary, estimates are made of the raw score mean and variance on each of the Achievement Tests for the same standard reference group. This group is defined as one having a mean of 500 and standard deviation of 100 on both SAT-Verbal and SAT-Mathematical, and a Verbal-Mathematical covariance of 4,000. After these estimates are made, each pair of estimates (mean and variance) is defined as 500 and 10,000 (that is, 100 for the standard deviation) in accordance with equation 7 (Schultz & Angoff, 1956; also Angoff, 1961a).

It should be noted that from the point of view of their derivation, equations 23 to 26 are extensions of equations 18 to 21, which depend on the assumption that the subgroups taking the different forms are only randomly different. The comparable scores problem that is being

<hr>

[19] Actually there is a degree of approximation here. The SAT-Verbal was defined as described above, in April 1941; the SAT-Mathematical was not defined until April 1942, and this was done by assigning it the same mean and standard deviation as were found on the SAT-Verbal at that April 1942 administration.

considered here necessarily fails to satisfy that assumption, and, therefore, the estimates required for it must be derived from other assumptions, such as those basic to equations 30 to 33. However, in spite of these differences in assumptions, equations 23 to 26 are computationally precisely equivalent to the formulas needed for the comparable scores problem and may be considered appropriate for that use.

The scaling of the four original language Achievement Tests of the College Board (French, German, Latin, and Spanish) will illustrate the way in which the use of two anchor test variables may be extended to three. In a study conducted by L. R Tucker (Angoff, 1961b) data were collected that made it clear that the various foreign languages were studied for characteristically different amounts of time in secondary school. In order to reflect its role in the comparability among the language Achievement Tests, the number of years of language study was therefore added to SAT-Verbal and SAT-Mathematical as a third "anchor test" and used in equations involving three predictors, as shown in equations 56 and 57. These equations, providing estimates of mean and variance for the standard reference group on language test X, for example, are computationally parallel to equations 23 and 25, respectively, but extended to three variables.

$$\hat{\mu}_x = M_{x_\alpha} + b_{xv.mn_\alpha}(\mu_v - M_{v_\alpha})$$
$$+ b_{xm.vn_\alpha}(\mu_m - M_{m_\alpha})$$
$$+ b_{xn.vm_\alpha}(\mu_n - M_{n_\alpha}), \quad [56]$$

and

$$\sigma_x^2 = s_{x_\alpha}^2 + b_{xv.mn_\alpha}^2(\sigma_v^2 - s_{v_\alpha}^2)$$
$$+ b_{xm.vn_\alpha}^2(\sigma_m^2 - s_{m_\alpha}^2)$$
$$+ b_{xn.vm_\alpha}^2(\sigma_n^2 - s_{n_\alpha}^2)$$
$$+ 2b_{xv.mn_\alpha}b_{xm.vn_\alpha}(\sigma_{vm} - s_{vm_\alpha}) \quad [57]$$
$$+ 2b_{xv.mn_\alpha}b_{xn.vm_\alpha}(\sigma_{vn} - s_{vn_\alpha})$$
$$+ 2b_{xm.vn_\alpha}b_{xn.vm_\alpha}(\sigma_{mn} - s_{mn_\alpha}),$$

where n, the only new symbol used here, refers to the number of years of language training. Clearly, not all the members of the standard reference group had chosen to take a foreign

language test, and population values involving years of language training were not available for them. However, since the matrix of the means, the variances, and the covariance for SAT-Verbal and SAT-Mathematical for the total *observed* group taking one or more languages was found to be very close to the population values (500, 10,000, and 4,000, respectively), the statistics involving years of language training (n) observed for the total group studying any one (or more than one) language were taken as population values for the purposes of equations 56 and 57.

If the desired definition of comparability involves all moments, not only the first two, analogous curvilinear methods that are applicable to the problem of optional tests and make use of the relationship with an anchor test can be worked out, corresponding to the curvilinear method of equating outlined in design IV above (p. 581). It also should be observed here that another procedure similar in intent to the procedure just described is Flanagan's scaled score system for the Cooperative Tests (Flanagan, 1939), which made use of the Stanford Achievement Test and the Otis Self-Administering Test of Mental Ability as "anchor" tests for the "50-point" for each of the Cooperative Achievement Tests. (See the section in this chapter on scaling.)

One of the characteristics of the College Board method stems from the fact that correlations between the Achievement Tests and the SAT vary from test to test, with the result that the estimates of mean and variance given in equations 23 to 26 are affected by the *different amounts of regression* of the parenthetical terms as well as by the values of the parenthetical terms themselves. This differential regression in turn affects the placement of the scale for each test on the underlying scale structure for the entire battery. On the other hand, such a result is precisely what should occur, since information on the anchor test (the SAT) should be used only to the extent that it is relevant to performance on the subject-matter test.

There is one type of comparability that is particularly applicable to selection situations in which scores on different tests are available for different subgroups of the applicant body. In some such situations the applicants may have the choice of taking one or another of the selection tests; in other situations, as in bilingual cultures, where the tests are not equally appropriate for all applicants, there is in effect no choice possible for many applicants; the situation essentially determines the choice of test for them. Nevertheless, once accepted, the students are called upon to engage in a mixed competition in which there is an attempt made to disregard linguistic and cultural differences among students and to evaluate their performances in terms of what purports, at least, to be a common scale. In such situations, scores on the two (or more) tests are made comparable by defining as "equivalent" those scores on the two (or more) tests that predict the same score on the criterion measure. The relationship used for this comparability is one of those given earlier in the section on equating and calibration for the same situation but involving parallel forms: $Y = AX + B$, where $A = b_{ux}/b_{uy}$ and

$$B = \frac{1}{b_{uy}} (D_{ux} - D_{uy}),$$

where $D_{ux} = M_{u_\alpha} - b_{ux} M_{x_\alpha}$ and $D_{uy} = M_{u_\beta} - b_{uy} M_{y_\beta}$ (equations 44 and 45).

Ideally, the two tests should correlate equally with the criterion. If they correlate unequally with the criterion then those applicants who offer as part of their credentials the test with the higher correlation and who score low on their test will be disadvantaged relative to the applicants who are at the same rank position but who offer the other test for admission. On the other hand, if they score high on their test they will be at an advantage relative to the applicants at the same rank position who offer the other test.

Scores on two tests may also be defined as comparable if they are *predicted* by the same score on a third variable. This procedure would be appropriate if one attempted, for example, to establish comparability among the grading systems employed in the various departments of a university and/or in various universities. In this situation, the test that had been adminis-

tered for selection or just after matriculation at the university (or universities) might be used as the anchor test. The relationship for this comparability was also given in the section on equating and calibration, involving parallel forms (equations 42 and 43): $Y = AX + B$, where $A = b_{yu}/b_{xu}$ and $B = D_{yu} - A D_{xu}$, and where $D_{xu} = M_{x_\alpha} - b_{xu} M_{u_\alpha}$ and $D_{yu} = M_{y_\beta} - b_{yu} M_{u_\beta}$. Here too the comparability is affected by the difference in the correlations, r_{xu} and r_{yu}, but the advantages and disadvantages to the applicant go in the opposite direction. A student who takes the test with the *higher* correlation with the third variable and scores low on his test will have an advantage over those who are at the same rank position but who offer the other test. On the other hand, if that student scores high on his test he will be disadvantaged relative to the students at the same rank position who take the other test.

There is another method of defining comparability which appears to be direct and easy to apply and comprehend but which has grave limitations. This is the method that defines as the comparable Y score for each value of X the score on variable Y that would be predicted for that X score in the usual regression sense, that is by the equation, $Y = AX + B$, where $A = b_{yx}$ and $B = M_y - b_{yx} M_x$. The difficulty with this procedure is that scores on Test Y will therefore be regressed relative to the original distribution of Y scores, that is they will have a reduced standard deviation, not equal to s_y, but equal to $r_{xy} s_y$ instead. The lower the correlation between Tests X and Y, the narrower will be the distribution of predicted Y scores. If the purpose of deriving comparable scores, as would probably be the case with this method, is to merge and compare scores earned on Test Y by some individuals with Y scores converted from Test X, taken by other individuals, then clearly this method is inappropriate. Moreover, it necessarily introduces bias, since, as a result of the regression method, individuals scoring below the mean on Test X would be given higher scores on Test Y, closer to the mean; and individuals scoring above the mean on Test X would be given lower scores on Test Y, also closer to the mean. Thus, if applicants were given the option, say in a selection competition, of taking Test X or Test Y, it would be to an applicant's best—and unfair—advantage to take Test X if he were a low-ability student and to take Test Y if he were a high-ability student. For obvious reasons, any procedure that is susceptible to strategic manipulations unrelated to the applicant's ability should be avoided. Finally, it should be pointed out that this regression method as a method of comparability suffers from the fact that its solution is not uniquely given. Rather than one, there are two lines possible, each unidirectional, one for predicting Y from X and the other for predicting X from Y. These lines are often equally defensible and appropriate, and for that reason they do not permit a clear choice. Yet they serve separate purposes and they yield different results. For example, the best estimate, by this procedure, of a person's score on Test Y, given his score of 74 on Test X, may be 68, but unless the correlation between Tests X and Y is perfect, the best estimate of his score on Test X, given that his score on Test Y is 68, is *not* 74. Because of the lack of symmetry in this method (i.e. two separate unidirectional lines) and because of the regression effect, which does not permit the merging of obtained and converted scores, it would probably be advisable to avoid using this method of deriving comparable scores.

There appear to be two principal purposes for which comparable scores are derived. One is to merge and compare, and otherwise treat as interchangeable, scores on different tests for different examinees. Typical examples of comparability that serve this purpose are those derived for the different Advanced Tests of the Graduate Record Examinations, the different Achievement Tests of the College Board, and aptitude and achievement tests that are couched in different languages for students of different language background. The other purpose is to develop profiles across a battery of tests of different function. These profiles are used to study the patterns of performance for individuals and to identify relative strengths and weaknesses in different areas, presumably for differential diagnosis, guidance, and placement.

Whatever the purpose of the comparable scores, normative or ipsative, it is crucial to keep in mind the characteristics of the group on which the comparability is established and to interpret the results for individuals in terms of that group. It is meaningless to ask in the abstract whether a person is a better athlete than a student, whether he is more handsome than intelligent, more heavy than tall, or indeed, better in verbal than in mathematical tasks. It is quite meaningful, however, to ask these questions about his characteristics *in relation to a particular reference group*. But it must be kept in mind that, depending on the reference group that is chosen, the conclusions drawn from the comparison could be quite different. Thus an individual could be "better in verbal than in mathematical" if he is being compared with a male reference group but "better in mathematical than verbal" if he is being compared with a female reference group. This nonuniqueness of comparable scores derives from the fact that the measures in question are measures of different function; there is no unique single conversion table that can be derived for tests of different function, and there is no single conversion table that is applicable to all types of groups. This is so for the reason that different types of groups necessarily show different types of profiles, i.e. patterns of means, on tests of different function. Indeed, because they reveal group characteristics and are closely dependent on the groups on which they are based, conversions across tests of different function are themselves another way of expressing group profiles.

The matter of "equating" nonparallel tests has been reviewed in some detail by Angoff (1966). As was pointed out here too, the problem of conversion from one form to a parallel[20] form of a test may be thought of simply as a problem of transforming systems of units, directly analogous to the conversion of centigrade to Fahrenheit, centimeters to inches, and

[20] As mentioned earlier in the section on equating and calibration, the operational definition of parallelism here is essentially the one developed by Wilks (1946) and extended by Votaw (1948): two tests may be considered parallel if, after conversion to the same scale, their means, standard deviations, and correlations with any and all outside criteria are equal (Gulliksen, 1950).

so on. This kind of conversion, across systems of units for two instruments that measure precisely the same function, is unique. There is only one conversion, except for random error, however it is derived and however it is applied. But in the case of comparable scores for tests of different function, there would be as many conversions as there are groups for whom the tests are appropriate and as many conversions as there are situations for which the tests are appropriate. As Flanagan (1951) has pointed out, even two tests that purported to measure competence in the same subject (say, biology) but differed in emphasis, might show a pattern of performance for students in New York that was quite different from the pattern they exhibited for students in Los Angeles, and this pattern might well be a reflection of the patterns of curricular emphasis in the two cities.

The failure of nonparallel tests to yield a single set of comparable scores is apparent too when one considers a number of tests, each designed to measure competence in a different subject-matter area (e.g. spelling, arithmetic, reading, social studies) but over a range of grade levels. If one were to establish a system of comparable scores for these tests based on a group of students at grade 3, one would almost necessarily find that the scores were no longer comparable at grades 4 and 5 and still further in disagreement at grades 6, 7, and 8. The failure of the system to retain its comparability throughout the grades is the inevitable result of different growth rates, however the comparability is defined; and the differential growth rates are themselves, as Lindquist (1953) has pointed out, necessarily the result of arbitrary decisions to introduce the subject-matter concepts in the grades at certain fixed points in time and to progress in the subjects in a particular sequence at a particular rate. Any change in the pedagogic pattern, also arbitrary, would render entirely inapplicable whatever system of comparability had been established and would call for a totally new derivation in terms of the new pedagogic pattern.

Although tables of comparable scores bring with them problems that exist over and beyond the problems of equated scores for tests of similar function, they are nevertheless extremely useful, indeed indispensable in many situations. Nevertheless, it is easy to overlook their sources of error. Some of these errors are random and are associated with any equating enterprise; others are associated with the fact that they deal with tests of different function and, because they are systematic and predictable, can only be taken as errors of bias.

Frequently the situation is one in which the tests and the use for which the table of comparable scores is required cannot be questioned or altered but must be dealt with directly. In such instances it may be possible at least to choose the kind of group to use in forming a conversion table. Three such groups are: (a) the national norms group; (b) a set of differentiated norms groups; and (c) the local norms group. Comparable scores based on a "sample of convenience," one for which data just happen to be available, are of little, if any, value.

Of the various kinds of comparable scores, the one based on differentiated norms is probably the most defensible. This procedure will yield a number of conversion tables, each based on, and appropriate for, a different norms group. Each conversion, like a profile, will be descriptive of the group on which it is based and applicable only to that group. The user will be forced to choose the appropriate table with care, keeping in mind the group for which he intends to use it and the purpose for which it is to be applied.

The local norms approach to comparable scores is similar to the one involving differentiated norms and is in general as highly recommended for the purpose of comparable scores as are local norms distributions themselves for the purpose of evaluating relative status. Here the cautions that need to be exercised are: (a) that the group has not been directly selected on either of the scores involved in the conversion; (b) that there are sufficient cases to yield reliable conversions; and (c) that the conversions be applied only in the institution (school or college) where they were developed or in institutions known to be similar to it.

The national norms approach is probably the least satisfactory of all, except when the tests in question are closely similar in function. Its principal advantage, however, is that it is the most readily applied method of obtaining rough conversion tables, if for no other reason than the fact that national norms for tests are generally readily available. The significant concern here is that the norms groups for the various tests may not have been selected in the same fashion in order to satisfy, even approximately, the requirement that the reference group for all tests be the same, or at least, randomly equivalent. The sources of unreliability in norms samples are numerous enough and large enough to introduce serious errors in tables of comparable scores.

If the methods of equating parallel forms are adapted to the problem of comparable scores for nonparallel tests, then it is pertinent to ask: (a) How similar are the tests for which comparable scores are to be developed? (b) How appropriate is the group on which the table of comparable scores is based when one considers the person or the group for whom the table is to be used? Once these questions are answered it would then be necessary to consider the purpose for which the table is to be used and the nature of the decisions that would be based on it in order to evaluate the degree of error that could be tolerated. Clearly, for some decisions, those that are not crucial and those that can be corrected if later found to be incorrect, the demand for precision is not great, while for other decisions and uses, those in which the careers of individuals are at stake, only the highest degree of precision is permitted. Each situation must be evaluated on its own merit, with full awareness that statistical solutions are fundamentally no more precise than the data they are based on and no more defensible than the methods used to derive them.

REFERENCES

Angoff, W. H. Test reliability and effective test length. *Psychometrika*, 1953, **18**, 1–14.

Angoff, W. H. Measurement and scaling. In C. W. Harris (Ed.), *Encyclopedia of educational research.* (3rd ed.) New York: Macmillan, 1960. Pp. 807–817.

Angoff, W. H. Basic equations in scaling and equating. In S. S. Wilks (Ed.), *Scaling and equating College Board tests.* Princeton, N. J.: Educational Testing Service, 1961. Pp. 120–129. (a)

Angoff, W. H. Language training study: 1947. In S. S. Wilks (Ed.), *Scaling and equating College Board tests.* Princeton, N. J.: Educational Testing Service, 1961. Pp. 130–143. (b)

Angoff, W. H. Scales with nonmeaningful origins and units of measurement. Symposium: Standard scores for aptitude and achievement tests. *Educational and Psychological Measurement*, 1962, **22**, 27–34.

Angoff, W. H. Can useful general-purpose equivalency tables be prepared for different college admissions tests? In A. Anastasi (Ed.), *Testing problems in perspective.* Washington: American Council on Education, 1966. Pp. 251–264.

Angoff, W. H. How we calibrate College Board scores. *College Board Review*, 1968, No. 68, 11–14.

Angoff, W. H. (Ed.) *The College Board technical manual: A description of research and development for the College Board Scholastic Aptitude Test and Achievement Tests.* Princeton, N. J.: Educational Testing Service, 1970, in press.

Angoff, W. H. Test scores and norms. In L. C. Deighton (Ed.), *Encyclopedia of Education.* New York: Macmillan. In preparation.

Angoff, W. H. & Waite, A. Study of double part-score equating for the Scholastic Aptitude Test. In S. S. Wilks (Ed.), *Scaling and Equating College Board Tests.* Princeton, N. J.: Educational Testing Service, 1961. Pp. 73–85.

Beggs, D. L., & Hieronymus, A. N. Uniformity of growth in the basic skills throughout the school year and during the summer. *Journal of Educational Measurement*, 1968, **5**, 91–97.

Birnbaum, A. Chaps. 17–20. In Lord, F. M., & Novick, M. R. *Statistical theories of mental test scores.* Reading, Mass.: Addison-Wesley Publishing Co., 1968.

Cattell, R. B. Psychological measurement: Normative, ipsative, interactive. *Psychological Review*, 1944, **51**, 292–303.

Cleary, T. A., & Hilton, T. L. An investigation of item bias. *Educational and Psychological Measurement*, 1968, **28**, 61–75.

Conrad, H. S. Norms. In W. S. Monroe (Ed.), *Encyclopedia of educational research.* (Rev. ed.) New York: Macmillan, 1950. Pp. 795–802.

Cooperative School and College Ability Tests: Manual for interpreting scores. Princeton, N. J.: Educational Testing Service, 1956.

Cooperative School and College Ability Tests: Handbook for SCAT series II. Princeton, N. J.: Educational Testing Service, 1967. 54 pp.

Cornell, F. G. Sampling methods. In C. W. Harris

(Ed.), *Encyclopedia of educational research.* (3rd ed.) New York: Macmillan, 1960. Pp. 1181–1183.

Cureton, E. E. The accomplishment quotient technic. *Journal of Experimental Education*, 1937, **5**, 315–326.

Cureton, E. E. Minimum requirements in establishing and reporting norms on educational tests. *Harvard Educational Review*, 1941, **11**, 287–300.

Cureton, E. E., & Tukey, J. W. Smoothing frequency distributions, equating tests, and preparing norms. *American Psychologist*, 1951, **6**, 404. (Abstract)

Davenport, K. S., & Remmers, H. H. Factors in state characteristics related to average A-12 V-12 test scores. *Journal of Educational Psychology*, 1950, **41**, 110–115.

Ebel, R. L. Content standard test scores. Symposium: Standard scores for aptitude and achievement tests. *Educational and Psychological Measurement*, 1962, **22**, 15–25.

Fan, C.-t. On the applications of the method of absolute scaling. *Psychometrika*, 1957, **22**, 175–183.

Flanagan, J. C. *The Cooperative Achievement Tests: A bulletin reporting the basic principles and procedures used in the development of their system of scaled scores.* New York: American Council on Education, Cooperative Test Service, 1939.

Flanagan, J. C. (Ed.) *The aviation psychology program in the Army Air Forces.* (Report No. 1) Washington: Government Printing Office, 1948.

Flanagan, J. C. Units, scores, and norms. In E. F. Lindquist (Ed.), *Educational measurement.* Washington: American Council on Education, 1951. Pp. 695–763,

Flanagan, J. C. Selecting appropriate score scales for tests. (Discussion) In *Proceedings of the 1952 Invitational Conference on Testing Problems.* Princeton, N. J.: Educational Testing Service, 1953. Pp. 29–33.

Flanagan, J. C. Symposium: Standard scores for achievement tests. (Discussion) *Educational and Psychological Measurement*, 1962, **22**, 35–39.

Flanagan, J. C., Dailey, J. T., Shaycoft, M. F., Gorham, W. A., Orr, D. B., & Goldberg, I. *The talents of American youth: I. Design for a study of American youth.* Boston: Houghton Mifflin, 1962.

Gardner, E. F. Determination of units of measurement which are consistent with inter- and intra-grade differences in ability. Unpublished doctoral dissertation, Harvard University, Graduate School of Education, 1947.

Gardner, E. F. Value of norms based on a new type of scale unit. In *Proceedings of the 1948 Invitational Conference on Testing Problems.* Princeton, N. J.: Educational Testing Service, 1949. Pp. 67–74.

Gardner, E. F. Comments on selected scaling techniques with a description of a new type of scale. *Journal of Clinical Psychology*, 1950, **6**, 38–43.

Gardner, E. F. Normative standard scores. Symposium: Standard scores for aptitude and achievement tests. *Educational and Psychological Measurement*, 1962, **22**, 7–14.

Gardner, E. F. The importance of reference groups in scaling procedure. In A. Anastasi (Ed.), *Testing problems in perspective.* Washington: American Council on Education, 1966. Pp. 272–280.

Gulliksen, H. *Theory of mental tests.* New York: Wiley, 1950.

Guttman, L. The basis for scalogram analysis. In S. A. Stouffer et al., *Studies in social psychology in World War II.* Vol. IV. *Measurement and prediction.* Princeton, N. J.: Princeton University Press, 1950. Pp. 60–90.

Harris, C. W. (Ed.) *Problems in measuring change.* Madison: University of Wisconsin Press, 1963.

Hull, C. L. The conversion of test scores into series which shall have any assigned mean and degree of dispersion. *Journal of Applied Psychology*, 1922, **6**, 298–300.

Keats, J. A. A statistical theory of objective test scores. Hawthorn, Victoria: Australian Council for Educational Research, October 1951.

Keats, J. A., & Lord, F. M. A theoretical distribution for mental test scores. *Psychometrika*, 1962, **27**, 59–72.

Kelley, T. L. Ridge-route norms. *Harvard Educational Review*, 1940, **10**, 309–314.

Kelley, T. L. *Fundamentals of statistics.* Cambridge, Mass.: Harvard University Press, 1947.

Kish, L. *Survey sampling.* New York: Wiley, 1965.

Lawley, D. N. On problems connected with item selection and test construction. *Proceedings of the Royal Society of Edinburgh*, 1942–43, 61(Section A, Part III), 273–287.

Lazarsfeld, P. F. Chaps. 10 & 11. In S. A. Stouffer et al., *Studies in social psychology in World War II.* Vol. IV. *Measurement and prediction.* Princeton, N. J.: Princeton University Press, 1950.

Lennon, R. T. Equating nonparallel tests. *Journal of Educational Measurement*, 1964, **1**, 15–18.

Lennon, R. T. Norms: 1963. In A. Anastasi (Ed.), *Testing problems in perspective.* Washington: American Council on Education, 1966. Pp. 243–250.

Levine, R. S. Equating the score scales of alternate forms administered to samples of different ability. Educational Testing Service *Research Bulletin*, 1955, No. 23.

Levine, R. S. Estimated national norms for the Scholastic Aptitude Test. Educational Testing Service *Statistical Report*, 1958, No. 1.

Lindquist, E. F. Factors determining reliability of test norms. *Journal of Educational Psychology*, 1930, **21**, 512–520.

Lindquist, E. F. Sampling in educational research. *Journal of Educational Psychology*, 1940, **31**, 561–574.

Lindquist, E. F. Selecting appropriate score scales for tests. (Discussion) In *Proceedings of the 1952 Invitational Conference on Testing Problems*. Princeton, N. J.: Educational Testing Service, 1953. Pp. 34–40.

Lindquist, E. F. Norms by schools. In A. Anastasi (Ed.), *Testing problems in perspective*. Washington: American Council on Education, 1966. Pp. 269–271.

Lindquist, E. F., & Hieronymus, A. N. *Iowa Tests of Basic Skills: Manual for administrators, supervisors, and counselors*. New York: Houghton Mifflin, 1964.

Lord, F. M. Notes on comparable scales for test scores. Educational Testing Service *Research Bulletin*, 1950, No. 48.

Lord, F. M. A theory of test scores. *Psychometric Monographs*, 1952, No. 7. (a)

Lord, F. M. The scale proposed for the Academic Ability Test. Educational Testing Service *Research Memorandum*, 1952, No. 3. (b)

Lord, F. M. On the statistical treatment of football numbers. *American Psychologist*, 1953, **8**, 750–751.

Lord, F. M. Equating test scores—a maximum likelihood solution. *Psychometrika*, 1955, **20**, 193–200. (a)

Lord, F. M. The standard error of norms and the standard error of measurement. Educational Testing Service *Research Memorandum*, 1955, No. 16. (b)

Lord, F. M. A survey of observed test-score distributions with respect to skewness and kurtosis. *Educational and Psychological Measurement*, 1955, **15**, 383–389. (c)

Lord, F. M. The measurement of growth. *Educational and Psychological Measurement*, 1956, **16**, 421–437.

Lord, F. M. Do tests of the same length have the same standard errors of measurement? *Educational and Psychological Measurement*, 1957, **17**, 510–521.

Lord, F. M. Further problems in the measurement of growth. *Educational and Psychological Measurement*, 1958, **18**, 437–451.

Lord, F. M. Test norms and sampling theory.

Journal of Experimental Education, 1959, **27**, 247–263.

Lord, F. M. Large-sample covariance analysis when the control variable is fallible. *Journal of the American Statistical Association*, 1960, **55**, 307–321.

Lord, F. M. Estimating norms by item-sampling. *Educational and Psychological Measurement*, 1962, **22**, 259–267.

Lord, F. M. Elementary models for measuring change. In C. W. Harris (Ed.), *Problems in measuring change*. Madison: University of Wisconsin Press, 1963. Pp. 21–38.

Lord, F. M., & Novick, M. R. *Statistical theories of mental test scores*. Reading, Mass.: Addison-Wesley Publishing Co., 1968. Chaps. 17–20.

Lorge, I., Thorndike, R. L., & Hagen, E. *Technical manual for the Lorge-Thorndike Intelligence Tests, Multi-Level Edition*. Boston: Houghton Mifflin, 1966.

McCall, W. A. *Measurement*. New York: Macmillan, 1939.

McGee, V. E. Towards a maximally efficient system of braiding for Scholastic Aptitude Test equating. In S. S. Wilks (Ed.), *Scaling and equating College Board tests*. Princeton, N. J.: Educational Testing Service, 1961. Pp. 86–96.

McNemar, Q. *The revision of the Stanford-Binet scale*. New York: Houghton Mifflin, 1942.

McNemar, Q. On growth measurement. *Educational and Psychological Measurement*, 1958, **18**, 47–55.

Manning, W. H., & DuBois, P. H. Correlational methods in research on human learning. *Perceptual and Motor Skills*, 1962, **15**, 287–321.

Mollenkopf, W. G. A study of secondary school characteristics as related to test scores. Educational Testing Service *Research Bulletin*, 1956, No. 6.

Pearson, K. On the relationship of intelligence to size and shape of head, and to other physical and mental characters. *Biometrika*, 1906, **5**, 105–146.

Rasch, G. *Probabilistic models for some intelligence and educational tests*. Copenhagen, Denmark: The Danish Institute for Educational Research, 1960.

Schrader, W. B. Norms. In C. W. Harris (Ed.), *Encyclopedia of educational research*. (3rd ed.) New York: Macmillan, 1960. Pp. 922–927.

Schultz, M. K., & Angoff, W. H. The development of new scales for the Aptitude and Advanced Tests of the Graduate Record Examinations.

Journal of Educational Psychology, 1956, **47,** 285–294.

Science Research Associates. Iowa Tests of Educational Development: Technical report (unpublished manuscript). Chicago: Science Research Associates, 1966.

Seashore, H., Wesman, A., & Doppelt, J. The standardization of the Wechsler Intelligence Scale for Children. *Journal of Consulting Psychology,* 1950, **14,** 99–110.

Stevens, S. S. Mathematics, measurements, and psychophysics. In S. S. Stevens (Ed.), *Handbook of experimental psychology.* New York: Wiley, 1951. Pp. 1–49.

Swineford, F., & Fan, C.-t. A method of score conversion through item statistics. *Psychometrika,* 1957, **22,** 185–188.

Terman, L. M., & Merrill, M. A. *Measuring intelligence.* New York: Houghton Mifflin, 1937.

Terman, L. M., & Merrill, M. A. *Stanford-Binet Intelligence Scale.* New York: Houghton Mifflin, 1960.

Thorndike, E. L., Bregman, E. O., Cobb, M. V., & Woodyard, E. *The measurement of intelligence.* New York: Columbia University, Teachers College, Bureau of Publications, 1927.

Thorndike, R. L. Community variables as predictors of intelligence and academic achievement. *Journal of Educational Psychology,* 1951, **42,** 321–338.

Thorndike, R. L. *The concepts of over- and underachievement.* New York: Columbia University, Teachers College, Bureau of Publications, 1963.

Thorndike, R. L. Intellectual status and intellectual growth. *Journal of Educational Psychology,* 1966, **57,** 121–127.

Thurstone, L. L. A method of scaling psychological and educational tests. *Journal of Educational Psychology,* 1925, **16,** 433–451.

Thurstone, L. L. The mental age concept. *Psychological Review,* 1926, **33,** 268–278.

Thurstone, L. L. A law of comparative judgment. *Psychological Review,* 1927, **34,** 273–286.

Thurstone, L. L. The absolute zero in intelligence measurement. *Psychological Review,* 1928, **35,** 175–197. (a)

Thurstone, L. L. Attitudes can be measured. *American Journal of Sociology,* 1928, **33,** 529–554. (b)

Thurstone, L. L. Primary mental abilities. *Psychometric Monographs,* 1938, No. 1.

Thurstone, L. L. The calibration of test items. *American Psychologist,* 1947, **2,** 103–104.

Thurstone, L. L., & Chave, E. J. *The measurement of attitude.* Chicago: University of Chicago, 1929.

Toops, H. A. A proposal for a standard million in compiling norms. *Ohio College Association Bulletin,* No. 125. (c. 1939)

Torgeson, W. S. *Theory and methods of scaling,* New York: Wiley, 1958.

Tucker, L. R Academic Ability Test. Educational Testing Service *Research Memorandum,* 1951, No. 17.

Tucker, L. R Scales minimizing the importance of reference groups. In *Proceedings of the 1952 Invitational Conference on Testing Problems.* Princeton, N. J.: Educational Testing Service, 1953. Pp. 22–28.

Tucker, L. R, Damarin, F., Messick, S. A base-free measure of change. *Psychometrika,* 1966, **31,** 457–473.

Votaw, D. F., Jr. Testing compound symmetry in a normal multivariate distribution. *Annals of Mathematical Statistics,* 1948, **19,** 447–473.

Wilks, S. S. Sample criteria for testing equality of means, equality of variances, and equality of covariances in a normal multivariate distribution. *Annals of Mathematical Statistics,* 1946, **17,** 257–281.

Wilks, S. S. (Ed.) *Scaling and equating College Board Tests.* Princeton, N. J.: Educational Testing Service, 1961.

Wright. B. D. Sample-free test calibration and person measurement. In *Proceedings of the 1967 Invitational Conference on Testing Problems.* Princeton, N. J.: Educational Testing Service, 1968. Pp. 85–101.

16. Techniques for Considering Multiple Measurements

William W. Cooley
University of Pittsburgh

Previous chapters have described how to plan, write, try out, reproduce, administer, process, and evaluate instruments that measure aspects of human behavior relevant to education. Subsequent chapters discuss applications of the resulting measurement instruments in such educational situations as learning and instruction, guidance, selection, placement, and the evaluation of educational programs. In all such applications it is almost inevitable that more than one measure is involved in any particular problem area. The purpose of this chapter is to introduce some of the techniques in current use for the simultaneous consideration of multiple measurements that allow inferences to be made either about individuals or about groups of individuals.

The use of multiple measures in education has its basis in trait-and-factor psychology, which has developed procedures for considering the basic behavioral differences that occur among individuals. An excellent summary of the ways in which traits are viewed by psychologists recently has been offered by Lohnes (1966).

We define a trait as an enduring pattern of behaviors which is exhibited by all people, but in varying degrees. We describe human personality as a system of traits, so that a personality is the overall organization of the enduring patterns of behaviors exhibited by a person. What characterizes a person as an individual, different from every other individual, is not the elements of his personality so much as the unique profile of degrees of intensity of those elements. In this theory, the traits which are the elements of personality are common to all people, but are developed in different people to different degrees. These degrees of strength or weakness of a trait in different people are measur-

able, so that the trait profile which characterizes a particular personality can be represented in scientific research by a set of scores [p. 30].

Educators require a multiple-trait approach to considering individual differences for several reasons. One of these is the consideration that schools are trying to modify behavior along more than one dimension (for example, verbal *and* arithmetic skills). Also, educators recognize that dimensions of motivation as well as ability must be considered in such problems as predicting how well a student will do in a particular curriculum.

The necessity of a multiple-trait approach also can be seen when one considers such problems as describing talent within a school population. If two traits are correlated .10, only about 15 percent of those scoring among the top 10 percent on one trait will score among the top 10 percent on the other.[1] If the two traits correlate .50, about one-third of those in the top 10 percent on one trait will score similarly on the other. Even if the two traits correlate as high as .80, only about one-half of the students scoring in the top 10 percent on one trait will do so on the other. Figure 16.1 illustrates this point for a correlation of .80. Because different tests can place an individual in quite different intervals, educators frequently use more than one test for such important considerations as school guidance, instructional grouping and diagnosis, evaluation, college selection, or scholarship awards.

One problem with the trait approach has

---

[1] Assuming a bivariate normal distribution for the two measures.

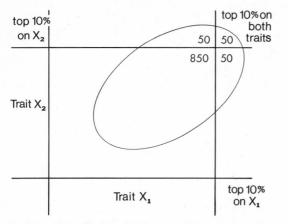

FIG. 16.1. Overlap among top 10 percent on two traits correlated .80 ($N = 1000$).

been the vast proliferation of trait names that have been offered by psychologists and educators. An early summary by Allport and Odbert (1936) found over 17,000 trait names in the English language. This abundance, of course, causes extreme confusion since the same trait may receive different names when used by different people under different conditions. It also is possible to find the same name referring to quite different traits, which adds to the confusion.

Another problem with the trait approach is really a matter of unfinished business. McNemar (1964) pointed this out very strongly in his presidential address to the American Psychological Association in which he said that the necessity of multiple measures in the area of mental ability really has not been demonstrated very convincingly. His plea for a return to the concept of general intelligence was based primarily on the lack of sufficient evidence for the utility of the primary mental abilities approach of Thurstone and others.

As one reads through the test reviews in Buros' *Mental Measurements Yearbook*, the common theme that runs through the criticism of available batteries is the need for validation studies, studies that demonstrate the extent to which multiple measures contribute to improved prediction and understanding of human behavior and that also demonstrate the relationships between different profiles and different kinds of future behavior.

These two problems, the proliferation of traits and the validation of traits, must be attacked, or there will continue to be "more and more factors of less and less importance [McNemar, 1964, p. 872]." In addition, educators need help in sorting out sets of useful, valid traits from this vast array of possible traits.

A temptation here is to set forth some rules to be used in deciding which common traits educators should use. However, one of the most fruitless activities in any science is for one scientist to set forth a set of rules which he then insists all others should follow. A more reasonable approach is to work toward the development of a system of traits that minimizes the previously existing problems and then hope that educators will see the logic in this approach and begin to adopt it. For example, one could argue that a necessary and sufficient condition for a trait to be worthy of consideration is that it provide an *independent* contribution to the prediction of some socially important behavioral criterion from such areas as school performance, vocational development, marriage, citizenship, mental illness, etc. If a group decided that this really made sense and began to develop a system of traits with these operating principles, they would eventually have an operational, parsimonious, and pragmatic system that educators surely would begin to adopt.

THE PARALLEL-STALK MODEL

Although multiple measures have been used in education for some time, the application of mathematical procedures for systematically extracting information from profiles is relatively recent. Earlier efforts at profile representation and interpretation used the parallel-stalk model illustrated in figure 16.2. This figure represents the scores for student Johnny on five different traits. The fact that the connecting lines between the parallel stalks had no meaning did not seem to bother most users, since they did help to emphasize the variations in Johnny's scores. If the means for the five traits on a reference group appropriate for Johnny are all equal to five and the traits are school achievement scales, it is then inferred by the profile inter-preter that Johnny is not doing as well on tests X_1 and X_2 as he is on tests X_3, X_4, and X_5.

One very serious shortcoming of such within-profile contrasts, especially in the achievement area, is the unreliability of differ-ence scores. This unreliability is partly the re-sult of the high correlations among the traits measured by the battery. Some publishers "solve" this problem by not reporting these correlations! Where they are available, or the user computes them himself, it becomes clear that it is almost impossible to talk about the differences an individual exhibits from trait to trait because of the extremely low reliability of the differences between highly correlated traits. Thus, the test manual for almost every high school achievement battery asks the teacher or counselor to be sure to notice differences within student profiles. The plea is to notice that Johnny is higher on reading than he is on spelling, for example, while failing to point out that, given a correlation of .7 between these two tests and given the reliabilities for the two scales of .8, the reliability of the *difference* be-tween standard scores on those two tests is only about .33.

The relationship between the reliabilities of two tests and the reliability of the difference

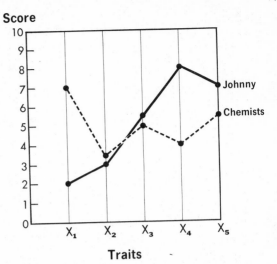

FIG. 16.3 Comparison of Johnny's profile with that for chemists.

between their standard scores is given by the equation

$$r_{dd} = \frac{r_{xx} + r_{yy} - 2r_{xy}}{2 - 2r_{xy}},$$

where r_{dd} is the reliability of the difference be-tween scores on tests X and Y, r_{xx} and r_{yy} are the two test reliabilities, and r_{xy} is the correlation between X and Y.

Relatively independent measures are re-quired if differences within individuals from trait to trait are to be reliable. As can be seen from examination of this equation, if the two traits in question are uncorrelated, the reliabil-ity of the difference scores will be the same as the average reliability of the traits being com-pared. To provide a battery that measures a set of highly related traits and to then encourage educators to make interpretations regarding trait differences for students without even re-porting the typical correlations among these traits is certainly an irresponsible practice.

Another problem with the parallel-stalk method is the difficulty of comparing profiles. For example, it may be desirable to compare Johnny's profile with a set of profiles represent-ing the members of a particular reference group. If Johnny is an aspiring chemist, he might be interested in knowing whether or not he re-sembles former students who became success-

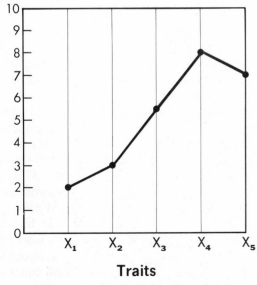

FIG. 16.2. Johnny's profile on five different traits

Trait X_2

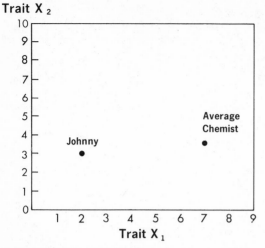

FIG. 16.4. Comparison of profiles in a two-dimensional trait space.

ful, satisfied chemists. Comparison of Johnny's profile with the average profile of a group of former students who became chemists (illustrated in figure 16.3) is not too revealing. It is difficult to decide just how closely he resembles chemists, or how much variation there is among chemists, or whether Johnny more closely resembles mediocre chemists or very successful chemists, or whether Johnny would be "better off" as a salesman, etc. It should be obvious that the practice of staring at the ups and downs of profiles displayed on parallel stalks is an inadequate approach to making inferences about profiles of individuals and groups. A better model is needed.

THE TRAIT-SPACE MODEL

About 1950 a new geometry for the profile problem began to be used by Cattell (1950), Cronbach (1950), Tiedeman, Bryan, and Rulon (1951), and others. This new model, which is referred to here as the Trait-Space Model, views profiles as vectors in a multidimensional space defined by p traits. Figure 16.4 illustrates a two-dimensional trait space, where traits X_1 and X_2 serve to locate Johnny and the average chemist as points in that space. The development of this new model was a rather creative act. The model was not obvious because of the difficulty of visualizing what one does when there are more than two or three such traits.

Also, there was the problem of correlation among the traits. How can a space defined by axes at right angles be used to describe profile distances if the traits are correlated? The trait-space model for handling profiles made it possible to apply the mathematics of multidimensional spaces to these and other aspects of the profile problem. Then the availability of the computer by the 1950s made this multivariate approach feasible. Before considering the utility of this p-dimensional model for analyzing profiles, it is perhaps useful to introduce the relationship between the geometric model and the matrix algebra that is used to manipulate profile data.

In figure 16.4, Johnny's score of 2 on X_1 and 3 on X_2 located him as a point in a two-dimensional space defined by the axes X_1 and X_2. This information is represented algebraically as a row or column of numbers, generally enclosed in brackets, called a *vector*. Thus Johnny's vector is [2 3] for the data of figure 16.4 and [2 3 6 8 7] for his five scores represented by the profile in figure 16.3. The first vector locates

---

TABLE 16.1

Roster of Scores for 10 Chemists on Five Variables

ROSTER MATRIX

Chemist	Score on Test				
	1	2	3	4	5
1	7	4	3	8	0
2	4	1	8	3	4
3	6	3	5	6	9
4	8	6	1	4	4
5	8	5	7	1	8
6	7	2	9	9	6
7	5	3	3	1	9
8	9	5	8	2	7
9	7	4	5	6	6
10	8	2	2	3	8

Symbolically:

$$\mathbf{X} = \begin{bmatrix} X_{11} & X_{12} & \cdots & X_{1p} \\ X_{21} & X_{22} & \cdots & X_{2p} \\ \cdot & \cdot & X_{ij} & \cdot \\ \cdot & \cdot & & \cdot \\ \cdot & \cdot & & \cdot \\ X_{N1} & X_{N2} & \cdots & X_{Np} \end{bmatrix} = [X_{ij}]$$

$$\text{where } \begin{aligned} i &= 1, N \\ j &= 1, p \end{aligned}$$

TABLE 16.2

Some Illustrative Basic Matrix Operations

Given:

$$A = \begin{bmatrix} 3 & 2 \\ 1 & 5 \end{bmatrix} \qquad B = \begin{bmatrix} 1 & 4 \\ 3 & 2 \end{bmatrix} \qquad C = \begin{bmatrix} 1 & 2 \\ 5 & 3 \\ 4 & 1 \end{bmatrix}$$

(A and B are matrices with four elements; C, a matrix with six elements.)

$$V' = \begin{bmatrix} 4 & 2 & 6 \end{bmatrix} \qquad V = \begin{bmatrix} 4 \\ 2 \\ 6 \end{bmatrix} \qquad I = \begin{bmatrix} 1 & 0 & 0 \\ 0 & 1 & 0 \\ 0 & 0 & 1 \end{bmatrix}$$

(V is a vector with three elements, written vertically, and V' is the transpose, i.e. the same elements written horizontally. I is the identity matrix, all zeros except the ones in the diagonal.)

Then:

$$A + B = \begin{bmatrix} 4 & 6 \\ 4 & 7 \end{bmatrix}$$

(corresponding elements are added)

$$A - B = \begin{bmatrix} 2 & -2 \\ -2 & 3 \end{bmatrix}$$

(corresponding elements are subtracted)

$$V' \cdot V = \begin{bmatrix} 4 & 2 & 6 \end{bmatrix} \cdot \begin{bmatrix} 4 \\ 2 \\ 6 \end{bmatrix} = \begin{bmatrix} 4 \cdot 4 + 2 \cdot 2 + 6 \cdot 6 \end{bmatrix} = 56$$

(vector multiplication)

$$A \cdot B = \begin{bmatrix} (3 \cdot 1 + 2 \cdot 3) & (3 \cdot 4 + 2 \cdot 2) \\ (1 \cdot 1 + 5 \cdot 3) & (1 \cdot 4 + 5 \cdot 2) \end{bmatrix} = \begin{bmatrix} 9 & 16 \\ 16 & 14 \end{bmatrix}$$

(matrix multiplication)

$$I \cdot C = C \qquad \begin{bmatrix} 1 & 0 & 0 \\ 0 & 1 & 0 \\ 0 & 0 & 1 \end{bmatrix} \cdot \begin{bmatrix} 1 & 2 \\ 5 & 3 \\ 4 & 1 \end{bmatrix} = \begin{bmatrix} 1 & 2 \\ 5 & 3 \\ 4 & 1 \end{bmatrix}$$

(multiplication by an identity matrix)

(identity matrix)

$$C'C = \begin{bmatrix} 1 & 5 & 4 \\ 2 & 3 & 1 \end{bmatrix} \cdot \begin{bmatrix} 1 & 2 \\ 5 & 3 \\ 4 & 1 \end{bmatrix} = \begin{bmatrix} 42 & 21 \\ 21 & 14 \end{bmatrix}$$

(premultiplying the matrix C by its transpose)

$$A \cdot A^{-1} = I \qquad (A^{-1} \text{ is the inverse of A})$$

$$\begin{bmatrix} 3 & 2 \\ 1 & 5 \end{bmatrix} \cdot \begin{bmatrix} 5/13 & -1/13 \\ -2/13 & 3/13 \end{bmatrix} = \begin{bmatrix} 1.0 & 0.0 \\ 0.0 & 1.0 \end{bmatrix}$$
$$\qquad A \qquad\qquad A^{-1} \qquad\qquad\quad I$$

(multiplying a matrix by its inverse yields an identity matrix)

$$|A| = (3 \cdot 5 - 2 \cdot 1) = 13$$

($|A|$ is the determinant of A)

Characteristic roots and vectors of A:

Given $(A - \lambda_i I)v = 0$, then:

$$\lambda_1 = 5.7 \qquad v_1 = \begin{bmatrix} .57 \\ .82 \end{bmatrix} \qquad v_2 = \begin{bmatrix} .60 \\ .80 \end{bmatrix} \qquad \sum \lambda_i = 8.0$$
$$\lambda_2 = 2.3 \qquad\qquad\qquad\qquad\qquad\qquad\qquad\qquad \text{trace of } A = 8.0$$
eigenvalues $\qquad\qquad$ eigenvectors $\qquad\qquad$ (trace is sum of diagonal elements, $3 + 5$ for A)

Johnny in a two-dimensional trait space, the latter vector in a five-dimensional trait space. Each individual has a location unique for him in a trait space. People with similar profiles will tend to occupy similar regions of the space. A set of scores for 10 chemists would be represented by 10 vectors. Taken together as an array of 10 rows and 5 columns they compose a 10 by 5 matrix (table 16.1). The general form for a matrix of scores, in which X_{ij} is the score of the ith person on the jth test, is shown below both in an expanded and a highly condensed symbolism.

Multivariate procedures for handling profiles utilize the mathematics of matrices and vectors. Although matrix algebra cannot be

TABLE 16.3

Variance-Covariance Matrix

(from table 16.1 data)

Numerical Example:

$$\mathbf{D} = \begin{bmatrix} 2.09 & 1.45 & -0.39 & -0.07 & 0.11 \\ 1.45 & 2.25 & -1.15 & -0.75 & -0.45 \\ -0.39 & -1.15 & 7.09 & 0.57 & 0.89 \\ -0.07 & -0.75 & 0.57 & 7.21 & -3.53 \\ 0.11 & -0.45 & 0.89 & -3.53 & 7.09 \end{bmatrix}$$

Symbolically

$$\mathbf{D} = \begin{bmatrix} s_1^2 & s_1 s_2 r_{12} & s_1 s_3 r_{13} & \cdots & s_1 s_t r_{1t} \\ s_2 s_1 r_{21} & s_2^2 & & & \\ \vdots & & \ddots & & \\ s_t s_1 r_{t1} & \cdots & \cdots & \cdots & s_t^2 \end{bmatrix}$$

s_i^2 = variance for variable i

$s_i s_j r_{ij}$ = covariance for variable i and j

taught here, it can be illustrated. The student not familiar with these techniques will need to become familiar with matrix algebra if he expects to do further work with profiles along the lines indicated in the balance of this chapter. Good introductions to matrix algebra are found in Ayres (1962), Hohn (1964), and Horst (1963).

Matrix algebra provides very powerful rules for manipulating (adding, multiplying, etc.) arrays of numbers (i.e. matrices and vectors) and a notational scheme for conveniently denoting them. Table 16.2 illustrates some of the basic matrix operations used in profile analysis. The roster of scores in table 16.1 is a matrix which can be represented by the single boldface character **X**. A few matrix manipulations allow one to go from the roster matrix **X** to the variance-covariance matrix **D** of table 16.3 and the correlation matrix **R** of table 16.4. The vector of group means, called the *centroid* [6.9 3.5 5.1 4.3 6.1], and the variance-covariance matrix **D** are necessary and sufficient estimators of the location and shape of the population represented by the sample, assuming that the population is multivariate normal. The multivariate normal distribution is the *p*-dimensional analog of the univariate normal distribution. (See

Morrison, 1967, for a good discussion of this distribution and for why it is so useful and valid in the behavioral sciences.)

The trait-space model permits one to add to the conceptualizations of trait and personality introduced earlier. The trait profile that characterizes a particular personality now can be represented as a point in a *p*-dimensional space. An individual's personality can be defined as his location in that space, the location determined by the total pattern of the *p* behavioral measures that are available for that individual. People who have similar patterns of trait scores will occupy the same region of this space. The trait scores sample and summarize behavior, and people who behave similarly are thought to have similar personalities. This is a more general and more operational concept of personality than generally is proposed. It allows for the inclusion of both dimensions of maximum performance (ability) and typical performance (motives).

In this context, a trait is operationally defined in terms of some specific measurement procedure. That is why the terms *trait* and *measure* are used synonymously in this discussion. To describe a dimension of individual differences that is a function of several different measures, the term *factor* is used. Procedures for determining factors are considered later in this chapter.

Centours and Probabilities

In order to deal with profiles more efficiently, it is important to be able to deal with a

TABLE 16.4

Correlation Matrix

$$\mathbf{R} = \begin{bmatrix} 1.00 & 0.67 & -0.10 & -0.02 & 0.03 \\ 0.67 & 1.00 & -0.29 & -0.19 & -0.11 \\ -0.10 & -0.29 & 1.00 & 0.08 & 0.13 \\ -0.02 & -0.19 & 0.08 & 1.00 & -0.49 \\ 0.03 & -0.11 & 0.13 & -0.49 & 1.00 \end{bmatrix}$$

$$\mathbf{R} = \begin{bmatrix} 1.00 & r_{12} & r_{13} & \cdots & r_{1t} \\ r_{21} & 1.00 & r_{23} & \cdots & r_{2t} \\ r_{31} & r_{32} & 1.00 & \cdots & r_{3t} \\ \vdots & \vdots & \vdots & \cdots & \vdots \\ r_{t1} & r_{t2} & r_{t3} & \cdots & 1.00 \end{bmatrix}$$

p-dimensional space and describe and locate points in that space with respect to other points and with respect to the coordinate system. One useful statistic for describing the location of a particular point with respect to a swarm of points is called the *centour* (*cen*tile con*tour*). The centour is most easily illustrated for the one-dimensional case. Given a sample from a univariate normal population, with sample estimates of M_x and s_x^2 for the mean and variance, the statistic

$$\chi_1^2 = \frac{(X_i - M_x)^2}{s_x^2} \qquad [1]$$

distributes approximately as χ^2 with one degree of freedom for sample points from that population. The inverse cumulative probability associated with each χ^2 is called the centour for that point. It represents the estimated proportion of the population that lies further from the population mean than does the point X_i. For example, Johnny had a score of 2.0 on the trait for which the mean for chemists was 6.9 and s_x equaled 1.45. Therefore,

$$\chi^2 = \frac{(2.0 - 6.9)^2}{2.09} = 11.49.$$

The inverse cumulative probability for a χ^2 equal to 11.49 is less than .001, so less than one in 1,000 chemists would be expected to lie further from the chemist mean than does Johnny.

For the multidimensional case involving p traits, equation 1 generalizes to $\chi_p^2 = x_i' D^{-1} x_i$, where x_i' is a row vector whose p elements are the deviations of individual i from the p sample means, and D^{-1} is the inverse of the $p \times p$ variance-covariance matrix. Johnny's centour in the distribution for chemists (for $p = 5$) is less than one, based upon a χ_5^2 equal to 21.1. This means that less than 1 percent of the chemists look less like the average chemist than does Johnny. Note that when $p = 1$ the matrix equation of χ_p^2 becomes identical to the preceding equation.

Geometrically, the centour in a two-dimensional space defines an ellipse beyond which a certain proportion of the population is expected to lie. Returning to the profiles given

TABLE 16.5

Scores, Chi Squares and Centours for the 10 Chemists

Chem-ist	Scores on Tests					Chi Squares (ndf = 5)	Cen-tours
	1	2	3	4	5		
1	7	4	3	8	0	5.65	34
2	4	1	8	3	4	7.57	19
3	6	3	5	6	9	4.27	51
4	8	6	1	4	4	4.33	50
5	8	5	7	1	8	3.33	65
6	7	2	9	9	6	5.60	35
7	5	3	3	1	9	4.80	44
8	9	5	8	2	7	4.69	46
9	7	4	5	6	6	1.00	96
10	8	2	2	3	8	8.77	12
Means	6.9	3.5	5.1	4.3	6.1		
Standard Deviations	1.4	1.5	2.7	2.7	2.7		

in figure 16.4 for Johnny and the chemists, the chemists' dispersion

$$\begin{bmatrix} 2.09 & 1.45 \\ 1.45 & 2.25 \end{bmatrix}$$

and centroid [6.9 3.5] in the space defined by X_1 and X_2 produce a χ^2 for Johnny of

$$\chi^2 = [4.9 \ .5] \cdot \begin{bmatrix} 2.09 & 1.45 \\ 1.45 & 2.25 \end{bmatrix}^{-1} \cdot \begin{bmatrix} 4.9 \\ .5 \end{bmatrix} = 18.3.$$

This χ^2 with two degrees of freedom has an inverse cumulative probability of $<.01$. This means that less than 1 percent of the chemists lie outside of the ellipse that passed through Johnny's point. This result indicates that Johnny is slightly more similar to chemists if one considers only X_1 and X_2, than if all five dimensions are used as was done in the previous calculation. In the three-dimensional space, a given χ_3^2 traces an ellipsoid, and, where $p > 3$, the figure is termed a hyperellipsoid, but the concept of the centour in terms of proportions lying further from the centroid remains the same.

Table 16.5 presents the centours for the 10 chemists. Since centours are the inverse cumulative probabilities (expressed as a percentage) of the χ^2, high centours are associated with low values of χ^2. The higher the centour the more that individual resembles the average chemist;

that is, the more closely his score profile resembles the mean profile for chemists.

Probability of Group Membership

A frequently encountered profile problem is concerned with the comparison of the profile of an individual with a set of reference groups, where group membership of the individual is to be inferred from his trait profile. This problem is most easily introduced by using the simple case of one trait and a mixed population consisting of only two groups.

A histogram, representing samples from two groups, A and B, is plotted on trait X in figure 16.5. The shaded area indicates the frequency of sample A at a particular score on X, the unshaded area the frequency for sample B. Note for example that about one-third of those with a score of 2 on X are members of group A. If the measurement of trait X was taken antecedent to group membership, then a score of 2 on X would indicate probable membership in group B, since two-thirds of those with that score do join group B.

Although the histogram is useful for illustrating the basic approach to the profile problem that is being introduced here, graphical procedures are relatively unmanageable if one is dealing with a large number of groups on a large number of traits. Moving from X as a

discrete to a continuous variable and introducing the assumption that the trait X is normally distributed within groups A and B, it is possible to begin to see how to shift from a graphical approach to a mathematical approach. The familiar equation for determining the probability density a of the normal curve at any point X_i along trait X for group A can be written:

$$a = \frac{1}{\sigma_a \sqrt{2\Pi}} e^{-(X_i - \mu_a)^2 / 2\sigma_a^2}.$$

The parameters μ and σ^2 are generally estimated from the sample mean and variance of group A on variable X. Thus, given the mean and standard deviation for sample A on X, it is possible to estimate the height of the A curve at X_i and by similar equation the height of the B curve at that same point.[2] Figure 16.6 illustrates the densities a and b.

This comparison of heights of curves represents a comparison of the density function for groups A and B on variable X. What one is doing is comparing the density of group A with the density of group B at point X_i. This comparison of densities then yields the probability that an individual with score X_i is a member of group A, and similarly the probability for group B. That is

$$P_A = \frac{a}{a + b} \quad \text{and} \quad P_B = \frac{a}{a + b},$$

where $P_A + P_B = 1.00$.

The next step in this generalization is to examine the density function for the bivariate normal distribution.

$$a = \frac{1}{2\Pi\sigma_1\sigma_2\sqrt{1 - \rho_{12}^2}}$$

$$\cdot \exp\left[\frac{1}{2(1 - \rho_{12}^2)} \left(\frac{x_1^2}{\sigma_1^2} + \frac{x_2^2}{\sigma_2^2} - \frac{2\rho_{12}x_1x_2}{\sigma_1\sigma_2} \right) \right]$$

where $X_1 = (X_{1i} - \mu_1)$ and X_{1i} is the score for individual i on test 1. Here it is clear that the major

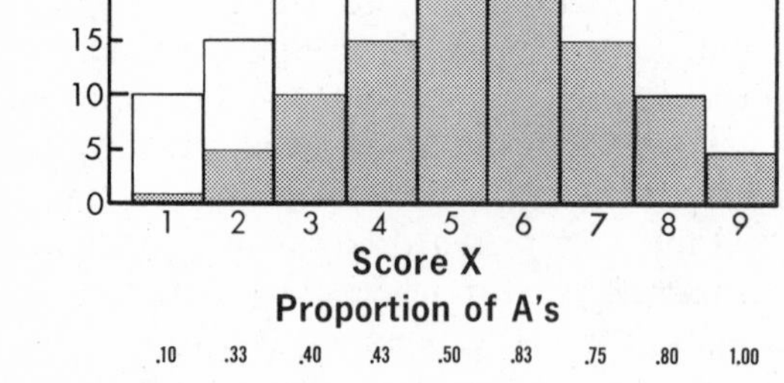

Frequency

FIG. 16.5. Distributions for groups A and B on trait X (group A shaded).

[2] This substitution of sample estimates into the equations for the theoretical distribution is appropriate only for large samples. For a discussion of corrections for number of degrees of freedom, see Geisser (1964).

Frequency

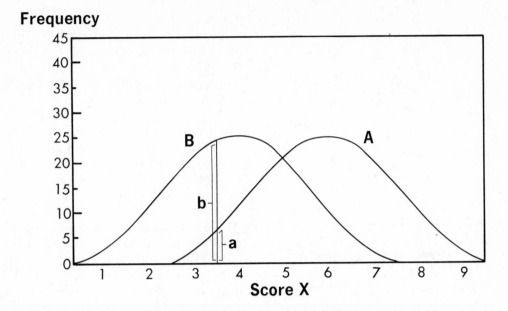

FIG. 16.6. Distributions for groups A and B

changes are from one mean and standard deviation to two means and two standard deviations for the two variables, X_1 and X_2. Also added is the correlation between the variates, ρ_{12}. Figure 16.7 illustrates the bivariate distributions for two populations, A and B. Substituting the sample estimates for population A into the bivariate normal equation, the density of As at point X_{1i}, X_{2i} is obtained. The resulting densities for A and B can then be compared as before to obtain the probability that

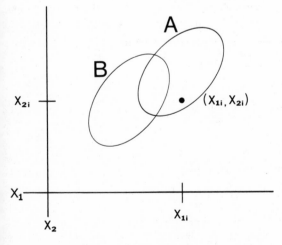

FIG. 16.7. Bivariate normal distributions for populations A and B.

individual i is a member of group A or group B. The generalization of this approach to more than two dimensions is facilitated by moving to a matrix notation for describing the density function for multivariate normal populations.

If $\mathbf{D}$ represents the $p \times p$ variance-covariance matrix for group A and x_i represents the column vector of deviations for individual i from the p group A means, then the multivariate normal density function is proportional to

$$a = \frac{1}{|\mathbf{D}|^{1/2}} \exp(-x_i' \mathbf{D}^{-1} x_i/2) \qquad [2]$$

where $|\mathbf{D}|^{1/2}$ is the square root of the determinant of $\mathbf{D}$. Again, once the density at point i is determined for both groups A and B in this multivariate space, then the probabilities of being in A and B are directly determinable as before. Generalizing this approach from two groups to k groups simply requires the determination of k densities. Once they are determined, the probability that i is a member of group A is a ratio of the density of group A at point x_i to the sum of the densities of all k groups.

The preceding discussion assumes that the groups composing the mixed population occur

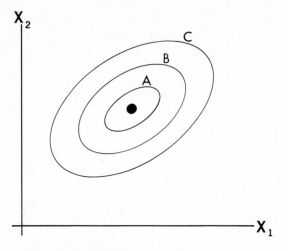

FIG. 16.8. Ellipses representing three centours (A = 80th, B = 50th, C = 20th).

just been described (see, for example, Rulon, Tiedeman, Tatsuoka, & Langmuir, 1967). In figure 16.8, let ellipses A, B, and C represent the 80th, 50th, and 20th centours respectively. The region lying *within* ellipse A can be represented as ($x^2 \leq .45$), which is the space in which x^2 is less than or equal to .45, the x^2 (ndf = 2) associated with the centour equal to 80. Similarly, the space lying *outside* ellipse B could be represented as ($x^2 \geq 1.39$). Thus any point whose x^2 was equal to or greater than 1.39 would lie in the region of the space not included within ellipse B.

While the centour is useful for defining regions with respect to a single population, the classification probabilities permit one to consider two or more populations. In the two-group case represented in Figure 16.9, the region of the space in which the density of the group A points is greater than the group B points can be expressed ($P_A > P_B$). For the general case of g groups, the region of the space where the group j density is higher than any other group is ($P_j > P_k$), where j and k go from one to g and $j \neq k$. Again,

$$\sum_{j=1}^{g} P_j = 1.00.$$

in equal numbers in that population. If they do not and if the proportions of the mix are known, then the proportion can be included in each equation for describing density. If q_a is the proportion of As in the population and q_b is the proportion of Bs, then $q_a + q_b = 1.00$ for the two-group case. The q values can then be placed in the density equations in the numerator for the coefficient of e. Use of unity in the numerator of equation 2 was based on the assumption that the number in each group was the same for that mixed population.

Regions in the Trait Space

A scheme for considering regions in the trait space has been developed that builds upon the centour and probability concepts which have

Most classification problems can be dealt with by using some variation of these procedures. If the task is to predict eventual group membership, basing that prediction on the highest P_j will maximize the number of correct

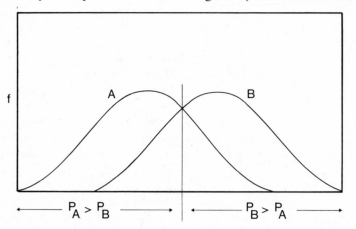

FIG. 16.9. Regions for two populations in one-dimensional space

predictions. This procedure assumes that the same processes that determined group membership for the norming groups continue to operate for the sample for which predictions are being made.

Distances in the Trait Space

Every high school geometry student has learned how to determine the distance between two points given their coordinates in a two-dimensional space. The Pythagorean theorem directs him to take the square root of the sum of squared differences between corresponding coordinates. Going back to figure 16.4, the "distance" between Johnny and the average chemist then would be $\sqrt{(6.9-2)^2+(3.5-3)^2} = \sqrt{24.26} = 4.92$. But *not* every high school geometry student recognizes that this theorem also applies to spaces defined by more than two axes and that it assumes that the scale for each axis is in comparable units and that the measurements represented by those axes are at right angles.

A generalization of this simple distance measure to include the case of multiple dependent measures was offered some time ago by Mahalanobis (1936) but has only recently become a recognized tool in profile analysis (see, for example, Overall, 1964). If x' is the row vector of differences between the two score vectors X_1 and X_2, and d is the desired distance between them, then d^2, where $d^2 = x'x$, is the squared distance using the Pythagorean theorem directly. Mahalanobis has shown that the dependencies can be taken into account by introducing the variance-covariance matrix D yielding the matrix equation $d^2 = x'D^{-1}x$.

That equation should look familiar. It is the equation used to produce the χ^2s upon which the centour is based. Thus $d^2 = \chi^2$, and the square root of χ^2 is a measure of distance between any two points drawn from the set of points whose dispersion is D. In computing Johnny's centour his squared distance from the chemist centroid was found to be 18.3 in the two-dimensional space. This value is smaller than the 24.26 found for d^2 when the correlation between those two measures was not taken into account. This shorter distance ($\sqrt{18.3}$) is the same as would be obtained by first transforming the space to independent axes of equal variance and then applying the Pythagorean theorem in that new orthogonal space. (Jones, 1968, provides a good discussion of this point.)

To eliminate arbitrary differences in scale, the measures can be standardized so that D becomes R and the difference in score vectors is expressed in standard score form (z). Notice also that if the measures are uncorrelated then R becomes an identity matrix and d^2 becomes $z'Iz = z'z$, and one is back to Pythagoras again. The generalized distance measure, d^2, is applicable to distances between two individuals, two groups, or a group and an individual. What is required, of course, is an estimate of the population dispersion from which the groups and/or individuals are drawn.

REDUCING DIMENSIONALITY

Multivariate analysis provides a variety of techniques for reducing the number of dimensions needed for studying the ways in which groups or individuals differ. Rulon and associates (1967, p. 203), in musing about the size of the bookshelf a counselor would need to store the centour tables required for an 8-group 17-variable centour application (60^{13} five-foot shelves), pointed to the need to reduce the number of variates used for *finding* centours in a set of tables. Of course with today's computer capability and availability, it is possible to compute a centour much faster than finding it in a table, as Rulon and associates proposed. Where computer facilities are available, centours and probabilities of group membership can be computed directly in the test space as they are needed for selection or guidance situations. Reducing dimensionality is useful, however, for improved understanding of the basic ways in which groups and individuals differ, and, since these techniques play such a large role in measurement applications, some of the major procedures for reducing dimensionality will be summarized and illustrated here.

Principal Components

Suppose variables X_1 and X_2 are very highly correlated. The 10th centour might appear as

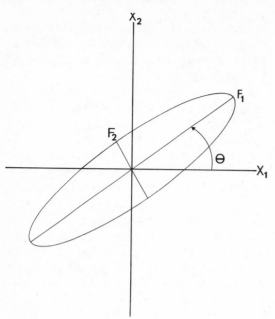

FIG. 16.10. Rotation of axes through angle θ

the ellipse in figure 16.10. If axis X_1 is rotated through an angle θ to position F_1, and X_2 similarly rotated to F_2, then all sample points can now be described in terms of two new coordinates, F_1 and F_2. Notice that most of the information regarding the ways in which those individuals differ is contained in their location along axis F_1. The information not preserved if the dimensionality is treated as one is their perpendicular distances from F_1, namely their location on the F_2 axis. Principal components analysis is the major technique used to account for as much as possible of the differences among a set of individuals on a set of measures using a limited number of dimensions.

Algebraically, the principal components solution is obtained by extracting the p characteristic roots (eigenvalues) and vectors (eigenvectors) of the correlation matrix $\mathbf{R}$. In matrix notation the general equation is $(\mathbf{R} - \lambda_i \mathbf{I})\mathbf{v}_i = 0$ where λ_i is one of the p possible roots of $\mathbf{R}$, and $\mathbf{v}_i$ is the corresponding normalized vector. The normalized vector is transformed to coefficients for computing component scores (F_i) by multiplying the p elements of $\mathbf{v}_i$ by $1/\sqrt{\lambda_i}$. The resulting coefficients c_i transform standardized scores of the original variables to component scores of unit variance. Given a student's

column vector of standard scores $\mathbf{z}'$, the vector product $c_1 \mathbf{z}' = F_1$.

The sum of the λs is equal to p, which is the trace of $\mathbf{R}$. This is also the total variance, since each test variance is equal to one, as represented in the correlation matrix with unities in the main diagonal. The proportion of total test variance accounted for by component i is determined by λ_i/P. The λs are arranged so that they become successively smaller as i goes from one to p, so the first m components account for $100 \left(\sum_{i=1}^{m} \lambda_i \right)/P$ percent of the total variance in the original set of measures.

Lohnes (1966) provided a good demonstration of the utility of the principal components approach in his work with the Project Talent test battery. He reduced a 60-dimensional space, defined by the 60 correlated Project Talent ability measures, to 11 independent components. Although these 11 components left about one-third of the total variance of the 60 ability measures not accounted for, follow-up studies indicated that for the types of criterion measures that are likely to be of interest in longitudinal studies such as Project Talent, the two-thirds of the variance that is explained by the first 11 components does as good a job of prediction as does the full set of 60 variables.

Although the principal components method is generally considered as one of several variations of factor analysis, some feel the distinction between factor analysis and components analysis is basic and must be preserved (see, for example, Harris, 1964). One difference is that components analysis emphasizes accounting for as much of the total variance as possible with the fewest number of factors, while factor analysis is more concerned with "explaining" the correlations among the observed measurements by identifying hypothetical sources of common variation (factors) among the correlated variates.

Operationally, the major difference is whether or not unities are used as the diagonal elements of $\mathbf{R}$. The correlation matrix $\mathbf{R}$ is a variance-covariance matrix of standardized scores, with variances indicated in the principal diagonal of $\mathbf{R}$ (all equal to 1.00) and with covariances as the off-diagonal elements of **R**. The variance unique to each variable can be removed from the analysis prior to factor extraction. This is done by estimating the proportion of variance, which is common to (or predictable from) the rest of the set of variables, and substituting these communalities, as they are called, for the unit variances on the diagonal of **R**. A variety of procedures is then available for extracting common factors from this adjusted correlation matrix (Cattell, 1966; Fruchter, 1954; Harman, 1967; Harris, 1967; Horst, 1965).

It is sometimes puzzling to the uninitiated how it is possible for different factor analysts to arrive at different factor descriptions of the same domain. This is largely due to the fact that there are many options open to the factor analyst. For example, it is possible to obtain oblique factors, in which case the resulting factors are correlated. Whether or not to produce oblique or orthogonal factors is more a function of the investigator's theoretical orientation, or the purposes of the analysis, than anything intrinsic in the data for which he is attempting to provide a factor model.

Also there is the question of how many factors are adequate to the task of explaining the relationships among the observed variables. Some investigators prefer a statistical inference solution; others simply select those factors that are easily interpreted in terms of the nature and number of observed variables that are highly related to the obtained factors. Of course all of these decisions regarding the number of factors, the form of rotation, and the interpretation of factors are troublesome for all "brands" of factor analysis, including the use of principal components.

The most frequently used factor analytic technique begins with the principal components of the correlation matrix followed by a VARIMAX rotation to simplify the interpretation of those factors that appear necessary to explain the observed relationships. A small numerical example can best illustrate these procedures.

The correlation matrix (**R**) of table 16.6 displays the relationships among nine variables. The nine roots (eigenvalues) of **R** are listed in table 16.7. A sharp drop in the size of these values can be seen after the third root. The sum of the first three roots is 7.91; and $7.91/9.00 = .88$, which indicates that 88 percent of the total variance is accounted for by the first three components. An examination of the correlations between the three main components and the nine variables (principal components structure in table 16.7) also indicates that all of the variables have high communalities using the first three components. These observed communalities are the sum of the squared correlations across rows of the structure, so they represent the proportion of each variable's variance that is explained by the first three components. These kinds of considerations lead to the conclusion that three factors are adequate to describe the ways in which individuals differ on the nine measured traits. A three-dimensional space preserves most of the information contained in the nine-dimensional space.

TABLE 16.6

Correlation Matrix for Factor Analysis Example

Trait	1	2	3	4	5	6	7	8	9
1	1.00	.16	.80	.14	.10	.13	.75	.03	.09
2	.16	1.00	.05	.18	.86	.15	.13	.89	.14
3	.80	.05	1.00	.06	.03	−.10	.73	.04	−.06
4	.14	.18	.06	1.00	−.08	.82	.07	.08	.77
5	.10	.86	.03	−.08	1.00	.01	−.01	.84	.12
6	.13	.15	−.10	.82	.01	1.00	.20	−.02	.85
7	.75	.13	.73	.07	−.01	.20	1.00	.11	.05
8	.03	.89	.04	.08	.84	−.02	.11	1.00	.10
9	.09	.14	−.06	.77	.12	.85	.05	.10	1.00

TABLE 16.7

Results of Factor Analysis

Eigenvalues of R	Trait	Principal Components Structure			Communalities
		1	2	3	
3.08	1	.52	.14	−.75	.87
2.46	2	.75	−.57	.22	.93
2.37	3	.39	.06	−.84	.86
.37	4	.58	.64	.32	.85
.33	5	.62	.68	.22	.90
.23	6	.58	.67	.35	.92
.11	7	.49	.15	−.74	.81
.04	8	.66	−.66	.22	.91
.01	9	.59	.58	.42	.87

$$9.00 = \sum_{i=1}^{t} \lambda_i$$

Trait	Rotated Factor Structure			Communalities
	1	2	3	
1	.06	.09	.92	.87
2	.95	.13	.09	.93
3	.01	−.08	.93	.86
4	.02	.92	.07	.85
5	.95	−.02	.00	.90
6	.01	.96	.05	.92
7	.04	.09	.90	.81
8	.95	.02	.03	.91
9	.09	.93	.01	.87

The problem with the components structure is that it is not easily interpreted. Once it is decided that the nine-dimensional space can be represented by three orthogonal factors, the three components can be rotated without losing any information about the relative location of the N sample points.

The VARIMAX rotated structure is reported at the bottom of table 16.7. Here it is seen that factor 1 is highly related to traits 2, 5, and 8; factor 2 to traits 4, 6, and 9; and factor 3 to traits 1, 3, and 7. One then goes on to consider and describe the derived factors in terms of their associated traits (i.e. test variables).

Of course, measures of human traits do not usually form such nice neat factors. If they did there would not be such a wide variety of factor analytic techniques available. In fact they would not even be necessary, since inspection of the correlation matrix (table 16.6) yields the same three factors. The example does serve to illustrate the basic aspects of factor analysis in a manner that helps the uninitiated see their relevance to the original observations.

Discriminant Analysis

Component and factor analysis are techniques to be applied when the concern is *individual* differences. If, however, the object is to identify the basic ways in which *groups* differ, then discriminant analysis is appropriate. Figure 16.11 illustrates the simplest case, two groups and two variables. If the two distributions representing groups A and B are projected on to F_1, then a maximum of information regarding group differences is preserved if the F_1 axis is perpendicular to the line of minimum overlap, M.

Algebraically, multiple group discriminant functions are found by obtaining the characteristic roots (λ) and vectors (v) of the matrix equation $(\mathbf{W}^{-1}\mathbf{A} - \lambda\mathbf{I})\mathbf{v} = 0$, where $\mathbf{W}$ and $\mathbf{A}$ are deviation sums of squares and cross products matrices for within and among groups, respectively. The resulting transformation vector, v, when applied to the original measures produces a discriminant score that maximizes group centroid separation and minimizes within-group dispersion. That is, the ratio of among-

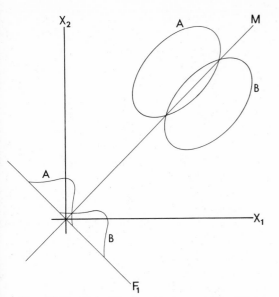

FIG. 16.11. Projection from test space (X_1, X_2) to discriminant space (F_1).

to within-group dispersion is maximized in the resulting reduced space (on F_1 in figure 16.11). With p traits and g groups the maximum number of discriminant functions needed to describe group differences is either p or $g-1$, whichever is smaller.

As an example, consider the problem of distinguishing between those college chemistry majors who became professional chemists and those who became high school chemistry teachers after graduating from college. Suppose five tests were administered to a sample of college chemistry majors, and then through follow-up questionnaires, their present occupations and career plans were determined. When

TABLE 16.8
Roster of Scores for 10 Chemistry Teachers on Five Variables

Teacher	Variable				
	1	2	3	4	5
1	4	5	2	3	7
2	7	8	4	5	6
3	8	7	4	9	5
4	2	4	1	5	3
5	7	6	5	8	8
6	8	9	3	7	5
7	1	2	3	9	4
8	4	5	6	8	7
9	7	8	2	6	7
10	8	6	5	8	6

the individuals were classified into the two categories, chemist or chemistry teacher, there were the 10 chemists of table 16.1 and the 10 teachers of table 16.8.

Since there are only two groups, one discriminant function is the maximum number possible. Solving for the characteristic root and vector of the matrix product $\mathbf{W}^{-1}\mathbf{A}$ yields $\lambda = 5.304$ and $\mathbf{v}' = [-.34\ .40\ -.01\ .14\ .09]$. The vector product $\mathbf{v}'\mathbf{x}_i$, where again $\mathbf{x}_i$ is a column vector of deviations from the grand means for individual i, locates each individual on the discriminant axis. The elements of $\mathbf{v}$ have been scaled so that the discriminant scores have unit variance. The central limits theorem lends confidence that discriminant scores will tend to be normally distributed. Figure 16.12 illustrates the two distributions on that discriminant axis.

The interpretation of the discriminant function is based upon an examination of the correlations between the original five test scores

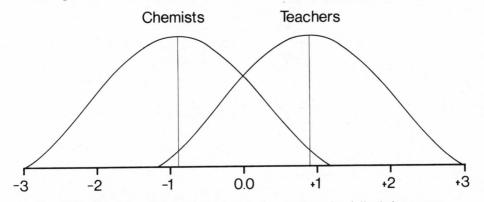

FIG. 16.12. Chemists and chemistry teachers in the one-dimensional discriminant space

TABLE 16.9

Weights and Correlations for the Discriminant Function

Variable	Discriminant Weight	Correlation
1	−.34	−.31
2	.40	.60
3	−.01	−.36
4	.14	.49
5	.09	−.07

and each student's discriminant score. The five correlations are found in table 16.9, along with the weights making up v, the transformation vector. The correlations reveal that predictors 2 and 4 are positively correlated with the discriminant function while 1 and 3 are negatively related. If, for example, variables 2 and 4 were measuring traits from the affective domain, such as primary orientation toward people, and 1 and 3 were nonverbal mental ability measures, the "results" of this hypothetical example of discriminant analysis would be consistent with the results of several career development investigators (e.g. Cooley, 1964; Lee, 1961; Roe & Siegelman, 1964).

An example from Project Talent research (Cooley, 1966) illustrates how useful discriminant analysis can be in the construction of a relatively simple map of a complicated set of data. The research question concerned the extent to which 19 ability tests from the Project Talent battery could describe the kinds of career plan changes that were likely to take place over a five-year period among late adolescent males. Ninth-grade male students were classified into one of six groups according to their career plans. The six category classification scheme is summarized in table 16.10, which includes illustrative occupations that would fall in each of the six cells. The same students were subsequently contacted through mailed questionnaires one year after graduation from high school. The follow-up plans also were classified in this six-category scheme. Contrasting ninth-grade plans with follow-up plans resulted in the 6×6 frequency distribution that is provided in table 16.11. For example, 2,379 boys planned to have careers in the physical sciences at ninth grade; in the follow-up there were only 1,307 boys with plans to become physical scientists and of them 965 were from the original 2,379. Thus the entries in the main diagonal of table 16.11 show the frequency with which plans remained unchanged, whereas the off-diagonal frequencies indicate the nature and extent of the changes that took place between grade nine and one year after high school graduation.

Table 16.11 then can be thought of as an array of 36 groups, 6 of which are groups representing stable plans and 30 representing some type of change in plans. Using 19 ability measures as predictors of group membership, a 36-group discriminant analysis was performed

TABLE 16.10

Six-Category Classification Scheme

	SCIENCE-TECHNOLOGY		NONTECHNICAL	
	(1)	(2)	(3)	(4)
	Physical	*Biological-Medical*	*Nonbusiness*	*Business*
College	Mathematician Physical scientist Engineer Scientific aide	Biological scientist Nurse Physician Pharmacist Dentist Medical technician	Social scientist Social worker Clergyman Teacher	Accountant Lawyer Businessman Government Salesman
		(5)		(6)
Noncollege		Aviation Engineering aide Medical technician Skilled worker Structural worker		Government Salesman Accountant Service worker Businessman Office worker

TABLE 16.11

Career Group Self-Predictions
(Grade 9 Males)

Grade 9 Plans	Follow-up Plans 1	2	3	4	5	6	Grade 9 Totals
1. Physical science	965	291	378	545	121	79	2,379
2. Biological-Medical	106	377	173	213	29	37	935
3. Humanities	49	47	261	120	36	19	532
4. Business (C)	57	50	140	440	24	39	750
5. Technical	94	28	67	97	316	128	730
6. Business (NC)	36	27	72	178	93	125	531
Follow-up totals	1,307	820	1,091	1,593	619	427	5,857

42 percent hits (underlined cells define "hits")

which attempted to see the relationship between ability profiles and the types of career plan changes that took place during that period. The analysis resulted in only two significant discriminant functions out of a maximum of 19 mathematically possible. One was primarily a function of the academic achievement measures in the battery and the other was a bipolar function contrasting verbal ability measures against nonverbal ability measures. Of course, the interpretations of these discriminant functions are based on the correlations between the original 19 measures and the resulting two discriminant functions. Each of the 36 group centroids can be located in this two-dimensional discriminant plane; this is shown in figure 16.13. The centroids of the six stable groups are indicated with small open circles, and the 30 change groups are solid circles. Figure 16.13 shows how the groups that changed from one career plan to another more closely resembled the stable group in the new career plan than the career plan group they left. This type of analysis permits one to examine the combinations of attri-

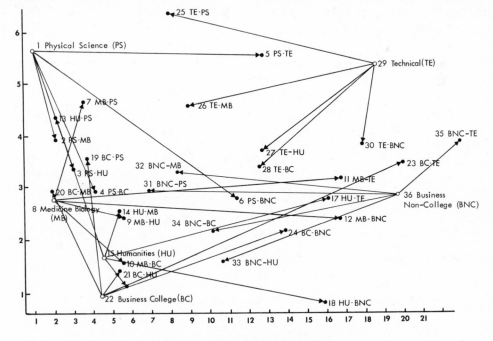

FIG. 16.13. The 36 centroids in the ability space

butes that tend to indicate stability in career field, which implies a criterion of success and satisfaction. That is, it seems safe to assume that those who stay with a particular career plan are at least achieving some minimum level of success and satisfaction.

Multiple Regression

The most frequently used linear function of the original measures is derived by multiple regression analysis. Here the task is to find a set of coefficients for the p traits, considered as predictors, that will maximize the correlation between the criterion measure to be predicted and the linear composite (i.e. weighted sum) of the p traits. The coefficients for the desired linear function are called the standardized partial regression coefficients (b) and are derived from the matrix operation $b = R^{-1}r_c$, where R is the $p \times p$ matrix of the correlations among the predictors, r_c is a column vector of correlations between the criterion and each of the p predictors, and b is a column vector of the desired coefficients. Given a vector z_i of standard scores for individual i, the prediction $\hat{z}_{c_i}$ on the standardized criterion is simply the vector product $b'z_i = \hat{z}_{c_i}$. The multiple correlation ($R_{c \cdot 1,2,\ldots t}$) is then the product-moment correlation between the observed criterion z_c, and the prediction $\hat{z}_c$.

The square of the multiple correlation coefficient is found by forming the vector product $b'r_c = R^2_{c \cdot 1,2,\ldots p}$.

To illustrate this procedure, assume that the five measures on the 10 chemists were made while they were in college and that a sixth measure, grade point average in graduate school, was available as a criterion for each of them. Table 16.4 reported the correlations among the predictors, matrix R. Table 16.12 reports the correlation between each predictor and the criterion (X_c) as vector r_c. Multiplying the inverse of matrix R by the vector r_c yields the regression coefficients b in table 16.12. The resulting multiple correlation of .62 indicates the extent of the linear relationship between the predictors and the criterion. The prediction is the weighted sum of standard scores as indicated in the multiple regression equation of table 16.12. The regression equation also is written in raw score form in the equation below the standardized form. The correlations between each predictor and the criterion z_c indicate that predictors 1 and 3 had the highest degree of relationship with the criterion. The coefficients in b indicate that variables 1 and 2 were the most useful predictors, given this particular set of five predictors and 10 observations.

TABLE 16.12

Multiple Correlation Results for Chemists

Predictor	Correlations with Criterion (r_c)	Standardized Regression Coefficients (b)	Correlation with Prediction ($r_c(1/R_{c \cdot 12345})$)
1	.36	.69	.59
2	−.09	−.47	−.15
3	.28	.19	.45
4	.15	.11	.24
5	.15	.11	.25

Multiple correlation coefficient: $b'r_c = .62 = R_{c \cdot 12345}$

Prediction equations for individual i

Multiple regression equation (for standard scores): $\hat{z}_{c_i} = .69z_{1i} - .47z_{2i} + .19z_{3i} + .11z_{4i} + .11z_{5i}$

Multiple regression equation (for observed scores):
$\hat{X}_{c_i} = 1.027X_{1i} - .669X_{2i} + .152X_{3i} + .089X_{4i} + .091X_{5i} - 1.259$

Criterion data

Vector of observed values of the criterion: $X'_c = [3 \quad 4 \quad 2 \quad 4 \quad 5 \quad 8 \quad 4 \quad 6 \quad 9 \quad 7]$

Mean of $X_c = 5.20$
Standard deviation = 2.14

Multiple regression has been used widely in education to predict student success in school, primarily for purposes of selection in higher education. Given several predictors of academic performance, regression analysis has certain advantages over alternatives such as the frequently used cutoff scores for each predictor. For example, it allows a high score on one predictor to compensate for a low score on another in a manner not possible using the multiple cutoff approach.

Of course, there are difficulties as well as advantages, not the least of which is obtaining a reliable and valid measure of criterion performance in the first place. It is far easier to determine if an individual is a member of a certain group than to determine his degree of success in that group. Rulon et al. (1967) recently have summarized some of the other difficulties inherent in applying multiple regression techniques in selection and classification situations.

In the case of career guidance, for example, multiple regression techniques have not proven to be particularly useful for helping a student decide among alternative careers. The difficulty is partly one of defining success adequately and partly one of obtaining reliable and relevant assessments of the aspects of success that one has identified. But even where reliable, valid measures are available, there is the problem of predictors. To develop a regression equation suitable for some population (e.g. grade 12 males in the United States in 1968), it is necessary for both predictors and criteria to be available for a representative sample from the population. If the regression equations are to predict over the time interval from the guidance situation (e.g. grade 13) to the point in the career where degree of success can be established (perhaps 10 years later) expensive longitudinal studies are required. Even if they are conducted there is the question of whether the prediction equations developed are appropriate for the "new crop" of 12th graders 10 years later. Schools and the labor market are not very stable. Even if one decides the equations are still valid, how are they to be used? Are students to be encouraged to enter the occupation in which

they are most likely to succeed? If so, they will tend to enter the less demanding occupations. Also, critical variables for a given occupation often do not show up in a regression equation because the group is relatively homogeneous with respect to that trait as a result of institutional and self-selection.

Another difficulty with multiple regression has been brought to light by a number of investigations that have shown that multiple regression coefficients tend not to "hold up" in cross-validation studies (e.g. Burket, 1964; Herzberg, 1969; Marks, 1966). That is, predictor weights derived by multiple regression in one sample produce predictions for new samples that do not correlate nearly as well with the criteria as they did in the original sample. In fact, rather simple alternatives to regression weights, such as using the elements of r_c directly (or even just unit weights!) frequently outperform the b weights on cross validation. Of course this problem diminishes as the ratio of sample size to number of predictors gets larger (e.g. at least 10 or 20 to 1). Herzberg (1969) and Burket (1964) provide a basis for a general multivariate research strategy that begins with a principal components analysis prior to a concern for prediction to an interval scale (as in multiple regression) or a nominal scale (as in classification).

Canonical Correlation

If there are two sets of measures on the same subjects and one is interested in deriving dimensions from one set that are maximally correlated with derived dimensions from another set, then canonical correlation is an appropriate multivariate procedure. The method is similar to extracting the principal components of each of two sets of variables and then rotating these two sets of components so that one component from the first set is maximally correlated with one from the second set. Then the second largest correlation is found, and so on, until each component from the smaller of the two sets of variables has a corresponding component in the other set.

Algebraically, canonical correlations are derived from the partitioned matrix—

$$R = \begin{bmatrix} R_{11} & | & R_{12} \\ \hline R_{21} & | & R_{22} \end{bmatrix}$$

where submatrix R_{11} contains the correlations among the variables of one of the two sets; R_{22}, the correlations among the traits of the second set; and R_{12}, the correlations between the two sets, with $R'_{12} = R_{21}$. The two sets may contain different numbers of variables. Then the matrix equation $\{(R_{22}^{-1}R_{21}R_{11}^{-1}R_{12} - \lambda_1 I)v_{21} = 0\}$ is solved for λ_1 and v_{21}, which are the characteristic roots and vectors of the matrix product $[R_{22}^{-1}R_{21}R_{11}^{-1}R_{12}]$. The vector v_{21} contains the weights for the second set. A corresponding set of weights for the first set is obtained from $R_{11}^{-1}R_{12}v_{21} = v_{11}$. Applying v_{11} to standard scores of the variables of the first set and v_{21} to the second set, a pair of canonical variates is formed that has a correlation coefficient equal to $\sqrt{\lambda_1}$. This is the maximum correlation possible between the two linear functions, one from each of the two sets of variables.

After this first pair of canonical variates is extracted, a second pair is determined that is orthogonal to the first. Computationally, v_{22} is the vector associated with λ_2, and v_{12} is found in the same manner as v_{11}. The remaining possible canonical relationships are similarly determined. If the data are arranged so that the order of R_{22} is always less than or equal to the order of R_{11}, then the order of R_{22} represents the maximum number of canonical relationships.

Canonical correlation could be used to relate the five predictor measures of the aspiring chemists of the example to three later measures of performance criteria. The results for a numerical example are summarized in table 16.13. Matrix R_{12} reports the product moment correlations between the 15 possible pairs of the five predictors (as rows) and three criteria (as columns). R_{22} is the matrix of correlations among the three criteria. Matrix R_{11} was previously reported as table 16.4.

The two sets of canonical weights of table 16.13 have v_{1j} as columns of the first set and v_{2j} as columns of the second set, where j goes from one to three, corresponding to the three possible canonical correlations in this example. These

TABLE 16.13

Canonical Correlation Results

CORRELATION MATRICES

$$R_{12} = \begin{bmatrix} .36 & .37 & -.11 \\ -.09 & .08 & -.14 \\ .28 & .52 & .55 \\ .15 & .38 & .69 \\ .15 & -.07 & -.33 \end{bmatrix} \quad R_{22} = \begin{bmatrix} 1.00 & .22 & .01 \\ .22 & 1.00 & .51 \\ .01 & .51 & 1.00 \end{bmatrix}$$

CANONICAL WEIGHTS

	First Set				Second Set		
	1	2	3		1	2	3
1	.15	−1.23	−.25	1	.30	−.56	−.82
2	.12	.71	1.11	2	.30	−.67	.95
3	.69	−.02	.40	3	.74	.79	−.45
4	.72	.34	−.23				
5	.04	−.14	−.20				

Canonical Correlations: (1) .92 (2) .70 (3) .24

CANONICAL STRUCTURE

	First Set				Second Set		
	1	2	3		1	2	3
1	.15	−.76	.45	1	.38	−.70	−.61
2	−.11	−.16	.89	2	.75	−.40	.54
3	.70	−.09	.07	3	.90	.44	.03
4	.73	.30	−.30				
5	−.24	−.43	−.17				

vectors are scaled so that the canonical variates have unit variance.

If the first columns of weights for the first set are applied to the standardized predictors and the first columns for the second set are applied to the standardized criterion, then the resulting pair of canonical variates will correlate .92. Similarly, using the second and third columns of weights, two other pairs of canonical variates can be formed, correlating .70 and .24 respectively. As can be seen in R_{12}, the highest bivariate correlation between these two sets is for predictor number 4 and criterion number 3 (.69).

Interpretation of these canonical relationships is done by examining the structure at the bottom of table 16.13. Once again, structure represents the correlations between the original variables and the derived linear functions of them. For example, the first canonical relationship is between a factor that is primarily a function of predictors 3 and 4 and a factor primarily defined by criteria 2 and 3.

Computing the structure in all applications of multivariate linear reduction has greatly reduced the difficulty of interpreting multivariate results. The structure A can be computed directly from the standardized coefficients V and the correlations among the original measures (R), since $A = RV$.

Some Project Talent research provided an example of an application of canonical correlation (Cooley, 1967). Measures of vocational interests and abilities were available for a sample of boys at both grade 9 and grade 12. The canonical relationships among these four sets of variables (grade 9 interests and abilities and grade 12 interests and abilities) contributed to a description of how responses to a vocational interest inventory change during high school and how those changes are related to grade 9 abilities. It was found that in some ways interest profiles change during high school to be more consistent with earlier abilities, while in other ways the abilities profile changes as a function of interests.

A good single source for additional research examples of multivariate applications is Cattell (1966). See also the Project Talent monographs listed in the references and Cooley and Lohnes (1962). Small numerical examples were used in this chapter in order to simplify presentation of the major multivariate techniques in use today.

APPLICATION CONSIDERATIONS

In considering possible techniques for analyzing profiles, it makes a difference whether one is attempting to optimize institutional benefits (personnel psychology) or those of the individual (personal psychology). A very extensive personnel psychology has been developed while there is a very limited personal psychology. Elaborate models have been developed for the military establishment and industry for selection and assignment. Those techniques tend to have little direct application to central educational problems such as diagnosing student instructional difficulties or facilitating career guidance. Even where applications have been related to education the primary concern has been from the point of view of the educational institution rather than the individual student.

There is some hope for the future. It is not surprising that concerns for institutional benefits dominated previous research since industry and the Department of Defense supported most of the activity in this area. Now that support is available from other agencies with a greater concern for the welfare of the individual, the stage is set for more progress in that area.

REFERENCES

Allport, G. W., & Odbert, H. S. Trait-names: A psycholexical study. *Psychological Monographs*, 1936, **47**(1, Whole No. 211).

Ayres, F., Jr. *Theory and problems of matrices.* New York: Schaum, 1962.

Burket, G. R. A study of reduced rank models for multiple prediction. *Psychometric Monographs*, 1964, No. 12.

Buros, O. K. *The 6th mental measurements yearbook.* Highland Park, N.J.: Gryphon Press, 1965.

Cattell, R. B. *Personality: A systematic theoretical and factual study.* New York: McGraw-Hill, 1950.

Cattell, R. B. (Ed.) *Handbook of multivariate experimental psychology.* Chicago: Rand McNally, 1966.

Cooley, W. W. Current research on the career development of scientists. *Journal of Counseling Psychology*, 1964, **11**, 88–93.

Cooley, W. W. Predicting career plan changes. *Project Talent One-Year Follow-Up Studies* Pittsburgh: University of Pittsburgh, 1966.

Cooley, W. W. Interactions among interests, abilities, and career plans. *Journal of Applied Psychology* 1967, **51**, Monogr. Suppl. No. 640.

Cooley, W. W., & Lohnes, P. R. *Multivariate procedures for the behavioral sciences.* New York: Wiley, 1962.

Cooley, W. W., & Lohnes, P. R. *Predicting development of young adults.* Pittsburgh: University of Pittsburgh, Project Talent, 1968.

Cooley, W. W., & Lohnes, P. R. *Multivariate data analysis.* New York: Wiley, 1970.

Cronbach, L. J. Statistical methods for multi-score tests. *Journal of Clinical Psychology*, 1950, **6**, 21–26.

Cronbach, L. J., & Gleser, G. C. Assessing similarity between profiles. *Psychological Bulletin*, 1953, **50**, 456–473.

Fruchter, B. *Introduction to factor analysis*. Princeton, N.J.: Van Nostrand, 1954.

Geisser, S. Posterior odds for multivariate normal classifications. *The Journal of the Royal Statistical Society Series B* (*Methodological*), 1964, **26**(1), 69–76.

Harman, H. H. *Modern factor analysis*. Chicago: University of Chicago Press, 1967.

Harris, C. W. Some recent developments in factor analysis. *Educational and Psychological Measurement*, 1964, **24**, 193–206.

Harris, C. W. On factors and factor scores. *Psychometrika*, 1967, **32**(4).

Herzberg, P. A. The parameters of cross-validation. *Psychometrika* (Monogr. Suppl. 16), 1969, **34**.

Hohn, F. E. *Elementary matrix algebra*. New York: Macmillan, 1964.

Horst, P. A. *Matrix algebra for social scientists*. New York: Holt, Rinehart & Winston, 1963.

Horst, P. A. *Factor analysis of data matrices*. New York: Holt, Rinehart & Winston, 1965.

Jones, K. J. Problems of grouping individuals and the method of modality. *Behavioral Science*, 1968, **13**, 496–511.

Lee, E. C. Career development of science teachers. Unpublished doctoral dissertation, Harvard Graduate School of Education, 1961.

Lohnes, P. R. *Measuring adolescent personality*. Pittsburgh: University of Pittsburgh, Project Talent, 1966.

McNemar, Q. Lost: Our intelligence? Why? *American Psychologist*, 1964, **19**, 871–882.

Mahalanobis, P. C. On the generalized distance in statistics. *Proceedings from National Institute of Science, India*, 1936, **12**, 49–58.

Marks, M. R. Two kinds of regression weights which are better than betas in crossed samples. Paper presented at the American Psychological Association convention, 1966.

Morrison, D. F. *Multivariate statistical methods*. New York: McGraw-Hill, 1967.

Nunnally, J. The analysis of profile data. *Psychological Bulletin*, 1962, **59**, 311–319.

Overall, J. E. Note on multivariate methods for profile analysis. *Psychological Bulletin*, 1964, **61**, 195–198.

Roe, A., & Siegelman, M. *The origin of interests*. Washington: American Personnel and Guidance Association, 1964.

Rulon, P. J., Tiedeman, D. V., Tatsuoka, M. M., & Langmuir, C. R. *Multivariate statistics for personnel classification*. New York: Wiley, 1967.

Tiedeman, D. V. A geometric model for the profile problem. In A. Anastasi (Ed.), *Testing problems in perspective*. Washington: American Council on Education, 1966. Pp. 331–354.

Tiedeman, D. V., Bryan, J. G., & Rulon, P. J. *The utility of the airman classification battery for assignment of airmen to eight air force specialities*. Cambridge, Mass.: Educational Research Corporation, 1951.

Application of Tests to Educational Problems

PART FOUR

17. Measurement in Learning and Instruction

Robert Glaser and Anthony J. Nitko
University of Pittsburgh

With respect to the educational process, *learning* is defined as the acquisition of behavior brought about by the school environment, the instructional means designed by the educator, and the educational system. Ideally, the learner interacts with the instructional environment, changes it, and is changed in turn by the consequences of his actions. The particular properties of the behavior acquired by the learner depend upon the details of the educational environment that is designed and provided. What is taught and how it is taught depend upon the objectives and values of the school system; what and how, however, are not separable entities. The instructional environment can influence the student's behavior more or less directly: it can enable the student to acquire certain kinds of performance, and it can teach him to teach himself. Fostering, nurturing, guiding, influencing, and controlling human behavior is the practical objective of the educational enterprise. Educational environments, designed and provided by society, influence and control student behavior; they cannot do otherwise since the existence of any environment, whether it be a culture, a home, or a school, shapes behavior in intended and unintended ways. Many facets of human behavior are involved: the learning of subject-matter content and of skills and processes involved in using it, e.g. retention, transfer, problem solving, critical thinking, creating, ways of processing information, and attitudes and motivation toward these activities. The design of an educational environment is a complex and subtle enterprise, and different kinds of environments encourage and optimize certain kinds of behavior and minimize and discourage others.

Testing and measurement represent one of the critical components of the educational environment—*they provide the essential information for the development, operation, and evaluation of this enterprise.* To be useful, this information must be relevant to the specific instructional system with which one is concerned. That is, information requirements are derived from and specified by an analysis of a particular educational environment and are unique to it. Different educational environments will have different informational requirements. This is not to say, however, that a particular instructional system needs information only about itself. The values and goals of some systems will require information about other systems. It should be clear then that, since testing and measurement provide unique and relevant information, the design of testing and measurement procedures must be preceded by the specification of the particular instructional system (and the information requirements) for which these procedures are intended. What needs to be measured is then known, insofar as possible, and a testing program can be designed to satisfy these requirements. In short, measurement procedures need to be designed with the information requirements of a specific instructional system in mind.

The fundamental task of testing and measurement (in education) is to provide information for making basic, essential decisions with respect to education's instructional design and operation. Four activities of instructional design influence measurement requirements: *analy-*

sis of the subject-matter domain under consideration, diagnosis of the characteristics of the learner, design of the instructional environment, and *evaluation of learning outcomes.*

The fundamental task of testing and measurement in education is to provide information for making decisions with respect to the above stages of instructional design and operation. In the analysis of the subject-matter domain, subject-matter experts are assisted in analyzing their domains in terms of the performance competencies which compose them. Representative instances are analyzed according to the properties of the content involved and the ways in which a student must respond to and process this content. The structural characteristics of the domain are laid out according to its conceptual hierarchies and operating rules in terms of increasing complexity of student performance. Major concerns center around the analysis and definition of instructionally relevant performance, including the specification of educational objectives, translating these objectives into some kind of assessable performance, and performing studies and gathering data about the facilitating or inhibiting effects of particular curriculum sequences. The kind of analysis that goes on at this time is a significant determinant of the subsequent stages of instructional design. Learning is analyzed in terms of its subject-matter content and also in terms of the behavioral repertoires or behavioral processes that are being learned. These properties of content and process define the nature of measuring instruments and the nature of instruction.

The second activity—diagnosis of the characteristics of the learner—involves measurement of the behavior with which a student enters into instruction, including (*a*) the extent to which the student has already acquired what is to be learned, (*b*) the extent to which he has the necessary prerequisites, and (*c*) the characteristics of the way in which he learns that interact with the available instructional alternatives. These measurements provide information about the *existing preinstructional behavior* of the learner as distinguished from the performance competence to be achieved.

When attempting to provide this kind of information, one is concerned with the problems that arise in the measurement of individual differences. However, for instructional purposes, the concern reduces to those differences that are especially relevant to the kind of instructional system that has been devised. No doubt, different individual capabilities require different modes of instruction. The general problem is the interaction between individual differences and the instructional environment (see Cronbach's discussion, pp. 499–503; see also pp. 701–729). It is increasingly apparent that for effective instruction, measurements must be made of differences in learning characteristics. The kinds of measurements that need to be taken will differ depending upon the options available in the instructional system. Characteristics that will predict the success of students in a relatively fixed environment will be different from those predicting success of students in a system where there are multiple paths to the same end.

Once the nature of the task to be learned and the entering characteristics of the learner are described, the third activity—designing the instructional environment—can take place. The design of the instructional environment involves the specification of the conditions under which learning can occur. These conditions allow the learner to progress from an entering-behavior state to the terminal state in which he has acquired the educational goals described as subject-matter competence and the desired outcomes of instruction. This requires the design and construction of the teaching procedures, materials, and tests that are to be employed in the educational process. Also included are provisions for conditions that will result in the motivation to use, maintain, and extend the competence that is taught. The information required for the design and construction of the learning environment has two purposes. One is information for making decisions about how instruction is to proceed; the other is information required for modifying the design of instructional procedures, materials, and equipment. With regard to the first, as instruction proceeds, information for instructional decisions must be provided to the teacher, the student, and possibly to a machine, each of which assists in guiding the student through the course of instruction. In the light of present educational innovation, it is highly likely that the job of the teacher will be influenced by procedures which allow assessment decisions to be made increasingly by the student himself and also by computer testing and related instructional devices. (The design of tests for use by the student in self-assessment has been seriously neglected in the past by educational test constructors.) With respect to the second kind of information, testing and measurement activities also will be required to support the adoption of innovative techniques and to support the maintenance of worthwhile existing techniques. Just as, at the present time, commercially available tests must present evidence about their development and documentation of their effectiveness, so will instructional techniques—whether they be procedures or devices—need to be accompanied by information describing their construction and improvement and documenting their effectiveness.

Finally, the fourth activity—evaluating learning outcomes—provides information including (*a*) the extent to which the acquired behavior of the learner approaches performance criteria and (*b*) the extent to which the values espoused by the designers of the system and associated with this performance have been attained. Thus, the primary requirement is for measurement of what has been learned. The *what is learned* becomes fundamental since the instructional process requires information about the details of the performance of the learner in order to know how instruction should proceed. *What* includes both content and process and is defined, insofar as possible, with reference to prespecified performance criteria. When this performance has been attained by an individual learner to the degree required by the designers of the instructional system, then the learner is said to have attained *mastery* of the instructional goal. Interpretations of measurements that provide such information may be termed *absolute interpretations* (see pp. 446–447); tests constructed with this kind of mea-

surement in mind are called criterion-referenced tests (a more formal definition of criterion-referenced tests is developed and their construction requirements are discussed on pp. 652–661). Performance referenced only by norms does not define *what* is learned; therefore, appropriate information is not provided about what individuals can do and how they behave. The information necessary for instructional decision making is essentially descriptive of present performance (that is, at the time of testing) and is not predictive in the sense of predictive validity. The major predictive concern in the measurement of learning outcomes is the relationship between proximate and ultimate educational objectives, and this is more of a learning transfer problem than a correlational one.[1]

To recapitulate, learning in the educational sense can be defined as a process of transition of the learner from an initial entering state to a specified arbitrary terminal state. Instruction and teaching are the practices in schools by which conditions are provided to enable this transition to occur. Measurement in instruction and learning is concerned with providing data, assessments, and information about the nature of learner performance and about the nature of instructional conditions. The assessment of student performance is used to guide the implementation of appropriate instructional conditions, and the measurement of the conditions is used to indicate whether the conditions are, indeed, realized. In addition to guiding the instructional process, measurement is used to evaluate its total effectiveness. All these measurements are used for making decisions in the course of developing and improving an instructional system, in the course of its operation, and, after it has occurred, for evaluating its overall outcomes.

The Approach of This Chapter

As the above introductory comments suggest, measurement in learning and instruction should be discussed in light of certain instructional design requirements and specific models

[1] The correlation coefficient has been the chief "measure" of the predictive validity of a test in the past.

or systems of instruction. This chapter approaches its task in this way: it initially considers three general classes of instructional models found in current educational practice. One particular model for adapting instruction to individual differences is described, and its testing and measurement implications are discussed. The description of the instructional model is followed by considerations relevant to (a) analysis of performance domains, (b) individual assignments to instructional alternatives, and (c) subsequent measurement of what is learned by means of criterion-referenced tests. These topics are discussed in terms of the measurements required to make instructional decisions about individual learners. The last section of this chapter briefly discusses the important topic of evaluating and improving an instructional system and its components. At that point group data play a more central role.

The reader should note that at times in the first part of this chapter, measurements and tests that provide information relevant to absolute interpretations are called for (see pp. 446–47). The design, construction, and use of such tests require a more detailed discussion than can be provided in the course of a more general treatment of the overall testing requirements needed in the particular instructional model examined. As a consequence, a separate section (pp. 655–61) dealing with criterion-referenced tests is provided after the measurement implications of the particular instructional model are discussed. It is hoped that these initial considerations of the measurements that are required in the context of an instructional system will serve as an "advance organizer" on the subject of criterion-referenced testing. (The reader who feels that his needs are best served by first examining the more detailed treatment of this type of test may read the later section first without loss of continuity.)

In order to place the topics of this chapter into perspective, a brief review is needed of the way in which the relationships among the disciplines of psychological measurement, experimental psychology, and the field of educa-

tional practice have influenced the state of measurement in learning and instruction.

Some History

A significant complication in the field of measurement in learning and instruction results from the historical routes of two major fields of psychology—the measurement of individual differences and the experimental psychology of learning. It is well documented that early scientific psychology began with these two as apparently separate disciplines. This history can be traced from the Titchener-Baldwin controversy in the 1890s, through Cronbach's (1957) address on "The Two Disciplines of Scientific Psychology," through the 1967 book edited by Gagné on *Learning and Individual Differences*. Throughout the years, the importance of coordination between the two fields has been recognized but with sustained work by only a few individuals. The requirements inherent in developing a scientific base for instruction make this coordination mandatory, with changes in traditional practices being required in each field. E. L. Thorndike (1914) raised the problem in his *Educational Psychology*, pointing to experiments that showed the effect of equal learning opportunity, i.e. equal practice, on producing increases or decreases in individual differences. Woodrow (1938) pointed out that the divergence or convergence of individual differences with practice depended upon the shape of the learning curve and the position of individuals on it as a result of their prior task-relevant experience. In addition, Woodrow indicated that the influence of individual differences in the course of practice might also be a function of the way in which the task changes during practice. Recent work on this problem has been carried out in a series of studies, by Fleishman (1967), that show that final scores in a learning task are dependent upon a different pattern of abilities than initial scores.

A classic article by Woodrow (1946) pointed out the lack of relationship between general ability measures, such as intelligence, and learning variables. Woodrow's findings, from both the laboratory and the classroom, contradicted the assumption that the ability to learn, in the sense of ability to improve with practice, is related to measured intelligence. Correlations between intelligence and gain generally were not statistically significant. Woodrow interpreted his results by assuming that a score at any stage of practice consists of a general factor, G, and specific factors, these latter changing with practice. As a result, there can be a high and undiminishing correlation between the general factor and scores at all stages of practice; it is also possible for the correlation between G and gain to be negligible when gain is the result of a high degree of specificity resulting from task characteristics and individual differences in performing these tasks. The line of work generated by Woodrow has been reflected in the active interest in this problem by DuBois (1965) and by Gulliksen and his students, e.g. Duncanson (1964) and Stake (1961).

On the side of learning theory, Hull (1945), in developing his theory of learning, initially gave serious attention to individual differences in learning. He pointed out that the study of behavior has two tasks: the first is deriving primary laws as displayed by the modal or average organism under given conditions; the second is the problem of innate behavioral differences under identical environmental conditions. Most neglected, said Hull, is the relationship between the two approaches. Although Hull acknowledged environmental and historical sources of individual differences, his main concern was with individual differences that are innate and constitutional. His approach, however, was applicable to both sources. As is known, he adopted the point of view of the natural sciences, of physics in particular, where a scientific law is expressed in terms of an equation of a particular form and the empirical constants in the equation are determined by observed conditions that vary with individual events but do not change the general form of the law. Hull's notion was that individual differences find expression in these empirical constants. Many years later, a few psychologists followed up Hull's notions with respect to individual differences as influencing learning equation parameters (Noble, Noble, & Alcock, 1958; Reynolds & Adams, 1954; Spence, 1956, 1960; Zeaman & Kaufman, 1955). This small amount of work represents a major part of the attention paid by learning theorists to individual differences. In contrast, however, at least two approaches to the study of behavior attack the problem of individual differences in learning by attempting to develop techniques that produce lawful individual functions. This is the procedure adopted by Skinner (1938; Ferster & Skinner, 1957) and described in detail by Sidman (1960) in his book on the tactics of scientific research. In a different way, it is also the approach being employed by recent information-processing and computer simulation approaches to the analysis of complex cognitive tasks (Reitman, 1965; Simon & Newell, 1964).

The history of work on learning and individual differences shows clearly the dearth of basic information required for attacking certain critical problems in the design of instruction. The basic problems are those that revolve around issues inherent in adapting educational alternatives (learning conditions) to individual differences at the beginning of a course of instruction and those that appear during learning. Because of the relative insularities of the psychometric field and learning theory, no base of research information and theory is readily available. A major inadequacy of the factor-analytic psychometric approach is the lack of a theoretical framework for the selection of reference tests and learning measures. Global notions of general intelligence are obviously no longer useful scientific concepts for describing learner characteristics because such global measures tend to neglect and obscure specific individual differences. Rather, what is more important for instruction is to determine initial patterns of ability and competence that interact with learning. In the experimental and theoretical study of learning, resistance to discovering what may be hidden in error variance needs to be overcome. Unique factor variance, if it exists, needs to be examined and accounted for, not only in terms of error, but also in terms of what implications it may have for learning and instruction. As has been indicated (pp. 499–503), learner-treatment interactions must be sought in experiments that study the learning effects of various instructional treatments. Examination of ordinal and disordinal interactions provides the data upon which learning experiences that are adaptive to individual differences can be designed. Increased attention must be paid to initial baseline characteristics of the learner prior to experimental treatment, and statements of principles of learning need to incorporate parameters reflecting individual differences.

Another major contributor to the lack of integration between individual differences and educational alternatives has been the state of educational practice itself. While educators have recognized the need for adapting to individual differences and various ungraded and track systems have been devised, the degree of adaptation has never been enough to force answers to the underlying problem of the interactions between individual differences and educational alternatives. However, new approaches to individualizing education are being attempted. The requirements for instructional design that these attempts raise will influence both educational practice and the underlying research and knowledge requirements.

INSTRUCTIONAL MODELS

As indicated, the purpose of measurement for instruction can best be illustrated in terms of a particular model for an educational system since different patterns of instruction have different measurement requirements. In general, the model should recognize that the educational process is concerned with behavioral change and that instruction provides the conditions to foster the processes by which change takes place. Teaching always begins with a particular behavioral state, assesses the characteristics of this state, and implements instructional procedures accordingly; assessment of the changing state of the learner provides information for further use and allocation of instructional methods and resources. Guidance of the instructional process can take place by

the student, the teacher, and/or an automaton. The model should further recognize that an educational system should permit the exercise of individual talents and offer the opportunity for students to develop and excel at every level of ability. It is therefore necessary for an educational system to arrange for the individualized treatment of students. Educators have been aware of this necessity, and their concern with adapting to the needs of the student is a familiar theme which provides the justification for many current educational innovations (Heathers, 1969).

Several major patterns of adapting to individual differences can be identified in education if one examines past and present educational practices and examines future possibilities (Cronbach, 1967). These patterns can be described in terms of the extent to which educational goals and instructional methods have been varied for the handling of individual differences as they appear in the school. One pattern occurs where both educational goals and instructional methods are relatively fixed and inflexible. Individual differences are taken into account chiefly by dropping students along the way. The underlying rationale involved is that every child should "go as far as his abilities warrant." However, a weeding-out process is assumed which is reached earlier or later by different individuals. With this pattern, it is also possible to vary "time to learn" required for different students. When this is done, an individual is permitted to stay in school until he learns certain essential educational outcomes to a specified criterion of achievement. To some extent, this latter practice is carried out in the old policy of keeping a child in the first grade until he can read his primer and in the more recent nongraded primary unit that some children complete in three years and some in four.

A second pattern of adaptation to individual differences is one in which the prospective future role of a student is determined, and, depending upon this role, he is provided with an appropriate curriculum. When this system is in operation, students are channeled into different courses such as academic courses, vocational courses, or business courses; vocationally oriented students get one kind of mathematics and academically oriented students get a different kind of mathematics. Adapting to individual differences by this pattern assumes that an educational system has provision for optional educational objectives, but within each option the instructional program is relatively fixed.

A third pattern of adaptation to individual differences varies instructional treatments: different students are taught by different instructional procedures, and the sequence of educational goals is not necessarily common to all students. This pattern can be implemented in different ways. At one extreme, a school can provide a main fixed instructional sequence, and students are branched from this track for remedial work; when the remedial work is successfully completed, the student is put back into the general track. At the other extreme, there is seemingly the more ideal situation. A school carries out an instructional program that begins by providing detailed diagnosis of the student's learning habits and attitudes, achievements, skills, cognitive style, etc. On the basis of this analysis of the student's characteristics, he is guided through a course of instruction specifically tailored to him. Conceivably, in this procedure, students learn in different ways, e.g. some by their own discovery and some by more structured methods.

In light of the current experimentation in schools on procedures for adapting to individual differences, it seems likely that in the near future, patterns falling between these two latter extremes will be developed and adopted by many schools. The quality of the various systems developed will depend upon the answers to many questions of research and practical implementation. Particularly, the difficult question of the interaction between the characteristics of a student at a particular point in his learning and appropriate methods of instruction is raised for intensive study. Proof will have to be forthcoming that the instructional methods devised for adapting to individual student differences result in significantly greater

attainment of educational goals than less intricate classroom practices or classroom practices where the average best method is employed.

The Instructional Model Considered in This Chapter

At the present time, it seems possible to develop educational methods that are more sensitive to individual differences than procedures have been in the past. Educational systems for accomplishing this will no doubt take many forms and have many nuances as they are developed. The general components of one model are presented here as a basis for examining the measurement and evaluation tasks that it demands. In terms of the three educational patterns of individual difference adaptation described above, it would seem that this model falls somewhere between the extremes of the third, i.e. between remedial branching and unique tailoring. It should be pointed out that in an educational pattern adaptive to individual differences, measurement and evaluation tasks come about primarily because certain events occur that require data and information for both operation and for research-and-development decision making. These events can be categorized into the following six components (Glaser, 1970):

1. *Outcomes of learning are specified in terms of the behavioral manifestations of competence and the conditions under which it is to be exercised.* This is the platitudinous assertion of the fundamental necessity for describing the foreseeable outcomes of instruction in terms of certain measurable products and assessable student performance, while at the same time keeping in mind that what is easily measured is not necessarily synonymous with the goals of instruction. In addition, analysis and definition must be made of the performance domain intended to be taught and learned. The "structure" of the domain is specified in terms of its subgoal competencies and possible paths along which students can progress to attain learning objectives.

2. *Detailed diagnosis is made of the initial*

state of a learner entering a particular instructional situation. A description of student performance characteristics relevant to the instruction at hand is necessary to pursue further education. Without the assessment of initial learner characteristics, carrying out an educational procedure is a presumption. It is like prescribing medication for an illness without first examining the symptoms. In the early stages of a particular educational period, instructional procedures will adapt to the findings of the initial assessment, generally reflecting the accumulated performance capabilities resulting from the long-term behavior history of the learner. The history that is specifically measured is relevant to the next immediate educational step that is to be taken.

3. *Educational alternatives are provided that are adaptive to the classifications resulting from the initial student educational profiles.* These alternative instructional procedures are assigned selectively to the student or made available to him for his selection. They are available through the teacher and/or through materials or automated devices with which the student works.

4. *As the student learns, his performance is monitored and repeatedly assessed at longer or shorter intervals appropriate to what is being taught.* In early skill learning, assessment is almost continuous. Later on, as competence grows, problems grow larger; as the student becomes increasingly self-sustaining, assessment occurs less frequently. This monitoring serves several purposes: it provides a basis for knowledge of results and appropriate reinforcement contingencies to the learner and a basis for adaptation to learner demands. This learning history accumulated in the course of instruction is called short-term history and, in addition to information from the long-term history, provides information for assignment of the next instructional unit. The short-term history also provides information about the effectiveness of the instructional material itself.

5. *Instruction and learning proceed in a cybernetic fashion, tracking the performance and selections of the student.* Assessment and performance are interlinked, one determining the nature and requirement for the other. Instruc-

tion proceeds as a function of the relationship among measures of student performance, available instructional alternatives, and learning criteria that are chosen to be optimized. The question of which criteria are to be optimized becomes critical. Is it retention, transfer, the magnitude of difference between pre- and post-test scores, motivation to continue learning including the ability to do so with minimal instructional guidance, or is it all of these? If tracking of the instructional process permits instruction to become precise enough, then a good job can be done to optimize some gains and minimize others unless the presence of the latter gains is desired, expressed, and assessed. The outcomes of learning measured at any point in instruction are referenced to and evaluated in terms of competence criteria and the values to be optimized; provision is always made for the ability of humans to surpass expectations.

6. *The system collects information in order to improve itself, and inherent in the system's design is its capability for doing this.* A major defect in the implementation of educational innovations has been the lack of the cumulative attainment of knowledge, on the basis of which the next innovation is better than the one that preceded it.

Given that the changing trends in education will lead to an instructional model somewhat like that just described, the remaining sections of this chapter consider the implications for the nature of measurement and evaluation procedures.

ANALYSIS AND DEFINITION OF PERFORMANCE DOMAINS

In an educational system, the specification and measurement of the outcomes of learning in terms of observable human performance determine how the system operates. Vague statements of the desired educational outcomes leave little concrete information about what the teacher and the student are to look for and what the designers of the system are to strive to attain. Furthermore, performance standards specified in advance need not impose conformities nor stifle freedom of inquiry. Interaction between the specification of outcomes and instructional procedures provides the basis for redefining objectives. The need for constant revision of objectives is as inherent in a well-designed educational system as is the initial need for defining them. There is a sustained process of clarifying goals, working toward them, evaluating progress, reexamining the objectives, modifying instructional procedures, and clarifying the objectives in light of evaluated experience. This process should indicate the inadequacies and omissions in a curriculum. The fear of many educators that detailed specification of objectives limits them to "trivial" behaviors only—those that can be forced into measurable and observable terms—is an incorrect notion. Rather, one should think of them as amendable approximations of ideals. For example, if complex reasoning and open-endedness are desirable aspects of human behavior, then they need to be recognizable and assessable goals. Failure to state such goals or specification of them in a vague and general way detracts from their being seriously considered as attainable and may force us to settle for only what can be easily expressed and measured.

The analysis and classification of behavior to be learned is an increasingly prominent feature in the psychology of learning, being fostered both by experimental and theoretical requirements and by attempts at practical applications (Bruner, 1964; Gagné, 1965a, b; Glaser, 1962; Melton, 1964; Miller, 1965). This trend has come about because all-inclusive theories and schools are no longer major psychological influences and have been replaced by more miniature systems resulting from the analysis of certain behavioral processes and classes of behavior. The working assumption is that the various classes of behaviors that human beings display have different characteristics that need to be specifically analyzed. The implication of this for the analysis of instructionally relevant performance domains is that school learning must be analyzed both for its subject-matter content and its behavioral repertoire.

The increasing movement of individuals be-

tween laboratory study and educational problems contributes to the need for behavioral analysis. In the laboratory, a task performed by a subject has special properties built into it for particular scientific interests; the task is so designed that its properties are clear enough for experimental investigation. In contrast, the behavior presented by school learning is not designed for the laboratory and needs to be analyzed so that it can be subjected to study. The necessity for this kind of "task analysis" adds a new requirement to the study of learning and instruction, e.g. recent work in psychology on taxonomies, behavioral categories, and the analysis of behavioral processes (Gagné, 1965b; Melton, 1964; Reitman, 1965; Simon & Paige, 1966). In education, this is seen in the recent concerns about "behavioral objectives" and the definition of educational tasks. Techniques for the analysis of performance and for the derivation of assessment procedures based on these analyses are very much in the early stage of development, and at the present time this is a growing area of activity among learning and educational psychologists (Gagné, 1970; Gibson, 1965; Glaser, 1962; Hively, 1966a; Kersh, 1965; Schutz, Baker, & Gerlach, 1964). Increasingly, there will be more formal analyses of the way in which the content and psychological processes inherent in school learning influence and determine the nature of measurement and instruction.

Subject-Matter Structure and Component Task Analysis

Prominent in the analysis of performance domains is the concern with the structure of the subject matter (e.g. Bruner, 1964; Gagné, 1962; Taba, 1966). As educational tasks or goals are analyzed, they imply a series of subgoals through which instruction must proceed. The arrangement of these subgoals is a function of the subject matter being taught, the approach of the course designer to the subject matter, and also the way in which the student elects, or his performance advises, that instruction should proceed. Different students may follow different paths through the subject matter so that for any particular individual, some subgoals may be omitted, added to, re-combined, or rearranged. Subgoals provide nodes at which information about performance can be obtained and instructional decisions can be made. There are few techniques available for the analysis of learning tasks and their struc-tures. One procedure that seems most promis-ing is that developed out of Gagné's work on learning hierarchies (Gagné, 1962, 1968; Gagné, Mayor, Garstens, & Paradise, 1962; Gagné & Paradise, 1961). The term *learning hierarchy* refers to a set of component tasks or perfor-mances leading to a particular instructional objective. These component tasks have an ordered relationship to one another. Beginning with a statement of some "terminal" objective of instruction, the attempt is made to analyze this terminal performance into component tasks in a structure such that lower level tasks gener-ate positive transfer to higher level ones. The set of ordered performances forms a hierarchy that can assist in the design of instruction and its assessment.

Figure 17.1 reproduces one of these hier-archies pertaining to the addition of integers (Gagné et al., 1962). In the framework of in-struction in "modern math," children learn two distinguishable terminal capabilities: one of these, shown on the right, is simply finding sums of positive and negative numbers; a second, shown on the left, constitutes a dem-onstration of the logical validity of adding any pair of integers, using the properties of the number system to effect this demonstration.

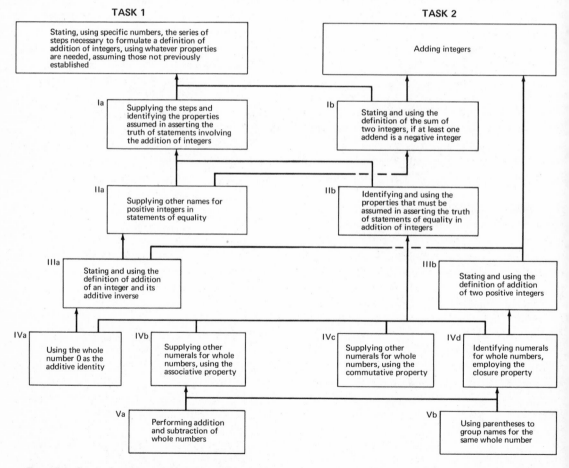

Fɪɢ. 17.1. Curriculum hierarchy on the addition of integers. (Gagné et al., "Factors in Acquiring Knowledge of a Mathematical Task," *Psychological Monographs*, Vol. 76, Part 1, 1962, Fig. 1, p. 4 (Whole No. 526). Copyright 1962 by the American Psychological Association, and reproduced by permission.)

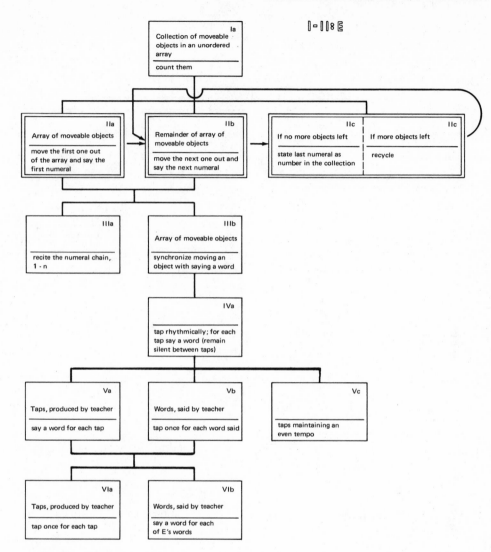

FIG. 17.2. Curriculum hierarchy for counting a collection of movable objects. (By permission of L. B. Resnick.)

For both these tasks, an analysis revealed a set of subordinate capabilities shown in the figure, some in common and some not in common, ranging down to some relatively simple skills that the children were presumed to possess at the beginning of instruction. Figures 17.2 and 17.3 show hierarchies of less complex behavior developed with kindergarten children which are somewhat easier to follow (Resnick & Wang, personal communication). In figure 17.2 the terminal behavior is counting a movable set of objects; in figure 17.3 the terminal behavior is the capability to place an object in the appro-

priate cell of a two-dimensional matrix. In each of these two figures the row of double-lined boxes connected by arrows shows the behavioral sequence that accomplishes the terminal performance. The boxes below this show the hierarchical skills leading to this performance sequence. The analysis of learning hierarchies, or *component task analysis*, begins with any desired instructional objective, behaviorally stated, and asks in effect: To perform this behavior what prerequisite or component behaviors must the learner be able to perform? For each behavior so identified, the same ques-

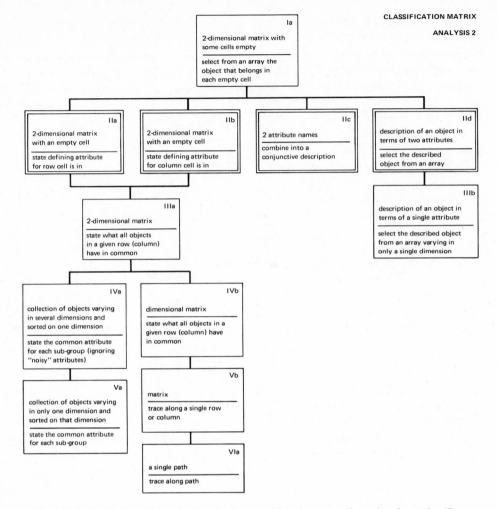

FIG. 17.3. Curriculum hierarchy for placing an object in a two-dimensional matrix. (By permission of L. B. Resnick.)

tion is asked, thus generating a hierarchy of objectives based on testable prerequisites. The analysis can begin at any level and always specifies what comes earlier in the curriculum. The importance of the backward analytic procedure for instruction is that it provides a method for identifying critical prior behaviors—behaviors whose absence not only may be difficult to diagnose but also may be significant impediments to future learning. In practical applications, a component task analysis can stop when the behaviors identified are the ones that the course designer believes can be safely assumed in the student population. Thus, this kind of analysis attempts to provide ordered sets of

tasks for inclusion in a curriculum and also to specify the skills a student needs to enter a curriculum successfuly.

The kinds of performances identified in this manner are generated not only by the logic of the subject matter but also by the psychological structure of the subject matter—psychological structure being roughly defined, in this context, as an ordering of behaviors in a sequence of prerequisite tasks so that competence in an early task in the sequence facilitates the learning of later tasks in the sequence. The relationship between tasks is hierarchical in the sense that competence at a higher level implies successful performance at lower levels. When analyzed in this way, it may not always be the case that the logical subject-matter relationships in a knowledge structure defined by scholars in the field are the same as the described psychological structure (Glaser, 1962; Suppes, 1966). In the case where one works with task hierarchies for which there is no established subject-matter organization, such as the kind of behavior that might be taught to four- or five-year-olds, the nature of the structure of the component tasks is an interesting psychological problem (Resnick, 1967; Resnick & Wang, 1969).

A persistent question that is raised concerns how much of education can be analyzed into hierarchical structures. At this stage of development of instructional design techniques, the answer to the question is very much an open, experimental matter. The technique has hardly been explored. Three things should be pointed out, however. First, it should be recognized that hierarchies or structures that might be developed for the more complex behaviors need not be unique. That is, it may well be that several such hierarchies exist, each of which is "valid" with different kinds of learners, but none of which taken singly is valid for all learners. Second, the analysis of learning objectives into component and prerequisite behaviors does not guarantee an immediately complete and viable structure and sequence. As is pointed out below, such hierarchies stand very much as hypotheses subject to empirical investigation. Third, regardless of the precision and specificity with which learning sequences are identified, in actual practice there is always a functioning sequence. If one is "teaching" a complex behavior, he must begin somewhere and proceed through some sequence of steps. He, thus, has at least an implicit or intuitive structure and sequence within which he operates. The point here is that techniques, such as employed by Gagné and by Resnick for example, provide one means of making explicit the behaviors to be learned and the sequence in which these behaviors might be acquired. It would appear that as these behavioral analysis techniques are improved, much more of the content and process of school subject matter can be analyzed for the purpose of instruction.

Hierarchy Validation

Once analyzed, the hierarchical analysis stands as a hypothesis of ordering that requires data to test its validity. If tests are developed for each of the component tasks described, then data are obtained by which patterns of responding to the subordinate tasks can be ascertained. Indices, somewhat like those obtained in a Guttman-type scale analysis, can be computed to determine the sequential dependencies in the hierarchy (Resnick & Wang, 1969). In contrast to a typical simplex structure, a hierarchical analysis usually presents an intricate tree structure for which new measures of branching and ordering need to be devised. Validation of a hierarchy also can be carried out experimentally by controlled transfer experiments that determine the facilitation in the acquisition of higher ordered tasks as a function of the attainment of lower ones. The empirical tryout of the hypotheses represented by a task hierarchy seems to be an important endeavor for instructional design. Suggestions about how determinations of hierarchy validity might be made have been discussed in preliminary papers by Gagné (1968), Resnick (1967), and Resnick and Wang (1969). One example is a study by Cox and Graham (1966) using elementary arithmetic tasks. They investigated a task ordering used for instruction, showed how an initially hypothesized ordering might be improved, and suggested a revised order that might be more useful to consider in designing the curriculum.

What kinds of information do such structures provide for the design of instruction? The basic implication is that no objective is taught to the learner until he has, in one way or another, met the prerequisites for that objective. However, the prerequisite learnings can be attained in a variety of ways: they can be learned one at a time or they can be learned many at once in large leaps. The instructional process would seem to be facilitated by continuous identification of the furthest skill along the hierarchy that a student can perform at any moment, or, if a student is unsuccessful at a particular objective, by determining the most immediate subobjective at which he is successful. This type of upward and downward branching seems to take more advantage of the relations between the student's performance level and psychological structure of the subject matter. Thus, the hierarchies as they are derived indicate only the relation of subordination or sequential performance capability. They do not necessarily specify instructional procedures, i.e. how tasks should be learned or what tasks should be taught at the same time. Each analysis says what behaviors are to be observed and tested for, even though it may take a significant amount of instruction to get from one component task to another. As a result, essential information is provided with respect to assessing performance, since the instructor or instructional device is told what observations are relevant to determining the status of learned performance. A hierarchical analysis provides a good map on which the attainment, in performance terms, of an individual student may be located. The uses of such hierarchies in designing a testing program for a particular instructional system are discussed below.

PLACEMENT, DIAGNOSIS, AND ASSIGNMENT TO INSTRUCTIONAL TREATMENT

The model of adaptive, individualized instruction outlined previously points to the necessity for specifying foreseeable instructional outcomes and for designing sequences of instructional subgoals that are compatible with the structure of the subject matter and that facilitate attainment of these outcomes. These specified sequences and hierarchies can be considered as a kind of "curricular lattice" through which the progress of individual students can be assessed in their attainment of the instructional goals. If adaptive instruction is at all effective, both the *rate* and *manner* of progress through the curriculum sequence will vary from individual to individual. The purpose of this section is to examine the particular measurement requirements involved.

Initial Placement Testing

To facilitate discussion, schematic representations of two types of hierarchical sequences are illustrated in figure 17.4. Briefly, the lettered boxes in these illustrations represent instructionally relevant behaviors that are prerequisite to each other. Thus, in the linear sequence, A is prerequisite to B, B is prerequisite to C, etc. In this sequence, D represents the terminal instructional outcome for this segment of the instructional sequence. The boxes in the tree-structure sequence have a similar relationship, with the exception that parallel columns of boxes are considered to be sequentially independent of each other from a

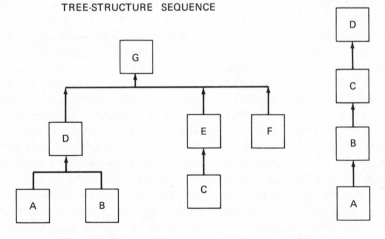

FIG. 17.4. Two possible hierarchies of sequence of instruction

learning sequence point of view. Thus, behaviors A and B are both considered prerequisite to D, but A and B are not prerequisite to each other. Similarly, D, E, and F are all prerequisite to G (the terminal instructional outcome for this sequence), but the temporal sequence of instruction is not specified. Thus, E may be learned before D, F learned before D, etc., but C must be learned before E.

With respect to the individualization of instruction, such a hierarchical specification provides a map on which an individual student may be located before actual instruction begins (i.e. before providing the learning experiences so that the learner may acquire the next sequence of behaviors). Thus, given that little is known about an individual learner who is to acquire the terminal curriculum objective of the sequence, the first decision that must be made about him answers the question, Where in this sequence of learning experiences should this individual begin his study? The problem is to locate or place the student with respect to his position in the learning sequence. This first decision, or placement decision, specifies the initial requirements for a testing program designed to facilitate the adaptation of instruction to the individual learner. At this point, the information required of measuring instruments with respect to a given segment of the instructional sequence is primarily achievement information. These tests provide information concerning the knowledge and skills already possessed by the individual before he begins an instructional sequence. The term *placement test* in this discussion will be reserved for the type of test that provides this kind of information—namely, long-term achievement information that is specifically obtained to facilitate the initial placement decision. It should be noted that the use of the terms *placement* and *placement decision* is somewhat different from the use of those terms in chapter 14 (see pp. 499–500). Although here and in chapter 14 (pp. 499–503) the concern is with making decisions about all examinees (i.e. there is clearly no screening-out or selection decision), the discrepancy between the two uses of the terms follows from the no-

tion of treatment allocation. That is, at this point in the instructional decision-making process, one is assuming that all of the students being measured by the placement test need to be located at some point in the given curriculum sequence and that the decision has not been made concerning the teaching technique (i.e. the instructional treatment) to which an individual is to be assigned in order that he may acquire the next sequential behavior. This latter decision is called a *diagnostic decision* in the discussion below (pp. 643–45), and it would seem that some of the statistical characteristics of those tests described in chapter 14 (pp. 499–503) are more applicable to these latter (diagnostic) instruments. If one either is experimenting with an instructional sequence or has several viable sequences leading to the same terminal instructional goal to which an individual may be allocated, then such procedures as outlined in chapter 14 are important for examining test validities. As an example, consider the two versions of the instructional sequence illustrated at the top of figure 17.5. Suppose both were viable sequences for different kinds of students. Suppose one had a predictor test, administered it to a group of students, and assigned the students to one of the two sequences at random. Then if the regression functions of the outcome measure on the predictor variable appeared as in (i) of figure 17.5, one would have some evidence to conclude that Sequence I is a better sequence overall regardless of scores on the predictor test. On the other hand, if the regression functions appeared as in (ii) of figure 17.5, one would use Sequence I for all those who had $Z > Z_i$ on the predictor test, and Sequence II for all others. However, one would still need to locate a student within the particular sequence allocated in order to maximally adapt instruction to individual needs. In this chapter, it is this latter type of decision that will be called a *placement decision*.

Achievement information obtained in this way is specific to a particular curriculum sequence, to each prerequisite instructional objective within a given sequence, and to a

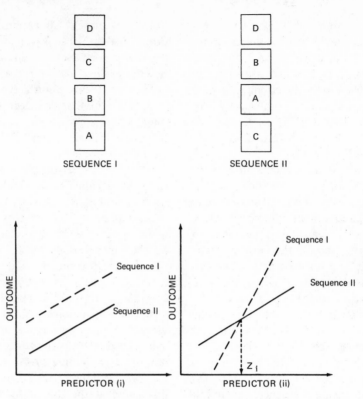

F̲ɪɢ̲. 17.5. Illustration of alternative instructional sequences and some regression functions that may be useful in deciding a predictor test's value in making decisions concerning sequence allocation.

learner's performance in relation to the given sequence and its prerequisites. Thus, tests designed to provide information for placement decisions in an adaptive instructional system must be constructed with a particular curriculum map in mind. It appears impossible to employ a test based on a vaguely defined domain of content to provide the information that is required to make an adaptive placement decision of the type considered here. Furthermore, to be useful in placing an individual learner, these tests must yield more than a single global score reflecting achievement over the entire domain of instruction. Information must be provided concerning the specific knowledge and skills already mastered, partially learned, or not yet mastered by the individual learner. Such placement tests also must provide information about an individual learner's performance that is referenced to the curriculum sequence with which he is faced. This means that the information provided by these placement tests must be

accessible to the placement decision maker in a criterion-referenced form, rather than in a norm-referenced form. For example, in a given group, Johnny's score on a test designed to measure a particular instructional objective may be at the 99th percentile; yet he may well have to be given instruction on the objective. This is so because percentile ranks and, in general, norm-derived scores, are referenced to the group and not referenced to a curriculum sequence as defined here, and the objective may be one that *no one* in the group has mastered.

It is probable that in situations where little is known about an individual learner's performance and where the curriculum sequence consists of a large number of instructional objectives, a single placement test is not an efficient device for reliably providing all the information that is needed. In certain instructional systems which have attempted adaptive individualization of instruction, an entire curriculum area (such as elementary mathematics is structured and sequenced, and placement testing is sequentially performed. For example, Cox and Boston (1967), reporting on the testing procedures employed with Individually Prescribed Instruction (IPI) (Glaser, 1967; Lindvall & Bolvin, 1967), demonstrated the use of a sequential testing procedure. In this situation, elementary school mathematics is sequenced in terms of units of instruction. Within each unit is a sequence of instructional objectives that are to be mastered by an individual learner. Initial placement is accomplished in a two-stage testing procedure. A student new to the system is given a test over a broad range of the curriculum sequence, and scores on the test are referenced to specific units within the sequence. The first decision that is made concerns unit placement; at the second stage of testing, placement is made, within the unit sequence, to a specific instructional objective. Stage one, broad-range placement to a unit, need occur only once at the beginning of a course of study. When the student completes an instructional unit, he is given a stage-two placement test for the next sequential unit; thus, he is placed within each successive segment of the curriculum sequence. A similar procedure was reported by Rahmlow (1969) with respect to a series of programmed instruction units in mathematics.

Some of the statistical characteristics and decision rules that are applicable to these placement tests are discussed in detail in the section of this chapter dealing with criterion-referenced tests (pp. 652–61). The test characteristics necessary for this type of placement test, if they are to be efficient measuring instruments, depend heavily on the validity of the proposed curriculum sequence. For example, if there were no extant sequence, it would be necessary to test an examinee on every objective (node or "box") in the curriculum. If there is a viable sequence, however, the situation improves considerably. One could then devise a sequential testing procedure (see pp. 651–52 concerning branch-testing procedures) in which only some nodes are tested, and passing items on those nodes would indicate that earlier nodes in the sequence would be passed by the examinee as

well (because of the hierarchical dependencies that exist).

Such a procedure was employed by Ferguson (1969) in designing a computer-assisted placement test for a unit of instruction in the IPI arithmetic curriculum. The hierarchies with which he worked are presented in figure 17.6. Figure 17.6 represents two sequences of instructional objectives, for a total of 18 instructional objectives in all. (As shown in table 17.1, objective number 3 is the same in both sequences.) Each one of the 18 instructional objectives defined a relatively homogeneous domain or universe of test items or test tasks. The problem was to place an individual at a single "box" or objective in each sequence in such a manner that if he were tested on all those objectives below that location he would demonstrate mastery[2] on the items, and if he were tested on all those objectives above that location he would demonstrate lack of mastery on these items. Ferguson found that the most efficient testing procedure for accomplishing this was to begin testing with items of "medium difficulty,"[3] for example, items sampled from the universe defined by objective 8 in figure 17.6. If the pupil demonstrated mastery of this objective he was branched to items dealing with an objective that was more difficult. The branching was either to the most difficult untested objective in the hierarchy (objective 13) or to one midway between the initial objective tested and the most difficult untested objective (objective 11), depending on the pupil's response pattern leading to the mastery decision. If an examinee failed to demonstrate mastery of objective 8 he was

[2] The term "mastery" means that an examinee makes a sufficient number of correct responses on the sample of test items presented to him in order to support the generalization (from this sample of items to the domain or universe of items implied by an instructional objective) that he has attained the desired, pre-specified degree of proficiency with respect to the domain. In certain situations, this can be considered as a simple or compound hypothesis testing situation.

[3] Note that "item difficulty" has a meaning in this context only in reference to the sequence or hierarchy which is employed. It is not used in the same way as in classical measurement theory (see Lord & Novick, 1968, pp. 328–329), although such uses coincide when a group of individuals who are heterogeneous with respect to the sequence are tested.

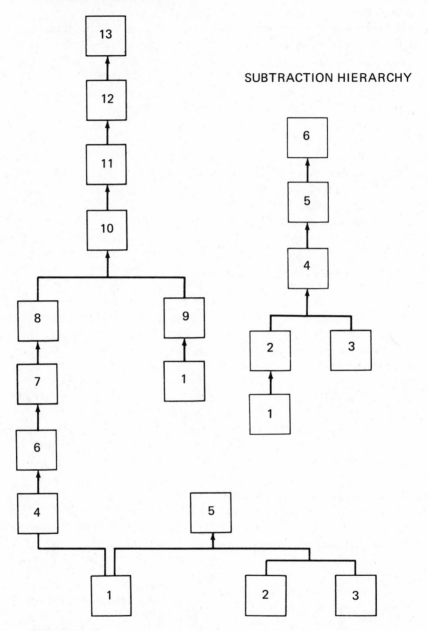

FIG. 17.6. Hierarchies of objectives for an arithmetic unit in addition and subtraction. (Adapted from Ferguson, 1969.)

branched to an easier set of items. A set of branching rules similar to those for mastery decisions was used, but branching was downward either to the easiest objective or to one midway between the initial and the easiest objective. Testing proceeded until a decision was made about each objective, but each objective was not specifically tested since branching to more difficult objectives implied without formal testing that easier (or lower) objectives had been mastered. If the hypothesized hierarchy is an accurate description of the prerequisite relation

TABLE 17.1

Objectives for Computer-Assisted Branched Testing for Addition-Subtraction

Subtraction Hierarchy

1 Solves subtraction problems related to single-digit combinations by multiples of ten.

2 Solves subtraction problems with no borrowing. Three- and four-digit combinations.

3 Solves subtraction problems from memory for two-digit sums less than or equal to twenty.

4 Subtracts two-digit numbers with borrowing from the tens' place.

5 Subtracts three-digit numbers with borrowing from the tens' *or* hundreds' place.

6 Subtracts three-digit numbers with borrowing from the tens' *and* hundreds' place.

Addition Hierarchy

1 Solves addition problems from memory for sums less than or equal to twenty.

2 Solves subtraction problems from memory for sums less than or equal to nine.

3 Solves subtraction problems from memory for two-digit sums less than or equal to twenty.

4 Solves addition problems related to single-digit combinations by multiples of ten.

5 Finds the missing addend for problems with three single-digit addends.

6 Does column addition with no carrying. Two addends with three- and four-digit combinations.

7 Does column addition with no carrying. Three- or four-digit numbers with three to five addends.

8 Adds two-digit numbers with carrying to the tens' *or* hundreds' place. Two addends.

9 Finds the sums for column addition using three to five single-digit addends.

10 Adds two-digit numbers with carrying to the tens' *or* hundreds' place. Three or four addends.

11 Adds two-digit numbers with carrying to the tens' *and* hundreds' place. Two to four addends.

12 Adds three-digit numbers with carrying to the tens' *or* hundreds' place. Two to four addends.

13 Adds three-digit numbers with carrying to the tens' *and* hundreds' place. Two to four addends.

between objectives, this latter assumption will be substantiated on the basis of empirical results (Ferguson, 1969).

Assignment to Instructional Alternatives

The specification of the structure and sequence of instructional goals and subgoals is a necessary but not a sufficient condition for the adaptation of instruction to the individual. Hierarchical curriculum sequences, as described here, specify neither the rate nor the manner of progress of the individual learner through the sequence but do indicate what observations to make in assessing learning. Further information is required to determine to which of the available instructional alternatives (i.e. methods or kinds of instruction) different students should be assigned. In terms of instructional content, the placement of learners at various points in the curriculum sequence according to their placement profile provides certain information about the content of instruction or about how instruction should proceed. However, as has been indicated, this procedure is not sufficient for determining the process or mode of instruction. In terms of decisions to be made, the information required is that which answers the question, Given that this student has been located at a particular point in the curriculum sequence, what is the instructional alternative that will best adapt to his individual requirements and thus maximize his attainment of the next instructionally relevant objective? Such decisions are in a real sense diagnostic decisions,[4] in that diagnosis implies both content and nature of the instructional procedure. In this sense, tests designed to provide this kind of information may be called diagnostic tests. It is probably true that a single test of the conventional type now published and used in the schools will not be able to provide all the data relevant to the instructional technique assignment decisions required in an adaptive instructional system.

---

[4] As indicated in chapter 14, these decisions are termed placement decisions. The distinction between the use of these terms in that chapter and in this one has been pointed out (p. 639).

Assignment decisions about instructional alternatives are made on the basis of placement and diagnostic information; that is, a student is assigned, guided to, or allowed to select a means of instruction. A fundamental question concerns the nature of the instructional alternatives available. What are they? Where do they come from? How are they developed? On what basis do different instructional treatments differ so as to be adaptive to individual requirements? In most of the contemporary educational environments, adaptation takes place on the basis of class grouping and perhaps special work with individual students where this is possible. Certain adaptive mechanisms are left up to the student so that some students have to work harder or spend more time on their homework than others. If a school permits a more individualized setting, then other opportunities for providing different instructional alternatives can be made available. Instructional alternatives can be adaptive to the student's present level of achievement and such aspects as his mastery of prerequisites, his retention of previous learning, the speed at which he learns including the amount of practice he requires, and his ability to learn in structured or less structured situations. Treatments differing in those respects that are shown to be related to measured aspects of entering behavior might be able to provide a significant beginning for effective adaptation to individual differences. However, in designing instructional alternatives, it is difficult to know how to use other variables that come out of learning theory (such as requirements for reinforcement, distribution of practice, use of mediation and coding mechanisms, and stimulus and modality variables [e.g. verbal, spatial, auditory, and visual presentation]), and more needs to be known about their interaction with individual differences. A study by Rosner, Richman, and Scott (1969), for example, indicated that there might be relatively high incidence of clinically significant perceptual-motor dysfunction among both special education and regular classroom pupils. Such individual differences should be examined to determine their relationships to educational outcomes (e.g. early reading) and their importance for designing instruction and instructional materials. Another example might be found in the work by Bormuth (1968). Here the reading difficulty (as determined by the cloze readability scale [Bormuth, 1970]) of a passage was examined in relationship to the amount of new information a subject acquired from reading the passage. Preliminary results indicated that passages that were "slightly difficult" for the subject resulted in more acquisition of new information than either "too easy," "just right," or "too difficult." If such findings could be demonstrated as generalizable (over populations of subjects and curriculum areas), then this might indicate that written instructional materials, say in social studies, need to be adjusted on an individual basis in order to be maximally effective, i.e. adaptive. Several versions of a text, for example, might be needed.

If one assumes that measures of entering behavior can be obtained and that instructional treatments are available, then at the present state of knowledge, empirical work must take place to determine those measures most efficient for assigning individuals to classes of instructional alternatives. The task is to determine those measures with the highest discriminating potential for allocating between instructional alternatives. Such measures should have sharply different regression slopes for different instructional alternatives to be most useful (see pp. 499–503). As a result of initial placement and diagnostic decisions, the group of students involved is reduced to subsets, allocable to the various available instructional treatments. These initial decisions will be corrected by further assignments as learning proceeds so that the allocation procedure becomes a multistage decision process that defines an individualized instructional path.

Typically, aptitude test batteries have been used to predict scholastic success where the instructional system is relatively nonadaptive. The aptitudes generally measured in education are very much the product of the kind of educational environment in which the aptitude tests have been validated. The basic assumption underlying nonadaptive instruction is that not all pupils can learn a given instructional task to a specified degree of mastery. Adaptive instruction, on the other hand, seeks to design instruction that assures that a given level of mastery is attained by most students. Such models as that proposed by Carroll (1963) and discussed by Bloom (1969) indicate that aptitude takes on a different meaning in adaptive instruction. Other models of adaptive individualized instruction have also been proposed, for example, the IPI project (Lindvall & Bolvin, 1967) and Project Plan (Flanagan, 1967, 1969).

Adaptive instruction demands a different approach to the prediction of success. If the decision to be made is what kind of instruction to provide the learner, then little information is obtained from the usual kind of aptitude measurement. The behaviors that need to be measured are those that are predictive of immediate instructional success within a particular instructional technique. It can be postulated that if the criteria for aptitude test validation had been immediate learning success rather than some long-range performance criteria, the nature of today's generally accepted aptitude batteries would be quite different. This postulation seems likely since factorial studies of the changing composition of abilities over the course of learning (Fleishman, 1965, 1967) show that different abilities are involved at the beginning and end of the course of learning. While it may be useful to forecast over the long range, an adaptive instructional model also requires measures that are closely related to more immediate learning criteria, i.e. success in initial instructional steps. Current types of measured aptitude may be limited in that they are operationally designed to predict over the long period, given reasonably nonadaptive forms of educational treatment. Evidence for this lack of utility of general psychometric measures with respect to instructional decisions comes from the line of studies dealing with correlations between psychometric variables and learning measures (see p. 628). The identification of the kinds of "aptitude" variables that can be used to place individuals or to rec-ommend to individuals certain kinds of learning experiences is a vast new area in the field of measurement related to instructional decision making.

As has been indicated, aptitude measures are not the only consideration when individuals are allocated to alternate learning experiences to accomplish the same instructional goals. Another aspect of diagnosis includes the analysis of the errors in student responses. One example of a situation in which errors are analyzed and directly related to instructional treatment is found in a series of tests developed by Nesbit (1966). In arithmetic operations involving the addition and subtraction of fractions, children were first given a relatively broad-range test spanning the topic. Those children who erred on any of the items were administered a second test. Their errors on the second test were analyzed and the teacher was provided with both a list of the types of error committed by each child and a description of the specific instructional activities designed to overcome this error. Thus, not only performance omissions (i.e. lack of mastery of the domain of instructionally relevant tasks) were identified, but also performance characteristics (i.e. such as error-type identification) and individualized treatment (i.e. learning activities structured around new tasks to be learned and the child's cause of present difficulty) were provided. Increased testing activities of this sort are to be encouraged if adaptive instruction is to be realized.

Continuous Monitoring and Assessment of Instructional Outcomes

In the adaptive instructional model, as the student proceeds with his course of instruction, his performance is monitored and assessed at established test and decision points. Achievement measures are obtained similar to those used to assess initial placement; in addition, the opportunity is available for assessment to be made of the student's learning characteristics. (Suggestions for the latter have been mentioned above: learning rate, need for practice, ability to retain previous learning, situations in which he seems to learn best, etc.) This achievement- and learning-style information is updated as the student progresses, and it provides the primary information for the decision making required to guide student learning. As this continuous measurement is in effect over a period of time, it would incorporate and supersede initial achievement and aptitude information. If appropriately and subtly done, teaching, instruction, and testing would fade into one another. Testing information would be used for the student, teacher, or automaton to make decisions about future instruction, and to a large extent the evaluative, "course grade" function of testing would be deemphasized.

Achievement measurement in this context is necessarily criterion-referenced measurement. The information obtained from a test tells whether a learning criterion has been achieved, and if it has not, further tells in what respect criterion performance has not been attained. Various levels of criterion mastery are set as the student progresses. Generally, some level of mastery is set by the requirements of the subject matter, the student population, etc. Implicit in the instructional model are defined criteria of competence. The basic task for instruction is to provide the methods that will enable most students in a particular course to attain mastery.

Of unique interest in instructional measurement, as instruction proceeds, are the measurements of learning aptitudes and learning styles that can be made. In today's education, assessments of these kinds are, to a large extent, made by observation and judgment of the teacher—when the teacher has the opportunity to observe, is a good observer, and has the appropriate flexibility to implement the results of these judgments. Probably, these observations and judgments can be significantly improved by providing the teacher with observational instruments and by training the teacher in their use. The significant problem in this context is to develop measures of learning characteristics that are useful in practical instruction. As the student learns, it should be possible to devise learning experiences in which measures are obtained that provide information to the student and the teacher about the student's learning

"style." This is an area in which there has been much lip service and which is done intuitively at the present time. The development of appropriate measurement procedures, which might be called learning process psychometrics, seems to be of critical importance (Cronbach, 1967).

As the student learns, then, information is obtained about how he learns and what he learns; instructional assignments, self-made or teacher-made, take place; and assessment is made of a student's performance at particular decision points. There is a three-way relationship among measures of learning, instructional alternatives, and criteria for assessing performance. Since measures of learning and instructional alternatives are evaluated in terms of how well they assist in helping the student attain educational goals, then the criterion measures become quite critical. Depending upon the measures used, some instructional outcomes will be maximized and others minimized; some kinds of student performance may be minimized inadvertently unless they are expressed and explicitly assessed. In this regard, it seems almost inescapable that development of more fully criterion-referenced measures, measures that reflect a student's performance in relation to standards of attainment derived from a behavioral analysis of the curriculum area under consideration, be advanced. In addition, serious attempts must be made to measure what has been heretofore so difficult: such aspects as transfer of knowledge to new situations, problem solving, and self-direction—those aspects of learning and knowledge that are basic to an individual's capability for continuous growth and development.

Two further points are appropriate here. First, information about learning relevant to an adaptive model should come primarily from the interaction effects generally neglected in studies of learning. As Cronbach and Gleser (1965) have pointed out, the learning experimentalist assumes a fixed population and hunts for the treatment with the highest average and least variability. The correlational psychologist has, by and large, assumed a fixed treatment and hunted for the aptitude that maximizes the slope of the function relating outcome to measured aptitude. The present instructional model assumes that there are strong interactions between treatment variables and measurements of individuals; and unless one treatment is clearly the best for everyone, as may rarely be the case, treatments or instructional alternatives should be differentiated in a way to maximize their interaction with performance criteria. If this assumption is correct, then individual performance measures that have strong interactions with learning variables and their associated instructional alternatives are of greater importance than measures that do not show these interactions. This forces an examination of the slope of the regression function in learning experiments, so that this interaction can be evaluated (see chapter 14). Intensive experimental research is required to determine the extent to which instructional treatments need to be qualified by individual-difference interactions. The search for such interactions has been a major effort in the field of medical diagnosis and treatment and seems to be becoming one in education (Lubin, 1961).

Second, the continuous pattern of assessment and instructional prescription, and assessment and instructional prescription again, can be represented as a multistage decision process where decisions are made sequentially and decisions made early in the process affect decisions made subsequently. The task of instruction is to prescribe the most effective sequences. Problems of this kind in other fields, such as electrical engineering, economics, and operations research, have been tackled by mathematical procedures applied to optimization problems. Essentially, optimization procedures involve making decisions by choosing a quantitative measure of effectiveness and determining the best solution according to this criterion with appropriate constraints. A quantitative model is then developed into which values can be placed to indicate the outcome that is produced when various values are introduced.

Groen and Atkinson (1966) pointed out the kind of quantitative model that deals with this kind of analysis. They suggested a multistage process that can be considered as a discrete N-stage process; at any given time, the state of the system, i.e. the learner, can be characterized. This state, which is probably multivariate and described by a state vector, is followed by a decision that also may be multivariate; the state is transformed into the new updated state. The process consists of N successive stages where at each of the N-1 stages a decision is made. The last stage, the end of a lesson unit, is a terminal stage where no decision is made other than whether the terminal criteria have been attained. The optimization problem in this process is to find a decision procedure for determining which instructional alternatives to present at each stage, given the instructional alternatives available, the set of possible student responses to the previous lesson unit, and specification of the criteria to be optimized for the terminal stage. This decision procedure defines an instructional strategy and is determined by the functional relationship between (a) the long- and short-range history of the student and (b) student performance at each stage and at the terminal stage. Figure 17.7 illustrates this type of N-stage instructional process as Groen and Atkinson visualized its application in computer-assisted instruction. A more general flow diagram is presented in figure 17.8. This figure illustrates the instructional stages for the IPI project. To be made useful for the type of analysis described above, the procedure illustrated by figure 17.8 would probably need to be broken down into finer stages.

Groen and Atkinson pointed out that one way to find an optimal strategy is to enumerate every path of the decision tree generated by the multistage process, but that this can be improved upon by the use of adequate learning models which can reduce the number of possible paths that can be considered. In order to reduce these paths still further, dynamic programming procedures (Bellman, 1957; Bellman & Dreyfus, 1962), might be useful for discovering optimal strategies and hence for providing a set of techniques for reducing the portion of the tree that must be searched. This technique involves the maximization or optimization of the utility of a sequence of N decisions (or stages of instruction). This is accom-

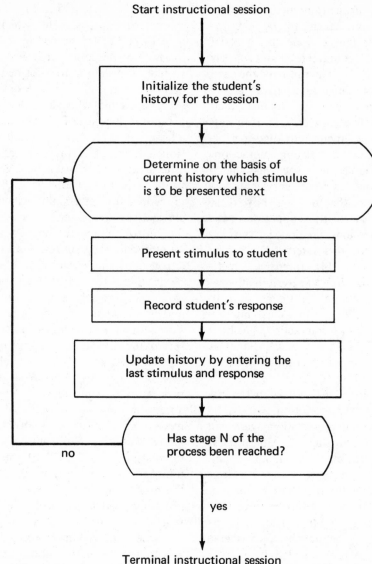

Start instructional session

Initialize the student's
history for the session

Determine on the basis of
current history which stimulus
is to be presented next

Present stimulus to student

Record student's response

Update history by entering the
last stimulus and response

Has stage N of the
process been reached?

no

yes

Terminal instructional session

FIG. 17.7. Flow diagram for an instructional system. (Groen & Atkinson, "Models for Optimizing the Learning Process," *Psychological Bulletin*, Vol. 66, 1966, Fig. 1, p. 311. Copyright 1966 by the American Psychological Association and reproduced by permission.)

plished by employing a mathematical function that depends on the maximized utility of the $(N-1)^{th}$ decision in the sequence. The utility of a sequence may be defined, for example, in terms of a score on a test that is administered at the completion of the Nth stage of instruction. Thus, at each of the stages in the sequence of instruction, the learner is presented with the types of instruction that will maximize criterion per-

formance. The kind of instruction presented at the jth stage of the sequence is determined as a function of the maximized utility of the instructional decision made at the $(j-1)^{th}$ stage. This is an interesting approach for instructional theory and psychometrics, although some initial experimentation has not been overwhelmingly successful (Groen & Atkinson, 1966).

In order to carry out such an approach, two

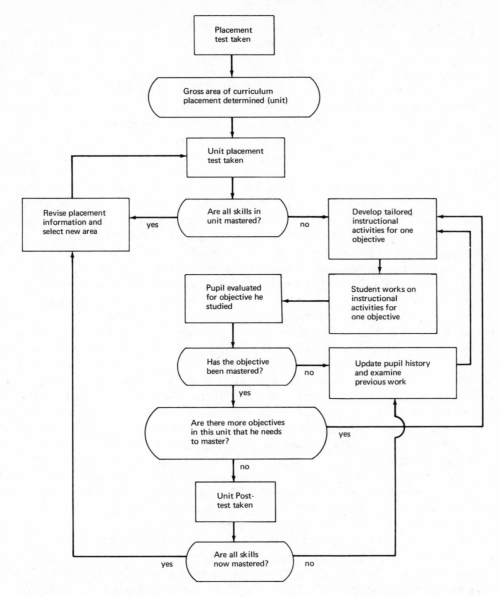

FIG. 17.8. Instructional process flowchart for the IPI procedure. (Adapted from Lindvall, Cox, & Bolvin, 1970, in press.)

fundamental efforts are required: first, quantitative knowledge of how the system variables interact must be obtained, and, second, agreed-upon measures of system effectiveness must be established. Upon the completion of these steps requiring, respectively, knowledge and value judgment, optimization procedures can be carried out. It has been shown that relative to the total effort needed to achieve a rational decision, the optimization procedure itself often requires little work when these first two steps are properly done (Wilde & Beightler, 1967). Thus, two ever-present tasks must still be confronted: (a) knowledge and description of the instructional process and (b) the development of valid performance measures.

Management of Test-Provided Information

It is apparent from the preceding discussion in this chapter that the type of information required from a comprehensive testing program in an adaptive system of individualized instruction must be easily generated and readily accessible to the student and the instructor. This means that a measuring, information-providing system must be designed and embedded as a component of the overall instructional system. Once embedded into the system, instruction and testing become less distinct and more mutually supporting.

The information generated as a student progresses through a curriculum sequence must be processed and analyzed so that future decision making is facilitated. Thus, testing programs designed to provide the information required to make the four kinds of adaptive decisions—initial placement, individual diagnosis, individual monitoring, and outcome assessment —must also make provisions for reporting results in a usable form to students and instructors. It would seem further that the burden of designing and constructing such tests, of processing response data, and of providing preliminary analysis of test data must be handled by someone other than the classroom teacher. If instructional outcomes and available sequences are specified in advance, there appears to be no reason why tests and other information-generating instruments cannot be predesigned and made available to the student and the instructor as needed. That is, tests can be predesigned and coded to particular segments of the curriculum sequence in much the same manner that texts and other instructional materials are predesigned. Since the model for individualized instruction considered here (see pp. 631–32) provides for the capacity of the system to update and improve itself as more is learned about its operation, tests and other instructional materials can be updated and reintroduced without disrupting the instructional system. The instructor, then, can be freed of his duties as "materials producer" and can better perform his role as instructional decision maker.

In an individualized system, the amount of data needed for decision making increases in direct relation to the number of students. Traditionally, group-based information has been the primary form of data used in classroom decision making. When all students are working on the same task, the task (e.g. page number, chapter, etc.) is the only bit of information needed to characterize the group. On the other hand, when every individual is allowed to progress at his own rate and to work on different tasks, then one needs distinct information about each student (Cooley, 1970, in press). The kind of information required also varies in the two situations. In the group teaching situation, the information emphasis is on what is taught at any particular point in time. When instruction is adaptive, the information emphasis shifts to what is learned by each student.

With the increased amount and kind of information that is required for adaptive instruction, it seems almost inevitable that a computer system be integrated with the measurement and instructional system in order to manage the individualized school. Such a management system has as its goals to increase the effectiveness of the adaptive instructional model and to maximize teacher productivity in operating in the system. Systems for computer-managed instruction have been described by Bratten (1968), Brudner (1968), and Flanagan (1969). One such computer management system is being developed in connection with an individualized elementary school and is described in detail elsewhere (Cooley & Glaser, 1969). In this system, the instructor can interrogate the computer to obtain a variety of information relevant to making instructional decisions. For example, in curriculum sequences blocked off as units, the instructor is able to obtain a listing of all the performance data available for a particular student who has been working in that unit. This would include test data specific to the unit which were collected prior to instruction (placement data); within-unit performance data and test data (monitoring data); and posttest data over the unit after instruction has been completed (evaluative data). Teacher analysis of these data is used to diagnose and prescribe further work for the student. Another example of information that the instructor can obtain from the computer is a listing of the class members showing where in the curriculum sequence each student is working and how long he has been working at that lesson unit. In this manner, the instructor is able to monitor class progress and to identify quickly students who are working at a particular point in a sequence for an inordinate length of time; such students may need assignment to new instructional materials, small group instruction, personal tutoring, or other modifications of their instructional environment.

Branch Testing

In recent years, the advance of instructional technology and the introduction of the computer as an instructional device have spurred serious interest among test constructors in realtime alteration of the manner in which tests are administered and scored—that is, on-the-spot adaptation of the sequences of items, number of items, or manner of presentation of items while testing is in progress. In particular, interest has been generated for a procedure known as branch testing or tailored testing. In this testing procedure, the item(s) to which an examinee is to respond next is determined by his responses on the preceding item(s). This procedure makes it possible for each examinee to be administered a different set of items that are best suited to measuring his characteristics. Thus, tests can be considered "tailored" to the individual. Rules for determining which items to administer next are termed branching rules.

It would seem that tests that are administered in this branching or tailoring mode have great applicability to the four general types of testing problems encountered in the instructional model described above. One application of branching previously mentioned concerns placement testing (Cox & Boston, 1967; Ferguson, 1969; Rahmlow, 1969). Another application was mentioned in connection with diagnostic testing (Nesbit, 1966). In this section, the topic of branch testing is considered somewhat more broadly to examine the flavor of this type of testing procedure and its possible instructional applications. In another section of the chapter (pp. 640–43), the possibility of using sequential analysis techniques (Wald, 1947) with certain types of test items is discussed.

Most studies dealing with the effectiveness of the branch-testing procedure have been concerned with the measurement of mental ability, that is, the location of an examinee on a continuum of a hypothetical variable or trait (examples of such studies include Angoff & Huddleston, 1958—using the CEEB; Bayroff & Seeley, 1967—using the AFQT; Cleary, Linn, & Rock, 1968—using the SCAT and STEP). The various strategies or types of branching that have been reported can be subdivided into two broad classes (Cleary et al., 1968): (a) those procedures that employ two distinct test sections that route an examinee and measure him, respectively; and (b) those that measure and route examinees simultaneously (i.e. without distinct test sections to route and measure separately). Within each of these classes, various techniques are employed to construct the routing and/or measuring test, thus giving rise to several branching strategies.

Although these various strategies have been enumerated and described in the literature, little work has been done concerning the instructional implications and possibilities of using branch testing. In a paper entitled "Some Theory for Tailored Testing," Lord (1970) spoke directly to this point.

It should be clear that there are important differences between testing for instructional purposes and testing for measurement purposes. The virtue of an instructional test lies ultimately in its effectiveness in changing the examinee. At the end, we would like him to be able to answer every test item correctly. A measuring instrument, on the other hand, should not alter the trait being measured. Moreover . . . measurement is most effective when the examinee knows the answers to only about half of the test items. The discussion here [i.e. the test theory of tailored testing] will be concerned exclusively with measurement problems and not at all with instructional testing [p. 2].

Lord showed that from the measurement point of view, gains from tailored testing are slight except for low ability and high ability examinees. However, as Green (1970) has indicated in commenting on Lord's paper, branching (particularly under computer control) may have advantages: possible substantial savings in testing time, branching from broad areas of the achievement domain to narrow areas for in-depth analysis, measuring more complex behavior, measuring response latencies, sequencing responses, and sequencing items on the basis of what the measure shows—to name a few. Of particular relevance, when an instructional system is considered, is the point Green makes that considerations of measurement per se are wasteful in the overall decision-making process. Failing to consider the interrelationship between measurement and decision making neglects the importance of deciding what additional data need to be collected before adequate decisions can be made. The integration of measurement into the decision process has been discussed by Cronbach and Gleser (1965) in the context of selection and placement. It has, however, barely been explored with respect to instruction and with assistance from computers.

Branching strategies for instruction are best based on rules determined by a combination of psychological theory and subject-matter organization. For example, in a procedure suggested by Gagné (1970) for assessing the learning of principles, one can distinguish between a principle and concepts that make up the principle. A two-stage testing procedure is employed in which the first item set measures whether or not an individual possesses the concepts. If the individual is successful on these items, he is branched to another set which tests whether or not he has learned the principle. If one tested only the principle and the student's response was inadequate, it would not be known whether the learner (a) did not learn either the principle or the concepts or (b) learned the concepts but not the principle. Another possibility concerns tasks involving use of two or more principles. The two-stage measurement procedure would let one discriminate between examinees who (a) knew one principle and not the other, (b) knew the second principle but not the first, (c) knew none of the principles, (d) knew all the principles but were unable to put them together, and (e) knew all the principles and could put them together correctly to solve the task.

A further conception of branch testing can include the notion of measuring the process by which a learner solves a problem (e.g. Newell & Forehand, 1968). That is, the examinee is given the task and must interact with and interrogate the computer to determine courses of action or to solicit further information necessary to solve the problem or complete the task. These procedures are not new conceptions in testing (see Glaser, Damrin, & Gardner, 1954; McGuire, 1968), but the feasibility of such procedures for measurement seems much greater with computer technology. Moreover, significant advances in measurement in an adaptive instructional system will come about, not in the notion of increased precision of measuring the same things currently measured, but as a result of measurement procedures based upon analyses of subject-matter task structure and the behavioral processes involved in performing these tasks.

CRITERION-REFERENCED TESTING

Tests that measure instructional outcomes and that are used for making instructional decisions demand special characteristics—characteristics that are different from the mental test model that has been successfully applied in aptitude testing work. That there is a pressing need for the development of achievement or performance measurement theory and technique has been pointed out (Cronbach, 1963; Ebel, 1962; Flanagan, 1951; Glaser, 1963), and although preliminary work has begun, no substantial literature is extant. In this section some considerations in the development of performance tests are discussed. Of particular significance are: (a) the generation of items from statements of educational objectives; (b) interpretation of a test score in terms of test content and performance criteria, as well as in terms of norms referenced to the scores of other examinees; and (c) interpretation of test scores so that they have meaning beyond the performance sample actually assessed and so that test scores can be generalized to the performance domain that the test subset represents.

At the heart of the issue concerning the two types of tests discussed in this section is the matter of deriving meaning from test scores.

The score or number assigned to the individual as a result of a measurement procedure is basically inert and must be related semantically to the behavior of the individual who is measured (Lord & Novick, 1968). There are many semantic interpretations that are possible in educational measurement, but, for the most part, educational test authors have concentrated on interpreting the test score of an individual primarily by relating it to the test scores of other individuals. Such interpretations, which have been called norm-referenced interpretations throughout this chapter, have serious limitations when they are employed with achievement tests that are used in instructional systems seeking to be adaptive to the individual. These limitations were discussed in an earlier section. A complete discussion of why such interpretations have come to be so prevalent in educational measurement is beyond the scope of this chapter, but it can be pointed out that the concentration of psychological test theory on trait variability and on the relative differences between individuals, the reluctance of educators to specify precisely their desired goals in terms of observable behavior, the reliance of measurement specialists on the mental test model, and the desire of test constructors to build tests that are applicable to many different instructional systems for a variety of purposes have contributed in no small part to the development and use of these norm-referenced interpretations.

The type of semantic interpretation of test scores that is required by the system of adaptive individualized instruction described in this chapter may be termed a criterion-referenced interpretation. *A criterion-referenced test is one that is deliberately constructed to yield measurements that are directly interpretable in terms of specified performance standards.* Performance standards are generally specified by defining a class or domain of tasks that should be performed by the individual. Measurements are taken on representative samples of tasks drawn from this domain, and such measurements are referenced directly to this domain for each individual measured.

Criterion-referenced tests are not designed to facilitate individual difference comparisons such as the relative standing of an examinee in a norm group or population, nor are they designed to facilitate interpretations about an examinee's relative standing with respect to a hypothetical variable such as reading ability. Rather, they are specifically constructed to support generalizations about an individual's performance relative to a specified domain of tasks, e.g. letter discrimination, letter blending, following written directions. (In the instructional context, such a domain of tasks may be termed a *domain of instructionally relevant tasks.* The insertion of the qualifiers "instructionally relevant" serves to delimit the domain to those tasks, the learning of which is the goal of instruction. The term *tasks* includes both content and process.)

When the term *criterion-referenced test* is used (e.g. by Glaser, 1963; Glaser & Cox, 1968; Glaser & Klaus, 1962; Lindvall & Nitko, 1969), it has a somewhat different meaning from the two more prevalent uses of the terms criterion or criterion tests in educational and psychological measurement literature. One of these usages involves the notion that scores on an achievement measuring instrument (X) correlate with scores derived from a second measurement situation (Y), this second situation being, for example, scores on another achievement test or performance ratings such as grades. With this usage, the Y scores are often termed criterion scores, and the degree to which the achievement test approximates, or relates to, the criterion is often expressed by the product-moment correlation, r_{XY}. Because achievement test scores have the potential for correlating with a variety of other measures, relationships to multiple criteria are often reported. A second prevalent interpretation of the term criterion in achievement measurement concerns the imposition of an acceptable score magnitude as an index of attainment. The phrases "working to criterion level" and "mastery is indicated by obtaining a score equivalent to 80 percent of the items correct" are indicative of this type of interpretation of criterion. Often both of these uses of the term criterion are applied to a single measuring instrument: a test may serve to define the criterion to be measured, and students may be selected according to some cut-off score on it.

Norm-Referenced Tests vs. Criterion-Referenced Tests

As Popham and Husek (1969) indicated, the distinction between a norm-referenced test and a criterion-referenced test cannot be made by simple inspection of a particular instrument. The distinction is found by examining (a) the purpose for which the test was constructed, (b) the manner in which it was constructed, (c) the specificity of the information yielded about the domain of instructionally relevant tasks, (d) the generalizability of test performance information to the domain, and (e) the use to be made of the obtained test information.

Since criterion-referenced tests are specifically designed to provide information that is directly interpretable in terms of specified performance standards, this means that performance standards must be established prior to test construction and that the purpose of testing is to assess an individual's status with respect to these standards.

One source of confusion between the type of test discussed here and the typical achievement test of traditional usage resides in the notion of defining task domains and sampling from them in order to obtain test items. Arguments are often put forth that any achievement test defines a criterion in the sense that it is representative of desired outcomes and that one can determine the particular skills (tasks) an individual can perform by simply examining his responses to the items on the test. The problem is, of course, that, in practice, desired outcomes have seldom been specified in performance terms prior to test construction. Furthermore, the items that finally appear on a test typically have been subjected to a rather rigorous sifting procedure designed to maximize the test constructor's conception of what the final distribution of test scores should be like and how the items of the test should function statistically. Ease of administration and scoring are often

other determinants of what the final test task will be. As Lindquist (1968) has noted, many valuable test tasks have been sacrificed through the machine-scoring restrictions of current test practices. These and other test construction practices often lead to tests composed of tasks that tend to distort interpretations about the capabilities of the examinee with respect to a clearly defined domain of performance standards.

The distinction between norm-referenced and criterion-referenced tests can often be determined by examining the specificity of the information that can be obtained by the test in relation to the domain of relevant tasks. Logical transition from the test to the domain and back again from the domain should be readily accomplished for criterion-referenced tests, so that there is little difficulty in identifying with some degree of confidence the class of tasks that can be performed. This means that the task domain measured by criterion-referenced tests must be defined in terms of observable behavior and that the test is a representative sample of the performance domain from which competence is inferred.

Thus, the attainment of "reading ability" can only be inferred to have occurred. The basis for this inference is observable performance on the specified domain of tasks into which reading ability has been analyzed, such as reading aloud, identifying an object described in a text, rephrasing sentences, carrying out a written instruction, reacting emotionally to described events, and so on. Criterion-referenced tests seek to provide information regarding whether such kinds of performance can or cannot be demonstrated by an individual learner and not how much reading ability an examinee possesses along a hypothetical ability dimension. What is implied is some analysis of task structure in which each task description includes criteria of performance. This means that within a particular instructional context a test constructor is seldom free to choose at will the type of task he is to include in his test. This has been already delimited by definition of the domain of relevant tasks that describe the outcomes of learning. It also means that a scoring system must be devised that will preserve information about which tasks an individual can perform. Scores such as percentile ranks, stanines, and grade equivalents preserve norm-group information but lose the specificity of criterion information (Lindvall & Nitko, 1969).

A criterion-referenced test must also be generalizable to the task domain that the specific test tasks represent. One does not have to go very far in a curriculum sequence before the number of tasks that the learner is to perform becomes very large. To take a simple example, in an elementary arithmetic sequence, column addition appears relatively early. An instructionally relevant domain might consist of correct performance on all 3-, 4-, and 5-addend problems with the restriction that each addend be a single-digit integer from 0 through 9. The relevant domain of tasks consists of 111,000 addition problems. The measurement problem for criterion-referenced test constructors is how to build a test of reasonable length so that generalizations can be made about which specific problem types an individual learner can or cannot perform. Norm-referenced test constructors do not have such a problem, since judicious selection of items will result in variable scores that spread out individuals, thus allowing one to say, "Johnny can do more than Suzy." The question of what Johnny can or cannot do is left unanswered. Examination of an individual's item responses provides only a tenuous basis for inference when norm-referenced tests are used (Lindquist & Hieronymus, 1964). Yet, if instruction is to be adaptive to the individual learner, this information must be obtained. Is it specific number combinations which trouble Johnny? Is it problems that involve partial sums of a certain magnitude? Is it failure to apply the associative principle to simplify the calculation? These and many more such questions need to be answered in order to guide the instructional process.

The use to which achievement test information is put is another determinant of whether criterion-referenced or norm-referenced tests are needed. Both kinds of tests are used to make decisions about individuals, but the nature of the decisions determines the information re- quired. In situations where there is a constraint on the number of individuals who can be admitted and in which some degree of selectivity is necessary, then comparisons among individuals are necessary and, hence, norm-referenced information is used. On the other hand, in educational situations where the requirement is to obtain information about the competencies possessed by a single individual before instruction can be provided, then criterion-referenced information is needed. Generally, in existing instructional systems that are relatively nonadaptive, admission decisions are made on a group basis and use norm-referenced data. As the feasibility of adaptive, individualized instruction increases, knowledge of an individual learner's position in the group becomes less important than knowledge of the competencies that the individual does or does not possess. Hence, it is likely that educational measurement will require criterion-referenced information in addition to norm-referenced information.

Item Construction

The major problem involved in constructing items for criterion-referenced tests is the design of test tasks that are clearly members of the relevant domain. In their ideal form, the tasks to be performed are representative samples of tasks that are the objectives of instruction at a particular stage in the instructional sequence. Two points need to be considered here. The first is the place of ultimate vs. proximate instructional objectives and their relation to instructionally relevant tasks. The second is the generation of test items from descriptions of instructional objectives.

Ultimate and proximate objectives

The distinction between and discussion of ultimate and proximate educational objectives were thoughtfully done by Lindquist (1951) in the previous edition of this volume. Such a distinction and its consequences for educational measurement are especially important to note. Educational practice generally assumes that the knowledge and capabilities with which the student leaves the classroom are related to the educational goals envisioned by the teacher. This assumption implies that the long-range goals that the students are to attain in the future are known and that the behavior with which they leave a particular course actually contributes to the attainment of these goals. What is closer to reality is that the long-term relationship between what the student is taught and the way he is eventually required to behave in society or in his job is not very clear. In contrast to the ultimate goals of education, the proximate objectives consist of the terminal behavior that a student displays at the end of a specific instructional situation. It should be noted that proximate objectives are not defined as the materials of instruction nor as the particular set of test items that has been used in the instructional situation. For example, at the end of a course in spelling one might reasonably expect a student to be able to spell certain classes of words from dictation. During the course, certain of these words might have been used as examples or as practice exercises. The instructor would be interested in the student's performance with respect to the class or domain of words as a proximate objective of instruction and not the particular words used in instruction. Thus, to assess a student's performance with respect to a domain, one also may need to consider the transfer relationship between the items in the domain and the preceding instruction.

It is this proximate behavior that is the only tangible evidence on which the teacher can operate and by which both the teacher and the student can determine that adequate instruction is being carried out. However, as Lindquist (1951) pointed out, proximate objectives are ephemeral things: specific content changes with reorganization of subject matter and methods of teaching; and different instructors in the same subject want to develop generalized understandings in their students, but each may use quite different subject-matter areas, examples, and materials. Nevertheless, specific end-of-course behaviors are learned by students and tested for by instructors, both operating under the assumption that these behaviors facilitate the attainment of ultimate objectives

(although many would not wish to judge the effectiveness of an educational system on the basis of attainment of proximate objectives). The proximate objectives, however, do determine the nature of an instructional institution, the way students and instructors act, and the way in which the success of the teachers, students, and institution is evaluated. In this sense, the present discussion is limited to measurement of those behaviors that are under the control of the educational institution and that the student learns or is expected to learn.

Generation of test tasks

The job of the test constructor is considerably simplified if instructional goals and subgoals are initially specified in terms of relevant tasks that the learner can be expected to perform. Those tasks that are relevant to specific stages in the curriculum sequence, such as one of the "boxes" in figure 17.4, form the basis for the tasks to be included in criterion-referenced tests. In recent years, the trend in curriculum design has been to state instructional goals and subgoals in terms of behavioral objectives. Statements of behavioral objectives then must be translated into specific test tasks that, when successfully completed by the individual learner, form the basis for the inference that the behavior has been acquired by the learner. As instructional sequences become complex, this domain of instructionally relevant tasks becomes quite large, but, as Hively (1966b) has indicated, they can often be grouped into classes in such a manner that the general form of a class of tasks can be specified.

Recent developments in the analysis of behavior are helpful in analyzing performance into component tasks. For example, learning hierarchy analysis provides one means of distinguishing between components and more complex behavior. Something like Gagné's (1970) suggestion for a two-stage testing operation is required to measure the presence or absence of the complex behavior and then the presence or absence of the underlying prerequisites or components. The essential point is that adequate measurement must provide unambiguous information about the kinds of behaviors that

Descriptive Title	Sample Item	General Form	Generation Rules[a]
Basic fact; minuend > 10.	13 −6 ──	A −B ──	1. $A = 1a; B = b$ 2. $(a < b) \in U$ 3. $\{H, V\}$
Simple borrow; one-digit subtrahend.	53 −7 ──	A −B ──	1. $A = a_1 a_2; B = b$ 2. $a_1 \in U - \{1\}$ 3. $(b > a_2) \in U_0$
Borrow across 0.	403 −138 ──	A −B ──	1. $N \in \{3, 4\}$ 2. $A = a_1 a_2 \cdots; B = b_1 b_2 \cdots$ 3. $(a_1 > b_1), (a_3 < b_3),$ $(a_4 \geq b_4) \in U_0$ 4. $b_2 \in U_0$ 5. $a_2 = 0$ 6. $P\{\{1, 2, 3\}, \{4\}\}$
Equation; missing subtrahend.	42− ─ =25	A− ─ =B	1. $A = a_1 a_2; B = b_1 b_2$ 2. $a_1 \in U$ 3. $a_2, b_1, b_2 \in U_0$ 4. Check: $0 < B < A$

[a] Explanation of notation:

Capital letters $A, B, \cdots$ represent numerals.
Small letters (with or without subscripts), a, b, a_1, b_2, etc., represent digits.
$x \in \{ \cdots \}$: Choose at random a replacement for x from the given set.
$a, b, c, \in \{ \cdots \}$: All of a, b, c are chosen from the given set *with replacement*.
N_A: Number of digits in numeral A.
N: Number of digits in each numeral in the problem.
$a_1, a_2, \cdots \in \{ \cdots \}$: Generate all the a_i necessary. In general " $\cdots$ " means continue the pattern established.
$(a < b) \in \{ \cdots \}$: Choose two numbers at random *without* replacement; let a be the smaller.
$\{H, V\}$: Choose a horizontal or vertical format.
$P\{A, B, \cdots \}$: Choose a permutation of the elements in the set. (If the set consists of subscripts, permute those subscripted elements.)
Set operations are used as normally defined. Note that $A - B = A \cap \bar{B}$. Ordered pairs are also used as usual.
Check: If a check is not fulfilled, regenerate all elements involved in the *check* statement (and any elements dependent upon them).
Special sets:
$U = \{1, 2, \cdots, 9\}$
$U_0 = \{0, 1, \cdots, 9\}$

FIG. 17.9. Examples of item forms from the subtraction universe. (Reprinted by permission from Hively et al., "A 'universe-defined' system of Arithmetic Achievement Tests," *Journal of Educational Measurement*, 1968.)

learners can and cannot perform so that instruction can appropriately proceed. Other examples are Hively's (1966a) analysis and Gibson's (1965) analytical experiments of elementary reading behavior that begin to examine the specific components of reading behavior so that the task domain can be identified for teaching and testing purposes. Another interesting approach has been presented by Gane and Woolfenden (1968) using a repetitive mechanical task. Their approach was to express performance in terms of an algorithm or flow chart so that not only were the component tasks specified, but also the sequence of performance was described. As detailed analyses of

school subject matters become increasingly prevalent, the test constructor will be able to judge more easily whether a test task is properly a member of the domain of tasks so that what is taught and learned can be accurately assessed.

Specification of the domain of tasks necessitates more than simply giving examples of the desired tasks. It has been suggested that what is needed is a general "item form" accompanied by a list of task generation rules (Hively, 1966b; Hively, Patterson, & Page, 1968). An illustration of such item forms is reproduced in figures 17.9 and 17.10. Figure 17.9 presents examples of item forms for subtraction tasks in arithmetic skills. A title

Purpose: To test the ability to solve an equality necessitating application of Theorem A,[1] Postulate B,[2] and Postulate C.[3] The solution set is to be non-empty and bounded by integers.

Task Format: $a-b|c+(-1)^f d| \geq e$

Generation Rules:

1. $c \epsilon \{x, y, z\}$
2. $b \epsilon \{2, 3, 4, 5\}$
3. $f \epsilon \{0, 1\}$
4. $d \epsilon \{1, 2, 3, \cdots, 9\}$
5. $g \epsilon \{kb | k \epsilon \{1, 2, \cdots, 5\}$ and $kb \neq b\}$
6. $e \epsilon \{1, 2, 3, \cdots, 20\}$
7. $a = g + e$

Explanation of Generation Rules

1. c is the variable of the inequality; x, y, or z may be used.
2. b, the coefficient of the absolute value term, can vary from 2 to 5.
3. $(-1)^f$ allows the sign of the constant within the absolute value term to vary.
4. The constant d can vary from 1 to 9.
5. g is a multiple of b, up to $5b$, and not equal to b.
6. e is any natural number from 1 to 20.
7. $a = g + e$. In solving the problem, one will arrive at the step $a - e \geq b|c+(-1)^f d|$. Since $a - e = g$, and g is a multiple of b, a cancellation step is required next. It is this pattern that must remain constant across the form.

---

[1] *Theorem 1.* If a is a real number and $a > 0$, then $|x| < a$ if and only if $-a < x < a$. [Use $\leq$, where x is of the form $(y \pm b)$.]
[2] *Postulate 1.* If a, b, c are real numbers such that $a < b$, then $a + c < b + c$. [Applied where c is a constant and also where c is the absolute value term.]
[3] *Postulate 2.* If a, b, c are real numbers such that $a < b$ and $0 < c$, then $ac < bc$.

FIG. 17.10. Illustration of Hively's task format and task generation rules. (From Hively, 1966b.) Reprinted by permission.

---

at the left of the table roughly describes a component task of the subtraction domain. A sample item is given in the next column as it would appear on a test. A general form, together with generation rules, given in the next two columns, defines the set of test items that represent the test task. Specifically, the general form and the rules for generating a set of test items has been called by Hively an item form. A collection of item forms constitutes a domain or universe from which tests and test items may be drawn. Such a procedure as this delimits and clearly specifies the domain of tasks to be learned, and the test constructor can then produce test tasks that clearly represent this domain. Judgments can be made relatively easily concerning the "content validity"

of the test. Consider the item form in figure 17.10 concerned with a specific ability in algebra performance. In this case an item requiring the solution of the inequality $18 \geq 12 - 2|y+3|$, is *not* a member of the domain specified by figure 17.10 since there is no application of Postulate 2 to $-2|y+3|$. A similar approach to defining item tasks has been presented by Osburn (1968). Osburn attempted to define a general item type and then to further analyze the general type into more specific item forms so that a hierarchical arrangement of test tasks was generated. His suggestion included the specification of verbal replacement sets as well as the numerical type depicted by Hively's example. Osburn's example of an item form and a verbal replacement set for one of the variable elements of the item form is reproduced in figure 17.11. It would seem that provisions for verbal replacement sets such as these might remove much of the "sterility" that might be encountered by a fixed verbal format while, at the same time, maintaining a clear link to a general class of items to be included in a particular test.

Bormuth, in a book entitled *On the Theory of Achievement Test Items* (1970), developed the idea that tests that are made using current test construction procedures cannot unequivocally be claimed to represent the properties of instruction nor to be objectively reproducible. He suggested that a test item is defined as a property of the test writer and not as a property of the instruction. A score on an achievement test which is made by the procedures currently in use must be interpreted as the student's responses to the test writer's responses to the instruction. Since little knowledge is available of the factors which determine the test writer's behaviors, the relationship of the student's score to the instruction must be regarded as essentially undefinable. Hence, it seems that what is required is a fundamental change in the conception of a test item, of how it is defined, and of how responses to it are described. The solution Bormuth offers is to suggest that linguistic analysis can be used to make explicit the methods by which items are derived from statements of instructional objectives. Trans-

Item Form

Given $(ND:\mu, \sigma)$ and $(Region\ ND:\mu, \sigma)$. If one sample point (P) is randomly selected from $(ND:\mu, \sigma)$, what is the probability that (P) is in $(Region\ ND:\mu, \sigma)$?

Possible Replacement Set for $(ND:\mu, \sigma)$*

1. A fair penny is tossed (N) times and the number of heads is recorded.
2. John's true score on a certain test is (T) and the standard error of the test is (SE).
3. An urn contains (P) white balls and (Q) red balls. (N) balls are randomly selected with replacement and the number of white balls is noted.
4. The Wechsler Adult Intelligence Scale is standardized over the general population to mean of 100 and a standard deviation of 15.
5. A rat presses a bar an average of (P) times per minute when a light is on, and (Q) times per minute when the light is off. Under both conditions the distribution of bar presses is approximately normal with a standard deviation of (SD).
6. Sam takes a test consisting of (R) (K)-alternative multiple choice items and guesses on all items.
7. A certain batch of ball bearings is known to contain 20 per cent defectives. (N) ball bearings are shipped to a customer.
8. A certain test contains (R) items that are all of equal difficulty, $P = (X)$, for a population of 9th grade students.
9. A white die is rolled (N) times and the number of times the (Y)-face turns up is noted.
10. A certain firm produces packaged butter. Quality control has shown that the average weight per package is 16.5 ounces with a standard deviation of .5 ounces.

* Before this item form can be used to generate items, suitable numerical replacement sets need to be defined.

FIG. 17.11. An example of a verbal replacement set for a variable element in an item form. (Reprinted by permission of and adapted from Osburn, "Item Sampling for Achievement Testing," *Educational and Psychological Measurement*, 1968.)

formational rules (analogous to linguistic transformations) are used to specify definitions of types of items that could be formed. Like the notion of item forms, a reasonable degree of objectivity and replicability is introduced into item construction procedures.

This brief discussion on item construction has indicated some recent developments for consideration by achievement test constructors concerned with creating test tasks that reliably represent instructional objectives. It is apparent, of course, that these techniques could be applied to tests that are not criterion referenced. However, further development and

the application of such techniques seem essential to the construction of criterion-referenced tests and for the development of achievement testing theory.

Test Construction

When the domain of instructionally relevant tasks has been analyzed and described, specific test tasks must be selected for inclusion on the final form of the test. Item selection and analysis techniques have, of course, been designed with this in mind. The requirements for norm-referenced or group-based item parameters are treated extensively in the literature. The issues of item and test parameters are not clear. For example, many of the item and test statistics employed with norm-referenced tests are dependent on the observed variance of the total test scores. Criterion-referenced tests, on the other hand, when employed in instructional situations may display little variance in total test scores. For example, instruction in many arithmetic skills, by its very nature, does not seek to "spread out" the examinees but seeks to reach criterion levels of general competence. If a test were administered prior to instructional treatment and again after instructional treatment, examinee scores on the posttest would show an increase in mean performance and a decrease in performance variation as each student attained skill mastery. In theory, adaptive instruction seeks to ensure that all individuals in the population show certain levels of mastery in the instructional domain, while not excluding differences in achievement beyond the general level of mastery established. Thus, on those instructional tasks where mastery criteria have been established, if posttest items show great variation in difficulty in the population that has been instructed, and items on the posttest are instructionally relevant tasks, then instruction has been inadequate.

For criterion-referenced tests, the empirical estimation of reliability is not clear. As Popham and Husek (1969) indicated, estimates of internal consistency and test-retest coefficients are often inappropriate because of their dependency on total-test score variability. Mastery-level performance for all individuals instructed reduces variance-based estimates considerably. Thus, these estimation techniques may be inappropriate when applied in situations that reflect adaptative instruction. Tests used in these circumstances could be both internally consistent and stable, yet estimates of these indices that are dependent on score variability may not reflect this.

On the assumption that test tasks are samples from the domain of relevant tasks, the problem of ascertaining an individual's status in a task domain might be conceptualized as an item-sampling problem; that is, tasks are sampled and examined in relation to a single individual. The purpose of the test is to determine the proportion of the tasks in the domain that he can perform. Techniques developed for acceptance sampling and sequential testing (for example, see Lindgren & McElrath, 1966, for an elementary discussion) might be investigated for use in this context. For example, if ϕ represents the "true" proportion of incorrectly performed tasks in the domain for an examinee under consideration, the probability function related to accepting the individual as a "master" of the domain (given ϕ) can be specified and, for a fixed observed cut-off score, probabilities of accepting the individual's test-demonstrated performance as evidence for sufficient mastery of the domain can be computed for each true value of ϕ. One could determine risk in the testing situation for both the examinee and the instructor by specifying in advance the proportion of mastery of the domain required before decisions concerning the continuation or termination of instruction are made. That is, specify criterion error proportions ϕ_1 and ϕ_2 such that if the examinee's error proportion $\phi \leq \phi_1$ he has had sufficient instruction relative to the domain, and if $\phi \geq \phi_2$ more (perhaps different) instruction is indicated. The instructor's "risk" would be allowing a learner to terminate instruction on this particular domain and get on with new instruction. Examinee "risk" would be forcing the student to continue instruction in the domain when he has already mastered it. The results of some preliminary investigations have been presented by Kriewall and Hirsch (1969) in connection with instruction in elementary mathematics.

In situations where the test length, i.e. the number of test items, can vary from person to person, it may be possible to employ the sequential likelihood-ratio test (Wald, 1947). The procedure allows specification of error rates in advance of testing for given "hypotheses" about the proportion of instructionally relevant tasks (test items) that can be successfully completed by the examinee at a given point in time. A discussion of this technique is found in many elementary statistical texts. In achievement testing applications, this procedure would take on the following character: A student needs to be evaluated on a given, relatively large, domain of tasks. The problem is to determine whether the proportion of correctly performed tasks is sufficient to terminate instruction with respect to this domain and to allow him to advance to instruction on a new domain of tasks. If the proportion of correctly performed tasks is not sufficient for mastery, instruction with respect to the domain is to be continued.

The following proportions are specified in advance of testing:

$\phi_1 =$ the minimum acceptable proportion of tasks mastered in the domain. This proportion is considered the minimum criterion achievement level for mastery of the domain.

$\phi_2 =$ an alternative proportion of domain tasks mastered below which the criterion achievement level is not obtained (i.e. the maximum proportion correct that will still result in a nonmastery decision).

In the testing situation, ϕ_1 functions as the null hypothesis to be tested against the alternative ϕ_2. Type I and Type II error rates are then specified for classifying the examinee as having mastery or nonmastery. A Type I error occurs when it is decided that a student needs instruction with respect to the domain, when in fact his true proportion of successfully performed tasks is sufficient for mastery. A Type II error is committed when the student is allowed to terminate instruction, when in fact the true proportion of the tasks he can perform is insufficient for mastery. Acceptance and rejection criteria are then established consistent with the Type I and Type II error rates specified. An examinee continues taking the test until a mastery or nonmastery decision can be made. The acceptance and rejection criteria change after each item is attempted and scored; that is, after each item a decision is made to stop testing and declare mastery, continue testing, or to stop testing and declare nonmastery. This procedure was used successfully by Ferguson (1969) in his work on branch testing. Items were generated by a computer and presented to the examinee via a teletype terminal. This preliminary study indicated that the sequential sampling technique, coupled with subject-matter branching rules, reduced testing time considerably and yielded reliable mastery decisions with respect to the domains sampled.

These techniques seem interesting but certainly need to be explored further, both theoretically and empirically, before they can be recommended as being useful in the instructional context. They have been discussed briefly here primarily to stimulate further inquiry.

FORMATIVE EVALUATION

The sixth element of the instructional model considered in this chapter states that in the system, information is collected in order to improve it, and this capability is inherent in the system's design. Information feedback for this purpose is an essential aspect of increasing rationality in decision making relevant to the design of educational programs. Of particular significance in this regard is the recent emphasis on *formative evaluation* (Cronbach, 1963; Lindvall, Cox, & Bolvin, 1970; Scriven, 1967). Formative evaluation refers to the data provided during the development and design stages of instructional procedures and materials; these data provide the information used for subsequent redesign of instructional techniques. Information provided to the student or to the teacher only for the conduct of ongoing instruction is not formative in this sense, although the term formative evaluation has been used to include both kinds of information (e.g.

Bloom, 1969b). Formative evaluation, however, can be included in the intermediate stages of development as well as in later stages of continuous improvement and revision. Throughout, formative evaluation focuses on the specific outcomes of various aspects of instruction so that information is provided about the intended or unintended results of these techniques. In its best sense, formative evaluation precludes the one-shot trial of an innovation on the basis of which a decision is made to accept or reject a new instructional program.

This type of formative evaluation is like the high degree of telemetering instrumentation required for the design of new hardware systems. In the early stages of design, a great deal of instrumentation is devoted to measuring and assessing the characteristics of the various functions that the system carries out and their outcomes. As the system's components become more reliable and information is obtained about their effects, less and less measurement for evaluation is necessary. At this latter point, the only information required is that used for the carrying out of normal operations and for possible eventual improvement. As an example, consider an instructional system, such as IPI, in which one aspect of adaptation to individual differences is the writing of a tailored or individual lesson plan for each student for each skill he is to learn. Such a tailored plan is called a *prescription*. In the initial and intermediate stages of design and development, it is necessary to collect and analyze teacher prescriptions in order to determine if they are indeed individualized and adaptive to students (Bolvin, 1967). This information is then fed back to system developers (research and development personnel) and to teachers as operators of the system. If it is discovered that prescriptions are not individualized, decisions need to be made concerning whether the system or the operators are the cause. That is, does the system fail to provide the necessary data and alternative instructional procedures or do teachers fail to consider relevant student data and existing alternative instructional treatments? The relationships between the prescriptive component and other components need to be examined as well. For example, does the testing and measurement component provide the necessary data relevant to adaptive prescriptions? Such considerations are system evaluations that are formative in nature and serve as a basis for future redesign and development. They serve to direct examination not only to outcome variables, such as student achievement and rate of progress, but also to the conditions that influence these variables.

The formative evaluation implied by the sixth element of the proposed model requires: (*a*) a planned and specially designed instructional program, (*b*) goals that are considered as desirable outcomes of the program, and (*c*) methods for determining the degree to which the planned program achieves the desired goals. Evaluation studies are generated by concern with the discrepancies among stated, measured, and attained goals; with the discrepancies among the stated means for achieving goals and the actual implemented means; and with an analysis of why implemented means have not resulted in expressed goals. Formative evaluation studies attempt to find out why a program or aspects of a program are or are not effective. The answers require detailed analysis of such factors as the attributes of the program itself (e.g. teaching procedures, instructional materials, testing instruments, classroom management practices), the population of students involved, the situational and community context in which it takes place, and the different effects produced by the program (e.g. cognitive, attitudinal, affective, unintended, and positive or negative side effects). Evaluation can take place along many dimensions and in terms of multiple decision criteria such as learning outcomes, costs, necessity for teacher retraining, community acceptance, etc. The information obtained is feedback to the system and serves to redefine or improve it.

Principles and practices involved in evaluation studies have recently been discussed in detail by many writers: by Suchman (1967) with respect to public service and social action programs in general; by Gagné (1967a), Scriven (1967) and Tyler (1967), with respect to curriculum; by an NSSE yearbook with respect to education in general (Tyler, 1969); by Lindvall and associates (1970) for individualized educational programs in particular; and others. Campbell and Stanley (1963) described various aspects of the internal validity of educational experiments. Such considerations are important for formative evaluation procedures carried out to yield information relevant to redesign and development since they relate directly to the interpretation of the effects of the instructional procedure. Bracht and Glass (1968) have discussed the external validity of educational studies, *external* being defined as the extent to which an experiment can be generalized to different subjects, settings, and experimenters. These authors have presented a detailed examination of the threats to external validity that cause a study to be specific to a limited population or a particular set of environmental factors.

Without going into specific procedures and techniques of evaluation studies, certain general aspects especially appropriate to learning and instruction can be mentioned in this chapter.

Long- and Short-Range Objectives

As has been said previously, a significant problem in the evaluation of instructional systems concerns the relationships among means, proximate instructional objectives, and long-range goals. A program may be unsuccessful for at least two reasons: either (*a*) because it was unsuccessful in developing techniques that produced the desired end-of-course goals or (*b*) because, although it was successful in putting a program into operation and in attaining proximate objectives, these objectives were not related to ultimate expressed goals. Seldom is an instructional enterprise in a position to study the relationship between proximate and ultimate objectives. Programs usually are evaluated in terms of the immediate criteria of school accomplishment or, possibly, accomplishment in the next higher level of education. Concern for some evaluation of long-range goals has been indicated in Project Talent (Flanagan, 1964) and the National Assessment Study (Frymier, 1967; Tyler, 1966). For the most part, however, formative evaluation studies concentrate on essentially immediate objectives assuming a relationship between proximate and ultimate goals.

Preinnovation Baseline Data

The problem of control groups and comparative studies has been extensively discussed in the literature of educational research (e.g. Campbell & Stanley, 1963). Establishing controls in the light of the many interacting factors that influence school settings and populations is a major difficulty in the conduct of evaluation studies. In recent years, particularly in special education, techniques suggested by the work of Skinner have been used with individual children in which the learner is used as his own control. These techniques are described by Wolf and Risley (1970, in press) and, in the context of basic scientific research in behavior, by Sidman (1960). It is of interest to consider these techniques in the context of formative evaluation. An essential aspect of the design used in these studies is the establishment of baselines. The use of baseline logic proceeds by asking the question, Does the instructional treatment substantially affect the baseline rate of the learner's behavior? The question implies that a change occurs and that sufficient information is obtained to attribute the change to the instructional procedure. For this purpose, measures of relevant aspects of the learner's behavior are obtained prior to the introduction of new instructional techniques. The new techniques are then introduced and change is observed in relation to the previously obtained baseline measures. Assuming that measurement of baseline aspects had been in effect long enough to indicate that the measures were reasonably stable and that the changes after the instructional treatment were significant, it still might be difficult to attribute the change to the specifics of the new instructional procedures. To pin down cause and effect, some form of control comparison is desirable, and possible designs, in educational settings, that provide sufficient information for making an estimate of change have been suggested by Wolf and Risley (1969). Related also is the discussion by Camp-

bell and Stanley (1963) of the time-series experiment and the equivalent time-samples design.

The importance of using such techniques as these is that evaluation studies generally have not reported preinnovation baseline data, and the detailed assessment of the students, teachers, and school environment prior to the introduction of new instructional techniques seems fundamental to effective evaluation.

The Independent Variable

The formative evaluation implied by the sixth element of the model assesses the effect of practices derived from elements one through five. The practices are introduced for the attainment of expressed objectives. Not only must the degree to which objectives are attained be ascertained, but also the effectiveness with which the practices are carried out must be determined. Appropriate values of the dependent variable, i.e. attainment of objectives, it is assumed, will result from effective implementation of the independent variable, i.e. the practices developed to implement the first five elements of the model. However, in most educational studies, more attention is paid to assessing outcomes than to the adequacies of implementation. Certainly, the latter is a prior requirement. In order to accomplish this, it is necessary for the designers of an instructional program to provide specific criteria that indicate just how the program should function and how specific features of the program should look when the program is in actual operation. A listing of the criteria for the satisfactory functioning of these items provides a checklist for evaluating the degree to which adequate implementation has taken place.

Determining the effectiveness of the independent variable is one major requirement of the instructional model described in this chapter. Assessments of the operation of the program are needed in order to provide information for redesigning and improving its implementation. The other major aspect is whether or not adequate implementation can indeed accomplish program objectives. In reality, in the day-to-day development of instructional programs, the distinction between these two aspects is not clear. As one assesses whether teaching, materials, equipment, and general school practices are operating appropriately, information is also obtained about how they affect instructional objectives. One usually does not wait to get near-perfect implementation and then proceed to measure instructional outcomes. In the stages of formative evaluation, both aspects proceed together. It is only after some degree of stability is attained and a program has been developed that it seems reasonable to move into a second phase of evaluation. In this second stage, every effort is made to ensure that the implementation criteria are met for the most part, and, when they are, goals of the program can be evaluated more definitely. An example of the specification of items in the operation of an instructional program has been described by Lindvall and associates (1970) for the IPI program. Such a specification is geared to evaluating the program's implementation. Basic program operations have been broken down into the following classes: characteristics of instructional objectives, testing procedures, the prescribing of instruction, instructional materials and devices, teacher activities, student activities, and classroom management procedures. Figure 17.12 shows each of these classes of operations in outline form. The operations listed are those that need to be observed and assessed and for which criteria must be stated, at a particular stage of development of the program, so as to indicate adequate or inadequate implementation. Such a list of specifications provides the basis for the development of telemetering procedures that are used by instructional developers to monitor the implementation of the independent variables and to determine the effects of instructional techniques.

Particular comment should be made on instructional materials and devices that appear to be a new element for evaluation in present-day instructional programs. Some general principles involved have been described by Lumsdaine (1965) and by Mechner (1965). An examination of the product development process and the training of personnel in the field (Popham,

1967) and examples of its effectiveness have been documented (Flanagan, 1966; Mechner, 1967). The evaluation of materials and devices has many facets that need to be examined, such as the sequencing and content of instruction, format and packaging, the ability of the student to follow directions for use, the student's ability to manipulate and work with materials and devices of a particular design, and the way in which the teacher employs these techniques. Procedures are being developed for product design and evaluation along a number of lines. For example, with respect to computer-assisted instruction, Bunderson (1970) has described components of a prescriptive model for designing CAI programs. An interesting technique for evaluating material in programmed instructional texts has been described by Holland (1967); and the evaluation hierarchies in specific subject matters have been described by Gagné (1970) and by Resnick and Wang (1969).

In much the same manner as test designers obtain data on test characteristics in order to improve test functioning, data on instructional techniques need to be obtained. Just as the design-trial-redesign cycle has been used in the development of programmed instructional materials, formative evaluation proceeds for educational systems in general. It seems likely that techniques employed for instruction will eventually, where applicable, be developed with the same degree of analysis and documentation as is now done for well-received test batteries. The history of evaluation in the testing movement is clear: as tests came to be increasingly used and abused, professional societies stepped in to issue statements of standards for quality control, and schools of education provided courses in tests and measurement for users. At the present time, test producers provide manuals documenting the development and specific utility of the tests under particular conditions and with particular populations. Vis-à-vis the present technology of test construction, design and evaluation with respect to instruction will have to develop its own theories and practices growing out of a convergence of the fields of individual differences, learning, and perfor-

INSTRUCTIONAL OBJECTIVES that:

(a) can be used by lesson writers, test developers, and teachers without ambiguity.

(b) are in prerequisite order as evidenced by pupil mastery and progression.

(c) permit lesson writers to develop sequences of lessons that have no missing steps nor overlapping steps and with which pupils can make progress.

(d) are such that persons can agree as to what the pupil is to be taught and on what he is to be tested.

(e) are inclusive enough so that no important gaps in abilities taught are discovered.

THE TESTING PROGRAM:

(a) is used to place pupils at correct points in the instructional continua.

(b) provides valid diagnosis of pupil needs.

(c) provides a valid assessment of mastery of objectives and of units.

(d) is administered so that the pupil is taking CET's and unit tests at proper times.

(e) provides data that are found useful by the teachers for developing valid prescriptions.

(f) provides data that are meaningful to the student.

INSTRUCTIONAL PRESCRIPTIONS:

(a) are based upon proper use of test results and specified prescription writing procedures.

(b) provide learning experiences that are a challenge but permit regular progress.

(c) vary from pupil to pupil depending upon individual differences.

(d) permit pupil to proceed at his best rate.

(e) are interpreted and used correctly by the pupil.

(f) are modified as required.

THE INSTRUCTIONAL MATERIALS AND DEVICES:

(a) are easily identified with the proper objective.

(b) have demonstrated instructional effectiveness.

(c) are used by pupils largely in individual independent study.

(d) are used by pupils in individualized packages.

(e) keep the pupil actively involved.

(f) require a minimum of direct teacher help to pupils.

(g) are shown to teach more effectively as they are revised.

THE TEACHER CLASSROOM ACTIVITIES are such that:

(a) there is little delay in the pupil's getting help when he needs it.

(b) teacher assistance to pupils is largely on an individual basis.

(c) the teacher will spend some class time in examining pupil work and in developing prescriptions.

(d) positive reinforcement of desirable behavior is employed.

(e) teachers give the students considerable freedom.

(f) little time is spent on lectures (etc.) to the group and individual or small group tutoring is employed.

PUPIL CLASSROOM ACTIVITIES are such that:

(a) pupils work largely on an individual and independent basis.

(b) pupils are studying with a minimum of wasted time.

(c) pupils secure needed materials in an efficient manner.

(d) pupils help each other on occasion.

CLASSROOM MANAGEMENT PROCEDURES are such that:

(a) teacher aides score papers and record results in an efficient manner.

(b) pupils score some work pages.

(c) pupils procure own lesson materials.

(d) pupils decide when to have lessons scored.

FIG. 17.12. Basic operational elements in development and evaluation of a system for IPI. (Reprinted by permission of Rand McNally & Co. from Lindvall et al., "Evaluation as a Tool in Curriculum Development," AERA Monograph Series on Curriculum Evaluation, 1970, in press.)

mance analysis. Some departure will be required in the standard rules of test development and use (Cronbach, 1963).

Sustaining Mechanisms

At the later stages of formative evaluation or following an encouraging evaluation study, a significant concern often is whether or not the effects of the experimental instructional technique will hold up as a continuing state of af-

fairs. One aspect of this is the so-called Hawthorne effect. In the classic Hawthorne study (Roethlisberger & Dickson, 1939), an evaluation of a program designed to increase worker productivity found that the specific operational independent variables, such as change in illumination, rest periods, and hours of work, were spuriously effective; that is, productivity tended to increase no matter what change was made. The investigators concluded that the actual independent variable causing change was interest and concern on the part of the management. A well-executed evaluation study should be able to detect such effects. Factors that result in only the temporary maintenance of effects may be extremely subtle and may not be immediately apparent. The maintenance of effects requires environmental support for the new program. Frequently, when teachers are trained in the new curricula and techniques that they bring to their classrooms, conditions are provided in which the new program can proceed, but eventually conventional forces of the environment resume their potency and the innovation is stifled. An example of this is the series of events that followed the introduction of programmed texts into conventional school settings. A study by Carlson (1965) described some of the effects of the lack of a supporting environment for this new instructional technique. One of the unanticipated consequences he described was a restriction of individual differences in learning rate. Although an important anticipated consequence of programmed instruction was that students could be able to learn at their own rates, there were forces operating that minimized the differences in individual rates of achievement. As the program progressed, and as individual students began to vary widely in levels of achievement and rates of progress, the teacher "corrected" for this by either consciously or unconsciously pacing the students. The output of the fast students was restricted so that the same troublesome point could be explained to a number of students at one time, and the slow students were allowed to have access to programs outside of class time while average and fast students were not allowed extraclass access. This had the net effect of minimizing the range of student progress. In addition, "enrichment materials" were supplied to the fast students that also contributed to a condition of minimum spread. In this and other respects, when programmed instruction materials were introduced into a school for further evaluation, sustaining mechanisms were not provided that would permit the impact of this new instructional technique to result in its anticipated consequences.

Adaptation to Individual Differences

The key issue in instructional systems that attempt to individualize instruction is evaluation of the effectiveness of techniques designed for adapting instruction to individual differences. The instructional model employed as an organizing basis for this chapter is an attempt to present a set of general requirements for individualizing instruction. However, the success of any model for individualization is limited by certain constraints. If the operational plan is carried out satisfactorily, then the limitations become ones of technical capability and the extent of knowledge about human behavior. This revolves about several basic issues: the extent to which, in any particular subject matter, learning hierarchies or other orderly structures can be identified and validated; the extent to which individual differences in background and learning characteristics that interact with instructional variables can be identified and measured; and the extent to which alternative instructional techniques and educational experiences can be developed that are adaptive to these measured individual characteristics. These issues are significant areas for basic research in the areas of human performance analysis, the measurement of individual differences, and the functional relationship between these differences and the details of the learning process. The tasks of formative evaluation are to assess technological developments based upon what fundamental knowledge is available, to force improved application, and to provide questions for basic research. The extent to which systems of individualized education are successful in adapting to the nuances of individual differences is a function of this knowledge. The criterion against which systems for individualized instruction need to be evaluated is the extent to which they optimize the use of different measures of behavior and different alternatives for learning in order to provide different instructional paths. It is possible to overdifferentiate and underdifferentiate in adapting to individual differences, and evaluation should indicate where multiple paths are more effective in attaining educational goals than a conventional system which is aimed at the average student. As more knowledge is obtained, the number of paths available for different individuals will be determined by knowledge of the relationships among learning, the analysis of learned performance, and measures of individual differences.

REFERENCES

Angoff, W. H., & Huddleston, E. M. The multilevel experiment: A study of a two-level test system for the College Board Scholastic Aptitude Test. Educational Testing Service *Statistical Report*, 1958, No. 21.

Bayroff, A. G., & Seeley, L. C. An exploratory study of branching tests. U. S. Army BSRL, Technical Research Note 188, June 1967.

Bellman, R. *Dynamic programming*. Princeton, N.J.: Princeton University Press, 1957.

Bellman, R., & Dreyfus, S. E. *Applied dynamic programming*. Princeton, N.J.: Princeton University Press, 1962.

Bloom, B. S. Some theoretical issues relating to educational evaluation. In R. Tyler (Ed.), *Educational evaluation: New roles, new means.* 68th Yearbook, Part II. Chicago: National Society for the Study of Education, 1969. Pp. 26–50.

Bloom, B. S. Learning for mastery. In J. T. Hastings & G. F. Madaus (Eds.), *Formative and summative evaluation of student learning.* New York: McGraw-Hill, 1970, in press.

Bolvin, J. O. Evaluating teacher functions. Paper presented at meeting of the American Educational Research Association, New York, February 1967.

Bormuth, J. R. Empirical determinants of the instructional reading level. Paper presented at the International Reading Association Conference, Boston, April 1968.

Bormuth, J. R. *On the theory of achievement test items*. Chicago: University of Chicago Press, 1970.

Bracht, G. H., & Glass, G. V. The external validity of experiments. *American Educational Research Journal*, 1968, **5,** 437–474.

Bratten, J. E. *Educational applications of information management systems.* Santa Monica, Calif.: System Development Corporation, June 1968.

Brudner, H. J. Computer-managed instruction. *Science*, 1968, **162,** 970–976.

Bruner, J. S. Some theorems on instruction illustrated with reference to mathematics. In E. Hilgard (Ed.), *Theories of learning and instruction.* 63rd Yearbook, Part I. Chicago: University of Chicago, National Society for the Study of Education, 1964. Pp. 306–335.

Bunderson, C. V. The computer and instructional design. In W. Holtzman (Ed.), *Computer-assisted instruction, testing, and guidance.* New York: Harper & Row, 1970, in press.

Campbell, D. T., & Stanley, J. C. Experimental and quasi-experimental designs for research on teaching. In N. L. Gage (Ed.), *Handbook of research on teaching.* Chicago: Rand McNally, 1963. Pp. 171–246.

Carlson, R. C. *Adoption of educational innovations.* Eugene, Ore.: University of Oregon, Center for the Advanced Study of Educational Administration, 1965.

Carroll, J. B. A model of school learning. *Teachers College Record*, 1963, **64,** 723–733.

Cleary, T. A., Linn, R. L., & Rock, D. A. An exploratory study of programmed tests. *Educational and Psychological Measurement*, 1968, **28,** 347–349.

Cooley, W. W. Computer-assisted instructional management. In *Encyclopedia of education.* New York: Macmillan, 1970, in press.

Cooley, W. W., & Glaser, R. The computer and individualized instruction. *Science*, 1969, **166,** 574–582.

Cox, R. C., & Boston, M. E. Diagnosis of pupil achievement in the Individually Prescribed Instruction project. (Working Paper 15.) Pittsburgh, Pa.: University of Pittsburgh, Learning Research and Development Center, 1967.

Cox, R. C., & Graham, G. T. The development of a sequentially scaled achievement test. *Journal of Educational Measurement*, 1966, **3,** 147–150.

Cronbach, L. J. The two disciplines of scientific psychology. *American Psychologist*, 1957, **12,** 671–684.

Cronbach, L. J. Course improvement through evaluation. *Teachers College Record*, 1963, **64,** 672–683.

Cronbach, L. J. How can instruction be adapted to individual differences? In R. M. Gagné (Ed.), *Learning and individual differences.* Columbus, Ohio: Charles E. Merrill, 1967. Pp. 23–29.

Cronbach, L. J., & Gleser, G. C. *Psychological tests and personnel decisions.* Urbana: University of Illinois Press, 1965.

Dubois, P. H. The design of correlational studies in training. In R. Glaser (Ed.), *Training research and education.* New York: Wiley, 1965. Pp. 63–86.

Duncanson, J. P. *Intelligence and the ability to*

learn. Princeton, N.J.: Educational Testing Service, 1964.

Ebel, R. L. Content-standard test scores. *Educational and Psychological Measurement*, 1962, **22**, 15–25.

Ferster, C. B., & Skinner, B. F. *Schedules of reinforcement*. New York: Appleton-Century-Crofts, 1957.

Ferguson, R. L. The development, implementation, and evaluation of a computer-assisted branched test for a program of individually prescribed instruction. Unpublished doctoral dissertation, University of Pittsburgh, 1969.

Flanagan, J. C. Units, scores, and norms. In E. F. Lindquist (Ed.), *Educational measurement*. Washington: American Council on Education, 1951. Pp. 695–763.

Flanagan, J. C. The identification, development, and utilization of human talents: The American high school student. Pittsburgh, Pa.: University of Pittsburgh, 1964. [USOE Cooperative Research Project No. 635]

Flanagan, J. C. The assessment of the effectiveness of educational programs. Unpublished paper circulated May 1966. (mimeo)

Flanagan, J. C. Functional education for the seventies. *Phi Delta Kappan*, 1967, **49**, 27–32.

Flanagan, J. C. Program for learning in accordance with needs. *Psychology in the Schools*, 1969, **6**, 133–136.

Fleishman, E. A. The description and prediction of perceptual-motor skill learning. In R. Glaser (Ed.), *Training research and education*. New York: Wiley, 1965. Pp. 137–175.

Fleishman, E. A. Individual differences and motor learning. In R. M. Gagné (Ed.), *Learning and individual differences*. Columbus, Ohio: Charles E. Merrill, 1967. Pp. 165–191.

Frymier, J. R. National assessment. In F. T. Wilhelm (Ed.), *Evaluation as feedback and guide*. Washington: Association for Supervision and Curriculum Development and National Education Association, 1967. Pp. 249–259.

Gagné, R. M. The acquisition of knowledge. *Psychological Review*, 1962, **69**, 355–365.

Gagné, R. M. The analysis of instructional objectives for the design of instruction. In R. Glaser (Ed.), *Teaching machines and programed learning. II: Data and directions*. Washington: National Education Association, 1965. Pp. 21–65. (a)

Gagné, R. M. *The conditions of learning*. New York: Holt, Rinehart & Winston, 1965. (b)

Gagné, R. M. Curriculum research and the promotion of learning. In *Perspectives of curriculum evaluation*. (AERA Monograph Series on Curriculum Evaluation, No. 1.) Chicago: Rand McNally, 1967. Pp. 19–38. (a)

Gagné, R. M. (Ed.) *Learning and individual differences*. Columbus, Ohio: Charles E. Merrill, 1967. (b)

Gagné, R. M. Learning hierarchies. *Educational Psychologist*, 1968, **6**(November), 1–9.

Gagné, R. M. Instructional variables and learning outcomes. In M. C. Wittrock & D. Wiley (Eds.), *Evaluation of instruction*. New York: Holt, Rinehart & Winston, 1970.

Gagné, R. M., Mayor, J. R., Garstens, H. L., & Paradise, N. E. Factors in acquiring knowledge of a mathematical task. *Psychological Monographs*, 1962, **76** (7, Whole No. 526).

Gagné, R. M., & Paradise, N. E. Abilities and learning sets in knowledge acquisition. *Psychological Monographs*, 1961, **75** (14, Whole No. 578).

Gane, C. P., & Woolfenden, P. J. Algorithms and the analysis of skilled behavior. *Industrial Training International*, July 1968.

Gibson, E. J. Learning to read. *Science*, 1965, **148**, 1066–1072.

Glaser, R. Some research problems in automated instruction: Instructional objectives and subject-matter structure. In J. E. Coulson (Ed.), *Programmed learning and computer-based instruction*. New York: Wiley, 1962. Pp. 67–85.

Glaser, R. Instructional technology and the measurement of learning outcomes. *American Psychologist*, 1963, **18**, 519–521.

Glaser, R. Adapting the elementary school curriculum to individual performance. In *Proceedings of the 1967 Invitational Conference on Testing Problems*. Princeton, N.J.: Educational Testing Service, 1967. Pp. 3–36.

Glaser, R. Evaluation of instruction and changing educational models. In M. C. Wittrock & D. E. Wiley (Eds.), *Evaluation of instruction*. New York: Holt, Rinehart, & Winston, 1970.

Glaser, R., & Cox, R. C. Criterion-referenced testing for the measurement of educational outcomes. In R. Weisgerber (Ed.), *Instructional process and media innovation*. Chicago: Rand McNally, 1968. Pp. 545–550.

Glaser, R., & Klaus, D. J. Proficiency measurement: Assessing human performance. In R. Gagné (Ed.), *Psychological principles in system development*. New York: Holt, Rinehart, & Winston, 1962. Pp. 419–474.

Glaser, R., Damrin, D. E., & Gardner, F. M. The tab item: A technique for the measurement of proficiency in diagnostic problem solving tasks. *Educational and Psychological Measurement*, 1954, **14**, 283–293.

Green, B. F. Comments on tailored testing. In W. Holtzman (Ed.), *Computer-assisted instruction, testing, and guidance*. New York: Harper & Row, 1970, in press.

Groen, G. J., & Atkinson, R. C. Models for

optimizing the learning process. *Psychological Bulletin*, 1966, **66**, 309–320.

Heathers, G. Grouping. In *Encyclopedia of educational research*. (4th ed.) New York: Macmillan, 1969. Pp. 559–570.

Hively, W. A framework for the analysis of elementary reading behavior. *American Educational Research Journal*, 1966, **3**, 89–103. (a)

Hively, W. Preparation of a programmed course in algebra for secondary school teachers: A report to the National Science Foundation. Minnesota State Department of Education, Minnesota National Laboratory, 1966. (b)

Hively, W., Patterson, H. L., & Page, S. A "universe-defined" system of arithmetic achievement tests. *Journal of Educational Measurement*, 1968, **5**, 275–290.

Holland, J. G. A quantitative measure for programmed instruction. *American Educational Research Journal*, 1967, **4**, 87–101.

Hull, C. L. The place of innate individual and species differences in a natural-science theory of behavior. *Psychological Review*, 1945, **52**, 55–60.

Kersh, B. Y. Programing classroom instruction. In R. Glaser (Ed.), *Teaching machines and programed learning. II: Data and directions*. Washington: National Education Association, 1965. Pp. 321–368.

Kriewall, T. E., & Hirsch, E. The development and interpretation of criterion-referenced tests. Paper presented at meeting of the American Educational Research Association, Los Angeles, February 1969.

Lindgren, B. W., & McElrath, G. W. *Introduction to probability and statistics*. (2nd ed.) New York: Macmillan, 1966.

Lindquist, E. F. Preliminary considerations in objective test construction. In E. F. Lindquist (Ed.), *Educational measurement*. Washington: American Council on Education, 1951, Pp. 119–158.

Lindquist, E. F. *The impact of machines on educational measurement*. Bloomington, Ind.: Phi Delta Kappa International, 1968.

Lindquist, E. F., & Hieronymus, A. N. *Teachers manual: Iowa tests of basic skills*. Boston: Houghton-Mifflin, 1964.

Lindvall, C. M., & Bolvin, J. O. Programed instruction in the schools: An application of programing principles in "Individually Prescribed Instruction." In P. Lange (Ed.), *Programed instruction*. 66th Yearbook, Part II. Chicago: National Society for the Study of Education, 1967. Pp. 217–254.

Lindvall, C. M., Cox, R. C., & Bolvin, J. O. Evaluation as a tool in curriculum development: The IPI evaluation program. (AERA Monograph Series on Curriculum Evaluation.) Chicago: Rand McNally, 1970.

Lindvall, C. M., & Nitko, A. J. Criterion-referenced tests: A rationale for their development and an empirical investigation of their use. Paper presented at meeting of the National Council on Measurement in Education, Los Angeles, February 1969.

Lord, F. M. Some test theory for tailored testing. In W. Holtzman (Ed.), *Computer-assisted instruction, testing, and guidance*. New York: Harper & Row, 1970, in press.

Lord, F. M., & Novick, M. R. *Statistical theories of mental test score*. Reading, Mass.: Addison-Wesley, 1968.

Lubin, A. The interpretation of significant interaction. *Educational and Psychological Measurement*, 1961, **21**, 807–817.

Lumsdaine, A. A. Assessing the effectiveness of instructional programs. In R. Glaser (Ed.), *Teaching machines and programed learning. II: Data and directions*. Washington: National Education Association, 1965. Pp. 267–320.

McGuire, C. H. An evaluation model for professional education—medical education. In *Proceedings of the 1967 Invitational Conference on Testing Problems*. Princeton, N.J.: Educational Testing Service, 1968. Pp. 37–52.

Mechner, F. Science education and behavioral technology. In R. Glaser (Ed.), *Teaching machines and programed learning. II: Data and directions*. Washington: National Education Association, 1965. Pp. 441–507.

Mechner, F. Behavioral analysis and instructional sequencing. In P. Lange (Ed.), *Programed instruction*. 66th Yearbook, Part II. Chicago: National Society for the Study of Education, 1967. Pp. 81–103.

Melton, A. W. *Categories of human learning*. New York: Academic Press, 1964.

Miller, R. B. Analysis and specification of behavior for training. In R. Glaser (Ed.), *Training research and education*. New York: Wiley, 1965. Pp. 31–62.

Nesbit, M. Y. The CHILD program: Computer help in learning diagnosis of arithmetic scores. (Curriculum Bulletin 7-E-B.) Miami, Fla.: Dade County Board of Public Instruction, 1966.

Newell, A., & Forehand, G. On process measurement, computer simulation and theoretical models. In H. H. Harmon, C. E. Helm, & D. E. Loye (Eds.), *Computer-assisted testing: Proceedings of a conference on CAT*. Princeton, N.J.: Educational Testing Service, 1968.

Noble, C. E., Noble, J. L., & Alcock, W. T. Prediction of individual differences in human trial-and-error learning. *Perceptual and Motor Skills*, 1958, **8**, 151–172.

Osburn, H. G. Item sampling for achievement testing. *Educational and Psychological Measurement*, 1968, **28,** 95–104.

Popham, W. J. Instructional product development: Two approaches to training. *AV Communication Review*, 1967, **15,** 402–411.

Popham, W. J., & Husek, T. R. Implications of criterion-referenced measurement. *Journal of Educational Measurement*, 1969, **6,** 1–9.

Rahmlow, H. F. A measurement design to facilitate optimum efficiency in diagnosing student needs. Paper presented at meeting of the National Council on Measurement in Education, Los Angeles, February 1969.

Reitman, W. *Cognition and thought.* New York: Wiley, 1965.

Resnick, L. B. Design of an early learning curriculum. (Working Paper 16.) Pittsburgh, Pa.: University of Pittsburgh, Learning Research and Development Center, 1967.

Resnick, L. B., & Wang, M. C. Approaches to the validation of learning hierarchies. Paper presented at the Eighteenth Annual Western Regional Conference on Testing Problems, San Francisco, May 1969.

Reynolds, B., & Adams, J. A. Psychomotor performance as a function of initial level of ability. *American Journal of Psychology*, 1954, **67,** 268–277.

Roethlisberger, F. J., & Dickson, W. J. *Management and the worker.* Cambridge, Mass.: Harvard University Press, 1939.

Rosner, J., Richman, V., & Scott, R. H. The identification of children with perceptual-motor dysfunction. (Working Paper 47.) Pittsburgh, Pa.: University of Pittsburgh, Learning Research and Development Center, 1969.

Schutz, R. E., Baker, R. L., & Gerlach, V. S. *Measurement procedures in programmed instruction.* Tempe: Arizona State University, Classroom Learning Laboratory, 1964.

Scriven, M. The methodology of evaluation. In *Perspectives of curriculum evaluation.* (AERA Monograph Series on Curriculum Evaluation, No. 1.) Chicago: Rand McNally, 1967. Pp. 39–83.

Sidman, M. *Tactics of scientific research.* New York: Basic Books, 1960.

Simon, H. A., & Newell, A. Information processing in computer and man. *American Scientist*, 1964, **52,** 281–300.

Simon, H. A., & Paige, J. M. Cognitive processes in solving algebra word problems. In B. Kleinmuntz

(Ed.), *Problem solving.* New York: Wiley, 1966. Pp. 51–119.

Skinner, B. F. *The behavior of organisms: An experimental analysis.* New York: Appleton-Century-Crofts, 1938.

Spence, K. W. *Behavior theory and conditioning.* New Haven, Conn.: Yale University Press, 1956.

Spence, K. W. *Behavior theory and learning.* Englewood Cliffs, N.J.: Prentice-Hall, 1960.

Stake, R. E. Learning parameters, aptitudes, and achievement. *Psychometric Monographs*, 1961, No. 9.

Suchman, E. A. *Evaluation research: Principles and practice in public service & social action programs.* New York: Russell Sage Foundation, 1967.

Suppes, P. Mathematical concept formation in children. *American Psychologist*, 1966, **21,** 139–150.

Taba, H. Teaching strategies and cognitive functioning in elementary school children. San Francisco: San Francisco State College, 1966. [Cooperative Research Project No. 2404.]

Thorndike, E. L. *Educational psychology.* Vol. III. New York: Columbia University, Teachers College, 1914.

Tyler, R. W. The objectives and plans for a national assessment of educational progress. *Journal of Educational Measurement*, 1966, **3,** 1–4.

Tyler, R. W. Changing concepts of educational evaluation. In *Perspectives of curriculum evaluation.* (AERA Monograph Series on Curriculum Evaluation, No. 1.) Chicago: Rand McNally, 1967. Pp. 13–18.

Tyler, R. W. (Ed.) *Educational evaluation: New roles, new means.* 68th Yearbook, Part II. Chicago: National Society for the Study of Education, 1969.

Wald, A. *Sequential analysis.* New York: Wiley, 1947.

Wilde, D. J., & Beightler, C. S. *Foundations of optimization.* Englewood Cliffs, N.J.: Prentice-Hall, 1967.

Wolf, M. M., & Risley, T. R. Reinforcement: Applied research. *The nature of reinforcement.* Columbus, Ohio: Charles E. Merrill, 1970, in press.

Woodrow, H. A. The effect of practice on groups of different initial ability. *Journal of Educational Psychology*, 1938, **29,** 268–278.

Woodrow, H. A. The ability to learn. *Psychological Review*, 1946, **53,** 147–158.

Zeaman, D., & Kaufman, H. Individual differences and theory in a motor learning task. *Psychological Monographs*, 1955, **69**(6, Whole No. 391).

18. Use of Measurement in Student Planning and Guidance

J. A. Davis
Educational Testing Service, Southeastern Office

STUDENT USE OF MEASUREMENT INFORMATION

It would seem that measures of individual traits or competencies should be useful not only for the teacher or other educational agents who intervene in the life and development of students but also for the student himself. Points are reached in the educational process where the student or his parents have some options or where at the very least the teacher or the educational system does not exercise complete control. Even before these points are reached, the student's attitudes and conduct in the learning situation are a product not only of the situation itself but also of his perception of who and what he is, what he enjoys, and what he can or cannot do. All of these perceptions affect his responses to the ongoing learning situation.

The essential promise of measurement for use in student planning is twofold. First, it should provide a more systematic, objective, precise, and valid set of evaluations than that provided by the residue of the welter of experiences and formal or subtle evaluations gone before. It provides an opportunity for verifying, refuting, or amending previously held convictions. Second, measurement promises new information relevant to the quality and style of the individual's performance in future situations or information that may not be too easy for him to extract from prior experiences. A fringe benefit of each of these promises is the identification and highlighting of some of the traits and qualities that study of individual development has shown are important to consider in planning, in a context that specifies the nature of that importance (e.g. the validity question).

In examining how measurement may indeed live up to the first promise, one must ask what is wrong with using the "residue" of self-evaluations from experiences gone before in the life and education of the student. Should not any planning be heavily based on prior experience? Does the competent guidance specialist or teacher not lean heavily on prior evaluations to determine if a measure is creditable?

There are several problems which may limit or interfere with the evaluative attitudes the student holds toward himself as a function of prior experiences and their built-in evaluation procedures. First, these experiences may not be consistent, or they may be contradictory to other experiences outside the school. Or, the particular needs of the student may interfere with his assessment of himself or with his acceptance of evaluations.

More important for guidance purposes, however, is the fact that the student's experience has been restricted to a limited set of teachers, texts, tasks, and evaluation procedures. Also, he acquires a personal interpretation of evaluations by observing where he stands among others in his family, class, or school. In future educational or life situations, the authority, content, evaluation procedures, and comparative groups may change. Measurement provides a mechanism for utilizing new (and, hopefully, better for planning purposes) authority, content, and evaluation procedures and for extending the comparative base to new groups.

The great bulk of the ongoing evaluational program of the school is concerned with the monitoring and management of student progress. Some formal measures may be taken purely for teacher use toward the more effective attainment of instructional goals, yet have utility for the student for planning purposes. In addition, the science of measurement, wherein the utility of measures is frequently predicated on predictive validity, may yield instruments that are not particularly appropriate to weave into the evaluational fabric of the educational program but that bear on questions important for the student to consider in planning.

The use of measurement in student planning and guidance, then, is predicated on the assumptions that options appear in the educational process wherein the student must make his own decisions and live with them and that measurement may afford useful information that he does not already have.

PROVISION OF MEASUREMENT
INFORMATION TO THE STUDENT

In the routine conduct of an educational program, the curriculum, texts, and teachers determine what is to be measured. The range of standings on a measure that is found in a particular class or school determines, by and large, the qualitative meanings given to different standings. These standings are generally communicated to students (and to their parents) with minimal ado through the provision of scored or graded tests and the report card. The A through F or other conventional schemas acquire meaning for the student through his general observation of how others, particularly the teachers and school officials, seem to view the ratings or what actions they take as a consequence of them. It must be recognized that this measurement is obtained primarily to aid the school and its staff in planning educational treatment.

The provision of measurement information to the student for *his* use in planning, however, requires a special kind of intervention if it is to be maximally effective or, for that matter, if it is not to be dangerously misleading in some instances. This intervention requires a good working knowledge of the principles of measurement, applied carefully and rigorously in the performance of two essential tasks. The first of these is the selection of qualities to be measured and the instruments or procedures for providing the measures, with special attention to what the student may find useful for his needs and purposes. The second essential task

requiring the highest order of knowledge of measurement is the effective communication to the student of the true meanings and limitations of the measures provided. It is to the performance of these two tasks that discussion now turns.

SELECTION OF MEASURES
FOR THE STUDENT'S USE

The considerations in selecting measures for student use in planning are quite simple and straightforward:

1. What are the alternatives he faces? What decisions must he make?

2. What information about himself, these alternatives, and the consequences of various decisions does he need to make an informed choice or to guide him at subsequent choice points?

3. When are the strategic times for communicating this information? At what points in the decision-making process is it needed if the best use is to be made of it?

4. Of the needed information, what parts may be provided by tests or other measures?

5. Considering the level of the student and the difficulty of the concepts encompassed by the relevant measures, how comprehensible will the measurement information be? Can the validity of the measure be described faithfully in terms of constructs that the student may be able to manipulate, or can projections be made to probable performance on criteria that the student can understand and appreciate?

6. Are there adequate opportunities for transmitting the data and interpretations to the student, for testing his understanding of it, and for observing the quality of the use he makes of it?

As reasonable as these considerations may seem, they are frequently ignored in practice. Too often, measures are drawn only from those already available, wherein measures have been selected for institutional rather than individual purposes. Measurement information is frequently transmitted at times chosen because they do not interfere too greatly with the instructional program or at the point where immediate decisions are required by the program.

The best models for test interpretation have come from the field of counseling and guidance, where communication is viewed as a one-to-one matter; yet, few institutions have sufficient guidance staff to permit much time with individual students. Relevant information beyond that available from measurement (sometimes that needed to place measurement information in a proper perspective) is underemphasized. These realities and the reasons for them need to be kept in mind as the steps in selecting measures for student use in planning are examined.

Alternatives Facing the Student

There are two kinds of situations in which the student may be confronted with alternatives and where formal consideration, planning, and decision may be necessary. The first kind of situation is where there are clear options among alternative courses or programs. In the elementary school, such options are generally confined to such extracurricular activities as band or school clubs, although as one nears the high school stage some specific course options may be made available. The start of high school frequently involves a choice between programs (e.g. academic versus vocational) and almost always choices among courses within programs.

The most highly touted choice point during the years spanned by the elementary and secondary schools is, of course, that which comes at the end of this educational program. Particular attention to the alternatives the student faces at this point is reasonable; the school will lose its direct control over the student when he is gone, yet depend on the lives and contributions of its graduates for the test of the ultimate validity of its program. There is not only the need to prevent cancellation of educational benefits by inept and frequently irreversible choices, but also the need to maintain some focus on the alternatives graduates select and on their performance in these alternatives, with a view to the continuing improvement of the educational program.

The number of options at the end of secondary school expands suddenly and tremendously. For some, the choice will be among vocations and entry strategies; for others, among various opportunities for continuing education or training. The current national emphasis on financial aid to students and on the adjustment of entrance standards or the provision to offer special remedial work to accommodate cultural minorities means that for more students than ever before there is a choice between work or college. A period in the armed services may represent still another option.

In helping a student select among these alternatives, a cardinal rule to follow is that few if any students are aware of the tremendous diversity of options. They have had little chance to observe many work roles; the numbers of institutions of further education they can name is sharply limited. Many students see military service as a postponement strategy or rationalize that it may provide time, maturity, and the same set of fresh options they already have.

In understanding these alternatives well enough to deal with the selection of measurement information to transmit to the student, the intervening agent must develop and rely on several sources. The most immediately available are the various published materials about educational and vocational opportunities. A second source of information can be developed by a program of follow-up studies of graduates, both where they go and how they perform. And, although the alternatives the student himself perceives come without guarantee of completeness or accuracy of perception, these should also be known.

Options among alternative courses and programs (or, to some extent, among vocational or retraining opportunities) continue to occur for the student. In practice, however, the responsibility for aiding the student passes more and more, if to anyone, to the academic adviser or instructor, the placement official, or the employment agency, where measurement specialization is absent or limited. Options and choice-points continue to exist, however, and, although the student's accumulating experience may make professional assistance less urgent, good cases can be made for it. Frequently in the college or work situation, measurement specialists may find or create roles, as well as enjoy more leisure to study internal options and the characteristics and performance of the incumbents.

There are other situations where the options for the student are of a more subtle kind. These are the situations where planning and choice is not directed to alternative courses, programs, or activities but rather to alternative responses to a situation wherein the student is entrapped. These are more frequently apparent when the student experiences visible difficulties but may occur when progress seems normal. The classic situation is when the student appears to be achieving at levels below that of his peers in ability. The case can be made, however, that the criteria by which students are evaluated have flaws. Is the student responding to his work in such a way that skills and knowledge will be retained beyond the marking period? Are his response styles appropriate and efficient? Is he growing in interest and appreciation for his subjects in particular and for learning in general?

Observation of students is useful in determining the alternative responses; influencing or changing these responses through the transmission of measurement information to students is difficult, for the responses are generally the result of many experiences gone before. Nevertheless, the measurement specialist may be able to use tests not only to diagnose response styles but also to help the student detect and explore other modes of response.

Information Needed by the Student in Planning

Too frequently, the measurement specialist in practice is sensitive only to the kinds of information measurement may provide. A prime example is the matter of choice of college, where rank on ability among entering freshmen, or even probability of survival, may be communicated, without regard for information on program, cost, or housing pattern. This limitation probably occurs because the measurement specialist is just that or because his expertise is too completely demanded for purely testing activities.

Absence of concern for the total body of information that the student may find useful in planning is dangerous. Tests and other measures of human performance tend to be viewed by the lay public as possessing more authority than their actual reliability and validity would indicate and may distract the student from other considerations. The measurement specialist who uses tests in guidance activities is not immune to this hazard; for example, in precollege counseling where only normative information is available on entering college freshmen Scholastic Aptitude Test performance in a set of colleges, he finds it easy to overlook the fact that attrition standards of the colleges (which may vary from 5 to 80 percent) have real implications for a candidate's probability of survival. For his own as well as the student's total perspective, then, the intervening agent should attempt to inventory all the information that may be useful in a given planning situation.

Strategic Times for Communicating Information

Although the management of educational programs encourages the formulation of the concept of choice points, the study of human development and decision making indicates that it is more useful to consider choice as a *process* rather than as an *event*. Careful planning is achieved over time, rather than in a blinding flash of insight or sudden acquisition of new information. This is because almost any planning involves multiple considerations of uncertain hierarchy and because, as long as there are errors of measurement and errors of estimate, tests most appropriately provide hypotheses for further testing.

Too frequently, the pressures in the educational program make measurement and other aid to student planning an emergency last-minute exercise when choices must be made. It may be far more efficient to anticipate some choice points with a considerable time margin. The use of the Preliminary Scholastic Aptitude Test (directed toward high school juniors), or similar data that may be obtained even earlier, may serve to narrow the search of the student for an appropriate college, as well as permit more time for other considerations to be infused into his planning.

If educational personnel tend to be guilty of delaying aid beyond the times that are most suitable, students tend to behave even more badly on this score. The younger, or the less mature, that the individual is, the more difficult it is for him to take seriously an action that he must take some time in the future. The implication is that the intervening agent who would see measurement information used wisely and well may need to concern himself with interesting and motivating students in the options they will face. For example, college days need not be scheduled for, or oriented toward, only those who must complete their applications in the next three months. It is well to note, too, that popular prejudices that sometimes interfere with realistic aspirations grow with age and unguided experience; early elementary school children may be better able to see the honest satisfactions that can be experienced in both arc welding and business management than are high school students who have developed firm status hierarchies. Early exposure to relevant information may keep some channels and options open.

Identification of Measures That May Add Pertinent Information

Too frequently, tests and other measures are invoked in the student planning situation simply because measurement seems modern and scientific or because testing gives the intervening agent something to do to which the student may respond appreciatively. The position must be taken that the intervening agent should first examine the alternatives in a planning situation, then determine what information is needed, and then decide if measurement fills any gaps.

Going at the problem this way (rather than first asking what measurement may provide and then asking what else is needed) may seem awkward and hardly within the purview of the measurement specialist. It is true that good measurement practice may reveal in part what information is relevant and what is not. Yet, the measurement specialist is peculiarly susceptible to becoming impacted with the technology he practices, for he deals constantly with situations in which there appear to be great discrepancies between facts and popular conceptions. Special effort seems necessary if he is to be sure that he is dispensing pertinent information.

There is some justification for this kind of caution in that measurement information is restricted to the limits of its demonstrated validity. Even if the major core of validity information is predictive in nature, the criterion may have flaws; and the assumption that the student being measured is like the members of the validation sample in all important ways is always tenuous. And, of course, the options in some planning situations are such that there are no formal measures with reasonable certainty of validity. For example, there is little that tests might provide the exceptional young lady with early acceptance at Vassar who is trying to decide whether to invest a last elective in home economics or typing.

The kinds of information that measurement may add draw precisely from the specific validities of the measures used. Measures based essentially on content validity may bear on adequacy of preparation, both in terms of desirable prior achievement and readiness and in terms of tool skills. Where there has been a predictive study, or where the measures have been applied to groups involved in the planning options, the measurement may provide insights into the nature of the new groups and the probable feel of the competition, as well as probabilities of success. If measures are interpreted skillfully, the student may discover some of the problems he may expect and where he may need special care or effort to offset these potential liabilities.

Comprehensibility of the Measurement Information

Not enough is known about the kinds of concepts that students can manipulate meaningfully at various ages or levels of development. Yet, careful questioning will show that the average ten-year-old has some difficulty even distinguishing between ability, achievement, and interest. Some of the constructs that are "old hat" to measurement specialists or teachers are quite difficult for younger students or those of limited verbal ability (some personality variables or cognitive styles are good cases in point). The probable level of readiness of the student to understand and apply measurement information appropriately must be reckoned with, or the necessary communication cannot take place.

Opportunities for Transmitting Measurement Information to Students

It has been noted in passing that the best model for transmitting information to the student is the direct, personal, and usually private counseling situation. This provides an opportunity, if only a fleeting one, to check on understanding and to observe the beginning struggle of the student to apply the information. A persistent problem in most situations, however, is providing time for one or more individual conferences to take place with many students.

Several easements have appeared and can be used in some instances. One of these is group interpretation, where it has been found that under skillful direction the members of the group may be quite effective in detecting and showing one another important limitations in the significance of test results. Another is expansion of the team of interpreters beyond guidance personnel and into the rank and file of teachers. Since most school staffs vary in their knowledge of measurement, the more skilled among them need to devote time to in-service training and to the contrivance of aids to interpretation.

Many test publishers now provide formal score report forms and supporting materials for use in transmitting scores to students and their parents. Two arguments for their use are that reputable publishers can utilize top measurement talent and extensive pilot testing in contriving presentation forms and accompanying interpretative materials and that a good record that the student may keep may hold the specific meanings over time better than memory of an interview in which many things were discussed.

Nevertheless, any such materials should be examined carefully to determine their suitability, clarity, and integrity with regard to the limitations of the data presented. For example, do the presentations describe clearly what was measured, in ways that would inhibit ready over-generalizing, or do they give little more than the names of the tests? Are limitations, such as those that might accrue in an achievement test from sampling items from texts used elsewhere, spelled out? Are scores shown in a way that illustrates unmistakably the error of measurement? Are comparison groups clearly defined, and do they have any real relevance for the student?

Even when the muster of this kind of inspection is passed, the careful teacher or counselor should still test the prepared interpretations with a range of real students to determine if more elaboration is needed to sharpen understandings or to correct misinterpretations by the student. It is always desirable for any materials to be backed up by opportunities for some give and take between students and the teacher or counselor—both before and after the student has shared the information with his parents or others.

INTERPRETATION OF MEASUREMENT INFORMATION TO THE STUDENT

The essential problem in transmitting measurement information to the student in such a way that he may make sound use of it is the problem of teaching, usually in limited time, the basic principles of measurement. A factor that makes this less than impossible is that a good, illustrative, and personal example—the student's score—is available for use in the teaching situation. The student does not need to know how to compute an error of measurement or a validity coefficient, but rather, faced with a particular datum, what it means for him.

Care in setting the stage for the presentation of measurement information is helpful. To the layman, tests have a terrible authority and preciseness. Illustration of the error of measurement can afford a first step in stripping some of that authority away. Most students can understand, if it is pointed out, that test authors vary in what they consider important to include in a test.

Another helpful strategy is the transmission to the student of the nature of what he may expect. The point that clear and sharp answers are not likely to emerge, that measurement data may bring new complexities into planning, should be made before committing the student to testing. The notion that measurement provides most appropriately a source of hypotheses for further testing can be demonstrated by citing a range of possible scores and following each score with a "What if you . . ." kind of question.

An essential preliminary to the interpretation of measurement information is the matter of helping the student phrase the proper questions. He is seldom very expert in this; his stated concerns follow such patterns as How good am I on thus-and-so? or Which college should I choose according to the tests? Answers to the latter question are difficult if not impossible to come by; the simple answer to the former question of "You scored in the top five percent" may satisfy the student and leave him chafing to go home, but is, of course, incomplete and meaningless so far as specific decisions are concerned.

Phrasing good questions for measurement information to answer is primarily a matter of casting them in the form and content that the particular validity bases of the measures to be used actually possess. Where these questions fall short of the total problem, the student and the intervening agent may phrase other questions and speculate how and where the answers may be found.

Upon obtaining a measurement, most students will require help in understanding the system in which the score is reported. For most purposes, a percentile system, together with a clear description of the normative group, is readily comprehensible. The use of a graphic representation of the normal distribution curve is also frequently helpful. This can serve to illustrate that there are many peers for the average student, or that absolute differences between the 50th and the 55th percentile are not the

same as those between the 90th and the 95th percentile. The chart designed by and available from the Psychological Corporation (see Gronlund, 1968, p. 120) is a useful visual aid.

Special care should be exercised to relate scores to meaningful normative groups. Great care has been exercised by some test developers to contrive score distributions based on national samples. However, the student lives within, and will later come in contact or compete with, less than that total range of humanity. The normative groups most useful for institutional or program evaluation may not be particularly relevant (in fact, may be terribly misleading) to the student for his planning purposes.

The simplest example is the student at a selective preparatory school who is concerned with his chances in an Ivy League College and who is told that he is in the top five percent of the general population in scholastic aptitude. If the total class of the college is within that same range, the student learns nothing of where he would stand in the class. Another example is the student who is a member of a cultural minority group where scores on some measures may be sharply restricted and for whom national grade-level norms are used.

It is important not only to choose carefully and describe faithfully the normative group on which a standing is based but also to provide some indication of the standings of other groups. Most students are but vaguely aware of how much difference there is, say, in averages on scholastic ability for the general population as opposed to high school seniors or college graduates, or, for that matter, in averages for entering freshmen at different colleges. Normative bases should be used that reflect the levels that the student occupies or may move into, but sometimes he needs the perspective that the performance of quite divergent groups may illustrate.

There is now fairly good agreement that such formulations as the IQ or the grade-level equivalent have severe limitations as indices on which scores may be transmitted to students. Although there is a built-in normative reference, the comparison groups are concealed. Particular scores become a kind of ultimate end in themselves. Grade-level equivalents have the problems that similar standings may be obtained by getting a lot of simple material correct or by performing well on the more difficult items; they also conceal the normal range of grade-level equivalents found in any given class.

Knowing one's standing on a measure, the error in the measurement, and the nature and performance of one or more normative groups is not enough. The student must place some value on his performance, must form some expectancies of his success in one or more concrete situations in the future. What are the implications of his standing? What does his score mean for him? This, of course, is the central and crucial question of validity.

In the case of *content* validity, the meaning of the measure draws heavily on the review of the kinds of behavior sampled by the test, on what authority and from what item pool the sample was drawn, and on the credibility and generalizability of that authority. (The content should, of course, be amenable to easy description and represent something as much in the "going currency" of the layman as of the measurement specialist.) Typical questions the measures may answer include: What is my competency in solving problems in algebra? What levels of French vocabulary can I handle? Do I have a good basis for beginning a study of calculus? Do I need to review the rules of grammar? The student needs some help in most cases in judging the adequacy, for his purposes, of the particular definition of a content area or in understanding how this definition differs from those probably less formal definitions he has had before.

A measure with construct validity, so far as the problem of interpretation to a student is concerned, is simply one with a more complex or technical kind of content validity. As construct validation is a never-ending proposition, it is directed toward the education of the measurement specialist rather than toward the student. Some constructs are relatively straightforward (psychologists are in agreement as to their definition), and the construct can be

readily communicated by stating the elements in the definition. Other constructs are more complex, or encompass behavior of vague practical relevance in planning, or differ in important ways from the popular use of the language with which they are described. The interpretation of such measures is therefore a matter of helping the student become his own clinician and preparing him to continue on his own the defining of and searching for meaning of the construct.

Measures with concurrent validity are particularly useful for providing a description of prospective environments—or more precisely, some characteristics of the inhabitants of those environments. Questions need to be raised as to whether these patterns are the function of experience in the environment, or of natural or artificial selectivity; and, the point needs to be made that handicaps are offset by assets, and that there are tolerances to accommodate a variety of people.

Measures with predictive validity, though troublesome unfortunately to some guidance specialists of purely clinical bent, probably lend themselves to the most honest and communicable interpretation. With the advent of modern data-processing methods, more and more prediction information is available in a usable form such as an expectancy table. Here, the focus can be directly on a statement of the implications for future situations, because specific criteria are bound to the measure and the error of estimate provides the probability that various levels of criterion performance will be attained. The "norms" are no longer scores of some varied group that also suffered the measurement, but individuals with standings like the student and of an observable range of criterion performance. The fact that a particular variance in performance is observed among a group of individuals with like scores is a dramatic and creditable demonstration of the bounds of authority of the test. Schrader ("A Taxonomy of Expectancy Tables," in Payne and McMorris, 1967, pp. 209–215) has provided an excellent example of expectancy tables and their use.

Although such interpretation, when specific validity studies make it possible, would seem almost flawless, there are some problems or cautions that the intervening agent should share with the student. One of these is the criterion problem: other criteria than the one employed may be reasonable. In vocational situations, one cannot be sure that criteria will remain fairly similar between one company and another or one supervisor and another. There may be particular handicaps, hidden to the intervening agent and the student, that the student has but which were not shared by others in the validation sample. With the pace of change in instructional methods or levels of students accommodated that exists in the current decade, expectancy tables may become outdated rather quickly.

All of these considerations strengthen some propositions advanced earlier. A measurement is best considered a source of hypotheses for further testing; information provided by measurement alone is seldom, if ever, sufficient for planning. Other information about the nature of the alternatives themselves and their consequences must be introjected, and the specific authority of the measure determined by continuing experience. When the measurement specialist can lead the student to the point where he begins to conduct his own continuing inquiry into the personal validity of the scores he has received, the highest order of success in interpretation has been achieved.

REFERENCES

Berdie, R. F., Layton, W. L., Swanson, E. O., & Hagenah, T. *Testing in guidance and counseling*. New York: McGraw-Hill, 1963.

Chauncey, H., & Dobbin, J. E. *Testing: Its place in education today*. New York: Harper & Row, 1963.

Davis, F. B. *Educational measurements and their interpretation*. Belmont, Calif.: Wadsworth, 1964.

Froehlich, C. P., & Hoyt, K. B. *Guidance testing*. Chicago: Science Research Associates, 1959.

Goldman, L. *Using tests in counseling*. New York: Appleton-Century-Crofts, 1961.

Gronlund, N. E. (Ed.) *Readings in measurement and evaluation*. New York: Macmillan, 1968.

Payne, D. A., & McMorris, R. F. (Eds.) *Educational and psychological measurement*. Waltham, Mass.: Blaisdell, 1967.

Weitz, H. *Behavior change through guidance*. New York: Wiley, 1964.

19. Use of Measurement in Selection and Placement

John R. Hills
Florida State University

CONCEPT OF UTILITY
AND DECISION THEORY

Applications to specific problems of educational selection and placement of the developments discussed in the preceding chapters are the subject of this chapter. The implications and results both from classical procedures and procedures based on decision theory will be examined. Such an examination requires consideration of the concept of utility.

Utility for Society and for Institutions

Decision theory is based on the notion that an institution should make decisions in such a way that the institution gets the most out of its resources. The "most" that it wants to get is what one speaks of when one uses the word "utility." Ordinarily one might say, it gets the most satisfaction, the most benefit, the most payoff. Sometimes the utility can be expressed as money, i.e. decisions are made so that the net income is the greatest that can be derived from applying the resources to the possible alternative courses of action. Other possible scales of utility might, for educational institutions, be such things as the sum of students' scores on standardized tests that the institution is willing to accept as measures of its effectiveness. Or utility might be judged by the average grades of students, or by the number who become National Merit Scholars or Rhodes Scholars or who enter graduate school, or by the number who enter the major state university.

Utility, then, reflects the satisfaction resulting from an action or set of actions. Individuals and organizations may have different points of view about utilities of certain outcomes. In industry, the utility or payoff may be measured in dollars. A rejected applicant contributes zero dollars. In education, society as a whole may view a student who is rejected by a university but who instead goes to a junior college as having definite positive utility (see Cronbach, 1957, p. 680). On the other hand, the university to which the student applied may consider its utility to be derived from the student's progress in understanding, his later ability to contribute to society, and similar things as they reflect favorably on the sound use of the university's resources. A student who is not admitted to the university cannot reflect credit on that university in this way and thus has zero utility for the university. In this sense, educational selection is similar to military or industrial selection.[1]

Utility for Individuals

The individual student also must consider utility as he makes decisions. Individual decisions and institutional decisions both can be based on decision theory models, but the models are not identical. The individual decisions perhaps are best thought of in the frame of reference of counseling, while the institutional decisions are best thought of in the frames of reference of selection, placement, and classification. (For discussion of these terms, the reader is advised to review their presentation by Cronbach in chapter 14, pp. 492–503; see also Cronbach & Gleser, 1965.) A fundamental difference between individual and institutional decisions is that the institution can think of making many similar decisions and averaging its experience across decisions. For instance, it might consider 1,000 candidates for 100 places in an entering freshman class. While it might be wrong in one direction for some of the 100 chosen, it will probably be wrong in the other direction for others, and these errors will tend to balance out. By contrast, the individual cannot reasonably think of making the same deci-

---

[1] A comprehensive mathematical treatment of decision theory related to testing is given by Cronbach and Gleser (1965); see also pages 495–496 of chapter 14.

sion 1,000 times. He is going to decide now which college to attend. If he is wrong, he is wrong from now on. He can change his mind, but he cannot balance this college-choice error against 1,000 other times he might try different colleges.

Individual decisions

Since decision making by the individual is not discussed later in this chapter, how he might proceed using decision theory is described here briefly. The reader will be able to contrast the individual's approach with the institution's approach, upon which the remainder of the chapter centers.

The individual might approach making his decision by a procedure such as the following. The information that the individual is seeking as he makes his decision is what course of action can be expected to yield for him the greatest value or utility. Obtaining that information requires that some other information be known or estimated. The individual must consider what courses of action are open for his reasonable consideration, what the possible outcomes of each of those courses of action might be, what the utility of each possible outcome might be in terms of his values, and how likely each possible outcome would be if that course of action is taken. By summing the products of probabilities multiplied by utilities for each course of action, the individual can compare the expected values of the various courses of action and choose the one with the greatest expected value.

To illustrate, consider a student attempting to choose which college to attend. Suppose that he has narrowed the choice down to three possibilities, colleges I, II, and III. In each of these, the possible outcomes for the individual are grade averages A, B, C, D, and F, for the purpose of this illustration. The probability of occurrence of each of these outcomes at each institution can be calculated through use of the appropriate regression equations for predicting grades from previous performances and test scores. A judgmental scaling method can be used to obtain estimates of the value the student places on obtaining each level of average grade at each institution. The products of value-

placed-on-each-level-of-grade multiplied by probability-of-obtaining-that-level-of-grade can be summed for each college. The colleges then can be compared on the basis of expected value, the one with the largest sum being chosen as the best alternative. A procedure such as this has been described in detail by Hills (1964b); it is based on procedures used in business as described by Schlaifer (1959). With this brief nod to individual decisions, the discussion returns to the chapter's primary concern—the making of decisions by institutions.

SELECTION

Colleges have learned to become selective. Arguments have been presented that there should be no selection in education. For example, Smith (1956) expressed the point of view that the solution to the problem of increasing numbers of applicants for college is not selection if there is any way to expand facilities so that all applicants can be admitted. He based this conclusion on the fact that out of 1,006 graduating students from the University of Kansas on 6 June 1955, 208 had scored below the 50th percentile (University of Kansas incoming students' and national norms) on the *American Council on Education Psychological Examination* and on the *Cooperative English Test*. Smith (1956) asserted that these people would have been jobless if they had not been admitted to college, since "a college degree is necessary to succeed in most fields of endeavor [p. 2]."

There are many hidden assumptions in Smith's argument. However, even the obvious assumptions that (*a*) if selection is introduced the first step should be to reject half of the applicants, (*b*) joblessness is the fate of the person who does not graduate from college, and (*c*) selection should be based on separate consideration of two tests which happen to be available, ignoring any measure of previous performance, are enough to vitiate Smith's case. This apparently was recognized when, in 1962, a panel of educational experts helping Kansas to plan for its next generation suggested that the state institutions had been too generous about admitting and retaining poorly qualified students.

Some colleges learned to be selective many years ago. Others are just beginning to discover that they cannot practice "open" admissions, that they cannot admit anyone who applies. Few colleges exist which do not use some device, such as requiring the equivalent of high school graduation or establishing a minimum age, to prevent just anyone of any age and background from walking into classes. However, there are colleges which do not view themselves as being selective but refer to themselves as being competitive in admissions. By this they mean that they do not have strict and explicit admissions requirements that apply equally to all applicants. They pick and choose among those who meet their minimum requirements and perhaps occasionally choose someone who does not even meet those minimums. Those colleges tend to refer to colleges that operate on a strict explicit policy as being selective, as contrasted with competitive, in admissions.

Sound Admissions

Whether an institution is open, selective, or competitive in admissions, it seems that certain characteristics must inhere in a sound admissions program. The program must be orderly. The proper steps must be taken in the proper sequence and on time, and they must be done reliably one term after another. The program should be fully specified and clear so that all who are involved or who may become involved can follow all the steps without faltering. To be sound, the program must be rational (i.e. it must be designed to achieve carefully determined objectives), and the design must be logical and thoroughly planned to eliminate any nonessentials while including all essentials in their proper places. Finally, the program must be modifiable on the basis of observations of its operation and its success in meeting the specified objectives efficiently.

Institutional commitments

As an institution decides to develop a sound selection program in order to meet its goals (which may include or be congruent with the goals of the students), the institution must make certain commitments. It decides to do things in one way or another, or to allow confusion to reign in which case it does not have a sound program. There are at least six issues on which the institution must take such a stand: (a) the kind of benefits it desires, (b) whether it will adapt its treatment of students according to the characteristics of the students in order to achieve the benefits most efficiently (e.g. whether to have remedial programs), (c) whether it will recruit applicants or restrict itself to certain kinds of applicants, (d) what measures it will use in making admissions decisions, (e) how those measures will be combined if more than one is used, and (f) where the decision point will be (on whatever measure or measures are used), above which an applicant will be admitted and below which he will be rejected. Each of these is defined more fully below and then examined in more detail later.

Most institutions behave as though they desired to select those candidates who would survive their programs of instruction, i.e. graduate. Some, however, would admit that they select those who can be expected to survive even part of their programs. Some of these institutions believe that even brief exposure to the college climate is so beneficial to members of their candidate pool that it is better to admit people who will have a high probability of failure than to reject them and thereby deny them even the brief experience of college attendance. Others may believe that if prediction of success is not perfect, everyone should be given a chance.

Still other institutions behave as though the desired benefit is having their dormitories and cafeterias sufficiently full that money is not lost on their operation. Admissions policy here is a matter of economics rather than education. Other institutions may be concerned not just with the graduation of those whom they admit but also with their graduation as cultured ladies and gentlemen. Among these there are those institutions that would carefully choose young ladies and gentlemen in the admissions process in order to be sure that their product would display refined tastes. There may also be institutions who choose uncultured youth from the applicant pool with the deliberate intention of changing them into models of enlightenment. The benefit to these institutions is the growth of the candidate.

Whatever the determination, in order for the institution to select intelligently it must take a stand concerning the kind of benefit it wants to maximize on the average in its institutional selection decisions. Unfortunately, many institutions have not made deliberate and explicit decisions about this basic issue.

A second commitment concerns whether the institution feels that its program is a "fixed" one determined by its end product and by the limits of a two- or four-year program. An engineering school may often view itself in just this way. Such an institution may believe that it is unreasonable for the institution to attempt to accommodate itself to applicants who cannot be expected to accomplish the objective within the specified time period. It would then be unsympathetic to the idea of introducing remedial courses for students who were inadequately prepared, or introducing more courses in a sequence, resulting in a longer curriculum for those who could reach the objective but only through more time and effort than the optimum. By way of contrast, other institutions may take the view that their goal is to reach the objective with all of their students regardless of how long it takes or what kinds of teaching are necessary. They might attempt to evaluate each new group of students to see what their needs are and might design academic experiences to meet those needs. This will be called "adapting the treatments to the students" in the context of the discussions later of decision theory as applied to selection and placement.

A third commitment the institution must make concerns the sources of its applicants. The institution can leave the matter to chance; it can consider whoever comes. However, many institutions are not free to take that course. State-supported colleges and universities are often under obligation or pressure to serve primarily the students whose parents are residents of the state and who thus have contributed to the tax support of the institutions. Other institutions are particularly ob-

ligated to students of one religion, one sex, or one restricted geographical area, such as a county or city. Beyond those considerations, there is also the issue of whether the institution will actively recruit candidates. From the point of view of decision theory, even when available selection tests are not very efficient, utility can be increased through improved recruiting for a constant-sized student body. This permits use of a more stringent criterion of quality for the students who will be admitted (Cronbach & Gleser, 1965, pp. 39–41), and this lower selection ratio has the same effect on increasing average utility that a higher selection-procedure validity would produce.

On the other hand, a college also may use its public image as a selection device. The admissions policy and selection machinery provide direct selection, in Clark's (1959) terms, but the public relations office provides indirect selection by controlling the image of the institution so that students select themselves in ways desired by the college. In one sense, the direct selection can be dispensed with if the indirect procedure results in recruiting the kind of students the college wants. However, there are some problems. With indirect selection the college cannot tell much about its selection ratio, and it will often have only a vague idea of how to combine its public-relations-selection program with its recruiting program to get the desired results. Besides that, there is the problem that images are inherently more resistant to change than are institutions. They often lag far behind the reality of the campus. An admissions procedure that does not depend heavily on self-selection is much more controllable.

A fourth commitment the institution must make concerns the measures it will utilize in making its decisions. Traditionally, test scores of some kind have been very widely used. Even wider in use, perhaps, are records of previous academic performance, recommendations by former teachers or administrators, and the information found on application forms. The institution must make a deliberate and informed choice of the material to use if it desires to have a sound selection program. The amount of material to be gathered and processed directly affects the cost of making each selection decision. The greater the cost of information gathering for a given validity, the less will be the average utility of that information to the institution. Eventually one could do so much testing and information gathering that the whole measurement program would cost more than it is worth.

A fifth commitment involves the manner in which the measures will be combined into a form from which consistent decisions can be made on the various candidates. Two models are in common use, the regression model and the cutting-score model. Each has different implications and produces different results. Aside from these formal models, there are also informal procedures which are usually part of selection decisions. One must consider whether the decisions will be made on a statistical basis, a clinical basis, or some combination.

A final commitment that must be made in a sound admissions program concerns the location of the specific decision point or points on the admissions measure or measures, the point above which a candidate is selected and below which he is rejected. The choice of this point can be made on the basis of the desired yield of entrants, on the basis of a predetermined level of minimum acceptable talent, or on the basis of a minimum probability of success with which the institution is willing to struggle, success being defined in terms of the institution's goals. If one considers educational selection as a form of placement, the choice point can be the point at which rejection is more beneficial to society (rather than to the institution) than acceptance would be. The decision point can be very precise, or it can be a decision area within which additional variables or even random factors are permitted to operate. Sometimes the gray area will involve a special additional set of measurements in the form of a try-out program, such as being accepted on probation or for a special trial period (e.g. the summer term in college). In the decision-theory frame of reference, all acceptances in a decision process are really temporary in that additional measurements are taken during the period when the

accepted candidate is performing. These measurements are used to decide whether he will later be rejected after all, i.e. "flunked" out or, perhaps, counseled out.

There are, then, six issues upon which an institution must commit itself if it will operate a sound selection program: the criteria (kind of benefit), whether it will adapt treatments, the source of applicants, the predictors, the means of combining predictors, and the cutting point for rejection. Now each of these will be considered in detail.

Criteria for Admissions Decisions

As will be remembered from other discussions of the criterion problem (see pp. 484–92), it is seldom, if ever, possible to measure the criterion of interest directly. The institution, in this discussion so far, is thought of as wanting to maximize certain benefits to itself. These may be such mundane considerations as keeping its financial accounts balanced, but more often they involve considerations such as developing understanding, knowledge, creativity, and ability to contribute to society on the part of the student. Somehow these must be represented in a useful way, and usually it is necessary to resort to observations which will be accepted as practically useful indicators of attainment on the criterion scale. Thus, grade point average might be used as an indicator of attainment of understanding and knowledge, or even of success in college. Some other criteria are more difficult to represent for many students, e.g. creativity or ability to contribute to society. Some of the indicators that often are used are discussed next.

Traditionally the criterion which researchers chose as being the relevant one for educational selection was the grade average in subsequent course work. There have been hundreds (or perhaps thousands) of studies of the validity of various kinds of measures for predicting academic grades. Grades have been chosen as the criterion of success in school and college regardless of what the catalog of the institution said it was trying to accomplish with the students it admitted and regardless of whether grades represent level of competence or represent personality, discipline, effort or represent a combination of these and other characteristics.

Grades are alluring as a criterion because they are usually easily obtainable, readily quantifiable, and of great importance in making other decisions such as whether students graduate or not, whether they are allowed to remain in school or not, whether they are given honors, whether they are allowed to take advanced or special courses, and so on. Clearly, regardless of what institutions say about what they desire to accomplish with students, they behave as though they valued most the students who obtained high grades, whatever that signifies. (We ignore here the value placed on students who win athletic contests!)

In spite of its wide use, the grade point average has been vigorously criticized on a number of grounds. A few of the recurring issues may be listed and briefly considered.

1. Grades are stated to be a poor representation of educational utility because they are contaminated with irrelevant factors, such as diligence (in preparing long papers), handwriting and general verbal ability (Klein & Hart, 1968), or a personal attractiveness and skill in interacting with the instructor.

2. Grading standards tend to vary by instructor, department, and level within the institution. Instructor differences introduce a certain amount of unreliability into the grade point average, but an educational culture that grades more leniently in some departments or more leniently as one goes up through the years of college and graduate school suffers from systematic biases that make interpretation of results for different groups or at different educational levels extremely difficult.

3. Some administrative practices, such as counting only the second grade when a course is repeated or disregarding grades on more than the minimum required number of credits, further reduce the comparability of meaning of the indicator from person to person and group to group.

4. In certain graduate and professional schools, the spread of grades is so reduced that individual differences in grade point average become quite unreliable. Undergraduate college grades also have been criticized as being unreliable, but evidence hardly bears this out (Hills, 1957) and the pooled average of grades in a number of courses appears to be a reasonably stable indicator.

5. In general, the empirical character and philosophical bases of grading practices in an institution are implicit and unexamined, so that no one really knows how grades are being arrived at or how they are related to the goals and objectives of the institution. What constitutes utility for the institution has not been seriously examined, so there has been no systematic attempt to develop consistent grading practices that are closely related to that concept of utility.

Dissatisfaction with grade point average has led to the occasional use of other indicators of the utility of an individual or group as institutional output. Several may be mentioned.

1. Ratings by faculty members have occasionally been obtained. Research with rating procedures in industry, civil service, and education have indicated strengths and especially weaknesses (see, for example, Campbell & Fiske, 1959; Davis, 1964, 1966; Guilford, 1954, ch. 11). In the academic situation, they tend to be difficult to obtain, of low reliability, and highly redundant with grades.

2. In some situations, licensing tests or other standard evaluations by an external agency represent a relevant indicator of utility. Especially in professional programs, board examinations or the equivalent have a kind of self-evident relevance to the goals of the instructional program.

3. Performance measures, as in architecture or design (Skager, Klein, & Schultz, 1967), may sometimes be set up to constitute a type of synthesis of the learning the student is expected to achieve and the objectives of the educational program.

4. The goals of the institution may lie in part outside of class, and there may be some attempt to assemble information on accomplishments in nonacademic areas and to predict

these performances (Richards, Holland, & Lutz, 1966). However, main interest in studying such accomplishments has been found in an outside agency rather than in college faculties, so one can question how much reality these achievements have as expressions of utility for the college.

5. Persistence at the institution until graduation (as opposed to transferring out) may be mentioned as one practical indicator of utility for some institutions. At a somewhat selfish and institution-centered level, it may be preferable to admit a student who will elect to stay to the end of his program in preference to one who will elect to transfer out leaving a vacancy in a class and a sense of rejection in the institution.

Adaptation of Treatment

An institution may choose whether it will operate a fixed-treatment program or an adaptive-treatment program. If students are to be chosen for one specified treatment that cannot be modified (e.g. a uniform freshman-year curriculum with no remedial or honors programs), then, assuming a linear relationship between payoff and predictor variables, Cronbach and Gleser (1965, pp. 41, 309) showed that it is always desirable to test at least twice as many bona fide applicants as will be accepted, if the predictor variables are worth using at all.

However, this is not precisely the case if the institution chooses to operate an adaptive-treatment program; that is the institution may deliberately adjust its program to fit the characteristics of its entering freshmen. If the group is unusually able, the institution may speed up its program or start at a higher level, attempting to graduate the group sooner or more highly educated. Regardless of whether the institution explicitly decides to operate an adaptive-treatment program, the faculty members as individuals may alter their instruction to suit the people they find in their classes. This is another form of adaptation. Probably this kind of adaptation occurs often in institutions (Hills, 1967; Hills & Gladney, 1968; Webb, 1959). Cronbach and Gleser (1965, p. 48) made the fairly reasonable assumptions that

1. each treatment will have its own payoff function relating expected payoff to score,
2. payoff functions are linear, and continuous,
3. payoff is related to treatment and to score by a saddle-shaped surface described in detail in their discussion,[2]

and they assumed for purposes of development that all treatments and payoffs have in common only a single aptitude factor. They then found that in adaptive treatment the optimum selection ratio (proportion of applicants who are accepted) will depend on the parameters of the function relating payoff to treatment and to score on the underlying aptitude factor. Thus an institution's decision about whether to adapt its treatment of students will have important bearings on its use of predictor variables and on the optimum selection ratio to maximize the gain in utility to be obtained through considering predictors at all.

Sources of Applicants

From the preceding discussion it is clear that colleges' sources of applicants are factors to consider in developing sound selection programs. While it is theoretically helpful to know that utility can be maximized by use of a specific selection ratio depending upon the circumstances of selection, to take advantage of this a college must be able to adjust its recruiting practices to produce sufficient applicants so that its selection ratio properly fits the number of students it desires, which is considered as relatively fixed. Many small colleges and junior colleges that serve a local area admit nearly all applicants. In such cases, any money spent on testing for admissions purposes simply may be wasted.

[2] A payoff function is the functional relationship or curve stating how much benefit (payoff) a person with a given score is expected to contribute through production or other outcome. The general type of payoff function assumed by Cronbach and Gleser is stated as $e_{st} = m_{st}s + c + bm_{st} - am_{st}^2$, where e_{st} is the payoff from treatment t applied to persons with true aptitude score s, m_{st} is the slope of the function relating payoff to true score when treatment t is applied, and a, b, and c are parameters of the saddle surface. Their magnitude varies depending on which treatments and what aptitude are being considered.

A second effect of recruiting which should be considered is the fact that, if, in order to increase the applicant population, the nature of the institution is misrepresented or exaggerated, the institution may be decreasing its selection ratio for entrants at the expense of increasing the number of dropouts later. Some colleges could profitably consider some form of "negative recruiting," i.e. spelling out the nature of the institution accurately in order to reduce the number of students who apply because of a faulty image. An institution that seeks academic rigor along with a national athletic reputation may have a difficult time getting students and counselors to realize that a student who chooses the college because of the notoriety of its team must do more than attend football games in order to survive the academic rigors of the institution. Those who would come primarily because they identify with the team might better be directed elsewhere. They may soon find themselves disenchanted, perhaps in academic difficulty, and possibly with no place to turn since most other colleges do not welcome their sister institution's failures.

Prediction Measures

The fourth type of issue to be dealt with is the choice of predictive devices that will be used in picking applicants for admission. Before discussing specific alternatives, it may be profitable to examine some general considerations that underlie any final choice. First, the cost of the selection process must be subtracted from any test-produced gain in utility in order to determine the net gain in utility. This implies that the greatest gain in utility can be obtained by using the least expensive measures that yield comparable results. Furthermore, it suggests that if useful predictions can be made from data that are collected for other purposes and therefore add nothing additional to costs, such data have the potential of providing appreciable net gain. Thus it behooves one to consider first the readily available data as predictors. A second, fundamental idea is that predictors cannot be considered in isolation from each other. If one starts out with a readily available predictor of some validity (such as high school grades), then an additional measure has value only to the extent that it adds validity beyond that provided by the initial predictor, and each additional measure must be evaluated by its ability to improve upon the existing team, i.e. by its "incremental validity" (Sechrest, 1963).

With these ideas in mind, consideration turns to some of the kinds of measures that are often examined or used in educational selection. Often readily available are previous academic grades. Usually institutions request applicants to fill out an application form that provides biographical data. Many institutions also require scores on some admissions test. Some desire to interview each applicant. Some ask the applicant for references; some obtain ratings of the applicant; some obtain measures of personality variables; and some use still other miscellaneous devices. What has been the experience generally with such prediction efforts?

Previous grades

In practical terms, for educational selection one usually has readily available a transcript of the candidate's previous work. Many studies have found that the record of performance in high school is the most valid single predictor of performance in college as reflected in the criterion of college grades. This is not surprising. The high school record is a work sample of college performance, in a sense, and it also capitalizes on being similar in form to the criterion to be predicted. As Vernon (1958) has pointed out, measures can show correlation due to their similarity in form as well as to similarity in content or to dependence on common underlying attributes. Thus, ratings might predict other ratings better than test scores would be expected to predict those ratings, tests should be the best predictors of test scores, and, by the same token grades should be the best predictors of grades, as typically they are. In setting up an academic selection system then, the first kind of a predictor to look for is some readily available work sample from previous performance. The best work samples usually will be the ones closest to the criterion in time and form. One should expect much higher correlations between freshman and sophomore grades in college than between sophomore college grades and high school average. Once the student is in college, probably the best predictor of later undergraduate grades will be the average of earlier college grades. Any attempt to improve on the level of prediction available from the conveniently accessible work sample must be evaluated in terms of the increment to validity that is provided.

It is sometimes thought that adjusting the high school record of performance to remove from it the influence of differences in standards among high schools would be useful in improving predictions of college success. Several studies have indicated that this is a forlorn hope when test scores are already used along with the unadjusted high school grades as predictors. The most extensive of these studies was conducted by Lindquist (1963) in connection with the American College Testing Program (see also Linn, 1966). Apparently the test scores serve in a regression equation to counteract the influence of differential grading standards in the high schools—in effect, they "equate" the high school grades from various schools.

Studies have shown that the predictions of college grades can be made relatively early in the high school career and that prediction on the basis of the first three years of high school performance and test scores is about as accurate as prediction from all four years of high school and test scores. Further studies have shown that the high school record does not need to be purified by restricting it to academic courses as long as test scores are used together with high school grades in multiple prediction. The high school record and aptitude test scores are a very robust prediction team. (Discussion and data concerning these findings appear in Hills, Gladney, & Klock, 1967).

Many institutions use rank-in-class instead of high school grade average to represent previous academic performance. The two seem to serve about equally well as predictors, especially when they are used in conjunction with other predictors such as admissions test scores. There

is the virtue of simplicity in grade point averages. Any single student's grade average does not depend upon the performance of other students in the same way that rank does. Therefore, there is no need to wait until all students have finished high school to obtain a transcript with a reasonably complete representation of his high school performance in terms of grade point average. To obtain such an indication in terms of rank-in-class requires that the school rank all students at any point in time to provide information for any one student, a rather unattractive proposition for a school with hundreds or thousands of students.

Biographical data

Usually an applicant not only will provide a transcript but also will fill out an application form providing personal data about himself, his family, and perhaps his aspirations or expectations. While these data may be well used for specific purposes, such as finding tuba players and tackles, this source of information for academic selection and placement often lies untapped in the files of educational institutions. Results are mixed concerning the value of such "biodata," and some methodological problems are regularly overlooked in studies in this area.

Cross validation— The important concept of incremental validity—the fact that any new predictor must add to the predictive efficiency already available if it is to be of practical significance—has already been described (see, for example, Hilton & Myers, 1967; Hood & Swanson, 1965, p. 119). It also should be noted that any predictor must survive the scrutiny of cross validation in order to be of use; that is, one must take two random samples from a population for which the predictor is judged to be interesting, determine the regression coefficients for one of the samples, and apply those coefficients to the other sample in order accurately to estimate the validity of the predictor. The validity coefficient that one might obtain from applying the regression coefficients to the sample from which they were obtained will be spuriously high. Cross validation is especially crucial for instruments, such as a biographical data blank, in which the selection of items to be keyed has been determined empirically from the initial sample.

Operational validation— Not only must one examine predictors from the vantage point of cross validity, but he also must consider their operational validity. In operation, one does not have nice random samples with which to deal. He usually has, at best, incidental samples. Any differences between samples, such as entering freshmen from one year to the next, will tend to lower the validity of predictors. Thus operational validity will tend to be lower than cross validity. Not only that, but to the extent that a predictor might become invalidated, operational validity may quickly shrink to zero. For instance, if it is noted that all students who elect to take a certain advanced placement test get higher freshman grades than would otherwise be predicted, use of that information as a predictor could be expected to result in students' learning of its use and in their permitting that knowledge to alter their choice of the advanced placement test they take. When that happens the operational validity of the information about choice of advanced placement test disappears.

Generality of findings— One characteristic of studies of biographical data as predictors has been that what seems to work in one situation cannot be depended on to work in the same way in what seems to be a very similar situation (see, for instance, Henry, 1966, pp. 93–95). This makes it very difficult to recommend specific biographical items as potentially good predictors for particular situations. When an item of biographical data does work, often it is difficult to figure out what makes it effective. There is no theoretical underpinning for successes in the area. This lack is so noticeable that a foundation is attempting to encourage preliminary theoretical development in the area (Glennon & Albright, 1966).

Unpublished negative findings— Handicapping research and theory development in this area is the fact that negative results with biographical data seldom are published, but positive results more often find their way into the literature. Instances have been reported privately to the author of large-scale studies of biographical data which were never even prepared for publication because the investigator was certain that the effort of preparation would be unrewarded by publication: he found no potentially useful biographical data predictors.

Effects of prior selection— Some studies that appear to display relatively satifactory incremental validity are misleading because they have not properly accounted for the fact that other available predictors, such as previous grades and test scores, already have been used in the selection of the subjects on whom the validity of biographical data was examined. Once a variable has been used in selection, other unused variables will tend to appear superior in predictive efficiency due to the restricted range of the variable already used in selection (see, for example, Anastasi, Meade, & Schneiders, 1960).

Absolute vs. differential prediction— Some attempts to use biographical data as predictors may have been less successful than they might otherwise have been because they concentrated on selecting contributors to absolute prediction rather than contributors to differential prediction (see Horst, 1954, 1955; P. Lunneborg & C. Lunneborg, 1966).

Academic vs. nonacademic prediction— Finally, it may be that nonintellective predictors are most appropriate and useful for nonintellective criteria (Richards et al., 1966). Fishman (1959), however, has suggested that study of nonintellective measures (such as biographical data) as predictors of intellective criteria has not been adequately rationalized. Only limited facets have been explored though many hundreds of studies have been reported.

The conclusion about the usefulness of biographical data for educational selection and placement must, then, be a guarded one. Sometimes biographical data appear to be useful (e.g.

Abel, 1966; Henry, 1966; C. Lunneborg & P. Lunneborg, 1966; P. Lunneborg & C. Lunneborg, 1966; Owens & Henry, 1966; Richards et al., 1966). At other times they do not appear to be so promising (e.g. Anastasi et al., 1960; Henry, 1966; Hilton & Myers, 1967; Hood & Swanson, 1965, p. 119; Nichols, 1966; Schwarz & Krug, 1961; Skager et al., 1967; Webb, 1960). Often what appears to be promising loses its appeal when scrutinized for methodological inadequacies.

Admissions test scores

The record of previous performance and the information from application blanks are data readily available for academic selection. However, additional data have often been found to be useful, and the most useful have usually been scores on admissions tests. Like previous performance records, and unlike biographical data, the record is so full of the reports of incremental validity from scholastic aptitude test scores that a report of their failure would be more interesting to an editor than another report of their value.

Illustrative findings with aptitude tests— One of the most widely used sets of test scores, and one with a long history of use, is the Scholastic Aptitude Test of the College Entrance Examination Board. Hills (1964d) provides an example of what can be expected from this very carefully constructed, secure test of two sorts of aptitude, verbal and mathematical, when combined with high school performance as a predictor of freshman grades in a wide variety of colleges. (These colleges were all the publicly supported colleges in the state of Georgia.) Averaging by sex over 19 colleges and a five-year period to include 175 sets of data involving 27,961 students, it is reported that the average correlation between high school performance and first-year college grade average is .55. Including the SAT scores raises the average multiple correlation to .65. This is a 40 percent increase in the proportion of criterion variance accounted for (Horst, 1966, p. 371).

The multiple correlations obtained from the use of a different admissions test, that of the American College Testing Program, in a different part of the United States are of about the same magnitude (Munday, 1965). That program uses four test scores and four different evaluations of high school performance, making a total of eight predictor variables, as contrasted to the three or fewer included in Hills's studies.

A college need not use nationwide, securely administered admissions tests, such as the SAT or ACT programs, in order to obtain this level of incremental validity. It probably can obtain much the same results from any of a wide variety of aptitude tests commercially available (Swanson, Merwin, & Berdie, 1963). And, of course, there is no guarantee that a specific college will obtain the average multiple correlation of .65 that is reported. Some institutions have higher correlations, some have lower, and there are substantial fluctuations from year to year, especially with classes of fewer than 500 students. In general, the multiple correlations will be higher for females than males (Hills, 1964d), but this is not always true (Dickerson, 1965). Within the kinds of students found in public colleges, restriction in range due to selection or sociocultural factors seems not to influence the magnitude of the multiple correlations to any practically significant degree (Hills, 1964d; Munday, 1965). Such findings may not, however, be typical of highly selective private colleges; unfortunately, large compilations of recent data over several years reported by college are not readily available for such institutions.

Achievement tests— Achievement tests are often thought of as potential additional test contributors to prediction from high school performance and aptitude test scores. It should be remembered that there is not a very clear distinction between aptitude and achievement in educational testing. One measures aptitude by determining how much a student has achieved. There is no way to get at a college applicant's intelligence uncontaminated by his approximately 18 years of experience and training. The principal difference between the two constructs is that the achievement test is confined to a single subject matter more completely than is the aptitude test. However, it usually will be found that verbal aptitude tests are highly correlated with English achievement tests, mathematical aptitude tests are highly correlated with mathematics achievement tests, and, indeed, verbal and mathematical aptitude tests often are correlated with each other at the level of about .60 or higher. It probably would be difficult for a measurement or subject-matter expert to sort into separate groups accurately the items from aptitude and achievement tests in similar areas.

This similarity shows up in an interesting way. One might ask, for instance, how much would the use of the College Board's achievement tests increase the multiple correlation to be obtained from use of the high school performance record and the College Board's aptitude test (the SAT). Unpublished analyses of many sets of data collected by a number of investigators at various colleges show that on the average the increase is very small, on the order of .03.

A series of unpublished studies conducted by Kenneth Wilson of the College Research Center at Vassar College indicates that using high school performance (rank-in-class), aptitude tests, and the average of scores on achievement tests in a battery, the achievement test average will have a higher standard partial regression weight (Beta weight) than will the aptitude tests, and, indeed, the weights for the aptitude tests will probably not be significantly different from zero. (This finding could be in part due to restriction in range as a result of selection based more heavily on the aptitude than the achievement tests.) It seems very likely that the contribution of achievement tests to multiple prediction that already involves high school performance and aptitude measures generally will be modest or inconsequential, as illustrated with these data from the College Board's substantial program.

Stability of prediction— Long-term statewide systematic study of prediction of college grades from test scores and high school performance has been reassuring in many respects (Hills et al., 1967). It has been shown that prediction equations from one year are generally sound for use in immediately succeeding years (operational validation), but after two or three years one needs to check to be sure that drift has not made the old weights unacceptable (Hills, Bush, & Klock, 1966). It also has been shown that the predictions of first-year grades are related to performance over the two-year period of a junior college and the four-year period of a senior college. The average correlation between predicted freshman grades and obtained cumulative averages at graduation seems to fall in the upper .50s or lower .60s. It appears that separate prediction equations often are not required for different departments or majors, especially when there is not a contrast between science versus nonscience departments. There is some indication that institutions that have strong technical programs, such as engineering, and that also have strong liberal arts programs may well need separate prediction equations because of the differential emphasis on mathematics. Prediction equations should regularly be developed separately by sex, though. Females often obtain higher grades than males of the same aptitude (Hills, Masters, & Emory, 1961; Stanley & Porter, 1967). They also are reported to be more predictable than men (Hills, 1964d; Seashore, 1961).

Methodological problems— One should note that there are certain subtleties of conducting studies of prediction on the basis of test scores (and other variables) which can cause data to be misleading to the unwary. For instance, in Hills and his collaborators' studies, the predictions were made for those who survived the first year of college. If they had been made for those who survived only the first term, higher correlations might have been found because many of the weak students might drop out after the first term and thus restrict the range of the criterion and the predictor scores. On the other hand, first-term grades as a criterion might not be as reliable as first-year grades, which would tend to make the first-term criterion less predictable.

Again, in Hills's and his collaborators' data

there were colleges which were highly selective in admissions policy and others which were essentially nonselective. Lower correlations would be expected in the institutions that had already used the test scores as a basis for admitting students. Other colleges which might be even more selective than the most selective of those Hills and his colleagues studied might find markedly lower correlations than were found in Georgia.

It is interesting, however, to note that in the Georgia data it was not found that attrition over four years of college produced lower standard deviations of test scores than were obtained for end-of-freshman-year data. There was appreciable attrition, but it apparently took place all along the continuum of aptitude test scores. This may be related to the relatively high correlations found in those institutions between test scores obtained before admission and cumulative average grades at graduation.

Interviews

From years of evidence it seems that in gathering information to be used as a basis for sound educational selection the first step should be to include an evaluation of past performance, such as grades, and the second step to add to that one or more scores from tests of academic aptitude or achievement. Beyond that, many things have been tried with little consistent evidence of incremental validity. The use of biographical data for incremental prediction in educational selection has been examined above. A very common procedure in college admissions is to require that each candidate be interviewed by a representative of the institution. The evidence on the value of interview findings as incremental predictors is very discouraging and has been for years (Cronbach & Gleser, 1965, p. 145; Kelly, 1954; Ward, 1955).

Study of the interview (Webster, 1964) is beginning to shed some light on the interviewing process. Perhaps eventually it will be known why the interview is so ineffective and even how to conduct effective interviews. The findings available now are that the decisions that are made in the selection interview are usually made within the first 30 seconds of the inter-

view, even though the interviews under study lasted, on the average, 15 minutes. Early impressions are very important, and the interview tends to be a search for negative evidence—anything unfavorable that appears in the interview is likely to lead to rejection. Interviews often become sales pitches during the latter minutes when the interviewer has already decided to recommend acceptance of the applicant, but if rejection is the decision, the interviewer is less pleasant. Interviewers tend to differ in their response styles, particularly in their category widths, i.e. their tolerance in accepting candidates. This may be one cause of differences between the decisions of different interviewers. It appears that unfavorable impressions are much more important than favorable impressions in determining the final decisions that will be made. Furthermore, interviewers are sensitive to adaptation level—a poor applicant tends to make the applicant who follows him look good, and a good applicant handicaps the person who follows him. As these findings are verified by other laboratories, and as the decision process becomes better understood, the interview may become useful as a selection tool; at present, however, the contribution of the interview is to public relations rather than to improved selection.

Interviews as wideband procedures— Discussions of interviews and similar techniques as "wideband" procedures, as presented, for example, by Cronbach and Gleser (1965, pp. 144-148) may tempt one as justification for continued use of interviews in educational selection. The idea is that information that is of modest validity for many different decisions if used for each of them may be more beneficial (of greater utility) than information that is highly relevant for but one decision. The interview is a good device for obtaining information on a variety of topics, and great variety can be introduced without increasing the cost proportionately. Thus, an interview might be more justifiable than a long reliable admissions test which is relevant only for predicting grade point average.

This justification of interviews for educational selection is weakened by the situation in which interviewing is usually done. The problem is that the information from the interview is seldom used for a variety of decisions. If each of the applicant's prospective teachers participated in the interview and could derive information from it as to how best to handle the applicant, the wide band-width potential of the interview might be realized; but the involvement of all those faculty in interviewing each applicant would raise the cost unbearably. As things stand, the information from the interview probably never leaves the admissions office and is related only to one decision—admission. The low fidelity and high cost of the interview make its use irrational for most educational selection situations.

References and ratings

Most educational institutions require that in some form or other an applicant present with his application material statements from other people concerning his qualifications or personal characteristics. These personal references may take the form of letters, ratings on formal rating scales, telephone conversations, or other devices. Since so much of these kinds of data is collected routinely and since references absorb so much time and effort both from the candidates and from those who provide the comments, it is surprising how little is known about their value. Boulger and Colmen (1964) reported that in a recent 15-year period (1949–1963) there was only one study concerning research on references indexed in *Psychological Abstracts* under headings where such research might be expected. A few unpublished studies can be unearthed (e.g. Boulger & Colmen, 1964). What findings there are tend to be disappointing.

As was noted above, the evaluations by those who provide personal references for applicants may be obtained in the form of ratings. Many other variables can take this form also. Criteria also can be in the form of ratings. Probably any general statement about ratings as predictors is hazardous without specifying the characteristics being rated. However, there is no empirical basis for expecting ratings to provide

appreciable incremental validity. Examples of disappointing results are found in Gough, Hall, and Harris (1963) and Smith (1966).

Personality variables

In the first edition of *Educational Measurement* (Lindquist, 1951), Chauncey and Frederiksen were optimistic enough to say, "While some improvement in prediction of college success may come from further refinement of the aptitude and achievement tests, it would seem that the greatest advances may come through a thorough exploration of the measurement of personal qualities [p. 97]." In the years since that was written little of the promise has been fulfilled. Smith (1966) wrote, "But to *predict* performance from independent measures of personality is quite another matter, in regard to which the entire experience of personnel psychology must caution us against optimism [p. 562]." And Cronbach and Snow (1969) stated, "Despite the extended efforts of psychologists pursuing diverse traditions, it appears that each of the methods of testing and conceptualizing personality that has been exploited during the past two decades is open to serious criticism. It is hard to see that any one of the several lines of effort . . . has moved forward during this period [p. 149]."

While it still seems logical that temperament and personality should play an important role in academic performance and be useful traits to include in a prediction battery, there is little encouraging evidence to report. Webb (1965) has been able to cross-validate Fricke's (1963) findings that the empirically derived Achiever Personality score from the Opinion, Attitude and Interest Survey adds to the predictability of freshman grades at Emory University when the other predictors are high school performance and scores from the College Board's SAT. The increment is about .05 to multiple correlations of about .55, not a great amount, but a 20 percent improvement and enough to be of some importance (Horst, 1966, p. 371). There is no sign of the "big breakthrough" here, despite a great amount of effort being devoted to the problem (Lavin, 1965). Perhaps part of the reason is that the high school performance measure and the criterion already may share elements of personality measurement that are important for prediction. In other words, this hypothesis is that the personality traits that are important for obtaining high grades in college also were important in obtaining high grades in high school. The high school record already is reflecting these personality traits, so no new measure of them yields a sizable increment of validity. Even when the criterion of academic success is thought to be heavily laden with creativity, personality measures selected to be related to creativity are not consistently related to the criteria (Skager et al., 1967).

Work samples

Skager and his colleagues, in trying to predict performance in a design school, suggested that they overlooked one possibility, that of using work samples of drawing performance as predictors of drawing performance (Skager et al., 1967, pp. 13–14). While that may be appropriate in predicting unusual criteria such as design grades or the nonintellective criteria of Richards and his colleagues (1966), for the usual academic criterion of grades in later course work the high school record already is perhaps the best work sample possible.

Perhaps at this point it would be well to summarize the results from the area that has been discussed here, that of "noncognitive" predictors. Fishman's (1959) excellent discussion of the area provides a statement from 1959 that still seems appropriate. After having reviewed 168 recent studies of noncognitive predictors Fishman commented, "I hope that I am being fair when I say that up until now this approach has *rarely* produced anything startling in terms of the magnitude of multiples and in terms of 'gains' in prediction above and beyond what is attainable via the use of intellective predictors alone [p. 62]."

Methods of Data Combination

After the institution has decided what it values as an objective or a set of objectives and after it decides what sorts of measures to use in trying to predict which students have the highest probabilities of reaching those objectives, it must decide how to use the predictors to yield values that will be used to determine who will or will not be admitted. Three main alternatives need to be considered: (*a*) setting a minimum score (cutting score) on each variable below which a candidate will be rejected, (*b*) combining the two or more variables into a single score, usually by a linear combination, and admitting those with the highest composite scores, or (*c*) allowing an admissions officer to study the record for each applicant, weighting the evidence with respect to the applicant as his clinical judgment dictates and arriving at a decision as to whether or not he should be admitted.

Multiple cutting scores

A common procedure, perhaps unfortunately, is for the institution to decide that anyone who scores below some specific value on a predictor measure should not be admitted. If there are several predictors, a cutoff score is set for each of them. The procedure attracts users because it seems so simple. The admissions officer merely has to remember the cutting score on each variable. Any candidate who does not meet any cutoff can be told immediately that he is rejected. The cutoffs can be published, also, thus clearly informing candidates of their eligibility.

The most unfortunate thing about the procedure is that its administrative simplicity makes it readily available for uninformed and thoughtless use. Cutoff scores can be set arbitrarily without adequate evidence on the validity of the variable that is being used for selection or of the yield of admitted candidates that can be expected for any given set of minimum scores. For example, the author knows of several instances in which colleges picked cutoffs that sounded nice and put them into effect only to discover late in the admissions season that they were far too high and had the effect of nearly wiping out the entering freshman class. The result in each case was a desperate attempt to find enough live bodies to fill the class regardless of their quality or potential as students. The seemingly simple method backfired seriously. (It also happens that an available measure may erroneously be assumed to be valid. The combination of invalid measure and arbitrary cutoff is, perhaps, the nadir of sophistication in selection.)

The rationale underlying the multiple cutoff method is that high aptitude of one kind does not offset low aptitude of another. Thus, a person with high verbal skills but with mathematical skills below the cutoff would be rejected. Experience suggests, however, that in education at least, and especially in institutions with varied curricula, lack of one kind of talent can often be compensated for by possession of another relevant talent. Guilford (1965, p. 430) suggested that if such compensatory effects were not common, there would be much more shrinkage than is usually found in the relationships between criteria and composite predictor scores that assume compensation.

The rationale for separate cutting scores becomes less defensible as the scores become less reliable and as separate scores become more highly correlated. The rationale that each ability must be present in a minimum amount can only be defended in relation to *true score* on the underlying abilities. Errors of measurement, which are unrelated to the true ability level, must serve to muddy the relationship between test performance and academic criterion measure. Lord (1962) has elaborated the mathematical relationships involved, showing that as the correlation between predictors increases and as their reliability decreases, fixed cutoff scores become less and less optimal for selecting the desired candidates. To achieve the theoretical optimum, the user of cutoff scores would have to vary the cutoff on one variable depending upon the level of score on the other variable much as he would if he were assuming compensation and using a combination of the two or more scores from the beginning. Thus, the mathematically proper use of cutting scores on fallible predictors becomes quite as complex as a linear equation for combining scores.

Multiple cutoff procedures may be quite as effective as linear combination under some circumstances, as a study by Grimsley (1949) indicated. However, in that study, the multiple cutting-score procedure showed up to best advantage in identifying the best 10 to 15 percent of applicants rather than in discriminating within the lower half of the group, the part of the distribution in which most educational selection occurs.

Multiple regression

Among those who operate educational selection programs with some sophistication, linear multiple regression methods are probably the most common means of combining predictor data. The multiple regression procedure is based on the assumption that high aptitude of one relevant kind can compensate for lower aptitude of another kind. In this way multiple regression differs from the multiple cutoff procedure just described. While the exact multiple regression analysis yields a prediction equation that minimizes squared errors of prediction, it has been recognized for a long time that regression weights could be simplified dramatically with little practical loss of predictive accuracy (Guilford, 1965, p. 423). A single-digit approximation to exact regression weights will yield a composite score whose validity coefficient differs from that determined by exact weights only in the third or fourth decimal place. This produces an important gain for the practical application of multiple regression methods to educational selection because simplifications in the equations make the procedure feasible for operation by clerical personnel and usable in counseling as well as selection contexts where calculators or computers are not handily available.

It must be recognized, of course, that the widespread availability of computer services seems imminent. If the day ever comes when admissions officers, personnel departments, counselors, and others who make personnel decisions have ready access to all the promised developments, at that time discussions of what procedures are useful because they provide simplifications will be passé. Those who have highly developed computer facilities find that the simplifications are unimportant in use—the computer takes only slightly longer to do things in the complicated way. And, indeed, once this is recognized, highly complicated procedures can be put into effect. Some agencies already provide through computer use such things as predicted grades for all applicants to particular colleges that avail themselves of such a service, and they also provide various summarizations of information on applicants such as might be used by an admissions committee in evaluating individual applicants.

The day of such widespread computer utilization is not at hand yet. Many admissions officers, most counselors, and most applicants must think in terms of doing the data manipulations for particular instances by hand. For them, the simplifications that can be introduced are still important and will continue to be important for probably another decade at least. Such simplifications may be most significant for the making of individual decisions, as described early in this chapter, because the individual applicants have so little experience with making decisions based on actuarial data that anything very complex may confuse more than it enlightens. It seems pointless to go to any great effort to train individuals to be able to use computers with such data for decision making when only one decision they make can be handled this way.

As examples of the simplifications that are possible, Hills (1964a) has described a procedure for converting the typical multiple regression equation into a simple expectancy table that is usable by counselees themselves. Hills and his colleagues published tables of this sort for all the colleges in Georgia in order to improve counseling about college attendance in that state (Hills, Klock, & Bush, 1965). They supplied similar data to the college admissions offices of the state so that admissions officers and counselors could operate from the same basic data, combined in the same manner. Also the American College Testing Program Research Service employs a procedure to simplify the use of regression results for expeditious use in counseling (American College Testing Program, undated).

Besides the simplification available through using integral regression weights or special tables for combining predictor variables, a further simplification results from deletion of variables that do not provide useful incre-

mental validity. Thus, in many of the tables for Georgia colleges one of the three available predictors received a weight so close to zero that it could safely be ignored in predicting grades or admission. In the ACT Program's Texas *Counselor's Guide*, noncontributing variables have not been similarly deleted but are evident in that nearly all students receive a score within one or two points of the same value regardless of their scores on these variables. Deletion of such unnecessary detail can simplify the use of regression procedures to the extent that they are not very different in practical use from multiple cutoff methods. Even simple graphical procedures can be prepared when only two predictors are required (Guilford, 1965, pp. 397–398). These have been found to be very useful in college admissions offices.

It must be understood in this connection that, due to intercorrelations among variables, while one often discovers a number of variables that may be correlated with the criterion, only a few of them will make practically or statistically significant contributions to prediction accuracy when used in multiple regression. The variables that do not provide a useful increment should be ignored, but that does not imply that low or high scores on those variables are meaningless. It only implies that they do not add to the information already present in the system of predictors.

Occasionally a negative regression weight will occur. Usually it will be small and will not reappear on replication. However, if a statistically and practically significant negative weight does develop repeatedly for a variable (e.g. Hills et al. 1961b, p. 11), that variable should be used as a suppressor variable (Guilford, 1965, pp. 405–406). The difficulty with such variables is that the counselee or applicant finds it hard to understand that high performance on that variable can possibly be detrimental. What he fails to comprehend is that the different variables are functioning as a team in multiple regression. If one score has too much reasoning variance to match the proportion of reasoning variance in the criterion, another variable with reasoning variance may get a negative weight in order to obtain the proper balance. Taken by itself, the second variable might have a positive correlation with the criterion, but as a member of a team it functions best with a negative weight. To explain this satisfactorily to a person unfamiliar with factor analysis is as difficult as explaining to a novice why a T-formation quarterback always seems to get the ball and run backward away from the goal line. Perhaps it is fortunate that suppressor variables do not often appear in academic selection situations.

Clinical vs. actuarial prediction

Often in educational selection as it is practiced, various kinds of data are collected, such as test scores and biographical data, and, though statistical predictions may be computed, finally a human judge makes a decision as to which candidates will be rejected. The judge pays only as much attention to the data as he cares to, and he may interview or otherwise observe the candidate in order to gather additional data. A question arises as to whether having the additional data gathered by the judge (who might be called a clinician in order to put this discussion into the frame of reference of the professional literature) yields incremental validity. Another question is whether the clinician (admissions officer) can make better decisions on the basis of his experience than can be made by means of statistical or actuarial prediction equations. These problems have received considerable attention over the years and have been discussed comprehensively in a recent report by Sawyer (1966).

Though the issues are not yet resolved fully, it seems clear that the mechanical statistical combination of data is practically never improved upon by modification by clinical judgment. That is, given a specific set of data and a criterion, combining those data by means of a statistical procedure, such as a multiple regression equation, always yields as accurate predictions, and in some studies more accurate predictions, as does letting a clinician or judge examine those same data and make predictions from them. In fact, according to Sawyer's (1966) review of the literature, the clinicians do not improve on the statistical predictions even

when they are given the statistical predictions as part of the data they may consider.

On the other hand, there is some evidence in Sawyer's review to suggest that the clinical judge may have something to contribute from his observations. The best methods, in terms of the proportion of studies in which these methods were compared with other methods and equalled or exceeded the accuracy of the other methods, were methods that combined data mechanically but included clinicians' observations as part of the data to be combined. Thus if expert judges are to be used in the selection process, present data suggest that they not be allowed to make the final evaluations upon which decisions are made but that they be used as expert observers producing data that can be introduced into prediction equations or other statistical combination procedures that generate the final evaluations. In other words, if subjective evaluation of applicants is to be introduced into the selection process, through use of interview or other techniques, it is important that these evaluations be recorded systematically in such a form that subsequent analysis can be carried out to determine the extent to which such evaluations actually contribute to the prediction of relevant criteria. The relevant evaluations can then be entered as data in the prediction equation that will produce estimates of performance in a mechanical manner. Those applicants who exceed a cutoff point on the estimates of performance should be accepted with no further human intervention.

Even these conclusions must be tempered. While the current data, which Sawyer stated he believed to be inadequate for final disposal of the issues, suggest that the clinical judge may add something to the measurement side of prediction, one must determine in any particular situation whether the amount of increase in accuracy of prediction yielded through the judge's observations justifies the expense of use of the judge's time for this purpose. In many situations, a judge who was sufficiently knowledgeable or experienced to make a contribution in data gathering for prediction purposes would be so important that his time would be even more valuable for other purposes. If whatever he did in making his observations could be codified so that a less sophisticated person could substitute for him, it could probably be codified so that a mechanical device could substitute for him also, thus converting this kind of information gathering into a mechanical procedure instead of a clinical procedure (Helm, 1967). Even when the expert is required and can make a contribution to the information used to make predictions, his contribution may be a rather modest increment to the validity obtained without the inclusion of his judgments. The value of this increment including the expenditure of faculty thereby saved must be balanced against the expense of exhausting the expert's time for the purpose of interviewing or observing applicants.

Methods of Setting Cutoff Scores

If there is to be selection, there must be a means for deciding for each applicant whether he is accepted or rejected. This implies one or more cutoff points or scores below which the decision is rejection. In this section, methods of setting cutoff scores based on classical procedures and based on decision theory are discussed. The classical procedures include the prediction of categories from measurements, with and without consideration of base rates, and the method of predicted yield. The decision theory procedures are different for fixed and adaptive treatments.

Before proceeding to a discussion of those methods, some of the philosophical and situational problems that impinge on the setting of cutoff scores need to be considered. As was noted in the beginning of this chapter, whether selection is legitimate at all depends on one's point of view. People also differ in their attitude toward whether what is called selection in education is really selection or whether it should be thought of as placement, which also has been discussed earlier.

Another area in which people's opinions differ concerns grading standards—considered at this point because it is with reference to grades, as criteria or as reflectors of utility, that cutoffs are set. An extreme illustration may most clearly pose the problem. Suppose an institution that has been admitting all high school graduates miraculously is able to commence admitting only high school valedictorians. Suppose that the institution has been giving grades in a distribution of 5 percent Fs, 20 percent Ds, 50 percent Cs, 20 percent Bs, and 5 percent As in the past (a distribution that has nothing to recommend it, incidentally). Now it has an entering class that, by comparison with previous years, would have no members performing as poorly as those who formerly obtained C, D, or F grades. Should the institution no longer use grades other than A and B? If so, can it claim to be doing an adequate job of evaluating its students and informing them about their progress, rewarding unusual success, accurately describing their achievements to prospective employers, and so on? Some would argue that the answer should be in the affirmative; others would argue in the negative—or at least they would behave as though they believed that something similar to the old distribution of grades should be maintained for the new group of highly selected students (see especially, Webb, 1959).

To pose the problem another way, suppose that a selective institution decides to open a branch campus offering the first two years of college work. To obtain the cooperation of the community in which the branch is located, suppose that the institution finds that it must go along with describing the branch as opening new opportunities for the high school graduates of the community, much as would a junior college. In all likelihood this would have, as a result, an entering class at the branch that represents a much wider range of academic aptitude than occurs on the selective main campus. Should the persons whose academic achievements do not meet the standards of the main campus be dismissed from the branch? If so, the failure rate will be strikingly high and community support will be lost. The resolution of problems such as these are not technical matters, but they must be recognized as real and important considerations by the expert who would apply educational measurement to problems of selection and placement. (Relevant discussions appear in Aiken, 1963; Ebel, 1965, pp.

424–435; Gulliksen, 1950, pp. 299–304; Hills, 1964c; Hills, 1967; Hills & Gladney, 1968; Marks, 1967; Webb, 1959.)

One more situational problem that impinges on selection and placement is that of restrictions based on the extent of facilities or finances. These restrictions result in quotas for the selection or placement process that override technical considerations. Their presence may be the determining factor in where a cutoff is set.

Classical approach

Predicting categories from measurements— If a single selection variable is used, or if a multiple regression equation is to be used in order to combine the data from several selection variables, and if the goal that is set is to admit those students who will survive to graduate (or survive the freshman year, or attain some similar criterion), one is in the position of predicting categories or attributes from measurements. Standard statistics texts (e.g. Guilford, 1965) discuss this problem. One procedure is to draw the overlapping frequency distributions of the predictor variable for the successful and unsuccessful groups.

If these distribution curves intersect, the point of intersection (at which point an individual has a 50–50 chance of success) might be chosen as the cutoff point. Persons with more favorable scores would be admitted, and those with less favorable scores and consequently better than an even chance of failure would be rejected. A formula can be used to determine this point analytically rather than graphically (Guilford, 1965, p. 385).

If the success ratio in an educational program is high—for example, if 95 percent of all applicants would be successful in completing it—then a test that attempts to identify the 5 percent that will fail may make so many errors that it would be preferable to accept everyone, saving the testing time and money. Helmstadter (1964) described a simple routine for calculating the number of errors that would be made by using a particular cutting score and comparing this with the number of errors that would be made by admitting everyone. The "base rate" can be an important factor in determining whether a test or other selection variable is of any value.

Predicted yield— Thorndike (1949) has outlined a useful procedure called the method of predicted yield. Hills and Klock (1965) have presented details of essentially the same procedure specifically applied to the problem of selective admission to college. In essence, the admissions officer starts to solve the cutoff problem with certain data at hand, namely, the number of applications accepted for the previous year and the number of freshmen who entered the previous year. These numbers indicate the rate of success the college has in enrolling the students it accepts. (Rates vary, in the author's experience, from about .6 to over .9, with the lower ratios usually being associated with the institutions whose students obtain *higher* mean scores on admissions tests. Students applying to those more prestigious institutions are more likely to be self-selected on aptitude and to receive multiple acceptances.) The admissions officer also must have at hand his estimate of the number of applications the institution will receive for the coming year (often a very complex estimation problem) and the number of entering freshmen that are desired, i.e. the quota. The procedure assumes a fixed quota to be met and attempts to set a cutting score that will meet the quota while at the same time maintaining standards at as high a level as possible. The percentile point for the cutoff on the predictor distribution based on the previous year's applicants can be obtained from the equation (Hills & Klock, 1965, 1967)

$$p = 100 - \frac{100ux}{vw},$$

where

u is the number of applications accepted for the previous year,

v is the number of applications anticipated for the coming year,

w is the number of freshmen who entered in the previous year, and

x is the number of entering freshmen desired for the coming year.

Of course, if a multiple regression procedure is used in prediction, for determining the predictor distribution one must use the regression equation for the coming year applied to last year's applicants. This procedure is based on the assumption that the quality of applicants and the percentage of those accepted who finally enroll is stable from one year to the next. It should be realized that separate cutoff points can be generated in this manner for different classifications of students, such as men and women, students to be permitted to live in dormitories, and so on.

Decision theory approach

As the reader will recall from chapter 14, as one looks at selection problems from the point of view of decision theory he considers the payoff in utility and the gain in utility from various decision strategies and from the use of various kinds of information in making the decisions.

Fixed treatment cutoff— A cutoff score is determined in terms of the selection ratio, i.e. the proportion of applicants to be selected. The cutting score that gives the greatest gain in utility per man tested for fixed treatment (see p. 683) has been shown (Cronbach & Gleser, 1965) to be the value of y' that satisfies the equation

$$\xi(y') - y'\phi(y') = \frac{C_y}{\sigma_e r_{ye}},$$

where

$\xi(y')$ is the ordinate of the normal curve at the cutting score, y',

$\phi(y')$ is the proportion who score above y',

C_y is the average cost of testing one person,

σ_e is the standard deviation of the evaluated criterion on the population from which subjects will be selected, and

r_{ye} is the correlation of the test with the evaluated criterion on the population from which subjects will be selected.

This cutting score assumes that (*a*) the payoff has a linear regression on test score, (*b*) the payoff for rejected candidates is zero, and (*c*) the test scores are normally distributed with mean of zero and standard deviation of unity.

Of course, in most educational selection situations this formula cannot readily be used to set cutoff scores because the payoff function is often not known. However, as was observed earlier, Cronbach and Gleser (1965, pp. 41, 309) pointed out that in this situation it is always desirable to test at least twice as many men as will be accepted if a test is worth using at all. Thus, the cutoff should be set to reject at least half of the applicants if gain in utility per man tested is to be maximized in a selection situation where the treatment (curriculum) is fixed (see p. 686). As pointed out earlier, if the size of an entering class is considered to be fixed this condition can often be achieved only by increasing the supply of applicants (without at the same time lowering their quality).

Adaptive treatment cutoff— In education it may not be very realistic to think of the treatments that students are given as fixed and unresponsive to the level of students who are selected. Often the faculty will adjust their teaching approach to some extent to fit the students who appear in their classes. This is the situation referred to earlier (pp. 683–86) as selection with adaptive treatment. The utility for those selected is always greater with adaptive treatment (if the treatment is indeed adaptive, and not maladaptive) unless the fixed treatment happens to be the optimum treatment for the whole group selected. In order to fix cutoff scores properly when treatment is adaptive, however, it appears that one would have to have information on the nature of the payoff surface characteristic of a particular situation.

As has been noted, for some purposes it may be appropriate to think of the educational "selection" problem as really a case of educational placement. That is, the applicant either gets placed into one educational experience, say a senior college to which he applies, or, if rejected there, he may also apply to a junior college and be accepted. If one considers the issue in this light, the cutoff scores can be located by determining the points at which the regression lines of payoff on test score cross for the various educational treatments (Cronbach, 1957, pp. 680–681). This is a topic that will be discussed later in connection with the general discussion of placement. One question that might well be raised at this point, however, is whether there is indeed a crossing point for the payoff functions of the various treatments. For instance, if for some applicants payoff was increased by placing them in a junior college transfer-oriented program instead of enrolling them directly into a senior college, then one should expect their senior college performance after transfer to be superior to that obtained by equally able students who entered senior colleges directly. The experience with junior college transfers, as summarized by Hills (1965), does not encourage one to believe that such superiority in performance is very common.

Summary

To summarize, the discussion so far has tried to place the selection and placement problems in a perspective relating society, institutions, and individuals as they make decisions based on information. It was noted that what an institution thinks of as selection, society may view as placement, and that an institution can think about decisions about individuals in ways that individuals cannot employ as they think about institutions.

A sound admissions program was defined as orderly, fully specified and clear, rational, logical, thoroughly planned, and modifiable. In developing such a program, an institution takes a stance on a number of issues, including the kind of benefit or utility it desires to achieve with its operations, whether it will be adaptive in its treatment of students, to what extent it will recruit applicants for its classes, what measures it will use in making its admissions decisions, how those measures will be combined, and where the cutting score will be placed. Various kinds of benefit (criteria) and various possible measures for making decisions were examined in detail, and the setting of cutoff scores was discussed in terms of both classical and decision theory procedures.

PLACEMENT

Initial Considerations

In the beginning of this chapter reference was made to Cronbach's definition of selection as being one kind of classification problem, that in which one of the classes of assignment was rejection. Classification is the broad term to include a variety of personnel assignment problems (cf. Cronbach & Gleser, 1965, chap. 2). Specifically, it includes the assignment of personnel to different treatments when there are several different predictor variables and several different treatments. Placement refers to a more restricted matter, the assignment of personnel to different treatments along a single dimension when there is only a single predictor dimension, though this may be a composite derived from a procedure such as multiple regression (Cronbach & Gleser, 1965, p. 13). Placement may include selection if one of the placements possible is rejection, in which case utility for each rejectee is considered to be zero. The principal difference between the earlier part of the chapter and this second part is that here personnel decisions will be considered in which there is more than one treatment available for those who are accepted. (Of course, if rejection is not permitted, everyone is accepted and is assigned to at least one of two or more available treatments.)

Fixed vs. adaptive treatments

The several treatments may be considered to be fixed, in that they are established a priori without regard to a particular group of students. That is, it might be institutional policy to offer in the ninth grade a fast-moving algebra section, one or more sections of "regular" algebra, and one or more sections of business arithmetic. Or it might be possible to have adaptive treatment conditions, in which the nature of the options to be offered would be determined after examination of, and in relation to, the current group of students. Thus, how rapidly the advanced section moved would be based on input information about the achievements and abilities of the students.

Fixed vs. adaptive quotas

Another aspect that can vary is the quota of cases that will be assigned to each treatment. It may be fixed; that is the college president may say that the institution can afford only two sections of 45 students each in remedial English, no matter how many need remediation or how badly they need it. Or the mathematics department may decide that first-year class sizes should be as near to 20 students each as possible, so the quotas for different treatments are all approximately equal. On the other hand, the quotas may be adaptable, free to be adjusted so as to maximize utility.

A common placement procedure in education is that in which the treatments are fixed, the quotas are also fixed, and there are a limited number of categories into which accepted applicants can be placed. Thus there may be a specified number of faculty available to teach mathematics, a predetermined number of these are to be assigned to teach remedial or noncredit mathematics, and new freshman students may be limited to the alternatives of enrolling in remedial mathematics, in analytic geometry, in differential calculus, or in no mathematics at all.

Placement according to achievement vs. according to learning rate

One approach to placement consists of trying to locate the student at the proper point in a sequence of courses according to how much he already knows. A student may be exempted from, and perhaps given credit for, courses below the level into which he is placed. Another approach consists of placing the student according to how fast he might be expected to learn. Thus some students might be placed in an accelerated mathematics course not because they have already been exposed to prerequisite ideas but because the course content was going to be covered at a rapid pace and perhaps at an abstract level. Others might conceivably be assigned to a decelerated course that would

cover the same ground but more slowly using many concrete examples. What is being done in this kind of placement is assigning the student to a particular mode of instruction or approach to content.

Purpose of placement

The above kinds of placement are attempts to situate the student in the course or treatment that will challenge him but will not overwhelm him—to prevent his wasting time or being bored on the one hand and to prevent his failure due to lack of preparation or lack of sufficient repetition or explication on the other. It appears that there are two ways of doing this. However, both are cases of attempting to place him in an instructional setting that will maximize payoff. This is, then, what placement is all about. In the paragraphs below some of the currently used placement techniques and their problems are described, followed by discussion of the implications of a decision theory approach to placement and its problems.

Current Placement Procedures
Use of placement tests

At the college level, most placement centers around English, foreign languages, and mathematics instruction. Procedures vary, but a quite common approach is to administer a subject-matter test during the senior year in high school or sometime before the initial registration for college classes and decide on the basis of that test into which treatment level or kind of instruction to assign the student in that subject. Certain tests are offered by publishers with this in mind, such as the Advanced Placement Program, the College-Level Examination Program, the Comparative Guidance and Placement Program, and the entire battery of Achievement Tests of the College Entrance Examination Board (Dyer, 1964, p. 9). The particular set of test elements of the American College Testing Program's admission test was chosen with the idea of use for this kind of placement in college courses (Lindquist & McCarrel, 1959, pp. 3, 12, 21–22). Other tests also are used for this purpose, such as the Iowa Tests of Educational Development, the Nelson-

Denny Reading Test, and Modern Language Association–Cooperative Foreign Language Tests, other published tests, and, perhaps most often, tests prepared by local institutions.

At the very least sophisticated level of college placement, test scores may not be used at all. The institution may make its placement decision on the basis of an overall impression of the student's vita including, perhaps, recommendations of his high school teachers in related subjects.

When test scores are involved, however, the administrative framework for instruction may be so irrational as to make the tests relatively useless. It is not uncommon to find that a college merely has a certain arbitrary number of spaces in remedial and advanced courses, and it places the lowest-scoring group of applicants into the remedial slots and the highest-scoring group into the advanced slots, the remainder being assigned to the routine teaching sections.

Problems in the evaluation of placement tests— Hopefully a college will at least place students on the basis of tests with names that appear to be relevant to the courses in which students are being placed, but it would be less than typically the case if the college investigated the semantic soundness (see chapter 14) of the tests it is using for placement. The content and validities of a test cannot be judged by its name. Some tests might be as useful for placement in a course with quite a different name as for placement in a course with a name similar to that of the test. An English test may be as effective for placement in social studies as in English. That is to say, some tests used for placement may be rather general learning ability tests rather than specific measures of achievement in a subject matter.

Often the college will not even think to evaluate for an "unplaced" group of students the correlational relationships between performance on the placement tests and performance in the courses into which students are to be placed by those tests—or, if such an investigation is made and the correlations are found to be disappointingly low, the college will go right ahead with placement based on those tests. After all, what else is it to do when the students are there, the faculty have been assigned to and prepared for remedial and advanced courses, and classes start tomorrow?

Sometimes college departments do not bother to check the published tests that might be suitable instruments for placement but move directly to developing their own instruments— perhaps merely using final examinations for previous offerings of the course. The effectiveness of these local tests often is unchallenged and unevaluated year after year.

At a more sophisticated level, some colleges diligently search for tests that will be effective placement devices, and, if they find none on the market, the faculty in the relevant departments develop their own tests and study their effectiveness. Usually the measures of effectiveness that are employed are (*a*) the correlations between the test and success in the courses and (*b*) some consideration of the usefulness of the test in setting cutoff levels for assignment of students to treatments.

One of the difficulties that is experienced in practical operation is that the decision to place students is often made before the research on how to place students soundly is finished, or even commenced. There is usually great reluctance to place all students randomly into the routine and alternate treatments for a year or two while the placement instrument is being evaluated. If that is not done, it is very hard to evaluate the instrument because the basic question to be asked is how well this instrument would predict in advance which students would have trouble with the routine course or would be able to handle a more (or less) advanced or accelerated or a differently presented course.

Once the students, on the basis of scores, are placed into different levels or kinds of courses, it is not easy to evaluate what might have happened in the absence of such placement because grading practices cannot be counted on to remain constant. Some remedial faculty, for instance, will take the position that since these students already have been determined to be inadequate, it is only reasonable to expect but a few of them to do satisfactory work in the course. Other remedial faculty will take the opposite position that since the course is there to help the students, there is no point in failing them. They could have been rejected for admission if that was what was intended. Therefore the faculty grade more generously. Furthermore, the grading standards in the routine course might change if the remedial-level students were enrolled in it. (Grades could be equated, or test scores could be used as the criterion to alleviate this problem, but these are not commonly employed procedures.)

With all of this potential wobble, it is difficult to determine how well the placement test would have functioned in the total group. Corrections for range restriction may be of some help in evaluating the correlations that might have been obtained for the total group, but such correction procedures do not give one a very clear picture of the optimum point at which to set the cutoff scores for assignment to different treatments. Bivariate frequency distributions, rather than correlation coefficients, are the data used in setting cutoff scores.[3]

Advanced placement
through high school preparation

A different approach to placement into advanced courses is that of arranging for the college course to be taught in the high school. This is the essence of the College Board's Advanced Placement Program. A high school agrees to follow a certain specified course syllabus that has been developed by a committee concerned with what is taught in such a course at the college level. Then at the end of the course the students in such courses all over the country are given a common Advanced Placement test in that subject. These tests are read and carefully graded by a national committee of readers. The scores are made available to colleges.

Colleges vary in the standards they set for acceptance of grades on Advanced Placement tests; and they also vary as to whether they merely exempt the student from taking the

same course in college, exempt him and give him credit, or exempt him, give him credit, and give him credit with a grade. It is apparently rare for a college to be completely rational in making these decisions even with such a well thought-out program as this (Casserly, Peterson, & Coffman, 1965). A college reasonably could administer these tests to its own students in these courses and give credit to any high school student who scored as well as the lowest scoring college student who received credit for the course. That would be applying the same standards to both groups. (It should be pointed out that for this to be effective, great effort would have to be expended to obtain grades on these essays comparable in quality, especially reliability, to those demanded by the College Board Advanced Placement Examinations.) So far as can readily be determined, virtually no college operates in this fashion, and colleges are generally quite arbitrary in deciding such questions as to what levels of performance to give exemptions, credits, and college grades.

Complex placement procedures

In several institutions, complex and flexible placement procedures based on years of accumulated experience seem to operate, though their effectiveness is seldom, if ever, carefully evaluated. In one, the admissions officer of an institute of technology (who functioned in that capacity for over 40 years) personally examined each applicant's record with regard to mathematics. Based on his experience with (a) previous students from particular high schools and high school teachers, (b) scores on the SAT and achievement tests in mathematics, and (c) mathematics courses and teachers in the institute of technology, this admissions officer assigned each applicant to the mathematics course that seemed most appropriate. The student could enter that course. If he passed it, he got credit for that course and for all prior courses in the mathematics sequence. If he found himself in difficulty in the course to which he was assigned, he could arrange with the admissions officer and the department head to drop back to a more appropriate course. If he found the assigned course too easy, he could

---

[3] Cronbach and Snow (1969, p. 22) suggested that it may be possible to avoid the need for random assignment by examining discontinuities in within-group regressions. This possibility deserves elaboration.

likewise arrange to advance to a higher course in the sequence. Whatever course he passed gave him automatic credit for the preceding courses.

A procedure such as this has much to recommend it, but it has several serious flaws, probably the worst of which is that it is not written down anywhere. This procedure was severely disrupted when the admissions officer retired, and it may take 20 or 30 more years for his replacement to gain enough experience to operate a similar procedure effectively. Of course, there are other problems, too, such as changes in faculty and courses in the high schools and the institute that upset the procedure now and then. But with flexibility on the part of the student, these are minor perturbations. If such a procedure were systematized, the decision process could be handled by a computer or a clerk (Helm, 1967), with systematic updating as continuous research revealed shifts in parameters. Often, however, with procedures such as these it is nearly impossible to obtain the cooperation and support necessary to effect the systematization. The author knows of none which has been documented in written form, though several that claim to be functioning have been described to him.

Computerized sequential placement testing

It would be only a modest further step in such a procedure to take advantage of modern technology and use computer-assisted testing to provide some of the information for a procedure such as the above. Branching tests could be developed covering the various topics to be studied in each course. Each student could take the necessary number and sequence of items to determine whether he had sufficient mastery of each topic to enter courses at various levels. For many of the students, mastery would be high enough or low enough that relatively few items would be needed to fix their levels. For borderline students, more items would be needed. But these additional items would be used only when needed (Cronbach & Gleser, 1965, especially pp. 94–95). Further use of the computer in the form of computer-assisted instruction (or some other form of programmed

learning) might very quickly bring up to a satisfactory level certain kinds of deficiencies that might otherwise prove troublesome for a person who was generally adequately prepared for a specific course level. But such procedures are not yet being used, or if used, are quite rare. One which has recently been funded for development is Project PLAN (Flanagan, 1967).

In summary, as a minimum—one that is not always reached at the present time—an institution undertaking a program of testing for placement purposes could be expected to carry out the following steps:

1. Define clearly and explicitly the alternative treatments that are planned, with respect both to their content and to their objectives.

2. Examine critically available published tests to determine whether any appear relevant to the differences between the treatments, and which seem most relevant.

3. If it appears necessary to develop a local test, design it specifically with the goal of identifying the differences that are relevant to the first point.

4. Conduct follow-up studies of students assigned to the different treatments to appraise their success and satisfaction in the program.

Ideally, as suggested earlier, for a year or two some students should be assigned to the "regular" and some to the "special" treatments on a random basis, so that a determination can be made of success in each treatment group in relation to performance on the measures being used for placement. Some of the problems arising in the conduct of such studies are considered in later sections of this chapter, together with the manner in which results from the study may appropriately be used to guide placement decisions.

Effectiveness of Placement Procedures

The superficial foundation for current placement and remedial practices in American education is seldom discussed with students and their parents, a condition which parades under a flag of altruism but smacks of fraud. Before examining specific studies of the effectiveness of placement, one must consider relevant criteria.

Grades as criteria

If a placement procedure is to be worthwhile, it must be worthwhile for something. The usual criterion has something to do with successfully passing a course or with the level of achievement in a course. That is, if too many students fail or get low grades in a course, then a better procedure would have placed more of them in a prior course. Or one might say that the students who have been placed in a prior course and complete it successfully should be prepared successfully to complete the subsequent course. That is the purpose for their having been placed where they were. If these students cannot move ahead after being placed in a prior or remedial course, then placement was not successful. And if too many fail the routine course when placement is operating, again the placement is not successful—it was introduced to prevent unnecessary failure. Furthermore, there should not be undue numbers of students placed in advanced courses who are unable to complete them satisfactorily. On the other hand, if advanced placement is functioning properly, few students in the routine courses should be obtaining high grades while loafing.

Persistence as a criterion

The importance of grades as a functional criterion cannot be denied, but there are other criteria which are also relevant in the placement context. One of importance is persistence. If the students are subjected to courses for which they are so poorly prepared that frustration and failure seem unavoidable, they are likely to drop out of those courses and perhaps out of the institution. Also, if they are placed in courses which merely repeat what they have already done or which move so slowly as to bore them, they are likely to judge their time and money poorly spent and seek other avenues for their investment. One objective of placement, then, in addition to that of successful performance in a course, is completion of that and other courses in the institution. A sound placement program should reduce withdrawal rates from courses into which students are placed and from the institution.

Satisfaction as a criterion

Another criterion which is not often considered but which seems an important aspect of sound placement is implicit in the persistence criterion and could be evaluated explicitly. That is the criterion of student satisfaction. If placement in such areas as mathematics is successful, the student should be placed at the level for which he is prepared, he should proceed at the pace which is appropriate for him, and he should be able to reach any level in the usual lower-division mathematics sequence which he desires or which is required for his other objectives. This should be a very satisfying learning experience for anyone seriously interested in higher education. If the student is dissatisfied with his experience in mathematics, it is likely that his placement in the sequence has been improper (Gagné, 1965, especially pp. 175–181; Dunn, 1966). One check on whether placement is operating properly would then be whether students were satisfied with the placement that they experienced. Their suggestions might be valuable data in revising placement procedures (see Casserly, 1968).

Evaluation of placement measures

As noted, institutions often use a test as a device upon which to base placement. In many cases there is little or no evaluation of the appropriateness of the test that is used except perhaps to see that it has a reasonable name. More evaluation than that is in order. The semantic soundness and the content and criterion-related validity of the test should be questioned (see chapter 14). Another consideration is also in order here, though, and that is the question of whether the test is more effective than other already available data would be. The author has witnessed situations in which a test given specifically for placement in English could not be demonstrated to be sufficiently more effective for placement in English courses (using the criteria and methods accepted by the institution) than the SAT Verbal scores which were already available due to their use in admission. The additional effort and cost of the placement test were wasted (unless, perhaps, it served a public relations function that alone justified the cost). Though it was not studied, there was good reason to believe that using the average of high school grades, or the average of grades in English courses, would have been as effective as either of the test scores. (In this context, see Gelso & Wilson, 1967; Wilson & Gelso, 1967.) For some reason, though, there seems to be a halo about test scores for placement that causes some faculty members to believe that no other kind of data deserve consideration.

Evaluation of treatments

Not only are the folkways about the virtue of tests over other measures for placement subject to question, but also there seems to be a folk myth that the best placement for persons inadequately prepared for a course is into a lower-level course. This never seems to be checked against the possiblity that as effective a procedure as the usual remedial course would be merely to have the student take the routine course twice. He might learn enough from his first experience with it to make the second time through quite easy, and the course might be easier the second time through than it would be after the typical remedial course. It is unknown what this type of placement would do for such criteria as satisfaction or persistence, but if the procedure was explained carefully and if the administrative procedures were adjusted so that poor performance the first time through a course was judged no more harshly than the taking of a remedial course, these criteria might not suffer unduly.

Remedial courses

It does not seem to be widely realized that remedial courses are generally not very effective in improving subsequent grades or reducing withdrawal when soundly evaluated. Ahmann and Glock (1959) published an outstanding study of a remedial procedure. They evaluated a course in applied mathematics for freshmen males in the College of Agriculture at Cornell University. The purpose of the special course was to prepare the students so that the faculty members would not have to go back over elementary mathematics before going on to the

appropriate topics for their science and mathematics courses. The special course was very carefully developed through cooperative efforts of the experimenters and the faculty. It was a full three-semester hour course taught in sections of 25 students.

The Cornell Mathematics Test was used as a placement instrument and as one of the criteria of the study. The test had been developed in cooperation with the agriculture and physical science faculties who suggested items and topics for inclusion, edited the items, and rated them for importance. The test showed evidence of content, concurrent, and construct validity. On the basis of scores on this test, the top 20 percent of the class was excluded from the study. The remaining students were randomly assigned to the remedial course or to a control group who received no formal instruction in mathematics.

The principal criteria were final course grades in eight introductory courses involving mathematics and six cumulative grade averages. The statistical treatment was analysis of covariance with performance on the Ohio State Psychological Examination and the Cornell Mathematics Test as covariates.

The results were devastating. Though the students and their faculty advisors agreed by a large majority that the course was valuable and should be offered, and though over half of the instructors thought the course would be worthwhile for agriculture freshmen and over 90 percent thought it would be worthwhile for those poorly prepared in mathematics, and though over 70 percent of the students thought that they were at least fairly well prepared in mathematics due to the course, there were only two significant results from the analyses of covariance, and these were in the opposite direction from that desired. They both involved chemistry courses in which the control subjects obtained higher grades than the subjects who took the special course. Further study showed that the students' scores on the Cornell Mathematics Test had indeed risen, with the rise being significantly greater for the experimental subjects. But comparisons of dropout rates at various periods (dropout being defined as leaving the university with a cumulative grade point average below 70) showed that the cumulative attrition was not different for the control and experimental subjects by the end of the third semester. In both groups the loss was 25 percent.

It is not easy to locate sound evaluations of remedial procedures such as this. However, informal discussion with admissions officers and college counseling center personnel leads the writer to believe that remediation is relatively ineffective. One admissions officer, who asked that his institution not be identified, stated that a 10-year study had shown that no student who was placed in a remedial course during that period had graduated from the institution.

The lack of published data concerning sound evaluations of remedial procedures is paralleled by the lack of data evaluating placement procedures. Review of the literature in this area yields few published studies. The College Entrance Examination Board provides a whole series of Achievement Tests on a worldwide administrative basis several times a year. They are often suggested for use in college placement. Even such agencies as this have in the past conducted but few studies of the effectiveness of their tests for placement purposes.

A review of the Validity Studies Section of the journal *Educational and Psychological Measurement*, a logical place to expect such studies to be published, reveals a dearth of data. Informal reviews of other appropriate original sources yield the same result. One suspects that two factors might underlie this lack of published evaluative data. One is that such studies seem inherently to be of primarily local interest. It is unlikely that a placement procedure will be generally applicable because institutions, their faculties, and their clienteles differ so widely. Thus the person conducting such a study is less likely to prepare it for publication, and the editor who receives a manuscript on such a study is less likely to publish it than something of greater apparent generality. The second factor which might lie behind the lack of published studies is that they may regularly not be very

impressive. The ones in which the author has participated have been very disappointing and have been relegated to the files of the institutions which were involved. This may well have been the case with many other placement studies.

Examples of the vague sorts of descriptions about placement, which are commonly available, appeared in the American Council on Education's publication, *College Testing: A Guide to Practices and Programs* (American Council on Education, Committee on Measurement and Evaluation, 1959). In a 10-page chapter on "The Use of Tests in Course Placement or Accreditation," no evidence is given that placement is effective; and there is no discussion of precisely how placement is done, how tests are chosen, how cutoff scores are set, or other particulars that one needs to know in order to introduce an effective placement program. Little of this kind of information, and no evaluation of the effectiveness of placement, can be found in the descriptions of specific college and university testing programs which form the last 70 pages of the ACE's book.

Illustrative reported studies

A few interesting studies have been reported (not necessarily published). Abramson (1959) reported a very competent study of the effect of special grouping of able students in high school on their performance in college. He selected four schools to represent different practices and theories concerning the grouping of students of high ability. In one, there was no centrally organized method for grouping students. In another, high-ability students were selected for honor classes in one or two major subjects. In the third, high-ability students were selected for membership in an "honor school," and they were assigned to honor classes for most of their subjects. The fourth case was a special high school to which only high-ability students were admitted on the basis of a special examination.

After careful study Abramson remarked:

The major conclusion that may be drawn from this inquiry is that college freshmen and sophomore grade-point averages, honors, and course grades were not influenced by ability grouping as it existed in the 1953–1954 and 1954–1955 school years in the high schools included in the study [p. 13].

He further concluded:

The administrative problems created in the high school by the programming of "honor" classes and by the maintenance of subordinate organizations for high-ability pupils cannot be considered as providing a return in the form of marked differences in the future academic success of the graduates of these schools in the course of their college program [pp. 13–14].

At the College Board's Southern Regional Meeting in 1967, J. E. Mickler reported on the University of Alabama's placement procedure. Their testing program for entering students has involved as much as 12 hours of testing time. High school course grades also are used in placement. As many as 70 predictors are used for some purposes. The possible treatments for various students are very complex. A student may start at any of five levels of mathematics, three levels of chemistry, four levels of English, or two levels of French or Spanish. Grades are the only criterion reported on. With all this elaborate structure, Mickler presented no evidence that grades in later courses, persistence in courses or in the institution, or student satisfaction were enhanced due to the placement operation (cf. p. 706). One wonders whether it is encouraging to hear him say that expansion of the program is anticipated because, among other things, it has "the solid support of the central administration."

A study by Francis (1966) at the University of Missouri illustrated well the inadequacies of some current conceptions of the placement problem. Francis reported in detail the intercorrelations, multiple correlations, regression equations, and standard errors of estimate for predicting grades in Calculus I and Calculus II from grades and test scores, but he showed no recognition of the need for evidence concerning whether placement on the basis of such variables is effective in producing better performance, more satisfaction, or longer persistence in the course or the institution.

An unpublished study by Gelso and Trowell (1967) carried the placement question through to a reasonable criterion and discovered that the plan for placement in history at South Georgia College, a public junior college in Douglas, if anything, reverses the order of courses. In this instance, the courses History 110 and History 111 are considered by the faculty to be logically sequential though it is recognized that the students' understanding of the material in History 111 is not dependent on their understanding of the material in History 110. The question that was raised was whether students would obtain higher grades in 111 if it was taken after 110. Of two groups of students, one took the courses in the logically sequential order (110 followed by 111), and one took the courses in the reverse order (111 followed by 110). Instead of the logical order producing higher grades in the second course, the results indicated that there were no significant differences, but the mean grades were higher in *both* 110 and 111 if the courses were taken in the logically incorrect order, 111 followed by 110. Although Gelso and Trowell did determine that the groups were equivalent on predicted freshman average grade, they were not able to assign students randomly to sequences. There might then be relevant variables operating that were not controlled by finding only minute differences between groups in predicted averages. At any rate, the study shows the importance of checking on a placement procedure that seems to be logically sound.

Dunn's (1966) study, mentioned earlier, uses the student's reported satisfaction as the explicit criterion for placement. At the University of Arkansas students may be placed in one of five mathematics courses depending on their scores on a 60-question multiple-choice test primarily drawn from basic algebra. After some years of use of the placement procedure, a questionnaire was administered to freshmen nearing the end of their second semester of college mathematics to obtain information about their degree of satisfaction with their placement. The questionnaire asked what their placement had been; what grade they had obtained; whether they had to work hard to get that grade; whether their placement was too advanced, not advanced enough, not interesting, or just right; whether they had been placed most suitably and where they should have been placed if the placement was not just right. While one might wish for corroborative evidence, this set of questions permitted Dunn to generate groups of students who, according to self-report, had been properly placed and to evaluate the placement test in terms of correct classifications of students to these ideal groups. (It would have been illuminating to know the base rate of correct classification without the test. See Meehl & Rosen, 1955.) Dunn found that the cutoff scores that were in use for assigning students to various mathematics courses gave rather high probabilities of misclassification. However, when new cutoffs were generated to minimize the maximum probability of misclassification, the chances of misclassification were still approximately two out of three. Even when the test was broken into subsets of questions, the subsets optimized, and optimal weights assigned to the sets, Dunn reported that there was little improvement in classification accuracy. He concluded that the reason for this was the lack of variety among the test items—that a greater variety of questions was needed to discriminate among various levels of mathematical sophistication.

Setting Cutoff Scores by Classical Procedures

One of the difficult problems facing institutions that attempt to use placement as it has been described above is the setting of the cutoff score on a predictor or weighted combination of predictors that determines into which treatment a particular student will be placed. In Dunn's (1966) report of mathematics placement at the University of Arkansas, the cutoff scores being used when he commenced his study were:

Above 45 (out of 60 items): Enroll in Math 255 or 128;

Between 26 and 44: Enroll in Math 120;

Between 15 and 25: Enroll in Math 115;

Below 14: Enroll in Math 102.

Though Dunn did not say so, the fact that these cutoff points are spaced so neatly at 15, 25 and 45 suggests that they were chosen arbi-

trarily. Such arbitrariness is often evident in the placement practices of schools and colleges.

Quotas

The first primitive advance over completely arbitrary choice often is choice of cutoff points so that certain quotas are met; i.e. so that the weakest students fill all the available spaces in the remedial sections and the strongest fill all the spaces in the advanced sections. The advance is primitive because no arbitrary quota is sensible in placement. The procedure would be tolerable from the individual's point of view if the correlation between the placement test and the criterion were positive and perfect, or nearly so. However, that situation is not likely to occur in practice. Correlations between placement test scores and criteria such as grades are more likely to be around .5 than any number greater than that, and often they will not be that high (see, for instance, Goolsby, 1966b).

If the placement test does not have a very high correlation with the grade criterion, but if students are placed in the remedial sections on the basis of such a placement test, one is guilty of suggesting to students that he has accurately determined what is wrong with them and is giving them the proper treatments for their difficulties, when in fact the whole procedure may be very doubtful from the placement instrument through the remediation.

If the cutoff points for assigning students to remedial courses are based on quotas and if the placement test *does* have a very high correlation with the grade criterion, one may experience additional problems. Suppose that not all those who clearly require remediation according to the placement test are assigned to the remedial sections because the quota is too small. The others have been accepted for admission already, so they must be placed somewhere. The only location available is the regular sections—which is the same as deliberately dooming many of them to failure.

From the institution's point of view, an additional problem that arises with modest or low correlations between placement tests and criteria is that in such cases a suitable cutoff point cannot be found that assigns more than a very few persons to special sections, such as the remedial sections, and also assigns to such sections more of those who would fail the standard course than would pass that course.

For instance, at Southern Technical Institute in Georgia the use of the College Board's Achievement Test in English was examined for the purpose of placing students into regular or remedial English. The grades obtained by students in freshman English were tabulated for low score intervals on the achievement test to attempt to locate a cutoff score. The institution's desire was to assign a reasonable number of students to remedial English and that these would be predominantly those students who would fail the freshman English course if they were to attempt it without further preparation. As table 19.1 shows, any cutoff

TABLE 19.1

Bivariate Grouped Frequency Distribution of College Board English Achievement Test Score vs. Grades in Regular Freshman English

($r = .41$ $N = 710$)

CEEB ENGLISH ACHIEVEMENT TEST SCORE	FRESHMAN ENGLISH GRADE					
	F	D	C	B	A	Total
340–700	9	77	273	173	27	559
320–339	7	9	34	8	1	59
300–319	1	12	25	9	0	47
275–299	3	5	20	2	0	30
250–274	1	8	3	1	0	13
225–249	0	1	1	0	0	2
Total	21	112	356	193	28	710

score would assign more students to the remedial course who passed freshman English than who failed it. Even very low cutoff scores would place students into the remedial course who would obtain even Cs and Bs in the regular course. This finding is due to two things: (*a*) the relatively low (but not atypical) degree of relationship between scores on the test and success in English and (*b*) the grading practice of the institution that results in only three or four percent of the class obtaining grades of A or of F. Similar conditions are widespread in colleges in the United States.

By a method discussed earlier in connection with selection, one can seek to determine a cutoff score so that more of the people who would fail the regular course than would pass that course are assigned to a lower-level course. That method is to plot the frequency distributions of the failing students and of the passing students and to set the cutoff score at the point where these distributions cross, if such a point exists.

Probability of attainment of selected criterion level

Other points could be chosen for the cutoff. Educational Testing Service and the College Entrance Examination Board recommend (CEEB, 1967) that for placing students into sequential courses or courses in which different sections of students are taught at different levels of instruction, a common course examination or adjusted grade be used as the criterion. They propose that the cutoff score for a placement test be based on the probability of attaining a given level on the criterion. Thus, suppose that a common examination were to be used for all entering freshmen who took English, regardless of whether it was remedial, regular, or advanced. Those students who were predicted to have at least 50 chances in 100 of earning a score that would be associated with a grade above F in the regular course and who were predicted to have less than 50 chances in 100 of earning a score that would be associated with a grade above B in the regular course, might be assigned to take the regular course. The students above and below those cutoff points would be assigned to advanced or remedial sections, respectively, in order to avoid boredom, on the one hand, and failure, on the other.

Highest-level course with selected level of predicted achievement

For placement in courses of different content within a field, the College Board recommends that a prediction equation be developed for each course and each student be placed in the highest-level course for which he has a predicted grade at a predetermined point. Thus, if there were three mathematics courses of different content to which a freshman could be assigned, his predicted performances in each course would be obtained, and he might be assigned to the highest-level course in which he was predicted to obtain a passing grade. These, then, are two more principles for setting cutoff points, i.e. (*a*) setting the cutoff according to a predetermined probability of obtaining a specified grade and (*b*) setting the cutoff at a predetermined grade level and assigning the student to the highest-level course for which his predicted grade reaches that level.

These methods of placement are not without some difficulties. The College Board's (1967) report gives no guidance at all concerning the levels of probabilities or the predetermined levels of performance that should be used in their procedures. The institution is left to be arbitrary, or to use some principle such as has been described before—that of assigning to the remedial course more of the prospective failures than of the prospective passes in the regular course. Since the College Board's publication does not mention the matter of the possibility of an improper balance of potential successes and failures below any chosen cutoff point, it is likely that the institution that uses the College Board's publication without additional instruction will indeed be arbitrary in selecting cutoff scores. This cannot be readily defended as a sound procedure.

The upper end causes the same sorts of problems as have been discussed and illustrated for the low end of the placement scale, though they may not be so damaging to students. At the low end, one wants to provide remediation for those who could not pass the regular course otherwise; at the high end, one wants to exempt those who already know enough of the subject matter that they can be expected to obtain the highest grades, i.e. those who are adequately prepared for work at a higher level. In either case, one needs a placement test that correlates very highly with grades in order to find a cutoff point that will admit to the special treatment more of the desired cases than the undesired cases and that will also admit enough cases to make provision of a special treatment worthwhile.

Task analysis

An approach which seems not to be widely used in organizing remediation or advancement, but that would seem logically sound if successive course work depends on mastery of that which has preceded, would be through task analysis (Gagné, 1962). The particular tasks involved in subsequent learning could be isolated and related to their prerequisites. Each prerequisite could be specifically taught so that all prerequisites would be available before advanced learning was introduced. The problems with this approach lie in the analyses of the tasks, of course; but perhaps more important is the fact that, for it to operate effectively, the whole educational system would have to be revised toward far greater flexibility than now exists. Such a revision will take place only as unusual force is applied to overcome great inertia.

Decision Theory and Educational Placement

After examining placement procedures that are being used and the problems associated with them, after discovering that there is very little published literature describing successful (or even unsuccessful) placement procedures and their associated curricular components, and after becoming acquainted with some of the problems of setting up operational programs based on the classical approaches to placement, one develops a feeling that what is being done is not very sound or successful and that there must be a better way. One way that has not yet received much more than theoretical or logical exploration, but that seems promising at this point, is the use of the decision theory model (Cronbach & Gleser, 1965, especially chap. 5).

The principal characteristic of the decision theory approach that is distinctly different from the more customary views about placement is the set of ideas that people have different degrees of various traits and that various traits are differently associated with success in specific learning situations. Ideally education should be organized so that there would be available a variety of ways of approaching a subject matter, and people should be assigned to the ways (treatments) according to their traits so that learning would be most efficient. The ways people differ might be their past experiences with the subject matter (their level of specific prerequisite training), their aptitudes, their cognitive styles, their personality traits, their attitudes, or such other characteristics as are found to be relevant to performance on the learning task. The ways that the subject matter might be approached (treatments) might involve not only the level of prerequisite knowledge required but also such things as the mode of presentation, the manner and attitude of the teacher, the degree to which independent vs. group study was emphasized or provided for, the kind of teaching aids used and the extent of their use, and so on.

Illustration of the decision theory approach

To illustrate and contrast this approach with the traditional approach to placement, consider a placement procedure that might be used in English. Suppose that the English department of a junior college complains that many of the entering freshmen do not know grammar and punctuation, have limited writing skills, and really do not know how to read fluently. Without such skills as these they simply cannot be expected to be able to write satisfactory term papers in the introductory English literature course. So a special noncredit remedial English course is proposed to develop these skills in those students who lack them, and a placement test is provided to determine which students should be assigned to the remedial course. How should this program be operated and how should it be evaluated?

Now, according to traditional thinking, the course in what will probably be dubbed "bonehead English" will be deemed successful to the extent that its "graduates" are able to compete in the standard freshman introductory English literature course on a par with those assigned directly to the course. Their "holes" have been patched, so to speak (cf. Carroll, 1967, p. 42; Cronbach, 1967, p. 27). Statistically, if the remedial program is working soundly one should not be able to distinguish between the distributions of introductory English literature grades of the students who have passed remedial English and those who were not assigned to remedial English but went directly into the regular freshman course.

Decision theory analysis— In terms of the decision theory model, there are two treatments in connection with freshman English. One is two courses long, consisting of remedial English followed by regular freshman English. The other is one course long, that single course being regular freshman English. There is also a placement test to determine which students will be assigned to each of the treatments.

Now, suppose that a student who has already mastered the skills in grammar, punctuation, writing, and reading will not be benefited by taking the extra course. Further, suppose that he may be so bored by that treatment that he will do less well in the second part of the sequence, the regular freshman English literature part, which is the basic interest, than he would have done if he entered that course directly. Suppose, on the other hand, that the student who has not mastered the basic English skills will be very handicapped by the one-course treatment but may be given a great advantage in regular freshman English by the two-course treatment.

The situation may be illustrated by the schema in figure 19.1. The lines in the figure are the regression lines of final grades in regular freshman English literature on placement test scores. It can be seen that if a student's score on the placement test is above (to the right of) the crossing point he can be expected to obtain higher grades in the regular freshman English literature course if he is placed in the one-course sequence. (He avoids boredom.) However, if his placement test score is below the crossing point, he will obtain higher grades in the regular English part of the instruction if he takes the two-course treatment. (His difficulties are corrected before facing the regular course.)

The English teacher can be expected to object at this point on the grounds that the remediation cannot be so boring as actually to

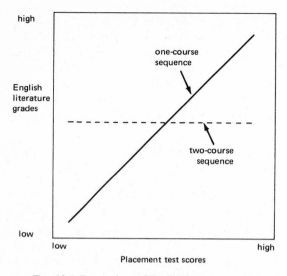

FIG. 19.1. Regressions of English literature grades on placement test scores where placement is effective.

handicap a person for the regular course. Assuming linearity of regression (which may be hazardous at this point), this position hypothesizes that the schema in figure 19.2 more accurately depicts the situation. The teacher's assertion is that, within the range of students available to this junior college, the two-course sequence is better for all students and that everyone should be assigned to remedial English if the institution indeed desires that each student

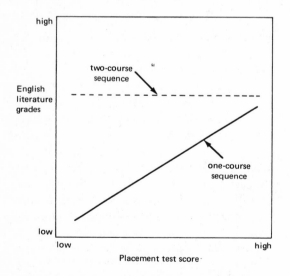

FIG. 19.2. Regressions of English literature grades on placement test scores where placement is ineffective.

should attain the highest level of competence in English that can be provided for.

However, this argument ignores the additional investment in time of student and teacher that is involved in reaching this level. Extra time and labor must be counted as a *cost* and must be subtracted from the payoff to get the *net* utility of a treatment. From this point of view, figure 19.1 is very likely the more appropriate representation.

Notice the striking thing that this model says about the placement test. *For placement to be worthwhile the placement test must have different regression slopes for the various treatments* (see also chap. 14, pp. 499–501). The traditional model does not recognize this necessity, and, indeed, traditional practice in colleges fails to recognize it also. The author cannot recall ever having witnessed a claim that a commercial or locally developed placement test was efficacious because it had different regression coefficients for different available treatments.

Traditional tests and decision theory placement

As Cronbach has pointed out earlier (p. 500), a test that measures ability in general or correlates highly with a general ability test is likely to be of little value in placement under this model because very similar regression slopes are likely to result for all treatments. The interaction between trait and treatment is the key to the model. In educational terms, such an interaction is no more than recognizing and capitalizing on the fact (see evidence later in this chapter) that different students can best be taught by different methods.

This approach suggests that the institution should seek or attempt to create strong trait-treatment interactions involving the subject matters wherein placement is a concern. For instance, in a subject matter such as mathematics, English, or a foreign language, one might attempt to invent several different approaches in accordance with his hypotheses as to the bases of different types of students' difficulties. He then might attempt to develop a test that would have different regression slopes for the different treatments. Students would be assigned to the treatments according to the locations of their scores on the test in relationship to the crossing point of the regression lines. It might or might not be the case that one of the effective treatments would be the same as what is now done under the label of remediation or advanced placement in that subject matter.

It is not clear yet what can be done toward making such a model work in practice. The finding of interactions between instructional methods and individual differences may be difficult and frustrating (Carroll, 1967; Cronbach, 1967). For example, Goolsby (1966a) attempted to develop diverse social studies tests such as might be helpful in placing students. His seven social studies tests, selected to maximize differences in the character of the content of the items in each test, had intercorrelations with each other ranging from .63 to .95. There would appear to be a general ability factor running through such a set of tests to produce such high intercorrelations even though the tests were deliberately picked and constructed to be different from each other while remaining within the content of eighth grade social studies.

Implications of the decision theory model

Cronbach and Gleser (1965) have presented an extensive theoretical analysis of decision theory as it applies to the placement problem. The interested reader should refer to their book for details, including the mathematical arguments. Here it is intended to extract only some of their conclusions that will be of interest to the practitioner who might consider exploring this approach.[4] To do so, it is necessary

[4] The models that have been developed for applying decision-theory approach to personnel decisions involve a number of assumptions that may not be met in practice. The first is that one have an acceptable measure of benefit or utility. That grades are a direct measure of utility and that the conventional numerical equivalents fairly represent the utility attached to each grade is quite a hazardous assumption, but one that is implicit in most treatments of grades. A second assumption, though one that is subject to empirical verification, is that for each possible treatment the relationship between predictor and utility is linear. A third assumption is that placement into different treatments can appropriately be

that a few points be clarified in order to simplify later considerations. First, when one speaks about the validity of a test for a treatment, it will simplify matters if one considers the correlation between scores on the test, y, and payoff, e, from the treatment, t, to be made up of two elements—(a) the correlation between the test scores and an underlying trait, s, and (b) the correlation between that underlying trait and the payoff. Thus,

$$r_{ye_t} = r_{ys}r_{se_t}$$

This assumes that y and e have nothing in common but s. The correlation r_{ye_t} is the correlation one obtains when he compares scores on a placement test with grades in freshman English, assuming that the numbers associated with various levels of grades (typically, 0, 1, 2, 3, and 4) accurately reflect the importance or value (payoff) those grades have for the institution. (That assumption seems very hazardous, as will be seen below.)

Regression slopes for different treatments— Now, it is of course the case that with r_{ys} constant for a set of test scores and an underlying trait (such as an ability factor one obtains through factor analysis), r_{ye_t} can vary from one treatment to another because r_{se_t} may not be the same for various treatments. Furthermore, the regression slopes, m, for different treatments can differ because they also depend on σ_{e_t}, according to the expression,

$$m_{y_t} = r_{ys}r_{se_t}\sigma_{e_t} = r_{ye_t}\sigma_{e_t},$$

where test scores, y, and the underlying trait, s, are measured on scales with mean of zero and unit standard deviation.

Slopes depend on r_{se_t} and on σ_{e_t}— The fact that for placement to be effective the regression lines must cross for different treatments indicates that the different treatments should have

made on the basis of a single predictor composite measuring a common "ability," and that this ability mediates the relationship between predictor and indicator of utility. The presentation that follows is based upon this simplified model.

different values for m_{y_t}. Since r_{ys} is assumed to be constant, the differences in the m values must come from differences in the relationship, r_{se_t}, between the underlying trait, s, and the payoff, e_t, or from differences in values of σ_{e_t}. The latter could be the case. For instance, assume that the numbers associated with grades (such as four points for an A, three points for a B, two points for a C, one point for a D, and zero for an F) are the payoff values. Then a treatment that resulted in a wide spread of grades would have a large σ_{e_t}. A treatment that had a narrow spread (perhaps all As, even) would have a small σ_{e_t}.

Let us pause to examine the assumption about the payoff scale of grades because it will clarify the meaning of utility and emphasize the importance of the practical problem of developing an adequate value scale when making decisions. If the typical numbers associated with grades (F$=0$, D$=1$, C$=2$, B$=3$, and A$=4$) are used as the utility scale for these grades, it implies that an institution values equally two students with grades of C and two students, one of whom has an A average and one of whom has an F average. That may be the case, but it also may be the case that an institution does not worry very much about students who fail—they are more or less expected, for instance, in the academic programs of many open-door junior colleges. Such institutions may value As, or above average grades, disproportionately highly and should, perhaps, use numbers such as 0, 0, 1, 2, and 3 to represent grades from F to A. Then an A and an F ($3+0=3.0$) would be equivalent to two C+'s ($1.5+1.5=3.0$). On the other hand, some institutions may be very concerned about failures, expect them to be rare, and be distressed when they occur. (This may be common in professional schools such as medical schools.) They might more properly express grades numerically as 0, 11, 12, 13, and 14, for F to A, respectively. An A and an F student ($14+0=14$) would then be equivalent in value to the institution of two students with grades below D ($7+7=14$), and this might better reflect the institution's values or utilities attached to such performances.

Institutions seldom, if ever, have thought through their grading systems from this point of view. Usually the numbers assigned grades are merely a convenience to make averaging simple. Thus, to use the numbers 0, 1, 2, 3, and 4 to represent the utilities of grades of F to A for an institution is hazardous, but one cannot make decisions without reflecting some value scale. This one was used merely to simplify the illustration.

Fixed treatments and fixed quotas— In a placement situation in which the treatments have been fixed (certain courses in mathematics will be taught regardless of what kinds of students are available) and in which quotas are fixed (certain predetermined proportions of students or numbers of students will be assigned to each of the various mathematics courses), certain things are known. It is known how many and what kind of treatments there will be, and it is known that the cutoff points on the test score, y, must be set to obtain certain numbers or proportions of students. Those points can be chosen once a frequency distribution of y scores for the entering students is available, or they can be estimated from previous students' data as described earlier under the topic of selection. What decision theory contributes in this situation is the demonstration (Cronbach & Gleser, 1965, app. 1) that here the gain in utility (i.e. the expected payoff from a set of decisions) is a linear function of r_{ys}, that is of the correlation between the placement test scores and the underlying trait. This is to be contrasted with the common interpretation of the importance of a validity coefficient being judged by r^2 rather than r.

Fixed treatments and adaptive quotas— When there are fixed treatments but quotas can be adjusted according to the kinds of students one has to work with, a procedure for setting cutting scores is needed. In this case, the setting of cutting scores is simply that which was discussed earlier—placing them where the regression lines of grades (or other payoffs) on test scores cross. Each student is assigned to the treatment that has the highest payoff for his test score.

In the case of fixed treatments and adaptive quotas the utility function depends on the particular treatments used; it is not a simple linear function of r_{ys}.

The optimum strategy for placement depends upon two types of factors: (a) the size of the difference in average payoff over all persons for the different treatments and (b) the size of the differences in slope m, for the different treatments, which in turn depends upon the value of r_{ys}. If one treatment is on average substantially better than the others, it will tend to be only for the extremes of ability that the alternate treatments will be superior. By the same token, if differences in slopes, m, are small, it will only be at the extremes that the regression lines for the alternate treatments will intersect the one that is best on average. Conversely, when treatments are nearly equal on average, and/or when differences in slope of the regression of payoff on predictor are marked, the regressions will intersect near the mean, and it will be advantageous to assign many students to the nonaverage treatments.

As an illustration, consider a college that has a more or less fixed curriculum. For example, suppose that remedial English is taught in about the same way from year to year, or that changes in remedial English are based on teacher preferences rather than on characteristics of the students to be taught, and suppose that the same is the case with the other English courses. Assume that this college has three possible fixed treatments in English for entering freshmen. One is remedial, one is regular (i.e. English I), and the third is the second regular course (i.e. English II). Additionally say that these two regular English courses are the English requirement for graduation, so that it is reasonable to use as the criterion (i.e. utility function) grades in the second regular English course.

Now think of the correlations between placement test scores and grades in English II for students in three groups, those who take remedial English and English I before taking English II, those who take English I before taking English II, and those who take no other English before taking English II. For placement

to be effective those correlations should differ (assuming for simplicity that the standard deviations of English II grades are the same for the three groups). Those correlations have been labeled r_{ye_t}, where t stands for the three different treatments. Remember that r_{ye_t} is the product of multiplying the correlation r_{ys} (between the test, y, and the underlying ability, s—which might be the ability to read, in this case) by the correlation r_{se_t} (between the ability and grades in English II), the latter correlation being different for each treatment.

Thus, the extent to which a test permits useful placement is a joint function of how well the test measures the relevant underlying trait and how markedly the validity of the trait differs for different treatments. For a specified trait, i.e. a specified r_{se} for each of the treatments, the extent to which r_{ye_t} can differ is limited by the size of r_{ys}.

But these r_{ye_t}'s represent the slopes of the regression lines for the three treatments (assuming equal σ_{e_t}'s as stated above). With r_{ye_t}'s that do not differ very much from one treatment to another, the regression lines approach being parallel. In such cases, the cutting scores for assigning persons to the different treatments will tend to assign more cases to the middle group (i.e. to the treatment suitable for the average entering freshman). Suppose, in this example, a reading test had been used as the basis for placing students in alternate treatments, and suppose that it had been found that the slope of the regression line of grades on test score was only slightly different for those who had started with remedial English, those who had started with English I, and those who had started with English II. This could mean either that (a) reading ability has little differential validity for the three treatments (possibly being quite valid for all three though not differentiating) or (b) the test used is not a good measure of reading ability. The remedy is quite different in the two cases. In the first case, some other type of measure that has more differential validity must be found; in the second, a better reading test must be found. But so long as the situation exists, the regression lines will intersect only near the extremes, and optimal strategy will dictate that most students receive the average treatment.

Adaptive treatments with fixed quotas— In order to consider adaptive treatment situations, it is necessary to make some assumptions about the relationship between payoff and underlying ability under various treatments. Cronbach and Gleser (1965) chose to elaborate the simplest mathematical function that covers a reasonable variety of nontrivial relationships, represented by the equation

$$e_{st} = m_{st}s + c + bm_{st} - am_{st}^2,$$

in which e_{st} is the payoff for a given level of ability s in a given treatment t, m_{st} is the slope of the payoff function and is equal to $\sigma_{st}r_{set}$, and the parameters a, b, and c differ for different underlying abilities or different treatments. They must be determined empirically. Using this payoff relationship, which Cronbach and Gleser (1965) believed to be quite satisfactory as a working assumption, led them to useful conclusions about some aspects of the problem of placement under adaptive treatment conditions.

If a college can be so flexible as to provide adaptive treatments—i.e. to evaluate the incoming students and use treatments especially suited to them (which requires extensive and careful study of various prior groups in order to generate adequate information on which treatments are suited to what kinds of students)—it is found that utility is a function of r_{ys}^2 (the square of the correlation between the placement test score and the underlying trait). This is similar to the traditional interpretation of validity coefficients, but it contrasts with the interpretation when treatments are fixed.

Adaptive treatments with adaptive quotas— When quotas can be adjusted with adaptive treatments, questions arise concerning such matters as how different the various treatments should be, how many of them there should be, and how the cutting scores should be set. Cronbach and Gleser's (1965) theorizing revealed that the higher the value of r_{ys} the more the

various treatments should differ in their essential nature. In proportion as the test places students accurately with respect to their possession of the underlying trait, and that trait has differential validity for the range of possible treatments, it is fruitful to provide markedly different educational programs for them. If r_{ys} is relatively low, the various treatments should be rather similar.

Cronbach and Gleser's calculations indicated that, with regard to the number of different treatments that should be introduced, over a wide variety of conditions most of the benefit will be obtained from the use of not more than four or five different treatments. It is interesting that Cronbach and Gleser's development suggests that the value of increased r_{ys} (i.e. improved test validity) for their model is not justification of more different treatments but rather greater distinction between treatments. As they said: "With a good test people may be divided into ten groups and given ten sharply distinct treatments, that is, treatments suited to quite different levels of aptitude. With a poor test people may still be divided into ten groups, but the ten treatments should not be extremely different [pp. 64–65]."

The locations of cutting scores in the case of a fixed number of adaptive treatments and adjustable quotas also do not depend on the size of the correlation coefficients. In fact, Cronbach and Gleser (1965, p. 61) provided a table giving the cutting scores on y in standard score values and their percentile equivalents for up to six treatments. These scores are located halfway between the test score (y) means for the groups assigned to adjacent treatments.

An illustration

It is helpful to think through these implications in terms of a concrete, if fictitious, example. For this purpose consider mathematics placement. Suppose, then, that through study of payoff as it relates to characteristics of students in the various treatments that are to be available, it is found that payoff is related to only one factor, s. Suppose further that it has been possible to identify this factor, and it turns out to be the aptitude factor called by factor analysts, *Number*, found clearly in many factor analyses (French, 1951). This factor represents facility in manipulating numbers in any form, and it is found in tests whose items involve numbers. Suppose further that one chooses as a measure of this aptitude, s, the Numerical Operations test from the Guilford-Zimmerman Aptitude Survey (Guilford & Zimmerman, 1956). Scores on this test become the variable y. The factor loading of the Numerical Operations test, y, on the Number factor, s, is the correlation r_{ys}, which can be estimated as approximately .75 (French, 1951).

Now for the sake of the illustration, suppose there is available as a criterion a comprehensive test of performance in those aspects of mathematics that represent the common objectives of the freshman program. This is assumed to be equally appropriate for all students and acceptable as a uniform measure of payoff. There *must* be some common indicator of utility if the different treatments are to be compared. Suppose that when all students are placed in the regular freshman mathematics course, the correlation (r_{ye_t}) between scores on the Numerical Operations test and the criterion comprehensive achievement test is .50. Then, knowing r_{ys} and r_{ye_t}, one can compute the correlation r_{se_t} between the number factor and this performance for this treatment to be .67. For some other treatment, such as a remedial treatment, the r_{ye_t} and r_{se_t} values might be different but r_{ys} remains the same.

Assume that for a specially designed remedial program, perhaps one that emphasized numerical facility for example, the Numerical Operations test correlated with the comprehensive achievement test only .30. Assume further that when entering freshmen were assigned at random to the two treatments they received final scores with means and standard deviations as follows:

	Mean	SD	r_{ye_t}
Regular course	100	20	.50
Remedial course	95	10	.30

Thus, the remedial course is not as effective for the average freshman, but it results in a smaller spread of final scores and results in fewer very low scores.

Given the two treatments described above, to illustrate *fixed treatments with fixed quotas* assume that each freshman will be assigned to either the regular or the special mathematics course. Teachers have been assigned to the courses, syllabi and materials have been prepared, and the courses will be given in the specified way no matter what the nature of the newly admitted freshman class. Suppose further that the administration has fixed as a quota that the 20 percent of the incoming class who are likely to benefit most from it will be assigned to the special remedial treatment.

The conditions set forth for the illustration lead to the regression lines shown in figure 19.3. Clearly, the 20 percent to enter the remedial program should be those lowest on Numerical Operations. If the new class is comparable to previous classes, a score cutting off the lowest 20 percent would fall as shown in figure 19.3. In the example, as it was set up, a policy of assigning 20 percent to the remedial treatment turns out to be very nearly the optimal one since the cutting score intersects the two regression lines very nearly at their intersection. If the fixed quota had been 10 percent, a number of poorer students, who would have performed better on average as a result of the remedial course, would have had to be assigned to the regular course; if the quota had been 30 percent, the reverse would have been the case.

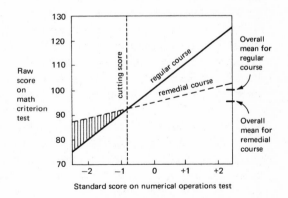

FIG. 19.3. Regressions of mathematics criterion scores on Numerical Operations placement test standard scores for two treatment groups in mathematics.

The gain in utility from using the remedial course for placement of less able students is represented by the shaded area in figure 19.3. If one were able to replace the test that was actually used with a perfect measure of the same ability factor, so that r_{ys} was 1.00 instead of .75, the steepness of both the regression lines would have been increased by one-third, and the distance between them and the shaded area by the same ratio. Thus, the gain from this type of placement is a linear function of r_{ys}.

In the example given, the quota assigned to each treatment was very nearly optimal. But suppose to illustrate *fixed treatments with adaptive quotas* that the next freshman class was more able so far as Numerical Operations is concerned, and only 10 percent fell below the score level at which the two regression lines had been found to intersect. Then optimal assignment would require that quotas be changed (if treatments are firmly fixed and not subject to change), so that only 10 percent are assigned to the remedial treatment.

Now if the administration were to allow three treatments—a remedial group, a regular group, and an advanced group—one would need to carry out an experiment with random assignment and plot the three regression lines on one graph. If the treatments were appropriately designed, it would be expected that the three lines would cross, perhaps as in figure 19.4. With adaptive quotas, each student would be assigned to that treatment for which the regression line showed the highest predicted achievement, given his Numerical Operations test score. In figure 19.4 the outcome with remedial treatment is shown as completely unrelated to Numerical Operations score, the outcome with regular treatment as moderately related, and the outcome with advanced treatment as highly related. If a better test of the numerical factor were obtained, the two higher treatments could be expected to show steeper regressions, and the intersection points to move toward each other on the horizontal scale. That is, with a more discriminating test, it would be advantageous to assign a larger percentage to the extreme treatments. This is a general relationship that can be expected to hold uniformly.

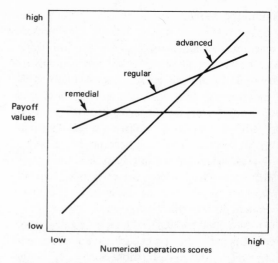

FIG. 19.4. Regressions of payoff from mathematics criterion scores on Numerical Operations placement test scores for three treatments.

To illustrate *adaptive treatment with fixed quotas* consider that the administration specifies that there are to be three variations of the mathematics course, one for the bottom 20 percent on Numerical Operations score, one for the middle 60 percent, and one for the top 20 percent. The faculty might be directed to produce the very best course they could for each group. A proper solution to this problem would depend upon how really different the groups were, and this in turn would depend upon how well the Numerical Operations score measured the underlying Number factor, that is, upon r_{ys}. At one extreme, if the test had no correlation with the relevant underlying factor, groups picked on the test would have no real difference on that factor, and no difference in treatment would be called for. At the other extreme, if the test was a perfect measure of the factor, the groups would show the maximum possible difference, given the specified quotas, and a maximum difference in treatment would be appropriate.

The different treatments would be designed to maximize achievement in the limited segment of the ability range receiving that treatment, without regard to the rest of the entering group, by providing materials and procedures that were especially suitable for this segment. The remedial treatment, perhaps one emphasizing computational skills, could be expected to minimize the disadvantage of the less able, while providing little of benefit to the more able, and as a result the regression would be flat or the variability of criterion scores small or both. The advanced treatment designed for the top group, possibly one giving an abstract and theoretical approach, should show just the reverse pattern, i.e. steep regression and/or wide dispersion of criterion scores.

As a final exploitation of the illustration, to wit, *adaptive treatment with adaptive quotas*, the situation in which the greatest utility is to be derived, suppose the administration authorizes the mathematics faculty to adjust not only the courses that they offer but also the number taking each. The questions that now arise are (*a*) how many different variations of the course should be offered, (*b*) how much should each one differ from the others, and (*c*) how many students should be assigned to each.

On the first question, in theory the ideal for maximizing payoff on the criterion test would be for *each* discriminable level of student to have a course tailored to his unique ability level. However, even if this were technically and administratively possible, the Cronbach and Gleser theoretical model indicates that payoff would be little better than for three or perhaps four levels of instruction. Diminishing returns set in very rapidly beyond this point, even when each course is ideally tailored to the ability level of its clientele.

On the second question, the theoretical model indicates that the ideal proportions to be assigned to each treatment remain the same irrespective of r_{ys}, the correlation between the placement test and the underlying trait. Given the model that Cronbach and Gleser (1965) developed, with a set of three treatments, the cutting scores should be set to assign 26 percent of students to each of the extreme treatments and 48 percent to the middle one. Similar percentages have been calculated for other numbers of treatments.

On the third question, as discussed in the previous section on fixed quotas, once the number of treatments and the quotas for each have been decided, the amount of difference in treatments does depend on the genuine amount of difference between the groups, and this in turn

is a function of the degree to which the available test is a good measure of the relevant differentiating trait. At the extreme, when the test is quite poor as an indicator, the actual difference between groups on the relevant trait will be so little that the size of gains from more finely differentiated treatments may seem too small to justify the effort and cost of providing a number of differentiated programs.

Examples of trait-treatment interactions

Not a great amount of investigation has yet been reported specifically seeking, inventing, and evaluating test scores that have different regression slopes for different instructional procedures aimed at the same end product. A body of related work on the problem has been critically reviewed by Cronbach and Snow (1969). A few studies will be described below to illustrate salient points and problems. Some of the studies concern the operation of more than one variable and thus fall into the realm of classification problems rather than clear placement problems. They have been included here to clarify important points.

Placement of early-school children via personality variables— Placement based on trait-treatment interactions may be appropriate at the early school level. Grimes and Allinsmith (1961) studied the interactions between personality traits (compulsivity and anxiety) and overachievement in reading when children in the first three grades were taught by the phonics method vs. the whole-word method. They found that in schools using the whole-word method, there was little difference in degree of over- or underachievement for students of different levels of compulsivity, but, that in schools using the phonics methods, the highly compulsive students overachieved much more than the medium and low compulsive students. The relationship between compulsivity and over-achievement in these schools appeared to be positive, linear, and statistically significant at the .01 level.

In the case of the anxiety variable, it was found that in the phonics schools degree of anxiety made little difference, but that in the whole-word schools there was a negative linear relationship between anxiety and overachievement, significant at the .01 level. There was also a higher-order interaction between compulsivity, anxiety, and teaching method, with the students who were high on both compulsivity and anxiety performing by far the best in relationship to their intelligence in the phonics schools but next to the worst in the whole-word schools.

If such findings are replicated, placement of first and second graders into classes in which reading is taught by different methods may be clearly indicated. It is worth emphasizing that from these findings the placement in this situation would be based on measures of personality variables rather than aptitude variables. The kinds of trait-treatment interactions important for placement may involve variables not customarily measured in routine educational testing programs and may involve variables that will not be found in lists of "placement" tests. Some institutions might find alarming the prospect of making important decisions about students on the basis of scores from tests so unlike those to which they and the parents of their students have become accustomed.

Placement of college students related to student characteristics— Snow, Tiffin, and Seibert (1965) deliberately set out to follow Cronbach's (1957) suggestion that interactions between treatment and learner variables be specifically sought in order to improve instruction. They studied the interactions between learner characteristics and filmed vs. live presentations of demonstrations in an introductory college physics course. Learner variables studied were prior knowledge of physics, attitude toward instructional films, attitude toward entertainment films, attitude toward physics, ascendancy, responsibility, emotional stability, sociability, total personality self-evaluation, numerical aptitude, verbal aptitude, academic achievement, past experience with instructional films, past experience with entertainment films, and past use of college library films. The criteria for achievement in physics were immediate recall on five-minute tests taken right after the demonstration and delayed recall on items included in five hour-long course examinations.

All test questions formed part of the students' final course grades.

Considering that 28 separate $2 \times 3 \times 3$ factorial designs were analyzed, relatively few significant interactions were found, and these were not cross validated, so the results must be taken as preliminary evidence. It appears that interactions are more common in connection with immediate than delayed recall, and it appears that in this kind of study, three-way interactions are most common, with previous knowledge of physics being prevalent as one of the variables.

Other variables that entered into interactions with filmed vs. live method were attitude toward instructional films, numerical aptitude, verbal aptitude, past use of the college's film library, ascendance, and responsibility. The latter two variables were the only ones that were involved in interactions that did not involve the third variable of previous knowledge of physics. The interactions in this study tended to be complex and nonlinear, so they cannot easily be described, probably cannot easily be used, and require extensive verification through other studies. They do suggest, however, a difference in teaching method that might be important and a variety of personal variables that might be well to include in other investigations of trait-treatment interactions.

Placement of college students related to teacher characteristics— A series of studies undertaken at the University of Michigan under the direction of McKeachie and Milholland and their colleagues (McKeachie, 1961) examined the characteristics of teachers as they related to characteristics of students in classes in French, mathematics, and psychology.[5]

One study considered whether male students who were high on need for Achievement would obtain better course grades in college courses in French, mathematics, or psychology in which the teacher set high achievement standards and encouraged competition. They hypothesized that men in the middle range of need for Achievement would perform poorly in such

[5] Additional data in the form of multilithed brief reports of these studies were obtained through personal correspondence with W. J. McKeachie.

courses. (Notice that previous attempts to use need for Achievement scores as a measure for women have been so unsuccessful that they are not expected to be of much value here. This, itself, is an interaction which may be of importance and seems to be well confirmed.) However, the outcome of this study was negative. No significant interaction between need for Achievement and achievement cues in the classroom was found.

In another study the interaction between need for Affiliation and teacher warmth was studied as it related to grades and test scores of students in these same college course areas. Mixed results were obtained. In some courses for some criteria for one sex, interactions were found. In others there were no interactions, and sometimes the interactions were opposite from the hypothesized direction.

In a third study, interactions between need for Power and student assertiveness in discussion sections in these same courses were studied. No interactions were found for women at all. For men there was an interaction between assertiveness and need for Power as those variables influenced the criterion of grades, but this was not true for scores on objective examinations on course content.

Another study considered personality-test scores of students and teachers and ratings of teachers by each other and by students. The subjects in this study were introductory psychology students, and the criterion was an objective test in psychology. Scores on the psychology test were adjusted for aptitude through use of scores on a standardized aptitude test. Only one significant interaction between trait and treatment as they influenced the criterion was observed. Men high in sophistication as measured by the personality test did best on the psychology examination when taught by teachers rated *low* in culture. Cultured teachers were most effective with men scoring in the lower two-thirds of the distribution of sophistication scores.

Matching student and teacher characteristics— Finally, Milholland conducted a study in which all the gleanings from the above studies and others were integrated in an attempt to assign introductory psychology students to sections such that they matched their teachers in a manner to enhance performance. The teacher attributes that were varied from one section of psychology to another were teacher's use of achievement cues, teacher's skill, and teacher's culture. The student attributes were College Board SAT scores; scores from the Opinion, Attitude and Interest Survey; TAT pictures to measure needs for Achievement, Affiliation, and Power; the sophistication scale of Cattell's 16PF; the Alpert-Haber Achievement Anxiety Test; a study-habits inventory; and two attitude questionnaires. (Unfortunately, it was found that the time required to score the TAT protocols precluded using these scores for placement. This is one of the problems which must be recognized in planning a placement-testing program.)

In one course in psychology it was possible to schedule two sections of the class at each class hour and to control assignment between the two sections. For another psychology course, even this freedom of matching was not available since there were too few students to permit two sections every hour. This again illustrates one of the practical problems of trying to capitalize on trait-treatment interactions.

Possibly because of the severe limitations on the study, it was found that there were no differences in achievement for those students who matched their teachers well as contrasted with those who did not match their teachers at all. For both sexes the matching seemed to have a positive effect on objective test scores and a negative effect on grades but neither was significantly different from zero.

A variety of studies with attempts at replication— Another major project directed toward the study of interactions between traits and treatments has been conducted at Florida State University by Kropp, Nelson, and King (1967). This extensive series of studies is too broad to present here. The investigators used aptitude measures from the Primary Mental Abilities battery and from the Guilford Structure of Intellect model (Guilford & Hoepfner, 1966); they used a variety of content including reading material, mathematics material, concept-formation tasks, and chemistry course work. Some of their learning material was from common school tasks; some was prepared especially for the experiments. They used subjects ranging from elementary school through graduate school students. While they found a considerable amount of support for the existence of aptitude-treatment interactions, their studies do not yield much that is appropriate for immediate practical application to educational placement. They did more to attempt to replicate their findings than any other investigators considered, but replication was not always successful.

It does seem from their work that reasoning abilities have interactions with amounts of redundancy in reading passages to be learned by sixth graders, and cognition of semantic classes and convergent production of semantic relations (perhaps similar to what has been called a reasoning ability) have useful interactions with symbolic vs. semantic presentations of college-level mathematical concepts. However, these relationships involved relatively brief learning sequences, not the typical several-month-long learning period with which one is usually involved in educational placement.

Deliberate reduction in significance of a trait— An experiment done in connection with training computer programmers for the Navy is of especial interest. In it a deliberate attempt was made to create a treatment in which the regression of performance on an aptitude variable would be reduced to zero, thus generating a strong aptitude-treatment interaction. Ford and Meyer (1966) realized that previous studies had found very high relationships (*r*s in the .70s) between scores on mathematical aptitude and performance on computer flow-charting problems. They set out to develop a set of programmed instruction materials that would help the lower mathematics-aptitude students.

Through process analysis of the skills needed for the flow-charting task, it was discovered that the students of lower mathematics aptitude had two major difficulties. They could not get started on the design problem, and they had not mastered the definitions and rules of the special flow-charting language. The programmed instruction materials were revised specifically to alleviate these difficulties, a process that nearly doubled the length of the instructional program. After that revision it was found that the students of lower mathematical aptitude performed as well on practical flow-chart design problems as students higher in mathematical aptitude. (It did take the students of lower mathematical aptitude 65 percent longer to complete the revised programmed instruction sequence, but they also had required longer on the original training material while achieving lower performance levels.) Here, then, is a recognition and development of a trait-treatment interaction important for placement. However, it might be that the high aptitude students can complete either program in the same amount of time and reach the same level of proficiency after either sequence. If that is the case, one should advise *all* students to take the revised learning materials, rather than advising different learning materials for persons of different levels of mathematical aptitude.

Problems in the use of trait-treatment interactions

In examining the literature on trait-treatment interactions and their use in educational placement, occasional note has been made of problems to be faced in operational settings. It may be well to make a number of these problems explicit before leaving this discussion. The work of McKeachie and his colleagues (1961), Kropp and his colleagues (1967), and an unpublished paper on placement delivered by S. C. Webb to the February 1967 Regional Meeting of the College Entrance Examination Board held in New Orleans are particularly useful to alert one to pitfalls. Areas of potential difficulty have been roughly classified below into problems involving faculty, tests, administration, and theory.

Faculty— Faculty members play two somewhat different roles in relation to the development and operation of a placement program to take advantage of trait-treatment interactions. On the one hand, their help is needed in identifying relevant traits and designing modified treatments. On the other, they are the persons who must apply the treatments not only during an initial experimental period but also through the years as the differentiated treatments become a part of the institution's continuing operational procedure. It remains to be seen how well they will fill the two roles. Some faculty members will probably recognize the significance of this approach and be excited about participating in an effort to do something constructive with it. It seems likely that many individual faculty members will resist the idea because of its novelty and because it will tax their knowledge and understanding of their own subject matter, of teaching procedures, and of the nature of their fellow men. Some of the areas of difficulty can be anticipated.

1. It may be that the faculty will have difficulty suggesting variables that can be expected to interact with various instructional procedures.

2. It may often be the case that the faculty member cannot describe his own treatment of his material well enough for the generation of reasonable hypotheses about variables that might interact.

3. The development of measures of interacting variables may be a process that requires the cooperation of the faculty members who are in charge of specific instructional sequences. Test development can be expected to be rather difficult in this area. It remains to be seen whether faculty in general will be willing to invest the effort required to produce useful measures of interacting variables.

4. Faculty may not readily adjust to the modification of their classroom procedures in unorthodox ways, i.e. other than by watering down the content or lengthening the treatment through additional explanations, examples, drill, etc. But unorthodox modifications may be what are necessary, especially if the interacting variables are in the personality domain. It may be the teacher's attitude that must be modified for some kinds of students. Or it may be the entire classroom structure. Or a complete reorientation may be demanded, as, for example, the teaching of creeping in order to improve reading (Delacato, 1963; but see Glass, 1966). Such unfamiliar demands on faculty can be expected to be viewed with suspicion. If accepted they will surely make unusual demands on faculty time.

5. It may be that difficulty will be experienced in inventing lengthy sequences of instruction based on a consistent and specific instructional treatment. Kropp and his colleagues (1967) found this to be the case. Probably the practice in the past has been for teachers to vary their treatments, intuitively recognizing interactions between traits and treatments and taking them into account by providing a variety of treatments so that all traits would be accommodated. If a group is assembled homogeneous with respect to the relevant trait, a consistent treatment adapted to the group should be more efficient. However, it may be difficult for teachers to reduce the spontaneous variation that they may have intuitively introduced into their treatments in the past in order to accommodate the range of characteristics represented.

6. Even if faculty members can develop and consistently use specific kinds of teaching treatments, they may not be willing to teach quarter after quarter or year after year in exactly the same way. For that matter, teachers may change with experience in subtle ways that are very important in connection with trait-treatment interactions. (If such changes were not expected, there would be no value associated with experience in teaching.) However, if study finds this year that Mr. Jones is very effective with students who are high in trait X, any change Mr. Jones makes next year based on his experience may be for the worse. Thus with human teachers, as contrasted to programmed instruction or computer-assisted instruction, effective exploitation of trait-treatment interactions may require continuous evaluative monitoring.

7. A final problem to be mentioned which involves faculty is that of development of a criterion that is appropriate for all the various treatments. Course grades will not serve as this criterion unless those course grades are anchored by a common test or other reference variable. Some faculty will object strenuously to

use of common criteria. Some will view it as an invasion of their teaching privacy. Some will not be cooperative or interested in helping to develop such common criteria. Others, however, will recognize that if their teaching is in a school setting rather than a private tutoring setting, they cannot logically demand or expect to use idiosyncratic criteria ignoring the objectives of the institution of which they are a part.

Tests— The relationship of the faculty to the necessary test development for placement based on trait-treatment interactions has been mentioned above. There are other technical aspects of measurement that deserve attention.

1. The "placement tests" that are now available commercially will probably not be relevant for placement based on interactions. Those tests were not designed with different treatments in mind, and they were validated (if at all) against course grades or test scores without regard to the kind of instruction that produced those grades or scores.

It may be that one can never expect commercial publishers to produce tests suitable for placement based on trait-treatment interactions. The number of kinds of treatments that are discovered and used may be so great that the trait measures also will be very specific and thus generate little sales volume. However, some kinds of trait-treatment combinations may be found to be generally useful. Their widespread adoption would create the demand for a commercial test product that could be profitable. In fact, if such combinations are found, the commercially satisfactory development may be an entire trait-treatment package, including the measure or measures of relevant traits, preselected cutoff scores, the method of teaching (perhaps in a computer program or other programmed materials), and the evaluative criterion measure. An approach like this is being attempted in project PLAN (Flanagan, 1967).

2. If suitable commercial measures are not available, then the institutions that desire to place students on the basis of interactions will have to develop their own placement tests. This will require measurement sophistication of a high order. The unsophisticated test constructor will probably tend to produce a general ability measure that will fail to have the necessary interactions with different treatments. Beyond that, there are severe reliability requirements on placement measures. As in selection, it is desirable to have as few obtained scores near the cutting score as possible. Administratively this keeps down the number of persons who complain about being only one or two points away from the placement they favor. This is achieved through having either a test with a very flat distribution or a distribution skewed so that the cutting point is in a portion of the distribution with low density. Flat distributions are obtained by having wide standard deviations of obtained scores in relation to the number of items. This results from high item intercorrelations, and high item intercorrelations are basic to high internal consistency reliability.

Since attempting to achieve high reliability is likely to result in long tests, and since testing time for placement is at a premium when it must be done during orientation or during the first few class periods in an educational setting, alternatives such as sequential tests or peaked tests (Cronbach & Warrington, 1952) are possible solutions.

If two or more trait measures are used, as in the Kropp, Nelson, and King studies (1967), the reliability of the difference scores (see pages 385–86) between the two traits must be high, a result not easily achieved if the traits are positively correlated. Furthermore, internal-consistency reliability, while necessary, is not sufficient. The traits and their measures must also be stable over substantial periods of time—at least as long as is required to process the students through the related learning sequence. If day-to-day variability in the trait or its measure is great, one cannot expect to obtain, replicate, or generalize trait-treatment interactions.

3. To the extent that interactions are found involving personality traits, the usability of such traits in other than counseling situations depends upon improved measures of those traits. It remains to be seen whether measures that depend for their accuracy upon the cooperation of the student in revealing himself as accurately as possible can be expected to function properly

in placement. Not much progress has yet been made in developing highly reliable personality measures that eliminate the effects of social desirability, faking, antagonism of the examinee or his parents, etc. (Messick, 1964). Projective techniques, such as the TAT measures used by McKeachie, Milholland, and their collaborators (McKeachie, 1961), are so awkward to score as to be nearly useless unless elaborate administrative provisions are instituted. Even some of the ability traits present measurement problems. The Structure of Intellect model (Guilford & Hoepfner, 1966) contains some traits that are so recently recognized that operationally satisfactory measures of those traits are not yet conveniently available. This model may eventually, however, be one of the most useful sources of trait-treatment interaction hypotheses (Kropp et al., 1967; but see also Cronbach & Snow, 1969, pp. 61–66).

4. Of course the fundamental problem, which might be classified under this heading, is that so little actually is known at the present time concerning which traits interact with what kinds of treatments in educational settings relevant to placement.

Administration— The administrators of an institution will have to face the possibility of drastic changes if placement is effective. In the past, their problem has been as simple as deciding how many faculty members could be assigned to remedial or advanced work and assigning classroom space, then letting the chips fall where they would. If placement on the basis of trait-treatment interactions were successful, it might be that marked student progress would take place very rapidly. For instance, suppose that it was discovered that one of the principal problems with certain students in mathematics was a fear of numbers. Further, suppose that a measure that would detect and evaluate this antipathy was developed, and that a treatment was developed that would reduce or eliminate it in a matter of six weeks of concentrated effort. (Some other illustration could easily be advanced.) The administration would have to figure out what to do with such students at the end of six weeks when they were all ready to go

into college mathematics, but there would not be a mathematics class ready for them until the next term started.

1. One administrative problem, then, is that of introducing sufficient flexibility into scheduling that effective placement can be exploited to its fullest.

2. Other new flexibilities will be required if personality variables are used in placement for which the scoring is time consuming and difficult. For instance, if McKeachie and Milholland were to use their TAT measures operationally, those measures would have to be administered in early preassessment sessions in order to permit scoring. What would the administration do with students who wished to enroll but missed the preassessment sessions? Would it exclude people from admission to the state university because they had failed to take a projective personality test? Administrative problems with state legislators can be foreseen in such a case.

3. Still more flexibility will be required if a variety of treatments are to be provided within individual subject matters and in such a manner that students can fit the proper treatment into their course planning. In other words, in the past placement in mathematics usually involved no more than one kind of remediation. Each student was either assigned to that treatment or to the regular course. Suppose that study of trait-treatment interactions reveals that there are really three or four different kinds of maladies in mathematics, each requiring a different kind of treatment. Provision for each treatment would probably have to be made available several times a day in order for each student to have an opportunity to schedule his proper treatment. Suppose further that special treatments were to be provided in a wide variety of subjects. It is not difficult to pose a very complex scheduling problem. If this complexity is ignored or a fitting to it is only roughly approximated, one may expect the kind of inconsequential results observed by Milholland.

4. If there are to be many treatments, it is implied that there will be many placement measures. The work of Snow and his colleagues (1965) suggested that some of the trait-treat-

ment interactions will be curved rather than linear, and they may involve higher-order interactions. The Michigan investigations suggested that achievement controlled for aptitude may be important in placement considerations. This all suggests that a very sophisticated and complex placement or classification procedure may be required. It may require a computer to coordinate all the various aspects in a workable manner.

5. One more problem for the administration will be the matter of quotas. For effective placement, the quotas may have to be adaptable, set according to the students who are available to be placed. For the administration to have to become adaptive to providing the kind of education needed by the students instead of providing a set of programs and letting the students get the best education they can out of it, will require extensive adjustment in many cases. For example, the matters of budgeting and staffing will have to await their final resolution until placement has been completed. This is not administratively convenient—and perhaps not even possible. One question, then, is whether the compromises that are necessary to permit placement to be administered will destroy the benefit to be expected from placement. (And maybe that is partly what has resulted in placement as it is now practiced having so little to show for itself.)

6. Placement for maximum educational payoff may not be acceptable to the students. If the payoff is not in better grades, the students may not desire to be placed into the treatment that will maximize what they learn. This may pose a problem for the administration in the form of concern for getting students to accept their placement—or it may pose an alternative problem in the form of concern for getting better systems of evaluation of and rewards for learning.

Theory— While Cronbach and Gleser (1965) took a great stride in the development of decision theory as applied to psychological testing in their pioneer book, it must have been apparent as one read the foregoing hypothetical illustrations of applications to educational placement that there are serious gaps still in the theory that is needed for realistic problems.

1. There is in Cronbach and Gleser's work the development of theory based on one particular model of the relationship between payoff and aptitude across varied treatments. It has not been empirically established how well this model fits practical educational placement problems or what other models might fit better and might have different implications from those explicated for the Cronbach-Gleser model.

2. The parameter values even for the Cronbach-Gleser model are not sufficiently well known in enough varied situations to be able to evaluate its adequacy or to estimate what might be reasonable or typical values of the parameters in educational applications.

3. It is not clear how values can be assigned satisfactorily to educational outcomes on a scale commensurate with that of costs of measurement permitting the subtraction of those costs in evaluating utility. Cronbach and Gleser (1965, p. 121) call this the Achilles' heel of decision theory.

4. Different treatments may vary widely in their costs. These costs are not specifically introduced into the Cronbach-Gleser formulations, but they may loom large in practical applications. A fully adequate treatment of any procedure for making educational decisions must include the costs of implementing those decisions in arriving at the net benefit from the procedure.

5. There is no clear, coherent, and practicable decision theory development of the classification problem. There seems to be a greater need for sound development and clear description of the theoretical underpinning and implications of this problem in education than for the problem of placement. In considering educational placement, one soon begins to think of using different underlying abilities for different treatments—and this is the more general and more difficult problem of classification.

Concluding Evaluation of the Placement Problem

By this time, so many problems have been posed and such an apparition of complexity raised that a natural response is to reject the decision theory approach and retreat to the good old simple days. However, it appears to the author that those good old days never existed but were a figment of inadequate analysis. This is the reason that one can find almost no sound studies demonstrating the effectiveness of placement as it is often naively done, with no consideration of the interaction between traits and treatments as they affect criteria. Once one accepts the correctness of the fundamental idea that different students can be taught most effectively through the use of different methods, the rest of the decision theory rationale seems inescapable. But this fundamental idea is just as basic to placement as it is currently done as it is to placement as it should be done taking advantage of decision theory as an intellectual tool. Thus there appears to be no retreat available.

The appropriate questions are related to exploration of ways to advance. Can some salient trait-treatment interactions highly relevant to educational placement be found? Can advantage be taken of only a few of the possibilities, thus reducing complexity, without giving up most of the potential gain? If not, is it possible to recognize, accept, and adapt to the idea that effective educational placement is not feasible, at least not on the microscopic level of within-institutional placement? Perhaps the only feasible kind of effective placement will be on the macroscopic level—e.g. placement into college vs. trade school vs. no further formal education, etc. Or perhaps the key lies in classification, based on consideration of several different traits and several different treatments at once, rather than placement based on a single underlying variable. The most important contribution of the decision theory frame of reference at present may be its heuristic effect in opening these kinds of questions for study.

REFERENCES

Abel, W. H. Attrition and the student who is certain. *Personnel and Guidance Journal*, 1966, **44,** 1042–1045.

Abramson, D. S. *The effect of special grouping of high-ability students in high school upon their achievement in college.* New York: Board of Education of the City of New York, Bureau of Educational Program Research and Statistics, 1959. [Publication No. 144]

Ahmann, J. S., & Glock, M. D. An evaluation of the effectiveness of a freshman mathematics course. *Journal of Educational Psychology*, 1959, **50,** 41–45.

Aiken, L. R., Jr. The grading behavior of a college faculty. *Educational and Psychological Measurement*, 1963, **23,** 319–322.

American College Testing Program. *Counselor's guide to selected Texas colleges.* Iowa City: ACT, undated (produced in 1964).

American Council on Education, Committee on Measurement and Evaluation. *College testing: A guide to practices and programs.* Washington: ACE, 1959.

Anastasi, A., Meade, M. J., & Schneiders, A. A. *The validation of a biographical inventory as a predictor of college success.* New York: College Entrance Examination Board, 1960.

Boulger, J. R., & Colmen, J. G. Differentiating validity of reference sources for predicting success as a Peace Corps volunteer. Peace Corps Division of Research *Research Notes*, 1964, No. 10.

Campbell, D. T., & Fiske, D. W. Convergent and divergent validation by the multitrait-multimethod matrix. *Psychological Bulletin*, 1959, **56,** 81–105.

Carroll, J. B. Instructional methods and individual differences: Discussion of Dr. Cronbach's paper. In R. M. Gagné (Ed.), *Learning and individual differences.* Columbus, Ohio: Charles E. Merrill, 1967. Pp. 40–44.

Casserly, P. L. To see ourselves as others see us. Educational Testing Service *Research Memorandum*, 1968, No. 12.

Casserly, P. L., Peterson, R. E., & Coffman, W. E. College decisions on advanced placement. II. An interview survey of advanced placement policies and practices at 63 colleges. Educational Testing Service *Research Bulletin*, 1965, No. 41.

Clark, B. R. College image and student selection. In *Selection and educational differentiation.* Berkeley, Calif.: Center for the Study of Higher Education, 1959. Pp. 155–168.

College Entrance Examination Board. *Designing validity studies and collecting data.* New York: CEEB, 1967.

Cronbach, L. J. The two disciplines of psychology. *American Psychologist*, 1957, **12,** 671–684.

Cronbach, L. J. How can instruction be adapted to individual differences? In R. M. Gagné (Ed.), *Learning and individual differences*. Columbus, Ohio: Charles E. Merrill, 1967. Pp. 23–29.

Cronbach, L. J., & Gleser, G. *Psychological tests and personnel decisions*. (2nd ed.) Urbana: University of Illinois Press, 1965.

Cronbach, L. J., & Snow, R. E. *Final report: Individual differences in learning ability as a function of instructional variables*. Stanford, Calif.: Stanford University, School of Education, 1969.

Cronbach, L. J., & Warrington, W. G. Efficiency of multiple-choice tests as a function of spread of item difficulties. *Psychometrika*, 1952, **17**, 124–147.

Davis, J. A. Faculty perceptions of students: I. The development of the Student Rating Form. Educational Testing Service *Research Bulletin*, 1964, No. 10.

Davis, J. A. Faculty perceptions of students: VI. Characteristics of students for whom there is faculty agreement on desirability. Educational Testing Service *Research Bulletin*, 1966, No. 28.

Delacato, C. H. *The diagnosis and treatment of speech and reading problems*. Springfield, Ill.: Charles C Thomas, 1963.

Dickerson, A. D. An investigation of the relative accuracy with which the academic success of college-level men and women can be predicted. Unpublished master's thesis, University of Texas, 1965.

Domino, G. Differential prediction of academic achievement in conforming and independent settings. *Journal of Educational Psychology*, 1968, **59**, 256–260.

Dunn, J. E. A study of the University of Arkansas mathematics entrance examination as a placement device. *Journal of Experimental Education*, 1966, **34**, 63–68.

Dyer, H. S. The College Board achievement tests. *College Board Review*, 1964, **54**, 6–10.

Ebel, R. L. *Measuring educational achievement*. Englewood Cliffs, N. J.: Prentice-Hall, 1965.

Edgerton, H. S. Adapting training methods to trainee aptitudes. U. S. Department of the Navy, Office of Naval Research *Research Review*, 1958 (October).

Fishman, J. A. Nonintellective factors as predictors, as criteria, and as contingencies in selection and guidance of college students: A sociopsychological analysis. In T. R. McConnell (Ed.), *Selection and educational differentiation*. Berkeley, Calif.: Center for Study of Higher Education, 1959. Pp. 55–73.

Flanagan, J. C. Functional education for the seventies. *Phi Delta Kappan*, 1967, **49**, 27–32.

Ford, J. D., Jr., & Meyer, J. K. Training in computer flow charting using programmed instruction: Eliminating the effects of mathematics aptitude upon achievement. U. S. Naval Personnel Research Activity *Technical Bulletin*, 1966, No. 10.

Francis, R. L. A placement study in analytic geometry and calculus. *Educational and Psychological Measurement*, 1966, **26**, 1041–1046.

French, J. W. The description of aptitude and achievement tests in terms of rotated factors. *Psychometric Monograph*, 1951, No. 5.

Fricke, B. G. *Opinion, attitude, and interest survey handbook*. Ann Arbor: University of Michigan, Evaluation and Examination Division, 1963.

Gagné, R. M. The acquisition of knowledge. *Psychological Review*, 1962, **69**, 355–365.

Gagné, R. M. *The conditions of learning*. New York: Holt, Rinehart & Winston, 1965.

Gelso, C. J., & Trowell, C. The effect of the order in which History 110 and 111 are taken on performance in these courses. South Georgia College *Research Report*, 1967, No. 4. (mimeo)

Gelso, C. J., & Wilson, R. The prediction of grades in College Algebra. South Georgia College *Research Report*, 1967, No. 1. (mimeo)

Glass, G. V. *A critique of experiments on the role of neurological organization in reading performance*. Urbana: University of Illinois, College of Education, 1966. [Curriculum Laboratory Working Paper No. 6]

Glennon, J. R., & Albright, L. E. *A catalog of life history items*. Greensboro, N. C.: Richardson Foundation, 1966.

Goolsby, T. M., Jr. Differentiating between measures of different outcomes in the social studies. *Journal of Educational Measurement*, 1966, **3**, 219–222. (a)

Goolsby, T. M., Jr. The validity of a comprehensive college sophomore test battery for use in selection, placement, and advisement. *Educational and Psychological Measurement*, 1966, **26**, 977–983. (b)

Gough, H. C., Hall, W. B., & Harris, R. E. Admissions procedures as forecasters of performance in medical training. *Journal of Medical Education*, 1963, **38**, 983–998.

Grimes, J. W., & Allinsmith, W. Compulsivity, anxiety, and school achievement. *Merrill-Palmer Quarterly of Behavior and Development*, 1961, **7**, 247–271.

Grimsley, G. A comparative study of the Wherry-Doolittle and a multiple cutting-score method. *Psychological Monographs*, 1949, **63** (Whole No. 2).

Guilford, J. P. *Psychometric methods*. (2nd ed.) New York: McGraw-Hill, 1954.

Guilford, J. P. *Fundamental statistics in psychology and education*. (4th ed.) New York: McGraw-Hill, 1965.

Guilford, J. P., & Hoepfner, R. Structure of intellect factors and their tests. *Reports from the Psychological Laboratory of the University of Southern California*, 1966, No. 31.

Guilford, J. P., & Zimmerman, W. S. *Guilford-Zimmerman aptitude survey*. Beverly Hills, Calif.: Sheridan Supply, 1956.

Gulliksen, H. O. *Theory of mental tests*. New York: Wiley, 1950.

Helm, C. E. The natural-language approach to psychometrics. In J. C. Stanley (Ed.), *Proceedings of the 1966 Invitational Conference on Testing Problems*. Princeton, N. J.: Educational Testing Service, 1967. Pp. 80–86.

Helmstadter, G. C. *Principles of psychological measurement*. New York: Appleton-Century-Crofts, 1964.

Henry, E. R. *Research conference on the use of autobiographical data as psychological predictors*. Greensboro, N. C.: Richardson Foundation, 1966.

Hills, J. R. Factor-analyzed abilities and success in college mathematics. *Educational and Psychological Measurement*, 1957, **17**, 615–622.

Hills, J. R. College expectancy tables for high school counselors. *Personnel and Guidance Journal*, 1964, **42**, 479–483. (a)

Hills, J. R. Decision theory and college choice. *Personnel and Guidance Journal*, 1964, **43**, 17–22. (b)

Hills, J. R. The effect of admissions policy on college grading standards. *Journal of Educational Measurement*, 1964, **2**, 115–118. (c)

Hills, J. R. Prediction of college grades for all public colleges of a state. *Journal of Educational Measurement*, 1964, **1**, 155–159. (d)

Hills, J. R. Transfer shock: The academic performance of the junior college transfer. *Journal of Experimental Education*, 1965, **33**, 201–216.

Hills, J. R. Housing and grading practices. *Florida Journal of Educational Research*, 1967, **9**, 57–60.

Hills, J. R., Bush, M. L., & Klock, J. A. Keeping college prediction equations current. *Journal of Educational Measurement*, 1966, **3**, 33–34.

Hills, J. R., Emory, L. B., Franz, G., & Crowder, D. G. Admissions and guidance research in the University System of Georgia. *Personnel and Guidance Journal*, 1961, **39**, 452–457. (a)

Hills, J. R., & Gladney, M. B. Factors influencing grading standards. *Journal of Educational Measurement*, 1968, **5**, 31–40.

Hills, J. R., & Klock, J. A. Setting cutoff scores in selective admissions. *Journal of Educational Measurement*, 1965, **2**, 97–102.

Hills, J. R., & Klock, J. A. Setting cutoff scores in selective admissions. *Journal of Educational Measurement*, 1967, **4**, 263.

Hills, J. R., Klock, J. A., & Bush, M. L. *Counselor's guide to Georgia colleges*. (2nd ed.) Atlanta: Regents of the University System of Georgia, 1965.

Hills, J. R., Masters, P. B., & Emory, L. B. *Supplement: Counselor's guide to Georgia colleges*. Atlanta: Regents of the University System of Georgia, 1961.

Hilton, T. L., & Myers, A. E. Growth study II. Personal background, experience, and school achievement: An investigation of the contribution of questionnaire data to academic prediction. *Journal of Educational Measurement*, 1967, **4**, 69–80.

Hood, A. B., & Swanson, E. O. *What type of college for what type of student?* Minneapolis: University of Minnesota Student Counseling Bureau, 1965. (Cooperative Research Project No. 2182 [OE-4-10-014])

Horst, P. A technique for the development of a differential prediction battery. *Psychological Monographs*, 1954, **68**(Whole No. 380).

Horst, P. A technique for the development of a multiple absolute prediction battery. *Psychological Monographs*, 1955, **69**(Whole No. 390).

Horst, P. *Psychological measurement and prediction*. Belmont, Calif.: Wadsworth, 1966.

Kelly, E. L. Theory and techniques of assessment. *Annual Review of Psychology*, 1954, **5**, 286–290.

Klein, S. P., & Hart, F. M. The nature of essay grades in law school. Educational Testing Service *Research Bulletin*, 1968, No. 6.

Kropp, R. P., Nelson, W. A., & King, F. J. Identification and definition of subject-matter content variables related to human aptitudes. Final Report, Project No. 2914, U. S. Department of Health, Education, and Welfare, Office of Education, Bureau of Research, January 1967.

Lavin, D. E. *The prediction of academic performance*. New York: Russell Sage Foundation, 1965.

Lindquist, E. F. (Ed.) *Educational measurement*. Washington: American Council on Education, 1951.

Lindquist, E. F. An evaluation of a technique for scaling high school grades to improve prediction of college success. *Educational and Psychological Measurement*, 1963, **23**, 623–646.

Lindquist, E. F., & McCarrel, T. *ACT: The American College Testing program*. Iowa City: Measurement Research Center, 1959.

Linn, R. L. Grade adjustments for prediction of academic performance: A review. *Journal of Educational Measurement*, 1966, **3**, 313–329.

Lord, F. M. Cutting scores and errors of measurement. *Psychometrika*, 1962, **27**, 19–30.

Lunneborg, C. E., & Lunneborg, P. W. The prediction of different criteria of law school performance. *Educational and Psychological Measurement*, 1966, **26**, 935–944.

Lunneborg, P. W., & Lunneborg, C. E. The differential prediction of college grades from biographical information. *Educational and Psychological Measurement*, 1966, **26**, 917–925.

McKeachie, W. J. Motivation, teaching methods, and college learning. In M. R. Jones (Ed.), *Nebraska symposium on motivation, 1961*. Lincoln: University of Nebraska Press, 1961.

Marks, E. A comparison of the entering freshman classes of 1957 through 1966. *Georgia Institute of Technology Research Memorandum*, 1967, No. 4.

Meehl, P. E., & Rosen, A. Antecedent probability and the efficiency of psychometric signs, patterns, or cutting scores. *Psychological Bulletin*, 1955, **52**, 194–216.

Messick, S. Personality measurement and college performance. In A. G. Wesman (Ed.), *Proceedings of the 1963 Invitational Conference on Testing Problems*. Princeton, N. J.: Educational Testing Service, 1964. Pp. 110–129.

Munday, L. Predicting college grades in predominantly Negro colleges. *Journal of Educational Measurement*, 1965, **2**, 157–160.

Nichols, R. C. Nonintellective predictors of achievement in college. *Educational and Psychological measurement*, 1966, **26**, 899–915.

Owens, W. A., & Henry, E. R. *Biographical data in industrial psychology: A review and evaluation.* Greensboro, N. C.: Richardson Foundation, 1966.

Richards, J. M., Holland, J. L., & Lutz, S. W. The prediction of student accomplishment in college. *ACT Research Reports*, 1966, No. 13.

Sawyer, J. Measurement *and* prediction, clinical *and* statistical. *Psychological Review*, 1966, **66**, 178–200.

Schlaifer, R. *Probability and statistics for business decisions*. New York: McGraw-Hill, 1959.

Schwarz, P. A., & Krug, R. E. *Development of tests for Peace Corps selection*. Pittsburgh: American Institute for Research, 1961. (Brief printed summary.)

Seashore, H. G. Women are more predictable than men. Presidential address, Division 17, American Psychological Association, New York, September 1961.

Sechrest, L. Incremental validity: A recommendation. *Educational and Psychological Measurement*, 1963, **23**, 153–158.

Skager, R. W., Klein, S. P., & Schultz, C. B. The prediction of academic and artistic achievement at a school of design. *Journal of Educational Measurement*, 1967, **4**, 105–117.

Smith, G. B. Who should be eliminated? A study of selective admission to college. *Kansas Studies in Education*, 1956, 7(1).

Smith, M. B. Explorations in competence: A study of Peace Corps teachers in Ghana. *American Psychologist*, 1966, **21**, 555–566.

Snow, R. E., Tiffin, J., & Seibert, W. F. Individual differences and instructional film effects. *Journal of Educational Psychology*, 1965, **56**, 315–326.

Stanley, J. C., & Porter, A. C. Correlation of Scholastic Aptitude Test scores with grades for Negroes versus whites. *Journal of Educational Measurement*, 1967, **4**, 199–218.

Swanson, E. O., Merwin, J. C., & Berdie, R. F. A follow-up in Minnesota colleges showing the relationship of college grades to high school rank and test scores in the Minnesota College State-Wide Testing Program. University of Minnesota Office of Dean of Students *Research Bulletin*, 1963, **5**(1).

Thorndike, R. L. *Personnel selection*. New York: Wiley, 1949.

Vernon, P. E. Educational testing and test-form factors. Educational Testing Service *Research Bulletin*, 1958, No. 3.

Ward, L. B. The interview as an assessment technique. In *College admissions*. Vol. 2. New York: College Entrance Examination Board, 1955. Pp. 62–71.

Webb, S. C. Measured changes in college grading standards. *College Board Review*, 1959, **39**, 27–30.

Webb, S. C. The comparative validity of two biographical inventory keys. *Journal of Applied Psychology*, 1960, **44**, 177–183.

Webb, S. C. Two cross validations of the Opinion, Attitude, and Interest Survey. *Educational and Psychological Measurement*, 1965, **25**, 517–523.

Webster, E. C. *Decision making in the employment interview*. Montreal, Que.: Eagle, 1964.

Wilson, R., & Gelso, C. J. The prediction of grades in college algebra: A continuation and extension. South Georgia College *Research Report*, 1967, No. 3. (mimeo)

20. The Evaluation of Educational Programs

Alexander W. Astin
American Council on Education

Robert J. Panos
National Computer Systems

The purpose of this chapter is to review some of the conceptual and methodological issues concerning the evaluation of educational programs.[1] Although evaluation in educational research traditionally has been identified with curriculum evaluation, for the purposes of this discussion an educational "program" is conceived as any ongoing educational activity which is designed to produce specified changes in the behavior of the individuals who are exposed to it. Thus, an educational program could be a particular method of instruction, a single classroom lesson, a complete course of study, a programmed textbook, the environment of a college, a special remedial program, an apprenticeship or internship, or an entire school system.

In the minds of many educators and researchers, the task of evaluating educational programs has come to be closely associated with the construction and administration of achievement tests. While measuring the student's achievement or progress is clearly an important element in the evaluative process, this chapter attempts to present a somewhat broader model of the problem of evaluating educational programs. It is the authors' belief that using this model in the design of future evaluative studies will avoid some of the limitations that have characterized many of the evaluative studies conducted in the past.

Evaluation involves the collection of information concerning the impact of an educational program.[2] While there are many possible uses for such information, it is assumed that *the fundamental purpose of evaluation is to produce information which can be used in educational decision making.* These decisions may be concerned with the continuation, termination, or modification of an existing program, or with the development and possible adoption of some new program. Whatever the particular decision may involve, evaluation is most likely to produce useful information if it is based on an understanding of the nature of the educational decision-making process itself.

THE NATURE OF EDUCATIONAL DECISIONS

The need for rendering an educational decision implies the existence of two fundamental conditions: some recognized educational *objective* or set of objectives and at least two alternative *means* for accomplishing these objectives. Although the objectives of educational programs are many and varied, the ultimate objectives of education usually are concerned with the student's learning and personal development, the teacher's scholarly work, or the general cultural development of the community. However, since the relative importance of various educational objectives may change with time, it may be important for those who are responsible for conducting evaluative studies to

[1] In this chapter there has been no attempt made to present a comprehensive review of the literature in the broad fields commonly known as "educational evaluation" or "curriculum evaluation." Reading of much of this literature leads the authors to the conclusion that a somewhat broader conceptual model of the evaluative process is needed. In developing this chapter, we have, of course, drawn heavily upon many of the ideas of other writers. Whenever possible, we have attempted to identify and cite these relevant earlier sources.

[2] Scriven (1967) makes a distinction between "formative" evaluation, which is conducted in conjunction with the development of new educational programs, and "summative" evaluation, which is used to assess the effectiveness of existing programs. Although the authors' analysis is concerned primarily with problems of "summative" evaluation, the basic conceptual and methodological issues appear to be equally relevant to problems of "formative" evaluation.

attempt to incorporate a relatively broad and diverse set of potential objectives in their analyses.

Any educational decision involves a choice among the available alternative means by which the desired objectives may be achieved. In the context of a school system, for example, these means might include the deliberate organization of certain learning experiences (e.g. curricula, teaching methods), the manipulative structuring of the physical environment (e.g. design and location of classrooms, buildings, playgrounds), or the establishment of certain rules and regulations. Viewed in this way, *every administrative decision is predicated on a belief in the existence of a causal relationship between some educational objective and a particular means selected to achieve that objective.* In short, the decision maker believes that of all the means available, the one selected is "best" in the sense that it is most likely to result in the desired outcome.

Although these assumptions concerning means-ends relationships are often not made explicit, they nevertheless underlie every administrative decision. Take, for example, the apparently minor question of where to locate a new gymnasium on the school grounds. If several alternative sites are available, a decision must be made about which one to use. If the principal or superintendent decides to locate the building on site A rather than on sites B or C, his choice is obviously not a random one (although others on his staff may regard it as such). His decision to build on site A is based on the assumption that, with respect to some outcome, the consequences of building on site A will be superior to the consequences of building on the other sites. The outcome may be an educational one (he believes that the ultimate benefits to the students will be greater if the building is located on site A), an intermediate economic one (the total costs of constructing and maintaining the building will be less), or some combination. Such economic criteria become educational only to the extent that the decision maker is willing to assume that the total educational output will be improved by trading off an economy at one point for an increased expenditure somewhere else.

Which set of criteria—educational, economic, or other—the administrator uses as a basis for his decision is a question that involves a complex system of subjective weighting and value judgments.[3] While the optimal weighting in the above situation would depend on the nature and mission of the particular school and the value systems of those who are responsible for its operation, it is important to recognize that the decision (build on site A) is based necessarily on an assumption that the chosen alternative, in relation to the other possible alternatives, is more likely to bring about certain outcomes that are judged to have value in terms of the goals of the educational program.[4]

Rational educational decisions are typically rendered by consulting the available information that is considered to be relevant both to the desired outcomes and to the various means under consideration. A major function of evaluation is to extend this fund of information, in order that the decision maker may better anticipate the consequences of the alternative means that he is considering. In the sections that follow the nature of educational programs is discussed, and then some of the evaluative procedures that can be used to produce information for use in making decisions concerning these programs are examined.

THE NATURE OF AN EDUCATIONAL PROGRAM

Any educational program can be conceived as comprising three conceptually distinct components: *outputs, inputs* and *operations.*[5] To be maximally useful in decision making, evaluation

---

[3] An introduction to the philosophical problems posed by the valuational components of rational choice can be found in Hemple (1965, chap. 3). A theoretical discussion of methods of quantitatively combining valuational components appears in Carnap (1950, pp. 264–279). A recent expository discussion of the problems concerning the assignment of values to outcomes has been presented by Cronbach and Gleser (1965, pp. 121–132).

[4] The problem of rational choice in the face of alternative outcomes has been systematically examined from such diverse viewpoints as the stochastic theory of decision making (Wald, 1947), game theory (Neumann & Morgenstern, 1947), and inductive logic (Carnap, 1950).

[5] The three components of the authors' model, which were first proposed in earlier work (Astin, 1965; Astin & Panos, 1966), closely resemble Stake's (1967) three evaluative components: antecedents, transactions, and outcomes.

should provide information concerning all three of these program components and their interrelationships.

Educational Outputs

Outputs refer to the ends or objectives of the educational program. Other terms commonly used to refer to educational outputs are criteria, goals, outcomes, achievements, and dependent variables. Although these outcomes are usually expressed at high levels of abstraction (e.g. the development of capacity for critical thinking), most educational programs are designed also to affect relatively more concrete outcomes which can be directly observed or measured. More specifically, reference is made here to the students' achievements, knowledge, skills, aptitude for future learning, values, personality, interpersonal relations, and other behaviors that are likely to be influenced by the educational program. It has already been suggested that other goals, such as reducing the costs of operating the program or recruiting high quality educational personnel are, at best, intermediate—they are intended as means of achieving student-oriented educational objectives. Unfortunately, this point often seems to be overlooked in designing or implementing many educational programs: intermediate objectives such as greater economy of operation may be pursued so vigorously by those responsible for the program as to become regarded as ends in themselves, that is, as ultimate objectives. This situation is understandable when one considers that such intermediate objectives, and the means for achieving them and for assessing their achievement or non-achievement, are often much more clearly specified than are the more ultimate objectives of education. It is much easier, for example, for a school administrator to demonstrate that he has reduced the per pupil costs of running his institution than it is for him to show that he has facilitated his students' learning by introducing a new, less costly curriculum. Similarly, it is a relatively simple clerical task to show that the percentage of teachers with graduate degrees has been increased by vigorous recruiting but quite another thing to demonstrate that the students' development also has been enhanced

by the (supposed) improvement in the overall quality of instruction.

An analysis of relevant educational outputs should include not only those outcomes that the program is specifically designed to influence, but also the possible "side effects" of the program. For example, the introduction of a "track" system or similar procedure for ability grouping may—as intended—increase the overall level of achievement of the students in a school system, but it might also increase the incidence of, say, disciplinary problems. Unless the possibility of such unintended outcomes is taken into account in the conduct of an evaluative study, the conclusions drawn from the study can be highly misleading.

Educational objectives, because they are derived from a variety of sources—administrators, teachers, students, governing boards, subject-matter specialists, and the society at large—and because they develop gradually, are initially poorly defined and sometimes apparently contradictory. Nevertheless, it is only as clearly stated educational objectives are achieved that the relevant operational or behavioral manifestations of these objectives, that is, measures of educational progress, can be developed.

Some writers (e.g. Atkin, 1963; Eisner, 1967) have expressed a concern that the quest for operationally defined measures of educational outputs may, if pursued too vigorously and uncritically, inhibit innovation in the design of educational programs. Another, perhaps more basic, concern is that the value judgments inherent in the specification of outcome criteria may conflict with the presumed scientific objectivity of the evaluative researcher. In this regard it is important to recognize the distinction between specifying desired educational objectives, which is fundamentally a nonobjective, nonvalidatable procedure involving value judgments (Astin, 1964), and the empirical determination of how these objectives or outcomes are affected by the educational program under study. It would appear that scientific objectivity and detachment is essential primarily in the performance of this latter function. One protection for the evaluative researcher in selecting his measure of educational outcomes is to use multiple criteria representing a diversity of educational objectives and values, some of which may be mutually exclusive or even contradictory. In this manner, the subjective weighting of the various outcomes can be left to those individual decision makers who are in a position to act on the basis of the findings. In short, the use of multiple outcome criteria represents a recognition of the fact that the relative social importance attached to various outcomes may change with time and that students, teachers, administrators, policy makers, and other consumers of the results of evaluative research may attach quite different values to different types of outcomes.

Educational Inputs

Inputs are the talents, skills, aspirations, and other potentials for growth and learning that the student brings with him into the educational program. Other terms that are sometimes used in reference to the student's input characteristics are pretests, selection criteria, control variables, antecedent variables, interacting variables, motivations, and aptitudes. These inputs are, in a sense, the human raw materials with which the educational program has to deal. Inputs normally include not only the personal characteristics of the individual pupils but also those of their family and of the culture in which they live—such features as the valuation of school learning, the emphasis placed on effort and achievement, and the abstractness, correctness, and complexity of language usage.[6] Although the point is apparently overlooked in many evaluative studies, the inputs to some educational programs are vastly different from the inputs to other programs, even though the various programs may have similar or even identical educational objectives.

Student input characteristics are an important consideration in educational evaluation for at least two reasons. First, the student's ultimate level of performance in terms of the relevant output criteria may often be circumscribed by certain of his input characteristics, no

[6] Characteristics of the students' community can, under certain circumstances, be regarded also a part of the educational operations (see the next section).

matter what the nature of the particular educational program might be. Thus, the work of Bruner (1961), Piaget (1950), Erikson (1950), and others suggests that not even the most imaginative and stimulating science curriculum would be likely to produce an understanding of certain scientific concepts within a group of students who had not yet attained the psychological level of mastery needed to integrate the newer concepts with those they had already learned. Secondly, to the extent that the educational environment reflects the characteristics of the students themselves, it can be influenced dramatically by the nature of the student input: for example, the educational environment of an urban elementary school attended mostly by children from poor families is likely to be quite different from the environment of an elementary school attended primarily by suburban children from affluent families, even if both schools have identical curricula, physical plants, faculty-student ratios, and so on.

The preceding observations highlight the importance of measuring those student input characteristics that reasonably can be expected to affect either the environment of the educational program or the later student outcomes that are relevant to the goals of the program. Note that the student's input characteristics can affect his output performance directly (i.e. individual differences in performance tend to show some stability with time) or indirectly by means of interactions with the educational operations (i.e. different types of students may be affected differently by a given program). Since the relevance of any input measure thus largely is determined by the particular outcomes being evaluated, it is important to define these outcomes as early as possible in the evaluative process. Otherwise, the input information that is obtained at the time the student enters the program may not be appropriate in terms of the output measures that are eventually used.

Educational Operations

Operations refer to those characteristics of the educational program that are capable of affecting the relevant student outputs. In the broadest sense, the term *operations* encompasses a wide range of terms: environmental experiences, means, independent variables, educational interventions, experimental treatments, learning experiences, learning strategies, curricula, teacher style, and instructional techniques. In other words, educational operations comprise the entire array of environmental variables that characterize a particular educational program—the means to the achievement of the educational ends.

In the broadest sense, the educational operations also include the community attitudes and other aspects of the social context in which the educational program is carried out. Frequently the effects of such contextual factors cannot be assessed directly, because the educational program is being evaluated within a single school or community. However, if the evaluative study is replicated simultaneously in several different social settings, some of the effects of the social context can be assessed.

Although adequate measures of educational operations or environments are essential to good evaluative research, the measurement of educational environments is much less well developed than is the measurement of educational inputs and outputs (Astin, Panos, & Creager, 1966). Typically, an educational program is "measured" only in a relatively crude, nominal sense: program A versus no program; or, program A versus program B. These dichotomous or categorical distinctions may reflect the fact that educational programs are usually developed and implemented in their entirety, rather than as a sequence of separate and distinct operations.

The principal use of measures of educational operations in evaluative research is to provide an analytic frame of reference within which to interpret the observed impact of an educational program on the relevant student outputs in terms of specific environmental or "treatment" variables. While it may be of some value to know simply that one program has a better overall outcome than another, such information is of little functional use either in improving existing programs or in developing new ones (Cahen, 1967; Cronbach, 1963). For example, the knowledge that students attending school A

achieve a higher overall score on a standardized achievement test in mathematics than do students attending school B is of limited help to the decision maker in choosing between their respective mathematics curricula, *even if the two schools are similar with regard to student input.* Lacking information about other possible differences between the educational environments of the two schools, the administrator does not have a secure basis for assuming that the mathematics curriculum at school A is superior to the one at school B. Perhaps the students at school A perform better in mathematics, not because of the mathematics curriculum per se, but because school A provides more opportunities than does school B for the student to apply his mathematical knowledge in other subjects. Or, perhaps, school A simply has better mathematics teachers. In short, merely adopting the apparently "better" program (mathematics curriculum at school A) may not result in the desired changes in student outcomes (mathematics achievement), if other, confounded differences between the two school environments have brought about the observed difference in student performance. Furthermore, even if it were possible to show that such differences in the performances of the student populations are attributable to differences in their curricula, it is often difficult to determine which of the specific differences between the two curricula are responsible for the observed effects.

Interactions among the Components

The interrelationships of educational inputs, outputs, and operations are shown schematically in figure 20.1. Since the purpose of educational decision making is to select those educational operations that are most likely to

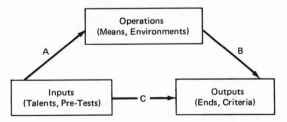

Fig. 20.1. Components of an educational program.

maximize the student's performance on the desired outcomes, the decision maker's causal assumptions necessarily involve relationship B in figure 20.1. Consequently, the principal purpose of evaluation is to provide information concerning how the various alternative educational operations under consideration are likely to affect the student's performance. From a methodological point of view, however, a thorough knowledge of relationships A or C may be required before one can adequately interpret any observed relationship B.

With respect to C—the relationship between input and output—the experience of many years of research in predicting human performance shows that the student's output performance will be determined, in part, by his input characteristics. More simply: the student's talents and aspirations, before he is ever exposed to the educational program, will in part determine what he learns and how he develops after completing the program.

But it is the presence of relationship A that may complicate the design of an evaluative study, particularly when the students have not been assigned at random to the various environments that are being compared. It has already been noted that the quality of the educational environment can be affected by the student input. The student input, therefore, is likely to be related both to output and to the educational operations. Given this dual relationship, it is possible for a significant relationship B to be mediated simply by differential student inputs to the alternative educational programs that are being compared, rather than by the differential effects of the program themselves.

Figure 20.1 suggests that there are at least three different ways in which input can influence output:

1. The direct effect of input on output (arrow C). Although this effect is usually reflected in the correlation between initial and final status on some educational outcome, it should be noted that the student's performance on certain outcome measures can be directly affected by input characteristics other than his initial status on the measure (men may differ from women, for example, in the average amount of change over time that they show on the measure).

2. The indirect effect of input via the educational operations (relationships A and C). It has already been noted that the environment of an educational program can be greatly influenced by the input characteristics of the pupils. Strictly speaking, this is an *inter*personal rather than *intra*personal effect such as described in point 1 (above), since the student's outcome performance is being influenced by the input characteristics of his fellow students.

3. Interactions between inputs and operations. These interactions refer to situations where the effects of an educational program are not the same for different types of students. Program A, for example, may be very effective for highly motivated students but less effective than Program B for the less motivated students. Although such interaction effects are subsumed under relationship C in figure 20.1, they could be portrayed more explicitly by an additional box representing *combinations* of inputs and operations. This additional box could be formed by the junction of the two new arrows (from inputs and operations), and connected directly to outputs by means of a third arrow.

This discussion makes it clear that the interpretation of an observed relationship between the student's output performance and the type of educational program (operation) to which he has been exposed is necessarily ambiguous if no control has been exercised over differential student inputs. Some of the research strategies for dealing with this problem are discussed later.

THE ROLE OF EVALUATION

The major function of evaluation is to provide the decision maker with relevant information about the inputs, outputs, and operations of the program under consideration. In attempting to understand how such information is used—or can be used—in rendering educational decisions, it is important to recognize that any item of information can be classified on the basis of how it is collected—that is, of its source. At least four different classes of information can be identified: folklore, anecdotal information, descriptive information, and research information. *Folklore* refers to any widely accepted but empirically untested assumption concerning a causal relationship between an educational program or operation and an educational outcome. For example, one familiar item of folklore in higher education is the notion that the quality of the educational environment is a function of the faculty-student ratio. The "best" ratio, in this view, is the highest one. Because of economic constraints on the possible size of the faculty, people disagree over what the upper limit should be; but it is generally assumed that the fewer the number of students per faculty member, the better will be the overall outcome, where the outcome is defined by such goals as the development of the student's intellectual skills, critical thinking, character, citizenship, and the like. The point is that these assumed cause-effect relationships have not been subjected to objective tests.

Because educational folklore is often concerned with the means and objectives of common educational problems, it frequently is used as a basis for decision making. It should be made clear that to label a particular educational belief as folklore is not to suggest that it is necessarily false; rather, it is to emphasize that it has not been subjected to an empirical test under conditions where it is open to being refuted.

Anecdotal information is sometimes the initial source of folklore and so the two are closely related. Anecdotal information differs, however, from folklore in that it is not generally current or widely accepted. In utilizing anecdotal information, the decision maker generalizes from one particular situation to another which he judges to be similar. Unfortunately, such generalization is based on gross judgments of similarity. More importantly, using anecdotal information may limit the alternatives that the decision maker is willing to consider. We had better not try that here; you know what happened at school X when they tried it—in one form or another—is probably not as infrequent to educational decision making as educators would like to believe. For example, the highly publicized student unrest that began at the Berkeley campus of the University of California in 1964 was early subjected to a plethora of anecdotal "explanation." In general, these anecdotal accounts attributed the emergence of the student protests, at least in part, to the depersonalizing effects of the large, complex university. Other "explanations" of the Berkeley incidents are, of course, possible. However, to the extent that this interpretation of the trouble at Berkeley gains general acceptance, such anecdotes may gradually become part of the educational folklore, and decisions about the administration of other large institutions thus may be made with the intention of "avoiding another Berkeley." The problem with anecdotal information, as with folklore, is that the implied relationships between educational means and ends have not been empirically tested.

Descriptive information, unlike folklore and anecdotes, does not involve any explicit statements of causal relationships. Thus, one can describe the content and methodology of an elementary school curriculum in natural science without making any assumptions about the *impact* of this curriculum on the student. The description may be entirely qualitative, or it may involve quantitative features such as the proportion of time devoted to certain subtopics, the number and frequency of examinations or review exercises, and so forth. One also can describe or measure the actual performance of the students in terms of their scores on some standardized test of achievement in natural science, once again without coming to any conclusions about how their performance has been affected by the curriculum. Many administrators, however, tend to regard evaluative research as the collection and display of purely descriptive information. Frequently, requests for such information are made without any consideration of the fact that the data are ultimately to be used in making causal inferences. Since descriptive data do not provide the causal link, the decision maker explicitly—or, more often, implicitly—does (see method I, below).

Since both folklore and anecdotes involve assumptions about the differential effects of certain educational operations, they represent forms of "evaluation" that can be (and often are) used in decision making. *Research* information also involves a statement of a causal relationship between an educational operation and an educational outcome. The critical distinction between research information and folklore or anecdotes is that research information is derived from data collected under conditions where relationships other than those obtained (or sought after) were possible. For example, in an empirical test of the effects of the faculty-student ratio on student achievement, it would be possible to find no relationship, or even a negative one. It is important to note that research information is the only source of information available to the decision maker that is subject to the scientific test of replication.

In spite of its apparent usefulness in evaluation, the quality of research information can vary greatly. For example, one can perform empirical "tests" of the existence of certain causal relationships under conditions where the variables are inadequately controlled and the results consequently ambiguous. Such research information may be highly misleading, since it is subject to several plausible rival interpretations (see methods I–IV, below). Conversely, useful research information is obtained under conditions where all known plausible rival interpretations of the observed relationship have been considered in the analysis.

The importance of adequately designed research is well illustrated by the history of research on "PhD productivity" of colleges and universities. The earliest studies indicated that the graduates of certain colleges and universities were much more likely than were the graduates of other institutions to win fellowships for graduate study and to go on to obtain the PhD degree (Knapp & Goodrich, 1952; Knapp & Greenbaum, 1953). More importantly, the "highly productive" institutions, when compared with the less productive ones, were found to have higher faculty-student ratios, larger libraries, more scholarship and research funds, and other resources usually assumed to be indicative of institutional "excellence" and prestige. In short, these early studies seemed to show

that such institutional resources (operations) are conducive to the development of the student's motivation to seek advanced training (output). Among other things, this research evidence offered empirical confirmation for the folklore about the determinants of "quality" in higher education. Taken at face value, and assuming that the output under study (motivation to seek advanced training) was relevant to the goals of the institution, these findings offered empirical support for the administrator's attempts to increase the size of his faculty, library, and similar institutional resources.

But the validity of these earlier studies came to be doubted when it was found that the relatively highly productive institutions enroll greater proportions of academically able students than do the less productive institutions (Holland, 1957). Intellectually advantaged students are, of course, more likely than average students both to win graduate fellowships and to be interested in pursuing the doctorate upon graduation, *even if their institution exerts no special influence during the undergraduate years.* These doubts were subsequently confirmed by a series of studies (Astin, 1962, 1963a, 1963b) in which differential undergraduate student inputs to the diverse educational programs were controlled. Thus, when the abilities, career plans, and socioeconomic backgrounds of the entering students were taken into account, an institution's output of PhDs was revealed to be largely a function of the characteristics of its entering students, rather than of its institutional resources. Moreover, certain types of institutions that were earlier described as "highly productive" of PhDs turned out to be underproductive in relation to their student inputs. In addition, the apparent "effects" of library size, faculty-student ratio, and other similar measures of educational operations disappeared.

The administrative lesson to be learned from these studies is clear: inadequately designed evaluative research may result in highly misleading causal interpretations. Unfortunately, the temptation to base educational decisions on such results is great, especially when the causal means-end relationships seem to confirm the folklore.

THE DESIGN OF EVALUATIVE STUDIES

Ideally, any evaluative study involves the collection and analysis of information regarding inputs, outputs, and operations. While the realities of the educational decision-making process frequently limit the quality and amount of such information that reasonably can be collected, the usefulness of many evaluative studies could be greatly increased by recognizing more fully the importance of adequate design. In this section, some of the methodologies typically used in evaluative studies are reviewed, with particular attention directed at discussing the relevance and possible usefulness of the obtained results in decision making.

Method I: Description of Educational Operations

This is perhaps the least complex and most widely used method of evaluation. It consists essentially of a logical analysis or simply a detailed description of the content of the educational program being evaluated.[7] For example, the principal of a high school might "evaluate" the social studies course taught by one of his staff by examining the syllabus of the course with regard to content sequence and organization of lessons, reading assignments, and so forth. Another example of this method of evaluation would be the procedures typically followed by the regional accrediting associations for colleges and universities. The accreditation process usually involves the collection of descriptive information concerning institutional characteristics such as faculty-student ratios, teaching loads, size of the library, physical plant, required and elective courses, and the percentage of PhDs on the faculty. Occasionally accreditation also may involve the collection of data on inputs (e.g. the aptitude test scores or high school grades of the students who are admitted) or outputs (e.g. the percentage of students going on to graduate or professional school), although descriptive information on the nature of certain educational

operations provides the principal basis for evaluation.

An example from higher education of a large-scale evaluative study using this method is Cartter's (1966) survey in which the "quality" of graduate programs was shown to be highly related to the scholarly productivity and reputation of the faculty in each department.

Perhaps the most well-known series of evaluations using this method are Conant's (1959, 1963, 1967) assessments of the quality of American high schools and American teachers colleges.

The principal limitation of this method of evaluation is that the descriptive information that is produced is not, by itself, useful in decision making, because it provides no direct evidence about the impact or effect of the measured operations on relevant educational outcomes. Thus, in the absence of such causal information, the decision maker must *supply* it by assumption. In the field of curriculum evaluation, for example, the use of this method makes it necessary to assume that "what is taught is what is learned." In more complex evaluations using this method, such as accreditation in higher education, the decision maker must often rely on the folklore (e.g. the supposed educational value of the faculty-student ratio) in order to make use of the descriptive information about educational operations. In the recent study of graduate education, for example, it would be necessary to assume that the educational benefit to the student is proportional to the professional scholarly reputation of the faculty, in order to employ the departmental ratings as measures of the "quality" of the graduate program.

To the extent that folklore concerning the effects of various educational operations is replaced by research information (e.g. if it could be shown that the graduate student's learning and professional development is actually enhanced by attending a "high quality" institution), decision makers have a much sounder basis for using the descriptive information obtained by this method. More importantly, since research information could help to sort out which of the many educational operations

---

[7] In some respects this method resembles what Scriven (1967) has termed "intrinsic" evaluation or the "noninferential study of what goes on in the classroom [pp. 49–50]."

makes what difference in terms of the various outputs, the task of evaluation by this method would be greatly simplified: the decision maker would need descriptive data concerning only those operations that reasonably could be expected to affect the outputs that are relevant to his educational goals.

Method II: Measurement of Educational Outputs

It has already been noted that many measurement specialists are inclined to define evaluation almost exclusively in terms of the assessment of educational outcomes. Placing primary emphasis on the measurement of outcomes necessarily results in focusing upon test development and the test itself, so that it is not surprising that an entire philosophy of evaluation has come to be associated with the process of achievement testing (Tyler, 1951). In a sense, this method of evaluation is concerned usually with absolute standards of performance: Do students who complete this program meet certain minimal standards?

One of the most frequent applications of this method is in the evaluation of schools or school systems. Typical output measures might include the percentage of dropouts, the percentage of students who subsequently go on to complete the next higher level of education successfully, or the students' average performance on standardized tests of educational achievement. However, if such measures are used in a *relative* rather than absolute sense (e.g. if the students' scores are evaluated in terms of percentiles based on national norms), the evaluation being performed is actually of a different type (see method III, below), since the program under study is being compared with other programs. In this latter instance, the "measure" of the educational operations is of the simple nominal type: this program versus all other programs combined.

The most extensive contemporary evaluative study using method II is the National Assessment of Educational Progress sponsored by the Carnegie Corporation of New York (Ebel, 1966; Merwin, 1966; Tyler, 1966). The principal aim of the project is to develop a comprehensive battery of measures of educational progress

which will be administered to a national sample of children and adults. While this program is oriented primarily toward the measurement of achievement at various age levels, there will be some interest in comparing the achievement levels of subgroups of students defined in terms of variables like geographic region, type of community, size of school, and so on. If such comparisons are to be used to identify environmental factors that influence the student's educational progress, this study would be an example of method III.

An advantage of evaluation studies using this method is that they focus attention on the fundamental problems of defining and measuring those outputs that are relevant to the goals of the educational program.[8] The major weakness of method II is that the obtained information concerning educational outcomes is not designed to evaluate how the student has been affected by the particular educational program being studied. Since there is no information bearing directly on the *relationship* between the educational operation and the measured educational outputs, the decision maker is once again forced to supply such causal information by assumption. Typically, this amounts to assuming that what is measured is what has been learned.

Methods II and IV represent versions of what Scriven (1967) calls "noncomparative" evaluation. The present authors' general view of the nature of evaluative research is that the impact of any educational practice or program can be assessed only by comparison with some alternative practice or program. They prefer this "comparative" concept of evaluative research for two closely related reasons. First, even in the classical randomized experiment with experimental and control groups, the "control" subjects are not placed either in cold

---

[8] Some educators equate the term *evaluation* with the choice of output or criterion measures. Note that the decision to use a particular output measure is based essentially on value judgments about what the appropriate goals of the program are and not on any assumption about the effectiveness of the program. In the context of this chapter, *evaluation* refers to the problem of determining how these outputs are affected by the program.

storage or in a state of suspended animation; rather, they are simultaneously exposed to a variety of (often poorly defined) environmental experiences. Second, educational decision making, as the discussion of this chapter already has attempted to show, necessarily involves a choice between *alternatives*. If the decision concerns a possible change in existing practices or the possible adoption of some new program, the "alternative" which is most analogous to the "control group" is to maintain the status quo. (Some of the interpretive problems associated with "comparative" evaluation studies are discussed in the next section.)

Method III: Measurement of Operations and Outputs

In this method of evaluation, information is collected concerning the operations and outputs of the educational program and their interrelationships. One example of this type of evaluation already has been examined in the earlier discussion of studies on PhD productivity of colleges. A somewhat simpler application of this method would be to compare the effects on the student's achievement of two different methods of teaching a particular course. The criterion measure in this case might be the students' scores on some standardized achievement test administered after completion of the course; the "measurement" of the educational operations would consist simply of a dichotomy —method A versus method B. A more extensive measurement of the educational operations would require using several classes which could be ordered systematically (from highest to lowest) on those operations that may be of interest (e.g. class size, amount of lecture versus discussion, age of instructor, percentage of time devoted to independent study, amount of assigned reading, frequency of examinations, and so on). Although this latter type of refinement is more cumbersome and expensive, it has the advantage of facilitating the *interpretation* of any observed effects in terms of specific operations.

Two examples of recent evaluative studies using this method are the *International Study of Achievement in Mathematics* (Husén, 1967) and the U. S. Office of Education's survey, *Equality of Educational Opportunity* (Coleman et al. 1966). In the international study, the principal educational outcome—achievement in mathematics—was measured in terms of a paper-and-pencil multiple-choice test of mathematics achievement, which was administered to students in 12 different countries. The major goal of the project was to evaluate differences in student achievement in mathematics among and within the 12 countries in terms of operations such as school expenditure, level of teacher training, type of school organization, level of technological development, and degree of urbanization. One of the major purposes of the equal opportunities survey was to assess the impact of de facto segregation in the schools (the educational operation) on the student outcomes as measured by standardized achievement tests (the educational output).

One advantage of evaluative studies utilizing this design is that empirical data are obtained concerning the relationship between educational outputs and educational operations. The principal limitation of this design, as has already been pointed out in the discussion of studies of PhD productivity, is that no information about educational inputs is collected. Thus, *unless the students have been randomly assigned to the various educational programs*, it is virtually impossible to interpret unambiguously any observed relationship between educational operations and educational outputs without resorting to the current folklore.[9] For example, the USOE survey showed that Negro students in predominantly Negro schools tend to achieve at a lower level than do Negro students in predominantly white schools. Was this difference a result of de facto segregation, or was it simply a reflection of the fact that, perhaps, Negroes who enroll at predominantly white schools have greater potential for achievement than do Negroes who enroll at predominantly Negro

[9] It is important to note that this method of evaluation does not produce ambiguous information concerning the relationship between outputs and operations, as long as the students have been assigned to the various educational operations (schools, teaching methods, etc.) at random. In such true experiments, information on inputs serves to increase the precision of the evaluation but not its validity.

schools? A more important practical question from the point of view of educational decision making is whether these data warrant the conclusion that the average achievement of those Negro students who now attend predominantly Negro schools will be increased if they are indiscriminantly distributed within predominantly white schools. In the absence of any data on differential student inputs to the two types of schools, there is no way to resolve this ambiguity from the available data (Nichols, 1966).

Method IV: Measurement of Educational Inputs and Outputs

This method of evaluation involves the measurement of educational inputs and outputs. Students are assessed at the time they enter the program (input) and again at some subsequent point in time following exposure to the program (output). The principal goal of this method is to assess the impact of the program in terms of *changes* in the student that are revealed by comparing his input and output performances. Because of this focus on evaluating change over time, it is generally desirable to have input and output measures that are comparable.

This method is frequently employed to evaluate the effectiveness of remedial or other special educational programs. The effectiveness of a program that is designed to increase the student's proficiency in reading, for example, might be evaluated by administering standard tests of reading speed and comprehension before and after the course. The output measure also might be readministered at some later time, in order to determine if the observed short-term changes in speed and comprehension persist over longer periods of time.

An example of this method is the series of studies of student change conducted at Vassar College (Sanford, 1956). The purpose of this evaluative study was to determine how the student's personality development is affected by his undergraduate college experience. A battery of personality tests was administered at the time of matriculation, again during the sophomore and junior years, and also at the time of graduation. The impact of the college years was evaluated in terms of temporal changes as revealed by comparing students' responses to the same test items at these several points in time.

The advantage of this method of evaluation is that it focuses attention on the longitudinal nature of student change and development by viewing the student's output performance in relation to his input characteristics. Its major weakness is that it produces no information bearing directly on the question of whether or not the program that is being evaluated actually has contributed to these student changes. Would changes that were observed in the Vassar students during the four years have occurred if the students had attended a different kind of college or no college at all?[10] Consequently, data obtained using this method can be used to evaluate the impact of a program only if the decision maker is willing to make certain assumptions about what would have happened to the students if they had been exposed to a different set of operations. Typically, he assumes that the observed changes were due to the impact of the educational program and that the changes would not have occurred if the student had not been exposed to the program.

Whether or not such assumptions are warranted in the absence of any additional empirical information depends to some extent on the nature of the evaluative study being performed. For example, in the case where all students show some increase in reading speed and comprehension while taking a special six-week program in reading acceleration, it may be reasonable to assume that the students would not have shown such changes during the same period of time if they had not had the same course.[11] The assumption that they would have changed differently if they had taken a *different* type of program, of course, would be much more difficult to defend. That is, in the absence of any prior specification and measurement of the educational operations, ex post facto causal explanations of the observed changes in relation

---

[10] The situation here is identical to the one encountered in experimentation when no control group is used.

[11] Of course, if the students were assigned to the remedial course *because* they initially had low scores on the reading test, the apparent increases may be attributable to regression artifacts rather than to the effects of the course.

to the educational program may be gratuitous. Evidence from more recent studies (Plant, 1965), for example, suggests that the personality changes observed in the Vassar students may not have been primarily a function of the college experience but may instead have been simply maturational or developmental changes that are likely to occur in most students during these years, regardless of where (or whether) they attend college.

Method V: Measurement of Educational Inputs, Outputs, and Operations

This method of evaluation utilizes information from all three major components of the educational program. Its principal advantages are that the observed relationships between educational operations and educational outputs can be evaluated relative to educational inputs and that changes in the students who are exposed to a given educational program can be compared with changes in students who are exposed to one or more different programs. Although this type of information is more directly functional in decision making than is the information produced by any of the other methods of evaluation, method V has been used infrequently in evaluative research.

An obvious obstacle to the use of this design in evaluative studies is the time and expense required to collect longitudinal information (inputs and outputs) from students, especially on a large scale utilizing representative samples. Perhaps the most important obstacle, however, is that the collection of adequate input data requires that the relevant goals or outputs of the program and the procedures for their measurement be specified before the evaluative study is ever begun. Furthermore, the use of this method requires that some operations other than those of the program that is being evaluated be specified beforehand and that comparable input and output data from the students who will be exposed to these alternative operations also be collected. In its simplest form, this other group of students would consist of a control group that would be studied concurrently with the experimental group of students who are exposed to the program being evaluated.

In addition to its usefulness in educational decision making, evaluative information obtained with this method is of potential value in the formulation and refinement of educational theory. Too often, theories of learning and instruction are developed from an inadequate body of knowledge, and well-designed evaluative research can be of significant value in providing a better empirical base both for testing existing theories and for the development of new ones.

Since the potential number of input, output, and environmental variables that might be included in any evaluative study is very large, if not infinite, the implementation of this method in practice requires careful planning and a judicious selection of variables. Output measures must, of course, be relevant to the goals of the educational program. However, they must also be diverse enough to satisfy the varied objectives of educators, students, and parents, to assess possible side effects of the program and—at the same time—sufficiently objective and concise so as to be administratively feasible. Input measures would, ideally, be selected on the basis of existing theory and knowledge concerning human qualities that affect performance; lacking such a body of theory, researchers should strive, at minimum, to include "pretests" on each output measure among their array of input measures. Measures of educational operations, however, represent perhaps the weakest element in the researcher's armamentarium. At a minimum, the researcher should obtain a detailed narrative documentation of the programs being evaluated. Ideally, of course, the number of program units (teachers, classes, schools, etc.) would be large enough to permit the researcher to order them in terms of quantifiable attributes.

Some Methodological Problems

Most evaluative research using one of the five methods described above involves the use of "quasi-experimental" designs (Campbell & Stanley, 1963), since reality constraints typically preclude classical experimentation in social settings (Campbell, 1957). *True experiments* are characterized by the random assignment of the experimental units (students) to the different treatment conditions (educational operations). Since randomization is, in the strictest sense, both necessary and sufficient to enable the decision maker to interpret causally the relationship between the educational operations and the outputs, it thus eliminates the necessity of taking into account the possible effect of variables not considered as part of the experiment and assures the validity of the application of tests of statistical significance.

Perhaps the major limitation of classical experimentation in social settings is that it is rarely feasible to replicate the experimental conditions on any substantial scale. These conditions would include the populations from which the samples of teachers and students were selected, the method of sampling, the geographic and social context in which the experiment was conducted, interactions between teachers and methods, and other unreplicable factors that may have influenced the findings. If the possibility of adequate replication is open to serious question, the value of the experimental findings is more theoretical than practical, since the decision maker cannot be sure of the generalizability of the results to his particular situation. Furthermore, it is seldom possible or desirable to assign the experimental units of concern in education (students) randomly to various educational experiences.

Quasi-experimental designs are useful when randomization is either not feasible or not desirable, but where sufficient controls of either the educational operations or the student inputs are introduced in the design to rule out plausible alternative explanations of the findings. Campbell and Stanley (1963) have described a number of research designs which reduce the chances that causal interpretations of the observed relationships between the educational operations and outputs will be invalid. For the most part, these research designs require the three types of information that are available from method V, although some of the designs are appropriate when information is lacking either on environments (method IV) or inputs (method III).

The principal advantage of quasi-experimental designs in evaluative research is that they permit the investigator to conduct in situ evaluations of the relative impact of educational programs on student development, thereby minimizing the problems of replication and artificiality that typically characterize true experiments. Two necessary conditions for the conduct of such natural experiments are: (a) the existence of two or more independent sets of educational operations that can be meaningfully compared (these might be different schools or different methods of instruction); and (b) an imperfect matching of the student inputs with the educational programs, so that the confounding of inputs and operations is only partial (e.g. it would not be possible to compare the effects of a school for girls and a school for boys on some output measure that is related to sex). Assuming that these conditions are present, quasi-experimental procedures permit the simultaneous comparison of the impact of any number of concurrent educational programs. If the number of programs being evaluated is sufficiently large to enable the investigator to order their educational operations on measurable dimensions (such as classroom size or per student expenditures), the relative impact of these more specific operations also can be estimated. Knowledge of the specific educational operations that account for the observed impact of any educational program is, of course, important both in the improvement of existing programs and in the development of new ones.

The major limitation of quasi-experimental studies is that the investigator can never be certain that he has adequately controlled every possible source of input bias. Most frequently, these biases involve the input characteristics of the student that determine, in part, the particular educational program to which he is eventually exposed. The investigator's principal concern here is to measure and control adequately any input characteristic that is likely to influence (a) the student's chances of being selected into a particular program and (b) his subsequent output performance.

In short, whether the investigator chooses to use experimental or quasi-experimental procedures necessarily depends on many practical and technical considerations. Assuming that the logistics of the evaluation problem gives him a choice between these two approaches, his decision should probably be determined by weighing the relative disadvantages of not being able to replicate the experimental conditions in practice against not being sure all relevant biasing inputs can be adequately controlled.

In spite of its apparent appropriateness to our evaluative model, the simple "pretest-posttest" covariance design is probably not adequate for dealing with many evaluative problems where the assignment of students to the different programs is nonrandom. It is likely, for example, that the student's posttest performance may be affected by input factors that are not reflected in his pretest performance. Perhaps the safest approach under these circumstances is to employ multiple covariates, including both a pretest measure and measures of any other input characteristics that may be nonrandomly distributed among the different programs.

Another limitation of the covariance model as traditionally applied in empirical research is that the different "treatments" (educational programs) are conceived of in qualitative rather than quantitative terms. As has already been noted, several writers have questioned the usefulness of the findings from such studies because they do not necessarily show *which* of the many differences in the specific operations of the various programs accounted for the observed difference in performance. One possible approach to this interpretive problem is to study a great many varied programs simultaneously. Each individual program thus is treated in a manner somewhat analogous to the treatment of individual persons in the study of individual differences. Measures of specific environmental ("personality") differences among the various programs can be developed and subsequently related to the differential effects of the programs on the students' performance.[12] Such analyses, which are likely to employ multiple part and partial correlational techniques rather than

covariance analysis, make it possible to interpret the differential effects of the programs in terms of more specific environmental variables. While such studies tend to be extremely expensive because of the large number of variables, programs, and students involved, it has been demonstrated that they are feasible (Astin & Panos, 1969).

A major problem in the use of covariance or partial correlational analyses is posed by the *error of measurement* in the input variable (i.e. in the covaried or partialled variable). If the groups being compared differ initially with respect to the input variable, the investigator runs the risk of finding a spurious environmental or treatment "effect," which is, in reality, a statistical artifact resulting from errors of measurement in the input variable. Since these errors attenuate the observed relationship between the input and output measure, the investigator essentially "undercorrects" for the initial input differences if he bases his analysis simply on these observed relationships. For a fuller discussion of this problem and a suggested remedy, see Tucker, Damerin, and Messick (1966).

OTHER USES OF EVALUATION

In the foregoing discussion the major function of evaluation has been defined as the production of information concerning the differential impact of educational programs on the development of students. Although such information is obtained primarily as an aid to the decision maker, the information and the evaluative process itself have many other potential applications. These other potential uses of evaluation and evaluative information, some of which have been described in detail by Tyler (1951), will be only briefly summarized here.

Information on Outputs

In addition to its usefulness in evaluation, information on the outputs of an educational program can be helpful both in the instructional process and in the administration of the educational program. A potentially valuable exercise, for example, is the specification and definition of relevant educational outcomes and the development of measures for assessing

---

[12] An important methodological consideration here is to employ the *student*, rather than the program, as the unit of analysis in controlling for differential input characteristics. If the program is used as the unit of analysis (i.e. if each student input characteristic is first aggregated by program before its effects are controlled), the researcher runs the risk of partialling out some or perhaps all of the differential environmental effects (Astin, 1963a).

these outcomes. Active participation by administrative and instructional staff in this process often serves as a means of clarifying unique educational objectives and also increases the likelihood that the output measures that are eventually selected will be relevant to the longer range educational goals of the program (Bloom, 1956).

While output information is not, by itself, a sufficient basis for evaluating the impact of a given program, the availability of such information does make it possible to determine whether desired changes have taken place in the student or whether certain absolute standards of performance are being met. Such information can be of considerable use to the teacher and administrator in educational planning, particularly if the feedback is relatively immediate. Students who are not developing satisfactorily in a particular program can thus be given special assistance, and teachers whose students do not appear to be progressing can be encouraged to modify their techniques. Such diagnostic and remedial use of evaluative information obtained from an ongoing program is of ever greater potential value if it is coupled with appropriate student input information. While such information on student change does not, as has been pointed out already, necessarily prove causation, it must be remembered that day-to-day educational decisions very often cannot await the completion of controlled longitudinal studies and that the existence of objective data on the educational progress of the students can be a valuable guide in the rendering of these decisions.

Information on Inputs

The systematic collection of information on the student inputs to an educational program may often prove to be a source of enlightenment both to teachers and to administrators, quite apart from the later use of such information in longitudinal evaluative studies. Although it may be difficult to imagine how an educational program could be intelligently planned and implemented in the absence of any real knowledge of the kinds of students who will be exposed to it, there are undoubtedly many programs that have operated for some time with only meager data on the needs, talents, aspirations, and backgrounds of their students.

Some of the more obvious uses of input information are in setting realistic objectives for the program, in designing or modifying the specific educational operations, and in sorting or assigning students to appropriate experiences within the program. Another potentially important application of input information is in monitoring the characteristics of successive classes of students entering the program. Such information makes it possible to detect changes that might require certain adjustments in the goals or operations of the program.

Information on Operations

Information concerning educational operations could be of considerable use in educational administration and instruction, although the descriptive information that is typically available is of relatively limited value. A potentially more useful kind of information would be *comparative* data based on a comprehensive taxonomy of educational environments (Astin, 1968; Creager & Astin, 1968). Such a taxonomic system would permit the educator to view his particular set of educational operations in the context of other programs with similar objectives. From a larger perspective, the existence of objective taxonomic information on several programs permits the educational planner to view the characteristics of an entire educational system in terms of its diversities and similarities and to identify gaps in the system where certain innovative practices might be tried out.

Objective information on the specific operations of an educational program is most useful, of course, when the probable impact of those operations on various educational outcomes already has been determined by longitudinal evaluative research.

SUMMARY

This chapter has presented a model for evaluating educational programs. The major aspects of the model are summarized and discussed below.

1. The principal purpose of evaluation is to produce information that can guide decisions concerning the adoption or modification of an educational program.

2. Since administrative decisions implicitly assume the existence of certain causal relationships between the alternative means or programs under consideration and the desired ends or objectives of the program, evaluation is most useful in decision making if it produces information concerning these causal relationships.

3. For purposes of evaluation, any educational program can be regarded as comprising three fundamental components: student *inputs*, (the personal characteristics of the students as they enter the program), student *outputs* (the later behavior of the student with respect to the objectives of the program), and educational *operations* (the environmental characteristics of the program). Evaluation is concerned with determining the differential effects of educational operations on educational outputs. Many of the evaluative studies that have been conducted in the past have not produced results that are directly relevant to decision making because one or more of the three basic informational components have been either poorly assessed or missing from the analysis. In particular, many studies have been of limited value because they have relied exclusively on output information (measures of educational outcomes) and have thus failed to produce empirical information on the *relationships* among the educational outputs, inputs, and operations.

4. At least four sources of information about the effects of educational operations on student development can be identified: *folklore, anec-* *dotal information, descriptive information, and research information.* Folklore and anecdotes represent empirically untested statements concerning causal relationships between certain educational operations and outputs. Since descriptive data are not directly concerned with explicit causal relationships, the causal inferences must be furnished by assumption in order to use such data in decision making. Research, on the other hand, yields objective empirical data concerning the effects of educational operations; data are collected under conditions where effects other than those actually obtained (or sought after) are possible. Unlike folklore and anecdotes, research information is subject to the scientific test of replication. One of the objectives of educational measurement is to replace the existing folklore with research information.

5. The extent to which the results of evaluative research can be regarded as relevant to any decision problem is dependent on a number of considerations, including the appropriateness of the particular operations and outputs being studied, and the methodology used to obtain the research information. Although a great variety of research designs and methods have been used in evaluative studies, potentially the most useful design is one which includes objective data on the characteristics of the educational operations and longitudinal data on student inputs and outputs. The confidence that the decision maker can place in causal interpretations of the resulting findings is dependent on the extent to which all plausible rival interpretations have been considered in the analysis.

REFERENCES

Astin, A. W. "Productivity" of undergraduate institutions. *Science*, 1962, **136**, 129–35.

Astin, A. W. Differential college effects on the motivation of talented students to obtain the Ph.D. *Journal of Educational Psychology*, 1963, **54**, 63–71. (a)

Astin, A. W. Undergraduate institutions and the production of scientists. *Science*, 1963, **141**, 334–338. (b)

Astin, A. W. Criterion-centered research. *Educa-* *tional and Psychological Measurement*, 1964, **24**, 807–822.

Astin, A. W. *Who goes where to college*. Chicago: Science Research Associates, Inc., 1965.

Astin, A. W. *The college environment*. Washington: American Council on Education, 1968.

Astin, A. W. & Panos, R. J. A national research data bank for higher education. *Educational Record*, 1966, **47**, 5–17.

Astin, A. W., & Panos, R. J. *The educational and*

vocational development of college students. Washington: American Council on Education, 1969.

Astin, A. W., Panos, R. J., & Creager, J. A. A program of longitudinal research on the higher educational system. *ACE Research Reports*, 1966, **1**(1).

Atkin, J. M. Some evaluation problems in a course content improvement project. *Journal of Research in Science Teaching*, 1963, **1**, 129–132.

Atkin, J. M. Using behaviorally-stated objectives for designing the curriculum: A cautionary note. Paper presented at annual meeting of the American Educational Research Association, Chicago, 1968.

Bloom, B. S. (Ed.) *Taxonomy of educational objectives.* Handbook I. *The cognitive domain.* New York: David McKay, 1956.

Bruner, J. S. *The process of education.* Cambridge, Mass.: Harvard University Press, 1961.

Cahen, L. S. The role of long term studies in curriculum evaluation. Princeton, N. J.: Educational Testing Service, 1967. (mimeo)

Campbell, D. T. Factors relevant to the validity of experiments in social settings. *Psychological Bulletin*, 1957, **54**, 297–312.

Campbell, D. T., & Stanley, J. C. Experimental and quasi-experimental designs for research on teaching. In N. L. Gage (Ed.), *Handbook of research on teaching.* Chicago: Rand McNally, 1963. Pp. 171–246.

Carnap, R. *Logical foundations of probability.* Chicago: University of Chicago Press, 1950.

Cartter, A. M. *Graduate education: A study of the assessment of quality.* Washington: American Council on Education, 1966.

Coleman, J. S., et al. *Equality of educational opportunity.* Washington: U. S. Department of Health, Education, and Welfare, Office of Education, 1966.

Conant, J. B. *The American high school today: A first report to interested citizens.* New York: McGraw-Hill, 1959.

Conant, J. B. *The education of American teachers.* New York: McGraw-Hill, 1963.

Conant, J. B. *The comprehensive high school; A second report to interested citizens.* New York: McGraw-Hill, 1967.

Creager, J. A., & Astin, A. W. Alternative methods of describing characteristics of colleges and universities. *Educational and Psychological Measurement*, 1968, **28**, 719–734.

Cronbach, L. J. Course improvement through education. *Teachers College Record*, 1963, **64**, 672–683.

Cronbach, L. J., & Gleser, G. C. *Psychological tests and personnel decisions.* Urbana: University of Illinois Press, 1965.

Ebel, R. L. Some measurement problems in a national assessment of educational progress. *Journal of Educational Measurement*, 1966, **3**, 11–18.

Eisner, E. W. Educational objectives: Help or hindrance? *The School Review*, 1967, **75**, 250–260.

Erikson, E. H., *Childhood and society.* New York: W. W. Norton, 1950.

Hemple, C. G. *Aspects of scientific explanation.* New York: Free Press, 1965.

Holland, J. L. Undergraduate origins of American scientists. *Science*, 1957, **126**, 433–437.

Husén, T. (Ed.) *International study of achievement in mathematics.* New York: Wiley, 1967. (Stockholm: Almquist & Wiksell)

Knapp, R. H., & Goodrich, H. B. *Origins of the American scientists.* Chicago: University of Chicago Press, 1952.

Knapp, R. H., & Greenbaum, J. J. *The younger American scholar: His collegiate origins.* Chicago: University of Chicago Press, 1953.

Merwin, J. C. The progress of exploration toward a national assessment of educational progress. *Journal of Educational Measurement*, 1966, **3**, 5–10.

Neumann, J. von, & Morgenstern, O. *Theory of games and economic behavior.* Princeton, N. J.: Princeton University Press, 1947.

Nichols, R. C. Schools and the disadvantaged. *Science*, 1966, **154**, 1312–1314.

Piaget, J. *The psychology of intelligence.* New York: Harcourt, Brace, 1950.

Plant, W. T. Longitudinal changes in intolerance and authoritarianism for subjects differing in amount of college education over four years. *Genetic Psychology Monographs*, 1965, **72**, 247–287.

Sanford, N. Personality development during the college years. *Personnel and Guidance Journal*, 1956, **35**, 74–80.

Scriven, M. The methodology of evaluation. In *Perspectives of curriculum evaluation: AERA monograph series on curriculum evaluation.* Chicago: Rand McNally, 1967. Pp. 39–83.

Stake, R. E. An emerging theory of evaluation—borrowings from many methodologies. Paper presented at the annual meeting of the American Educational Research Association, New York, 1967.

Tucker, L. R., Damarin, F., & Messick, S. A base-free measure of change. *Psychometrika*, 1966, **31**, 457–473.

Tyler, R. W. The functions of measurement in improving instruction. In E. F. Lindquist (Ed.), *Educational measurement*. Washington: American Council on Education, 1951. Pp. 47–67.

Tyler, R. W. The objectives and plans for a national assessment of educational progress. *Journal of Educational Measurement*, 1966, **3**, 1–4.

Wald, A. *Sequential analysis*. New York: Wiley, 1947.

Index

Index